ENGINEERING MATHEMATICS – I

(With Large No. of MCQ's & Solved Problems)

FOR

F. E. : FIRST YEAR DEGREE COURSE IN ENGINEERING

ACCORDING TO NEW REVISED SYLLABUS OF
SAVITRIBAI PHULE PUNE UNIVERSITY
(EFFECTIVE FROM ACADEMIC YEAR - 2012 – 2013)
COMMON FOR ALL DEGREE ENGINEERING COURSES

Dr. M. Y. GOKHALE
M. Sc. (Pure Maths.), M. Sc. (App. Maths.)
Ph. D. (I. I. T., Mumbai)
Professor and Head, Deptt. of Mathematics,
Maharashtra Institute of Technology,
PUNE.

Dr. N. S. MUJUMDAR
M. Sc., M. Phil., Ph. D. (Maths.)
Professor in Mathematics,
JSPM's Rajarshi Shahu
College of Engineering,
Tathawade, PUNE.

Prof. S. S. KULKARNI
M. Sc. (Maths.) (I. I. T. Mumbai)
Eminent Professor of Mathematics,
PUNE.

Prof. A. N. SINGH
M. A. (Mathematics Gold Medalist)
Formerly Head of Mathematics, Deptt.
D. Y. Patil College of Engineering,
Pimpri, PUNE.

Prof. K. R. ATAL
M. Sc. (Mathematics)
Lecturer (Selection Grade) Deptt. of Applied Sciences,
Pune Institute of Computer Technology,
Dhankawdi, PUNE

N2751

ENGINEERING MATHEMATICS-I　　　　　　　　　　　ISBN 978-93-80725-16-1

Fourth Edition : June 2015

© : Authors

The text of this publication, or any part thereof, should not be reproduced or transmitted in any form or stored in any computer storage system or device for distribution including photocopy, recording, taping or information retrieval system or reproduced on any disc, tape, perforated media or other information storage device etc., without the written permission of Authors with whom the rights are reserved. Breach of this condition is liable for legal action.

Every effort has been made to avoid errors or omissions in this publication. In spite of this, errors may have crept in. Any mistake, error or discrepancy so noted and shall be brought to our notice shall be taken care of in the next edition. It is notified that neither the publisher nor the authors or seller shall be responsible for any damage or loss of action to any one, of any kind, in any manner, therefrom.

Published By :	CTP	Printed By :
NIRALI PRAKASHAN Abhyudaya Pragati, 1312, Shivaji Nagar, Off J.M. Road, PUNE – 411005 Tel - (020) 25512336/37/39, Fax - (020) 25511379 Email : niralipune@pragationline.com		**REPRO INDIA LTD.** Mumbai

☞ **DISTRIBUTION CENTRES**

PUNE
Nirali Prakashan : 19, Budhwar Peth, Jogeshwari Mandir Lane, Pune 411002, Maharashtra
Tel : (020) 2445 2044, 66022708, Fax : (020) 2445 1538
Email : bookorder@pragationline.com, niralilocal@pragationline.com

Nirali Prakashan : S. No. 28/27, Dhyari, Near Pari Company, Pune 411041
Tel : (020) 24690204 Fax : (020) 24690316
Email : dhyari@pragationline.com, bookorder@pragationline.com

MUMBAI
Nirali Prakashan : 385, S.V.P. Road, Rasdhara Co-op. Hsg. Society Ltd.,
Girgaum, Mumbai 400004, Maharashtra
Tel : (022) 2385 6339 / 2386 9976, Fax : (022) 2386 9976
Email : niralimumbai@pragationline.com

☞ **DISTRIBUTION BRANCHES**

JALGAON
Nirali Prakashan : 34, V. V. Golani Market, Navi Peth, Jalgaon 425001,
Maharashtra, Tel : (0257) 222 0395, Mob : 94234 91860

KOLHAPUR
Nirali Prakashan : New Mahadvar Road, Kedar Plaza, 1st Floor Opp. IDBI Bank
Kolhapur 416 012, Maharashtra. Mob : 9850046155

NAGPUR
Pratibha Book Distributors : Above Maratha Mandir, Shop No. 3, First Floor,
Rani Jhanshi Square, Sitabuldi, Nagpur 440012, Maharashtra
Tel : (0712) 254 7129

DELHI
Nirali Prakashan : 4593/21, Basement, Aggarwal Lane 15, Ansari Road, Daryaganj
Near Times of India Building, New Delhi 110002 Mob : 08505972553

BENGALURU
Pragati Book House : House No. 1, Sanjeevappa Lane, Avenue Road Cross,
Opp. Rice Church, Bengaluru – 560002.
Tel : (080) 64513344, 64513355,Mob : 9880582331, 9845021552
Email:bharatsavla@yahoo.com

CHENNAI
Pragati Books : 9/1, Montieth Road, Behind Taas Mahal, Egmore,
Chennai 600008 Tamil Nadu, Tel : (044) 6518 3535,
Mob : 94440 01782 / 98450 21552 / 98805 82331,
Email : bharatsavla@yahoo.com

niralipune@pragationline.com | www.pragationline.com

Also find us on www.facebook.com/niralibooks

PREFACE TO THE FOURTH EDITION

We are glad and excited to announce that the Third Edition of this book received an overwhelming response from the engineering student community, compelling us to release its Fourth Edition within a very short period of time.

This thoroughly revised Fourth Edition has been updated with additional matter, many solved problems, including solutions to all university examination problems and numerous exercises for practice.

Special care has been taken to maintain high degree of accuracy in the theory and numericals throughout the book.

We take this opportunity to express our sincere thanks to Dineshbhai Furia of Nirali Prakashan, a reputed pioneer in the publication field. Our special thanks to Jignesh Furia for their effective cooperation and great care in bringing out this revised edition. We also appreciate the efforts of M. P. Munde and the entire staff of Engineering Books Deptt. of Nirali Prakashan namely Mrs. Deepali Lachake (Co-ordinator) and Mrs. Shilpa Kale for bringing this book to the students in a timely manner.

We sincerely hope that this "Fourth Edition" will also be warmly received by all concerned as in the past.

Valuable suggestions from our esteemed readers to improve the book are most welcome and highly appreciated.

PUNE —Authors

PREFACE TO THE FIRST EDITION

Our text books on **Engineering Mathematics-I** have occupied place of pride among engineering student's community for more than fifteen years now. All the teachers of this group of authors have been teaching mathematics in engineering colleges for the past several years. Difficulties of engineering students are well understood by the authors and that is reflected in the text material.

As per the policy of the University, Engineering Syllabi is revised every five years. Last revision was in the year 2008. New revision is coming little earlier, as university has introduced **online** system of examination from this year.

As per the new system, two **online** examinations will be conducted at the end of first month and second month in the first semester. First **online** examination will be based on first and second units and second examination will cover third and fourth units. Both the **online** examinations will have objective types of questions with multiple choices. End semester examination will be based on all the six units and that will be conducted in traditional way.

New text book is written, taking in to account all the new features that have been introduced. New entrants to the engineering field will definitely find this book, complete in all respect. Students will find the subject matter presentation quite lucid. There are large number of illustrative examples and well graded exercises. Addition of multiple choice questions will be very useful to the students, especially for **online** examinations.

We take this opportunity to express our sincere thanks to Shri. Dineshbhai Furia of Nirali Prakashan, pioneer in all fields of education. Thanks are also due to Shri. Jignesh Furia, whose dynamic leadership is helpful to all the authors of Nirali Prakashan.

We specially appreciate the efforts of Shri. M. P. Munde and entire staff of Nirali Prakashan for making the publication of this book possible, well in time.

We also thankful to Mr. Santosh Bare for DTP and Mrs. Angha Kaware for Proof Reading.

We have no doubt that like our earlier texts, student's community will respond favourably to this new venture.

The advice and suggestions of our esteemed readers to improve the text are most welcomed, and will be highly appreciated.

Pune   Authors

SYLLABUS

Unit : 1 (09 Hrs.)

Matrices : Rank, Normal Form, System of Linear Equations, Linear Dependence and Independence, Linear and Orthogonal Transformations. Eigen Values, Eigen Vectors, Cayley – Hamilton Theorem. Application to Problems in Engineering (Translation and Rotation of Matrix).

Unit : 2 (09 Hrs)

Complex Numbers and Applications : Argand Diagram, De'Moivre's theorem and its application to find roots of Algebraic Equations. Hyperbolic Functions, Inverse Hyperbolic Functions, Logarithm of Complex Numbers, Separation into Real and Imaginary parts, Application to Problems in Engineering.

Unit : 3 (08 Hrs.)

Infinite Series : Infinite Sequences, Infinite Series, Alternating Series, Tests for Convergence, Absolute and Conditional Convergence, Range of Convergence.

Differential Calculus : Successive Differentiation, Leibnitz's Theorem.

Unit : 4 (09 Hrs.)

Expansion of Functions : Taylor's Series and Maclaurin's Series.

Differential Calculus : Indeterminate Forms, L'Hospital's Rule, Evaluation of Limits.

Unit : 5 (09 Hrs.)

Partial Differentiation and Applications : Partial Derivatives, Euler's Theorem on Homogeneous Functions, Implicit Functions, Total Derivatives, Change of Independent Variables.

Unit : 6 (09 Hrs)

Jacobian : Jocobians and their applications. Errors and Approximations.

Maxima and Minima : Maxima and Minima of Functions of two variables, Lagrange's Method of undetermined multipliers.

● ● ●

CONTENTS

Unit : I

1. Matrices — 1.1 – 1.32
2. System of Linear Algebraic Equations — 2.1 – 2.56
3. Eigen Values, Eigne Vectors — 3.1 – 3.64

Unit : II

4. Complex Numbers — 4.1 – 4.72
5. Hyperbolic Functions, Logarithms of Complex Numbers — 5.1 – 5.46

Unit : III

6. Infinite Series — 6.1 – 6.96
7. Successive Differentiation — 7.1 – 7.50

Unit : IV

8. Taylor's and Maclaurin's Theorem — 8.1 – 8.42
9. Indeterminate Forms — 9.1 – 9.42

Unit : V

10. Partial Differentiation and Applications — 10.1 – 10.86

Unit : VI

11. Jacobians, Errors and Approximations, Maxima and Minima — 11.1 – 11.84

- Model Question Paper : First Online Exam (25 Marks) — M.1 – M.2
- Model Question Paper : Second Online Exam (25 Marks) — M.3 – M.4
- Model Question Paper : Theory Exam (50 Marks) — M.5 – M.6
- University Question Papers (Dec. 2012 to May 2015) — UQP.1 – UQP.14

CHAPTER ONE

MATRICES

1.1 INTRODUCTION

Before giving formal definition of a matrix, let us consider some examples from practical field. These examples will give some physical insight into the topic of matrices that we are going to discuss in next few sections.

Ex. 1 : There are m cement factories and cement is to be supplied to n cities. The transportation cost of supplying one truck load of cement from i^{th} factory or location to the jth city or destination is C_{ij} and is presented in tabular form such as,

Table A

		City			
	j \ i	1	2	3	4
Factory	1	200	400	600	450
	2	300	550	750	1000
	3	100	300	600	500
	4	250	350	700	800
	5	300	490	760	810

Above table shows that, transportation cost from the factory i = 3 to the city j = 4 is Rs. 500/-. Similarly from the factory i = 5 to the city j = 2 is Rs. 490/- and so on. Arrangement of numbers in table A in the form of 5 rows and 4 columns, is unique and shifting of numbers (or elements) from one position to the other is not permissible. Interchange of two rows or columns is also not possible. Every element or number at the intersection of ith row and j^{th} column has fixed meaning.

Ex. 2 : Second example we take from game theory. Consider the coin matching game in which two players participate. Each player calls either a Head H or a Tail T. If the outcomes match H, H or T, T. A wins Rs. 100 from B, otherwise B wins Rs. 100 from A or it results in loss of Rs. 100 for player A.

Outcome of this game can be represented in tabular form as shown below

Table B

		B	
		H	T
A	H	100	−100
	T	−100	100

Table B represents a fixed arrangement of numbers in the form of rows and columns. It is clear that either the two rows or two columns cannot be interchanged.

In the above two examples, we have come across fixed arrangement of numbers in the form of rows and columns. These two examples are chosen for easy understanding of the students. Such fixed arrangement of numbers with associated meanings, arise in almost every branch of engineering.

With this background, we are in a position to start the study of matrices, with formal definition of a matrix.

1.2 DEFINITION OF A MATRIX

An arrangement of certain numbers in an array of m rows and n columns, such as

$$A = \begin{bmatrix} a_{11} & a_{12} & a_{13} & \cdots & a_{1n} \\ a_{21} & a_{22} & a_{23} & \cdots & a_{2n} \\ \vdots & \vdots & \vdots & \vdots & \vdots \\ a_{m1} & a_{m2} & a_{m3} & \cdots & a_{mn} \end{bmatrix}$$

is called as m × n matrix (read as m by n). In the above arrangement, all horizontal lines correspond to rows and vertical lines correspond to columns.

m denotes total number of rows in A, n denotes total number of columns in A. Thus order of A is written as $A_{m \times n}$. In short, matrix A can also be denoted by

$$A = \{a_{ij}\}_{m \times n}$$ where a_{ij} denotes an element belonging to the ith row and j^{th} column where i = 1, 2, 3, ... m; j = 1, 2, 3 ... n.

$$A_{3 \times 2} = \begin{bmatrix} 1 & 2 \\ 2 & 4 \\ 3 & 6 \end{bmatrix}, \quad A_{3 \times 4} = \begin{bmatrix} 1 & 2 & 4 & 0 \\ -1 & 3 & 1 & 1 \\ 0 & 4 & 0 & 2 \end{bmatrix}, \quad A_{3 \times 3} = \begin{bmatrix} 1 & 2 & 3 \\ 3 & 1 & 4 \\ 0 & 1 & 2 \end{bmatrix}$$

Different notations used for enclosing the elements of matrix are [ ], ( ), || ||, { }.

It must be noted that matrix represents the arrangement of numbers and it satisfies certain rules and laws of operations. It cannot be evaluated like a determinant. While determinant represents certain number or is a notation to denote certain expression, matrix is an entity in the form of arrangement of numbers, which cannot be disturbed.

Elements a_{11}, a_{22}, a_{33} ... etc. are said to be on leading diagonal or principal diagonal and they are termed as diagonal elements.

1.3 TYPES OF MATRICES

1. Row or Column matrices : A matrix of order $1 \times n$ i.e. having only one row and n columns, is known as *row matrix* or *row vector*.

e.g. $A = [a_{11}\ a_{12}\ a_{13}\ \ldots\ a_{1n}]$, $B_{14} = [-2, 1, 0, 3]$

A matrix of order $m \times 1$ i.e. having only one column and m rows, is known as *column matrix* or *column vector*.

e.g. $A = \begin{bmatrix} a_{11} \\ a_{21} \\ a_{31} \\ \ldots \\ a_{m1} \end{bmatrix}$, $B_{31} = \begin{bmatrix} 0 \\ 1 \\ 2 \end{bmatrix}$

2. Zero or Null matrix : A matrix containing all zero elements is known as zero or null matrix and it is denoted by Z.

e.g. $Z_{34} = \begin{bmatrix} 0 & 0 & 0 & 0 \\ 0 & 0 & 0 & 0 \\ 0 & 0 & 0 & 0 \end{bmatrix}$

3. Square matrix : A matrix containing no. of rows = no. of columns is known as square matrix.

$A_{3 \times 3} = \begin{bmatrix} 1 & 2 & 3 \\ 0 & 1 & -1 \\ 1 & 2 & -2 \end{bmatrix}$, $A_{2 \times 2} = \begin{bmatrix} 0 & 1 \\ -1 & 2 \end{bmatrix}$

4. Transpose of matrix : A matrix obtained by interchanging rows and columns of a matrix A is called transpose of A. It is denoted by A' or A^* or A^T.

If $A = \begin{bmatrix} 1 & 2 & 3 \\ 2 & 1 & 4 \\ 0 & 1 & 2 \\ 1 & 1 & -1 \end{bmatrix}$ then $A^T = \begin{bmatrix} 1 & 2 & 0 & 1 \\ 2 & 1 & 1 & 1 \\ 3 & 4 & 2 & -1 \end{bmatrix}$

5. Symmetric matrix : A square matrix A is said to be symmetric matrix if $A = A'$

i.e. $A = \begin{bmatrix} 1 & 2 & -1 \\ 2 & 1 & 3 \\ -1 & 3 & 2 \end{bmatrix}$ Also $A = \begin{bmatrix} a & h & g \\ h & b & f \\ g & f & c \end{bmatrix}$

In a symmetric matrix, $a_{ij} = a_{ji}$ for all i, j.

i.e. $a_{12} = a_{21}$
$a_{13} = a_{31}$
$a_{23} = a_{32}$

6. Skew symmetric matrix : A is said to be skew symmetric if $A = -A'$. Here $a_{ij} = -a_{ji}$ for all i, j.

> **Note :** Diagonal elements of skew symmetric matrix are zero because $a_{ii} = -a_{ii}$
> $\therefore \quad 2a_{ii} = 0 \quad$ or $\quad a_{ii} = 0.$

i.e. $\quad A = \begin{bmatrix} 0 & 1 & 2 \\ -1 & 0 & 3 \\ -2 & -3 & 0 \end{bmatrix}$ is skew symmetric matrix.

7. Diagonal matrix : If a square matrix contains all non-diagonal elements as zeroes then it is called as diagonal matrix.

e.g. $\quad A = \begin{bmatrix} 1 & 0 & 0 \\ 0 & 2 & 0 \\ 0 & 0 & 3 \end{bmatrix}$

8. Scalar matrix : If a square matrix has all diagonal elements equal i.e. $a_{11} = a_{22} = a_{33}$ ... then it is called scalar matrix.

e.g. $\quad A = \begin{bmatrix} 2 & 0 & 0 \\ 0 & 2 & 0 \\ 0 & 0 & 2 \end{bmatrix}$

9. Unit matrix : It is a diagonal matrix, where all the diagonal elements are unity and it is denoted by I_n. Unit matrix is also called an identity matrix.

e.g. $\quad I_3 = \begin{bmatrix} 1 & 0 & 0 \\ 0 & 1 & 0 \\ 0 & 0 & 1 \end{bmatrix}, \quad I_4 = \begin{bmatrix} 1 & 0 & 0 & 0 \\ 0 & 1 & 0 & 0 \\ 0 & 0 & 1 & 0 \\ 0 & 0 & 0 & 1 \end{bmatrix}$

10. Upper triangular matrix : It is a square matrix in which all the elements below the principal diagonal are zeroes.

e.g. $\quad A = \begin{bmatrix} 1 & 2 & 3 \\ 0 & 2 & 1 \\ 0 & 0 & 1 \end{bmatrix}$

11. Lower triangular matrix : It is a square matrix in which all the elements above principal diagonal are zeroes.

e.g. $\quad A = \begin{bmatrix} 3 & 0 & 0 \\ 2 & 2 & 0 \\ 1 & 2 & 1 \end{bmatrix}$

1.4 DETERMINANT OF A MATRIX

If A is a square matrix then $|A|$ = determinant of A.

If
$$A = \begin{bmatrix} 2 & 3 & 1 \\ 1 & 2 & 3 \\ -1 & 1 & 0 \end{bmatrix}$$

then
$$|A| = \begin{vmatrix} 2 & 3 & 1 \\ 1 & 2 & 3 \\ -1 & 1 & 0 \end{vmatrix}$$

Expansion: $|A| = 2(0-3) - 3(0+3) + 1(1+2) = -6 - 9 + 3 = -12$

1.5 MINOR OF AN ELEMENT OF |A|

Let
$$|A| = \begin{vmatrix} a_1 & b_1 & c_1 \\ a_2 & b_2 & c_2 \\ a_3 & b_3 & c_3 \end{vmatrix}$$

Then minor of an element of $|A|$ is a determinant obtained by omitting the row and the column in which the element is present.

$$\text{minor of } a_1 = \begin{vmatrix} b_2 & c_2 \\ b_3 & c_3 \end{vmatrix} \qquad \text{minor of } a_3 = \begin{vmatrix} b_1 & c_1 \\ b_2 & c_2 \end{vmatrix}$$

$$\text{minor of } b_2 = \begin{vmatrix} a_1 & c_1 \\ a_3 & c_3 \end{vmatrix} \qquad \text{minor of } c_3 = \begin{vmatrix} a_1 & b_1 \\ a_2 & b_2 \end{vmatrix}$$

In general, minor of an element a_{ij} is denoted by M_{ij}.

1.6 COFACTOR OF AN ELEMENT a_{ij} IN |A|

Cofactor of an element a_{ij} in $|A|$ is denoted by A_{ij}. It is a minor of a_{ij} associated with proper sign.

e.g.
$$A_{ij} = (-1)^{i+j} M_{ij}$$

$$|A| = \begin{vmatrix} a_{11} & a_{12} & a_{13} \\ a_{21} & a_{22} & a_{23} \\ a_{31} & a_{32} & a_{33} \end{vmatrix}$$

$$A_{11} = (-1)^{1+1} M_{11} = \begin{vmatrix} a_{22} & a_{23} \\ a_{32} & a_{33} \end{vmatrix}$$

$$A_{21} = (-1)^{2+1} \begin{vmatrix} a_{12} & a_{13} \\ a_{32} & a_{33} \end{vmatrix}$$

1.7 ADJOINT OF A MATRIX

Adjoint of a square matrix A is the transpose of the matrix formed by the cofactors of the elements of the given matrix A.

$$A = \begin{bmatrix} a_{11} & a_{12} & a_{13} \\ a_{21} & a_{22} & a_{23} \\ a_{31} & a_{32} & a_{33} \end{bmatrix}, \text{Adj } A = \begin{bmatrix} A_{11} & A_{21} & A_{31} \\ A_{12} & A_{22} & A_{32} \\ A_{13} & A_{23} & A_{33} \end{bmatrix}$$

e.g. $A = \begin{bmatrix} 1 & 2 & 3 \\ 0 & -1 & -3 \\ 4 & 5 & -4 \end{bmatrix}, A' = \begin{bmatrix} 1 & 0 & 4 \\ 2 & -1 & 5 \\ 3 & -3 & -4 \end{bmatrix}$

C.F. of 1 = 19   C.F. of 0 = 23   C.F. of 4 = –3
C.F. of 2 = – 12   C.F. of –1 = –16   C.F. of 5 = 3
C.F. of 3 = 4   C.F. of –3 = 3   C.F. of –4 = –1

$$\text{adj } A = \begin{bmatrix} 19 & 23 & -3 \\ -12 & -16 & 3 \\ 4 & 3 & -1 \end{bmatrix}$$

Note : For a square matrix A, if $|A| = 0$ then A is called a *singular matrix*.
If $|A| \neq 0$ then A is called a *non-singular matrix*.

1.8 INVERSE OF A

If A is a square matrix and $|A| \neq 0$ i.e. A is a non-singular matrix then

$$A^{-1} = \frac{1}{|A|} \text{ adj } A.$$

1.9 OPERATIONS OF MATRICES

1. **Equality of two matrices :** If two matrices A and B have same order and all the elements of A and B in the corresponding positions are equal then A = B.

e.g. $A = \begin{bmatrix} 1 & 2 \\ 3 & 4 \end{bmatrix}, B = \begin{bmatrix} 1 & 2 \\ 3 & 4 \end{bmatrix} \quad \therefore A = B$

2. **Multiplication of matrix by scalar :**

If $A = \begin{bmatrix} 1 & 2 & 3 \\ 3 & -1 & 2 \end{bmatrix}$ then $2A = \begin{bmatrix} 2 & 4 & 6 \\ 6 & -2 & 4 \end{bmatrix}$ and $(-1) A = \begin{bmatrix} -1 & -2 & -3 \\ -3 & 1 & -2 \end{bmatrix}$

3. **Sum of matrices :** If A and B have same order then we define A + B as a matrix obtained by addition of corresponding elements of A and B.

i.e. $A = \begin{bmatrix} 1 & 2 \\ 1 & 1 \end{bmatrix}, B = \begin{bmatrix} 2 & 3 \\ 4 & 5 \end{bmatrix} \quad \therefore A + B = \begin{bmatrix} 1+2 & 2+3 \\ 1+4 & 1+5 \end{bmatrix} = \begin{bmatrix} 3 & 5 \\ 5 & 6 \end{bmatrix}$

Similarly $\quad A - B = A + (-1) B = \begin{bmatrix} 1-2 & 2-3 \\ 1-4 & 1-5 \end{bmatrix} = \begin{bmatrix} -1 & -1 \\ -3 & -4 \end{bmatrix}$

Also
$$A + B + C = [A + B] + C; \quad A + B = B + A$$
$$A + (B + C) = (A + B) + C; \quad K(A + B) = KA + KB$$
$$(K_1 + K_2) A = K_1 A + K_2 A$$
$$A + Z = A = Z + A$$

where Z is a null matrix of the same order as A.

4. Multiplication of matrices : If *columns of A = rows of B,* then product AB exists and it is computed as

$$A = \begin{bmatrix} 1 & 2 & 3 \\ 2 & 3 & 4 \end{bmatrix}_{2 \times 3}, \quad B = \begin{bmatrix} 2 & 1 & 1 \\ -1 & 2 & 1 \\ 3 & 4 & 1 \end{bmatrix}_{3 \times 3}$$

$$AB = \begin{bmatrix} 1(2) + 2(-1) + 3(3) & 1(1) + 2(2) + 3(4) & 1(1) + 2(1) + 3(1) \\ 2(2) + 3(-1) + 4(3) & 2(1) + 3(2) + 4(4) & 2(1) + 3(1) + 4(1) \end{bmatrix} = \begin{bmatrix} 9 & 17 & 6 \\ 13 & 24 & 9 \end{bmatrix}_{2 \times 3}$$

Note :
1. In general, $AB \neq BA$.
2. $AB = 0$ does not imply $A = 0$ or $B = 0$.
   e.g. $A = \begin{bmatrix} 1 & 2 \\ 1 & 2 \end{bmatrix}, B = \begin{bmatrix} 2 & 6 \\ -1 & -3 \end{bmatrix}$. Here $AB = \begin{bmatrix} 0 & 0 \\ 0 & 0 \end{bmatrix}$ But $A \neq 0, B \neq 0$
3. If $AB = AC$ does not imply, $B = C$.
4. $A(BC) = (AB)C$
5. $A(B + C) = AB + AC, \quad (A + B) C = AC + BC$
6. $K(AB) = (KA) B = A (KB)$
7. $A^2 = AA, \quad A^3 = A^2 A$
   $A^m A^n = A^{m+n}$
   $(A^m)^n = A^{mn}$
8. $(A')' = A$
9. $(AB)' = B' A'$
10. $(A + B)' = A' + B'$
11. If A is a square matrix then it can be written as $A = \frac{1}{2} (A + A') + \frac{1}{2} (A - A')$.

Thus square matrix A can always be expressed as the sum of a symmetric and skew symmetric matrix.

For $\quad (A + A')' = A' + (A')' = A' + A = A + A'$
$\quad\quad\quad (A - A')' = A' - (A')' = A' - A = -(A - A')$

which shows that $A + A'$ is symmetric and $A - A'$ is skew symmetric.

12. $(AB)^{-1} = B^{-1} A^{-1}$
13. $(A^{-1})' = (A')^{-1}$
14. $|AB| = |A| \cdot |B|$.

1.10 ELEMENTARY TRANSFORMATIONS OF MATRIX

Definitions : The following three types of transformations, performed on any non-zero matrix A, are called elementary transformations :

1. The interchange of ith and j^{th} rows denoted by R_{ij}.

   The interchange of ith and j^{th} columns denoted by C_{ij}.

2. The multiplication of each element of ith row by a non-zero scalar k is denoted by kR_i.

   The multiplication of each element of ith column by a non-zero scalar k is denoted by kC_i.

3. Multiplication of every element of jth row by scalar k and adding to the corresponding element of ith row is denoted by $(R_i + kR_j)$.

Multiplication of every element of jth column by scalar k and adding to the corresponding element of ith column is denoted by $C_i + k\,C_j$.

1.11 THE RANK OF A MATRIX

The matrix is said to be of *rank r* if there is

1. At least one minor of the order r which is not equal to zero and
2. Every minor of the order (r + 1) is equal to zero.

   The rank of matrix A is the maximum order of its non-vanishing minor and it is denoted as $\rho(A) = r$.

If a matrix has a non-zero minor of order r, then $\rho(A) \geq r$.

If a matrix has all the minors of order (r + 1) as zeroes, then $\rho(A) \leq r$.

If A is an $m \times n$ matrix then $\rho(A) \leq$ minimum of m and n.

Elementary transformations of a matrix do not alter the rank and order of a matrix.

If matrix B is obtained from A by subjecting it to any elementary row or column transformations then we write A ~ B [A is equivalent to B]. B is called equivalent matrix. Note that elementary transformations do not alter the rank of a matrix, hence we use the sign of equivalence. Note that ranks of A and B are same.

1.12 TYPE I : FINDING THE RANK BY REDUCING THE MATRIX A TO ECHELON FORM

Echelon or Cannonical form of A matrix : Let a matrix A be of order $m \times n$ i.e. $A_{m \times n}$.

Then the cannonical or echelon form of 'A' is a matrix in which

1. One or more elements in each of the *first r rows are non-zero and the elements in the remaining rows are zeroes.*

2. In the first r rows, the first non-zero element in each row appears in a column to the right of the first non-zero element of the preceding row.

Matrix A must be reduced to the form such as $\begin{bmatrix} 1 & 2 & 3 & 4 & 5 \\ 0 & 1 & 2 & 3 & 4 \\ 0 & 0 & 1 & 2 & 3 \\ 0 & 0 & 0 & 0 & 0 \end{bmatrix}$

by performing only row transformations.

For finding the rank of a matrix, Echelon form is very useful as it shows the maximum order of non-vanishing minor and thus the rank is immediately obtained.

To determine the rank of matrix $A_{m \times n}$ reduce it to echelon form and if

m = total no. of rows in A and k = total no. of rows which contain all zero elements.

then $\rho(A) = m - k$. Also if k = 0 then $\rho(A) = m$.

Ex. 1 : *Find the rank of A, where* $A = \begin{bmatrix} 1 & 2 & -1 & 3 \\ 3 & 4 & 0 & -1 \\ -1 & 0 & -2 & 7 \end{bmatrix}$

Sol. : $A = \begin{bmatrix} 1 & 2 & -1 & 3 \\ 3 & 4 & 0 & -1 \\ -1 & 0 & -2 & 7 \end{bmatrix}$

Perform $R_2 - 3R_1$; $R_3 + R_1$ ~ $\begin{bmatrix} 1 & 2 & -1 & 3 \\ 0 & -2 & 3 & -10 \\ 0 & 2 & -3 & 10 \end{bmatrix}$

Perform $R_3 + R_2$ ~ $\begin{bmatrix} 1 & 2 & -1 & 3 \\ 0 & -2 & 3 & -10 \\ 0 & 0 & 0 & 0 \end{bmatrix}$

Here m = total no. of rows = 3
k = total no. of rows which contain all zero elements = 1.
∴ $\rho(A) = m - k = 3 - 1 = 2$ ∴ $\rho(A) = 2$

Ex. 2 : *Find the rank of* $A = \begin{bmatrix} 2 & 3 & -1 & -1 \\ 1 & -1 & -2 & -4 \\ 3 & 1 & 3 & -2 \\ 6 & 3 & 0 & -7 \end{bmatrix}$

Sol. : $A = \begin{bmatrix} 2 & 3 & -1 & -1 \\ 1 & -1 & -2 & -4 \\ 3 & 1 & 3 & -2 \\ 6 & 3 & 0 & -7 \end{bmatrix}$

Perform R_{12} ~ $\begin{bmatrix} 1 & -1 & -2 & -4 \\ 2 & 3 & -1 & -1 \\ 3 & 1 & 3 & -2 \\ 6 & 3 & 0 & -7 \end{bmatrix}$

Perform $R_2 - 2R_1$, $R_3 - 3R_1$, $R_4 - 6R_1$ ~ $\begin{bmatrix} 1 & -1 & -2 & -4 \\ 0 & 5 & 3 & 7 \\ 0 & 4 & 9 & 10 \\ 0 & 9 & 12 & 17 \end{bmatrix}$

Perform $R_2 - R_3$ ~ $\begin{bmatrix} 1 & -1 & -2 & -4 \\ 0 & 1 & -6 & -3 \\ 0 & 4 & 9 & 10 \\ 0 & 9 & 12 & 17 \end{bmatrix}$

Perform $R_3 - 4R_2$, $R_4 - 9R_2$ ~ $\begin{bmatrix} 1 & -1 & -2 & -4 \\ 0 & 1 & -6 & -3 \\ 0 & 0 & 33 & 22 \\ 0 & 0 & 66 & 44 \end{bmatrix}$

Perform $\frac{1}{11}R_3$, $\frac{1}{22}R_4$ ~ $\begin{bmatrix} 1 & -1 & -2 & -4 \\ 0 & 1 & -6 & -3 \\ 0 & 0 & 3 & 2 \\ 0 & 0 & 3 & 2 \end{bmatrix}$

Perform $R_4 - R_3$ ~ $\begin{bmatrix} 1 & -1 & -2 & -4 \\ 0 & 1 & -6 & -3 \\ 0 & 0 & 3 & 2 \\ 0 & 0 & 0 & 0 \end{bmatrix}$

Here $m = 4$, $k = 1$

$\therefore \quad \rho(A) = m - k = 4 - 1 = 3$ Hence $\rho(A) = 3$.

EXERCISE 1.1

Hint : (For the problems 1 to 10 use echelon form)

Find the rank of A

1. $\begin{bmatrix} 1 & 2 & -2 & 3 \\ 2 & 5 & -4 & 6 \\ -1 & -3 & 2 & -2 \\ 2 & 4 & -1 & 6 \end{bmatrix}$ **Ans.** $\rho(A) = 4$

2. $\begin{bmatrix} 3 & -2 & 0 & -1 \\ 0 & 2 & 2 & 7 \\ 1 & -2 & -3 & 2 \\ 0 & 1 & 2 & 1 \end{bmatrix}$ **Ans.** $\rho(A) = 4$

3. $\begin{bmatrix} 2 & -2 & 0 & 6 \\ 4 & 2 & 0 & 2 \\ 1 & -1 & 0 & 3 \\ 1 & -2 & 1 & 2 \end{bmatrix}$ **Ans.** $\rho(A) = 3$

4. $\begin{bmatrix} 3 & 4 & 1 & 1 \\ 2 & 4 & 3 & 6 \\ -1 & -2 & 6 & 4 \\ 1 & -1 & 2 & -3 \end{bmatrix}$ **Ans.** $\rho(A) = 4$

5. $\begin{bmatrix} 0 & 1 & -3 & -1 \\ 1 & 0 & 1 & 1 \\ 3 & 1 & 0 & 2 \\ 1 & 1 & -2 & 0 \end{bmatrix}$ **Ans.** $\rho(A) = 2$

6. $\begin{bmatrix} 1 & -1 & 2 & 3 \\ 4 & 1 & 0 & 2 \\ 0 & 3 & 1 & 4 \\ 0 & 1 & 0 & 2 \end{bmatrix}$ **Ans.** $\rho(A) = 4$

7. $\begin{bmatrix} 6 & 1 & 3 & 8 \\ 4 & 2 & 6 & -1 \\ 10 & 3 & 9 & 7 \\ 16 & 4 & 12 & 15 \end{bmatrix}$ **Ans.** $\rho(A) = 2$

8. $\begin{bmatrix} 1 & 2 & 3 & 4 \\ 2 & 1 & 4 & 3 \\ 3 & 0 & 5 & -10 \end{bmatrix}$ **Ans.** $\rho(A) = 3$

9. $\begin{bmatrix} 4 & 2 & -1 & 2 \\ 1 & -1 & 2 & 1 \\ 2 & 2 & -2 & 0 \end{bmatrix}$ **Ans.** $\rho(A) = 3$

10. $\begin{bmatrix} 2 & -2 & -2 & 0 & 2 \\ 3 & -1 & -1 & 4 & 1 \\ 0 & -1 & 0 & 1 & 2 \\ 1 & 1 & 3 & 2 & -2 \\ 2 & 2 & 4 & 6 & -3 \end{bmatrix}$

Ans. $\rho(A) = 4$.

1.13 TYPE II : FINDING THE RANK BY REDUCING THE MATRIX A TO THE NORMAL FORM

Normal form of matrix "A" :

Definition : By performing elementary transformations, any *non-zero* matrix A can be reduced to one of the following four forms, called the *normal form* of A.

(1) $[I_r]$ (2) $[I_r \quad 0]$ (3) $\begin{bmatrix} I_r \\ 0 \end{bmatrix}$ (4) $\begin{bmatrix} I_r & 0 \\ 0 & 0 \end{bmatrix}$.

where I_r is unit matrix or identity matrix and 0 denotes null matrix.

Note :

1. The number r so obtained is called the rank of A.
2. Rank of A is denoted by $\rho(A) = r$.
3. Elementary transformations do not alter the rank of a matrix.
4. Use both elementary row and column transformations.

Ex. 1 : *Reduce the following matrix to its normal form and hence find its rank, where*

$$A = \begin{bmatrix} 2 & 3 & -1 & -1 \\ 1 & -1 & -2 & -4 \\ 3 & 1 & 3 & -2 \\ 6 & 3 & 0 & -7 \end{bmatrix}$$

(Dec. 2007)

Sol. :

$$A = \begin{bmatrix} 2 & 3 & -1 & -1 \\ 1 & -1 & -2 & -4 \\ 3 & 1 & 3 & -2 \\ 6 & 3 & 0 & -7 \end{bmatrix}$$

By R_{12}

$$\sim \begin{bmatrix} 1 & -1 & -2 & -4 \\ 2 & 3 & -1 & -1 \\ 3 & 1 & 3 & -2 \\ 6 & 3 & 0 & -7 \end{bmatrix}$$

By $R_2 - 2R_1$, $R_3 - 3R_1$, $R_4 - 6R_1$

$$\sim \begin{bmatrix} 1 & -1 & -2 & -4 \\ 0 & 5 & 3 & 7 \\ 0 & 4 & 9 & 10 \\ 0 & 9 & 12 & 17 \end{bmatrix}$$

By $C_2 + C_1$, $C_3 + 2C_1$, $C_4 + 4C_1$

$$\sim \begin{bmatrix} 1 & 0 & 0 & 0 \\ 0 & 5 & 3 & 7 \\ 0 & 4 & 9 & 10 \\ 0 & 9 & 12 & 17 \end{bmatrix}$$

By $R_2 - R_3$

$$\sim \begin{bmatrix} 1 & 0 & 0 & 0 \\ 0 & 1 & -6 & -3 \\ 0 & 4 & 9 & 10 \\ 0 & 9 & 12 & 17 \end{bmatrix}$$

By $R_3 - 4R_2$, $R_4 - 9R_2$

$$\sim \begin{bmatrix} 1 & 0 & 0 & 0 \\ 0 & 1 & -6 & -3 \\ 0 & 0 & 33 & 22 \\ 0 & 0 & 66 & 44 \end{bmatrix}$$

By $C_3 + 6C_2$, $C_4 + 3C_2$

$$\sim \begin{bmatrix} 1 & 0 & 0 & 0 \\ 0 & 1 & 0 & 0 \\ 0 & 0 & 33 & 22 \\ 0 & 0 & 66 & 44 \end{bmatrix}$$

By $\frac{1}{33} C_3$, $\frac{1}{22} C_4$

$$\sim \begin{bmatrix} 1 & 0 & 0 & 0 \\ 0 & 1 & 0 & 0 \\ 0 & 0 & 1 & 1 \\ 0 & 0 & 2 & 2 \end{bmatrix}$$

By $R_4 - 2R_3$

$$\sim \begin{bmatrix} 1 & 0 & 0 & 0 \\ 0 & 1 & 0 & 0 \\ 0 & 0 & 1 & 1 \\ 0 & 0 & 0 & 0 \end{bmatrix}$$

By $C_4 - C_3$

$$\sim \left[\begin{array}{ccc|c} 1 & 0 & 0 & 0 \\ 0 & 1 & 0 & 0 \\ 0 & 0 & 1 & 0 \\ \hline 0 & 0 & 0 & 0 \end{array}\right]$$

$A = \begin{bmatrix} I_3 & 0 \\ 0 & 0 \end{bmatrix}$ which is the required Normal Form of A. Hence $\rho(A) = 3$.

Ex. 2 : *Reduce the following matrix to the normal form and find the rank.* **(Dec. 96)**

$$A = \begin{bmatrix} 2 & -4 & 3 & 1 & 0 \\ 1 & -2 & 1 & -4 & 2 \\ 0 & 1 & -1 & 3 & 1 \\ 4 & -7 & 4 & -4 & 5 \end{bmatrix}$$

Sol. :
$$A = \begin{bmatrix} 2 & -4 & 3 & 1 & 0 \\ 1 & -2 & 1 & -4 & 2 \\ 0 & 1 & -1 & 3 & 1 \\ 4 & -7 & 4 & -4 & 5 \end{bmatrix}$$

By R_{12}

$$\sim \begin{bmatrix} 1 & -2 & 1 & -4 & 2 \\ 2 & -4 & 3 & 1 & 0 \\ 0 & 1 & -1 & 3 & 1 \\ 4 & -7 & 4 & -4 & 5 \end{bmatrix}$$

By $R_2 - 2R_1$, $R_4 - 4R_1$

$$\sim \begin{bmatrix} 1 & -2 & 1 & -4 & 2 \\ 0 & 0 & 1 & 9 & -4 \\ 0 & 1 & -1 & 3 & 1 \\ 0 & 1 & 0 & 12 & -3 \end{bmatrix}$$

By $C_2 + 2C_1$, $C_3 - C_1$, $C_4 + 4C_1$, $C_5 - 2C_1$

$$\sim \begin{bmatrix} 1 & 0 & 0 & 0 & 0 \\ 0 & 0 & 1 & 9 & -4 \\ 0 & 1 & -1 & 3 & 1 \\ 0 & 1 & 0 & 12 & -3 \end{bmatrix}$$

By R_{23}

$$\sim \begin{bmatrix} 1 & 0 & 0 & 0 & 0 \\ 0 & 1 & -1 & 3 & 1 \\ 0 & 0 & 1 & 9 & -4 \\ 0 & 1 & 0 & 12 & -3 \end{bmatrix}$$

By $R_4 - R_2$

$$\sim \begin{bmatrix} 1 & 0 & 0 & 0 & 0 \\ 0 & 1 & -1 & 3 & 1 \\ 0 & 0 & 1 & 9 & -4 \\ 0 & 0 & 1 & 9 & -4 \end{bmatrix}$$

By $C_3 + C_2,\ C_4 - 3C_2,\ C_5 - C_2$

$$\sim \begin{bmatrix} 1 & 0 & 0 & 0 & 0 \\ 0 & 1 & 0 & 0 & 0 \\ 0 & 0 & 1 & 9 & -4 \\ 0 & 0 & 1 & 9 & -4 \end{bmatrix}$$

By $R_4 - R_3$

$$\sim \begin{bmatrix} 1 & 0 & 0 & 0 & 0 \\ 0 & 1 & 0 & 0 & 0 \\ 0 & 0 & 1 & 9 & -4 \\ 0 & 0 & 0 & 0 & 0 \end{bmatrix}$$

By $C_4 - 9C_3,\ C_5 + 4C_3$

$$\sim \left[\begin{array}{ccc|cc} 1 & 0 & 0 & 0 & 0 \\ 0 & 1 & 0 & 0 & 0 \\ 0 & 0 & 1 & 0 & 0 \\ \hline 0 & 0 & 0 & 0 & 0 \end{array} \right]$$

$$\sim \begin{bmatrix} I_3 & 0 \\ 0 & 0 \end{bmatrix} \text{ which is the required normal form of A.}$$

$\therefore \quad \rho(A) = 3$

Ex. 3 : *Reduce the following matrix to its normal form and hence find its rank where*

$$A = \begin{bmatrix} 1 & 1 & 1 \\ 2 & -3 & 4 \\ 3 & -2 & 3 \end{bmatrix}$$

Sol. :

$$A = \begin{bmatrix} 1 & 1 & 1 \\ 2 & -3 & 4 \\ 3 & -2 & 3 \end{bmatrix}$$

By $R_2 - 2R_1$, $R_3 - 3R_1$
$$\sim \begin{bmatrix} 1 & 1 & 1 \\ 0 & -5 & 2 \\ 0 & -5 & 0 \end{bmatrix}$$

By $C_2 - C_1$, $C_3 - C_1$
$$\sim \begin{bmatrix} 1 & 0 & 0 \\ 0 & -5 & 2 \\ 0 & -5 & 0 \end{bmatrix}$$

By $\frac{-1}{5}(C_2)$, $\frac{1}{2}(C_3)$
$$\sim \begin{bmatrix} 1 & 0 & 0 \\ 0 & 1 & 1 \\ 0 & 1 & 0 \end{bmatrix}$$

By $R_3 - R_2$
$$\sim \begin{bmatrix} 1 & 0 & 0 \\ 0 & 1 & 1 \\ 0 & 0 & -1 \end{bmatrix}$$

By $C_3 - C_2$
$$\sim \begin{bmatrix} 1 & 0 & 0 \\ 0 & 1 & 0 \\ 0 & 0 & -1 \end{bmatrix}$$

By $-1(R_3)$
$$\sim \begin{bmatrix} 1 & 0 & 0 \\ 0 & 1 & 0 \\ 0 & 0 & 1 \end{bmatrix}$$

$$\sim [I_3]$$

$$\therefore \rho(A) = 3$$

Ex. 4 : *Reduce the following matrix to its normal form and hence find its rank where*

$$A = \begin{bmatrix} 1 & 1 & -1 & 1 \\ 1 & -1 & 2 & -1 \\ 3 & 1 & 0 & 1 \end{bmatrix} \quad \text{(Dec. 2006)}$$

Sol. :
$$A = \begin{bmatrix} 1 & 1 & -1 & 1 \\ 1 & -1 & 2 & -1 \\ 3 & 1 & 0 & 1 \end{bmatrix}$$

By $R_2 - R_1$, $R_3 - 3R_1$
$$\sim \begin{bmatrix} 1 & 1 & -1 & 1 \\ 0 & -2 & 3 & -2 \\ 0 & -2 & 3 & -2 \end{bmatrix}$$

By $R_3 - R_2$

$$\sim \begin{bmatrix} 1 & 1 & -1 & 1 \\ 0 & -2 & 3 & -2 \\ 0 & 0 & 0 & 0 \end{bmatrix}$$

By $C_2 - C_1,\ C_3 + C_1,\ C_4 - C_1$

$$\sim \begin{bmatrix} 1 & 0 & 0 & 0 \\ 0 & -2 & 3 & -2 \\ 0 & 0 & 0 & 0 \end{bmatrix}$$

By $\dfrac{-1}{2} C_2,\ \dfrac{1}{3} C_3,\ \dfrac{-1}{2} C_4$

$$\sim \begin{bmatrix} 1 & 0 & 0 & 0 \\ 0 & 1 & 1 & 1 \\ 0 & 0 & 0 & 0 \end{bmatrix}$$

By $C_3 - C_2,\ C_4 - C_2$

$$\sim \left[\begin{array}{cc|cc} 1 & 0 & 0 & 0 \\ 0 & 1 & 0 & 0 \\ \hline 0 & 0 & 0 & 0 \end{array}\right]$$

$$\sim \begin{bmatrix} I_2 & 0 \\ 0 & 0 \end{bmatrix}$$

Hence $\rho(A) = 2$

Ex. 5 : *Reduce to normal form the matrix A and find its rank.*

$$A = \begin{bmatrix} 3 & 2 & 5 & 7 & 12 \\ 1 & 1 & 2 & 3 & 5 \\ 3 & 3 & 6 & 9 & 15 \end{bmatrix} \quad \textbf{(Dec. 2005)}$$

Sol. :

$$A = \begin{bmatrix} 3 & 2 & 5 & 7 & 12 \\ 1 & 1 & 2 & 3 & 5 \\ 3 & 3 & 6 & 9 & 15 \end{bmatrix}$$

By R_{12}

$$\sim \begin{bmatrix} 1 & 1 & 2 & 3 & 5 \\ 3 & 2 & 5 & 7 & 12 \\ 3 & 3 & 6 & 9 & 15 \end{bmatrix}$$

By $R_2 - 3R_1,\ R_3 - 3R_1$

$$\sim \begin{bmatrix} 1 & 1 & 2 & 3 & 5 \\ 0 & -1 & -1 & -2 & -3 \\ 0 & 0 & 0 & 0 & 0 \end{bmatrix}$$

By $C_2 - C_1,\ C_3 - 2C_1,\ C_4 - 3C_1,\ C_5 - 5C_1$

$$\sim \begin{bmatrix} 1 & 0 & 0 & 0 & 0 \\ 0 & -1 & -1 & -2 & -3 \\ 0 & 0 & 0 & 0 & 0 \end{bmatrix}$$

Engineering Mathematics - I — Matrices

By – (R_2)

$$\sim \begin{bmatrix} 1 & 0 & 0 & 0 & 0 \\ 0 & 1 & 1 & 2 & 3 \\ 0 & 0 & 0 & 0 & 0 \end{bmatrix}$$

By $C_3 - C_2$, $C_4 - 2C_2$, $C_5 - 3C_2$

$$\sim \left[\begin{array}{cc|ccc} 1 & 0 & 0 & 0 & 0 \\ 0 & 1 & 0 & 0 & 0 \\ \hline 0 & 0 & 0 & 0 & 0 \end{array} \right]$$

$$\sim \begin{bmatrix} I_2 & : & 0 \\ 0 & : & 0 \end{bmatrix}$$

Hence $\rho(A) = 2$

EXERCISE 1.2

Reduce the following matrix to its normal form and hence find its rank.

(1) $\begin{bmatrix} 1 & 2 & -2 & 3 \\ 2 & 5 & -4 & 6 \\ -1 & -3 & 2 & -2 \\ 2 & 4 & -1 & 6 \end{bmatrix}$

Ans. $\rho(A) = 4$ **(Dec. 94, 95)**

(2) $\begin{bmatrix} 3 & -2 & 0 & -1 \\ 0 & 2 & 2 & 7 \\ 1 & -2 & -3 & 2 \\ 0 & 1 & 2 & 1 \end{bmatrix}$

Ans. $\rho(A) = 4$ **(Dec. 93)**

(3) $\begin{bmatrix} 2 & 3 & -1 & -1 \\ 1 & -1 & -2 & -4 \\ 3 & 1 & 3 & -2 \\ 6 & 3 & 0 & -7 \end{bmatrix}$

Ans. $\rho(A) = 3$ **(May 93)**

(4) $\begin{bmatrix} 3 & 4 & 1 & 1 \\ 2 & 4 & 3 & 6 \\ -1 & -2 & 6 & 4 \\ 1 & -1 & 2 & -3 \end{bmatrix}$

Ans. $\rho(A) = 4$ **(Dec. 91, 92)**

(5) $\begin{bmatrix} 1 & 2 & 1 & 0 \\ -2 & 4 & 3 & 0 \\ 1 & 0 & 2 & -8 \end{bmatrix}$

Ans. $\rho(A) = 3$

(6) $\begin{bmatrix} 1 & 2 & -1 & 3 \\ 3 & 4 & 0 & -1 \\ -1 & 0 & -2 & 7 \end{bmatrix}$

Ans. $\rho(A) = 2$

(7) $\begin{bmatrix} 3 & 2 & -1 & 5 \\ 5 & 1 & 4 & -2 \\ 1 & -4 & 11 & -19 \end{bmatrix}$

Ans. $\rho(A) = 2$

(8) $\begin{bmatrix} 1 & 3 & 6 & -1 \\ 1 & 4 & 5 & 1 \\ 1 & 5 & 4 & 3 \end{bmatrix}$

Ans. $\rho(A) = 2$

(9) $\begin{bmatrix} 1 & 2 & 1 & 0 \\ 3 & 2 & 1 & 2 \\ 2 & -1 & 2 & 5 \\ 5 & 6 & 3 & 2 \\ 1 & 3 & -1 & -3 \end{bmatrix}$

Ans. $\rho(A) = 3$ **(Dec. 2003)**

(10) $\begin{bmatrix} 6 & 1 & 3 & 8 \\ 4 & 2 & 6 & -1 \\ 10 & 3 & 9 & 7 \\ 16 & 4 & 12 & 15 \end{bmatrix}$

Ans. $\rho(A) = 2$

(11) $\begin{bmatrix} 3 & 1 & 2 & 1 \\ 2 & 0 & 3 & 2 \\ 1 & 2 & 3 & 4 \\ 3 & 1 & 4 & 1 \\ 2 & 4 & 6 & 8 \end{bmatrix}$

Ans. $\rho(A) = 4$ **(June 92)**

(12) $\begin{bmatrix} 1 & -1 & 2 & 3 \\ 4 & 1 & 0 & 2 \\ 0 & 3 & 1 & 4 \\ 0 & 1 & 0 & 2 \end{bmatrix}$

Ans. $\rho(A) = 4$

(13) $\begin{bmatrix} 1 & 2 & 3 & 0 \\ 2 & 4 & 3 & 2 \\ 3 & 2 & 1 & 3 \\ 6 & 8 & 7 & 5 \end{bmatrix}$

Ans. $\rho(A) = 3$

(14) $\begin{bmatrix} 0 & 1 & 2 & -2 \\ 4 & 0 & 2 & 6 \\ 2 & 1 & 3 & 1 \end{bmatrix}$

Ans. $\rho(A) = 2$ **(June 90)**

(15) $\begin{bmatrix} 1 & 2 & 3 & -2 \\ 2 & -2 & 1 & 3 \\ 3 & 0 & 4 & 1 \end{bmatrix}$

Ans. $\rho(A) = 2$

(16) $\begin{bmatrix} 1 & 2 & 3 & 4 \\ 2 & 1 & 4 & 3 \\ 3 & 0 & 5 & -10 \end{bmatrix}$

Ans. $\rho(A) = 3$

(17) $\begin{bmatrix} 1 & 2 & -1 & 2 \\ -2 & -5 & 3 & 0 \\ 1 & 0 & 1 & 10 \end{bmatrix}$

Ans. $\rho(A) = 2$ **(May 2010)**

(18) $\begin{bmatrix} 1 & 1 & 1 & -1 \\ 1 & 2 & 3 & 4 \\ 3 & 4 & 5 & 2 \end{bmatrix}$

Ans. $\rho(A) = 2$

(19) $\begin{bmatrix} 1 & 2 & 3 \\ 3 & 1 & 2 \end{bmatrix}$

Ans. $\rho(A) = 2$

(20) $\begin{bmatrix} 2 & 1 & -3 & -6 \\ 3 & -3 & 1 & 2 \\ 1 & 1 & 1 & 2 \end{bmatrix}$

Ans. $\rho(A) = 3$ **(Dec. 91)**

(21) $\begin{bmatrix} 2 & -2 & 0 & 6 \\ 4 & 2 & 0 & 2 \\ 1 & -1 & 0 & 3 \\ 1 & -2 & 1 & 2 \end{bmatrix}$

Ans. $\rho(A) = 3$

(22) $\begin{bmatrix} 2 & 3 & 4 & 5 \\ 3 & 4 & 5 & 6 \\ 4 & 5 & 6 & 7 \\ 9 & 10 & 11 & 12 \end{bmatrix}$

Ans. $\rho(A) = 2$ **(May 2008)**

1.14 TYPE III : FINDING NON-SINGULAR MATRICES P AND Q SUCH THAT PAQ IS IN NORMAL FORM

Ex. 1 : *Find non-singular matrices P and Q such that* $A = \begin{bmatrix} 1 & 2 & 3 & 4 \\ 2 & 1 & 4 & 3 \\ 3 & 0 & 5 & -10 \end{bmatrix}$

is reduced to normal form. Also find the rank of A.

Sol. : Total number of rows = 3. $\therefore$ Consider unit matrix I_3
Total number of columns = 4 $\therefore$ Consider unit matrix I_4.
$\therefore$ Write
$$A_{3 \times 4} = I_3 \, A \, I_4$$
$$A = I_3 \, A \, I_4$$

$$\begin{bmatrix} 1 & 2 & 3 & 4 \\ 2 & 1 & 4 & 3 \\ 3 & 0 & 5 & -10 \end{bmatrix} = \begin{bmatrix} 1 & 0 & 0 \\ 0 & 1 & 0 \\ 0 & 0 & 1 \end{bmatrix} A \begin{bmatrix} 1 & 0 & 0 & 0 \\ 0 & 1 & 0 & 0 \\ 0 & 0 & 1 & 0 \\ 0 & 0 & 0 & 1 \end{bmatrix}$$

Our aim is to reduce A to normal form by using elementary transformations.

Note 1 : Perform row transformations only on left hand side matrix A and on I_3 keep I_4 unaltered.

Note 2 : If we want to perform column transformations then perform it on left hand side matrix A and on I_4 keep I_3 unaltered.

By $R_2 - 2R_1$, $R_3 - 3R_1$
$$\begin{bmatrix} 1 & 2 & 3 & 4 \\ 0 & -3 & -2 & -5 \\ 0 & -6 & -4 & -22 \end{bmatrix} = \begin{bmatrix} 1 & 0 & 0 \\ -2 & 1 & 0 \\ -3 & 0 & 1 \end{bmatrix} A \begin{bmatrix} 1 & 0 & 0 & 0 \\ 0 & 1 & 0 & 0 \\ 0 & 0 & 1 & 0 \\ 0 & 0 & 0 & 1 \end{bmatrix}$$

By $C_2 - 2C_1$, $C_3 - 3C_1$, $C_4 - 4C_1$
$$\begin{bmatrix} 1 & 0 & 0 & 0 \\ 0 & -3 & -2 & -5 \\ 0 & -6 & -4 & -22 \end{bmatrix} = \begin{bmatrix} 1 & 0 & 0 \\ -2 & 1 & 0 \\ -3 & 0 & 1 \end{bmatrix} A \begin{bmatrix} 1 & -2 & -3 & -4 \\ 0 & 1 & 0 & 0 \\ 0 & 0 & 1 & 0 \\ 0 & 0 & 0 & 1 \end{bmatrix}$$

By $R_3 - 2R_2$
$$\begin{bmatrix} 1 & 0 & 0 & 0 \\ 0 & -3 & -2 & -5 \\ 0 & 0 & 0 & -12 \end{bmatrix} = \begin{bmatrix} 1 & 0 & 0 \\ -2 & 1 & 0 \\ 1 & -2 & 1 \end{bmatrix} A \begin{bmatrix} 1 & -2 & -3 & -4 \\ 0 & 1 & 0 & 0 \\ 0 & 0 & 1 & 0 \\ 0 & 0 & 0 & 1 \end{bmatrix}$$

By $-R_2$, $-R_3$
$$\begin{bmatrix} 1 & 0 & 0 & 0 \\ 0 & 3 & 2 & 5 \\ 0 & 0 & 0 & 12 \end{bmatrix} = \begin{bmatrix} 1 & 0 & 0 \\ 2 & -1 & 0 \\ -1 & 2 & -1 \end{bmatrix} A \begin{bmatrix} 1 & -2 & -3 & -4 \\ 0 & 1 & 0 & 0 \\ 0 & 0 & 1 & 0 \\ 0 & 0 & 0 & 1 \end{bmatrix}$$

By $C_2 - C_3$

$$\begin{bmatrix} 1 & 0 & 0 & 0 \\ 0 & 1 & 2 & 5 \\ 0 & 0 & 0 & 12 \end{bmatrix} = \begin{bmatrix} 1 & 0 & 0 \\ 2 & -1 & 0 \\ -1 & 2 & -1 \end{bmatrix} A \begin{bmatrix} 1 & 1 & -3 & -4 \\ 0 & 1 & 0 & 0 \\ 0 & -1 & 1 & 0 \\ 0 & 0 & 0 & 1 \end{bmatrix}$$

By $C_3 - 2C_2, C_4 - 5C_2$

$$\begin{bmatrix} 1 & 0 & 0 & 0 \\ 0 & 1 & 0 & 0 \\ 0 & 0 & 0 & 12 \end{bmatrix} = \begin{bmatrix} 1 & 0 & 0 \\ 2 & -1 & 0 \\ -1 & 2 & -1 \end{bmatrix} A \begin{bmatrix} 1 & 1 & -5 & -9 \\ 0 & 1 & -2 & -5 \\ 0 & -1 & 3 & 5 \\ 0 & 0 & 0 & 1 \end{bmatrix}$$

By $\frac{1}{12} R_3$

$$\begin{bmatrix} 1 & 0 & 0 & 0 \\ 0 & 1 & 0 & 0 \\ 0 & 0 & 0 & 1 \end{bmatrix} = \begin{bmatrix} 1 & 0 & 0 \\ 2 & -1 & 0 \\ \frac{-1}{12} & \frac{1}{6} & \frac{-1}{12} \end{bmatrix} A \begin{bmatrix} 1 & 1 & -5 & -9 \\ 0 & 1 & -2 & -5 \\ 0 & -1 & 3 & 5 \\ 0 & 0 & 0 & 1 \end{bmatrix}$$

By C_{34}

$$\begin{bmatrix} 1 & 0 & 0 & : & 0 \\ 0 & 1 & 0 & : & 0 \\ 0 & 0 & 1 & : & 0 \end{bmatrix} = \begin{bmatrix} 1 & 0 & 0 \\ 2 & -1 & 0 \\ \frac{-1}{12} & \frac{1}{6} & \frac{-1}{12} \end{bmatrix} A \begin{bmatrix} 1 & 1 & -9 & -5 \\ 0 & 1 & -5 & -2 \\ 0 & -1 & 5 & 3 \\ 0 & 0 & 1 & 0 \end{bmatrix}$$

$$[I_3 : 0] = PAQ$$

Here PAQ is in normal form. $\rho(A) = 3$

$$P = \begin{bmatrix} 1 & 0 & 0 \\ 2 & -1 & 0 \\ \frac{-1}{12} & \frac{1}{6} & \frac{-1}{12} \end{bmatrix}, \quad Q = \begin{bmatrix} 1 & 1 & -9 & -5 \\ 0 & 1 & -5 & -2 \\ 0 & -1 & 5 & 3 \\ 0 & 0 & 1 & 0 \end{bmatrix}$$

Here P and Q are non-singular matrices.

Note : P and Q are not unique.

Check :

$$PA = \begin{bmatrix} 1 & 0 & 0 \\ 2 & -1 & 0 \\ \frac{-1}{12} & \frac{1}{6} & \frac{-1}{12} \end{bmatrix} \begin{bmatrix} 1 & 2 & 3 & 4 \\ 2 & 1 & 4 & 3 \\ 3 & 0 & 5 & -10 \end{bmatrix} = \begin{bmatrix} 1 & 2 & 3 & 4 \\ 0 & 3 & 2 & 5 \\ 0 & 0 & 0 & 1 \end{bmatrix}$$

$$PAQ = (PA)(Q)$$

$$= \begin{bmatrix} 1 & 2 & 3 & 4 \\ 0 & 3 & 2 & 5 \\ 0 & 0 & 0 & 1 \end{bmatrix} \begin{bmatrix} 1 & 1 & -9 & -5 \\ 0 & 1 & -5 & -2 \\ 0 & -1 & 5 & 3 \\ 0 & 0 & 1 & 0 \end{bmatrix} = \begin{bmatrix} 1 & 0 & 0 & : & 0 \\ 0 & 1 & 0 & : & 0 \\ 0 & 0 & 1 & : & 0 \end{bmatrix}$$

$$= [I_3 : 0]$$

$\therefore \quad PAQ = I$

Ex. 2 : *For the matrix A, find non-singular matrices P and Q, such that, PAQ is in the normal form.* $A = \begin{bmatrix} 2 & 1 & -3 & -6 \\ 3 & -3 & 1 & 2 \\ 1 & 1 & 1 & 2 \end{bmatrix}$. **(May 2009)**

Sol. : Part 1 : Order of $A = 3 \times 4$.

Total number of rows in $A = 3$. $\therefore$ Consider unit matrix I_3.

Total number of columns in $A = 4$ $\therefore$ Consider unit matrix I_4.

$$\text{Write } A_{3 \times 4} = I_3 A I_4$$

$$\begin{bmatrix} 2 & 1 & -3 & -6 \\ 3 & -3 & 1 & 2 \\ 1 & 1 & 1 & 2 \end{bmatrix} = \begin{bmatrix} 1 & 0 & 0 \\ 0 & 1 & 0 \\ 0 & 0 & 1 \end{bmatrix} A \begin{bmatrix} 1 & 0 & 0 & 0 \\ 0 & 1 & 0 & 0 \\ 0 & 0 & 1 & 0 \\ 0 & 0 & 0 & 1 \end{bmatrix}$$

By R_{13}

$$\begin{bmatrix} 1 & 1 & 1 & 2 \\ 3 & -3 & 1 & 2 \\ 2 & 1 & -3 & -6 \end{bmatrix} = \begin{bmatrix} 0 & 0 & 1 \\ 0 & 1 & 0 \\ 1 & 0 & 0 \end{bmatrix} A \begin{bmatrix} 1 & 0 & 0 & 0 \\ 0 & 1 & 0 & 0 \\ 0 & 0 & 1 & 0 \\ 0 & 0 & 0 & 1 \end{bmatrix}$$

By $R_2 - 3R_1, R_3 - 2R_1$

$$\begin{bmatrix} 1 & 1 & 1 & 2 \\ 0 & -6 & -2 & -4 \\ 0 & -1 & -5 & -10 \end{bmatrix} = \begin{bmatrix} 0 & 0 & 1 \\ 0 & 1 & -3 \\ 1 & 0 & -2 \end{bmatrix} A \begin{bmatrix} 1 & 0 & 0 & 0 \\ 0 & 1 & 0 & 0 \\ 0 & 0 & 1 & 0 \\ 0 & 0 & 0 & 1 \end{bmatrix}$$

By $C_2 - C_1, C_3 - C_1, C_4 - 2C_1$

$$\begin{bmatrix} 1 & 0 & 0 & 0 \\ 0 & -6 & -2 & -4 \\ 0 & -1 & -5 & -10 \end{bmatrix} = \begin{bmatrix} 0 & 0 & 1 \\ 0 & 1 & -3 \\ 1 & 0 & -2 \end{bmatrix} A \begin{bmatrix} 1 & -1 & -1 & -2 \\ 0 & 1 & 0 & 0 \\ 0 & 0 & 1 & 0 \\ 0 & 0 & 0 & 1 \end{bmatrix}$$

By $-R_2, -R_3$ and then followed by R_{23}

$$\begin{bmatrix} 1 & 0 & 0 & 0 \\ 0 & 1 & 5 & 10 \\ 0 & 6 & 2 & 4 \end{bmatrix} = \begin{bmatrix} 0 & 0 & 1 \\ -1 & 0 & 2 \\ 0 & -1 & 3 \end{bmatrix} A \begin{bmatrix} 1 & -1 & -1 & -2 \\ 0 & 1 & 0 & 0 \\ 0 & 0 & 1 & 0 \\ 0 & 0 & 0 & 1 \end{bmatrix}$$

By $R_3 - 6R_2$

$$\begin{bmatrix} 1 & 0 & 0 & 0 \\ 0 & 1 & 5 & 10 \\ 0 & 0 & -28 & -56 \end{bmatrix} = \begin{bmatrix} 0 & 0 & 1 \\ -1 & 0 & 2 \\ 6 & -1 & -9 \end{bmatrix} A \begin{bmatrix} 1 & -1 & -1 & -2 \\ 0 & 1 & 0 & 0 \\ 0 & 0 & 1 & 0 \\ 0 & 0 & 0 & 1 \end{bmatrix}$$

By $C_3 - 5C_2$, $C_4 - 10C_2$ $\begin{bmatrix} 1 & 0 & 0 & 0 \\ 0 & 1 & 0 & 0 \\ 0 & 0 & -28 & -56 \end{bmatrix} = \begin{bmatrix} 0 & 0 & 1 \\ -1 & 0 & 2 \\ 6 & -1 & -9 \end{bmatrix} A \begin{bmatrix} 1 & -1 & 4 & 8 \\ 0 & 1 & -5 & -10 \\ 0 & 0 & 1 & 0 \\ 0 & 0 & 0 & 1 \end{bmatrix}$

By $-\dfrac{1}{28} R_3$ $\begin{bmatrix} 1 & 0 & 0 & 0 \\ 0 & 1 & 0 & 0 \\ 0 & 0 & 1 & 2 \end{bmatrix} = \begin{bmatrix} 0 & 0 & 1 \\ -1 & 0 & 2 \\ \dfrac{-6}{28} & \dfrac{1}{28} & \dfrac{9}{28} \end{bmatrix} A \begin{bmatrix} 1 & -1 & 4 & 8 \\ 0 & 1 & -5 & -10 \\ 0 & 0 & 1 & 0 \\ 0 & 0 & 0 & 1 \end{bmatrix}$

By $C_4 - 2C_3$ $\begin{bmatrix} 1 & 0 & 0 & 0 \\ 0 & 1 & 0 & 0 \\ 0 & 0 & 1 & 0 \end{bmatrix} = \begin{bmatrix} 0 & 0 & 1 \\ -1 & 0 & 2 \\ \dfrac{-6}{28} & \dfrac{1}{28} & \dfrac{9}{28} \end{bmatrix} A \begin{bmatrix} 1 & -1 & 4 & 0 \\ 0 & 1 & -5 & 0 \\ 0 & 0 & 1 & -2 \\ 0 & 0 & 0 & 1 \end{bmatrix}$

$[\, I_3 \;:\; 0 \,] \;=\; PAQ$

PAQ is in normal form. P, Q are non-singular matrices.

$\rho(A) \;=\; 3$

EXERCISE 1.3

Find non-singular matrices P and Q such that PAQ is in normal form. Hence find the rank of A where,

(1) $A = \begin{bmatrix} 2 & 3 & 1 & 4 \\ 1 & 2 & 2 & 3 \\ 0 & -1 & -3 & -2 \end{bmatrix}$

Hint: $A_{3 \times 4} = I_3 A I_4$ Ans. $\rho(A) = 2$

(2) $A = \begin{bmatrix} 3 & 2 & -1 & 5 \\ 5 & 1 & 4 & -2 \\ 1 & -4 & 11 & -19 \end{bmatrix}$

Ans. $\rho(A) = 2$

(3) $A = \begin{bmatrix} 1 & 2 & 3 & -2 \\ 2 & -2 & 1 & 3 \\ 3 & 0 & 4 & 1 \end{bmatrix}$

Hint: $A_{3 \times 4} = I_3 A I_4$ Ans. $\rho(A) = 2$

(4) $A = \begin{bmatrix} 1 & 2 & 0 & -1 \\ 3 & 4 & 1 & 2 \\ -2 & 3 & -2 & 5 \end{bmatrix}$

Ans. $\rho(A) = 3$

(5) $A = \begin{bmatrix} 1 & 2 & 3 \\ 3 & 1 & 2 \end{bmatrix}$

Hint: $A_{2 \times 3} = I_2 A I_3$ Ans. $\rho(A) = 2$

(6) $A = \begin{bmatrix} 1 & 3 & 6 & -1 \\ 1 & 4 & 5 & 1 \\ 1 & 5 & 4 & 3 \end{bmatrix}$

Ans. $\rho(A) = 2$

(7) $A = \begin{bmatrix} 4 & 2 & -1 & 2 \\ 1 & -1 & 2 & 1 \\ 2 & 2 & -2 & 0 \end{bmatrix}$ (8) $A = \begin{bmatrix} 1 & 2 & 1 & 0 \\ -2 & 4 & 3 & 0 \\ 1 & 0 & 2 & -8 \end{bmatrix}$

Hint : $A_{3 \times 4} = I_3 A I_4$ **Ans.** $\rho(A) = 3$ **Ans.** $\rho(A) = 3$ **(Dec. 2004)**

(9) $A = \begin{bmatrix} 0 & 1 & 2 & -2 \\ 4 & 0 & 2 & 6 \\ 2 & 1 & 3 & 1 \end{bmatrix}$ (10) $A = \begin{bmatrix} 1 & 2 & -1 & 3 \\ 3 & 4 & 0 & -1 \\ -1 & 0 & -2 & 7 \end{bmatrix}$

Hint : $A_{3 \times 4} = I_3 A I_4$ **Ans.** $\rho(A) = 2$ **Ans.** $\rho(A) = 2$

1.15 COMPUTATION OF INVERSE BY ADJOINT METHOD

Adjoint method.

If   (1) A is a square matrix.

(2) $|A| \neq 0$ then there exists A^{-1} and it is given by

$$A^{-1} = \frac{1}{|A|} \text{ adj. A.}$$

Ex. 1 : *Find A^{-1} by using adjoint method for* $A = \begin{bmatrix} 1 & 1 & 1 \\ 1 & 2 & 3 \\ 1 & 4 & 9 \end{bmatrix}$.

Sol. : $|A| = 1(18-12) - 1(9-3) + 1(4-2) = 6 - 6 + 2 = 2$

$$A' = \begin{bmatrix} 1 & 1 & 1 \\ 1 & 2 & 4 \\ 1 & 3 & 9 \end{bmatrix}$$

C.F. of 1 = 6   C.F. of 1 = −5   C.F. of 1 = 1
C.F. of 1 = −6   C.F. of 2 = 8   C.F. of 4 = −2
C.F. of 1 = 2   C.F. of 3 = −3   C.F. of 9 = 1

$$\text{Adj. A} = \begin{bmatrix} 6 & -5 & 1 \\ -6 & 8 & -2 \\ 2 & -3 & 1 \end{bmatrix}$$

$$A^{-1} = \frac{1}{2} \begin{bmatrix} 6 & -5 & 1 \\ -6 & 8 & -2 \\ 2 & -3 & 1 \end{bmatrix}$$

Ex. 2 : *Find A^{-1} by using adjoint method* $A = \begin{bmatrix} 1 & 2 & -2 \\ -1 & 3 & 0 \\ 0 & -2 & 1 \end{bmatrix}$.

Sol. :

$$|A| = 1(3+0) - 2(-1-0) - 2(2-0) = 1$$

$$A' = \begin{bmatrix} 1 & -1 & 0 \\ 2 & 3 & -2 \\ -2 & 0 & 1 \end{bmatrix}$$

C.F. of 1 = 3 C.F. of –1 = 2 C.F. of 0 = 6
C.F. of 2 = 1 C.F. of 3 = 1 C.F. of –2 = 2
C.F. of –2 = 2 C.F. of 0 = 2 C.F. of 1 = 5

$$\text{Adj. } A = \begin{bmatrix} 3 & 2 & 6 \\ 1 & 1 & 2 \\ 2 & 2 & 5 \end{bmatrix}$$

$$A^{-1} = \frac{1}{1} \begin{bmatrix} 3 & 2 & 6 \\ 1 & 1 & 2 \\ 2 & 2 & 5 \end{bmatrix} = \begin{bmatrix} 3 & 2 & 6 \\ 1 & 1 & 2 \\ 2 & 2 & 5 \end{bmatrix}$$

Note : Students are advised to remember adjoint method for finding A^{-1} since we will be using this method for solving system of linear non-homogeneous equations.

EXERCISE 1.4

Find A^{-1} by using adjoint method.

(1) $A = \begin{bmatrix} 9 & 7 & 3 \\ 5 & -1 & 4 \\ 3 & 5 & 1 \end{bmatrix}$ **Ans.** $A^{-1} = \frac{-1}{56} \begin{bmatrix} -21 & 8 & 31 \\ 7 & 0 & -21 \\ 28 & -24 & -44 \end{bmatrix}$

(2) $A = \begin{bmatrix} 3 & -3 & 4 \\ 2 & -3 & 4 \\ 0 & -1 & 1 \end{bmatrix}$ **Ans.** $A^{-1} = \begin{bmatrix} 1 & -1 & 0 \\ -2 & 3 & -4 \\ -2 & 3 & -3 \end{bmatrix}$

(3) $A = \begin{bmatrix} 2 & -2 & 3 \\ 3 & -1 & 2 \\ 1 & 2 & -1 \end{bmatrix}$ **Ans.** $A^{-1} = \frac{1}{5} \begin{bmatrix} -3 & 4 & -1 \\ 5 & -5 & 5 \\ 7 & -6 & 4 \end{bmatrix}$

(4) $A = \begin{bmatrix} 2 & 3 & 4 \\ 4 & 3 & 1 \\ 1 & 2 & 4 \end{bmatrix}$ **Ans.** $A^{-1} = \frac{1}{5} \begin{bmatrix} -10 & 4 & 9 \\ 15 & -4 & -14 \\ -5 & 1 & 6 \end{bmatrix}$

(5) $A = \begin{bmatrix} 2 & -1 & 3 \\ 0 & 2 & 0 \\ 2 & 1 & 1 \end{bmatrix}$ Ans. $A^{-1} = \dfrac{1}{8} \begin{bmatrix} -2 & -4 & 6 \\ 0 & 4 & 0 \\ 4 & 4 & -4 \end{bmatrix}$

(6) $A = \begin{bmatrix} 1 & 3 & 7 \\ 4 & 2 & 3 \\ 1 & 2 & 1 \end{bmatrix}$ Ans. $A^{-1} = \dfrac{1}{35} \begin{bmatrix} -4 & 11 & -5 \\ -1 & -6 & 25 \\ 6 & 1 & -10 \end{bmatrix}$

1.16 TO OBTAIN A^{-1} BY FINDING NON-SINGULAR MATRICES P AND Q SUCH THAT PAQ IS IN NORMAL FORM

Special Note :

If A is a *square matrix* then we get two non-singular matrices P and Q such that PAQ = I. Also $A^{-1} = QP$ provided A is a non-singular matrix.

e.g. : (1) For $A_{2 \times 2}$ we write $A_{2 \times 2} = I_2 \, A \, I_2$ (2) For $A_{3 \times 3}$ we write $A_{3 \times 3} = I_3 \, A \, I_3$.

Ex. 1 : *Find non-singular matrices P and Q such that PAQ is in the normal form.*

Also find the rank of A. Hence obtain A^{-1}, $A = \begin{bmatrix} 2 & 3 & 4 \\ 4 & 3 & 1 \\ 1 & 2 & 4 \end{bmatrix}$.

Sol. : $A = \begin{bmatrix} 2 & 3 & 4 \\ 4 & 3 & 1 \\ 1 & 2 & 4 \end{bmatrix}$

Total number of rows = 3 $\therefore$ Consider unit matrix I_3.
Total number of columns = 3 $\therefore$ Consider unit matrix I_3.
$\therefore$ Write $A_{3 \times 3} = I_3 \, A \, I_3$

$\begin{bmatrix} 2 & 3 & 4 \\ 4 & 3 & 1 \\ 1 & 2 & 4 \end{bmatrix} = \begin{bmatrix} 1 & 0 & 0 \\ 0 & 1 & 0 \\ 0 & 0 & 1 \end{bmatrix} A \begin{bmatrix} 1 & 0 & 0 \\ 0 & 1 & 0 \\ 0 & 0 & 1 \end{bmatrix}$

By R_{13}
$\begin{bmatrix} 1 & 2 & 4 \\ 4 & 3 & 1 \\ 2 & 3 & 4 \end{bmatrix} = \begin{bmatrix} 0 & 0 & 1 \\ 0 & 1 & 0 \\ 1 & 0 & 0 \end{bmatrix} A \begin{bmatrix} 1 & 0 & 0 \\ 0 & 1 & 0 \\ 0 & 0 & 1 \end{bmatrix}$

By $R_2 - 4R_1, R_3 - 2R_1$
$\begin{bmatrix} 1 & 2 & 4 \\ 0 & -5 & -15 \\ 0 & -1 & -4 \end{bmatrix} = \begin{bmatrix} 0 & 0 & 1 \\ 0 & 1 & -4 \\ 1 & 0 & -2 \end{bmatrix} A \begin{bmatrix} 1 & 0 & 0 \\ 0 & 1 & 0 \\ 0 & 0 & 1 \end{bmatrix}$

By $C_2 - 2C_1, C_3 - 4C_1$
$\begin{bmatrix} 1 & 0 & 0 \\ 0 & -5 & -15 \\ 0 & -1 & -4 \end{bmatrix} = \begin{bmatrix} 0 & 0 & 1 \\ 0 & 1 & -4 \\ 1 & 0 & -2 \end{bmatrix} A \begin{bmatrix} 1 & -2 & -4 \\ 0 & 1 & 0 \\ 0 & 0 & 1 \end{bmatrix}$

By $-R_2, -R_3$
$$\begin{bmatrix} 1 & 0 & 0 \\ 0 & 5 & 15 \\ 0 & 1 & 4 \end{bmatrix} = \begin{bmatrix} 0 & 0 & 1 \\ 0 & -1 & 4 \\ -1 & 0 & 2 \end{bmatrix} A \begin{bmatrix} 1 & -2 & -4 \\ 0 & 1 & 0 \\ 0 & 0 & 1 \end{bmatrix}$$

By R_{23}
$$\begin{bmatrix} 1 & 0 & 0 \\ 0 & 1 & 4 \\ 0 & 5 & 15 \end{bmatrix} = \begin{bmatrix} 0 & 0 & 1 \\ -1 & 0 & 2 \\ 0 & -1 & 4 \end{bmatrix} A \begin{bmatrix} 1 & -2 & -4 \\ 0 & 1 & 0 \\ 0 & 0 & 1 \end{bmatrix}$$

By $R_3 - 5R_2$
$$\begin{bmatrix} 1 & 0 & 0 \\ 0 & 1 & 4 \\ 0 & 0 & -5 \end{bmatrix} = \begin{bmatrix} 0 & 0 & 1 \\ -1 & 0 & 2 \\ 5 & -1 & -6 \end{bmatrix} A \begin{bmatrix} 1 & -2 & -4 \\ 0 & 1 & 0 \\ 0 & 0 & 1 \end{bmatrix}$$

By $C_3 - 4C_2$
$$\begin{bmatrix} 1 & 0 & 0 \\ 0 & 1 & 0 \\ 0 & 0 & -5 \end{bmatrix} = \begin{bmatrix} 0 & 0 & 1 \\ -1 & 0 & 2 \\ 5 & -1 & -6 \end{bmatrix} A \begin{bmatrix} 1 & -2 & 4 \\ 0 & 1 & -4 \\ 0 & 0 & 1 \end{bmatrix}$$

By $-\frac{1}{5} R_3$
$$\begin{bmatrix} 1 & 0 & 0 \\ 0 & 1 & 0 \\ 0 & 0 & 1 \end{bmatrix} = \begin{bmatrix} 0 & 0 & 1 \\ -1 & 0 & 2 \\ -1 & \frac{1}{5} & \frac{6}{5} \end{bmatrix} A \begin{bmatrix} 1 & -2 & 4 \\ 0 & 1 & -4 \\ 0 & 0 & 1 \end{bmatrix}$$

$$I_3 = PAQ$$

PAQ is in normal form.

$$P = \begin{bmatrix} 0 & 0 & 1 \\ -1 & 0 & 2 \\ -1 & \frac{1}{5} & \frac{6}{5} \end{bmatrix} \text{ and } Q = \begin{bmatrix} 1 & -2 & 4 \\ 0 & 1 & -4 \\ 0 & 0 & 1 \end{bmatrix}$$

Here P and Q are non-singular matrices.

$$\rho(A) = 3.$$

Check : $\quad PAQ = I$

$$PA = \begin{bmatrix} 0 & 0 & 1 \\ -1 & 0 & 2 \\ -1 & \frac{1}{5} & \frac{6}{5} \end{bmatrix} \begin{bmatrix} 2 & 3 & 4 \\ 4 & 3 & 1 \\ 1 & 2 & 4 \end{bmatrix} = \begin{bmatrix} 1 & 2 & 4 \\ 0 & 1 & 4 \\ 0 & 0 & 1 \end{bmatrix}$$

$$PAQ = \begin{bmatrix} 1 & 2 & 4 \\ 0 & 1 & 4 \\ 0 & 0 & 1 \end{bmatrix} \begin{bmatrix} 1 & -2 & 4 \\ 0 & 1 & -4 \\ 0 & 0 & 1 \end{bmatrix} = \begin{bmatrix} 1 & 0 & 0 \\ 0 & 1 & 0 \\ 0 & 0 & 1 \end{bmatrix}$$

To find A^{-1}, we use
$$PAQ = I_3$$
$$A^{-1} = QP$$

$$A^{-1} = \begin{bmatrix} 1 & -2 & 4 \\ 0 & 1 & -4 \\ 0 & 0 & 1 \end{bmatrix} \begin{bmatrix} 0 & 0 & 1 \\ -1 & 0 & 2 \\ -1 & \frac{1}{5} & \frac{6}{5} \end{bmatrix} = \begin{bmatrix} -2 & 4/5 & 9/5 \\ 3 & -4/5 & -14/5 \\ -1 & 1/5 & 6/5 \end{bmatrix}$$

Ex. 2 : If $A = \begin{bmatrix} 3 & -3 & 4 \\ 2 & -3 & 4 \\ 0 & -1 & 1 \end{bmatrix}$, find two non-singular matrices P and Q, such that PAQ = I, where 'I' is the unit matrix and hence find A^{-1}. **(May 2005, 2006)**

Sol. : Order of A is 3×3. Write $A_{3 \times 3} = I_3 \, A \, I_3$

$$\begin{bmatrix} 3 & -3 & 4 \\ 2 & -3 & 4 \\ 0 & -1 & 1 \end{bmatrix} = \begin{bmatrix} 1 & 0 & 0 \\ 0 & 1 & 0 \\ 0 & 0 & 1 \end{bmatrix} A \begin{bmatrix} 1 & 0 & 0 \\ 0 & 1 & 0 \\ 0 & 0 & 1 \end{bmatrix}$$

By $R_1 - R_2$
$$\begin{bmatrix} 1 & 0 & 0 \\ 2 & -3 & 4 \\ 0 & -1 & 1 \end{bmatrix} = \begin{bmatrix} 1 & -1 & 0 \\ 0 & 1 & 0 \\ 0 & 0 & 1 \end{bmatrix} A \begin{bmatrix} 1 & 0 & 0 \\ 0 & 1 & 0 \\ 0 & 0 & 1 \end{bmatrix}$$

By $R_2 - 2R_1$
$$\begin{bmatrix} 1 & 0 & 0 \\ 0 & -3 & 4 \\ 0 & -1 & 1 \end{bmatrix} = \begin{bmatrix} 1 & -1 & 0 \\ -2 & 3 & 0 \\ 0 & 0 & 1 \end{bmatrix} A \begin{bmatrix} 1 & 0 & 0 \\ 0 & 1 & 0 \\ 0 & 0 & 1 \end{bmatrix}$$

By $-C_2$
$$\begin{bmatrix} 1 & 0 & 0 \\ 0 & 3 & 4 \\ 0 & 1 & 1 \end{bmatrix} = \begin{bmatrix} 1 & -1 & 0 \\ -2 & 3 & 0 \\ 0 & 0 & 1 \end{bmatrix} A \begin{bmatrix} 1 & 0 & 0 \\ 0 & -1 & 0 \\ 0 & 0 & 1 \end{bmatrix}$$

By R_{23}
$$\begin{bmatrix} 1 & 0 & 0 \\ 0 & 1 & 1 \\ 0 & 3 & 4 \end{bmatrix} = \begin{bmatrix} 1 & -1 & 0 \\ 0 & 0 & 1 \\ -2 & 3 & 0 \end{bmatrix} A \begin{bmatrix} 1 & 0 & 0 \\ 0 & -1 & 0 \\ 0 & 0 & 1 \end{bmatrix}$$

By $R_3 - 3R_2$
$$\begin{bmatrix} 1 & 0 & 0 \\ 0 & 1 & 1 \\ 0 & 0 & 1 \end{bmatrix} = \begin{bmatrix} 1 & -1 & 0 \\ 0 & 0 & 1 \\ -2 & 3 & -3 \end{bmatrix} A \begin{bmatrix} 1 & 0 & 0 \\ 0 & -1 & 0 \\ 0 & 0 & 1 \end{bmatrix}$$

By $C_3 - C_2$
$$\begin{bmatrix} 1 & 0 & 0 \\ 0 & 1 & 0 \\ 0 & 0 & 1 \end{bmatrix} = \begin{bmatrix} 1 & -1 & 0 \\ 0 & 0 & 1 \\ -2 & 3 & -3 \end{bmatrix} A \begin{bmatrix} 1 & 0 & 0 \\ 0 & -1 & 1 \\ 0 & 0 & 1 \end{bmatrix}$$

$$I_3 = PAQ$$

PAQ is in normal form.
$$\rho(A) = 3$$
To find A^{-1}, we use $A^{-1} = QP$

$$A^{-1} = \begin{bmatrix} 1 & 0 & 0 \\ 0 & -1 & 1 \\ 0 & 0 & 1 \end{bmatrix} \begin{bmatrix} 1 & -1 & 0 \\ 0 & 0 & 1 \\ -2 & 3 & -3 \end{bmatrix}$$

$$A^{-1} = \begin{bmatrix} 1 & -1 & 0 \\ -2 & 3 & -4 \\ -2 & 3 & -3 \end{bmatrix}$$

EXERCISE 1.5

Find non-singular matrices P and Q such that PAQ is in normal form. Hence find the rank of A and also find A^{-1}.

(1) $A = \begin{bmatrix} 2 & -2 & 3 \\ 3 & -1 & 2 \\ 1 & 2 & -1 \end{bmatrix}$ **(May 2007)** **Ans.** $A^{-1} = \dfrac{1}{5}\begin{bmatrix} -3 & 4 & -1 \\ 5 & -5 & 5 \\ 7 & -6 & 4 \end{bmatrix}$

(2) $A = \begin{bmatrix} 1 & 1 & 1 \\ 1 & 2 & 3 \\ 1 & 4 & 9 \end{bmatrix}$ **Ans.** $A^{-1} = \dfrac{1}{2}\begin{bmatrix} 6 & -5 & 1 \\ -6 & 8 & -2 \\ 2 & -3 & 1 \end{bmatrix}$

(3) $A = \begin{bmatrix} 1 & 2 & -2 \\ -1 & 3 & 0 \\ 0 & -2 & 1 \end{bmatrix}$ **Ans.** $A^{-1} = \begin{bmatrix} 3 & 2 & 6 \\ 1 & 1 & 2 \\ 2 & 2 & 5 \end{bmatrix}$

(4) $A = \begin{bmatrix} 1 & 3 & 3 \\ 1 & 4 & 3 \\ 1 & 3 & 4 \end{bmatrix}$ **Ans.** $A^{-1} = \begin{bmatrix} 7 & -3 & -3 \\ -1 & 1 & 0 \\ -1 & 0 & 1 \end{bmatrix}$

MULTIPLE CHOICE QUESTIONS

Type I : Rank and Normal Form :

1. If a matrix A has at least one minor of order r is non zero and every minors of order (r + 1) are zero then (1)
   (A) rank of matrix A ≥ r
   (B) rank of matrix A = r
   (C) rank of matrix A ≤ r
   (D) none of these

2. For matrix A order m × n, the rank r of matrix A is (1)
   (A) r ≥ minimum of m and n
   (B) r ≥ maximum of m and n
   (C) r ≤ minimum of m and n
   (D) r ≤ maximum of m and n

3. If a matrix A has all its minors of order (r + 1) are zero then (1)
   (A) rank of matrix A ≥ r
   (B) rank of matrix A = r
   (C) rank of matrix A ≤ r
   (D) none of these

4. For non-singular matrix A of order n × n, rank r of A is (1)
   (A) r > n
   (B) r = n
   (C) r < n
   (D) none of these

5. The rank of matrix of order m × n is (1)
   (A) highest order of its non-vanishing minor
   (B) smallest order of its non-vanishing minor
   (C) highest order of its vanishing minor
   (D) smallest order of its vanishing minor

6. The rank of matrix does not alter by (1)
   (A) elementary row transformation
   (B) elementary column transformation
   (C) taking transpose
   (D) all the above

7. Which of the following is not elementary transformation ? (1)
   (A) $C_i + 4C_j$
   (B) $R_i - 2R_j$
   (C) $\dfrac{R_i}{R_j}$
   (D) $kR_i, k \neq 0$

8. Normal form of matrix $A = \begin{bmatrix} 1 & 0 & 0 \\ 0 & 1 & 0 \\ 0 & 0 & 0 \end{bmatrix}$ is (1)
   (A) $\begin{bmatrix} I_2 & 0 \\ 0 & 0 \end{bmatrix}$
   (B) $[I_3]$
   (C) $[I_2 \ 0]$
   (D) $\begin{bmatrix} I_1 & 0 \\ 0 & 0 \end{bmatrix}$

9. By performing elementary transformations if any non-zero matrix A of order 4 × 5 is reduced to the normal form $\begin{bmatrix} I_2 & 0 \\ 0 & 0 \end{bmatrix}$ then the rank of A is equal to (1)
   (A) 4
   (B) 2
   (C) 5
   (D) 1

10. By performing elementary transformations if any non-zero matrix A of order 4 × 4 is reduced to the normal form $[I_4]$ then the rank of A is equal to (1)

    (A) 4 (B) 2
    (C) 5 (D) 1

11. By performing elementary transformations if any non-zero matrix A of order 3 × 4 is reduced to the normal form $[I_3, 0]$ then the rank of A is equal to (1)

    (A) 4 (B) 2
    (C) 3 (D) 1

12. By performing elementary transformations if any non-zero matrix A of order 4 × 3 is reduced to the normal form $\begin{bmatrix} I_3 \\ 0 \end{bmatrix}$ then the rank of A is equal to (1)

    (A) 4 (B) 2
    (C) 3 (D) 1

13. If A is non-singular matrix, there exist two non-singular matrices P and Q such that PAQ is in normal form, then A^{-1} is equal to (1)

    (A) PQ (B) $P^{-1}Q^{-1}$
    (C) QP (D) $Q^{-1}P^{-1}$

14. Normal form of matrix $A = \begin{bmatrix} 1 & 0 \\ 0 & 2 \end{bmatrix}$ is (2)

    (A) $[I_2 \ 0]$ (B) $[I_2]$
    (C) $[I_3]$ (D) $\begin{bmatrix} I_1 \\ 0 \end{bmatrix}$

15. Normal form of matrix $A = \begin{bmatrix} 1 & 0 & 0 \\ 0 & 0 & 1 \\ 1 & 0 & 0 \end{bmatrix}$ is (2)

    (A) $[I_2 \ 0]$ (B) $[I_3]$
    (C) $[I_1 \ 0]$ (D) $\begin{bmatrix} I_2 & 0 \\ 0 & 0 \end{bmatrix}$

16. The rank of matrix $A = \begin{bmatrix} 4 & 0 & 0 \\ 0 & 3 & 0 \\ 0 & 0 & 5 \end{bmatrix}$ is equal to (2)

    (A) 4 (B) 3
    (C) 5 (D) 1

17. The rank of matrix $A = \begin{bmatrix} 1 & 2 & 3 \\ 3 & 1 & 2 \end{bmatrix}$ is equal to (2)

    (A) 4   (B) 3
    (C) 2   (D) 1

18. The rank of matrix $A = \begin{bmatrix} 1 & 1 & 1 \\ 2 & 2 & 2 \\ 3 & 3 & 3 \end{bmatrix}$ is equal to (2)

    (A) 4   (B) 3
    (C) 2   (D) 1

19. The rank of matrix $A = \begin{bmatrix} 1 & 2 & 3 \\ 2 & 2 & 2 \\ 3 & 3 & 3 \end{bmatrix}$ is equal to (2)

    (A) 4   (B) 3
    (C) 2   (D) 1

20. The rank of matrix $A = \begin{bmatrix} 1 & 2 & 3 & 4 & 5 \\ 0 & 1 & 2 & 3 & 4 \\ 0 & 0 & 1 & 2 & 3 \\ 0 & 0 & 0 & 0 & 0 \end{bmatrix}$ is equal to (2)

    (A) 4   (B) 3
    (C) 5   (D) 1

21. The rank of matrix $A = \begin{bmatrix} 1 & 3 & 8 & 6 \\ 2 & 6 & -1 & 4 \\ 3 & 9 & 7 & 10 \end{bmatrix}$ is equal to (2)

    (A) 4   (B) 3
    (C) 2   (D) 1

22. The rank of matrix $A = \begin{bmatrix} 1 & 0 & 1 & 1 \\ 3 & 1 & 0 & 2 \\ 1 & 1 & -2 & 0 \end{bmatrix}$ is equal to (2)

    (A) 2   (B) 1
    (C) 3   (D) 4

23. The rank of matrix $A = \begin{bmatrix} 1 & 3 & 6 \\ 1 & 4 & 5 \\ 1 & 5 & 4 \end{bmatrix}$ is equal to (2)

   (A) 3 (B) 1
   (C) 4 (D) 2

24. The rank of matrix $A = \begin{bmatrix} 1 & 1 & 1 \\ 2 & -3 & 4 \\ 3 & -2 & 3 \end{bmatrix}$ is equal to (2)

   (A) 1 (B) 3
   (C) 2 (D) 4

25. The rank of matrix $A = \begin{bmatrix} 1 & 1 & 1 & 1 \\ 2 & 3 & 4 & 5 \\ 0 & 1 & 2 & 3 \\ 0 & 1 & 2 & 3 \end{bmatrix}$ is equal to (2)

   (A) 1 (B) 4
   (C) 3 (D) 2

Answers

1. (B)	5. (A)	9. (B)	13. (C)	17. (C)	21. (C)	25. (D)
2. (C)	6. (D)	10. (A)	14. (B)	18. (D)	22. (A)	
3. (C)	7. (C)	11. (C)	15. (D)	19. (C)	23. (D)	
4. (B)	8. (A)	12. (C)	16. (B)	20. (B)	24. (B)	

CHAPTER TWO

SYSTEM OF LINEAR ALGEBRAIC EQUATIONS

2.1 SOLUTION OF SIMULTANEOUS EQUATIONS BY MATRICES

Consider a system of 'm' linear equations in 'n' unknowns $x_1, x_2, x_3 \ldots x_n$.

$a_{11} x_1 + a_{12} x_2 + \ldots + a_{1n} x_n = b_1$
$a_{21} x_1 + a_{22} x_2 + \ldots + a_{2n} x_n = b_2$
$\vdots \qquad \vdots \qquad \vdots \qquad \vdots$
$a_{m1} x_1 + a_{m2} x_2 + \ldots + a_{mn} x_n = b_m$

The above system of equations can be written in compact form by using matrix notation

$$\begin{bmatrix} a_{11} & a_{12} & \ldots & a_{1n} \\ a_{21} & a_{22} & \ldots & a_{2n} \\ \vdots & \vdots & & \vdots \\ \vdots & \vdots & \vdots & \\ a_{m1} & a_{m2} & \ldots & a_{mn} \end{bmatrix} \begin{bmatrix} x_1 \\ x_2 \\ \vdots \\ \vdots \\ x_n \end{bmatrix} = \begin{bmatrix} b_1 \\ b_2 \\ \vdots \\ \vdots \\ b_m \end{bmatrix}$$

i.e. $AX = B$, where coefficient matrix A is

$$A = \begin{bmatrix} a_{11} & a_{12} & \ldots & a_{1n} \\ a_{21} & a_{22} & \ldots & a_{2n} \\ \vdots & \vdots & & \vdots \\ \vdots & \vdots & \vdots & \\ a_{m1} & a_{m2} & \ldots & a_{mn} \end{bmatrix}, X = \begin{bmatrix} x_1 \\ x_2 \\ \vdots \\ \vdots \\ x_n \end{bmatrix}, B = \begin{bmatrix} b_1 \\ b_2 \\ \vdots \\ \vdots \\ b_m \end{bmatrix}$$

When the system $AX = B$ has a solution i.e. set of values of $x_1, x_2, \ldots x_n$ satisfy *simultaneously all m equations* then the system is said to be *consistent*, otherwise the system is called *inconsistent*.

2.2 AUGMENTED MATRIX (A, B)

Definition : If $AX = B$ is a system of m equations in n unknowns then the matrix written as (A, B) is called as the augmented matrix.

Hence, $(A, B) = \begin{bmatrix} a_{11} & a_{12} & \ldots & a_{1n} & : & b_1 \\ a_{21} & a_{22} & \ldots & a_{2n} & : & b_2 \\ \vdots & & & & : & \\ \vdots & & & & : & \\ a_{m1} & a_{m2} & \ldots & a_{mn} & : & b_m \end{bmatrix}$

2.3 NON-HOMOGENEOUS EQUATIONS

For the system of equations AX = B if matrix B is not a null or zero matrix then the system AX = B is known as non-homogeneous system of equations.

2.4 HOMOGENEOUS EQUATIONS

For the system of equations AX = B if matrix B is a null or zero matrix i.e. Z then the system AX = Z is known as homogeneous system of equations.

e.g. (1) $\left.\begin{array}{l} x + y + z = 3 \\ x - y + 2z = 4 \\ 2x + 3y - z = 0 \end{array}\right\}$ (2) $\left.\begin{array}{l} x + y + z = 0 \\ 2x + 3y - 4z = 0 \\ x - y + 2z = 0 \end{array}\right\}$

Non-homogeneous equations   Homogeneous equations

2.5 CONDITION FOR CONSISTENCY OF NON-HOMOGENEOUS EQUATIONS

Consider a system of 'm' equations in 'n' unknowns given by AX = B.

Let m = total number of equations, n = total number of unknowns.

Case 1: Let m ≠ n (i.e. no. of equations different from number of unknowns).

(1) If rank of the coefficient matrix A = rank of the augmented matrix (A, B), then the system AX = B is said to be **consistent**. In other words, if $\rho(A) = \rho(A, B)$ then system is consistent.

(2) **No solution:** If $\rho(A) \neq \rho(A, B)$ then system is said to be **inconsistent** and possesses no solution.

(3) **A Unique solution:** If $\rho(A) = \rho(A, B) = n =$ total number of unknowns, then system AX = B possesses *a unique solution* (only one solution).

(4) **An infinite number of solutions:** If $\rho(A) = \rho(A, B) < n$ then system possesses *an infinite number of solutions* which can be represented parametrically by employing some parameter t.

Note: If $\rho(A) = \rho(A, B) = r < n$ then r unknowns can be expressed in terms of remaining (n – r) unknowns.

Case 2: Let m = n. No. of equations = No. of unknowns > 3.

(1) $\rho(A) = \rho(A, B) = n$ system is *consistent* and possesses a unique solution.

(2) $\rho(A) \neq \rho(A, B)$ system is *inconsistent* and possesses *no solution*.

(3) $\rho(A) = \rho(A, B) = r < n$ then system is *consistent* and possesses an *infinite number of solutions*.

Case 3: Let m = n. No. of equations = no. of unknowns = 3. i.e. 3 equations in 3 unknowns. We have AX = B. Find |A|.

(1) If $|A| \neq 0$ system is consistent, then A^{-1} exists and system possesses *a unique solution* given by $X = A^{-1} B$.

(2) If $|A| = 0$ then system is either inconsistent or possesses an infinite number of solutions and this is decided by applying the method of reduction. Write augmented matrix (A, B).

Now, if $\rho(A) = \rho(A, B) < n$ then system possesses *an infinite number of solutions*.

If $\rho(A) \neq \rho(A, B)$ then system is inconsistent and possesses *no solution*.

Problems on Non-homogeneous equations are mainly divided in the following types.

Type 1 : $AX = B$ is non-homogeneous where $m \neq n$, $m = n = 4$. Here system is mainly consistent.

Type 2 : This is also another special type. $AX = B$ is non-homogeneous.

where $m \neq n$, $m = n$ with

1. Coefficient matrix A containing some λ or a.

2. RHS matrix B containing some K or λ or μ.

Type 3 : $AX = B$ is non-homogeneous where $m \neq n$, $m = n$. Here system is mainly inconsistent.

Type 4 : $AX = B$ is non-homogeneous where $m = n = 3$, covering application of matrix inversion method if $|A| \neq 0$. Also if $|A| = 0$ we will apply method of reduction with $\rho(A) = \rho(A, B) < n \Rightarrow$ an infinite number of solutions. $\rho(A) \neq \rho(A, B)$ no solution (inconsistent).

The results related to consistency of Non-homogeneous system of equations can be remembered by using following flow chart.

2.6 CHART 1 AND CHART 2

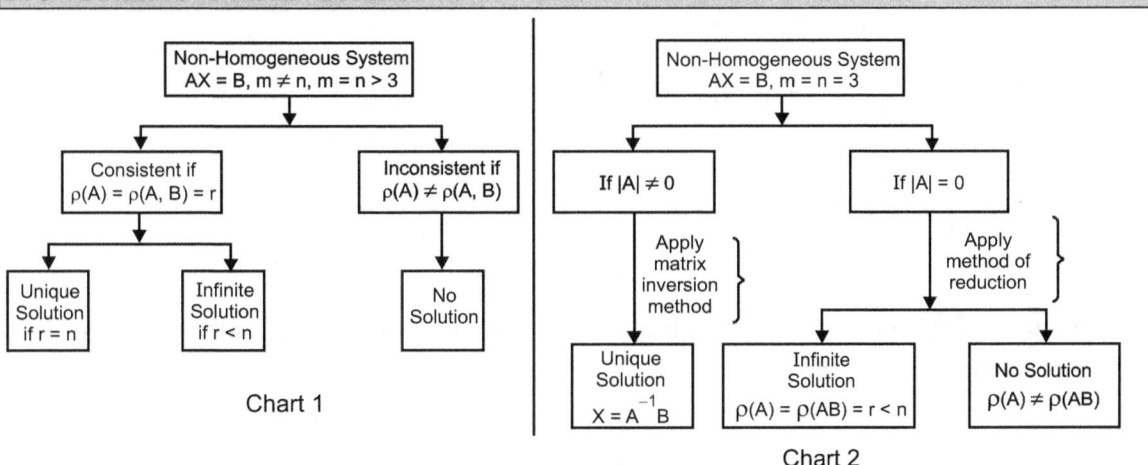

Chart 1

Chart 2

Note : While solving system of non-homogeneous or homogeneous equations, for an augmented matrix (A, B) or (A, Z) respectively, we will perform only elementary row transformations.

2.7 TYPE 1 : EXAMPLES ON NON-HOMOGENEOUS SYSTEM OF EQUATIONS BY USING METHOD OF REDUCTION

Ex. 1 : *Solve the system of equations by matrix method*

$$2x_1 + x_2 - x_3 + 3x_4 = 8$$
$$x_1 + x_2 + x_3 - x_4 + 2 = 0$$
$$3x_1 + 2x_2 - x_3 = 6$$
$$4x_2 + 3x_3 + 2x_4 + 8 = 0$$

Sol. : Given system of equations in matrix form can be written as

$$\begin{bmatrix} 2 & 1 & -1 & 3 \\ 1 & 1 & 1 & -1 \\ 3 & 2 & -1 & 0 \\ 0 & 4 & 3 & 2 \end{bmatrix} \begin{bmatrix} x_1 \\ x_2 \\ x_3 \\ x_4 \end{bmatrix} = \begin{bmatrix} 8 \\ -2 \\ 6 \\ -8 \end{bmatrix}$$

i.e. $AX = B.$

Consider an augmented matrix.

$$(A, B) = \begin{bmatrix} 2 & 1 & -1 & 3 & | & 8 \\ 1 & 1 & 1 & -1 & | & -2 \\ 3 & 2 & -1 & 0 & | & 6 \\ 0 & 4 & 3 & 2 & | & -8 \end{bmatrix}$$

Step 1 : Get $a_{11} = 1$

Perform R_{12}

$$\begin{bmatrix} 1 & 1 & 1 & -1 & | & -2 \\ 2 & 1 & -1 & 3 & | & 8 \\ 3 & 2 & -1 & 0 & | & 6 \\ 0 & 4 & 3 & 2 & | & -8 \end{bmatrix}$$

Step 2 : Make a_{21}, a_{31} equal to zero. (**Hint :** Use row transformation).

Perform $R_2 - 2R_1$, $R_3 - 3R_1$

$$\sim \begin{bmatrix} 1 & 1 & 1 & -1 & | & -2 \\ 0 & -1 & -3 & 5 & | & 12 \\ 0 & -1 & -4 & 3 & | & 12 \\ 0 & 4 & 3 & 2 & | & -8 \end{bmatrix}$$

Step 3 : Note that without making $a_{22} = 1$, we can get a_{32}, a_{42} equal to zero. For this purpose, use again row transformation.

Perform $R_3 - R_2$, $R_4 + 4R_2$

$$\sim \begin{bmatrix} 1 & 1 & 1 & -1 & | & -2 \\ 0 & -1 & -3 & 5 & | & 12 \\ 0 & 0 & -1 & -2 & | & 0 \\ 0 & 0 & -9 & 22 & | & 40 \end{bmatrix}$$

Step 4 : Again keep a_{33} as it is and make $a_{43} = 0$.

Perform $R_4 - 9R_3$

$$\sim \begin{bmatrix} 1 & 1 & 1 & -1 & | & -2 \\ 0 & -1 & -3 & 5 & | & 12 \\ 0 & 0 & -1 & -2 & | & 0 \\ 0 & 0 & 0 & 40 & | & 40 \end{bmatrix}$$

Step 5 : This is reduced to echelon form.

$$\rho(A) = \rho(A, B) = 4 - 0 = 4 = \text{total number of variables}$$

Hence system possesses a unique solution and it is given as follows.

By R_4 $40 x_4 = 40,$ $\therefore x_4 = 1$
By R_3 $-x_3 - 2x_4 = 0,$ $\therefore x_3 = -2$
By R_2 $-x_2 - 3x_3 + 5x_4 = 12,$ $\therefore x_2 = -3(-2) + 5(1) - 12 = -1$
By R_1 $x_1 + x_2 + x_3 - x_4 = -2,$ $\therefore x_1 = -2 + 1 + 2 + 1 = 2$

Hence the solution set is $x_1 = 2$, $x_2 = -1$, $x_3 = -2$, $x_4 = 1$

Step 6 : Always check your answer (i.e. values of x_1, x_2, x_3, x_4) by substituting in one of the equation. i.e. $2x_1 + x_2 - x_3 + 3x_4 = 8$ $\therefore$ $2(2) - 1 + 2 + 3 = 8$ $\therefore$ $8 = 8$

Ex. 2 : *Is the following system of equations consistent ? If so solve it.*

$$x + y + z = 6$$
$$x - y + 2z = 5$$
$$3x + y + z = 8$$
$$2x - 2y + 3z = 7$$

(May 2011)

Sol. : Given system of equations in matrix form can be written as

$$\begin{bmatrix} 1 & 1 & 1 \\ 1 & -1 & 2 \\ 3 & 1 & 1 \\ 2 & -2 & 3 \end{bmatrix} \begin{bmatrix} x \\ y \\ z \end{bmatrix} = \begin{bmatrix} 6 \\ 5 \\ 8 \\ 7 \end{bmatrix}$$

i.e. $AX = B$

Consider an augmented matrix

$$(A, B) = \begin{bmatrix} 1 & 1 & 1 & | & 6 \\ 1 & -1 & 2 & | & 5 \\ 3 & 1 & 1 & | & 8 \\ 2 & -2 & 3 & | & 7 \end{bmatrix}$$

Perform $R_2 - R_1,\ R_3 - 3R_1,\ R_4 - 2R_1$

$$\sim \begin{bmatrix} 1 & 1 & 1 & | & 6 \\ 0 & -2 & 1 & | & -1 \\ 0 & -2 & -2 & | & -10 \\ 0 & -4 & 1 & | & -5 \end{bmatrix}$$

Perform $R_3 - R_2$, $R_4 - 2R_2$

$$\sim \begin{bmatrix} 1 & 1 & 1 & | & 6 \\ 0 & -2 & 1 & | & -1 \\ 0 & 0 & -3 & | & -9 \\ 0 & 0 & -1 & | & -3 \end{bmatrix}$$

Perform $R_3 - 3R_4$

$$\sim \begin{bmatrix} 1 & 1 & 1 & | & 6 \\ 0 & -2 & 1 & | & -1 \\ 0 & 0 & 0 & | & 0 \\ 0 & 0 & -1 & | & -3 \end{bmatrix}$$

$\rho(A) = 4 - 1 = 3 \quad \rho(A, B) = 4 - 1 = 3$

$\rho(A) = \rho(A, B) \quad \therefore$ System is consistent.

$\rho(A) = \rho(A, B) = 3 =$ no. of variables $\therefore$ System possesses a unique solution given as

By $R_4 \quad -z = -3, \quad z = 3$
By $R_2 \quad -2y + z = -1, \quad 2y = 4, \quad y = 2$
By $R_1 \quad x + y + z = 6, \quad x = 6 - 2 - 3 = 1 \quad \therefore \quad x = 1$

Hence the solution is $x = 1 \quad y = 2 \quad z = 3$.

Ex. 3 : *By considering the ranks of relevant matrices, examine for consistency the system of equations :*

$2x - y - z = 2$

$x + 2y + z = 2$

$4x - 7y - 5z = 2$ *and solve them if found consistent.* **(Dec. 2004, May 2010, Dec. 2014)**

Sol. : Given system of equations in matrix form can be written as

$$\begin{bmatrix} 2 & -1 & -1 \\ 1 & 2 & 1 \\ 4 & -7 & -5 \end{bmatrix} \begin{bmatrix} x \\ y \\ z \end{bmatrix} = \begin{bmatrix} 2 \\ 2 \\ 2 \end{bmatrix}$$

i.e. $\quad AX = B$

Consider an augmented matrix,

$$(A, B) = \begin{bmatrix} 2 & -1 & -1 & | & 2 \\ 1 & 2 & 1 & | & 2 \\ 4 & -7 & -5 & | & 2 \end{bmatrix}$$

Perform R_{12}

$$\sim \begin{bmatrix} 1 & 2 & 1 & | & 2 \\ 2 & -1 & -1 & | & 2 \\ 4 & -7 & -5 & | & 2 \end{bmatrix}$$

Perform $R_2 - 2R_1$, $R_3 - 4R_1$

$$\sim \begin{bmatrix} 1 & 2 & 1 & | & 2 \\ 0 & -5 & -3 & | & -2 \\ 0 & -15 & -9 & | & -6 \end{bmatrix}$$

Perform $R_3 - 3R_2$

$$\sim \begin{bmatrix} 1 & 2 & 1 & | & 2 \\ 0 & -5 & -3 & | & -2 \\ 0 & 0 & 0 & | & 0 \end{bmatrix}$$

$\rho(A) = 3 - 1 = 2$, $\rho(A, B) = 3 - 1 = 2$
$\rho(A) = \rho(A, B)$ ∴ System is consistent.
$\rho(A) = \rho(A, B) = 2 < 3$, number of variables, system possesses an infinite number of solutions given as follows.

By R_2 $-5y - 3z = -2$ Let $z = t$ $y = \dfrac{2 - 3t}{5}$

By R_1 $x + 2y + z = 2$ $x = 2 - \dfrac{4 - 6t}{5} - t = \dfrac{10 - 4 + 6t - 5t}{5} = \dfrac{6 + t}{5}$

Hence solution set is $x = \dfrac{6 + t}{5}$, $y = \dfrac{2 - 3t}{5}$, $z = t$.

Ex. 4 : *Examine for consistency the following set of equations and obtain the solution if consistent.*

$$2x_1 + x_2 - x_3 + 3x_4 = 11$$
$$x_1 - 2x_2 + x_3 + x_4 = 8$$
$$4x_1 + 7x_2 + 2x_3 - x_4 = 0$$
$$3x_1 + 5x_2 + 4x_3 + 4x_4 = 17$$

Sol. : Given system of equations in matrix form can be written as

$$\begin{bmatrix} 2 & 1 & -1 & 3 \\ 1 & -2 & 1 & 1 \\ 4 & 7 & 2 & -1 \\ 3 & 5 & 4 & 4 \end{bmatrix} \begin{bmatrix} x_1 \\ x_2 \\ x_3 \\ x_4 \end{bmatrix} = \begin{bmatrix} 11 \\ 8 \\ 0 \\ 17 \end{bmatrix}$$

i.e. $AX = B$

Consider an augmented matrix

$$(A, B) = \begin{bmatrix} 2 & 1 & -1 & 3 & | & 11 \\ 1 & -2 & 1 & 1 & | & 8 \\ 4 & 7 & 2 & -1 & | & 0 \\ 3 & 5 & 4 & 4 & | & 17 \end{bmatrix}$$

By R_{12}

$$\sim \begin{bmatrix} 1 & -2 & 1 & 1 & | & 8 \\ 2 & 1 & -1 & 3 & | & 11 \\ 4 & 7 & 2 & -1 & | & 0 \\ 3 & 5 & 4 & 4 & | & 17 \end{bmatrix}$$

By $R_2 - 2R_1$, $R_3 - 4R_1$, $R_4 - 3R_1$

$$\sim \begin{bmatrix} 1 & -2 & 1 & 1 & | & 8 \\ 0 & 5 & -3 & 1 & | & -5 \\ 0 & 15 & -2 & -5 & | & -32 \\ 0 & 11 & 1 & 1 & | & -7 \end{bmatrix}$$

By $R_3 - 3R_2$, $R_4 - R_2$

$$\sim \begin{bmatrix} 1 & -2 & 1 & 1 & | & 8 \\ 0 & 5 & -3 & 1 & | & -5 \\ 0 & 0 & 7 & -8 & | & -17 \\ 0 & 6 & 4 & 0 & | & -2 \end{bmatrix}$$

By $R_4 - \dfrac{6}{5} R_2$

$$\sim \begin{bmatrix} 1 & -2 & 1 & 1 & | & 8 \\ 0 & 5 & -3 & 1 & | & -5 \\ 0 & 0 & 7 & -8 & | & -17 \\ 0 & 0 & \dfrac{38}{5} & \dfrac{-6}{5} & | & 4 \end{bmatrix}$$

By $R_4 - \dfrac{38}{35} R_3$

$$\sim \begin{bmatrix} 1 & -2 & 1 & 1 & | & 8 \\ 0 & 5 & -3 & 1 & | & -5 \\ 0 & 0 & 7 & -8 & | & -17 \\ 0 & 0 & 0 & \dfrac{262}{35} & | & \dfrac{786}{35} \end{bmatrix}$$

Here $\rho(A) = 4 - 0 = 4$, $\rho(A, B) = 4 - 0 = 4$

$\rho(A) = \rho(A, B) = 4 = 4$, number of variables.

System is consistent and possesses a unique solution.

By R_4 $\dfrac{262}{35} x_4 = \dfrac{786}{35}$ $x_4 = 3$

By R_3 $7x_3 - 8x_4 = -17$ $7x_3 = -17 + 24 = 7$ $x_3 = 1$

By R_2 $5x_2 - 3x_3 + x_4 = -5$ $5x_2 = -5 + 3 - 3 = -5$ $x_2 = -1$

By R_1 $x_1 - 2x_2 + x_3 + x_4 = 8$ $x_1 = -2 - 1 - 3 + 8 = 2$ $x_1 = 2$.

Required solution set is $x_1 = 2$, $x_2 = -1$, $x_3 = 1$, $x_4 = 3$.

EXERCISE 2.1

Hint: Use method discussed in type 1.

Examine for consistency and if consistent then solve it.

(1) $2x_1 + x_2 - 5x_3 + x_4 = 8$
$x_1 + 3x_2 - 6x_4 = -15$
$2x_2 - x_3 + 2x_4 = -5$
$x_1 + 4x_2 - 7x_3 + 6x_4 = 0$
Ans. $x_1 = 3$, $x_2 = -4$, $x_3 = -1$, $x_4 = 1$.

(2) $4x - 2y + 6z = 8$
$x + y - 3z = -1$
$15x - 3y + 9z = 21$
Ans. $x = 1$, $y = 3t - 2$, $z = t$

(3) $2x_1 - 3x_2 + 5x_3 = 1$
$3x_1 + x_2 - x_3 = 2$
$x_1 + 4x_2 - 6x_3 = 1$ **(May 2007)**
Ans. $x_1 = \dfrac{7-2t}{11}$, $x_2 = \dfrac{1+17t}{11}$, $x_3 = t$

(4) $3x + 3y + 2z = 1$
$x + 2y = 4$
$10y + 3z = -2$
$2x - 3y - z = 5$
Ans. $x = 2$, $y = 1$, $z = -4$

(5) $3x + y + 2z = 3$
$2x - 3y - z = -3$
$x + 2y + z = 4$
Ans. $x = 1$, $y = 2$, $z = -1$

(6) $5x + 3y + 7z = 4$
$3x + 26y + 2z = 9$
$7x + 2y + 10z = 5$
Ans. $x = \dfrac{7-16t}{11}$, $y = \dfrac{3+t}{11}$, $z = t$

(7) $2x_1 + x_2 + 2x_3 + x_4 = 6$
$6x_1 - 6x_2 + 6x_3 + 12x_4 = 36$
$4x_1 + 3x_2 + 3x_3 - 3x_4 = -1$
$2x_1 + 2x_2 - x_3 + x_4 = 10$ **(Dec. 2003)**
Ans. $x_1 = 2$, $x_2 = 1$, $x_3 = -1$, $x_4 = 3$

(8) $x + 2y + 2z = 1$
$2x + 2y + 3z = 3$
$x - y + 3z = 5$
Ans. $x = 1$, $y = -1$, $z = 1$

(9) $2x + z = 4$
$x - 2y + 2z = 7$
$3x + 2y = 1$
Ans. $x = 2 - \dfrac{t}{2}$, $y = -\dfrac{5}{2} + \dfrac{3t}{4}$, $z = t$,

(10) $2x_1 + x_2 + 5x_3 + x_4 = 5$
$x_1 + x_2 - 3x_3 - 4x_4 = -1$
$3x_1 + 6x_2 - 2x_3 + x_4 = 8$
$2x_1 + 2x_2 + 2x_3 - 3x_4 = 2$
Ans. $x_1 = 2$, $x_2 = \dfrac{1}{5}$, $x_3 = 0$, $x_4 = \dfrac{4}{5}$

(11) $x + 2y + z = -1$
$6x + y + z = -4$
$2x - 3y - z = 0$
$-x - 7y - 2z = 7$
$x - y = 1$
Ans. $x = -1$, $y = -2$, $z = 4$

(12) $x + y + z = 6$
$2x + y + 3z = 13$
$5x + 2y + z = 12$
$2x - 3y - 2z = -10$
Ans. $x = 1$, $y = 2$, $z = 3$

(13) $2x + 3y + 4z = 11$
$x + 5y + 7z = 15$
$3x + 11y + 13z = 25$
Ans. $x = 2$, $y = -3$, $z = 4$

(14) $x + y + z = 4$
$2x + 5y - 2z = 3$
Ans. $x = \dfrac{17-7t}{3}$, $y = \dfrac{-5+4t}{3}$, $z = t$

2.8 TYPE 2 : NON-HOMOGENEOUS EQUATIONS WITH
(I) COEFFICIENT MATRIX A CONTAINING SOME λ OR a.
(II) R.H.S. MATRIX B CONTAINING SOME K OR λ OR μ

In this type follow the important steps involved.

Step 1 : Write given system in matrix notation AX = B.

Step 2 : Write augmented matrix (A, B).

Step 3 : Reduce it to echelon form.

Step 4 : Discuss the cases for unique solution, no solution and an infinite number of solutions depending on selection of arbitrary constants. Carefully note down the following solved examples.

Ex. 1 : *Find for what values of k, the set of equations*

$$2x - 3y + 6z - 5t = 3$$
$$y - 4z + t = 1$$
$$4x - 5y + 8z - 9t = k$$

has (1) No solution, (2) An infinite number of solutions. **(May 2004)**

Sol. : Step 1 : Given system in matrix form can be written as,

$$\begin{bmatrix} 2 & -3 & 6 & -5 \\ 0 & 1 & -4 & 1 \\ 4 & -5 & 8 & -9 \end{bmatrix} \begin{bmatrix} x \\ y \\ z \\ t \end{bmatrix} = \begin{bmatrix} 3 \\ 1 \\ k \end{bmatrix}$$

Step 2 : Consider an augmented matrix,

$$(A, B) = \begin{bmatrix} 2 & -3 & 6 & -5 & | & 3 \\ 0 & 1 & -4 & 1 & | & 1 \\ 4 & -5 & 8 & -9 & | & k \end{bmatrix}$$

Step 3 : Now we will reduce (A, B) to echelon form.

Perform $R_3 - 2R_1$

$$\sim \begin{bmatrix} 2 & -3 & 6 & -5 & | & 3 \\ 0 & 1 & -4 & 1 & | & 1 \\ 0 & 1 & -4 & 1 & | & k-6 \end{bmatrix}$$

Perform $R_3 - R_2$

$$\sim \begin{bmatrix} 2 & -3 & 6 & -5 & | & 3 \\ 0 & 1 & -4 & 1 & | & 1 \\ 0 & 0 & 0 & 0 & | & k-7 \end{bmatrix}$$

Important step :

Step 4 : One can easily check that $\rho(A) = 3 - 1 = 2$. To find $\rho(A, B)$ we have to put down some condition on k – 7. This involves two cases.

Let us discuss case 1.

Case 1 : If $k - 7 = 0$ i.e. $k = 7$ then above system will become

$$\begin{bmatrix} 2 & -3 & 6 & -5 & | & 3 \\ 0 & 1 & -4 & 1 & | & 1 \\ 0 & 0 & 0 & 0 & | & 0 \end{bmatrix}$$

$\therefore$ $\rho(A) = \rho(A, B) = 3 - 1 = 2 < 4$

$\therefore$ System will possess an infinite number of solutions.

i.e. if $k = 7$ system possesses an infinite number of solutions.

Case 2 : If $k - 7 \neq 0$ i.e. $k \neq 7$. In this case, we have to select value of k other than 7 say $k = 1$ (you can choose any value) then above system becomes

$$\begin{bmatrix} 2 & -3 & 6 & -5 & | & 3 \\ 0 & 1 & -4 & 1 & | & 1 \\ 0 & 0 & 0 & 0 & | & -6 \end{bmatrix}$$

Note that $\rho(A) = 3 - 1 = 2 \quad \rho(A, B) = 3 - 0 = 3 \quad \rho(A) \neq \rho(A, B)$

$\therefore$ For $k \neq 7$ system possesses no solution.

Ex. 2 : *Show that if $\mu \neq 0$ the system of equations*

$2x + y = a$

$x + \mu y - z = b$

$y + 2z = c$

has unique solution for every choice of a, b, c. If $\mu = 0$, determine the relation satisfied by a, b, c such that the system is inconsistent. Find the general solution by taking $\mu = 0$, $a = 1$, $b = 1$, $c = -1$.

Sol. : Part 1 : The above system of equations in matrix form can be written as

$$\begin{bmatrix} 2 & 1 & 0 \\ 1 & \mu & -1 \\ 0 & 1 & 2 \end{bmatrix} \begin{bmatrix} x \\ y \\ z \end{bmatrix} = \begin{bmatrix} a \\ b \\ c \end{bmatrix}$$

Here 3 equations in 3 unknowns are there, hence we will apply another method. (For details, please see type 4).

$$|A| = \begin{vmatrix} 2 & 1 & 0 \\ 1 & \mu & -1 \\ 0 & 1 & 2 \end{vmatrix} = 2(2\mu + 1) - 1(2)$$

$$|A| = 4\mu$$

If $\mu \neq 0$ $\therefore$ $|A| \neq 0$ the system $AX = B$ always possesses a unique solution for every choice of a, b, c.

Part 2: If $\mu = 0$ then

$$\begin{bmatrix} 2 & 1 & 0 \\ 1 & 0 & -1 \\ 0 & 1 & 2 \end{bmatrix} \begin{bmatrix} x \\ y \\ z \end{bmatrix} = \begin{bmatrix} a \\ b \\ c \end{bmatrix}$$

Perform R_{12}, $\quad$ (A, B) $\sim \begin{bmatrix} 1 & 0 & -1 & | & b \\ 2 & 1 & 0 & | & a \\ 0 & 1 & 2 & | & c \end{bmatrix}$

Perform $R_2 - 2R_1$ $\quad \sim \begin{bmatrix} 1 & 0 & -1 & | & b \\ 0 & 1 & 2 & | & a-2b \\ 0 & 1 & 2 & | & c \end{bmatrix}$

Perform $R_3 - R_2$ $\quad \sim \begin{bmatrix} 1 & 0 & -1 & | & b \\ 0 & 1 & 2 & | & a-2b \\ 0 & 0 & 0 & | & c-a+2b \end{bmatrix}$ ... (1)

If $\mu = 0$ and $c - a + 2b \ne 0$ then $\rho(A) = 3 - 1 = 2$, $\rho(A, B) = 3 - 0 = 3$.

$\rho(A) \ne \rho(A, B)$ system is inconsistent.

Hence if $\mu = 0$ and $c - a + 2b \ne 0$ then system possesses no solution.

Part 3: If $\mu = 0$, $c - a + 2b = 0$ then $\rho(A) = \rho(A, B) = 2 < 3$. System possesses an infinite number of solutions.

Hence, system is consistent if $\mu = 0$ and $c - a + 2b = 0$.

Part 4: Take $\mu = 0$, $a = 1$, $b = 1$, $c = -1$. Substituting in equation (1), we get

$$(A, B) \sim \begin{bmatrix} 1 & 0 & -1 & | & 1 \\ 0 & 1 & 2 & | & -1 \\ 0 & 0 & 0 & | & 0 \end{bmatrix}$$

$\rho(A) = \rho(A, B) = 2 < 3$, system possesses an infinite no. of solutions.

By R_2 $\quad y + 2z = -1 \quad$ let $z = t \quad y = -1 - 2t$

By R_1 $\quad x - z = 1 \quad\quad\quad\quad\quad\quad x = 1 + t$

Hence if $\mu = 0$, $a = 1$, $b = 1$, $c = -1$ then solution set is $x = 1 + t$, $y = -1 - 2t$, $z = t$.

Ex. 3: *Investigate for what values of λ and μ, the system of simultaneous equations*

$x + y + z = 6$

$x + 2y + 3z = 10$

$x + 2y + \lambda z = \mu$

have (1) No solution. (2) A unique solution. (3) An infinite number of solutions.

Sol. : The above system in matrix form can be written as

$$\begin{bmatrix} 1 & 1 & 1 \\ 1 & 2 & 3 \\ 1 & 2 & \lambda \end{bmatrix} \begin{bmatrix} x \\ y \\ z \end{bmatrix} = \begin{bmatrix} 6 \\ 10 \\ \mu \end{bmatrix}$$

i.e. $\quad AX = B$

$$(A, B) = \begin{bmatrix} 1 & 1 & 1 & | & 6 \\ 1 & 2 & 3 & | & 10 \\ 1 & 2 & \lambda & | & \mu \end{bmatrix}$$

Perform $R_2 - R_1$, $R_3 - R_1$

$$\sim \begin{bmatrix} 1 & 1 & 1 & | & 6 \\ 0 & 1 & 2 & | & 4 \\ 0 & 1 & \lambda-1 & | & \mu-6 \end{bmatrix}$$

Perform $R_3 - R_2$

$$\sim \begin{bmatrix} 1 & 1 & 1 & | & 6 \\ 0 & 1 & 2 & | & 4 \\ 0 & 0 & \lambda-3 & | & \mu-10 \end{bmatrix}$$

Case 1 : For no solution : This will happen only when $\rho(A) \neq \rho(A, B)$

When $\lambda - 3 = 0$ and $\mu - 10 \neq 0$

i.e. $\lambda = 3$, $\mu \neq 10$ then $\rho(A) = 3 - 1 = 2$, $\rho(A, B) = 3 - 0 = 3$

$\rho(A) \neq \rho(A, B)$, system possesses no solution.

Hence for $\lambda = 3$, $\mu \neq 10$ then system possesses no solution.

Case 2 : For a unique solution : This will happen only when $\rho(A) = \rho(A, B) = 3 =$ number of variables.

i.e. When $\lambda - 3 \neq 0$ but μ can take any value then $\rho(A) = 3 - 0 = 3$,

$\rho(A, B) = 3 - 0 = 3$.

$\rho(A) = \rho(A, B) = 3 =$ number of variables, system possesses a unique solution.

Hence for $\lambda \neq 3$ and μ can take any value then system possesses a unique solution.

Case 3 : For an infinite number of solutions : This will happen only when

$\rho(A) = \rho(A, B) = 2 < 3$ (number of variables)

i.e. when $\lambda - 3 = 0$, $\mu - 10 = 0$

i.e. $\lambda = 3$, $\mu = 10$.

Then $\rho(A) = \rho(A, B) = 3 - 1 = 2 < 3$. System is consistent and possesses an infinite number of solutions.

Hence if $\lambda = 3$, $\mu = 10$ then system possesses an infinite number of solutions.

Ex. 4 : *Use matrix method to determine the values of λ for which the equations*

$x + 2y + z = 3$

$x + y + z = \lambda$

$3x + y + 3z = \lambda^2$ *are consistent and solve them for these values of λ.* **(May 09, 13)**

Sol.: In matrix form, the above system can be written as

$$\begin{bmatrix} 1 & 2 & 1 \\ 1 & 1 & 1 \\ 3 & 1 & 3 \end{bmatrix} \begin{bmatrix} x \\ y \\ z \end{bmatrix} = \begin{bmatrix} 3 \\ \lambda \\ \lambda^2 \end{bmatrix}$$

$$(A, B) = \begin{bmatrix} 1 & 2 & 1 & | & 3 \\ 1 & 1 & 1 & | & \lambda \\ 3 & 1 & 3 & | & \lambda^2 \end{bmatrix}$$

Perform $R_2 - R_1, R_3 - 3R_1$

$$\sim \begin{bmatrix} 1 & 2 & 1 & | & 3 \\ 0 & -1 & 0 & | & \lambda - 3 \\ 0 & -5 & 0 & | & \lambda^2 - 9 \end{bmatrix}$$

Perform $R_3 - 5R_2$

$$\sim \begin{bmatrix} 1 & 2 & 1 & | & 3 \\ 0 & -1 & 0 & | & \lambda - 3 \\ 0 & 0 & 0 & | & \lambda^2 - 5\lambda + 6 \end{bmatrix}$$

If $\lambda^2 - 5\lambda + 6 = 0$ $(\lambda - 2)(\lambda - 3) = 0$

$\lambda = 2, \lambda = 3$ then given system is consistent and possesses an infinite no. of solutions.

For $\lambda = 2$, $(A, B) = \begin{bmatrix} 1 & 2 & 1 & | & 3 \\ 0 & -1 & 0 & | & -1 \\ 0 & 0 & 0 & | & 0 \end{bmatrix}$

By R_2 $-y = -1$ $y = 1$
By R_1 $x + 2y + z = 3$ $x + z = 1$ $z = t$ $x = 1 - t$
For $\lambda = 2$, $x = 1 - t, y = 1, z = t$

For $\lambda = 3$, $(A, B) = \begin{bmatrix} 1 & 2 & 1 & | & 3 \\ 0 & -1 & 0 & | & 0 \\ 0 & 0 & 0 & | & 0 \end{bmatrix}$

By R_2 $-y = 0$ $y = 0$
By R_1 $x + 2y + z = 3$ $x + z = 3$ $z = t$ $x = 3 - t$
For $\lambda = 3$, $x = 3 - t$, $y = 0$, $z = t$.

EXERCISE 2.2

1. Investigate for what values of a & b, the system of simultaneous equations:
    $2x - y + 3z = 2$
    $x + y + 2z = 2$
    $5x - y + az = b$
    have (1) No solution. (2) A unique solution. (3) An infinite number of solutions. **(Dec. 2006)**

Ans. a = 8, b ≠ 6; system possesses no solution.

  a ≠ 8, b may have any value, system possesses a unique system.

  a = 8, b = 6 then system possesses an infinite number of solutions.

2. Investigate the values of λ and μ so that the equations
$$2x + 3y + 5z = 9$$
$$7x + 3y - 2z = 8$$
$$2x + 3y + \lambda z = \mu$$
have (1) No solution. (2) A unique solution. (3) An infinite number of solutions.

Ans. λ = 5, μ ≠ 9, system possesses no solution.

  λ ≠ 5 and for any value of μ, system possesses a unique solution.

  λ = 5, μ = 9 then system possesses an infinite number of solutions.

3. Investigate for what values of k the equations
$$x + y + z = 1$$
$$2x + y + 4z = k$$
$$4x + y + 10z = k^2$$
have infinite number of solutions ? Hence, find solutions.

Ans. k = 1, 2. **(Dec. 2005, May 2006)**

4. Show that the system
$$3x + 4y + 5z = \alpha$$
$$4x + 5y + 6z = \beta$$
$$5x + 6y + 7z = \gamma$$
is consistent only when α, β, γ are in arithmetic progression. **(May 05, 14)**

5. Show that the following system of equations
$$3x + 4y + 5z = a$$
$$4x + 5y + 6z = b$$
$$5x + 6y + 7z = c$$
will be consistent only when a + c = 2b. **(May 2008)**

2.9 TYPE 3 : PROBLEMS ON NON-HOMOGENEOUS EQUATIONS WHERE SYSTEM IS INCONSISTENT

Ex. 1 : *Solve or establish the inconsistency of the following system of equations*
$$2x - 3y + 7z = 5$$
$$3x + y - 3z = 13$$
$$2x + 19y - 47z = 32$$

Sol. : The above system in matrix form can be written as

$$\begin{bmatrix} 2 & -3 & 7 \\ 3 & 1 & -3 \\ 2 & 19 & -47 \end{bmatrix} \begin{bmatrix} x \\ y \\ z \end{bmatrix} = \begin{bmatrix} 5 \\ 13 \\ 32 \end{bmatrix}$$

$$(A, B) = \begin{bmatrix} 2 & -3 & 7 & | & 5 \\ 3 & 1 & -3 & | & 13 \\ 2 & 19 & -47 & | & 32 \end{bmatrix}$$

Perform $R_1 - R_3$, $R_2 - R_3$

$$\sim \begin{bmatrix} 0 & -22 & 54 & | & -27 \\ 1 & -18 & 44 & | & -19 \\ 2 & 19 & -47 & | & 32 \end{bmatrix}$$

Perform R_{12}

$$\sim \begin{bmatrix} 1 & -18 & 44 & | & -19 \\ 0 & -22 & 54 & | & -27 \\ 2 & 19 & -47 & | & 32 \end{bmatrix}$$

Perform $R_3 - 2R_1$

$$\sim \begin{bmatrix} 1 & -18 & 44 & | & -19 \\ 0 & -22 & 54 & | & -27 \\ 0 & 55 & -135 & | & 70 \end{bmatrix}$$

Perform $\frac{1}{5} R_3$

$$\sim \begin{bmatrix} 1 & -18 & 44 & | & -19 \\ 0 & -22 & 54 & | & -27 \\ 0 & 11 & -27 & | & 14 \end{bmatrix}$$

Perform $R_2 + 2R_3$

$$\sim \begin{bmatrix} 1 & -18 & 44 & | & -19 \\ 0 & 0 & 0 & | & 1 \\ 0 & 11 & -27 & | & 14 \end{bmatrix}$$

Perform R_{23}

$$\sim \begin{bmatrix} 1 & -18 & 44 & | & -19 \\ 0 & 11 & -27 & | & 14 \\ 0 & 0 & 0 & | & 1 \end{bmatrix}$$

$\rho(A) = 3 - 1 = 2,$ $\qquad \rho(A, B) = 3 - 0 = 3,$ $\qquad \rho(A) \neq \rho(A, B)$

$\therefore$ System is inconsistent. $\quad \therefore$ No solution exists.

Ex. 2 : *Examine for consistency and solve, if consistent.*

$x + y + z = 3$
$2x - y + 3z = 1$
$4x + y + 5z = 2$
$3x - 2y + z = 4$

Sol. : The above system in matrix form can be written as

$$\begin{bmatrix} 1 & 1 & 1 \\ 2 & -1 & 3 \\ 4 & 1 & 5 \\ 3 & -2 & 1 \end{bmatrix} \begin{bmatrix} x \\ y \\ z \end{bmatrix} = \begin{bmatrix} 3 \\ 1 \\ 2 \\ 4 \end{bmatrix}$$

$$(A, B) = \begin{bmatrix} 1 & 1 & 1 & | & 3 \\ 2 & -1 & 3 & | & 1 \\ 4 & 1 & 5 & | & 2 \\ 3 & -2 & 1 & | & 4 \end{bmatrix}$$

Perform $R_2 - 2R_1, R_3 - 4R_1, R_4 - 3R_1$

$$\sim \begin{bmatrix} 1 & 1 & 1 & | & 3 \\ 0 & -3 & 1 & | & -5 \\ 0 & -3 & 1 & | & -10 \\ 0 & -5 & -2 & | & -5 \end{bmatrix}$$

Perform $R_3 - R_2, -\dfrac{1}{5} R_4$

$$\sim \begin{bmatrix} 1 & 1 & 1 & | & 3 \\ 0 & -3 & 1 & | & -5 \\ 0 & 0 & 0 & | & -5 \\ 0 & 1 & \dfrac{2}{5} & | & 1 \end{bmatrix}$$

Perform R_{24}

$$\sim \begin{bmatrix} 1 & 1 & 1 & | & 3 \\ 0 & 1 & \dfrac{2}{5} & | & 1 \\ 0 & 0 & 0 & | & -5 \\ 0 & -3 & 1 & | & -5 \end{bmatrix}$$

Perform $R_4 + 3R_2$

$$\sim \begin{bmatrix} 1 & 1 & 1 & | & 3 \\ 0 & 1 & \dfrac{2}{5} & | & 1 \\ 0 & 0 & 0 & | & -5 \\ 0 & 0 & \dfrac{11}{5} & | & -2 \end{bmatrix}$$

Perform R_{34}

$$\sim \begin{bmatrix} 1 & 1 & 1 & | & 3 \\ 0 & 1 & \dfrac{2}{5} & | & 1 \\ 0 & 0 & \dfrac{11}{5} & | & -2 \\ 0 & 0 & 0 & | & -5 \end{bmatrix}$$

$\rho(A) = 4 - 1 = 3,$ $\quad \rho(A, B) = 4 - 0 = 4 \quad \rho(A) \neq \rho(A, B)$

$\therefore$ System is inconsistent. $\quad \therefore$ No solution exists.

EXERCISE 2.3

(1) Examine for consistency and solve, if consistent.

$x_1 + x_2 + 2x_3 + x_4 = 5$

$2x_1 + 3x_2 - x_3 - 2x_4 = 2$

$4x_1 + 5x_2 + 3x_3 = 7$ **Ans.** System is inconsistent

(2) Examine for consistency and solve, if consistent.

$2x + 6y + 11 = 0$

$6x + 20y - 6z + 3 = 0$

$6y - 18z + 1 = 0$ **Ans.** System is inconsistent

2.10 TYPE 4 : PROBLEMS ON NON-HOMOGENEOUS EQUATIONS BY USING MATRIX INVERSION METHOD

Problems involving $|A| \neq 0$ with 3 equations in 3 unknowns.

Ex. 1 : *Solve, by matrix inversion, the system*

$x + y + z = 0$

$2x + 3y - z = -5$

$x - y + z = 4$

Sol. : Step 1 : m = no. of equations = 3, n = no. of unknowns = 3.

We will apply method of matrix inversion. The above system of equations in matrix form can be written as

$$\begin{bmatrix} 1 & 1 & 1 \\ 2 & 3 & -1 \\ 1 & -1 & 1 \end{bmatrix} \begin{bmatrix} x \\ y \\ z \end{bmatrix} = \begin{bmatrix} 0 \\ -5 \\ 4 \end{bmatrix}$$

i.e. AX = B.

Step 2 : $|A| = \begin{vmatrix} 1 & 1 & 1 \\ 2 & 3 & -1 \\ 1 & -1 & 1 \end{vmatrix}$

$= 1(3-1) - 1(2+1) + 1(-2-3) = 2 - 3 - 5$

$|A| = -6 \neq 0$

System is consistent. Also A^{-1} exists, system possesses a unique solution given by $X = A^{-1}B$.

Step 3 : $A^{-1} = \dfrac{1}{|A|}$ adj. A $\quad \therefore$ adj. A $= \begin{bmatrix} 2 & -2 & -4 \\ -3 & 0 & 3 \\ -5 & 2 & 1 \end{bmatrix}$

$$A^{-1} = \frac{1}{-6} \begin{bmatrix} 2 & -2 & -4 \\ -3 & 0 & 3 \\ -5 & 2 & 1 \end{bmatrix}$$

$$X = \frac{1}{-6} \begin{bmatrix} 2 & -2 & -4 \\ -3 & 0 & 3 \\ -5 & 2 & 1 \end{bmatrix} \begin{bmatrix} 0 \\ -5 \\ 4 \end{bmatrix} = \frac{1}{-6} \begin{bmatrix} -6 \\ 12 \\ -6 \end{bmatrix}$$

$$\begin{bmatrix} x \\ y \\ z \end{bmatrix} = \begin{bmatrix} 1 \\ -2 \\ 1 \end{bmatrix} \quad \text{i.e. } x = 1, \ y = -2, \ z = 1$$

Ex. 2: *Solve, by matrix inversion, the system*

$$x + 2y - z = 2$$
$$3x + 8y + 2z = 10$$
$$4x + 9y - z = 12$$

Sol.: Step 1: $m = 3$, $n = 3$. In matrix form

$$\begin{bmatrix} 1 & 2 & -1 \\ 3 & 8 & 2 \\ 4 & 9 & -1 \end{bmatrix} \begin{bmatrix} x \\ y \\ z \end{bmatrix} = \begin{bmatrix} 2 \\ 10 \\ 12 \end{bmatrix}$$

$$AX = B$$

Step 2:

$$|A| = \begin{vmatrix} 1 & 2 & -1 \\ 3 & 8 & 2 \\ 4 & 9 & -1 \end{vmatrix} = 1(-26) - 2(-11) - 1(-5)$$

$$|A| = 1 \neq 0$$

System is consistent. Also A^{-1} exists, system possesses a unique solution given by

$$X = A^{-1} B$$

Step 3:

$$A^{-1} = \frac{1}{|A|} \text{adj. } A$$

$$\therefore \quad \text{adj. } A = \begin{bmatrix} -26 & -7 & 12 \\ 11 & 3 & -5 \\ -5 & -1 & 2 \end{bmatrix}$$

$$\therefore \quad X = \frac{1}{1} \begin{bmatrix} -26 & -7 & 12 \\ 11 & 3 & -5 \\ -5 & -1 & 2 \end{bmatrix} \begin{bmatrix} 2 \\ 10 \\ 12 \end{bmatrix}$$

$$\begin{bmatrix} x \\ y \\ z \end{bmatrix} = \begin{bmatrix} 22 \\ -8 \\ 4 \end{bmatrix} \quad \therefore x = 22, \ y = -8, \ z = 4$$

EXERCISE 2.4

Solve, by matrix inversion, the systems

(1) $x + y + z = 3$
$x + 2y + 3z = 4$
$x + 4y + 9z = 6$ (Dec. 2012)
Ans. $x = 2, y = 1, z = 0$

(2) $3x - y + 4z = 3$
$x + 2y - 3z = -2$
$6x + 5y + z = -3$
Ans. $x = \frac{4}{7}, y = \frac{-9}{7}, z = 0$

(3) $9x + 7y + 3z = 6$
$5x - y + 4z = 1$
$3x + 5y + z = 2$
Ans. $x = 1, y = 0, z = -1$

(4) $3x + y + 2z = 3$
$2x - 3y - z = -3$
$x + 2y + z = 4$
Ans. $x = 1, y = 2, z = -1$

(5) $2x + 3y + 4z = 11$
$x + 5y + 7z = 15$
$3x + 11y + 13z = 25$
Ans. $x = 2, y = -3, z = 4$

(6) $x + 2y + z = -1$
$6x + y + z = -4$
$2x - 3y - z = 0$
Ans. $x = -1, y = -2, z = 4$

(7) Using the loop current method on a circuit, the following equations are obtained :

$7i_1 - 4i_2 = 12$
$-4i_1 + 12i_2 - 6i_3 = 0$
$-6i_2 + 14i_3 = 0$

By matrix method, solve for i_1, i_2 and i_3. **Ans.** $i_1 = \frac{396}{175}, i_2 = \frac{24}{25}, i_3 = \frac{72}{175}$

2.11 PROBLEMS INVOLVING |A| = 0

Ex. 1 : *Examine for consistency and if consistent then solve,*

$x + y + z = 1$
$x + 2y + 4z = 2$
$x + 4y + 10z = 4$

Sol. : Step 1 : Here $m = 3, n = 3$.

In matrix form,

$$\begin{bmatrix} 1 & 1 & 1 \\ 1 & 2 & 4 \\ 1 & 4 & 10 \end{bmatrix} \begin{bmatrix} x \\ y \\ z \end{bmatrix} = \begin{bmatrix} 1 \\ 2 \\ 4 \end{bmatrix}$$

Step 2 : $|A| = \begin{vmatrix} 1 & 1 & 1 \\ 1 & 2 & 4 \\ 1 & 4 & 10 \end{vmatrix} = 4 - 6 + 2$ $\therefore |A| = 0$

Step 3 : Consider

$$(A, B) = \begin{bmatrix} 1 & 1 & 1 & | & 1 \\ 1 & 2 & 4 & | & 2 \\ 1 & 4 & 10 & | & 4 \end{bmatrix}$$

Perform $R_2 - R_1, R_3 - R_1$

$$\sim \begin{bmatrix} 1 & 1 & 1 & | & 1 \\ 0 & 1 & 3 & | & 1 \\ 0 & 3 & 9 & | & 3 \end{bmatrix}$$

Perform $R_3 - 3R_2$

$$\sim \begin{bmatrix} 1 & 1 & 1 & | & 1 \\ 0 & 1 & 3 & | & 1 \\ 0 & 0 & 0 & | & 0 \end{bmatrix}$$

$\rho(A) = \rho(A, B) = 2 < 3$. System is consistent and possesses an infinite number of solutions.

By R_2 $y + 3z = 1$, $z = t$, $y = 1 - 3t$
By R_1 $x + y + z = 1$, $x = 1 - 1 + 3t - t = 2t$

$\therefore$ $x = 2t$, $y = 1 - 3t$, $z = t$ is the solution set.

Ex. 2 : *Examine for consistency and solve, if consistent*

$2x - 3y + 5z = 1$

$3x + y - z = 2$

$x + 4y - 6z = 1$

Sol. : Step 1 : The above system of equations in matrix form can be written as

$$(A, B) = \begin{bmatrix} 2 & -3 & 5 & | & 1 \\ 3 & 1 & -1 & | & 2 \\ 1 & 4 & -6 & | & 1 \end{bmatrix}$$

Step 2 :

$$|A| = \begin{vmatrix} 2 & -3 & 5 \\ 3 & 1 & -1 \\ 1 & 4 & -6 \end{vmatrix} = 2(-2) + 3(-17) + 5(11)$$

$|A| = 0$

Step 3 : We will apply method of reduction.

$$(A, B) = \begin{bmatrix} 2 & -3 & 5 & | & 1 \\ 3 & 1 & -1 & | & 2 \\ 1 & 4 & -6 & | & 1 \end{bmatrix}$$

Perform R_{13}
$$\sim \begin{bmatrix} 1 & 4 & -6 & | & 1 \\ 3 & 1 & -1 & | & 2 \\ 2 & -3 & 5 & | & 1 \end{bmatrix}$$

Perform $R_2 - 3R_1,\ R_3 - 2R_1$
$$\sim \begin{bmatrix} 1 & 4 & -6 & | & 1 \\ 0 & -11 & 17 & | & -1 \\ 0 & -11 & 17 & | & -1 \end{bmatrix}$$

Perform $R_3 - R_2$
$$\sim \begin{bmatrix} 1 & 4 & -6 & | & 1 \\ 0 & -11 & 17 & | & -1 \\ 0 & 0 & 0 & | & 0 \end{bmatrix}$$

$\rho(A) = \rho(A, B) = 3 - 1 = 2 < 3$

System possesses an infinite number of solutions.

By R_2 $\quad 11y + 17z = -1,\ y = t,\ z = \dfrac{-1 + 11t}{17}$

By R_1 $\quad x + 4y - 6z = 1,\ x = 1 - 4t + \dfrac{66t - 6}{17} = \dfrac{11 - 2t}{17}$

Hence the required solution set is $x = \dfrac{11 - 2t}{17},\ y = t,\ z = \dfrac{-1 + 11t}{17}$

EXERCISE 2.5

(1) Examine for consistency and solve, if consistent
$2x - y + 3z = 1$
$3x + 2y + z = 3$
$x - 4y + 5z = -1$
Ans. $x = \dfrac{5 - 7t}{7},\ y = \dfrac{3 + 7t}{7},\ z = t.$

(2) Examine for consistency and solve, if consistent
$5x + 3y + 7z = 4$
$3x + 26y + 2z = 9$
$7x + 2y + 10z = 5$
Ans. $x = 5 - 16t,\ y = t,\ z = 11t - 3.$

2.12 CONDITION FOR CONSISTENCY OF HOMOGENEOUS EQUATIONS

Consider a system of 'm' linear equations in 'n' unknowns $x_1, x_2, x_3, \ldots, x_n$:

$a_{11} x_1 + a_{12} x_2 + \ldots + a_{1n} x_n = 0$
$a_{21} x_1 + a_{22} x_2 + \ldots + a_{2n} x_n = 0$
$\quad \vdots \qquad\quad \vdots \qquad\quad \vdots$
$\quad \vdots \qquad\quad \vdots \qquad\quad \vdots$
$a_{m1} x_1 + a_{m2} x_2 + \ldots + a_{mn} x_n = 0$

This system in matrix notation can be written as

$$\begin{bmatrix} a_{11} & a_{12} & \cdots & a_{1n} \\ a_{21} & a_{22} & \cdots & a_{2n} \\ \vdots & & & \\ \vdots & & & \\ a_{m1} & a_{m2} & \cdots & a_{mn} \end{bmatrix} \begin{bmatrix} x_1 \\ x_2 \\ \vdots \\ \vdots \\ x_n \end{bmatrix} = \begin{bmatrix} 0 \\ 0 \\ \vdots \\ \vdots \\ 0 \end{bmatrix}$$

i.e. $\quad AX = Z$

where $\quad A =$ Coefficient matrix, $B =$ Null or zero matrix

The augmented matrix,

$$(A, B) = \begin{bmatrix} a_{11} & a_{12} & \cdots & a_{1n} & : & 0 \\ a_{21} & a_{22} & \cdots & a_{2n} & : & 0 \\ \vdots & \vdots & & \vdots & : & \vdots \\ \vdots & \vdots & & \vdots & : & \vdots \\ a_{m1} & a_{m2} & \cdots & a_{mm} & : & 0 \end{bmatrix}$$

We note that since $\rho(A) = \rho(A, Z)$, therefore the homogeneous system is always consistent.

For $\quad AX = Z$

Let $\quad m =$ total number of equations,

$\quad n =$ total number of unknowns

Case 1 : Let $m \neq n$, $m = n > 3$.

(No. of equations is different from no. of unknowns or 4 equations in 4 unknowns)

(1) If $\rho(A) = \rho(A, Z) = n$, no. of variables then system possesses a *unique solution* $x_1 = 0, x_2 = 0 \ldots x_n = 0$ which is also called as *trivial solution*.

(2) If $\rho(A) = \rho(A, Z) = r < n$, then system possesses an infinite number of solutions (called as non-trivial solution), where 'r' unknowns can be expressed in terms of remaining $(n - r)$ unknowns to which whatever values can be assigned.

Case 2 : Let $m = n = 3$ (No. of equations = no. of unknowns = 3 i.e. 3 equations in 3 unknowns). We have $AX = Z$.

Find $|A|$

(1) If $|A| \neq 0$, system possesses a unique solution, $X = A^{-1}Z$

i.e. $x_1 = 0 \ldots x_n = 0$. Hence is known as trivial solution.

(2) If $|A| = 0$ then apply method of reduction. $\rho(A) = \rho(A, Z) = r < n$ then system possesses *an infinite number of solutions (non-trivial solution)*.

Problems on homogeneous equations are mainly divided in the following types :

Type 1 : $AX = Z$ $m \neq n$, $m = n = 4$.

$\rho(A) = \rho(A, Z) = n$ $\Rightarrow$ unique solution i.e. trivial solution

$\rho(A) = \rho(A, Z) = r < n$ $\Rightarrow$ an infinite number of solutions.

i.e. non-trivial solution.

Type 2 : $AX = Z$ $m = n = 3$.

If $|A| \neq 0$ $\Rightarrow$ unique equation i.e. trivial solution.

If $|A| = 0$ $\Rightarrow$ an infinite number of solutions by using method of reduction.

2.13 CHART 3

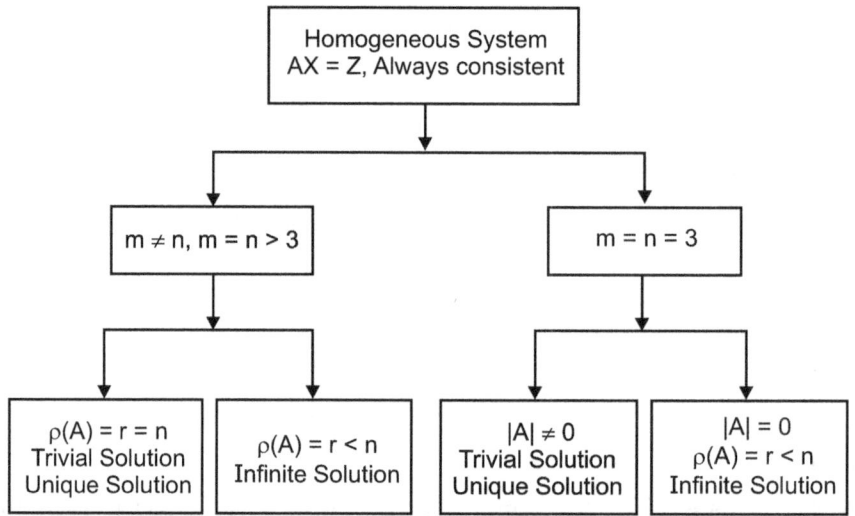

2.14 TYPE 1 : EXAMPLES ON HOMOGENEOUS SYSTEM OF EQUATIONS BY USING METHOD OF REDUCTION

Ex. 1 : *Examine for non-trivial solution, the following set of equations and solve them.*

$4x - y + 2z + t = 0$

$2x + 3y - z - 2t = 0$

$7y - 4z - 5t = 0$

$2x - 11y + 7z + 8t = 0$

Sol. : Step 1 : The above system in matrix form can be written as

$$\begin{bmatrix} 4 & -1 & 2 & 1 \\ 2 & 3 & -1 & -2 \\ 0 & 7 & -4 & -5 \\ 2 & -11 & 7 & 8 \end{bmatrix} \begin{bmatrix} x \\ y \\ z \\ t \end{bmatrix} = \begin{bmatrix} 0 \\ 0 \\ 0 \\ 0 \end{bmatrix}$$

$AX = Z$

Step 2 : Consider an augmented matrix,

$$(A, Z) = \begin{bmatrix} 4 & -1 & 2 & 1 & | & 0 \\ 2 & 3 & -1 & -2 & | & 0 \\ 0 & 7 & -4 & -5 & | & 0 \\ 2 & -11 & 7 & 8 & | & 0 \end{bmatrix}$$

Perform $R_1 - 2R_2, R_4 - R_2$

$$\sim \begin{bmatrix} 0 & -7 & 4 & 5 & | & 0 \\ 2 & 3 & -1 & -2 & | & 0 \\ 0 & 7 & -4 & -5 & | & 0 \\ 0 & -14 & 8 & 10 & | & 0 \end{bmatrix}$$

Perform R_{12}

$$\sim \begin{bmatrix} 2 & 3 & -1 & -2 & | & 0 \\ 0 & -7 & 4 & 5 & | & 0 \\ 0 & 7 & -4 & -5 & | & 0 \\ 0 & -14 & 8 & 10 & | & 0 \end{bmatrix}$$

Perform $R_3 + R_2, R_4 - 2R_2$

$$\sim \begin{bmatrix} 2 & 3 & -1 & -2 & | & 0 \\ 0 & -7 & 4 & 5 & | & 0 \\ 0 & 0 & 0 & 0 & | & 0 \\ 0 & 0 & 0 & 0 & | & 0 \end{bmatrix}$$

$$\rho(A) = \rho(A, Z) = 4 - 2 = 2 < 4$$

System possesses an infinite number of solutions which can be expressed in terms of 2 parameters say a, b.

By R_2 $\quad -7y + 4z + 5t = 0$

Let $t = a, z = b$ $\therefore 7y = 4b + 5a, \quad y = \dfrac{4b + 5a}{7}$

By R_1 $\quad 2x + 3y - z - 2t = 0 \quad\quad x = \dfrac{-12b - 15a}{14} + \dfrac{b}{2} + a = \dfrac{-5b - a}{14}$

Hence the required solution set is $x = \dfrac{-5b - a}{14}$, $y = \dfrac{4b + 5a}{7}$, $z = b$, $t = a$.

Ex. 2 : *Solve the following system of equations*

$x + 2y + 3z = 0$
$2x + 3y + z = 0$
$4x + 5y + 4z = 0$
$x + y - 2z = 0$

Sol. : Step 1 : In matrix form, the above system can be written as

$$\begin{bmatrix} 1 & 2 & 3 \\ 2 & 3 & 1 \\ 4 & 5 & 4 \\ 1 & 1 & -2 \end{bmatrix} \begin{bmatrix} x \\ y \\ z \end{bmatrix} = \begin{bmatrix} 0 \\ 0 \\ 0 \\ 0 \end{bmatrix}$$

$$(A, B) = \begin{bmatrix} 1 & 2 & 3 & | & 0 \\ 2 & 3 & 1 & | & 0 \\ 4 & 5 & 4 & | & 0 \\ 1 & 1 & -2 & | & 0 \end{bmatrix}$$

Perform $R_2 - 2R_1$, $R_3 - 4R_4$, $R_4 - R_1$

$$\sim \begin{bmatrix} 1 & 2 & 3 & | & 0 \\ 0 & -1 & -5 & | & 0 \\ 0 & -3 & -8 & | & 0 \\ 0 & -1 & -5 & | & 0 \end{bmatrix}$$

Perform $R_3 - 3R_2$, $R_4 - R_2$

$$\sim \begin{bmatrix} 1 & 2 & 3 & | & 0 \\ 0 & -1 & -5 & | & 0 \\ 0 & 0 & 7 & | & 0 \\ 0 & 0 & 0 & | & 0 \end{bmatrix}$$

$\rho(A) = \rho(A, Z) = 4 - 1 = 3$
= no. of variables.

∴ System possesses a unique solution (i.e.) trivial solution

By R_3 $7z = 0$ $z = 0$
By R_2 $-y - 5z = 0$ $y = 0$
By R_1 $x + 2y + 3z = 0$ $x = 0$

Hence $x = y = z = 0$ is a trivial solution.

EXERCISE 2.6

Examine for non-trivial solutions, the following set of equations and solve them.

(1) $2x_1 - 2x_2 + 5x_3 + 3x_4 = 0$
   $4x_1 - x_2 + x_3 + x_4 = 0$
   $3x_1 - 2x_2 + 3x_3 + 4x_4 = 0$
   $x_1 - 3x_2 + 7x_3 + 6x_4 = 0$
   Ans. $x_1 = \dfrac{5t}{9}$, $x_2 = 4t$, $x_3 = \dfrac{7t}{9}$, $x_4 = t$

(2) $2x_1 + x_2 + 3x_3 + 6x_4 = 0$
   $3x_1 - x_2 + x_3 + 3x_4 = 0$
   $-x_1 - 2x_2 + 3x_3 = 0$
   $-x_1 - 4x_2 - 2x_3 - 7x_4 = 0$
   Ans. $x_1 = -t$, $x_2 = -t$, $x_3 = -t$, $x_4 = t$

(3) $x + y + 2z = 0$
   $x + 2y + 3z = 0$
   $x + 3y + 4z = 0$
   $3x + 4y + 7z = 0$
   Ans. $x = -t$, $y = -t$, $z = t$

(4) $x + y + 3z = 0$
   $x - y + z = 0$
   $-x + 2y = 0$
   $x - y + z = 0$
   Ans. $x = -2t$, $y = -t$, $z = t$

(5) $x_1 + 3x_2 + 4x_3 - 6x_4 = 0$
    $x_2 + 6x_3 = 0$
    $2x_1 + 2x_2 + 2x_3 - 3x_4 = 0$
    $x_1 + x_2 - 4x_3 - 4x_4 = 0$

Ans. $x_1 = 2t$, $x_2 = -6t$, $x_3 = t$, $x_4 = -2t$

(6) $x_1 + 2x_2 - 3x_4 = 0$
    $2x_1 - x_2 + x_3 + 7x_4 = 0$
    $4x_1 + 3x_2 + 2x_3 + 2x_4 = 0$

Ans. $x_1 = \dfrac{-9t}{5}$, $x_2 = \dfrac{12t}{5}$, $x_3 = -t$, $x_4 = t$

2.15 TYPE 2 : EXAMPLES ON HOMOGENEOUS SYSTEM OF EQUATIONS WITH 3 EQUATIONS IN 3 UNKNOWNS

Ex. 1 : *Examine for non-trivial solutions*
$5x + 2y - 3z = 0$
$3x + y + z = 0$
$2x + y + 6z = 0$

Sol. : Step 1 : The above system in matrix form can be written as

$$\begin{bmatrix} 5 & 2 & -3 \\ 3 & 1 & 1 \\ 2 & 1 & 6 \end{bmatrix} \begin{bmatrix} x \\ y \\ z \end{bmatrix} = \begin{bmatrix} 0 \\ 0 \\ 0 \end{bmatrix}$$

Step 2 :
$$|A| = \begin{vmatrix} 5 & 2 & -3 \\ 3 & 1 & 1 \\ 2 & 1 & 6 \end{vmatrix} = 25 - 32 - 3$$

$|A| = -10 \neq 0$

Step 3 : $|A| \neq 0 \Rightarrow$ system possesses a unique solution
$X = A^{-1}Z$ i.e. $x = y = z = 0$

Hence system possesses a trivial solution.

Ex. 2 : *Show that the system of equations*
$ax + by + cz = 0$
$bx + cy + az = 0$
$cx + ay + bz = 0$
has a non-trivial solution only if $a + b + c = 0$ or if $a = b = c$.
Find the non-trivial solutions when the condition is satisfied.

Sol. : Step 1 : The above system in matrix form can be written as

$$\begin{bmatrix} a & b & c \\ b & c & a \\ c & a & b \end{bmatrix} \begin{bmatrix} x \\ y \\ z \end{bmatrix} = \begin{bmatrix} 0 \\ 0 \\ 0 \end{bmatrix}$$

i.e. $AX = Z$

Step 2 :
$$|A| = \begin{vmatrix} a & b & c \\ b & c & a \\ c & a & b \end{vmatrix}$$

If $|A| = 0$, system possesses a non-trivial solution.

$$a(bc - a^2) - b(b^2 - ac) + c(ab - c^2) = 0$$

i.e. $\quad a^3 + b^3 + c^3 - 3abc = 0$

Recalling from algebra, the standard factors are

$$(a + b + c)(a^2 + b^2 + c^2 - ab - bc - ac) = 0$$

Note : $x^3 + y^3 + z^3 - 3xyz = (x + y + z)(x^2 + y^2 + z^2 - xy - yz - zx)$

We have two possibilities : (1) either $a + b + c = 0$ or

(2) $(a^2 + b^2 + c^2 - ab - bc - ca) = 0$

i.e. $\quad a^2 - ab + b^2 - bc + c^2 - ac = 0$

$\frac{1}{2}[(a^2 - 2ab + b^2) + (b^2 - 2bc + c^2) + (c^2 - 2ac + a^2)] = 0$ (Carefully note down the adjustments)

$\frac{1}{2}[(a-b)^2 + (b-c)^2 + (c-a)^2] = 0 \quad$ i.e. $(a-b)^2 + (b-c)^2 + (c-a)^2 = 0$

Requires $a - b = 0$, $b - c = 0$, $c - a = 0$, i.e. $a = b = c$.

Hence system possesses a non-trivial solution only if $a + b + c = 0$ or if $a = b = c$.

Step 3 : If $a + b + c = 0$ then the given system is equivalent to only two distinct equations

$$ax + by + cz = 0$$
$$bx + cy + az = 0$$

Solving by Cramer's rule, $\quad \dfrac{x}{\begin{vmatrix} b & c \\ c & a \end{vmatrix}} = \dfrac{-y}{\begin{vmatrix} a & c \\ b & a \end{vmatrix}} = \dfrac{z}{\begin{vmatrix} a & b \\ b & c \end{vmatrix}}$

$$\frac{x}{ab - c^2} = \frac{-y}{a^2 - bc} = \frac{z}{ac - b^2} = t \text{ (say)}$$

$\therefore \quad x = (ab - c^2) t \qquad y = (bc - a^2) t \qquad z = (ac - b^2) t$

Step 4 : If $a = b = c$ the given system is equivalent to only one equation.

e.g. $\qquad\qquad\qquad ax + by + cz = 0 \qquad a = b = c$

$\qquad\qquad\qquad\qquad a(x + y + z) = 0$

$\because \quad a \neq 0 \qquad \therefore \quad x + y + z = 0$

$z = t, \; y = s \quad \therefore \quad x = -s - t$

Hence

If $a + b + c = 0$ then $x = (ab - c^2)t$, $y = (bc - a^2)t$, $z = (ca - b^2)t$ is the solution.

If $a = b = c$ then $x = -s - t$, $y = s$, $z = t$ is the solution.

Ex. 3 : *For different values of k, discuss the nature of solution of the following equations*

$$x + 2y - z = 0$$
$$3x + (k + 7)y - 3z = 0$$
$$2x + 4y + (k - 3)z = 0.$$

Sol. : Step 1 : Above system in matrix form can be written as

$$\begin{bmatrix} 1 & 2 & -1 \\ 3 & k+7 & -3 \\ 2 & 4 & k-3 \end{bmatrix} \begin{bmatrix} x \\ y \\ z \end{bmatrix} = \begin{bmatrix} 0 \\ 0 \\ 0 \end{bmatrix}$$

i.e. $AX = Z$

Step 2 :

$$|A| = \begin{vmatrix} 1 & 2 & -1 \\ 3 & k+7 & -3 \\ 2 & 4 & k-3 \end{vmatrix}$$

$$|A| = [(k+7)(k-3) + 12] - 2(3k - 9 + 6) - 1(12 - 2k - 14)$$
$$= k^2 + 4k - 9 - 6k + 6 + 2 + 2k$$
$$= k^2 - 1$$

Case 1 : If $|A| \neq 0$ i.e. $k^2 - 1 \neq 0$, i.e. $k = \pm 1$ the system possesses a unique solution.

i.e. trivial solution $x = y = z = 0$

Case 2 : If $|A| = 0$ i.e. $k^2 - 1 = 0$, i.e. $k = 1$, $k = -1$, system possesses a non-trivial solution.

For $k = 1$, $(A, Z) = \begin{bmatrix} 1 & 2 & -1 & | & 0 \\ 3 & 8 & -3 & | & 0 \\ 2 & 4 & -2 & | & 0 \end{bmatrix}$

Perform $R_2 - 3R_1$, $R_3 - 2R_1$ $\sim \begin{bmatrix} 1 & 2 & -1 & | & 0 \\ 0 & 2 & 0 & | & 0 \\ 0 & 0 & 0 & | & 0 \end{bmatrix}$

$\rho(A) = \rho(A, Z) = 3 - 1 = 2 < 3.$

∴ System possesses an infinite number of solutions.

By R_2, $2y = 0$, $y = 0$
By R_1, $x + 2y - z = 0$, $x - z = 0$, $z = t$, $x = t$.

For $k = -1$ $(A, Z) = \begin{bmatrix} 1 & 2 & -1 & | & 0 \\ 3 & 6 & -3 & | & 0 \\ 2 & 4 & -4 & | & 0 \end{bmatrix}$

Perform $R_2 - 3R_1$, $R_3 - 2R_1$

$$\sim \begin{bmatrix} 1 & 2 & -1 & | & 0 \\ 0 & 0 & 0 & | & 0 \\ 0 & 0 & -2 & | & 0 \end{bmatrix}$$

$\rho(A) = \rho(A, Z) = 3 - 1 = 2 < 3$

System possesses an infinite number of solutions.

By R_3 $-2z = 0$ $z = 0$

By R_1 $x + 2y - z = 0$ $x + 2y = 0$, $y = t$, $x = -2t$

For $k = 1$, $x = t$, $y = 0$, $z = t$.   For $k = -1$, $x = -2t$, $y = t$, $z = 0$.

Ex. 4 : *Show that the system of equations*

$x_1 + 2x_2 + 3x_3 = \lambda x_1$

$3x_1 + x_2 + 2x_3 = \lambda x_2$

$2x_1 + 3x_2 + x_3 = \lambda x_3$

can possess a non-trivial solution only if $\lambda = 6$. Obtain the general solution for real values of λ.

Sol. : Step 1 : The above system of equations in matrix form can be written as

$$\begin{bmatrix} (1-\lambda) & 2 & 3 \\ 3 & (1-\lambda) & 2 \\ 2 & 3 & (1-\lambda) \end{bmatrix} \begin{bmatrix} x_1 \\ x_2 \\ x_3 \end{bmatrix} = \begin{bmatrix} 0 \\ 0 \\ 0 \end{bmatrix}$$

i.e. $AX = Z$

Step 2 : $|A| = \begin{vmatrix} 1-\lambda & 2 & 3 \\ 3 & 1-\lambda & 2 \\ 2 & 3 & 1-\lambda \end{vmatrix}$

$= \lambda^3 - 3\lambda^2 - 15\lambda - 18$

$\lambda = \pm 1, \pm 2, \pm 3, \ldots\ldots\ldots$

$\lambda = 6$ satisfies this equation.

6	1	−3	−15	−18
		6	18	18
	1	3	3	0

$|A| = (\lambda - 6)(\lambda^2 + 3\lambda + 3)$.

If $|A| = 0$, system possesses a non-trivial solution.

i.e. $\lambda = 6$ is the only real value of λ.

∴ Put $\lambda = 6$ $(A, Z) = \begin{bmatrix} -5 & 2 & 3 & | & 0 \\ 3 & -5 & 2 & | & 0 \\ 2 & 3 & -5 & | & 0 \end{bmatrix}$

Perform $R_1 + 2R_3$, $R_2 - R_3$ $\sim \begin{bmatrix} -1 & 8 & -7 & | & 0 \\ 1 & -8 & 7 & | & 0 \\ 2 & 3 & -5 & | & 0 \end{bmatrix}$

Perform $R_1 + R_2$, $R_3 - 2R_2$ $\sim \begin{bmatrix} 0 & 0 & 0 & | & 0 \\ 1 & -8 & 7 & | & 0 \\ 0 & 19 & -19 & | & 0 \end{bmatrix}$

$\rho(A) = \rho(A, Z) = 3 - 1 = 2 < 3$

System possesses an infinite number of solutions.

By R_3 $19x_2 - 19x_3 = 0$ $x_3 = t,$ $x_2 = t$

By R_2 $x_1 - 8x_2 + 7x_3 = 0$ $x_1 = t$

For real value of $\lambda = 6$, $x_1 = x_2 = x_3 = t$

EXERCISE 2.7

Examine for non-trivial solutions :

(1) $x + 2y + 3z = 0$
    $2x + 3y + z = 0$
    $4x + 5y + 4z = 0$
    Ans. $|A| = -7 \neq 0$,
    trivial solution $x = y = z = 0$

(2) $4x_1 - x_2 + x_3 = 0$
    $x_1 + 2x_2 - x_3 = 0$
    $3x_1 + x_2 + 5x_3 = 0$
    Ans. $|A| = 47 \neq 0$,
    trivial solution $x_1 = x_2 = x_3 = 0$

(3) $2x - y + 3z = 0$
    $3x + 2y + z = 0$
    $x - 4y + 5z = 0$
    Ans. $|A| = 0$, $x = t$, $y = -t$, $z = t$

(4) $x + 3y + z = 0$
    $2x - 2y - 6z = 0$
    $3x + y - 5z = 0$
    Ans. $|A| = 0$, $x = 2t$, $y = -t$, $z = t$

(5) $x + 2y = 0$
    $2x - y + z = 0$
    $4x + 3y + 2z = 0$
    Ans. $|A| = -5 \neq 0$, $x = y = z = 0$.

2.16 VECTOR, LINEAR DEPENDENT AND INDEPENDENT VECTORS

We define n dimensional vector as an ordered set of n elements $x_1, x_2, ..., x_n$ and is denoted by
$$x = \begin{bmatrix} x_1 \\ x_2 \\ \vdots \\ \vdots \\ x_n \end{bmatrix}, \quad x = [x_1, x_2, ..., x_n].$$

The elements $x_1, x_2, ..., x_n$ are called components of x.

2.17 DEFINITION OF LINEAR DEPENDENT VECTORS

Let $x_1, x_2, ..., x_n$ be a system of n row (or column) matrices of the same order (also called vectors).

If there exist n scalars $c_1, c_2, c_3, ... c_n$, **not all zero,**

such that $c_1 x_1 + c_2 x_2 + ... + c_n x_n = 0$,

then the system of n vectors is called as *linearly dependent*.

2.18 DEFINITION OF LINEAR INDEPENDENT VECTORS

Let $x_1, x_2, ..., x_n$ be a system of n row (or column) matrices of the *same order* (also called vectors).

The system of n vectors $x_1, x_2, ..., x_n$ is said to be *linearly independent*, if every relation of the type $c_1 x_1 + c_2 x_2 + ... + c_n x_n = 0$ implies $c_1 = c_2 = c_3 ... c_n = 0$.

2.19 PROBLEMS ON LINEARLY DEPENDENT, INDEPENDENT VECTORS

Ex. 1 : *Examine for linear dependence or independence of vectors (2, –1, 3, 2), (1, 3, 4, 2) and (3, –5, 2, 2). Find a relation between them if dependent.* **(May 2004, 2009, 2014)**

Sol. : Step 1 : Let the given vectors be $x_1 = (2, -1, 3, 2)$, $x_2 = (1, 3, 4, 2)$ and $x_3 = (3, -5, 2, 2)$. Consider the matrix equation $c_1 x_1 + c_2 x_2 + c_3 x_3 = 0$

$c_1(2, -1, 3, 2) + c_2(1, 3, 4, 2) + c_3(3, -5, 2, 2) = (0, 0, 0, 0)$.

i.e.
$$2c_1 + c_2 + 3c_3 = 0$$
$$-c_1 + 3c_2 - 5c_3 = 0$$
$$3c_1 + 4c_2 + 2c_3 = 0$$
$$2c_1 + 2c_2 + 2c_3 = 0$$

which is a homogeneous system of equations.

Step 2 : In matrix form,

$$\begin{bmatrix} 2 & 1 & 3 \\ -1 & 3 & -5 \\ 3 & 4 & 2 \\ 2 & 2 & 2 \end{bmatrix} \begin{bmatrix} c_1 \\ c_2 \\ c_3 \end{bmatrix} = \begin{bmatrix} 0 \\ 0 \\ 0 \\ 0 \end{bmatrix}$$

$$(A, Z) = \begin{bmatrix} 2 & 1 & 3 & | & 0 \\ -1 & 3 & -5 & | & 0 \\ 3 & 4 & 2 & | & 0 \\ 2 & 2 & 2 & | & 0 \end{bmatrix}$$

Perform $R_1 + R_2$, $R_3 + 3R_2$, $R_4 + 2R_2$

$$\sim \begin{bmatrix} 1 & 4 & -2 & | & 0 \\ -1 & 3 & -5 & | & 0 \\ 0 & 13 & -13 & | & 0 \\ 0 & 8 & -8 & | & 0 \end{bmatrix}$$

Perform $R_2 + R_1$, $\frac{1}{13}R_3$, $\frac{1}{8}R_4$

$$\sim \begin{bmatrix} 1 & 4 & -2 & | & 0 \\ 0 & 7 & -7 & | & 0 \\ 0 & 1 & -1 & | & 0 \\ 0 & 1 & -1 & | & 0 \end{bmatrix}$$

Perform $R_2 - 7R_3$, $R_4 - R_3$

$$\sim \begin{bmatrix} 1 & 4 & -2 & | & 0 \\ 0 & 0 & 0 & | & 0 \\ 0 & 1 & -1 & | & 0 \\ 0 & 0 & 0 & | & 0 \end{bmatrix}$$

Perform R_{23}

$$\sim \begin{bmatrix} 1 & 4 & -2 & | & 0 \\ 0 & 1 & -1 & | & 0 \\ 0 & 0 & 0 & | & 0 \\ 0 & 0 & 0 & | & 0 \end{bmatrix}$$

$\rho(A) = \rho(A, Z) = 4 - 2 = 2 < 3$

∴ System possesses a non-trivial solution.

By R_2 $c_2 - c_3 = 0$, $c_3 = t$, $c_2 = t$

By R_1 $c_1 + 4c_2 - 2c_3 = 0$, $c_1 = -2t$

Note that we got all c_1, c_2, c_3 non-zero, therefore, x_1, x_2, x_3 are linearly dependent.

Step 3 : From the matrix equation $c_1 x_1 + c_2 x_2 + c_3 x_3 = 0$

i.e. $-2t\, x_1 + t\, x_2 + t\, x_3 = 0$ or $2x_1 = x_2 + x_3$ which is the required relation among them.

Step 4 : Final check : $2x_1 = x_2 + x_3$

$2\,(2, -1, 3, 2) = (1, 3, 4, 2) + (3, -5, 2, 2)$

$(4, -2, 6, 4) = (4, -2, 6, 4)$

Ex. 2 : *Show that $\vec{x_1}\ \vec{x_2}\ \vec{x_3}$ are linearly independent and $\vec{x_4}$ depends upon them where*

$\vec{x_1} = (1, 2, 4)$, $\vec{x_2} = (2, -1, 3)$, $\vec{x_3} = (0, 1, 2)$, $\vec{x_4} = (-3, 7, 2)$. **(Dec. 2005)**

Sol. : Part 1 : First we will show that $x_1\ x_2\ x_3$ are linearly independent. Consider the matrix equation $\quad c_1 x_1 + c_2 x_2 + c_3 x_3 = 0$

$c_1(1, 2, 4) + c_2(2, -1, 3) + c_3(0, 1, 2) = (0, 0, 0)$

$$c_1 + 2c_2 = 0$$
$$2c_1 - c_2 + c_3 = 0$$
$$4c_1 + 3c_2 + 2c_3 = 0$$

In matrix form

$$\begin{bmatrix} 1 & 2 & 0 \\ 2 & -1 & 1 \\ 4 & 3 & 2 \end{bmatrix} \begin{bmatrix} c_1 \\ c_2 \\ c_3 \end{bmatrix} = \begin{bmatrix} 0 \\ 0 \\ 0 \end{bmatrix} \quad \therefore\ |A| = \begin{vmatrix} 1 & 2 & 0 \\ 2 & -1 & 1 \\ 4 & 3 & 2 \end{vmatrix} \quad |A| = -5 \neq 0$$

$\therefore\quad$ Above system possesses a unique solution i.e. trivial solution $c_1 = 0$, $c_2 = 0$, $c_3 = 0$

$\therefore\quad$ Vectors x_1, x_2, x_3 are linearly independent.

Part 2 : We will check linear dependence for x_1, x_2, x_3 and x_4.

Consider the matrix equation $\ c_1 x_1 + c_2 x_2 + c_3 x_3 + c_4 x_4 = 0$

$c_1(1, 2, 4) + c_2(2, -1, 3) + c_3(0, 1, 2) + c_4(-3, 7, 2) = (0, 0, 0)$

$$c_1 + 2c_2 - 3c_4 = 0$$
$$2c_1 - c_2 + c_3 + 7c_4 = 0$$
$$4c_1 + 3c_2 + 2c_3 + 2c_4 = 0$$

In matrix form, $\quad \begin{bmatrix} 1 & 2 & 0 & -3 \\ 2 & -1 & 1 & 7 \\ 4 & 3 & 2 & 2 \end{bmatrix} \begin{bmatrix} c_1 \\ c_2 \\ c_3 \\ c_4 \end{bmatrix} = \begin{bmatrix} 0 \\ 0 \\ 0 \end{bmatrix}$

$$(A, Z) = \begin{bmatrix} 1 & 2 & 0 & -3 & | & 0 \\ 2 & -1 & 1 & 7 & | & 0 \\ 4 & 3 & 2 & 2 & | & 0 \end{bmatrix}$$

Perform $R_2 - 2R_1$, $R_3 - 4R_1$ $\quad \sim \begin{bmatrix} 1 & 2 & 0 & -3 & | & 0 \\ 0 & -5 & 1 & 13 & | & 0 \\ 0 & -5 & 2 & 14 & | & 0 \end{bmatrix}$

Perform $R_3 - R_2$

$$\sim \begin{bmatrix} 1 & 2 & 0 & -3 & | & 0 \\ 0 & -5 & 1 & 13 & | & 0 \\ 0 & 0 & 1 & 1 & | & 0 \end{bmatrix}$$

$$\rho(A) = \rho(A, Z) = 3 - 0 = 3 < 4$$

System possesses a non-trivial solution.

By R_3 $\qquad c_3 + c_4 = 0, \qquad c_4 = t, \qquad c_3 = -t$

By R_2 $\qquad -5c_2 + c_3 + 13c_4 = 0, \qquad c_2 = \dfrac{12}{5}t$

By R_1 $\qquad c_1 + 2c_2 - 3c_4 = 0, \qquad c_1 = -\dfrac{9}{5}t$

Since c_1, c_2, c_3, c_4 are non-zero, therefore, x_1, x_2, x_3, x_4 are linearly dependent.

From the matrix equation $c_1 x_1 + c_2 x_2 + c_3 x_3 + c_4 x_4 = 0$

$$-\dfrac{9}{5}t\, x_1 + \dfrac{12}{5} t\, x_2 - t\, x_3 + t\, x_4 = 0$$

$-9x_1 + 12x_2 - 5x_3 + 5x_4 = 0$ or $9x_1 + 5x_3 = 12x_2 + 5x_4$

which is the required relation among them.

Ex. 3: *Define linear dependence and independence of vectors. Examine for linear dependence of vectors $(1, 2, -1, 0)$, $(1, 3, 1, 2)$, $(4, 2, 1, 0)$, $(6, 1, 0, 1)$ and find a relation between them if dependent.* **(May 2005, 2009)**

Sol. : Part 1 : For definition refer article 2.4.

Part 2 : Let the given vectors be

$x_1 = (1, 2, -1, 0), \; x_2 = (1, 3, 1, 2), \; x_3 = (4, 2, 1, 0), \; x_4 = (6, 1, 0, 1)$

Consider the matrix equation $c_1 x_1 + c_2 x_2 + c_3 x_3 + c_4 x_4 = 0$

$c_1 (1, 2, -1, 0) + c_2 (1, 3, 1, 2) + c_3 (4, 2, 1, 0) + c_4 (6, 1, 0, 1) = 0$

$$\begin{aligned} c_1 + c_2 + 4c_3 + 6c_4 &= 0 \\ 2c_1 + 3c_2 + 2c_3 + c_4 &= 0 \\ -c_1 + c_2 + c_3 &= 0 \\ 2c_2 + c_4 &= 0 \end{aligned}$$

In matrix form, $\begin{bmatrix} 1 & 1 & 4 & 6 \\ 2 & 3 & 2 & 1 \\ -1 & 1 & 1 & 0 \\ 0 & 2 & 0 & 1 \end{bmatrix} \begin{bmatrix} c_1 \\ c_2 \\ c_3 \\ c_4 \end{bmatrix} = \begin{bmatrix} 0 \\ 0 \\ 0 \\ 0 \end{bmatrix}$

$$(A, Z) = \begin{bmatrix} 1 & 1 & 4 & 6 & | & 0 \\ 2 & 3 & 2 & 1 & | & 0 \\ -1 & 1 & 1 & 0 & | & 0 \\ 0 & 2 & 0 & 1 & | & 0 \end{bmatrix}$$

Perform $R_2 - 2R_1$, $R_3 + R_1$

$$\sim \begin{bmatrix} 1 & 1 & 4 & 6 & | & 0 \\ 0 & 1 & -6 & -11 & | & 0 \\ 0 & 2 & 5 & 6 & | & 0 \\ 0 & 2 & 0 & 1 & | & 0 \end{bmatrix}$$

Perform $R_3 - 2R_2$, $R_4 - 2R_2$

$$\sim \begin{bmatrix} 1 & 1 & 4 & 6 & | & 0 \\ 0 & 1 & -6 & -11 & | & 0 \\ 0 & 0 & 17 & 28 & | & 0 \\ 0 & 0 & 12 & 23 & | & 0 \end{bmatrix}$$

Perform $R_4 - \dfrac{12}{17} R_3$

$$\sim \begin{bmatrix} 1 & 1 & 4 & 6 & | & 0 \\ 0 & 1 & -6 & -11 & | & 0 \\ 0 & 0 & 17 & 28 & | & 0 \\ 0 & 0 & 0 & \dfrac{55}{17} & | & 0 \end{bmatrix}$$

$$\rho(A) = \rho(A, Z) = 4 - 0 = 4$$

∴ System possesses a unique solution i.e. trivial solution. $c_1 = c_2 = c_3 = c_4 = 0$.
∴ x_1, x_2, x_3, x_4 are linearly independent.
Hence there does not exist any relation among them.

Ex. 4 : *Find the rank of the matrix* $\begin{bmatrix} 1 & 1 & -1 & 1 \\ 1 & -1 & 2 & -1 \\ 3 & 1 & 0 & 1 \end{bmatrix}$

Discuss and find the relation of linear dependence amongst its row vectors.

Sol. : Part 1 :

$$A = \begin{bmatrix} 1 & 1 & -1 & 1 \\ 1 & -1 & 2 & -1 \\ 3 & 1 & 0 & 1 \end{bmatrix}$$

Perform $R_2 - R_1$, $R_3 - 3R_1$

$$\sim \begin{bmatrix} 1 & 1 & -1 & 1 \\ 0 & -2 & 3 & -2 \\ 0 & -2 & 3 & -2 \end{bmatrix}$$

Perform $R_3 - R_2$

$$\sim \begin{bmatrix} 1 & 1 & -1 & 1 \\ 0 & -2 & 3 & -2 \\ 0 & 0 & 0 & 0 \end{bmatrix}$$

$\rho(A) = 3 - 1 = 2$ ∴ $\rho(A) = 2$

Part 2 : Let the row vectors be $x_1 = (1, 1, -1, 1)$, $x_2 = (1, -1, 2, -1)$, $x_3 = (3, 1, 0, 1)$
Consider the matrix equation $c_1 x_1 + c_2 x_2 + c_3 x_3 = 0$.
$c_1(1, 1, -1, 1) + c_2(1, -1, 2, -1) + c_3(3, 1, 0, 1) = (0, 0, 0, 0)$

$$c_1 + c_2 + 3c_3 = 0$$
$$c_1 - c_2 + c_3 = 0$$
$$-c_1 + 2c_2 = 0$$
$$c_1 - c_2 + c_3 = 0$$

In matrix form, $\begin{bmatrix} 1 & 1 & 3 \\ 1 & -1 & 1 \\ -1 & 2 & 0 \\ 1 & -1 & 1 \end{bmatrix} \begin{bmatrix} c_1 \\ c_2 \\ c_3 \end{bmatrix} = \begin{bmatrix} 0 \\ 0 \\ 0 \\ 0 \end{bmatrix}$

Perform $R_2 - R_1$, $R_3 + R_1$, $R_4 - R_1$, $(A, Z) = \begin{bmatrix} 1 & 1 & 3 & | & 0 \\ 0 & -2 & -2 & | & 0 \\ 0 & 3 & 3 & | & 0 \\ 0 & -2 & -2 & | & 0 \end{bmatrix}$

Perform $R_3 + \dfrac{3}{2} R_2$, $R_4 - R_2$ $\sim \begin{bmatrix} 1 & 1 & 3 & | & 0 \\ 0 & -2 & -2 & | & 0 \\ 0 & 0 & 0 & | & 0 \\ 0 & 0 & 0 & | & 0 \end{bmatrix}$

$\rho(A) = \rho(A, Z) = 4 - 2 = 2 < 3$ System possesses a non-trivial solution
By R_2 $-2c_2 - 2c_3 = 0$ $c_2 + c_3 = 0$, $c_3 = t$, $c_2 = -t$
By R_1 $c_1 + c_2 + 3c_3 = 0$ $c_1 = -2t$
Since we have c_1, c_2, c_3 non-zero $\therefore$ x_1, x_2, x_3 are linearly dependent.
From the matrix equation $c_1 x_1 + c_2 x_2 + c_3 x_3 = 0$
$-2t x_1 - t x_2 + t x_3 = 0$ $\therefore$ $-2x_1 - x_2 + x_3 = 0$
i.e. $2x_1 + x_2 = x_3$ is the required relation.

EXERCISE 2.8

Examine for linear dependence or independence the following system of vectors. If dependent, find the relation between them.

(1) $x_1 = (1, -1, 1)$, $x_2 = (2, 1, 1)$, $x_3 = (3, 0, 2)$ **(Dec. 2004)**
Ans. Dependent, $x_1 + x_2 = x_3$

(2) $x_1 = (1, 1, 1, 3)$, $x_2 = (1, 2, 3, 4)$, $x_3 = (2, 3, 4, 7)$ **(Dec. 2006)**
Ans. Dependent, $x_1 + x_2 = x_3$

(3) $x_1 = (1, 2, 3)$, $x_2 = (2, -2, 6)$ **Ans.** Independent

(4) $x_1 = (3, 1, -4)$, $x_2 = (2, 2, -3)$, $x_3 = (0, -4, 1)$ **(Dec. 2003, May 2010)**
Ans. Dependent, $2x_1 = 3x_2 + x_3$

(5) $x_1 = (2, 3, 4, -2)$, $x_2 = (-1, -2, -2, 1)$, $x_3 = (1, 1, 2, -1)$

(May 2007) Ans. Dependent, $x_1 + x_2 = x_3$

(6) $x_1 = (2, 2, 7, -1)$, $x_2 = (3, -1, 2, 4)$, $x_3 = (1, 1, 3, 1)$ **(Dec. 12) Ans.** Independent

(7) $x_1 = (2, 1, -1, 1)$, $x_2 = (1, 2, 1, -1)$, $x_3 = (1, 1, 2, 1)$ **Ans.** Independent

(8) $x_1 = (1, -2, -3, 4)$, $x_2 = (-2, 4, -1, 3)$, $x_3 = (-1, 2, 7, 6)$ **Ans.** Independent

(9) $x_1 = (1, 2, 4)^T$, $x_2 = (3, 7, 10)^T$ **Ans.** Independent

(10) $x_1 = (2, 2, 1)^T$, $x_2 = (1, 3, 1)^T$, $x_3 = (1, 2, 2)^T$.   **Ans.** Independent

(11) $x_1 = \begin{pmatrix} 1 \\ 2 \\ 3 \end{pmatrix}$, $x_2 = \begin{pmatrix} 3 \\ -2 \\ 1 \end{pmatrix}$, $x_3 = \begin{pmatrix} 1 \\ -6 \\ -5 \end{pmatrix}$ **(May 2014)**   **Ans.** Dependent, $2x_1 + x_3 = x_2$

(12) Find the rank of $A = \begin{bmatrix} 1 & 2 & 3 & -2 \\ 2 & -2 & 1 & 3 \\ 3 & 0 & 4 & 1 \end{bmatrix}$ and the relation of linear dependence among row vectors. **(May 2006)**

Ans. $\rho(A) = 2$, Dependent, $x_1 + x_2 = x_3$

2.20 LINEAR TRANSFORMATIONS

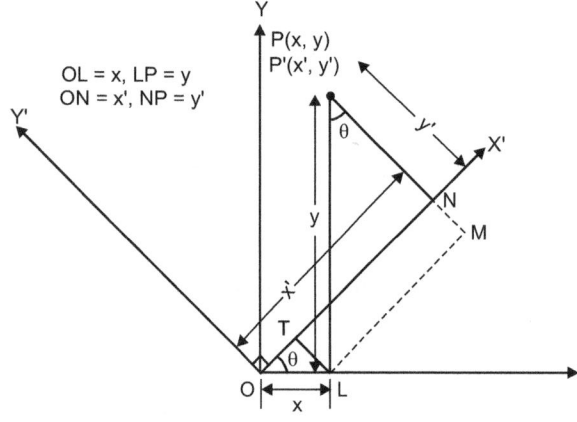

Fig. 2.1

$OL = x$, $LP = y$
$ON = x'$, $NP = y'$

Here $P(x, y)$ corresponds to the rectangular system XOY. $P'(x', y')$ corresponds to the rectangular system X'OY'.

The coordinates (x', y') can be connected to the co-ordinates (x, y) by the relations.

From Fig. 2.1,
$$x' = ON = OT + TN$$
$$= OL \cos \theta + LP \sin \theta$$
$$x' = x \cos \theta + y \sin \theta$$

$OL = x$, $LP = y$, $\angle TOL = \theta$, $TN = LM$

From $\angle TOL$, $\cos \theta = \dfrac{OT}{OL} = \dfrac{OT}{x}$ $\therefore$ $OT = x \cos \theta$

$\angle LPM = \theta$, $\sin \theta = \dfrac{LM}{LP} = \dfrac{TN}{y}$ $\therefore$ $TN = y \sin \theta$

Also $y' = PN = PM - MN = LP \cos \theta - OL \sin \theta$

$y' = y \cos \theta - x \sin \theta$

In $\angle LPM$, $\cos \theta = \dfrac{PM}{LP} = \dfrac{PM}{y}$ $\therefore$ $y \cos \theta = PM$

∠ TOL, $\sin\theta = \dfrac{TL}{OL} = \dfrac{MN}{x}$ ∴ $MN = x\sin\theta$

$(\because MN = TL)$

∴ $\qquad x' = x\cos\theta + y\sin\theta$ ... (1)

$\qquad y' = y\cos\theta - x\sin\theta$

i.e. $\qquad y' = -x\sin\theta + y\cos\theta$ ... (2)

(1) and (2) in a compact form in matrix notation can be written as

$$\begin{bmatrix} x' \\ y' \end{bmatrix} = \begin{bmatrix} \cos\theta & \sin\theta \\ -\sin\theta & \cos\theta \end{bmatrix} \begin{bmatrix} x \\ y \end{bmatrix}$$

i.e. $\qquad X' = AX$ ... (3)

Equation (3) transforms the variables x, y to the variables x', y' and exhibits a simple example of the linear transformation.

The transformation $X' = AX$ given by equation (3) is called *linear transformation in two dimensions*.

We have a more general transformation as $\left. \begin{array}{l} x' = a_1 x + b_1 y \\ y' = a_2 x + b_2 y \end{array} \right\}$

i.e. $\qquad \begin{bmatrix} x' \\ y' \end{bmatrix} = \begin{bmatrix} a_1 & b_1 \\ a_2 & b_2 \end{bmatrix} \begin{bmatrix} x \\ y \end{bmatrix}$

$\qquad X' = AX$

Also $\qquad x' = a_1 x + a_2 y + a_3 z$

$\qquad y' = b_1 x + b_2 y + b_3 z$

$\qquad z' = c_1 x + c_2 y + c_3 z$

i.e. $\qquad \begin{bmatrix} x' \\ y' \\ z' \end{bmatrix} = \begin{bmatrix} a_1 & a_2 & a_3 \\ b_1 & b_2 & b_3 \\ c_1 & c_2 & c_3 \end{bmatrix} \begin{bmatrix} x \\ y \\ z \end{bmatrix}$

$\qquad X' = AX$ ... (4)

The transformation $X' = AX$ given by equation (4) is called *linear transformation* from (x, y, z) to (x', y', z') in *three dimensions*.

A general linear transformation is represented by

$$\left. \begin{array}{l} y_1 = a_{11}x_1 + a_{12}x_2 + \ldots + a_{1n}x_n \\ y_2 = a_{21}x_1 + a_{22}x_2 + \ldots + a_{2n}x_n \\ \vdots \\ \vdots \\ y_n = a_{n1}x_1 + a_{n2}x_2 + \ldots + a_{nn}x_n \end{array} \right\} \quad \ldots(5)$$

i.e. in matrix notation, (5) can be written as

$$\begin{bmatrix} y_1 \\ y_2 \\ \vdots \\ \vdots \\ y_n \end{bmatrix} = \begin{bmatrix} a_{11} & a_{12} & \cdots & a_{1n} \\ a_{21} & a_{22} & \cdots & a_{2n} \\ \vdots & & & \vdots \\ & \vdots & & \\ a_{n1} & a_{n2} & \cdots & a_{nn} \end{bmatrix} \begin{bmatrix} x_1 \\ x_2 \\ \vdots \\ \vdots \\ x_n \end{bmatrix}$$

i.e. $Y = AX$ gives linear transformation from n variables $x_1 x_2 \ldots x_n$ to the variables $y_1 y_2 \ldots y_n$ i.e. the transformation of the vector X to the vector Y.

This transformation is called linear because $Y_1 = AX_1$ and $Y_2 = AX_2$ implies $aY_1 + bY_2 = A[aX_1 + bX_2]$ for all values of a and b.

Thus, if $X = \begin{bmatrix} 1 \\ -1 \end{bmatrix}$ and $A = \begin{bmatrix} 2 & -1 \\ 1 & 2 \end{bmatrix}$ then $Y = \begin{bmatrix} y_1 \\ y_2 \end{bmatrix} = \begin{bmatrix} 2 & -1 \\ 1 & 2 \end{bmatrix} \begin{bmatrix} 1 \\ -1 \end{bmatrix}$

$$\begin{bmatrix} y_1 \\ y_2 \end{bmatrix} = \begin{bmatrix} 3 \\ -1 \end{bmatrix}$$

So that $(1, -1) \to (3, -1)$ under the transformation defined by A.

The relation $Y = AX$ expresses $y_1 y_2 \ldots y_n$ in terms of $x_1 x_2 \ldots x_n$. It may be noted that *every square matrix defines a linear transformation.*

'A' is called the matrix of transformation. $|A|$ is known as the modulus of transformation.

If $|A| = 0$, then the transformation matrix A is called as *singular* and the linear transformation is also called as *singular*.

If $|A| \neq 0$, then the transformation matrix A is called as *non-singular* and the linear transformation is also called as *non-singular* or *regular*.

For a non-singular transformation $Y = AX$, since 'A' is non-singular (i.e. $|A| \neq 0$), A^{-1} exists and we can write the inverse transformation, which carries the vector Y back into the vector X, as

$$X = A^{-1}Y.$$

If a transformation from $(x_1 x_2 \ldots x_n)$ to $(y_1 y_2 \ldots y_n)$ is given by $Y = AX$ and another transformation from $(y_1 y_2 \ldots y_n)$ to $(z_1 z_2 \ldots z_n)$ is given by $Z = BY$, then the transformation from $(x_1 x_2 \ldots x_n)$ to $(z_1 z_2 \ldots z_n)$ is given by

$$Z = BY = B(AX)$$
$$Z = (BA)X$$

A non-singular linear transformation carries linearly independent vectors into linearly independent vectors.

A non-singular linear transformation carries linearly dependent vectors into linearly dependent vectors.

2.21 PROBLEMS ON LINEAR TRANSFORMATIONS

Ex. 1 : *Given the transformation* $Y = \begin{bmatrix} 2 & 1 & 1 \\ 1 & 1 & 2 \\ 1 & 0 & -2 \end{bmatrix} \begin{bmatrix} x_1 \\ x_2 \\ x_3 \end{bmatrix}$. *Find the co-ordinates $(x_1\ x_2\ x_3)$ in X corresponding to $(1, 2, -1)$ in Y.* **(May 2004, May 2010)**

Sol. : $Y = AX$ i.e. $AX = Y$

$$\begin{bmatrix} 2 & 1 & 1 \\ 1 & 1 & 2 \\ 1 & 0 & -2 \end{bmatrix} \begin{bmatrix} x_1 \\ x_2 \\ x_3 \end{bmatrix} = \begin{bmatrix} 1 \\ 2 \\ -1 \end{bmatrix}$$

This is non-homogeneous system of equations with $m = n = 3$

$$|A| = \begin{vmatrix} 2 & 1 & 1 \\ 1 & 1 & 2 \\ 1 & 0 & -2 \end{vmatrix} = -4 + 4 - 1$$

$$|A| = -1 \neq 0$$

System possesses a unique solution $X = A^{-1}Y$.

$$A^{-1} = \frac{1}{|A|} \text{adj. } A$$

$$\text{adj } A = \begin{bmatrix} -2 & 2 & 1 \\ 4 & -5 & -3 \\ -1 & 1 & 1 \end{bmatrix} \quad \therefore A^{-1} = \frac{1}{-1} \begin{bmatrix} -2 & 2 & 1 \\ 4 & -5 & -3 \\ -1 & 1 & 1 \end{bmatrix} = \begin{bmatrix} 2 & -2 & -1 \\ -4 & 5 & 3 \\ 1 & -1 & -1 \end{bmatrix}$$

$$X = A^{-1}Y = \begin{bmatrix} 2 & -2 & -1 \\ -4 & 5 & 3 \\ 1 & -1 & -1 \end{bmatrix} \begin{bmatrix} 1 \\ 2 \\ -1 \end{bmatrix}$$

$$\begin{bmatrix} x_1 \\ x_2 \\ x_3 \end{bmatrix} = \begin{bmatrix} -1 \\ 3 \\ 0 \end{bmatrix}. \text{ Hence } (-1, 3, 0) \text{ corresponds to } (1, 2, -1) \text{ in Y.}$$

Ex. 2 : *Express each of the transformations* $\begin{matrix} x_1 = 3y_1 + 2y_2 \\ x_2 = -y_1 + 4y_2 \end{matrix} \}$ *and* $\begin{matrix} y_1 = z_1 + 2z_2 \\ y_2 = 3z_1 \end{matrix} \}$ *in the matrix form and find the composite transformation which expresses x_1, x_2 in terms of z_1, z_2.*

Sol. : The transformation $\begin{matrix} x_1 = 3y_1 + 2y_2 \\ x_2 = -y_1 + 4y_2 \end{matrix} \}$ in matrix form can be written as

$$\begin{bmatrix} x_1 \\ x_2 \end{bmatrix} = \begin{bmatrix} 3 & 2 \\ -1 & 4 \end{bmatrix} \begin{bmatrix} y_1 \\ y_2 \end{bmatrix}$$

$$X = AY$$

Also the transformation $\left.\begin{matrix} y_1 = z_1 + 2z_2 \\ y_2 = 3z_1 \end{matrix}\right\}$ in matrix form can be written as

$$\begin{bmatrix} y_1 \\ y_2 \end{bmatrix} = \begin{bmatrix} 1 & 2 \\ 3 & 0 \end{bmatrix} \begin{bmatrix} z_1 \\ z_2 \end{bmatrix}$$

$$Y = BZ$$

∴ Required composite transformation is

$$X = AY = \begin{bmatrix} 3 & 2 \\ -1 & 4 \end{bmatrix} \begin{bmatrix} y_1 \\ y_2 \end{bmatrix} = \begin{bmatrix} 3 & 2 \\ -1 & 4 \end{bmatrix} \begin{bmatrix} 1 & 2 \\ 3 & 0 \end{bmatrix} \begin{bmatrix} z_1 \\ z_2 \end{bmatrix}$$

$$\begin{bmatrix} x_1 \\ x_2 \end{bmatrix} = \begin{bmatrix} 9 & 6 \\ 11 & -2 \end{bmatrix} \begin{bmatrix} z_1 \\ z_2 \end{bmatrix}$$

∴ $\left.\begin{matrix} x_1 = 9z_1 + 6z_2 \\ x_2 = 11z_1 - 2z_2 \end{matrix}\right\}$ is the required transformation.

Ex. 3 : *A transformation from the variables $x_1\ x_2\ x_3$ to $y_1\ y_2\ y_3$ is given by $Y = AX$ and another transformation from $y_1\ y_2\ y_3$ to $z_1\ z_2\ z_3$ is given by $Z = BY$, where*

$$A = \begin{bmatrix} 2 & 1 & 0 \\ 0 & 1 & -2 \\ -1 & 2 & 1 \end{bmatrix}, B = \begin{bmatrix} 1 & 1 & 1 \\ 1 & 2 & 3 \\ 1 & 3 & 5 \end{bmatrix}.$$

Obtain the transformation from $x_1\ x_2\ x_3$ to $z_1\ z_2\ z_3$.

Sol. : Given transformation is $Y = AX$ and $Z = BY$.

∴ The required composite transformation is

$$Z = BY$$
$$Z = B(AX) = (BA)X$$

$$\begin{bmatrix} z_1 \\ z_2 \\ z_3 \end{bmatrix} = \begin{bmatrix} 1 & 1 & 1 \\ 1 & 2 & 3 \\ 1 & 3 & 5 \end{bmatrix} \begin{bmatrix} 2 & 1 & 0 \\ 0 & 1 & -2 \\ -1 & 2 & 1 \end{bmatrix} \begin{bmatrix} x_1 \\ x_2 \\ x_3 \end{bmatrix}$$

$$= \begin{bmatrix} 1 & 4 & -1 \\ -1 & 9 & -1 \\ -3 & 14 & -1 \end{bmatrix} \begin{bmatrix} x_1 \\ x_2 \\ x_3 \end{bmatrix}$$

$z_1 = x_1 + 4x_2 - x_3,\ z_2 = -x_1 + 9x_2 - x_3,\ z_3 = -3x_1 + 14x_2 - x_3.$

Ex. 4 : *Find a linear operator in two dimensions which maps the vectors (1, 1) and (3, −2) into the vectors (2, 1) and (1, 2) respectively.*

Sol. : The linear transformation must be

$$Y = AX$$

$$\begin{bmatrix} y_1 \\ y_2 \end{bmatrix} = \begin{bmatrix} a_1 & b_1 \\ a_2 & b_2 \end{bmatrix} \begin{bmatrix} x_1 \\ x_2 \end{bmatrix}$$

(1, 1) maps to → (2, 1) in Y $(x_1, x_2) \to (y_1, y_2)$ in Y

We have
$$\begin{bmatrix} 2 \\ 1 \end{bmatrix} = \begin{bmatrix} a_1 & b_1 \\ a_2 & b_2 \end{bmatrix} \begin{bmatrix} 1 \\ 1 \end{bmatrix}$$

By assuming the transformation matrix $A = \begin{bmatrix} a_1 & b_1 \\ a_2 & b_2 \end{bmatrix}$ $\therefore \left. \begin{array}{l} a_1 + b_1 = 2 \\ a_2 + b_2 = 1 \end{array} \right\}$

Also (3, –2) maps to → (1, 2) $(x_1, x_2) \to (y_1, y_2)$

i.e.
$$\begin{bmatrix} 1 \\ 2 \end{bmatrix} = \begin{bmatrix} a_1 & b_1 \\ a_2 & b_2 \end{bmatrix} \begin{bmatrix} 3 \\ -2 \end{bmatrix} \quad \text{i.e.} \left. \begin{array}{l} 3a_1 - 2b_1 = 1 \\ 3a_2 - 2b_2 = 2 \end{array} \right\}$$

∴ Solving $\left. \begin{array}{l} a_1 + b_1 = 2 \\ 3a_1 - 2b_1 = 1 \end{array} \right\}$ we get $a_1 = 1, \ b_1 = 1$.

Also solving $\left. \begin{array}{l} a_2 + b_2 = 1 \\ 3a_2 - 2b_2 = 2 \end{array} \right\}$ we get $a_2 = \frac{4}{5}, \ b_2 = \frac{1}{5}$

∴ $A = \begin{bmatrix} 1 & 1 \\ \frac{4}{5} & \frac{1}{5} \end{bmatrix}$ is the required matrix of transformation.

EXERCISE 2.9

(1) Given the transformation $Y = \begin{bmatrix} 4 & -5 & 1 \\ 3 & 1 & -2 \\ 1 & 4 & 1 \end{bmatrix} \begin{bmatrix} x_1 \\ x_2 \\ x_3 \end{bmatrix}$

Find the co-ordinates (x_1, x_2, x_3) corresponding to (2, 9, 5) in Y.

Ans. $|A| = 72$, $A^{-1} = \frac{1}{72} \begin{bmatrix} 9 & 9 & 9 \\ -5 & 3 & 11 \\ 11 & -21 & 19 \end{bmatrix}$ $x_1 = 2, \ x_2 = 1, \ x_3 = -1$.

(2) Given the transformation $Y = \begin{bmatrix} 1 & 1 & -2 \\ 2 & -1 & 1 \\ 3 & 1 & -1 \end{bmatrix} \begin{bmatrix} x_1 \\ x_2 \\ x_3 \end{bmatrix}$.

Find the co-ordinates (x_1, x_2, x_3) corresponding to (3, 0, 8) in Y.

Ans. $x_1 = \frac{8}{5}, \ x_2 = 5, \ x_3 = \frac{9}{5}$.

(3) Given the transformation $Y = \begin{bmatrix} 1 & -2 & 3 \\ 2 & 0 & -3 \\ 1 & 1 & 1 \end{bmatrix} \begin{bmatrix} x_1 \\ x_2 \\ x_3 \end{bmatrix}$

Find the co-ordinates (x_1, x_2, x_3) corresponding to $(2, 3, 0)$ in Y. **(May 2008)**

Ans. $x_1 = \dfrac{21}{19}$, $x_2 = \dfrac{-16}{19}$, $x_3 = \dfrac{-5}{19}$.

(4) Express each of the transformations $\left.\begin{array}{l} x_1 = 3y_1 + 5y_2 \\ x_2 = -y_1 + 7y_2 \end{array}\right\}$ and $\left.\begin{array}{l} y_1 = z_1 + 3z_2 \\ y_2 = 4z_1 \end{array}\right\}$ in the matrix form and find the composite transformation which express x_1, x_2 in terms of z_1, z_2. **(May 2004)**

Ans. $X = \begin{bmatrix} 23 & 9 \\ 27 & -3 \end{bmatrix} Z$, i.e. $\begin{array}{l} x_1 = 23z_1 + 9z_2 \\ x_2 = 27z_1 - 3z_2 \end{array}$.

(5) A transformation from the variables x_1, x_2, x_3 to y_1, y_2, y_3 is given by $X = AY$ and another transformation from y_1, y_2, y_3 to z_1, z_2, z_3 is given by $Y = BZ$, where

$A = \begin{bmatrix} 1 & 1 & -1 \\ 0 & 1 & 1 \\ 2 & 1 & 3 \end{bmatrix}$ and $B = \begin{bmatrix} 1 & 2 & -1 \\ 1 & 0 & 1 \\ 2 & 1 & 1 \end{bmatrix}$. Obtain the transformation from x_1, x_2, x_3 to z_1, z_2, z_3.

Ans. $X = \begin{bmatrix} 0 & 1 & -1 \\ 3 & 1 & 2 \\ 9 & 7 & 2 \end{bmatrix} Z$.

(6) Show that the transformation
$$\begin{array}{l} y_1 = x_1 + x_2 + x_3 \\ y_2 = 2x_1 + 3x_2 + 4x_3 \\ y_3 = x_1 - x_2 + x_3 \end{array}$$
is regular. Write down the inverse transformations. Also find the co-ordinates (x_1, x_2, x_3) corresponding to $(6, 20, 2)$ in Y.

Ans. Regular, $X = A^{-1}Y$, $x_1 = 1$, $x_2 = 2$, $x_3 = 3$.

2.22 ORTHOGONAL TRANSFORMATION AND ORTHOGONAL MATRIX

Definition: The linear transformation $Y = AX$ where

$Y = \begin{bmatrix} y_1 \\ y_2 \\ \vdots \\ y_n \end{bmatrix}$, $A = \begin{bmatrix} a_{11} & a_{12} & \cdots & a_{1n} \\ a_{21} & a_{22} & \cdots & a_{2n} \\ \vdots & & & \\ a_{n1} & a_{n2} & \cdots & a_{nn} \end{bmatrix}$, $X = \begin{bmatrix} X_1 \\ X_2 \\ \vdots \\ X_n \end{bmatrix}$ is said to be orthogonal,

if it transforms $x_1^2 + x_2^2 + \ldots + x_n^2$ into $y_1^2 + y_2^2 + \ldots + y_n^2$.

If $Y = AX$ is an orthogonal transformation then the matrix A of this transformation is called an orthogonal matrix.

We have, $\quad X'X = [x_1 \ x_2 \ ... \ x_n] \begin{bmatrix} X_1 \\ X_2 \\ \vdots \\ \vdots \\ X_n \end{bmatrix}$

$$X'X = x_1^2 + x_2^2 + x_3^2 + ... + x_n^2$$

Since $\quad Y = AX$ transformation is orthogonal

$\therefore \quad x_1^2 + x_2^2 + ... + x_n^2 \quad$ transforms into $y_1^2 + y_2^2 + ... + y_n^2$

$\therefore$
$$X'X = x_1^2 + x_2^2 + ... + x_n^2$$
$$X'X = y_1^2 + y_2^2 + ... + y_n^2$$
$$X'X = Y'Y$$
$$\quad\quad = (AX)'(AX) \quad\quad (\because Y = AX)$$
$$\quad\quad = X'A'(AX) \quad\quad (\because (AB)' = B'A')$$
$$X'X = X'(A'A)X$$

which holds only when $A'A = I$

i.e. $\quad\quad A'A = A^{-1}A \quad\quad (\because A^{-1}A = I)$

$\quad\quad A' = A^{-1}$

2.23 ORTHOGONAL MATRIX

Hence a square matrix A is said to be orthogonal if $AA' = A'A = I$

If A is orthogonal then $A^{-1} = A'$

2.24 PROBLEMS ON ORTHOGONAL MATRIX

Ex. 1 : *If A is an orthogonal matrix, prove that* $|A| = \pm 1$.

Sol. : Given that A is an orthogonal matrix $\therefore AA' = I$

$\therefore \quad\quad |AA'| = |I|$

$\quad\quad |A||A'| = 1 \quad\quad\quad$ But $\ |A'| = |A|$

$\quad\quad |A||A| = 1$

$\quad\quad [|A|]^2 = 1$

$\quad\quad |A| = \pm 1$

Ex. 2 : *If A is orthogonal matrix then show that A^{-1} is also orthogonal. Further, show that A' is also orthogonal.*

Sol. : Part 1 : Given A is orthogonal. $AA' = I$

$$(AA')^{-1} = I^{-1}$$
$$(A')^{-1} A^{-1} = I \qquad \because (AB)^{-1} = B^{-1} A^{-1}$$

Also $\qquad (A^{-1})' = (A')^{-1}$

$\therefore \quad (A^{-1})' A^{-1} = I \implies A^{-1}$ is also orthogonal.

Part 2 : A is orthogonal $\therefore AA' = I$

$$(AA')' = I'$$
$$(A')' A' = I \;[\because (AB)' = B'A'] \implies A' \text{ is orthogonal.}$$

Ex. 3 : *Show that* $A = \dfrac{1}{3}\begin{bmatrix} 1 & 2 & 2 \\ 2 & 1 & -2 \\ 2 & -2 & 1 \end{bmatrix}$ *is orthogonal.* **(May 2007)**

Sol. : We have by definition A is orthogonal if
$$AA' = A'A = I$$

$$AA' = \frac{1}{3}\begin{bmatrix} 1 & 2 & 2 \\ 2 & 1 & -2 \\ 2 & -2 & 1 \end{bmatrix} \frac{1}{3}\begin{bmatrix} 1 & 2 & 2 \\ 2 & 1 & -2 \\ 2 & -2 & 1 \end{bmatrix}$$

$$AA' = \frac{1}{9}\begin{bmatrix} 9 & 0 & 0 \\ 0 & 9 & 0 \\ 0 & 0 & 9 \end{bmatrix} = \begin{bmatrix} 1 & 0 & 0 \\ 0 & 1 & 0 \\ 0 & 0 & 1 \end{bmatrix}$$

$AA' = I \implies A$ is orthogonal

Ex. 4 : *Show that* $A = \begin{bmatrix} \cos\theta & 0 & \sin\theta \\ 0 & 1 & 0 \\ -\sin\theta & 0 & \cos\theta \end{bmatrix}$ *is an orthogonal matrix.*

(Dec. 2005, 2007; May 2011)

Sol. : We have by definition A is orthogonal if $AA' = A'A = I$

$$AA' = \begin{bmatrix} \cos\theta & 0 & \sin\theta \\ 0 & 1 & 0 \\ -\sin\theta & 0 & \cos\theta \end{bmatrix} \begin{bmatrix} \cos\theta & 0 & -\sin\theta \\ 0 & 1 & 0 \\ \sin\theta & 0 & \cos\theta \end{bmatrix}$$

$$= \begin{bmatrix} \cos^2\theta + \sin^2\theta & 0 & -\sin\theta\cos\theta + \cos\theta\sin\theta \\ 0 & 1 & 0 \\ -\sin\theta\cos\theta + \cos\theta\sin\theta & 0 & \sin^2\theta + \cos^2\theta \end{bmatrix}$$

$$= \begin{bmatrix} 1 & 0 & 0 \\ 0 & 1 & 0 \\ 0 & 0 & 1 \end{bmatrix} \quad \text{Hence A is orthogonal matrix.}$$

Ex. 5 : *Determine the values of a, b, c when* $\begin{bmatrix} 0 & 2b & c \\ a & b & -c \\ a & -b & c \end{bmatrix}$ *is orthogonal.*

(May 05, 09; Dec. 2010)

Sol. : If A is orthogonal then it requires
$$AA' = I$$

$$AA' = \begin{bmatrix} 0 & 2b & c \\ a & b & -c \\ a & -b & c \end{bmatrix} \begin{bmatrix} 0 & a & a \\ 2b & b & -b \\ c & -c & c \end{bmatrix}$$

$$= \begin{bmatrix} 4b^2 + c^2 & 2b^2 - c^2 & -2b^2 + c^2 \\ 2b^2 - c^2 & a^2 + b^2 + c^2 & a^2 - b^2 - c^2 \\ -2b^2 + c^2 & a^2 - b^2 - c^2 & a^2 + b^2 + c^2 \end{bmatrix}$$

But $\quad AA' = I$

$\therefore \quad 4b^2 + c^2 = 1, \quad 2b^2 - c^2 = 0$

$\therefore \quad 6b^2 = 1 \quad\quad b^2 = \dfrac{1}{6} \quad \therefore b = \pm \dfrac{1}{\sqrt{6}}$

$\quad\quad\quad c^2 = \dfrac{1}{3} \quad\quad \therefore c = \pm \dfrac{1}{\sqrt{3}}$

Also $\quad a^2 + b^2 + c^2 = 1, \quad a^2 = \dfrac{1}{2}, \quad a = \pm \dfrac{1}{\sqrt{2}}$

$\therefore \quad a = \pm \dfrac{1}{\sqrt{2}}, \quad b = \pm \dfrac{1}{\sqrt{6}}, \quad c = \pm \dfrac{1}{\sqrt{3}}$

Ex. 6 : *Is* $A = \begin{bmatrix} 2 & 2 & 1 \\ -2 & 1 & 2 \\ 1 & -2 & 2 \end{bmatrix}$ *orthogonal ? If not, can it be converted into an orthogonal matrix ?*

(May 2006)

Sol. : Part 1 : A is said to be orthogonal if $AA' = I$

$$AA' = \begin{bmatrix} 2 & 2 & 1 \\ -2 & 1 & 2 \\ 1 & -2 & 2 \end{bmatrix} \begin{bmatrix} 2 & -2 & 1 \\ 2 & 1 & -2 \\ 1 & 2 & 2 \end{bmatrix}$$

$$AA' = \begin{bmatrix} 9 & 0 & 0 \\ 0 & 9 & 0 \\ 0 & 0 & 9 \end{bmatrix} \neq I_3 \therefore \text{A is not orthogonal.}$$

Part 2 : However, matrix A can be converted into an orthogonal matrix by making each row element of A of unit magnitude.

Let $X_1 = [\, 2 \;\; 2 \;\; 1 \,] \quad \therefore$ its magnitude is $\sqrt{(2)^2 + (2)^2 + (1)^2} = 3$

Hence normalised vector $\bar{X}_1 = \left[\dfrac{2}{3} \;\; \dfrac{2}{3} \;\; \dfrac{1}{3} \right]$

Similarly $X_2 = [-2 \ 1 \ 2]$ having magnitude $\sqrt{(-2)^2 + (1)^2 + (2)^2} = 3$

$\therefore \quad \bar{X}_2 = \left[\dfrac{-2}{3} \ \dfrac{1}{3} \ \dfrac{2}{3} \right]$

Also $X_3 = [1 \ -2 \ 2]$ having magnitude $\sqrt{(-2)^2 + (1)^2 + (2)^2} = 3$

$\therefore \quad \bar{X}_3 = \left[\dfrac{1}{3} \ -\dfrac{2}{3} \ \dfrac{2}{3} \right]$

Now write $B = \begin{bmatrix} \bar{X}_1 \\ \bar{X}_2 \\ \bar{X}_3 \end{bmatrix} = \begin{bmatrix} 2/3 & 2/3 & 1/3 \\ -2/3 & 1/3 & 2/3 \\ 1/3 & -2/3 & 2/3 \end{bmatrix} = \dfrac{1}{3}\begin{bmatrix} 2 & 2 & 1 \\ -2 & 1 & 2 \\ 1 & -2 & 2 \end{bmatrix}$

$BB' = \dfrac{1}{3}\begin{bmatrix} 2 & 2 & 1 \\ -2 & 1 & 2 \\ 1 & -2 & 2 \end{bmatrix} \dfrac{1}{3}\begin{bmatrix} 2 & -2 & 1 \\ 2 & 1 & -2 \\ 1 & 2 & 2 \end{bmatrix} = \dfrac{1}{9}\begin{bmatrix} 9 & 0 & 0 \\ 0 & 9 & 0 \\ 0 & 0 & 9 \end{bmatrix} = I_3 \Rightarrow B$ is orthogonal

EXERCISE 2.10

Verify whether the following matrix is orthogonal or not, if so write A^{-1} (1 to 9).

(1) $A = \dfrac{1}{3}\begin{bmatrix} -2 & 1 & 2 \\ 2 & 2 & 1 \\ 1 & -2 & 2 \end{bmatrix}$ **Ans. Yes**

(2) $A = \dfrac{1}{3}\begin{bmatrix} 2 & 1 & 2 \\ -2 & 2 & 1 \\ 1 & 2 & -2 \end{bmatrix}$ **Ans. Yes**

(3) $A = \begin{bmatrix} \cos\theta & \sin\theta \\ -\sin\theta & \cos\theta \end{bmatrix}$ **Ans. Yes**

(4) $A = \dfrac{1}{13}\begin{bmatrix} -12 & -5 \\ 5 & -12 \end{bmatrix}$ **Ans. Yes**

(5) $A = \begin{bmatrix} \dfrac{1}{\sqrt{2}} & 0 & \dfrac{1}{\sqrt{2}} \\ 0 & 1 & 0 \\ \dfrac{1}{\sqrt{2}} & 0 & -\dfrac{1}{\sqrt{2}} \end{bmatrix}$ **Ans. Yes**

(6) $A = \begin{bmatrix} \dfrac{1}{\sqrt{2}} & \dfrac{1}{\sqrt{6}} & \dfrac{1}{\sqrt{3}} \\ 0 & \dfrac{-2}{\sqrt{6}} & \dfrac{1}{\sqrt{3}} \\ \dfrac{1}{\sqrt{2}} & \dfrac{1}{\sqrt{6}} & \dfrac{1}{\sqrt{3}} \end{bmatrix}$ **Ans. Yes**

(7) $A = \begin{bmatrix} \dfrac{1}{\sqrt{6}} & \dfrac{1}{\sqrt{2}} & \dfrac{1}{\sqrt{3}} \\ \dfrac{2}{\sqrt{6}} & 0 & \dfrac{-1}{\sqrt{3}} \\ \dfrac{1}{\sqrt{6}} & \dfrac{-1}{\sqrt{2}} & \dfrac{1}{\sqrt{3}} \end{bmatrix}$ **Ans. Yes**

(8) $A = \begin{bmatrix} \dfrac{1}{\sqrt{3}} & 0 & \dfrac{2}{\sqrt{6}} \\ \dfrac{1}{\sqrt{3}} & \dfrac{1}{\sqrt{2}} & \dfrac{-1}{\sqrt{6}} \\ \dfrac{-1}{\sqrt{3}} & \dfrac{1}{\sqrt{2}} & \dfrac{1}{\sqrt{6}} \end{bmatrix}$ **Ans. Yes**

(9) $A = \dfrac{1}{3}\begin{bmatrix} 1 & 2 & 2 \\ 2 & -2 & 1 \\ 2 & 1 & -2 \end{bmatrix}$ **Ans.** Yes

(10) $A = \dfrac{1}{9}\begin{bmatrix} -8 & 4 & 1 \\ 1 & 4 & -8 \\ 4 & 7 & 4 \end{bmatrix}$ **Ans.** Yes (Dec. 2006)

(11) $A = \begin{bmatrix} \dfrac{1}{\sqrt{14}} & \dfrac{2}{\sqrt{5}} & \dfrac{3}{\sqrt{70}} \\ \dfrac{2}{\sqrt{14}} & \dfrac{-1}{\sqrt{5}} & \dfrac{6}{\sqrt{70}} \\ \dfrac{3}{\sqrt{14}} & 0 & \dfrac{-5}{\sqrt{70}} \end{bmatrix}$ **Ans.** Yes

(12) $A = \begin{bmatrix} \dfrac{1}{\sqrt{14}} & 0 & \dfrac{-13}{\sqrt{182}} \\ \dfrac{2}{\sqrt{14}} & \dfrac{3}{\sqrt{13}} & \dfrac{2}{\sqrt{182}} \\ \dfrac{3}{\sqrt{14}} & \dfrac{-2}{\sqrt{13}} & \dfrac{3}{\sqrt{182}} \end{bmatrix}$ **Ans.** Yes

(13) $A = \begin{bmatrix} \dfrac{4}{\sqrt{18}} & 0 & \dfrac{1}{3} \\ \dfrac{1}{\sqrt{18}} & \dfrac{1}{\sqrt{2}} & \dfrac{-2}{3} \\ \dfrac{-1}{\sqrt{18}} & \dfrac{1}{\sqrt{2}} & \dfrac{2}{3} \end{bmatrix}$ **Ans.** Yes

(14) $A = \dfrac{1}{3}\begin{bmatrix} 2 & 2 & 1 \\ -2 & 1 & 2 \\ 1 & -1 & 2 \end{bmatrix}$ **Ans.** not orthogonal

(15) $\begin{bmatrix} \cos\phi\cos\theta & \sin\phi & \cos\phi\sin\theta \\ -\sin\phi\cos\theta & \cos\phi & -\sin\phi\sin\theta \\ -\sin\theta & 0 & \cos\theta \end{bmatrix}$ **Ans.** Yes.

(16) If $A = \begin{bmatrix} 1/3 & 2/3 & a \\ 2/3 & 1/3 & b \\ 2/3 & -2/3 & c \end{bmatrix}$ is orthogonal, find a, b, c. **(Dec. 03, May 09, Dec. 2009)**

Ans. $a = \pm\dfrac{2}{3}$, $b = \mp\dfrac{2}{3}$, $c = \pm\dfrac{1}{3}$.

(17) $\dfrac{1}{13}\begin{bmatrix} -12 & -5 \\ 5 & -12 \end{bmatrix}$ **Ans.** Yes

(18) $\dfrac{1}{15}\begin{bmatrix} 5 & -14 & 2 \\ -10 & -5 & -10 \\ 10 & 2 & -11 \end{bmatrix}$ **Ans.** Yes

(19) Show the transformation

$y_1 = \dfrac{2}{3}x_1 + \dfrac{1}{3}x_2 + \dfrac{2}{3}x_3$, $y_2 = -\dfrac{2}{3}x_1 + \dfrac{2}{3}x_2 + \dfrac{1}{3}x_3$, $y_3 = \dfrac{1}{3}x_1 + \dfrac{2}{3}x_2 - \dfrac{2}{3}x_3$

is orthogonal.

MULTIPLE CHOICE QUESTIONS

Type I : System of Linear Equations and Linear Dependence and Independence

1. Homogeneous system of linear equations (1)
   - (A) is always consistent
   - (B) is always inconsistent
   - (C) has always infinite solution
   - (D) none of these

2. Non-homogeneous system of linear equations AX = B is consistent if (1)
   - (A) rank of A = rank of (A | B)
   - (B) rank of A ≠ rank of (A | B)
   - (C) rank of A > number of unknowns
   - (D) none of these

3. Non-homogeneous system of linear equations AX = B is inconsistent if (1)
   - (A) rank of A = rank of (A | B)
   - (B) rank of A ≠ rank of (A | B)
   - (C) rank of A > number of unknowns
   - (D) none of these

4. For consistent m × n non-homogeneous system of linear equations AX = B, if rank of A = r = number of unknowns, then the system possesses (1)
   - (A) unique solution
   - (B) no solutions
   - (C) infinitely many solutions
   - (D) n – r solutions

5. An n × n homogeneous system of linear equations AX = 0 is given. If the rank of A is r < n, then the system has (1)
   - (A) n – 2r independent solutions
   - (B) r independent solutions
   - (C) no solution
   - (D) n – r independent solutions

6. For consistent m × n non-homogeneous system of linear equations AX = B if rank of A = r < number of unknowns, then the system possesses (1)
   - (A) unique solution
   - (B) no solutions
   - (C) infinitely many solutions
   - (D) n – r solutions

7. The condition for unique solution of m × n non-homogeneous system of linear equations AX = B is (1)
   - (A) rank of A = r = number of unknowns
   - (B) rank of A = r < number of unknowns
   - (C) rank of A = r > number of unknowns
   - (D) none of the above

8. The condition for infinitely many solutions of m × n non-homogeneous system of linear equations AX = B is (1)

   (A) rank of A = r = number of unknowns
   (B) rank of A = r < number of unknowns
   (C) rank of A = r > number of unknowns
   (D) not defined

9. An n × n non-homogeneous system of linear equations AX = B with A is non-singular matrix has (1)

   (A) unique solution   (B) no solutions
   (C) infinitely many solutions (D) n − r solutions

10. An n × n homogeneous system of linear equations AX = 0 with A is non-singular matrix has (1)

    (A) n − r solutions   (B) non-trivial solution
    (C) infinitely many solutions (D) trivial solution

11. An n × n homogeneous system of linear equations AX = 0 with A is singular matrix has (1)

    (A) trivial solution   (B) non-trivial solution
    (C) no solution   (D) n − r solutions

12. Given system of linear equations 3x + 2y + z = 0, x + 4y + z = 0, 2x + y + 4z = 0 has (2)

    (A) no solution   (B) only trivial solution
    (C) infinite solutions   (D) none of these

13. Given system of linear equations x + 2y + 3z = 0, 2x + 3y + z = 0, 4x + 5y + 4z = 0 has (2)

    (A) only trivial solution (B) no solution
    (C) infinite solutions   (D) none of these

14. Given system of linear equations x − 4y + 5z = 0, 2x − y + 3z = 0, 3x + 2y + z = 0 has (2)

    (A) no solution   (B) only trivial solution
    (C) infinite solutions   (D) none of these

15. Given system of linear equations x + 3y + z = 0, 2x − 2y − 6z = 0, 3x + y − 5z = 0 has (2)

    (A) no solution   (B) only trivial solution
    (C) infinite solutions   (D) none of these

16. Given system of linear equations $x + y + z = 1$, $x + 2y + 4z = 2$, $x + 4y + 10z = 4$ has (2)
    (A) unique solution
    (B) no solutions
    (C) infinitely many solutions
    (D) n – r solutions

17. Given system of linear equations $x - 4y + 5z = -1$, $2x - y + 3z = 1$, $3x + 2y + z = 3$ has (2)
    (A) unique solution
    (B) no solutions
    (C) infinitely many solutions
    (D) n – r solutions

18. Given system of linear equations $x + y + z = 3$, $x + 2y + 3z = 4$, $x + 4y + 9z = 6$ has (2)
    (A) n – r solutions
    (B) no solutions
    (C) infinitely many solutions
    (D) unique solution

19. For what value of k, the homogeneous system $x + 2y - z = 0$, $3x + 8y - 3z = 0$, $2x + 4y + (k - 3)z = 0$ has infinitely many solutions? (2)
    (A) k = 0
    (B) k = 1
    (C) k = 2
    (D) k = 3

20. For what value of λ, the system of linear equations $x + y + z = 6$, $x + 2y + 3z = 10$, $x + 2y + \lambda z = 10$ has infinitely many solutions? (2)
    (A) λ = 1
    (B) λ = 3
    (C) λ = –3
    (D) λ = 10

21. For the values of μ ≠ 8, the system of linear equations $2x - y + 3z = 2$, $x + y + 2z = 2$, $5x - y + \mu z = 2$ has (2)
    (A) unique solution
    (B) no solutions
    (C) infinitely many solutions
    (D) x = 0, y = 0, z = 0

22. For $C_1X_1 + C_2X_2 + C_3X_3 = 0$ where X_1, X_2, X_3 non-zero vectors and C_1, C_2, C_3 are constants then X_1, X_2, X_3 are linearly independent if (1)
    (A) $C_1 \neq 0, C_2 \neq 0, C_3 \neq 0$
    (B) $C_1 \neq 0, C_2 = 0, C_3 = 0$
    (C) $C_1 \neq 0, C_2 \neq 0, C_3 = 0$
    (D) $C_1 = 0, C_2 = 0, C_3 = 0$

23. For $C_1X_1 + C_2X_2 + C_3X_3 = 0$ where X_1, X_2, X_3 non-zero vectors and C_1, C_2, C_3 are constants then X_1, X_2, X_3 are linearly dependent if (1)
    (A) $C_1 = 0, C_2 = 0, C_3 = 0$
    (B) not all C_1, C_2, C_3 are zero
    (C) $C_1 = \infty, C_2 = \infty, C_3 = \infty$
    (D) none of these

24. The vectors $X_1 = (1, 2, 3)$, $X_2 = (2, 4, 6)$ are (1)
    (A) linearly dependent
    (B) linearly independent
    (C) mutually orthogonal
    (D) none of these

25. The vectors $X_1 = (1, 1, 1)$, $X_2 = (2, 2, 2)$, $X_3 = (3, 3, 3)$ are (1)
    (A) linearly independent
    (B) linearly dependent
    (C) mutually orthogonal
    (D) none of these

Type II : Linear Transformation and Orthogonal Transformations

26. For the linear transformation $Y = AX$ if $|A| = 0$ then the transformation is (1)
    - (A) nonsingular
    - (B) orthogonal
    - (C) singular
    - (D) none of these

27. For the linear transformation $Y = AX$ if $|A| \neq 0$ then the transformation is (1)
    - (A) nonsingular
    - (B) orthogonal
    - (C) singular
    - (D) none of these

28. If $Y = AX$ and $Z = BY$ be two linear transformations then the composite transformation which takes X to Z is given by (1)
    - (A) $Z = (AB) X$
    - (B) $Z = (BA) X$
    - (C) $X = (BA) Z$
    - (D) $X = (AB) Z$

29. If $Y = AX$ is non-singular linear transformations then its inverse transformation is (1)
    - (A) $X = A^{-1}Y$
    - (B) $Y = A^{-1}X$
    - (C) $X = YA^{-1}$
    - (D) does not exist

30. For square matrix A to be an orthogonal matrix (1)
    - (A) $AA^T = I$
    - (B) $AA^T = A^{-1}$
    - (C) $A^2 = I$
    - (D) $A = A^T$

31. If A is an orthogonal matrix then A^{-1} equals to (1)
    - (A) A
    - (B) A^T
    - (C) A^2
    - (D) I

32. If A is an orthogonal matrix then determinant of A is (1)
    - (A) 0
    - (B) ± 3
    - (C) ± 2
    - (D) ± 1

33. If A is an orthogonal matrix then
    - (A) A^T is orthogonal
    - (B) A^{-1} is orthogonal
    - (C) $\det (A) = \pm 1$
    - (D) all are correct

34. If $Y = AX$ is an orthogonal linear transformations then the matrix A is (1)
    - (A) nonsingular
    - (B) orthogonal
    - (C) singular
    - (D) none of these

35. For an orthogonal matrix $A = \begin{bmatrix} \cos\theta & \sin\theta \\ -\sin\theta & \cos\theta \end{bmatrix}$, A^{-1} is (1)
    - (A) $\begin{bmatrix} \cos\theta & \sin\theta \\ -\sin\theta & -\cos\theta \end{bmatrix}$
    - (B) $\begin{bmatrix} -\cos\theta & \sin\theta \\ -\sin\theta & \cos\theta \end{bmatrix}$
    - (C) $\begin{bmatrix} \cos\theta & \sin\theta \\ -\sin\theta & \cos\theta \end{bmatrix}$
    - (D) $\begin{bmatrix} \cos\theta & -\sin\theta \\ \sin\theta & \cos\theta \end{bmatrix}$

36. For an orthogonal matrix $A = \dfrac{1}{3}\begin{bmatrix} -2 & 1 & 2 \\ 2 & 2 & 1 \\ 1 & -2 & 2 \end{bmatrix}$, A^{-1} is (1)

(A) $\dfrac{1}{3}\begin{bmatrix} -2 & 1 & 2 \\ 2 & 2 & 1 \\ 1 & -2 & 2 \end{bmatrix}$

(B) $\dfrac{1}{3}\begin{bmatrix} 2 & -1 & -2 \\ -2 & -2 & -1 \\ -1 & 2 & -2 \end{bmatrix}$

(C) $\dfrac{1}{3}\begin{bmatrix} -2 & 2 & 1 \\ 1 & 2 & -2 \\ 2 & 1 & 2 \end{bmatrix}$

(D) does not exist

37. For an orthogonal matrix $A = \dfrac{1}{\sqrt{2}}\begin{bmatrix} 1 & 0 & 1 \\ 0 & 1 & 0 \\ 1 & 0 & -1 \end{bmatrix}$, A^{-1} is (1)

(A) $\dfrac{1}{\sqrt{2}}\begin{bmatrix} -1 & 0 & -1 \\ 0 & -1 & 0 \\ -1 & 0 & -1 \end{bmatrix}$

(B) $\begin{bmatrix} 1 & 0 & 1 \\ 0 & 1 & 0 \\ 1 & 0 & 1 \end{bmatrix}$

(C) $\dfrac{1}{\sqrt{2}}\begin{bmatrix} 1 & 0 & 1 \\ 0 & 1 & 0 \\ 1 & 0 & -1 \end{bmatrix}$

(D) does not exist

38. For an orthogonal matrix $A = \dfrac{1}{13}\begin{bmatrix} -12 & -5 \\ 5 & -12 \end{bmatrix}$, A^{-1} is (2)

(A) $\dfrac{1}{13}\begin{bmatrix} -12 & -5 \\ 5 & -12 \end{bmatrix}$

(B) $\dfrac{1}{13}\begin{bmatrix} -12 & 5 \\ -5 & -12 \end{bmatrix}$

(C) $\begin{bmatrix} -12 & -5 \\ 5 & -12 \end{bmatrix}$

(D) does not exist

39. The matrix of linear transformations $y_1 = 2x_1 + x_2 + x_3$, $y_2 = x_1 + x_2 + 2x_3$, $y_3 = x_1 - 2x_3$ (2)

(A) $\begin{bmatrix} 2 & 1 & 1 \\ 1 & 1 & 2 \\ 1 & 0 & -2 \end{bmatrix}$

(B) $\begin{bmatrix} 2 & 1 & 1 \\ 1 & 1 & 2 \\ 0 & 0 & 0 \end{bmatrix}$

(C) $\begin{bmatrix} 2 & 1 & 1 \\ 1 & 1 & 0 \\ 1 & 1 & -2 \end{bmatrix}$

(D) $\begin{bmatrix} 2 & 1 & 1 \\ 1 & 0 & 2 \\ 1 & 0 & 0 \end{bmatrix}$

40. The linear transformation $Y = \begin{bmatrix} 4 & -5 & 1 \\ 3 & 1 & -2 \\ 1 & 4 & 1 \end{bmatrix} \begin{bmatrix} x_1 \\ x_2 \\ x_3 \end{bmatrix}$ is (2)

    (A) nonsingular (B) composite
    (C) singular (D) none of these

41. The linear transformation $Y = \begin{bmatrix} 2 & -1 & 3 \\ 3 & 2 & 1 \\ 1 & -4 & 5 \end{bmatrix} \begin{bmatrix} x_1 \\ x_2 \\ x_3 \end{bmatrix}$ is (2)

    (A) nonsingular (B) orthogonal
    (C) singular (D) none of these

42. For the transformation $\begin{bmatrix} y_1 \\ y_2 \\ y_3 \end{bmatrix} = \begin{bmatrix} 2 & 1 & 1 \\ 1 & 1 & 2 \\ 1 & 0 & -2 \end{bmatrix} \begin{bmatrix} x_1 \\ x_2 \\ x_3 \end{bmatrix}$ coordinates (y_1, y_2, y_3) in Y corresponding to $(-1, 3, 0)$ in X are (2)

    (A) $(-1, -2, -1)$ (B) $(1, 2, -1)$
    (C) $(1, 1, 1)$ (D) $(-1, -2, 1)$

43. Whether the matrix $A = \begin{bmatrix} \cos\theta & \sin\theta \\ -\sin\theta & \cos\theta \end{bmatrix}$ is orthogonal ? (2)

    (A) yes (B) no
    (C) can't say (D) none of these

44. For what values of k, the matrix $A = \begin{bmatrix} \frac{1}{2} & k \\ -k & \frac{1}{2} \end{bmatrix}$ is an orthogonal matrix. (2)

    (A) $\pm\frac{\sqrt{3}}{2}$ (B) $\pm\frac{3}{4}$
    (C) $\pm\frac{1}{2}$ (D) ± 1

45. For what value of b, the matrix $A = \frac{1}{13}\begin{bmatrix} b & -5 \\ 5 & b \end{bmatrix}$ is an orthogonal ? (2)

    (A) ± 5 (B) ± 13
    (C) ± 12 (D) ± 16

46. For what values of λ, the matrix $A = \frac{1}{3}\begin{bmatrix} \lambda & 2 & 2 \\ 2 & 1 & -2 \\ 2 & -2 & 1 \end{bmatrix}$ is an orthogonal ? (2)

    (A) ± 2 (B) ± 4
    (C) ± 3 (D) ± 1

47. The linear transformation $Y = \begin{bmatrix} 0 & 1 \\ -1 & 0 \end{bmatrix} \begin{bmatrix} x_1 \\ x_2 \end{bmatrix}$ is (2)

   (A) composite (B) orthogonal
   (C) singular   (D) none of these

48. If the linear transformation $Y = \begin{bmatrix} \dfrac{1}{2} & \dfrac{\sqrt{3}}{2} \\ -\dfrac{\sqrt{3}}{2} & \dfrac{1}{2} \end{bmatrix} \begin{bmatrix} x_1 \\ x_2 \end{bmatrix}$ is an orthogonal linear transformation then its inverse transformation is (2)

   (A) $X = \begin{bmatrix} \dfrac{1}{2} & \dfrac{\sqrt{3}}{2} \\ -\dfrac{\sqrt{3}}{2} & \dfrac{1}{2} \end{bmatrix} \begin{bmatrix} y_1 \\ y_2 \end{bmatrix}$

   (B) $Y = \begin{bmatrix} \dfrac{1}{2} & -\dfrac{\sqrt{3}}{2} \\ \dfrac{\sqrt{3}}{2} & \dfrac{1}{2} \end{bmatrix} \begin{bmatrix} x_1 \\ x_2 \end{bmatrix}$

   (C) $X = \begin{bmatrix} -\dfrac{1}{2} & -\dfrac{\sqrt{3}}{2} \\ -\dfrac{\sqrt{3}}{2} & -\dfrac{1}{2} \end{bmatrix} \begin{bmatrix} y_1 \\ y_2 \end{bmatrix}$

   (D) $X = \begin{bmatrix} \dfrac{1}{2} & -\dfrac{\sqrt{3}}{2} \\ \dfrac{\sqrt{3}}{2} & \dfrac{1}{2} \end{bmatrix} \begin{bmatrix} y_1 \\ y_2 \end{bmatrix}$

Answers

1. (A)	11. (B)	21. (A)	31. (B)	41. (C)
2. (A)	12. (B)	22. (D)	32. (D)	42. (B)
3. (B)	13. (A)	23. (B)	33. (D)	43. (A)
4. (A)	14. (C)	24. (A)	34. (B)	44. (A)
5. (D)	15. (C)	25. (B)	35. (D)	45. (C)
6. (C)	16. (C)	26. (C)	36. (C)	46. (D)
7. (A)	17. (C)	27. (A)	37. (C)	47. (B)
8. (B)	18. (D)	28. (B)	38. (B)	48. (D)
9. (A)	19. (B)	29. (A)	39. (A)	
10. (D)	20. (B)	30. (A)	40. (A)	

CHAPTER THREE
EIGEN VALUES, EIGEN VECTORS

3.1 INTRODUCTION

As far as the engineering applications are concerned, eigen value problems are among the most important problems in connection with matrices, and the student should follow our present discussion with particular attention. We first define the basic concepts and explain them in terms of typical examples.

Let A be a n × n square matrix and Y and X are two non-zero column vectors such that

$$Y = AX$$

$$\begin{bmatrix} y_1 \\ y_2 \\ \vdots \\ \vdots \\ y_n \end{bmatrix} = \begin{bmatrix} a_{11} & a_{12} & \cdots & a_{1n} \\ a_{21} & a_{22} & \cdots & a_{2n} \\ \vdots & \vdots & & \vdots \\ \vdots & \vdots & & \vdots \\ a_{n1} & a_{n2} & \cdots & a_{nn} \end{bmatrix} \begin{bmatrix} x_1 \\ x_2 \\ \vdots \\ \vdots \\ x_n \end{bmatrix}$$

Y = AX means 'A' transforms vector X to vector Y

It is an interesting and important problem to determine which vectors, if any, are left unchanged in direction. Since two non-trivial vectors have the same direction if one is a non-zero scalar multiple of the other, this is equivalent to determine those vectors X whose images Y are given by

$$Y = \lambda X$$

In other words, our aim is to find X and λ which will satisfy the requirement that transformation of X due to matrix A is λX.

Important Point :

Hence, it is interesting to consider the transformation for a given matrix A which gives $Y = \lambda X$.

i.e. Vector X is transformed into a vector Y which has the same direction as X but has different magnitude.

∴ $Y = \lambda X$

$AX = \lambda X$ (∵ Y = AX)

$AX = \lambda IX$ (∵ X = IX)

$AX - \lambda IX = 0$ i.e. $(A - \lambda I) X = 0$

(3.1)

$$\begin{bmatrix} a_{11}-\lambda & a_{12} & a_{13} & \cdots & a_{1n} \\ a_{21} & a_{22}-\lambda & a_{23} & \cdots & a_{2n} \\ \vdots & \vdots & \vdots & & \vdots \\ \vdots & \vdots & \vdots & & \vdots \\ a_{n1} & a_{n2} & a_{n3} & \cdots & a_{nn}-\lambda \end{bmatrix} \begin{bmatrix} x_1 \\ x_2 \\ \vdots \\ \vdots \\ x_n \end{bmatrix} = \begin{bmatrix} 0 \\ 0 \\ \vdots \\ \vdots \\ 0 \end{bmatrix} \quad \ldots (1)$$

As we know that, this system of homogeneous linear equations will have a non-trivial solution, $(X \neq 0)$ if $|A - \lambda I| = 0$.

(Recall that $AX = Z$ will have non-trivial solution if $|A| = 0$)

$$D(\lambda) = |A - \lambda I| = \begin{vmatrix} a_{11}-\lambda & a_{12} & \cdots & a_{1n} \\ a_{21} & a_{22}-\lambda & \cdots & a_{2n} \\ \vdots & \vdots & & \vdots \\ \vdots & \vdots & & \vdots \\ a_{n1} & a_{n2} & \cdots & a_{nn}-\lambda \end{vmatrix} = 0$$

This is obviously a polynomial equation of degree n in the parameter λ.

$\therefore \quad D(\lambda) = |A - \lambda I| = a_0 \lambda^n + a_1 \lambda^{n-1} + a_2 \lambda^{n-2} + \ldots + a_n = 0 \quad \ldots (2)$

This polynomial equation of degree n in λ can be factorised into n linear factors as

$$D(\lambda) = |A - \lambda I| = (\lambda - \lambda_1)(\lambda - \lambda_2)(\lambda - \lambda_3) \ldots (\lambda - \lambda_n) = 0$$

3.2 CHARACTERISTIC DETERMINANT

We call $D(\lambda) = \begin{vmatrix} a_{11}-\lambda & a_{12} & \cdots & a_{1n} \\ a_{21} & a_{22}-\lambda & \cdots & a_{2n} \\ \vdots & \vdots & & \vdots \\ \vdots & \vdots & & \vdots \\ a_{n1} & a_{n2} & \cdots & a_{nn}-\lambda \end{vmatrix}$ as the characteristic determinant

3.3 CHARACTERISTIC MATRIX OF A

The matrix $[A - \lambda I] = \begin{bmatrix} a_{11}-\lambda & a_{12} & \cdots & a_{1n} \\ a_{21} & a_{22}-\lambda & \cdots & a_{2n} \\ \vdots & \vdots & & \vdots \\ \vdots & \vdots & & \vdots \\ a_{n1} & a_{n2} & \cdots & a_{nn}-\lambda \end{bmatrix}$

where I is an unit matrix of order n, is called characteristic matrix of A.

3.4 CHARACTERISTIC POLYNOMIAL OF A

$$D(\lambda) = |A - \lambda I| = a_0 \lambda^n + a_1 \lambda^{n-1} + a_2 \lambda^{n-2} + \ldots + a_n$$

is known as characteristic polynomial of matrix A.

3.5 CHARACTERISTIC EQUATION OF A

$$D(\lambda) = |A - \lambda I| = 0$$

i.e. $a_0 \lambda^n + a_1 \lambda^{n-1} + a_2 \lambda^{n-2} + \ldots + a_n = 0$ is called characteristic equation of A.

Obviously, the degree of the characteristic equation of a matrix is equal to the order of that matrix.

3.6 CHARACTERISTIC ROOTS OR EIGEN VALUES

$$D(\lambda) = |A - \lambda I| = (\lambda - \lambda_1)(\lambda - \lambda_2) \ldots (\lambda - \lambda_n) = 0$$

where $\lambda = \lambda_1, \lambda_2, \lambda_3, \ldots \lambda_n$ are called characteristic roots or eigen values or proper values or latent roots of the matrix A.

3.7 SPECTRUM OF A

The set of all characteristic roots of the matrix A is called spectrum of A.

3.8 CHARACTERISTIC VECTOR OR EIGEN VECTOR

For every characteristic root, $(A - \lambda I) X = 0$ will have a non-trivial solution.

Let X_i be the solution vector of $(A - \lambda I) X = 0$ corresponding to the characteristic root λ_i, then X_i is called characteristic vector or Eigen vector or latent vector associated with the root λ_i.

Definition of Eigen value and Eigen vector :

Any non-zero vector X is said to be a characteristic vector (or eigen vector) of a matrix A, if there exists a number λ such that $AX = \lambda X$.

Also then λ is said to be a characteristic root (or eigen value) of the matrix A corresponding to the characteristic vector X.

Note :

1. The eigen values of a square matrix 'A' are the roots of the corresponding characteristic equation $a_0 \lambda^n + a_1 \lambda^{n-1} + \ldots + a_n = 0$.
2. An $n \times n$ matrix has at least one eigen value and at most n numerically different eigen values.
3. Eigen value : In German it is "Eigen wert" : "Eigen" means "Proper", "Wert" means "Value".
4. The word "Eigen vector" is a mixture of German and English.

   The German prefix, "Eigen" can be translated as "Proper" or "Characteristic".

   Hence "Eigen values" are also called "Proper values" or "Characteristic Values".

   In the older literature, eigen values are sometimes called "Latent roots" or "Pole".

3.9 PROPERTIES OF EIGEN VALUES

1. **Trace of A :** The sum of the entries on the main diagonal of an n × n matrix A is called the trace of A; thus

   Trace of A $= a_{11} + a_{22} + a_{33} + \ldots + a_{nn}$

2. The sum of the eigen values of a matrix is the sum of the elements of the principal diagonal i.e. Trace of A $= a_{11} + a_{22} + \ldots + a_{nn} = \lambda_1 + \lambda_2 + \ldots + \lambda_n$.

3. The eigen values of an upper or lower triangular matrix are the elements on its main diagonal.

4. The product of the eigen values of a matrix equals the determinant of the matrix. i.e. $\lambda_1 \times \lambda_2 \times \lambda_3 \times \ldots \times \lambda_n = |A|$.

5. If $\lambda_1, \lambda_2 \ldots \lambda_n$ are eigen values of A then $\dfrac{1}{\lambda_1}, \dfrac{1}{\lambda_2} \ldots \dfrac{1}{\lambda_n}$ are eigen values of A^{-1}.

6. The matrix KA has the eigen values $K\lambda_1, K\lambda_2, \ldots K\lambda_n$.

7. The matrix A^m (m a non-negative integer) has the eigen values $\lambda_1^m, \lambda_2^m, \ldots \lambda_n^m$.

8. **Spectral shift :** The matrix (A – KI) has the eigen values $\lambda_1 - K, \lambda_2 - K, \ldots \lambda_n - K$.

9. The eigen values of a symmetric matrix are real.

10. The eigen values of A and A' are the same.

11. The inverse A^{-1} exists iff $\lambda_j \neq 0$, $j = 1, 2, 3, \ldots n$.

3.10 PROPERTIES OF EIGEN VECTORS

1. If X is an eigen vector of a matrix A corresponding to an eigen value λ, so is KX with any $K \neq 0$.

   Thus, the eigen vector corresponding to an eigen value is not unique.

   Proof : $AX = \lambda X$ $\therefore$ $K(AX) = K(\lambda X)$

   $A(KX) = \lambda(KX) \Rightarrow$ KX is also eigen vector of A

2. Let $\lambda_1, \lambda_2, \ldots \lambda_n$ be distinct eigen values of an n × n matrix then corresponding eigen vectors $X_1, X_2, \ldots X_n$ form a linearly independent set.

   i.e. $X_1, X_2, \ldots X_n$ are linearly independent. (Refer chapter 2 for linear independence of vectors).

3. Corresponding to n distinct eigen values, we get n independent eigen vectors. But when two or more eigen values are equal, it may or may not be possible to get linearly independent eigen vectors corresponding to the repeated roots.

4. An n × n matrix may have n linearly independent eigen vectors or it may have fewer than n.

5. Eigen vector of a square matrix cannot correspond to two distinct eigen values.

6. **Orthogonal eigen vectors :** Two eigen vectors X_1 and X_2 are said to be orthogonal if $X_1' X_2 = 0$.

   e.g. $X_1 = \begin{bmatrix} 1 \\ 2 \\ 3 \end{bmatrix}$, $X_2 = \begin{bmatrix} 3 \\ 0 \\ -1 \end{bmatrix}$

   $\therefore X_1' X_2 = \begin{bmatrix} 1 & 2 & 3 \end{bmatrix} \begin{bmatrix} 3 \\ 0 \\ -1 \end{bmatrix} = 1(3) + 2(0) + 3(-1) = 0$

   $\therefore X_1 X_2$ are orthogonal.

7. Eigen vectors of a symmetric matrix corresponding to different eigen values are orthogonal.

   Note : Eigen values may be zero; an eigen vector may not be the zero vector.

3.11 METHOD OF FINDING EIGEN VALUES OF A

1. Let A be a matrix of order 3×3 say $A = \begin{bmatrix} 4 & 0 & 0 \\ 0 & 5 & 0 \\ 0 & 0 & 6 \end{bmatrix}$ then write down directly the eigen values of A as $\lambda = 4, 5, 6$.

2. If $A = \begin{bmatrix} 1 & -2 & -1 \\ 0 & 3 & 2 \\ 0 & 0 & 5 \end{bmatrix}$ then eigen values are $\lambda = 1, 3, 5$.

3. If $A = \begin{bmatrix} 1 & 0 & 0 \\ -1 & 2 & 0 \\ 4 & 0 & 3 \end{bmatrix}$ then eigen values are $\lambda = 1, 2, 3$.

4. For a square matrix of order 2×2 say $A = \begin{bmatrix} a_{11} & a_{12} \\ a_{21} & a_{22} \end{bmatrix}$, the characteristic equation of A is $|A - \lambda I| = 0$ i.e. $\begin{vmatrix} a_{11} - \lambda & a_{12} \\ a_{21} & a_{22} - \lambda \end{vmatrix} = 0$

Now the expansion of this determinant is written by using a *short cut method* as follows.

Important Step : $\lambda^2 - S_1 \lambda + |A| = 0$
where $\quad S_1 =$ Sum of minors of order one along main diagonal of A
$\quad\quad S_1 = a_{11} + a_{22}$. Also $|A| = \begin{vmatrix} a_{11} & a_{12} \\ a_{21} & a_{22} \end{vmatrix} = a_{11} a_{22} - a_{12} a_{21}$

5. For a square matrix of order 3×3 say $A = \begin{bmatrix} a_{11} & a_{12} & a_{13} \\ a_{21} & a_{22} & a_{23} \\ a_{31} & a_{32} & a_{33} \end{bmatrix}$ the characteristic equation of A is $|A - \lambda I| = 0$ i.e. $\begin{vmatrix} a_{11} - \lambda & a_{12} & a_{13} \\ a_{21} & a_{22} - \lambda & a_{23} \\ a_{31} & a_{32} & a_{33} - \lambda \end{vmatrix} = 0$.

Important Step : $\lambda^3 - S_1 \lambda^2 + S_2 \lambda - |A| = 0$
where
S_1 = Sum of minors of order one along main diagonal of A
$S_1 = a_{11} + a_{22} + a_{33}$
S_2 = Sum of minors of order two of the diagonal element of A
S_2 = minor of a_{11} + minor of a_{22} + minor of a_{33}

$S_2 = \begin{vmatrix} a_{22} & a_{23} \\ a_{32} & a_{33} \end{vmatrix} + \begin{vmatrix} a_{11} & a_{13} \\ a_{31} & a_{33} \end{vmatrix} + \begin{vmatrix} a_{11} & a_{12} \\ a_{21} & a_{22} \end{vmatrix}$

$|A| = a_{11}(a_{22}a_{33} - a_{23}a_{32}) - a_{12}(a_{21}a_{33} - a_{23}a_{31}) + a_{13}(a_{21}a_{32} - a_{22}a_{31})$

Important Note : We can check the eigen values obtained are correct or wrong by using the following formula :

(1) For $A_{2 \times 2}$, we must have $\lambda_1 + \lambda_2 = a_{11} + a_{22}$ and $\lambda_1 \cdot \lambda_2 = |A|$.

(2) For $A_{3 \times 3}$, we must have $\lambda_1 + \lambda_2 + \lambda_3 = a_{11} + a_{22} + a_{33}$ and $\lambda_1 \cdot \lambda_2 \cdot \lambda_3 = |A|$.

Cramer's Rule : Consider $a_1 x + b_1 y + c_1 z = 0$
$a_2 x + b_2 y + c_2 z = 0$

Thus by using Cramer's rule, we have $\dfrac{x}{\begin{vmatrix} b_1 & c_1 \\ b_2 & c_2 \end{vmatrix}} = \dfrac{-y}{\begin{vmatrix} a_1 & c_1 \\ a_2 & c_2 \end{vmatrix}} = \dfrac{z}{\begin{vmatrix} a_1 & b_1 \\ a_2 & b_2 \end{vmatrix}}$.

Now problems of determining Eigen values and Eigen vectors are mainly divided into the following types.

Type 1 : A is non-symmetric with non-repeated Eigen values.

Type 2 : A is non-symmetric with repeated Eigen values.

Type 3 : A is symmetric with non-repeated Eigen values where Eigen vectors are orthogonal to each other.

Type 4 : A is symmetric with repeated Eigen values.

Type 5 : A may be symmetric/non-symmetric having only two eigen vectors. With $\lambda = \lambda_1$, with $\lambda = \lambda_2 = \lambda_3$.

Type 6 : A may be symmetric / non-symmetric having only one eigen vector corresponding to $\lambda = \lambda_1 = \lambda_2 = \lambda_3$.

3.12 TYPE 1 : 'A' IS NON-SYMMETRIC, EIGEN VALUES ARE NON-REPEATED

Ex. 1 : *Find the Eigen values and Eigen vectors of the following matrix*

$$A = \begin{bmatrix} 1 & 0 & -1 \\ 1 & 2 & 1 \\ 2 & 2 & 3 \end{bmatrix}.$$

(May 2009, May 2015)

Sol. : Step 1 : The characteristic equation of A is $|A - \lambda I| = 0$ i.e. $\begin{vmatrix} 1-\lambda & 0 & -1 \\ 1 & 2-\lambda & 1 \\ 2 & 2 & 3-\lambda \end{vmatrix} = 0.$

$$\lambda^3 - S_1\lambda^2 + S_2\lambda - |A| = 0$$

where $\quad S_1 = 1 + 2 + 3, \quad S_1 = 6$

$$S_2 = \begin{vmatrix} 2 & 1 \\ 2 & 3 \end{vmatrix} + \begin{vmatrix} 1 & -1 \\ 2 & 3 \end{vmatrix} + \begin{vmatrix} 1 & 0 \\ 1 & 2 \end{vmatrix} = 4 + 5 + 2, \; S_1 = 11$$

$$|A| = 1(6-2) - 1(2-4) = 6$$

∴ The characteristic equation of A is $\lambda^3 - 6\lambda^2 + 11\lambda - 6 = 0$ ... (1)

Step 2 : To find the roots of (1), we note that sum of coefficients $= 0$

$\lambda - 1 = 0$ must be the factor of (1). Now use synthetic division

```
1 |  1    -6    11    -6
  |       1    -5     6
  -----------------------
     1    -5     6     0
```

The factors are $(\lambda - 1)(\lambda^2 - 5\lambda + 6) = 0$
$(\lambda - 1)(\lambda - 2)(\lambda - 3) = 0$

Hence $\lambda = 1, \lambda = 2, \lambda = 3$ are the required Eigen values of A.

Note that $\lambda_1 + \lambda_2 + \lambda_3 = a_{11} + a_{22} + a_{33}$ i.e. $1 + 2 + 3 = 1 + 2 + 3$

Step 3 : Let $\lambda_1 = 1, \lambda_2 = 2, \lambda_3 = 3$ be the Eigen values of A.

To find the Eigen vectors for the corresponding Eigen values, we will consider the matrix equation $(A - \lambda I)X = 0,$ where $X = \begin{bmatrix} x \\ y \\ z \end{bmatrix}.$

$$\begin{bmatrix} 1-\lambda & 0 & -1 \\ 1 & 2-\lambda & 1 \\ 2 & 2 & 3-\lambda \end{bmatrix} \begin{bmatrix} x \\ y \\ z \end{bmatrix} = \begin{bmatrix} 0 \\ 0 \\ 0 \end{bmatrix} \qquad \ldots (2)$$

Step 4 : For Eigen value $\lambda = \lambda_1 = 1,$ let the corresponding Eigen vector be

$X_1 = \begin{bmatrix} x \\ y \\ z \end{bmatrix}.$

Put $\lambda = \lambda_1 = 1$ ∴ The matrix equation (2) will become

$$\begin{bmatrix} 0 & 0 & -1 \\ 1 & 1 & 1 \\ 2 & 2 & 2 \end{bmatrix} \begin{bmatrix} x \\ y \\ z \end{bmatrix} = \begin{bmatrix} 0 \\ 0 \\ 0 \end{bmatrix}$$ i.e. $AX = Z$

which is Homogeneous system of equations.

By R_1, $\quad 0(x) + 0(y) - 1(z) = 0 \quad$ ∴ $\quad z = 0$
By R_2, $\quad x + y + z = 0 \quad\quad x + y = 0 \quad$ Let $y = t,\ x = -t$

Hence for $\lambda_1 = 1$, the corresponding Eigen vector is $X_1 = \begin{bmatrix} -t \\ t \\ 0 \end{bmatrix} = t \begin{bmatrix} -1 \\ 1 \\ 0 \end{bmatrix}$.

By considering the particular solution (vector), we have for $\lambda_1 = 1$, $X_1 = \begin{bmatrix} -1 \\ 1 \\ 0 \end{bmatrix}$.

Step 5 : For Eigen value $\lambda = \lambda_2 = 2$, let the corresponding Eigen vector be $X_2 = \begin{bmatrix} x \\ y \\ z \end{bmatrix}$.

Put $\lambda = \lambda_2 = 2$ ∴ The matrix equation (2) will become $\begin{bmatrix} -1 & 0 & -1 \\ 1 & 0 & 1 \\ 2 & 2 & 1 \end{bmatrix} \begin{bmatrix} x \\ y \\ z \end{bmatrix} = \begin{bmatrix} 0 \\ 0 \\ 0 \end{bmatrix}$

i.e. $AX = Z$ which is Homogeneous system of equations.

By R_1, $\quad\quad -x - z = 0 \quad\quad$ Let $z = t$ ∴ $x = -t$

By R_3, $\quad\quad 2x + 2y + z = 0,\ y = \dfrac{t}{2}$ ∴ $X_2 = \begin{bmatrix} -t \\ \frac{t}{2} \\ t \end{bmatrix}$ or $\begin{bmatrix} -2t \\ t \\ 2t \end{bmatrix}$ or $t \begin{bmatrix} -2 \\ 1 \\ 2 \end{bmatrix}$

Hence for $\lambda_2 = 2$, the corresponding Eigen vector is $X_2 = \begin{bmatrix} -2 \\ 1 \\ 2 \end{bmatrix}$.

Step 6 : For Eigen value $\lambda = \lambda_3 = 3$, let the corresponding Eigen vector be $X_3 = \begin{bmatrix} x \\ y \\ z \end{bmatrix}$. Put $\lambda = \lambda_3 = 3$

∴ The matrix equation (2) will become $\begin{bmatrix} -2 & 0 & -1 \\ 1 & -1 & 1 \\ 2 & 2 & 0 \end{bmatrix} \begin{bmatrix} x \\ y \\ z \end{bmatrix} = \begin{bmatrix} 0 \\ 0 \\ 0 \end{bmatrix}$

i.e. $\quad\quad AX = Z$ which is Homogeneous system of equations.

By R_1, $\quad -2x - z = 0 \quad$ Let $x = t, \ z = -2t$
By R_3, $\quad 2x + 2y = 0 \quad x + y = 0, \ y = -t$

$$X_3 = \begin{bmatrix} t \\ -t \\ -2t \end{bmatrix} \text{ or } t \begin{bmatrix} 1 \\ -1 \\ -2 \end{bmatrix}$$

Hence for $\lambda_3 = 3$, the corresponding Eigen vector is $X_3 = \begin{bmatrix} 1 \\ -1 \\ -2 \end{bmatrix}$.

Step 7: $\lambda_1 = 1 \to X_1 = \begin{bmatrix} -1 \\ 1 \\ 0 \end{bmatrix}, \ \lambda_2 = 2 \to X_2 = \begin{bmatrix} -2 \\ 1 \\ 2 \end{bmatrix}, \ \lambda_3 = 3 \to X_3 = \begin{bmatrix} 1 \\ -1 \\ -2 \end{bmatrix}$.

Ex. 2: *Determine the Eigen values and Eigen vectors of the following matrix*

$$A = \begin{bmatrix} 4 & 6 & 6 \\ 1 & 3 & 2 \\ -1 & -4 & -3 \end{bmatrix}.$$

Sol.: Step 1: The characteristic equation of A is $|A - \lambda I| = 0$

i.e. $\begin{bmatrix} 4-\lambda & 6 & 6 \\ 1 & 3-\lambda & 2 \\ -1 & -4 & -3-\lambda \end{bmatrix} = 0$

$\lambda^3 - S_1\lambda^2 + S_2\lambda - |A| = 0 \quad$ where $S_1 = 4 + 3 - 3 = 4$

$$S_2 = \begin{vmatrix} 3 & 2 \\ -4 & -3 \end{vmatrix} + \begin{vmatrix} 4 & 6 \\ -1 & -3 \end{vmatrix} + \begin{vmatrix} 4 & 6 \\ 1 & 3 \end{vmatrix}$$

$S_2 = -1 - 6 + 6 = -1$

$|A| = 4(-1) - 6(-1) + 6(-1) = -4$

∴ The characteristic equation of A is $\lambda^3 - 4\lambda^2 - \lambda + 4 = 0$ ... (1)

Step 2: To find the roots of (1), we note that sum of coefficients = 0.

∴ $(\lambda - 1) = 0$ must be the factor of (1).

Now use synthetic division

$$\begin{array}{c|cccc} 1 & 1 & -4 & -1 & 4 \\ & & +1 & -3 & -4 \\ \hline & 1 & -3 & -4 & 0 \end{array}$$

∴ The factors are $(\lambda - 1)(\lambda^2 - 3\lambda - 4) = 0$

$(\lambda - 1)(\lambda + 1)(\lambda - 4) = 0$

Hence $\lambda = -1, \ \lambda = 1, \ \lambda = 4$ are the required Eigen values of A.

Note that $\lambda_1 + \lambda_2 + \lambda_3 = a_{11} + a_{22} + a_{33}$ i.e. $-1 + 1 + 4 = 4 + 3 - 3$

Step 3 : Let $\lambda_1 = -1$, $\lambda_2 = 1$, $\lambda_3 = 4$ be the Eigen values of A.

To find the Eigen vectors for the corresponding Eigen values we will consider the matrix equation $(A - \lambda I) X = 0$, where

$$X = \begin{bmatrix} x \\ y \\ z \end{bmatrix} \text{ i.e. } \begin{bmatrix} 4-\lambda & 6 & 6 \\ 1 & 3-\lambda & 2 \\ -1 & -4 & -3-\lambda \end{bmatrix} \begin{bmatrix} x \\ y \\ z \end{bmatrix} = \begin{bmatrix} 0 \\ 0 \\ 0 \end{bmatrix} \quad \ldots (2)$$

Step 4 : For $\lambda = \lambda_1 = -1$, let the corresponding eigen vector be $X_1 = \begin{bmatrix} x \\ y \\ z \end{bmatrix}$.

Put $\lambda = \lambda_1 = -1$ in (2). The matrix equation (2) will become

$$\begin{bmatrix} 5 & 6 & 6 \\ 1 & 4 & 2 \\ -1 & -4 & -2 \end{bmatrix} \begin{bmatrix} x \\ y \\ z \end{bmatrix} = \begin{bmatrix} 0 \\ 0 \\ 0 \end{bmatrix}$$

which is homogeneous system of equations. Consider first two equations
$$5x + 6y + 6z = 0$$
$$x + 4y + 2z = 0$$

Solving by Cramer's rule, $\dfrac{x}{\begin{vmatrix} 6 & 6 \\ 4 & 2 \end{vmatrix}} = \dfrac{-y}{\begin{vmatrix} 5 & 6 \\ 1 & 2 \end{vmatrix}} = \dfrac{z}{\begin{vmatrix} 5 & 6 \\ 1 & 4 \end{vmatrix}}$

$\dfrac{x}{-12} = \dfrac{-y}{4} = \dfrac{z}{14}$ or $\dfrac{x}{-6} = \dfrac{y}{-2} = \dfrac{z}{7} = t$ $\therefore$ $x = -6t$, $y = -2t$, $z = 7t$

For $\lambda_1 = -1$, $X_1 = \begin{bmatrix} -6t \\ -2t \\ 7t \end{bmatrix}$ or $t \begin{bmatrix} -6 \\ -2 \\ 7 \end{bmatrix}$

Hence for $\lambda_1 = -1$, the corresponding Eigen vector is $X_1 = \begin{bmatrix} -6 \\ -2 \\ 7 \end{bmatrix}$.

Step 5 : For $\lambda = \lambda_2 = 1$, let the corresponding Eigen vector be $X_2 = \begin{bmatrix} x \\ y \\ z \end{bmatrix}$

Put $\lambda = \lambda_2 = 1$ in (2) $\therefore$ The matrix equation (2) will become

$$\begin{bmatrix} 3 & 6 & 6 \\ 1 & 2 & 2 \\ -1 & -4 & -4 \end{bmatrix} \begin{bmatrix} x \\ y \\ z \end{bmatrix} = \begin{bmatrix} 0 \\ 0 \\ 0 \end{bmatrix}$$
$$AX = Z$$

which is Homogeneous system of equations. Here first two equations are identical.

∴ Consider last two equations
$$x + 2y + 2z = 0$$
$$-x - 4y - 4z = 0$$

Solving by Cramer's rule, $\dfrac{x}{\begin{vmatrix} 2 & 2 \\ -4 & -4 \end{vmatrix}} = \dfrac{-y}{\begin{vmatrix} 1 & 2 \\ -1 & -4 \end{vmatrix}} = \dfrac{z}{\begin{vmatrix} 1 & 2 \\ -1 & -4 \end{vmatrix}}$.

$\dfrac{x}{0} = \dfrac{-y}{-2} = \dfrac{z}{-2}$ or $\dfrac{x}{0} = \dfrac{y}{1} = \dfrac{z}{-1} = t$ i.e. $x = 0$, $y = t$, $z = -t$

For $\lambda_2 = 1$, $X_2 = \begin{bmatrix} 0 \\ t \\ -t \end{bmatrix}$ or $t \begin{bmatrix} 0 \\ 1 \\ -1 \end{bmatrix}$

Hence for $\lambda_2 = 1$, the corresponding eigen vector is $X_2 = \begin{bmatrix} 0 \\ 1 \\ -1 \end{bmatrix}$

Step 6 : For $\lambda = \lambda_3 = 4$, let the corresponding Eigen vector be $X_3 = \begin{bmatrix} x \\ y \\ z \end{bmatrix}$

Put $\lambda = \lambda_3 = 4$ in (2).

∴ The matrix equation (2) will become

$\begin{bmatrix} 0 & 6 & 6 \\ 1 & -1 & 2 \\ -1 & -4 & -7 \end{bmatrix} \begin{bmatrix} x \\ y \\ z \end{bmatrix} = \begin{bmatrix} 0 \\ 0 \\ 0 \end{bmatrix}$ i.e. $AX = Z$

which is Homogeneous system of equations.
By R_1 $6y + 6z = 0$, $y + z = 0$ Let $z = t$, $y = -t$
By R_2 $x - y + 2z = 0$, $x = -3t$

For $\lambda_3 = 4$, $X_3 = \begin{bmatrix} -3t \\ -t \\ t \end{bmatrix}$ or $t \begin{bmatrix} -3 \\ -1 \\ 1 \end{bmatrix}$. Hence for $\lambda_3 = 4$, the Eigen vector is

$X_3 = \begin{bmatrix} -3 \\ -1 \\ 1 \end{bmatrix}$.

Step 7 : $\lambda_1 = -1 \to X_1 = \begin{bmatrix} -6 \\ -2 \\ 7 \end{bmatrix}$; $\lambda_2 = 1 \to X_2 = \begin{bmatrix} 0 \\ 1 \\ -1 \end{bmatrix}$; $\lambda_3 = 4 \to X_3 = \begin{bmatrix} -3 \\ -1 \\ 1 \end{bmatrix}$.

Ex. 3 : *Find the Eigen values and Eigen vectors of the following matrix* $A = \begin{bmatrix} 14 & -10 \\ 5 & -1 \end{bmatrix}$.

(May 2006)

Sol. : Step 1 : The characteristic equation of A is $|A - \lambda I| = 0$ i.e. $\begin{vmatrix} 14 - \lambda & -10 \\ 5 & -1 - \lambda \end{vmatrix} = 0$

$(14 - \lambda)(-1 - \lambda) + 50 = 0$ or $\lambda^2 - 13\lambda + 36 = 0$ or $(\lambda - 9)(\lambda - 4) = 0$

OR $\lambda^2 - S_1 \lambda + |A| = 0$, where $S_1 = 14 - 1 = 13$ and $|A| = -14 + 50 = 36$

$\therefore \quad \lambda^2 - 13\lambda + 36 = 0$

Hence $\lambda = 9$, $\lambda = 4$ are the required Eigen values of A.

Note that $\lambda_1 + \lambda_2 = a_{11} + a_{22}$ i.e. $9 + 4 = 14 - 1$

Step 2 : Let $\lambda_1 = 9$, $\lambda_2 = 4$ be the Eigen values of A.

To find the Eigen vectors for the corresponding Eigen values, we will consider the matrix equation $(A - \lambda I) X = 0$,

where $X = \begin{bmatrix} x \\ y \end{bmatrix}$ i.e. $\begin{bmatrix} 14 - \lambda & -10 \\ 5 & -1 - \lambda \end{bmatrix} \begin{bmatrix} x \\ y \end{bmatrix} = \begin{bmatrix} 0 \\ 0 \end{bmatrix}$ ... (1)

Step 3 : For $\lambda = \lambda_1 = 9$, let the corresponding Eigen vector be $X_1 = \begin{bmatrix} x \\ y \end{bmatrix}$.

Put $\lambda = \lambda_1 = 9$ in equation (1).

$\therefore$ The matrix equation (1) will become $\begin{bmatrix} 5 & -10 \\ 5 & -10 \end{bmatrix} \begin{bmatrix} x \\ y \end{bmatrix} = \begin{bmatrix} 0 \\ 0 \end{bmatrix}$

By R_1 $\qquad 5x - 10y = 0, \qquad x - 2y = 0$. We set $y = t$, $x = 2t$

For $\lambda_1 = 9$, $X_1 = \begin{bmatrix} 2t \\ t \end{bmatrix}$ or $t \begin{bmatrix} 2 \\ 1 \end{bmatrix}$. Hence for $\lambda_1 = 9$ the Eigen vector is $X_1 = \begin{bmatrix} 2 \\ 1 \end{bmatrix}$.

Step 4 : For $\lambda = \lambda_2 = 4$, let the corresponding Eigen vector be $X_2 = \begin{bmatrix} x \\ y \end{bmatrix}$.

Put $\lambda = \lambda_2 = 4$ in equation (1).

$\therefore$ The matrix equation (1) will become $\begin{bmatrix} 10 & -10 \\ 5 & -5 \end{bmatrix} \begin{bmatrix} x \\ y \end{bmatrix} = \begin{bmatrix} 0 \\ 0 \end{bmatrix}$

By R_1 $\qquad 10x - 10y = 0$, $x - y = 0$, $x = y$. We set $y = t$, $x = t$

For $\lambda_2 = 4$ $\qquad X_2 = \begin{bmatrix} t \\ t \end{bmatrix}$ or $t \begin{bmatrix} 1 \\ 1 \end{bmatrix}$.

Hence for $\lambda_2 = 4$ the Eigen vector is $X_2 = \begin{bmatrix} 1 \\ 1 \end{bmatrix}$.

Step 5 : $\lambda_1 = 9 \rightarrow \qquad X_1 = \begin{bmatrix} 2 \\ 1 \end{bmatrix}$, $\lambda_2 = 4 \rightarrow X_2 = \begin{bmatrix} 1 \\ 1 \end{bmatrix}$

EXERCISE 3.1

Matrix A is Non-symmetric, Eigen values are different.

Find the Eigen values and the corresponding Eigen vectors for the following matrices.

(1) $\begin{bmatrix} 9 & -1 & 9 \\ 3 & -1 & 3 \\ -7 & 1 & -7 \end{bmatrix}$ **Ans.** $\lambda^3 - \lambda^2 - 2\lambda = 0;\ -1, 0, 2;\ \begin{bmatrix} 1 \\ 1 \\ -1 \end{bmatrix}, \begin{bmatrix} 1 \\ 0 \\ -1 \end{bmatrix}, \begin{bmatrix} 4 \\ 1 \\ -3 \end{bmatrix}$

(2) $\begin{bmatrix} -2 & -8 & -12 \\ 1 & 4 & 4 \\ 0 & 0 & 1 \end{bmatrix}$ **Ans.** $\lambda^3 - 3\lambda^2 + 2\lambda = 0;\ 0, 1, 2;\ \begin{bmatrix} 4 \\ -1 \\ 0 \end{bmatrix}, \begin{bmatrix} 4 \\ 0 \\ -1 \end{bmatrix}, \begin{bmatrix} 2 \\ -1 \\ 0 \end{bmatrix}$

(3) $\begin{bmatrix} 2 & -2 & 3 \\ 1 & 1 & 1 \\ 1 & 3 & -1 \end{bmatrix}$ **(May 04) Ans.** $\lambda^3 - 2\lambda^2 - 5\lambda + 6 = 0;\ -2, 1, 3;\ \begin{bmatrix} 11 \\ 1 \\ -14 \end{bmatrix}, \begin{bmatrix} 1 \\ -1 \\ -1 \end{bmatrix}, \begin{bmatrix} 1 \\ 1 \\ 1 \end{bmatrix}$

(4) $\begin{bmatrix} 1 & 4 \\ 2 & 3 \end{bmatrix}$ **Ans.** $\lambda^2 - 4\lambda - 5 = 0;\ 5, -1;\ \begin{bmatrix} 1 \\ 1 \end{bmatrix}, \begin{bmatrix} -2 \\ 1 \end{bmatrix}$

(5) $\begin{bmatrix} 4 & 2 & -2 \\ -5 & 3 & 2 \\ -2 & 4 & 1 \end{bmatrix}$ **Ans.** $\lambda^3 - 8\lambda^2 + 17\lambda - 10 = 0;\ 1, 2, 5;\ \begin{bmatrix} 2 \\ 1 \\ 4 \end{bmatrix}, \begin{bmatrix} 1 \\ 1 \\ 2 \end{bmatrix}, \begin{bmatrix} 0 \\ 1 \\ 1 \end{bmatrix}$

(Dec. 07, May 13)

(6) $\begin{bmatrix} -1 & 1 & 2 \\ 0 & -2 & 1 \\ 0 & 0 & -3 \end{bmatrix}$ **Ans.** $\lambda^3 + 6\lambda^2 + 11\lambda + 6 = 0;\ -1, -2, -3;\ \begin{bmatrix} 1 \\ 0 \\ 0 \end{bmatrix}, \begin{bmatrix} 1 \\ -1 \\ 0 \end{bmatrix}, \begin{bmatrix} 1 \\ 2 \\ -2 \end{bmatrix}$

(7) $\begin{bmatrix} 1 & -2 \\ -5 & 4 \end{bmatrix}$ **Ans.** $\lambda^2 - 5\lambda - 6 = 0;\ 6, -1;\ \begin{bmatrix} 2 \\ -5 \end{bmatrix}, \begin{bmatrix} 1 \\ 1 \end{bmatrix}$

(8) $\begin{bmatrix} 5 & 4 \\ 1 & 2 \end{bmatrix}$ **Ans.** $\lambda^2 - 7\lambda + 6 = 0;\ 1, 6;\ \begin{bmatrix} 1 \\ -1 \end{bmatrix}, \begin{bmatrix} 4 \\ 1 \end{bmatrix}$

(9) $\begin{bmatrix} 1 & 1 & -2 \\ -1 & 2 & 1 \\ 0 & 1 & -1 \end{bmatrix}$ **(Dec. 2012) Ans.** $\lambda^3 - 2\lambda^2 - \lambda + 2 = 0;\ -1, 2, 1;\ \begin{bmatrix} 1 \\ 0 \\ 1 \end{bmatrix}, \begin{bmatrix} 1 \\ 3 \\ 1 \end{bmatrix}, \begin{bmatrix} 3 \\ 2 \\ 1 \end{bmatrix}$

(10) $\begin{bmatrix} -9 & 2 & 6 \\ 5 & 0 & -3 \\ -16 & 4 & 11 \end{bmatrix}$ **Ans.** $\lambda^3 - 2\lambda^2 - \lambda + 2 = 0;\ 1, -1, 2;\ \begin{bmatrix} 1 \\ -1 \\ 2 \end{bmatrix}, \begin{bmatrix} 2 \\ -1 \\ 3 \end{bmatrix};\ \begin{bmatrix} 2 \\ -1 \\ 4 \end{bmatrix}$

(11) $\begin{bmatrix} 11 & -4 & -7 \\ 7 & -2 & -5 \\ 10 & -4 & -6 \end{bmatrix}$ (Dec. 2012) **Ans.** $\lambda^3 - 3\lambda^2 + 2\lambda = 0;\ 0, 1, 2;\ \begin{bmatrix} 1 \\ 1 \\ 1 \end{bmatrix}, \begin{bmatrix} 1 \\ -1 \\ 2 \end{bmatrix}, \begin{bmatrix} 2 \\ 1 \\ 2 \end{bmatrix}$

(12) $\begin{bmatrix} 2 & -1 & 1 \\ 1 & 2 & -1 \\ 1 & -1 & 2 \end{bmatrix}$ **Ans.** $\lambda^3 - 6\lambda^2 + 11\lambda - 6 = 0;\ 1, 2, 3;\ \begin{bmatrix} 0 \\ 1 \\ 1 \end{bmatrix}, \begin{bmatrix} 1 \\ 1 \\ 1 \end{bmatrix}, \begin{bmatrix} 1 \\ 0 \\ 1 \end{bmatrix}$

(May 2010, Dec. 2010)

(13) $\begin{bmatrix} 2 & 2 & 0 \\ 2 & 1 & 1 \\ -7 & 2 & -3 \end{bmatrix}$ **Ans.** $\lambda^3 - 13\lambda + 12 = 0;\ 1, 3, -4;\ \begin{bmatrix} 2 \\ -1 \\ -4 \end{bmatrix}, \begin{bmatrix} 2 \\ 1 \\ -2 \end{bmatrix}, \begin{bmatrix} 1 \\ -3 \\ 13 \end{bmatrix}$

(14) $\begin{bmatrix} 8 & -8 & -2 \\ 4 & -3 & -2 \\ 3 & -4 & 1 \end{bmatrix}$ **Ans.** $\lambda^3 - 6\lambda^2 + 11\lambda - 6 = 0;\ 1, 2, 3;\ \begin{bmatrix} 4 \\ 3 \\ 2 \end{bmatrix}, \begin{bmatrix} 3 \\ 2 \\ 1 \end{bmatrix}, \begin{bmatrix} 2 \\ 1 \\ 1 \end{bmatrix}$

(15) $\begin{bmatrix} 6 & 10 & 6 \\ 0 & 8 & 12 \\ 0 & 0 & 2 \end{bmatrix}$ **Ans.** $\lambda^3 - 16\lambda^2 + 76\lambda - 96 = 0;\ 6, 8, 2;\ \begin{bmatrix} 1 \\ 0 \\ 0 \end{bmatrix}, \begin{bmatrix} 5 \\ 1 \\ 0 \end{bmatrix}, \begin{bmatrix} 7 \\ -4 \\ 2 \end{bmatrix}$

(16) $\begin{bmatrix} 15 & 0 & -15 \\ -3 & 6 & 9 \\ 5 & 0 & -5 \end{bmatrix}$ **Ans.** $\lambda^3 - 16\lambda^2 + 60\lambda = 0;\ 10, 6, 0;\ \begin{bmatrix} 3 \\ 0 \\ 1 \end{bmatrix}, \begin{bmatrix} 0 \\ 1 \\ 0 \end{bmatrix}, \begin{bmatrix} 1 \\ -1 \\ 1 \end{bmatrix}$

(17) $\begin{bmatrix} 3 & 1 & 4 \\ 0 & 2 & 6 \\ 0 & 0 & 5 \end{bmatrix}$ **Ans.** $\lambda^3 - 10\lambda^2 + 31\lambda - 30 = 0;\ 3, 2, 5;\ \begin{bmatrix} 1 \\ 0 \\ 0 \end{bmatrix}, \begin{bmatrix} -1 \\ 1 \\ 0 \end{bmatrix}, \begin{bmatrix} 3 \\ 2 \\ 1 \end{bmatrix}$

(18) $\begin{bmatrix} 2 & -3 & 1 \\ 3 & 1 & 3 \\ -5 & 2 & -4 \end{bmatrix}$ **Ans.** $\lambda^3 + \lambda^2 - 2\lambda = 0;\ 0, 1, -2;\ \begin{bmatrix} 10 \\ 3 \\ -11 \end{bmatrix}, \begin{bmatrix} 1 \\ 0 \\ -1 \end{bmatrix}, \begin{bmatrix} 4 \\ 3 \\ -7 \end{bmatrix}$

(19) $\begin{bmatrix} 1 & 0 & 0 \\ 0 & 3 & -3 \\ 0 & -1 & 3 \end{bmatrix}$ **Ans.** $\lambda^3 - 7\lambda^2 + 12\lambda - 6 = 0;\ 1, 2, 4;\ \begin{bmatrix} 1 \\ 0 \\ 0 \end{bmatrix}, \begin{bmatrix} 0 \\ 1 \\ 1 \end{bmatrix}, \begin{bmatrix} 0 \\ 1 \\ -1 \end{bmatrix}$

(20) $\begin{bmatrix} 4 & 0 & 1 \\ -2 & 1 & 0 \\ -2 & 0 & 1 \end{bmatrix}$ **Ans.** $\lambda^3 - 6\lambda^2 + 11\lambda - 6 = 0;\ 1, 2, 3;\ \begin{bmatrix} 0 \\ 1 \\ 0 \end{bmatrix}, \begin{bmatrix} -1 \\ 2 \\ 2 \end{bmatrix}, \begin{bmatrix} -1 \\ 1 \\ 1 \end{bmatrix}$

(21) $\begin{bmatrix} 1 & 2 & 4 \\ -2 & -4 & 2 \\ 2 & 4 & 3 \end{bmatrix}$ **Ans.** $\lambda^3 - 25\lambda = 0;\ 5, 0, -5;\ \begin{bmatrix} 1 \\ 0 \\ 1 \end{bmatrix}, \begin{bmatrix} 2 \\ -1 \\ 0 \end{bmatrix}, \begin{bmatrix} 0 \\ 2 \\ -1 \end{bmatrix}$

(22) $\begin{bmatrix} 0 & 2 & 0 \\ 3 & -2 & 3 \\ 0 & 3 & 0 \end{bmatrix}$ **Ans.** $\lambda^3 + 2\lambda^2 - 15\lambda = 0$; 3, 0, –5; $\begin{bmatrix} 2 \\ 3 \\ 3 \end{bmatrix}, \begin{bmatrix} 1 \\ 0 \\ -1 \end{bmatrix}, \begin{bmatrix} 2 \\ -5 \\ 3 \end{bmatrix}$

(23) $\begin{bmatrix} 1 & 6 & 1 \\ 1 & 2 & 0 \\ 0 & 0 & 3 \end{bmatrix}$ **Ans.** $\lambda^3 - 6\lambda^2 + 5\lambda + 12 = 0$; –1, 3, 4; $\begin{bmatrix} 3 \\ -1 \\ 0 \end{bmatrix}, \begin{bmatrix} 1 \\ -1 \\ 4 \end{bmatrix}, \begin{bmatrix} 2 \\ 1 \\ 0 \end{bmatrix}$

(24) $\begin{bmatrix} 1 & 1 & 1 \\ 1 & 2 & 3 \\ -1 & 1 & 0 \end{bmatrix}$ **Ans.** $\lambda^3 - 3\lambda^2 - \lambda + 3 = 0$; 1, –1, 3; $\begin{bmatrix} 2 \\ 1 \\ -1 \end{bmatrix}, \begin{bmatrix} 0 \\ -1 \\ 1 \end{bmatrix}, \begin{bmatrix} 4 \\ 7 \\ 1 \end{bmatrix}$

(25) $\begin{bmatrix} 1 & 1 & 0 \\ 1 & -1 & 2 \\ 0 & 1 & 1 \end{bmatrix}$ **Ans.** $\lambda^3 - \lambda^2 - 4\lambda + 4 = 0$; 1, 2, –2; $\begin{bmatrix} 2 \\ 0 \\ -1 \end{bmatrix}, \begin{bmatrix} 1 \\ 1 \\ 1 \end{bmatrix}, \begin{bmatrix} 1 \\ -3 \\ 1 \end{bmatrix}$

(26) $\begin{bmatrix} 3 & 5 \\ -2 & -4 \end{bmatrix}$ **Ans.** $\lambda^2 + \lambda - 2 = 0$; 1, –2; $\begin{bmatrix} -5 \\ 2 \end{bmatrix}, \begin{bmatrix} -1 \\ 1 \end{bmatrix}$

(27) $\begin{bmatrix} 0 & 1 & 0 \\ 0 & 0 & 1 \\ 80 & -68 & 16 \end{bmatrix}$ **Ans.** $\lambda^3 - 16\lambda^2 + 68\lambda - 80 = 0$; 2, 4, 10; $\begin{bmatrix} 1 \\ 2 \\ 4 \end{bmatrix}, \begin{bmatrix} 1 \\ 4 \\ 16 \end{bmatrix}, \begin{bmatrix} 1 \\ 10 \\ 100 \end{bmatrix}$

(28) $\begin{bmatrix} 15 & -4 & -3 \\ -10 & 12 & -6 \\ -20 & 4 & -2 \end{bmatrix}$ **Ans.** $\lambda^3 - 25\lambda^2 + 50\lambda + 1000 = 0$; –5, 10, 20; $\begin{bmatrix} 1 \\ 2 \\ 4 \end{bmatrix}, \begin{bmatrix} 1 \\ 2 \\ -1 \end{bmatrix}, \begin{bmatrix} -2 \\ 1 \\ 2 \end{bmatrix}$

(29) $\begin{bmatrix} 13 & -3 & 5 \\ 0 & 4 & 0 \\ -15 & 9 & -7 \end{bmatrix}$ **Ans.** $\lambda^3 - 10\lambda^2 + 8\lambda + 64 = 0$; –2, 4, 8; $\begin{bmatrix} 1 \\ 0 \\ -3 \end{bmatrix}, \begin{bmatrix} 1 \\ -2 \\ -3 \end{bmatrix}, \begin{bmatrix} 1 \\ 0 \\ -1 \end{bmatrix}$

(30) $\begin{bmatrix} 1 & 20 & 0 \\ -1 & 7 & 1 \\ 3 & 0 & -2 \end{bmatrix}$ **Ans.** $\lambda^3 - 6\lambda^2 + 11\lambda - 6 = 0$; 1, 2, 3; $\begin{bmatrix} 1 \\ 0 \\ 1 \end{bmatrix}, \begin{bmatrix} 20 \\ 1 \\ 15 \end{bmatrix}, \begin{bmatrix} 10 \\ 1 \\ 6 \end{bmatrix}$

3.13 TYPE 2 : 'A' IS NON-SYMMETRIC, EIGEN VALUES ARE REPEATED

Ex. 1 : *Find Eigen values and Eigen vectors of the matrix* $A = \begin{bmatrix} -17 & 18 & -6 \\ -18 & 19 & -6 \\ -9 & 9 & -2 \end{bmatrix}$.

Sol. : Step 1 : The characteristic equation of A is $|A - \lambda I| = 0$,

$$\begin{vmatrix} -17-\lambda & 18 & -6 \\ -18 & 19-\lambda & -6 \\ -9 & 9 & -2-\lambda \end{vmatrix} = 0$$

$$\lambda^3 - S_1\lambda^2 + S_2\lambda - |A| = 0, \text{ where } S_1 = -17 + 19 - 2 = 0$$

$$S_2 = \begin{vmatrix} 19 & -6 \\ 9 & -2 \end{vmatrix} + \begin{vmatrix} -17 & -6 \\ -9 & -2 \end{vmatrix} + \begin{vmatrix} -17 & 18 \\ -18 & 19 \end{vmatrix} = 16 - 20 + 1 = -3$$

$$|A| = -17(16) - 18(-18) - 6(9) = -2$$

∴ The characteristic equation of A is $\lambda^3 - 3\lambda + 2 = 0$ ... (1)

Step 2 : For the factors of equation (1), we note that sum of coefficients = 0

∴ $(\lambda - 1) = 0$ must be the factor of (1).

By using synthetic division

```
 1 | 1   0   -3    2
   |     1    1   -2
   |_____
     1    1   -2    0
```

$(\lambda - 1)(\lambda^2 + \lambda - 2) = 0$

i.e. $(\lambda - 1)(\lambda + 2)(\lambda - 1) = 0$

Hence $\lambda = 1, 1, -2$ are the required eigen values of A.

Note that $\lambda_1 + \lambda_2 + \lambda_3 = a_{11} + a_{22} + a_{33}$ i.e. $1 + 1 - 2 = -17 + 19 - 2$

(Always denote non-repeated Eigen value by λ_1 and remaining two by $\lambda_2 = \lambda_3$)

Step 3 : Let $\lambda_1 = -2$, $\lambda_2 = 1 = \lambda_3$, be the Eigen values of A.

To find the Eigen vectors for the corresponding Eigen values, we will consider the matrix equation $(A - \lambda I) X = 0$.

where $X = \begin{bmatrix} x \\ y \\ z \end{bmatrix}$ i.e. $\begin{bmatrix} -17-\lambda & 18 & -6 \\ -18 & 19-\lambda & -6 \\ -9 & 9 & -2-\lambda \end{bmatrix} \begin{bmatrix} x \\ y \\ z \end{bmatrix} = \begin{bmatrix} 0 \\ 0 \\ 0 \end{bmatrix}$ ... (2)

Step 4 : For $\lambda = \lambda_1 = -2$, let the Eigen vector be $X_1 = \begin{bmatrix} x \\ y \\ z \end{bmatrix}$.

Put $\lambda = \lambda_1 = -2$

∴ The matrix equation (2) will become

$\begin{bmatrix} -15 & 18 & -6 \\ -18 & 21 & -6 \\ -9 & 9 & 0 \end{bmatrix} \begin{bmatrix} x \\ y \\ z \end{bmatrix} = \begin{bmatrix} 0 \\ 0 \\ 0 \end{bmatrix}$ i.e. AX = Z

which is homogeneous system of equations. Consider the first two equations.

$-15x + 18y - 6z = 0$, $-18x + 21y - 6z = 0$

i.e. $-5x + 6y - 2z = 0$, $-6x + 7y - 2z = 0$

By Cramer's rule $\dfrac{x}{\begin{vmatrix} 6 & -2 \\ 7 & -2 \end{vmatrix}} = \dfrac{-y}{\begin{vmatrix} -5 & -2 \\ -6 & -2 \end{vmatrix}} = \dfrac{z}{\begin{vmatrix} -5 & 6 \\ -6 & 7 \end{vmatrix}}$ i.e. $\dfrac{x}{2} = \dfrac{y}{2} = \dfrac{z}{1} = t$

$$x = 2t, \quad y = 2t, \quad z = t$$

For $\lambda_1 = -2$, we have Eigen vector $X_1 = \begin{bmatrix} 2 \\ 2 \\ 1 \end{bmatrix}$

Step 5: For $\lambda = \lambda_2 = 1$, let the Eigen vector be $X_2 = \begin{bmatrix} x \\ y \\ z \end{bmatrix}$.

Put $\lambda = \lambda_2 = 1$, ∴ the matrix equation (2) will become

$\begin{bmatrix} -18 & 18 & -6 \\ -18 & 18 & -6 \\ -9 & 9 & -3 \end{bmatrix} \begin{bmatrix} x \\ y \\ z \end{bmatrix} = \begin{bmatrix} 0 \\ 0 \\ 0 \end{bmatrix}$ i.e. AX = Z which is homogeneous system of equations.

The above system essentially gives a single equation $-18x + 18y - 6z = 0$
i.e. $\quad -3x + 3y - z = 0$

Important Step: Let $z = 0 \quad \therefore -3x + 3y = 0 \quad x = y$

Let $y = t \quad \therefore x = t \quad$ Hence for $\lambda_2 = 1$, $X_2 = \begin{bmatrix} 1 \\ 1 \\ 0 \end{bmatrix}$

Step 6: Now $\lambda = \lambda_3 = 1 = \lambda_2 \quad \therefore$ we arrive at same equation
$\quad -18x + 18y - 6z = 0$
i.e. $\quad -3x + 3y - z = 0$

Since the matrix is non-symmetric, the corresponding Eigen vectors X_2 and X_3 must be linearly independent.

This can be done by choosing $y = 0 \quad \therefore -3x - z = 0$

Let $x = t, \; z = -3t \quad \therefore$ For $\lambda_3 = 1$, the Eigen vector be $X_3 = \begin{bmatrix} 1 \\ 0 \\ -3 \end{bmatrix}$.

Carefully note down the procedure of finding X_2 and X_3 for repeated Eigen value $\lambda_2 = \lambda_3 = 1$.

Step 7: Hence

$$\lambda_1 = -2 \to X_1 = \begin{bmatrix} 2 \\ 2 \\ 1 \end{bmatrix}, \quad \lambda_2 = 1 \to X_2 = \begin{bmatrix} 1 \\ 1 \\ 0 \end{bmatrix}, \quad \lambda_3 = 1 \to X_3 = \begin{bmatrix} 1 \\ 0 \\ -3 \end{bmatrix}$$

Ex. 2 : *Find the Eigen values and the corresponding Eigen vectors for the following matrix*

$$A = \begin{bmatrix} 1 & -6 & -4 \\ 0 & 4 & 2 \\ 0 & -6 & -3 \end{bmatrix}.$$

Sol. : Step 1 : The characteristic equation $|A - \lambda I| = 0$ i.e. $\begin{vmatrix} 1-\lambda & -6 & -4 \\ 0 & 4-\lambda & 2 \\ 0 & -6 & -3-\lambda \end{vmatrix} = 0$

$\lambda^3 - S_1 \lambda^2 + S_2 \lambda - |A| = 0$, where $S_1 = 1 + 4 - 3 = 2$

$S_2 = \begin{vmatrix} 4 & 2 \\ -6 & -3 \end{vmatrix} + \begin{vmatrix} 1 & -4 \\ 0 & -3 \end{vmatrix} + \begin{vmatrix} 1 & -6 \\ 0 & 4 \end{vmatrix} = 0 - 3 + 4 = 1$

$|A| = 1(0) = 0$

Hence the characteristic equation of A is $\lambda^3 - 2\lambda^2 + \lambda = 0$ ... (1)

Step 2 : For the factors of equation (1), we have $\lambda^3 - 2\lambda^2 + \lambda = 0$

$\lambda(\lambda^2 - 2\lambda + 1) = 0, \quad \lambda(\lambda - 1)^2 = 0$

Hence $\lambda = 0, \lambda = 1, 1$ are the required Eigen values of A

[Note that if $|A| = 0$ then $\lambda = 0$ is one root of equation (1)].

Note that $\lambda_1 + \lambda_2 + \lambda_3 = a_{11} + a_{22} + a_{33}$ i.e. $0 + 1 + 1 = 1 + 4 - 3$.

Step 3 : Again denoting the non-repeated Eigen value by $\lambda_1 = 0$ and $\lambda_2 = \lambda_3 = 1$.

To find the Eigen vectors for the corresponding Eigen values, we will consider the matrix equation

$$(A - \lambda I) X = 0$$

where $X = \begin{bmatrix} x \\ y \\ z \end{bmatrix}$ i.e. $\begin{bmatrix} 1-\lambda & -6 & -4 \\ 0 & 4-\lambda & 2 \\ 0 & -6 & -3-\lambda \end{bmatrix} \begin{bmatrix} x \\ y \\ z \end{bmatrix} = \begin{bmatrix} 0 \\ 0 \\ 0 \end{bmatrix}$ ... (2)

Step 4 : For $\lambda = \lambda_1 = 0$, let the corresponding Eigen vector be $X_1 = \begin{bmatrix} x \\ y \\ z \end{bmatrix}$.

Put $\lambda = \lambda_1 = 0$, ∴ the matrix equation (2) will become $\begin{bmatrix} 1 & -6 & -4 \\ 0 & 4 & 2 \\ 0 & -6 & -3 \end{bmatrix} \begin{bmatrix} x \\ y \\ z \end{bmatrix} = \begin{bmatrix} 0 \\ 0 \\ 0 \end{bmatrix}$

$AX = Z$, which is Homogeneous system of equations. Consider first two equations

$x - 6y - 4z = 0$

$0x + 4y + 2z = 0$

Solving by Cramer's rule,
$$\dfrac{x}{\begin{vmatrix} -6 & -4 \\ 4 & 2 \end{vmatrix}} = \dfrac{-y}{\begin{vmatrix} 1 & -4 \\ 0 & 2 \end{vmatrix}} = \dfrac{z}{\begin{vmatrix} 1 & -6 \\ 0 & 4 \end{vmatrix}}$$

$$\dfrac{x}{4} = \dfrac{y}{-2} = \dfrac{z}{4}, \quad \dfrac{x}{2} = \dfrac{y}{-1} = \dfrac{z}{2} = t$$

$$x = 2t, \quad y = -t, \quad z = 2t$$

For $\lambda_1 = 0$, $\quad X_1 = \begin{bmatrix} 2 \\ -1 \\ 2 \end{bmatrix}$

Step 5: For $\lambda = \lambda_2 = 1$, let the corresponding Eigen vector be $X_2 = \begin{bmatrix} x \\ y \\ z \end{bmatrix}$.

Put $\lambda = \lambda_2 = 1$, ∴ the matrix equation (2) will become $\begin{bmatrix} 0 & -6 & -4 \\ 0 & 3 & 2 \\ 0 & -6 & -4 \end{bmatrix} \begin{bmatrix} x \\ y \\ z \end{bmatrix} = \begin{bmatrix} 0 \\ 0 \\ 0 \end{bmatrix}$

By R_2 $\quad 0.x + 3y + 2z = 0 \quad$ Let $z = t, \; y = -\dfrac{2}{3}t$

i.e. $z = 3t, \; y = -2t$ and x can take any value, say $x = t$

∴ For $\lambda_2 = 1$, $\quad X_2 = \begin{bmatrix} 1 \\ -2 \\ 3 \end{bmatrix}$

Step 6: For $\lambda = \lambda_3 = 1 = \lambda_2$, we arrive at same equation
$\quad 0.x + 3y + 2z = 0$

Let $\quad z = t, \quad y = -\dfrac{2}{3}t$

i.e. $\quad z = 3t, \quad y = -2t$

Again the matrix is non-symmetric.

∴ The corresponding Eigen vectors X_2 and X_3 must be linearly independent.
This can be done by choosing $x = 2t, \; y = -2t, \; z = 3t$.

∴ For $\lambda_3 = 1$, $\quad X_3 = \begin{bmatrix} 2 \\ -2 \\ 3 \end{bmatrix}$

Step 7: Hence

$$\lambda_1 = 0 \to X_1 = \begin{bmatrix} 2 \\ -1 \\ 2 \end{bmatrix}, \; \lambda_2 = 1 \to X_2 = \begin{bmatrix} 1 \\ -2 \\ 3 \end{bmatrix}, \; \lambda_3 = 1 \to X_3 = \begin{bmatrix} 2 \\ -2 \\ 3 \end{bmatrix}$$

EXERCISE 3.2

A is Non-symmetric, Repeated Eigen values.

Find the Eigen values and Eigen vectors of the following matrices.

(1) $\begin{bmatrix} 2 & 1 & 1 \\ 2 & 3 & 2 \\ 3 & 3 & 4 \end{bmatrix}$ **Ans.** $\lambda^3 - 9\lambda^2 + 15\lambda - 7 = 0;\ 7, 1, 1;\ \begin{bmatrix} 1 \\ 2 \\ 3 \end{bmatrix}, \begin{bmatrix} 0 \\ 1 \\ -1 \end{bmatrix}, \begin{bmatrix} 1 \\ 0 \\ -1 \end{bmatrix}$

(2) $\begin{bmatrix} 2 & 2 & 1 \\ 1 & 3 & 1 \\ 1 & 2 & 2 \end{bmatrix}$ **Ans.** $\lambda^3 - 7\lambda^2 + 11\lambda - 5 = 0;\ 5, 1, 1;\ \begin{bmatrix} 1 \\ 1 \\ 1 \end{bmatrix}, \begin{bmatrix} 2 \\ -1 \\ 0 \end{bmatrix}, \begin{bmatrix} 1 \\ 0 \\ -1 \end{bmatrix}$

(3) $\begin{bmatrix} -2 & 2 & -3 \\ 2 & 1 & -6 \\ -1 & -2 & 0 \end{bmatrix}$ **(Dec. 06)** **Ans.** $\lambda^3 + \lambda^2 - 21\lambda - 45 = 0;\ 5, -3, -3;\ \begin{bmatrix} 1 \\ 2 \\ -1 \end{bmatrix}, \begin{bmatrix} 2 \\ -1 \\ 0 \end{bmatrix}, \begin{bmatrix} 3 \\ 0 \\ 1 \end{bmatrix}$

(4) $\begin{bmatrix} 2 & 1 & 1 \\ 1 & 2 & 1 \\ 0 & 0 & 1 \end{bmatrix}$ **Ans.** $\lambda^3 - 5\lambda^2 + 7\lambda - 3 = 0;\ 3, 1, 1;\ \begin{bmatrix} 1 \\ 1 \\ 0 \end{bmatrix}, \begin{bmatrix} 1 \\ -1 \\ 0 \end{bmatrix}, \begin{bmatrix} 0 \\ 0 \\ 1 \end{bmatrix}$

(5) $\begin{bmatrix} -9 & 4 & 4 \\ -8 & 3 & 4 \\ -16 & 8 & 7 \end{bmatrix}$ **Ans.** $\lambda^3 - \lambda^2 - 5\lambda - 3 = 0;\ 3, -1, -1;\ \begin{bmatrix} 1 \\ 1 \\ 2 \end{bmatrix}, \begin{bmatrix} 1 \\ 1 \\ 1 \end{bmatrix}, \begin{bmatrix} 0 \\ 1 \\ -1 \end{bmatrix}$

(6) $\begin{bmatrix} 1 & 0 & 0 \\ 2 & 0 & 1 \\ 3 & 1 & 0 \end{bmatrix}$ **Ans.** $\lambda^3 - \lambda^2 - \lambda + 1 = 0;\ -1, 1, 1;\ \begin{bmatrix} 0 \\ -1 \\ 1 \end{bmatrix}, \begin{bmatrix} 0 \\ 1 \\ 1 \end{bmatrix}, \begin{bmatrix} 1 \\ 0 \\ 0 \end{bmatrix}$

3.14 TYPE 3 : 'A' IS SYMMETRIC, EIGEN VALUES ARE NON-REPEATED

Note : Eigen vectors are orthogonal to each other.

Ex. 1 : *Find the Eigen values and Eigen vectors of the following matrix*

$$\begin{bmatrix} -2 & 5 & 4 \\ 5 & 7 & 5 \\ 4 & 5 & -2 \end{bmatrix}.$$

Sol. : Step 1 : Here note that 'A' is a symmetric matrix, Eigen vectors X_1, X_2, X_3 are orthogonal to each other.

Step 2 : The characteristic equation of A is $|A - \lambda I| = 0$.

$$\begin{vmatrix} -2-\lambda & 5 & 4 \\ 5 & 7-\lambda & 5 \\ 4 & 5 & -2-\lambda \end{vmatrix} = 0$$

$\lambda^3 - S_1 \lambda^2 + S_2 \lambda - |A| = 0$, where $S_1 = -2 + 7 - 2 = 3$

$$S_2 = \begin{vmatrix} 7 & 5 \\ 5 & -2 \end{vmatrix} + \begin{vmatrix} -2 & 4 \\ 4 & -2 \end{vmatrix} + \begin{vmatrix} -2 & 5 \\ 5 & 7 \end{vmatrix}$$

$= -39 - 12 - 39 = -90$

$|A| = -2(-39) - 5(-30) + 4(-3) = 78 + 150 - 12 = 216$

Hence the characteristic equation of A is $\lambda^3 - 3\lambda^2 - 90\lambda - 216 = 0$ ... (1)

Step 3 : For the factors of $\lambda^3 - 3\lambda^2 - 90\lambda - 216 = 0$, try $\lambda = \pm 1, \pm 2, \pm 3$.

$\lambda = -3$ satisfies equation (1) $\therefore$ we divide by $\lambda = -3$. Hence using synthetic division,

```
-3 | 1    -3    -90    -216
   |      -3     18     216
   | 1    -6    -72      0
```

$\therefore \quad (\lambda + 3)(\lambda^2 - 6\lambda - 72) = 0$

$(\lambda + 3)(\lambda - 12)(\lambda + 6) = 0$

$\lambda = -3, -6, 12$ are the Eigen values of A.

Note that $\lambda_1 + \lambda_2 + \lambda_3 = a_{11} + a_{22} + a_{33}$ i.e. $-3 - 6 + 12 = -2 + 7 - 2$

Step 4 : Let $\lambda_1 = -3, \lambda_2 = -6, \lambda_3 = 12$ are the Eigen values.

To find the Eigen vectors, we will consider the matrix equation $(A - \lambda I)X = 0$.

where $X = \begin{bmatrix} x \\ y \\ z \end{bmatrix}$ i.e. $\begin{bmatrix} -2-\lambda & 5 & 4 \\ 5 & 7-\lambda & 5 \\ 4 & 5 & -2-\lambda \end{bmatrix} \begin{bmatrix} x \\ y \\ z \end{bmatrix} = \begin{bmatrix} 0 \\ 0 \\ 0 \end{bmatrix}$ ... (2)

Step 5 : For $\lambda = \lambda_1 = -3$, let the corresponding Eigen vector be $X_1 = \begin{bmatrix} x \\ y \\ z \end{bmatrix}$.

Put $\lambda = \lambda_1 = -3$ $\therefore$ the matrix equation (2) will become $\begin{bmatrix} 1 & 5 & 4 \\ 5 & 10 & 5 \\ 4 & 5 & 1 \end{bmatrix} \begin{bmatrix} x \\ y \\ z \end{bmatrix} = \begin{bmatrix} 0 \\ 0 \\ 0 \end{bmatrix}$

$AX = Z$ which is homogeneous system of equations. Consider the first two equations :

$x + 5y + 4z = 0$

$5x + 10y + 5z = 0$

By using Cramer's rule, $\dfrac{x}{\begin{vmatrix} 5 & 4 \\ 10 & 5 \end{vmatrix}} = \dfrac{-y}{\begin{vmatrix} 1 & 4 \\ 5 & 5 \end{vmatrix}} = \dfrac{z}{\begin{vmatrix} 1 & 5 \\ 5 & 10 \end{vmatrix}}$

$$\dfrac{x}{-15} = \dfrac{y}{15} = \dfrac{z}{-15}$$

$$\dfrac{x}{1} = \dfrac{y}{-1} = \dfrac{z}{1} = t \quad \text{i.e.} \quad x = t, \ y = -t, \ z = t$$

Hence for $\lambda_1 = -3$ the Eigen vector is $X_1 = \begin{bmatrix} 1 \\ -1 \\ 1 \end{bmatrix}$

Step 6 : For $\lambda = \lambda_2 = -6$, let the corresponding Eigen vector be $X_2 = \begin{bmatrix} x \\ y \\ z \end{bmatrix}$.

Put $\lambda = \lambda_2 = -6$ ∴ the matrix equation (2) will become $\begin{bmatrix} 4 & 5 & 4 \\ 5 & 13 & 5 \\ 4 & 5 & 4 \end{bmatrix} \begin{bmatrix} x \\ y \\ z \end{bmatrix} = \begin{bmatrix} 0 \\ 0 \\ 0 \end{bmatrix}$

$$AX = Z$$

which is homogeneous system of equations. Consider the first two equations :

$$4x + 5y + 4z = 0$$
$$5x + 13y + 5z = 0$$

By Cramer's rule, $\dfrac{x}{\begin{vmatrix} 5 & 4 \\ 13 & 5 \end{vmatrix}} = \dfrac{-y}{\begin{vmatrix} 4 & 4 \\ 5 & 5 \end{vmatrix}} = \dfrac{z}{\begin{vmatrix} 4 & 5 \\ 5 & 13 \end{vmatrix}}$

$$\dfrac{x}{-27} = \dfrac{-y}{0} = \dfrac{z}{27} \quad \text{i.e.} \quad \dfrac{x}{-1} = \dfrac{y}{0} = \dfrac{z}{1}$$

Hence for $\lambda_2 = -6$, the Eigen vector is $X_2 = \begin{bmatrix} -1 \\ 0 \\ 1 \end{bmatrix}$.

Step 7 : For $\lambda = \lambda_3 = 12$, let the corresponding Eigen vector be $X_3 = \begin{bmatrix} x \\ y \\ z \end{bmatrix}$.

Put $\lambda = \lambda_3 = 12$, ∴ the matrix equation (2) will become

$$\begin{bmatrix} -14 & 5 & 4 \\ 5 & -5 & 5 \\ 4 & 5 & -14 \end{bmatrix} \begin{bmatrix} x \\ y \\ z \end{bmatrix} = \begin{bmatrix} 0 \\ 0 \\ 0 \end{bmatrix}$$

$$AX = Z$$

which is homogeneous system of equations. Consider the first two equations :
$$-14x + 5y + 4z = 0$$
$$5x - 5y + 5z = 0$$
i.e. $\quad x - y + z = 0$

Solving $\quad -14x + 5y + 4z = 0$
$$x - y + z = 0$$

By Cramer's rule, $\dfrac{x}{\begin{vmatrix} 5 & 4 \\ -1 & 1 \end{vmatrix}} = \dfrac{-y}{\begin{vmatrix} -14 & 4 \\ 1 & 1 \end{vmatrix}} = \dfrac{z}{\begin{vmatrix} -14 & 5 \\ 1 & -1 \end{vmatrix}}$

$$\frac{x}{9} = \frac{y}{18} = \frac{z}{9}$$

$$\frac{x}{1} = \frac{y}{2} = \frac{z}{1} = t \quad \text{i.e. } x = t, \ y = 2t, \ z = t$$

For $\lambda_3 = 12$ $\qquad X_3 = \begin{bmatrix} 1 \\ 2 \\ 1 \end{bmatrix}$

Step 8 : Hence Eigen values and Eigen vectors are

$$\lambda_1 = -3 \to X_1 = \begin{bmatrix} 1 \\ -1 \\ 1 \end{bmatrix}, \ \lambda_2 = -6 \to X_2 = \begin{bmatrix} -1 \\ 0 \\ 1 \end{bmatrix}, \ \lambda_3 = 12 \to X_3 = \begin{bmatrix} 1 \\ 2 \\ 1 \end{bmatrix}$$

Step 9 : Check : X_1, X_2, X_3 are orthogonal to each other.

$X_1' \, X_2 = 0 \quad \text{i.e. } (1 \ -1 \ 1) \begin{bmatrix} -1 \\ 0 \\ 1 \end{bmatrix} = 0$

$X_2' \, X_3 = 0 \quad \text{i.e. } (-1 \ 0 \ 1) \begin{bmatrix} 1 \\ 2 \\ 1 \end{bmatrix} = 0$

$X_3' \, X_1 = 0 \quad \text{i.e. } (1 \ 2 \ 1) \begin{bmatrix} 1 \\ -1 \\ 1 \end{bmatrix} = 0$

Hence X_1, X_2, X_3 are orthogonal.

Ex. 2 : *Find Eigen values and Eigen vectors of the following matrix*

$$A = \begin{bmatrix} 5 & 0 & 1 \\ 0 & -2 & 0 \\ 1 & 0 & 5 \end{bmatrix}.$$

Sol. : Step 1 : Here note that 'A' is a symmetric matrix. Eigen vectors X_1, X_2, X_3 are orthogonal to each other.

Step 2 : The characteristic equation of A is $|A - \lambda I| = 0$ i.e. $\begin{vmatrix} 5-\lambda & 0 & 1 \\ 0 & -2-\lambda & 0 \\ 1 & 0 & 5-\lambda \end{vmatrix} = 0$.

where
$$\lambda^3 - S_1 \lambda^2 + S_2 \lambda - |A| = 0$$
$$S_1 = 5 - 2 + 5 = 8$$
$$S_2 = \begin{vmatrix} -2 & 0 \\ 0 & 5 \end{vmatrix} + \begin{vmatrix} 5 & 1 \\ 1 & 5 \end{vmatrix} + \begin{vmatrix} 5 & 0 \\ 0 & -2 \end{vmatrix}$$
$$= -10 + 24 - 10 = 4$$
$$|A| = 5(-10) + 1(2) = -48$$

Hence the characteristic equation of A is $\lambda^3 - 8\lambda^2 + 4\lambda + 48 = 0$ ... (1)

Step 3 : For the factors of $\lambda^3 - 8\lambda^2 + 4\lambda + 48 = 0$

Try $\lambda = \pm 1, \pm 2, \ldots \lambda = -2$ satisfies equation (1) $\therefore$ we divide by $\lambda = -2$. Hence using synthetic division

```
-2 | 1   -8    4    48
   |     -2   20   -48
   |_____
     1   -10   24    0
```

$(\lambda + 2)(\lambda^2 - 10\lambda + 24) = 0$
$(\lambda + 2)(\lambda - 4)(\lambda - 6) = 0$

$\lambda = -2, 4, 6$ are the Eigen values of A.

Note that $\lambda_1 + \lambda_2 + \lambda_3 = a_{11} + a_{22} + a_{33}$ i.e. $-2 + 4 + 6 = 5 - 2 + 5$

Step 4 : Let $\lambda_1 = -2, \lambda_2 = 4, \lambda_3 = 6$ are the Eigen values.

To find the Eigen vectors, we will consider the matrix equation

$$\begin{bmatrix} 5-\lambda & 0 & 1 \\ 0 & -2-\lambda & 0 \\ 1 & 0 & 5-\lambda \end{bmatrix} \begin{bmatrix} x \\ y \\ z \end{bmatrix} = \begin{bmatrix} 0 \\ 0 \\ 0 \end{bmatrix} \quad \ldots (2)$$

Step 5 : For $\lambda = \lambda_1 = -2$, let the corresponding Eigen vector be $X_1 = \begin{bmatrix} x \\ y \\ z \end{bmatrix}$.

Put $\lambda = \lambda_1 = -2$ $\therefore$ the matrix equation (2) will become $\begin{bmatrix} 7 & 0 & 1 \\ 0 & 0 & 0 \\ 1 & 0 & 7 \end{bmatrix} \begin{bmatrix} x \\ y \\ z \end{bmatrix} = \begin{bmatrix} 0 \\ 0 \\ 0 \end{bmatrix}$

$AX = Z$ which is homogeneous system of equations. Consider first and last equations.
$$7x + z = 0$$
$$x + 7z = 0$$

$$\frac{x}{\begin{vmatrix} 0 & 1 \\ 0 & 7 \end{vmatrix}} = \frac{-y}{\begin{vmatrix} 7 & 1 \\ 1 & 7 \end{vmatrix}} = \frac{z}{\begin{vmatrix} 7 & 0 \\ 1 & 0 \end{vmatrix}}$$

$$\frac{x}{0} = \frac{y}{-48} = \frac{z}{0} \quad \text{i.e.} \quad \frac{x}{0} = \frac{y}{1} = \frac{z}{0} = t$$

$x = 0,\ y = t,\ z = 0\ $ or $\ \lambda_1 = -2 \qquad X_1 = \begin{bmatrix} 0 \\ 1 \\ 0 \end{bmatrix}$

Step 6 : For $\lambda = \lambda_2 = 4$, let the corresponding Eigen vector be $X_2 = \begin{bmatrix} x \\ y \\ z \end{bmatrix}$.

Put $\lambda = \lambda_2 = 4$ ∴ the matrix equation (2) will become $\begin{bmatrix} 1 & 0 & 1 \\ 0 & -6 & 0 \\ 1 & 0 & 1 \end{bmatrix} \begin{bmatrix} x \\ y \\ z \end{bmatrix} = \begin{bmatrix} 0 \\ 0 \\ 0 \end{bmatrix}$

$AX = Z$ which is homogeneous system of equations. Consider the first two equations :

$$x + 0.y + z = 0$$
$$0.x - 6y + 0.z = 0$$

By Cramer's rule, $\dfrac{x}{\begin{vmatrix} 0 & 1 \\ -6 & 0 \end{vmatrix}} = \dfrac{-y}{\begin{vmatrix} 1 & 1 \\ 0 & 0 \end{vmatrix}} = \dfrac{z}{\begin{vmatrix} 1 & 0 \\ 1 & -6 \end{vmatrix}}$

$$\frac{x}{6} = \frac{y}{0} = \frac{z}{-6}$$

$$\frac{x}{1} = \frac{y}{0} = \frac{z}{-1} = t$$

∴ For $\lambda_2 = 4$, Eigen vector is $X_2 = \begin{bmatrix} 1 \\ 0 \\ -1 \end{bmatrix}$

Step 7 : For $\lambda = \lambda_3 = 6$, let the corresponding Eigen vector be $X_3 = \begin{bmatrix} x \\ y \\ z \end{bmatrix}$.

Put $\lambda = \lambda_3 = 6$ ∴ the matrix equation (2) will become $\begin{bmatrix} -1 & 0 & 1 \\ 0 & -8 & 0 \\ 1 & 0 & -1 \end{bmatrix} \begin{bmatrix} x \\ y \\ z \end{bmatrix} = \begin{bmatrix} 0 \\ 0 \\ 0 \end{bmatrix}$

$AX = Z$ which is homogeneous system of equations. Consider the first two equations

$$-x + 0.y + z = 0$$
$$0.x - 8y + 0.z = 0$$

By Cramer's rule, $\dfrac{x}{\begin{vmatrix} 0 & 1 \\ -8 & 0 \end{vmatrix}} = \dfrac{-y}{\begin{vmatrix} -1 & 1 \\ 0 & 0 \end{vmatrix}} = \dfrac{z}{\begin{vmatrix} -1 & 0 \\ 0 & -8 \end{vmatrix}}$

$$\dfrac{x}{8} = \dfrac{y}{0} = \dfrac{z}{8}$$

$$\dfrac{x}{1} = \dfrac{y}{0} = \dfrac{z}{1} = t$$

$x = t,\ y = 0,\ z = t,$ $\therefore$ For $\lambda_3 = 6$, the Eigen vector is $X_3 = \begin{bmatrix} 1 \\ 0 \\ 1 \end{bmatrix}$

Step 8: Hence Eigen values and corresponding Eigen vectors of A are

$$\lambda_1 = -2 \rightarrow X_1 = \begin{bmatrix} 0 \\ 1 \\ 0 \end{bmatrix},\ \lambda_2 = 4 \rightarrow X_2 = \begin{bmatrix} 1 \\ 0 \\ -1 \end{bmatrix},\ \lambda_3 = 6 \rightarrow X_3 = \begin{bmatrix} 1 \\ 0 \\ 1 \end{bmatrix}$$

EXERCISE 3.3

'A' is symmetric, Eigen values are non-repeated.

Find the Eigen values and the corresponding Eigen vectors for the following matrices.

(1) $\begin{bmatrix} 2 & 4 & -6 \\ 4 & 2 & -6 \\ -6 & -6 & -15 \end{bmatrix}$ **Ans.** $\lambda^3 + 11\lambda^2 - 144\lambda - 324 = 0;\ -2, 9, -18;\ \begin{bmatrix} 1 \\ -1 \\ 0 \end{bmatrix}, \begin{bmatrix} 2 \\ 2 \\ -1 \end{bmatrix}, \begin{bmatrix} 1 \\ 1 \\ 4 \end{bmatrix}$

(2) $\begin{bmatrix} 7 & 0 & -2 \\ 0 & 5 & -2 \\ -2 & -2 & 6 \end{bmatrix}$ **Ans.** $\lambda^3 - 18\lambda^2 + 99\lambda - 162 = 0;\ 3, 6, 9;\ \begin{bmatrix} 1 \\ 2 \\ 2 \end{bmatrix}, \begin{bmatrix} 2 \\ -2 \\ 1 \end{bmatrix}, \begin{bmatrix} 2 \\ 1 \\ -2 \end{bmatrix}$

(3) $\begin{bmatrix} 7 & -2 & -2 \\ -2 & 1 & 4 \\ -2 & 4 & 1 \end{bmatrix}$ **Ans.** $\lambda^3 - 9\lambda^2 - 9\lambda + 81 = 0;\ -3, 3, 9;\ \begin{bmatrix} 0 \\ 1 \\ -1 \end{bmatrix}, \begin{bmatrix} 1 \\ 1 \\ 1 \end{bmatrix}, \begin{bmatrix} -2 \\ 1 \\ 1 \end{bmatrix}$

(4) $\begin{bmatrix} 8 & -6 & 2 \\ -6 & 7 & -4 \\ 2 & -4 & 3 \end{bmatrix}$ **Ans.** $\lambda^3 - 18\lambda^2 + 45\lambda = 0;\ 0, 3, 15;\ \begin{bmatrix} 1 \\ 2 \\ 2 \end{bmatrix}, \begin{bmatrix} 2 \\ 1 \\ -2 \end{bmatrix}, \begin{bmatrix} 2 \\ -2 \\ 1 \end{bmatrix}$

(5) $\begin{bmatrix} 3 & -1 & 1 \\ -1 & 5 & -1 \\ 1 & -1 & 3 \end{bmatrix}$ **Ans.** $\lambda^3 - 11\lambda^2 + 36\lambda - 36 = 0;\ 2, 3, 6;\ \begin{bmatrix} -1 \\ 0 \\ 1 \end{bmatrix}, \begin{bmatrix} 1 \\ 1 \\ 1 \end{bmatrix}, \begin{bmatrix} 1 \\ -2 \\ 1 \end{bmatrix}$

(6) $\begin{bmatrix} 2 & 2 & 0 \\ 2 & 2 & 0 \\ 0 & 0 & 1 \end{bmatrix}$ **Ans.** $\lambda^3 - 5\lambda^2 + 4\lambda = 0$; 0, 1, 4; $\begin{bmatrix} 1 \\ -1 \\ 0 \end{bmatrix}, \begin{bmatrix} 0 \\ 0 \\ 1 \end{bmatrix}, \begin{bmatrix} 1 \\ 1 \\ 0 \end{bmatrix}$

(7) $\begin{bmatrix} 4 & 0 & 0 \\ 0 & 8 & 0 \\ 0 & 0 & 6 \end{bmatrix}$ **Ans.** $\lambda^3 - 18\lambda^2 + 104\lambda - 192 = 0$; 4, 8, 6; $\begin{bmatrix} 1 \\ 0 \\ 0 \end{bmatrix}, \begin{bmatrix} 0 \\ 1 \\ 0 \end{bmatrix}, \begin{bmatrix} 0 \\ 0 \\ 1 \end{bmatrix}$

(8) $\begin{bmatrix} 1 & 0 & -4 \\ 0 & 5 & 4 \\ -4 & 4 & 3 \end{bmatrix}$ **Ans.** $\lambda^3 - 9\lambda^2 - 9\lambda + 81 = 0$; 3, -3, 9; $\begin{bmatrix} 2 \\ 2 \\ -1 \end{bmatrix}, \begin{bmatrix} 2 \\ -1 \\ 2 \end{bmatrix}, \begin{bmatrix} -1 \\ 2 \\ 2 \end{bmatrix}$

(9) $\begin{bmatrix} 2 & 0 & -1 \\ 0 & 2 & 0 \\ -1 & 0 & 2 \end{bmatrix}$ **Ans.** $\lambda^3 - 6\lambda^2 + 11\lambda - 6 = 0$; 1, 2, 3; $\begin{bmatrix} 1 \\ 0 \\ 1 \end{bmatrix}, \begin{bmatrix} 0 \\ 1 \\ 0 \end{bmatrix}, \begin{bmatrix} 1 \\ 0 \\ -1 \end{bmatrix}$

(10) $\begin{bmatrix} 6 & 2 & -2 \\ 2 & 6 & -2 \\ -2 & -2 & 10 \end{bmatrix}$ **Ans.** $\lambda^3 - 22\lambda^2 + 144\lambda - 288 = 0$; 4, 6, 12; $\begin{bmatrix} 1 \\ -1 \\ 0 \end{bmatrix}, \begin{bmatrix} 1 \\ 1 \\ 1 \end{bmatrix}, \begin{bmatrix} 1 \\ 1 \\ -2 \end{bmatrix}$

(11) $\begin{bmatrix} 3 & 2 & -1 \\ 2 & 3 & -1 \\ -1 & -1 & 4 \end{bmatrix}$ **Ans.** $\lambda^3 - 10\lambda^2 + 27\lambda - 18 = 0$; 1, 3, 6; $\begin{bmatrix} 1 \\ -1 \\ 0 \end{bmatrix}, \begin{bmatrix} 1 \\ 1 \\ 2 \end{bmatrix}, \begin{bmatrix} 1 \\ 1 \\ -1 \end{bmatrix}$

3.15 TYPE 4 : 'A' IS SYMMETRIC, EIGEN VALUES ARE REPEATED

Ex. 1 : *Find the Eigen values and Eigen vectors for the following matrix*

$$A = \begin{bmatrix} 0 & 1 & 1 \\ 1 & 0 & 1 \\ 1 & 1 & 0 \end{bmatrix}.$$

Sol. : Step 1 : Here note that 'A' is a symmetric matrix. Eigen vectors X_1, X_2, X_3 are orthogonal to each other.

Step 2 : The characteristic equation of A is $|A - \lambda I| = 0$ $\begin{vmatrix} 0-\lambda & 1 & 1 \\ 1 & 0-\lambda & 1 \\ 1 & 1 & 0-\lambda \end{vmatrix} = 0.$

$$\lambda^3 - S_1\lambda^2 + S_2\lambda - |A| = 0$$
$$S_1 = 0 + 0 + 0 = 0$$
$$S_2 = \begin{vmatrix} 0 & 1 \\ 1 & 0 \end{vmatrix} + \begin{vmatrix} 0 & 1 \\ 1 & 0 \end{vmatrix} + \begin{vmatrix} 0 & 1 \\ 1 & 0 \end{vmatrix}$$
$$= -1 - 1 - 1 = -3$$
$$|A| = -1(-1) + 1(1) = 2$$

Hence the characteristic equation of A is $\lambda^3 - 3\lambda - 2 = 0$ ... (1)

Step 3 : For the factors of equation (1), we try $\lambda = \pm 1, \pm 2, \ldots$ and $\lambda = -1$, satisfies equation (1). By using synthetic division

```
-1 | 1   0   -3   -2
   |    -1    1    2
   -----------------------
     1  -1   -2    0
```

$(\lambda + 1)(\lambda^2 - \lambda - 2) = 0$

$(\lambda + 1)(\lambda - 2)(\lambda + 1) = 0$

$\lambda = 2, -1, -1$ are the Eigen values.

Note that $\lambda_1 + \lambda_2 + \lambda_3 = a_{11} + a_{22} + a_{23}$ i.e. $2 - 1 - 1 = 0 + 0 + 0$

Step 4 : Again denoting the non-repeated Eigen value by $\lambda_1 = 2$, and the remaining two by

$$\lambda_2 = \lambda_3 = -1$$

To find the corresponding Eigen vectors, we will consider the matrix equation

$(A - \lambda I) X = 0$, where $X = \begin{bmatrix} x \\ y \\ z \end{bmatrix}$ i.e. $\begin{bmatrix} 0-\lambda & 1 & 1 \\ 1 & 0-\lambda & 1 \\ 1 & 1 & 0-\lambda \end{bmatrix} \begin{bmatrix} x \\ y \\ z \end{bmatrix} = \begin{bmatrix} 0 \\ 0 \\ 0 \end{bmatrix}$ ... (2)

Step 5 : For $\lambda = \lambda_1 = 2$, let the corresponding Eigen vector be $X_1 = \begin{bmatrix} x \\ y \\ z \end{bmatrix}$.

Put $\lambda = \lambda_1 = 2$ ∴ the matrix equation (2) will become $\begin{bmatrix} -2 & 1 & 1 \\ 1 & -2 & 1 \\ 1 & 1 & -2 \end{bmatrix} \begin{bmatrix} x \\ y \\ z \end{bmatrix} = \begin{bmatrix} 0 \\ 0 \\ 0 \end{bmatrix}$

$$AX = Z$$

which is homogeneous system of equations. Consider the first two equations :

$$-2x + y + z = 0$$
$$x - 2y + z = 0$$

By Cramer's rule, $\dfrac{x}{\begin{vmatrix} 1 & 1 \\ -2 & 1 \end{vmatrix}} = \dfrac{-y}{\begin{vmatrix} -2 & 1 \\ 1 & 1 \end{vmatrix}} = \dfrac{z}{\begin{vmatrix} -2 & 1 \\ 1 & -2 \end{vmatrix}}$

$$\frac{x}{3} = \frac{y}{3} = \frac{z}{3}$$

$$\frac{x}{1} = \frac{y}{1} = \frac{z}{1} = t$$

For $\lambda_1 = 2$ Eigen vector is $X_1 = \begin{bmatrix} 1 \\ 1 \\ 1 \end{bmatrix}$.

Step 6 : For $\lambda = \lambda_2 = -1$, let the corresponding Eigen vector be $X_2 = \begin{bmatrix} x \\ y \\ z \end{bmatrix}$.

Put $\lambda = \lambda_2 = -1$, $\therefore$ the matrix equation (2) will become $\begin{bmatrix} 1 & 1 & 1 \\ 1 & 1 & 1 \\ 1 & 1 & 1 \end{bmatrix} \begin{bmatrix} x \\ y \\ z \end{bmatrix} = \begin{bmatrix} 0 \\ 0 \\ 0 \end{bmatrix}$

$AX = Z$ which is homogeneous system of equations.

This system leads to a single equation $x + y + z = 0$

Important Step :

Let $z = 0$, $y = t$ $\quad\therefore\quad x = -t$

$\therefore$ For $\lambda_2 = -1$, $\quad X_2 = \begin{bmatrix} -1 \\ 1 \\ 0 \end{bmatrix}$

Step 7 : For $\lambda = \lambda_3 = -1 = \lambda_2$, we will assume that corresponding Eigen vector be

$$X_3 = \begin{bmatrix} l \\ m \\ n \end{bmatrix}$$

Here for $\lambda_3 = -1$ system leads to the same equation $x + y + z = 0$ and we must choose X_3 such that X_1, X_2, X_3 are orthogonal. $\therefore$ Let $X_3 = \begin{bmatrix} l \\ m \\ n \end{bmatrix}$ be the Eigen vector.

Since X_1, X_3 are orthogonal which requires $X_1' X_3 = 0$ i.e. $[1 \ 1 \ 1] \begin{bmatrix} l \\ m \\ n \end{bmatrix} = 0$

$l + m + n = 0$ ... (3)

Also X_2, X_3 are orthogonal which requires $X_2' X_3 = 0$ i.e. $[-1 \ 1 \ 0] \begin{bmatrix} l \\ m \\ n \end{bmatrix} = 0$

$-l + m + 0.n = 0$ ... (4)

Solving (3) and (4) by Cramer's rule,

$l + m + n = 0$
$-l + m + 0.n = 0$

$$\frac{l}{\begin{vmatrix} 1 & 1 \\ 1 & 0 \end{vmatrix}} = \frac{-m}{\begin{vmatrix} 1 & 1 \\ -1 & 0 \end{vmatrix}} = \frac{n}{\begin{vmatrix} 1 & 1 \\ -1 & 1 \end{vmatrix}}$$

$$\frac{l}{-1} = \frac{m}{-1} = \frac{n}{2}$$

$$\frac{l}{1} = \frac{m}{1} = \frac{n}{-2} = t, \quad l = t, \; m = t, \; n = -2t$$

∴ For $\lambda_3 = -1$, $\quad X_3 = \begin{bmatrix} 1 \\ 1 \\ -2 \end{bmatrix}$

Step 8 : Hence Eigen values and Eigen vectors are

$$\lambda_1 = 2 \rightarrow X_1 = \begin{bmatrix} 1 \\ 1 \\ 1 \end{bmatrix}, \quad \lambda_2 = -1 \rightarrow X_2 = \begin{bmatrix} -1 \\ 1 \\ 0 \end{bmatrix}, \quad \lambda_3 = -1 \rightarrow X_3 = \begin{bmatrix} 1 \\ 1 \\ -2 \end{bmatrix}$$

Ex. 2 : *Find the Eigen values and Eigen vectors of the following matrix*

$$A = \begin{bmatrix} 1 & 2 & 3 \\ 2 & 4 & 6 \\ 3 & 6 & 9 \end{bmatrix}.$$

Sol. : Step 1 : Here note that 'A' is a symmetric matrix. Eigen vectors X_1, X_2, X_3 are orthogonal to each other.

Step 2 : The characteristic equation of A is $|A - \lambda I| = 0$

$$\begin{vmatrix} 1-\lambda & 2 & 3 \\ 2 & 4-\lambda & 6 \\ 3 & 6 & 9-\lambda \end{vmatrix} = 0$$

$$\lambda^3 - S_1 \lambda^2 + S_2 \lambda - |A| = 0$$

where $\quad S_1 = 1 + 4 + 9 = 14$

$$S_2 = \begin{vmatrix} 4 & 6 \\ 6 & 9 \end{vmatrix} + \begin{vmatrix} 1 & 3 \\ 3 & 9 \end{vmatrix} + \begin{vmatrix} 1 & 2 \\ 2 & 4 \end{vmatrix} = 0 + 0 + 0 = 0$$

$$|A| = 1(0) - 2(0) + 3(0) = 0$$

Hence the characteristic equation of A is $\lambda^3 - 14\lambda^2 = 0$ ... (1)

Step 3 : Factors of (1) :

$$\lambda^3 - 14\lambda^2 = 0$$
$$\lambda^2 (\lambda - 14) = 0$$

$\lambda = 14, 0, 0$ are the Eigen values of A.

Note that $\quad \lambda_1 + \lambda_2 + \lambda_3 = a_{11} + a_{22} + a_{33}$

$$14 + 0 + 0 = 1 + 4 + 9$$

Step 4 : Let the non-repeated Eigen value be $\lambda_1 = 14$ and $\lambda_2 = 0 = \lambda_3$.

To find the corresponding Eigen vectors, we will consider the matrix equation

$(A - \lambda I) X = 0$ where $X = \begin{bmatrix} x \\ y \\ z \end{bmatrix}$ i.e. $\begin{bmatrix} 1-\lambda & 2 & 3 \\ 2 & 4-\lambda & 6 \\ 3 & 6 & 9-\lambda \end{bmatrix} \begin{bmatrix} x \\ y \\ z \end{bmatrix} = \begin{bmatrix} 0 \\ 0 \\ 0 \end{bmatrix}$ ... (2)

Step 5 : For $\lambda = \lambda_1 = 14$, let the corresponding Eigen vector be $X_1 = \begin{bmatrix} x \\ y \\ z \end{bmatrix}$.

Put $\lambda = \lambda_1 = 14$, ∴ the matrix equation (2) will become

$\begin{bmatrix} -13 & 2 & 3 \\ 2 & -10 & 6 \\ 3 & 6 & -5 \end{bmatrix} \begin{bmatrix} x \\ y \\ z \end{bmatrix} = \begin{bmatrix} 0 \\ 0 \\ 0 \end{bmatrix}$

$AX = Z$ which is homogeneous system of equations. Consider the last two equations :

$$2x - 10y + 6z = 0$$
i.e. $\quad x - 5y + 3z = 0$
and $\quad 3x + 6y - 5z = 0$

By Cramer's rule, $\dfrac{x}{\begin{vmatrix} -5 & 3 \\ 6 & -5 \end{vmatrix}} = \dfrac{-y}{\begin{vmatrix} 1 & 3 \\ 3 & -5 \end{vmatrix}} = \dfrac{z}{\begin{vmatrix} 1 & -5 \\ 3 & 6 \end{vmatrix}}$

$$\dfrac{x}{7} = \dfrac{y}{14} = \dfrac{z}{21}$$

$$\dfrac{x}{1} = \dfrac{y}{2} = \dfrac{z}{3} = t \quad \text{i.e.} \quad x = t, \ y = 2t, \ z = 3t$$

∴ For $\lambda_1 = 14$, the Eigen vector is $X_1 = \begin{bmatrix} 1 \\ 2 \\ 3 \end{bmatrix}$

Step 6 : For $\lambda = \lambda_2 = 0$, let the corresponding Eigen vector be $X_2 = \begin{bmatrix} x \\ y \\ z \end{bmatrix}$.

Put $\lambda = \lambda_2 = 0$ ∴ the matrix equation (2) will become $\begin{bmatrix} 1 & 2 & 3 \\ 2 & 4 & 6 \\ 3 & 6 & 9 \end{bmatrix} \begin{bmatrix} x \\ y \\ z \end{bmatrix} = \begin{bmatrix} 0 \\ 0 \\ 0 \end{bmatrix}$

$AX = Z$ which is homogeneous system of equations.

This system leads to a single equation $x + 2y + 3z = 0$.

Important Step :

Let $z = 0$, $y = t$, $\therefore x = -2t$

$\therefore$ For $\lambda_2 = 0$ $\quad X_2 = \begin{bmatrix} -2 \\ 1 \\ 0 \end{bmatrix}$

Step 7 : For $\lambda = \lambda_3 = 0 = \lambda_2$ again system leads to the same equation

$$x + 2y + 3z = 0$$

$\therefore$ We must choose X_3 such that X_1, X_2, X_3 are orthogonal. Hence we will assume the Eigen vector as $X_3 = \begin{bmatrix} l \\ m \\ n \end{bmatrix}$.

Since X_1, X_3 are orthogonal which requires

$$X_1' X_3 = 0 \text{ i.e. } \begin{bmatrix} 1 & 2 & 3 \end{bmatrix} \begin{bmatrix} l \\ m \\ n \end{bmatrix} = 0$$

$$l + 2m + 3n = 0 \qquad \ldots (3)$$

Also X_2, X_3 are orthogonal which requires

$$X_2' X_3 = 0 \text{ i.e. } \begin{bmatrix} -2 & 1 & 0 \end{bmatrix} \begin{bmatrix} l \\ m \\ n \end{bmatrix} = 0$$

$$-2l + m + 0.n = 0 \qquad \ldots (4)$$

Solving (3) and (4) by Cramer's rule,

$$l + 2m + 3n = 0$$
$$-2l + m + 0.n = 0$$

$$\frac{l}{\begin{vmatrix} 2 & 3 \\ 1 & 0 \end{vmatrix}} = \frac{-m}{\begin{vmatrix} 1 & 3 \\ -2 & 0 \end{vmatrix}} = \frac{n}{\begin{vmatrix} 1 & 2 \\ -2 & 1 \end{vmatrix}}$$

$$\frac{l}{-3} = \frac{m}{-6} = \frac{n}{5}$$

$$\frac{l}{3} = \frac{m}{6} = \frac{n}{-5} = t$$

$$l = 3t, \ m = 6t, \ n = -5t$$

$\therefore$ For $\lambda_3 = 0$, $\quad X_3 = \begin{bmatrix} 3 \\ 6 \\ -5 \end{bmatrix}$

Step 8 : Hence Eigen values and Eigen vectors are

$$\lambda_1 = 14 \to X_1 = \begin{bmatrix} 1 \\ 2 \\ 3 \end{bmatrix}, \quad \lambda_2 = 0 \to X_2 = \begin{bmatrix} -2 \\ 1 \\ 0 \end{bmatrix}, \quad \lambda_3 = 0 \to X_3 = \begin{bmatrix} 3 \\ 6 \\ -5 \end{bmatrix}$$

EXERCISE 3.4

Find the Eigen values and the corresponding Eigen vectors of the following matrices.

(1) $\begin{bmatrix} 6 & -2 & 2 \\ -2 & 3 & -1 \\ 2 & -1 & 3 \end{bmatrix}$ **Ans.** $\lambda^3 - 12\lambda^2 + 36\lambda - 32 = 0$; 8, 2, 2; $\begin{bmatrix} 2 \\ -1 \\ 1 \end{bmatrix}, \begin{bmatrix} 0 \\ 1 \\ 1 \end{bmatrix}, \begin{bmatrix} 1 \\ 1 \\ -1 \end{bmatrix}$

(May 2008)

(2) $\begin{bmatrix} 7 & -2 & 1 \\ -2 & 10 & -2 \\ 1 & -2 & 7 \end{bmatrix}$ **Ans.** $\lambda^3 - 24\lambda^2 + 180\lambda - 432 = 0$; 12, 6, 6; $\begin{bmatrix} 1 \\ -2 \\ 1 \end{bmatrix}, \begin{bmatrix} 1 \\ 0 \\ -1 \end{bmatrix}, \begin{bmatrix} 1 \\ 1 \\ 1 \end{bmatrix}$

(3) $\begin{bmatrix} 2 & -1 & 1 \\ -1 & 2 & -1 \\ 1 & -1 & 2 \end{bmatrix}$ **Ans.** $\lambda^3 - 6\lambda^2 + 9\lambda - 4 = 0$; 4, 1, 1; $\begin{bmatrix} 1 \\ -1 \\ 1 \end{bmatrix}, \begin{bmatrix} 1 \\ 1 \\ 0 \end{bmatrix}, \begin{bmatrix} -1 \\ 1 \\ 2 \end{bmatrix}$

(4) $\begin{bmatrix} 2 & 0 & 1 \\ 0 & 3 & 0 \\ 1 & 0 & 2 \end{bmatrix}$ **Ans.** $\lambda^3 - 7\lambda^2 + 15\lambda - 9 = 0$; 1, 3, 3; $\begin{bmatrix} 1 \\ 0 \\ -1 \end{bmatrix}, \begin{bmatrix} 1 \\ 1 \\ 1 \end{bmatrix}, \begin{bmatrix} 1 \\ -2 \\ 1 \end{bmatrix}$

(5) $\begin{bmatrix} 4 & -1 & 1 \\ -1 & 4 & -1 \\ 1 & -1 & 4 \end{bmatrix}$ **Ans.** $\lambda^3 - 12\lambda^2 + 45\lambda - 54 = 0$; 6, 3, 3; $\begin{bmatrix} 1 \\ -1 \\ 1 \end{bmatrix}, \begin{bmatrix} 1 \\ 1 \\ 0 \end{bmatrix}, \begin{bmatrix} -1 \\ 1 \\ 2 \end{bmatrix}$

(6) $\begin{bmatrix} 3 & 1 & 1 \\ 1 & 3 & -1 \\ 1 & -1 & 3 \end{bmatrix}$ **Ans.** $\lambda^3 - 9\lambda^2 + 24\lambda - 16 = 0$; 1, 4, 4; $\begin{bmatrix} -1 \\ 1 \\ 1 \end{bmatrix}, \begin{bmatrix} 0 \\ 1 \\ -1 \end{bmatrix}, \begin{bmatrix} 2 \\ 1 \\ 1 \end{bmatrix}$

(May 2007)

(7) $\begin{bmatrix} 1 & 2 & 2 \\ 2 & 1 & 2 \\ 2 & 2 & 1 \end{bmatrix}$ **Ans.** $\lambda^3 - 3\lambda^2 - 9\lambda - 5 = 0$; 5, -1, -1; $\begin{bmatrix} 1 \\ 1 \\ 1 \end{bmatrix}, \begin{bmatrix} 1 \\ -1 \\ 0 \end{bmatrix}, \begin{bmatrix} 1 \\ 1 \\ -2 \end{bmatrix}$

(8) $\begin{bmatrix} 2 & 1 & 1 \\ 1 & 2 & -1 \\ 1 & -1 & 2 \end{bmatrix}$ **Ans.** $\lambda^3 - 6\lambda^2 + 9\lambda = 0$; 0, 3, 3; $\begin{bmatrix} -1 \\ 1 \\ 1 \end{bmatrix}, \begin{bmatrix} 1 \\ 1 \\ 0 \end{bmatrix}, \begin{bmatrix} 1 \\ -1 \\ 2 \end{bmatrix}$

(9) $\begin{bmatrix} 1 & 1 & -1 \\ 1 & 1 & -1 \\ -1 & -1 & 1 \end{bmatrix}$ **Ans.** $\lambda^3 - 3\lambda^2 = 0; 3, 0, 0;$ $\begin{bmatrix} 1 \\ 1 \\ -1 \end{bmatrix}, \begin{bmatrix} 1 \\ 0 \\ 1 \end{bmatrix}, \begin{bmatrix} -1 \\ 1 \\ 0 \end{bmatrix}$

($|A| = 0 \Rightarrow \lambda = 0$ is one root, it is repeated).

(10) $\begin{bmatrix} 3 & -1 & 1 \\ -1 & 3 & -1 \\ 1 & -1 & 3 \end{bmatrix}$ **Ans.** $\lambda^3 - 9\lambda^2 + 24\lambda - 20 = 0; 5, 2, 2;$ $\begin{bmatrix} 1 \\ -1 \\ 1 \end{bmatrix}, \begin{bmatrix} 1 \\ 1 \\ 0 \end{bmatrix}, \begin{bmatrix} -1 \\ 0 \\ 1 \end{bmatrix}$

(Dec. 2004)

(11) $\begin{bmatrix} -2 & 2 & 3 \\ 2 & 1 & 6 \\ 3 & 6 & 6 \end{bmatrix}$ **Ans.** $\lambda^3 - 5\lambda^2 - 57\lambda - 99 = 0; 11, -3, -3;$ $\begin{bmatrix} 1 \\ 2 \\ 3 \end{bmatrix}, \begin{bmatrix} -2 \\ 1 \\ 0 \end{bmatrix}, \begin{bmatrix} -3 \\ 0 \\ 1 \end{bmatrix}$

3.16 TYPE 5 : EXAMPLES INVOLVING ONLY TWO EIGEN VECTORS FOR $\lambda_1, \lambda_2 = \lambda_3$

Ex. 1 : *Find the Eigen values and the corresponding Eigen vectors of the following matrix*

$A = \begin{bmatrix} 1 & 2 & 2 \\ 0 & 2 & 1 \\ -1 & 2 & 2 \end{bmatrix}.$

Sol. : Step 1 : The characteristic equation of A is

$$|A - \lambda I| = 0 \quad \begin{vmatrix} 1-\lambda & 2 & 2 \\ 0 & 2-\lambda & 1 \\ -1 & 2 & 2-\lambda \end{vmatrix} = 0$$

$$\lambda^3 - S_1\lambda^2 + S_2\lambda - |A| = 0$$

where $S_1 = 1 + 2 + 2 = 5$

$S_2 = \begin{vmatrix} 2 & 1 \\ 2 & 2 \end{vmatrix} + \begin{vmatrix} 1 & 2 \\ -1 & 2 \end{vmatrix} + \begin{vmatrix} 1 & 2 \\ 0 & 2 \end{vmatrix} = 2 + 4 + 2 = 8$

$|A| = 1(2) - 1(-2) = 4$

The characteristic equation of A is $\lambda^3 - 5\lambda^2 + 8\lambda - 4 = 0$ ... (1)

Step 2 : Factors : Sum of coefficients $= 0$

$\therefore \quad (\lambda - 1) = 0$ must be the factor of equation (1). By using synthetic division,

```
1 | 1   -5    8   -4
  |      1   -4    4
  |_____
    1   -4    4    0
```

$(\lambda - 1)(\lambda^2 - 4\lambda + 4) = 0$

$(\lambda - 1)(\lambda - 2)^2 = 0$

Hence $\lambda = 1, \lambda = 2,$ are the required Eigen values of A.

Note that $\lambda_1 + \lambda_2 + \lambda_3 = a_{11} + a_{22} + a_{33}$ i.e. $1 + 2 + 2 = 1 + 2 + 2$

Step 3 : Let $\lambda_1 = 1$, $\lambda_2 = 2 = \lambda_3$ be the Eigen values of A.

To find the corresponding Eigen vectors of A, we will consider the matrix equation

$(A - \lambda I) X = 0$, where $X = \begin{bmatrix} x \\ y \\ z \end{bmatrix}$ i.e. $\begin{bmatrix} 1-\lambda & 2 & 2 \\ 0 & 2-\lambda & 1 \\ -1 & 2 & 2-\lambda \end{bmatrix} \begin{bmatrix} x \\ y \\ z \end{bmatrix} = \begin{bmatrix} 0 \\ 0 \\ 0 \end{bmatrix}$ ... (2)

Step 4 : For $\lambda = \lambda_1 = 1$, let the Eigen vector be $X_1 = \begin{bmatrix} x \\ y \\ z \end{bmatrix}$.

Put $\lambda = \lambda_1 = 1$ ∴ the matrix equation (2) will become $\begin{bmatrix} 0 & 2 & 2 \\ 0 & 1 & 1 \\ -1 & 2 & 1 \end{bmatrix} \begin{bmatrix} x \\ y \\ z \end{bmatrix} = \begin{bmatrix} 0 \\ 0 \\ 0 \end{bmatrix}$

AX = Z which is homogeneous system of equations. Consider the last two equations :

$$0x + y + z = 0$$
$$-x + 2y + z = 0$$

$$\frac{x}{\begin{vmatrix} 1 & 1 \\ 2 & 1 \end{vmatrix}} = \frac{-y}{\begin{vmatrix} 0 & 1 \\ -1 & 1 \end{vmatrix}} = \frac{z}{\begin{vmatrix} 0 & 1 \\ -1 & 2 \end{vmatrix}}$$

$$\frac{x}{-1} = \frac{y}{-1} = \frac{z}{1}$$

$$\frac{x}{1} = \frac{y}{1} = \frac{z}{-1} = t \qquad x = t, \ y = t, \ z = -t$$

∴ For $\lambda_1 = 1$, $X_1 = \begin{bmatrix} 1 \\ 1 \\ -1 \end{bmatrix}$ is the corresponding Eigen vector.

Step 5 : For $\lambda = \lambda_2 = 2$, let the Eigen vector be $X_2 = \begin{bmatrix} x \\ y \\ z \end{bmatrix}$.

Put $\lambda = \lambda_2 = 2$ ∴ the matrix equation (2) will become $\begin{bmatrix} -1 & 2 & 2 \\ 0 & 0 & 1 \\ -1 & 2 & 0 \end{bmatrix} \begin{bmatrix} x \\ y \\ z \end{bmatrix} = \begin{bmatrix} 0 \\ 0 \\ 0 \end{bmatrix}$.

By R_1 $-x + 2y + 2z = 0$
By R_2 $z = 0$
By R_3 $-x + 2y = 0$

Let $y = 1$ ∴ $x = 2$ ∴ For $\lambda_2 = 2$, $X_2 = \begin{bmatrix} 2 \\ 1 \\ 0 \end{bmatrix}$

Note : We get one characteristic vector corresponding to repeated root $\lambda_2 = 2 = \lambda_3$

Reason : For $\lambda_2 = 2$, consider again the homogeneous system $AX = Z$.

i.e. $\begin{bmatrix} -1 & 2 & 2 \\ 0 & 0 & 1 \\ -1 & 2 & 0 \end{bmatrix} \begin{bmatrix} x \\ y \\ z \end{bmatrix} = \begin{bmatrix} 0 \\ 0 \\ 0 \end{bmatrix}$

$(A, Z) = \begin{bmatrix} -1 & 2 & 2 & | & 0 \\ 0 & 0 & 1 & | & 0 \\ -1 & 2 & 0 & | & 0 \end{bmatrix}$

Perform $R_3 - R_1$ $\sim \begin{bmatrix} -1 & 2 & 2 & | & 0 \\ 0 & 0 & 1 & | & 0 \\ 0 & 0 & -2 & | & 0 \end{bmatrix}$

Perform $R_3 + 2R_2$ $\sim \begin{bmatrix} -1 & 2 & 2 & | & 0 \\ 0 & 0 & 1 & | & 0 \\ 0 & 0 & 0 & | & 0 \end{bmatrix}$

$\rho(A, Z) = \rho(A) = 3 - 1 = 2 < 3$

∴ System possesses $n - r = 3 - 2 = 1$ i.e. only one independent solution.

∴ For $\lambda_2 = 2 = \lambda_3$ we get only one characteristic vector $X_2 = \begin{bmatrix} 2 \\ 1 \\ 0 \end{bmatrix}$.

Ex. 2 : *Find the Eigen values and Eigen vectors of the following matrix*

$$A = \begin{bmatrix} 4 & 6 & 6 \\ 1 & 3 & 2 \\ -1 & -5 & -2 \end{bmatrix}.$$ **(May 2005)**

Sol. : Step 1 : The characteristic equation of A is $|A - \lambda I| = 0$ $\begin{vmatrix} 4-\lambda & 6 & 6 \\ 1 & 3-\lambda & 2 \\ -1 & -5 & -2-\lambda \end{vmatrix} = 0$

$\lambda^3 - S_1 \lambda^2 + S_2 \lambda - |A| = 0$

where $S_1 = 4 + 3 - 2 = 5$

$S_2 = \begin{vmatrix} 3 & 2 \\ -5 & -2 \end{vmatrix} + \begin{vmatrix} 4 & 6 \\ -1 & -2 \end{vmatrix} + \begin{vmatrix} 4 & 6 \\ 1 & 3 \end{vmatrix} = 4 - 2 + 6 = 8$

$|A| = 4(4) - 6(0) + 6(-2) = 4$

∴ The characteristic equation of A is $\lambda^3 - 5\lambda^2 + 8\lambda - 4 = 0$ ... (1)

Step 2 : For the factors we note that sum of coefficients = 0

$\therefore \quad \lambda - 1 = 0$ must be the factor of (1). By using synthetic division

$$\begin{array}{r|rrrr} 1 & 1 & -5 & 8 & -4 \\ & & 1 & -4 & 4 \\ \hline & 1 & -4 & 4 & 0 \end{array}$$

$$(\lambda - 1)(\lambda^2 - 4\lambda + 4) = 0$$
$$(\lambda - 1)(\lambda - 2)^2 = 0$$

$\therefore \qquad \lambda = 1, 2, 2$ are the Eigen values.

Note that $\lambda_1 + \lambda_2 + \lambda_3 = a_{11} + a_{22} + a_{33}$ i.e. $1 + 2 + 2 = 4 + 3 - 2$

Step 3 : Let $\lambda_1 = 1, \lambda_2 = 2 = \lambda_3$ be the Eigen values.

To find the corresponding Eigen vector, we will consider the matrix equation

$$(A - \lambda I) X = 0, \text{ where } X = \begin{bmatrix} x \\ y \\ z \end{bmatrix} \text{ i.e. } \begin{bmatrix} 4-\lambda & 6 & 6 \\ 1 & 3-\lambda & 2 \\ -1 & -5 & -2-\lambda \end{bmatrix} \begin{bmatrix} x \\ y \\ z \end{bmatrix} = \begin{bmatrix} 0 \\ 0 \\ 0 \end{bmatrix} \quad \ldots (2)$$

Step 4 : For $\lambda = \lambda_1 = 1$, let the Eigen vector be $X_1 = \begin{bmatrix} x \\ y \\ z \end{bmatrix}$.

Put $\lambda = \lambda_1 = 1$ $\therefore$ the matrix equation (2) will become $\begin{bmatrix} 3 & 6 & 6 \\ 1 & 2 & 2 \\ -1 & -5 & -3 \end{bmatrix} \begin{bmatrix} x \\ y \\ z \end{bmatrix} = \begin{bmatrix} 0 \\ 0 \\ 0 \end{bmatrix}$.

$AX = Z$ which is homogeneous system of equations. Consider last two equations :

$$x + 2y + 2z = 0 \quad \text{and} \quad x + 5y + 3z = 0$$

By Cramer's rule,

$$\frac{x}{\begin{vmatrix} 2 & 2 \\ 5 & 3 \end{vmatrix}} = \frac{-y}{\begin{vmatrix} 1 & 2 \\ 1 & 3 \end{vmatrix}} = \frac{z}{\begin{vmatrix} 1 & 2 \\ 1 & 5 \end{vmatrix}}$$

$$\frac{x}{-4} = \frac{y}{-1} = \frac{z}{3}$$

Hence for $\lambda_1 = 1$, $\qquad X_1 = \begin{bmatrix} 4 \\ 1 \\ -3 \end{bmatrix}$

Step 5 : For $\lambda = \lambda_2 = 2$, let the corresponding Eigen vector be $X_2 = \begin{bmatrix} x \\ y \\ z \end{bmatrix}$.

Put $\lambda = \lambda_2 = \lambda_3$ $\therefore$ the matrix equation (2) will become $\begin{bmatrix} 2 & 6 & 6 \\ 1 & 1 & 2 \\ -1 & -5 & -4 \end{bmatrix} \begin{bmatrix} x \\ y \\ z \end{bmatrix} = \begin{bmatrix} 0 \\ 0 \\ 0 \end{bmatrix}$

AX = Z which is a homogeneous system of equations. Consider first two equations:

$$2x + 6y + 6z = 0$$

i.e. $\quad x + 3y + 3z = 0 \quad$ and $\quad x + y + 2z = 0$

By Cramer's rule, $\quad \dfrac{x}{\begin{vmatrix} 3 & 3 \\ 1 & 2 \end{vmatrix}} = \dfrac{-y}{\begin{vmatrix} 1 & 3 \\ 1 & 2 \end{vmatrix}} = \dfrac{z}{\begin{vmatrix} 1 & 3 \\ 1 & 1 \end{vmatrix}}$

$$\frac{x}{3} = \frac{y}{1} = \frac{z}{-2}$$

Hence for $\lambda_2 = 2$, $\quad X_2 = \begin{bmatrix} 3 \\ 1 \\ -2 \end{bmatrix}$

Note : We get one characteristic vector corresponding to repeated root $\lambda_2 = 2 = \lambda_3$.

EXERCISE 3.5

$\left(\text{For } \lambda_2 = \lambda_3 \text{ repeated eigen value we are getting only one Eigen vector say } X_2 = \begin{bmatrix} x \\ y \\ z \end{bmatrix} \right)$

Find Eigen values and the Eigen vectors of the following matrices :

(1) $\begin{bmatrix} 3 & 10 & 5 \\ -2 & -3 & -4 \\ 3 & 5 & 7 \end{bmatrix}$ **Ans.** $\lambda^3 - 7\lambda^2 + 16\lambda - 12 = 0; \ 3, 2, 2; \ \begin{bmatrix} 1 \\ 1 \\ -2 \end{bmatrix}, \begin{bmatrix} 5 \\ 2 \\ -5 \end{bmatrix}$

(2) $\begin{bmatrix} 1 & 2 & 2 \\ 0 & 2 & 1 \\ -1 & 2 & 2 \end{bmatrix}$ **Ans.** $\lambda^3 - 5\lambda^2 + 8\lambda - 4 = 0; \ 1, 2, 2; \ \begin{bmatrix} 1 \\ 1 \\ -1 \end{bmatrix}, \begin{bmatrix} 2 \\ 1 \\ 0 \end{bmatrix}$

(3) $\begin{bmatrix} 1 & 2 & 3 \\ 0 & 2 & 3 \\ 0 & 0 & 2 \end{bmatrix}$ **Ans.** $\lambda^3 - 5\lambda^2 + 8\lambda - 4 = 0; \ 1, 2, 2; \ \begin{bmatrix} 1 \\ 0 \\ 0 \end{bmatrix}, \begin{bmatrix} 2 \\ 1 \\ 0 \end{bmatrix}$

3.17 TYPE 6 : EXAMPLES INVOLVING ONLY ONE EIGEN VECTOR FOR $\lambda_1 = \lambda_2 = \lambda_3$

Ex. 1 : *Find the characteristic roots and the corresponding characteristic vectors for the following matrix* $A = \begin{bmatrix} 0 & 1 & 0 \\ 0 & 0 & 1 \\ 1 & -3 & 3 \end{bmatrix}$.

Sol. : Step 1 : The characteristic equation of A is $|A - \lambda I| = 0$.

$$\begin{vmatrix} 0-\lambda & 1 & 0 \\ 0 & 0-\lambda & 1 \\ 1 & -3 & 3-\lambda \end{vmatrix} = 0$$

$$\lambda^3 - S_1\lambda^2 + S_2\lambda - |A| = 0$$

where $\quad S_1 = 0 + 0 + 3 = 3$

$$S_2 = \begin{vmatrix} 0 & 1 \\ -3 & 3 \end{vmatrix} + \begin{vmatrix} 0 & 0 \\ 1 & 3 \end{vmatrix} + \begin{vmatrix} 0 & 1 \\ 0 & 0 \end{vmatrix} = 3 + 0 + 0 = 3$$

$$|A| = 1$$

The characteristic equation of A is $\lambda^3 - 3\lambda^2 + 3\lambda - 1 = 0$ ... (1)

Step 2 : For the factors we know that equation (1) is a perfect cube $(\lambda - 1)^3 = 0$

Hence $\lambda = 1, 1, 1$ are the three repeated Eigen values of A.

Note that $\quad \lambda_1 + \lambda_2 + \lambda_3 = a_{11} + a_{22} + a_{33}$

$$1 + 1 + 1 = 0 + 0 + 3$$

Step 3 : Let $\lambda_1 = 1$ be the Eigen value.

To find the Eigen vector we will consider the matrix equation

$(A - \lambda I) X = 0$, where $X = \begin{bmatrix} x \\ y \\ z \end{bmatrix}$ i.e. $\begin{vmatrix} 0-\lambda & 1 & 0 \\ 0 & 0-\lambda & 1 \\ 1 & -3 & 3-\lambda \end{vmatrix} \begin{bmatrix} x \\ y \\ z \end{bmatrix} = \begin{bmatrix} 0 \\ 0 \\ 0 \end{bmatrix}$ ... (2)

Step 4 : For $\lambda = \lambda_1 = 1$, let the corresponding Eigen vector be $X_1 = \begin{bmatrix} x \\ y \\ z \end{bmatrix}$.

Put $\lambda = \lambda_1 = 1$, ∴ the matrix equation (2) will become $\begin{bmatrix} -1 & 1 & 0 \\ 0 & -1 & 1 \\ 1 & -3 & 2 \end{bmatrix} \begin{bmatrix} x \\ y \\ z \end{bmatrix} = \begin{bmatrix} 0 \\ 0 \\ 0 \end{bmatrix}$

$$AX = Z$$

which is homogeneous system of equations. Consider the first two equations :

$$-x + y + 0z = 0$$
$$0x - y + z = 0$$

By Cramer's rule, $\dfrac{x}{\begin{vmatrix} 1 & 0 \\ -1 & 1 \end{vmatrix}} = \dfrac{-y}{\begin{vmatrix} -1 & 0 \\ 0 & 1 \end{vmatrix}} = \dfrac{z}{\begin{vmatrix} -1 & 1 \\ 0 & -1 \end{vmatrix}}$

$$\dfrac{x}{1} = \dfrac{y}{1} = \dfrac{z}{1}$$

Hence for $\lambda_1 = 1$ the Eigen vector is $X_1 = \begin{bmatrix} 1 \\ 1 \\ 1 \end{bmatrix}$.

Note : Only one characteristic vector has been obtained for $\lambda_1 = 1$ which is repeated thrice.

Reason :

For $\lambda_1 = 1$, consider the matrix equation $AX = Z$ i.e. $\begin{bmatrix} -1 & 1 & 0 \\ 0 & -1 & 1 \\ 1 & -3 & 2 \end{bmatrix} \begin{bmatrix} x \\ y \\ z \end{bmatrix} = \begin{bmatrix} 0 \\ 0 \\ 0 \end{bmatrix}$

Consider an augmented matrix $(A, Z) \sim \begin{bmatrix} -1 & 1 & 0 & | & 0 \\ 0 & -1 & 1 & | & 0 \\ 1 & -3 & 2 & | & 0 \end{bmatrix}$

Perform $R_3 + R_1$ $\sim \begin{bmatrix} -1 & 1 & 0 & | & 0 \\ 0 & -1 & 1 & | & 0 \\ 0 & -2 & 2 & | & 0 \end{bmatrix}$

Perform $R_3 - 2R_2$ $\sim \begin{bmatrix} -1 & 1 & 0 & | & 0 \\ 0 & -1 & 1 & | & 0 \\ 0 & 0 & 0 & | & 0 \end{bmatrix}$

$\rho(A, Z) = \rho(A) = 3 - 1 = 2 < 3$

∴ System possesses $n - r = 3 - 2 = 1$ i.e. only one linearly independent solution.

∴ For $\lambda_1 = \lambda_2 = \lambda_3 = 1$, we get only one characteristic vector $X_1 = \begin{bmatrix} 1 \\ 1 \\ 1 \end{bmatrix}$.

EXERCISE 3.6

Find Eigen values and Eigen vectors of the following matrices.

(1) $\begin{bmatrix} -3 & -7 & -5 \\ 2 & 4 & 3 \\ 1 & 2 & 2 \end{bmatrix}$ **Ans.** $\lambda^3 - 3\lambda^2 + 3\lambda - 1 = 0$; 1, 1, 1; $\begin{bmatrix} -3 \\ 1 \\ 1 \end{bmatrix}$

(2) $\begin{bmatrix} 2 & 1 & 0 \\ 0 & 2 & 1 \\ 0 & 0 & 2 \end{bmatrix}$ **Ans.** $\lambda^3 - 6\lambda^2 + 12\lambda - 8 = 0$; 2, 2, 2; $\begin{bmatrix} 1 \\ 0 \\ 0 \end{bmatrix}$

3.18 ADDITIONAL EXAMPLES ON EIGEN VALUES & EIGEN VECTORS

Ex. 1 : *If λ is an eigen value of matrix A, show that λ^n is eigen value of A^n.*

Sol. : Since λ is an eigen value of A, we have $AX = \lambda X$ ... (1)

Premultiply by A, $\quad A^2X = \lambda AX$
$\quad\quad\quad\quad\quad\quad\quad A^2X = \lambda(\lambda X)$ by (1)
$\quad\quad\quad\quad\quad\quad\quad A^2X = \lambda^2 X$

Premultiply by A, $\quad A^3X = \lambda^2(AX)$
$\quad\quad\quad\quad\quad\quad\quad\quad\quad = \lambda^2(\lambda X)$ by (1)
$\quad\quad\quad\quad\quad\quad\quad A^3X = \lambda^3 X$

Thus premultiply (1) by A^{n-1},
$\quad\quad\quad\quad\quad\quad\quad A^n X = \lambda(A^{n-1}X)$
$\quad\quad\quad\quad\quad\quad\quad\quad\quad = \lambda(\lambda^{n-1}X)$
$\quad\quad\quad\quad\quad\quad\quad A^n X = \lambda^n X \Rightarrow \lambda^n$ is an eigen value of A^n

---

Ex. 2 : *If λ is an eigen value of matrix A, show that $\dfrac{|A|}{\lambda}$ is eigen value of adj A.*

Sol. : We have $\quad A(\text{adj } A) = |A| I$
or $\quad\quad\quad\quad\quad \text{Adj } A = |A| A^{-1}$ ... (1)

As λ is an eigen value of A, we have
$\quad\quad\quad\quad\quad AX = \lambda X$

Premultiplying by A^{-1}, we get,
$\quad\quad\quad\quad\quad A^{-1}(AX) = \lambda A^{-1} X$
$\quad\quad\quad\quad\quad\quad\quad X = \lambda A^{-1} X$

i.e. $\quad\quad\quad\quad\quad A^{-1}X = \dfrac{1}{\lambda} X$ ... (2)

i.e. $\dfrac{1}{\lambda}$ is eigen value of A^{-1}.

Now post multiply by X the result (1)
$\quad\quad\quad\quad (\text{adj } A) X = |A| A^{-1}X = |A| \dfrac{1}{\lambda} X$ by (2)
$\quad\quad\quad\quad (\text{adj } A) X = \dfrac{|A|}{\lambda} X$

$\therefore \dfrac{|A|}{\lambda}$ is the eigen value of adj A.

Ex. 3 : *Show that if $\lambda_1 \lambda_2 \ldots \lambda_n$ are the eigen values of a matrix 'A' then $\dfrac{1}{\lambda_1}, \dfrac{1}{\lambda_2} \ldots \dfrac{1}{\lambda_n}$ are eigen values of A^{-1}.*

Sol. : As λ_r (r = 1, 2, ... n) are eigen values of 'A',

$\therefore \quad\quad\quad\quad\quad A X_r = \lambda_r X_r$ ... (1)

Premultiply (1) by A^{-1}

$$A^{-1} A X_r = \lambda_r A^{-1} X_r$$
$$X_r = \lambda_r A^{-1} X_r$$
$$\frac{1}{\lambda_r} X_r = A^{-1} X_r$$

$\therefore \quad A^{-1} X_r = \frac{1}{\lambda_r} X_r \Rightarrow \frac{1}{\lambda_r}$ (r = 1, 2, ... n) are eigen values of A^{-1}.

Ex. 4 : *If λ is an eigen value of a orthogonal matrix then show that $\frac{1}{\lambda}$ is also its eigen value.*

Sol. : Let A be an orthogonal matrix.

$\therefore \quad AA' = A'A = I$ Also $A^{-1} = A'$

Let λ be an eigen value of A.

$\therefore \quad AX = \lambda X$
$$(A^{-1} A) X = \lambda (A^{-1} X)$$
$$IX = \lambda (A^{-1} X)$$
$$\frac{1}{\lambda} X = A^{-1} X \quad \text{But} \quad A^{-1} = A'$$

$\therefore \quad A'X = \frac{1}{\lambda} X \Rightarrow \frac{1}{\lambda}$ is eigen value of A'

$\Rightarrow \frac{1}{\lambda}$ is also eigen value of A, because A and A' have same eigen values.

Ex. 5 : *Find the spectrum of the matrix* $\begin{bmatrix} 4 & 0 & 1 \\ -2 & 1 & 0 \\ -2 & 0 & 1 \end{bmatrix}$. **(May 2011)**

Sol. : Let $A = \begin{bmatrix} 4 & 0 & 1 \\ -2 & 1 & 0 \\ -2 & 0 & 1 \end{bmatrix}$

The characteristic equation of A is $|A - \lambda I| = 0$ i.e. $\begin{vmatrix} 4-\lambda & 0 & 1 \\ -2 & 1-\lambda & 0 \\ -2 & 0 & 1-\lambda \end{vmatrix} = 0$.

where $\lambda^3 - S_1 \lambda^2 + S_2 \lambda - |A| = 0$

$S_1 = 4 + 1 + 1 = 6$

$S_2 = \begin{vmatrix} 1 & 0 \\ 0 & 1 \end{vmatrix} + \begin{vmatrix} 4 & 1 \\ -2 & 1 \end{vmatrix} + \begin{vmatrix} 4 & 0 \\ -2 & 1 \end{vmatrix}$

$= 1 + 6 + 4 = 11$

$|A| = 4(1) + 1(2) = 6$

$\therefore \quad \lambda^3 - 6\lambda^2 + 11\lambda - 6 = 0$ ... (1)

Sum of the coefficients = 0 ∴ $\lambda = 1$ must be the factor of (1).

By using synthetic division

```
1 | 1   -6   11   -6
  |      1   -5    6
  |_____
    1   -5    6    0
```

$(\lambda - 1)(\lambda^2 - 5\lambda + 6) = 0$

$(\lambda - 1)(\lambda - 2)(\lambda - 3) = 0$

∴ $\lambda = 1, 2, 3$ are the eigen values of A   ∴ Spectrum of A is {1, 2, 3}

Ex. 6 : *Show that* $A = \begin{bmatrix} 0 & a & b \\ a & 0 & c \\ b & c & 0 \end{bmatrix}$, $B = \begin{bmatrix} 0 & b & a \\ b & 0 & c \\ a & c & 0 \end{bmatrix}$ *have the same characteristic equation.*

Sol. : The characteristic equation of A is $|A - \lambda I| = 0$.

$$\begin{vmatrix} 0-\lambda & a & b \\ a & 0-\lambda & c \\ b & c & 0-\lambda \end{vmatrix} = 0$$

$\lambda^3 - 0 \cdot \lambda^2 + [-c^2 - b^2 - a^2]\lambda - [-a(-bc) + b(ac)] = 0$

$\lambda^3 - (a^2 + b^2 + c^2)\lambda - 2abc = 0$ ... (1)

The characteristic equation of B is $|B - \lambda I| = 0$

$$\begin{vmatrix} 0-\lambda & b & a \\ a & 0-\lambda & c \\ b & c & 0-\lambda \end{vmatrix} = 0$$

$\lambda^3 - 0 \cdot \lambda^2 + [-c^2 - a^2 - b^2]\lambda - [-b(-ac) + a(bc)] = 0$

$\lambda^3 - (a^2 + b^2 + c^2)\lambda - 2abc = 0$ ... (2)

From (1) and (2), it is clear that the characteristic equation of A and B is same.

3.19 CAYLEY – HAMILTON THEOREM

Statement : Every square matrix satisfies its own characteristic equation.

The theorem states that if $|A - \lambda I| = 0$ i.e.

$a_0 \lambda^n + a_1 \lambda^{n-1} + \ldots + a_{n-1} \lambda + a_n = 0$ is characteristic equation of a square matrix A, then A satisfies this equation i.e.

$a_0 A^n + a_1 A^{n-1} + \ldots + a_{n-1} A + a_n I = 0$

Proof : Since the elements of $A - \lambda I$ are at most of first degree in λ, the elements of adj. $(A - \lambda I)$ are polynomials in λ of degree $(n-1)$ or less. We can, therefore, split up adj. $(A - \lambda I)$ into a number of matrices each containing the same power of λ and write

$$\text{adj.}(A - \lambda I) = B_0 + B_1 \lambda + B_2 \lambda^2 + \ldots + B_{n-1} \lambda^{n-1}$$

Also, we know that if M is a square matrix then
$$M \, (\text{adj. } M) = |M| \times I$$
$\therefore$ Put $\quad M = (A - \lambda I)$
$\therefore \quad (A - \lambda I) \, [\text{adj.} \, (A - \lambda I)] = |A - \lambda I| \times I$

$(A - \lambda I) \, [B_0 + B_1 \lambda + B_2 \lambda^2 + \ldots + B_{n-1} \lambda^{n-1}] = [a_0 \lambda^n + a_1 \lambda^{n-1} + \ldots + a_{n-1} \lambda + a_n] \times I$

$AB_0 + (AB_1 - B_0) \lambda + (AB_2 - B_1) \lambda^2 + \ldots - B_{n-1} \lambda^n = a_0 I \lambda^n + a_1 I \lambda^{n-1} + \ldots + a_{n-1} I \lambda + a_n I$

Equating coefficients of like powers of λ on both sides, we have

$$AB_0 = a_n I$$
$$AB_1 - B_0 = a_{n-1} I$$
$$AB_2 - B_1 = a_{n-2} I$$
$$\vdots$$
$$\vdots$$
$$-B_{n-1} = a_0 I$$

Premultiplying these equations by $I, A, A^2, A^3, \ldots A^n$ respectively, we have

$$AB_0 = a_n I$$
$$A^2 B_1 - A B_0 = a_{n-1} AI$$
$$A^3 B_2 - A^2 B_1 = a_{n-2} A^2 I$$
$$-A^n B_{n-1} = a_0 A^n I$$

Now adding these equations and noting that the terms on left hand side cancel in pairs, we get,

$a_n I + a_{n-1} AI + a_{n-2} A^2 I + \ldots + a_0 A^n I = 0$

i.e. $a_0 A^n + a_1 A^{n-1} + \ldots + a_{n-2} A^2 + a_{n-1} A + a_n = 0$ ...(1)

Hence the proof.

From equation (1), $\quad A^n = \dfrac{-1}{a_0} [a_1 A^{n-1} + a_2 A^{n-2} + \ldots + a_{n-1} A + a_n]$

Therefore with the help of Cayley – Hamilton theorem, the nth power of any square matrix can be expressed as a linear combination of lower powers of A.

To find A^{-1} by using Cayley–Hamilton theorem, we require A to be non-singular matrix then A^{-1} exists and can be obtained as follows.

Multiplying equation (1) by A^{-1}, we get

$a_0 A^{-1} A^n + a_1 A^{-1} A^{n-1} + \ldots + a_{n-2} A^{-1} A^2 + a_{n-1} A^{-1} A + a_n A^{-1} = 0$

$\therefore \quad A^{-1} = -\dfrac{1}{a_n} [a_{n-1} I + a_{n-2} A + a_{n-3} A^2 + \ldots + a_1 A^{n-2} + a_0 A^{n-1}]$

which is the required expression for A^{-1}.

For problems on Cayley-Hamilton theorem, we will use the following important steps.

(1) Find characteristic equation of A.

For $A_{2 \times 2}$ it is $\lambda^2 - S_1 \lambda + |A| = 0$

For $A_{3 \times 3}$ it is $\lambda^3 - S_1 \lambda^2 + S_2 \lambda - |A| = 0$

(2) By Cayley–Hamilton theorem, we get,

$A^2 - S_1 A + |A| = 0$

or $A^3 - S_1 A^2 + S_2 A - |A| = 0$ ... (1)

(3) Find A^2, A^3 and verify it by using equation (1).

(4) For $A_{2 \times 2}$, to find A^3 we multiply equation (1) by A i.e.

$A^3 = S_1 A^2 - A(|A|)$

For $A_{3 \times 3}$, to find A^4 we multiply equation (1) by A

i.e. $A^4 = S_1 A^3 - S_2 A^2 + A(|A|)$.

(5) To find A^{-1} we must have $|A| \neq 0$. Hence for $A_{2 \times 2}$, we multiply equation (1) by A^{-1} to get,

$$A^{-1} = \frac{1}{|A|}[-A + S_1 \cdot I]$$

For $A_{3 \times 3}$ we multiply equation (1) by A^{-1} to get

$$A^{-1} = \frac{1}{|A|}[A^2 - S_1 A + S_2 \cdot I]$$

Ex. 1 : *Verify Cayley-Hamilton theorem for* $A = \begin{bmatrix} 1 & 2 & -2 \\ -1 & 3 & 0 \\ 0 & -2 & 1 \end{bmatrix}$ *and use it to find* A^4 *and* A^{-1}.

Sol. : Step 1 : The characteristic equation of A is $|A - \lambda I| = 0$ $\begin{vmatrix} 1-\lambda & 2 & -2 \\ -1 & 3-\lambda & 0 \\ 0 & -2 & 1-\lambda \end{vmatrix} = 0$.

$\lambda^3 - S_1 \lambda^2 + S_2 \lambda - |A| = 0$

$S_1 = 1 + 3 + 1 = 5$

$S_2 = \begin{vmatrix} 3 & 0 \\ -2 & 1 \end{vmatrix} + \begin{vmatrix} 1 & -2 \\ 0 & 1 \end{vmatrix} + \begin{vmatrix} 1 & 2 \\ -1 & 3 \end{vmatrix}$

$= 3 + 1 + 5 = 9$

$|A| = 1(3) + 1(-2) = 1$

Hence the characteristic equation of A is $\lambda^3 - 5\lambda^2 + 9\lambda - 1 = 0$.

Step 2 : By using Cayley-Hamilton theorem, we have $A^3 - 5A^2 + 9A - I = 0$ ... (1)

Step 3 : To verify Cayley-Hamilton theorem, we first obtain A^2 and A^3 as follows :

$$A^2 = \begin{bmatrix} 1 & 2 & -2 \\ -1 & 3 & 0 \\ 0 & -2 & 1 \end{bmatrix} \begin{bmatrix} 1 & 2 & -2 \\ -1 & 3 & 0 \\ 0 & -2 & 1 \end{bmatrix} = \begin{bmatrix} -1 & 12 & -4 \\ -4 & 7 & 2 \\ 2 & -8 & 1 \end{bmatrix}$$

$$A^3 = A^2 A = \begin{bmatrix} -1 & 12 & -4 \\ -4 & 7 & 2 \\ 2 & -8 & 1 \end{bmatrix} \begin{bmatrix} 1 & 2 & -2 \\ -1 & 3 & 0 \\ 0 & -2 & 1 \end{bmatrix} = \begin{bmatrix} -13 & 42 & -2 \\ -11 & 9 & 10 \\ 10 & -22 & -3 \end{bmatrix}$$

By using equation (1),

$$A^3 - 5A^2 + 9A - I = \begin{bmatrix} -13 & 42 & -2 \\ -11 & 9 & 10 \\ 10 & -22 & -3 \end{bmatrix} - 5 \begin{bmatrix} -1 & 12 & -4 \\ -4 & 7 & 2 \\ 2 & -8 & 1 \end{bmatrix}$$

$$+ 9 \begin{bmatrix} 1 & 2 & -2 \\ -1 & 3 & 0 \\ 0 & -2 & 1 \end{bmatrix} - \begin{bmatrix} 1 & 0 & 0 \\ 0 & 1 & 0 \\ 0 & 0 & 1 \end{bmatrix}$$

$$= \begin{bmatrix} 0 & 0 & 0 \\ 0 & 0 & 0 \\ 0 & 0 & 0 \end{bmatrix}$$

Hence Cayley-Hamilton theorem is verified.

Step 4 : To find A^4 we multiply equation (1) by A.

$A^4 - 5A^3 + 9A^2 - AI = 0$

$A^4 = 5A^3 - 9A^2 + A$

$$= 5 \begin{bmatrix} -13 & 42 & -2 \\ -11 & 9 & 10 \\ 10 & -22 & -3 \end{bmatrix} - 9 \begin{bmatrix} -1 & 12 & -4 \\ -4 & 7 & 2 \\ 2 & -8 & 1 \end{bmatrix} + \begin{bmatrix} 1 & 2 & -2 \\ -1 & 3 & 0 \\ 0 & -2 & 1 \end{bmatrix}$$

$$= \begin{bmatrix} -55 & 104 & 24 \\ -20 & -15 & 32 \\ 32 & -40 & -23 \end{bmatrix}$$

Step 5 : To find A^{-1} we multiply equation (1) by A^{-1}.

$A^2 - 5A + 9I - A^{-1}I = 0$

$A^{-1} = A^2 - 5A + 9I$

$$= \begin{bmatrix} -1 & 12 & -4 \\ -4 & 7 & 2 \\ 2 & -8 & 1 \end{bmatrix} - 5 \begin{bmatrix} 1 & 2 & -2 \\ -1 & 3 & 0 \\ 0 & -2 & 1 \end{bmatrix} + \begin{bmatrix} 9 & 0 & 0 \\ 0 & 9 & 0 \\ 0 & 0 & 9 \end{bmatrix} = \begin{bmatrix} 3 & 2 & 6 \\ 1 & 1 & 2 \\ 2 & 2 & 5 \end{bmatrix}$$

Ex. 2 : *Verify Cayley-Hamilton theorem for* $A = \begin{bmatrix} 1 & 1 & 3 \\ 1 & 3 & -3 \\ -2 & -4 & -4 \end{bmatrix}$ *and use it to find* A^{-1}.

Sol. : Step 1 : The characteristic equation of A is

$$|A - \lambda I| = 0 \quad \begin{vmatrix} 1-\lambda & 1 & 3 \\ 1 & 3-\lambda & -3 \\ -2 & -4 & -4-\lambda \end{vmatrix} = 0.$$

$$\lambda^3 - S_1 \lambda^2 + S_2 \lambda - |A| = 0$$

$$S_1 = 1 + 3 - 4 = 0$$

$$S_2 = \begin{vmatrix} 3 & -3 \\ -4 & -4 \end{vmatrix} + \begin{vmatrix} 1 & 3 \\ -2 & -4 \end{vmatrix} + \begin{vmatrix} 1 & 1 \\ 1 & 3 \end{vmatrix}$$

$$= -24 + 2 + 2 = -20$$

$$|A| = 1(-24) + 10 + 6 = -8$$

Hence the characteristic equation of A is $\lambda^3 - 20\lambda + 8 = 0$.

Step 2 : By Cayley-Hamilton theorem, we have

$$A^3 - 20A + 8I = 0 \qquad \ldots (1)$$

Step 3 : To verify equation (1) we require A^3.

Now, $A^2 = \begin{bmatrix} 1 & 1 & 3 \\ 1 & 3 & -3 \\ -2 & -4 & -4 \end{bmatrix} \begin{bmatrix} 1 & 1 & 3 \\ 1 & 3 & -3 \\ -2 & -4 & -4 \end{bmatrix} = \begin{bmatrix} -4 & -8 & -12 \\ 10 & 22 & 6 \\ 2 & 2 & 22 \end{bmatrix}$

$A^3 = \begin{bmatrix} -4 & -8 & -12 \\ 10 & 22 & 6 \\ 2 & 2 & 22 \end{bmatrix} \begin{bmatrix} 1 & 1 & 3 \\ 1 & 3 & -3 \\ -2 & -4 & -4 \end{bmatrix} = \begin{bmatrix} 12 & 20 & 60 \\ 20 & 52 & -60 \\ -40 & -80 & -88 \end{bmatrix}$

$A^3 - 20A + 8I = \begin{bmatrix} 12 & 20 & 60 \\ 20 & 52 & -60 \\ -40 & -80 & -88 \end{bmatrix} - 20 \begin{bmatrix} 1 & 1 & 3 \\ 1 & 3 & -3 \\ -2 & -4 & -4 \end{bmatrix} + \begin{bmatrix} 8 & 0 & 0 \\ 0 & 8 & 0 \\ 0 & 0 & 8 \end{bmatrix}$

$= \begin{bmatrix} 0 & 0 & 0 \\ 0 & 0 & 0 \\ 0 & 0 & 0 \end{bmatrix}$

Hence Cayley–Hamilton theorem is verified.

Step 4 : To find A^{-1} we multiply equation (1) by A^{-1}.

$$A^2 - 20I + 8A^{-1} = 0$$

$$A^{-1} = \frac{1}{8}[20I - A^2] = \frac{1}{8} \left\{ \begin{bmatrix} 20 & 0 & 0 \\ 0 & 20 & 0 \\ 0 & 0 & 20 \end{bmatrix} - \begin{bmatrix} -4 & -8 & -12 \\ 10 & 22 & 6 \\ 2 & 2 & 22 \end{bmatrix} \right\} = \frac{1}{8} \begin{bmatrix} 24 & 8 & 12 \\ -10 & -2 & -6 \\ -2 & -2 & -2 \end{bmatrix}$$

Ex. 3 : *Verify Cayley–Hamilton theorem for* $A = \begin{bmatrix} 2 & 1 & 1 \\ 0 & 1 & 0 \\ 1 & 1 & 2 \end{bmatrix}$ *and use it to find the matrix* $A^8 - 5A^7 + 7A^6 - 3A^5 + A^4 - 5A^3 + 8A^2 - 2A + I.$ **(May 2005, Dec. 2005)**

Sol. : Step 1 : The characteristic equation of A is $|A - \lambda I| = 0$

$$\begin{vmatrix} 2-\lambda & 1 & 1 \\ 0 & 1-\lambda & 0 \\ 1 & 1 & 2-\lambda \end{vmatrix} = 0$$

$\lambda^3 - S_1 \lambda^2 + S_2 \lambda - |A| = 0$

where $\quad S_1 = 2 + 1 + 2 = 5$

$S_2 = \begin{vmatrix} 1 & 0 \\ 1 & 2 \end{vmatrix} + \begin{vmatrix} 2 & 1 \\ 1 & 2 \end{vmatrix} + \begin{vmatrix} 2 & 1 \\ 0 & 1 \end{vmatrix} = 2 + 3 + 2 = 7$

$|A| = 2(2) - 1(0) + 1(-1) = 3$

Hence the characteristic equation of A is

$\lambda^3 - 5\lambda^2 + 7\lambda - 3 = 0$

Step 2 : By Cayley-Hamilton theorem, 'A' satisfies its own characteristic equation i.e. we have $A^3 - 5A^2 + 7A - 3I = 0$ ... (1)

Step 3 : Verification : To verify

$A^3 - 5A^2 + 7A - 3I = 0$

Let $\quad A^2 = \begin{bmatrix} 2 & 1 & 1 \\ 0 & 1 & 0 \\ 1 & 1 & 2 \end{bmatrix} \begin{bmatrix} 2 & 1 & 1 \\ 0 & 1 & 0 \\ 1 & 1 & 2 \end{bmatrix} = \begin{bmatrix} 5 & 4 & 4 \\ 0 & 1 & 0 \\ 4 & 4 & 5 \end{bmatrix}$

$A^3 = \begin{bmatrix} 5 & 4 & 4 \\ 0 & 1 & 0 \\ 4 & 4 & 5 \end{bmatrix} \begin{bmatrix} 2 & 1 & 1 \\ 0 & 1 & 0 \\ 1 & 1 & 2 \end{bmatrix} = \begin{bmatrix} 14 & 13 & 13 \\ 0 & 1 & 0 \\ 13 & 13 & 14 \end{bmatrix}$

$A^3 - 5A^2 + 7A - 3I = \begin{bmatrix} 14 & 13 & 13 \\ 0 & 1 & 0 \\ 13 & 13 & 14 \end{bmatrix} - 5\begin{bmatrix} 5 & 4 & 4 \\ 0 & 1 & 0 \\ 4 & 4 & 5 \end{bmatrix} + 7\begin{bmatrix} 2 & 1 & 1 \\ 0 & 1 & 0 \\ 1 & 1 & 2 \end{bmatrix} - \begin{bmatrix} 3 & 0 & 0 \\ 0 & 3 & 0 \\ 0 & 0 & 3 \end{bmatrix}$

$= \begin{bmatrix} 0 & 0 & 0 \\ 0 & 0 & 0 \\ 0 & 0 & 0 \end{bmatrix}$

Hence Cayley–Hamilton theorem is verified.

Step 4 : Now the given expression can be written as
$A^8 - 5A^7 + 7A^6 - 3A^5 + A^4 - 5A^3 + 8A^2 - 2A + I$

$= A^5(A^3 - 5A^2 + 7A - 3) + A(A^3 - 5A^2 + 7A - 3) + A^2 + A + I$

$= A^2 + A + I$ [By using equation (1) $\because A^3 - 5A^2 + 7A - 3 = 0$]

$$= \begin{bmatrix} 5 & 4 & 4 \\ 0 & 1 & 0 \\ 4 & 4 & 5 \end{bmatrix} + \begin{bmatrix} 2 & 1 & 1 \\ 0 & 1 & 0 \\ 1 & 1 & 2 \end{bmatrix} + \begin{bmatrix} 1 & 0 & 0 \\ 0 & 1 & 0 \\ 0 & 0 & 1 \end{bmatrix}$$

$$= \begin{bmatrix} 8 & 5 & 5 \\ 0 & 3 & 0 \\ 5 & 5 & 8 \end{bmatrix}$$

Ex. 4: *Find the characteristic equation for* $A = \begin{bmatrix} 1 & 4 \\ 2 & 3 \end{bmatrix}$ *and use it to find the simplified expression for* $A^5 + 5A^4 - 6A^3 + 2A^2 - 4A + 7I$.

Sol. : **Step 1**: The characteristic equation of A is $|A - \lambda I| = 0$ $\begin{vmatrix} 1-\lambda & 4 \\ 2 & 3-\lambda \end{vmatrix} = 0$

$$\lambda^2 - S_1 \lambda + |A| = 0$$

where
$$S_1 = 1 + 3 = 4$$
$$|A| = 3 - 8 = -5$$
$$\lambda^2 - 4\lambda - 5 = 0 \text{ which is the required characteristic equation of A.}$$

Step 2: By Cayley-Hamilton theorem $A^2 - 4A - 5I = 0$ ... (1)

Step 3: To verify it we require A^2

$$\therefore \quad A^2 = \begin{bmatrix} 1 & 4 \\ 2 & 3 \end{bmatrix} \begin{bmatrix} 1 & 4 \\ 2 & 3 \end{bmatrix} = \begin{bmatrix} 9 & 16 \\ 8 & 17 \end{bmatrix}$$

$$\therefore \quad A^2 - 4A - 5I = \begin{bmatrix} 9 & 16 \\ 8 & 17 \end{bmatrix} - 4 \begin{bmatrix} 1 & 4 \\ 2 & 3 \end{bmatrix} - \begin{bmatrix} 5 & 0 \\ 0 & 5 \end{bmatrix} = \begin{bmatrix} 0 & 0 \\ 0 & 0 \end{bmatrix}$$

Step 4: From (1), $A^2 = 4A + 5I$

$$A^3 = 4A^2 + 5A = 4(4A + 5I) + 5A = 21A + 20I$$
$$A^4 = 21A^2 + 20A = 21(4A + 5I) + 20A = 104A + 105I$$
$$A^5 = 104A^2 + 105A = 104(4A + 5I) + 105A = 521A + 520I$$

$\therefore \quad A^5 + 5A^4 - 6A^3 + 2A^2 - 4A + 7I$

$$= 521A + 520I + 5(104A + 105I) - 6(21A + 20I)$$
$$\quad + 2(4A + 5I) - 4A + 7I$$

$$= 919A + 942I = 919 \begin{bmatrix} 1 & 4 \\ 2 & 3 \end{bmatrix} + \begin{bmatrix} 942 & 0 \\ 0 & 942 \end{bmatrix}$$

$$= \begin{bmatrix} 1861 & 3676 \\ 1838 & 3699 \end{bmatrix}$$

EXERCISE 3.7

Verify Cayley-Hamilton theorem for the following matrix A and use it to find A^4 and A^{-1}.

(1) $A = \begin{bmatrix} 2 & -1 & 1 \\ -1 & 2 & -1 \\ 1 & -1 & 2 \end{bmatrix}$ Ans. $A^3 - 6A^2 + 9A - 4I = 0$, $A^{-1} = \dfrac{1}{4} \begin{bmatrix} 3 & 1 & -1 \\ 1 & 3 & 1 \\ -1 & 1 & 3 \end{bmatrix}$

(May 2004, Dec. 2006)

(2) $A = \begin{bmatrix} 1 & 3 & 7 \\ 4 & 2 & 3 \\ 1 & 2 & 1 \end{bmatrix}$ Ans. $A^3 - 4A^2 - 20A - 35I = 0$, $A^{-1} = \dfrac{1}{35} \begin{bmatrix} -4 & 11 & -5 \\ -1 & -6 & 25 \\ 6 & 1 & -10 \end{bmatrix}$

(3) $A = \begin{bmatrix} 8 & -8 & -2 \\ 4 & -3 & -2 \\ 3 & -4 & 1 \end{bmatrix}$ Ans. $A^3 - 6A^2 + 11A - 6I = 0$, $A^{-1} = \dfrac{1}{6} \begin{bmatrix} -11 & 16 & 10 \\ -10 & 14 & 8 \\ -7 & 8 & 8 \end{bmatrix}$

(4) $A = \begin{bmatrix} 1 & 0 & 1 \\ 0 & 1 & 0 \\ 0 & 0 & 1 \end{bmatrix}$ (May 2009) Ans. $A^3 - 3A^2 + 3A - I = 0$, $A^{-1} = \begin{bmatrix} 1 & 0 & -1 \\ 0 & 1 & 0 \\ 0 & 0 & 1 \end{bmatrix}$

(5) $A = \begin{bmatrix} 1 & 0 & 2 \\ 0 & 2 & 1 \\ 2 & 0 & 3 \end{bmatrix}$ Ans. $A^3 - 6A^2 + 7A + 2I = 0$, $A^{-1} = \begin{bmatrix} -3 & 0 & 2 \\ -1 & 1/2 & 1/2 \\ 2 & 0 & -1 \end{bmatrix}$

(6) $A = \begin{bmatrix} 1 & 2 & 0 \\ 2 & -1 & 0 \\ 0 & 0 & -1 \end{bmatrix}$ Also find A^{-1}. (May 2006)

Ans. $A^3 + A^2 - 5A - 5I = 0$, $A^{-1} = \dfrac{1}{5} \begin{bmatrix} 1 & 2 & 0 \\ 2 & -1 & 0 \\ 0 & 0 & -5 \end{bmatrix}$

$A^{-2} = \dfrac{1}{5}[A + I - 5A^{-1}] = \dfrac{1}{5} \begin{bmatrix} 1 & 0 & 0 \\ 0 & 1 & 0 \\ 0 & 0 & 1 \end{bmatrix}$

(7) $A = \begin{bmatrix} 1 & 0 & -2 \\ 2 & 2 & 4 \\ 0 & 0 & 2 \end{bmatrix}$ (May 2014) Ans. $A^3 - 5A^2 + 8A - 4I = 0$, $A^{-1} = \dfrac{1}{4} \begin{bmatrix} 4 & 0 & 4 \\ -4 & 2 & -8 \\ 0 & 0 & 2 \end{bmatrix}$

(8) $A = \begin{bmatrix} 0 & 1 & 2 \\ 1 & 2 & 3 \\ 3 & 1 & 1 \end{bmatrix}$ Ans. $A^3 - 3A^2 - 8A + 2I = 0$, $A^{-1} = \dfrac{1}{2} \begin{bmatrix} 1 & -1 & 1 \\ -8 & 6 & -2 \\ 5 & -3 & 1 \end{bmatrix}$

(Dec. 2003, May 2007)

(9) $A = \begin{bmatrix} 2 & 2 & 0 \\ 2 & 1 & 1 \\ -7 & 2 & -3 \end{bmatrix}$ **Ans.** $A^3 - 13A + 12I = 0$, $A^{-1} = \dfrac{1}{12} \begin{bmatrix} 5 & -6 & -2 \\ 1 & 6 & 2 \\ -11 & 18 & 2 \end{bmatrix}$

(10) $A = \begin{bmatrix} 1 & 0 & -1 \\ 1 & 2 & 1 \\ 2 & 2 & 3 \end{bmatrix}$ **Ans.** $A^3 - 6A^2 + 11A - 6I = 0$, $A^{-1} = \dfrac{1}{6} \begin{bmatrix} 4 & -2 & 2 \\ -1 & 5 & -2 \\ -2 & -2 & 2 \end{bmatrix}$

(11) $A = \begin{bmatrix} 1 & 2 & 2 \\ 0 & 2 & 1 \\ -1 & 2 & 2 \end{bmatrix}$ **Ans.** $A^3 - 5A^2 + 8A - 4I = 0$, $A^{-1} = \dfrac{1}{4} \begin{bmatrix} 2 & 0 & -2 \\ -1 & 4 & -1 \\ 2 & -4 & 2 \end{bmatrix}$

(Dec. 2004, May 2010)

(12) $A = \begin{bmatrix} 2 & 1 & 1 \\ 1 & 2 & 1 \\ 0 & 0 & 1 \end{bmatrix}$ (May 11) **Ans.** $A^3 - 5A^2 + 7A - 3I = 0$, $A^{-1} = \dfrac{1}{3} \begin{bmatrix} 2 & -1 & -1 \\ -1 & 2 & -1 \\ 0 & 0 & 3 \end{bmatrix}$

(13) $A = \begin{bmatrix} 1 & 1 & -2 \\ -1 & 2 & 1 \\ 0 & 1 & -1 \end{bmatrix}$ **Ans.** $A^3 - 2A^2 - A + 2I = 0$, $A^{-1} = \dfrac{1}{2} \begin{bmatrix} 3 & 1 & -5 \\ 1 & 1 & -1 \\ 1 & 1 & -3 \end{bmatrix}$

(14) $A = \begin{bmatrix} 0 & 1 & 0 \\ 0 & 0 & 1 \\ 1 & -3 & 3 \end{bmatrix}$ **Ans.** $A^3 - 3A^2 + 3A - I = 0$, $A^{-1} = \begin{bmatrix} 3 & -3 & 1 \\ 1 & 0 & 0 \\ 0 & 1 & 0 \end{bmatrix}$

(15) $A = \begin{bmatrix} 2 & -1 & 1 \\ 1 & 2 & -1 \\ 1 & -1 & 2 \end{bmatrix}$ **Ans.** $A^3 - 6A^2 + 11A - 6I = 0$, $A^{-1} = \dfrac{1}{6} \begin{bmatrix} 3 & 1 & -1 \\ -3 & 3 & 3 \\ -3 & 1 & 5 \end{bmatrix}$

(16) $A = \begin{bmatrix} 1 & 2 & 2 \\ 2 & 1 & 2 \\ 2 & 2 & 1 \end{bmatrix}$ **Ans.** $A^3 - 3A^2 - 9A - 5I = 0$, $A^{-1} = \dfrac{1}{5} \begin{bmatrix} -3 & 2 & 2 \\ 2 & -3 & 2 \\ 2 & 2 & -3 \end{bmatrix}$

(17) $A = \begin{bmatrix} 1 & 1 & 0 \\ 0 & 0 & 1 \\ 2 & 1 & -1 \end{bmatrix}$ **Ans.** $A^3 - 2A - I = 0$, $A^{-1} = \begin{bmatrix} -1 & 1 & 1 \\ 2 & -1 & -1 \\ 0 & 1 & 0 \end{bmatrix}$

(18) $A = \begin{bmatrix} 3 & 1 & 4 \\ 0 & 2 & 6 \\ 0 & 0 & 5 \end{bmatrix}$ **Ans.** $A^3 - 10A^2 + 31A - 30I = 0$, $A^{-1} = \dfrac{1}{30} \begin{bmatrix} 10 & -5 & -2 \\ 0 & 15 & -18 \\ 0 & 0 & 6 \end{bmatrix}$

(19) $A = \begin{bmatrix} -2 & 2 & -3 \\ 2 & 1 & -6 \\ -1 & -2 & 0 \end{bmatrix}$ Ans. $A^3 + A^2 - 21A - 45I = 0$, $A^{-1} = \dfrac{1}{45}\begin{bmatrix} -12 & 6 & -9 \\ 6 & -3 & -18 \\ -3 & -6 & -6 \end{bmatrix}$

(20) $A = \begin{bmatrix} 1 & 0 & -4 \\ 0 & 5 & 4 \\ -4 & 4 & 3 \end{bmatrix}$ Ans. $A^3 - 9A^2 - 9A + 81I = 0$, $A^{-1} = \dfrac{-1}{81}\begin{bmatrix} -1 & -16 & 20 \\ -16 & -13 & -4 \\ 20 & -4 & 5 \end{bmatrix}$

(21) $A = \begin{bmatrix} -4 & 5 & 5 \\ -5 & 6 & 5 \\ -5 & 5 & 6 \end{bmatrix}$. Also find A^5.

Ans. $A^3 - 8A^2 + 13A - 6I = 0$, $A^{-1} = \dfrac{1}{6}\begin{bmatrix} 11 & -5 & -5 \\ 5 & 1 & -5 \\ 5 & -5 & 1 \end{bmatrix}$

(22) $A = \begin{bmatrix} 1 & 1 & 2 \\ 3 & 1 & 1 \\ 2 & 3 & 1 \end{bmatrix}$. Find A^{-1}, A^{-2}, A^{-3}. **(Dec. 2009)** Ans. $A^3 - 3A^2 - 7A - 11 = 0$

$A^{-1} = \dfrac{1}{11}\begin{bmatrix} -2 & 5 & -1 \\ -1 & -3 & 5 \\ 7 & -1 & -2 \end{bmatrix}$, $A^{-2} = \dfrac{1}{11}(A - 3I - 7A^{-1})$, $A^{-3} = \dfrac{1}{121}\begin{bmatrix} -8 & -24 & 29 \\ 40 & -1 & -24 \\ -27 & 40 & -8 \end{bmatrix}$

(23) $A = \begin{bmatrix} 1 & 2 \\ 1 & 1 \end{bmatrix}$. Find A^{-1}, A^{-2}, A^{-3}.

Ans. $A^2 - 2A - I = 0$, $A^{-1} = \begin{bmatrix} -1 & 2 \\ 1 & -1 \end{bmatrix}$, $A^{-2} = \begin{bmatrix} 3 & -4 \\ -2 & 3 \end{bmatrix}$, $A^{-3} = \begin{bmatrix} -7 & 10 \\ 5 & -7 \end{bmatrix}$

(24) $A = \begin{bmatrix} 1 & 2 & 4 \\ -1 & 0 & 3 \\ 3 & 1 & -2 \end{bmatrix}$. Find A^{-1}. Ans. $A^3 + A^2 - 15A - 7I = 0$, $A^{-1} = \dfrac{1}{7}\begin{bmatrix} -3 & 8 & 6 \\ 7 & -14 & -7 \\ -1 & 5 & 2 \end{bmatrix}$

MULTIPLE CHOICE QUESTIONS

Type I : Eigen Values and Eigen Vectors

1. The characteristic equation for the square matrix A is (1)
   (A) $|A - \lambda I| = 0$
   (B) $|A + \lambda I| = 0$
   (C) $|A^2 - \lambda I| = 0$
   (D) none of these

2. If $\lambda_1, \lambda_2, \lambda_3$ are eigen values of nonsingular matrix A then eigen values of A^{-1} are (1)
   (A) $\dfrac{1}{\lambda_1}, \dfrac{1}{\lambda_2}, \dfrac{1}{\lambda_3}$
   (B) $\lambda_1, \lambda_2, \lambda_3$
   (C) $\lambda_1^2, \lambda_2^2, \lambda_3^2$
   (D) $-\lambda_1, -\lambda_2, -\lambda_3$

3. If $\lambda_1, \lambda_2, \lambda_3$ are eigen values of matrix A then trace of A is equal to (1)

   (A) $\dfrac{1}{\lambda_1}+\dfrac{1}{\lambda_2}+\dfrac{1}{\lambda_3}$

   (B) $\lambda_1 + \lambda_2 + \lambda_3$

   (C) $\lambda_1^2 + \lambda_2^2 + \lambda_3^2$

   (D) $\lambda_1 \times \lambda_2 \times \lambda_3$

4. The sum of the eigen values of a matrix is equal to (1)

   (A) rank of the matrix
   (B) determinant of the matrix
   (C) trace of the matrix
   (D) none of these

5. The product of the eigen values of a matrix is equal to (1)

   (A) trace of the matrix
   (B) determinant of the matrix
   (C) rank of the matrix
   (D) none of these

6. The eigen values of a upper triangular matrix are (1)

   (A) its principal diagonal elements
   (B) 0, 0, 0
   (C) 1, 1, 1
   (D) none of these

7. The eigen values of a lower triangular matrix are (1)

   (A) its principal diagonal elements
   (B) 0, 0, 0
   (C) 1, 1, 1
   (D) none of these

8. If an eigen value of a square matrix A is $\lambda = 0$ then (1)

   (A) A is nonsingular
   (B) A is orthogonal
   (C) A is singular
   (D) none of these

9. Eigen vectors of a real symmetric matrix A are orthogonal if the eigen values are (1)

   (A) repeated
   (B) nonrepeated
   (C) complex
   (D) none of these

10. Eigen vectors corresponding to distinct eigen values of a real symmetric matrix A are (1)

    (A) linearly dependent
    (B) equal
    (C) orthogonal
    (D) none of these

11. If $\lambda_1, \lambda_2, \lambda_3$ are eigen values of matrix A of order three then eigen values of matrix A^m are (1)

    (A) $\dfrac{1}{\lambda_1^m}, \dfrac{1}{\lambda_2^m}, \dfrac{1}{\lambda_3^m}$

    (B) $\lambda_1^m \lambda_2^m + \lambda_2^m \lambda_3^m + \lambda_1^m \lambda_3^m$

    (C) $-\lambda_1^m, -\lambda_2^m, -\lambda_3^m$

    (D) $\lambda_1^m, \lambda_2^m, \lambda_3^m$

12. If $\lambda_1, \lambda_2, \lambda_3$ are eigen values of matrix A of order three and k is any non-zero constant, then the eigen values of matrix kA are (1)

    (A) $\dfrac{\lambda_1}{k}, \dfrac{\lambda_2}{k}, \dfrac{\lambda_3}{k}$ (B) $\lambda_1, \lambda_2, \lambda_3$

    (C) $-k\lambda_1, -k\lambda_2, -k\lambda_3$ (D) $k\lambda_1, k\lambda_2, k\lambda_3$

13. The eigen values of the matrix $A = \begin{bmatrix} 8 & -4 \\ 2 & 2 \end{bmatrix}$ are (2)

    (A) $\lambda = 4, 5$ (B) $\lambda = -4, -6$

    (C) $\lambda = 4, 6$ (D) none of these

14. The eigen values of the matrix $A = \begin{bmatrix} 1 & -2 \\ -5 & 4 \end{bmatrix}$ are (2)

    (A) $\lambda = -6, 1$ (B) $\lambda = 2, 3$

    (C) $\lambda = 6, -1$ (D) none of these

15. For matrix $A = \begin{bmatrix} 1 & 0 & 0 \\ -1 & 2 & 0 \\ 4 & 0 & 3 \end{bmatrix}$, the eigen values of A are (2)

    (A) $-1, -2, -3$ (B) $2, 2, 2$
    (C) $2, -3, 1$ (D) $1, 2, 3$

16. For matrix $A = \begin{bmatrix} 1 & -2 & -1 \\ 0 & 3 & 2 \\ 0 & 0 & 5 \end{bmatrix}$, the eigen values of A are (2)

    (A) $1, -2, -1$ (B) $1, -3, -5$
    (C) $-1, -3, -5$ (D) $1, 3, 5$

17. For matrix $A = \begin{bmatrix} -1 & 0 & 0 \\ 2 & -3 & 0 \\ 1 & 4 & 2 \end{bmatrix}$, the eigen values of A^2 are (2)

    (A) $-1, -9, -4$ (B) $1, 9, 4$
    (C) $-1, -3, 2$ (D) $1, 3, -2$

18. If A is any non-zero matrix of order 2×2 with trace of $A = -1$ and $|A| = -2$ then the eigen values of A are (2)

    (A) 2 and -1 (B) -3 and 2
    (C) -2 and -1 (D) -2 and 1

19. The sum and product of the eigen values of the matrix $A = \begin{bmatrix} 2 & 2 & 1 \\ 1 & 3 & 1 \\ 1 & 2 & 2 \end{bmatrix}$ are respectively (2)

    (A) 7 and 7   (B) 7 and 5
    (C) 5 and 6   (D) 5 and 8

20. If $\lambda_1, \lambda_2, \lambda_3$ are eigen values of matrix $\begin{bmatrix} -2 & -9 & 5 \\ -5 & -10 & 7 \\ -9 & -21 & 14 \end{bmatrix}$ then $\lambda_1 + \lambda_2 + \lambda_3$ is equal to (2)

    (A) −16   (B) 2
    (C) −6   (D) −14

21. Two of the eigen values of 3 × 3 matrix whose determinant is equal to 4 are −1 and 2. The third eigen value of the matrix is equal to (2)

    (A) 1   (B) −1
    (C) −2   (D) 2

22. The characteristic equation of the matrix $\begin{bmatrix} 3 & 5 \\ -2 & -4 \end{bmatrix}$ is (2)

    (A) $\lambda^2 - \lambda + 2 = 0$ (B) $\lambda^3 + \lambda^2 + \lambda - 2 = 0$
    (C) $\lambda^2 - \lambda - 2 = 0$ (D) $\lambda^2 + \lambda - 2 = 0$

23. The characteristic equation of the matrix $\begin{bmatrix} 3 & 1 & 1 \\ -1 & 5 & -1 \\ 1 & -1 & 3 \end{bmatrix}$ is (2)

    (A) $\lambda^3 - 11\lambda^2 + 38\lambda - 40 = 0$ (B) $\lambda^3 - 11\lambda^2 + 38\lambda + 40 = 0$
    (C) $\lambda^3 + 11\lambda^2 + 38\lambda + 40 = 0$ (D) $\lambda^3 + 11\lambda^2 + 38\lambda + 40 = 0$

24. If the characteristic equation for the matrix A is $\lambda^3 - 6\lambda^2 + 11\lambda - 6 = 0$ then the eigen values of the matrix A are (2)

    (A) 1, 2, 3   (B) −1, −2, −3
    (C) 1, 2, −3   (D) none of these

25. If the characteristic equation for the matrix A is $\lambda^3 - 2\lambda^2 + \lambda = 0$ then the eigen values of the matrix A are (2)

    (A) 0, 1, 1   (B) 0, −1, −1
    (C) 0, 2, 2   (D) none of these

26. If the characteristic equation for the matrix A is $\lambda^3 - 3\lambda^2 + 3\lambda - 1 = 0$ then the eigen values of the matrix A are (2)
    (A) 1, –1, –1
    (B) 1, 2, 3
    (C) 1, 1, 1
    (D) none of these

27. The eigen vector X_1 corresponding to eigen value $\lambda_1 = 1$ for the matrix
    $A = \begin{bmatrix} 4 & 6 & 6 \\ 1 & 3 & 2 \\ -1 & -4 & -3 \end{bmatrix}$ is obtained by solving (2)

    (A) $\begin{bmatrix} 3 & 6 & 6 \\ 1 & 2 & 2 \\ -1 & -4 & -4 \end{bmatrix} \begin{bmatrix} x_1 \\ x_2 \\ x_3 \end{bmatrix} = \begin{bmatrix} 0 \\ 0 \\ 0 \end{bmatrix}$
    (B) $\begin{bmatrix} 5 & 6 & 6 \\ 1 & 4 & 2 \\ -1 & -4 & -2 \end{bmatrix} \begin{bmatrix} x_1 \\ x_2 \\ x_3 \end{bmatrix} = \begin{bmatrix} 0 \\ 0 \\ 0 \end{bmatrix}$

    (C) $\begin{bmatrix} 3 & 5 & 5 \\ 0 & 2 & 1 \\ -2 & -5 & -4 \end{bmatrix} \begin{bmatrix} x_1 \\ x_2 \\ x_3 \end{bmatrix} = \begin{bmatrix} 0 \\ 0 \\ 0 \end{bmatrix}$
    (D) none of these

Type II : Cayley Hamilton Theorem

28. Cayley Hamilton theorem states that (1)
    (A) sum of eigen values is equal to trace of matrix
    (B) the product of the eigen values of a matrix is equal to determinant of the matrix
    (C) every square matrix satisfies its own characteristic equation
    (D) eigen values of a matrix and its transpose is same

29. If the characteristic equation of matrix A of order 2×2 is $\lambda^2 - 2\lambda - 1 = 0$. Then by Cayley Hamilton theorem (1)
    (A) $A^2 + 2A + I = 0$
    (B) $A^2 + 2A - I = 0$
    (C) $A^2 - 2A + I = 0$
    (D) $A^2 - 2A - I = 0$

30. If the characteristic equation of matrix A of order 3×3 is $\lambda^3 - 5\lambda^2 + 9\lambda - 1 = 0$. Then by Cayley Hamilton theorem (1)
    (A) $A^3 - 5A^2 - 9A - I = 0$
    (B) $A^3 + 5A^2 + 9A + I = 0$
    (C) $A^3 - 5A^2 + 9A - I = 0$
    (D) $5A^2 - 9A - I = 0$

31. If the characteristic equation of matrix A of order 2×2 is $\lambda^2 - 9\lambda - 1 = 0$. Then by Cayley Hamilton theorem, A^{-1} is equal to (2)
    (A) $A - 9I$
    (B) $A + 9I$
    (C) $-A - 9I$
    (D) $A^2 - 9A - I$

32. If the characteristic equation of matrix A of order 3×3 is $\lambda^3 - 3\lambda^2 + 3\lambda - 1 = 0$. Then by Cayley Hamilton theorem, A^{-1} is equal to (2)
    (A) $A^3 - 3A^2 + 3A - I$
    (B) $A^2 - 3A - 3I$
    (C) $3A^2 - 3A - I$
    (D) $A^2 - 3A + 3I$

33. Cayley Hamilton theorem is verified for the matrix $A = \begin{bmatrix} 1 & 1 & 0 \\ 0 & 0 & 1 \\ 2 & 1 & -1 \end{bmatrix}$, using (2)
    (A) $A^3 + 2A - I = 0$
    (B) $A^3 + 2A + I = 0$
    (C) $A^3 - 2A + I = 0$
    (D) $A^3 - 2A - I = 0$

34. Using Cayley Hamilton theorem, A^{-1} for the matrix $A = \begin{bmatrix} 1 & 4 \\ 2 & 3 \end{bmatrix}$ is calculated from (2)
    (A) $\frac{1}{5}(-A - 4I)$
    (B) $\frac{1}{5}(A - 4I)$
    (C) $\frac{1}{5}(A + 4I)$
    (D) $\frac{1}{5}(4I - A)$

35. Using Cayley Hamilton theorem, A^{-1} for the matrix $A = \begin{bmatrix} 1 & 2 \\ 1 & 1 \end{bmatrix}$ is calculated from (2)
    (A) $A + 2I$
    (B) $A - 2I$
    (C) $-A + 2I$
    (D) $-A - 2I$

36. Using Cayley Hamilton theorem, A^3 for the matrix $A = \begin{bmatrix} 1 & 4 \\ 2 & 3 \end{bmatrix}$ is calculated from (2)
    (A) $4A^2 + 5A$
    (B) $5A - 4A^2$
    (C) $-4A^2 - 5A$
    (D) $4A^2 - 5A$

37. If $\lambda^3 - 5\lambda^2 + 9\lambda - 1 = 0$ is characteristic equation of a matrix A then by Cayley Hamilton theorem, A^4 is calculated from (2)
    (A) $5A^3 - 9A^2 + A$
    (B) $5A^3 + 9A^2 + A$
    (C) $-5A^3 - 9A^2 - A$
    (D) $-9A^2 + A$

38. The given characteristic equation of matrix A of order 2×2 is $\lambda^2 - 3\lambda + 2 = 0$. Using Cayley Hamilton theorem, simplified expression of $A^3 - 3A^2 + 5A - 5I$ is (2)
    (A) $3A - 5I$
    (B) $-5A + 3I$
    (C) $5A - 3I$
    (D) none of these

39. The given characteristic equation of matrix A of order 3 × 3 is $\lambda^3 - 6\lambda^2 + 9\lambda - 4 = 0$. Using Cayley Hamilton theorem, simplified expression of $A^5 - 6A^4 + 9A^3 - 4A^2 + 5A - 3I$ is (2)

   (A) $5A + 3I$
   (B) $-5A + 3I$
   (C) $5A - 3I$
   (D) none of these

Answers

1. (A)	9. (B)	17. (B)	25. (A)	33. (D)
2. (A)	10. (C)	18. (D)	26. (C)	34. (B)
3. (B)	11. (D)	19. (B)	27. (A)	35. (B)
4. (C)	12. (D)	20. (B)	28. (C)	36. (A)
5. (B)	13. (C)	21. (C)	29. (D)	37. (A)
6. (A)	14. (C)	22. (D)	30. (C)	38. (A)
7. (A)	15. (D)	23. (A)	31. (A)	39. (C)
8. (C)	16. (D)	24. (A)	32. (D)	

3.20 MATRIX TRANSFORMATION

Matrix transformations, translational or rotational are used in Computer Aided Designs [CAD]. Computer graphics principles are applied for the generation of images of designs. The model of a design is represented using real valued numbers in two or three dimensions. The aim of computer graphics in CAD is to perform the transformation from design model to an efficient display. One of the major steps in the process is to map or transform the lines or curves from the coordinate system in which they are defined i.e. the model coordinate system to the coordinate system of the screen. It is also required to map or transform the vectors from the model coordinate system to the coordinate system of the display screen. The user may wish to show multiple views of the model on the same screen. This is achieved through the concepts of windows and viewports. The window is an imaginary rectangular frame of variable size or shape through which the user looks on to the model. The viewport is the area of the screen on which the contents of the window are displayed as an image. The general process of mapping or transformation from the model coordinate system to the screen coordinate system is known as viewing transformation. This transformation requires scaling, rotation and translation to be applied to the model coordinate definition of the picture. The windowing transformation is a particular case in which no rotation is applied.

Windowing transformation consists of scaling and translation.

Scaling : If (x, y, z) are the coordinates of a point P with reference to ox, oy, oz as coordinate axes (see Fig. 3.1) and (X, Y, Z) are the coordinates of a point P with reference to OX, OY, OZ as coordinate axes and if t is the scaling factor, then,

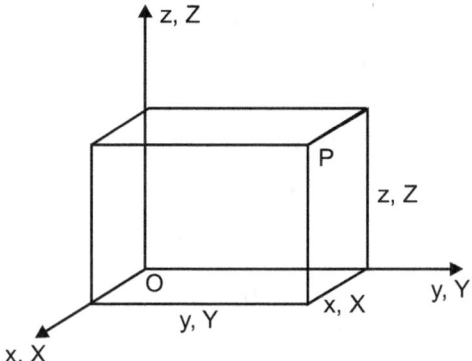

Fig. 3.1

$$X = tx$$
$$Y = ty \qquad \ldots (1)$$
$$Z = tz$$

or in matrix form

$$\begin{bmatrix} X \\ Y \\ Z \end{bmatrix} = \begin{bmatrix} t & 0 & 0 \\ 0 & t & 0 \\ 0 & 0 & t \end{bmatrix} \begin{bmatrix} x \\ y \\ z \end{bmatrix}$$

Translation : If (x, y, z) are the coordinates of the point P w.r.t. ox, oy, oz and (X, Y, Z) are the coordinates of the point P w.r.t. O'X, O'Y, O'Z (See Fig. 3.2), where O' has coordinates (dx, dy, dz) w.r.t. ox, oy, oz then,

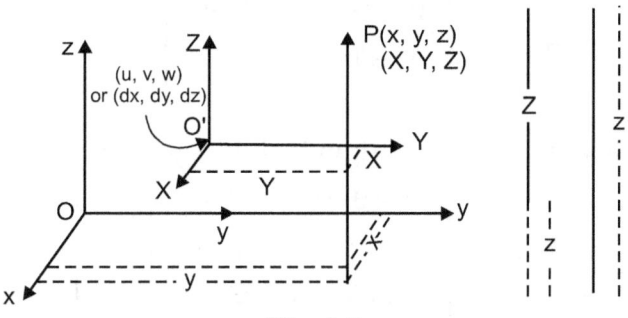

Fig. 3.2

$$X = x - dx \qquad X = x - u$$
$$Y = y - dy \quad \text{OR} \quad Y = y - v \qquad \ldots (2)$$
$$Z = z - dz \qquad Z = z - w$$

To express these relations in matrix transformation form, we use homogeneous coordinates.

This involves representing the position of a point w.r.t. ox, oy, oz by (ux, uy, uz, u) instead of (x, y, z) and instead of representing the point by (X, Y, Z), we represent it as (uX, uY, uZ, u) where the scale factor u is normally taken as unity. Now relations (2) can be written in matrix form as

$$\begin{bmatrix} X \\ Y \\ Z \\ 1 \end{bmatrix} = \begin{bmatrix} 1 & 0 & 0 & -dx \\ 0 & 1 & 0 & -dy \\ 0 & 0 & 1 & -dz \\ 0 & 0 & 0 & 1 \end{bmatrix} \begin{bmatrix} x \\ y \\ z \\ 1 \end{bmatrix}$$

OR
$$\begin{bmatrix} X \\ Y \\ Z \end{bmatrix} = \begin{bmatrix} 1 & 0 & 0 & -u \\ 0 & 1 & 0 & -v \\ 0 & 0 & 1 & w \\ 0 & 0 & 0 & 1 \end{bmatrix} \begin{bmatrix} x \\ y \\ z \\ 1 \end{bmatrix}$$

(1) If we combine the rotation about z-axis and translation then we get the new co-ordinates as [i.e. if the rotation is about z-axis by angle θ and origin is shifted to (u, v, w) then]

$$\begin{bmatrix} X \\ Y \\ Z \\ 1 \end{bmatrix} = \begin{bmatrix} \cos\theta & \sin\theta & 0 & -u \\ -\sin\theta & \cos\theta & 0 & -v \\ 0 & 0 & 1 & -w \\ 0 & 0 & 0 & 1 \end{bmatrix} \begin{bmatrix} x \\ y \\ z \\ 1 \end{bmatrix}$$

(2) If rotation is about x-axis and origin is shifted to (u v w) then

$$\begin{bmatrix} X \\ Y \\ Z \\ 1 \end{bmatrix} = \begin{bmatrix} 1 & 0 & 0 & -u \\ 0 & \cos\theta & \sin\theta & -v \\ 0 & -\sin\theta & \cos\theta & -w \\ 0 & 0 & 0 & 1 \end{bmatrix} \begin{bmatrix} x \\ y \\ z \\ 1 \end{bmatrix}$$

(3) If rotation is about y-axis and origin is shifted to (u, v, w) then

$$\begin{bmatrix} X \\ Y \\ Z \\ 1 \end{bmatrix} = \begin{bmatrix} \cos\theta & 0 & -\sin\theta & -u \\ 0 & 1 & 0 & -v \\ +\sin\theta & 0 & \cos\theta & -w \\ 0 & 0 & 0 & 1 \end{bmatrix} \begin{bmatrix} x \\ y \\ z \\ 1 \end{bmatrix}$$

Rotation :

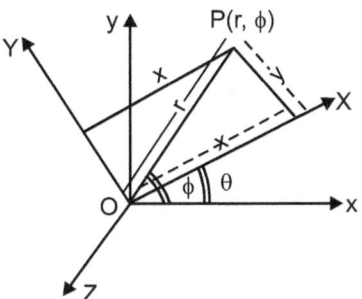

Fig. 3.3

Consider a point P whose coordinates w.r.t. ox, oy, oz are (x, y, z) and w.r.t. OX, OY, OZ are (X, Y, Z). Consider rotation taking place about the z-axis of the model coordinate system as shown in Fig. 3.3. It is clear that z coordinates in both systems will remain same.

Let (r, ϕ) be polar coordinates of the point P in xoy plane.

$$\therefore \quad x = r\cos\phi, \quad y = r\sin\phi \qquad \ldots (4)$$

If angle of rotation of the axes is θ, then

$$X = r\cos(\phi - \theta), \quad Y = r\sin(\phi - \theta)$$

$$\therefore \quad X = r[\cos\phi\cos\theta + \sin\phi\sin\theta] \qquad \ldots (5)$$

$$Y = r[\sin\phi\cos\theta - \cos\phi\sin\theta]$$

$$\therefore \quad X = (r\cos\phi)\cos\theta + (r\sin\phi)\sin\theta \qquad \ldots (6)$$

$$Y = (r\sin\phi)\cos\theta - (r\cos\phi)\sin\theta$$

$$\therefore \quad X = x\cos\theta + y\sin\theta \qquad \ldots (7)$$

$$Y = -x\sin\theta + y\cos\theta$$

$$Z = z \quad \text{[As rotation is about z-axis]}$$

Relation (7) can be put in matrix form as

$$\begin{bmatrix} X \\ Y \\ Z \end{bmatrix} = \begin{bmatrix} \cos\theta & \sin\theta & 0 \\ -\sin\theta & \cos\theta & 0 \\ 0 & 0 & 1 \end{bmatrix} \begin{bmatrix} x \\ y \\ z \end{bmatrix} \qquad \ldots (8)$$

Similarly, for rotation about x-axis, we shall obtain

$$X = x \qquad \ldots (9)$$

$$Y = y\cos\theta + z\sin\theta$$

$$Z = -y\sin\theta + z\cos\theta$$

or, in matrix form,

$$\begin{bmatrix} X \\ Y \\ Z \end{bmatrix} = \begin{bmatrix} 1 & 0 & 0 \\ 0 & \cos\theta & \sin\theta \\ 0 & -\sin\theta & \cos\theta \end{bmatrix} \begin{bmatrix} x \\ y \\ z \end{bmatrix} \quad \ldots (10)$$

And rotation about y-axis will give

$$Y = y$$
$$X = -z\sin\theta + x\cos\theta \quad \ldots (11)$$
$$Z = z\cos\theta + x\sin\theta$$

or, in matrix form,

$$\begin{bmatrix} X \\ Y \\ Z \end{bmatrix} = \begin{bmatrix} \cos\theta & 0 & -\sin\theta \\ 0 & 1 & 0 \\ \sin\theta & 0 & \cos\theta \end{bmatrix} \begin{bmatrix} x \\ y \\ z \end{bmatrix} \quad \ldots (12)$$

Ex. 1 : *Co-ordinates of a point P are (50, 50, 50). Origin is shifted to the point (5, –2, 3). Rotation is about z-axis through 45°. Find the co-ordinates of P in new co-ordinate system.*

Sol. : As the rotation is about z-axis and translation is (u, v, w), thus the rotation and translation together in matrix form is given by

$$\begin{bmatrix} X \\ Y \\ Z \\ 1 \end{bmatrix} = \begin{bmatrix} \cos\theta & \sin\theta & 0 & -u \\ -\sin\theta & \cos\theta & 0 & -v \\ 0 & 0 & 1 & -w \\ 0 & 0 & 0 & 1 \end{bmatrix} \begin{bmatrix} x \\ y \\ z \\ 1 \end{bmatrix}$$

Substituting x = 50, y = 50, z = 50, u = 5, v = –2, w = 3, θ = 45°, we get

$$\begin{bmatrix} X \\ Y \\ Z \\ 1 \end{bmatrix} = \begin{bmatrix} 1/\sqrt{2} & 1/\sqrt{2} & 0 & -5 \\ -1/\sqrt{2} & 1/\sqrt{2} & 0 & 2 \\ 0 & 0 & 1 & -3 \\ 0 & 0 & 0 & 1 \end{bmatrix} \begin{bmatrix} 50 \\ 50 \\ 50 \\ 1 \end{bmatrix}$$

Thus,

$$X = \frac{50}{\sqrt{2}} + \frac{50}{\sqrt{2}} + 0 - 5$$

$$Y = \frac{-50}{\sqrt{2}} + \frac{50}{\sqrt{2}} + 0 + 2$$

$$Z = 0 + 0 + 50 - 3$$

$$1 = 1$$

∴ $X = 65.71, Y = 2, Z = 47$.

Ex. 2 : *Centre of the arc of the circle is (10, 10, 0) in a given coordinate system. Origin is shifted to the point (2, 0, 0) along with coordinate axes and then rotation is carried about x-axis through 60°. Find the coordinates of the centre in new coordinate system.*

Sol. : Let (x, y, z) be the coordinates of the centre in old system and X, Y, Z be the coordinates of the centre in new system.

Using relations (10), (3) and homogeneous coordinates, we get, considering only rotation

$$\begin{bmatrix} X \\ Y \\ Z \\ 1 \end{bmatrix} = \begin{bmatrix} 1 & 0 & 0 & 0 \\ 0 & \cos 60° & \sin 60° & 0 \\ 0 & -\sin 60° & \cos 60° & 0 \\ 0 & 0 & 0 & 1 \end{bmatrix} \begin{bmatrix} x \\ y \\ z \\ 1 \end{bmatrix} \quad \ldots (1)$$

Considering only translation

or
$$\begin{bmatrix} X \\ Y \\ Z \\ 1 \end{bmatrix} = \begin{bmatrix} 1 & 0 & 0 & -2 \\ 0 & 1 & 0 & 0 \\ 0 & 0 & 1 & 0 \\ 0 & 0 & 0 & 1 \end{bmatrix} \begin{bmatrix} x \\ y \\ z \\ 1 \end{bmatrix} \quad \ldots (2)$$

Combining transformations (1) and (2),

$$\begin{bmatrix} X \\ Y \\ Z \\ 1 \end{bmatrix} = \begin{bmatrix} 1 & 0 & 0 & -2 \\ 0 & 0.50 & 0.866 & 0 \\ 0 & -0.866 & 0.5 & 0 \\ 0 & 0 & 0 & 1 \end{bmatrix} \begin{bmatrix} x \\ y \\ z \\ 1 \end{bmatrix} \quad \ldots (3)$$

Now putting x = 10, y = 10, z = 0 in (3) and simplifying, we get,

$$X = 10 - 2 = 8$$

$$Y = 5$$

$$Z = -8.66$$

∴   Coordinates of centre in new system are (8, 5, – 8.66).

Ex. 3 : *Centre of arc of the circle is (10, 10, 10). Origin is (0, 0, 0), rotation is about through an angle 60°. Find the centre of arc of the circle in new co-ordinate system.*

Sol. : As the rotation is about x-axis, thus

$$\begin{bmatrix} X \\ Y \\ Z \end{bmatrix} = \begin{bmatrix} 1 & 0 & 0 \\ 0 & \cos\theta & \sin\theta \\ 0 & -\sin\theta & \cos\theta \end{bmatrix} \begin{bmatrix} x \\ y \\ z \end{bmatrix}$$

Given : $x = 10, y = 10, z = 10$ and $\theta = 60°$

As the origin is (0, 0, 0),

$$\begin{bmatrix} X \\ Y \\ Z \end{bmatrix} = \begin{bmatrix} 1 & 0 & 0 \\ 0 & \cos 60 & \sin 60 \\ 0 & -\sin 60 & \cos 60 \end{bmatrix} \begin{bmatrix} 10 \\ 10 \\ 10 \end{bmatrix}$$

$$\begin{bmatrix} X \\ Y \\ Z \end{bmatrix} = \begin{bmatrix} 1 & 0 & 0 \\ 0 & 1/2 & \sqrt{3}/2 \\ 0 & -\sqrt{3}/2 & 1/2 \end{bmatrix} \begin{bmatrix} 10 \\ 10 \\ 10 \end{bmatrix}$$

$X = 10, Y = 13.66, Z = -3.66$

EXERCISE 3.8

1. Coordinates of a point P are (50, 50, 50). Origin is shifted to the point (5, –2, 3) with axes transferred parallel to themselves. Rotation is carried out about z-axis through 45°. Find the coordinates of the point P in new coordinate system.
   [Ans. (65.7, 2, 47)]

2. Centre of the arc of the circle in a given coordinate system is (100, 100, 100). Origin is shifted to the point (–10, –5, 2). Rotation is carried out about y-axis through an angle of 30°. Find the centre of the arc of the circle in new coordinate system. **[Ans. (46.66, 105, 134.66)]**

   Note : The use of homogeneous coordinates has many applications in computer graphics, in addition to the generations of viewing transformations, already discussed. Translational and rotational transformations are also very useful in robotics and in mechanisms analysis. Discussion of these usages is beyond the scope of this work.

3. Centre of the arc of the circle is (10, 10, 10) in a given co-ordinate system. Origin (0 0 0) and then rotation is carried about x-axis through 60°. Find the co-ordinates of centre in the new co-ordinate system. **[Ans. (10, 5, – 8.66)]**

4. Centre of the arc of the circle is (10, 10, 10). Origin is shifted to the point (2, 0, 0) along with co-ordinate axes and then rotation is carried out about x-axis through 60°. Find co-ordinates of the centre in new co-ordinate system.
   [Ans. (8, 5, – 8.66)]

5. Centre of arc of the circle in a given co-ordinate system is (100, 100, 100). Origin is shifted to the point (–10, –5, 2). Rotation is carried out about y-axis through an angle of 30°. Find the centre in new co-ordinate system. **[Ans. (46.66, 105, 134.76)]**

CHAPTER FOUR

COMPLEX NUMBERS

4.1 INTRODUCTION

Study of complex numbers becomes essential to Engineering students, because of their frequent occurrence in problems dealing with electrical circuits, mechanical vibrating systems, etc.

Complex numbers are encountered in the solution of an algebraic equation $ax^2 + bx + c = 0$ (where a, b, c are real numbers). The solution of such an equation is given by

$$x = \frac{-b \pm \sqrt{b^2 - 4ac}}{2a}$$

The real number system cannot explain the solution for the case $b^2 < 4ac$ as it involves a negative quantity (or a negative real number) under the radical sign. Since the square of a real number (positive or negative) is a positive real number, therefore, the square root of a negative real number is termed as an imaginary number (there is no real number whose square is negative).

For example, $\sqrt{-2}$, $\sqrt{-3.5}$, $\sqrt{-4}$, etc. are all imaginary numbers. If we introduce an entity $i = \sqrt{-1}$ and postulate that $i^2 = -1$, the above imaginary numbers can be written as

$$\sqrt{-2} = \sqrt{(-1) \times (2)} = \sqrt{(-1)} \times \sqrt{(2)} = i\sqrt{2}$$
$$\sqrt{-4} = \sqrt{(-1) \times (4)} = \sqrt{(-1)} \times \sqrt{(4)} = i\,2$$

In general, we can write

$$\sqrt{-a^2} = \sqrt{(-1) \times (a^2)} = \sqrt{(-1)} \times \sqrt{(a)^2} = i\,a$$

Combination of real and imaginary numbers constitute the complex number system.

In this chapter, we shall develop the algebra and geometry of complex numbers and study their properties.

4.2 DEFINITION

A number of the form $x + iy$, where x, y are any real numbers is defined as a complex number.

If $z = x + iy$, then x is called real part of z and y is called the imaginary part of z and are denoted by Re (z) = x, Im (z) = y.

If $x = 0$ and $y \neq 0$, then $z = 0 + iy = iy$ is called purely imaginary number.

If $x \neq 0$ and $y = 0$, then $z = x + i0 = x$ is a real number. Because of this property the complex number system is considered as an extension of real number system.

4.3 ALGEBRA OF COMPLEX NUMBERS

In performing operations with complex numbers, we can proceed as in the algebra of real numbers, replacing i^2 by -1 when it occurs.

If $z_1 = x_1 + iy_1$ and $z_2 = x_2 + iy_2$ are any two complex numbers, we define following rules and laws of operations.

1. **Equality :** Two complex numbers z_1 and z_2 are said to be equal if and only if their corresponding real and imaginary parts are equal, i.e. if $x_1 = x_2$ and $y_1 = y_2$.

2. **Addition :**
$$z_1 + z_2 = (x_1 + iy_1) + (x_2 + iy_2) = (x_1 + x_2) + i(y_1 + y_2)$$

3. **Subtraction :**
$$z_1 - z_2 = (x_1 + iy_1) - (x_2 + iy_2) = (x_1 - x_2) + i(y_1 - y_2)$$

4. **Multiplication :**
$$z_1 \cdot z_2 = (x_1 + iy_1) \cdot (x_2 + iy_2) = (x_1 x_2 - y_1 y_2) + i(x_1 y_2 + y_1 x_2)$$

5. **Division :**
$$\frac{z_1}{z_2} = \frac{(x_1 + iy_1)}{(x_2 + iy_2)} = \frac{(x_1 + iy_1)}{(x_2 + iy_2)} \cdot \frac{(x_2 - iy_2)}{(x_2 - iy_2)}$$
$$= \frac{(x_1 x_2 + y_1 y_2)}{\left(x_2^2 + y_2^2\right)} + i \frac{(y_1 x_2 - x_1 y_2)}{\left(x_2^2 + y_2^2\right)}$$

6. **Commutative law of Addition and Multiplication :**
$$z_1 + z_2 = z_2 + z_1, \qquad z_1 z_2 = z_2 z_1$$

7. **Associative law of Addition and Multiplication :**
$$z_1 + (z_2 + z_3) = (z_1 + z_2) + (z_3) \qquad \text{(where } z_3 = x_3 + iy_3\text{)}$$
$$z_1 (z_2 z_3) = (z_1 z_2) z_3$$

8. **Distributive law :**
$$z_1 (z_2 + z_3) = z_1 z_2 + z_1 z_3$$

4.4 GRAPHICAL OR GEOMETRICAL REPRESENTATION OF COMPLEX NUMBERS (ARGAND DIAGRAM)

Let $z = x + iy$ be a complex number. It can be uniquely determined by order pair (x, y) of real numbers. Since there exists one-one correspondence between the ordered pairs of real numbers and point on the plane, every complex number can be represented by a unique point $P(x, y)$ (Fig. 4.1) with reference to rectangular axes X'OX and Y'OY. Complex numbers of the form $x + i0$ (i.e. real numbers) are represented by points $(x, 0)$ on the x-axis which is called real axis. Complex numbers of the form $0 + iy$ (i.e purely imaginary numbers) are represented by points $(0, y)$ on the y-axis which is called imaginary axis.

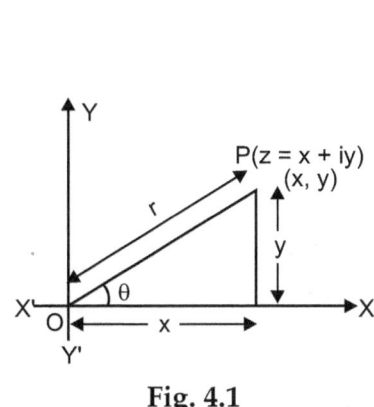

Fig. 4.1

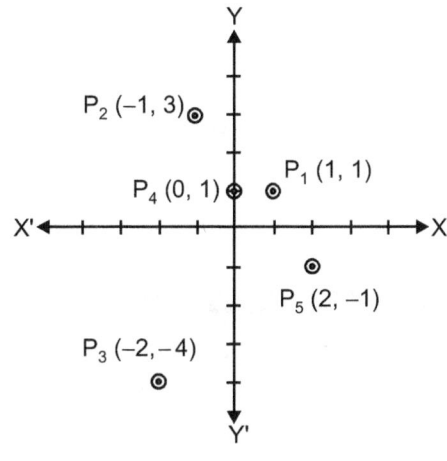

Fig. 4.2

As an illustration, the complex numbers $z_1 = 1 + i$, $z_2 = -1 + 3i$, $z_3 = -2 - 4i$, $z_4 = i$ and $z_5 = 2 - i$ are represented by the points $P_1(1, 1)$, $P_2(-1, 3)$, $P_3(-2, -4)$, $P_4(0, 1)$ and $P_5(2, -1)$ respectively (Fig. 4.2). The method of representing complex numbers by points in a plane was introduced by J.R. Argand and such representation is called *Argand diagram*.

A complex number $z = x + iy$ can also be represented by the vector **OP** whose initial point is the origin and whose terminal point P is the point (x, y).

Here after we shall refer to the complex number $z = x + iy$ as

(1) the point z whose co-ordinates are (x, y)

(2) the vector **OP** from O to P(x, y).

4.5 COMPLEX CONJUGATE NUMBERS

The complex conjugate, or simply the conjugate, of a complex number $z = x + iy$ is defined as the number $\bar{z} = x - iy$.

For example, the conjugate of $z = 5 + 2i$ is $\bar{z} = 5 - 2i$ (Fig. 4.3), which is the reflection of the point z in the x-axis.

Furthermore, by addition and subtraction, we obtain the relationships $z + \bar{z} = 2x$ and $z - \bar{z} = 2iy$. This yields the important formulae :

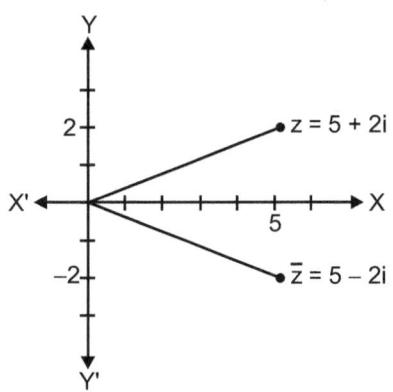

Fig. 4.3

$$\text{Re}(z) = \frac{1}{2}(z+\bar{z}), \qquad \text{Im}(z) = \frac{1}{2i}(z-\bar{z})$$

We also have,
$$\overline{(z_1+z_2)} = \bar{z}_1+\bar{z}_2, \qquad \overline{(z_1-z_2)} = \bar{z}_1-\bar{z}_2$$

$$\overline{z_1 z_2} = \bar{z}_1 \bar{z}_2, \qquad \overline{\left(\frac{z_1}{z_2}\right)} = \frac{\bar{z}_1}{\bar{z}_2}$$

4.6 ABSOLUTE VALUE

The absolute value, or the modulus of a complex number $z = x + iy$ is defined by non-negative real number $\sqrt{x^2+y^2}$ and is denoted by $|z|$.

Thus $\qquad |z| = \sqrt{x^2+y^2} = \sqrt{z\bar{z}} \ (\geq 0)$

For example, $\quad |-4+2i| = \sqrt{(-4)^2+(2)^2} = \sqrt{20} = 2\sqrt{5}$

Geometrically, $|z|$ is the distance of the point $P(x, y)$ from the origin. Consequently, $|z_1 - z_2|$ is the distance between the points z_1 and z_2. This is also evident from the definition, since

$$|z_1-z_2| = |(x_1-x_2)+i(y_1-y_2)| = \sqrt{(x_1-x_2)^2+(y_1-y_2)^2}$$

For example, the condition $|z-i| = 5$ requires that the point z to be on the circle of radius 5 with centre at (0, 1).

The statement $|z_1| > |z_2|$ means that the point z_1 is farther from the origin than the point z_2 because absolute values are real numbers. However, the statement $z_1 > z_2$ or $z_1 < z_2$ are meangingless, unless z_1 and z_2 are both real.

4.7 POLAR FORM OF COMPLEX NUMBERS

In Article 4.4 we have seen that complex number $z = x + iy$ can be represented by the point whose cartesian co-ordinates are (x, y). Since the point P in a plane is also associated with the numbers (r, θ) called polar co-ordinates of the point P, where $x = r \cos \theta, y = r \sin \theta$ (Fig. 4.1).

We can write $z = x + iy = r(\cos \theta + i \sin \theta)$ where $x = r \cos \theta$ and $y = r \sin \theta$. Squaring and adding we get $x^2 + y^2 = r^2$ or $r = \sqrt{x^2+y^2}$. The non-negative square root of $x^2 + y^2$ is defined as modulus of the complex number z and is denoted by the symbol $|z|$. Thus we have $|z| = r = \sqrt{x^2+y^2}$.

Again $\qquad \dfrac{y}{x} = \dfrac{r \sin \theta}{r \cos \theta} = \tan \theta \quad \therefore \quad \theta = \tan^{-1}\left(\dfrac{y}{x}\right)$

Angle θ is called the amplitude or argument of the complex number z and we write
$$\text{amp}(z) = \theta \quad \text{or} \quad \arg(z) = \theta$$

θ is determined from the relations

$$\cos \theta = \frac{x}{r} \quad \text{and} \quad \sin \theta = \frac{y}{r} \quad \text{where } r = \sqrt{x^2+y^2}$$

Thus if $z \neq 0$, the value of arg $(z) = \theta$ can be found from equations $\cos \theta = x/r$, $\sin \theta = y/r$. Arg (z) is multivalued function, since the trignometric functions $\cos \theta$ and $\sin \theta$ both have the period 2π radians, and so we could also write

$$z = r(\cos \theta + i \sin \theta) = r\{\cos(\theta + 2n\pi) + i \sin(\theta + 2n\pi)\} \quad \text{for } n = 0, 1, 2, \ldots$$

Geometrically, if OP (Fig. 4.1) be turned in an anticlockwise direction through multiples of angles 2π, the points P(x, y) for all such rotations, will have the same position as before and hence for all such positions of OP, the point P always represents the same complex number.

Hence arg $(z) = \theta + 2n\pi$, $n = 0, 1, 2, \ldots$ where $\theta + 2n\pi$ is known as *general value of amplitude* of z and the value θ that lies between $-\pi$ to π is called *principal value of the amplitude*.

For $z \neq 0$, we can also determine arg (z) from the formula $\theta = \arg(z) = \tan^{-1}\dfrac{y}{x}$ and knowing quadrant in which z lies. We must pay attention to the quadrant, since $\tan \theta$ has period π and not 2π, so that the arg (z) and arg $(-z)$ have the same tangent. For example, if $\theta_1 = \arg(1 + i)$ and $\theta_2 = \arg(-1 - i)$, then we have $\tan \theta_1 = \tan \theta_2 = 1$.

As an illustration let us express the numbers (i) $1 \pm i$, (ii) $1 \pm \sqrt{3}\, i$ in the form $r(\cos \theta + i \sin \theta)$.

(i) Let $\quad 1 + i = r(\cos \theta + i \sin \theta)$

By equating real and imaginary parts, we get

$$r \cos \theta = 1, \quad r \sin \theta = 1 \quad \therefore \quad r = \sqrt{2}$$

and $\quad \cos \theta = \dfrac{1}{\sqrt{2}}, \quad \sin \theta = \dfrac{1}{\sqrt{2}} \quad \therefore \quad \theta = \dfrac{\pi}{4}$

Here $\quad |1 + i| = r = \sqrt{2}$ and Amp $(1 + i) = \dfrac{\pi}{4}$

Now $\quad 1 - i = r(\cos \theta + i \sin \theta)$ gives

$$r \cos \theta = 1, \quad r \sin \theta = -1 \quad \therefore \quad r = \sqrt{2}$$

and $\quad \cos \theta = \dfrac{1}{\sqrt{2}}, \quad \sin \theta = \dfrac{-1}{\sqrt{2}} \quad \therefore \quad \theta = -\dfrac{\pi}{4}$

Since θ lies in the fourth quadrant and $\cos\left(-\dfrac{\pi}{4}\right) = \cos\left(\dfrac{\pi}{4}\right) = \dfrac{1}{\sqrt{2}}$

$$\sin\left(-\dfrac{\pi}{4}\right) = -\sin\dfrac{\pi}{4} = \dfrac{-1}{\sqrt{2}}$$

Thus $\quad 1 - i = \sqrt{2}\left\{\cos\left(\dfrac{-\pi}{4}\right) + i \sin\left(\dfrac{-\pi}{4}\right)\right\} = \sqrt{2}\left\{\cos\dfrac{\pi}{4} - i \sin\dfrac{\pi}{4}\right\}$

$\therefore \quad 1 \pm i = \sqrt{2}\left\{\cos\dfrac{\pi}{4} \pm i \sin\dfrac{\pi}{4}\right\}$

(ii) Let $1 + i\sqrt{3} = r(\cos\theta + i\sin\theta)$

$\therefore \quad r\cos\theta = 1, \quad r\sin\theta = \sqrt{3} \quad \therefore \quad r = 2$

and $\cos\theta = \dfrac{1}{2}, \quad \sin\theta = \dfrac{\sqrt{3}}{2} \quad \therefore \quad \theta = \dfrac{\pi}{3}$

$\therefore \quad 1 + i\sqrt{3} = 2\left(\cos\dfrac{\pi}{3} + i\sin\dfrac{\pi}{3}\right)$

Similarly, we can establish that

$$1 - i\sqrt{3} = 2\left\{\cos\left(\dfrac{-\pi}{3}\right) + i\sin\left(\dfrac{-\pi}{3}\right)\right\} = 2\left\{\cos\dfrac{\pi}{3} - i\sin\dfrac{\pi}{3}\right\}$$

As an exercise, students are advised to express the numbers $-1 + i, -1 - i, -1 - i\sqrt{3}$ in the form $r(\cos\theta + i\sin\theta)$.

Remark : Principal value of argument :

For $z \neq 0$, we determine principal value of argument using formula $\theta = \arg(z) = \tan^{-1}\dfrac{y}{x}$ and knowing quadrant in which z lies.

The formula $\theta = \tan^{-1}\left(\dfrac{y}{x}\right)$ is applicable only if x and y both are positive. Depending upon the quadrant in which complex number z [i.e. point (x, y)] lies, following formulae can be used to determine $\arg(z)$.

(1) First quadrant (i.e. if $x > 0, y > 0$) :

$$\theta = \arg(z) = \tan^{-1}\left(\dfrac{y}{x}\right)$$

(2) Second quadrant (i.e. if $x < 0, y > 0$) :

$$\theta = \arg(z) = \pi - \tan^{-1}\left(\left|\dfrac{y}{x}\right|\right)$$

(3) Third quadrant (i.e. if $x < 0, y < 0$) :

$$\theta = \arg(z) = \tan^{-1}\left(\left|\dfrac{y}{x}\right|\right) \pm \pi$$

(4) Fouth quadrant (i.e. if $x > 0, y < 0$) :

$$\theta = \arg(z) = -\tan^{-1}\left(\left|\dfrac{y}{x}\right|\right)$$

We also note that

(i) If z lies in first or second quadrant then $0 \leq \theta \leq \pi$.

(ii) If z lies in third or fourth quadrant then $-\pi < \theta < 0$.

4.8 EXPONENTIAL FORM OF COMPLEX NUMBER

When x is a real, we know that

$$e^x = 1 + x + \frac{x^2}{2!} + \frac{x^3}{3!} + \frac{x^4}{4!} + \ldots \ldots \quad \ldots (1)$$

$$\cos x = 1 - \frac{x^2}{2!} + \frac{x^4}{4!} - \frac{x^6}{6!} + \ldots \ldots \quad \ldots (2)$$

$$\sin x = x - \frac{x^3}{3!} + \frac{x^5}{5!} - \frac{x^7}{7!} + \ldots \ldots \quad \ldots (3)$$

Assuming that this is true for all values of x (real or complex) replacing x by ix in (1), we get

$$e^{ix} = 1 + ix + \frac{i^2 x^2}{2!} + \frac{i^3 x^3}{3!} + \frac{i^4 x^4}{4!} + \ldots \ldots$$

$$e^{ix} = \left(1 - \frac{x^2}{2!} + \frac{x^4}{4!} \ldots\right) + i\left(x - \frac{x^3}{3!} + \frac{x^5}{5!} \ldots\right) \quad \left\{\begin{array}{l} \because i^2 = -1,\; i^3 = -i \\ i^4 = 1,\; i^5 = i \end{array}\right.$$

$$e^{ix} = \cos x + i \sin x \quad \ldots (4)$$

Similarly, $\quad e^{-ix} = \cos x - i \sin x \quad \ldots (5)$

These are known as **Euler's Formulae.**

Thus the complex number z has following forms :

$$z = x + iy \text{ (Cartesian form)}$$
$$= r(\cos\theta + i\sin\theta) \text{ (Polar form)}$$
$$= r e^{i\theta} \text{ (Exponential form)}$$

As an illustration, let us express the following numbers into real and imaginary parts.

(i) $e^{5 + i\pi/2}$ (ii) $e^{(5+3i)^2}$

(i) Let $\quad z = e^{5+i\pi/2} = e^5\left[\cos\frac{\pi}{2} + i\sin\frac{\pi}{2}\right] = e^5(0 + i) = i e^5$

$\therefore \quad$ Re (z) = 0, $\quad$ Im (z) = e^5

(ii) Let $\quad z = e^{(5+3i)^2} = e^{(25 + 9i^2 + 30i)} = e^{16 + 30i} = e^{16}(\cos 30 + i \sin 30)$

$\therefore \quad$ Re (z) = $e^{16} \cos 30$, $\quad$ Im (z) = $e^{16} \sin 30$

4.9 GRAPHICAL (GEOMETRICAL) REPRESENTATION OF $z_1 + z_2$

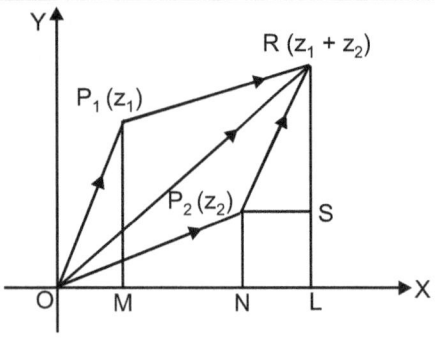

Fig. 4.4

In Fig. 4.4, P_1, P_2 represent the complex numbers $z_1 = x_1 + iy_1$, $z_2 = x_2 + iy_2$ respectively. Complete the parallelogram OP_1RP_2. Draw P_1M, P_2N, RL perpendiculars on X-axis and P_2S perpendicular on RL.

Since P_1, P_2 represent $z_1 = x_1 + iy_1$ & $z_2 = x_2 + iy_2$ respectively. Also $OM = x_1$, $MP_1 = y_1$, $ON = x_2$, $NP_2 = y_2$ and $OL = OM + ML$.

Now ML is the projection of P_1R on x-axis which is equal to ON the projection of OP_2 on X-axis.

∴ $OL = OM + ON = x_1 + x_2$

Similarly $LR = LS + SR$

$= NP_2 + MP_1$ [$SR = MP_1$ by reasoning as before]

$= y_2 + y_1$

Thus R will have cartesian coordinates $(x_1 + x_2, y_1 + y_2)$ and therefore point R or vector **OR** will represent the complex number

$$z_1 + z_2 = (x_1 + iy_1) + (x_2 + iy_2)$$
$$= (x_1 + x_2) + i(y_1 + y_2)$$

The parallelogram law of vectors is valid in complex number addition, for

$$OR = OP_1 + P_1R = OP_1 + OP_2$$

The operation of subtraction is also evident from Fig. 4.4.

$$P_1R = OR - OP_1 = z_1 + z_2 - z_1 = z_2$$

But $P_1R = OP_2 = z_2$

Thus z_2 is obtained by subtracting z_1 from $z_1 + z_2$.

4.10 GRAPHICAL (GEOMETRICAL) REPRESENTATION OF $z_1 \cdot z_2$

Let $z_1 = x_1 + iy_1 = r_1(\cos\theta_1 + i\sin\theta_1)$

and $z_2 = x_2 + iy_2 = r_2(\cos\theta_2 + \sin\theta_2)$

∴ $z_1 \cdot z_2 = r_1 \cdot r_2 \{(\cos\theta_1 + i\sin\theta_1)(\cos\theta_2 + i\sin\theta_2)\}$

$= r_1 \cdot r_2 \{(\cos\theta_1 \cos\theta_2 - \sin\theta_1 \sin\theta_2) + i(\sin\theta_1 \cos\theta_2 + \cos\theta_1 \sin\theta_2)\}$

$= r_1 \cdot r_2 \{\cos(\theta_1 + \theta_2) + i\sin(\theta_1 + \theta_2)\}$

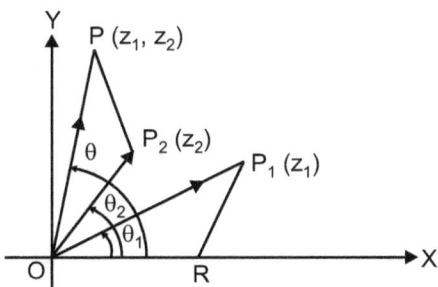

Fig. 4.5

Thus $|z_1 \cdot z_2| = r_1 r_2$ and $\text{Amp}(z_1 \cdot z_2) = \theta_1 + \theta_2$

$\therefore \quad \text{Amp}(z_1 \cdot z_2) = \text{Amp}(z_1) + \text{Amp}(z_2)$

In Fig. 4.5, P_1 represents $z_1 = r_1(\cos\theta_1 + i\sin\theta_1)$ and P_2 represents $z_2 = r_2(\cos\theta_2 + i\sin\theta_1)$. So that, $OP_1 = r_1$, $OP_2 = r_2$. Let $OR = 1$. Construct the triangle OP_2P similar to the triangle ORP_1 such that $\angle ORP_1 = \angle OP_2P$ & $\angle P_1OR = \angle POP_2 = \theta_1$.

We will establish that the point P represents $z_1 z_2$.

Let P represent $z = r(\cos\theta + i\sin\theta)$. From the similarity of triangles ORP_1 and OP_2P,

$$\frac{OP}{OP_1} = \frac{OP_2}{OR} \quad \text{i.e.} \quad \frac{r}{r_1} = \frac{r_2}{1} \qquad \therefore \; r = r_1 r_2$$

Thus $\quad |z| = r = r_1 r_2 = |z_1||z_2|$

Also $\quad \theta = \angle POX = \angle POP_2 + \angle P_2OX$

But $\quad \angle POP_2 = \angle P_1OR = \theta_1$ and $\angle P_2OX = \theta_2 \qquad \therefore \; \theta = \theta_1 + \theta_2$

OR $\quad \text{Amp}(z) = \text{Amp}(z_1) + \text{Amp}(z_2)$

Hence, P represents $z_1 z_2$.

Hence the product of the complex number is a complex number whose modulus is the product of their moduli and whose amplitude is the sum of their amplitudes.

Remark : The effect of multiplying complex number z_1 by z_2 is to turn the position vector $OP_1(z_1)$ through an angle θ_2 (i.e. by principal value of amplitude of z_2) and alter its length by the multiplying factor r_2.

4.11 GRAPHICAL (GEOMETRICAL) REPRESENTATION OF $\dfrac{z_1}{z_2}$

As before, let $z_1 = r_1(\cos\theta_1 + i\sin\theta_1)$ and $z_2 = r_2(\cos\theta_2 + i\sin\theta_2)$

$\therefore$
$$\frac{z_1}{z_2} = \frac{r_1(\cos\theta_1 + i\sin\theta_1)}{r_2(\cos\theta_2 + i\sin\theta_2)} = \frac{r_1}{r_2} \frac{(\cos\theta_1 + i\sin\theta_1)(\cos\theta_2 - i\sin\theta_2)}{(\cos\theta_2 + i\sin\theta_2)(\cos\theta_2 - i\sin\theta_2)}$$

$$= \frac{r_1}{r_2}\left[\frac{(\cos\theta_1\cos\theta_2 + \sin\theta_1\sin\theta_2) + i(\sin\theta_1\cos\theta_2 - \cos\theta_1\sin\theta_2)}{\cos^2\theta_2 + \sin^2\theta_2}\right]$$

$$= \frac{r_1}{r_2}[\cos(\theta_1 - \theta_2) + i\sin(\theta_1 - \theta_2)]$$

Thus $\left|\dfrac{z_1}{z_2}\right| = \dfrac{r_1}{r_2} = \dfrac{|z_1|}{|z_2|}$

and $\text{Amp}\left(\dfrac{z_1}{z_2}\right) = \theta_1 - \theta_2 = \text{Amp}(z_1) - \text{Amp}(z_2)$

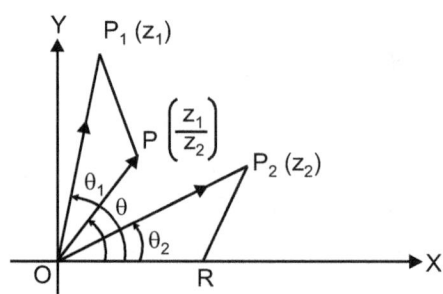

Fig. 4.6

In Fig. 4.6, P_1 represents z_1 and P_2 represents z_2 so that $OP_1 = r_1$ and $OP_2 = r_2$ such that $\angle P_1OX = \theta_1$, $\angle P_2OX = \theta_2$. Let $OR = 1$. Construct the triangle $\Delta\, OP_1P$ similar to $\Delta\, OP_2R$ such that $\angle OP_1P = \angle OP_2R$ and $\angle P_1OP = \angle P_2OR = \theta_2$

It will be shown that P represents $\dfrac{z_1}{z_2}$.

Let P represent $z = r(\cos\theta + i\sin\theta)$ then $OP = r$ and $\angle POX = \theta$.

From the similar triangles OP_1P and OP_2R,

$$\dfrac{OP}{OR} = \dfrac{OP_1}{OP_2} \text{ i.e. } \dfrac{r}{1} = \dfrac{r_1}{r_2} \qquad \therefore r = \dfrac{r_1}{r_2}$$

Thus $|z| = r = \dfrac{r_1}{r_2} = \dfrac{|z_1|}{|z_2|}$

Also $\angle P_1OX = \angle P_1OP + \angle POX$

i.e. $\theta_1 = \theta_2 + \theta$ $\qquad \therefore \theta = \theta_1 - \theta_2$

or $\text{Amp } z = \text{Amp } z_1 - \text{Amp } z_2$

which shows that P represents $\dfrac{z_1}{z_2}$.

Hence the modulus of the quotient of two complex numbers is the quotient of their moduli and amplitude of the quotient is the difference of their amplitudes.

Remark : The effect of division of z_1 by z_2 is to turn the position vector $OP_1(z_1)$ through an angle θ_2 in clockwise direction and alter its length by the multiplying factor $\dfrac{1}{r_2}$.

Some Useful Results :

(1) $(\cos \alpha + i \sin \alpha)(\cos \beta + i \sin \beta) = \cos(\alpha + \beta) + i \sin(\alpha + \beta)$

(2) $\dfrac{\cos \alpha + i \sin \alpha}{\cos \beta + i \sin \beta} = \cos(\alpha - \beta) + i \sin(\alpha - \beta)$

(3) $\dfrac{1}{\cos \theta + i \sin \theta} = \cos \theta - i \sin \theta$

(4) $\dfrac{1}{\cos \theta - i \sin \theta} = \cos \theta + i \sin \theta$

(5) $\dfrac{1}{i} = -i$.

4.12 ILLUSTRATIONS ON BASIC DEFINITIONS

Ex. 1 : *Find the modulus and amplitude (argument) of* $\dfrac{(3 - i\sqrt{2})^2}{1 + 2i}$.

Sol. :
$$\dfrac{(3 - i\sqrt{2})^2}{1 + 2i} = \dfrac{9 - 2 - (6\sqrt{2})i}{1 + 2i} = \dfrac{(7 - 6\sqrt{2}\,i)}{(1 + 2i)} \cdot \dfrac{(1 - 2i)}{(1 - 2i)}$$

$$= \dfrac{(7 - 12\sqrt{2}) - i(6\sqrt{2} + 14)}{5} = x + iy \text{ say}$$

$\therefore \quad$ Modulus $= \sqrt{x^2 + y^2} = \sqrt{\left(\dfrac{7 - 12\sqrt{2}}{5}\right)^2 + \left(\dfrac{6\sqrt{2} + 14}{5}\right)^2}$

$$= \dfrac{11\sqrt{5}}{5}$$

and $\quad$ Amplitude $= \tan^{-1}\dfrac{y}{x} = \tan^{-1}\left(\dfrac{6\sqrt{2} + 14}{12\sqrt{2} - 7}\right)$.

[Note that θ lies in the third quadrant.]

Ex. 2 : *Find the modulus and amplitude of the following :*

(a) $\tan \alpha - i$, (b) $1 - \cos \alpha + i \sin \alpha$.

Sol. : (a) Let $z = \tan \alpha - i = \dfrac{\sin \alpha}{\cos \alpha} - i = \dfrac{1}{\cos \alpha}(\sin \alpha - i \cos \alpha)$

$$= \sec \alpha \left[\cos\left(\dfrac{\pi}{2} - \alpha\right) - i \sin\left(\dfrac{\pi}{2} - \alpha\right)\right]$$

$$= \sec \alpha \left[\cos\left(\alpha - \dfrac{\pi}{2}\right) + i \sin\left(\alpha - \dfrac{\pi}{2}\right)\right]$$

$$= r[\cos \theta + i \sin \theta]$$

$\therefore \quad$ Modulus $z = r = \sec \alpha$ and Amplitude $z = \theta = \alpha - \dfrac{\pi}{2}$

(b) Let $z = 1 - \cos \alpha + i \sin \alpha = 2 \sin^2 \alpha/2 + 2i \sin \alpha/2 \cos \alpha/2$

$$= 2 \sin \alpha/2 \, (\sin \alpha/2 + i \cos \alpha/2)$$

$$= 2 \sin \alpha/2 \, [\cos(\pi/2 - \alpha/2) + i \sin(\pi/2 - \alpha/2)]$$

∴ Modulus $z = 2 \sin \alpha/2$ and Amplitude $z = \pi/2 - \alpha/2$.

Ex. 3 : *If x and y are real, solve the equation* $\dfrac{iy}{ix+1} - \dfrac{3y+4i}{3x+y} = 0$.

Sol. : $\dfrac{iy}{(ix+1)} - \dfrac{(3y+4i)}{(3x+y)} = \dfrac{iy(3x+y) - (3y+4i)(ix+1)}{(ix+1)(3x+y)}$

$$= \dfrac{(-3y+4x) + i(3xy + y^2 - 3xy - 4)}{(ix+1)(3x+y)} = 0, \text{ (given)}$$

∴ $(-3y + 4x) = 0$ and $(y^2 - 4) = 0$

∴ $x = \pm \dfrac{3}{2}, \quad y = \pm 2$

Ex. 4 : *Find z if $|z+i| = |z|$ and* $\arg\left(\dfrac{z+i}{z}\right) = \dfrac{\pi}{4}$. **(Dec. 2006)**

Sol. : We have $\left|\dfrac{z+i}{z}\right| = 1$ and $\arg\left(\dfrac{z+i}{z}\right) = \dfrac{\pi}{4}$

∴ $\dfrac{z+i}{z} = \cos\dfrac{\pi}{4} + i \sin\dfrac{\pi}{4}$

∴ $z + i = z\left(\cos\dfrac{\pi}{4} + i \sin\dfrac{\pi}{4}\right)$

∴ $z\left(1 - \cos\dfrac{\pi}{4} - i \sin\dfrac{\pi}{4}\right) = -i$

∴ $z = \dfrac{i}{\left(\cos\dfrac{\pi}{4} - 1\right) + i \sin\dfrac{\pi}{4}}$

$$= \dfrac{i}{\left(\cos\dfrac{\pi}{4} - 1\right) + i \sin\dfrac{\pi}{4}} \times \dfrac{\left(\cos\dfrac{\pi}{4} - 1\right) - i \sin\dfrac{\pi}{4}}{\left(\cos\dfrac{\pi}{4} - 1\right) - i \sin\dfrac{\pi}{4}}$$

$$= \dfrac{\sin\dfrac{\pi}{4} + i\left(\cos\dfrac{\pi}{4} - 1\right)}{\left(\cos\dfrac{\pi}{4} - 1\right)^2 + \sin^2\dfrac{\pi}{4}} = \dfrac{\sin\dfrac{\pi}{4} + i\left(\cos\dfrac{\pi}{4} - 1\right)}{1 + 1 - 2\cos\dfrac{\pi}{4}}$$

$$= \dfrac{1}{2}\left[\dfrac{\sin\dfrac{\pi}{4}}{1 - \cos\dfrac{\pi}{4}} - i\right] = \dfrac{1}{2}\left[\dfrac{2 \sin\dfrac{\pi}{8} \cos\dfrac{\pi}{8}}{2 \sin^2\dfrac{\pi}{8}} - i\right]$$

∴ $z = \dfrac{1}{2}\left[\cot\dfrac{\pi}{8} - i\right]$

Another method : Let $z = x + iy$ $\therefore$ $|z + i| = |z|$ gives

$$x^2 + (y + 1)^2 = x^2 + y^2 \therefore y = -\frac{1}{2}$$

and $\arg\left(\dfrac{z+i}{z}\right) = \dfrac{\pi}{4}$ gives $\tan^{-1}\left(\dfrac{y+1}{x}\right) - \tan^{-1}\left(\dfrac{y}{x}\right) = \dfrac{\pi}{4}$

$$\tan^{-1}\left(\frac{1}{2x}\right) - \tan^{-1}\left(-\frac{1}{2x}\right) = \frac{\pi}{4} \qquad \left(\because y = -\frac{1}{2}\right)$$

$$2 \tan^{-1}\left(\frac{1}{2x}\right) = \frac{\pi}{4}$$

$$\tan\left[2 \tan^{-1}\left(\frac{1}{2x}\right)\right] = 1$$

$$\frac{2(1/2x)}{1 - (1/2x)^2} = 1$$

$$4x^2 - 4x - 1 = 0 \text{ gives } x = \frac{1}{2} \pm \frac{1}{\sqrt{2}}$$

$\therefore$ $\qquad z = \left(\dfrac{1}{2} \pm \dfrac{1}{\sqrt{2}}\right) - i\dfrac{1}{2}$.

Ex. 5 : *Show that* $\left|\dfrac{z}{|z|} - 1\right| \leq |\arg z|$. **(May 2009)**

Sol. : Let $\qquad z = r(\cos\theta + i\sin\theta) = |z|(\cos\theta + i\sin\theta)$

$\therefore \qquad \left|\dfrac{z}{|z|} - 1\right| = \left|\dfrac{|z|(\cos\theta + i\sin\theta)}{|z|} - 1\right|$

$\qquad\qquad = |\cos\theta + i\sin\theta - 1| = |(\cos\theta - 1) + i\sin\theta|$

$\qquad\qquad = \sqrt{(\cos\theta - 1)^2 + \sin^2\theta} = \sqrt{2(1 - \cos\theta)}$

$\qquad\qquad = 2\sin\dfrac{\theta}{2}$

$\qquad\qquad \leq 2\left|\dfrac{\theta}{2}\right|$

$\qquad\qquad = |\theta|$

$\therefore \qquad \left|\dfrac{z}{|z|} - 1\right| \leq |\arg z| \qquad\qquad \{\because |\theta| = |\arg z|\}$

Ex. 6 : Given $\dfrac{1}{\rho} = \dfrac{1}{L_p i} + C_p i + \dfrac{1}{R}$, where L, p, R are real. Express ρ in the form $A e^{i\theta}$ giving the values of A, θ.

Sol. :

$$\dfrac{1}{\rho} = \dfrac{1}{L_p i} + C_p i + \dfrac{1}{R}$$

$$= \dfrac{1}{R} - \dfrac{i}{L_p} + C_p i \qquad \left\{\because \dfrac{1}{i} = -i\right\}$$

$$= \dfrac{1}{R} - i\left(\dfrac{1}{L_p} - C_p\right)$$

Let $\quad \rho = A e^{i\theta} \qquad \therefore \dfrac{1}{\rho} = \dfrac{1}{A e^{i\theta}} = \dfrac{1}{A} e^{-i\theta}$

$\therefore \qquad \dfrac{1}{A} e^{-i\theta} = \dfrac{1}{R} - i\left(\dfrac{1}{L_p} - C_p\right)$

$\therefore \qquad \dfrac{1}{A}(\cos\theta - i\sin\theta) = \dfrac{1}{R} - i\left(\dfrac{1}{L_p} - C_p\right)$

Equating real and imaginary parts,

$$\dfrac{1}{A}\cos\theta = \dfrac{1}{R} \qquad \ldots (1)$$

$$\dfrac{1}{A}\sin\theta = \dfrac{1}{L_p} - C_p \qquad \ldots (2)$$

Squaring (1) and (2) and adding, we get

$$\dfrac{1}{A^2}(\cos^2\theta + \sin^2\theta) = \dfrac{1}{R^2} + \left(\dfrac{1}{L_p} - C_p\right)^2$$

or $\qquad \dfrac{1}{A} = \sqrt{\dfrac{1}{R^2} + \left(\dfrac{1}{L_p} - C_p\right)^2}$

or $\qquad A = \dfrac{1}{\sqrt{\dfrac{1}{R^2} + \left(\dfrac{1}{L_p} - C_p\right)^2}}$

Also, on dividing (2) by (1), we get

$$\tan\theta = \dfrac{\left(\dfrac{1}{L_p} - C_p\right)}{\dfrac{1}{R}} = R\left(\dfrac{1}{L_p} - C_p\right)$$

or $\qquad \theta = \tan^{-1}\left[R\left(\dfrac{1}{L_p} - C_p\right)\right]$

$\therefore \qquad \rho = A e^{i\theta}$

Ex. 7 : If $(a_1 + i b_1) \cdot (a_2 + i b_2) \ldots\ldots (a_n + i b_n) = A + i B$, prove that

(a) $\tan^{-1}\left(\dfrac{b_1}{a_1}\right) + \tan^{-1}\left(\dfrac{b_2}{a_2}\right) + \ldots\ldots + \tan^{-1}\left(\dfrac{b_n}{a_n}\right) = \tan^{-1}\left(\dfrac{B}{A}\right)$.

(b) $\left(a_1^2 + b_1^2\right) \cdot \left(a_2^2 + b_2^2\right) \ldots\ldots \left(a_n^2 + b_n^2\right) = A^2 + B^2$.

Sol. : Let
$(a_1 + ib_1) = r_1 (\cos \theta_1 + i \sin \theta_1)$
$(a_2 + ib_2) = r_2 (\cos \theta_2 + i \sin \theta_2)$
....
....
$(a_n + ib_n) = r_n (\cos \theta_n + i \sin \theta_n)$

$\therefore$ $r_1 = \sqrt{a_1^2 + b_1^2}$ and $\theta_1 = \tan^{-1}\dfrac{b_1}{a_1}$

$r_2 = \sqrt{a_2^2 + b_2^2}$ and $\theta_2 = \tan^{-1}\dfrac{b_2}{a_2}$

....
....

$r_n = \sqrt{a_n^2 + b_n^2}$ and $\theta_n = \tan^{-1}\dfrac{b_n}{a_n}$

If $A + iB = r (\cos \theta + i \sin \theta)$

then $r = \sqrt{A^2 + B^2}$ and $\theta = \tan^{-1}\dfrac{B}{A}$

Hence $(a_1 + ib_1) \cdot (a_2 + ib_2) \ldots\ldots (a_n + ib_n) = A + iB$ takes the polar form
$(r_1 r_2 \ldots\ldots r_n) [\cos (\theta_1 + \theta_2 \ldots\ldots \theta_n) + i \sin (\theta_1 + \theta_2 \ldots \theta_n)] = r (\cos \theta + i \sin \theta)$

$\therefore$ $\theta_1 + \theta_2 + \ldots + \theta_n = \theta$

or $\tan^{-1}\dfrac{b_1}{a_1} + \tan^{-1}\dfrac{b_2}{a_2} + \tan^{-1}\dfrac{b_3}{a_3} + \ldots + \tan^{-1}\dfrac{b_n}{a_n} = \tan^{-1}\dfrac{B}{A}$ which proves part (a).

Also $r_1 r_2 \ldots\ldots r_n = r$

$\therefore$ $r_1^2 r_2^2 \ldots\ldots r_n^2 = r^2$

or $\left(a_1^2 + b_1^2\right)\left(a_2^2 + b_2^2\right) \ldots\ldots \left(a_n^2 + b_n^2\right) = A^2 + B^2$ which proves part (b).

Ex. 8 : If z_1 and z_2 are two complex numbers such that $|z_1 + z_2| = |z_1 - z_2|$ then show that the amp $\left(\dfrac{z_1}{z_2}\right) = \dfrac{\pi}{2}$. **(Dec. 2009)**

Sol. : Let $z_1 = r_1 (\cos \theta_1 + i \sin \theta_1)$ and $z_2 = r_2 (\cos \theta_2 + i \sin \theta_2)$

$\therefore$ $z_1 + z_2 = (r_1 \cos \theta_1 + r_2 \cos \theta_2) + i (r_1 \sin \theta_1 + r_2 \sin \theta_2)$

$|z_1 + z_2|^2 = (r_1 \cos \theta_1 + r_2 \cos \theta_2)^2 + (r_1 \sin \theta_1 + r_2 \sin \theta_2)^2$

$= r_1^2 + r_2^2 + 2 r_1 r_2 \cos (\theta_1 - \theta_2)$

and
$$z_1 - z_2 = (r_1 \cos \theta_1 - r_2 \cos \theta_2) + i(r_1 \sin \theta_1 - r_2 \sin \theta_2)$$
$$|z_1 - z_2|^2 = (r_1 \cos \theta_1 - r_2 \cos \theta_2)^2 + (r_1 \sin \theta_1 - r_2 \sin \theta_2)^2$$
$$= r_1^2 + r_2^2 - 2r_1 r_2 \cos(\theta_1 - \theta_2)$$

Given that $|z_1 + z_2|^2 = |z_1 - z_2|^2$

$\therefore \ r_1^2 + r_2^2 + 2r_1 r_2 \cos(\theta_1 - \theta_2) = r_1^2 + r_2^2 - 2r_1 r_2 \cos(\theta_1 - \theta_2)$

$\therefore \quad 4 r_1 r_2 \cos(\theta_1 - \theta_2) = 0$

$\therefore \quad \cos(\theta_1 - \theta_2) = 0 \qquad \{\because r_1 \neq 0, r_2 \neq 0\}$

$\therefore \quad \theta_1 - \theta_2 = \pi/2$

$\therefore \quad \text{amp}(z_1) - \text{amp}(z_2) = \pi/2$

or $\quad \text{amp}\left(\dfrac{z_1}{z_2}\right) = \pi/2$

Ex. 9 : *Prove that* $e^{2ai \cot^{-1} b} \left[\dfrac{bi - 1}{bi + 1}\right]^{-a} = 1.$

Sol. :
$$\dfrac{bi - 1}{bi + 1} = \dfrac{i\left(b - \dfrac{1}{i}\right)}{i\left(b + \dfrac{1}{i}\right)} = \dfrac{b + i}{b - i} \qquad \left\{\because \dfrac{1}{i} = -i\right\} \qquad \ldots \text{(i)}$$

Let $\quad b + i = r e^{i\theta}$
$\quad \quad b - i = r e^{-i\theta}$ $\qquad \ldots$ (ii)

where $r^2 = b + 1$, $\quad \theta = \tan^{-1} \dfrac{1}{b} = \cot^{-1} b$,

$$\left[\dfrac{bi - 1}{bi + 1}\right]^{-a} = \left[\dfrac{b + i}{b - i}\right]^{-a} = \left[\dfrac{r e^{i\theta}}{r e^{-i\theta}}\right]^{-a}$$
$$= \left(e^{2i\theta}\right)^{-a} = e^{-2ai\theta} \qquad \text{[From (ii)]}$$
$$= e^{-2ai \cot^{-1} b} \qquad \ldots \text{(iii)}$$

$\therefore \quad e^{2ai \cot^{-1} b} \left[\dfrac{bi - 1}{bi + 1}\right]^{-a} = e^{2ai \cot^{-1} b} \cdot e^{-2ai \cot^{-1} b} \qquad \text{[From (iii)]}$
$$= e^0 = 1$$

Ex. 10 : *Prove that*

$$\dfrac{1 + \cos \alpha + i \sin \alpha}{1 - \cos \alpha + i \sin \alpha} = \cot \dfrac{\alpha}{2} e^{i(\alpha - \pi/2)}$$

Sol. : L.H.S. $= \dfrac{(1 + \cos \alpha) + i \sin \alpha}{(1 - \cos \alpha) + i \sin \alpha} = \dfrac{2 \cos^2 \alpha/2 + i\, 2 \sin \alpha/2 \cos \alpha/2}{2 \sin^2 \alpha/2 + i\, 2 \sin \alpha/2 \cos \alpha/2}$

$$= \dfrac{2 \cos \alpha/2 \,(\cos \alpha/2 + i \sin \alpha/2)}{2 \sin \alpha/2 \,(\sin \alpha/2 + i \cos \alpha/2)}$$

$$= \cot \alpha/2 \; \frac{e^{i\alpha/2}}{\left\{\cos\left(\frac{\pi}{2}-\frac{\alpha}{2}\right)+i\sin\left(\frac{\pi}{2}-\frac{\alpha}{2}\right)\right\}}$$

$$= \cot \alpha/2 \; \frac{e^{i\alpha/2}}{e^{i(\pi/2-\alpha/2)}}$$

$$= \cot \alpha/2 \; e^{i(\alpha/2-\pi/2+\alpha/2)}$$

$$= \cot \alpha/2 \; e^{i(\alpha-\pi/2)}$$

Ex. 11 : If $p = \cos\theta + i\sin\theta$ and $q = \cos\phi + i\sin\phi$, show that

$$\frac{(p+q)(pq-1)}{(p-q)(pq+1)} = \frac{\sin\theta+\sin\phi}{\sin\theta-\sin\phi}.$$

Sol. :

$$p + q = \cos\theta + \cos\phi + i(\sin\theta + \sin\phi)$$

$$= 2\cos\left(\frac{\theta-\phi}{2}\right)\cos\left(\frac{\theta+\phi}{2}\right) + i\,2\cos\left(\frac{\theta-\phi}{2}\right)\sin\left(\frac{\theta+\phi}{2}\right)$$

$$= 2\cos\left(\frac{\theta-\phi}{2}\right)\left[\cos\left(\frac{\theta+\phi}{2}\right) + i\sin\left(\frac{\theta+\phi}{2}\right)\right]$$

$$p - q = (\cos\theta - \cos\phi) + i(\sin\theta - \sin\phi)$$

$$= -2\sin\left(\frac{\theta-\phi}{2}\right)\sin\left(\frac{\theta+\phi}{2}\right) + i\,2\sin\left(\frac{\theta-\phi}{2}\right)\cos\left(\frac{\theta+\phi}{2}\right)$$

$$= 2\sin\left(\frac{\theta-\phi}{2}\right)\left[-\sin\left(\frac{\theta+\phi}{2}\right) + i\cos\left(\frac{\theta+\phi}{2}\right)\right]$$

$$= 2i\sin\left(\frac{\theta-\phi}{2}\right)\left[\cos\left(\frac{\theta+\phi}{2}\right) + i\sin\left(\frac{\theta+\phi}{2}\right)\right] \quad \{\because i^2 = -1\}$$

$$pq + 1 = [(\cos\theta\cos\phi - \sin\theta\sin\phi) + i(\cos\theta\sin\phi + \sin\theta\cos\phi)] + 1$$

$$= \cos(\theta+\phi) + i\sin(\theta+\phi) + 1$$

$$= 2\cos\left(\frac{\theta+\phi}{2}\right)\cos\left(\frac{\theta+\phi}{2}\right) + i\,2\cos\left(\frac{\theta+\phi}{2}\right)\sin\left(\frac{\theta+\phi}{2}\right)$$

$$pq + 1 = 2\cos\left(\frac{\theta+\phi}{2}\right)\left[\cos\left(\frac{\theta+\phi}{2}\right) + i\sin\left(\frac{\theta+\phi}{2}\right)\right]$$

Similarly,

$$pq - 1 = 2i\sin\left(\frac{\theta+\phi}{2}\right)\left[\cos\left(\frac{\theta+\phi}{2}\right) + i\sin\left(\frac{\theta+\phi}{2}\right)\right]$$

$\therefore$ L.H.S. $= \dfrac{(p+q)(pq-1)}{(p-q)(pq+1)} = \dfrac{\cos\dfrac{\theta-\phi}{2} \; i\sin\dfrac{\theta+\phi}{2}}{i\sin\dfrac{\theta-\phi}{2} \; \cos\dfrac{\theta+\phi}{2}}$

$$= \frac{2 \sin \frac{\theta + \phi}{2} \cos \frac{\theta - \phi}{2}}{2 \cos \frac{\theta + \phi}{2} \sin \frac{\theta - \phi}{2}} = \frac{\sin \theta + \sin \phi}{\sin \theta - \sin \phi} = \text{R.H.S.}$$

EXERCISE 4.1

1. Express in the form a + ib.
   (i) $\frac{1}{(2+i)^2} - \frac{1}{(2-i)^2}$, (ii) $\sqrt{\frac{1+i}{1-i}}$, (iii) $\frac{i^4 + i^9 + i^{16}}{2 - i^8 + i^{10} - i^{15}}$, (iv) $\frac{(4+5i)^2}{(2+3i)^2}$.

   Ans. (i) $\frac{-8i}{25}$, (ii) $\frac{1}{\sqrt{2}} + \frac{i}{\sqrt{2}}$, (iii) $1 - 2i$, (iv) $\frac{525}{169} - \frac{92i}{169}$.

2. Find the modulus and principal value of amplitude of the following
   (i) $\frac{2 + 6\sqrt{3}\,i}{5 + \sqrt{3}\,i}$, (ii) $\frac{(1+2i)^5}{(3-4i)(2-11i)}$, (iii) $1 + \sin \alpha + i \cos \alpha$,
   (iv) $\left(\frac{4-5i}{2+3i}\right)\left(\frac{3+2i}{7+i}\right)$.

   Ans. (i) $r = 2$, $\theta = \pi/3$, (ii) $r = 1$, $\theta = \pi/2$,
   (iii) $r = \sqrt{2} (\cos \alpha/2 + \sin \alpha/2)$, $\theta = \left(\frac{\pi}{4} - \frac{\alpha}{2}\right)$ (iv) $r = 0.9055$, $\theta = \tan^{-1}(-7.2)$

3. If $(\alpha + i\beta) = \frac{1}{a + ib}$, prove that $(\alpha^2 + \beta^2)(a^2 + b^2) = 1$.

4. If $z = x + iy$, $Z = X + iY$, show that if $z = \frac{Z-1}{Z+1}$, then $x^2 + y^2 = \frac{(X-1)^2 + Y^2}{(X+1)^2 + Y^2}$.

5. If $x^2 + y^2 = 1$, prove that $\frac{1 + x + iy}{1 + x - iy} = x + iy$.

6. If $a = \cos \theta + i \sin \theta$, prove that $1 + a + a^2 = (1 + 2\cos \theta)(\cos \theta + i \sin \theta)$
   [Hint: Use the result $1 + \cos 2\theta = 2\cos^2 \theta$].

7. If $a^2 + b^2 + c^2 = 1$, $b + ic = (1 + a)z$, then prove that $\frac{a + ib}{1 + c} = \frac{1 + iz}{1 - iz}$.

   $\left[\text{Hint}: iz = \frac{ib - c}{1 + a}\right]$

8. Express $\frac{1}{(x+iy)^2} + \frac{1}{(x-iy)^2}$ in the form (a + ib) giving the values of a, b in terms of x and y.

   Ans. $a = \frac{2(x^2 - y^2)}{(x^2 + y^2)^2}$, $b = 0$.

9. If $|z| = 1$, $z \neq 1$, prove that $\frac{z-1}{z+1}$ is purely imaginary number. **(May 2002)**

10. Find the complex number z if $\arg(z+1) = \dfrac{\pi}{6}$ and $\arg(z-1) = \dfrac{2\pi}{3}$. **(May 09, Dec. 14)**

   [Hint: Given, $\tan^{-1}\dfrac{y}{x+1} = \dfrac{\pi}{6}$ and $\tan^{-1}\dfrac{y}{x-1} = \dfrac{2\pi}{3}$, solve for x and y]

   Ans. $z = 1/2 + i\sqrt{3}/2$

11. Find z if $\arg(z+2i) = \dfrac{\pi}{4}$, $\arg(z-2i) = \dfrac{3\pi}{4}$. **(May 2007, May 2010)**

   [Hint: Given : $\tan^{-1}\dfrac{y+2}{x} = \dfrac{\pi}{4}$ and $\tan^{-1}\dfrac{y-2}{x} = \tan\dfrac{3\pi}{4}$, solve for x and y]

   Ans. $z = 2$.

12. Solve the equation $z^2 + 2(1+2i)z - (11+2i) = 0$ where $z = x + iy$ and verify that sum of the roots is $-2(1+2i)$ and product is $-(11+2i)$.

   Ans. $2 - i,\ -4 - 3i$.

13. If $|i+z| = |i-z|$, show that z is real. **(May 2008)**

14. If $(1+ai)(1+bi)(1+ci) = p + iq$, prove that **(May 2014)**
   (i) $p \cdot \tan[\tan^{-1}a + \tan^{-1}b + \tan^{-1}c] = q$
   (ii) $(1+a^2)(1+b^2)(1+c^2) = p^2 + q^2$.

   [Hint: Let $1+ai = r_1 e^{i\theta_1}$, $1+bi = r_2 e^{i\theta_2}$, $1+ci = r_3 e^{i\theta_3}$, $p+iq = r e^{i\theta}$ and proceed further as in solved Ex. 7.]

15. If $p = a + ib$, $q = a - ib$ where a and b are real, prove that $p\,e^p + q\,e^q$ is real.

   Ans. $p\,e^p + q\,e^q = 2e^a(a\cos b - b\sin b)$ which is a real quantity.

16. If $r_1 e^{i\theta_1} + r_2 e^{i\theta_2} = Re^{i\phi}$, find R and ϕ.

   Ans. $R = \sqrt{r_1^2 + r_2^2 + 2r_1 r_2 \cos(\theta_1 - \theta_2)}$, $\phi = \tan^{-1}\dfrac{r_1 \sin\theta_1 + r_2 \sin\theta_2}{r_1 \cos\theta_1 + r_2 \cos\theta_2}$

17. If $a = \cos\alpha + i\sin\alpha$, $b = \cos\beta + i\sin\beta$, $c = \cos\gamma + i\sin\gamma$, then prove that

   $$\dfrac{(b+c)(c+a)(a+b)}{abc} = 8\cos\dfrac{\beta-\gamma}{2}\cos\dfrac{\gamma-\alpha}{2}\cos\dfrac{\alpha-\beta}{2}.$$

4.13 ILLUSTRATIONS ON ARGAND DIAGRAM

Ex. 1: If $z = \sqrt{3} + i$, represent z, z^3, $\dfrac{4}{z}$ on Argand diagram.

Sol.: Given, $z = \sqrt{3} + i$ ($\sqrt{3} = 1.73$ approximately)

∴ z will be represented by the point (1.73, 1)

$$z^3 = (\sqrt{3}+i)^3 = (\sqrt{3}+i)^2 (\sqrt{3}+i)$$
$$= (2 + 2\sqrt{3}\,i)(\sqrt{3}+i)$$
$$= 2(1+\sqrt{3}\,i)(\sqrt{3}+i) = 8i$$

∴ z^3 will be represented by the point $(0, 8)$

$$\frac{4}{z} = \frac{4}{\sqrt{3}+i} = 4\frac{(\sqrt{3}-i)}{(\sqrt{3}+i)(\sqrt{3}-i)}$$

$$= \frac{\sqrt{3}-i}{3+1} = \sqrt{3}-i \quad (\sqrt{3} = 1.73 \text{ approximately})$$

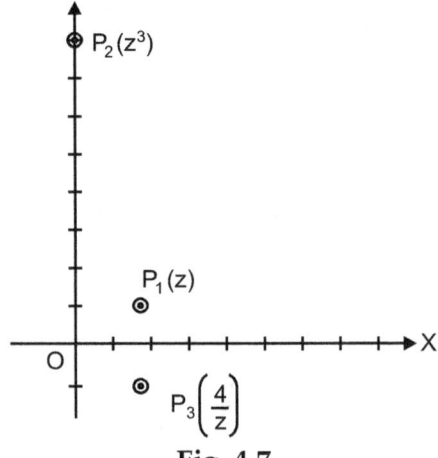

Fig. 4.7

∴ $\frac{4}{z}$ will be represented by the point $(1.73, -1)$. Points P_1, P_2, P_3 which represent $z, z^3, \frac{4}{z}$ respectively are shown on the Argand diagram.

Ex. 2 : *Find the locus of z satisfying*
  (i) $|z-2| = 3$, (ii) $|z-i| = 6$, (iii) $|z-5-6i| = 4$,
  (iv) $|z-3| + |z+3| = 10$, (v) $amp \frac{z-1}{z+1} = \frac{\pi}{4}$.

Sol. : (i) Let $\quad z = x + iy$

∴ $\quad |z-2| = 3 \Rightarrow |x+iy-2| = 3$

$\quad\quad\quad\quad\quad\quad \Rightarrow |(x-2)+iy| = 3$

$\quad\quad\quad\quad\quad\quad \Rightarrow (x-2)^2 + y^2 = 9 \quad \{\because |z|^2 = x^2+y^2\}$

which is a circle with centre $(2, 0)$ and radius 3.

(ii) Let $\quad z = x + iy$

∴ $\quad |z-i| = 6 \Rightarrow |x+iy-i| = 6$

$\quad\quad\quad\quad\quad \Rightarrow |x+i(y-1)| = 6$

$\quad\quad\quad\quad\quad \Rightarrow x^2 + (y-1)^2 = 36$

which is a circle with centre $(0, 1)$ and radius 6.

(iii) Let $z = x + iy$

$\therefore |z - 5 - 6i| = 4 \Rightarrow |x + iy - 5 - 6i| = 4$

$\Rightarrow |(x - 5) + i(y - 6)| = 4$

$\Rightarrow (x - 5)^2 + (y - 6)^2 = 16$

which is a circle with centre (5, 6) and radius 4.

Remark : We note that if z is a variable point and z_0 is the fixed point then $|z - z_0| = k$ represents a circle with centre at z_0 and radius k.

(iv) Let $z = x + iy$

$\therefore |z - 3| + |z + 3| = 10 \Rightarrow |x + iy - 3| + |x + iy + 3| = 10$

$\Rightarrow |(x - 3) + iy| + |(x + 3) + iy| = 10$

$\Rightarrow \sqrt{(x - 3)^2 + y^2} + \sqrt{(x + 3)^2 + y^2} = 10$

$\Rightarrow \sqrt{(x - 3)^2 + y^2} = 10 - \sqrt{(x + 3)^2 + y^2}$

squaring both the sides

$\Rightarrow (x - 3)^2 + y^2 = 100 + (x + 3)^2 + y^2 - 20\sqrt{(x + 3)^2 + y^2}$

$\Rightarrow 20\sqrt{(x + 3)^2 + y^2} = (x + 3)^2 - (x - 3)^2 + 100$

$\Rightarrow 5\sqrt{(x + 3)^2 + y^2} = 25 + 3x$

again squaring on both sides

$\Rightarrow 25[(x + 3)^2 + y^2] = (25 + 3x)^2$

$\Rightarrow 25[x^2 + y^2 + 6x + 9] = 625 + 150x + 9x^2$

$\Rightarrow 16x^2 + 25y^2 = 400$

$\Rightarrow \dfrac{x^2}{25} + \dfrac{y^2}{16} = 1$ which represents a ellipse.

Geometrically, $|z + 3| + |z - 3| = 10$ represents ellipse, since the sum of the distances from any point P(z) on the ellipse to the foci A (–3, 0), B (3, 0) is equal to 10 (= 2a, the major axis). (i.e. AP + BP = 10).

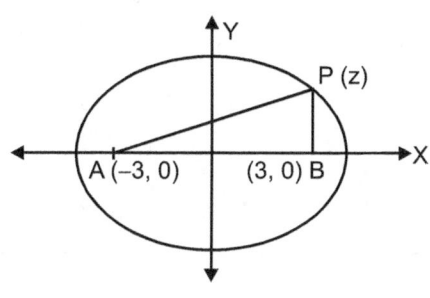

Fig. 4.8

(v) amp $\left(\dfrac{z - 1}{z + 1}\right) = \dfrac{\pi}{4}$

Let $z = x + iy$

$$\therefore \quad \text{amp} \frac{z-1}{z+1} = \frac{\pi}{4} \Rightarrow \text{amp}(z-1) - \text{amp}(z+1) = \frac{\pi}{4}$$

$$\Rightarrow \text{amp}(x-1+iy) - \text{amp}(x+1+iy) = \frac{\pi}{4}$$

$$\Rightarrow \tan^{-1}\frac{y}{x-1} - \tan^{-1}\frac{y}{x+1} = \frac{\pi}{4}$$

$$\Rightarrow \tan^{-1}\frac{\frac{y}{x-1} - \frac{y}{x+1}}{1 + \frac{y}{x-1}\frac{y}{x+1}} = \frac{\pi}{4}$$

$$\Rightarrow \frac{xy + y - xy + y}{x^2 - 1 + y^2} = \tan\frac{\pi}{4} = 1$$

$$\Rightarrow x^2 + y^2 - 1 = 2y$$

$$\Rightarrow (x-0)^2 + (y-1)^2 = 2$$

which is a circle with centre at $(0, 1)$ and radius $\sqrt{2}$.

Ex. 3 : If $\dfrac{z-1}{z+i}$ is purely imaginary, find the locus of z. **(Dec. 2010)**

Sol. : Let
$$z = x + iy$$

$$\therefore \quad \frac{z-1}{z+i} = \frac{x+iy-1}{x+iy+i} = \frac{(x-1)+iy}{x+i(y+1)}$$

$$= \frac{(x-1)+iy}{x+i(y+1)} \cdot \frac{x-i(y+1)}{x-i(y+1)}$$

$$= \text{Purely imaginary}$$

$\therefore$ The real part of $\dfrac{z-1}{z+i} = 0$.

i.e. $\quad \dfrac{x(x-1) + y(y+1)}{x^2 + (y+1)^2} = 0$

i.e. $\quad x(x-1) + y(y+1) = 0$

or $\quad \left(x - \dfrac{1}{2}\right)^2 + \left(y + \dfrac{1}{2}\right)^2 = \left(\dfrac{1}{\sqrt{2}}\right)^2$

which is a circle with centre $\left(\dfrac{1}{2}, -\dfrac{1}{2}\right)$ and radius $\dfrac{1}{\sqrt{2}}$.

Ex. 4 : *The centre of a regular hexagon is (2 – i) and one of its vertices is (–1 + i). Find the two adjacent vertices of the hexagon.*

Sol. : Let C the centre and A is one of the vertices of hexagon with respect to origin O, be represented by complex numbers.

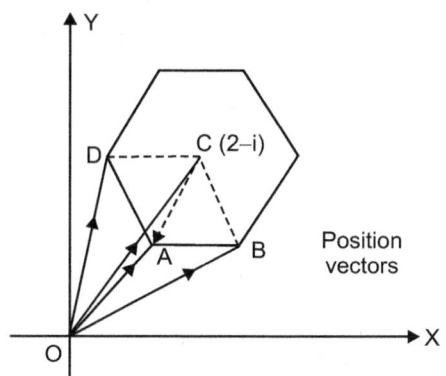

Fig. 4.9

$$OC = 2 - i \quad \text{and} \quad OA = (-1 + i)$$

$$\therefore \quad CA = OA - OC$$
$$= (-1 + i) - (2 - i)$$
$$= (-3 + 2i) \quad \ldots \text{(i)}$$

Since hexagon is regular $|CA| = |CB| = |CD|$ and angle subtended by each side at the centre is $\frac{\pi}{3}$. Hence vector **CB** can be obtained by rotating **CA** through an angle $\frac{\pi}{3}$ in the anti-clockwise (i.e. positive sense) direction (i.e. by increasing the amplitude by an angle $\frac{\pi}{3}$).

$$\therefore \quad CB = CA \left\{ \cos \frac{\pi}{3} + i \sin \frac{\pi}{3} \right\} = (-3 + 2i) \left(\frac{1}{2} + i \frac{\sqrt{3}}{2} \right)$$
$$= \left(-\frac{3}{2} - \sqrt{3} \right) + i \left(1 - \frac{3\sqrt{3}}{2} \right) \quad \ldots \text{(ii)}$$

Similarly, vector **CD** can be obtained by rotating **CA** through an angle $\frac{\pi}{3}$ in clockwise (negative sense) direction (i.e. decreasing the amplitude by an angle $\frac{\pi}{3}$).

$$\therefore \quad CD = CA \left\{ \cos \left(-\frac{\pi}{3} \right) + \sin \left(-\frac{\pi}{3} \right) \right\}$$
$$= CA \left\{ \cos \left(\frac{\pi}{3} \right) - i \sin \left(\frac{\pi}{3} \right) \right\} \quad \left\{ \begin{array}{l} \because \quad \cos(-\theta) = \cos \theta \\ \text{and} \quad \sin(-\theta) = -\sin \theta \end{array} \right\}$$
$$= (-3 + 2i) \left(\frac{1}{2} - i \frac{\sqrt{3}}{2} \right) = \left(-\frac{3}{2} + \sqrt{3} \right) + i \left(1 + \frac{3\sqrt{3}}{2} \right) \quad \ldots \text{(iii)}$$

Hence, (ii) and (iii) represent the position vectors B and D respectively w.r.t. origin C. Now the position vectors of B and D with respect to origin O, are given by

$$OB = OC + CB$$
$$= (2-i) + \left\{\left(-\frac{3}{2}-\sqrt{3}\right) + i\left(1-\frac{3\sqrt{3}}{2}\right)\right\}$$
$$= \left(\frac{1}{2}-\sqrt{3}\right) - i\frac{3\sqrt{3}}{2} \qquad \ldots \text{(iv)}$$

and
$$OD = OC + CD$$
$$= (2-i) + \left\{\left(-\frac{3}{2}+\sqrt{3}\right) + i\left(1+\frac{3\sqrt{3}}{2}\right)\right\}$$
$$= \left(\frac{1}{2}+\sqrt{3}\right) + i\frac{3\sqrt{3}}{2} \qquad \ldots \text{(v)}$$

Hence (iv) and (v) represent vertices B and D.

Ex. 5 : *If z_1, z_2, z_3 represent vertices of an equilateral triangle, prove that :*
$$z_1^2 + z_2^2 + z_3^2 = z_1 z_2 + z_2 z_3 + z_3 z_1$$

Sol. : z_1, z_2, z_3 represent the vertices of an equilateral triangle (Fig. 4.10).

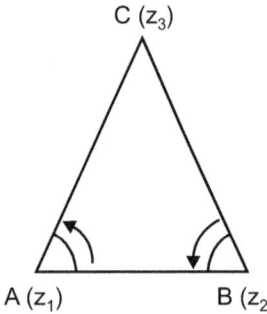

Fig. 4.10

$$AC = z_3 - z_1$$
$$AB = z_2 - z_1$$
$$AC = AB\left(\cos\frac{\pi}{3} + i\sin\frac{\pi}{3}\right)$$

{AC is obtained by rotating AB through an angle $\pi/3$}

$$\therefore \quad (z_3 - z_1) = (z_2 - z_1)\left(\cos\frac{\pi}{3} + i\sin\frac{\pi}{3}\right) \qquad \ldots \text{(i)}$$

$$BA = BC\left(\cos\frac{\pi}{3} + i\sin\frac{\pi}{3}\right)$$

$$\therefore \quad (z_1 - z_2) = (z_3 - z_2)\left(\cos\frac{\pi}{3} + i\sin\frac{\pi}{3}\right) \qquad \ldots \text{(ii)}$$

Dividing (i) by (ii),

$$\frac{z_3 - z_1}{z_1 - z_2} = \frac{z_2 - z_1}{z_3 - z_2}$$

$$\therefore \quad (z_3 - z_1)(z_3 - z_2) = (z_2 - z_1)(z_1 - z_2)$$

$$\therefore \quad z_1^2 + z_2^2 + z_3^2 = z_1 z_2 + z_2 z_3 + z_3 z_1 \text{ which is a required result.}$$

Ex. 6 : *A square lies above real axis in Argand diagram, and two of its adjacent vertices are the origin and the point $5 + 6i$. Find the complex numbers representing other vertices.*

(Dec. 2005, 2008, 2010, 2012, Dec. 2014)

Sol. :

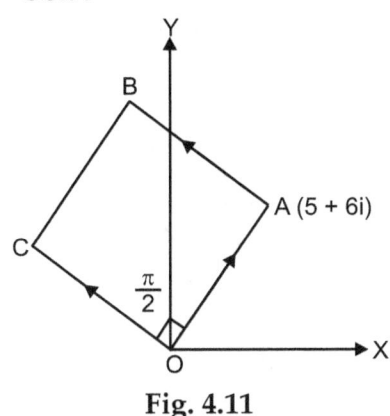

Fig. 4.11

Let **OA** = 5 + 6i

Vector **OC** is obtained from vector **OA** by rotating it through right angle in anti-clockwise sense.

∴ $\mathbf{OC} = \mathbf{OA}\left(\cos\frac{\pi}{2} + i\sin\frac{\pi}{2}\right)$

$= (5 + 6i)\, i = -6 + 5i$

Also $\mathbf{AB} = \mathbf{OC} = -6 + 5i$

∴ $\mathbf{OB} = \mathbf{OA} + \mathbf{AB}$

$= 5 + 6i - 6 + 5i = -1 + 11i$

Thus C and B are represented by complex numbers $-6 + 5i$ and $-1 + 11i$ respectively.

Ex. 7 : *On Argand diagram, the circumcentre of an equilateral triangle represents the complex number $1 + i$. If one vertex represents the complex number $-1 + 3i$, find the complex number represented by the other two vertices.* **(Dec. 2004, 2006)**

Sol. : Let, **OA** and **OG** represent complex numbers $-1 + 3i$ and $+1 + i$, the circumcentre G and vertex A.

∴ $\mathbf{GA} = \mathbf{OA} - \mathbf{OG} = (-1 + 3i) - (1 + i)$

$= (-2 + 2i)$

Since $|\mathbf{GA}| = |\mathbf{GB}| = |\mathbf{GC}|$, the complex numbers with respect to G as origin, representing vertices B, C are given by GB and GC, which are obtained by rotating GA through $\frac{2\pi}{3}$ in anti-clockwise (positive sense) for B and clockwise (negative sense) direction for C.

∴ $\mathbf{GB} = \mathbf{GA}\left(\cos\frac{2\pi}{3} + i\sin\frac{2\pi}{3}\right)$

$= (-2 + 2i)\left(-\frac{1}{2} + i\frac{\sqrt{3}}{2}\right)$

$= (1 - \sqrt{3}) - i(1 + \sqrt{3})$

and $\mathbf{GC} = \mathbf{GA}\left[\cos\left(\frac{-2\pi}{3}\right) + i\sin\left(\frac{-2\pi}{3}\right)\right]$

$= (-2 + 2i)\left(-\frac{1}{2} - i\frac{\sqrt{3}}{2}\right)$

$= (1 + \sqrt{3}) - i(1 - \sqrt{3})$

Also $\mathbf{OB} = \mathbf{OG} + \mathbf{GB} = (2 - \sqrt{3}) - i\sqrt{3}$

and $\mathbf{OC} = \mathbf{OG} + \mathbf{GC} = (2 + \sqrt{3}) + i\sqrt{3}$

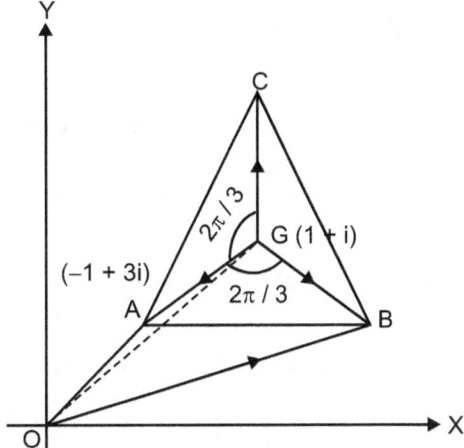

Fig. 4.12

Thus complex numbers of vertices B, C with respect to origin 'O'.

Ex. 8 : If z_1, z_2 and the origin O represent on the Argand diagram, vertices of an equilateral triangle, show that
(Dec. 2007, May 2011)

$$\frac{1}{z_1^2} + \frac{1}{z_2^2} = \frac{1}{z_1 z_2}$$

Sol. : OB is obtained by rotating OA in anticlockwise direction through an angle $\pi/3$.

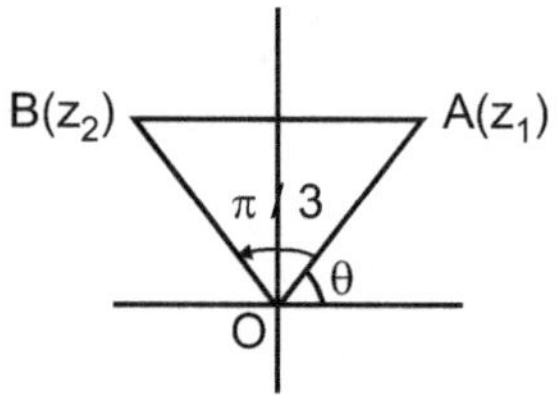

∴ $OB = OA\, e^{i\pi/3}$

i.e. $z_2 = z_1\, e^{i\pi/3}$

∴ $\dfrac{z_2}{z_1} = e^{i\pi/3}$ ... (i)

Fig. 4.13

Similarly, OA is obtained by rotating OB in clockwise direction through an angle $\pi/3$.

∴ $OA = OB\, e^{-i\pi/3}$

i.e. $z_1 = z_2\, e^{-i\pi/3}$ ... (ii)

∴ $\dfrac{z_1}{z_2} = e^{-i\pi/3}$

Adding (i) and (ii),

$$\frac{z_1}{z_2} + \frac{z_2}{z_1} = 2\cos\frac{\pi}{3} = 1$$

On multiplying by $\dfrac{1}{z_1 z_2}$ on both sides,

$$\frac{1}{z_1^2} + \frac{1}{z_2^2} = \frac{1}{z_1 z_2}$$

Alternative Method :

Let modulus and amplitude of z_1 be r and θ respectively, then

$$z_1 = r(\cos\theta + i\sin\theta)$$

∴ $z_2 = r(\cos\theta + i\sin\theta)\left(\cos\dfrac{\pi}{3} + i\sin\dfrac{\pi}{3}\right)$

i.e. $z_2 = r\left\{\cos\left(\theta + \dfrac{\pi}{3}\right) + i\sin\left(\theta + \dfrac{\pi}{3}\right)\right\}$

∴ $z_1 z_2 = [r(\cos\theta + i\sin\theta)]\left[r\left\{\cos\left(\theta + \dfrac{\pi}{3}\right) + i\sin\left(\theta + \dfrac{\pi}{3}\right)\right\}\right]$

          $= r^2\left\{\cos\left(2\theta + \dfrac{\pi}{3}\right) + i\sin\left(2\theta + \dfrac{\pi}{3}\right)\right\}$

and $z_1^2 + z_2^2 = \{r(\cos\theta + i\sin\theta)\}^2 + \left[r\left\{\cos\left(\theta + \dfrac{\pi}{3}\right) + i\sin\left(2\theta + \dfrac{2\pi}{3}\right)\right\}\right]^2$

$= r^2\left[\{\cos 2\theta + i\sin 2\theta\} + \left\{\cos\left(2\theta + \dfrac{2\pi}{3}\right) + i\sin\left(2\theta + \dfrac{2\pi}{3}\right)\right\}\right]$

$= r^2\left[\left\{\cos 2\theta + \cos\left(2\theta + \dfrac{2\pi}{3}\right)\right\} + i\left\{\sin 2\theta + \sin\left(2\theta + \dfrac{2\pi}{3}\right)\right\}\right]$

$= r^2\left[\left\{2\cos\left(\dfrac{4\theta + \dfrac{2\pi}{3}}{2}\right)\cos\left(\dfrac{-\dfrac{2\pi}{3}}{2}\right)\right\} + i\left\{2\sin\left(\dfrac{4\theta + \dfrac{2\pi}{3}}{2}\right)\cos\left(\dfrac{-\dfrac{2\pi}{3}}{2}\right)\right\}\right]$

$= r^2\left[\cos\left(2\theta + \dfrac{\pi}{3}\right)\cdot(1) + i\sin\left(2\theta + \dfrac{\pi}{3}\right)\cdot(1)\right] \qquad \left(\because 2\cos\dfrac{\pi}{3} = 1\right)$

$= z_1 z_2$

i.e. $\quad z_1^2 + z_2^2 = z_1 z_2$

$\therefore \quad \dfrac{1}{z_1^2} + \dfrac{1}{z_2^2} = \dfrac{1}{z_1 z_2}$

Ex. 9 : *If z_1 and z_2 are the roots of the equation $z^2 - az + a^2 = 0$ where a is a complex number, show that the points z_1 and z_2 are the vertices of an equilateral triangle described on opposite sides of the line joining O to point a.* **(May 2005, 2007)**

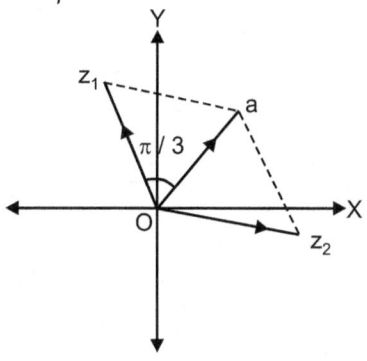

Fig. 4.14

Sol. : Roots of the given equation $z^2 - az + a^2 = 0$ are $\left(\dfrac{1}{2} \pm \dfrac{\sqrt{3}}{2}i\right)a$

Let $\qquad z_1 = \left(\dfrac{1}{2} + \dfrac{\sqrt{3}}{2}i\right)a \qquad$ and $\qquad z_2 = \left(\dfrac{1}{2} - \dfrac{\sqrt{3}}{2}i\right)a$

Since $\qquad \left|\dfrac{1}{2} + \dfrac{\sqrt{3}}{2}i\right| = 1, \qquad \left|\dfrac{1}{2} - \dfrac{\sqrt{3}}{2}i\right| = 1$

and $\qquad \text{Amp}\left(\dfrac{1}{2} + \dfrac{\sqrt{3}}{2}i\right) = \dfrac{\pi}{3}, \qquad \text{Amp}\left(\dfrac{1}{2} - \dfrac{\sqrt{3}}{2}i\right) = -\dfrac{\pi}{3}$

Therefore, $\qquad |z_1| = |a|, \qquad\qquad |z_2| = |a| \qquad\qquad \dots\text{(i)}$

Also, $\quad \text{Amp } z_1 = \text{Amp} \left[\left(\frac{1}{2} + \frac{\sqrt{3}}{2} i \right) (a) \right]$

$= \text{Amp} \left(\frac{1}{2} + \frac{\sqrt{3}}{2} i \right) + \text{Amp } (a) = \frac{\pi}{3} + \text{Amp } (a) \quad \ldots \text{(ii)}$

and $\quad \text{Amp } z_2 = \text{Amp} \left[\left(\frac{1}{2} - \frac{\sqrt{3}}{2} i \right) (a) \right]$

$= \text{Amp} \left(\frac{1}{2} - \frac{\sqrt{3}}{2} i \right) + \text{Amp } (a) = -\frac{\pi}{3} + \text{Amp } (a) \quad \ldots \text{(iii)}$

Hence from (i), (ii) and (iii), z_1 and z_2 are the vertices of an equilateral triangle described on opposite sides of the line Oa.

Ex. 10 : *If p is real and complex number $\frac{1+i}{2+ip} + \frac{2+3i}{3+i}$ is represented on Argand's diagram by a point on a line $y = x$, show that $p = -5 \pm \sqrt{21}$.*

Sol. : Let $z = x + iy$ be the given complex number.

$\therefore \quad z = x + iy = \frac{1+i}{2+ip} + \frac{2+3i}{3+i}$

$= \left(\frac{1+i}{2+ip} \right) \left(\frac{2-ip}{2-ip} \right) + \left(\frac{2+3i}{3+i} \right) \left(\frac{3-i}{3-i} \right)$

$= \frac{(2+p) + i(2-p)}{4+p^2} + \frac{9+7i}{10}$

$= \frac{(20+10p) + i(20-10p) + (36+9p^2) + i(28+7p^2)}{10(4+p^2)}$

$= \frac{(56+10p+9p^2)}{10(4+p^2)} + \frac{i(48-10p+7p^2)}{10(4+p^2)}$

Since the number lies on the line $y = x$

$\therefore \quad$ Real part of $z =$ Imaginary part z

$\therefore \quad 56 + 10p + 9p^2 = 48 - 10p + 7p^2$

i.e. $\quad 2p^2 + 20p + 8 = 0$

i.e. $\quad p^2 + 10p + 4 = 0$

$\therefore \quad p = \frac{-10 \pm \sqrt{100 - 16}}{2}$

$\therefore \quad p = -5 \pm \sqrt{21}$

Ex. 11 : *Prove that the two triangles whose vertices are represented by complex numbers a_1, a_2, a_3 and b_1, b_2, b_3 respectively are similar if*

$$\begin{vmatrix} a_1 & b_1 & 1 \\ a_2 & b_2 & 1 \\ a_3 & b_3 & 1 \end{vmatrix} = 0$$

Sol. : Let ABC and PQR be the two triangles whose vertices are represented by (a_1, a_2, a_3) and (b_1, b_2, b_3), then the triangles are similar if

$$\frac{\overline{AB}}{\overline{AC}} = \frac{\overline{PQ}}{\overline{PR}} \quad \text{i.e.} \quad \frac{a_2 - a_1}{a_3 - a_1} = \frac{b_2 - b_1}{b_3 - b_1}$$

i.e. $(a_2 - a_1)(b_3 - b_1) - (a_3 - a_1)(b_2 - b_1) = 0$

i.e. $$\begin{vmatrix} a_1 & b_1 & 1 \\ a_2 & b_2 & 1 \\ a_3 & b_3 & 1 \end{vmatrix} = 0$$

EXERCISE 4.2

1. Find locus of z satisfying :

   (i) $1 < |z + 2i| \leq 3$, (ii) $\pi/6 \leq \text{amp}(z) \leq \frac{\pi}{3}$, (iii) $|z + 1| + |z - 1| < 3$,

   (iv) $|z - 3| - |z + 3| = 4$ **(May 2004)**, (v) $\text{Re}(z^2) = 1$, (vi) $|z + 1| = |z - i|$.

   Ans. (i) Annular region of circles with centre $(0, -2)$ and radii 1 and 3.
   (ii) Region bounded by and including the lines $\theta = \pi/6$ and $\theta = \pi/3$.
   (iii) Interior of the ellipse having foci ± 1 and major axis 3 unit $(20x^2 + 36y^2 = 45)$.
   (iv) Hyperbola $5x^2 - 4y^2 = 20$
   (v) Rectangular hyperbola $x^2 - y^2 = 1$.
   (vi) Straight line $y = -x$.

2. Show that the points $-1, +1, 3 + 4i, \dfrac{1}{3 + 4i}$ on Argand's diagram lie on a circle.

   Find its radius and represent centre on Argand diagram.

[**Hint :** Let A (-1), B $\left(\dfrac{1}{3+4i}\right) = \left(\dfrac{3-4i}{25}\right)$, C $(+1)$, D $(3+4i)$, then centre must lie on the perpendicular bisector of AC i.e on y-axis. Let centre be $(0, a)$ and equation of the circle be $x^2 + (y-a)^2 = r^2$; $a = 3$, $r = \sqrt{10}$]

Ans. Centre $= 3i$, Radius $= \sqrt{10}$.

3. Find the locus of a point z if z_1 and z_2 are two given complex numbers such that $|z - z_1| = |z - z_2|$.

    Ans. Locus of P is the right bisector of AB.

4. Show that the equation of a circle on a line segment joining z_1 and z_2 as diameter is $|z - z_1|^2 + |z - z_2|^2 = |z_1 - z_2|^2$.

    [**Hint :** Let A $= z_1$, B $= z_2$ and P (z) is any point on the circle, then $\angle$ APB, being angle in a semi circle is right angle.]

5. On Argand's diagram, the circumcentre of an equilateral triangle represents the complex number $1 + i$. If one vertex represents the complex number $-1 + 3i$, find complex numbers represented by the other two vertices.

    Ans. $(1 + i) + (-2 + 2i)\, e^{i\,2\pi/3}$, $(1 + i) + (-2 + 2i)\, e^{-i\,2\pi/3}$.

6. Show that the points $i, -i, 2 - i, 2 + i$ are the vertices of a square.

7. A square lies entirely in second quadrant. If one of the side join the points -2 and $2i$, find the complex numbers representing other vertices.

    Ans. $-2 + 4i, -4 + 2i$.

8. The centre of a regular hexagon is at the origin and one vertex is given by $1 + i$ on Argand's diagram. Find the remaining vertices.

    Ans. $\sqrt{2}\left\{\cos\left(\dfrac{\pi}{4} + k\dfrac{\pi}{3}\right) + i\sin\left(\dfrac{\pi}{4} + k\dfrac{\pi}{3}\right)\right\}$, where $k = 1, 2, 3, 4$.

9. Two opposite vertices of a square are represented by complex numbers $(9 + 12i)$ and $(-5 + 10i)$. Find the complex number representing the other two vertices of the square. **(Dec. 2009, May 2010)**

    Ans. $(1 + 18i)$ and $(3 + 4i)$.

10. The vertices of a triangle ABC are $1 + 2i$, $4 - 2i$, $1 - 6i$. Prove that ABC is isosceles triangle and find the lengths of the sides.

    Ans. $5, 5, 8$.

11. If z_1, z_2, z_3, z_4 are vertices of a parallelogram, then prove that

    $z_1 - z_2 + z_3 - z_4 = 0$.

12. If z_1, z_2, z_3 are vertices of isosceles triangle right angled at the vertex z_2, prove that $z_1^2 + 2z_2^2 + z_3^2 = 2z_2(z_1 + z_2)$. **(May 2008, 2015)**

    [**Hint**: Perpendicular from vertex $B(z_2)$ bisect the line joining $A(z_1)$ and $C(z_3)$.

    $\therefore$ Foot of perpendicular from (D) is $\frac{z_1 + z_3}{2}$. $\overline{DC} = \overline{DB}\ e^{-i\pi/2}$ and $\overline{DA} = \overline{DB}\ e^{i\pi/2}$].

13. The points A, P, Q in the Argand's diagram represent the complex numbers 2, z, z² respectively. If P described a circle on OA as diameter, find the locus of Q, O being the origin.

    [**Hint**: Let $P = r(\cos\theta + i\sin\theta)$, Point A = 2 lies on the real axis, $\angle XOP = \theta$. In semi circle $\angle OPA$ = right angle, therefore OP = OA $\cos\theta \Rightarrow r = 2\cos\theta$. Let $Q = r_1(\cos\theta_1 + i\sin\theta_1)$].

    Ans. Locus of Q is cardioide $r = 2(1 + \cos\theta)$.

14. If $z_1 + z_2 + z_3 = 0$ and $|z_1| = |z_2| = |z_3| = k$, prove that $\frac{1}{z_1} + \frac{1}{z_2} + \frac{1}{z_3} = 0$.

    [**Hint**: Let $z_1 = x_1 + iy_1$, $z_2 = x_2 + iy_2$, $z_3 = x_3 + iy_3$, then

    $z_1 + z_2 + z_3 = 0 \Rightarrow x_1 + x_2 + x_3 = 0 = y_1 + y_2 + y_3$

    $\therefore \quad \frac{1}{z_1} + \frac{1}{z_2} + \frac{1}{z_3} = \frac{\overline{z_1}}{z_1\overline{z_1}} + \frac{\overline{z_2}}{z_2\overline{z_2}} + \frac{\overline{z_3}}{z_3\overline{z_3}} = \frac{\overline{z_1}}{|z_1|^2} + \frac{\overline{z_2}}{|z_2|^2} + \frac{\overline{z_3}}{|z_3|^2}$

    $= \frac{(x_1 - iy_1) + (x_2 - iy_2) + (x_3 - iy_3)}{k^2} = 0.$]

15. Find the locus of the point P(z) satisfying $z = z_1 + t(z_2 - z_1)$ where z_1, z_2 are complex numbers and t is real.

    [**Hint**: $z = x + iy$, $z_1 = x_1 + iy_1$, $z_2 = x_2 + iy_2$ $\therefore x - x_1 = t(x_2 - x_1)$ and $y - y_1 = t(y_2 - y_1)$. Thus locus is a straight line.]

16. If $z = x + iy$ where x and y are real, show that

    (a) when $\frac{z+i}{z+2}$ is real, the locus of the point (x, y) is a straight line.

    (b) when $\frac{z+i}{z+2}$ is purely imaginary, the locus of the point (x, y) is a circle of radius $\frac{1}{2}\sqrt{5}$. Find the complex number representing the centre of this circle.

    [**Hint**: $\frac{z+i}{z+2} = \frac{(x^2 + y^2 + 2x + y) + i(x + 2y + 2)}{(x+2)^2 + y^2}$

    For part (a), $x + 2y + 2 = 0$ and for part (b), $x^2 + y^2 + x + y = 0$, $(-1, -1/2)$ is centre and $r = \sqrt{1 + \frac{1}{4}}$, complex number representing the centre is $-1 - \frac{1}{2}i$].

17. If $x + iy = \dfrac{3}{2 + \cos\theta + i\sin\theta}$, prove that the locus of (x, y) is the circle $x^2 + y^2 = 4x - 3$.

   [**Hint**: We have $x = \dfrac{6 + 3\cos\theta}{5 + 4\cos\theta}$, $y = \dfrac{-3\sin\theta}{5 + 4\cos\theta}$

   $\cos\theta = \dfrac{6 - 5x}{4x - 3}$, $\sin\theta = \dfrac{-3y}{4x - 3}$, Use $\sin^2\theta + \cos^2\theta = 1$].

18. In an "Argand" diagram, the points A, B, C and D are respectively z^{-1}, 1, z and z^2, where z is a complex number. If $|z - 1| = 1$, show that **AB** is parallel to **OC** and **BC** is parallel to **OD**, where O is the origin. **(May 2006)**

   [**Hint**: C $(z) = x + iy$, B $(z) = 1$, A $(z^{-1}) = \dfrac{x - iy}{x^2 + y^2}$, D $(z^2) = (x^2 - y^2 + i\,2xy)$. Also $|z - 1| = 1$ gives $x^2 + y^2 = 2x$. Show that slope **AB** = slope **OC** and slope **BC** = slope **OD**].

19. If $P_1(z_1)$, $P_2(z_2)$ and $P_3(z_3)$ be three points in the Argand plane then prove that $\angle P_1P_2P_3 = \text{amp}\left(\dfrac{z_3 - z_2}{z_1 - z_2}\right)$ and P_1, P_2 and P_3 are collinear if $\dfrac{z_3 - z_2}{z_1 - z_2}$ is real.

   [**Hint**: Let $\mathbf{P_2P_3} = z_3 - z_2$, $\mathbf{P_2P_1} = z_1 - z_2$, let $z_3 - z_2 = r_2(\cos\theta_2 + i\sin\theta_2)$ and $z_1 - z_2 = r_1(\cos\theta_1 + i\sin\theta_1)$. If $\dfrac{z_3 - z_2}{z_1 - z_2}$ is real, then $\theta_1 = \theta_2$ $\therefore$ P_1, P_2 and P_3 are collinear.]

20. If z_1, z_2, z_3 are complex numbers such that their representative points are collinear, prove that they satisfy a relation of the form $az_1 + bz_2 + cz_3 = 0$ where a, b, c are real and $a + b + c = 0$.

   [**Hint**: Let C divide AB in the ratio $b : a$ ($a \ne b$)

   $\therefore z = \dfrac{az_1 + bz_2}{a + b}$ and use $a + b = -c$]

21. If $z_1\, z_2$ are given complex numbers, find the numbers z_3 and z_4 so that the points z_3, z_4 and z_1, z_4 are opposite corners of a square.

   [**Hint**: Let **OA** $(z_1) = x_1 + iy_1$, **OC** $(z_2) = (x_2 + iy_2)$. Mid point E of AC

   OC $= \left(\dfrac{x_1 + y_2}{2} + i\dfrac{y_1 + y_2}{2}\right)$ $\therefore$ **EC** = **OC** − **OE** $= \dfrac{x_2 - x_1}{2} + i\dfrac{y_2 - y_1}{2}$

   $\because$ |**EC**| = |**EB**| = |**ED**| $\therefore$ ED = EC $c^{i\pi/2}$ and EB EC $e^{-i\pi/2}$ and

   OD = **OE** + **ED** and **OB** = **OE** + **EB**.

22. If $\dfrac{z - 2i}{2z - 1}$ is purely imaginary, prove that the locus of z in the Argand's diagram is a circle. Find centre and radius. **(Dec. 2003, 2008; May 2013)**

4.14 POWERS OF COMPLEX NUMBERS : DEMOIVRE'S THEOREM

Demoivre's theorem states that for any real number n, one of the values of $(\cos \theta + i \sin \theta)^n$ is $\cos n\theta + i \sin n\theta$.

Proof : To prove the theorem, we are required to consider three cases.

Case I : n, positive integer

By direct multiplication, we have

$$(\cos \theta_1 + i \sin \theta_1)(\cos \theta_2 + i \sin \theta_2)$$
$$= (\cos \theta_1 \cos \theta_2 - \sin \theta_1 \sin \theta_2) + i(\sin \theta_1 \cos \theta_2 + \cos \theta_1 \sin \theta_2)$$
$$= \cos(\theta_1 + \theta_2) + i \sin(\theta_1 + \theta_2)$$

Again $(\cos \theta_1 + i \sin \theta_1)(\cos \theta_2 + i \sin \theta_2)(\cos \theta_3 + i \sin \theta_3)$
$$= \{\cos(\theta_1 + \theta_2) + i \sin(\theta_1 + \theta_2)\}(\cos \theta_3 + i \sin \theta_3)$$
$$= \cos(\theta_1 + \theta_2 + \theta_3) + i \sin(\theta_1 + \theta_2 + \theta_3)$$

Continuing this process, we can write

$$(\cos \theta_1 + i \sin \theta_1)(\cos \theta_2 + i \sin \theta_2)(\cos \theta_3 + i \sin \theta_3) \ldots \ldots (\cos \theta_n + i \sin \theta_n)$$
$$= \cos(\theta_1 + \theta_2 + \theta_3 + \ldots \theta_n) + i \sin(\theta_1 + \theta_2 + \theta_3 + \ldots \theta_n)$$

Putting $\theta_1 = \theta_2 = \theta_3 = \ldots = \theta$

we get $(\cos \theta + i \sin \theta)^n = \cos n\theta + i \sin n\theta$

Case II : n, negative integer

Let $n = -m$, where m is positive integer.

$\therefore \quad (\cos \theta + i \sin \theta)^n = (\cos \theta + i \sin \theta)^{-m} = \dfrac{1}{(\cos \theta + i \sin \theta)^m}$

$$= \dfrac{1}{(\cos m\theta + i \sin m\theta)} \quad \ldots \text{(by case I)}$$

$$= \dfrac{(\cos m\theta - i \sin m\theta)}{(\cos m\theta + i \sin m\theta)(\cos m\theta - i \sin m\theta)}$$

$$= \dfrac{\cos(-m)\theta + i \sin(-m)\theta}{\cos^2 m\theta + \sin^2 m\theta}$$

$$= \cos n\theta + i \sin n\theta \quad \ldots \text{(as } n = -m\text{)}$$

Case III : n rational number of the form $\dfrac{p}{q}$.

Let $n = \dfrac{p}{q}$ where q is positive integer and p is integer positive or negative.

Consider,

$$\left(\cos \dfrac{\theta}{q} + i \sin \dfrac{\theta}{q}\right)^q = \cos\left(q \cdot \dfrac{\theta}{q}\right) + i \sin\left(q \cdot \dfrac{\theta}{q}\right)$$

$$= \cos \theta + i \sin \theta \quad \ldots \text{(by case I)}$$

Thus $\cos \dfrac{\theta}{q} + i \sin \dfrac{\theta}{q}$ is such that its qth power is $\cos \theta + i \sin \theta$.

Hence $\cos\frac{\theta}{q} + i\sin\frac{\theta}{q}$ is one of the qth roots of $\cos\theta + i\sin\theta$.

i.e. $(\cos\theta + i\sin\theta)^{1/q} = \cos\frac{\theta}{q} + i\sin\frac{\theta}{q}$

Raising both sides to the power p

i.e. $(\cos\theta + i\sin\theta)^{p/q} = \left(\cos\frac{\theta}{q} + i\sin\frac{\theta}{q}\right)^p$

$= \cos\frac{p\theta}{q} + i\sin\frac{p\theta}{q}$ (by cases I and II)

$\therefore \quad (\cos\theta + i\sin\theta)^n = \cos n\theta + i\sin n\theta \quad \ldots \left(as\ n = \frac{p}{q}\right)$

which proves the Demoivre's theorem.

Remark : Demoivre's theorem has many applications such as (i) simplification of complex expressions, (ii) to obtain roots of complex numbers, (iii) to prove certain trigonometrical identities and many others.

4.15 ILLUSTRATIONS ON DEMOIVRE'S THEOREM

Ex. 1 : *Simplify using Demoivre's theorem, the expression*

$$\frac{(\cos 2\theta - i\sin 2\theta)^7 (\cos 3\theta + i\sin 3\theta)^{-5}}{(\cos 4\theta + i\sin 4\theta)^{12} (\cos 5\theta - i\sin 5\theta)^{-6}}$$

Sol. : $\cos 2\theta - i\sin 2\theta = \cos(-2\theta) + i\sin(-2\theta)$

$= (\cos\theta + i\sin\theta)^{-2}$,

$\cos 3\theta + i\sin 3\theta = (\cos\theta + i\sin\theta)^3$,

$\cos 4\theta + i\sin 4\theta = (\cos\theta + i\sin\theta)^4$,

$\cos 5\theta - i\sin 5\theta = \cos(-5\theta) + i\sin(-5\theta) = (\cos\theta + i\sin\theta)^{-5}$

The given expression is equal to

$$\frac{(\cos\theta + i\sin\theta)^{-14} (\cos\theta + i\sin\theta)^{-15}}{(\cos\theta + i\sin\theta)^{48} (\cos\theta + i\sin\theta)^{30}}$$

$= (\cos\theta + i\sin\theta)^{-14-15-48-30}$

$= (\cos\theta + i\sin\theta)^{-107}$

$= \cos(-107\theta) + i\sin(-107\theta)$

$= \cos 107\theta - i\sin 107\theta$

Ex. 2 : *Express $(1 + 7i)(2 - i)^{-2}$ in the form $r(\cos\theta + i\sin\theta)$ and prove that its fourth power is a real negative number.*

Sol. : Let $z = \dfrac{(1+7i)}{(2-i)^2} = \dfrac{(1+7i)}{4-4i-1}$

$= \dfrac{1+7i}{3-4i} \times \dfrac{3+4i}{3+4i} = \dfrac{-25+25i}{25}$

$= -1 + i$

Let $\quad z = -1+i = r(\cos\theta + i\sin\theta)$

$\therefore \quad r\cos\theta = -1, \quad r\sin\theta = 1$

$\therefore \quad r = \sqrt{2}, \quad \theta = \dfrac{3\pi}{4}$

$\therefore \quad z = \sqrt{2}\left(\cos\dfrac{3\pi}{4} + i\sin\dfrac{3\pi}{4}\right)$

and $\quad z^4 = \left[\sqrt{2}\left(\cos\dfrac{3\pi}{4} + i\sin\dfrac{3\pi}{4}\right)\right]^4$

$\qquad = (\sqrt{2})^4 (\cos 3\pi + i\sin 3\pi) = 4(-1)$

$\qquad = -4$ which is a real negative number.

Ex. 3 : *Find the modulus and principle value of the argument of* $\dfrac{(1+i\sqrt{3})^{13}}{(\sqrt{3}-i)^{11}}$.

Sol. : Let $\quad 1 + i\sqrt{3} = r(\cos\theta + i\sin\theta) \quad \begin{cases} \because\ r\cos\theta = 1,\ r\sin\theta = \sqrt{3} \\ \therefore\ r = 2,\ \theta = \pi/3 \end{cases}$

$\qquad\qquad\qquad = 2\left(\cos\dfrac{\pi}{3} + i\sin\dfrac{\pi}{3}\right)$

and $\quad \sqrt{3} - i = r(\cos\theta + i\sin\theta) \quad \begin{cases} \because\ r\cos\theta = \sqrt{3},\ r\sin\theta = -1 \\ \therefore\ r = 2,\ \theta = -\pi/6 \end{cases}$

$\qquad\qquad\qquad = 2(\cos\pi/6 - i\sin\pi/6)$

$\therefore \quad \dfrac{(1+i\sqrt{3})^{13}}{(\sqrt{3}-i)^{11}} = \dfrac{[2(\cos\pi/3 + i\sin\pi/3)]^{13}}{[2(\cos\pi/6 - i\sin\pi/6)]^{11}}$

$\qquad = \dfrac{2^{13}\left(\cos\dfrac{13\pi}{3} + i\sin\dfrac{13\pi}{3}\right)}{2^{11}\left(\cos\dfrac{11\pi}{6} - i\sin\dfrac{11\pi}{6}\right)}$

$\qquad = 2^2\left[\left(\cos\dfrac{13\pi}{3} + i\sin\dfrac{13\pi}{3}\right)\left(\cos\dfrac{11\pi}{6} - i\sin\dfrac{11\pi}{6}\right)^{-1}\right]$

$\qquad = 4\left[\left(\cos\dfrac{13\pi}{3} + i\sin\dfrac{13\pi}{3}\right)\left(\cos\dfrac{11\pi}{6} + i\sin\dfrac{11\pi}{6}\right)\right]$

$\qquad = 4\left[\cos\left(\dfrac{13\pi}{3} + \dfrac{11\pi}{6}\right) + i\sin\left(\dfrac{13\pi}{3} + \dfrac{11\pi}{6}\right)\right]$

$\qquad = 4\left[\cos\dfrac{37\pi}{6} + i\sin\dfrac{37\pi}{6}\right]$

$\qquad = 4\left[\cos\left(6\pi + \dfrac{\pi}{6}\right) + i\sin\left(6\pi + \dfrac{\pi}{6}\right)\right]$

$\qquad = 4\left[\cos\dfrac{\pi}{6} + i\sin\dfrac{\pi}{6}\right]$

Hence the modulus is 4 and principle value of argument is $\dfrac{\pi}{6}$.

Ex. 4 : *Simplify* $(\sin\theta + i\cos\theta)^n$.

Sol. : We can not apply Demoivre's theorem directly as it is not in the standard form $(\cos\theta + i\sin\theta)^n$.

$$\therefore \quad (\sin\theta + i\cos\theta)^n = \left\{\cos\left(\frac{\pi}{2}-\theta\right) + i\sin\left(\frac{\pi}{2}-\theta\right)\right\}^n$$

$$= \cos\left(\frac{n\pi}{2}-n\theta\right) + i\sin\left(\frac{n\pi}{2}-n\theta\right)$$

Ex. 5 : *Prove that* $\left[\dfrac{1+\sin\theta+i\cos\theta}{1+\sin\theta-i\cos\theta}\right]^n = \cos\left(\dfrac{n\pi}{2}-n\theta\right) + i\sin\left(\dfrac{n\pi}{2}-n\theta\right)$.

Sol. : L.H.S. $= \left[\dfrac{1+\cos\left(\frac{\pi}{2}-\theta\right)+i\sin\left(\frac{\pi}{2}-\theta\right)}{1+\cos\left(\frac{\pi}{2}-\theta\right)-i\sin\left(\frac{\pi}{2}-\theta\right)}\right]^n$

$$= \left[\dfrac{2\cos^2\left(\frac{\pi}{4}-\frac{\theta}{2}\right)+2i\sin\left(\frac{\pi}{4}-\frac{\theta}{2}\right)\cos\left(\frac{\pi}{4}-\frac{\theta}{2}\right)}{2\cos^2\left(\frac{\pi}{4}-\frac{\theta}{2}\right)-2i\sin\left(\frac{\pi}{4}-\frac{\theta}{2}\right)\cos\left(\frac{\pi}{4}-\frac{\theta}{2}\right)}\right]^n$$

Cancelling common factor $2\cos\left(\dfrac{\pi}{4}-\dfrac{\theta}{2}\right)$ in numerator and denominator, we obtain

$$\text{L.H.S.} = \left[\dfrac{\cos\left(\frac{\pi}{4}-\frac{\theta}{2}\right)+i\sin\left(\frac{\pi}{4}-\frac{\theta}{2}\right)}{\cos\left(\frac{\pi}{4}-\frac{\theta}{2}\right)-i\sin\left(\frac{\pi}{4}-\frac{\theta}{2}\right)}\right]^n$$

$$= \dfrac{\cos\left(\frac{n\pi}{4}-\frac{n\theta}{2}\right)+i\sin\left(\frac{n\pi}{4}-\frac{n\theta}{2}\right)}{\cos\left(\frac{n\pi}{4}-\frac{n\theta}{2}\right)-i\sin\left(\frac{n\pi}{4}-\frac{n\theta}{2}\right)} \qquad \text{... (By Demoivre's theorem)}$$

$$= \left[\cos\left(\frac{n\pi}{4}-\frac{n\theta}{2}\right)+i\sin\left(\frac{n\pi}{4}-\frac{n\theta}{2}\right)\right]\cdot\left[\cos\left(\frac{n\pi}{4}-\frac{n\theta}{2}\right)-i\sin\left(\frac{n\pi}{4}-\frac{n\theta}{2}\right)\right]^{-1}$$

$$= \left[\cos\left(\frac{n\pi}{4}-\frac{n\theta}{2}\right)+i\sin\left(\frac{n\pi}{4}-\frac{n\theta}{2}\right)\right]\cdot\left[\cos\left(\frac{n\pi}{4}-\frac{n\theta}{2}\right)+i\sin\left(\frac{n\pi}{4}-\frac{n\theta}{2}\right)\right]$$

$$= \cos\left(\frac{n\pi}{2}-n\theta\right)+i\sin\left(\frac{n\pi}{2}-n\theta\right)$$

$$= \text{R.H.S.}$$

Ex. 6 : Prove that $[(\cos\theta - \cos\phi) + i(\sin\theta - \sin\phi)]^n +$

$[(\cos\theta - \cos\phi) - i(\sin\theta - \sin\phi)]^n = 2^{n+1} \sin^n \dfrac{\theta-\phi}{2} \cos \dfrac{n(\theta+\phi+\pi)}{2}$.

Sol. : Since, $\cos\theta - \cos\phi = 2\sin\dfrac{\theta+\phi}{2}\sin\dfrac{\phi-\theta}{2}$

and $\sin\theta - \sin\phi = 2\cos\dfrac{\theta+\phi}{2}\sin\dfrac{\theta-\phi}{2}$

$\therefore$ $(\cos\theta - \cos\phi) + i(\sin\theta - \sin\phi)$

$= -2\sin\dfrac{\theta+\phi}{2}\sin\dfrac{\theta-\phi}{2} + i2\cos\dfrac{\theta+\phi}{2}\sin\dfrac{\theta-\phi}{2}$

$= 2\sin\dfrac{\theta-\phi}{2}\left[-\sin\dfrac{\theta-\phi}{2} + i\cos\dfrac{\theta+\phi}{2}\right]$

$= 2\sin\dfrac{\theta-\phi}{2}\left[\cos\left(\dfrac{\pi}{2}+\dfrac{\theta+\phi}{2}\right) + i\sin\left(\dfrac{\pi}{2}+\dfrac{\theta+\phi}{2}\right)\right]$

$\therefore$ $[(\cos\theta - \cos\phi) + i(\sin\theta - \sin\phi)]^n$

$= 2^n \sin^n\dfrac{\theta-\phi}{2}\left[\cos\left(\dfrac{\pi}{2}+\dfrac{\theta+\phi}{2}\right) + i\sin\left(\dfrac{\pi}{2}+\dfrac{\theta+\phi}{2}\right)\right]^n$

$= 2^n \sin^n\dfrac{\theta-\phi}{2}\left[\cos\left(\dfrac{n\pi}{2}+\dfrac{n(\theta+\phi)}{2}\right) + i\sin\left(\dfrac{n\pi}{2}+\dfrac{n(\theta+\phi)}{2}\right)\right]$ ... (1)

[By using Demoivre's theorem]

Similarly,

$[(\cos\theta - \cos\phi) - i(\sin\theta - \sin\phi)]^n$

$= 2^n \sin^n\dfrac{\theta-\phi}{2}\left[\cos\left(\dfrac{n\pi}{2}+\dfrac{n(\theta+\phi)}{2}\right) - i\sin\left(\dfrac{n\pi}{2}+\dfrac{n(\theta+\phi)}{2}\right)\right]$ ... (2)

Adding (1) and (2), we get the required result.

Ex. 7 : Prove that $(x+iy)^{m/n} + (x-iy)^{m/n} = 2(x^2+y^2)^{m/2n} \cdot \cos\left(\dfrac{m}{n}\tan^{-1}\dfrac{y}{x}\right)$.

Sol. : Let $x + iy = r(\cos\theta + i\sin\theta)$

$\therefore$ $x = r\cos\theta,\quad y = r\sin\theta$

$\therefore$ $r^2 = x^2 + y^2$ or $r = \sqrt{x^2+y^2}$

and $\tan\theta = \dfrac{y}{x}$ or $\theta = \tan^{-1}\dfrac{y}{x}$

Now, $x + iy = r(\cos\theta + i\sin\theta)$

$(x+iy)^{m/n} = r^{m/n}\left\{\cos\left(\dfrac{m}{n}\theta\right) + i\sin\left(\dfrac{m}{n}\theta\right)\right\}$

$$x - iy = r(\cos\theta - i\sin\theta) = r\{\cos(-\theta) + i\sin(-\theta)\}$$

$$\therefore \quad (x - iy)^{m/n} = r^{m/n}\left\{\cos\left(-\frac{m}{n}\theta\right) + i\sin\left(-\frac{m}{n}\theta\right)\right\}$$

$$= r^{m/n}\left\{\cos\frac{m}{n}\theta - i\sin\frac{m}{n}\theta\right\}$$

$$\therefore (x+iy)^{m/n} + (x-iy)^{m/n} = 2r^{m/n}\cos\left(\frac{m}{n}\theta\right) = 2(x^2+y^2)^{m/2n}\cos\left(\frac{m}{n}\tan^{-1}\frac{y}{x}\right)$$

Ex. 8 : If $x_r = \cos\left(\dfrac{\pi}{2^r}\right) + i\sin\left(\dfrac{\pi}{2^r}\right)$, show that $x_1 \cdot x_2 \cdot x_3 \ldots x_\infty = -1$.

Sol. : We have
$$x_1 = \cos\left(\frac{\pi}{2}\right) + i\sin\left(\frac{\pi}{2}\right)$$

$$x_2 = \cos\frac{\pi}{2^2} + i\sin\frac{\pi}{2^2}$$

$$x_3 = \cos\frac{\pi}{2^3} + i\sin\frac{\pi}{2^3}$$

... .

$$x_r = \cos\frac{\pi}{2^r} + i\sin\frac{\pi}{2^r}$$

$$\therefore \quad x_1 \cdot x_2 \cdot x_3 \ldots \ldots x_\infty = \left[\left(\cos\frac{\pi}{2} + i\sin\frac{\pi}{2}\right)\left(\cos\frac{\pi}{2^2} + i\sin\frac{\pi}{2^2}\right)\left(\cos\frac{\pi}{2^3} + i\sin\frac{\pi}{2^3}\right)\right.$$

$$\left.\ldots\ldots\left(\cos\frac{\pi}{2^r} + i\sin\frac{\pi}{2^r}\right)\ldots\ldots\right]$$

$$= \cos\left(\frac{\pi}{2} + \frac{\pi}{2^2} + \frac{\pi}{2^3} + \ldots + \frac{\pi}{2^r} + \ldots\right)$$

$$+ i\sin\left(\frac{\pi}{2} + \frac{\pi}{2^2} + \frac{\pi}{2^3} + \ldots + \frac{\pi}{2^r} + \ldots\right)$$

Now, $\dfrac{\pi}{2} + \dfrac{\pi}{2^2} + \dfrac{\pi}{2^3} + \ldots + \dfrac{\pi}{2^r} + \ldots \infty$ is the sum of a geometric infinite series with first term $\dfrac{\pi}{2}$ and common ratio $\dfrac{1}{2}$.

$\therefore$ Its sum is given by $\dfrac{\pi/2}{1 - 1/2} = \pi$

$\therefore \quad x_1 \cdot x_2 \cdot x_3 \ldots x_\infty = \cos\pi + i\sin\pi = -1$

Ex. 9 : Prove that if n is any positive integer and
$$(1 + x)^n = P_0 + P_1 + P_2 x^2 + \ldots + P_n x^n + \ldots$$

then
(i) $P_0 - P_2 + P_4 \ldots = 2^{n/2}\cos\dfrac{n\pi}{4}$

(ii) $P_0 + P_4 + P_8 \ldots = 2^{n-2} + 2^{(n/2)-1}\cos\dfrac{n\pi}{4}$.

Sol. : To prove part (i), put $x = i$

$$\therefore \quad (1 + i)^n = P_0 + P_1 + P_2 + P_2 i^2 + P_3 i^3 + P_4 i^4 \ldots$$

Now, $\quad 1 + i = r(\cos \theta + i \sin \theta)$

$\therefore \quad r \cos \theta = 1, \; r \sin \theta = 1$ that gives $r = \sqrt{2}$ and $\theta = \dfrac{\pi}{4}$.

$$\therefore \quad 1 + i = \sqrt{2}\left(\cos \frac{\pi}{4} + i \sin \frac{\pi}{4}\right)$$

and $\quad (1 + i)^n = 2^{n/2}\left(\cos \dfrac{n\pi}{4} + i \sin \dfrac{n\pi}{4}\right)$

$$\therefore \quad 2^{n/2}\left(\cos \frac{n\pi}{4} + i \sin \frac{n\pi}{4}\right) = P_0 + P_1 i - P_2 - P_3 i + P_4 \ldots$$

Equating real parts

$$2^{n/2} \cos \frac{n\pi}{4} = P_0 - P_2 + P_4 \ldots \qquad \ldots (1)$$

which proves result (i).

To prove part (ii), first put $x = 1$.

$$\therefore \quad (1 + x)^n = (1 + 1)^n = P_0 + P_1 + P_2 \ldots P_n$$

$$\therefore \quad 2^n = P_0 + P_1 + P_2 + P_3 + P_4 \ldots P_n \qquad \ldots (2)$$

Again putting $x = -1$,

$$0 = P_0 - P_1 + P_2 - P_3 + P_4 \ldots \qquad \ldots (3)$$

Adding (2) and (3),

$$2^n = 2(P_0 + P_2 + P_4 \ldots)$$
$$2^{n-1} = P_0 + P_2 + P_4 \ldots \qquad \ldots (4)$$

Adding (1) and (4),

$$2^{n/2} \cos \frac{n\pi}{4} + 2^{n-1} = 2(P_0 + P_4 + P_8 \ldots)$$

$$\therefore \quad 2^{(n/2)-1} \cos \frac{n\pi}{4} + 2^{n-2} = P_0 + P_4 + P_8 \ldots$$

which proves desired result (ii).

Ex. 10 : If $\alpha = 1 + i$, $\beta = 1 - i$ and $\cot \phi = x + 1$, prove that

$$\dfrac{(x + \alpha)^n - (x + \beta)^n}{\alpha - \beta} = \sin n\phi \, \text{cosec}^n \phi \qquad \text{(Dec. 2004, May 2014)}$$

Sol. : $\quad x + \alpha = x + 1 + i = \cot \phi + i$

$$= \dfrac{\cos \phi + i \sin \phi}{\sin \phi}$$

$$\therefore \quad (x+\alpha)^n = \left(\frac{\cos\phi + i\sin\phi}{\sin\phi}\right)^n = \frac{\cos n\phi + i\sin n\phi}{\sin^n\phi} \quad \ldots (1)$$

Similarly, $\quad x + \beta = x + 1 - i = \cot\phi - i = \dfrac{\cos\phi - i\sin\phi}{\sin\phi}$

$$\therefore \quad (x+\beta)^n = \left(\frac{\cos\phi - i\sin\phi}{\sin\phi}\right)^n$$

$$= \frac{\cos n\phi - i\sin n\phi}{\sin^n\phi} \quad \ldots (2)$$

and $\quad \alpha - \beta = (1+i) - (1-i)$

$$= 2i \quad \ldots (3)$$

From (1), (2) and (3),

$$\frac{(x+\alpha)^n - (x+\beta)^n}{\alpha - \beta} = \frac{(\cos n\phi + i\sin n\phi) - (\cos n\phi - i\sin n\phi)}{2i\sin^n\phi}$$

$$= \frac{2i\sin n\phi}{2i\sin^n\phi}$$

$$= \sin n\phi \, \mathrm{cosec}^n\phi$$

Ex. 11 : *Prove that*

$$(1 - e^{i\theta})^{-1/2} + (1 - e^{-i\theta})^{-1/2} = \left(1 + \mathrm{cosec}\,\frac{\theta}{2}\right)^{1/2}$$

Sol. : $\quad (1 - e^{i\theta}) = (1 - \cos\theta - i\sin\theta) = \left(2\sin^2\dfrac{\theta}{2} - 2i\sin\dfrac{\theta}{2}\cos\dfrac{\theta}{2}\right)$

$$= \left(2\sin\dfrac{\theta}{2}\right)\left(\sin\dfrac{\theta}{2} - i\cos\dfrac{\theta}{2}\right)$$

$$= \left(2\sin\dfrac{\theta}{2}\right)\left[\cos\left(\dfrac{\pi}{2} - \dfrac{\theta}{2}\right) - i\sin\left(\dfrac{\pi}{2} - \dfrac{\theta}{2}\right)\right]$$

$$= \left(2\sin\dfrac{\theta}{2}\right)(e^{-i\phi}), \quad \phi = \dfrac{\pi}{2} - \dfrac{\theta}{2}$$

$$\therefore \quad (1 - e^{i\theta})^{-1/2} = \left(2\sin\dfrac{\theta}{2}\right)^{-1/2}(e^{-i\phi})^{-1/2} = \left(2\sin\dfrac{\theta}{2}\right)^{-1/2} e^{i\phi/2} \quad \ldots (1)$$

Similarly, $\quad (1 - e^{-i\theta}) = (1 - \cos\theta + i\sin\theta) = \left(2\sin^2\dfrac{\theta}{2} + 2i\sin\dfrac{\theta}{2}\cos\dfrac{\theta}{2}\right)$

$$= \left(2\sin\dfrac{\theta}{2}\right)\left(\sin\dfrac{\theta}{2} + i\cos\dfrac{\theta}{2}\right)$$

$$= \left(2\sin\dfrac{\theta}{2}\right)(e^{i\phi}), \quad \phi = \dfrac{\pi}{2} - \dfrac{\theta}{2}$$

$$\therefore \quad (1 - e^{-i\theta})^{-1/2} = \left(2 \sin \frac{\theta}{2}\right)^{-1/2} (e^{i\phi})^{-1/2}$$

$$= \left(2 \sin \frac{\theta}{2}\right)^{-1/2} e^{-i\phi/2} \qquad \ldots (2)$$

Hence from (1) and (2),

$$(1 - e^{i\theta})^{-1/2} + (1 - e^{-i\theta})^{-1/2} = \left(2 \sin \frac{\theta}{2}\right)^{-1/2} (e^{i\phi/2} + e^{-i\phi/2})$$

$$= \left(2 \sin \frac{\theta}{2}\right)^{-1/2} \left(2 \cos \frac{\phi}{2}\right)$$

$$= \frac{2 \cos \frac{\phi}{2}}{\left(2 \sin \frac{\theta}{2}\right)^{1/2}} = \left[\frac{4 \cos^2 \frac{\phi}{2}}{2 \sin \frac{\theta}{2}}\right]^{1/2}$$

$$= \left[\frac{1 + \cos \phi}{\sin \frac{\theta}{2}}\right]^{1/2} = \left(\frac{1 + \sin \frac{\theta}{2}}{\sin \frac{\theta}{2}}\right)^{1/2}, \quad \text{as } \phi = \frac{\pi}{2} - \frac{\theta}{2}$$

$$= \left(1 + \text{cosec} \frac{\theta}{2}\right)^{1/2}$$

Ex. 12 : If $\cos \alpha + \cos \beta + \cos \gamma = 0 = \sin \alpha + \sin \beta + \sin \gamma$ then show that

(a) $\cos 3\alpha + \cos 3\beta + \cos 3\gamma = 3 \cos (\alpha + \beta + \gamma)$,
$\sin 3\alpha + \sin 3\beta + \sin 3\gamma = 3 \sin (\alpha + \beta + \gamma)$

(b) $\cos 2\alpha + \cos 2\beta + \cos 2\gamma = 0 = \sin 2\alpha + \sin 2\beta + \sin 2\gamma$ **(May 2011)**

(c) $\cos^2 \alpha + \cos^2 \beta + \cos^2 \gamma = \frac{3}{2} = \sin^2 \alpha + \sin^2 \beta + \sin^2 \gamma$.

Sol. : Let $\quad a = \cos \alpha + i \sin \alpha = e^{i\alpha}, \ b = \cos \beta + i \sin \beta = e^{i\beta},$
$\qquad \qquad c = \cos \gamma + i \sin \gamma = e^{i\gamma}$

then $\quad a + b + c = e^{i\alpha} + e^{i\beta} + e^{i\gamma} = (\cos \alpha + \cos \beta + \cos \gamma) + i (\sin \alpha + \sin \beta + \sin \gamma)$

$\therefore \qquad a + b + c = 0 \qquad \ldots (1)$

and $\frac{1}{a} + \frac{1}{b} + \frac{1}{c} = e^{-i\alpha} + e^{-i\beta} + e^{-i\gamma}$

$\qquad \qquad = (\cos \alpha + \cos \beta + \cos \gamma) - i (\sin \alpha + \sin \beta + \sin \gamma) = 0$

Also, $\frac{1}{a} + \frac{1}{b} + \frac{1}{c} = 0 \Rightarrow ab + bc + ca = 0 \qquad \ldots (2)$

$\therefore \quad a^2 + b^2 + c^2 = (a + b + c)^2 - 2(ab + bc + ca) = 0 \qquad$ [by (1) and (2)]

i.e. $\quad a^2 + b^2 + c^2 = 0 \qquad \ldots (3)$

Again $a^3 + b^3 + c^3 - 3abc = (a + b + c)(a^2 + b^2 + c^2 - ab - bc - ca) = 0$ [by (1), (2), (3)]
$$a^3 + b^3 + c^3 - 3abc = 0 \qquad \ldots (4)$$

Part a, we have from (4),
$$a^3 + b^3 + c^3 = 3abc$$
$$e^{3i\alpha} + e^{3i\beta} + e^{3i\gamma} = 3e^{i(\alpha + \beta + \gamma)}$$
$$(\cos 3\alpha + \cos 3\beta + \cos 3\gamma) + i(\sin 3\alpha + \sin 3\beta + \sin 3\gamma)$$
$$= 3[\cos(\alpha + \beta + \gamma) + i\sin(\alpha + \beta + \gamma)]$$

Equating real and imaginary parts, we get
$$\cos 3\alpha + \cos 3\beta + \cos 3\gamma = 3\cos(\alpha + \beta + \gamma)$$
$$\sin 3\alpha + \sin 3\beta + \sin 3\gamma = 3\sin(\alpha + \beta + \gamma)$$

Part b, we have from (3),
$$a^2 + b^2 + c^2 = 0$$
$$(\cos 2\alpha + \cos 2\beta + \cos 2\gamma) + i(\sin 2\alpha + \sin 2\beta + \sin 2\gamma) = 0$$
hence $\cos 2\alpha + \cos 2\beta + \cos 2\gamma = 0$
$$\sin 2\alpha + \sin 2\beta + \sin 2\gamma = 0$$

Part c, we have from part b,
$$\cos 2\alpha + \cos 2\beta + \cos 2\gamma = 0$$
i.e. $(2\cos^2\alpha - 1) + (2\cos^2\beta - 1) + (2\cos^2\gamma - 1) = 0$

$\therefore \qquad \cos^2\alpha + \cos^2\beta + \cos^2\gamma = \dfrac{3}{2}$

$\therefore \qquad 1 - \sin^2\alpha + 1 - \sin^2\beta + 1 - \sin^2\gamma = \dfrac{3}{2}$

$\therefore \qquad \sin^2\alpha + \sin^2\beta + \sin^2\gamma = 3 - \dfrac{3}{2} = \dfrac{3}{2}$

$\therefore \qquad \cos^2\alpha + \cos^2\beta + \cos^2\gamma = \dfrac{3}{2} = \sin^2\alpha + \sin^2\beta + \sin^2\gamma$

Ex. 13 : If $x = \cos\alpha + i\sin\alpha$, $y = \cos\beta + i\sin\beta$, $z = \cos\gamma + i\sin\gamma$ and $u = \cos\delta + i\sin\delta$, prove that

(i) $xy + zu = 2\cos\left(\dfrac{\alpha + \beta - \gamma - \delta}{2}\right)\left[\cos\left(\dfrac{\alpha + \beta + \gamma + \delta}{2}\right) + i\sin\left(\dfrac{\alpha + \beta + \gamma + \delta}{2}\right)\right]$

(ii) $\dfrac{1}{(x - y)(z - u)}$

$= -\dfrac{1}{4}\operatorname{cosec}\left(\dfrac{\alpha - \beta}{2}\right)\operatorname{cosec}\left(\dfrac{\gamma - \delta}{2}\right)\left[\cos\left(\dfrac{\alpha + \beta + \gamma + \delta}{2}\right) - i\sin\left(\dfrac{\alpha + \beta + \gamma + \delta}{2}\right)\right]$

Sol. : (i)
$$xy + zu = [\cos(\alpha+\beta) + i\sin(\alpha+\beta)] + [\cos(\gamma+\delta) + i\sin(\gamma+\delta)]$$
$$= [\cos(\alpha+\beta) + \cos(\gamma+\delta)] + i[\sin(\alpha+\beta) + \sin(\gamma+\delta)]$$
$$= \left[2\cos\left(\frac{\alpha+\beta+\gamma+\delta}{2}\right)\cos\left(\frac{\alpha+\beta-\gamma-\delta}{2}\right)\right]$$
$$+ i\left[2\sin\left(\frac{\alpha+\beta+\gamma+\delta}{2}\right)\cos\left(\frac{\alpha+\beta-\gamma-\delta}{2}\right)\right]$$
$$= 2\cos\left(\frac{\alpha+\beta-\gamma-\delta}{2}\right)\left[\cos\left(\frac{\alpha+\beta+\gamma+\delta}{2}\right) + i\sin\left(\frac{\alpha+\beta+\gamma+\delta}{2}\right)\right]$$

(ii)
$$(x-y) = (\cos\alpha - \cos\beta) + i(\sin\alpha - \sin\gamma)$$
$$= \left[-2\sin\left(\frac{\alpha+\beta}{2}\right)\sin\left(\frac{\alpha-\beta}{2}\right)\right] + i\left[2\sin\left(\frac{\alpha-\beta}{2}\right)\cos\left(\frac{\alpha+\beta}{2}\right)\right]$$
$$= 2i\sin\left(\frac{\alpha-\beta}{2}\right)\left[\cos\left(\frac{\alpha+\beta}{2}\right) + i\sin\left(\frac{\alpha+\beta}{2}\right)\right]$$

Similarly,
$$(z-u) = 2i\sin\left(\frac{\gamma-\delta}{2}\right)\left[\cos\left(\frac{\gamma+\delta}{2}\right) + i\sin\left(\frac{\gamma+\delta}{2}\right)\right]$$

$$\therefore \quad \frac{1}{(x-y)(z-u)} =$$
$$-\frac{1}{4}\operatorname{cosec}\left(\frac{\alpha-\beta}{2}\right)\operatorname{cosec}\left(\frac{\gamma-\delta}{2}\right)\left[\cos\left(\frac{\alpha+\beta+\gamma+\delta}{2}\right) + i\sin\left(\frac{\alpha+\beta+\gamma+\delta}{2}\right)\right]^{-1}$$
$$= -\frac{1}{4}\operatorname{cosec}\left(\frac{\alpha-\beta}{2}\right)\operatorname{cosec}\left(\frac{\gamma-\delta}{2}\right)\left[\cos\left(\frac{\alpha+\beta+\gamma+\delta}{2}\right) - i\sin\left(\frac{\alpha+\beta+\gamma+\delta}{2}\right)\right]$$

Ex. 14 : If α and β are the roots of $z^2 \sin^2\theta - z\sin 2\theta + 1 = 0$, prove that
$$\alpha^n + \beta^n = 2\cos n\theta \operatorname{cosec}^n \theta \text{ where } n \text{ is a integer.} \qquad \textbf{(Dec. 2003, Dec. 2010)}$$

Sol. : Roots of given quadratic in z,
$$z = \frac{\sin 2\theta \pm \sqrt{\sin^2 2\theta - 4\sin^2\theta}}{2\sin^2\theta}$$
$$= \frac{2\sin\theta\cos\theta \pm \sqrt{4\sin^2\theta\cos^2\theta - 4\sin^2\theta}}{2\sin^2\theta} = \frac{\cos\theta \pm \sqrt{\cos^2\theta - 1}}{\sin\theta}$$
$$= (\cos\theta \pm i\sin\theta)\operatorname{cosec}\theta$$

Let $\quad \alpha = (\cos\theta + i\sin\theta)\operatorname{cosec}\theta, \quad \beta = (\cos\theta - i\sin\theta)\operatorname{cosec}\theta$

Then $\quad \alpha^n + \beta^n = [(\cos\theta + i\sin\theta)\operatorname{cosec}\theta]^n + [(\cos\theta - i\sin\theta)\operatorname{cosec}\theta]^n$
$$= (\cos n\theta + i\sin n\theta)\operatorname{cosec}^n\theta + (\cos n\theta - i\sin n\theta)\operatorname{cosec}^n\theta$$
$$= 2\cos n\theta \operatorname{cosec}^n\theta$$

Ex. 15 : If $z = -1 + i\sqrt{3}$ and n is an integer, prove that $2^{2n} + 2^n z^n + z^{2n}$ is zero, if n is not multiple of 3. **(Dec. 2009)**

Sol : $\quad z = -1 + i\sqrt{3} = 2\, e^{i\left(\frac{2\pi}{3}\right)}$

$\therefore\ 2^{2n} + 2^n z^n + z^{2n} = 2^{2n} + 2^n\, 2^n\, e^{i\left(\frac{2n\pi}{3}\right)} + 2^{2n} e^{i\left(\frac{4n\pi}{3}\right)}$

$\qquad = 2^{2n}\left[1 + e^{in(\pi - \pi/3)} + e^{in(\pi + \pi/3)}\right]$

$\qquad = 2^{2n}\left[1 + e^{in\pi}(e^{-in\pi/3} + e^{in\pi/3})\right]$

$\qquad = 2^{2n}\left[1 + (\cos n\pi + i\sin n\pi)\cdot 2\cos\dfrac{n\pi}{3}\right]$

$\qquad = 2^{2n}\left[1 + 2\cos n\pi \cdot \cos\dfrac{n\pi}{3}\right],\ n = 3k\pm 1\qquad$ [as $\sin n\pi = 0$]

$\qquad = 2^{2(3k+1)}\left[1 + 2(-1)^{3k+1}\cos(3k\pm 1)\dfrac{\pi}{3}\right]\qquad$ [as $\cos n\pi = (-1)^n$]

$\qquad = 2^{6k+2}\left[1 + 2(-1)^{3k+1}\cos\left(k\pi \pm \dfrac{\pi}{3}\right)\right]$

$\qquad = 2^{6k+2}\left[1 + 2(-1)^{3k+1}\cos k\pi \cos\dfrac{\pi}{3}\right]$

$\qquad = 2^{6k+2}\left[1 + 2(-1)^{4k+1}\dfrac{1}{2}\right]\qquad$ [as $\cos k\pi = (-1)^k$]

$\qquad = 2^{6k+2}\left[1 + 2(-1)\dfrac{1}{2}\right]$

$\qquad = 0,\quad$ if $n = 3k + 1$ (i.e. n is not a multiple of 3)

Ex. 16 : Prove that $\left(\dfrac{-1+i\sqrt{3}}{2}\right)^n + \left(\dfrac{-1-i\sqrt{3}}{2}\right)^n$ has the value -1 if $n = 3k \pm 1$ and 2 if $n = 3k$, where k is an integer. **(May 2005, May 2010)**

Sol. : $\quad \dfrac{-1+i\sqrt{3}}{2} = -\dfrac{1}{2} + i\dfrac{\sqrt{3}}{2} = \left(\cos\dfrac{2\pi}{3} + i\sin\dfrac{2\pi}{3}\right)$

$\therefore\ \left(\dfrac{-1+i\sqrt{3}}{2}\right)^n = \cos\dfrac{2n\pi}{3} + i\sin\dfrac{2n\pi}{3} \qquad \ldots (1)$

Similarly,

$\qquad \left(\dfrac{-1-i\sqrt{3}}{2}\right)^n = \cos\dfrac{2n\pi}{3} - i\sin\dfrac{2n\pi}{3} \qquad \ldots (2)$

Adding (1) and (2), we get

$\left(\dfrac{-1+i\sqrt{3}}{2}\right)^n + \left(\dfrac{-1-i\sqrt{3}}{2}\right)^n = 2\cos\dfrac{2n\pi}{3}$

Case I : If $n = 3k \pm 1$

$$\text{given expression} = 2\cos\left\{\frac{2\pi}{3}(3k \pm 1)\right\} = 2\cos\left(2k\pi \pm \frac{2\pi}{3}\right)$$

$$= 2\cos\left(\pm \frac{2\pi}{3}\right) = 2\cos\left(\frac{2\pi}{3}\right)$$

$$= 2\left(-\frac{1}{2}\right) = -1$$

Case II : If $n = 3k$

$$\text{given expression} = 2\cos\left(\frac{2\pi}{3} \cdot 3k\right) = 2\cos(2k\pi)$$

$$= 2(1) = 2$$

EXERCISE 4.3

1. Simplify using Demoivre's theorem :

    (i) $\dfrac{(\cos 3\theta + i\sin 3\theta)^8 \ (\cos 4\theta - i\sin 4\theta)^{-2}}{(\cos 2\theta - i\sin 2\theta)^4 (\cos \theta + i\sin \theta)^3}$, (ii) $\dfrac{(1+i)(1+\sqrt{3}\,i)}{i(1-\sqrt{3}\,i)}$,

    (iii) $\left(\dfrac{1}{\sqrt{2}} + \dfrac{i}{\sqrt{2}}\right)^{10} + \left(\dfrac{1}{\sqrt{2}} - \dfrac{i}{\sqrt{2}}\right)^{10}$

    Ans. (i) $\cos 37\theta + i\sin 37\theta$, (ii) $\sqrt{2}\left[\cos\dfrac{5\pi}{12} + i\sin\dfrac{5\pi}{12}\right]$, (iii) 0.

2. If $z_1 = e^{i\alpha}$, $z_2 = e^{i\beta}$, where $0 < \alpha < \dfrac{\pi}{2}$, $0 < \beta < \dfrac{\pi}{2}$, find modulus and argument of $\dfrac{1 + z_1^2}{1 - i z_1 z_2}$.

    Ans. Modulus $= \cos\alpha \sec\left(\dfrac{\pi}{4} - \dfrac{\alpha}{2} - \dfrac{\beta}{2}\right)$ and argument $= \left(\dfrac{\pi}{4} + \dfrac{\alpha - \beta}{2}\right)$.

3. Prove that $(1 + i\sqrt{3})^8 + (1 - i\sqrt{3})^8 = -256$.

4. If $2\cos\phi = x + \dfrac{1}{x}$ and $2\cos\Psi = y + \dfrac{1}{y}$, prove that **(May 2004, 2014, May 2015)**

    (i) $x^m y^n + \dfrac{1}{x^m y^n} = 2\cos(m\phi + n\Psi)$, (ii) $\dfrac{x^m}{y^n} + \dfrac{y^n}{x^m} = 2\cos(m\phi - n\Psi)$

    [Hint : Given $x^2 - 2\cos\theta\, x + 1 = 0$, solve for x.]

5. Prove that $(1 + \cos\theta + i\sin\theta)^n + (1 + \cos\theta - i\sin\theta)^n = 2^{n+1}\cos^n\dfrac{\theta}{2}\cos\dfrac{n\theta}{2}$.

6. If α, β are the roots of $x^2 - 2x + 2 = 0$, prove that $\alpha^n + \beta^n = 2^{n/2+1}\cos\dfrac{n\pi}{4}$.

7. If α, β are the roots of $t^2 - 2t + 2 = 0$, find the value of x such that
$$\frac{(x+\alpha)^n - (x+\beta)^n}{\alpha - \beta} = \frac{\sin n\theta}{\sin^n \theta}.$$

   [Hint: $\alpha = 1 + i$, $\beta = 1 - i$ $\therefore$ L.H.S. $= \frac{1}{2i}[(x+1+i)^n - (x+1-i)^n] = r^n \sin n\phi$
   $= \frac{\sin n\phi}{\sin^n \phi} =$ R.H.S.; for $x + 1 = r \cos \phi$, $1 = r \sin \phi$ $\therefore \phi = \theta$. Thus $x = r \cos \theta - 1 = \cot \theta - 1$.]

8. If $z = x + iy = r(\cos \theta + i \sin \theta)$, prove that $\sqrt{z} = \pm \frac{1}{\sqrt{2}}\left[\sqrt{r+x} \pm i\sqrt{r-x}\right]$.

   [Hint: Use $\cos \frac{\theta}{2} = \pm\sqrt{\frac{1+\cos \theta}{2}}$, $\sin \frac{\theta}{2} = \pm\sqrt{\frac{1-\cos \theta}{2}}$].

9. If $a = \cos 2\alpha + i \sin 2\alpha$, $b = \cos 2\beta + i \sin 2\beta$ and $c = \cos 2\gamma + i \sin 2\gamma$, prove that
   (i) $\sqrt{\frac{a}{b}} + \sqrt{\frac{b}{a}} = 2\cos(\alpha - \beta)$, (ii) $\sqrt{\frac{a}{b}} - \sqrt{\frac{b}{a}} = 2i\sin(\alpha - \beta)$,
   (iii) $\sqrt{\frac{ab}{c}} + \sqrt{\frac{c}{ab}} = 2\cos(\alpha + \beta - \gamma)$.

   [Hint: $\frac{a}{b} = e^{i2(\alpha - \beta)}$, $\frac{b}{a} = e^{-i2(\alpha - \beta)}$, $\frac{ab}{c} = e^{i2(\alpha + \beta - \gamma)}$, $\frac{c}{ab} = e^{-i2(\alpha + \beta - \gamma)}$].

10. If $\sin \alpha + \sin \beta + \sin \gamma = \cos \alpha + \cos \beta + \cos \gamma = 0$, prove that
    (i) $\cos(\beta + \gamma) + \cos(\gamma + \alpha) + \cos(\alpha + \beta) = 0$
    (ii) $\sin(\beta + \gamma) + \sin(\gamma + \alpha) + \sin(\alpha + \beta) = 0$

11. If $\sin \alpha + \sin \beta = 0 = \cos \alpha + \cos \beta$, prove that
    (i) $\cos 2\alpha + \cos 2\beta = 2\cos(\pi + \alpha + \beta)$
    (ii) $\sin 2\alpha + \sin 2\beta = 2\sin(\pi + \alpha + \beta)$.
    [Hint: Let $a = e^{i\alpha}$, $b = e^{i\beta}$, $a + b = 0$, $(a+b)^2 = 0$, $a^2 + b^2 = -2ab$]

12. If $\sin A + 2\sin B + 3\sin C = \cos A + 2\cos B + 3\cos C = 0$, prove that
    (i) $\sin 3A + 8\sin 3B + 27\sin 3C = 18\sin(A+B+C)$
    (ii) $\cos 3A + 8\cos 3B + 27\cos 3C = 18\cos(A+B+C)$

13. If $x = \cos \alpha + i \sin \alpha$, $y = \cos \beta + i \sin \beta$, prove that $\frac{x-y}{x+y} = i \tan \frac{\alpha - \beta}{2}$.

14. If $2\cos \theta = x + \frac{1}{x}$, prove that $\frac{x^{2n}+1}{x^{2n-1}+x} = \frac{\cos n\theta}{\cos(n-1)\theta}$.

    [Hint: $x = \cos \theta + i \sin \theta$, use Demoivre's theorem]

15. Find the value of $(3 + 4i)^{1/2} + (3 - 4i)^{1/2}$.
    [Hint: $3 + 4i = re^{i\theta}$]
    Ans. $2\sqrt{5} \cos\left(\frac{1}{2}\tan^{-1}\frac{4}{3}\right)$.

16. Prove that $\dfrac{1 + \sin\theta + i\cos\theta}{1 + \sin\theta - i\cos\theta} = \sin\theta + i\cos\theta$ and hence show that

$$\left(1 + \sin\dfrac{\pi}{5} + i\cos\dfrac{\pi}{5}\right)^5 + i\left(1 + \sin\dfrac{\pi}{5} - i\cos\dfrac{\pi}{5}\right)^5 = 0.$$

[Hint: Put $\theta = \dfrac{\pi}{5}$, $\dfrac{1 + \sin\dfrac{\pi}{5} + i\cos\dfrac{\pi}{5}}{1 + \sin\dfrac{\pi}{5} - i\cos\dfrac{\pi}{5}} = \sin\dfrac{\pi}{5} + i\cos\dfrac{\pi}{5} = \cos\left(\dfrac{\pi}{2} - \dfrac{\pi}{5}\right) + i\sin\left(\dfrac{\pi}{2} - \dfrac{\pi}{5}\right)$ raise to the power 5 on both sides and simplify.]

17. If $z = \cos\theta + i\sin\theta$, prove that $\dfrac{2}{1+z} = 1 - i\tan\dfrac{\theta}{2}$ and $\dfrac{1+z}{1-z} = i\cot\dfrac{\theta}{2}$.

[Hint: $\dfrac{1+z}{1-z} = \cot\dfrac{\theta}{2}\left[\dfrac{\cos\dfrac{\theta}{2} + i\sin\dfrac{\theta}{2}}{\sin\dfrac{\theta}{2} - i\cos\dfrac{\theta}{2}}\right] = i\cot\dfrac{\theta}{2}\left[\dfrac{\cos\dfrac{\theta}{2} + i\sin\dfrac{\theta}{2}}{i\sin\dfrac{\theta}{2} - i^2\cos\dfrac{\theta}{2}}\right] = i\cot\dfrac{\theta}{2}$]

18. If $\sin\Psi = i\tan\theta$, prove that $\cos\theta + i\sin\theta = \tan\left(\dfrac{\pi}{4} + \dfrac{\Psi}{2}\right)$.

[Hint: Let $\dfrac{\cos\theta}{i\sin\theta} = \dfrac{1}{\sin\Psi}$, By componendo and dividendo,

$\left(\dfrac{\cos\theta + i\sin\theta}{\cos\theta - i\sin\theta}\right) = \dfrac{1 + \sin\Psi}{1 - \sin\Psi}$].

4.16 APPLICATION OF DEMOIVRE'S THEOREM TO SOLVE ALGEBRAIC EQUATIONS

In proving Demoivre's theorem in article 4.14 Case III, we have seen that

$\cos\dfrac{\theta}{q} + i\sin\dfrac{\theta}{q}$ is one of the values of $(\cos\theta + i\sin\theta)^{1/q}$. The other values are obtained as follows :

$(\cos\theta + i\sin\theta)^{1/q} = \{\cos(2n\pi + \theta) + i\sin(2n\pi + \theta)\}^{1/q}$

where n is any positive integer

$$= \cos\dfrac{(2n\pi + \theta)}{q} + i\sin\dfrac{(2n\pi + \theta)}{q} \quad \text{... (By Demoivre's theorem)}$$

By giving n the successive values 0, 1, 2, 3, ... q – 1, we get q different values of $(\cos\theta + i\sin\theta)^{1/q}$.

These are $\cos\dfrac{\theta}{q} + i\sin\dfrac{\theta}{q}$, $\cos\left(\dfrac{2\pi + \theta}{q}\right) + i\sin\left(\dfrac{2\pi + \theta}{q}\right)$, $\cos\left(\dfrac{4\pi + \theta}{q}\right) + i\sin\left(\dfrac{4\pi + \theta}{q}\right)$ ...,

$\cos\left\{\dfrac{2(q-1)\pi + \theta}{q}\right\} + i\sin\left\{\dfrac{2(q-1)\pi + \theta}{q}\right\}$.

The highest value that is assigned to n is q – 1. The values q, q + 1, q + 2, ... if assigned to n give the same values corresponding to n = 0, 1, 2, ... etc. Thus $(\cos \theta + i \sin \theta)^{1/q}$ will have q different values. Using this property we can obtain q different values of $(x + iy)^{1/q}$ by expressing

$$x + iy = r(\cos \theta + i \sin \theta)$$
$$= r\{\cos(2n\pi + \theta) + i \sin(2n\pi + \theta)\}$$

Now,
$$(x + iy)^{1/q} = r^{1/q}[\cos(2n\pi + \theta) + i \sin(2n\pi + \theta)]^{1/q}$$
$$= r^{1/q}\left\{\cos\frac{(2n\pi + \theta)}{q} + i \sin\frac{(2n\pi + \theta)}{q}\right\}$$

Now, n = 0, 1, 2, ... q – 1 give q different values of $(x + iy)^{1/q}$. This can be used in solution of algebraic equations as illustrated in solved examples.

4.17 ILLUSTRATIONS ON ROOTS OF EQUATIONS

Ex. 1: *Solve the equation $x^3 - 1 = 0$.*

Sol.:
$$x^3 = 1 = \cos 0 + i \sin 0 = \cos(2n\pi) + i \sin(2n\pi)$$
$$\therefore \quad x = \{\cos(2n\pi) + i \sin(2n\pi)\}^{1/3}$$
$$= \cos\frac{2n\pi}{3} + i \sin\frac{2n\pi}{3} \quad \ldots \text{(By Demoivre's theorem)}$$

Putting n = 0, 1, 2, we get three roots of three equations as

$$x_0 = \cos 0 + i \sin 0 = 1$$
$$x_1 = \cos\frac{2\pi}{3} + i \sin\frac{2\pi}{3} = -\frac{1}{2} + i\frac{\sqrt{3}}{2}$$
$$x_2 = \cos\frac{4\pi}{3} + i \sin\frac{4\pi}{3} = -\frac{1}{2} - i\frac{\sqrt{3}}{2}$$

These are the roots of the equation $x^3 = 1$ or three different values of $(1)^{1/3}$, called cube roots of unity and are often denoted by 1, $\omega = \left(-1/2 + i\sqrt{3}/2\right)$ and $\omega^2 = \left(-1/2 - i\sqrt{3}/2\right)$. Also note that $1 + \omega + \omega^2 = 0$.

Ex. 2: *Find all the values of $(1 - i\sqrt{3})^{1/4}$.*

Sol.: Let $(1 - i\sqrt{3}) = r(\cos \theta + i \sin \theta)$
Equating real and imaginary parts, we get,
$$r \cos \theta = 1 \quad \text{and} \quad -\sqrt{3} = r \sin \theta$$
$$\therefore \quad r = 2 \quad \text{and} \quad \theta = -\frac{\pi}{3}$$
$$\therefore \quad (1 - i\sqrt{3}) = 2\left\{\cos\left(-\frac{\pi}{3}\right) + i \sin\left(-\frac{\pi}{3}\right)\right\}$$
$$= 2\left\{\cos\left(2n\pi - \frac{\pi}{3}\right) + i \sin\left(2n\pi - \frac{\pi}{3}\right)\right\}$$

$$\therefore \ (1-i\sqrt{3})^{1/4} = 2^{1/4}\left\{\cos\left(2n\pi - \frac{\pi}{3}\right) + i\sin\left(2n\pi - \frac{\pi}{3}\right)\right\}^{1/4}$$

$$= 2^{1/4}\left\{\cos\frac{\left(2n\pi - \frac{\pi}{3}\right)}{4} + i\sin\frac{\left(2n\pi - \frac{\pi}{3}\right)}{4}\right\} \quad \text{By Demoivre's theorem}$$

$$= 2^{1/4}\left\{\cos\frac{6n-1}{12}\pi + i\sin\frac{6n-1}{12}\pi\right\} \quad \text{where } n = 0, 1, 2 \text{ and } 3.$$

Hence the four values of $(1-i\sqrt{3})^{1/4}$ are

$$z_0 = 2^{1/4}\left\{\cos\left(-\frac{\pi}{12}\right) + i\sin\left(-\frac{\pi}{12}\right)\right\} = 2^{1/4}\left(\cos\frac{\pi}{12} - i\sin\frac{\pi}{12}\right)$$

$$= 2^{1/4}e^{-i\frac{\pi}{12}}$$

$$z_1 = 2^{1/4}\left\{\cos\frac{5\pi}{12} + i\sin\frac{5\pi}{12}\right\} = 2^{1/4}e^{i\frac{5\pi}{12}}$$

$$z_2 = 2^{1/4}\left\{\cos\frac{11\pi}{12} + i\sin\frac{11\pi}{12}\right\} = 2^{1/4}e^{i\frac{11\pi}{12}}$$

$$z_3 = 2^{1/4}\left\{\cos\frac{17\pi}{12} + i\sin\frac{17\pi}{12}\right\} = 2^{1/4}e^{i\frac{17\pi}{12}} \quad \text{Hence the values.}$$

Ex. 3 : *Show that the nth roots of unity form a geometric progression with common ratio $\left(\cos\frac{2\pi}{n} + i\sin\frac{2\pi}{n}\right)$ and show that the continued product of all n^{th} roots is $(-1)^{n+1}$.*

(Dec. 2005, May 2010)

Sol. : For n^{th} roots of unity,

let $\quad x = (1)^{1/n}$

$$x = 1^{1/n} = (\cos\theta + i\sin 0)^{1/n}$$

$$= \{\cos(2\pi k + 0) + i\sin(2\pi k + 0)\}^{1/n}$$

$$= \left\{\cos\left(\frac{2\pi k}{n}\right) + i\sin\left(\frac{2\pi k}{n}\right)\right\} \quad \text{where } k = 0, 1, 2, \ldots (n-1)$$

Thus roots are,

$k = 0, \quad x_0 = \{\cos 0 + i\sin 0\} = 1 = \left(\cos\frac{2\pi}{n} + i\sin n\frac{2\pi}{n}\right)^0$

$k = 1, \quad x_1 = \left\{\cos\frac{2\pi}{n} + i\sin\frac{2\pi}{n}\right\} = \left(\cos\frac{2\pi}{n} + i\sin\frac{2\pi}{n}\right)^1$

$k = 2, \quad x_2 = \left\{\cos\frac{4\pi}{n} + i\sin\frac{4\pi}{n}\right\} = \left(\cos\frac{2\pi}{n} + i\sin\frac{2\pi}{n}\right)^2$

$k = 3$, $\quad x_3 = \left\{\cos\dfrac{6\pi}{n} + i\sin\dfrac{6\pi}{n}\right\} = \left(\cos\dfrac{2\pi}{n} + i\sin\dfrac{2\pi}{n}\right)^3$

$\vdots \qquad\qquad \vdots$

$k = n-1 \quad x_{n-1} = \left\{\cos\dfrac{(n-1)2\pi}{n} + i\sin\dfrac{(n-1)2\pi}{n}\right\} = \left(\cos\dfrac{2\pi}{n} + i\sin\dfrac{2\pi}{n}\right)^{n-1}$

Therefore $x_0, x_1, x_2, \ldots x_{n-1}$ form G.P. with common ratio $\left(\cos\dfrac{2\pi}{n} + i\sin\dfrac{2\pi}{n}\right)$ and continued product of all n^{th} roots is $x_0, x_1, x_2, \ldots x_{n-1}$.

$$= \left(\cos\dfrac{2\pi}{n} + i\sin\dfrac{2\pi}{n}\right)^{0+1+2+3+\ldots+(n-1)}$$

$$= \left(\cos\dfrac{2\pi}{n} + i\sin\dfrac{2\pi}{n}\right)^{\frac{n(n-1)}{2}}$$

$\left\{\begin{array}{l}\text{Expression for sum of}\\ \text{first n terms of A.P.}\\ a, a+d, a+2d, \ldots \text{ is}\\ S_n = \dfrac{n}{2}[2a + (n-1)d]\\ \text{Here } a = 0, \ d = 1\end{array}\right.$

$$= \left[e^{i\frac{2\pi}{n}}\right]^{\frac{n(n-1)}{2}} = e^{i\pi(n-1)} = e^{in\pi}\, e^{-i\pi} = (-1)^n \cdot (-1) = (-1)^{n+1}$$

Ex. 4 : *Solve $x^4 - x^3 + x^2 - x + 1 = 0$.* **(May 2006, May 2011)**

Sol. : We can express

$$x^5 + 1 = (x^4 - x^3 + x^2 - x + 1)(x + 1) \qquad \ldots (1)$$

Consider the equation $x^5 + 1 = 0$

i.e. $\qquad x^5 = -1 = \cos\pi + i\sin\pi$

$\qquad\qquad = \cos(2n\pi + \pi) + i\sin(2n\pi + \pi)$

$\therefore \qquad x = \cos\dfrac{(2n+1)\pi}{5} + i\sin\dfrac{(2n+1)\pi}{5}$ $\qquad$ where $n = 0, 1, 2, 3, 4$

Putting $n = 0, 1, 2, 3, 4$ we get five roots of $x^5 + 1 = 0$ as

$x_0 = \cos\dfrac{\pi}{5} + i\sin\dfrac{\pi}{5} = e^{i\frac{\pi}{5}}, \qquad x_1 = \cos\dfrac{3\pi}{5} + i\sin\dfrac{3\pi}{5} = e^{i\frac{3\pi}{5}},$

$x_2 = \cos\pi + i\sin\pi = e^{i\pi} = -1, \ x_3 = \cos\dfrac{7\pi}{5} + i\sin\dfrac{7\pi}{5} = e^{i\frac{7\pi}{5}},$

$x_4 = \cos\dfrac{9\pi}{5} + i\sin\dfrac{9\pi}{5} = e^{i\frac{9\pi}{5}}$

Out of these $x_2 = -1$ corresponds to the factor $x + 1 = 0$ in (1). Hence x_0, x_1, x_3, x_4 are the roots of the given equation.

Ex. 5 : *Find all the values of $(1 + i)^{1/5}$; show that their product is $1 + i$.* **(May 04, 07, 09, 13)**

Sol. : Let $\quad 1 + i = r(\cos\theta + i\sin\theta)$

$\therefore \quad r\cos\theta = 1, \ r\sin\theta = -1$ i.e. $r = \sqrt{2}$ and $\theta = \dfrac{\pi}{4}$

$\therefore \quad 1 + i = \sqrt{2}\left(\cos\dfrac{\pi}{4} + i\sin\dfrac{\pi}{4}\right)$

$\qquad\qquad = 2^{1/2}\left\{\cos\left(2n\pi + \dfrac{\pi}{4}\right) + i\sin\left(2n\pi + \dfrac{\pi}{4}\right)\right\}$

$\qquad\qquad = 2^{1/2}\left\{\cos\dfrac{(8n+1)\pi}{4} + i\sin\dfrac{(8n+1)\pi}{4}\right\}$

$\therefore \quad (1+i)^{1/5} = 2^{1/10}\left\{\cos\dfrac{(8n+1)\pi}{20} + i\sin\dfrac{(8n+1)\pi}{20}\right\}$ where $n = 0, 1, 2, 3, 4$.

Putting $n = 0, 1, 2$ and 4, we get five values as

$x_0 = 2^{1/10}\left\{\cos\dfrac{\pi}{20} + i\sin\dfrac{\pi}{20}\right\}, \qquad x_1 = 2^{1/10}\left\{\cos\dfrac{9\pi}{20} + i\sin\dfrac{9\pi}{20}\right\}$

$x_2 = 2^{1/10}\left\{\cos\dfrac{17\pi}{20} + i\sin\dfrac{17\pi}{20}\right\}, \qquad x_3 = 2^{1/10}\left\{\cos\dfrac{25\pi}{20} + i\sin\dfrac{25\pi}{20}\right\}$

$x_4 = 2^{1/10}\left\{\cos\dfrac{33\pi}{20} + i\sin\dfrac{33\pi}{20}\right\}$

Product of these values is

$x_0 \cdot x_1 \cdot x_2 \cdot x_3 \cdot x_4 = 2^{5/10}\left\{\cos\left(\dfrac{\pi}{20} + \dfrac{9\pi}{20} + \dfrac{17\pi}{20} + \dfrac{25\pi}{20} + \dfrac{33\pi}{20}\right)\right.$

$\qquad\qquad\qquad\qquad\qquad \left. + i\sin\left(\dfrac{\pi}{20} + \dfrac{9\pi}{20} + \dfrac{17\pi}{20} + \dfrac{25\pi}{20} + \dfrac{33\pi}{20}\right)\right\}$

$\qquad\qquad = 2^{1/2}\left\{\cos\dfrac{85\pi}{20} + i\sin\dfrac{85\pi}{20}\right\}$

$\qquad\qquad = \sqrt{2}\left(\cos\dfrac{17\pi}{4} + i\sin\dfrac{17\pi}{4}\right)$

$\qquad\qquad = \sqrt{2}\left\{\cos\left(4\pi + \dfrac{\pi}{4}\right) + i\sin\left(4\pi + \dfrac{\pi}{4}\right)\right\}$

$\qquad\qquad = \sqrt{2}\left\{\cos\dfrac{\pi}{4} + i\sin\dfrac{\pi}{4}\right\}$

$\qquad\qquad = \sqrt{2}\left\{\dfrac{1}{\sqrt{2}} + i\dfrac{1}{\sqrt{2}}\right\} = 1 + i$

Ex. 6 : If $(1 + x)^6 + x^6 = 0$, show that $x = -\dfrac{1}{2} - \dfrac{i}{2} \cot \dfrac{\theta}{2}$

where $\theta = \dfrac{(2n + 1)\pi}{6}$, $n = 0, 1, 2, 3, 4, 5$.

Sol. : From given equation,
$$(1 + x)^6 = -x^6$$
$$\left(\dfrac{1 + x}{x}\right)^6 = -1 = \cos(2n\pi + \pi) + i\sin(2n\pi + \pi)$$

Raising to the power $\dfrac{1}{6}$

$$\dfrac{1 + x}{x} = \{\cos(2n + 1)\pi + i\sin(2n + 1)\pi\}^{1/6}$$

$$= \cos(2n + 1)\dfrac{\pi}{6} + i\sin(2n + 1)\dfrac{\pi}{6} \quad \text{[By Demoivre's theorem]}$$

$$= \cos\theta + i\sin\theta$$

where $\theta = \dfrac{(2n + 1)\pi}{6}$, $n = 0, 1, 2, 3, 4, 5$.

$\therefore \quad \dfrac{1}{x} = \cos\theta + i\sin\theta - 1$

or $\quad x = \dfrac{1}{\cos\theta + i\sin\theta - 1}$

i.e. $\quad x = \dfrac{1}{(\cos\theta - 1) + i\sin\theta} \times \dfrac{(\cos\theta - 1) - i\sin\theta}{(\cos\theta - 1) - i\sin\theta}$

$$= \dfrac{(\cos\theta - 1) - i\sin\theta}{(\cos\theta - 1)^2 + \sin^2\theta}$$

$$= \dfrac{(\cos\theta - 1) - i\sin\theta}{\cos^2\theta - 2\cos\theta + 1 + \sin^2\theta}$$

$$= \dfrac{(\cos\theta - 1) - i\sin\theta}{2(1 - \cos\theta)}$$

$$= -\dfrac{1}{2} - \dfrac{i\sin\theta}{4\sin^2\dfrac{\theta}{2}}$$

$$= -\dfrac{1}{2} - \dfrac{i\,2\sin\dfrac{\theta}{2}\cos\dfrac{\theta}{2}}{4\sin^2\dfrac{\theta}{2}}$$

$$= -\dfrac{1}{2} - \dfrac{i}{2}\cot\dfrac{\theta}{2}$$

which proves the required result.

Ex. 7 : *Find all the roots of $x^{12} - 1 = 0$ and identify the roots which are also the roots of $x^4 - x^2 + 1 = 0$.*

Sol. We have $x^{12} - 1 = 0$ $\therefore$ $(x^6 - 1)(x^6 + 1) = 0$

Therefore the roots of $x^{12} - 1 = 0$ are the roots of $(x^6 - 1) = 0$ and $(x^6 + 1) = 0$.

We have, $\quad x^6 = 1$

$$= \cos 0 + i \sin 0$$

$$= \cos(2n\pi) + i \sin(2n\pi)$$

$\therefore \quad x = \cos\left(\dfrac{2n\pi}{6}\right) + i \sin\left(\dfrac{2n\pi}{6}\right)$ (By Demoivre's theorem) ... (i)

where, $\quad n = 0, 1, 2, 3, 4, 5.$

Also $\quad x^6 = -1$

$$= \cos \pi + i \sin \pi$$

$$= \cos(2n\pi + \pi) + i \sin(2n\pi + \pi)$$

$\therefore \quad x = \cos\left(\dfrac{2n+1}{6}\right)\pi + i \sin\left(\dfrac{2n+1}{6}\right)\pi$ ... (ii)

where, $\quad n = 0, 1, 2, 3, 4, 5.$

Hence (i) and (ii) represent all the roots of $x^{12} - 1 = 0$.

Now to identify the roots which are also the roots of $x^4 - x^2 + 1 = 0$, we have,

$$(x^6 + 1) = (x^2 + 1)(x^4 - x^2 + 1) = 0$$

But roots of $x^2 + 1 = 0$ are $x = \pm i$.

Hence by excluding the roots $\pm i$ of $x^2 + 1 = 0$ in solution (ii), we get the required roots of $x^4 - x^2 + 1 = 0$.

Therefore from (ii), we have for $n = 0, 1, 2, 3, 4, 5$,

$$x_0 = \cos\dfrac{\pi}{6} + i \sin\dfrac{\pi}{6},$$

$$x_1 = \cos\dfrac{\pi}{2} + i \sin\dfrac{\pi}{2} = +i,$$

$$x_2 = \cos\dfrac{5\pi}{6} + i \sin\dfrac{5\pi}{6},$$

$$x_3 = \cos\dfrac{7\pi}{6} + i \sin\dfrac{7\pi}{6} = \cos\left(2\pi - \dfrac{5\pi}{6}\right) + i \sin\left(2\pi - \dfrac{5\pi}{6}\right)$$

$$= \cos\dfrac{5\pi}{6} - i \sin\dfrac{5\pi}{6},$$

$$x_4 = \cos\dfrac{9\pi}{6} + i \sin\dfrac{9\pi}{6} = \cos\dfrac{3\pi}{2} + i \sin\dfrac{3\pi}{2} = -i,$$

$$x_5 = \cos\frac{11\pi}{6} + i\sin\frac{11\pi}{6} = \cos\left(2\pi - \frac{\pi}{6}\right) + i\sin\left(2\pi - \frac{\pi}{6}\right)$$

$$= \cos\frac{\pi}{6} - i\sin\frac{\pi}{6}$$

Hence, four roots of $x^4 - x^2 + 1 = 0$ are $\cos\frac{\pi}{6} \pm i\sin\frac{\pi}{6}$, $\cos\frac{5\pi}{6} \pm i\sin\frac{5\pi}{6}$.

Ex. 8 : *Show that all the roots of* $(x+1)^7 = (x-1)^7$ *are given by* $\pm i\cot\left(\frac{r\pi}{7}\right)$ $r = 1, 2, 3,$ *why* $r \neq 0$. **(Dec. 2006)**

Sol. : Consider $(x+1)^7 = (x-1)^7$

Note that the term x^7 gets cancelled on both the sides after expansion, hence it is a sixth degree equation having six roots.

$$\frac{(x+1)^7}{(x-1)^7} = 1 = \cos 0 + i\sin 0 = \cos(2r\pi) + i\sin(2r\pi)$$

Raising both sides to the power $\frac{1}{7}$ and applying Demoivre's theorem on R.H.S.

$$\frac{x+1}{x-1} = \left\{\cos\frac{2r\pi}{7} + i\sin\frac{2r\pi}{7}\right\}$$

$$x + 1 = (x - 1)\left\{\cos\frac{2r\pi}{7} + i\sin\frac{2r\pi}{7}\right\}$$

To get the roots of the equation, we have to put $r = 0, 1, 2, 3, 4, 5, 6$.
but $r = 0$, gives $x + 1 = x - 1$ which is meaningless. $\therefore$ $r \neq 0$.
Hence, six roots of the equation correspond to $r = 1, 2, 3, 4, 5$ and 6.

Now, $\qquad \dfrac{x+1}{x-1} = \cos\dfrac{2r\pi}{7} + i\sin\dfrac{2r\pi}{7}$

$$\therefore \quad \frac{2x}{2} = \frac{1 + \cos\frac{2r\pi}{7} + i\sin\frac{2r\pi}{7}}{-1 + \cos\frac{2r\pi}{7} + i\sin\frac{2r\pi}{7}}$$

$$= \frac{2\cos^2\frac{r\pi}{7} + 2i\sin\frac{r\pi}{7}\cos\frac{r\pi}{7}}{-2\sin^2\frac{r\pi}{7} + 2i\sin\frac{r\pi}{7}\cos\frac{r\pi}{7}}$$

$$= \frac{2\cos\frac{r\pi}{7}\left\{\cos\frac{r\pi}{7} + i\sin\frac{r\pi}{7}\right\}}{-2\sin\frac{r\pi}{7}\left\{\sin\frac{r\pi}{7} - i\cos\frac{r\pi}{7}\right\}}$$

$$= -\cot\frac{r\pi}{7} \frac{\left\{\cos\frac{r\pi}{7} + i\sin\frac{r\pi}{7}\right\}\left\{\sin\frac{r\pi}{7} + i\cos\frac{r\pi}{7}\right\}}{\left\{\sin\frac{r\pi}{7} - i\cos\frac{r\pi}{7}\right\}\left\{\sin\frac{r\pi}{7} + i\cos\frac{r\pi}{7}\right\}}$$

$$= -\cot\frac{r\pi}{7}\left\{i\left(\sin^2\frac{r\pi}{7} + \cos^2\frac{r\pi}{7}\right)\right\}$$

∴ $x = -i\cot\frac{r\pi}{7}$

Putting $r = 1, 2, 3, 4, 5, 6$

$x_1 = -i\cot\frac{\pi}{7}$, $x_2 = -i\cot\frac{2\pi}{7}$, $x_3 = -i\cot\frac{3\pi}{7}$,

$x_4 = -i\cot\frac{4\pi}{7} = -i\cot\left(\pi - \frac{3\pi}{7}\right) = i\cot\frac{3\pi}{7}$,

$x_5 = -i\cot\frac{5\pi}{7} = -\cot\left(\pi - \frac{2\pi}{7}\right) = i\cot\frac{2\pi}{7}$,

$x_6 = -i\cot\frac{6\pi}{7} = -i\cot\left(\pi - \frac{\pi}{7}\right) = i\cot\frac{\pi}{7}$

Thus, all the roots are given by

$$x = \pm i\cot\frac{r\pi}{7} \quad \text{for } r = 1, 2, 3.$$

Ex. 9 : *Show that the roots of* $(x + 1)^6 + (x - 1)^6 = 0$ *are given by*

$-i\cot\frac{(2r + 1)\pi}{12}$, $r = 0, 1, 2, 3, 4, 5$.

Sol. : The given equation is

$$\left(\frac{x + 1}{x - 1}\right)^6 = -1$$

or $y^6 = -1$, where $y = \frac{x + 1}{x - 1}$

Now, $y^6 = \cos\pi + i\sin\pi$

$= \cos(2r\pi + \pi) + i\sin(2r\pi + \pi)$

$= \cos(2r + 1)\pi + i\sin(2r + 1)\pi$

∴ $y = \cos\frac{(2r + 1)\pi}{6} + i\sin\frac{(2r + 1)\pi}{6}$

where $r = 0, 1, 2, 3, 4, 5$

i.e. $\quad \dfrac{x+1}{x-1} = \cos\dfrac{(2r+1)\pi}{6} + i\sin\dfrac{(2r+1)\pi}{6}$

$\therefore \quad \dfrac{2x}{2} = \dfrac{\cos\dfrac{(2r+1)\pi}{6} + i\sin\dfrac{(2r+1)\pi}{6} + 1}{\cos\dfrac{(2r+1)\pi}{6} + i\sin\dfrac{(2r+1)\pi}{6} - 1}$

$= \dfrac{2\cos^2\dfrac{(2r+1)\pi}{6.2} + 2i\sin\dfrac{(2r+1)\pi}{6.2}\cos\dfrac{(2r+1)\pi}{6.2}}{-2\sin^2\dfrac{(2r+1)\pi}{6.2} + 2i\sin\dfrac{(2r+1)\pi}{6.2}\cos\dfrac{(2r+1)\pi}{6.2}}$

$= \dfrac{\cos\dfrac{(2r+1)\pi}{12}\left[\cos\dfrac{(2r+1)\pi}{12} + i\sin\dfrac{(2r+1)\pi}{12}\right]}{-\sin\dfrac{(2r+1)\pi}{12}\left[\sin\dfrac{(2r+1)\pi}{12} - i\sin\dfrac{(2r+1)\pi}{12}\right]}$

$= -\cot\dfrac{(2r+1)\pi}{12}\left[\dfrac{\cos\dfrac{(2r+1)\pi}{12} + i\sin\dfrac{(2r+1)\pi}{12}}{\sin\dfrac{(2r+1)\pi}{12} - i\cos\dfrac{(2r+1)\pi}{12}}\right]$

$\times \left[\dfrac{\sin\dfrac{(2r+1)\pi}{12} + i\cos\dfrac{(2r+1)\pi}{12}}{\sin\dfrac{(2r+1)\pi}{12} + i\cos\dfrac{(2r+1)\pi}{12}}\right]$ (rationalising)

$= -\cot\dfrac{(2r+1)\pi}{12}\left[i\left\{\sin^2\dfrac{(2r+1)\pi}{12} + \cos^2\dfrac{(2r+1)\pi}{7}\right\}\right]$

$= -i\cot\dfrac{(2r+1)\pi}{12}$

where $\quad r = 0, 1, 2, 3, 4, 5.$

Ex. 10 : *Find the cube roots of $(1 - \cos\theta - i\sin\theta)$.*

Sol. : We have to solve the equation $z^3 = k$ which give 3 roots.

Let $\quad z^3 = (1 - \cos\theta - i\sin\theta)$

$= 2\sin^2\dfrac{\theta}{2} - i\,2\sin\dfrac{\theta}{2}\cos\dfrac{\theta}{2}$

$= 2\sin\dfrac{\theta}{2}\left(\sin\dfrac{\theta}{2} - i\cos\dfrac{\theta}{2}\right)$

$= 2\sin\dfrac{\theta}{2}\left\{\cos\left(\dfrac{\theta}{2} - \dfrac{\pi}{2}\right) + i\sin\left(\dfrac{\theta}{2} - \dfrac{\pi}{2}\right)\right\}$

$= \left(2\sin\dfrac{\theta}{2}\right)\left\{\cos\left(2n\pi + \dfrac{\theta}{2} - \dfrac{\pi}{2}\right) + i\sin\left(2n\pi + \dfrac{\theta}{2} - \dfrac{\pi}{2}\right)\right\}$

$$\therefore \quad z = k^{1/3} = \left(2\sin\frac{\theta}{2}\right)^{1/3}\left\{\cos\left(2n\pi + \frac{\theta}{2} - \frac{\pi}{2}\right) + i\sin\left(2n\pi + \frac{\theta}{2} - \frac{\pi}{2}\right)\right\}^{1/3}$$

(Using Demoivre's theorem)

$$= \left(2\sin\frac{\theta}{2}\right)^{1/3}\left\{\cos\left(\frac{2n\pi + \frac{\theta}{2} - \frac{\pi}{2}}{3}\right) + i\sin\left(\frac{2n\pi + \frac{\theta}{2} - \frac{\pi}{2}}{3}\right)\right\}$$

where $n = 0, 1, 2$.

For $n = 0$, $\quad z_0 = \left(2\sin\frac{\theta}{2}\right)^{1/3}\left\{\cos\left(\frac{\theta}{6} - \frac{\pi}{6}\right) + i\sin\left(\frac{\theta}{6} - \frac{\pi}{6}\right)\right\}$

For $n = 1$, $\quad z_1 = \left(2\sin\frac{\theta}{2}\right)^{1/3}\left\{\cos\left(\frac{3\pi}{6} + \frac{\theta}{6}\right) + i\sin\left(\frac{3\pi}{6} + \frac{\theta}{6}\right)\right\}$

For $n = 2$, $\quad z_2 = \left(2\sin\frac{\theta}{2}\right)^{1/3}\left\{\cos\left(\frac{7\pi}{6} + \frac{\theta}{6}\right) + i\sin\left(\frac{7\pi}{6} + \frac{\theta}{6}\right)\right\}$

Ex. 11 : *Show that*

$$(x^5 - 1) = (x - 1)\left[x^2 + 2x\cos\left(\frac{\pi}{5}\right) + 1\right]\left[x^2 + 2x\cos\left(\frac{3\pi}{5}\right) + 1\right]$$

Sol. : We shall first solve $x^5 - 1 = 0$

i.e. $\quad x^5 = (1) = [\cos(2n\pi + 0) + i\sin(2n\pi + 0)]$

$\therefore \quad x = \cos\dfrac{2n\pi}{5} + i\sin\dfrac{2n\pi}{5}, \quad n = 0, 1, 2, 3, 4$

Thus the roots,

$n = 0$, $\quad x_0 = \cos 0 + i\sin 0 = 1$

$n = 1$, $\quad x_1 = \cos\dfrac{2\pi}{5} + i\sin\dfrac{2\pi}{5}$

$n = 2$, $\quad x_2 = \cos\dfrac{4\pi}{5} + i\sin\dfrac{4\pi}{5}$

$n = 3$, $\quad x_3 = \cos\dfrac{6\pi}{5} + i\sin\dfrac{6\pi}{5} = \cos\dfrac{4\pi}{5} - i\sin\dfrac{4\pi}{5}$

$n = 4$, $\quad x_4 = \cos\dfrac{8\pi}{5} + i\sin\dfrac{8\pi}{5} = \cos\dfrac{2\pi}{5} - i\sin\dfrac{2\pi}{5}$

$\therefore \quad x = 1, \quad \left(\cos\dfrac{2\pi}{5} \pm i\sin\dfrac{2\pi}{5}\right), \left(\cos\dfrac{4\pi}{5} \pm i\sin\dfrac{4\pi}{5}\right)$

Consider, $\quad x = \cos\dfrac{2\pi}{5} \pm i\sin\dfrac{2\pi}{5}$

$\Rightarrow \quad \left(x - \cos\dfrac{2\pi}{5}\right) = \pm i\sin\dfrac{2\pi}{5}$

$\Rightarrow \quad \left(x - \cos\dfrac{2\pi}{5}\right)^2 = \left(i\sin\dfrac{2\pi}{5}\right)^2$

$\Rightarrow \quad x^2 - 2x\cos\dfrac{2\pi}{5} + \cos^2\dfrac{2\pi}{5} = (-1)\sin^2\dfrac{2\pi}{5}$

$\Rightarrow \quad x^2 - 2x\cos\dfrac{2\pi}{5} + 1 = 0$

$\Rightarrow \quad x^2 - 2x\cos\left(\pi - \dfrac{3\pi}{5}\right) + 1 = 0$

$\Rightarrow \quad x^2 + 2x\cos\dfrac{3\pi}{5} + 1 = 0 \qquad \ldots \text{(i)}$

Similarly, $\quad x = \cos\dfrac{4\pi}{5} \pm i\sin\dfrac{4\pi}{5}$

$\Rightarrow \quad \left(x - \cos\dfrac{4\pi}{5}\right)^2 = \left(\pm i\sin\dfrac{4\pi}{5}\right)^2$

$\Rightarrow \quad x^2 - 2x\cos\dfrac{4\pi}{5} + \cos^2\dfrac{4\pi}{5} = (-1)\sin^2\dfrac{4\pi}{5}$

$\Rightarrow \quad x^2 - 2x\cos\dfrac{4\pi}{5} + 1 = 0$

$\Rightarrow \quad x^2 - 2x\cos\left(\pi - \dfrac{\pi}{5}\right) + 1 = 0$

$\Rightarrow \quad x^2 + 2x\cos\dfrac{\pi}{5} + 1 = 0 \qquad \ldots \text{(ii)}$

Also the factor corresponding to the root $x = 1$ is $(x - 1)$ $\qquad \ldots \text{(iii)}$

Hence from (i), (ii) and (iii), we get the required result.

Ex. 12 : *Show that* $\sqrt[n]{x + iy} + \sqrt[n]{x - iy}$ *has n real values and find those of*

$\sqrt[3]{1 + i\sqrt{3}} + \sqrt[3]{1 - i\sqrt{3}}$.

Sol. : Let $\quad x + iy = r(\cos\theta + i\sin\theta),\ x - iy = r(\cos\theta - i\sin\theta)$

$\therefore \quad (x + iy)^{1/n} = r^{1/n}\left[\cos\left(\dfrac{2k\pi + \theta}{n}\right) + i\sin\left(\dfrac{2k\pi + \theta}{n}\right)\right],$

where $k = 0, 1, 2, \ldots n - 1$.

and $(x - iy)^{1/n} = r^{1/n}\left[\cos\left(\dfrac{2k\pi + \theta}{n}\right) - i\sin\left(\dfrac{2k\pi + \theta}{n}\right)\right]$,

where $k = 0, 1, 2, \ldots n - 1$.

$\therefore \sqrt[n]{x + iy} + \sqrt[n]{x - iy} = 2r^{1/n}\cos\left(\dfrac{2k\pi + \theta}{n}\right)$, where $k = 0, 1, 2, \ldots n - 1$ ... (i)

The n real values of the expression are given by (i).

Now, $1 + i\sqrt{3} = 2\left(\cos\dfrac{\pi}{3} + i\sin\dfrac{\pi}{3}\right)$ [Here $r = 2, \theta = \dfrac{\pi}{3}$]

$1 - i\sqrt{3} = 2\left(\cos\dfrac{\pi}{3} - i\sin\dfrac{\pi}{3}\right)$

$\therefore \sqrt[3]{1 + i\sqrt{3}} + \sqrt[3]{1 - i\sqrt{3}} = (1 + i\sqrt{3})^{1/3} + (1 - i\sqrt{3})^{1/3}$

$= 2\,(2)^{1/3}\cos\dfrac{2k\pi + \dfrac{\pi}{3}}{3}$

$= 2^{4/3}\cos\dfrac{(6k + 1)\pi}{9}$ where $k = 0, 1, 2.$

which gives 3 real values of expression.

Ex. 13 : If z_1, z_2 are roots of the equation $az^2 + bz + c = 0$, where $b^2 - 4ac < 0$, obtain the value of $z_1^n + z_2^n$ in terms of a, b, c.

Sol. : We know that roots z_1, z_2 of quadratic equation are given by

$z_1 = \dfrac{-b}{2a} + \dfrac{\sqrt{b^2 - 4ac}}{2a}$, $z_2 = \dfrac{-b}{2a} - \dfrac{\sqrt{b^2 - 4ac}}{2a}$

let $b^2 - 4ac = -k^2$, then $(\because b^2 - 4ac < 0)$

$z_1 = -\dfrac{b}{2a} + i\dfrac{k}{2a} = re^{i\theta}$, $z_2 = \dfrac{-b}{2a} - i\dfrac{k}{2a} = re^{-i\theta}$

where, $r = \dfrac{1}{2a}\sqrt{b^2 + k^2} = \dfrac{1}{2a}\sqrt{b^2 + (4ac - b^2)} = \sqrt{\dfrac{c}{a}}$

and $\theta = \tan^{-1}\left(-\dfrac{k}{b}\right) = \tan^{-1}\left[\dfrac{\sqrt{4ac - b^2}}{-b}\right]$

$\therefore \quad z_1^n + z_2^n = r^n\,[e^{in\theta} + e^{-in\theta}]$

$= 2r^n\cos n\theta$

$= 2\left(\dfrac{c}{a}\right)^{n/2}\cos n\left[\tan^{-1}\dfrac{\sqrt{4ac - b^2}}{-b}\right]$

Ex. 14 : *Show that the points representing the roots of the equation* $z^3 = i(z-1)^3$ *on Argand's diagram are collinear.* **(May 2005)**

Sol. : We have $\left(\dfrac{z}{z-1}\right)^3 = i = \cos\left(2n\pi + \dfrac{\pi}{2}\right) + i\sin\left(2n\pi + \dfrac{\pi}{2}\right)$

$$= e^{i(2n\pi + \pi/2)}$$

$$\therefore \quad \dfrac{z}{z-1} = e^{\dfrac{i(2n\pi + \pi/2)}{3}} \qquad n = 0, 1, 2.$$

$$= e^{i\theta}, \qquad \text{where } \theta = \dfrac{4n+1}{6}\pi$$

$$\therefore \quad z = \dfrac{-e^{i\theta}}{1 - e^{i\theta}} = \dfrac{-e^{i\theta}}{1 - \cos\theta - i\sin\theta}$$

$$= \dfrac{-e^{i\theta}}{2\sin\dfrac{\theta}{2}\left(\sin\dfrac{\theta}{2} - i\cos\dfrac{\theta}{2}\right)}$$

$$= \dfrac{-e^{i\theta}}{2\sin\dfrac{\theta}{2}\left[\cos\left(\dfrac{\pi}{2} - \dfrac{\theta}{2}\right) - i\sin\left(\dfrac{\pi}{2} - \dfrac{\theta}{2}\right)\right]}$$

$$= \dfrac{-e^{i\theta} \, e^{i\left(\dfrac{\pi}{2} - \dfrac{\theta}{2}\right)}}{2\sin\dfrac{\theta}{2}} = -\dfrac{e^{i\pi/2} \, e^{i\theta/2}}{2\sin\dfrac{\theta}{2}}$$

$$= -\dfrac{i\left(\cos\dfrac{\theta}{2} + i\sin\dfrac{\theta}{2}\right)}{2\sin\dfrac{\theta}{2}}$$

$$= \dfrac{1}{2} - \dfrac{i}{2}\cot\dfrac{\theta}{2}, \qquad \text{where } \theta = \dfrac{4k+1}{6}\pi$$

For $k = 0, 1, 2$ we get three values of z. All these values have the same real part $1/2$. Hence the roots are collinear.

EXERCISE 4.4

1. Solve the following equations using Demoivre's theorem :
   (i) $x^2 - i = 0$, (ii) $x^3 + x^2 + x + 1 = 0$,
   (iii) $x^5 - x^4 + x^3 - x^2 + x - 1 = 0$, (iv) $x^9 - x^5 + x^4 - 1 = 0$ **(May 2009)**,
   (v) $x^{10} + 11x^5 + 10 = 0$, (vi) $x^4 + x^3 + x^2 + x + 1 = 0$

   Ans. (i) $\cos\dfrac{\pi}{4} + i\sin\dfrac{\pi}{4}$, $\cos\dfrac{5\pi}{4} + i\sin\dfrac{5\pi}{4}$,

   (ii) -1, $\cos\dfrac{\pi}{2} + i\sin\dfrac{\pi}{2}$, $-\cos\dfrac{\pi}{2} - i\sin\dfrac{\pi}{2}$,

(iii) $\cos\frac{r\pi}{3} + i\sin\frac{r\pi}{3}$, where $r = 0, 1, 2, 3, 4$, (iv) Factors are $(x^5 + 1)$, $(x^4 - 1)$,

(v) Factors are $(x^5 + 10)$, $(x^5 + 1)$, (vi) $(x - 1)(x^4 + x^3 + x^2 + x + 1) = x^5 - 1$.

2. Find the continued product of the four values of $\left(\frac{1}{2} + i\frac{\sqrt{3}}{2}\right)^{1/4}$. **(Dec. 2005)**

3. If α, β are complex cube roots of unity then prove that $\alpha^{3m} + \beta^{3m} = 2$, where m is any integer.

4. If ω is a complex cube root of unity, prove that $(1 - \omega)^6 = -27$.

5. Show that the roots of $x^5 = 1$ can be written as $1, \alpha, \alpha^2, \alpha^3, \alpha^4$. Hence show that $(1 - \alpha)(1 - \alpha^2)(1 - \alpha^3)(1 - \alpha^4) = 5$. **(May 2008, Dec. 2007)**

[**Hint** : $x = e^{i\frac{2n\pi}{5}}$, $n = 0, 1, 2, 3, 4$ i.e. $1, \alpha = e^{i\frac{2\pi}{5}}$, $\alpha^2 = e^{i\frac{4\pi}{5}}$, $\alpha^3 = e^{i\frac{6\pi}{5}}$, $\alpha^4 = e^{i\frac{8\pi}{5}}$ and $x^5 - 1 = (x - 1)(x^4 + x^3 + x^2 + x + 1) = 0$. Since $x = 1$ is one root of $x^5 - 1$, $\alpha, \alpha^2, \alpha^3, \alpha^4$ are roots of $x^4 + x^3 + x^2 + x + 1 = 0$. Put $x = 1$.]

6. If $1 + 2i$ is one root of the equation $x^4 - 3x^3 + 8x^2 - 7x + 5 = 0$, find the other roots.

[**Hint** : second root is $1 - 2i$ $\therefore$ $(x - 1 - 2i)(x - 1 + 2i)$ is the factor].

7. Solve $x^7 + x^4 + i(x^3 + 1) = 0$ **(Dec. 2003, 2012, May 2014)**

Ans. $\cos\frac{(4n+1)\pi}{8} + i\sin\frac{(2n+1)\pi}{8}$; $(n = 0, 1, 2, 3, 4,)$

$\cos\frac{(2n+1)\pi}{3} + i\sin\frac{(2n+1)\pi}{3}$; $(n = 0, 1, 2,)$

8. Solve $z^2 + z^{-2} = i$.

Ans. $\pm\frac{1}{2}(\sqrt{5} - 1)^{1/2}(1 - i)$

9. Show that the general value of θ which satisfy the equation $(\cos\theta + i\sin\theta)(\cos 2\theta + i\sin 2\theta) \ldots (\cos n\theta + i\sin n\theta) = 1$ is $\frac{4m\pi}{n(n+1)}$ where m is integer. [**Hint** : $e^{i\theta(1+2+\ldots n)} = e^{i2m\pi}$].

10. Solve $(2z - 1)^5 = 32z^5$.

Ans. $z = \left\{\dfrac{\sin\frac{n\pi}{5} + i\cos\frac{n\pi}{5}}{4\sin\frac{n\pi}{5}}\right\}$, $n = 1, 2, 3, 4$

[**Hint** : equation is of order 4 and not of 5]

11. If p, q are imaginary cube roots of unity, prove that

$pe^{px} + qe^{qx} = -e^{-x/2}\left[\sqrt{3}\sin\frac{\sqrt{3}}{2}x + \cos\frac{\sqrt{3}}{2}x\right]$.

[**Hint** : Cube roots of unity : $1, \omega = \dfrac{-1 + i\sqrt{3}}{2}, \omega^2 = \dfrac{-1 - i\sqrt{3}}{2}$, Let $p = \omega, q = \omega^2$].

12. Solve $16x^4 - 8x^3 + 4x^2 - 2x + 1 = 0$ (May 2008)

    [Hint: $(2x)^5 + 1 = (2x + 1)(16x^4 - 8x^3 + 4x^2 - 2x + 1)$]

    Ans. $x = \dfrac{1}{2}\left\{\cos(2n+1)\dfrac{\pi}{5} + i\sin(2n+1)\dfrac{\pi}{5}\right\}$, $n = 0, 1, 3, 4$.

13. Prove that the roots of the equation $x^2 - 2ax\cos\theta + a^2 = 0$ are also the roots of the equation $x^{2n} - 2a^n x^n \cos n\theta + a^{2n} = 0$, where n is positive integer.

    [Hint: Show that $x^2 - 2ax\cos\theta + a^2$ is a factor of $x^{2n} - 2a^n x^n \cos n\theta + a^{2n} = 0$].

14. Prove that all the roots of $x^4 + x^2 + 1 = x^3 + x$ are given by

    $\cos\dfrac{r\pi}{5} \pm i\sin\dfrac{r\pi}{5}$, where $r = 1, 3$.

15. Prove that $(x^2 - x^3)(x^4 - x) = \sqrt{5}$, where $x = \cos\dfrac{2\pi}{5} + i\sin\dfrac{2\pi}{5}$.

16. Find the roots common to $x^4 + 1 = 0$ and $x^6 - i = 0$.

    Ans. $\dfrac{-1+i}{\sqrt{2}}, \dfrac{1-i}{\sqrt{2}}$.

17. Prove that $(-1+i)^7 = -8(1+i)$

    [Hint: $-1 + i = \sqrt{2}\left(\cos\dfrac{3\pi}{4} + i\sin\dfrac{3\pi}{4}\right)$ $(1+i)^7 = 2^{7/2}\left(-\cos\dfrac{\pi}{4} - i\sin\dfrac{\pi}{4}\right) = 2^3(-1-i)$]

18. Show that

    (i) $1 + \cos\theta + \cos 2\theta + \ldots + \cos(n-1)\theta = \dfrac{1 - \cos\theta + \cos(n-1)\theta - \cos n\theta}{2(1 - \cos\theta)}$

    (ii) $\sin\theta + \sin 2\theta + \ldots + \sin(n-1)\theta = \dfrac{\sin\theta + \sin(n-1)\theta - \sin n\theta}{2(1 - \cos\theta)}$.

    $\left[\text{Hint}: 1 + z + z^2 + \ldots + z^{n-1} = \dfrac{1 - z^n}{1 - z}, \text{ put } z = \cos\theta + i\sin\theta, \text{ and use Demoivre's theorem}\right]$

19. Show that

    $x^7 + 1 = (x+1)\left(x^2 - 2x\cos\dfrac{\pi}{7} + 1\right)\left(x^2 - 2x\cos\dfrac{3\pi}{7} + 1\right)\left(x^2 - 2x\cos\dfrac{5\pi}{7} + 1\right)$

20. Find the 7th roots of unity and prove that the sum of their nth powers always vanish unless n be a multiple number of 7, n being an integer, and then the sum is 7.

    [Hint: $x_n = 1^{1/7} = e^{i\frac{2n\pi}{7}}$, $n = 0, 1, 2, 3, 4, 5, 6$. If $n = 7k$, sum = 7; If $n = 7k+1$, sum = 0}.

21. Solve by Demoivre's theorem $x^5 - (1+i) = 0$. Show that the product of the roots of the given equation is $(1+i)$. (Dec. 2004)

MULTIPLE CHOICE QUESTIONS

Type I : Problems on Basic Definition :

1. Polar form of the complex number $z = x + iy$ is (1)
   - (A) $r(\cos\theta + i\sin\theta)$
   - (B) $r(\cos\theta - i\sin\theta)$
   - (C) $(\cos\theta - i\sin\theta)$
   - (D) $(\cos\theta + i\sin\theta)$

2. Exponential form of the complex number $z = x + iy$ is (1)
   - (A) $re^{i\theta}$
   - (B) $e^{i\theta}$
   - (C) re^{θ}
   - (D) none of these

3. Modulus of the complex number $z = x + iy$ is (1)
   - (A) $\sqrt{x^2 - y^2}$
   - (B) $\tan^{-1}\dfrac{y}{x}$
   - (C) $\sqrt{x^2 + y^2}$
   - (D) none of these

4. Argument of the complex number $z = x + iy$ for $x > 0$, $y > 0$ is (1)
   - (A) $\tan^{-1}\dfrac{y}{x}$
   - (B) $\tan^{-1}\dfrac{x}{y}$
   - (C) $\sqrt{x^2 + y^2}$
   - (D) $\sqrt{x^2 - y^2}$

5. If $z = x + iy$ is the complex number then its complex conjugate $\bar{z}$ is equal to (1)
   - (A) $x - iy$
   - (B) $-x + iy$
   - (C) $-x - iy$
   - (D) none of these

6. On Argand's diagram, complex number $z = x + iy$ represents (1)
   - (A) point on xoy-plane
   - (B) line on xoy-plane
   - (C) circle on xoy-plane
   - (D) none of these

7. Two complex numbers z_1 and z_2 are comparable if (1
   - (A) z_1 and z_2 are real numbers
   - (B) z_1 and z_2 are complex numbers
   - (C) z_1 is complex number and z_2 is real number
   - (D) z_1 is real number and z_2 is complex number

8. If $z = 1 + i$ then arg (z) is equal to (1)
   - (A) $\dfrac{\pi}{4}$
   - (B) $\pi + \dfrac{\pi}{4}$
   - (C) $\pi - \dfrac{\pi}{4}$
   - (D) π

9. If $z = -1 + i$ then arg (z) is equal to (1)
    (a) $\dfrac{\pi}{4}$
    (B) $\pi + \dfrac{\pi}{4}$
    (C) $\pi - \dfrac{\pi}{4}$
    (D) π

10. If $z = -1 - i$ then arg (z) is equal to (1)
    (A) $\dfrac{\pi}{4}$
    (B) $\pi + \dfrac{\pi}{4}$
    (C) $\pi - \dfrac{\pi}{4}$
    (D) $\dfrac{\pi}{2}$

11. If $z = 1 - i$ then arg (z) is equal to (1)
    (A) $-\dfrac{\pi}{4}$
    (B) $\pi + \dfrac{\pi}{4}$
    (C) $\pi - \dfrac{\pi}{4}$
    (D) π

12. For any complex numbers z_1, z_2 arg $(z_1 \times z_2)$ is equal to (1)
    (A) arg $z_1 \times$ arg z_2
    (B) arg $z_1 +$ arg z_2
    (C) arg $z_1 -$ arg z_2
    (D) $\dfrac{\arg z_1}{\arg z_2}$

13. For any complex numbers z_1, z_2 the modulus of product $|z_1 \times z_2|$ is equal to (1)
    (A) $|z_1| \times |z_2|$
    (B) $|z_1| - |z_2|$
    (C) $\dfrac{|z_1|}{|z_2|}$
    (D) none of these

14. For any complex numbers z_1, z_2, arg $\left(\dfrac{z_1}{z_2}\right)$ is equal to (1)
    (A) arg $z_1 \times$ arg z_2
    (B) arg $z_1 +$ arg z_2
    (C) arg $z_1 -$ arg z_2
    (D) $\dfrac{\arg z_1}{\arg z_2}$

15. For any complex numbers z_1, z_2 the modulus of $\left|\dfrac{z_1}{z_2}\right|$ is equal to (1)
    (A) $\dfrac{|z_2|}{|z_1|}$
    (B) $|z_1| - |z_2|$
    (C) $\dfrac{|z_1|}{|z_2|}$
    (D) $|z_1| \times |z_2|$

16. Real part of the complex number $z = e^{5 + i\frac{\pi}{2}}$ is (2)
    (A) e^5
    (B) $-e^5$
    (C) 0
    (D) e^{-5}

17. Imaginary part of the complex number $z = e^{(5+3i)^2}$ is (2)

    (A) $e^{34} \sin 30$ (B) $e^{34} \cos 30$
    (C) $e^{16} \cos 30$ (D) $e^{16} \sin 30$

18. $x + iy$ form of the complex number $z = \dfrac{1}{(2+i)^2}$ is (2)

    (A) $\dfrac{1}{25}(3 + 4i)$ (B) $\dfrac{1}{25}(3 - 4i)$
    (C) $(2 + i)^{-2}$ (D) $\dfrac{1}{25}(-3 - 4i)$

19. $x + iy$ form of the complex number $z = \dfrac{1+i}{(1-i)^2}$ is (2)

    (A) $\dfrac{1}{2}(1 - i)$ (B) $\dfrac{1}{2}(-1 + i)$
    (C) $\dfrac{1}{2}(1 + i)$ (D) $\dfrac{1}{2}(-1 - i)$

20. $x + iy$ form of the complex number $z = \dfrac{2 + i6\sqrt{3}}{5 + i\sqrt{3}}$ is (2)

    (A) $(1 + i\sqrt{3})$ (B) $(1 - i\sqrt{3})$
    (C) $(-1 - i\sqrt{3})$ (D) $6 + i5\sqrt{3}$

21. Polar form of the complex number $\dfrac{1}{2} + i\dfrac{\sqrt{3}}{2}$ is (2)

    (A) $\cos\dfrac{\pi}{3} + i\sin\dfrac{\pi}{3}$ (B) $\cos\dfrac{\pi}{3} - i\sin\dfrac{\pi}{3}$
    (C) $\dfrac{1}{2}\left(\cos\dfrac{\pi}{3} + i\sin\dfrac{\pi}{3}\right)$ (D) $\dfrac{1}{2}\left(\cos\dfrac{\pi}{3} - i\sin\dfrac{\pi}{3}\right)$

22. If $z = x + iy$ then value of $\dfrac{z}{\bar{z}} + \dfrac{\bar{z}}{z}$ is equal to (2)

    (A) $2\left(\dfrac{x^2 + y^2}{x^2 - y^2}\right)$ (B) $\left(\dfrac{x^2 + y^2}{x^2 - y^2}\right)$
    (C) $2\left(\dfrac{x^2 - y^2}{x^2 + y^2}\right)$ (D) $\left(\dfrac{x^2 - y^2}{x^2 + y^2}\right)$

23. The smallest positive integer n for which $\left(\dfrac{1+i}{1-i}\right)^n = 1$ is (2)

    (A) $n = 1$ (B) $n = \dfrac{1}{4}$
    (C) $n = 4$ (D) $n = 2$

24. The smallest positive integer n for which $(1+i)^{2n} = (1-i)^{2n}$ is (2)
    (A) $n = 4$
    (B) $n = 8$
    (C) $n = 12$
    (D) $n = 2$

25. If $z = a\cos\theta + ia\sin\theta$ then $\dfrac{z}{\bar{z}} + \dfrac{\bar{z}}{z}$ is equal to (2)
    (A) $2\sin 2\theta$
    (B) $2\cos 2\theta$
    (C) $2\tan 2\theta$
    (D) $2\cot 2\theta$

26. If $(1 + ai)(1 + bi) = z$ then $\arg(z)$ is equal to (2)
    (A) $\tan^{-1}\left(\dfrac{a+b}{1-ab}\right)$
    (B) $\tan^{-1}\left(\dfrac{1-ab}{a+b}\right)$
    (C) $\sin^{-1}\left(\dfrac{a+b}{1-ab}\right)$
    (D) $\cos^{-1}\left(\dfrac{a+b}{1-ab}\right)$

27. If $(a_1 + ib_1)(a_2 + ib_2) = A + iB$ then which of the following is true? (2)
    (A) $\tan^{-1}\left(\dfrac{b_1}{a_1}\right) + \tan^{-1}\left(\dfrac{b_2}{a_2}\right) = \tan^{-1}\left(\dfrac{B}{A}\right)$
    (B) $\tan^{-1}\left(\dfrac{b_1}{a_1}\right) - \tan^{-1}\left(\dfrac{b_2}{a_2}\right) = \tan^{-1}\left(\dfrac{B}{A}\right)$
    (C) $\tan^{-1}\left(\dfrac{a_1}{b_1}\right) + \tan^{-1}\left(\dfrac{a_2}{b_2}\right) = \tan^{-1}\left(\dfrac{A}{B}\right)$
    (D) none of these

28. If $|z_1 + z_2|^2 = r_1^2 + r_2^2 + 2r_1 r_2 \cos(\theta_1 - \theta_2)$, $|z_1 - z_2|^2 = r_1^2 + r_2^2 - 2r_1 r_2 \cos(\theta_1 - \theta_2)$ and $|z_1 + z_2|^2 = |z_1 - z_2|^2$ then (2)
    (A) $\theta_1 + \theta_2 = \dfrac{\pi}{2}$
    (B) $\theta_1 - \theta_2 = 0$
    (C) $\theta_1 - \theta_2 = \dfrac{\pi}{2}$
    (D) none of these

29. If $(\alpha + i\beta) = \dfrac{1}{(a+ib)}$ then which of the following is correct? (2)
    (A) $(\alpha^2 - \beta^2)(a^2 - b^2) = 1$
    (B) $(\alpha^2 + \beta^2)(a^2 + b^2) = 1$
    (C) $\dfrac{(\alpha^2 + \beta^2)}{(a^2 + b^2)} = 1$
    (D) none of these

30. If z is a complex number such that if $|z| = 4$ and $\arg(z) = \dfrac{\pi}{3}$ then z is equal to (2)
    (A) $4\left(\dfrac{1}{2} + i\dfrac{\sqrt{3}}{2}\right)$
    (B) $4\left(\dfrac{1}{2} - i\dfrac{\sqrt{3}}{2}\right)$
    (C) $4\left(\dfrac{\sqrt{3}}{2} + i\dfrac{1}{2}\right)$
    (D) none of these

31. If $\alpha - i\beta = \dfrac{1}{a - ib}$ then which of the following is correct ? (2)

   (A) $(\alpha^2 - \beta^2)(a^2 - b^2) = 1$
   (B) $(\alpha^2 + \beta^2)(a^2 + b^2) = 1$
   (C) $\dfrac{(\alpha^2 + \beta^2)}{(a^2 + b^2)} = 1$
   (D) none of these

Type II : Problems on Argand's Diagram :

32. Locus of z satisfying $\arg(z) = \dfrac{\pi}{3}$ is (2)

   (A) straight line $y = \sqrt{3}\, x$
   (B) straight line $y = -\sqrt{3}\, x$
   (C) straight line $y = \dfrac{1}{\sqrt{3}}\, x$
   (D) straight line $y = -x$

33. Locus of z satisfying $|z + 1| = |z - i|$ is (2)
   (A) circle $(x - 1)^2 + (y + 1)^2 = 2$
   (B) parabola $y^2 = x$
   (C) straight line $y = +x$
   (D) straight line $y = -x$

34. Locus of z satisfying $\text{Re}(z^2) = 1$ is (2)
   (A) circle $(x - 1)^2 + (y + 1)^2 = 2$
   (B) hyperbola $x^2 - y^2 = 1$
   (C) ellipse $\dfrac{x^2}{1} + \dfrac{y^2}{2} = 1$
   (D) straight line $y = -x$

35. If z is a complex number for which $\dfrac{z + i}{z + 2}$ is purely real, then the locus of z is (2)

   (A) circle $x^2 + y^2 + x + y = 0$
   (B) hyperbola $x^2 - y^2 = 1$
   (C) ellipse $\dfrac{x^2}{1} + \dfrac{y^2}{2} = 1$
   (D) straight line $x + 2y + 2 = 0$

36. If z is a complex number for which $\dfrac{z + i}{z + 2}$ is purely imaginary, then the locus of z is (2)

   (A) circle $x^2 + y^2 + 2x + y = 0$
   (B) hyperbola $x^2 - y^2 = 1$
   (C) ellipse $\dfrac{x^2}{1} + \dfrac{y^2}{2} = 1$
   (D) straight line $x + 2y + 2 = 0$

37. If $z(z + i)$ is purely real number then the locus of z is (2)

   (A) $x = 0$ or $y = -\dfrac{1}{2}$
   (B) $x \neq 0$ and $y \neq -\dfrac{1}{2}$
   (C) $x = -\dfrac{1}{2}$ or $y = 0$
   (D) $x \neq 0$ and $y \neq 0$

38. If $\bar{z}(z + i)$ is purely imaginary number then locus of z is (2)
   (A) $x^2 + y^2 + y = 0$
   (B) $x^2 - y^2 - y = 0$
   (C) $x = 0$
   (D) none of these

39. By rotating vector $\overline{OA}$ in anticlockwise direction through an angle $\frac{\pi}{3}$, we get (2)

   (A) $\overline{OB} = \overline{OA}\, e^{i\frac{\pi}{3}}$
   (B) $\overline{OB} = \overline{OA}\, e^{-i\frac{\pi}{3}}$
   (C) $\overline{OB} = \overline{OA}\, e^{\frac{\pi}{3}}$
   (D) none of these

40. By rotating vector $OA = 2 - i$ in anticlockwise through angle $\frac{\pi}{3}$, we get (2)

   (A) $\left(1 + \frac{\sqrt{3}}{2}\right) + i\left(\sqrt{3} - \frac{1}{2}\right)$
   (B) $\left(1 + \frac{\sqrt{3}}{2}\right) - i\left(\sqrt{3} - \frac{1}{2}\right)$
   (C) $\left(1 - \frac{\sqrt{3}}{2}\right) + i\left(\sqrt{3} - \frac{1}{2}\right)$
   (D) $\left(1 - \frac{\sqrt{3}}{2}\right) - i\left(\sqrt{3} + \frac{1}{2}\right)$

41. By rotating vector $OA = 5 + 6i$ in anticlockwise direction through an angle $\frac{\pi}{2}$, we get
   (A) $5 - 6i$
   (B) $5i + 6$
   (C) $5i - 6$
   (D) $5 + 6i$

42. Locus of z satisfying $|z - 2| = 3$ is (2)
   (A) straight line passing through (2, 0) and (3, 0)
   (B) circle with centre (2, 0) and radius 3
   (C) circle with centre (2, 0) and radius $\sqrt{3}$
   (D) circle with centre (–2, 0) and radius 3

43. Locus of z satisfying $|z - i| = 6$ is (2)
   (A) straight line passing through (0, 1) and (6, 0)
   (B) circle with centre (0, 1) and radius $\sqrt{6}$
   (C) circle with centre (1, 0) and radius 6
   (D) circle with centre (0, 1) and radius 6

44. Locus of z satisfying $|z + 2 - i| = 2$ is (2)
   (A) $(x + 2)^2 + (y - 1)^2 = 4$
   (B) $(x - 2)^2 + (y + 1)^2 = 4$
   (C) $(x + 2)^2 + (y - 1)^2 = 2$
   (D) $(x - 2)^2 + (y + 1)^2 = 2$

45. Locus of z satisfying $|z - 3| + |z + 3| = 10$ is (2)
   (A) ellipse
   (B) circle
   (C) hyperbola
   (D) parabola

46. Locus of z satisfying $|z - 2i| + |z + 2i| = 5$ is the ellipse with major axis along
   (A) x-axis
   (B) y-axis (2)
   (C) y = x
   (D) y = –x

47. Locus of z satisfying $|z-3| + |z+3| = 10$ is the ellipse with major axis along (2)
    (A) x-axis
    (B) y-axis
    (C) y = x
    (D) y = –x

48. The complex number $\left(\dfrac{1+2i}{1-i}\right)$ lies in the (2)
    (A) first quadrant
    (B) second quadrant
    (C) third quadrant
    (D) fourth quadrant

Type III : Problems on Demoivre's Theorem and Applications :

49. The Demoivre's theorem states that for any real number n, one of the values of $(\cos\theta + i\sin\theta)^n$ is (1)
    (A) $\cos n\theta - i \sin n\theta$
    (B) $\cos^n \theta + i \sin^n \theta$
    (C) $\cos n\theta + i \sin n\theta$
    (D) none of these

50. If $x = \cos\theta + i\sin\theta$, then $x^n + \dfrac{1}{x^n}$ is equal to (2)
    (A) $2 \sin n\theta$
    (B) $2 \cos n\theta$
    (C) $2 (\cos n\theta + i \sin n\theta)$
    (D) none of these

51. Using Demoivre's theorem, simplified form of $\dfrac{\left(\sin\dfrac{\pi}{8} + i\cos\dfrac{\pi}{8}\right)^8}{\left(\sin\dfrac{\pi}{8} - i\cos\dfrac{\pi}{8}\right)^8}$ is equal to (2)
    (A) –1
    (B) 2i
    (C) 0
    (D) 1

52. Using Demoivre's theorem, simplified form of $(\sin\theta + i\cos\theta)^4$ is equal to (2)
    (A) $(\sin 4\theta + \cos 4\theta)$
    (B) $(\sin 4\theta - i \cos 4\theta)$
    (C) $(\cos 4\theta + i \sin 4\theta)$
    (D) $(\cos 4\theta - i \sin 4\theta)$

53. Using Demoivre's theorem, simplified form of $\dfrac{(1+i\sqrt{3})^6}{(1-i\sqrt{3})^6}$ is equal to (2)
    (A) $e^{-i4\pi}$
    (B) $e^{i4\pi}$
    (C) $e^{i2\pi}$
    (D) $e^{-i2\pi}$

54. Using Demoivre's theorem, simplified form of $\dfrac{(\sqrt{3}-i)^4}{(\sqrt{3}+i)^8}$ is equal to (2)
    (A) $\dfrac{1}{2^4} e^{-i2\pi}$
    (B) $\dfrac{1}{2^4} e^{i2\pi}$
    (C) $e^{i2\pi}$
    (D) $e^{-i2\pi}$

55. Using Demoivre's theorem, simplified form of $\dfrac{\left(1 + \cos\dfrac{\pi}{8} + i \sin\dfrac{\pi}{8}\right)^8}{\left(1 + \cos\dfrac{\pi}{8} - i \sin\dfrac{\pi}{8}\right)^8}$ is equal to
    (A) 1 + i
    (B) –1 (2)
    (C) 1 – i
    (D) 1

56. Using Demoivre's theorem, simplified form of $(1+i)^8 + (1-i)^8$ is equal to (2)
    (A) 2^8
    (B) 2^5
    (C) $2^4 \cos\dfrac{\pi}{4}$
    (D) $2^8 \cos\dfrac{\pi}{8}$

57. If $z = -1 + i$, then using Demoivre's theorem, z^4 is equal to (2)
    (A) -4
    (B) 4
    (C) $4i$
    (D) none of these

58. If $z = \dfrac{\sqrt{3}}{2} + i\dfrac{1}{2}$, then using Demoivre's theorem, z^{12} is equal to (2)
    (A) $-i$
    (B) -1
    (C) 1
    (D) i

59. Using Demoivre's theorem, exponential form of the expression $\left(\dfrac{\sqrt{3}}{2} + i\dfrac{1}{2}\right)^{1000}$ is
    (A) $e^{-i\frac{1000\pi}{6}}$
    (B) $e^{+i\frac{1000\pi}{6}}$ (2)
    (C) $e^{i\frac{1000\pi}{3}}$
    (D) none of these

60. If $\left[2\left(\cos\dfrac{\pi}{6} + i\sin\dfrac{\pi}{6}\right)\right]^6 = a + ib$, then (2)
    (A) $a = -2^6$ and $b = 0$
    (B) $a = 2^6$ and $b = 0$
    (C) $a = -2^6$ and $b = 1$
    (D) none of these

61. The roots of equation $x^3 - 1 = 0$ are (2)
    (A) $\cos\dfrac{(2k+1)\pi}{3} + i\sin\dfrac{(2k+1)\pi}{3}$, $k = 0, 1, 2$
    (B) $\cos\dfrac{(2k-1)\pi}{3} + i\sin\dfrac{(2k-1)\pi}{3}$, $k = 0, 1, 2$
    (C) $\cos\dfrac{2k\pi}{3} + i\sin\dfrac{2k\pi}{3}$, $k = 0, 1, 2$
    (D) none of these

62. The roots of equation $x^3 + 1 = 0$ are (2)
    (A) $\cos\dfrac{(2k+1)\pi}{3} + i\sin\dfrac{(2k+1)\pi}{3}$, $k = 0, 1, 2$
    (B) $\cos\dfrac{(2k-1)\pi}{3} + i\sin\dfrac{(2k-1)\pi}{3}$, $k = 0, 1, 2$
    (C) $\cos\dfrac{2k\pi}{3} + i\sin\dfrac{2k\pi}{3}$, $k = 0, 1, 2$
    (D) none of these

63. All the values of $(1 + i\sqrt{3})^{1/3}$ are (2)

   (A) $2^{1/3}\left[\cos\dfrac{(6k-1)\pi}{9} + i\sin\dfrac{(6k-1)\pi}{24}\right]$, $k = 0, 1, 2$

   (B) $2^{1/3}\left[\cos\dfrac{(6k+1)\pi}{9} - i\sin\dfrac{(6k+1)\pi}{9}\right]$, $k = 0, 1, 2$

   (C) $2^{1/3}\left[\cos\dfrac{(6k+1)\pi}{9} + i\sin\dfrac{(6k+1)\pi}{9}\right]$, $k = 0, 1, 2$

   (D) none of these

64. If the cube roots unity are 1, $\alpha = \left(\cos\dfrac{2\pi}{3} + i\sin\dfrac{2\pi}{3}\right)$ and $\beta = \left(\cos\dfrac{2\pi}{3} - i\sin\dfrac{2\pi}{3}\right)$ then the value of $1 + \alpha^{3n} + \beta^{3n}$, where n is any integer, is (2)

   (A) 0   (B) 1
   (C) 2   (D) 3

65. The nth roots of unity are given by $x_0 = e^{i0}$, $x_1 = e^{i\frac{2\pi}{n}}$, $x_2 = e^{i\frac{4\pi}{n}}$, ..., $x_{n-1} = e^{i\frac{2(n-1)\pi}{n}}$ then product of these roots $x_0 \cdot x_1 \cdot x_2 ..., x_{n-1}$ is (2)

   (A) -1 (B) $(-1)^n$
   (C) 0 (D) $(-1)^{n+1}$

66. All the values of $(i)^{1/3}$ are (2)

   (A) $\left[\cos\dfrac{(4k+1)\pi}{6} + i\sin\dfrac{(4k+1)\pi}{6}\right]$, $k = 0, 1, 2$

   (B) $\left[\cos\dfrac{(4k+1)\pi}{6} - i\sin\dfrac{(4k+1)\pi}{6}\right]$, $k = 0, 1, 2$

   (C) $\left[\cos\dfrac{(4k+1)\pi}{3} + i\sin\dfrac{(4k+1)\pi}{3}\right]$, $k = 0, 1, 2$

   (D) none of these

67. All the values of $(-i)^{1/3}$ are (2)

   (A) $\left[\cos\dfrac{(4k+1)\pi}{6} - i\sin\dfrac{(4k+1)\pi}{6}\right]$, $k = 0, 1, 2$

   (B) $\left[\cos\dfrac{(4k-1)\pi}{6} + i\sin\dfrac{(4k-1)\pi}{6}\right]$, $k = 0, 1, 2$

   (C) $\left[\cos\dfrac{(4k+1)\pi}{3} + i\sin\dfrac{(4k+1)\pi}{3}\right]$, $k = 0, 1, 2$

   (D) none of these

68. All the values of $(1 - i\sqrt{3})^{1/4}$ are (2)

   (A) $2^{1/4}\left[\cos\dfrac{(6k-1)\pi}{24} + i\sin\dfrac{(6k-1)\pi}{24}\right]$, $k = 0, 1, 2, 3$

   (B) $2^{1/4}\left[\cos\dfrac{(6k+1)\pi}{12} + i\sin\dfrac{(6k+1)\pi}{12}\right]$, $k = 0, 1, 2, 3$

   (C) $2^{1/4}\left[\cos\dfrac{(6k+1)\pi}{12} - i\sin\dfrac{(6k+1)\pi}{12}\right]$, $k = 0, 1, 2, 3$

   (D) none of these

69. All the values of $(1 + i)^{1/5}$ are (2)

   (A) $2^{1/10}\left[\cos\dfrac{(8k+1)\pi}{20} + i\sin\dfrac{(8k+1)\pi}{20}\right]$, $k = 0, 1, 2, 3, 4$

   (B) $2^{1/10}\left[\cos\dfrac{(8k-1)\pi}{20} + i\sin\dfrac{(8k-1)\pi}{20}\right]$, $k = 0, 1, 2, 3, 4$

   (C) $2^{1/10}\left[\cos\dfrac{2k\pi}{5} + i\sin\dfrac{2k\pi}{5}\right]$, $k = 0, 1, 2, 3, 4$

   (D) none of these

Answers

1. (A)	15. (C)	29. (B)	43. (D)	57. (A)
2. (A)	16. (C)	30. (A)	44. (A)	58. (C)
3. (C)	17. (D)	31. (B)	45. (A)	59. (B)
4. (A)	18. (B)	32. (A)	46. (B)	60. (A)
5. (A)	19. (B)	33. (D)	47. (A)	61. (C)
6. (A)	20. (A)	34. (B)	48. (B)	62. (A)
7. (A)	21. (A)	35. (D)	49. (C)	63. (C)
8. (A)	22. (C)	36. (A)	50. (B)	64. (D)
9. (C)	23. (C)	37. (A)	51. (D)	65. (D)
10. (B)	24. (D)	38. (A)	52. (D)	66. (A)
11. (A)	25. (B)	39. (A)	53. (B)	67. (B)
12. (B)	26. (A)	40. (A)	54. (A)	68. (C)
13. (A)	27. (A)	41. (C)	55. (B)	69. (A)
14. (C)	28. (C)	42. (B)	56. (B)	

CHAPTER FIVE

HYPERBOLIC FUNCTIONS, LOGARITHMS OF COMPLEX NUMBERS

5.1 CIRCULAR FUNCTIONS OF A COMPLEX VARIABLE

From Euler's formulae [sec. 4.8, Chap. 4], we have

$$e^{ix} = \cos x + i \sin x \qquad \ldots (1)$$

$$e^{-ix} = \cos x - i \sin x \qquad \ldots (2)$$

Adding (1) and (2), we get

$$\cos x = \frac{e^{ix} + e^{-ix}}{2} \qquad \ldots (3)$$

Similarly, subtracting (2) from (1), we get

$$\sin x = \frac{e^{ix} - e^{-ix}}{2i} \qquad \ldots (4)$$

(3) and (4) are the relations between circular and exponential functions (for x-real).

From (3) and (4), we can get corresponding expressions for tan x, cot x, sec x and cosec x.

On the basis of these equations, we extend the definitions of the sine and cosine (circular functions of real angle) into the **complex domain**. We define the circular functions of complex variable $z = x + iy$ by the equations

$$\cos z = \frac{e^{iz} + e^{-iz}}{2} \quad \text{and} \quad \sin z = \frac{e^{iz} - e^{-iz}}{2i} \qquad \ldots (5)$$

Although no geometrical meaning can be associated with relations (5) like cos x and sin x when x is a real number.

We can write similar expressions for other circular functions as

$$\tan z = \frac{\sin z}{\cos z} = \frac{e^{iz} - e^{-iz}}{i(e^{iz} + e^{-iz})}, \quad \cot z = \frac{\cos z}{\sin z} = \frac{i(e^{iz} + e^{-iz})}{e^{iz} - e^{-iz}}$$

$$\sec z = \frac{1}{\cos z} = \frac{2}{e^{iz} + e^{-iz}}, \quad \operatorname{cosec} z = \frac{1}{\sin z} = \frac{2i}{e^{iz} - e^{-iz}}$$

(5.1)

Since the exponential function is periodic ($e^{z + 2\pi i} = e^z e^{2\pi i} = e^z$) so are the circular functions:

$\cos(z \pm 2n\pi) = \cos z$, $\sin(z \pm 2n\pi) = \sin z$, $\tan(z \pm n\pi) = \tan z$, $\cot(z \pm n\pi) = \cot z$

where $n = 0, 1, 2, \ldots\ldots$

Thus $\sin z$ and $\cos z$ are periodic functions with period 2π and $\tan z$ is a periodic function with period π.

From the definitions, it follows that all the familiar trigonometric formulae for the real variable x hold good for the complex variable z.

5.2 HYPERBOLIC FUNCTIONS

We now define new class of functions (for x real or complex) known as Hyperbolic functions (closely related with circular functions).

Hyperbolic sine of x denoted by sinh x is defined as: $\sinh x = \dfrac{e^x - e^{-x}}{2}$ ... (6)

Hyperbolic cosine of x denoted by cosh x is defined as: $\cosh x = \dfrac{e^x + e^{-x}}{2}$ ... (7)

Other hyperbolic functions are obtained from (6) and (7) as

$\tanh x = \dfrac{\sinh x}{\cosh x} = \dfrac{e^x - e^{-x}}{e^x + e^{-x}}$, $\coth x = \dfrac{1}{\tanh x} = \dfrac{e^x + e^{-x}}{e^x - e^{-x}}$,

$\text{sech } x = \dfrac{1}{\cosh x} = \dfrac{2}{e^x + e^{-x}}$, $\text{cosech } x = \dfrac{1}{\sinh x} = \dfrac{2}{e^x - e^{-x}}$

From the definitions of sinh x and cosh x [i.e. from (6) and (7)] and using the series expansions:

$$e^x = 1 + x + \frac{x^2}{2!} + \frac{x^3}{3!} + \ldots \quad \text{and} \quad e^{-x} = 1 - x + \frac{x^2}{2!} - \frac{x^3}{3!} + \ldots$$

we get $\sinh x = x + \dfrac{x^3}{3!} + \dfrac{x^5}{5!} + \dfrac{x^7}{7!} + \ldots\ldots$, $\cosh x = 1 + \dfrac{x^2}{2!} + \dfrac{x^4}{4!} + \ldots\ldots$

The values of sinh x, cosh x, tanh x for $x = -\infty, 0, +\infty$ are obtained from the definition and are tabulated as:

x	sinh x	cosh x	tanh x
$-\infty$	$-\infty$	∞	-1
0	0	1	0
∞	∞	∞	1

Since $\sinh(-x) = -\sinh x$ and $\cosh(-x) = \cosh x$, sinh x is an odd function of x and cosh x is an even function of x.

Graph of Hyperbolic Functions

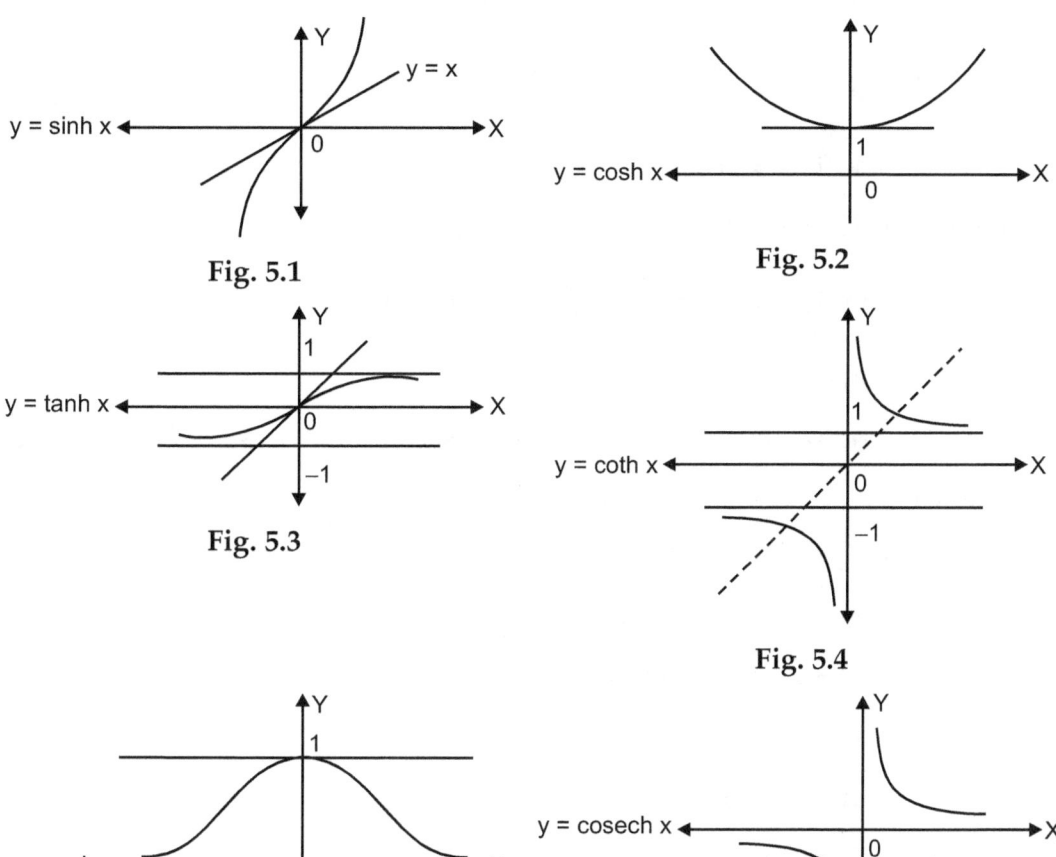

Fig. 5.1

Fig. 5.2

Fig. 5.3

Fig. 5.4

Fig. 5.5

Fig. 5.6

5.3 RELATION BETWEEN CIRCULAR AND HYPERBOLIC FUNCTIONS

Since for all values of x,

$$\sin x = \frac{e^{ix} - e^{-ix}}{2i}, \text{ replacing x by ix, we get}$$

$$\sin(ix) = \frac{e^{i(ix)} - e^{-i(ix)}}{2i} = \frac{e^{-x} - e^{+x}}{2i} = \frac{-(e^x - e^{-x})}{2i}$$

$$= i\left(\frac{e^x - e^{-x}}{2}\right) = i \sinh x$$

∴ $\sin(ix) = i \sinh x$ ... (8)

Similarly in the relation,

$$\cos x = \frac{e^{ix} + e^{-ix}}{2}, \text{ replacing } x \text{ by } ix, \text{ we get}$$

$$\cos(ix) = \frac{e^{i(ix)} + e^{-i(ix)}}{2} = \frac{e^x + e^{-x}}{2} = \cosh x$$

$\therefore \quad \cos(ix) = \cosh x$ ... (9)

Dividing (8) by (9), we get

$$\tan(ix) = \frac{\sin(ix)}{\cos(ix)} = \frac{i \sinh x}{\cosh x} = i \tanh x$$

$\therefore \quad \tan(ix) = i \tanh x$ ... (10)

Also, $\cot(ix) = -i \coth x$, $\sec(ix) = \operatorname{sech} x$ and $\operatorname{cosec}(ix) = -i \operatorname{cosech} x$

Again, if we replace x by ix in (8), we get

$$\sin i(ix) = i \sinh(ix)$$

i.e. $\sin(-x) = i \sinh(ix)$

i.e. $-\sin x = i \sinh(ix)$

i.e. $i^2 \sin x = i \sinh(ix)$

$\therefore \quad \sinh(ix) = i \sin x$ ... (11)

Similarly replacing x by ix in (9), we get

$$\cos i(ix) = \cosh(ix)$$

i.e. $\cos(-x) = \cosh(ix)$

$\therefore \quad \cosh(ix) = \cos x$ ... (12)

Dividing (11) by (12),

$\tanh(ix) = i \tan x$ ... (13)

Also, $\coth(ix) = -i \cot x$, $\operatorname{sech}(ix) = \sec x$ and $\operatorname{cosech}(ix) = -i \operatorname{cosec} x$.

Relations (8) to (13) are useful in separation of complex quantity into its real and imaginary parts.

It can also be seen that $\sinh(z)$ or $\sinh(x + iy)$ and $\cosh(z) = \cosh(x + iy)$ are periodic functions of period $2\pi i$.

5.4 FORMULAE OF HYPERBOLIC FUNCTIONS

Identities involving hyperbolic functions can be obtained from the corresponding formulae of circular (i.e. trigonometric) functions by replacing x by ix.

In the relation $\sin^2 x + \cos^2 x = 1$, replacing x by ix, we get

$$\sin^2(ix) + \cos^2(ix) = 1 \quad [\because \sin(ix) = i \sinh x, \cos(ix) = \cosh x]$$

i.e. $(i \sinh x)^2 + (\cosh x)^2 = 1$

$\therefore \quad \cosh^2 x - \sinh^2 x = 1$ ... (14)

Again consider $\sec^2 x = 1 + \tan^2(x)$

replacing x by ix, we get

$$\sec^2(ix) = 1 + \tan^2(ix) \quad [\because \sec(ix) = \text{sech } x, \tan(ix) = i \tanh x]$$

i.e. $\text{sech}^2 x = 1 - \tanh^2 x$

$\therefore \quad \text{sech}^2 x + \tanh^2 x = 1 \quad \text{or} \quad \text{sech}^2 x = 1 - \tanh^2 x$ ... (15)

Similarly, we can establish that

$\coth^2 x - \text{cosech}^2 x = 1$ ... (16)

In the relation, $\sin(A + B) = \sin A \cos B + \cos A \sin B$, put $A = ix$, $B = iy$

$$\sin i(x \pm y) = \sin(ix) \cos(iy) \pm \cos(ix) \sin(iy)$$

i.e. $i \sinh(x \pm y) = i \sinh x \cosh y \pm i \cosh x \sinh y$

$\therefore \quad \sinh(x \pm y) = \sinh x \cosh y \pm \cosh x \sinh y$ ... (17)

Similarly, we can establish that

$\cosh(x \pm y) = \cosh x \cosh y \pm \sinh x \sinh y$ ... (18)

On similar lines, following relations can also be established :

$\cosh 2x = \cosh^2 x + \sinh^2 x$ ... (19)

$\quad\quad\quad = 2 \cosh^2 x - 1$ ... (20)

$\quad\quad\quad = 1 + 2 \sinh^2 x$ ... (21)

$\sinh 2x = 2 \sinh x \cosh x$

$\sinh x + \sinh y = 2 \sinh \dfrac{x+y}{2} \cosh \dfrac{x-y}{2}$

$\sinh x - \sinh y = 2 \cosh \dfrac{x+y}{2} \sinh \dfrac{x-y}{2}$

$\cosh x + \cosh y = 2 \cosh \dfrac{x+y}{2} \cosh \dfrac{x-y}{2}$

$\cosh x - \cosh y = 2 \sinh \dfrac{x+y}{2} \sinh \dfrac{x-y}{2}$ ... (22)

$$\tanh(x \pm y) = \frac{\tanh x \pm \tanh y}{1 \pm \tanh x \tanh y} \qquad \ldots (23)$$

$$\sinh x = \frac{2 \tanh \frac{x}{2}}{1 - \tanh^2 \frac{x}{2}}$$

$$\cosh x = \frac{1 + \tanh^2 \frac{x}{2}}{1 - \tanh^2 \frac{x}{2}}$$

$$\tanh x = \frac{2 \tanh \frac{x}{2}}{1 + \tanh^2 \frac{x}{2}} \qquad \ldots (24)$$

$$\sinh 3x = 3 \sinh x + 4 \sinh^3 x, \quad \cosh 3x = 4 \cosh^3 x - 3 \cosh x \qquad \ldots (25)$$

Differentiation and Integration :

If $\quad y = \sinh x \quad \therefore \quad \dfrac{dy}{dx} = \dfrac{d}{dx}\left(\dfrac{e^x - e^{-x}}{2}\right) = \dfrac{e^x + e^{-x}}{2} = \cosh x$

If $\quad y = \cosh x \quad \therefore \quad \dfrac{dy}{dx} = \dfrac{d}{dx}\left(\dfrac{e^x + e^{-x}}{2}\right) = \dfrac{e^x - e^{-x}}{2} = \sinh x$

If $\quad y = \tanh x \quad \therefore \quad \dfrac{dy}{dx} = \dfrac{d}{dx}\left(\dfrac{e^x - e^{-x}}{e^x + e^{-x}}\right) = \left(\dfrac{2}{e^x + e^{-x}}\right)^2 = \operatorname{sech}^2 x$

From the above results, we can establish :

$$\int \cosh x \, dx = \sinh x$$

$$\int \sinh x \, dx = \cosh x$$

$$\int \operatorname{sech}^2 x \, dx = \tanh x$$

5.5 INVERSE HYPERBOLIC FUNCTION

Let $x = \sinh y$ then $y = \sinh^{-1} x$ is defined as inverse hyperbolic function of x.

Similarly, if $x = \cosh y$ then $y = \cosh^{-1} x$, $\tanh^{-1} x$, $\coth^{-1} x$, $\operatorname{sech}^{-1} x$ are similarly defined.

If $\qquad x = \sinh y = \dfrac{e^y - e^{-y}}{2}$ then multiplying throughout by e^y, we get

$$xe^y = \frac{e^{2y} - 1}{2}$$

$\therefore \qquad e^{2y} - 2xe^y - 1 = 0 \;$ which is a quadratic in e^y

$\therefore \qquad e^y = \dfrac{2x \pm \sqrt{4x^2 + 4}}{2} = x \pm \sqrt{x^2 + 1}$

Ignoring negative sign associated with $\sqrt{x^2+1}$
$$y = \log\left(x+\sqrt{x^2+1}\right)$$
$$\therefore \quad \sinh^{-1}x = \log\left(x+\sqrt{x^2+1}\right) \qquad \ldots (26)$$

Similarly, if $\quad x = \cosh y = \dfrac{e^y + e^{-y}}{2}$

$\therefore \quad e^{2y} - 2xe^y + 1 = 0$

which gives $\quad e^y = \dfrac{2x \pm \sqrt{4x^2-4}}{2} = x \pm \sqrt{x^2-1}$

Ignoring negative sign as before,
$$y = \log\left(x+\sqrt{x^2-1}\right)$$
$$\therefore \quad \cosh^{-1}x = \log\left(x+\sqrt{x^2-1}\right) \qquad \ldots (27)$$

Again, let $\quad x = \tanh y = \dfrac{e^y - e^{-y}}{e^y + e^{-y}}$

$\therefore \quad \dfrac{1+x}{1-x} = \dfrac{e^y - e^{-y} + e^y + e^{-y}}{e^y + e^{-y} - e^y + e^{-y}} = \dfrac{2e^y}{2e^{-y}} = e^{2y}$

$\therefore \quad 2y = \log\dfrac{1+x}{1-x} \quad \text{or} \quad y = \dfrac{1}{2}\log\dfrac{1+x}{1-x}$

$$\therefore \quad \tanh^{-1}x = \dfrac{1}{2}\log\dfrac{1+x}{1-x} \qquad \ldots (28)$$

Relations (26), (27) and (28) connect commonly used inverse hyperbolic functions with logarithmic functions.

We can also obtain mutual relations between inverse hyperbolic functions.

Let $\quad x = \sinh y \quad \therefore \quad y = \sinh^{-1}x$

Also $\quad x^2 = \sinh^2 y = \cosh^2 y - 1$

$\therefore \quad \cosh^2 y = 1 + x^2 \quad \text{or} \quad \cosh y = \sqrt{1+x^2}$

$\therefore \quad y = \cosh^{-1}\sqrt{1+x^2}$

Thus, $\quad \sinh^{-1}x = \cosh^{-1}\sqrt{1+x^2}$

Also from $\quad \cosh^2 y = 1 + x^2$, we get $\operatorname{sech}^2 y = \dfrac{1}{1+x^2}$

Now $\quad \operatorname{sech}^2 y = 1 - \tanh^2 y$

$\therefore \quad \tanh^2 y = 1 - \operatorname{sech}^2 y = 1 - \dfrac{1}{1+x^2} = \dfrac{x^2}{1+x^2}$

$\therefore \quad \tanh y = \dfrac{x}{\sqrt{1+x^2}} \quad \text{or} \quad y = \tanh^{-1}\dfrac{x}{\sqrt{1+x^2}}$

$\therefore \quad \sinh^{-1}x = \tanh^{-1}\dfrac{x}{\sqrt{1+x^2}}$

Similarly, other relations can also be obtained.

5.6 ILLUSTRATIONS ON BASIC DEFINITIONS

Ex. 1 : If $y = \log \tan x$, prove that

(i) $\sinh ny = \dfrac{1}{2}(\tan^n x - \cot^n x)$

(ii) $2 \cosh ny \operatorname{cosec} 2x = \cosh(n+1)y + \cosh(n-1)y$ **(May 2015)**

Sol. : (i) We have $y = \log \tan x$ $\therefore \tan x = e^y$ and $\cot x = e^{-y}$

$\tan^n x = e^{ny}$ and $\cot^n x = e^{-ny}$

$\therefore \dfrac{1}{2}(\tan^n x - \cot^n x) = \dfrac{1}{2}(e^{ny} - e^{-ny}) = \sinh ny$

(ii) R.H.S. $= \cosh(n+1)y + \cosh(n-1)y$ ... (1)

$= 2 \cosh ny \cosh y$

$\cosh y = \dfrac{e^y + e^{-y}}{2} = \dfrac{\tan x + \cot x}{2}$

$= \dfrac{\dfrac{\sin x}{\cos x} + \dfrac{\cos x}{\sin x}}{2}$

$= \dfrac{\sin^2 x + \cos^2 x}{2 \sin x \cos x} = \dfrac{1}{\sin 2x} = \operatorname{cosec} 2x$

Putting in (1), we get

R.H.S. $= 2 \cosh ny \operatorname{cosec} 2x$

$=$ L.H.S.

Ex. 2 : Find $\tanh x$ if $5 \sinh x - \cosh x = 5$. **(Dec. 2010)**

Sol. : Dividing the given relation by $\cosh x$, we get

$5 \tanh x - 1 = 5 \operatorname{sech} x$

Squaring on both sides, we get

$(5 \tanh x - 1)^2 = 25 \operatorname{sech}^2 x$

i.e. $25 \tanh^2 x + 1 - 10 \tanh x = 25(1 - \tanh^2 x)$

$50 \tanh^2 x - 10 \tanh x - 24 = 0$

i.e. $(5 \tanh x - 4)(5 \tanh x + 3) = 0$

$\therefore \tanh x = 4/5$ or $-3/5$

Ex. 3 : Show that $\operatorname{sech}^{-1}(\sin \theta) = \log \cot \dfrac{\theta}{2}$.

Sol. : Let $\operatorname{sech}^{-1}(\sin \theta) = x$

$\therefore \operatorname{sech} x = \sin \theta$

$\therefore \cosh x = \operatorname{cosec} \theta$

$\therefore x = \cosh^{-1}(\operatorname{cosec} \theta)$

$= \log\left(\operatorname{cosec} \theta + \sqrt{\operatorname{cosec}^2 \theta - 1}\right)$

$= \log(\operatorname{cosec} \theta + \cot \theta)$

$$= \log\left(\frac{1+\cos\theta}{\sin\theta}\right)$$

$$= \log\left(\frac{2\cos^2\frac{\theta}{2}}{2\sin\frac{\theta}{2}\cos\frac{\theta}{2}}\right)$$

$$= \log\cot\frac{\theta}{2}$$

Ex. 4 : If $y = \log\tan\left(\frac{\pi}{4} + \frac{x}{2}\right)$, prove that (i) $\tanh\frac{y}{2} = \tan\frac{x}{2}$, (ii) $\cosh y \cos x = 1$.

(Dec. 2007, May 2010)

Sol. : (i) We have

$$y = \log\tan(\pi/4 + x/2)$$

$$e^y = \tan(\pi/4 + x/2)$$

$$e^y = \frac{\tan\pi/4 + \tan x/2}{1 - \tan\pi/4 \, \tan x/2}$$

$$\frac{e^y}{1} = \frac{1 + \tan x/2}{1 - \tan x/2}$$

By Componendo and Dividendo, we get

$$\frac{e^y + 1}{e^y - 1} = \frac{2}{2\tan x/2}$$

$$\tan\frac{x}{2} = \frac{e^y - 1}{e^y + 1}$$

$$\tan\frac{x}{2} = \frac{e^{y/2} - e^{-y/2}}{e^{y/2} + e^{-y/2}} = \tanh\frac{y}{2}$$

$$\therefore \quad \tan\frac{x}{2} = \tanh\frac{y}{2}$$

(ii) Again,

$$\cosh y = \frac{1 + \tanh^2\frac{y}{2}}{1 - \tanh^2\frac{y}{2}}$$

$$= \frac{1 + \tan^2\frac{x}{2}}{1 - \tan^2\frac{x}{2}} \qquad \left\{\because \tanh\frac{y}{2} = \tan\frac{x}{2}\right\}$$

$$= \frac{1}{\cos x}$$

$$\therefore \quad \cosh y \cos x = 1$$

Ex. 5 : *Prove that* $\tan^{-1}\left[i\left(\dfrac{x-a}{x+a}\right)\right] = -\dfrac{i}{2}\log\left(\dfrac{a}{x}\right)$. **(May 2014)**

Sol. : Put $x = ae^y$ $\therefore e^y = \dfrac{x}{a}$ and $y = \log\dfrac{x}{a}$

$\therefore$ L.H.S. $= \tan^{-1}\left[i\left(\dfrac{ae^y - a}{ae^y + a}\right)\right]$

$= \tan^{-1}\left[i\left(\dfrac{e^{y/2} - e^{-y/2}}{e^{y/2} + e^{-y/2}}\right)\right] = \tan^{-1}\left(i\tanh\dfrac{y}{2}\right)$

$= \tan^{-1}\left(\tan i\dfrac{y}{2}\right)$ $\quad [\because \tan(iy) = i\tanh y]$

$= i\dfrac{y}{2} = \dfrac{i}{2}\log\dfrac{x}{a} = -\dfrac{i}{2}\log\dfrac{a}{x}$

Ex. 6 : If $\tan\left(\dfrac{x}{2}\right) = \tanh\left(\dfrac{u}{2}\right)$, *prove that (i) $\sinh u = \tan x$, (ii) $u = \log\tan\left(\dfrac{x}{2} + \dfrac{\pi}{4}\right)$*.

Sol. : (i) $\sinh u = \dfrac{2\tanh\dfrac{u}{2}}{1 - \tanh^2\dfrac{u}{2}} = \dfrac{2\tan x/2}{1 - \tan^2 x/2} = \tan x$

(ii) $\dfrac{u}{2} = \tanh^{-1}\left(\tan\dfrac{x}{2}\right)$

$\dfrac{u}{2} = \dfrac{1}{2}\log\left(\dfrac{1 + \tan\dfrac{x}{2}}{1 - \tan\dfrac{x}{2}}\right)$

$u = \log\tan\left(\dfrac{x}{2} + \dfrac{\pi}{4}\right)$

Ex. 7 : *If $\cosh x = \sec\theta$, then show that*

(i) $\theta = \dfrac{\pi}{2} - 2\tan^{-1}(e^{-x})$, (ii) $\tanh\dfrac{x}{2} = \pm\tan\dfrac{\theta}{2}$. **(Dec. 2009)**

Sol. : (i) We have $\cosh x = \sec\theta$

$\therefore \quad x = \cosh^{-1}(\sec\theta)$

$= \log(\sec\theta + \sqrt{\sec^2\theta - 1})$

$= \log(\sec\theta + \tan\theta)$

$= \log\left(\dfrac{1 + \sin\theta}{\cos\theta}\right)$

$\therefore \quad e^x = \dfrac{1 + \sin\theta}{\cos\theta}$

$$\therefore \quad e^{-x} = \frac{\cos\theta}{1+\sin\theta}$$

$$= \frac{\sin\alpha}{1+\cos\alpha} \qquad \text{where } \alpha = \frac{\pi}{2} - \theta$$

$$= \tan\frac{\alpha}{2}$$

$$\therefore \quad \alpha = 2\tan^{-1}(e^{-x})$$

$$\therefore \quad \theta = \frac{\pi}{2} - 2\tan^{-1}(e^{-x})$$

(ii) We have $\cosh x = \sec\theta$

$$\therefore \quad \frac{1+\tanh^2\frac{x}{2}}{1-\tanh^2\frac{x}{2}} = \frac{1+\tan^2\frac{\theta}{2}}{1-\tan^2\frac{\theta}{2}}$$

By comparing, we get

$$\tanh^2\frac{x}{2} = \tan^2\frac{\theta}{2}$$

$$\therefore \quad \tanh\frac{x}{2} = \pm\tan\frac{\theta}{2}$$

Ex. 8 : If $x = 2\cos\theta\cosh\phi$, $y = 2\sin\theta\sinh\phi$, prove that

(i) $\sec(\theta+i\phi) + \sec(\theta-i\phi) = \dfrac{4x}{x^2+y^2}$

(ii) $\sec(\theta+i\phi) - \sec(\theta-i\phi) = \dfrac{4iy}{x^2+y^2}$

Sol. :
$$x + iy = 2[\cos\theta\cosh\phi + i\sin\theta\sinh\phi]$$
$$= 2[\cos\theta\cos(i\phi) + \sin\theta\sin(i\phi)]$$
$$= 2\cos(\theta-i\phi) \quad [\because \cos(i\phi) = \cosh\phi \text{ and } \sin(i\phi) = i\sinh\phi]$$

Similarly, $\quad x - iy = 2\cos(\theta+i\phi)$

$$\therefore \quad \sec(\theta+i\phi) = \frac{2}{x-iy}, \quad \sec(\theta-i\phi) = \frac{2}{x+iy}$$

$$\therefore \quad \sec(\theta+i\phi) + \sec(\theta-i\phi) = \frac{2}{x-iy} + \frac{2}{x+iy} = \frac{2(x+iy-x+iy)}{x^2+y^2} = \frac{4x}{x^2+y^2}$$

and $\sec(\theta+i\phi) - \sec(\theta-i\phi) = \dfrac{2}{x-iy} - \dfrac{2}{x+iy} = \dfrac{2(x+iy-x+iy)}{x^2+y^2} = \dfrac{4iy}{x^2+y^2}$

Ex. 9 : *Prove that* $\tan^{-1}\left(\dfrac{\tan 2\theta + \tanh 2\phi}{\tan 2\theta - \tanh 2\phi}\right) + \tan^{-1}\left(\dfrac{\tan\theta - \tanh\phi}{\tan\theta + \tanh\phi}\right) = \tan^{-1}(\cot\theta\coth\phi)$

Sol. : Since $\tan^{-1}x + \tan^{-1}y = \tan^{-1}\dfrac{x+y}{1-xy}$

$$\text{L.H.S.} = \tan^{-1}\left[\dfrac{\left(\dfrac{\tan 2\theta + \tanh 2\phi}{\tan 2\theta - \tanh 2\phi}\right) + \left(\dfrac{\tan\theta - \tanh\phi}{\tan\theta + \tanh\phi}\right)}{1 - \left(\dfrac{\tan 2\theta + \tanh 2\phi}{\tan 2\theta - \tanh 2\phi}\right)\left(\dfrac{\tan\theta - \tanh\phi}{\tan\theta + \tanh\phi}\right)}\right]$$

$$= \tan^{-1}\left[\dfrac{\tan\theta\tan 2\theta + \tanh\phi\tanh 2\phi}{\tan 2\theta\tanh\phi - \tan\theta\tanh 2\phi}\right]$$

$$= \tan^{-1}\left[\dfrac{\tan\theta\left(\dfrac{2\tan\theta}{1-\tan^2\theta}\right) + \tanh\phi\left(\dfrac{2\tanh\phi}{1+\tanh^2\phi}\right)}{\tanh\phi\left(\dfrac{2\tan\theta}{1-\tan^2\theta}\right) + \tan\theta\left(\dfrac{2\tanh\phi}{1+\tanh^2\phi}\right)}\right]$$

$$= \tan^{-1}\left[\dfrac{(\tan^2\theta + \tanh^2\phi)}{\tan\theta\tanh\phi\,(\tan^2\theta + \tanh^2\phi)}\right]$$

$$= \tan^{-1}(\cot\theta\coth\phi)$$

Ex. 10 : *Prove that* $\cosh^{-1}\left(\dfrac{b + a\cos x}{a + b\cos x}\right) = \log\left[\dfrac{\sqrt{b+a} + \sqrt{b-a}\,\tan\dfrac{x}{2}}{\sqrt{b+a} - \sqrt{b-a}\,\tan\dfrac{x}{2}}\right]$.

Sol. : We know that,

$$\cosh^{-1}(z) = \log\left(z + \sqrt{z^2 - 1}\right) \qquad \ldots \text{(i)}$$

Let $\qquad z = \dfrac{b + a\cos x}{a + b\cos x}$

$\therefore \qquad z^2 - 1 = \left(\dfrac{b + a\cos x}{a + b\cos x}\right)^2 - 1 = \dfrac{(b + a\cos x)^2 - (a + b\cos x)^2}{(a + b\cos x)^2}$

$\qquad = \dfrac{(b^2 - a^2) + (a^2 - b^2)\cos^2 x}{(a + b\cos x)^2} = \dfrac{(b^2 - a^2)(1 - \cos^2 x)}{(a + b\cos x)^2}$

$\qquad = \dfrac{(b^2 - a^2)\sin^2 x}{(a + b\cos x)^2}$

Substituting in (i), we get

$\cosh^{-1}\left(\dfrac{b + a\cos x}{a + b\cos x}\right) = \log\left[\dfrac{b + a\cos x}{a + b\cos x} + \dfrac{\sqrt{b^2 - a^2}\,\sin x}{a + b\cos x}\right]$

$\qquad\qquad\qquad\qquad = \log\left[\dfrac{b + a\cos x + \sqrt{b^2 - a^2}\,\sin x}{a + b\cos x}\right]$

$$= \log\left[\frac{b + a\left(\frac{1-\tan^2 x/2}{1+\tan^2 x/2}\right) + \sqrt{b^2-a^2}\left(\frac{2\tan x/2}{1+\tan^2 x/2}\right)}{a + b\left(\frac{1-\tan^2 x/2}{1+\tan^2 x/2}\right)}\right]$$

$$= \log\left[\frac{b(1+\tan^2 x/2) + a(1-\tan^2 x/2) + 2\sqrt{b^2-a^2}\,(\tan x/2)}{a(1+\tan^2 x/2) + b(1-\tan^2 x/2)}\right]$$

$$= \log\left[\frac{(b+a) + (b-a)\tan^2 x/2 + 2\sqrt{b^2-a^2}\,\tan x/2}{(b+a) - (b-a)\tan^2 x/2}\right]$$

$$= \log\left[\frac{(\sqrt{b+a} + \sqrt{b-a}\,\tan x/2)^2}{(\sqrt{b+a} + \sqrt{b-a}\,\tan x/2)(\sqrt{b+a} - \sqrt{b-a}\,\tan x/2)}\right]$$

$$= \log\left[\frac{\sqrt{b+a} + \sqrt{b-a}\,\tan x/2}{\sqrt{b+a} - \sqrt{b-a}\,\tan x/2}\right]$$

EXERCISE 5.1

1. Prove that $\tanh^{-1}(\sin\theta) = \cosh^{-1}(\sec\theta)$.
2. Prove that $\sinh^{-1}(\tan\theta) = \log\tan(\pi/4 + \theta/2)$.
3. Prove that $(\cosh x + \sinh x)^n = (\cosh nx + \sinh nx)$, n being positive integer.

   (May 2011)

4. If $x = \tanh^{-1}(0.5)$, prove that $\sinh 2x = 4/3$.

   $$\left[\text{Hint}:\ \sinh 2x = \frac{2\tanh x}{1 - \tanh^2 x}\right]$$

5. Prove that $\cosh^5 x = \frac{1}{16}(\cosh 5x + 5\cosh 3x + 10\cosh x)$

   $$\left[\text{Hint}:\ \cosh^5 x = \frac{1}{32}(e^x + e^{-x})^5\right]$$

6. If $\cosh\alpha = \sec\beta$, prove that $\alpha = \pm\log(\sec\beta + \tan\beta)$.
7. If $\tan\alpha = \tan x \tanh y$ and $\tan\beta = \cot x \tanh y$, prove that $\tan(\alpha+\beta) = \sinh 2y \cosh 2x$.
8. Prove that $\sinh z$, $\cosh z$ are periodic functions and that $|\tanh z| \leq |$.

   [Hint: $\sinh(z + 2\pi i) = \sinh z \cosh(2\pi i) + i\cosh z \sinh(2\pi i)$
   $= \sinh z \cos 2\pi + i\cosh z \sin 2\pi$
   $= \sinh z$

   Also, $\quad -1 < |\tanh z| < 1$]

9. Show that $\operatorname{cosech} x + \coth x = \coth x/2$.
10. Prove that $\tanh^{-1} x = \sinh^{-1}\dfrac{x}{\sqrt{1-x^2}}$.

11. If $x = 2 \sin \alpha \cosh \beta$, $y = 2 \cos \alpha \sinh \beta$, prove that

    (i) $\text{cosec}(\alpha - i\beta) + \text{cosec}(\alpha + i\beta) = \dfrac{4x}{x^2 + y^2}$.

    (ii) $\text{cosec}(\alpha - i\beta) - \text{cosec}(\alpha + i\beta) = \dfrac{4iy}{x^2 + y^2}$.

    $\left[\textbf{Hint : } \text{cosec}(\alpha + i\beta) = \dfrac{1}{\sin(\alpha + i\beta)} = \dfrac{1}{\dfrac{x}{2} + i\dfrac{y}{2}} = \dfrac{2}{x + iy} \right].$

12. Prove that $(\cosh x - \sinh x)^n = \cosh nx - \sinh nx$.

13. If $\cosh x = \sec \theta$, then find the value of x and hence show that
    $\theta = \dfrac{\pi}{2} - 2 \tan^{-1}(e^{-x})$. **(May 2005, 2008)**

    [**Hint :** $x = \cosh^{-1}(\sec \theta) = \log[\sec \theta + \tan \theta] \Rightarrow e^{-x} = \dfrac{\cos \theta}{1 + \sin \theta}$, put $\theta = \dfrac{\pi}{2} - \alpha$

    $\therefore e^{-x} = \dfrac{\sin \alpha}{1 + \cos \alpha} = \tan \dfrac{\alpha}{2} \therefore \alpha = 2 \tan^{-1}(e^{-x})]$

14. Evaluate $\int \cosh^{-1}(2x)\, dx$.

    [**Hint :** $\int \log\left(2x + \sqrt{4x^2 - 1}\right) \cdot 1\, dx$, use integration by parts.]

15. Prove that $\cosh^2 x = \dfrac{1}{1 - \dfrac{1}{1 - \dfrac{1}{1 - \cosh^2 x}}}$.

5.7 SEPARATION OF REAL AND IMAGINARY PARTS OF COMPLEX QUANTITIES INVOLVING CIRCULAR & HYPERBOLIC FUNCTIONS

In this section we shall consider the important problem of separation into real and imaginary parts of a given complex quantity.

Consider $\sin(x + iy)$,

$$\sin(x + iy) = \sin x \cos(iy) + \cos x \sin(iy) \quad [\because \cos(iy) = \cosh y]$$

$$= \sin x \cosh y + i \cos x \sinh y \quad [\because \sin(iy) = i \sinh y]$$

Similarly, $\cos(x + iy) = \cos x \cosh y - i \sin x \sinh y$

Again, $\tan(x + iy) = \dfrac{\sin(x + iy)}{\cos(x + iy)}$

$$= \dfrac{2 \sin(x + iy)}{2 \cos(x + iy)} \cdot \dfrac{\cos(x - iy)}{\cos(x - iy)}$$

$$= \dfrac{\sin 2x + \sin(2iy)}{\cos 2x + \cos(2iy)}$$

$$= \dfrac{\sin 2x + i \sinh 2y}{\cos 2x + \cosh 2y}$$

$$\therefore \quad \tan(x+iy) = \frac{\sin 2x}{\cos 2x + \cosh 2y} + i\frac{\sinh 2y}{\cos 2x + \cosh 2y}$$

Similarly, $\quad \tan(x-iy) = \dfrac{\sin 2x}{\cos 2x + \cosh 2y} - i\dfrac{\sinh 2y}{\cos 2x + \cosh 2y}$

Thus, if $\tan(x+iy) = p+iq$ then $\tan(x-iy) = p-iq$

Students are advised to separate into real and imaginary parts of following complex quantities :

$$\cot(x+iy),\ \sec(x+iy),\ \operatorname{cosec}(x+iy)$$

Now, consider $\sinh(x+iy)$

$$\sinh(x+iy) = \sinh x \cosh(iy) + \cosh x \sinh(iy)$$
$$= \sinh x \cos y + i \cosh x \sin y \qquad [\because \cosh(iy) = \cos y \text{ and}$$
$$\sinh(iy) = i \sin y]$$

Similarly, $\quad \cosh(x+iy) = \cosh x \cos y + i \sinh x \sin y$

Again $\quad \tanh(x+iy) = \dfrac{\sinh(x+iy)}{\cosh(x+iy)}$

$$= \frac{2\sinh(x+iy)\cosh(x-iy)}{2\cosh(x+iy)\cosh(x-iy)}$$

$$= \frac{\sinh 2x + i\sinh(2iy)}{\cosh 2x + \cosh(2iy)}$$

$$= \frac{\sinh 2x + i\sin 2y}{\cosh 2x + \cos 2y}$$

$\therefore \quad \tanh(x+iy) = \dfrac{\sinh 2x}{\cosh 2x + \cos 2y} + i\dfrac{\sin 2y}{\cosh 2x + \cos 2y}$

Similarly, $\tanh(x-iy) = \dfrac{\sinh 2x}{\cosh 2x + \cos 2y} - i\dfrac{\sin 2y}{\cosh 2x + \cos 2y}$

Thus if $\tanh(x+iy) = p+iq$ then $\tanh(x-iy) = p-iq$.

Similarly $\coth(x+iy)$, $\operatorname{sech}(x+iy)$ and $\operatorname{cosech}(x+iy)$ can be separated into real and imaginary parts, which is left as exercise for the students.

Problems on separation of real and imaginary parts of $\tan(\alpha + i\beta)$ can be solved in the following manner.

Let $\quad \tan(\alpha + i\beta) = p + iq$ then $\tan(\alpha - i\beta) = p - iq \quad$ (as proved above)

Now, $\quad \tan 2\alpha = \tan[(\alpha + i\beta) + (\alpha - i\beta)]$

$$= \frac{\tan(\alpha + i\beta) + \tan(\alpha - i\beta)}{1 - \tan(\alpha + i\beta)\tan(\alpha - i\beta)}$$

$$= \frac{(p+iq) + (p-iq)}{1 - (p+iq)(p-iq)} = \frac{2p}{1 - p^2 - q^2}$$

which gives α in terms of p, q.

Similarly, $\tan(2i\beta) = \tan[(\alpha + i\beta) - (\alpha - i\beta)]$

$$\beta = \frac{\tan[(\alpha + i\beta) - (\alpha - i\beta)]}{1 + \tan(\alpha + i\beta)\tan(\alpha - i\beta)}$$

$\therefore \quad \tan(2i\beta) = \dfrac{(p+iq) - (p-iq)}{1 + (p+iq)(p-iq)} = \dfrac{2iq}{1 + p^2 + q^2}$

$\therefore \quad \tanh 2\beta = \dfrac{2q}{1 + p^2 + q^2}$

which gives β in terms of p and q.

5.8 ILLUSTRATIONS ON SEPARATION OF REAL & IMAGINARY PARTS

Ex. 1 : If $\tan(x + iy) = i$, where x and y are real, prove that x is indeterminate and y is infinite.

Sol. : We have,

$\tan(x + iy) = i$ ... (given)

then $\tan(x - iy) = -i$

Now $\tan 2x = \tan[(x + iy) + (x - iy)]$

$= \dfrac{\tan(x+iy) + \tan(x-iy)}{1 - \tan(x+iy)\tan(x-iy)}$

$\therefore \quad \tan 2x = \dfrac{i + (-1)}{1 - (i)(-i)} = \dfrac{0}{0}$

which shows that x is indeterminate.

Again $\tan(2iy) = [\tan(x+iy) - (x-iy)]$

$= \dfrac{\tan(x+iy) - \tan(x-iy)}{1 + \tan(x+iy)\tan(x-iy)}$

$= \dfrac{i-(-i)}{1 + i(-i)} = \dfrac{2i}{2} = i$

$\therefore \quad i \tanh 2y = i$ $\qquad [\because \tan(i2y) = i \tanh 2y]$

$\therefore \quad \tanh 2y = 1$

$\therefore \quad 2y = \tanh^{-1} 1 = \dfrac{1}{2} \log \dfrac{1+1}{1-1} = \infty$

Thus y is infinite.

Ex. 2 : If $\sin(\alpha + i\beta) = x + iy$, prove that (i) $\dfrac{x^2}{\cosh^2\beta} + \dfrac{y^2}{\sinh^2\beta} = 1$,

(ii) $\dfrac{x^2}{\sin^2\alpha} - \dfrac{y^2}{\cos^2\alpha} = 1$.

Sol. : We have, $\sin(\alpha + i\beta) = \sin\alpha \cos(i\beta) + \cos\alpha \sin(i\beta)$

$= \sin\alpha \cosh\beta + i\cos\alpha \sinh\beta$

$= x + iy$ ... (given)

Equating real and imaginary parts, we get
$$x = \sin\alpha \cosh\beta \quad \text{and} \quad y = \cos\alpha \sinh\beta \qquad \ldots (1)$$
$$\therefore \quad \frac{x}{\cosh\beta} = \sin\alpha, \quad \frac{y}{\sinh\beta} = \cos\alpha$$

Squaring and adding, we get
$$\frac{x^2}{\cosh^2\beta} + \frac{y^2}{\sinh^2\beta} = 1$$

Again from (1), we have
$$\frac{x}{\sin\alpha} = \cosh\beta \quad \text{and} \quad \frac{y}{\cos\alpha} = \sinh\beta$$

But $\cosh^2\beta - \sinh^2\beta = 1$

$$\therefore \quad \frac{x^2}{\sin^2\alpha} - \frac{y^2}{\cos^2\alpha} = 1$$

which proves the required result.

Ex. 3: If $\sinh(\theta + i\phi) = \cos\alpha + i\sin\alpha$, prove that $\sinh^4\theta = \cos^2\alpha = \cos^4\phi$. **(May 2006)**

Sol.: We have $\sinh(\theta + i\phi) = \cos\alpha + i\sin\alpha$

$\therefore \quad \sinh\theta \cosh i\phi + \cosh\theta \sinh i\phi = \cos\alpha + i\sin\alpha \qquad [\because \cosh iy = \cos y$

$\therefore \quad \sinh\theta \cos\phi + i\cosh\theta \sin\phi = \cos\alpha + i\sin\alpha \qquad \text{and } \sinh iy = i\sin y]$

Equating real and imaginary parts, we get
$$\sinh\theta \cos\phi = \cos\alpha \quad \text{and} \quad \cosh\theta \sin\phi = \sin\alpha$$
$$\therefore \quad \sinh^2\theta \cos^2\phi = \cos^2\alpha \quad \text{and} \quad \cosh^2\theta \sin^2\phi = \sin^2\alpha \qquad \ldots (1)$$
$$\therefore \quad \sinh^2\theta (1 - \sin^2\phi) = \cos^2\alpha \quad \text{and} \quad \cosh^2\theta \sin^2\phi = \sin^2\alpha$$

Adding the two results, we have
$$\sinh^2\theta + \sin^2\phi (\cosh^2\theta - \sinh^2\theta) = \sin^2\alpha + \cos^2\alpha$$
$$\therefore \quad \sin^2\phi = 1 - \sinh^2\theta \qquad [\because \cosh^2\theta - \sinh^2\theta = 1]$$
$$\therefore \quad 1 - \cos^2\phi = 1 - \sinh^2\theta$$
$$\therefore \quad \cos^2\phi = \sinh^2\theta$$
$$\therefore \quad \cos^4\phi = \sinh^4\theta \qquad \ldots (2)$$

Again from (1), $\cos^2\phi = \dfrac{\cos^2\alpha}{\sinh^2\theta}$ and $\sin^2\phi = \dfrac{\sin^2\alpha}{\cosh^2\theta}$

$$\therefore \quad \cos^2\phi + \sin^2\phi = \frac{\cos^2\alpha}{\sinh^2\theta} + \frac{\sin^2\alpha}{\cosh^2\theta}$$
$$\therefore \quad 1 = \frac{\cos^2\alpha \cosh^2\theta + \sin^2\alpha \sinh^2\theta}{\sinh^2\theta \cosh^2\theta}$$

$$\therefore \quad \sinh^2\theta \cosh^2\theta = \cos^2\alpha \cosh^2\theta + \sin^2\alpha \sinh^2\theta$$
$$= \cos^2\alpha \cosh^2\theta + (1 - \cos^2\alpha) \sinh^2\theta$$
$$= \cos^2\alpha \cosh^2\theta + \sinh^2\theta - \cos^2\alpha \sinh^2\theta$$
$$= \cos^2\alpha (\cosh^2\theta - \sinh^2\theta) + \sinh^2\theta$$
$$= \cos^2\alpha + \sinh^2\theta$$
$$\cos^2\alpha = \sinh^2\theta (\cosh^2\theta - 1) \qquad [\because \cosh^2\theta - \sinh^2\theta = 1]$$
$$= \sinh^2\theta \sinh^2\theta$$
$$\therefore \quad \cos^2\alpha = \sinh^4\theta \qquad \ldots (3)$$

From (2) and (3), we have,
$$\sinh^4\theta = \cos^2\alpha = \cos^4\phi$$

Note : We eliminate α and ϕ in the relations (1), to obtain results (2) and (3) respectively.

Ex. 4 : *If* $\cos(\alpha + i\beta) \cos(\gamma + i\delta) = 1$, *prove that*

(i) $\tanh^2\delta \cosh^2\beta = \sin^2\alpha,$ (ii) $\tanh^2\beta \cosh^2\delta = \sin^2\gamma.$

Sol. : We have
$$\cos(\alpha + i\beta) \cos(\gamma + i\delta) = 1$$
$$\therefore \quad \cos(\alpha + i\beta) = \sec(\gamma + i\delta) \qquad \ldots (1)$$
$$\therefore \quad \sin(\alpha + i\beta) = \sqrt{1 - \cos^2(\alpha + i\beta)}$$
$$= \sqrt{1 - \sec^2(\gamma + i\delta)}$$
$$= \sqrt{-\tan^2(\gamma + i\delta)}$$
$$= i \tan(\gamma + i\delta) \qquad \ldots (2)$$
$$\therefore \quad \tan(\alpha + i\beta) = \frac{\sin(\alpha + i\beta)}{\cos(\alpha + i\beta)} = \frac{i \tan(\gamma + i\delta)}{\sec(\gamma + i\delta)} \qquad \text{[by (1) and (2)]}$$
$$= i \sin(\gamma + i\delta)$$
$$= i (\sin\gamma \cos i\delta + \cos\gamma \sin i\delta)$$
$$= -\cos\gamma \sinh\delta + i \sin\gamma \cosh\delta \qquad \ldots (3)$$
$$\therefore \quad \tan(\alpha - i\beta) = -\cos\gamma \sinh\delta - i \sin\gamma \cosh\delta \qquad \ldots (4)$$

Now
$$\tan(2i\beta) = \tan[(\alpha + i\beta) - (\alpha - i\beta)]$$
$$= \frac{\tan(\alpha + i\beta) - \tan(\alpha - i\beta)}{1 + \tan(\alpha + i\beta) \tan(\alpha - i\beta)}$$
$$= \frac{2i \sin\gamma \cosh\delta}{1 + (\cos^2\gamma \sinh^2\delta + \sin^2\gamma \cosh^2\delta)} \qquad \text{[by (3) and (4)]}$$

$$\therefore \quad i \tanh 2\beta = \frac{i\, 2 \sin \gamma \cosh \delta}{\cosh^2 \delta + \sin^2 \gamma}$$

$$\therefore \quad \frac{2 \tanh \beta}{1 + \tanh^2 \beta} = \frac{2 \left(\dfrac{\sin \gamma}{\cosh \delta} \right)}{1 + \left(\dfrac{\sin \gamma}{\cosh \delta} \right)^2} \qquad \text{(dividing by } \cosh^2 \delta\text{)}$$

$$\therefore \quad \tanh \beta = \frac{\sin \gamma}{\cosh \delta}$$

$$\therefore \quad \tanh^2 \beta\ \cosh^2 \delta = \sin^2 \gamma \qquad \ldots (5)$$

which proves the second result. For the first result, consider $\cos (\gamma + i\delta) = \sec (\alpha + i\beta)$ and interchanging γ with α and δ with β in (5) we get $\tanh^2 \delta\ \cosh^2 \beta = \sin^2 \alpha$.

Ex. 5 : If $\sin^{-1}(\alpha + i\beta) = \lambda + i\mu$, prove that $\sin^2 \lambda$ and $\cosh^2 \mu$ are the roots of the equation $x^2 - (1 + \alpha^2 + \beta^2)\, x + \alpha^2 = 0$.

Sol. :
$$\sin^{-1}(\alpha + i\beta) = \lambda + i\mu$$
$$\alpha + i\beta = \sin(\lambda + i\mu)$$
$$\alpha + i\beta = \sin \lambda\ \cosh \mu + i \cos \lambda\ \sinh \mu$$
$$\therefore \quad \alpha = \sin \lambda \cosh \mu \ \text{ and } \ \beta = \cos \lambda\ \sinh \mu$$
$$\therefore \quad 1 + \alpha^2 + \beta^2 = 1 + \sin^2 \lambda\ \cosh^2 \mu + \cos^2 \lambda\ \sinh^2 \mu$$
$$= 1 + \sin^2 \lambda\ \cosh^2 \mu + (1 - \sin^2 \lambda)(\cosh^2 \mu - 1)$$
$$= 1 + \sin^2 \lambda\ \cosh^2 \mu + \cosh^2 \mu - \sin^2 \lambda\ \cosh^2 \mu + \sin^2 \lambda - 1$$
$$= \sin^2 \lambda + \cosh^2 \mu$$
$$\therefore \quad 1 + \alpha^2 + \beta^2 = \sin^2 \lambda + \cosh^2 \mu = \text{sum of roots} \qquad \ldots (1)$$
and
$$\alpha^2 = \sin^2 \lambda\ \cosh^2 \mu = \text{product of roots} \qquad \ldots (2)$$

From (1) and (2), it follows that $\sin^2 \lambda$ and $\cosh^2 \mu$ are the roots of the given quadratic equation.

Ex. 6 : If $\tan(\alpha + i\beta) = x + iy$, prove that
$$x^2 + y^2 + 2x \cot 2\alpha = 1 \quad \text{and} \quad x^2 + y^2 - 2y \coth 2\beta + 1 = 0 \qquad \textbf{(Dec. 2005)}$$

Sol. : We have, $\tan(\alpha + i\beta) = x + iy$

then $\tan(\alpha - i\beta) = x - iy$

Now,
$$\tan 2\alpha = \tan[(\alpha + i\beta) + (\alpha - i\beta)]$$
$$= \frac{\tan(\alpha + i\beta) + (\alpha - i\beta)}{1 - \tan(\alpha + i\beta) \tan(\alpha - i\beta)}$$
$$= \frac{x + iy + x - iy}{1 - (x + iy)(x - iy)} = \frac{2x}{1 - x^2 - y^2}$$

$$\therefore \quad 1 - x^2 - y^2 = 2x \cot 2\alpha$$
$$\therefore \quad x^2 + y^2 + 2x \cot 2\alpha = 1 \qquad \ldots (1)$$

Again
$$\tan 2i\beta = \tan[(\alpha + i\beta) - (\alpha - i\beta)]$$
$$= \frac{\tan(\alpha + i\beta) - \tan(\alpha - i\beta)}{1 + \tan(\alpha + i\beta)\tan(\alpha - i\beta)}$$
$$= \frac{(x + iy) - (x - iy)}{1 + (x + iy)(x - iy)} = \frac{2iy}{1 + x^2 + y^2}$$

$\therefore \quad \tanh 2\beta = \dfrac{2y}{1 + x^2 + y^2}$

$\therefore \quad x^2 + y^2 - 2y \coth 2\beta + 1 = 0 \qquad \ldots (2)$

(1) and (2) are the required results.

Ex. 7 : *Express* $\cos^{-1}\left(\dfrac{3i}{4}\right)$ *in the form a + ib.* **(Dec. 2007, May 2009, May 2010)**

Sol. : Let $\cos^{-1}\left(\dfrac{3i}{4}\right) = a + ib$

$\therefore \quad \cos(a + ib) = \dfrac{3i}{4}$

i.e. $\cos a \cos ib - \sin a \sin ib = \dfrac{3i}{4}$

$\cos a \cosh b - i \sin a \sinh b = \dfrac{3i}{4}$

Equating real and imaginary parts,

$\cos a \cosh b = 0 \qquad \ldots (1)$

and $\sin a \sinh b = -\dfrac{3}{4} \qquad \ldots (2)$

From (1), as $\cosh b \neq 0$

$\therefore \quad \cos a = 0$ i.e. $a = \dfrac{\pi}{2}$

From (2), $\sin a \sinh b = -\dfrac{3}{4}$

$\therefore \quad \sin\dfrac{\pi}{2} \sinh b = -\dfrac{3}{4} \qquad \left[\because a = \dfrac{\pi}{2}\right]$

$\therefore \quad \sinh b = -\dfrac{3}{4}$

$\therefore \quad b = \sinh^{-1}\left(-\dfrac{3}{4}\right)$

$= \log\left[-\dfrac{3}{4} + \sqrt{\dfrac{9}{16} + 1}\right] \quad \left[\because \sinh^{-1} x = \log(x + \sqrt{x^2 + 1})\right]$

$= \log\left[-\dfrac{3}{4} + \dfrac{5}{4}\right] = \log\dfrac{1}{2}$

i.e. $b = -\log 2$

$\therefore \quad \cos^{-1}\left(\dfrac{3i}{4}\right) = \dfrac{\pi}{2} - i\log 2$

Ex. 8 : If $\sin(\theta + i\phi) = \tan\alpha + i\sec\alpha$, show that $\cos 2\theta \cosh 2\phi = 3$. **(May 2007)**

Sol. : We have,
$$\sin(\theta + i\phi) = \sin\theta \cos(i\phi) + \cos\theta \sin(i\phi)$$
$$= \sin\theta \cosh\phi + i\cos\theta \sinh\phi$$

Equating real and imaginary parts,
$$\sin\theta \cosh\phi = \tan\alpha \text{ and } \cos\theta \sinh\phi = \sec\alpha$$

Now, $\sec^2\alpha = 1 + \tan^2\alpha$

$\therefore \cos^2\theta \sinh^2\phi = 1 + \sin^2\theta \cosh^2\phi$
$$= 1 + \sin^2\theta(1 + \sinh^2\phi)$$
$$= 1 + \sin^2\theta + \sin^2\theta \sinh^2\phi$$

$\therefore \cos^2\theta \sinh^2\phi - \sin^2\theta \sinh^2\phi = 1 + \sin^2\theta$

$$\sinh^2\phi \cos 2\theta = 1 + \sin^2\theta \qquad \ldots (1)$$

Again $\cosh 2\phi = 1 + 2\sinh^2\phi \qquad \therefore \sinh^2\phi = \dfrac{\cosh 2\phi - 1}{2}$

Putting in (1), we get

$$\dfrac{(\cosh 2\phi - 1)}{2} \cos 2\theta = 1 + \sin^2\theta$$

$\therefore \cosh 2\phi \cos 2\theta - \cos 2\theta = 2 + 2\sin^2\theta$

$\therefore \cosh 2\phi \cos 2\theta = \cos 2\theta + 2 + 2\sin^2\theta$
$$= 1 - 2\sin^2\theta + 2 + 2\sin^2\theta$$

$\therefore \cosh 2\phi \cos 2\theta = 3$ which is the required result.

Ex. 9 : If $\tan(\theta + i\phi) = \cos\alpha + i\sin\alpha$, prove that

(i) $\theta = \dfrac{n\pi}{2} + \dfrac{\pi}{4}$, (ii) $\phi = \dfrac{1}{2} \log \tan\left(\dfrac{\pi}{4} + \dfrac{\alpha}{2}\right)$. **(May 2007)**

Sol. : We have, $\tan(\theta + i\phi) = \cos\alpha + i\sin\alpha$

then $\tan(\theta - i\phi) = \cos\alpha - i\sin\alpha$

Now $\tan 2\theta = \tan[(\theta + i\phi) + (\theta - i\phi)]$

$\therefore \tan 2\theta = \dfrac{\tan(\theta + i\phi) + \tan(\theta - i\phi)}{1 - \tan(\theta + i\phi)\tan(\theta - i\phi)}$

$$= \dfrac{\cos\alpha + i\sin\alpha + \cos\alpha - i\sin\alpha}{1 - (\cos\alpha + i\sin\alpha)(\cos\alpha - i\sin\alpha)}$$

$$= \dfrac{2\cos\alpha}{1 - \cos^2\alpha - \sin^2\alpha} = \infty = \tan\left(n\pi + \dfrac{\pi}{2}\right)$$

$\therefore 2\theta = n\pi + \dfrac{\pi}{2}$ or $\theta = \dfrac{n\pi}{2} + \dfrac{\pi}{4}$

Again $\tan(2i\phi) = \tan[(\theta + i\phi) - (\theta - i\phi)]$

$$= \frac{\tan(\theta + i\phi) - \tan(\theta - i\phi)}{1 + \tan(\theta + i\phi)\tan(\theta - i\phi)}$$

$$= \frac{(\cos\alpha + i\sin\alpha) - (\cos\alpha - i\sin\alpha)}{1 + (\cos\alpha + i\sin\alpha)(\cos\alpha - i\sin\alpha)}$$

$$= \frac{2i\sin\alpha}{1 + \cos^2\alpha + \sin^2\alpha} = \frac{2i\sin\alpha}{2} = i\sin\alpha$$

$\therefore$ $i\tanh 2\phi = i\sin\alpha$ $\qquad [\because \tan(i2\phi) = i\tanh(2\phi)]$

$\therefore$ $\tanh 2\phi = \sin\alpha$

$2\phi = \tanh^{-1}(\sin\alpha)$

$\therefore$ $2\phi = \dfrac{1}{2}\log\dfrac{1+\sin\alpha}{1-\sin\alpha}$

$$= \frac{1}{2}\log\frac{\left(\cos^2\dfrac{\alpha}{2} + \sin^2\dfrac{\alpha}{2} + 2\sin\dfrac{\alpha}{2}\cos\dfrac{\alpha}{2}\right)}{\left(\cos^2\dfrac{\alpha}{2} + \sin^2\dfrac{\alpha}{2} - 2\sin\dfrac{\alpha}{2}\cos\dfrac{\alpha}{2}\right)}$$

$$= \frac{1}{2}\log\frac{\left(\cos\dfrac{\alpha}{2} + \sin\dfrac{\alpha}{2}\right)^2}{\left(\cos\dfrac{\alpha}{2} - \sin\dfrac{\alpha}{2}\right)^2} = \log\frac{\left(\cos\dfrac{\alpha}{2} + \sin\dfrac{\alpha}{2}\right)}{\left(\cos\dfrac{\alpha}{2} - \sin\dfrac{\alpha}{2}\right)}$$

$$= \log\frac{1 + \tan\dfrac{\alpha}{2}}{1 - \tan\dfrac{\alpha}{2}}$$

$2\phi = \log\tan\left(\dfrac{\pi}{4} + \dfrac{\alpha}{2}\right)$ $\qquad \left[\because \tan\dfrac{\pi}{4} = 1\right]$

$\therefore$ $\phi = \dfrac{1}{2}\log\tan\left(\dfrac{\pi}{4} + \dfrac{\alpha}{2}\right)$ $\qquad$ Hence the required result.

Ex. 10 : *If* $u + iv = \dfrac{1}{i}\log\left(\dfrac{1+ie^{i\theta}}{1-ie^{i\theta}}\right)$, *prove that* $u = \dfrac{\pi}{2}$ *and* $v = \log(\sec\theta + \tan\theta)$

Sol. : We have, $\quad u + iv = \dfrac{1}{i}\log\left(\dfrac{1+ie^{i\theta}}{1-ie^{i\theta}}\right)$

$$= \frac{2}{i}\tanh^{-1}(ie^{i\theta}) \qquad \left[\because \tanh^{-1}x = \frac{1}{2}\log\frac{1+x}{1-x}\right]$$

$\therefore$ $\dfrac{-v}{2} + i\dfrac{u}{2} = \tanh^{-1}(ie^{i\theta})$

$\therefore \qquad \tanh\left(-\dfrac{v}{2} + \dfrac{iu}{2}\right) = i \cdot e^{i\theta} = -\sin\theta + i\cos\theta$ ... (1)

$\therefore \qquad \tanh\left(-\dfrac{v}{2} - \dfrac{iu}{2}\right) = -\sin\theta - i\cos\theta$ ... (2)

Now $\qquad \tanh(-v) = \tanh\left[\left(-\dfrac{v}{2} + \dfrac{iu}{2}\right) + \left(-\dfrac{v}{2} - \dfrac{iu}{2}\right)\right]$

$= \dfrac{(-\sin\theta + i\cos\theta) + (-\sin\theta - i\cos\theta)}{1 + (-\sin\theta + i\cos\theta)(-\sin\theta - i\cos\theta)} = \dfrac{-2\sin\theta}{2}$

$= -\sin\theta$

$\therefore \qquad v = \tanh^{-1}(\sin\theta)$

$= \dfrac{1}{2}\log\left[\dfrac{1+\sin\theta}{1-\sin\theta}\right] = \dfrac{1}{2}\log\left[\dfrac{(1+\sin\theta)^2}{(1-\sin^2\theta)}\right]$

$= \dfrac{1}{2}\log\left[\dfrac{1+\sin\theta}{\cos\theta}\right]^2$

$= \log(\sec\theta + \tan\theta)$ ... (3)

Again $\qquad \tanh(iu) = \tanh\left[\left(-\dfrac{v}{2} + \dfrac{iu}{2}\right) - \left(-\dfrac{v}{2} - \dfrac{iu}{2}\right)\right]$

$= \dfrac{(-\sin\theta + i\cos\theta) - (-\sin\theta - i\cos\theta)}{1 - (-\sin\theta + i\cos\theta)(-\sin\theta - i\cos\theta)} = \dfrac{2i\cos\theta}{1-1}$

$\therefore \qquad i\tan u = \dfrac{i2\cos\theta}{0}$

i.e. $\qquad \tan u = \infty$

$\therefore \qquad u = \dfrac{\pi}{2}$ ... (4)

(3) and (4) are required results.

Ex. 11 : If $\tan\left(\dfrac{\pi}{4} + iv\right) = re^{i\theta}$, show that

(i) $r = 1$, (ii) $\tan\theta = \sinh 2v$, (iii) $\tanh v = \tan\theta/2$.

Sol. : We have, $\tan\left(\dfrac{\pi}{4} + iv\right) = \dfrac{\sin\left(\dfrac{\pi}{4} + iv\right)}{\cos\left(\dfrac{\pi}{4} + iv\right)} \times \dfrac{2\cos\left(\dfrac{\pi}{4} - iv\right)}{2\cos\left(\dfrac{\pi}{4} - iv\right)}$

$= \dfrac{\sin\dfrac{\pi}{2} + i\sinh 2v}{\cos\dfrac{\pi}{2} + \cosh 2v} = \dfrac{1 + i\sinh 2v}{\cosh 2v}$

$= re^{i\theta}$

$$\therefore \quad r = \frac{1}{\cosh^2 2v} + \frac{\sinh^2 2v}{\cosh^2 2v} = \frac{\cosh^2 2v}{\cosh^2 2v} = 1 \quad \ldots (1)$$

and
$$\tan\theta = \frac{\frac{\sinh 2v}{\cosh 2v}}{\frac{1}{\cosh 2v}} = \sinh 2v \quad \ldots (2)$$

Now $\sinh 2v = \tan\theta$

$\therefore \quad 2v = \sinh^{-1}(\tan\theta) = \log(\tan\theta + \sqrt{1+\tan^2\theta})$

$$= \log(\sec\theta + \tan\theta) = \log\left(\frac{1+\sin\theta}{\cos\theta}\right)$$

$$= \log\left[\frac{\left(\cos\frac{\theta}{2}+\sin\frac{\theta}{2}\right)^2}{\cos^2\frac{\theta}{2}-\sin^2\frac{\theta}{2}}\right] = \log\left[\frac{\cos\frac{\theta}{2}+\sin\frac{\theta}{2}}{\cos\frac{\theta}{2}-\sin\frac{\theta}{2}}\right]$$

$$= \frac{2}{2}\log\left[\frac{1+\tan\frac{\theta}{2}}{1-\tan\frac{\theta}{2}}\right] = 2\tanh^{-1}\left(\tan\frac{\theta}{2}\right)$$

$\therefore \quad v = \tanh^{-1}\left(\tan\frac{\theta}{2}\right)$

$\therefore \quad \tanh v = \tan\frac{\theta}{2} \quad \ldots (3)$

(1), (2) and (3) are the required results.

Ex. 12 : *If* $\cosh^{-1}(x+iy) + \cosh^{-1}(x-iy) = \cosh^{-1} a$ *then prove that*
$2(a-1)x^2 + 2(a+1)y^2 = a^2 - 1.$ **(May 2005)**

Sol. : Let $\cosh^{-1}(x+iy) = \alpha + i\beta$
then $\cosh^{-1}(x-iy) = \alpha - i\beta$
$\cosh^{-1}(x+iy) + \cosh^{-1}(x-iy) = 2\alpha$
$\therefore \quad \cosh^{-1} a = 2\alpha$ (by given relation)
$\therefore \quad a = \cosh 2\alpha \quad \ldots (1)$

Also, $x + iy = \cosh(\alpha + i\beta)$ then $x - iy = \cosh(\alpha - i\beta)$
By adding, $2x = \cosh(\alpha + i\beta) + \cosh(\alpha - i\beta)$
$2x = \cosh\alpha\cos\beta + i\sinh\alpha\sin\beta + \cosh\alpha\cos\beta - i\sinh\alpha\sin\beta$
$2x = 2\cosh\alpha\cos\beta$
$\therefore \quad x = \cosh\alpha\cos\beta \quad \ldots (2)$

By subtracting, $2iy = \cosh(\alpha + i\beta) - \cosh(\alpha - i\beta)$
$2iy = \cosh\alpha\cos\beta + i\sinh\alpha\sin\beta - \cosh\alpha\cos\beta + i\sinh\alpha\sin\beta$
$2iy = 2i\sinh\alpha\sin\beta$
$\therefore \quad y = \sinh\alpha\sin\beta \quad \ldots (3)$

Eliminating β between (2) and (3), we get

$$\frac{x^2}{\cosh^2 \alpha} = \cos^2 \beta, \quad \frac{y^2}{\sinh^2 \alpha} = \sin^2 \beta$$

$$\therefore \quad \frac{x^2}{\cosh^2 \alpha} + \frac{y^2}{\sinh^2 \alpha} = \cos^2 \beta + \sin^2 \beta$$

$$\frac{x^2}{\left(\frac{1+\cosh 2\alpha}{2}\right)} + \frac{y^2}{\left(\frac{\cosh 2\alpha - 1}{2}\right)} = 1$$

$$\frac{2x^2}{1+\cosh 2\alpha} + \frac{2y^2}{\cosh 2\alpha - 1} = 1$$

$$\frac{2x^2}{1+a} + \frac{2y^2}{a-1} = 1$$

$$2(a-1)x^2 + 2(a+1)y^2 = a^2 - 1$$

Ex. 13 : *Prove that* $\sin^{-1}(\csc \theta) = [2n + (-1)^n]\frac{\pi}{2} + i(-1)^n \log \cot\left(\frac{\theta}{2}\right)$. **(Dec. 2005)**

Sol. : Let $\sin^{-1}(\csc \theta) = x + iy$

$\therefore \quad \sin(x + iy) = \csc \theta$

or $\sin x \cos iy + \cos x \sin(iy) = \csc \theta$

$\sin x \cosh y + i \cos x \sinh y = \csc \theta$

Equating real and imaginary parts,

$\sin x \cosh y = \csc \theta$ and $\cos x \sinh y = 0$

Now $\cos x \sinh y = 0$ means $\cos x = 0$ or $\sinh y = 0$

but $\sinh y \neq 0$ as it implies $y \neq 0$ which is not true.

$\therefore \quad \cos x = 0$ or $x = \frac{\pi}{2}$

Consider $\sin x \cosh y = \csc \theta$

$\therefore \quad \cosh y = \csc \theta \quad \left[\because \sin \frac{\pi}{2} = 1\right]$

$\therefore \quad y = \cosh^{-1}(\csc \theta)$

$= \log\left(\csc \theta + \sqrt{\csc^2 \theta - 1}\right)$

$= \log(\csc \theta + \cot \theta) = \log\left(\frac{1}{\sin \theta} + \frac{\cos \theta}{\sin \theta}\right)$

$= \log\left(\frac{1+\cos \theta}{\sin \theta}\right) = \log \frac{2\cos^2 \frac{\theta}{2}}{2\sin\frac{\theta}{2}\cos\frac{\theta}{2}} = \log \cot \frac{\theta}{2}$

$\therefore \quad \sin^{-1}(\csc \theta) = x + iy = \frac{\pi}{2} + i \log \cot \frac{\theta}{2}$

Now considering general value, we get

$$\sin^{-1}(\text{cosec } \theta) = n\pi + (-1)^n \left\{ \frac{\pi}{2} + i \log \cot \frac{\theta}{2} \right\}$$

$[\because \sin^{-1} \alpha = n\pi + (-1)^n \sin^{-1} \alpha, \text{ where } \sin^{-1} \alpha \text{ lies between } -\pi/2 \text{ and } \pi/2]$

$$= n\pi + (-1)^n \frac{\pi}{2} + i(-1)^n \log \cot \frac{\theta}{2}$$

$$= 2\frac{n\pi}{2} + (-1)^n \frac{\pi}{2} + i(-1)^n \log \cot \frac{\theta}{2}$$

$$= [2n + (-1)^n] \frac{\pi}{2} + i(-1)^n \log \cot \frac{\theta}{2}$$

Ex. 14 : If $\cos\left(\frac{\pi}{4} + ia\right) \cdot \cosh\left(b + \frac{i\pi}{4}\right) = 1$ where a, b are real numbers, show that $2b = \log(2 + \sqrt{3})$. **(Dec. 2004)**

Sol. :
$$\cos\left(\frac{\pi}{4} + ia\right) \cdot \cosh\left(b + \frac{i\pi}{4}\right)$$

$$= \frac{2}{2} \cos\left(\frac{\pi}{4} + ia\right) \cos\left[i\left(b + \frac{i\pi}{4}\right)\right] \quad [\because \cosh x = \cos ix]$$

$$= \frac{1}{2} \left[\cos\left\{\frac{\pi}{4} + ia + ib + i^2\frac{\pi}{4}\right\} + \cos\left\{\frac{\pi}{4} + ia - ib - i^2\frac{\pi}{4}\right\} \right]$$

$$= \frac{1}{2} \left[\cos\{i(a+b)\} + \cos\left\{\frac{\pi}{2} + i(a-b)\right\} \right]$$

$$= \frac{1}{2} [\cosh(a+b) - \sin\{i(a-b)\}]$$

$$= \frac{1}{2} [\cosh(a+b) - i \sinh(a-b)]$$

$$= 1, \text{ given}$$

Equating real and imaginary parts,

$$\frac{1}{2} \cosh(a+b) = 1 \quad \ldots (1)$$

and $\sinh(a-b) = 0 \quad \ldots (2)$

From (2), $\sinh(a-b) = 0 \Rightarrow a = b$

Substituting in (1), $b + b = \cosh^{-1} 2$

$$2b = \log(2 + \sqrt{4-1}) \quad [\because \cosh^{-1} x = \log\{x + \sqrt{x^2-1}\}]$$

$$2b = \log(2 + \sqrt{3})$$

Ex. 15 : If $\dfrac{x + iy - c}{x + iy + c} = e^{u + iv}$, where x, y, u, v are real, show that

$$x = \frac{-c \sinh u}{\cosh u - \cos v}, \quad y = \frac{c \sin v}{\cosh u - \cos v}$$

and if $v = (2n+1)\dfrac{\pi}{2}$ where n is an integer, prove that $x^2 + y^2 = c^2$.

Sol. : Let $x + iy = z$ and $u + iv = w$

$$\therefore \quad \frac{z-c}{z+c} = e^w$$

$$\therefore \quad \frac{z}{c} = \left[\frac{1+e^w}{1-e^w}\right]$$

$$\therefore \quad \frac{x}{c} + \frac{iy}{c} = \frac{e^{-w/2} + e^{w/2}}{e^{-w/2} - e^{w/2}} = \frac{\cosh w/2}{-\sinh w/2}$$

$$\therefore \quad -\frac{x}{c} - \frac{iy}{c} = \frac{\cosh(u/2 + iv/2)}{\sinh(u/2 + iv/2)} \times \frac{2\sinh(u/2 - iv/2)}{2\sinh(u/2 - iv/2)}$$

$$= \frac{\sinh u + \sinh(-iv)}{\cosh u - \cosh(-iv)}$$

$$= \frac{\sinh u - i\sin v}{\cosh u - \cos v}$$

Equating real and imaginary parts, we get

$$x = \frac{-c\sinh u}{\cosh u - \cos v}, \quad y = \frac{c\sin v}{\cosh u - \cos v}$$

If $\quad v = (2n+1)\frac{\pi}{2}$

then $\quad \cos v = \cos(2n+1)\frac{\pi}{2} = 0$ and $\sin v = \pm 1$

$$\therefore \quad x = \frac{-c\sinh u}{\cosh u}, \quad y = \pm\frac{c}{\cosh u}$$

$$\therefore \quad x^2 + y^2 = \frac{c^2(\sinh^2 u + 1)}{\cosh^2 u}$$

$$\therefore \quad x^2 + y^2 = c^2$$

EXERCISE 5.2

1. If $\tan(x+iy) = \sin(u+iv)$ then prove that $\sin 2x \cot u = \sinh 2y \coth v$.

2. If $\operatorname{cosec}(x+iy) = u+iv$, prove that $(u^2+v^2)^2 = \frac{u^2}{\sin^2 x} - \frac{v^2}{\cos^2 x}$. **(Dec. 2005, 2014)**

3. If $\sin(\theta + i\phi) = \rho(\cos\alpha + i\sin\alpha)$, prove that
   $\rho^2 = 1/2(\cosh 2\phi - \cos 2\theta)$ and $\tanh \phi = \tan\alpha \tan\theta$

4. If $\sin(x+iy)\sin(\theta+i\phi) = 1$, prove that
   (i) $\tanh^2 y \cosh^2\phi = \cos^2\theta$, (ii) $\tanh^2\phi \cosh^2 y = \cos^2 x$.

5. If $a + ib = c\cot(\alpha + i\beta)$, then prove that
   $$\frac{a}{\sin 2\alpha} = \frac{-b}{\sinh 2\beta} = \frac{c}{2(\cosh^2\beta - \cos 2\alpha)}.$$

6. Prove that $\tan^{-1} z = \dfrac{i}{2} \log\left(\dfrac{i+z}{i-z}\right)$.

   [Hint: $\tan^{-1} z = u + iv \Rightarrow z = \tan[i(v - iu)]$]

7. Prove that $\sin^{-1}(ix) = i \log(x + \sqrt{1 + x^2})$.

8. If $\cos^{-1}(u + iv) = \alpha + i\beta$, prove that $\cos^2 \alpha$ and $\cosh^2 \beta$ are the roots of the quadratic $x^2 - x(1 + u^2 + v^2) + u^2 = 0$.

9. If $\tan(x + iy) = \alpha + i\beta$, prove that $\dfrac{1 - (\alpha^2 + \beta^2)}{1 + (\alpha^2 + \beta^2)} = \dfrac{\cos 2x}{\cosh 2y}$.

10. If $\tan(u + iv) = x + iy$, prove that the curves $u =$ constant and $v =$ constant are family of circles which are mutually orthogonal.

11. If $\tan z = \dfrac{i}{2}(1 - i)$, prove that $z = \dfrac{n\pi}{2} + \dfrac{1}{2}\tan^{-1} 2 - \dfrac{i}{4}\log 5$.

    [Hint: $\tan(x + iy) = \dfrac{1}{2} + \dfrac{i}{2}$, $\tan(x - iy) = \dfrac{1}{2} - \dfrac{i}{2}$, $\tan(2x) = 2$, $\tan(2iy) = \dfrac{2i}{3}$].

12. If $\tanh(a + ib) = x + iy$, prove that
    $1 + x^2 + y^2 = 2x \coth 2a$ and $x^2 + y^2 + 2y \cot 2b = 1$.

13. If $\cos(\theta + i\phi) = R e^{i\alpha}$, prove that $R^2 = \dfrac{1}{2}(\cos 2\theta + \cosh 2\phi)$
    and $\phi = \dfrac{1}{2} \log \dfrac{\sin(\theta - \alpha)}{\sin(\theta + \alpha)}$.

14. If $\sin(x + iy) = u + iv$, prove that   **(Dec. 2010)**
    $u^2 \csc^2 x - v^2 \sec^2 x = 1$ and $u^2 \operatorname{sech}^2 y + v^2 \operatorname{cosech}^2 y = 1$

15. If $x + iy = \cos(u + iv)$, prove that
    $(1 + x)^2 + y^2 = (\cosh v + \cos u)^2$ and $(1 - x)^2 + y^2 = (\cosh v - \cos u)^2$

16. If $x + iy = 2 \cosh(\lambda + i\pi/4)$, prove that $x^2 - y^2 = 2$.

17. If $\dfrac{u-1}{u+1} = \sin(x + iy)$, where $u = \alpha + i\beta$, show that the argument of u is $\theta + \phi$.

18. Find all the roots of $\sinh z = i$.   [Hint: $\sinh(x + iy) = i$, $x = 0$, $y = \pi/2$]

19. Prove that the values of $z (= x + iy)$ satisfying the equation
    $\sin(x + iy) = 3$ are given by $n\pi \pm (-1)^n \left\{\dfrac{\pi}{2} + i \log(3 + 2\sqrt{2})\right\}$

20. Show that all solutions of $\sin z = 2i \cos z$ are given by $z = \dfrac{n\pi}{2} + \dfrac{i}{2} \log 3$.

21. If $\csc\left(\dfrac{\pi}{4} + ix\right) = u + iv$, where x, u, v are real, show that
    $(u^2 + v^2)^2 = 2(u^2 - v^2)$.   **(May 2004, Dec. 2006)**

    [Hint: $\dfrac{1}{u+iv} = \dfrac{1}{\sqrt{2}}[\cosh x + i \sinh x]$ $\therefore$ $\dfrac{u - iv}{u^2 + v^2} = \dfrac{1}{\sqrt{2}}\cosh x + i\dfrac{1}{\sqrt{2}}\sinh x$].

22. If $\cosh(\theta + i\phi) = e^{i\alpha}$, prove that $\sin^2\alpha = \sin^4\phi = \sinh^4\theta$.

    [**Hint**: $\cosh(\theta + i\phi) = \cos\alpha + i\sin\alpha \Rightarrow \cosh\theta\cos\phi = \cos\alpha$ and $\sinh\theta\sin\phi = \sin\alpha$.
    Eliminating α and using $\cosh^2\theta = 1 + \sinh^2\theta$ and $\cos^2\phi = 1 - \sin^2\phi$, we obtain $\sinh^2\theta = \sin^2\phi \Rightarrow \sinh^4\theta + \sin^4\phi$. Next eliminating ϕ and using $\cos^2\alpha = 1 - \sin^2\alpha$ and $\cosh^2\theta = 1 + \sinh^2\theta \Rightarrow \sin^2\alpha = \sinh^4\theta$.]

23. Show that $\cos^{-1}(ix) = \dfrac{\pi}{2} - i\log(x + \sqrt{x^2+1})$.

    [**Hint**: $\cos^{-1}(ix) = y \Rightarrow \cos y = ix \Rightarrow \sin(\pi/2 - y) = ix \Rightarrow i\sin(\pi/2 - y) = i^2 x$.
    $\Rightarrow -x = \sinh(i\pi/2 - iy) \Rightarrow \sinh^{-1}(-x) = i\pi/2 - iy$ and proceed further.]

24. Separate into real and imaginary parts of the expression $\sin^{-1}(e^{i\theta})$.

    [**Hint**: $\sin(x + iy) = \cos\theta + i\sin\theta \Rightarrow \sin x\cosh y = \cos\theta$ and $\cos x\sinh y = \sin\theta$. Eliminating θ, and using $\cosh^2 y = 1 + \sinh^2 y$ and $\sin^2 x = 1 - \cos^2 x$, we obtain $\sinh y = \cos x$. Substituting in second relation; $\sinh y = \sqrt{\sin\theta}$ or $y = \sinh^{-1}\sqrt{\sin\theta}$ and $\cos^2 x = \sin\theta$ or $x = \cos^{-1}\sqrt{\sin\theta}$. **(May 2006)**

    Ans. $\sin^{-1}(e^{i\theta}) = \cos^{-1}\sqrt{\sin\theta} + i\log(\sqrt{\sin\theta} + \sqrt{1 + \sin\theta})$

5.9 LOGARITHMS OF COMPLEX NUMBERS

If u and z are two complex numbers such that

$$e^u = 1 + u + \frac{u^2}{2!} + \frac{u^3}{3!} + \cdots$$
$$= z$$

then u is defined to be the logarithm of z to the base e.

If $z = x + iy$ is any complex number, to find its logarithm, we express it in the general polar form as

$$\begin{aligned}
z &= x + iy \\
&= r(\cos\theta + i\sin\theta) \\
&= r[\cos(2n\pi + \theta) + i\sin(2n\pi + \theta)] \\
&= r\, e^{i(2n\pi + \theta)} \quad (r = \sqrt{x^2 + y^2};\ \theta = \tan^{-1} y/x)
\end{aligned}$$

$\therefore \qquad \text{Log } z = \log r + i(2n\pi + \theta) \qquad \ldots (1)$

or $\qquad \text{Log}(x + iy) = \log\sqrt{x^2 + y^2} + i\left(2n\pi + \tan^{-1}\dfrac{y}{x}\right) \qquad \ldots (2)$

This shows that the logarithm of a complex number $z = x + iy$ is a multivalued function (i.e. we get different values for the logarithm of $x + iy$ corresponding to $n = 0, 1, 2, 3, \ldots$).

The value of the logarithm given by (1) or (2) is called the general value of the logarithm.

In particular, if $n = 0$, we get

$\qquad \log z = \log r + i\theta \qquad \ldots (3)$

or $\qquad \log(x + iy) = \log\sqrt{x^2 + y^2} + i\tan^{-1}\dfrac{y}{x} \qquad \ldots (4)$

The value of the logarithm given by (3) or (4) is called the principal value of the logarithm.

Thus from (1) and (3), we can write

$$\text{Log } z = \log z + 2n\pi i \qquad \ldots (5)$$

While the general value of the logarithm is a multivalued function, the principal value of the logarithm is a single valued function.

Note that the general value of the logarithm of $z = x + iy$ is denoted by Log z (beginning with capital L) so as to distinguish it from its principal value which is denoted by log z.

While determining arg (z) from the formula $\theta = \arg(z) = \tan^{-1} \frac{y}{x}$, we must pay attention to the quadrant in which z lies, otherwise we can also find arg (z) = θ from the relations $x = r\cos\theta$, $y = r\sin\theta$.

5.10 ILLUSTRATIONS ON SEPARATION OF REAL & IMAGINARY PARTS

Ex. 1 : *Find General and Principal value of the logarithm of (i) $1 + i\sqrt{3}$, (ii) -5.*

Sol. : (i) Let $\qquad 1 + i\sqrt{3} = r(\cos\theta + i\sin\theta)$

$\therefore \qquad r = \sqrt{3+1} = 2, \quad \theta = \tan^{-1}\sqrt{3} = \frac{\pi}{3}$

$\therefore \qquad \text{Log}(1 + i\sqrt{3}) = \log 2 + i\left(2n\pi + \frac{\pi}{3}\right)$

and $\qquad \log(1 + i\sqrt{3}) = \log 2 + i\frac{\pi}{3}$

(ii) Let $\qquad -5 = 5(\cos\pi + i\sin\pi)$

$\therefore \qquad r = 5, \quad \theta = \pi$

$\qquad \text{Log}(-5) = \log 5 + i(2n\pi + \pi)$

$\qquad \qquad = \log 5 + i(2n+1)\pi$

and $\qquad \log(-5) = \log 5 + i\pi$

Ex. 2 : *Prove that* $\text{Log}\left\{\dfrac{(a-b) + i(a+b)}{(a+b) + i(a-b)}\right\} = i\left(2n\pi + \tan^{-1}\dfrac{2ab}{a^2-b^2}\right).$ (Dec. 2004)

Sol. : $\text{Log}\left\{\dfrac{(a-b) + i(a+b)}{(a+b) + i(a-b)}\right\}$

$= 2n\pi i + \log\left\{\dfrac{(a-b) + i(a+b)}{(a+b) + i(a-b)}\right\}$

$= 2n\pi i + \log\{(a-b) + i(a+b)\} - \log\{(a+b) + i(a-b)\}$

$= 2n\pi i + \left\{\log\sqrt{(a-b)^2 + (a+b)^2} + i\tan^{-1}\left(\dfrac{a+b}{a-b}\right)\right\}$

$\qquad\qquad - \left\{\log\sqrt{(a+b)^2 + (a-b)^2} + i\tan^{-1}\left(\dfrac{a-b}{a+b}\right)\right\}$

$$= 2n\pi i + i\left\{\tan^{-1}\left(\frac{a+b}{a-b}\right) - \tan^{-1}\left(\frac{a-b}{a+b}\right)\right\}$$

$$= 2n\pi i + i\tan^{-1}\left\{\frac{\left(\frac{a+b}{a-b}\right) - \left(\frac{a-b}{a+b}\right)}{1 + \left(\frac{a+b}{a-b}\right)\left(\frac{a-b}{a+b}\right)}\right\} = 2n\pi i + i\tan^{-1}\left\{\frac{\frac{(a+b)^2 - (a-b)^2}{a^2 - b^2}}{1+1}\right\}$$

$$= 2n\pi i + i\tan^{-1}\left\{\frac{4ab/(a^2-b^2)}{2}\right\} = 2n\pi i + i\tan^{-1}\left(\frac{2ab}{a^2-b^2}\right)$$

$$= i\left\{2n\pi + \tan^{-1}\left(\frac{2ab}{a^2-b^2}\right)\right\}.$$

Ex. 3 : *Show that* $\log \dfrac{\sin(x+iy)}{\sin(x-iy)} = 2i\tan^{-1}(\cot x \tanh y)$. **(May 2014)**

Sol. :

$$\log\frac{\sin(x+iy)}{\sin(x-iy)} = \log\sin(x+iy) - \log\sin(x-iy)$$

$$= \log\{\sin x \cos(iy) + \cos x \sin(iy)\} - \log\{\sin x \cos(iy) - \cos x \sin(iy)\}$$

$$= \log\{\sin x \cosh y + i\cos x \sinh y\} - \log\{\sin x \cosh y - \cos x \sinh y\}$$

$$= \log\sqrt{\sin^2 x \cosh^2 y + \cos^2 x \sinh^2 y} + i\tan^{-1}\left(\frac{\cos x \sinh y}{\sin x \cosh y}\right)$$

$$\quad - \log\sqrt{\sin^2 x \cosh^2 y + \cos^2 x \sinh^2 y} + i\tan^{-1}\left(\frac{\cos x \sinh y}{\sin x \cosh y}\right)$$

$$= 2i\tan^{-1}(\cot x \tanh y)$$

Ex. 4 : *Prove that* $\tan\left\{i\log\dfrac{a-ib}{a+ib}\right\} = \dfrac{2ab}{a^2-b^2}$. **(May 2009)**

Sol. :

$$\tan\left\{i\log\frac{a-ib}{a+ib}\right\} = \tan[i\{\log(a-ib) - \log(a+ib)\}]$$

$$= \tan\left[i\left\{\frac{1}{2}\log(a^2+b^2) - i\tan^{-1}\frac{b}{a}\right\} - i\left\{\frac{1}{2}\log(a^2+b^2) + i\tan^{-1}\frac{b}{a}\right\}\right]$$

$$= \tan\left\{2\tan^{-1}\frac{b}{a}\right\} = \tan 2\theta \qquad \left[\because \theta = \tan^{-1}\frac{b}{a} \text{ or } \tan\theta = \frac{b}{a}\right]$$

$$= \frac{2\tan\theta}{1-\tan^2\theta} = \frac{2\frac{b}{a}}{1-\frac{b^2}{a^2}} = \frac{2ab}{a^2-b^2}$$

Ex. 5 : *Prove that* $\log\left(\dfrac{1}{1-e^{i\theta}}\right) = \log\left(\dfrac{1}{2}\operatorname{cosec}\dfrac{\theta}{2}\right) + i\left(\dfrac{\pi}{2}-\dfrac{\theta}{2}\right)$.

Sol. : L.H.S. $= \log\left(\dfrac{1}{1-e^{i\theta}}\right)$

$= \log\left[\dfrac{1}{1-\cos\theta - i\sin\theta}\right]$

$= \log\left[\dfrac{1}{2\sin^2\dfrac{\theta}{2} - 2i\sin\dfrac{\theta}{2}\cos\dfrac{\theta}{2}}\right]$

$= \log\left[\dfrac{1}{2\sin\dfrac{\theta}{2}\left(\sin\dfrac{\theta}{2} - i\cos\dfrac{\theta}{2}\right)}\right]$

$= \log\left[\dfrac{1}{2\sin\dfrac{\theta}{2}\left\{\cos\left(\dfrac{\pi}{2}-\dfrac{\theta}{2}\right) - i\sin\left(\dfrac{\pi}{2}-\dfrac{\theta}{2}\right)\right\}}\right]$

$= \log\left(\dfrac{1}{2\sin\dfrac{\theta}{2}}\right) + \log\left[\dfrac{1}{\cos\left(\dfrac{\pi}{2}-\dfrac{\theta}{2}\right) - i\sin\left(\dfrac{\pi}{2}-\dfrac{\theta}{2}\right)}\right]$

$= \log\left(\dfrac{1}{2}\operatorname{cosec}\dfrac{\theta}{2}\right) + \log\left[\dfrac{1}{e^{-i\left(\dfrac{\pi}{2}-\dfrac{\theta}{2}\right)}}\right]$

$= \log\left(\dfrac{1}{2}\operatorname{cosec}\dfrac{\theta}{2}\right) + \log\left\{e^{i\left(\dfrac{\pi}{2}-\dfrac{\theta}{2}\right)}\right\}$

$= \log\left(\dfrac{1}{2}\operatorname{cosec}\dfrac{\theta}{2}\right) + i\left(\dfrac{\pi}{2}-\dfrac{\theta}{2}\right) =$ R.H.S.

Ex. 6 : *Prove that* $\log(e^{i\alpha}+e^{i\beta}) = \log\left(2\cos\dfrac{\alpha-\beta}{2}\right) + i\left(\dfrac{\alpha+\beta}{2}\right)$.

Sol. : $e^{i\alpha} + e^{i\beta} = (\cos\alpha + \cos\beta) + i(\sin\alpha + \sin\beta)$

$= 2\cos\dfrac{\alpha+\beta}{2}\cos\dfrac{\alpha-\beta}{2} + 2i\sin\dfrac{\alpha+\beta}{2}\cos\dfrac{\alpha-\beta}{2}$

$= \left(2\cos\dfrac{\alpha-\beta}{2}\right)\left[\cos\dfrac{\alpha+\beta}{2} + i\sin\dfrac{\alpha+\beta}{2}\right]$

$= \left(2\cos\dfrac{\alpha-\beta}{2}\right)e^{i\left(\dfrac{\alpha+\beta}{2}\right)}$

$= r\,e^{i\theta}$, where $r = \left(2\cos\dfrac{\alpha-\beta}{2}\right)$ and $\theta = \dfrac{\alpha+\beta}{2}$

$\therefore \quad \log(e^{i\alpha}+e^{i\beta}) = \log r + i\theta$

$= \log\left(2\cos\dfrac{\alpha-\beta}{2}\right) + i\left(\dfrac{\alpha+\beta}{2}\right)$

Ex. 7 : If $\log_e \log_e (x + iy) = p + iq$ then prove that
$$y = x \tan\{(\tan q) \log_e \sqrt{x^2 + y^2}\}.$$
(May 2013)

Sol. :
$$\log_e (x + iy) = \log \sqrt{x^2 + y^2} + i \tan^{-1}\frac{y}{x}$$
$$= A + iB \text{ (say)}.$$
$$\therefore \log_e \log_e (x + iy) = \log (A + iB)$$
$$= \log \sqrt{A^2 + B^2} + i \tan^{-1}\frac{B}{A}$$
$$= p + iq \text{ (given)}.$$

Equating real and imaginary parts, we get
$$p = \log \sqrt{A^2 + B^2} \text{ and } q = \tan^{-1}\frac{B}{A}$$
$$q = \tan^{-1}\frac{B}{A} \text{ gives } \frac{B}{A} = \tan q$$

$$\therefore \frac{\tan^{-1}\frac{y}{x}}{\log_e \sqrt{x^2 + y^2}} = \tan q \qquad \left[\because A = \log \sqrt{x^2 + y^2} \text{ and } B = \tan^{-1}\frac{y}{x}\right]$$

$$\therefore \tan^{-1}\frac{y}{x} = \tan q \log_e \sqrt{x^2 + y^2}$$
$$\frac{y}{x} = \tan\{\tan q \log_e \sqrt{x^2 + y^2}\}$$
$$\therefore y = x \tan\{\tan q \log_e \sqrt{x^2 + y^2}\}$$

Ex. 8 : Show that for any real numbers a and b, $e^{2ai \cot^{-1} b} \times \left\{\frac{bi - 1}{bi + 1}\right\}^{-a} = 1$.

Sol. :
$$\frac{bi - 1}{bi + 1} = \frac{i(b + i)}{i(b - i)} = \frac{b + i}{b - i}$$
$$\therefore \left\{\frac{bi - 1}{bi + 1}\right\}^{-a} = \left\{\frac{b + i}{b - i}\right\}^{-a} = z \text{ (say)}$$
$$\therefore \log z = -a \log \frac{b + i}{b - i}$$
$$= -a [\log (b + i) - \log (b - i)]$$
$$= -a [\log r + i\theta - \log r + i\theta]$$

where $r = \sqrt{1 + b^2}$, $\theta = \tan^{-1}\left(\frac{1}{b}\right)$

$$= -2ai\theta$$
$$\therefore z = e^{-2ai\theta} = e^{-2ai \tan^{-1}(1/b)}$$

Also $e^{2ai \cot^{-1}(b)} = e^{2ai \tan^{-1}(1/b)}$

$$\therefore \text{L.H.S.} = e^{2ai \tan^{-1}(1/b)} \times e^{-2ai \tan^{-1}(1/b)} = 1 = \text{R.H.S.}$$

EXERCISE 5.3

1. Find the General and Principal value of the logarithm of
   (i) $(1 + i)$, (ii) $(4 + 3i)$

   Ans. (i) $\text{Log}(1 + i) = \frac{1}{2}\log 2 + i\left(2n\pi + \frac{\pi}{4}\right)$, $\log(1 + i) = \frac{1}{2}\log 2 + i\pi/4$.

   (ii) $\text{Log}(4 + 3i) = \log 5 + i(2n\pi + \tan^{-1} 3/4)$,
   $\log(4 + 3i) = \log 5 + i \tan^{-1} 3/4$

2. Prove that $\log(1 + e^{2i\theta}) = \log(2\cos\theta) + i\theta$

3. Prove that $\log(1 + i\tan\alpha) = \log(\sec\alpha) + i\alpha$.

4. Prove that $\text{Log}\left(\frac{3-i}{3+i}\right) = 2i\left(n\pi - \tan^{-1}\frac{1}{3}\right)$.

5. Prove that $\text{Log}\left[\frac{\cos(x-iy)}{\cos(x+iy)}\right] = 2i\tan^{-1}(\tan x \tanh y)$.

6. If $p\log(a + ib) = (x + iy)\log m$, prove that $\frac{y}{x} = \frac{2\tan^{-1} b/a}{\log(a^2 + b^2)}$. **(May 2011)**

7. Prove that $\log(1 + re^{i\theta}) = \frac{1}{2}\log(1 + 2r\cos\theta + r^2) + i\tan^{-1}\frac{r\sin\theta}{1 + r\cos\theta}$.

   Deduce that $\log(1 + \cos\theta + i\sin\theta) = \log(2\cos\theta/2) + i\theta/2$.

8. Prove that $\cos\left[i\log\left(\frac{a+ib}{a-ib}\right)\right] = \frac{a^2 - b^2}{a^2 + b^2}$. **(May 2008, Dec. 2003)**

   [**Hint**: $\cos i\theta = \cosh\theta = \frac{e^\theta + e^{-\theta}}{2}$, $\theta = \log\left(\frac{a+ib}{a-ib}\right)$].

9. If $\log \sin(x + iy) = a + ib$, prove that $2e^{2a} = \cosh 2y - \cos 2x$. **(Dec. 2009)**

   [**Hint**: $\sin(x + iy) = e^{a+ib}$ $\therefore \sin(x - iy) = e^{a-ib}$].

10. Find all roots of the equation $\sinh z = i$.
    Ans. $i(2n + 1/2)\pi$.

11. Solve for z, if $e^z = 1 + i\sqrt{3}$.
    Ans. $z = \log 2 + i(2n\pi + \pi/3)$.

5.11 ILLUSTRATIONS ON SEPARATION OF REAL AND IMAGINARY PARTS OF EXPRESSIONS

$$(x + iy)^{(a+ib)}, \quad \text{Log}_{(a+ib)}(x + iy) \text{ and } \frac{(a+ib)^{x+iy}}{(p+iq)^{r+is}} = c + id.$$

(I) To separate into real and imaginary parts $(x + iy)^{(a+ib)}$, we write
$(x + iy)^{(a+ib)} = e^{(a+ib)\text{Log}(x+iy)}$.

(II) To separate into real and imaginary parts $\text{Log}_{(a+ib)}(x + iy)$, use change of base formula and write

$$\text{Log}_{(a+ib)}(x + iy) = \frac{\text{Log}(x + iy)}{\text{Log}(a + ib)}.$$

(III) If $\dfrac{(a+ib)^{x+iy}}{(p+iq)^{r+is}} = c+id$ is given, take logarithm of both sides and simplify, then use these to prove required results.

Type (I) $(x+iy)^{(a+ib)}$:

Ex. 1 : *Separate into real and imaginary parts of (i)* $(1+i)^{2-3i}$, *(ii)* i^{2i} *considering general and principal value.*

Sol. : (i) $(1+i)^{2-3i} = e^{\text{Log}(1+i)^{2-3i}} = e^{(2-3i)\text{Log}(1+i)}$

$$= e^{(2-3i)\left[\log\sqrt{1+1} + i(2n\pi + \tan^{-1} 1/1)\right]}$$

$$= e^{(2-3i)\left\{\tfrac{1}{2}\log 2 + i\left(2n\pi + \tfrac{\pi}{4}\right)\right\}}$$

$$= e^{\left\{\log 2 + 3\left(2n\pi + \tfrac{\pi}{4}\right)\right\}} \cdot e^{i\left\{-\tfrac{3}{2}\log 2 + 2\left(2n\pi + \tfrac{\pi}{4}\right)\right\}}$$

$$= e^{\left\{\log 2 + 3\left(2n\pi + \tfrac{\pi}{4}\right)\right\}} \cdot (\cos\phi + i\sin\phi)$$

where $\phi = -\dfrac{3}{2}\log 2 + 2\left(2n\pi + \dfrac{\pi}{4}\right)$

To consider only principal value, put n = 0

$\therefore \quad (1+i)^{(2-3i)} = e^{\log\left(2+\tfrac{3\pi}{4}\right)} \cdot (\cos\phi + i\sin\phi) \qquad$ where $\phi = \dfrac{-3}{2}\log 2 + \dfrac{\pi}{2}$

(ii) $\quad i^{2i} = e^{\text{Log } i^{2i}} = e^{2i \text{ Log } i}$

$$= e^{2i\{\log 1 + i(2n\pi + \tan^{-1} 1/0)\}}$$

$$= e^{2i\left\{i\left(2n\pi + \tfrac{\pi}{2}\right)\right\}}$$

$$= e^{-2\left\{2n\pi + \tfrac{\pi}{2}\right\}} \qquad\qquad \text{(general value)}$$

To consider only principal value, put n = 0

$\therefore \qquad i^{2i} = e^{-\pi}$

Ex. 2 : *Prove that i^i is wholly real and find its principal value. Also show that the value of i^i form a G.P.* **(May 2004, 2009)**

Sol. : $\qquad\qquad i^i = e^{i \text{ Log } i} \qquad\qquad \ldots (1)$

Now $\qquad\qquad i = \cos\dfrac{\pi}{2} + i\sin\dfrac{\pi}{2} \quad r=1, \ \theta = \dfrac{\pi}{2}$

$\therefore \qquad \text{Log } i = \log r + i(2n\pi + \theta) = \log 1 + i\left(2n\pi + \dfrac{\pi}{2}\right)$

$$= i\left(2n\pi + \dfrac{\pi}{2}\right)$$

Substituting in (1), we get

$$i^i = e^{i[i(2n\pi + \pi/2)]}$$

$$\therefore \quad i^i = e^{-(4n+1)\pi/2} \quad \text{which is wholly real.}$$

Putting $n = 0$, we get principal value of $i^i = e^{-\pi/2}$

Putting $n = 0, 1, 2, 3, \ldots$ the values of i^i are $e^{-\pi/2}, e^{-5\pi/2}, e^{-7\pi/2}, \ldots$
which form a G.P. whose common ratio is $e^{-2\pi}$.

Ex. 3 : *Separate into real and imaginary parts the expression* i^{i^i}.

Sol. :
$$i^{i^i} = e^{\text{Log}\{i^{i^i}\}} = e^{i^i \text{ Log } i} \qquad \ldots (1)$$

Now
$$i^i = e^{\text{Log } i^i} = e^{i \text{ Log } i} = e^{i\{\text{Log } 1 + i(2n\pi + \pi/2)\}}$$

$$= e^{i\{i(2n\pi + \frac{\pi}{2})\}} = e^{-(2n\pi + \frac{\pi}{2})}$$

Let
$$\text{Log } i = \left\{\log 1 + i\left(2m\pi + \frac{\pi}{2}\right)\right\} = i\left(2m\pi + \frac{\pi}{2}\right)$$

Substituting for i^i and Log i in (1), we get

$$i^{i^i} = e^{e^{-(2n\pi + \frac{\pi}{2})} \cdot i(2m\pi + \frac{\pi}{2})}$$

$$= e^{i\theta} \qquad \left[\text{where } \theta = \left(2m\pi + \frac{\pi}{2}\right) e^{-(2n\pi + \frac{\pi}{2})}\right]$$

$$= \cos\theta + i\sin\theta$$

Ex. 4 : *Considering the principal value, express in the form a + ib the expression* $(\sqrt{i})^{\sqrt{i}}$.
(Dec. 2005, 2007)

Sol. : Let $\quad z = (\sqrt{i})^{\sqrt{i}}$

Taking logarithm on both sides,

$$\log z = \sqrt{i} \log \sqrt{i}$$

$$= \left(\cos\frac{\pi}{2} + i\sin\frac{\pi}{2}\right)^{1/2} \left\{\frac{1}{2}\log\left(\cos\frac{\pi}{2} + i\sin\frac{\pi}{2}\right)\right\}$$

$$= \left(\cos\frac{\pi}{4} + i\sin\frac{\pi}{4}\right) \left\{\frac{1}{2}\log e^{i\frac{\pi}{2}}\right\}$$

$$= \left(\frac{1}{\sqrt{2}} + i\frac{1}{\sqrt{2}}\right) i\frac{\pi}{4} = -\frac{\pi}{4\sqrt{2}} + i\frac{\pi}{4\sqrt{2}} = a + ib \text{ (say)}$$

where $a = -\dfrac{\pi}{4\sqrt{2}}$ and $b = \dfrac{\pi}{4\sqrt{2}}$

$$\therefore \quad z = e^{a+ib} = e^a e^{ib}$$

$$= e^a (\cos b + i \sin b)$$

$$= e^{-\frac{\pi}{4\sqrt{2}}} \left(\cos\frac{\pi}{4\sqrt{2}} + i\sin\frac{\pi}{4\sqrt{2}}\right)$$

Ex. 5 : *Prove that the general value of $(1 + i \tan \alpha)^{-i}$ is $e^{2m\pi + \alpha} [\cos (\log \cos \alpha) + i \sin (\log \cos \alpha)]$.* **(Dec. 2006)**

Sol. : Let $\quad z = (1 + i \tan \alpha)^{-i}$

then $\quad \text{Log } z = -i \text{ Log } (1 + i \tan \alpha)$ ... (i)

Now, $\text{Log } (1 + i \tan \alpha) = \log \sqrt{1 + \tan^2 \alpha} + i \left[2m\pi + \tan^{-1} \left(\frac{\tan \alpha}{1} \right) \right]$

$\qquad = \log \sec \alpha + i (2m\pi + \alpha) = a + ib$

where $\quad a = \log \sec \alpha, \ b = 2m\pi + \alpha$

Substituting in (i),

$\quad \text{Log } z = -i (a + ib)$

$\qquad = b - ia$

$\therefore \quad z = e^{b-ia} = e^b \, e^{-ia} = e^b (\cos a - i \sin a)$

$\qquad = e^{(2m\pi + \alpha)} [\cos (\log \sec \alpha) - i \sin (\log \sec \alpha)]$

$\qquad = e^{(2m\pi + \alpha)} [\cos (-\log \cos \alpha) - i \sin (-\log \cos \alpha)]$

$\qquad = e^{(2m\pi + \alpha)} [\cos (\log \cos \alpha) + i \sin (\log \cos \alpha)]$

Ex. 6 : *Prove that real part of the principal value of $i^{\log (1+i)}$ is $e^{-\frac{\pi^2}{8}} \cos (\pi/4 \log 2)$.*
(Dec. 2004; May 2007, May 2011)

Sol. : We have, $i^{\log (1+i)} = e^{\log i^{\log (1+i)}}$

$\qquad = e^{\log (1+i) \log i}$

$\qquad = e^{(\log \sqrt{2} + i\pi/4)(i\pi/2)} \quad \left(\because \ \log i = i\frac{\pi}{2} \right)$

$\qquad = e^{\left(-\frac{\pi^2}{8} + i\frac{\pi}{4} \log 2 \right)} = e^{-\pi^2/8} \, e^{i(\pi/4 \log 2)}$

$\therefore$ Real part of $i^{\log (1+i)} = e^{-\pi^2/8} \cos \left(\frac{\pi}{4} \log 2 \right)$

Ex. 7 : *Prove that if $(1 + i \tan \alpha)^{(1 + i \tan \beta)}$ can have real values, one of them is $(\sec \alpha)^{(\sec^2 \beta)}$ considering only principal value.* **(May 2005)**

Sol. : $(1 + i \tan \alpha)^{(1 + i \tan \beta)} = e^{(1 + i \tan \beta) \log (1 + i \tan \alpha)}$ ... (1)

$\quad \log (1 + i \tan \alpha) = \log r + i\theta$

$\qquad = \log (\sec \alpha) + i\alpha$ ... (2)

Substituting from (2) in (1), we get

$(1 + i \tan \alpha)^{(1 + i \tan \beta)} = e^{(1 + i \tan \beta) [\log (\sec \alpha) + i\alpha]}$

$\qquad = e^{\{(\log \sec \alpha - \alpha \tan \beta)\}} \, e^{i (\alpha + \tan \beta \log \sec \alpha)}$ ... (3)

$\qquad = $ Real, if $\alpha + \tan \beta \log \sec \alpha = 0$ ... (4)

i.e. $\quad \alpha = -\tan \beta \log \sec \alpha$ ... (5)

Hence from (3), the real part of $(1 + i \tan \alpha)^{(1 + i \tan \beta)}$

$$= e^{\log \sec \alpha - \alpha \tan \beta}$$
$$= e^{\log \sec \alpha + \tan^2 \beta \log \sec \alpha} \qquad \text{[substituting from (5)]}$$
$$= e^{(\log \sec \alpha)(1 + \tan^2 \beta)}$$
$$= e^{(\sec^2 \beta)(\log \sec \alpha)} = e^{\log (\sec \alpha)^{(\sec^2 \beta)}} = (\sec \alpha)^{(\sec^2 \beta)}$$

Type II : $\text{Log}_{(a + ib)}(x + iy)$:

Ex. 8 : *Find general and principal value of the logarithm of $\text{Log}_2(-3)$.*

Sol. : $\log_2(3) = \dfrac{\text{Log}_e(-3)}{\text{Log}_e(2)}$ (Changing the base of logarithm to e)

Now $\quad -3 = 3(\cos \pi + i \sin \pi) \qquad \therefore \quad r = 3 \quad \text{and} \quad \theta = \pi$

and $\quad 2 = 2(\cos 0 + i \sin 0) \qquad \therefore \quad r = 3 \quad \text{and} \quad \theta = 0$

$\therefore \quad \dfrac{\text{Log}(-3)}{\text{Log}(2)} = \dfrac{\log 3 + i(2n\pi + \pi)}{\log 2 + i(2m\pi + 0)}$

$$= \dfrac{\log 3 + i(2n+1)\pi}{\log 2 + i(2m\pi)} \times \left\{\dfrac{\log 2 - 2m\pi i}{\log 2 - 2m\pi i}\right\}$$

$$= \dfrac{\{\log 3 \times \log 2 + 2m(2n+1)\pi^2\} + i\{(2n+1)\pi \log 2 - 2m\pi \log 3\}}{(\log 2)^2 + 4m^2\pi^2}$$

Principal value is obtained by putting $m = 0$, $n = 0$.

$$\dfrac{\log(-3)}{\log 2} = \dfrac{\log 3 \times \log 2 + \pi i \log 2}{(\log 2)^2} = \dfrac{\log 3 + \pi i}{(\log 2)}$$

Ex. 9 : *Show that $\text{Log}_i i = \dfrac{4n+1}{4m+1}$.*

Sol. : $\text{Log}_i(i) = \dfrac{\text{Log}_e(i)}{\text{Log}_e(i)}$ (note that Log i is multivated)

$$= \dfrac{\log 1 + i(2n\pi + \pi/2)}{\log 1 + i(2m\pi + \pi/2)} = \dfrac{(4n+1)}{(4m+1)} \qquad (\because i = e^{i\pi/2})$$

Ex. 10 : *Prove that* $\log_{(1-i)}(1+i) = \dfrac{\frac{1}{4}(\log 2)^2 - \frac{\pi^2}{16} + i\frac{\pi}{4}\log 2}{\frac{1}{4}(\log 2)^2 + \frac{\pi^2}{16}}$

Sol. : $\log_{(1-i)}(1+i) = \dfrac{\log(1+i)}{\log(1-i)} = \dfrac{\log \sqrt{2} + i\frac{\pi}{4}}{\log \sqrt{2} - i\frac{\pi}{4}}$

$$= \dfrac{\left(\frac{1}{2}\log 2 + i\frac{\pi}{4}\right)\left(\frac{1}{2}\log 2 + i\frac{\pi}{4}\right)}{\left(\frac{1}{2}\log 2 - i\frac{\pi}{4}\right)\left(\frac{1}{2}\log 2 + i\frac{\pi}{4}\right)} = \dfrac{\frac{1}{4}(\log 2)^2 - \frac{\pi^2}{16} + i\frac{\pi}{4}\log 2}{\frac{1}{4}(\log 2)^2 + \frac{\pi^2}{16}}$$

Type III : $\dfrac{(a+ib)^{(x+iy)}}{(p+iq)^{(r+is)}} = c+id$:

Ex. 11 : If $\dfrac{(1+i)^{x+iy}}{(1-i)^{x-iy}} = \alpha + i\beta$, prove that one value of $\tan^{-1}\dfrac{\beta}{\alpha}$ is $\dfrac{1}{2}\pi x + y\log 2$.

Sol. : Taking logarithm of both sides, we get

$(x+iy)\log(1+i) - (x-iy)\log(1-i) = \log(\alpha + i\beta)$ (Taking principal values)

i.e. $(x+iy)\left(\dfrac{1}{2}\log 2 + i\dfrac{\pi}{4}\right) - (x-iy)\left(\dfrac{1}{2}\log 2 - i\dfrac{\pi}{4}\right) = \log\sqrt{\alpha^2+\beta^2} + i\tan^{-1}\dfrac{\beta}{\alpha}$

$(\because 1+i = \sqrt{2}\, e^{i\pi/4})$

Equating imaginary parts of both sides, we get

$\tan^{-1}\dfrac{\beta}{\alpha} = \left(\dfrac{y}{2}\log 2 + \dfrac{\pi x}{4}\right) - \left(-\dfrac{y}{2}\log 2 - \dfrac{\pi x}{4}\right)$

$= \left(y\log 2 + \dfrac{\pi x}{2}\right)$

Ex. 12 : If $i^{(\alpha+i\beta)} = \alpha + i\beta$, prove that $\alpha^2 + \beta^2 = e^{-(4m+1)\pi\beta}$. **(May 2006)**

Sol. : Taking logarithm of both sides of $i^{(\alpha+i\beta)} = (\alpha + i\beta)$, we get

$(\alpha + i\beta)\,\text{Log}\,i = \text{Log}(\alpha + i\beta)$

i.e. $(\alpha + i\beta)\left[i\left(2m + \dfrac{1}{2}\right)\pi\right] = \dfrac{1}{2}\log(\alpha^2+\beta^2) + i\left(2n\pi + \tan^{-1}\dfrac{\beta}{\alpha}\right)$

$\left[\because \log i = \log 1 + i\left(2m\pi + \dfrac{\pi}{2}\right) = i\left(2m\pi + \dfrac{\pi}{2}\right)\right]$

$-\left(2m + \dfrac{1}{2}\right)\pi\beta + i\left(2m + \dfrac{1}{2}\right)\pi\alpha = \dfrac{1}{2}\log(\alpha^2+\beta^2) + i\left(2n\pi + \tan^{-1}\dfrac{\beta}{\alpha}\right)$

Equating real parts, we have

$-\left(2m + \dfrac{1}{2}\right)\pi\beta = \dfrac{1}{2}\log(\alpha^2+\beta^2)$

$\therefore \log(\alpha^2+\beta^2) = -(4m+1)\pi\beta$

$\therefore \alpha^2 + \beta^2 = e^{-(4m+1)\pi\beta}$

Ex. 13 : If $x^{x^{x^{\cdots\infty}}} = a(\cos\alpha + i\sin\alpha)$, show that the general value of x is

$r(\cos\theta + i\sin\theta)$,

where $\log r = \dfrac{(2n\pi + \alpha)\sin\alpha + (\cos\alpha)\log a}{a}$, $\theta = \dfrac{(2n\pi + \alpha)\cos\alpha - (\sin\alpha)\log a}{a}$

Sol. : Given expression is equivalent to

$x^{a(\cos\alpha + i\sin\alpha)} = a(\cos\alpha + i\sin\alpha)$

Taking logarithm of both sides

$a(\cos\alpha + i\sin\alpha)\,\text{Log}\,x = \text{Log}\{a(\cos\alpha + i\sin\alpha)\}$

or $a(\cos\alpha + i\sin\alpha)\,\text{Log}\{r(\cos\theta + i\sin\theta)\} = \text{Log}\{a(\cos\alpha + i\sin\alpha)\}$

$\because x = r(\cos\theta + i\sin\theta)$

$a(\cos\alpha + i\sin\alpha)\{\log r + i\theta\} = \log a + i(2n\pi + \alpha)$

or $\{a\cos\alpha\log r - a\sin\theta\} + i\{a\sin\alpha\log r + \theta a\cos\alpha\} = \log a + i(2n\pi + \alpha)$

Equating real and imaginary parts, we get,

$$a \cos \alpha \log r - a \theta \sin \alpha = \log a \qquad \ldots (1)$$
$$a \sin \alpha \log r + a \theta \cos \alpha = (2n\pi + \alpha) \qquad \ldots (2)$$

Multiplying (1) by $\cos \alpha$, (2) by $\sin \alpha$ and adding,

$$\therefore \quad a \log r = \cos \alpha \log a + (2n\pi + \alpha) \sin \alpha$$

$$\therefore \quad \log r = \frac{(2n\pi + \alpha) \sin \alpha + (\cos \alpha) \log a}{a} \qquad \ldots (3)$$

Similarly, multiplying (1) by $\sin \alpha$, (2) by $\cos \alpha$ and subtracting, we get

$$a\theta = (2n\pi + \alpha) \cos \alpha - (\sin \alpha) \log a$$

$$\theta = \frac{(2n\pi + \alpha) \cos \alpha - (\sin \alpha) \log a}{a} \qquad \ldots (4)$$

(3) and (4) are the required results.

Ex. 14 : *If $i^{i^{i \ldots ad \infty}} = A + iB$ considering principal values, prove that*

(i) $\tan \dfrac{\pi A}{2} = \dfrac{B}{A}$, (ii) $A^2 + B^2 = e^{-\pi B}$

Sol. : Given expression is equivalent to

$$i^{A + iB} = A + iB$$

Taking logarithm of both sides, we get

$$(A + iB) \log i = \log (A + iB)$$

$$(A + iB) (i\pi/2) = \frac{1}{2} \log (A^2 + B^2) + i \left(\tan^{-1} \frac{B}{A} \right)$$

(Taking principal values only)

Equating real and imaginary parts on both sides, we get

$$\frac{-B\pi}{2} = \frac{1}{2} \log (A^2 + B^2) \qquad \ldots (1)$$

$$\frac{A\pi}{2} = \tan^{-1} \frac{B}{A} \qquad \ldots (2)$$

From (1) and (2), we get

$$A^2 + B^2 = e^{-\pi B} \quad \text{and} \quad \tan \frac{\pi A}{2} = \frac{B}{A}$$

EXERCISE 5.4

1. Separate into real and imaginary parts of (i) $(1 + i)^{(1-i)}$, (ii) $(-i)^{-(1-i)}$.

    Ans. (i) $\sqrt{2} \; e^{(8n+1)\pi/4} (\cos \theta + i \sin \theta)$, where $\theta = (8n+1) \pi/4 - \dfrac{1}{2} \log 2$.

    (ii) $i \, e^{-(2kn\pi - \pi/2)}$

2. Separate into real and imaginary parts by considering only principal values $(1 + i\sqrt{3})^{(1 + i\sqrt{3})}$

    Ans. $2e^{-\pi/3} (\cos \theta + i \sin \theta)$, where $\theta = \pi/3 + \sqrt{3} \log 2$

3. Find general and principal value of logarithms of $\log_2(-5)$.

   Ans. $\dfrac{\{\log 5 \log 2 + 2n(2m+1)\pi^2\} + i\pi\{(2m+1)\log 2 - 2n \log 5\}}{(\log 2)^2 + 4n^2\pi^2}$

4. Prove that $\log_{10}(2) = \dfrac{\log 2 + 2m\pi i}{\log 10 + 2n\pi i}$.

5. Prove that $i^a = \cos\left[(4m+1)\dfrac{\pi}{2}a\right] + i\sin\left[(4m+1)\dfrac{\pi}{2}a\right]$.

6. Prove that $a^i = e^{-2n\pi}[\cos(\log a) + i\sin(\log a)]$

7. Prove that $(i)^{1-i} = (-i)^{i-1}$.

8. Prove that $\dfrac{(1+i)^{1-i}}{(1-i)^{1+i}} = \sin(\log 2) + i\cos(\log 2)$.

9. Prove that $\log_{(e^{i\beta})}(e^{i\alpha}) = \dfrac{2n\pi + \alpha}{2m\pi + \beta}$.

10. If $e^{ix} = i^y$, prove that $2x = (4n+1)\pi y$.

    [**Hint** : $ix = y \log i$]

11. Separate $(\sin\theta + i\cos\theta)^i$ into real and imaginary parts.

    Ans. $e^{\theta - \pi/2}$

12. If $\tan \log(x + iy) = a + ib$ and $a^2 + b^2 \neq 1$, then prove that

    $\tan \log(x^2 + y^2) = \dfrac{2a}{1 - a^2 - b^2}$ (Dec. 2006, 2012)

    [**Hint** : If $\tan(\log\sqrt{x^2+y^2} + i\tan^{-1}y/x) = a + ib$, then
    $\tan(\log\sqrt{x^2+y^2} - i\tan^{-1}y/x) = a - ib$ and
    use $\tan \log(x^2 + y^2) = \tan \log[(x+iy) + \log(x-iy)]$]

13. If $a^{\alpha + i\beta} = (x + iy)^{p + iq}$ then considering principal values, prove that

    $\alpha = \dfrac{p}{2}\log_a(x^2 + y^2) - q\tan^{-1}\dfrac{y}{x}\log_a e$ and $\log_a(x^2 + y^2) = \dfrac{2(\alpha p + \beta q)}{p^2 + q^2}$

    [**Hint** : $\log_a e = \dfrac{\log_e e}{\log_e a} = \dfrac{1}{\log_e a}$].

14. If $(a + ib)^p = m^{x + iy}$, prove that one of the values of y/x is $\dfrac{2\tan^{-1}(b/a)}{\log(a^2 + b^2)}$.

    [**Hint** : $p \log(a + ib) = (x + iy)\log m$,
    $p \log\sqrt{a^2 + b^2} = x \log m$ and $p \tan^{-1} b/a = y \log m$].   (Dec. 2003)

MULTIPLE CHOICE QUESTIONS

Type I : Hyperbolic functions :

1. Hyperbolic functions sinh x and cosh x are respectively (1)
   (A) even and odd
   (B) odd and even
   (C) odd and odd
   (D) even and even

2. e^z is a periodic function of period (1)
   (A) πi
   (B) 2π
   (C) $2\pi i$
   (D) none of these

3. Inverse hyperbolic function $\tanh^{-1} x$ is (1)
   (A) $\dfrac{1}{2} \log \dfrac{1+x}{1-x}$
   (B) $\dfrac{1}{2} \log \dfrac{1-x}{1+x}$
   (C) $\log \dfrac{1+x}{1-x}$
   (D) $\log \dfrac{1-x}{1+x}$

4. Inverse hyperbolic function $\cosh^{-1} x$ is (1)
   (A) $\log\left(x + \sqrt{x^2 - 1}\right)$
   (B) $\log\left(x + \sqrt{x^2 + 1}\right)$
   (C) $\log\left(x - \sqrt{x^2 - 1}\right)$
   (D) none of these

5. Inverse hyperbolic function $\sinh^{-1} x$ is (1)
   (A) $\log\left(x + \sqrt{x^2 - 1}\right)$
   (B) $\log\left(x + \sqrt{x^2 + 1}\right)$
   (C) $\log\left(x - \sqrt{x^2 - 1}\right)$
   (D) none of these

6. Which of the following is true ?
   (A) $\cosh^2 x + \sinh^2 x = 1$
   (B) $\cosh^2 x - \sinh^2 x = 1$
   (C) $\sinh^2 x - \cosh^2 x = 1$
   (D) $\cosh^2 x - \sinh^2 x = 2$

7. Which of the following is true ? (1)
   (A) $\cosh^2 x + \sinh^2 x = 1$
   (B) $\sinh(x+y) = \sinh x \cdot \cosh y + \cosh y \sinh x$
   (C) $\sinh^2 x - \cosh^2 x = 1$
   (D) $\cosh^2 x - \sinh^2 x = 2$

8. Which of the following is true ? (1)
   (A) $\sin(x+iy) = \sin x \cosh y - i \cos x \sinh y$
   (B) $\sin(x+iy) = i \sin x \cosh y + \cos x \sinh y$
   (C) $\sin(x+iy) = \sin x \cosh y + i \cos x \sinh y$
   (D) $\sin(x+iy) = i \sin x \cosh y - \cos x \sinh y$

9. If $y = \sinh x$ then $\dfrac{dy}{dx}$ is equal to (1)

   (A) $\sinh x$ (B) $\cosh x$
   (C) $-\sinh x$ (D) $-\cosh x$

10. If $y = \cosh x$ then $\dfrac{dy}{dx}$ is equal to (1)

    (A) $\sinh x$ (B) $\cosh x$
    (C) $-\sinh x$ (D) $-\cosh x$

11. $\int \sinh x\, dx$ is equal to (1)

    (A) $\sinh x$ (B) $\cosh x$
    (C) $-\sinh x$ (D) $-\cosh x$

12. $\int \cosh x\, dx$ is equal to (1)

    (A) $\sinh x$ (B) $\cosh x$
    (C) $-\sinh x$ (D) $-\cosh x$

13. If $\tan(x + iy) = p + iq$ then $\tan(x - iy)$ is equal to (1)

    (A) $p - iq$ (B) $p + iq$
    (C) $ip - q$ (D) $p - q$

14. Simplification of the expression $\cosh^3 x$ is (2)

    (A) $\dfrac{1}{4}[\cosh 3x + 3\cosh x]$ (B) $-\dfrac{1}{4}[\cosh 3x + 3\cosh x]$

    (C) $\dfrac{1}{4}[\sinh 3x - 3\sinh x]$ (D) none of these

15. Simplification of the expression $\sinh^3 x$ is (2)

    (A) $\dfrac{1}{4}[\cosh 3x + 3\cosh x]$ (B) $-\dfrac{1}{4}[\cosh 3x + 3\cosh x]$

    (C) $\dfrac{1}{4}[\sinh 3x - 3\sinh x]$ (D) none of these

16. The value of $\tanh\left(\log \sqrt{3}\right)$ is equal to (2)

    (A) 1   (B) 2
    (C) $\dfrac{1}{2}$ (D) none of these

17. The value of $\sinh^{-1}\left(-\dfrac{3}{4}\right)$ is equal to (2)

    (A) $-\log 2$ (B) $\log 2$
    (C) $-\dfrac{3}{4}$ (D) none of these

18. The value of $\cosh^{-1}\left(i\dfrac{3}{4}\right)$ is equal to (2)

    (A) $\log(2i)$
    (B) $\log(i)$
    (C) $i\dfrac{3}{4}$
    (D) none of these

19. If $\tan(x+iy) = i$ then x is equal to (2)

    (A) 0
    (B) 1
    (C) $\dfrac{0}{0}$
    (D) ∞

20. If $\sin(\alpha + i\beta) = x + iy$ then $\dfrac{x^2}{\cosh^2 \beta} + \dfrac{y^2}{\sinh^2 \beta}$ is equal to (2)

    (A) 1
    (B) 0
    (C) -1
    (D) ∞

21. If $\sin(\alpha + i\beta) = x + iy$ then $\dfrac{x^2}{\sin^2 \alpha} - \dfrac{y^2}{\cos^2 \alpha}$ is equal to (2)

    (A) 1
    (B) 0
    (C) -1
    (D) ∞

22. If $\cos a \cosh b - i \sin a \sinh b = \dfrac{3i}{4}$ then the value of a is (2)

    (A) 0
    (B) $\dfrac{3}{4}$
    (C) π
    (D) $\dfrac{\pi}{2}$

23. If $\tan \dfrac{x}{2} = \tanh \dfrac{u}{2}$ then the value of $\sinh u$ is equal to (2)

    (A) $\tanh \dfrac{x}{2}$
    (B) $\cosh \dfrac{x}{2}$
    (C) $\tan x$
    (D) $\cos x$

24. Simplification of the expression $\dfrac{1}{1 - \dfrac{1}{1 - \cosh^2 x}}$ is (2)

    (A) $\coth^2 x$
    (B) $\text{sech}^2 x$
    (C) $\tanh^2 x$
    (D) none of these

25. If $x = \tanh^{-1} \dfrac{1}{2}$ then the value of $\sinh 2x$ is equal to (2)

    (A) $\dfrac{3}{4}$
    (B) $\dfrac{4}{3}$
    (C) 2
    (D) $\dfrac{1}{2}$

26. If $x = \tanh^{-1}\frac{1}{2}$ then the value of cosh 2x is equal to (2)

   (A) $\frac{4}{3}$
   (B) $\frac{3}{5}$
   (C) $\frac{5}{3}$
   (D) $\frac{3}{4}$

Type II : Logarithms of Complex Numbers :

27. General value of logarithm of complex number (x + iy) is (1)

   (A) $\log(x+iy) = \log\sqrt{x^2+y^2} + i\tan^{-1}\frac{y}{x}$

   (B) $\log(x+iy) = \log\sqrt{x^2+y^2} + i\left(2n\pi + \tan^{-1}\frac{y}{x}\right)$

   (C) $\log(x+iy) = \log\sqrt{x^2+y^2} + i\tan^{-1}\frac{x}{y}$

   (D) $\log(x+iy) = \log\sqrt{x^2+y^2} - i\left(2n\pi + \tan^{-1}\frac{x}{y}\right)$

28. Principle value of logarithm of complex number (x + iy) is (1)

   (A) $\log(x+iy) = \log\sqrt{x^2+y^2} + i\tan^{-1}\frac{y}{x}$

   (B) $\log(x+iy) = \log\sqrt{x^2+y^2} + i\left(2n\pi + \tan^{-1}\frac{y}{x}\right)$

   (C) $\log(x+iy) = \log\sqrt{x^2+y^2} + i\tan^{-1}\frac{x}{y}$

   (D) $\log(x+iy) = \log\sqrt{x^2+y^2} - i\left(2n\pi + \tan^{-1}\frac{x}{y}\right)$

29. The general value of logarithm of complex number $\log(1 + i\tan\alpha)$ is (2)
   (A) $\log(\cot\alpha) + i(2n\pi + \alpha)$
   (B) $\log(\sec\alpha) - i(2n\pi + \alpha)$
   (C) $\log(\sec\alpha) + i(2n\pi + \alpha)$
   (D) $i(2n\pi + \alpha)$

30. The general value of logarithm of complex number $(1 + i\sqrt{3})$ is (2)

   (A) $\log 4 + i\left(2n\pi + \frac{\pi}{3}\right)$
   (B) $\log 2 + i\left(2n\pi + \frac{\pi}{6}\right)$
   (C) $\log 2 + i\left(2n\pi + \frac{\pi}{3}\right)$
   (D) $\log 4 + i\left(2n\pi - \frac{\pi}{4}\right)$

31. The value of $\log_{(1-i)}(1+i)$ is (2)

   (A) $\dfrac{\log\sqrt{2} + i\frac{\pi}{4}}{\log\sqrt{2} - i\frac{\pi}{4}}$
   (B) $\dfrac{\log\sqrt{2} - i\frac{\pi}{4}}{\log\sqrt{2} + i\frac{\pi}{4}}$

   (C) $\dfrac{\log 2 + i\frac{\pi}{4}}{\log 2 - i\frac{\pi}{4}}$
   (D) none of these

32. Principal value of logarithm of (–5) is (2)
    (A) –log 5 – iπ (B) –log 5 + iπ (C) log 5 – iπ (D) log 5 + iπ

33. The value of i^i is (2)
    (A) $\frac{\pi}{2}$ (B) $-\frac{\pi}{2}$ (C) $e^{\pi/2}$ (D) $e^{-\pi/2}$

34. The value of i^{1+i} is (2)
    (A) $e^{i\frac{\pi}{2}-\frac{\pi}{2}}$ (B) $e^{i\frac{\pi}{2}+\frac{\pi}{2}}$ (C) $e^{-i\frac{\pi}{2}-\frac{\pi}{2}}$ (D) none of these

35. The value of sin (log i^i) is (2)
    (A) 0 (B) 1 (C) –1 (D) i

36. If log [log (x + iy)] = p + iq then the value of $\tan^{-1}\left(\frac{y}{x}\right)$ is (2)
    (A) $e^p \cos q$ (B) $e^q \sin p$ (C) $e^q \cos p$ (D) $e^p \sin q$

37. The value of $\log\left(\frac{x+iy}{x-iy}\right)$ is equal to (2)
    (A) $2\sqrt{x^2+y^2}$ (B) $2\log\sqrt{x^2+y^2}$ (C) $2i \tan^{-1}\left(\frac{y}{x}\right)$ (D) $2 \tan^{-1}\left(\frac{y}{x}\right)$

38. The value of $\log\left(\frac{1-i\sqrt{3}}{1+i\sqrt{3}}\right)$ is equal to (2)
    (A) 2 log 4 (B) 2 log 2 (C) $2i\frac{\pi}{3}$ (D) $-2i\frac{\pi}{3}$

39. The value of $\tanh\left(\log\sqrt{5}\right)$ is equal to (2)
    (A) $\frac{3}{2}$ (B) $\frac{2}{3}$ (C) 0 (D) $\sqrt{5}$

40. If tan (x + iy) = α + iβ then (2)
    (A) $\tan 2x = \frac{2\alpha}{1-\alpha^2-\beta^2}$ (B) $\tan 2x = \frac{2\alpha}{1+\alpha^2+\beta^2}$
    (C) $\tan 2x = \frac{2\beta}{1-\alpha^2-\beta^2}$ (D) $\tan 2x = \frac{2\beta}{1+\alpha^2+\beta^2}$

41. If sinh z = i then (2)
    (A) x = 0, y = 0 (B) x = $\frac{\pi}{2}$, y = 0 (C) x = 0, y = $\frac{\pi}{2}$ (D) x = $\frac{\pi}{2}$, y = $\frac{\pi}{2}$

Answers

1. (B)	8. (C)	15. (C)	22. (D)	29. (C)	36. (D)
2. (C)	9. (B)	16. (C)	23. (C)	30. (C)	37. (C)
3. (A)	10. (A)	17. (A)	24. (C)	31. (A)	38. (D)
4. (A)	11. (B)	18. (A)	25. (B)	32. (D)	39. (B)
5. (B)	12. (A)	19. (C)	26. (C)	33. (D)	40. (A)
6. (B)	13. (A)	20. (A)	27. (B)	34. (A)	41. (C)
7. (B)	14. (A)	21. (A)	28. (A)	35. (C)	

CHAPTER SIX

INFINITE SERIES

6.1 INFINITE SEQUENCE

Any set of numbers $a_1, a_2, a_3, \ldots, a_n, \ldots$ such that to each positive integral value of n there corresponds a number a_n, is called a sequence.

A sequence is thus an aggregate whose members are arranged so as to correspond to the set $1, 2, 3, \ldots n, \ldots$ of positive integers.

A sequence is symbolically represented by $\{a_n\}$ or a_n.

e.g. The sequence $\{a_n\}$ defined by, $a_n = \dfrac{1}{n}$. $\therefore \{a_n\} = \left\{1, \dfrac{1}{2}, \dfrac{1}{3}, \dfrac{1}{4}, \dfrac{1}{5}, \ldots\right\}$

A sequence $\{a_n\}$ is said to be monotonically increasing if $a_{n+1} \geq a_n$ for every value of n; and monotonically decreasing if $a_{n+1} \leq a_n$ for every value of n.

If in the sequence the terms are alternately positive and negative, the sequence is called *alternating sequence*.

(i) Monotonic increasing sequence : $2, 4, 6, 8, 10, \ldots$

(ii) Monotonic decreasing sequence : $\dfrac{1}{2}, \dfrac{1}{2^2}, \dfrac{1}{2^3}, \dfrac{1}{2^4}, \ldots$

(iii) Alternating sequence : $1, -3, 5, -7, 9, \ldots, (-1)^{n+1}(2n-1), \ldots$

6.2 LIMIT OF A SEQUENCE

A sequence $\{a_n\}$ is said to tend to the limit l as $n \to \infty$ if, given a positive number ϵ, however small, we can find an integer m such that $|a_n - l| < \epsilon$ for all $n \geq m$.

Hence, $\underset{n \to \infty}{\text{Lt}} a_n = l$

If a sequence $\{a_n\}$ has a finite limit l, the sequence is said to be *convergent*; but if the limit is infinite, it is said to be *divergent*. If no limit exists, the sequence is said to be *oscillatory*.

(i) $\{a_n\} = \left\{1 + \dfrac{(-1)^n}{n}\right\}$

$\therefore \underset{n \to \infty}{\text{Lt}} a_n = \underset{n \to \infty}{\text{Lt}} \left[1 + \dfrac{(-1)^n}{n}\right] = 1.$

Here limit is finite $\Rightarrow$ sequence $\{a_n\}$ is convergent.

(ii) $\{a_n\} = \{n\}$

$\therefore \underset{n \to \infty}{\text{Lt}} a_n = \underset{n \to \infty}{\text{Lt}} n = \infty$

Here limit is infinite $\Rightarrow$ sequence $\{a_n\}$ is divergent.

(iii) $\{a_n\} = (-1)^n + \dfrac{1}{3n}$

This sequence oscillates between $+1$ or -1 as $n \to \infty$, hence the sequence is oscillatory.

6.3 BOUNDED SEQUENCE

1. Bounded above sequence : A sequence $\{a_n\}$ is said to be **bounded above** if there exists a real number M such that $a_n \leq M$ for all values of n.

Note that M is independent of n and M is called **upper bound**.

Least upper bound : A number M is called least upper bound of a sequence if M is the least of all the upper bounds.

For example, consider the sequence

$$\{a_n\} = \left\{\dfrac{n+1}{n}\right\}$$

$$\{a_n\} = 2, \dfrac{3}{2}, \dfrac{4}{3}, \dfrac{5}{4}, \ldots\ldots$$

Hence any number > 2 is an upper bound of a sequence $\{a_n\}$.

Also 2 is the least upper bound of a sequence $\{a_n\}$.

2. Bounded below sequence : A sequence $\{a_n\}$ is said to be **bounded below** if there exists a real number M such that $a_n \geq M$ for all values of n.

Note that M is independent of n and M is called **lower bound**.

Greatest lower bound : A number B is called greatest lower bound of a sequence if B is the greatest of all the lower bounds.

For example, consider the sequence

$$\{a_n\} = \left\{\dfrac{n+1}{n}\right\}$$

$$\{a_n\} = 2, 3/2, 4/3, 5/4, \ldots.$$

Hence any number < 1 is the lower bound of the sequence $\{a_n\}$. Also 1 is the greatest lower bound of a sequence $\{a_n\}$.

Important deductions :

1. Every convergent sequence is bounded.
2. A sequence may be bounded but it may not be convergent.

3. The necessary and sufficient condition for the convergence of a monotonic sequence is that it is bounded.
4. If a monotonic increasing sequence is not bounded above, it diverges to $+\infty$.
5. If a monotonic decreasing sequence is not bounded below, it diverges to $-\infty$.
6. If $\{a_n\}$ and $\{b_n\}$ are two convergent sequences, then sequence $\{a_n + b_n\}$ is also convergent.
7. If $\{a_n\}$ and $\{b_n\}$ are two convergent sequences such that $\underset{n \to \infty}{Lt}\, a_n = l$ and $\underset{n \to \infty}{Lt}\, b_n = m$ then sequence $\{a_n b_n\}$ is also convergent and converges to $l.m$. Sequence $\left\{\dfrac{a_n}{b_n}\right\}$ is also convergent and converges to $\dfrac{l}{m}$ $(m \neq 0)$.

6.4 CAUCHY'S GENERAL PRINCIPLE OF CONVERGENCE

A sequence $\{a_n\}$ is said to be convergent if and only if for any given $\epsilon > 0$ there exists a positive integer N such that $|a_m - a_n| < \epsilon$ for all $m, n \geq N$.

6.5 INFINITE SERIES

An expression of the form $u_1 + u_2 + \ldots + u_n + \ldots$ in which every term is followed by another, u_n being a function of the positive integral variable n, is called infinite series, and is denoted by $\sum\limits_{n=1}^{\infty} u_n$ or $\sum u_n$.

The sum of the first n terms of this series is denoted by
$$S_n = u_1 + u_2 + \ldots\ldots + u_n$$

Convergent series : A series $\sum\limits_{n=1}^{\infty} u_n$ is said to be convergent if S_n tends to a definite finite limit S as n tends to infinity.

The finite limit S of S_n is called the sum of the series and is written as
$$S = \lim_{n \to \infty} S_n.$$

Divergent series : A series $\sum\limits_{n=1}^{\infty} u_n$ is said to be divergent if S_n tends to $+\infty$ or $-\infty$ as n tends to infinity, i.e. if $\underset{n \to \infty}{Lt}\, S_n = \infty$ or $-\infty$.

Oscillatory series : A series $\sum\limits_{n=1}^{\infty} u_n$ is said to be an oscillatory series if S_n neither tends to a finite limit nor to $+\infty$ or $-\infty$ as n tends to infinity.

Note : Throughout this chapter the limits for infinite series will be taken as $n \to \infty$, so now we shall write "$\lim_{n \to \infty}$" as "lim" only.

General theorems : We will discuss some general theorems which will be very useful for further discussion.

I. The nature of a series remains unaltered if

(i) the signs of all the terms in a series are changed

(ii) a finite number of terms are added or omitted from an infinite series

(iii) each term of the series is multiplied or divided by the same fixed quantity which is not zero.

II. For a series $\sum_{n=1}^{\infty} u_n$ to be convergent, it is necessary but not sufficient that $\underset{n \to \infty}{Lt} u_n = 0$.

e.g. (i) $\sum_{n=1}^{\infty} \frac{1}{n} = 1 + \frac{1}{2} + \frac{1}{3} + \ldots + \frac{1}{n} + \ldots$

$\underset{n \to \infty}{Lt} \frac{1}{n} = 0$

But the series is divergent.

(ii) $\sum_{n=1}^{\infty} \frac{1}{\sqrt{n}} = 1 + \frac{1}{\sqrt{2}} + \frac{1}{\sqrt{3}} + \ldots + \frac{1}{\sqrt{n}} + \ldots$

$\underset{n \to \infty}{Lt} \frac{1}{\sqrt{n}} = 0$ But the series is divergent.

III. A series of positive terms is convergent if S_n is less than a fixed number for all values of n.

IV. A series of positive terms is divergent if each term after a fixed stage is greater than some fixed positive number.

Cor. : A series of positive terms is divergent if $\lim u_n > 0$.

V. If each term of a series $\sum_{n=1}^{\infty} u_n$ of positive terms does not exceed the corresponding term of a convergent series $\sum_{n=1}^{\infty} v_n$ of positive terms, then $\sum_{n=1}^{\infty} u_n$ is convergent.

If each term of $\sum\limits_{n=1}^{\infty} u_n$ exceeds (or equals) the corresponding term of a divergent series of positive terms, then $\sum\limits_{n=1}^{\infty} u_n$ is divergent.

VI. The sum of two divergent series may be convergent.
VII. Sum of a convergent and a divergent series is divergent.

ILLUSTRATIVE EXAMPLES

Ex. 1: *Test the convergence of the series*
$$\frac{1}{(m+1)(m+2)} + \frac{1}{(m+2)(m+3)} + \frac{1}{(m+3)(m+4)} + \ldots$$

Sol.: Here
$$u_n = \frac{1}{(m+n)(m+n+1)} = \frac{1}{m+n} - \frac{1}{m+n+1}$$

$$S_n = u_1 + u_2 + \ldots + u_n$$

$$= \left(\frac{1}{m+1} - \frac{1}{m+2}\right) + \left(\frac{1}{m+2} - \frac{1}{m+3}\right) + \left(\frac{1}{m+3} - \frac{1}{m+4}\right)$$

$$+ \ldots + \left(\frac{1}{m+n-1} - \frac{1}{m+n}\right) + \left(\frac{1}{m+n} - \frac{1}{m+n+1}\right)$$

$$S_n = \frac{1}{m+1} - \frac{1}{m+n+1}$$

$$\lim S_n = \lim \left(\frac{1}{m+1} - \frac{1}{m+n+1}\right) = \frac{1}{m+1}$$

which is a finite quantity.

Hence the given series is convergent.

Ex. 2: *Test the convergence of the series* $\frac{a}{b} + \frac{a+x}{b+x} + \frac{a+2x}{b+2x} + \ldots$ *where a and b are finite and positive and $x > 0$.*

Sol.: Omitting the first term, the nth term of the series is given by,
$$u_n = \frac{a+nx}{b+nx}$$

We have, $\lim\limits_{n \to \infty} u_n = \lim\limits_{n \to \infty} \frac{a+nx}{b+nx} = \lim\limits_{n \to \infty} \frac{x+(a/n)}{x+(b/n)} = \frac{x}{x} = 1$, which is > 0.

Since each term of the given series is positive and $\lim u_n > 0$, therefore the given series is divergent. By using general theorem IV.

Ex. 3: *Show that the series* $\sum\limits_{n=1}^{\infty} \left(1 + \frac{1}{n}\right)^n$ *is divergent.*

Sol.: Here each term of the given series is positive, and $u_n = \left(1 + \frac{1}{n}\right)^n$.

We have, $\lim\limits_{n \to \infty} u_n = \lim\limits_{n \to \infty} \left(1 + \frac{1}{n}\right)^n = e$, which is > 0.

∴ The given series is divergent.

Ex. 4 : *Show that the series* $\frac{1}{1+2^{-1}} + \frac{2}{1+2^{-2}} + \frac{3}{1+2^{-3}} + \ldots$ *is divergent.*

Sol. : Here each term of the given series is positive and $u_n = \frac{n}{1+2^{-n}}$.

We have, $\lim_{n \to \infty} u_n = \lim_{n \to \infty} \frac{n}{1+2^{-n}} = \lim_{n \to \infty} \frac{n}{1+(1/2)^n} = \infty$, which is > 0. $\therefore$ The given series is divergent.

Ex. 5 : *Test for convergence the series whose n^{th} term is $\frac{1}{1+1/n}$.*

Sol. : Here $u_n = \frac{1}{1+1/n}$

We have, $\lim_{n \to \infty} u_n = \lim_{n \to \infty} \frac{1}{1+(1/n)} = 1$, which is > 0.

$\therefore$ The given series is divergent.

Ex. 6 : *Prove that the series* $\frac{1}{\sqrt{2}} + \frac{2}{\sqrt{5}} + \frac{4}{\sqrt{(17)}} + \frac{8}{\sqrt{(65)}} + \ldots$ *is divergent.*

Sol. : Here, $u_n = \frac{2^{n-1}}{\sqrt{\{2^{2(n-1)} + 1\}}}$

$= \frac{2^{n-1}}{\sqrt{[2^{2(n-1)} \cdot \{1 + 1/2^{2(n-1)}\}]}}$

$= \frac{2^{n-1}}{2^{n-1}\sqrt{\left[1 + \frac{1}{2^{2(n-1)}}\right]}} = \frac{1}{\sqrt{\left[1 + \frac{1}{2^{2(n-1)}}\right]}}$

$\therefore \lim u_n = \frac{1}{\sqrt{[1+0]}} = 1$, which is > 0.

Hence, the given series $\sum u_n$ is divergent.

6.6 TEST OF CONVERGENCE AND DIVERGENCE

There are many series in which we cannot find out the sum of first n terms. Thus we cannot test the series for convergence or divergence by evaluating $\underset{n \to \infty}{Lt} S_n$. Hence, we shall describe some methods or tests to know whether the given series is convergent or divergent without finding out the sum of its first n terms.

I. Cauchy's n^{th} root test : The series $\sum_{n=1}^{\infty} u_n$ of positive terms is convergent if

$\underset{n \to \infty}{Lt} (u_n)^{1/n} < 1$ and divergent if $\underset{n \to \infty}{Lt} (u_n)^{1/n} > 1$.

If $\underset{n \to \infty}{Lt} (u_n)^{1/n} = 1$, the test fails.

ILLUSTRATIVE EXAMPLES

Ex. 1 : *Test the convergence of series* $\sum \left(1 + \frac{1}{n}\right)^{n^2}$.

Sol. : Here, $u_n = \left(1 + \frac{1}{n}\right)^{n^2}$

∴ $(u_n)^{1/n} = \left(1 + \frac{1}{n}\right)^n$

∴ $\text{Lim}(u_n)^{1/n} = \text{Lim}\left(1 + \frac{1}{n}\right)^n = e > 1.$ $\quad\left[\because \text{Lim}\left(1 + \frac{1}{n}\right)^n = e\right]$

Hence, by root test the series is divergent.

Ex. 2 : *Test the convergence of the following series* $1 + \frac{x}{2} + \frac{x^2}{3^2} + \frac{x^3}{4^3} + \ldots$.

Sol. : Neglecting the first term, we have,

$$u_n = \frac{x^n}{(n+1)^n} \text{ or } (u_n)^{1/n} = \frac{x}{n+1}$$

∴ $\text{Lim}(u_n)^{1/n} = \text{Lim}\frac{x}{n+1} = 0 < 1,$ for all values of x.

Hence, by root test the series is convergent for all values of x.

Ex. 3 : *Test the convergence of the following series* $\sum \left(1 + \frac{1}{n}\right)^{-n^2}$.

Sol. : Here, $u_n = \left(1 + \frac{1}{n}\right)^{-n^2}$

∴ $(u_n)^{1/n} = \left(1 + \frac{1}{n}\right)^{-n}$

∴ $\text{Lim}(u_n)^{1/n} = \text{Lim}\left(1 + \frac{1}{n}\right)^{-n} = \text{Lim}\frac{1}{\left(1 + \frac{1}{n}\right)^n}$

$= \frac{1}{e}$, which is < 1. $\quad\left[\because \text{Lim}\left(1 + \frac{1}{n}\right)^n = e\right]$

Hence, by n^{th} root test the series is convergent.

Ex. 4 : *Test the convergence of the following series :*

$$\frac{1^3}{3} + \frac{2^3}{3^2} + \frac{3^3}{3^3} + \frac{4^3}{3^4} + \frac{5^3}{3^4} + \ldots + \frac{n^3}{3^n} + \ldots$$

Sol. : Here $u_n = \frac{n^3}{3^n}$

∴ $(u_n)^{1/n} = \frac{n^{3/n}}{3}$

$$\therefore \quad \text{Lim}\ (u_n)^{1/n} = \left(\frac{n^{3/n}}{3}\right)$$

$$= \text{Lim}\ \frac{1}{3}\left(n^{1/n}\right)^3$$

$$= \frac{1}{3}\cdot 1 = \frac{1}{3} < 1 \qquad (\because \text{Lim}\ n^{1/n} = 1)$$

Hence, by n^{th} root test the series is convergent.

II. The P series $\sum\limits_{n=1}^{\infty} \dfrac{1}{n^p}$:

The series $\sum\limits_{n=1}^{\infty} \dfrac{1}{n^p} = \dfrac{1}{1^p} + \dfrac{1}{2^p} + \dfrac{1}{3^p} + \ldots + \dfrac{1}{n^p} + \ldots \ldots$

is convergent if $p > 1$ and divergent if $p \leq 1$.

Proof : Case (i) : Let $p > 1$. As the terms are all positive, we can group them as we like. Thus we can write the given series

$$\frac{1}{1^p} + \frac{1}{2^p} + \frac{1}{3^p} + \ldots = \frac{1}{1^p} + \left(\frac{1}{2^p} + \frac{1}{3^p}\right) + \left(\frac{1}{4^p} + \frac{1}{5^p} + \frac{1}{6^p} + \frac{1}{7^p}\right) + \left(\frac{1}{8^p} + \frac{1}{9^p} + \ldots + \frac{1}{15^p}\right) + \ldots$$

$$\ldots (1)$$

Now, since $p > 1$ $\therefore$ $3 > 2$ $\Rightarrow$ $3^p > 2^p$

$$\Rightarrow \frac{1}{3^p} < \frac{1}{2^p} \quad \therefore \quad \frac{1}{2^p} + \frac{1}{3^p} < \frac{1}{2^p} + \frac{1}{2^p} \quad \therefore \quad \frac{1}{2^p} + \frac{1}{3^p} < \frac{2}{2^p}$$

Similarly, $\quad \dfrac{1}{4^p} + \dfrac{1}{5^p} + \dfrac{1}{6^p} + \dfrac{1}{7^p} < \dfrac{1}{4^p} + \dfrac{1}{4^p} + \dfrac{1}{4^p} + \dfrac{1}{4^p} = \dfrac{4}{4^p}$

$$\frac{1}{8^p} + \frac{1}{9^p} + \ldots + \frac{1}{15^p} < \frac{8}{8^p}, \text{ and so on.}$$

$\therefore$ From (1), we have,

$$\frac{1}{1^p} + \frac{1}{2^p} + \frac{1}{3^p} + \ldots < \frac{1}{1^p} + \frac{2}{2^p} + \frac{4}{4^p} + \frac{8}{8^p} + \ldots$$

But the series on the R.H.S. is a geometric series whose common ratio is $\dfrac{2}{2^p} = \dfrac{1}{2^{p-1}}$ which is less than 1 as $p > 1$. Therefore the geometric series on the R.H.S. is convergent. Thus the given series is less than a convergent series.

Hence, the given series is convergent when $p > 1$.

Case (ii): Let p = 1 then the given series becomes

$$1 + \frac{1}{2} + \frac{1}{3} + \frac{1}{4} + \ldots = 1 + \frac{1}{2} + \left(\frac{1}{3} + \frac{1}{4}\right) + \left(\frac{1}{5} + \frac{1}{6} + \frac{1}{7} + \frac{1}{8}\right) + \left(\frac{1}{9} + \frac{1}{10} + \ldots + \frac{1}{16}\right) + \ldots \quad \ldots (2)$$

$\because \; 3 < 4 \quad \therefore \; \frac{1}{3} > \frac{1}{4} \quad \therefore \; \frac{1}{3} + \frac{1}{4} > \frac{1}{4} + \frac{1}{4}$

$\frac{1}{3} + \frac{1}{4} > \frac{1}{2} \; ; \; \frac{1}{5} + \frac{1}{6} + \frac{1}{7} + \frac{1}{8} > \frac{1}{8} + \frac{1}{8} + \frac{1}{8} + \frac{1}{8} = \frac{1}{2}$

$\frac{1}{9} + \frac{1}{10} + \ldots + \frac{1}{16} > \frac{1}{2}$, and so on.

∴ From (2), we have,

$$1 + \frac{1}{2} + \frac{1}{3} + \frac{1}{4} + \ldots > 1 + \frac{1}{2} + \frac{1}{2} + \frac{1}{2} + \ldots \quad \ldots (3)$$

But $1 + \frac{1}{2} + \frac{1}{2} + \ldots = 1 + (n-1)\frac{1}{2} = \frac{n+1}{2}$

which tends to ∞ as n → ∞, therefore the series on the R.H.S. of (3) is divergent. Thus the given series is greater than a divergent series. Hence, the given series is divergent when p = 1.

Case (iii): Let $p < 1$ then $\frac{1}{n^p} > \frac{1}{n}$ for n = 2, 3, 4, …

Thus the given series $\frac{1}{1^p} + \frac{1}{2^p} + \frac{1}{3^p} + \ldots$

is term by term greater than the series $1 + \frac{1}{2} + \frac{1}{3} + \frac{1}{4} + \ldots$, which is a divergent series as proved in case (ii). Hence, the given series is divergent when $p < 1$.

ILLUSTRATIVE EXAMPLES

Ex. 1: Test for convergence the following series (i) $\sum_{n=1}^{\infty} \frac{1}{n^2}$, (ii) $\sum_{n=1}^{\infty} \frac{1}{n^{1/3}}$

Sol.: (i) $\sum_{n=1}^{\infty} \frac{1}{n^2}$

∴ Comparing with $\sum_{n=1}^{\infty} \frac{1}{n^p}$, we have, p = 2 > 1 ∴ series is convergent.

(ii) $\sum_{n=1}^{\infty} \frac{1}{n^{1/3}}$

∴ Comparing with $\sum_{n=1}^{\infty} \frac{1}{n^p}$, we have, $p = \frac{1}{3} < 1$ ∴ series is divergent.

Convergence of a Geometric Series :

Consider the geometric series $a + ax + ax^2 + \ldots + ax^{n-1} + \ldots$

$\therefore \quad S_n = \dfrac{a(1-x^n)}{1-x}$ if $x < 1$

$\quad\quad S_n = \dfrac{a(x^n-1)}{x-1}$ if $x > 1$

Case I : $x < 1$ then $x^n \to 0$ as $n \to \infty$

$\therefore \quad \underset{n \to \infty}{Lt} S_n = \dfrac{a(1-0)}{1-x} = \dfrac{a}{1-x} =$ finite quantity

$\therefore$ Series is convergent.

Case II : $x > 1$ then $x^n \to \infty$ as $n \to \infty$

$\therefore \quad \underset{n \to \infty}{Lt} S_n = \dfrac{a(\infty - 1)}{x-1} = \infty$

$\therefore$ Series is divergent.

Case III : $x = 1 \quad \therefore S_n = a + a + \ldots$ to n terms

$\quad\quad\quad\quad = na$

which tends to ∞ or $-\infty$ as $n \to \infty$ according as a is positive or negative.

$\therefore$ Series is divergent.

Case IV : $x = -1$ then the series becomes $a - a + a - a + \ldots$, the sum of whose n terms oscillates between a and 0 according as n is odd or even.

$\therefore$ Series oscillates.

Case V : $x < -1$ then $\underset{n \to \infty}{Lt} S_n = \infty$ or $-\infty$ according as n is odd or even.

$\therefore$ Series oscillates.

$\therefore$ A geometric series $\sum_{n=1}^{\infty} ax^{n-1}$ with common ratio x is convergent if $|x| < 1$, divergent if $x \geq 1$ and oscillating if $x \leq -1$.

III. Comparison test : If $\sum_{n=1}^{\infty} u_n$ and $\sum_{n=1}^{\infty} v_n$ are two series of positive terms such that $\underset{n \to \infty}{Lt} \dfrac{u_n}{v_n}$ is finite and non-zero then the two series are either both convergent or both divergent.

Working rule to find the auxiliary series $\sum_{n=1}^{\infty} v_n$:

1. Find u_n and note that u_n contains the powers of n only which may be positive or negative, integral or fractional.

2. If u_n is in the form of a fraction then we take $v_n = \dfrac{n^p}{n^q} = \dfrac{1}{n^{q-p}}$, where p and q are respectively the highest indices of n in the numerator and denominator of u_n.

3. If u_n can be expanded in ascending powers of $\dfrac{1}{n}$ then to get v_n, we should retain only the lowest power of $\dfrac{1}{n}$.

ILLUSTRATIVE EXAMPLES

Ex. 1 : *Test for convergence the series whose n^{th} term is* $\dfrac{\sqrt{n}}{n^2 + 1}$.

Sol. : Here, $\quad u_n = \dfrac{\sqrt{n}}{n^2 + 1}$

∴ Let $\quad v_n = \dfrac{\sqrt{n}}{n^2} = \dfrac{1}{n^{3/2}}$,

i.e., the auxiliary series is $\sum v_n = \sum \dfrac{1}{n^{3/2}}$

Now, $\quad \text{Lim} \dfrac{u_n}{v_n} = \text{Lim} \left\{ \dfrac{\sqrt{n}}{n^2 + 1} \cdot n^{3/2} \right\}$

$= \lim \dfrac{n^2}{n^2 + 1}$

$= \lim \dfrac{1}{1 + 1/n^2} = 1$, which is finite and non-zero.

But the auxiliary series

$\sum v_n = \sum \dfrac{1}{n^{3/2}}$ is convergent $\qquad \left(\because P = \dfrac{3}{2} > 1 \right)$

Hence, by comparison test the series $\sum u_n$ is also convergent.

Ex. 2 : *Test for convergence the series whose n^{th} term is* $\dfrac{(2n^2 - 1)^{1/3}}{(3n^3 + 2n + 5)^{1/4}}$.

Sol. : Here, $\quad u_n = \dfrac{(2n^2 - 1)^{1/3}}{(3n^3 + 2n + 5)^{1/4}} = \dfrac{n^{2/3}(2 - 1/n^2)^{1/3}}{n^{3/4}(3 + 2/n^2 + 5/n^3)^{1/4}}$

$= \dfrac{1}{n^{1/12}} \dfrac{(2 - 1/n^2)^{1/3}}{(3 + 2/n^2 + 5/n^3)^{1/4}}$

Take, $v_n = \dfrac{1}{n^{1/12}}$

Then, $\dfrac{u_n}{v_n} = \dfrac{(2-1/n^2)^{1/3}}{(3+2/n^2+5/n^3)^{1/4}}$

$\therefore \lim\limits_{n \to \infty} \dfrac{u_n}{v_n} = \dfrac{2^{1/3}}{3^{1/4}}$ which is finite and non-zero.

Therefore, by comparison test, $\sum u_n$ and $\sum v_n$ are either both convergent or both divergent.

But v_n is the type $1/n^p$, where $p = 1/12$ i.e. < 1. Therefore, $\sum v_n$ is divergent. Hence $\sum u_n$ is also divergent.

Ex. 3 : *Test for convergence the series whose n^{th} term is $\dfrac{n^p}{(n+1)^q}$.*

Sol. : Here, $u_n = \dfrac{n^p}{(n+1)^q}$

$\therefore$ Let $v_n = \dfrac{n^p}{n^q} = \dfrac{1}{n^{q-p}}$

Now, $\lim \dfrac{u_n}{v_n} = \lim \left\{ \dfrac{n^p}{(n+1)^q} \cdot n^{q-p} \right\} = \lim \dfrac{1}{(1+1/n)^q}$

$= 1$ which is finite and non-zero.

But the auxiliary series,

$\sum v_n = \sum \dfrac{1}{n^{q-p}}$ is convergent if $q - p > 1$ i.e. if $p - q + 1 < 0$ and divergent if $q - p \leq 1$ i.e. if $p - q + 1 \geq 0$.

Hence by comparison test the given series $\sum u_n$ is convergent if $p - q + 1 < 0$ and divergent if $p - q + 1 \geq 0$.

Ex. 4 : *Test for convergence the series whose n^{th} term is $\dfrac{n}{(a+nb)^2}$.*

Sol. : Here, $u_n = \dfrac{n}{(a+nb)^2}$

$\therefore$ Let $v_n = \dfrac{n}{n^2} = \dfrac{1}{n}$

Now, $\lim \dfrac{u_n}{v_n} = \lim \dfrac{n}{(a+nb)^2} \cdot n$

$= \lim \dfrac{1}{(a/n+b)^2} = \dfrac{1}{b^2}$, which is finite and non-zero.

But the auxiliary series $\sum v_n = \sum \dfrac{1}{n}$ is divergent because here $p = 1$. Hence by comparison test, $\sum u_n$ is also divergent.

Ex. 5 : *Test for convergence the series whose n^{th} term is $\dfrac{1}{\sqrt{[n(n+1)]}}$.*

Sol. : Here,
$$u_n = \dfrac{1}{\sqrt{[n(n+1)]}}$$
$$= \dfrac{1}{\sqrt{[n^2(1+1/n)]}} = \dfrac{1}{n\sqrt{(1+1/n)}}$$

Take $v_n = \dfrac{1}{n}$, so that $\dfrac{u_n}{v_n} = \dfrac{1}{\sqrt{(1+1/n)}}$.

We have, $\lim \dfrac{u_n}{v_n} = \lim \dfrac{1}{\sqrt{(1+1/n)}} = 1$, which is finite and non-zero.

But the auxiliary series $\Sigma\, v_n$ is divergent because here p = 1. Hence by comparison test $\Sigma\, u_n$ is also divergent.

Ex. 6 : *Test the convergence of the series* $\dfrac{2}{1} + \dfrac{3}{8} + \dfrac{4}{27} + \dfrac{5}{64} + \ldots + \dfrac{n+1}{n^3} + \ldots$ **(May 09, 14)**

Sol. : Here, $\Sigma\, u_n = \dfrac{2}{1} + \dfrac{3}{8} + \dfrac{4}{27} + \dfrac{5}{64} + \ldots$

$$= \Sigma\, \dfrac{n+1}{n^3}$$

i.e. $u_n = \dfrac{n+1}{n^3}$

∴ Let $v_n = \dfrac{n}{n^3} = \dfrac{1}{n^2}$

Now, $\lim \dfrac{u_n}{v_n} = \lim \left\{ \dfrac{n+1}{n^3} \, n^2 \right\} = \lim \left\{ 1 + \dfrac{1}{n} \right\}$

= 1, which is finite and non-zero.

But the auxiliary series,
$$\Sigma\, v_n = \Sigma\, \dfrac{1}{n^2}$$
is convergent because here p = 2 > 1.

Hence by comparison test, the series $\Sigma\, u_n$ is also convergent.

Ex. 7 : *Test the convergence of the series* $\sqrt{\dfrac{1}{2^3}} + \sqrt{\dfrac{2}{3^3}} + \sqrt{\dfrac{3}{4^3}} + \ldots$. **(May 2009)**

Sol. : Here, $\Sigma\, u_n = \sqrt{\dfrac{1}{2^3}} + \sqrt{\dfrac{2}{3^3}} + \sqrt{\dfrac{3}{4^3}} + \ldots$

$$= \Sigma\, \sqrt{\left\{ \dfrac{n}{(n+1)^3} \right\}}$$

∴ $$u_n = \sqrt{\frac{n}{(n+1)^3}}$$

$$= \sqrt{\frac{n}{n^3(1+1/n)^3}} = \frac{1}{n}\sqrt{\frac{1}{(1+1/n)^3}}$$

Take $v_n = \dfrac{1}{n}$, so that

$$\lim \frac{u_n}{v_n} = \lim \sqrt{\frac{1}{(1+1/n)^3}} = 1,$$ which is finite and non-zero.

Therefore by comparison test Σu_n and Σv_n are either both convergent or both divergent.

But the auxiliary series $\Sigma v_n = \Sigma 1/n$ is divergent because here p = 1.

Hence, the given series Σu_n is also divergent.

Ex. 8 : *Test the convergence of the series* $\dfrac{14}{1^3} + \dfrac{24}{2^3} + \dfrac{34}{3^3} + \ldots + \dfrac{10n+4}{n^3} + \ldots$.

Sol. : Here $$u_n = \frac{10 \cdot n + 4}{n^3} = \frac{n\left(10 + \dfrac{4}{n}\right)}{n^3}$$

$$= \frac{\left(10 + \dfrac{4}{n}\right)}{n^2}$$

Take, $v_n = \dfrac{1}{n^2}$, so that

$$\lim \frac{u_n}{v_n} = \lim_{n \to \infty} (10 + 4/n) = 10$$

which is finite and non-zero. Therefore by comparison test Σu_n and Σv_n are either both convergent or both divergent. But the auxiliary series $\Sigma v_n = \Sigma 1/n^2$ is convergent because here p = 2 i.e. > 1.

Hence the given series Σu_n is also convergent.

Ex. 9 : *Test for convergence the series* $\dfrac{1}{1 \cdot 2 \cdot 3} + \dfrac{3}{2 \cdot 3 \cdot 4} + \dfrac{5}{3 \cdot 4 \cdot 5} + \ldots$.

Sol. : Here $$\Sigma u_n = \frac{1}{1 \cdot 2 \cdot 3} + \frac{3}{2 \cdot 3 \cdot 4} + \frac{5}{3 \cdot 4 \cdot 5} + \ldots$$

$$= \Sigma \frac{(2n-1)}{n(n+1)(n+2)}$$

i.e. $$u_n = \frac{(2n-1)}{n(n+1)(n+2)}$$

∴ Let $$v_n = \frac{n}{n \cdot n \cdot n} = \frac{1}{n^2}$$

Now, $$\lim \frac{u_n}{v_n} = \lim \frac{(2n-1) n^2}{n(n+1)(n+2)}$$

$$= \lim \frac{(2-1/n)}{(1+1/n)(1+2/n)}$$

$$= 2, \text{ which is finite and non-zero.}$$

But the auxiliary series $\sum v_n = \sum \frac{1}{n^2}$ is convergent because here $p = 2$ i.e. > 1.

Hence by comparison test, the given series is also convergent.

Ex. 10 : *Test for convergence the series* $\frac{1}{a \cdot 1^2 + b} + \frac{2}{a \cdot 2^2 + b} + \frac{3}{a \cdot 3^2 + b} + \ldots$.

Sol. : Here, $$\sum u_n = \frac{1}{a \cdot 1^2 + b} + \frac{2}{a \cdot 2^2 + b} + \frac{3}{a \cdot 3^2 + b} + \ldots$$

$$= \sum \left(\frac{n}{a \cdot n^2 + b}\right)$$

i.e. $$u_n = \frac{n}{an^2 + b} \quad \therefore \text{ let } v_n = \frac{n}{n^2} = \frac{1}{n}.$$

Now, $$\lim \frac{u_n}{v_n} = \lim \left(\frac{n}{an^2 + b} \cdot n\right)$$

$$= \lim \left(\frac{1}{a + b/n^2}\right)$$

$$= \frac{1}{a}, \text{ which is finite and non-zero.}$$

But the auxiliary series

$$\sum v_n = \sum \frac{1}{n} \text{ is divergent because here } p = 1.$$

Hence, by comparison test the given series is also divergent.

Ex. 11 : *Test for convergence the series* $\frac{1}{(x-d)^2} + \frac{1}{(x-2d)^2} + \frac{1}{(x-3d)^2} + \ldots$.

Sol. : Here, $$\sum u_n = \frac{1}{(x-d)^2} + \frac{1}{(x-2d)^2} + \frac{1}{(x-3d)^2} + \ldots$$

$$= \sum \frac{1}{(x-nd)^2}$$

i.e. $$u_n = \frac{1}{(x-nd)^2} \quad \therefore \text{ let } v_n = \frac{1}{n^2}$$

Now,
$$\lim \frac{u_n}{v_n} = \lim \left\{ \frac{1}{(x-nd)^2} \cdot n^2 \right\}$$
$$= \lim \left\{ \frac{1}{(x/n - d)^2} \right\} = \frac{1}{d^2}, \text{ which is finite and non-zero.}$$

But the auxiliary series $\sum v_n = \sum \frac{1}{n^2}$ is convergent because here p = 2 i.e. > 1. Hence by comparison test the given series is also convergent.

Ex. 12 : *Test the convergence of the series* $\frac{2^p}{1^q} + \frac{3^p}{2^q} + \frac{4^p}{3^q} + \ldots$

Sol. : Here,
$$\sum u_n = \frac{2^p}{1^q} + \frac{3^p}{2^q} + \frac{4^p}{3^q} + \ldots$$
$$= \sum \frac{(n+1)^p}{n^q},$$

i.e.
$$u_n = \frac{(n+1)^p}{n^q} \quad \therefore \text{ let } v_n = \frac{n^p}{n^q} = \frac{1}{n^{q-p}}.$$

Now,
$$\lim \frac{u_n}{v_n} = \lim \left\{ \frac{(n+1)^p}{n^q} \cdot n^{q-p} \right\}$$
$$= \lim (1 + 1/n)^p = 1, \text{ which is finite and non-zero.}$$

But the auxiliary series,
$$\sum v_n = \sum \frac{1}{n^{q-p}} \text{ is convergent if } q - p > 1 \text{ i.e. } p - q + 1 < 0,$$
and divergent if $q - p \leq 1$ i.e. $p - q + 1 \geq 0$.

Hence, by comparison test the given series $\sum u_n$ is also convergent if $p - q + 1 < 0$ and divergent if $p - q + 1 \geq 0$.

Ex. 13 : *Test the convergence of the series* $\frac{2}{1^p} + \frac{3}{2^p} + \frac{4}{3^p} + \frac{5}{4^p} + \ldots$.

Sol. : Here,
$$\sum u_n = \frac{2}{1^p} + \frac{3}{2^p} + \frac{4}{3^p} + \ldots$$
$$= \sum \left(\frac{n+1}{n^p} \right)$$

i.e.
$$u_n = \frac{n+1}{n^p} \quad \therefore \text{ Let } v_n = \frac{n}{n^p} = \frac{1}{n^{p-1}}$$

Now,
$$\lim \frac{u_n}{v_n} = \lim \left(\frac{n+1}{n^p} \cdot n^{p-1} \right)$$
$$= \lim (1 + 1/n) = 1, \text{ which is finite and non-zero.}$$

But the auxiliary series,

$$\Sigma v_n = \Sigma \frac{1}{n^{p-1}} \text{ is convergent if } p - 1 > 1 \text{ i.e. } p > 2,$$

and divergent if $p - 1 \leq 1$ i.e. if $p \leq 2$.

Hence, by comparison test the given series Σu_n is convergent if $p > 2$ and divergent if $p \leq 2$.

IV. D'Alembert's ratio test : If $\sum_{n=1}^{\infty} u_n$ is a series of positive terms then it is convergent if $\underset{n \to \infty}{Lt} \frac{u_n}{u_{n+1}} > 1$ and divergent if $\underset{n \to \infty}{Lt} \frac{u_n}{u_{n+1}} < 1$.

If $\underset{n \to \infty}{Lt} \frac{u_n}{u_{n+1}} = 1$, the test fails and a further investigation will be required.

ILLUSTRATIVE EXAMPLES

Ex. 1 : *Test for convergence the following series* $\Sigma \frac{n^2}{3^n}$.

Sol. :
$$u_n = \frac{n^2}{3^n} \quad \therefore \quad u_{n+1} = \frac{(n+1)^2}{3^{n+1}}$$

$$\frac{u_n}{u_{n+1}} = \frac{n^2}{3^n} \cdot \frac{3^{n+1}}{(n+1)^2} = 3 \cdot \left(\frac{n}{n+1}\right)^2 = \frac{3}{\left(1 + \frac{1}{n}\right)^2}$$

$$\underset{n \to \infty}{Lt} \frac{u_n}{u_{n+1}} = \underset{n \to \infty}{Lt} \frac{3}{\left(1 + \frac{1}{n}\right)^2} = 3 > 1.$$

∴ By ratio rest Σu_n is convergent.

Ex. 2 : *Find the nature of the following series* $\sum_{n=1}^{\infty} \frac{4 \cdot 7 \cdot 10 \cdots (3n+1)}{1 \cdot 2 \cdot 3 \cdots n}$.

Sol. :
$$u_n = \frac{4 \cdot 7 \cdot 10 \cdots (3n+1)}{n!} \quad \therefore \quad u_{n+1} = \frac{4 \cdot 7 \cdot 10 \cdots (3n+1)(3n+4)}{(n+1)!}$$

$$\frac{u_n}{u_{n+1}} = \frac{n+1}{3n+4} \quad \therefore \quad \underset{n \to \infty}{Lt} \frac{u_n}{u_{n+1}} = \frac{1}{3} < 1$$

∴ by ratio rest Σu_n is divergent.

Ex. 3 : *Test the convergence of the series* $1 + \frac{2^2}{2!} + \frac{3^2}{3!} + \frac{4^2}{4!} + \ldots$ **(May 2009)**

Sol. : Here, $u_n = \frac{n^2}{n!}$

and $$u_{n+1} = \frac{(n+1)^2}{(n+1)!}$$

Now, $$\frac{u_n}{u_{n+1}} = \frac{n^2}{n!} \cdot \frac{(n+1)!}{(n+1)^2}$$

$$= \frac{n^2(n+1)}{(n+1)^2} = \frac{n^2}{n+1} = \frac{n}{(1+1/n)}$$

$\therefore$ $$\lim \frac{u_n}{u_{n+1}} = \lim \frac{n}{(1+1/n)}$$

$$= \infty, \text{ which is} > 1.$$

Hence, by the ratio test the series $\sum u_n$ is convergent.

Ex. 4 : *Test for convergence the series* $\frac{1}{1+2} + \frac{2}{1+2^2} + \frac{3}{1+2^3} + \cdots$

Sol. : Here, $$u_n = \frac{n}{1+2^n}$$

and $$u_{n+1} = \frac{n+1}{1+2^{n+1}}$$

Now, $$\frac{u_n}{u_{n+1}} = \frac{n}{1+2^n} \cdot \frac{1+2^{n+1}}{n+1}$$

$$= \frac{n \cdot 2^{n+1}(1+1/2^{n+1})}{2^n(1+1/2^n) \cdot n(1+1/n)}$$

$$= 2 \frac{(1+1/2^{n+1})}{(1+1/2^n)(1+1/n)}$$

$\therefore$ $$\lim \frac{u_n}{u_{n+1}} = 2 \frac{(1+0)}{(1+0)(1+0)} = 2, \text{ which is} > 1.$$

Hence, by ratio test the series $\sum u_n$ is convergent.

Ex. 5 : *Test the convergence of the series whose n^{th} term is* $\frac{n^3+a}{2^n+a}$.

Sol. : Here, $$u_n = \frac{n^3+a}{2^n+a}$$

then $$u_{n+1} = \frac{(n+1)^3+a}{2^{n+1}+a}$$

Now, $$\frac{u_n}{u_{n+1}} = \frac{n^3+a}{2^n+a} \cdot \frac{2^{n+1}+a}{(n+1)^3+a}$$

$$= \frac{n^3(1+a/n^3) \cdot 2^{n+1}(1+a/2^{n+1})}{2^n(1+a/2^n) \cdot n^3\{(1+1/n)^3+a/n^3\}}$$

$$= 2 \cdot \frac{(1+a/n^3)(1+a/2^{n+1})}{(1+a/2^n)\{(1+1/n)^3+a/n^3\}}$$

$$\therefore \quad \lim \frac{u_n}{u_{n+1}} = 2 \frac{(1+0)(1+0)}{(1+0)\{(1+0)^3 + 0\}}$$

$$= 2, \text{ which is} > 1.$$

Hence, by ratio test the series $\sum u_n$ is convergent.

Ex. 6 : *Test for convergence the series whose n^{th} term is* $\frac{n^3}{(n-1)!}$.

Sol. : Here, $\qquad u_n = \frac{n^3}{(n-1)!}$

and $\qquad u_{n+1} = \frac{(n+1)^3}{n!}$

$$\therefore \quad \frac{u_n}{u_{n+1}} = \frac{n^3}{(n-1)!} \cdot \frac{n!}{(n+1)^3} = \frac{n^4}{(n+1)^3}$$

$$= \frac{n}{(1+1/n)^3}$$

$$\therefore \quad \lim \frac{u_n}{u_{n+1}} = \infty, \text{ which is} > 1.$$

Hence, by ratio test the series $\sum u_n$ is convergent.

Ex. 7 : *Test for convergence the series whose n^{th} term is* $\sqrt{\left\{\frac{2^n - 1}{3^n - 1}\right\}}$.

Sol. : Here, $\qquad u_n = \sqrt{\left(\frac{2^n - 1}{3^n - 1}\right)}$

and $\qquad u_{n+1} = \sqrt{\left(\frac{2^{n+1} - 1}{3^{n+1} - 1}\right)}$

Now, $\qquad \frac{u_n}{u_{n+1}} = \sqrt{\left(\frac{2^n - 1}{3^n - 1} \cdot \frac{3^{n+1} - 1}{2^{n+1} - 1}\right)}$

$$= \sqrt{\left\{\frac{2^n (1 - 1/2^n) \cdot 3^n (3 - 1/3^n)}{3^n (1 - 1/3^n) \cdot 2^n (2 - 1/2^n)}\right\}}$$

$$= \sqrt{\left(\frac{(1 - 1/2^n)(3 - 1/3^n)}{(1 - 1/3^n)(2 - 1/2^n)}\right)}$$

$$\therefore \quad \lim \frac{u_n}{u_{n+1}} = \sqrt{(3/2)}, \text{ which is} > 1.$$

Hence by ratio test the given series $\sum u_n$ is convergent.

Ex. 8 : *Test for convergence the series whose n^{th} term is $\dfrac{2^n}{n^3 + 1}$.*

Sol. : Here, $u_n = \dfrac{2^n}{n^3 + 1}$

and $u_{n+1} = \dfrac{2^{n+1}}{(n+1)^3 + 1}$

Now, $\dfrac{u_n}{u_{n+1}} = \dfrac{2^n}{n^3 + 1} \cdot \dfrac{(n+1)^3 + 1}{2^{n+1}}$

$= \dfrac{(1 + 1/n)^3 + 1/n^3}{(1 + 1/n^3) \cdot 2}$

$\lim \dfrac{u_n}{u_{n+1}} = \dfrac{1}{2}$, which is < 1.

Hence, by ratio test the given series is divergent.

V. Raabe's test : The series $\sum\limits_{n=1}^{\infty} u_n$ of positive terms : If $\underset{n \to \infty}{\text{Lt}}\; n\left(\dfrac{u_n}{u_{n+1}} - 1\right) = l$

then the series $\sum\limits_{n=1}^{\infty} u_n$ is convergent if $l > 1$ and divergent if $l < 1$.

If $l = 1$, the test fails.

Note : This test is generally applied when D'Alembert's ratio test fails.

ILLUSTRATIVE EXAMPLES

Ex. 1 : *Test for convergence the following series* $1 + \dfrac{1}{2} + \dfrac{1 \cdot 3}{2 \cdot 4} + \dfrac{1 \cdot 3 \cdot 5}{2 \cdot 4 \cdot 6} + \ldots$ **(May 2004)**

Sol. : $u_n = \dfrac{1 \cdot 3 \cdot 5 \ldots (2n-1)}{2 \cdot 4 \cdot 6 \ldots 2n} \quad \therefore \quad u_{n+1} = \dfrac{1 \cdot 3 \cdot 5 \ldots (2n-1)(2n+1)}{2 \cdot 4 \cdot 6 \ldots 2n (2n+2)}$

$\dfrac{u_n}{u_{n+1}} = \dfrac{2n+2}{2n+1} \quad \therefore \quad \underset{n \to \infty}{\text{Lt}} \dfrac{u_n}{u_{n+1}} = 1 \quad$ Ratio test fails.

Consider, $n\left(\dfrac{u_n}{u_{n+1}} - 1\right) = n\left(\dfrac{2n+2}{2n+1} - 1\right) = \dfrac{n}{2n+1}$

$\underset{n \to \infty}{\text{Lt}}\; n\left(\dfrac{u_n}{u_{n+1}} - 1\right) = \underset{n \to \infty}{\text{Lt}}\left(\dfrac{n}{2n+1}\right) = \dfrac{1}{2} < 1$

$\therefore$ By Raabe's test, $\sum u_n$ is divergent.

Ex. 2 : *Test for convergence the following series* $\sum \dfrac{1^2 \, 5^2 \, 9^2 \ldots (4n-3)^2}{4^2 \cdot 8^2 \cdot 12^2 \ldots (4n)^2}$. **(May 09, Dec. 09)**

Sol. : $u_n = \dfrac{1^2 \, 5^2 \ldots (4n-3)^2}{4^2 \, 8^2 \ldots (4n)^2} \quad \therefore \quad u_{n+1} = \dfrac{1^2 \, 5^2 \ldots (4n-3)^2 \, (4n+1)^2}{4^2 \, 8^2 \ldots (4n)^2 \, (4n+4)^2}$

$$\dfrac{u_n}{u_{n+1}} = \left(\dfrac{4n+4}{4n+1}\right)^2 \to 1, \text{ as } n \to \infty; \text{ Ratio test fails.}$$

$$\therefore \quad \lim_{n \to \infty} n\left(\dfrac{u_n}{u_{n+1}} - 1\right) = \lim_{n \to \infty} n\left(\dfrac{(4n+4)^2}{(4n+1)^2} - 1\right)$$

$$= \lim_{n \to \infty} n\left(\dfrac{24n+15}{16n^2+8n+1}\right)$$

$$= \lim_{n \to \infty} \left(\dfrac{24 + \dfrac{15}{n}}{16 + \dfrac{8}{n} + \dfrac{1}{n^2}}\right)$$

$$= \dfrac{24}{16} > 1$$

$\therefore$ By Raabe's test, $\sum u_n$ is convergent.

VI. Cauchy's condensation test : If the function $f(n)$ is positive for all positive integral values of n and continuously decreases as n increases, then the series $\sum\limits_{n=1}^{\infty} f(n)$ is convergent or divergent according as $\sum\limits_{n=1}^{\infty} a^n f(a^n)$ is convergent or divergent, "a" being a positive integer greater than unity.

Note : This test is applied when the series involves logarithmic expressions.

ILLUSTRATIVE EXAMPLE

Ex. 1 : *Test the convergence of the following series* $\dfrac{\log 2}{2} + \dfrac{\log 3}{3} + \dfrac{\log 4}{4} + \ldots$

Sol. : Let $f(n) = \dfrac{\log n}{n}$ which is positive for all positive integral values of n and decreases continually as n increases.

$$a^n f(a^n) = a^n \dfrac{\log a^n}{a^n} = n \log a$$

$$\sum a^n f(a^n) = \log a \sum n = \log a \, (1 + 2 + 3 + \ldots)$$

which is divergent as the series $1 + 2 + 3 + \ldots$ is divergent.

$\therefore$ By Cauchy's condensation test the given series,

$$\sum u_n = \sum \dfrac{\log n}{n} \text{ is also divergent.}$$

VII. The auxiliary series $\sum \dfrac{1}{n (\log n)^p}$:

The series $1 + \dfrac{1}{2 (\log 2)^p} + \dfrac{1}{3 (\log 3)^p} + \ldots\ldots + \dfrac{1}{n (\log n)^p} + \ldots$ is convergent if $p > 1$ and divergent if $p \leq 1$.

ILLUSTRATIVE EXAMPLES

Ex. 1 : *Test the convergence of the following series* $\sum_{n=2}^{\infty} \dfrac{1}{n \log n}$.

Sol. : $\sum u_n = \sum \dfrac{1}{n \log n}$ $\therefore$ Comparing with $\sum \dfrac{1}{n (\log n)^p}$, we have, $p = 1$.

$\therefore$ By using the auxiliary series $\sum \dfrac{1}{n (\log n)^p}$ the given series $\sum u_n$ is divergent.

Ex. 2 : *Test the convergence of the following series* $\sum \dfrac{n^{-1}}{\sqrt{\log n}}$.

Sol. : $\sum u_n = \dfrac{1}{n (\log n)^{1/2}}$

$\therefore$ Comparing with $\sum \dfrac{1}{n (\log n)^p}$ we have, $p = \dfrac{1}{2} < 1$ $\therefore$ by using the auxiliary series $\sum \dfrac{1}{n (\log n)^p}$ the given series $\sum u_n$ is divergent.

VIII. Gauss's test :

Let $\sum_{n=1}^{\infty} u_n$ be a series of positive terms and suppose that $\dfrac{u_n}{u_{n+1}}$ can be expressed in the form $\dfrac{u_n}{u_{n+1}} = 1 + \dfrac{l}{n} + \dfrac{b_n}{n^p}$, where $p > 1$ and b_n is bounded as $n \to \infty$ then $\sum_{n=1}^{\infty} u_n$ converges if $l > 1$ and diverges if $l \leq 1$.

ILLUSTRATIVE EXAMPLE

Ex. 1 : *Discuss the convergence or divergence of the series* $\dfrac{1^2}{2^2} + \dfrac{1^2 \cdot 3^2}{2^2 \cdot 4^2} + \dfrac{1^2 \cdot 3^2 \cdot 5^2}{2^2 \cdot 4^2 \cdot 6^2} + \ldots$

Sol. :
$$u_n = \left(\dfrac{1 \cdot 3 \cdot 5 \ldots (2n-1)}{2 \cdot 4 \cdot 6 \ldots 2n}\right)^2$$

$$u_{n+1} = \left(\dfrac{1 \cdot 3 \cdot 5 \ldots (2n-1)(2n+1)}{2 \cdot 4 \cdot 6 \ldots 2n \cdot (2n+2)}\right)^2$$

$$\frac{u_n}{u_{n+1}} = \left(\frac{2n+2}{2n+1}\right)^2 \to 1 \text{ as } n \to \infty \Rightarrow \text{Ratio test fails.}$$

$$n\left(\frac{u_n}{u_{n+1}} - 1\right) = n\left(\frac{(2n+2)^2}{(2n+1)^2} - 1\right)$$

$$= \frac{4n^2 + 3n}{4n^2 + 4n + 1} \to 1 \text{ as } n \to \infty \Rightarrow \text{Raabe's test fails.}$$

$$\therefore \quad \frac{u_n}{u_{n+1}} = \frac{4n^2 + 8n + 4}{4n^2 + 4n + 1} = 1 + \frac{4n+3}{4n^2 + 4n + 1}$$

$$= 1 + \frac{\frac{1}{n}(4n^2 + 4n + 1) - 1 - \frac{1}{n}}{4n^2 + 4n + 1}$$

$$= 1 + \frac{1}{n} - \frac{1 + \frac{1}{n}}{4n^2 + 4n + 1} = 1 + \frac{l}{n} + \frac{b_n}{n^p}$$

$\therefore \; l = 1, \qquad b_n = 1 + \dfrac{1}{n} \to 1 \text{ as } n \to \infty.$

∴ By Gauss's test the series is divergent.

IX. Logarithmic test : The series $\sum\limits_{n=1}^{\infty} u_n$ of positive terms is convergent or divergent according as $\underset{n \to \infty}{Lt}\left(n \log \dfrac{u_n}{u_{n+1}}\right) > 1$ or < 1.

Note : This test is an alternative to Raabe's test and is applied when D'Alembert's ratio test fails and when either

(i) n occurs as an exponent in $\dfrac{u_n}{u_{n+1}}$ or

(ii) taking logarithm of $\dfrac{u_n}{u_{n+1}}$ makes the evaluation of limits easier.

ILLUSTRATIVE EXAMPLES

Ex. 1 : *Test the series for convergence* $x + \dfrac{2^2 x^2}{2!} + \dfrac{3^3 x^3}{3!} + \dfrac{4^4 x^4}{4!} + \dfrac{5^5 x^5}{5!} + ...$

Sol : Here $\quad u_n = \dfrac{n^n}{n!} x^n$

and $\quad u_{n+1} = \dfrac{(n+1)^{n+1}}{(n+1)!} x^{n+1}$

Then,
$$\frac{u_n}{u_{n+1}} = \frac{n^n}{n!} \cdot \frac{(n+1)!}{(n+1)^{n+1}} \cdot \frac{1}{x}$$

$$= \frac{n^n(n+1)}{(n+1)^{n+1}} \cdot \frac{1}{x}$$

$$= \frac{1}{(1+1/n)^n} \cdot \frac{1}{x}$$

$$\therefore \quad \lim \frac{u_n}{u_{n+1}} = \lim \frac{1}{(1+1/n)^n} \cdot \frac{1}{x} = \frac{1}{ex}$$

∴ by ratio test the series is convergent if $1/ex > 1$, i.e., if $x < 1/e$ and the test fails when $1/ex = 1$, i.e., when $x = 1/e$.

When $x = \frac{1}{e}$, $\quad \frac{u_n}{u_{n+1}} = \frac{e}{(1+1/n)^n}$

Applying log test, we have,

$$\lim \left(n \log \frac{u_n}{u_{n+1}} \right) = \lim \left\{ n \log \frac{e}{(1+1/n)^n} \right\}$$

$$= \lim n \left[\log e - n \log(1 + 1/n) \right]$$

$$= \lim n \left[1 - n \left(\frac{1}{n} - \frac{1}{2n^2} + \frac{1}{3n^3} + \cdots \right) \right]$$

$$= \lim \left(\frac{1}{2} - \frac{1}{3n} + \cdots \right) = \frac{1}{2} < 1.$$

∴ The series is divergent.

Hence, the given series is convergent if $x < 1/e$ and divergent if $x \geq 1/e$.

X. De Morgan's or Bertrand's test : The series $\sum\limits_{n=1}^{\infty} u_n$ of positive terms is convergent or divergent according as $\underset{n \to \infty}{\text{Lt}} \left[\left\{ n \left(\frac{u_n}{u_{n+1}} - 1 \right) - 1 \right\} \log n \right] > 1$ or < 1.

Note : This test is to be applied when both D'Alembert's ratio test and Raabe's test fail.

Altr : The series $\sum\limits_{n=1}^{\infty} u_n$ is convergent or divergent according as

$$\underset{n \to \infty}{\text{Lt}} \left[\left(n \log \frac{u_n}{u_{n+1}} - 1 \right) \log n \right] > 1 \text{ or } < 1.$$

ILLUSTRATIVE EXAMPLE

Ex. 1 : Test the convergence of the series : $\dfrac{a}{b} + \dfrac{a(a+1)}{b(b+1)} + \dfrac{a(a+1)(a+2)}{b(b+1)(b+2)} + \ldots$

Sol. : Here, $u_n = \dfrac{a(a+1)(a+2)\ldots(a+n-1)}{b(b+1)(b+2)\ldots(b+n-1)}$

and $u_{n+1} = \dfrac{a(a+1)(a+2)\ldots(a+n-1)(a+n)}{b(b+1)\ldots(b+n-1)(b+n)}$

Then, $\dfrac{u_n}{u_{n+1}} = \dfrac{b+n}{a+n} = \dfrac{b/n+1}{a/n+1}$

$\therefore \lim \dfrac{u_n}{u_{n+1}} = \lim \left(\dfrac{b/n+1}{a/n+1}\right) = 1$

So that the ratio test fails.

Now, $n\left(\dfrac{u_n}{u_{n+1}} - 1\right) = n\left(\dfrac{b+n}{a+n} - 1\right)$

$= \dfrac{n(b-a)}{a+n} = \dfrac{b-a}{a/n+1}$

$\therefore \lim\left[n\left(\dfrac{u_n}{u_{n+1}} - 1\right)\right] = \dfrac{b-a}{1}$

$= (b-a)$

$\therefore$ by Raabe's test the series is convergent if $b - a > 1$ i.e., if $b > a + 1$, divergent if $b - a < 1$. i.e., if $b < a + 1$ and the test fails when $b - a = 1$, i.e. when $b = a + 1$.

When $b = a + 1$, then we have,

$$n\left(\dfrac{u_n}{u_{n+1}} - 1\right) = \dfrac{n}{a+n}$$

$\therefore \lim\left[\left\{n\left(\dfrac{u_n}{u_{n+1}} - 1\right) - 1\right\}\log n\right] = \lim\left[\left(\dfrac{n}{a+n} - 1\right)\log n\right]$

$= \lim\left[\left(\dfrac{-a}{a+n}\right)\log n\right]$

$= \lim\left[\left(\dfrac{-a}{a/n+1}\right)\cdot\dfrac{\log n}{n}\right]$

$= \dfrac{-a}{1}\cdot 0 = 0 < 1.$

$\therefore$ by DeMorgan's test the series $\sum u_n$ is divergent when $b = a + 1$.

Hence, the given series $\sum u_n$ is convergent if $b > a + 1$ and divergent if $b \leq a + 1$.

XI. Cauchy's integral test : Let $\sum_{n=1}^{\infty} u_n = \sum_{n=1}^{\infty} f(n)$ be a series of positive terms where $f(n)$ decreases as n increases and let $I = \int_{1}^{\infty} f(x)\, dx$ then

(i) If I is finite then $\sum_{n=1}^{\infty} u_n$ is convergent

(ii) If $I = \infty$ then $\sum_{n=1}^{\infty} u_n$ is divergent.

ILLUSTRATIVE EXAMPLE

Ex. 1 : *Show that the harmonic series of order p,* $\sum_{n=1}^{\infty} \dfrac{1}{n^p} = \dfrac{1}{1^p} + \dfrac{1}{2^p} + \dfrac{1}{3^p} + \ldots \infty$.

converges for $p > 1$ and diverges for $p \leq 1$.

Sol. : If $p \neq 1$,

$$\int_{1}^{\infty} \frac{dx}{x^p} = \lim_{m \to \infty} \int_{1}^{m} \frac{dx}{x^p}$$

$$= \lim_{m \to \infty} \left[\frac{x^{-p+1}}{-p+1} \right]_{1}^{m}$$

$$= \lim_{m \to \infty} \left[\frac{m^{1-p} - 1}{1-p} \right]$$

$$= \frac{1}{p-1} \text{ i.e. finite} \qquad \text{for } p > 1$$

$$= \infty \qquad\qquad\qquad \text{for } p < 1$$

If $p = 1$,

$$\int_{1}^{\infty} \frac{dx}{x} = \int_{1}^{\infty} \log x \to \infty, \text{ this proves the result.}$$

Ex. 2 : *Test for convergence the series* $\sum \dfrac{1}{n^2 + 1}$.

Sol. : Here, $u_n = \dfrac{1}{n^2 + 1} = f(n)$

$\therefore \qquad f(x) = \dfrac{1}{x^2 + 1}$

Engineering Mathematics – I Infinite Series

For $x \geq 1$, $f(x)$ is +ve and monotonic decreasing.

$\therefore$ Cauchy's Integral Test is applicable.

Now, $\quad \int_1^\infty f(x)\,dx = \int_1^\infty \dfrac{dx}{x^2+1} = [\tan^{-1} x]_1^\infty$

$$= \dfrac{\pi}{2} - \dfrac{\pi}{4}$$

$$= \dfrac{\pi}{4} = \text{finite}$$

$\Rightarrow \int_1^\infty f(x)\,dx$ converges and hence by integral test, $\sum u_n$ also converges.

6.7 ALTERNATING SERIES

An infinite series in which the terms are alternately positive and negative is called an alternating series.

e.g. $1 - \dfrac{1}{2} + \dfrac{1}{3} - \dfrac{1}{4} + \ldots = \sum_{n=1}^\infty (-1)^{n-1} \dfrac{1}{n}$ is an alternating series.

Leibnitz test (Alternating series test):

An infinite series $\sum_{n=1}^\infty (-1)^{n-1} u_n$ in which the terms are alternately positive and negative is convergent if

(i) each term of the series is numerically less than the preceding term and

(ii) $\underset{n \to \infty}{\text{Lt}}\; u_n = 0$.

ILLUSTRATIVE EXAMPLE

Ex. 1: *Examine the convergence of the series*

$$\dfrac{1}{2^2} - \dfrac{1}{3^3}(1+2) + \dfrac{1}{4^3}(1+2+3) - \dfrac{1}{5^3}(1+2+3+4) + \ldots$$

Sol.: It is an alternating series:

(i) $\quad u_n = \dfrac{1}{(n+1)^3} [1 + 2 + 3 + \ldots + n]$

$$= \dfrac{1}{(n+1)^3} \cdot \dfrac{n(n+1)}{2} = \dfrac{1}{2} \cdot \dfrac{n}{(n+1)^2}$$

$$u_{n+1} = \dfrac{1}{2} \cdot \dfrac{n+1}{(n+2)^2}$$

$$u_n - u_{n+1} = \frac{1}{2}\left[\frac{n}{(n+1)^2} - \frac{n+1}{(n+2)^2}\right] = \frac{1}{2} \frac{n(n+2)^2 - (n+1)^3}{(n+1)^2(n+2)^2}$$

$$= \frac{1}{2} \cdot \frac{n^2 + n - 1}{(n+1)^2(n+2)^2} > 0 \text{ for all } n.$$

$$\Rightarrow \qquad u_n > u_{n+1} \ \forall \ n.$$

(ii) $\displaystyle \lim_{n \to \infty} u_n = \lim_{n \to \infty} \frac{n}{2(n+1)^2} = \lim_{n \to \infty} \frac{\frac{1}{n}}{2\left(1+\frac{1}{n}\right)^2} = 0.$

Since, both the conditions of Lebnitz's test are satisfied, the given series is convergent.

Ex. 2 : *Show that the series* $1 - \frac{1}{2} + \frac{1}{3} - \frac{1}{4} + \frac{1}{5} - \ldots$ *is convergent.*

Sol. : The given series is $1 - \frac{1}{2} + \frac{1}{3} - \frac{1}{4} + \frac{1}{5} - \ldots$ i.e., $\Sigma (-1)^{n-1}(1/n)$ or say $\Sigma (-1)^{n-1} u_n$, where $u_n = 1/n$. In this series :

(i) The terms are alternately positive and negative.

(ii) Clearly $1 > \frac{1}{2} > \frac{1}{3} > \frac{1}{4} > \frac{1}{5} \ldots$ i.e., $u_1 > u_2 > u_3 > \ldots$

i.e., each term of the series is numerically less than the preceding term and

(iii) $\lim u_n = \lim \frac{1}{n} = \frac{1}{\infty} = 0.$

Thus all the three conditions of the Leibnitz's test are satisfied.
Hence, the given series is convergent.

Ex. 3 : *Test the convergence of the series* $1 - \frac{1}{\sqrt{2}} + \frac{1}{\sqrt{3}} - \frac{1}{\sqrt{4}} + \ldots$ **(Dec. 2014)**

Sol. : The given series

$$1 - \frac{1}{\sqrt{2}} + \frac{1}{\sqrt{3}} - \frac{1}{\sqrt{4}} + \ldots = \Sigma (-1)^{n-1} \cdot \frac{1}{\sqrt{n}}$$

$$= \Sigma (-1)^{n-1}, u_n \text{ say.}$$

Now we see that

(i) The terms of the given series are alternately positive and negative.

(ii) Clearly $1 > \frac{1}{\sqrt{2}} > \frac{1}{\sqrt{3}} > \frac{1}{\sqrt{4}} > \ldots$ i.e. $u_1 > u_2 > u_3 > \ldots$

i.e., each term of the series is numerically less than the preceding term and

(iii) $\lim u_n = \lim \frac{1}{\sqrt{n}} = \frac{1}{\infty} = 0.$

Thus all the three conditions of the Leibnitz's test are satisfied.
Hence, the given series is convergent.

6.8 ABSOLUTE CONVERGENCE

The series $\sum_{n=1}^{\infty} u_n$ which contains both the positive and negative terms is said to be absolutely convergent if the series $\sum_{n=1}^{\infty} |u_n|$ is convergent.

e.g. $\sum u_n = 1 - \frac{1}{2} + \frac{1}{2^2} - \frac{1}{2^3} + \ldots$ is an absolutely convergent series.

6.9 CONDITIONAL CONVERGENCE

If the alternating series $\sum_{n=1}^{\infty} u_n$ is convergent but the series $\sum_{n=1}^{\infty} |u_n|$ is divergent, then the series $\sum_{n=1}^{\infty} u_n$ is said to be conditionally convergent.

e.g. $\sum u_n = 1 - \frac{1}{2} + \frac{1}{3} - \frac{1}{4} + \ldots$ is convergent

and $\sum |u_n| = 1 + \frac{1}{2} + \ldots + \frac{1}{n} + \ldots$ is divergent.

Given series is conditionally convergent.

Important deductions :
1. In an absolutely convergent series with positive and negative terms, (i) the series formed by its positive terms alone is convergent, (ii) the series formed by its negative terms alone is convergent.
2. If the terms of an absolutely convergent series are rearranged, the series remains convergent and its sum is unaltered.

Summary of testing a series for convergence :

1. Let the given series $\sum_{n=1}^{\infty} u_n$ is a series with terms alternately positive and negative always apply Leibnitz's test.

2. Let the given series of positive terms be $\sum_{n=1}^{\infty} u_n$.

    Find : $\underset{n \to \infty}{Lt} u_n$.

    (a) If $\underset{n \to \infty}{Lt} u_n > 0 \Rightarrow$ series is divergent

    (b) $\underset{n \to \infty}{Lt} u_n = 0 \Rightarrow$ Series may or may not be convergent, needs further investigation.

3. $\underset{n \to \infty}{Lt} u_n = 0$ and u_n can be arranged as an algebraic fraction in n then apply comparison test.

4. If n occurs as an exponent in u_n and $\underset{n \to \infty}{Lt} (u_n)^{1/n}$ can be evaluated easily then apply Cauchy's n^{th} root test.

5. When u_n involves log n then Cauchy's condensation test may be applied.
   In case all the above tests fail, then adopt the following order.

6. D'Alembert's ratio test : Find $\underset{n \to \infty}{Lt} \dfrac{u_n}{u_{n+1}}$ then $\sum_{n=1}^{\infty} u_n$ is convergent or divergent according as this limit is > 1 or < 1.
   If this limit is = 1 $\Rightarrow$ this test fails.

   In this case, apply tests 7, 8, 9 or 10 depending upon the nature of u_n and $\dfrac{u_n}{u_{n+1}}$.

7. Comparison test : When ratio test fails, use comparison test.

8. Raabe's test : Find $\underset{n \to \infty}{Lt} n\left(\dfrac{u_n}{u_{n+1}} - 1\right)$.

   If this limit is > 1 or < 1 $\Rightarrow$ series is convergent or divergent. If this limit is = 1, apply test 10. If Raabe's test fails, use Gauss test.

9. Gauss test : Express $\dfrac{u_n}{u_{n+1}}$ in the form $\dfrac{u_n}{u_{n+1}} = 1 + \dfrac{l}{n} + \dfrac{b_n}{n^p}$ where p > 1, b_n is bounded as $n \to \infty$ then $\sum_{n=1}^{\infty} u_n$ converges if $l > 1$ and diverges if $l \leq 1$.

10. Logarithmic test : When $\dfrac{u_n}{u_{n+1}} - 1$ cannot be evaluated easily while $\log \dfrac{u_n}{u_{n+1}}$ can be easily evaluated then apply logarithmic test.
    Find $\underset{n \to \infty}{Lt} n \log \dfrac{u_n}{u_{n+1}}$. The series is convergent or divergent according as this limit is > 1 or < 1. If this limit = 1, apply test 11.

11. De Morgan's or Bertrand's test : Find $\underset{n \to \infty}{Lt} \left\{\left(n\left(\dfrac{u_n}{u_{n+1}} - 1\right) - 1\right) \log n\right\}$.

    The series is convergent or divergent according as this limit is > 1 or < 1.

12. Alternative to De Morgan's test : Find $\underset{n \to \infty}{Lt} \left[\left(n \log \dfrac{u_n}{u_{n+1}} - 1\right) \log n\right]$.

    The series is convergent or divergent according as this limit is > 1 or < 1.

6.10 WEIERSTRASS'S M-TEST

A series $\sum_{n=1}^{\infty} u_n(x)$ of functions converges uniformly and absolutely on an interval I if there exists a convergent series $\sum_{n=1}^{\infty} M_n$ of positive constants such that

$$|u_n(x)| \le M_n, \quad \forall\, n \in N \text{ and } \forall\, x \in I.$$

6.11 POWER SERIES AND RANGE OF CONVERGENCE

Definition : A series of the form

$$a_0 + a_1(x-c) + a_2(x-c)^2 + \ldots + a_n(x-c)^n + \ldots = \sum_{n=0}^{\infty} a_n(x-c)^n$$

where $a_0, a_1, a_2, \ldots, a_n$'s are independent of x, is called a **"power series"** in x.

Many functions can be expanded into power series which is valid only if the power series is convergent.

Range of convergence : If for all values of x between $x = l_1$ and $x = l_2$, the power series is convergent and beyond this range it is divergent for values of x then $l_1 \le x \le l_2$ is defined as the **range of convergence** of the power series $\sum_{n=0}^{\infty} a_n(x-c)^n$.

To determine the range of convergence of the power series we use ratio test.

$$\underset{n \to \infty}{Lt} \left| \frac{u_{n+1}}{u_n} \right| = \underset{n \to \infty}{Lt} \left| \frac{a_{n+1}(x-c)^{n+1}}{a_n(x-c)^n} \right| = \underset{n \to \infty}{Lt} \left| \frac{a_{n+1}}{a_n} \right| |x-c| = L$$

Let, $\quad \underset{n \to \infty}{Lt} \left| \frac{a_{n+1}}{a_n} \right| = M$

$\therefore \quad M\,|x-c| = L$

If $L < 1$ the series is convergent for $|x-c| < \dfrac{1}{M}$ and if $L > 1$ the series is divergent for $|x-c| > \dfrac{1}{M}$.

$\therefore$ The range of convergence for the power series is

$$-\frac{1}{M} < |x-c| < \frac{1}{M}$$

$\therefore \quad c - \dfrac{1}{M} < |x| < c + \dfrac{1}{M}$

Here the distance $\dfrac{1}{m}$ is called as **"circle of convergence"**.

ADDITIONAL SOLVED EXAMPLES

Ex. 1 : *Test the convergence of the series*
$$\left(\frac{2^2}{1^2} - \frac{2}{1}\right)^{-1} + \left(\frac{3^3}{2^3} - \frac{3}{2}\right)^{-2} + \left(\frac{4^4}{3^4} - \frac{4}{3}\right)^{-3} + \ldots$$

Sol. : Here, $\quad u_n = \left[\frac{(n+1)^{n+1}}{n^{n+1}} - \frac{n+1}{n}\right]^{-n}$

$\therefore \quad (u_n)^{1/n} = \left[\left(\frac{n+1}{n}\right)^{n+1} - \frac{n+1}{n}\right]^{-1}$

$\qquad = \left(\frac{n+1}{n}\right)^{-1} \left[\left\{\frac{n+1}{n}\right\}^n - 1\right]^{-1} = \left\{1 + \frac{1}{n}\right\}^{-1} \left[\left\{1 + \frac{1}{n}\right\}^n - 1\right]^{-1}$

$\therefore \quad \lim (u_n)^{1/n} = (1+0)^{-1} [e-1]^{-1}$

$\qquad = \frac{1}{e-1} < 1 \qquad\qquad (\because e = 2.718 \ldots)$

Hence, by root test the series is convergent.

Ex. 2 : *Test the convergence of the series* $1 + \frac{4}{2!} + \frac{4^2}{3!} + \frac{4^3}{4!} + \frac{4^4}{5!} + \frac{4^5}{6!} + \frac{4^6}{7!} + \ldots$

Sol. : Here, $\quad u_n = \frac{4^{n-1}}{n!} \quad$ and $\quad u_{n+1} = \frac{4^n}{(n+1)!}$

$\therefore \quad \frac{u_n}{u_{n+1}} = \frac{4^{n-1}}{n!} \cdot \frac{(n+1)!}{4^n} = \frac{n+1}{4}$

We have, $\quad \lim \frac{u_n}{u_{n+1}} = \lim \frac{n+1}{4} = \infty$, which is > 1.

$\therefore \quad$ By ratio test, the given series is convergent.

Ex. 3 : *Test the convergence of the series* $\frac{1}{3^p} + \frac{1}{5^p} + \frac{1}{7^p} + \frac{1}{9^p} + \ldots$

Sol. : Here, $\quad \Sigma u_n = \frac{1}{3^p} + \frac{1}{5^p} + \frac{1}{7^p} + \ldots = \Sigma \frac{1}{(2n+1)^p}$

So that, $\quad u_n = \frac{1}{(2n+1)^p}$

$\therefore$ let, $\quad v_n = \frac{1}{n^p}$

Now, $\quad \lim \frac{u_n}{v_n} = \lim \left\{\frac{1}{(2n+1)^p} \cdot n^p\right\} = \lim \frac{1}{(2+1/n)^p} = \frac{1}{2^p}$,

which is finite and non-zero.

But the auxiliary series $\Sigma v_n = \Sigma \frac{1}{n^p}$ is convergent if $p > 1$ and divergent if $p \leq 1$.

Hence, by comparison test the given series is convergent if $p > 1$ and divergent if $p \leq 1$.

Ex. 4 : *Test the convergence of the series* $\dfrac{1}{1+\sqrt{2}} + \dfrac{2}{1+2\sqrt{3}} + \dfrac{3}{1+3\sqrt{4}} + \ldots$ **(May 2011)**

Sol. : Here, $\sum u_n = \dfrac{1}{1+\sqrt{2}} + \dfrac{2}{1+2\sqrt{3}} + \dfrac{3}{1+3\sqrt{4}} + \ldots$

$$= \sum \dfrac{n}{1 + n\sqrt{(n+1)}}$$

i.e. $u_n = \dfrac{n}{1 + n\sqrt{(n+1)}}$

$\therefore$ let $v_n = \dfrac{n}{n\sqrt{n}} = \dfrac{1}{n^{1/2}}$

Now, $\lim \dfrac{u_n}{v_n} = \lim \left\{ \dfrac{n}{1 + n\sqrt{(n+1)}} \cdot n^{1/2} \right\} = \lim \left\{ \dfrac{1}{1/n^{3/2} + \sqrt{1 + 1/n}} \right\}$

$= 1$, which is finite and non-zero.

But the auxiliary series $\sum v_n = \sum \dfrac{1}{n^{1/2}}$ is divergent as here $p = \dfrac{1}{2} < 1$.

Hence by comparison test the given series is divergent.

Ex. 5 : *Test the series for convergence whose n^{th} term is given by,*
$$u_n = \sqrt{(n^3 + 1)} - \sqrt{n^3}$$

Sol. : Here, $u_n = \sqrt{(n^3 + 1)} - \sqrt{n^3}$

$$= n^{3/2} \left[\left(1 + \dfrac{1}{n^3}\right)^{1/2} - 1 \right]$$

$$= n^{3/2} \left[1 + \dfrac{1}{2n^3} + \dfrac{\frac{1}{2}\left(\frac{1}{2}-1\right)}{2!} \cdot \dfrac{1}{n^6} + \ldots - 1 \right] = \dfrac{1}{2n^{3/2}} - \dfrac{1}{8n^{9/2}} + \ldots$$

Taking the lowest power of $1/n$ in u_n, the auxiliary series is given by,

$$\sum v_n = \sum \dfrac{1}{n^{3/2}}$$

Now, $\lim \dfrac{u_n}{v_n} = \lim \left\{ \left(\dfrac{1}{2n^{3/2}} - \dfrac{1}{8n^{9/2}} + \ldots \right) \cdot n^{3/2} \right\} = \lim \left(\dfrac{1}{2} - \dfrac{1}{8n^3} + \ldots \right)$

$= \dfrac{1}{2}$, which is finite and non-zero.

But the auxiliary series $\sum v_n = \sum \dfrac{1}{n^{3/2}}$ is convergent as here $p = \dfrac{3}{2} > 1$.

Hence, by comparison test the given series $\sum u_n$ is convergent.

Ex. 6 : *Test the series whose n^{th} term is given by,*

Sol. : $u_n = \dfrac{\sqrt{(n+1)} - \sqrt{n}}{n^p} = \dfrac{\sqrt{n}}{n^p} \left[\left(1 + \dfrac{1}{n}\right)^{1/2} - 1 \right]$

$$= \frac{1}{n^{p-1/2}}\left[1 + \frac{1}{2n} + \frac{\frac{1}{2}\left(\frac{1}{2}-1\right)}{2!} \cdot \frac{1}{n^2} + \ldots - 1\right]$$

$$= \frac{1}{2n^{p+1/2}} - \frac{1}{8n^{p+3/2}} + \ldots$$

Taking the lowest power of $1/n$ in u_n the auxiliary series is given by,

$$\Sigma \, v_n = \Sigma \, \frac{1}{n^{p+1/2}}$$

Now, $$\lim \frac{u_n}{v_n} = \lim\left\{\left(\frac{1}{2n^{p+1/2}} - \frac{1}{8n^{p+3/2}} + \ldots\right) \cdot n^{p+1/2}\right\}$$

$$= \lim\left(\frac{1}{2} - \frac{1}{8n} + \ldots\right)$$

$$= \frac{1}{2}, \text{ which is finite and non-zero.}$$

But the auxiliary series $\Sigma \, v_n = \Sigma \, \frac{1}{n^{p+1/2}}$ is convergent if $p + \frac{1}{2} > 1$. i.e. if $p > \frac{1}{2}$ and divergent if $p + \frac{1}{2} \le 1$ i.e. if $p \le \frac{1}{2}$.

Hence, by comparison test the given series is convergent if $p > \frac{1}{2}$ and divergent if $p \le \frac{1}{2}$.

Ex. 7 : *Test the series whose n^{th} term is given by* $u_n = \sqrt{(n+1)} - \sqrt{(n-1)}$.

Sol. : Here, $\quad u_n = \sqrt{(n+1)} - \sqrt{(n-1)}$

$$= \sqrt{n\left[\left(1+\frac{1}{n}\right)^{1/2} - \left(1-\frac{1}{n}\right)^{1/2}\right]}$$

$$= \sqrt{n\left[\left\{1 + \frac{1}{2}\cdot\frac{1}{n} + \frac{\frac{1}{2}\left(\frac{1}{2}-1\right)}{2!} \cdot \frac{1}{n^2} + \frac{\frac{1}{2}\left(\frac{1}{2}-1\right)\left(\frac{1}{2}-2\right)}{3!} \cdot \frac{1}{n^3} + \ldots\right\}\right.}$$

$$\left.- \left\{1 - \frac{1}{2}\cdot\frac{1}{n} + \frac{\frac{1}{2}\left(\frac{1}{2}-1\right)}{2!} \cdot \frac{1}{n^2} - \frac{\frac{1}{2}\left(\frac{1}{2}-1\right)\left(\frac{1}{2}-2\right)}{3!} \cdot \frac{1}{n^3} + \ldots\right\}\right]$$

$$= \sqrt{n\left[2\left(\frac{1}{2n} + \frac{1}{16n^3} + \ldots\right)\right]}$$

$$= \frac{1}{n^{1/2}} + \frac{1}{8n^{5/2}} + \ldots$$

Taking the lowest power $\dfrac{1}{n}$ in u_n, the auxiliary series is given by,

$$\sum v_n = \sum \dfrac{1}{n^{1/2}}$$

Now, $\lim \dfrac{u_n}{v_n} = \lim \left\{\left(\dfrac{1}{n^{1/2}} + \dfrac{1}{8n^{5/2}} + \ldots\right) \cdot n^{1/2}\right\} = \lim \left(1 + \dfrac{1}{8n^2} + \ldots\right)$

$= 1$, which is finite and non-zero.

But the auxiliary series $\sum v_n = \sum \dfrac{1}{n^{1/2}}$ is divergent as here $p = \dfrac{1}{2} < 1$. Hence, by comparison test the given series is divergent.

Ex. 8 : *Test the series whose n^{th} term is given by*

$$u_n = \sqrt{(n^4 + 1)} - \sqrt{(n^4 - 1)} .$$

Sol. : Here, $u_n = \sqrt{(n^4 + 1)} - \sqrt{(n^4 - 1)}$

$= n^2 \left[\left(1 + \dfrac{1}{n^4}\right)^{1/2} - \left(1 - \dfrac{1}{n^4}\right)^{1/2}\right]$

$= n^2\left[\left\{1 + \dfrac{1}{2}\cdot\dfrac{1}{n^4} + \dfrac{\frac{1}{2}\cdot\left(\frac{1}{2}-1\right)}{2!}\cdot\dfrac{1}{n^8} + \dfrac{\frac{1}{2}\left(\frac{1}{2}-1\right)\left(\frac{1}{2}-2\right)}{3!}\dfrac{1}{n^{12}} + \ldots\right\}\right.$

$\left. - \left\{1 - \dfrac{1}{2}\cdot\dfrac{1}{n^4} + \dfrac{\frac{1}{2}\left(\frac{1}{2}-1\right)}{2!}\cdot\dfrac{1}{n^8} - \dfrac{\frac{1}{2}\left(\frac{1}{2}-1\right)\left(\frac{1}{2}-2\right)}{3!}\cdot\dfrac{1}{n^{12}} + \ldots\right\}\right]$

$= n^2\left[2\left\{\dfrac{1}{2n^4} + \dfrac{1}{16n^{12}} + \ldots\right\}\right]$

$= \dfrac{1}{n^2} + \dfrac{1}{8n^{10}} + \ldots$

Taking the lowest power of $1/n$ in u_n the auxiliary series is given by,

$$\sum v_n = \sum \dfrac{1}{n^2}$$

Now, $\lim \dfrac{u_n}{v_n} = \lim \left[\left\{\dfrac{1}{n^2} + \dfrac{1}{8n^{10}} + \ldots\right\} n^2\right]$

$= \lim \left\{1 + \dfrac{1}{8n^8} + \ldots\right\}$

$= 1$, which is finite and non-zero.

But the auxiliary series $\sum u_n = \sum \dfrac{1}{n^2}$ is convergent as here $p = 2 > 1$.

Hence by comparison test the given series is convergent.

Ex. 9 : *Test for convergence the following series* $\sum_{1}^{\infty} \left[\dfrac{\sqrt{(n^2+n+1)} - \sqrt{n^2-n+1}}{n} \right]$

(Dec. 2008)

Sol. : Here,
$$u_n = \dfrac{1}{n}\left[\sqrt{(n^2+n+1)} - \sqrt{(n^2-n+1)}\right]$$

$$= \dfrac{1}{n}\cdot n\left[\left\{1+\left(\dfrac{1}{n}+\dfrac{1}{n^2}\right)\right\}^{1/2} - \left\{1+\left(-\dfrac{1}{n}+\dfrac{1}{n^2}\right)\right\}^{1/2}\right]$$

$$= \left[\left\{1+\dfrac{1}{2}\left(\dfrac{1}{n}+\dfrac{1}{n^2}\right) - \dfrac{1}{8}\left(\dfrac{1}{n}+\dfrac{1}{n^2}\right)^2 + \ldots\right\}\right.$$

$$\left. -\left\{1+\dfrac{1}{2}\left(-\dfrac{1}{n}+\dfrac{1}{n^2}\right) - \dfrac{1}{8}\left(-\dfrac{1}{n}+\dfrac{1}{n^2}\right)^2 + \ldots\right\}\right]$$

$$= \dfrac{1}{n} - \dfrac{1}{2n^3} + \ldots$$

Taking the lowest power of $1/n$ in u_n, the auxiliary series is given by,

$$\sum v_n = \sum 1/n$$

Now, $\lim \dfrac{u_n}{v_n} = \lim \left(\dfrac{1}{n} - \dfrac{1}{2n^3} + \ldots\right)\cdot n = \lim\left(1 - \dfrac{1}{2n^2} + \ldots\right)$

$= 1$, which is finite and non-zero.

But the auxiliary series $\sum u_n = \sum 1/n$ is divergent as here $p = 1$.

Hence, by comparison test the given series is divergent.

Ex. 10 : *Test the series for convergence whose n^{th} term is given by* $u_n = \dfrac{1}{\sqrt{n}+\sqrt{(n+1)}}$.

Sol. : Here, $u_n = \dfrac{1}{\sqrt{n}+\sqrt{(n+1)}} = \dfrac{\sqrt{n}-\sqrt{(n+1)}}{n-(n+1)} = \sqrt{(n+1)} - \sqrt{n}$

$$= \sqrt{n}\left[\left(1+\dfrac{1}{n}\right)^{1/2} - 1\right]$$

$$= \sqrt{n}\left[1 + \dfrac{1}{2}\cdot\dfrac{1}{n} - \dfrac{1}{8}\cdot\dfrac{1}{n^2} + \ldots - 1\right]$$

$$= \dfrac{1}{2n^{1/2}} - \dfrac{1}{8n^{3/2}} + \ldots$$

Taking the lowest power of $1/n$ in u_n, the auxiliary series is given by $\sum v_n = \sum \dfrac{1}{n^{1/2}}$.

Now, $\lim \dfrac{u_n}{v_n} = \lim\left[\left\{\dfrac{1}{2n^{1/2}} - \dfrac{1}{8n^{3/2}} + \ldots\right\}\cdot n^{1/2}\right]$

$$= \lim\left\{\dfrac{1}{2} - \dfrac{1}{8n} + \ldots\right\}$$

$$= \dfrac{1}{2} \text{, which is finite and non-zero.}$$

But the auxiliary series $\sum v_n = \sum \frac{1}{n^{1/2}}$ is divergent as here $p = \frac{1}{2} < 1$.

Hence, by comparison test the given series is divergent.

Ex. 11 : *Test the series for convergence whose n^{th} term is given by,*

$$u_n = \frac{1}{n} - \log\left(\frac{n+1}{n}\right).$$

Sol. : Here, $u_n = \frac{1}{n} - \log\left\{\frac{n+1}{n}\right\} = \frac{1}{n} - \log\left\{1 + \frac{1}{n}\right\}$

$$= \frac{1}{n} - \left\{\frac{1}{n} - \frac{1}{2n^2} + \frac{1}{3n^3} - \cdots\right\} = \frac{1}{2n^2} - \frac{1}{3n^3} + \cdots$$

The lowest power of $\frac{1}{n}$ in u_n is $\frac{1}{n^2}$. Therefore to apply the comparison test the auxiliary series is taken as,

$$\sum v_n = \sum \frac{1}{n^2}$$

Now, $\lim \frac{u_n}{v_n} = \lim \left\{\frac{1}{2} - \frac{1}{3n} + \cdots\right\}$

$$= \frac{1}{2}, \text{ which is finite and non-zero.}$$

But auxiliary series $\sum v_n = \sum \frac{1}{n^2}$ is convergent as here $p = 2 > 1$.

Hence, by comparison test the given series is convergent.

Ex. 12 : *Test the series for convergence whose n^{th} term is* (Dec. 2012)

$$u_n = \left(\frac{1}{n}\right) \sin\left(\frac{1}{n}\right)$$

Sol. : Here, $u_n = \frac{1}{n} \sin \frac{1}{n} = \frac{1}{n}\left(\frac{1}{n} - \frac{1}{3!} \cdot \frac{1}{n^3} + \frac{1}{5!} \cdot \frac{1}{n^5} - \cdots\right)$

$$= \frac{1}{n^2} - \frac{1}{3!} \cdot \frac{1}{n^4} + \frac{1}{5! \, n^6} - \cdots$$

Taking the lowest power of $\frac{1}{n}$ in u_n, the auxiliary series is given by,

$$\sum v_n = \sum \frac{1}{n^2}.$$

Now, $\lim \frac{u_n}{v_n} = \lim \left\{1 - \frac{1}{3! \, n^2} + \frac{1}{5! \, n^4} - \cdots\right\} = 1$

which is finite and non-zero.

But the auxiliary series $\sum v_n = \sum \frac{1}{n^2}$ is convergent, as here $p = 2 > 1$.

Hence, by comparison test the given series is convergent.

Ex. 13 : *Test the series for convergence whose n^{th} term is*
$$u_n = \cos\left(\frac{1}{n}\right).$$

Sol. : Here, $u_n = \cos\left(\frac{1}{n}\right) = 1 - \frac{1}{2!}\cdot\frac{1}{n^2} + \frac{1}{4!}\cdot\frac{1}{n^4} - \ldots$

$$= \frac{1}{n^0} - \frac{1}{2!}\cdot\frac{1}{n^2} + \frac{1}{4!}\cdot\frac{1}{n^4} - \ldots$$

Taking the lowest power of $\frac{1}{n}$ in u_n, the auxiliary series is given by,

$$\Sigma\, v_n = \Sigma\, \frac{1}{n^0}$$

Now, $\quad \lim \dfrac{u_n}{v_n} = \lim\left\{1 - \dfrac{1}{2!}\dfrac{1}{n^2} + \dfrac{1}{4!\,n^4} - \ldots\right\}$

$\qquad\qquad = 1$, which is finite and non-zero.

But the auxiliary series $\Sigma\, v_n = \Sigma\, \dfrac{1}{n^0}$ is divergent as here $p = 0 < 1$.

Hence, by comparison test the given series is divergent.

Ex. 14 : *Test the series for convergence whose n^{th} term is*
$$u_n = \frac{1}{\sqrt{n}}\tan\left(\frac{1}{n}\right)$$

Sol. : Here, $u_n = \dfrac{1}{\sqrt{n}}\tan\left(\dfrac{1}{n}\right)$

$\qquad = \dfrac{1}{\sqrt{n}}\left(\dfrac{1}{n} + \dfrac{1}{3}\cdot\dfrac{1}{n^3} + \dfrac{2}{15}\cdot\dfrac{1}{n^5} + \ldots\right) \quad \left(\because \tan\theta = \theta + \dfrac{1}{3}\theta^3 + \dfrac{2}{15}\theta^5 + \ldots\right)$

$\qquad = \dfrac{1}{n^{3/2}} + \dfrac{1}{3n^{7/2}} + \ldots$

Taking the lowest power of $\frac{1}{n}$ in u_n, the auxiliary series is given by,

$$\Sigma\, v_n = \Sigma\, \frac{1}{n^{3/2}}$$

Now, $\quad \lim\dfrac{u_n}{v_n} = \lim\left(\dfrac{1}{n^{3/2}} + \dfrac{1}{3n^{7/2}} + \ldots\right) n^{3/2}$

$\qquad\qquad = \lim\left(1 + \dfrac{1}{3n^2} + \ldots\right)$

$\qquad\qquad = 1$, which is finite and non-zero.

But the auxiliary series $\Sigma\, u_n = \Sigma\, \dfrac{1}{n^{3/2}}$ is convergent as here $p = \dfrac{3}{2} > 1$.

Hence by comparison test the given series is convergent.

Ex. 15 : *Test the series for convergence whose n^{th} term is $u_n = \tan^{-1}\left(\frac{1}{n}\right)$.*

Sol. : Here,
$$u_n = \tan^{-1}\left(\frac{1}{n}\right)$$
$$= \frac{1}{n} - \frac{1}{3n^3} + \frac{1}{5n^5} - \ldots \qquad \left[\because \tan^{-1}x = x - \frac{x^3}{3} + \frac{x^5}{5}\ldots\right]$$

Taking the lowest power of $\frac{1}{n}$ in u_n, the auxiliary series is given by,

$$\Sigma \, v_n = \Sigma \, \frac{1}{n}$$

Now,
$$\lim \frac{u_n}{v_n} = \lim \left(1 - \frac{1}{3n^2} + \frac{1}{5n^4} - \ldots\right)$$
$$= 1, \text{ which is finite and non-zero.}$$

But the auxiliary series $\Sigma \, v_n = \Sigma \, \frac{1}{n}$ is divergent as here $p = 1$.

Hence, by comparison test the given series is divergent.

Ex. 16 : *Test for convergence the series* $\frac{1}{x} + \frac{1}{x-1} + \frac{1}{x+1} + \frac{1}{x-2} + \frac{1}{x+2} + \ldots\ldots,$ *x being a positive fraction.*

Sol. : Neglecting the first term, the given series is,

$$\Sigma \, u_n = \frac{1}{x-1} + \frac{1}{x+1} + \frac{1}{x-2} + \frac{1}{x+2} + \ldots$$
$$= \left\{\frac{1}{x-1} + \frac{1}{x+1}\right\} + \left\{\frac{1}{x-2} + \frac{1}{x+2}\right\} + \ldots$$
$$= \frac{2x}{x^2-1} + \frac{2x}{x^2-2^2} + \ldots = \Sigma \, \frac{2x}{x^2-n^2}$$

i.e.
$$u_n = \frac{2x}{x^2-n^2}$$

$\therefore$ Let
$$v_n = \frac{1}{n^2}$$

Now,
$$\lim \frac{u_n}{v_n} = \lim \left\{\frac{2x}{x^2-n^2} \cdot n^2\right\}$$
$$= \lim \left\{\frac{2x}{x^2/n^2-1}\right\}$$
$$= -2x, \text{ which is finite and non-zero.}$$

But the auxiliary series $\Sigma \, v_n = \Sigma \, \frac{1}{n^2}$ is convergent as here $p = 2 > 1$.

Hence by comparison test the given series is convergent.

Ex. 17 : *Test for convergence the series :*

$$\frac{1}{1+x} + \frac{x}{1+x^2} + \frac{x^2}{1+x^3} + \ldots + \frac{x^{n-1}}{1+x^n} + \ldots, \text{ where } x > 0.$$

Sol. : Here, $u_n = \dfrac{x^{n-1}}{1+x^n}$ and $u_{n+1} = \dfrac{x^n}{1+x^{n+1}}$

$$\therefore \quad \frac{u_n}{u_{n+1}} = \frac{x^{n-1}}{1+x^n} \cdot \frac{1+x^{n+1}}{x^n} = \frac{1}{x} \cdot \frac{1+x^{n+1}}{1+x^n}$$

Case I : Let $x < 1$. Then

$$\lim \frac{u_n}{u_{n+1}} = \lim \frac{1}{x} \frac{1+x^{n+1}}{1+x^n} \qquad \left[\because \lim x^n = 0 \text{ if } x < 1\right]$$

which is > 1 because $x < 1$.

$\therefore$ by ratio test the series is convergent in this case.

Case II : Let $x > 1$. Then,

$$\lim u_n = \lim \frac{x^{n-1}}{1+x^n} = \lim \frac{x^{n-1}}{x^n[1+1/x^n]}$$

$$= \lim \frac{1}{x[1+1/x^n]} \qquad \left[\because \lim 1/x^n = 0 \text{ if } x > 1\right]$$

$$= 1/x$$

which is > 0 because $x > 1$.

$\therefore$ The series $\Sigma\, u_n$ is divergent in this case.

Case III : Let $x = 1$.

When $x = 1$, the series is $\dfrac{1}{2} + \dfrac{1}{2} + \dfrac{1}{2} + \ldots$

$$\therefore \quad \lim S_n = \lim \left(\frac{n}{2}\right) = \infty$$

$\therefore$ The series is divergent when $x = 1$.

Hence, $\Sigma\, u_n$ is convergent if $x < 1$ and divergent if $x \geq 1$.

Ex. 18 : *Test the series for convergence whose n^{th} term is $u_n = \dfrac{1}{n^{(a+b/n)}}$.*

Sol. : Here, $u_n = \dfrac{1}{n^{(a+b/n)}}$

$$= \frac{1}{n^a \cdot n^{b/n}}$$

$\therefore$ Let the auxiliary series be $\Sigma\, v_n = \Sigma\left(\dfrac{1}{n^a}\right)$.

Now, $\lim \dfrac{u_n}{v_n} = \lim \left\{ \dfrac{1}{n^a \, n^{b/n}} \cdot n^a \right\} = \lim \left(\dfrac{1}{n^{b/n}} \right)$

$\qquad\qquad = \lim \dfrac{1}{(n^{1/n})^b}$

$\qquad\qquad = \dfrac{1}{(1)^b}$ $\qquad\qquad \left[\because \lim_{n \to \infty} n^{1/n} = 1 \right]$

$\qquad\qquad = 1$, which is finite and non-zero.

But the auxiliary series $\sum v_n = \sum (1/n^a)$ is convergent if $a > 1$ and divergent if $a \le 1$.

Hence, by comparison test the given series $\sum u_n$ is convergent if $a > 1$ and divergent if $a \le 1$.

Ex. 19 : *Test for convergence the series* $\dfrac{x}{1 \cdot 2} + \dfrac{x^2}{3 \cdot 4} + \dfrac{x^3}{5 \cdot 6} + \dfrac{x^4}{7 \cdot 8} + \ldots .$ **(May 2011)**

Sol. : Here, $\qquad u_n = \dfrac{x^n}{(2n-1) \cdot 2n}$, then $u_{n+1} = \dfrac{x^{n+1}}{(2n+1)(2n+2)}$

Now, $\qquad \dfrac{u_n}{u_{n+1}} = \dfrac{x^n}{(2n-1) \, 2n} \cdot \dfrac{(2n+1)(2n+2)}{x^{n+1}}$

$\qquad\qquad = \dfrac{(2 + 1/n)(2 + 2/n)}{(2 - 1/n) \cdot 2} \cdot \dfrac{1}{x}$

$\therefore \qquad \lim \dfrac{u_n}{u_{n+1}} = \dfrac{2 \cdot 2}{2 \cdot 2} \cdot \dfrac{1}{x}$

$\qquad\qquad = \dfrac{1}{x}$

$\therefore$ by ratio test the series is convergent if $1/x > 1$ i.e. if $x < 1$, divergent if $1/x < 1$ i.e. $x > 1$, and the test fails if $1/x = 1$ i.e. if $x = 1$.

Now, when $x = 1$, $\quad u_n = \dfrac{1}{(2n-1) \cdot 2n}$.

Let, $\qquad v_n = \dfrac{1}{n^2}$

$\therefore \qquad \lim \dfrac{u_n}{v_n} = \lim \dfrac{n^2}{(2n-1) \cdot 2n}$

$\qquad\qquad = \lim \dfrac{1}{(2 - 1/n) \cdot 2}$

$\qquad\qquad = \dfrac{1}{2 \cdot 2} = \dfrac{1}{4}$, which is finite and non-zero.

But the series $\sum v_n = \sum \frac{1}{n^2}$ is convergent because here $p = 2 > 1$.

∴ by comparison test $\sum u_n$ is convergent when $x = 1$.

Hence, the given series is convergent if $x \leq 1$ and divergent if $x > 1$.

Ex. 20 : *Test for convergence the series* $2x + \frac{3}{8} x^2 + \frac{4}{27} x^3 + \ldots + \frac{(n+1)}{n^3} \cdot x^n + \ldots$.

(May 2011)

Sol. : Here, $u_n = \frac{(n+1) x^n}{n^3}$, then $u_{n+1} = \frac{(n+2) x^{n+1}}{(n+1)^3}$

Now, $\frac{u_n}{u_{n+1}} = \frac{(n+1) x^n}{n^3} \cdot \frac{(n+1)^3}{(n+2) x^{n+1}}$

$= \frac{(1 + 1/n)^4}{(1 + 2/n)} \cdot \frac{1}{x}$

∴ $\lim \frac{u_n}{u_{n+1}} = \frac{1}{x}$,

∴ by ratio test the series is convergent if $1/x > 1$ i.e. if $x < 1$, divergent if $1/x < 1$ i.e. if $x > 1$ and the test fails when $x = 1$.

Now, when $x = 1$, then $u_n = \frac{n+1}{n^3}$.

To apply comparison test, take

$v_n = \frac{n}{n^3} = \frac{1}{n^2}$

∴ $\lim \frac{u_n}{v_n} = \lim \frac{n+1}{n^3} \cdot n^2$

$= \lim (1 + 1/n) = 1$, which is finite and non-zero.

But the series $\sum u_n = \sum 1/n^2$ is convergent because here $p = 2 > 1$.

∴ by comparison test $\sum u_n$ is also convergent when $x = 1$.

Hence, the given series is convergent if $x \leq 1$ and divergent if $x > 1$.

Ex. 21 : *Test for convergence the series* $\frac{1}{2\sqrt{1}} + \frac{x^2}{3\sqrt{2}} + \frac{x^4}{4\sqrt{3}} + \frac{x^6}{5\sqrt{4}} + \ldots$

Sol. : Here, $u_n = \frac{x^{2n-2}}{(n+1)\sqrt{n}}$, then $u_{n+1} = \frac{x^{2n}}{(n+2)\sqrt{n+1}}$

Now, $\frac{u_n}{u_{n+1}} = \frac{x^{2n-2}}{(n+1)\sqrt{n}} \cdot \frac{(n+2)\sqrt{(n+1)}}{x^{2n}}$

$= \frac{(1 + 2/n)}{(1 + 1/n)} \cdot \sqrt{\left(1 + \frac{1}{n}\right)} \cdot \frac{1}{x^2}$

∴ $\lim \dfrac{u_n}{u_{n+1}} = \dfrac{1}{1}\sqrt{1} \cdot \dfrac{1}{x^2} = \dfrac{1}{x^2}$

∴ by ratio test the given series is
convergent if $1/x^2 > 1$ i.e. if $x^2 < 1$.
divergent if $1/x^2 < 1$ i.e. if $x^2 > 1$ and the test fails when $x^2 = 1$.

Now, when $x^2 = 1$, $u_n = \dfrac{1}{(n+1)\sqrt{n}}$.

To apply comparison test, we have,

$$v_n = \dfrac{1}{n\sqrt{n}} = \dfrac{1}{n^{3/2}}$$

∴ $\lim \dfrac{u_n}{v_n} = \lim \dfrac{n^{3/2}}{(n+1)\sqrt{n}}$

$= \lim \dfrac{1}{(1+1/n)} = 1$, which is finite and non-zero.

Since, $\sum v_n = \sum 1/n^{3/2}$ is convergent as $p = 3/2 > 1$, therefore, by comparison test the given series is convergent when $x^2 = 1$.

Hence, the series is convergent if $x^2 \leq 1$ and divergent if $x^2 > 1$.

Ex. 22 : *Test the convergence of the series* $\dfrac{2x}{1^2} + \dfrac{3^2 x^2}{2^3} + \dfrac{4^3 x^3}{3^3} + \dfrac{5^4 x^4}{4^5} + \ldots$ **(Dec. 2008)**

Sol. : Here, $u_n = \dfrac{(n+1)^n}{n^{n+1}} x^n$

and $u_{n+1} = \dfrac{(n+2)^{n+1}}{(n+1)^{n+2}} \cdot x^{n+1}$

Then, $\dfrac{u_n}{u_{n+1}} = \dfrac{(n+1)^n (n+1)^{n+2}}{n^{n+1} (n+2)^{n+1}} \cdot \dfrac{1}{x}$

$= \dfrac{n^n (1+1/n)^n \cdot n^{n+2} (1+1/n)^{n+2}}{n^{n+1} \cdot n^{n+1} (1+2/n)^{n+1}} \cdot \dfrac{1}{x}$

$= \dfrac{(1+1/n)^n \cdot (1+1/n)^n (1+1/n)^2}{(1+2/n)^n (1+2/n)} \cdot \dfrac{1}{x}$

∴ $\lim \dfrac{u_n}{u_{n+1}} = \dfrac{e \cdot e \cdot 1}{e^2 \cdot 1} \cdot \dfrac{1}{x}$ $\left[\because \lim_{n \to \infty} \left(1 + \dfrac{x}{n}\right)^n = e^x \right]$

$= \dfrac{1}{x}$

∴ By ratio test the series is convergent if $1/x > 1$ i.e. $x < 1$, divergent if $1/x < 1$ if i.e. $x > 1$ and the test fails when $\frac{1}{x} = 1$ i.e. when $x = 1$.

When $x = 1$, we have $u_n = \frac{(n+1)^n}{n^{n+1}}$.

To apply comparison test in this case, we take,

$$v_n = \frac{n^n}{n^{n+1}} = \frac{1}{n}$$

Then, $\lim \frac{u_n}{v_n} = \lim \frac{(n+1)^n}{n^{n+1}} \cdot n$

$$= \lim (1 + 1/n)^n$$

$$= e$$

which is finite and non-zero.

But the auxiliary series $\sum v_n = \sum 1/n$ is divergent because here $p = 1$. Therefore, by comparison test $\sum u_n$ is also divergent when $x = 1$.

Hence, the given series is convergent if $x < 1$ and divergent if $x \geq 1$.

Ex. 23 : *Test the convergence of the series* $\sum \frac{x^n}{n + \sqrt{(1+n^2)}}$.

Sol. : Here, $u_n = \frac{x^n}{n + \sqrt{(1+n^2)}}$

∴ $u_{n+1} = \frac{x^{n+1}}{(n+1) + \sqrt{\{1 + (n+1)^2\}}}$

Then, $\frac{u_n}{u_{n+1}} = \frac{(n+1) + \sqrt{\{1 + (n+1)^2\}}}{n + \sqrt{(1+n^2)}} \cdot \frac{1}{x}$

$$= \frac{(1 + 1/n) + \sqrt{\{1/n^2 + (1 + 1/n^2)^2\}}}{1 + \sqrt{(1/n^2 + 1)}} \cdot \frac{1}{x}$$

$\lim \frac{u_n}{u_{n+1}} = \frac{(1+0)+1}{1+1} \cdot \frac{1}{x} = \frac{1}{x}$

∴ By ratio test the series is convergent if $1/x > 1$ i.e. if $x < 1$, divergent if $1/x < 1$ i.e. if $x > 1$ and the test fails when $1/x = 1$ i.e. when $x = 1$.

When $x = 1$, we have, $u_n = \frac{1}{n + \sqrt{(1+n^2)}}$

To apply comparison test in this case, we take $v_n = \frac{1}{n}$.

Now, $\dfrac{u_n}{v_n} = \lim \dfrac{n}{n + \sqrt{(1+n^2)}} = \lim \dfrac{1}{1 + \sqrt{(1/n^2+1)}}$
$= 1$, which is finite and non-zero.

Since the auxiliary series $\sum v_n = \sum 1/n$ is divergent as here $p = 1$, therefore by comparison test the given series $\sum u_n$ is also divergent when $x = 1$.

Hence, the given series is convergent if $x < 1$ and divergent if $x \geq 1$.

Ex. 24 : *Test for convergence the series* $1 + \dfrac{3}{4}x + \dfrac{5}{9}x^2 + \dfrac{7}{28}x^3 + \dfrac{9}{65}x^4 + \ldots$ **(May 2009)**

Sol. : Neglecting the first term 1, we have,

$$u_n = \dfrac{(2n+1)}{n^3+1} x^n \quad \text{and} \quad u_{n+1} = \dfrac{2n+3}{(n+1)^3+1} x^{n+1}$$

Then, $\dfrac{u_n}{u_{n+1}} = \dfrac{2n+1}{n^3+1} \cdot \dfrac{(n+1)^3+1}{2n+3} \cdot \dfrac{1}{x}$

$$= \dfrac{(2+1/n)}{(1+1/n^3)} \cdot \dfrac{(1+1/n)^3 + 1/n^3}{(2+3/n)} \cdot \dfrac{1}{x}$$

$\therefore \quad \lim \dfrac{u_n}{u_{n+1}} = \dfrac{2}{1} \cdot \dfrac{1+0}{2} \cdot \dfrac{1}{x} = \dfrac{1}{x}$

$\therefore$ by ratio test the series is convergent if $1/x > 1$ i.e. $x < 1$, divergent if $1/x < 1$ i.e. if $x > 1$ and the test fails when $1/x = 1$ i.e. when $x = 1$.

When $x = 1$, $\quad u_n = \dfrac{2n+1}{n^3+1}$

Take, $\quad v_n = \dfrac{n}{n^3} = \dfrac{1}{n^2}$

Now, $\quad \lim \dfrac{u_n}{v_n} = \lim \left(\dfrac{2n+1}{n^3+1} \cdot n^2\right) = \lim \left(\dfrac{2+1/n}{1+1/n^3}\right) = 2$

which is finite and non-zero.

But the auxiliary series $\sum v_n = \sum 1/n^2$ is convergent as here $p = 2 > 1$, therefore by comparison test the given series is also convergent when $x = 1$. Hence, the series is convergent if $x \leq 1$ and divergent if $x > 1$.

Ex. 25 : *Test for convergence the series* $\sum \left\{ \dfrac{(n+1)^3}{n^k + (n+2)^k} \right\}.$

Sol. : Here, $\quad u_n = \dfrac{(n+1)^3}{n^k + (n+2)^k}$

To apply comparison test, take

$$v_n = \dfrac{n^3}{n^k} = \dfrac{1}{n^{k-3}}$$

Now, $\lim \dfrac{u_n}{v_n} = \lim \dfrac{(n+1)^3}{n^k + (n+2)^k} \cdot n^{k-3}$

$= \lim \dfrac{(1+1/n)^3}{1 + (1+2/n)^k} = \dfrac{1}{1+1} = \dfrac{1}{2},$

which is finite and non-zero.

But the auxiliary series,

$$\Sigma v_n = \Sigma \dfrac{1}{n^{k-3}}$$

is convergent if $k - 3 > 1$ i.e. if $k > 4$ and divergent if $k - 3 \le 1$ i.e. if $k \le 4$.

Hence, by comparison test the given series is convergent if $k > 4$ and divergent if $k \le 4$.

Ex. 26 : *Test for convergence the series* $\sum\limits_{n=1}^{\infty} \dfrac{3n+1}{4n+3} x^n, > 0.$

Sol. : Here, $u_n = \dfrac{3n+1}{4n+3} x^n$

Then, $u_{n+1} = \dfrac{3(n+1)+1}{4(n+1)+3} x^{n+1}$

$= \dfrac{3n+4}{4n+7} x^{n+1}$

$\therefore \quad \dfrac{u_n}{u_{n+1}} = \dfrac{(3n+1)(4n+7)}{(4n+3)(3n+4)} \cdot \dfrac{x^n}{x^{n+1}}$

$= \dfrac{(3n+1)(4n+7)}{(4n+3)(3n+4)} \cdot \dfrac{1}{x}$

Now, $\lim \dfrac{u_n}{u_{n+1}} = \lim \dfrac{(3+1/n)(4+7/n)}{(4+3/n)(3+4/n)} \cdot \dfrac{1}{x}$

$= \dfrac{3 \cdot 4}{4 \cdot 3} \cdot \dfrac{1}{x} = \dfrac{1}{x}$

$\therefore$ by ratio test, the series Σu_n is convergent if $1/x > 1$ i.e. if $x < 1$ divergent if $1/x < 1$ i.e. if $x > 1$ and test fails if $1/x = 1$, i.e. if $x = 1$.

When $x = 1$, $u_n = \dfrac{3n+1}{4n+3}$.

In this case, we have,

$$\lim u_n = \lim \dfrac{3n+1}{4n+3} = \lim \dfrac{n(3+1/n)}{n(4+3/n)}$$

$$= \lim \frac{3 + 1/n}{4 + 3/n}$$

$$= \frac{3}{4}, \text{ which is} > 0.$$

∴ $\sum u_n$ is divergent when $x = 1$.

Hence, $\sum u_n$ is convergent if $x < 1$ and divergent if $x \geq 1$.

Ex. 27 : *Test the convergence of the series* $1 + \frac{2^2}{3 \cdot 4} + \frac{2^2 \cdot 4^2}{3 \cdot 4 \cdot 5 \cdot 6} + \frac{2^2 \cdot 4^2 \cdot 6^2}{3 \cdot 4 \cdot 5 \cdot 6 \cdot 7 \cdot 8} + \cdots$

Sol. : Neglecting the first term 1, we have,

$$u_n = \frac{2^2 \cdot 4^2 \cdot 6^2 \cdots (2n)^2}{3 \cdot 4 \cdot 5 \cdot 6 \cdot 7 \cdot 8 \cdots (2n)(2n+1)(2n+2)}$$

and

$$u_{n+1} = \frac{2^2 \cdot 4^2 \cdot 6^2 \cdots (2n)^2 (2n+2)^2}{3 \cdot 4 \cdot 5 \cdot 6 \cdot 7 \cdot 8 \cdots (2n+2)(2n+3)(2n+4)}$$

∴

$$\frac{u_n}{u_{n+1}} = \frac{(2n+3)(2n+4)}{(2n+2)^2} = \frac{(2 + 3/n)(2 + 4/n)}{(2 + 2/n)^2}$$

$$\lim \frac{u_n}{u_{n+1}} = \frac{2 \cdot 2}{(2)^2} = 1, \text{ so that the ratio test fails.}$$

Applying Raabe's test, we have,

$$\lim n \left(\frac{u_n}{u_{n+1}} - 1 \right) = \lim n \left[\frac{(2n+3)(2n+4)}{(2n+2)^2} - 1 \right]$$

$$= \lim n \left[\frac{6n + 8}{(2n+2)^2} \right] = \lim \left[\frac{6 + 8/n}{(2 + 2/n)^2} \right]$$

$$= \frac{6}{2^2} = \frac{3}{2} > 1.$$

Hence, the series is convergent.

Ex. 28 : *Test the convergence of the given series*

$$1 + \frac{3}{7} x + \frac{3 \cdot 6}{7 \cdot 10} x^2 + \frac{3 \cdot 6 \cdot 9}{7 \cdot 10 \cdot 13} x^3 + \frac{3 \cdot 6 \cdot 9 \cdot 12}{7 \cdot 10 \cdot 13 \cdot 16} x^4 + \cdots \quad \textbf{(May 2007, 2008)}$$

Sol. : Leaving the first term, we have, n^{th} term of the sequence 3, 6, 9, ... is $3 + (n-1)3 = 3n$ and n^{th} term of the sequence 7, 10, 13, ... is $7 + (n-1) = 3n + 4$.

∴

$$u_n = \frac{3 \cdot 6 \cdot 9 \cdots 3n}{7 \cdot 10 \cdot 13 \cdots (3n+4)} x^n.$$

then

$$u_{n+1} = \frac{3 \cdot 6 \cdot 9 \cdots 3n (3n+3)}{7 \cdot 10 \cdot 13 \cdots (3n+4)(3n+7)} x^{n+1}$$

Now, $\dfrac{u_n}{u_{n+1}} = \left(\dfrac{3n+7}{3n+3}\right) \cdot \dfrac{1}{x} = \left(\dfrac{3+7/n}{3+3/n}\right) \cdot \dfrac{1}{x}$

$\therefore \quad \lim \dfrac{u_n}{u_{n+1}} = \lim \left(\dfrac{3+7/n}{3+3/n}\right) \cdot \dfrac{1}{x} = \dfrac{3}{3} \cdot \dfrac{1}{x} = \dfrac{1}{x}$

$\therefore$ by ratio test, the series is convergent if $1/x > 1$ i.e. if $x < 1$, divergent if $1/x < 1$ i.e. if $x > 1$ and test fails if $1/x = 1$ i.e. if $x = 1$.

When $x = 1$, we have,

$$\dfrac{u_n}{u_{n+1}} = \dfrac{3n+7}{3n+3}$$

Applying Raabe's test we have,

$$\lim n \left(\dfrac{u_n}{u_{n+1}} - 1\right) = \lim n \left(\dfrac{3n+7}{3n+3} - 1\right) = \lim \dfrac{4n}{3n+3}$$

$$= \lim \dfrac{4}{3+3/n} = \dfrac{4}{3} > 1.$$

$\therefore$ The series is convergent when $x = 1$.

Hence, the given series is convergent if $x \leq 1$ and divergent if $x > 1$.

Ex. 29 : *Test the convergence of the series whose n^{th} term is $\left[\sqrt{(n^2+1)} - n\right] x^{2n}$.*

Sol. : Here, $u_n = \left[\sqrt{(n^2+1)} - n\right] x^{2n}$

$= n \left[(1 + 1/n^2)^{1/2} - 1\right] x^{2n}$

$= n \left[1 + \dfrac{1}{2} \cdot \dfrac{1}{n^2} + \dfrac{\dfrac{1}{2}\left(\dfrac{1}{2}-1\right)}{2!} \cdot \dfrac{1}{n^4} + \ldots - 1\right] x^{2n}$

$= \dfrac{1}{n} \left[\dfrac{1}{2} - \dfrac{1}{8n^2} + \ldots\right] x^{2n}$ ... (1)

$\therefore \quad u_{n+1} = \left(\dfrac{1}{n+1}\right)\left[\dfrac{1}{2} - \dfrac{1}{8(n+1)^2} + \ldots\right] x^{2n+2}$

$\therefore \quad \dfrac{u_n}{u_{n+1}} = \left(1 + \dfrac{1}{n}\right) \dfrac{\left[\dfrac{1}{2} - \dfrac{1}{8n^2} + \ldots\right]}{\left[\dfrac{1}{2} - \dfrac{1}{8(n+1)^2} + \ldots\right]} \cdot \dfrac{1}{x^2}$

$\therefore \quad \lim \dfrac{u_n}{u_{n+1}} = \dfrac{1}{x^2}$

$\therefore$ by D'Alembert's ratio test, the given series is convergent if $\dfrac{1}{x^2} > 1$ i.e., $x^2 < 1$ and divergent if $\dfrac{1}{x^2} < 1$ i.e. $x^2 > 1$.

If $1/x^2 = 1$, i.e. if $x^2 = 1$, the ratio rest fails and further investigation is required.

Now, when $x^2 = 1$, from (1), we have,

$$u_n = \frac{1}{n}\left[\frac{1}{2} - \frac{1}{8n^2} \cdots \right]$$

In this case to apply comparison test, we take $v_n = \frac{1}{n}$.

Then, $\quad \dfrac{u_n}{v_n} = \left[\dfrac{1}{2} - \dfrac{1}{8n^2} + \cdots \right]$

∴ $\quad \lim \dfrac{u_n}{v_n} = \dfrac{1}{2}$, which is finite and non-zero.

∴ by comparison test $\sum u_n$ and $\sum v_n$ are either both convergent or both divergent.

But for v_n, $p = 1$, so that $\sum v_n$ is divergent. Therefore, $\sum u_n$ is also divergent i.e., the given series is divergent when $x^2 = 1$.

Hence, the given series is convergent if $x^2 < 1$ and divergent if $x^2 \geq 1$.

Ex. 30 : *Test the convergence of series* $1 + \dfrac{1}{2} \cdot \dfrac{x^2}{4} + \dfrac{1 \cdot 3 \cdot 5}{2 \cdot 4 \cdot 6} \cdot \dfrac{x^4}{8} + \dfrac{1 \cdot 3 \cdot 5 \cdot 7 \cdot 9}{2 \cdot 4 \cdot 6 \cdot 8 \cdot 10} \cdot \dfrac{x^6}{12} + \cdots$

Sol. : Neglecting the first term 1, we have, n^{th} term of the sequence 1·3·5·9 ... is

$1 + (n-1)4 = 4n - 3$ and n^{th} term of the sequence 4, 8, 12, is $4 + (n-1)4 = 4n$.

∴ $\quad u_n = \dfrac{1 \cdot 3 \cdot 5 \cdots (4n-3)}{2 \cdot 4 \cdot 6 \cdots (4n-2)} \cdot \dfrac{x^{2n}}{4n}$

Then $\quad u_{n+1} = \dfrac{1 \cdot 3 \cdot 5 \cdots (4n-3)(4n-1)(4n+1)}{2 \cdot 4 \cdot 6 \cdots (4n-2)(4n)(4n+2)} \cdot \dfrac{x^{2n+2}}{(4n+4)}$

Now, $\quad \dfrac{u_n}{u_{n+1}} = \dfrac{4n(4n+2)}{(4n-1)(4n+1)} \cdot \dfrac{4n+4}{4n} \cdot \dfrac{1}{x^2}$

$= \dfrac{(4n+2)(4n+4)}{(4n-1)(4n+1)} \cdot \dfrac{1}{x^2}$

$= \dfrac{(4+2/n)(4+4/n)}{(4-1/n)(4+1/n)} \cdot \dfrac{1}{x^2}$

∴ $\quad \lim \dfrac{u_n}{u_{n+1}} = \dfrac{4 \cdot 4}{4 \cdot 4} \cdot \dfrac{1}{x^2} = \dfrac{1}{x^2}$

∴ by ratio test, the series $\sum u_n$ is convergent if $1/x^2 > 1$, i.e., if $x^2 < 1$, divergent if $1/x^2 < 1$, i.e., if $x^2 > 1$ and the test fails when $1/x^2 = 1$, i.e., when $x^2 = 1$.

When $x^2 = 1$,
$$\frac{u_n}{u_{n+1}} = \frac{(4n+2)(4n+4)}{(4n-1)(4n+1)}$$
$$= \frac{16n^2 + 24n + 8}{16n^2 - 1}$$

Applying Raabe's test, we have,
$$\lim n\left(\frac{u_n}{u_{n+1}} - 1\right) = \lim n\left(\frac{16n^2 + 24n + 8}{16n^2 - 1} - 1\right)$$
$$= \lim \frac{n(24n + 9)}{16n^2 - 1}$$
$$= \lim \frac{24 + 9/n}{16 - 1/n^2} = \frac{24}{16} = \frac{3}{2} > 1.$$

∴ The series is convergent, when $x^2 = 1$.

Hence, the given series is convergent if $x^2 \le 1$ and divergent if $x^2 > 1$.

Ex. 31 : *Test the convergence of the series* $\frac{x}{1} + \frac{1}{2} \cdot \frac{x^3}{3} + \frac{1 \cdot 3}{2 \cdot 4} \cdot \frac{x^5}{5} + \frac{1 \cdot 3 \cdot 5}{2 \cdot 4 \cdot 6} \cdot \frac{x^7}{7} + \ldots$

Sol. : Neglecting the first term, we have, n^{th} term of series 1, 3, 5, … is $1 + (n-1)2 = 2n - 1$ n^{th} term of the series 3, 5, 7 … is $3 + (n-1)2 = 2n + 1$.

∴
$$u_n = \frac{1 \cdot 3 \cdot 5 \ldots (2n-1)}{2 \cdot 4 \cdot 6 \ldots (2n)} \cdot \frac{x^{2n+1}}{(2n+1)}$$

then,
$$u_{n+1} = \frac{1 \cdot 3 \cdot 5 \ldots (2n-1)(2n+1)}{2 \cdot 4 \cdot 6 \ldots (2n)(2n+2)} \cdot \frac{x^{2n+2}}{(2n+3)}$$

Now,
$$\frac{u_n}{u_{n+1}} = \frac{(2n+2)(2n+3)}{(2n+1)^2} \cdot \frac{1}{x^2}$$
$$= \frac{(2 + 2/n)(2 + 3/n)}{(2 + 1/n)^2} \cdot \frac{1}{x^2}$$

∴
$$\lim \frac{u_n}{u_{n+1}} = \frac{2 \cdot 2}{2^2} \cdot \frac{1}{x^2} = \frac{1}{x^2}$$

∴ by ratio test, the series is convergent if $1/x^2 > 1$, i.e., if $x^2 < 1$, divergent if $1/x^2 < 1$, i.e., $x^2 > 1$ and the test fails when $1/x^2 = 1$, when $x^2 = 1$.

When $x^2 = 1$,
$$\frac{u_n}{u_{n+1}} = \frac{(2n+2)(2n+3)}{(2n+1)^2}$$

Applying Raabe's test, we have,
$$\lim n\left(\frac{u_n}{u_{n+1}} - 1\right) = \lim n\left[\frac{(2n+2)(2n+3)}{(2n+1)^2} - 1\right]$$

$$= \lim \frac{n(6n+5)}{(2n+1)^2}$$

$$= \lim \frac{6+5/n}{(2+1/n)^2}$$

$$= \frac{6}{2^2} = \frac{3}{2} > 1.$$

∴ The series is convergent when $x^2 = 1$.

Hence, the given series is convergent if $x^2 \leq 1$ and divergent if $x^2 > 1$.

Ex. 32 : *Test the series for convergence whose n^{th} term is $\frac{x^n}{a+\sqrt{n}}$.* (May 2009)

Sol. : Here, $u_n = \frac{x^n}{a+\sqrt{n}}$, then $u_{n+1} = \frac{x^{n+1}}{a+\sqrt{n+1}}$

Now, $\frac{u_n}{u_{n+1}} = \frac{a+\sqrt{(n+1)}}{a+\sqrt{n}} \cdot \frac{1}{x}$

$$= \frac{a/\sqrt{n} + \sqrt{(1+1/n)}}{(a/\sqrt{n})+1} \cdot \frac{1}{x}$$

∴ $\lim \frac{u_n}{u_{n+1}} = \frac{1}{x}$.

∴ by ratio test the series is convergent if $1/x > 1$, i.e. if $x < 1$, divergent if $1/x < 1$, i.e., if $x > 1$ and the test fails when $1/x = 1$, i.e., when $x = 1$.

When $x = 1$, $u_n = \frac{1}{a+\sqrt{n}} = \frac{1}{\sqrt{n}(1+a/\sqrt{n})}$

To apply comparison test in this case, we take $v_n = 1/\sqrt{n}$.

Now, $\lim \frac{u_n}{v_n} = \lim \frac{1}{\sqrt{n}(1+a/\sqrt{n})} \cdot \sqrt{n}$

$$= \lim \frac{1}{1+a/\sqrt{n}} = 1, \text{ which is finite and non-zero.}$$

∴ by comparison test $\sum u_n$ and $\sum v_n$ are either both convergent or both divergent. But $\sum v_n = \sum 1/n^{1/2}$ is divergent because here $P = \frac{1}{2} < 1$. Therefore, $\sum u_n$ is divergent when $x = 1$.

Hence, the given series is convergent if $x < 1$ and divergent if $x \geq 1$.

Ex. 33 : *Test the convergence of the series*

$$\frac{a}{a+3} + \frac{a(a+2)}{(a+3)(a+5)} x + \frac{a(a+2)(a+4)}{(a+3)(a+5)(a+7)} x^2 + \ldots$$

Sol. : Here, $\quad u_n = \dfrac{a(a+2)(a+4)\ldots(a+2n-2)}{(a+3)(a+5)\ldots(a+2n+1)} \cdot x^{n-1}$

and $\quad u_{n+1} = \dfrac{a(a+2)(a+4)\ldots(a+2n-2)(a+2n)}{(a+3)(a+5)\ldots(a+2n+1)(a+2n+3)} \cdot x^n$

Then, $\quad \dfrac{u_n}{u_{n+1}} = \left(\dfrac{a+2n+3}{a+2n}\right) \cdot \dfrac{1}{x}$

$$= \dfrac{2 + (a+3)/n}{2 + a/n} \cdot \dfrac{1}{x}$$

$\therefore \quad \lim \dfrac{u_n}{u_{n+1}} = \dfrac{2}{2} \cdot \dfrac{1}{x} = \dfrac{1}{x}.$

∴ by ratio rest the series is convergent if $1/x > 1$ i.e. if $x < 1$, divergent if $1/x < 1$, i.e., $x > 1$ and test fails when $1/x = 1$ i.e., when $x = 1$.

When $x = 1$, $\quad \dfrac{u_n}{u_{n+1}} = \dfrac{a+2n+3}{a+2n}$

Applying Raabe's test, we have,

$$\lim n\left(\dfrac{u_n}{u_{n+1}} - 1\right) = \lim n\left(\dfrac{a+2n+3}{a+2n} - 1\right)$$

$$= \lim \dfrac{3n}{a+2n}$$

$$= \lim \left(\dfrac{3}{a/n + 2}\right) = \dfrac{3}{2} > 1.$$

∴ The series is convergent when $x = 1$.

Hence, the given series is convergent if $x \leq 1$ and divergent if $x > 1$.

Ex. 34 : *Prove that the series* $\sum \dfrac{1 \cdot 2 \cdot 3 \ldots n}{4 \cdot 7 \ldots (3n+1)} x^n$ *converges when $0 < x < 3$ and diverges when $x \geq 3$.*

Sol. : Here, $\quad u_n = \dfrac{1 \cdot 2 \cdot 3 \cdot \ldots n}{4 \cdot 7 \cdot \ldots (3n+1)} x^n$

Then, $\quad u_{n+1} = \dfrac{1 \cdot 2 \cdot 3 \cdot \ldots n(n+1) x^{n+1}}{4 \cdot 7 \cdot \ldots (3n+1)(3n+4)}$

∴ $\quad \dfrac{u_n}{u_{n+1}} = \dfrac{3n+4}{n+1} \cdot \dfrac{1}{x} = \dfrac{3 + 4/n}{1 + 1/n} \cdot \dfrac{1}{x}$

We have, $\quad \lim \dfrac{u_n}{u_{n+1}} = \dfrac{3}{1} \cdot \dfrac{1}{x} = \dfrac{3}{x}$

∴ by ratio test the series is convergent if $3/x > 1$, i.e., if $x < 3$, divergent if $3/x < 1$ i.e., if $x > 3$ and the test fails when $3/x = 1$, i.e. when $x = 3$.

When $x = 3$, $\quad \dfrac{u_n}{u_{n+1}} = \dfrac{3n+4}{3(n+1)}$

Applying Raabe's test, we have,

$$\lim n\left(\dfrac{u_n}{u_{n+1}} - 1\right) = \lim n\left(\dfrac{3n+4}{3(n+1)} - 1\right) = \lim \dfrac{n}{3(n+1)}$$

$$= \lim \dfrac{1}{3(1+1/n)} = \dfrac{1}{3} < 1$$

∴ The series is divergent when $x = 3$.

Hence, the given series is convergent when $0 < x < 3$ and divergent when $x \geq 3$.

Ex. 35 : *Test the convergence of the series* $x \log x + x^2 \log 2x + \ldots + x^n \log nx + \ldots$

Sol. : Here, $\quad u_n = x^n \log nx$

and $\quad u_{n+1} = x^{n+1} \log(n+1)x$

Then, $\quad \dfrac{u_n}{u_{n+1}} = \dfrac{\log nx}{\log(n+1)x} \cdot \dfrac{1}{x} = \dfrac{\log nx}{\log\left\{nx\left(1+\dfrac{1}{n}\right)\right\}} \cdot \dfrac{1}{x}$

$$= \dfrac{\log nx}{\log nx + \log\left(1+\dfrac{1}{n}\right)} \cdot \dfrac{1}{x}$$

$$= \dfrac{\log nx}{\log nx + \dfrac{1}{n} - \dfrac{1}{2n^2} + \dfrac{1}{3n^3}} \cdot \dfrac{1}{x}$$

$$= \dfrac{1}{\left(1 + \dfrac{1}{n \log nx} - \dfrac{1}{2n^2 \log nx} + \ldots\right)} \cdot \dfrac{1}{x}$$

∴ $\quad \lim \dfrac{u_n}{u_{n+1}} = \dfrac{1}{x}$

∴ by ratio test the series is convergent if $1/x > 1$, i.e., if $x < 1$, divergent if $1/x < 1$, i.e. if $x > 1$ and test fails when $1/x = 1$ i.e. when $x = 1$.

When $x = 1$, we have $u_n = \log n$.

Now, $\quad \lim\limits_{n \to \infty} u_n = \lim\limits_{n \to \infty} \log n = \infty$, which is > 0.

∴ The given series is divergent when $x = 1$.

Hence, the series is convergent if $x < 1$ and divergent if $x \geq 1$.

Ex. 36 : *Test for convergence the series $x^2 (\log 2)^q + x^3 (\log 3)^q + x^4 (\log 4)^q + \ldots$.*

Sol. : Since $\log 1 = 0$, therefore the given series can be written as,

$$x (\log 1)^q + x^2 (\log 2)^q + x^3 (\log 3)^q + \ldots$$

$\therefore \qquad u_n = x^n (\log n)^q$ and $u_{n+1} = x^{n+1} [\log (n+1)]^q$

Now,
$$\frac{u_n}{u_{n+1}} = \left[\frac{\log n}{\log (n+1)}\right]^q \cdot \frac{1}{x}$$

$$= \left[\frac{\log n}{\log n (1 + 1/n)}\right]^q \cdot \frac{1}{x}$$

$$= \left[\frac{\log n}{\log n + \log (1 + 1/n)}\right]^q \cdot \frac{1}{x}$$

$$= \left[\frac{\log n}{\log n + 1/n - 1/2n^2 + \ldots}\right]^q \cdot \frac{1}{x}$$

$$= \left\{\frac{1}{1 + \dfrac{1}{n \log n} - \dfrac{1}{2n^2 \log n} + \ldots}\right\}^q \cdot \frac{1}{x}$$

$$= \left[1 + \left(\frac{1}{n \log n} - \frac{1}{2n^2 \log n} + \ldots\right)\right]^{-q} \cdot \frac{1}{x}$$

$$= \left[1 - q\left(\frac{1}{n \log n} - \frac{1}{2n^2 \log n} + \ldots\right)\right.$$

$$\left. + \frac{q(q+1)}{2!}\left(\frac{1}{n \log n} - \frac{1}{2n^2 \log n} + \ldots\right)^2 + \ldots\right] \cdot \frac{1}{x}$$

$$= \left[1 - \frac{q}{n \log n} + \frac{q}{2n^2}\left\{\frac{1}{\log n} + \frac{q+1}{(\log n)^2}\right\} + \ldots\right] \cdot \frac{1}{x}$$

$\therefore \qquad \lim \dfrac{u_n}{u_{n+1}} = \dfrac{1}{x}$

$\therefore$ by ratio test, the series is convergent if $1/x > 1$, i.e., if $x < 1$, divergent if $1/x < 1$, i.e., if $x > 1$ and the test fails when $1/x = 1$, i.e., when $x = 1$.

$$\frac{u_n}{u_{n+1}} = 1 - \frac{q}{n \log n} + \frac{q}{2n^2}\left\{\frac{1}{\log n} + \frac{q+1}{(\log n)^2}\right\} + \ldots$$

or
$$n\left(\frac{u_n}{u_{n+1}} - 1\right) = \frac{-q}{\log n} + \frac{q}{2n}\left\{\frac{1}{\log n} + \frac{q+1}{(\log n)^2}\right\} + \ldots$$

$\therefore \qquad \lim n\left(\dfrac{u_n}{u_{n+1}} - 1\right) = 0 < 1.$

$\therefore$ By Raabe's test the series is divergent when $x = 1$.

Hence, the given series is convergent if $x < 1$ and divergent if $x \geq 1$.

Ex. 37 : *Test for convergence the series*

$$\frac{(\log 2)^2}{2^2} + \frac{(\log 3)^2}{3^2} + \frac{(\log 4)^2}{4^2} + \ldots + \frac{(\log n)^2}{n^2} + \ldots$$

Sol. : The first term of the series may be taken as $\frac{(\log 1)^2}{1^2}$ because $\log 1 = 0$.

$\therefore\ $ n^{th} term of the series $= \frac{(\log n)^2}{n^2} = f(n)$ (Say)

Clearly $f(n)$ is positive for all positive integral value of n and decreases continually as n increases.

We have, $\quad a^n f(a^n) = \dfrac{a^n (\log a^n)^2}{(a^n)^2}$

$$= \frac{a^n \cdot n^2 (\log a)^2}{(a^n)^2}$$

$$= \frac{n^2 (\log a)^2}{a^n} \qquad a \text{ to be taken} > 1.$$

Consider the series $\sum a^n f(a^n) = \sum \{n^2 (\log a)^2 / a^n\} = \sum v_n$, say.

Here, $\quad v_n = \dfrac{n^2 (\log a)^2}{a^n}$, so that $v_{n+1} = \dfrac{(n+1)^2 (\log a)^2}{a^{n+1}}$

$\therefore\quad \dfrac{v_n}{v_{n+1}} = \dfrac{n^2 (\log a)^2}{a^n} \cdot \dfrac{a^{n+1}}{(n+1)^2 (\log a)^2} = \dfrac{a}{(1 + 1/n)^2}$

Now, $\quad \lim \dfrac{v_n}{v_{n+1}} = \lim \dfrac{a}{(1 + 1/n)^2} = a > 1.$

$\therefore\ $ by ratio test the series $\sum v_n = \sum a^n f(a^n)$ is convergent.

Hence, by Cauchy's condensation test the given series $\sum f(n)$ is also convergent.

Ex. 38 : *Test the series for convergence*

$$\frac{(1+a)(1+b)}{1 \cdot 2 \cdot 3} + \frac{(2+a)(2+b)}{2 \cdot 3 \cdot 4} + \frac{(3+a)(3+b)}{3 \cdot 4 \cdot 5} + \ldots$$

Sol. : Here, $\quad u_n = \dfrac{(n+a)(n+b)}{n(n+1)(n+2)} = \dfrac{(1+a/n)(1+b/n)}{n(1+1/n)(1+2/n)}$

To apply comparison test, we take $v_n = 1/n$.

Now, $\quad \lim \dfrac{u_n}{v_n} = \lim \dfrac{(1+a/n)(1+b/n)}{(1+1/n)(1+2/n)} = 1$

which is finite and non-zero.

Therefore, by comparison test $\sum u_n$ and $\sum v_n$ are either both convergent or both divergent.

But $\sum v_n = \sum 1/n$ is divergent because here $p = 1$.

Hence, $\sum u_n$ is also divergent.

Ex. 39 : *Test for convergence the series*

$$1 + \frac{\alpha\beta}{1\cdot\gamma}x + \frac{\alpha(\alpha+1)\,\beta(\beta+1)}{1\cdot 2\cdot\gamma(\gamma+1)}x^2 + \frac{\alpha(\alpha+1)(\alpha+2)\,\beta(\beta+1)(\beta+2)}{1\cdot 2\cdot 3\,\gamma(\gamma+1)(\gamma+2)}x^3 + \ldots\ldots$$

Sol. : Neglecting the first term 1, we have,

$$u_n = \frac{\alpha(\alpha+1)(\alpha+2)\ldots(\alpha+n-1)\,\beta(\beta+1)(\beta+2)\ldots(\beta+n-1)}{1\cdot 2\ldots n\cdot\gamma(\gamma+1)(\gamma+2)\ldots(\gamma+n-1)}x^n$$

and

$$u_{n+1} = \frac{\alpha(\alpha+1)\ldots(\alpha+n-1)(\alpha+n)\cdot\beta\cdot(\beta+1)\ldots(\beta+n-1)(\beta+n)}{1\cdot 2\ldots(n+1)\,\gamma(\gamma+1)\ldots(\gamma+n-1)(\gamma+n)}x^{n+1}$$

Then,

$$\frac{u_n}{u_{n+1}} = \frac{(n+1)(\gamma+n)}{(\alpha+n)(\beta+n)}\cdot\frac{1}{x}$$

$$= \frac{(1+1/n)(\gamma/n+1)}{(\alpha/n+1)(\beta/n+1)}\cdot\frac{1}{x}$$

$$\therefore\quad \lim\frac{u_n}{u_{n+1}} = \frac{1\cdot 1}{1\cdot 1}\cdot\frac{1}{x} = \frac{1}{x}$$

$\therefore$ by ratio test the series is convergent if $1/x > 1$, i.e., if $x < 1$, divergent if $1/x < 1$, i.e., if $x > 1$ and the test fails when $1/x = 1$ i.e., when $x = 1$.

When $x = 1$,

$$\frac{u_n}{u_{n+1}} = \frac{(n+1)(\gamma+n)}{(\alpha+n)(\beta+n)} = \frac{n^2+(\gamma+1)n+\gamma}{n^2+(\alpha+\beta)n+\alpha\beta}$$

Now,

$$n\left(\frac{u_n}{u_{n+1}}-1\right) = n\left[\frac{n^2+(\gamma+1)n+\gamma}{n^2+(\alpha+\beta)n+\alpha\beta}-1\right]$$

$$= \frac{n\,[(\gamma+1-\alpha-\beta)n+(\gamma-\alpha\beta)]}{n^2+(\alpha+\beta)n+\alpha\beta}$$

$$= \frac{(\gamma+1-\alpha-\beta)+(\gamma-\alpha\beta)/n}{1+(\alpha+\beta)/n+\alpha\beta/n^2}$$

$$\therefore\quad \lim n\left(\frac{u_n}{u_{n+1}}-1\right) = \left(\frac{\gamma+1-\alpha-\beta}{1}\right)$$

$$= \gamma+1-\alpha-\beta$$

$\therefore$ By Raabe's test, when $x = 1$, the series is convergent if $\gamma + 1 - \alpha - \beta > 1$, i.e., if $\gamma > \alpha + \beta$; divergent if $\gamma + 1 - \alpha - \beta < 1$, i.e., if $\gamma < \alpha + \beta$ and test fails when $\gamma + 1 - \alpha - \beta = 1$, i.e., when $\gamma = \alpha + \beta$ we have,

$$n\left(\frac{u_n}{u_{n+1}}-1\right) = \frac{n\{n+\alpha+\beta-\alpha\beta\}}{n^2+(\alpha+\beta)n+\alpha\beta}$$

$$\therefore \quad \lim\left[\left\{n\left(\frac{u_n}{u_{n+1}}-1\right)-1\right\}\log n\right] = \lim\left[\left\{\frac{n(n+\alpha+\beta-\alpha\beta)}{n^2+(\alpha+\beta)n+\alpha\beta}-1\right\}\log n\right]$$

$$= \lim\left[\frac{-\alpha\beta n - \alpha\beta}{n^2+(\alpha+\beta)n+\alpha\beta} \cdot \log n\right]$$

$$= \lim\left[\frac{-\alpha\beta(1+1/n)}{1+(\alpha+\beta)/n+\alpha\beta/n^2} \cdot \frac{\log n}{n}\right]$$

$$= \frac{-\alpha\beta}{1} \cdot 0 = 0 < 1.$$

∴ By DeMorgan's test the series is divergent in this case.

Hence, the series is convergent if $x < 1$, divergent if $x > 1$, and when $x = 1$, the series is convergent if $\gamma > \alpha + \beta$ and divergent if $\gamma \le \alpha + \beta$.

Ex. 40 : *Test for convergence the series* $x + x^{1+1/2} + x^{1+1/2+1/3} + x^{1+1/2+1/3+1/4} + \ldots$

Sol. : Here, $\quad u_n = x^{1+1/2+1/3+\ldots+1/n}$

and $\quad u_{n+1} = x^{1+1/2+1/3+\ldots+1/n+1/(n+1)}$

Then, $\quad \dfrac{u_n}{u_{n+1}} = \dfrac{1}{x^{1/(n+1)}}$

∴ $\quad \lim \dfrac{u_n}{u_{n+1}} = \dfrac{1}{x^0} = 1$, i.e. the ratio test fails.

Now, we shall apply log test.

We have, $\quad n \log \dfrac{u_n}{u_{n+1}} = n \log \dfrac{1}{x^{1/(n+1)}} = n \log \left(\dfrac{1}{x}\right)^{1/(n+1)} = \dfrac{n}{n+1} \log \dfrac{1}{x}$

$$= \frac{1}{(1+1/n)} \log \frac{1}{x}$$

∴ $\quad \lim n \log \dfrac{u_n}{u_{n+1}} = \log \dfrac{1}{x}$

∴ The series is convergent if $\log(1/x) > 1$ on $1/x > e$ and $x < 1/e$, divergent if $\log(1/x) < 1$ i.e., if $x > 1/e$, and the log test also fails if $\log(1/x) = 1$, i.e., if $x = 1/e$.

When $x = 1/e$, we have,

$$n \log \frac{u_n}{u_{n+1}} = \frac{n}{n+1}$$

$$\therefore \quad \lim\left[\left(n \log \frac{u_n}{u_{n+1}} - 1\right)\log n\right] = \lim\left[\left(\frac{n}{n+1} - 1\right)\log n\right]$$

$$= \lim\left(-\frac{\log n}{n+1}\right) = \lim\left(-\frac{\log n}{n} \cdot \frac{n}{n+1}\right)$$

$$= \lim\left(-\frac{\log n}{n} \cdot \frac{1}{1+1/n}\right) = 0 \cdot 1 = 0 < 1 \left(\because \lim \frac{\log n}{n} = 0\right)$$

Therefore, the series is divergent if $x = 1/e$.

Hence, the given series is convergent if $x < 1/e$ and divergent if $x \ge 1/e$.

Ex. 41 : *Test the convergence of the series* $1^p + \left(\frac{1}{2}\right)^p + \left(\frac{1\cdot 3}{2\cdot 4}\right)^p + \left(\frac{1\cdot 3\cdot 5}{2\cdot 4\cdot 6}\right)^p + \ldots$

Sol. : Neglecting the first term 1^p, we have,

$$u_n = \left[\frac{1\cdot 3\cdot 5 \ldots (2n-1)}{2\cdot 4\cdot 6 \ldots (2n)}\right]^p$$

and

$$u_{n+1} = \left[\frac{1\cdot 3\cdot 5 \ldots (2n-1)(2n+1)}{2\cdot 4\cdot 6 \ldots (2n)(2n+2)}\right]^p$$

Then,

$$\frac{u_n}{u_{n+1}} = \left(\frac{2n+2}{2n+1}\right)^p = \left(\frac{1+1/n}{1+1/2n}\right)^p$$

$$\lim \frac{u_n}{u_{n+1}} = \left(\frac{1}{1}\right)^p = 1, \text{ so that the ratio test fails.}$$

Now, we have,

$$\log \frac{u_n}{u_{n+1}} = \log \left(\frac{2n+2}{2n+1}\right)^p = \log \left(\frac{1+1/n}{1+1/2n}\right)^p$$

$$= p\left[\log(1+1/n) - \log(1+1/2n)\right]$$

$$= p\left[\left(\frac{1}{n} - \frac{1}{2n^2} + \frac{1}{3n^3} \ldots\right) - \left(\frac{1}{2n} - \frac{1}{2\cdot 2^2 n^2} + \frac{1}{3\cdot 2^3 n^3} - \ldots\right)\right]$$

$$= p\left[\left(1-\frac{1}{2}\right)\frac{1}{n} - \frac{1}{2}\left\{1-\frac{1}{4}\right\}\frac{1}{n^2} + \frac{1}{3}\left\{1-\frac{1}{8}\right\}\frac{1}{n^3} - \ldots\right]$$

$$= p\left[\frac{1}{2n} - \frac{3}{8n^2} + \frac{7}{24n^3} - \ldots\right]$$

$$\therefore \quad n \log \frac{u_n}{u_{n+1}} = p\left[\frac{1}{2} - \frac{3}{8n} + \frac{7}{24n^2} - \ldots\right]$$

Now, $\lim \left\{n \log \frac{u_n}{u_{n+1}}\right\} = \frac{p}{2}$

$\therefore$ By logarithmic test the series is convergent if $p/2 > 1$, i.e. if $p > 2$, divergent if $p/2 < 1$, i.e., if $p < 2$ and the test fails when $p/2 = 1$, i.e., when $p = 2$.

When $p = 2$, we have,

$$n \log \frac{u_n}{u_{n+1}} = 2\left[\frac{1}{2} - \frac{3}{8n} + \frac{7}{24n^2}\right]$$

$$= 1 - \frac{3}{4n} + \frac{7}{12n^2}$$

$$\therefore \lim \left[\left(n \log \frac{u_n}{u_{n+1}} - 1\right) \log n\right]$$

$$= \lim \left[\left\{-\frac{3}{4n} + \frac{7}{12n^2} - \ldots\right\} \log n\right]$$

$$= \lim\left[\left\{-\frac{3}{4} + \frac{7}{12n} - \ldots\right\} \cdot \frac{\log n}{n}\right]$$

$$= \left\{-\frac{3}{4}\right\} \cdot 0 = 0 < 1.$$

$\therefore$ The series is divergent when $p = 2$.

Hence, the given series is convergent if $p > 2$ and divergent if $p \leq 2$.

Ex. 42 : If $\dfrac{u_n}{u_{n+1}} = \dfrac{n^k + An^{k-1} + Bn^{k-2} + Cn^{k-3} + \ldots}{n^k + an^{k-1} + bn^{k-2} + cn^{k-3} + \ldots}$

where k is a positive integer, show that the series $\sum u_n$ is convergent if $A - a - 1 > 0$ and divergent if $A - a - 1 \leq 0$.

Sol. : We have,

$$\frac{u_n}{u_{n+1}} = \frac{n^k + An^{k-1} + Bn^{k-2} + Cn^{k-3} + \ldots}{n^k + an^{k-1} + bn^{k-2} + cn^{k-3} + \ldots}$$

$$= \frac{1 + A/n + B/n^2 + C/n^3 + \ldots}{1 + a/n + b/n^2 + c/n^3 + \ldots}$$

$\therefore \quad \lim \dfrac{u_n}{u_{n+1}} = \dfrac{1}{1} = 1$, so that the ratio test fails.

Now, $\quad n\left\{\dfrac{u_n}{u_{n+1}} - 1\right\} = n\left\{\dfrac{1 + A/n + B/n^2 + C/n^3 + \ldots}{1 + a/n + b/n^2 + c/n^3 + \ldots} - 1\right\}$

$$= n\left\{\frac{(A-a)/n + (B-b)/n^2 + (C-c)/n^3 + \ldots}{1 + a/n + b/n^2 + c/n^3 + \ldots}\right\}$$

$$= \frac{(A-a) + (B-b)/n + (C-c)/n^2 + \ldots}{1 + a/n + b/n^2 + c/n^3 + \ldots}$$

$\therefore \quad \lim n\left\{\dfrac{u_n}{u_{n+1}} - 1\right\} = \dfrac{A-a}{1} = A - a$

$\therefore$ By Raabe's test the series is convergent if $A - a > 1$, i.e., if $A - a - 1 > 0$, divergent if $A - a < 1$, i.e., if $A - a - 1 < 0$, and the test fails when $A - a = 1$, i.e. when $A - a - 1 = 0$.

When $A - a - 1 = 0$, we have,

$$n\left\{\frac{u_n}{u_{n+1}} - 1\right\} = \frac{1 + (B-b)/n + (C-c)/n^2 + \ldots}{1 + a/n + b/n^2 + c/n^3 + \ldots}$$

$\therefore \lim\left[\left\{n\left(\dfrac{u_n}{u_{n+1}} - 1\right) - 1\right\} \log n\right]$

$$= \lim\left[\left\{\left(\frac{1 + (B-b)/n + (C-c)/n^2 + \ldots}{1 + a/n + b/n^2 + \ldots}\right) - 1\right\} \log n\right]$$

$$= \lim \left[\frac{(B-b-a)/n + (C-c-b)/n^2 + \ldots}{1 + a/n + b/n^2 + \ldots} \cdot \log n \right]$$

$$= \lim \left[\frac{(B-b-a) + (C-c-b)/n + \ldots}{1 + a/n + b/n^2 + \ldots} \cdot \frac{\log n}{n} \right]$$

$$= \frac{B-b-a}{1} \cdot 0 = 0 < 1.$$

∴ By DeMorgan's test the series is divergent when $A - a - 1 = 0$.

Hence, the series is convergent if $A - a - 1 > 0$ and divergent if $A - a - 1 \leq 0$.

Ex. 43 : *Test the convergence of the series* $2 - \frac{3}{2} + \frac{4}{3} - \frac{5}{4} + \ldots$ *or* $\sum (-1)^{n+1} \left(\frac{n+1}{n} \right)$.

Sol. : The given series is

$$2 - \frac{3}{2} + \frac{4}{3} - \frac{5}{4} + \ldots = \sum (-1)^{n+1} \left(\frac{n+1}{n} \right)$$

$$= \sum (-1)^{n+1}, u_n \text{ say,}$$

where $u_n = \frac{n+1}{n}$

Here (i) The terms of the series are alternately positive and negative.

(ii) Clearly $2 > \frac{3}{2} > \frac{4}{3} > \frac{5}{4} > \ldots$ i.e. $u_1 > u_2 > u_3 > .$

i.e. each term of the series is numerically less than the preceding term and

(iii) $\lim u_n = \lim \left(\frac{n+1}{n} \right) = \lim \left(1 + \frac{1}{n} \right) = 1.$

Thus the third condition of the Leibnitz's test is not satisfied.

Hence, the given series can be written as,

$$2 - \frac{3}{2} + \frac{4}{3} - \frac{5}{4} + \ldots$$

i.e. $(1+1) - \left(1 + \frac{1}{2}\right) + \left(1 + \frac{1}{3}\right) - \left(1 + \frac{1}{4}\right) + \ldots$

i.e. $(1 - 1 + 1 - 1 + \ldots) + \left(1 - \frac{1}{2} + \frac{1}{3} - \frac{1}{4} + \ldots\right).$

Now the series in the second pair of brackets is convergent. The sum of this series is $\log (1 + 1)$ i.e., $\log 2$.

And the series in the first pair of brackets is oscillating as the sum of the n-terms of this series is 0 or 1 according as n is even or odd.

Hence, as n tends to infinity, the sum of the given series tends to $(0 + \log 2)$ or $(1 + \log 2)$ according as n is even or add. Therefore, the given series is an oscillatory series.

Ex. 44 : *Test the convergence of the series $1^{-p} - 2^{-p} + 3^{-p} \ldots$, when $p > 0$.*

Sol. : The given series is

$$1^{-p} - 2^{-p} + 3^{-p} - \ldots = \sum \frac{(-1)^{n-1}}{n^p}$$

$$= \sum (-1)^{n-1} u_n, \text{ (say)}$$

where $\quad u_n = \dfrac{1}{n^p}$

Here we see that

(i) The terms are alternately positive and negative.

(ii) $\therefore p > 0, \quad \therefore 1^p < 2^p < 3^p < \ldots$

or $\quad \dfrac{1}{1^p} > \dfrac{1}{2^p} > \dfrac{1}{3^p} \ldots\ldots$ or $\quad u_1 > u_2 > u_3 \ldots\ldots$

i.e. each term of the series is numerically less than the preceding term of the series.

and (iii) $\quad \lim u_n = \lim \dfrac{1}{n^p} = \dfrac{1}{\infty} = 0.$

Hence, by Lebnitz's test the series is convergent.

Ex. 45 : *Test the convergence of the series*

$$\log\left(\frac{1}{2}\right) - \log\left(\frac{2}{3}\right) + \log\left(\frac{3}{4}\right) - \log\left(\frac{4}{5}\right) + \ldots$$

Sol. : The given series,

$$\log\left(\frac{1}{2}\right) - \log\left(\frac{2}{3}\right) + \log\left(\frac{3}{4}\right) - \log\left(\frac{4}{5}\right) + \ldots$$

$$= -\log\left(\frac{2}{1}\right) + \log\left(\frac{3}{2}\right) - \log\left(\frac{4}{3}\right) + \log\left(\frac{5}{4}\right) - \ldots \quad \left[\because -\log x = \log x^{-1} = \log(1/x)\right]$$

$$= \sum (-1)^n \log\left(\frac{n+1}{n}\right) = \sum (-1)^n u_n, \text{ (say)},$$

where, $\quad u_n = \log\left\{\dfrac{n+1}{n}\right\}$

Now we see that,

(i) the terms of the series are alternately negative and positive,

(ii) $\because \dfrac{2}{1} > \dfrac{3}{2} > \dfrac{4}{3} > \dfrac{5}{3} \ldots$ and each of these is greater than unity.

$$\therefore \log\left(\frac{2}{1}\right) > \log\left(\frac{3}{2}\right) > \log\left(\frac{4}{3}\right) > \ldots \text{ or } u_1 > u_2 > u_3 > u_4 \ldots$$

i.e. each term of the series is numerically less than the preceding term.

and (iii) $\lim u_n = \lim \log \dfrac{n+1}{n} = \lim \log\left\{1 + \dfrac{1}{n}\right\}$

$= \log(1+0)$
$= \log 1 = 0$

Thus all the three conditions of Leibnitz's test are satisfied.
Hence, the given series is convergent.

Ex. 46 : *Test the convergence of the series* $1 - \dfrac{1}{2^2} + \dfrac{1}{3^2} - \dfrac{1}{4^2} + \dfrac{1}{5^2} - \ldots$

Sol. : The given series is

$$\sum (-1)^{n-1} \frac{1}{n^2} = \sum (-1)^n u_n, \text{ say}$$

where, $u_n = \dfrac{1}{n^2}$

Here we see that the terms of the series are alternately positive and negative, each term is numerically less than the preceding term and $\lim u_n = \lim (1/n^2) = 0$. Thus all the three conditions of the Leibnitz's test are satisfied. Therefore the series is convergent.

Ex. 47 : *Test the convergence of the series* $\dfrac{1}{x} - \dfrac{1}{x+a} + \dfrac{1}{x+2a} - \dfrac{1}{x+3a} + \ldots + x \text{ and } a > 0.$

Sol. : The given series is

$$\frac{1}{x} - \frac{1}{x+a} + \frac{1}{x+2a} - \frac{1}{x+3a} + \ldots = \sum_{n=1}^{\infty} \frac{(-1)^{n-1}}{x+(n-1)a} = \sum_{n=1}^{\infty} (-1)^{n-1} u_n, \text{ say}$$

where $u_n = \dfrac{1}{x+(n-1)a}$

Now we see that

(i) the terms of the series are alternately positive and negative,

(ii) $\therefore$ $x < x+a < x+2a < x+3a \ldots$

$\therefore \dfrac{1}{x} > \dfrac{1}{x+a} > \dfrac{1}{x+2a} > \dfrac{1}{x+3a} \ldots \text{ or } u_1 > u_2 > u_3 > u_4 \ldots$

i.e. each term of the series is numerically less than the preceding term

and (iii) $\lim u_n = \lim \dfrac{1}{x+(n-1)a}$

$= \lim \dfrac{1}{(x-a)+na} = \dfrac{1}{\infty} = 0.$

Thus all the three conditions of the Leibnitz's test for alternating series are satisfied.
Hence the series is convergent.

Ex. 48 : *Show that the following series is convergent* $\dfrac{1}{x+1} - \dfrac{1}{x+2} + \dfrac{1}{x+3} - ...,$ *except when x is a negative integer.*

Sol. : The given series is

$$\dfrac{1}{x+1} - \dfrac{1}{x+2} + \dfrac{1}{x+3} - ... = \Sigma \dfrac{(-1)^{n-1}}{x+n} = \Sigma (-1)^{n-1} u_n, \text{ (say)},$$

where, $\quad u_n = \dfrac{1}{x+n}$

Hence we see that

(i) If $x > -1$, the terms are alternately positive and negative from the beginning. If $x < -1$, excluding negative integers, then the terms are ultimately alternating in sign.

Since the removal of a finite number of terms does not affect convergence of the series, we may assume that the terms of the series are alternately positive and negative in both these cases.

(ii) Clearly $u_1 > u_2 > u_3 > u_4$ ... i.e. each term of the series is numerically less than the preceding term and

(iii) $\lim u_n = \lim \dfrac{1}{x+n} = \dfrac{1}{\infty} = 0.$

Hence, the series is convergent.

Ex. 49 : *Test the convergence of the series*

$\dfrac{1}{xy} - \dfrac{1}{(x+1)(y+1)} + \dfrac{1}{(x+2)(y+2)} - \dfrac{1}{(x+3)(y+3)} + ...$ *x and y being positive quantities.*

Sol. : The given series is

$$\dfrac{1}{xy} - \dfrac{1}{(x+1)(y+1)} + \dfrac{1}{(x+2)(y+2)} - \dfrac{1}{(x+3)(y+3)} + ...$$

$$= \sum_{n=1}^{\infty} \dfrac{(-1)^{n-1}}{(x+n-1)(y+n-1)} = \sum_{n=1}^{\infty} (-1)^{n-1} u_n, \text{ (say)},$$

where, $\quad u_n = \dfrac{1}{(x+n-1)(y+n-1)}$

Here we see that

(i) Since x, y are positive quantities, therefore the terms of the series are alternately positive and negative.

(ii) Since $x + 1 > x$ and $y + 1 > y$, therefore $(x+1)(y+1) > xy$,

or $\dfrac{1}{xy} > \dfrac{1}{(x+1)(y+1)}$ i.e., $u_1 > u_2$

Proceding similarly, we get,

$$u_1 > u_2 > u_3 > u_4 \ldots$$

i.e. each term of the series is numerically less than the preceding term and

(iii) $\lim u_n = \lim \dfrac{1}{(x+n-1)(y+n-1)} = \dfrac{1}{\infty} = 0.$

Hence, by Leibnitz's test, the given series is convergent.

Ex. 50 : *Prove that* $1 - \dfrac{1}{2} + \dfrac{1}{3} - \dfrac{1}{4} + \dfrac{1}{5} - \ldots$ *is convergent but not absolutely convergent.*

Sol. : Let the given series be $\sum u_n$

i.e.,
$$\sum u_n = 1 - \dfrac{1}{2} + \dfrac{1}{3} - \dfrac{1}{4} + \dfrac{1}{5} \ldots$$

$$= \sum \dfrac{(-1)^{n-1}}{n} \quad \text{where} \quad u_n = \dfrac{(-1)^{n-1}}{n}$$

Here the series $\sum u_n$ is convergent. (Refer Ex. 2 Article 6.7)

Now consider the series,

$$\sum |u_n| = 1 + \dfrac{1}{2} + \dfrac{1}{3} + \dfrac{1}{4} + \ldots$$

$$= \sum (1/n),$$

which is divergent, as here $p = 1$.

Hence, the given series is not absolutely convergent.

Ex. 51 : *Show that the series* $1 - \dfrac{1}{2^p} + \dfrac{1}{3^p} - \dfrac{1}{4^p} + \ldots$

is absolutely convergent if $p > 1$ and conditionally convergent if $0 < p \leq 1$.

Sol. : Let
$$\sum u_n = 1 - \dfrac{1}{2^p} + \dfrac{1}{3^p} - \dfrac{1}{4^p} \ldots$$

This series is convergent when $p > 0$.

Thus $\sum u_n$ is convergent if either $p > 1$ or if $0 < p \leq 1$.

Now consider the series,

$$\sum |u_n| = 1 + \dfrac{1}{2^p} + \dfrac{1}{3^p} + \dfrac{1}{4^p} + \ldots$$

$$= \sum \dfrac{1}{n^p},$$

which is convergent if $p > 1$ and divergent if $p \leq 1$,

i.e., $\sum |u_n|$ is convergent when $p > 1$ and divergent when $0 < p \leq 1$.

Thus when p > 1, both $\sum u_n$ and $\sum |u_n|$ are convergent.

Hence, the given series is absolutely convergent when p > 1.

But when $0 < p \leq 1$, $\sum u_n$ is convergent while $\sum |u_n|$ is divergent.

Hence, the given series is conditionally convergent when $0 < p \leq 1$.

Ex. 52 : *Test the convergence of the series* $1 - \frac{1}{\sqrt{2}} + \frac{1}{\sqrt{3}} - \frac{1}{\sqrt{4}} + \ldots$

Sol. : Let $\sum u_n = 1 - \frac{1}{\sqrt{2}} + \frac{1}{\sqrt{3}} - \frac{1}{\sqrt{4}} + \ldots = \sum \frac{(-1)^{n-1}}{\sqrt{n}}$

which is a convergent series. (Refer Ex. 3, Article 6.7)

Now consider the series,

$$\sum |u_n| = 1 + \frac{1}{\sqrt{2}} + \frac{1}{\sqrt{3}} + \ldots$$

$$= \sum \frac{1}{n^{1/2}},$$

which is divergent as here $p = \frac{1}{2} < 1$.

Hence, the given series is conditionally convergent.

Ex. 53 : *Test the convergence of the series* $1 - \frac{1}{2} + \frac{1}{4} - \frac{1}{8} + \ldots$ **(May 2004)**

Sol. : Let $\sum u_n = 1 - \frac{1}{2} + \frac{1}{4} - \frac{1}{8} + \ldots$

$$= \sum_{n=1}^{\infty} \frac{(-1)^{n-1}}{2^{n-1}}, \text{ so that } u_n = \frac{(-1)^{n-1}}{2^{n-1}}$$

Here we see that

(i) the terms are alternately positive and negative

(ii) each term is numerically less than the preceding term and

(iii) $\lim u_n = \lim \left(-\frac{1}{2}\right)^{n-1} = 0$.

∴ By Leibnitz's test for alternating series, $\sum u_n$ is convergent.

Now consider the series,

$$\sum |u_n| = 1 + \frac{1}{2} + \frac{1}{4} + \frac{1}{8} + \ldots$$

This is an infinite geometric series with common ratio $\frac{1}{2}$ which is < 1. Therefore, it is a convergent series. Since, both $\sum u_n$ and $\sum |u_n|$ are convergent, hence the given series $\sum u_n$ is absolutely convergent.

Ex. 54 : *Find whether the series* $1 - \dfrac{1}{2\sqrt{2}} + \dfrac{1}{3\sqrt{3}} - \dfrac{1}{4\sqrt{4}} + \ldots$ *is absolutely convergent.*

Sol. : Let
$$\Sigma\, u_n = 1 - \dfrac{1}{2\sqrt{2}} + \dfrac{1}{3\sqrt{3}} - \dfrac{1}{4\sqrt{4}} + \ldots$$

$$= \Sigma\, \dfrac{(-1)^{n-1}}{n\sqrt{n}}$$

Here we see that

(i) The terms are alternately positive and negative.

(ii) $u_1 > u_2 > u_3 \ldots$, (numerically) and (iii) $\lim u_n = \lim \dfrac{(-1)^{n-1}}{n\sqrt{n}} = 0$.

$\therefore$ By Leibnitz's test for alternating series $\Sigma\, u_n$ is convergent.

Now consider the series,

$$\Sigma\, |u_n| = 1 + \dfrac{1}{2\sqrt{2}} + \dfrac{1}{3\sqrt{3}} + \ldots$$

$$= \Sigma\, \dfrac{1}{n\sqrt{n}} = \Sigma\, \dfrac{1}{n^{3/2}},$$

which is clearly convergent as here $p = \dfrac{3}{2} > 1$.

Hence, the given series is absolutely convergent.

Ex. 55 : *Show that the series* $x - \dfrac{x^3}{3} + \dfrac{x^5}{5} \ldots$ *converges if and only if* $-1 \leq x \leq 1$.

Sol. : Let the given series be $\Sigma\, u_n$.

Then
$$u_n = (-1)^{n-1} \dfrac{x^{2n-1}}{2n-1}$$

and
$$u_{n+1} = (-1)^n \dfrac{x^{2n+1}}{2n+1}$$

$\therefore$
$$\left|\dfrac{u_n}{u_{n+1}}\right| = \dfrac{2n+1}{2n-1} \cdot \dfrac{1}{x^2}$$

Now,
$$\lim_{n \to \infty} \left|\dfrac{u_n}{u_{n+1}}\right| = \lim \left[\dfrac{(2+1/n)}{(2-1/n)} \cdot \dfrac{1}{x^2}\right] = \dfrac{1}{x^2}$$

$\therefore$ by D'Alembert's ratio test,

$\Sigma\, |u_n|$ converges if $1/x^2 > 1$.

i.e., $x^2 < 1$ i.e., $|x| < 1$ and diverges if $|x| > 1$. Since every absolutely convergent series is convergent, therefore the given series $\sum u_n$ converges when $|x| < 1$ i.e., $-1 < x < 1$.

When $x = 1$, the series $\sum u_n$ becomes $\left(1 - \frac{1}{3} + \frac{1}{5} - \frac{1}{7} + \ldots\right)$.

Which is again convergent by Leibnitz's test.

When $x > 1$ or when $x < -1$, obviously u_n does not tend to zero as $n \to \infty$. So the series $\sum u_n$ does not converge, when $|x| > 1$.

Hence the given series converges iff $-1 \leq x \leq 1$.

Ex. 56 : *Discuss the convergence of the logarithmic series*

$$x - \frac{x^2}{2} + \frac{x^3}{3} - \ldots + (-1)^{n-1}\frac{x^n}{n} + \ldots$$

Sol. : Let $\quad \sum u_n = x - \frac{x^2}{2} + \frac{x^3}{3} - \frac{x^4}{4} + \ldots$

The series $\sum u_n$ is absolutely convergent if the series $\sum |u_n|$ is convergent.

To discuss the convergence of $\sum |u_n|$ we shall apply ratio test.

We have, $\quad \dfrac{|u_n|}{|u_{n+1}|} = \left|\dfrac{u_n}{u_{n+1}}\right| = \left|\dfrac{x^n}{n} \cdot \dfrac{n+1}{x^{n+1}}\right| = \dfrac{n+1}{n} \cdot \dfrac{1}{|x|}$

$$= \left(1 + \frac{1}{n}\right) \cdot \frac{1}{|x|}$$

$\therefore \quad \lim \dfrac{|u_n|}{|u_{n+1}|} = \lim \left(1 + \dfrac{1}{n}\right) \dfrac{1}{|x|} = \dfrac{1}{|x|}$

So by ratio test the series $\sum |u_n|$ is convergent if $\dfrac{1}{|x|} > 1$.

i.e., if $|x| < 1$ i.e., if $-1 < x < 1$.

$\therefore$ The given series is absolutely convergent and hence also convergent if $-1 < x < 1$ i.e., if $|x| < 1$.

When $x = 1$, the given series is $1 - \frac{1}{2} + \frac{1}{3} - \frac{1}{4} + \ldots$

which converges by Leibnitz's test but convergence conditionally.

When $x = -1$, the given series is $-\left(1 + \frac{1}{2} + \frac{1}{3} + \frac{1}{4} + \ldots\right)$ which diverges to $-\infty$.

When $x > 1$ or $x < -1$ i.e., $|x| > 1$, obviously $\lim u_n \neq 0$ and so the series $\sum u_n$ does not converge.

Hence, the given series is convergent if $-1 < x \leq 1$. For $|x| < 1$ i.e., $-1 < x < 1$, it converges absolutely.

Ex. 57 : *Show that a series of positive terms, if convergent, is absolutely convergent. Prove that the series $2 \sin \frac{x}{3} + 4 \sin \frac{x}{9} + 8 \sin \frac{x}{27} + \ldots$. Converges absolutely for all finite values of x.*

Sol. : First part : Let $\sum u_n$ be a convergent series of positive terms. Since $u_n > 0$, therefore, $|u_n| = u_n$. So the series $\sum |u_n|$ is also convergent and hence the series $\sum u_n$ is absolutely convergent.

Second part : Let the given series be denoted by $\sum u_n$. Then

$$u_n = 2^n \sin(x/3^n), \text{ and } u_{n+1} = 2^{n+1} \sin(x/3^{n+1})$$

$$\therefore \quad \frac{u_n}{u_{n+1}} = \frac{1}{2} \cdot \sin(x/3^n) \cdot \frac{1}{\sin(x/3^{n+1})}$$

$$= \frac{1}{2} \cdot \frac{\sin(x/3^n)}{x/3^n} \cdot \frac{x/3^{n+1}}{\sin(x/3^{n+1})} \cdot 3$$

We shall test the convergence of the series $\sum |u_n|$.

We have, $\quad \dfrac{|u_n|}{|u_{n+1}|} = \left|\dfrac{u_n}{u_{n+1}}\right| = \dfrac{3}{2} \cdot \left|\dfrac{\sin(x/3^n)}{x/3^n}\right| \cdot \left|\dfrac{x/3^{n+1}}{\sin(x/3^{n+1})}\right|$

$$\therefore \quad \lim_{n \to \infty} \frac{|u_n|}{|u_{n+1}|} = \frac{3}{2} \text{ for all finite value of } x \text{ because } \lim_{n \to \infty} \frac{\sin(x/3^n)}{x/3^n} = 1.$$

Since $\displaystyle\lim_{n \to \infty} \frac{|u_n|}{|u_{n+1}|} > 1$ for all finite values of x, therefore by D'Alembert's ratio test, the series $\sum |u_n|$ is convergent for all finite values of x.

Hence, the series $\sum u_n$ converges absolutely for all finite values of x.

Ex. 58 : *Show that the series $1 + \dfrac{\alpha+1}{\beta+1} + \dfrac{(\alpha+1)(2\alpha+1)}{(\beta+1)(2\beta+1)} + \dfrac{(\alpha+1)(2\alpha+1)(3\alpha+1)}{(\beta+1)(2\beta+1)(3\beta+1)} + \ldots$*

converges if $\beta > \alpha > 0$ and diverges if $\alpha \geq \beta > 0$ [$\alpha > 0, \beta > 0$].

Sol. : Here, $\quad u_n = \dfrac{(\alpha+1)(2\alpha+1)\ldots[(n-1)\alpha+1]}{(\beta+1)(2\beta+1)\ldots[(n-1)\beta+1]}$

then $\quad u_{n+1} = \dfrac{(\alpha+1)(2\alpha+1)\ldots[(n-1)\alpha+1](n\alpha+1)}{(\beta+1)(2\beta+1)\ldots[(n-1)\beta+1](n\beta+1)}$

Now, $\quad \dfrac{u_n}{u_{n+1}} = \dfrac{n\beta+1}{n\alpha+1} = \dfrac{\beta+1/n}{\alpha+1/n}$

$\therefore \quad \lim \dfrac{u_n}{u_{n+1}} = \lim \dfrac{\beta+1/n}{\alpha+1/n} = \dfrac{\beta}{\alpha}$

∴ by ratio test the series is convergent if $\frac{\beta}{\alpha} > 1$ i.e. if $\beta > \alpha > 0$, divergent if $\frac{\beta}{\alpha} < 1$, i.e., if $\alpha > \beta > 0$, and the test fails if $\frac{\beta}{\alpha} = 1$ i.e., if $\beta = \alpha$. Now when $\beta = \alpha$, then the series becomes $1 + 1 + 1 + 1 + \ldots$ for which the sum of n terms $S_n = n$. ∵ $\lim S_n = \infty$.
∴ this series is convergent.

Hence, the given series is convergent if $\beta > \alpha > 0$ and divergent $\alpha \geq \beta > 0$.

Ex. 59 : *Test for convergence the series* $1 + 3x + 5x^2 + 7x^3 + \ldots$

Sol. : Here, $\quad u_n = (2n - 1) x^{n-1}$

and $\quad u_{n+1} = (2n + 1) x^n$

Now, $\quad \dfrac{u_n}{u_{n+1}} = \dfrac{(2n - 1) x^{n-1}}{(2n + 1) x^n} = \dfrac{(2 - 1/n)}{(2 + 1/n)} \cdot \dfrac{1}{x}$

∴ $\quad \lim \dfrac{u_n}{u_{n+1}} = \dfrac{2}{2} \cdot \dfrac{1}{x} = \dfrac{1}{x}$

by ratio test the series is convergent if $1/x > 1$.

i.e. if $1 > x$ or $x < 1$, the series is divergent if $1/x < 1$, i.e. if $x > 1$ and the test fails when $1/x = 1$, i.e. if $x = 1$.

Now, when $x = 1$, the series becomes $1 + 3 + 5 + 7 + \ldots$
The sum of n terms of this series is given by,

$$S_n = \frac{n}{2} [2.1 + (n - 1) \cdot 2] = n^2$$

∵ $\quad \lim S_n = \infty$, ∴ this series is divergent.

Hence, the given series is convergent if $x < 1$ and divergent if $x \geq 1$.

Ex. 60 : *Test for convergence the series* $1 + \dfrac{x}{2^2} + \dfrac{x^2}{3^2} + \dfrac{x^3}{4^2} + \ldots$

Sol. : Here, $\quad u_n = \dfrac{x^{n-1}}{n^2}$

and $\quad u_{n+1} = \dfrac{x^n}{(n + 1)^2}$

Now, $\quad \dfrac{u_n}{u_{n+1}} = \dfrac{x^{n-1}}{n^2} \cdot \dfrac{(n + 1)^2}{x^n}$

$\quad = (1 + 1/n)^2 \cdot \dfrac{1}{x}$

∴ $\quad \lim \dfrac{u_n}{u_{n+1}} = \lim (1 + 1/n)^2 \dfrac{1}{x} = \dfrac{1}{x}$

∴ By ratio test the series is convergent if $1/x > 1$, i.e., if $x < 1$, divergent if $1/x < 1$, i.e. if $x > 1$ and the test fails if $\frac{1}{x} = 1$ i.e. if $x = 1$.

Now when $x = 1$, then $u_n = \frac{1}{n^2}$.

∴ $\sum u_n = \sum \frac{1}{n^2}$ which is convergent because here $p = 2$ i.e. > 1.

Hence, the given series is convergent if $x \leq 1$ and divergent if $x > 1$.

Ex. 61 : *Test for convergence the series whose n^{th} term is $\frac{1}{x^n + x^{-n}}$.*

Sol. : Here, $u_n = \frac{1}{x^n + x^{-n}} = \frac{x^n}{x^{2n} + 1}$

and $u_{n+1} = \frac{x^{n+1}}{x^{2(n+1)} + 1}$

Now, $\frac{u_n}{u_{n+1}} = \frac{x^n}{x^{2n} + 1} \cdot \frac{x^{2n+2} + 1}{x^{n+1}}$

$= \frac{x^{2n+2} + 1}{x^{2n} + 1} \cdot \frac{1}{x}$

Here $\lim (u_n/u_{n+1})$ can be found only if we know that $x < 1$ or $x > 1$.

Let, $x < 1$.

Then $\lim \frac{u_n}{u_{n+1}} = \lim \frac{x^{2n+2} + 1}{x^{2n} + 1} \cdot \frac{1}{x}$

$= \frac{1}{x}$ $\quad [\because \lim x^{2n+2} = 0 \text{ if } x < 1]$

Now, if $x < 1$, then $1/x > 1$.

∴ If $x < 1$, we have $\lim (u_n/u_{n+1}) > 1$ and so by ratio test the series is convergent in this case.

Again let $x > 1$.

Then, $\lim \frac{u_n}{u_{n+1}} = \lim \frac{x^{2n+2}}{x^{2n} + 1} \cdot \frac{1}{x}$

$= \lim \frac{x^{2n+2}(1 + 1/x^{2n+2})}{x^{2n}(1 + 1/x^{2n})} \cdot \frac{1}{x}$

$= \lim x \frac{(1 + 1/x^{2n+2})}{(1 + 1/x^{2n})}$

$= x$ $\quad [\because \lim 1/x^{2n+2} = 0 \text{ if } x > 1]$

Thus when $x > 1$, we have $\lim (u_n/u_{n+1}) = x$ i.e. > 1 and so by ratio test the series is convergent in this case.

Again when $x = 1$, $u_n = \dfrac{1}{1+1} = \dfrac{1}{2}$ i.e. the series becomes $\dfrac{1}{2} + \dfrac{1}{2} + \dfrac{1}{2} + \ldots$

The sum of its n terms,

$$S_n = \dfrac{n}{2}$$

and $\lim S_n = \lim \dfrac{n}{2} = \infty$.

Therefore, the series is divergent when $x = 1$.

Hence, the given series is convergent when $x > 1$ or $x < 1$ and divergent when $x = 1$.

Ex. 62 : *Test the convergence of the series* $1 + \dfrac{x}{1!} + \dfrac{x^2}{2!} + \dfrac{x^3}{3!} + \ldots$

Sol. : Here $u_n = \dfrac{x^n}{n!}$

and $u_{n+1} = \dfrac{x^{n+1}}{(n+1)!}$

Now, $\dfrac{u_n}{u_{n+1}} = \dfrac{x^n}{n!} \cdot \dfrac{(n+1)!}{x^{n+1}}$

$= \dfrac{n+1}{x}$

$\therefore \quad \lim \dfrac{u_n}{u_{n+1}} = \infty$ for all values of x.

Thus for all values of x, $\lim (u_n/u_{n+1}) > 1$.

Hence, by ratio test the given series is convergent for all values of x.

Ex. 63 : *Test for convergence the series whose* n^{th} *term is* $\dfrac{(n+1) x^n}{n^2}$. **(Dec. 2010)**

Sol. : Here, $u_n = \dfrac{(n+1) x^n}{n^2}$

and $u_{n+1} = \dfrac{(n+2) x^{n+1}}{(n+1)^2}$

Now, $\dfrac{u_n}{u_{n+1}} = \dfrac{(n+1) x^n}{n^2} \cdot \dfrac{(n+1)^2}{(n+2) x^{n+1}}$

$= \dfrac{(1 + 1/n)^3}{1 + 2/n} \cdot \dfrac{1}{x}$

$= \dfrac{1}{x}$.

$\therefore$ By ratio test, the series is convergent if $1/x > 1$ i.e. if $x < 1$

Divergent if $1/x < 1$ i.e., if $x > 1$ and test fails if $1/x = 1$ i.e., if $x = 1$.

Now when $x = 1$, $u_n = \dfrac{n+1}{n^2}$.

Let $v_n = \dfrac{n}{n^2} = \dfrac{1}{n}$. So that the auxiliary series is

$$\Sigma v_n = \Sigma 1/n$$

We have, $\lim \dfrac{u_n}{v_n} = \lim \dfrac{n+1}{n^2} \cdot n$

$$= \lim (1 + 1/n) = 1$$

which is finite and non-zero.

Since the auxiliary series $\Sigma v_n = \Sigma 1/n$ is divergent as here $p = 1$.

∴ By comparison test the series Σu_n is also divergent when $x = 1$.

Hence, the given series is convergent if $x < 1$, and divergent if $x \geq 1$.

Ex. 64 : *Test for convergence the series whose n^{th} term is* $\dfrac{a^n}{x^n + a^n}$.

Sol. : Here, $u_n = \dfrac{a^n}{x^n + a^n}$

and $u_{n+1} = \dfrac{a^{n+1}}{x^{n+1} + a^{n+1}}$

Now, $\dfrac{u_n}{u_{n+1}} = \dfrac{a^n}{x^n + a^n} \cdot \dfrac{x^{n+1} + a^{n+1}}{a^{n+1}}$

$$= \dfrac{x^{n+1} + a^{n+1}}{a(x^n + a^n)}$$

Let $x > a$.

Then, $\lim \dfrac{u_n}{u_{n+1}} = \lim \dfrac{x^{n+1} + a^{n+1}}{a(x^n + a^n)}$

$$= \lim \dfrac{x^{n+1}[1 + (a/x)^{n+1}]}{ax^n[1 + (a/x^n)]}$$

$$= \lim \dfrac{x[1 + (a/x)^{n+1}]}{a[1 + (a/x)^n]}$$

$$= \dfrac{x}{a} \text{ which is } > 1.$$

∴ By ratio test the given series is convergent when $x > a$.

Let $x < a$.

Then, $\lim \dfrac{u_n}{u_{n+1}} = \lim \dfrac{a^{n+1}[1 + (x/a)^{n+1}]}{a \cdot a^n [1 + (x/a)^n]}$

$$= \lim \dfrac{[1 + (x/a)^{n+1}]}{[1 + (x/a)^n]} = 1$$

∴ The ratio test fails in this case.

But in this case, when $x < a$, we have,

$$\lim u_n = \frac{a^n}{x^n + a^n}$$

$$= \lim \frac{a^n}{a^n [1 + (x/a)^n]}$$

$$= \lim \frac{1}{[1 + (x/a)^n]}$$

$$= 1, \text{ which is } > 0.$$

∴ The given series is divergent when $x < a$.

Also when $x = a$, the series is $\frac{1}{2} + \frac{1}{2} + \ldots$, which is divergent.

Hence, the given series is convergent if $x > a$ and divergent if $x \leq a$.

Ex. 65 : *Test the convergence of series* $\sum_{n=1}^{\infty} \frac{x^n}{x + n}$.

Sol. : Here, $u_n = \frac{x^n}{x + n}$

and $u_{n+1} = \frac{x^{n+1}}{x + (n + 1)}$

Now, $\frac{u_n}{u_{n+1}} = \frac{x^n}{x + n} \cdot \frac{x + n + 1}{x^{n+1}}$

$$= \frac{1 + (x + 1)/n}{1 + x/n} \cdot \frac{1}{x}$$

∴ $\lim \frac{u_n}{u_{n+1}} = \frac{1}{x}$

∴ By ratio test the series is convergent if $1/x > 1$, i.e. if $x < 1$, divergent if $1/x < 1$, i.e. if $x > 1$ and the test fail when $x = 1$.

Now when $x = 1$, the $u_n = \frac{1}{1 + n}$.

We shall apply comparison test in this case take $v_n = 1/n$.

We have, $\lim \frac{u_n}{v_n} = \lim \frac{n}{n + 1} = \lim \frac{1}{1 + 1/n} = 1$ which is finite and non-zero.

But the series $\sum v_n = \sum 1/n$ is divergent when $x = 1$.

Hence, the given series is convergent if $x < 1$ and divergent if $x \geq 1$.

Ex. 66 : *Test the convergence of the series* $\sum \dfrac{n!\, x^n}{3 \cdot 5 \cdot 7 \ldots (2n+1)}$.

Sol. : Here, $u_n = \dfrac{n!\, x^n}{3 \cdot 5 \cdot 7 \ldots (2n+1)}$

$\therefore \quad u_{n+1} = \dfrac{(n+1)!\, x^{n+1}}{3 \cdot 5 \cdot 7 \ldots (2n+1)(2n+3)}$

Then, $\dfrac{u_n}{u_{n+1}} = \dfrac{2n+3}{(n+1)!} \cdot \dfrac{n!}{x} = \dfrac{2n+3}{n+1} \cdot \dfrac{1}{x}$

$\qquad = \left(\dfrac{2+3/n}{1+1/n}\right) \dfrac{1}{x}$

$\therefore \quad \lim \dfrac{u_n}{u_{n+1}} = \lim \left(\dfrac{2+3/n}{1+1/n}\right) \cdot \dfrac{1}{x} = \dfrac{2}{x}$

$\therefore$ By ratio test the series $\sum u_n$ is convergent if $2/x > 1$ i.e. if $x < 2$.

Divergent if $2/x < 1$ i.e. if $x > 2$ and the test fails when $2/x = 1$, i.e. when $x = 2$.

When $x = 2$, $\dfrac{u_n}{u_{n+1}} = \dfrac{2n+3}{2(n+1)}$

$\therefore \quad n\left(\dfrac{u_n}{u_{n+1}} - 1\right) = n\left(\dfrac{2n+3}{2n+2} - 1\right)$

$\qquad = \dfrac{n}{2(n+1)} = \dfrac{1}{2(1+1/n)}$

$\therefore \quad \lim n\left(\dfrac{u_n}{u_{n+1}} - 1\right) = \lim \dfrac{1}{2(1+1/n)} = \dfrac{1}{2}$, which is < 1.

$\therefore$ By Raabe's test, $\sum u_n$ is divergent when $x = 2$.

Hence, the given series $\sum u_n$ is convergent if $x < 2$ and divergent if $x \geq 2$.

Ex. 67 : *Test the convergence of the series* $\sum\limits_{n=1}^{\infty} \dfrac{1}{1 + \log n}$.

Sol. : Here, $u_n = \dfrac{1}{1 + \log n}$

and $u_{n+1} = \dfrac{1}{1 + \log(n+1)}$

Then, $\dfrac{u_n}{u_{n+1}} = \dfrac{1 + \log(n+1)}{1 + \log n} = \dfrac{1 + \log\{n(1+1/n)\}}{1 + \log n}$

$\qquad = \dfrac{1 + \log n + \log(1+1/n)}{1 + \log n}$

$$= \frac{\log en + \log(1+1/n)}{\log en}$$

$$= 1 + \frac{1}{\log en} \cdot \log(1+1/n)$$

$$= 1 + \frac{1}{\log en} \cdot \left(\frac{1}{n} - \frac{1}{2n^2} + \frac{1}{3n^3} \cdots\right)$$

$$= 1 + \frac{1}{n \log en} - \frac{1}{2n^2 \log en} + \cdots$$

$\therefore \quad \lim \frac{u_n}{u_{n+1}} = 1$, i.e. the ratio test fails.

Applying Raabe's test, we have,

$$\lim n\left(\frac{u_n}{u_{n+1}} - 1\right) = \lim n\left[\frac{1}{n \log en} - \frac{1}{2n^2 \log en} + \cdots\right]$$

$$= \lim\left(\frac{1}{\log en} - \frac{1}{2n \log en} + \cdots\right) = 0, \text{ which is } < 1.$$

Hence, the given series is divergent.

Ex. 68 : *Test the convergence of the series* $\frac{1}{\log 2} + \frac{1}{\log 3} + \frac{1}{\log 4} + \cdots$.

Sol. : Here let $f(n) = \frac{1}{\log n}$

Clearly f(n) is positive for all positive integrals values of n and decreases continuously as n increases.

Now, $\quad a^n f(a^n) = \frac{a^n}{(\log a^n)} = \frac{a^n}{n \log a}$

Consider the series,

$$\sum a^n f(a^n) = \sum \{a^n /(n \log a)\}$$
$$= \sum v_n \text{ (say)}$$

Here, $\quad v_n = \frac{a^n}{n \log a}$, and $v_{n+1} = \frac{a^{n+1}}{(n+1) \log a}$

$\therefore \quad \frac{v_n}{v_{n+1}} = \frac{n+1}{n} \cdot \frac{1}{a} = \left(1 + \frac{1}{n}\right) \cdot \frac{1}{a}$

$\therefore \quad \lim \frac{v_n}{v_{n+1}} = \frac{1}{a} < 1 \quad \text{as } a > 1.$

$\therefore$ By ratio test the series $\sum a^n f(a^n)$ is divergent.

Hence, by Cauchy's condensation test, the given series

$$\sum f(n) = \frac{1}{\log 2} + \frac{1}{\log 3} + \cdots \text{ is also divergent.}$$

Ex. 69 : *Test the convergence of the series* $\dfrac{1}{(\log 2)^p} + \dfrac{1}{(\log 3)^p} + \ldots + \dfrac{1}{(\log n)^p} + \ldots$

Sol. : Let $\quad f(n) = \dfrac{1}{(\log n)^p}$

which is positive for all positive integral values of n and decreases continually as n increases.

Now, $\quad a_n f(a^n) = \dfrac{a^n}{(\log a^n)^p} = \dfrac{a^n}{n^p (\log a)^p}$

Consider the series,

$$\sum a^n f(a^n) = \sum \dfrac{a^n}{n^p (\log a)^p} = \sum v_n, \text{ say.}$$

Here, $\quad v_n = \dfrac{a^n}{n^p (\log a)^p}$

and $\quad v_{n+1} = \dfrac{a^{n+1}}{(n+1)^p (\log a)^p}$

$\therefore \quad \dfrac{v_n}{v_{n+1}} = \dfrac{a^n}{n^p (\log a)^p} \cdot \dfrac{(n+1)^p (\log a)^p}{a^{n+1}}$

$$= \left(1 + \dfrac{1}{n}\right)^p \cdot \dfrac{1}{a}$$

$\therefore \quad \lim \dfrac{v_n}{v_{n+1}} = \dfrac{1}{a} < 1 \text{ as } a > 1$

$\therefore$ By ratio test, the series $\sum v_n = \sum a^n f(a^n)$ is divergent.

Hence by Cauchy's condensation test, the given series $\sum f(n)$ is also divergent.

Ex. 70 : *Test for convergence the series* $1 + \dfrac{x}{2} + \dfrac{2!}{3^2} x^2 + \dfrac{3!}{4^3} x^3 + \ldots$

Sol. : Here, $\quad u_n = \dfrac{(n-1)!}{n^{n-1}} x^{n-1}$

and $\quad u_{n+1} = \dfrac{n!}{(n+1)^n} x^n$

Then, $\quad \dfrac{u_n}{u_{n+1}} = \dfrac{(n-1)!}{n^{n-1}} \cdot \dfrac{(n+1)^n}{n!} \cdot \dfrac{1}{x}$

$$= \dfrac{(n+1)^n}{n^{n-1} \cdot n} \cdot \dfrac{1}{x}$$

$$= \left(1 + \dfrac{1}{n}\right)^n \cdot \dfrac{1}{x}$$

$$\lim \frac{u_n}{u_{n+1}} = \lim \left(1 + \frac{1}{n}\right)^n \cdot \frac{1}{x}$$

$$= \frac{e}{x} \qquad \left[\because \lim_{n \to \infty} \left(1 + \frac{1}{n}\right)^n = e\right]$$

∴ By ratio test the series is convergent if $e/x > 1$ i.e. if $x < e$, divergent if $e/x < 1$ i.e. if $x > e$ and the test fails when $e/x = 1$, i.e. when $x = e$.

When $x = e$, $\qquad \dfrac{u_n}{u_{n+1}} = \dfrac{1}{e}\left(1 + \dfrac{1}{n}\right)^n$

Applying log test, we have,

$$\lim \left(n \log \frac{u_n}{u_{n+1}}\right) = \lim \left[n \log \left\{\frac{1}{e}\left(1 + \frac{1}{n}\right)^n\right\}\right]$$

$$= \lim \left[n \left\{n \log \left(1 + \frac{1}{n}\right) - \log e\right\}\right]$$

$$= \lim \left[n \left\{n \left(\frac{1}{n} - \frac{1}{2n^2} + \frac{1}{3n^3} - \cdots\right) - 1\right\}\right]$$

$$= \lim \left[-\frac{1}{2} + \frac{1}{3n} \cdots\right]$$

$$= -\frac{1}{2} \text{, which is } < 1.$$

∴ The series is divergent when $x = e$.

Hence, the given series is convergent if $x < e$ and divergent if $x \geq e$.

Ex. 71 : *Test for convergence the series* $1 + \dfrac{2x}{2!} + \dfrac{3^2 x^2}{3!} + \dfrac{4^3 x^3}{4!} + \dfrac{5^4 x^4}{5!} + \cdots$

Sol. : Here, $\qquad u_n = \dfrac{n^{n-1}}{n!} x^{n-1}$

and $\qquad u_{n+1} = \dfrac{(n+1)^n}{(n+1)!} x^n$

Then, $\qquad \dfrac{u_n}{u_{n+1}} = \dfrac{n^{n-1}(n+1)!}{n!(n+1)^n} \cdot \dfrac{1}{x}$

$$= \frac{n^{n-1}(n+1)}{(n+1)^n} \cdot \frac{1}{x}$$

$$= \left(\frac{n}{n+1}\right)^{n-1} \cdot \frac{1}{x}$$

$$= \frac{1}{(1+1/n)^{n-1}} \cdot \frac{1}{x}$$

$$= \frac{1}{(1+1/n)^n} \cdot (1+1/n) \cdot \frac{1}{x}$$

$$\therefore \quad \lim \frac{u_n}{u_{n+1}} = \left\{ \frac{(1+1/n)}{(1+1/n)^n} \cdot \frac{1}{x} \right\}$$

$$= \frac{1}{ex}$$

$\therefore$ By ratio test the series is convergent if $1/ex > 1$, i.e. if $x < 1/e$, divergent if $1/ex < 1$, i.e. if $x > 1/e$ and the test fails when $1/ex = 1$, i.e., when $x = 1/e$.

When $x = 1/e$, $\quad \dfrac{u_n}{u_{n+1}} = \dfrac{e(1+1/n)}{(1+1/n)^n}$

Applying log test, we have

$$= \lim \left(n \log \frac{u_n}{u_{n+1}} \right)$$

$$= \lim \left[n \log \left\{ \frac{e(1+1/n)}{(1+1/n)^n} \right\} \right]$$

$$= \lim n \left[\log e + \log(1+1/n) - n \log(1+1/n) \right]$$

$$= \lim n \left[1 + \left(\frac{1}{n} - \frac{1}{2n^2} + \frac{1}{3n^3} \cdots \right) - n \left(\frac{1}{n} - \frac{1}{2n^2} + \frac{1}{3n^3} \cdots \right) \right]$$

$$= \lim n \left[\left(1 + \frac{1}{2} \right) \cdot \frac{1}{n} + \left\{ \frac{1}{2} + \frac{1}{3} \right\} \frac{1}{n^2} + \cdots \right]$$

$$= \lim \left[\frac{3}{2} + \frac{5}{6n} + \cdots \right]$$

$$= \frac{3}{2}, \text{ which is} > 1.$$

$\therefore$ The series is convergent when $x = 1/e$.

Hence, the given series is convergent if $x \leq 1/e$ and divergent if $x \geq 1/e$.

Ex. 72 : *Test the convergence of the series* $1 + \dfrac{2^2}{3^2} + \dfrac{2^2 \cdot 4^2}{3^2 \cdot 5^2} + \dfrac{2^2 \cdot 4^2 \cdot 6^2}{3^2 \cdot 5^2 \cdot 7^2} + \cdots$

Sol. : Neglecting the first term 1, we have,

$$u_n = \frac{2^2 \cdot 4^2 \cdot \ldots (2n)^2}{3^2 \cdot 5^2 \ldots (2n+1)^2}$$

then

$$u_{n+1} = \frac{2^2 \cdot 4^2 \cdot \ldots (2n)^2 (2n+2)^2}{3^2 \cdot 5^2 \ldots (2n+1)^2 (2n+3)^2}$$

Now,

$$\frac{u_n}{u_{n+1}} = \frac{(2n+3)^2}{(2n+2)^2} = \frac{(2+3/n)^2}{(2+2/n)^2}$$

$\therefore \quad \lim \dfrac{u_n}{u_{n+1}} = \lim \dfrac{(2+3/n)^2}{(2+2/n)^2}$

$$= \frac{2^2}{2^2} = 1$$

i.e., the ratio test fails.

∴ Applying Raabe's test, we have,

$$\lim n \left(\frac{u_n}{u_{n+1}} - 1\right) = \lim n \left\{\frac{(2n+3)^2}{(2n+2)^2} - 1\right\}$$

$$= \lim \frac{n(4n+5)}{(2n+2)^2} = \lim \frac{(4+5/n)}{(2+2/n)^2} = \frac{4}{2^2} = 1$$

∴ Raabe's test also fails.

Now, we apply De Morgan's test.

We have, $n\left(\dfrac{u_n}{u_{n+1}} - 1\right) = \dfrac{n(4n+5)}{(2n+2)^2}$

$$\therefore \lim \left[\left\{n\left(\frac{u_n}{u_{n+1}} - 1\right) - 1\right\} \log n\right]$$

$$= \lim \left[\left\{\frac{n(4n+5)}{(2n+2)^2} - 1\right\} \log n\right]$$

$$= \lim \left[\left\{\frac{-3n-4}{(2n+2)^2}\right\} \log n\right]$$

$$= \lim \left[\frac{-3-4/n}{(2+2/n)^2} \cdot \frac{\log n}{n}\right] = -\frac{3}{2^2} \infty \, 0 \quad \left[\because \log \frac{\log n}{n} = 0\right]$$

$$= 0, \text{ which is } < 1.$$

Hence, the given series $\sum u_n$ is divergent.

Ex. 73 : *Test the convergence of the following series* $\dfrac{1^2}{2^2} + \dfrac{1^2 \cdot 3^2}{2^2 \cdot 4^2} x + \dfrac{1^2 \cdot 3^2 \cdot 5^2}{2^2 \cdot 4^2 \cdot 6^2} x^2 + \ldots$

Sol. : Here, $\qquad u_n = \dfrac{1^2 \cdot 3^2 \ldots (2n-1)^2}{2^2 \cdot 4^2 \ldots (2n)^2} \cdot x^{n-1}$

and $\qquad u_{n+1} = \dfrac{1^2 \cdot 3^2 \ldots (2n-1)^2 \cdot (2n+1)^2}{2^2 \cdot 4^2 \ldots (2n)^2 (2n+2)^2} x^n$

Now, $\qquad \lim \dfrac{u_n}{u_{n+1}} = \lim \left\{\dfrac{2+2/n}{2+1/n}\right\}^2 \cdot \dfrac{1}{x} = \dfrac{2^2}{2^2} \cdot \dfrac{1}{x} = \dfrac{1}{x}$

∴ By ratio test the series $\sum u_n$ is convergent if $1/x > 1$, i.e. if $x < 1$, divergent if $1/x < 1$, i.e. if $x > 1$ and the test fails when $1/x = 1$, i.e., when $x = 1$.

When $x = 1$, we have,

$$\frac{u_n}{u_{n+1}} = \frac{(2n+2)^2}{(2n+1)^2}$$

$$\therefore \quad n\left\{\frac{u_n}{u_{n+1}} - 1\right\} = n\left\{\frac{(2n+2)^2}{(2n+1)^2} - 1\right\}$$

$$= \frac{n(4n+3)}{(2n+1)^2} = \frac{4+3/n}{(2+1/n)^2}$$

$$\therefore \quad \lim\left[n\left\{\frac{u_n}{u_{n+1}} - 1\right\}\right] = \lim\frac{4+3/n}{(2+1/n)^2} = \frac{4}{2^2} = 1$$

∴ Raabe's test fails when $x = 1$.

Now, $\quad n\left\{\frac{u_n}{u_{n+1}} - 1\right\} - 1 = \frac{n(4n+3)}{(2n+1)^2} - 1 = \frac{-n-1}{(2n+1)^2}$

$$\therefore \quad \lim\left[\left\{n\left(\frac{u_n}{u_{n+1}} - 1\right) - 1\right\}\log n\right]$$

$$= \lim\left[\left\{\frac{-n-1}{(2n+1)^2}\right\}\log n\right]$$

$$= \lim\left[\frac{-1-1/n}{(2+1/n)^2} \cdot \frac{\log n}{n}\right] = \frac{-1}{2^2} \cdot 0 = 0 < 1$$

∴ By De Morgan's test $\sum u_n$ is divergent when $x = 1$.

Hence, the given series $\sum u_n$ is convergent if $x < 1$ and divergent if $x \geq 1$.

Ex. 74 : *Test the convergence of the series* $1 + \frac{\alpha}{1 \cdot \beta}x + \frac{\alpha(\alpha+1)^2}{1 \cdot 2 \cdot \beta(\beta+1)}x^2 + \ldots$

Sol. : Neglecting the first term 1, we have,

$$u_n = \frac{\alpha(\alpha+1)^2(\alpha+2)^2 \ldots (\alpha+n-1)^2}{1 \cdot 2 \ldots n \cdot \beta(\beta+1) \ldots (\beta+n-1)} x^n$$

and $\quad u_{n+1} = \frac{\alpha(\alpha+1)^2(\alpha+2)^2 \ldots (\alpha+n-1)^2(\alpha+n)^2}{1 \cdot 2 \ldots n(n+1)\beta(\beta+1) \ldots (\beta+n-1)(\beta+n)} \cdot x^{n+1}$

Then, $\quad \frac{u_n}{u_{n+1}} = \frac{(n+1)(\beta+n)}{(\alpha+n)^2} \cdot \frac{1}{x}$

$$= \frac{(1+1/n)(\beta/n+1)}{(\alpha/n+1)^2} \cdot \frac{1}{x}$$

$$\therefore \quad \lim\frac{u_n}{u_{n+1}} = \frac{1}{x}$$

∴ By ratio test the given series is convergent if $1/x > 1$ i.e. if $x < 1$, divergent if $1/x < 1$ i.e. if $x > 1$ and the test fails when $1/x = 1$, i.e. when $x = 1$.

When $x = 1$, $\quad \frac{u_n}{u_{n+1}} = \frac{(n+1)(\beta+n)}{(\alpha+n)^2}$

Now, $n\left\{\dfrac{u_n}{u_{n+1}} - 1\right\} = n\left[\dfrac{(n+1)(\beta+n)}{(\alpha+n)^2} - 1\right] = \dfrac{n[(\beta - 2\alpha + 1)n - \alpha^2 + \beta]}{(\alpha+n)^2}$

$= \dfrac{(\beta - 2\alpha + 1) - \alpha^2/n + \beta/n}{(\alpha/n + 1)^2}$

$\therefore \quad \lim n\left\{\dfrac{u_n}{u_{n+1}} - 1\right\} = \dfrac{\beta - 2\alpha + 1}{1}$

$= \beta - 2\alpha + 1$

$\therefore$ By Raabe's test, when $x = 1$, the series is convergent if $\beta - 2\alpha + 1 > 1$ i.e. if $\beta > 2\alpha$, divergent if $\beta - 2\alpha + 1 < 1$ i.e. if $\beta < 2\alpha$ and the test fails when $\beta - 2\alpha + 1 = 1$, i.e. when $\beta = 2\alpha$.

When $\beta = 2\alpha$, we have,

$n\left\{\dfrac{u_n}{u_{n+1}} - 1\right\} = \dfrac{n(1 \cdot n - \alpha^2 + 2\alpha)}{(\alpha+n)^2}$

$\therefore \quad \lim\left\{n\left(\dfrac{u_n}{u_{n+1}} - 1\right) - 1\right\}\log n$

$= \lim\left[\left\{\dfrac{n(n - \alpha^2 + 2\alpha)}{(\alpha+n)^2} - 1\right\}\log n\right]$

$= \lim\left[\left\{\dfrac{-\alpha^2 n - \alpha^2}{(\alpha+n)^2}\right\}\log n\right] = \lim\left[\dfrac{-\alpha^2 - \alpha^2/n}{(\alpha/n + 1)^2} \cdot \dfrac{\log n}{n}\right]$

$= (-\alpha^2) \cdot 0 = 0 < 1$.

$\therefore$ When $x = 1$ and $\beta = 2\alpha$, then the series is divergent by De Morgan's test. Hence, the given series is convergent if $x < 1$, divergent if $x > 1$ and when $x = 1$, then the series is convergent if $\beta > 2\alpha$ and divergent if $\beta \leq 2\alpha$.

Ex. 75 : *Test the convergence of the given series*

$$\left\{\dfrac{1}{2\cdot 4}\right\}^{2/3} + \left\{\dfrac{1\cdot 3}{2\cdot 4\cdot 6}\right\}^{2/3} + \left\{\dfrac{1\cdot 3\cdot 5}{2\cdot 4\cdot 6\cdot 8}\right\}^{2/3} + \ldots$$

Sol. : Here, $u_n = \left[\dfrac{1\cdot 3\cdot 5 \ldots (2n-1)}{2\cdot 4\cdot 6 \ldots (2n+2)}\right]^{2/3}$

and $u_{n+1} = \left[\dfrac{1\cdot 3\cdot 5 \ldots (2n-1)(2n+1)}{2\cdot 4\cdot 6 \ldots (2n+2)(2n+4)}\right]^{2/3}$

Then, $\dfrac{u_n}{u_{n+1}} = \left\{\dfrac{2n+4}{2n+1}\right\}^{2/3} = \left\{\dfrac{1 + 2/n}{1 + 1/2n}\right\}^{2/3}$

$\therefore \quad \lim \dfrac{u_n}{u_{n+1}} = \left\{\dfrac{1}{1}\right\}^{2/3} = 1$

So that the ratio test fails.

Now, applying logarithmic test, we have,

$$\lim \left\{ n \log \frac{u_n}{u_{n+1}} \right\} = \lim \left[n \log \left\{ \frac{1 + 2/n}{1 + 1/2n} \right\}^{2/3} \right]$$

$$= \lim \frac{2n}{3} \left[\log \left\{ 1 + \frac{2}{n} \right\} - \log \left\{ 1 + \frac{1}{2n} \right\} \right]$$

$$= \lim \frac{2n}{3} \left[\left\{ \frac{2}{n} - \frac{1}{2} \cdot \frac{2^2}{n^2} + \frac{1}{3} \cdot \frac{2^3}{n^3} \cdots \right\} - \left\{ \frac{1}{2n} - \frac{1}{2} \cdot \frac{1}{2^2 n^2} + \frac{1}{3} \cdot \frac{1}{2^3 \cdot n^3} \cdots \right\} \right]$$

$$= \lim \frac{2n}{3} \left[\left\{ 2 - \frac{1}{2} \right\} \frac{1}{n} + \left\{ -2 + \frac{1}{8} \right\} \frac{1}{n^2} + \left\{ \frac{8}{3} - \frac{1}{24} \right\} \frac{1}{n^3} \right]$$

$$= \lim \left[1 - \frac{5}{4n} + \frac{7}{4n^2} \cdots \right] = 1.$$

So that the log test also fails. Therefore, we apply the next test given below.

We have, $\quad n \log \frac{u_n}{u_{n+1}} = 1 - \frac{5}{4n} + \frac{7}{4n^2} \cdots$

$$\therefore \quad \lim \left[\left\{ n \log \frac{u_n}{u_{n+1}} - 1 \right\} \log n \right]$$

$$= \lim \left[\left\{ \left(1 - \frac{5}{4n} + \frac{7}{4n^2} \cdots \right) - 1 \right\} \log n \right]$$

$$= \lim \left[-\frac{5}{4} \cdot \frac{\log n}{n} + \frac{7 \log n}{4n^2} \right]$$

$$= 0 < 1. \qquad \left[\because \lim \frac{\log n}{n} = 0 \right]$$

Hence, the given series is divergent.

Ex. 76 : *Determine absolute or conditional convergence of* $\sum \frac{(-1)^n n^2}{n^3 + 1}$

Sol. : $\quad |u_n| = \frac{n^2}{n^3 + 1}$

Use comparison test with $\sum v_n = \sum 1/n$.

$$\therefore \quad \lim_{n \to \infty} \left| \frac{u_n}{v_n} \right| = \lim_{n \to \infty} \frac{n^3}{n^3 + 1} = 1$$

and series $\sum v_n$ is divergent (p series with p = 1).

$\therefore \quad \sum |u_n|$ is divergent and $\sum u_n$ is not absolute convergent.

Now, $\sum u_n$ is alternating series where $u_n = \frac{n^2}{n^3 + 1}$

To prove $u_n > u_{n+1}$ i.e., to prove $\frac{n^2}{n^3 + 1} \geq \frac{(n+1)^2}{(n+1)^3 + 1}$

i.e. $n^2(n^3 + 3n^2 + 3n + 2) \geq (n^3 + 1)(n^2 + 2n + 1)$
i.e. $n^4 + 2n^3 + n^2 \geq 2n + 1$
i.e. $n^4 + (n^2 + 1)(2n + 1) \geq 0$
This is true for $n > 1$.

Now, $\lim_{n \to \infty} \dfrac{n^2}{n^3 + 1} = \lim_{n \to \infty} \dfrac{1}{n + \dfrac{1}{n^2}} = 0$

By Leibnitz test, $\sum u_n$ is convergent.

$\therefore$ $\sum u_n$ is conditionally convergent.

Ex. 77 : *Determine absolute or conditional convergence of* $\dfrac{1}{2} - \dfrac{2}{5} + \dfrac{3}{10} - \dfrac{4}{17} + \ldots$

Sol. : $\sum u_n = \sum (-1)^{n+1} \dfrac{n}{n^2 + 1}$

$|u_n| = \dfrac{n}{n^2 + 1}$

Using comparison test with $\sum v_n = \sum 1/n$, we get,

$\lim_{n \to \infty} \dfrac{|u_n|}{v_n} = 1$

$\therefore$ $\sum |u_n|$ is divergent since $\sum v_n$ is divergent.

$\therefore$ $\sum |u_n|$ is not absolute convergent.

Now, $\sum u_n$ is an alternating series with

$u_n = \dfrac{n}{n^2 + 1}$

To prove $\dfrac{n}{n^2 + 1} \geq \dfrac{n + 1}{(n + 1)^2 + 1}$

i.e. $n[n^2 + 2n + 2] \geq (n + 1)(n^2 + 1)$

$n^2 + n \geq 1$.

This is true for $n \geq 1$ and $\lim_{n \to \infty} u_n = \lim_{n \to \infty} \dfrac{n}{n^2 + 1} = 0$

$\therefore$ $\sum u_n$ is convergent by Leibnitz test.

$\therefore$ $\sum u_n$ is conditionally convergent.

Ex. 78 : *Find the range of convergence of* $\sum \dfrac{(x + 1)^n}{3^n \cdot n}$.

Sol. : $\sum \dfrac{(x + 1)^n}{3^n \cdot n}$

$$\lim_{n \to \infty} \left| \frac{u_{n+1}}{u_n} \right| = \lim_{n \to \infty} \left| \frac{(x+1)^{n+1}}{3^{n+1}(n+1)} \cdot \frac{3^n \cdot n}{(x+1)^n} \right| = \lim_{n \to \infty} \left| \frac{(x+1)}{3} \cdot \frac{n}{n+1} \right|$$

$$= \left| \frac{x+1}{3} \right|$$

Range of convergence $\left| \frac{x+1}{3} \right| < 1.$ i.e. $-1 < \frac{x+1}{3} < 1.$

When $x + 1 = -3$, the series becomes $\sum \frac{(-1)^n}{n}$ which is convergent.

When $x + 1 = 3$, the series becomes $\sum 1/n$ which is divergent.

The range of convergence is $-4 \leq x < 2$.

Ex. 79 : *Find the range of convergence of* $\sum \frac{x^n}{n!}$.

Sol. :
$$\lim_{n \to \infty} \left| \frac{u_{n+1}}{u_n} \right| = \lim_{n \to \infty} \left| \frac{x^{n+1}}{(n+1)!} \cdot \frac{n!}{x^n} \right|$$

$$= \lim_{n \to \infty} \left| \frac{x}{n+1} \right| < 1 \text{ for convergence}$$

i.e. $|x| \leq \infty$ i.e. $-\infty < x < \infty$.

The series converges for all values of x.

Ex. 80 : *Determine the range of convergence of* $\sum_{n=1}^{\infty} \frac{n+1}{2n+1} \cdot \frac{(x-3)^n}{2^n}$.

Sol. : Here,
$$\lim_{n \to \infty} \left| \frac{u_{n+1}}{u_n} \right| = \lim_{n \to \infty} \left| \left[\frac{n+2}{2n+3} \cdot \frac{(x-3)^{n+1}}{2^{n+1}} \cdot \frac{2^n(2n+1)}{(n+1)(x-3)^n} \right] \right|$$

$$= \lim_{n \to \infty} \left| \frac{(n+2)(2n+1)}{(2n+3)(n+1)} \right| \cdot \left| \frac{1}{2}(x-3) \right| < 1$$

for convergence ... (1)

But $\lim_{n \to \infty} \left| \frac{(n+2)(2n+1)}{(2n+3)(n+1)} \right| = \lim_{n \to \infty} \left| \frac{2n^2 + 5n + 2}{2n^2 + 5n + 3} \right| = 1$ as $n \to \infty$

∴ From (1) we have, $\frac{1}{2}|x-3| < 1$

∴ $|x-3| < 2$

$-2 < x - 3 < 2$ i.e. the range of convergence is $1 < x < 5$.

At $x = 1$, the series becomes

$$\sum_{n=1}^{\infty} \frac{n+1}{2n+1} \cdot \frac{(-2)^n}{2^n} = \sum_{n=1}^{\infty} (-1)^n \frac{n+1}{2n+1}$$ which is divergent.

At $x = 5$, the series is $\sum_{n=1}^{\infty} \dfrac{n+1}{2n+1} \dfrac{2^n}{2^n}$, which is divergent.

Hence the range of convergence is $1 < x < 5$.

Ex. 81 : *Test for convergence, state the test of convergence you use*
$$\left[\dfrac{2^2}{1^2} - \dfrac{2}{1}\right]^{-1} + \left[\dfrac{3^2}{2^2} - \dfrac{3}{2}\right]^{-2} + \left[\dfrac{4^2}{3^2} - \dfrac{4}{3}\right]^{-3} + \ldots$$

Sol. : We have,
$$u_n = \left[\dfrac{(n+1)^{n+1}}{n^{n+1}} - \dfrac{n+1}{n}\right]^{-n}$$
$$= \left[\dfrac{n+1}{n}\left\{\left(\dfrac{n+1}{n}\right)^n - 1\right\}\right]^{-n} \text{ so that}$$
$$(u_n)^{1/n} = \left[\dfrac{n+1}{n}\left\{\left(\dfrac{n+1}{n}\right)^n - 1\right\}\right]^{-1}$$
$$= \dfrac{1}{(1 + 1/n)\,[(1 + 1/n)^n - 1]}$$
$$\to \dfrac{1}{e-1} < 1 \text{ as } n \to \infty.$$

∴ By Cauchy's root test, the given series is convergent.

Ex. 82 : *Test for convergence* $\left(\dfrac{1}{2} - \dfrac{1}{\log 2}\right) - \left(\dfrac{1}{2} - \dfrac{1}{\log 2}\right) + \left(\dfrac{1}{2} - \dfrac{1}{\log 4}\right) + \ldots$

Sol. : $\left(\dfrac{1}{2} - \dfrac{1}{\log 2}\right) - \left(\dfrac{1}{2} - \dfrac{1}{\log 2}\right) + \left(\dfrac{1}{2} - \dfrac{1}{\log 4}\right) + \ldots$

This is an alternating series, each term is numerically less than the preceding term.

Here, $\qquad u_n = \dfrac{1}{2} - \dfrac{1}{\log(n+1)}$

We use n^{th} form test,
$$\lim_{n \to \infty} u_n = \lim_{n \to \infty} \dfrac{1}{2} - \dfrac{1}{\log(n+1)} = \dfrac{1}{2} \neq 0$$

∴ The series is divergent.

Ex. 83 : *Determine convergence of an alternating series and test* $\sum\limits_{n=1}^{\infty} \dfrac{\cos n\pi}{n^2 + 1}$ *for absolute and conditional convergence.*

Sol. : Here $\cos n\pi$ take value $-1, 1, -1, \ldots$ as n takes values from 1 to ∞.

Now, $\qquad \sum |u_n| = \sum\limits_{n=1}^{\infty} \left|\dfrac{\cos n\pi}{n^2 + 1}\right|$
$$= \sum_{n=1}^{\infty} \dfrac{1}{n^2 + 1}$$

Let, $v_n = \dfrac{1}{n^2}$ is a 'p' series with $p = 2 > 1$, which convergent.

∴ $\Sigma |u_n|$ is convergent.

∴ Σu_n is absolutely convergent.

EXERCISE 6.1

1. Test the following series for convergence whose n^{th} term is given by

    (1) $u_n = \sqrt{(n^2 + 1)} - n$ **(Ans. Div.)**

    (2) $u_n = (n^3 + 1)^{1/3} - n$.   **(Ans. Cgt.)**

    (3) $u_n = \dfrac{\sqrt{(n^2 + 1)} - n}{n^p}$.   **(Ans. Cgt. if $p > 0$, div. if $p \le 0$)**

    (4) $u_n = \sqrt{(n^3 + 1)} - \sqrt{(n^3 - 1)}$ **(Ans. Cgt.)**

    (5) $u_n = \sin(1/n)$ **(Ans. Div.)**

    (6) $u_n = \sin^2(1/n)$ **(Ans. Cgt.)**

    (7) $u_n = \cot^{-1} n$.   **(Ans. Div.)**

    (8) $u_n = \dfrac{1}{n(1 + 1/n)}$.

    (9) $\dfrac{n!}{n^n}$.   **(Ans. Cgt.)**

    (10) $\dfrac{3n - 1}{2^n}$ **(Ans. Cgt.)**

    (11) $\dfrac{x^{n-1}}{1 + x^n}$ **(Ans. Cgt. if $x < 1$, div. if $x \ge 1$)**

    (12) $\dfrac{n x^n}{n^2 + 1}$ **(Ans. Cgt. if $x < 1$, div. if $x \ge 1$)**

    (13) $\dfrac{1}{n \log n (\log \log n)}$ **(Ans. (Div.))**

    (14) $\sqrt{n \tan^{-1}\left(\dfrac{1}{n^3}\right)}$ **(Ans. Div.)**

2. Test for convergence the series

    (1) $1 + \dfrac{x}{2} + \dfrac{x^2}{15} + \ldots + \dfrac{x^n}{n^2 + 1} + \ldots$ **(Ans. Cgt. if $x \le 1$, div. if $x > 1$.**

    (2) $x + \dfrac{3}{5} x^2 + \dfrac{8}{10} x^3 + \dfrac{15}{17} x^4 + \ldots\ldots$ **(Ans. Cgt. if $x \le 1$, div. if $x \ge 1$)**

(3) $1 + \dfrac{2}{5} x + \dfrac{6}{9} x^2 + \dfrac{14}{17} x^3 + \ldots$ \hfill (**Ans.** Cgt. if $x < 1$, div. if $x \geq 1$)

(4) $2 + \dfrac{3}{2} x + \dfrac{4}{3} x^2 + \dfrac{5}{4} x^3 + \ldots$ where $x > 0$. \hfill (**Ans.** Cgt. if $x < 1$, div. if $x \geq 1$)

(5) $1 + \dfrac{1}{2} x + \dfrac{1 \cdot 3}{2 \cdot 4} x^2 + \dfrac{1 \cdot 3 \cdot 5}{2 \cdot 4 \cdot 6} x^3 + \ldots$ \hfill (**Ans.** Cgt. if $x < 1$, div. if $x \geq 1$)

(6) $x^2 + \dfrac{2^2}{3 \cdot 4} x^4 + \dfrac{2^2 \cdot 4^2}{3 \cdot 4 \cdot 5 \cdot 6} x^6 + \dfrac{2^2 \cdot 4^2 \cdot 6^2}{3 \cdot 4 \cdot 5 \cdot 6 \cdot 7 \cdot 8} x^8 + \ldots$

\hfill (**Ans.** Cgt. if $x^2 \leq 1$, div. if $x^2 > 1$)

(7) $1 + \dfrac{2^p}{2!} + \dfrac{3^p}{3!} + \dfrac{4^p}{4!} + \ldots$ \hfill (**Ans.** Cgt.)

(8) $\dfrac{1^2}{2^2} + \dfrac{1^2 \cdot 3^2}{2^2 \cdot 4^2} + \dfrac{1^2 \cdot 3^2 \cdot 5^2}{2^2 \cdot 4^2 \cdot 6^2} + \ldots$ \hfill (**Ans.** Div.)

(9) $\dfrac{1}{1^{1+1}} + \dfrac{1}{2^{1+1/2}} + \dfrac{1}{3^{1+1/3}} + \dfrac{1}{4^{1+1/4}} + \ldots$ \hfill (**Ans.** Div.)

(10) $1 + \dfrac{2x}{2!} + \dfrac{3^2 x^2}{3!} + \dfrac{4^3 x^3}{4!} + \ldots$ \hfill (**Ans.** Cgt. $x > 0$, div. $x < 0$)

(11) $1 + \dfrac{1}{2^2} + \dfrac{2^2}{3^3} + \dfrac{3^3}{4^4} + \dfrac{4^4}{5^5} + \ldots$ \hfill (**Ans.** Div.)

(12) $\dfrac{2}{7} + \dfrac{2 \cdot 5}{7 \cdot 10} + \dfrac{2 \cdot 5 \cdot 8}{7 \cdot 10 \cdot 13} + \ldots$ \hfill (**Ans.** Cgt.)

(13) $1 + \left(\dfrac{1}{2}\right)^p + \left(\dfrac{1 \cdot 3}{2 \cdot 4}\right)^p + \left(\dfrac{1 \cdot 3 \cdot 5}{2 \cdot 4 \cdot 6}\right)^p + \ldots$ \hfill (**Ans.** Cgt. if $p \geq 2$, div. if $p < 2$)

(14) $1 + \dfrac{x}{1} + \dfrac{1}{2} \cdot \dfrac{x^3}{3} + \dfrac{1 \cdot 3}{2 \cdot 4} \dfrac{x^5}{5} + \dfrac{1 \cdot 3 \cdot 5}{2 \cdot 4 \cdot 6} \dfrac{x^7}{7} + \ldots$

\hfill (**Ans.** Cgt. if $x^2 \leq 1$, div. if $x^2 > 1$)

(15) $1 + a + \dfrac{a(a+1)}{1 \cdot 2} + \dfrac{a(a+1)(a+2)}{1 \cdot 2 \cdot 3} + \ldots$ \hfill (**Ans.** Cgt. if $a \leq 0$, div. if $a > 0$)

(16) $\dfrac{1}{(2 \log 2)^p} + \dfrac{1}{(3 \log 3)^p} + \ldots + \dfrac{1}{(n \log n)^p} + \ldots$

\hfill (**Ans.** Cgt. if $p > 1$, div. if $p \leq 1$)

(17) $\dfrac{(a+x)}{1!} + \dfrac{(a+2x)^2}{2!} + \dfrac{(a+3x)^3}{3!} + \ldots$ \hfill (**Ans.** Cgt. if $x < \dfrac{1}{e}$, div. if $x \geq \dfrac{1}{e}$)

(18) $1 + \dfrac{1}{2} \cdot \dfrac{a}{b} + \dfrac{1 \cdot 3}{2 \cdot 4} \dfrac{a(a+1)}{b(b+1)} + \dfrac{1 \cdot 3 \cdot 5}{2 \cdot 4 \cdot 6} \cdot \dfrac{a(a+1)(a+2)}{b(b+1)(b+2)} + \ldots$

(19) $1 + \dfrac{a(1-a)}{1^2} + \dfrac{(1+a)a(1-a)(2-a)}{1^2 \cdot 2^2} + \dfrac{(2+a)(1+a)a(1-a)(2-a)(3-a)}{1^2 \cdot 2^2 \cdot 3^2} + \ldots$

\hfill (**Ans.** Div.)

(20) $\dfrac{1^2}{4^2} + \dfrac{1^2 \cdot 5^2}{4^2 \cdot 8^2} + \dfrac{1^2 \cdot 5^2 \cdot 9^2}{4^2 \cdot 8^2 \cdot 12^2} + \dfrac{1^2 \cdot 5^2 \cdot 9^2 \cdot 13^2}{4^2 \cdot 8^2 \cdot 12^2 \cdot 16^2} + \ldots$ \hfill (**Ans.** Cgt.)

3. Test the convergence of the series $\sum \dfrac{x^n}{(2n+1)^p}$. **(Ans.** Cgt. if $x < 1$, div. if $x > 1$,

    Cgt. if $x = 1$, $p > 1$, div. if $x = 1$, $p \leq 1$)

4. Test the convergence of the following series

    (1) $1 - \dfrac{1}{3} + \dfrac{1}{5} - \dfrac{1}{7} + \ldots$ **(Ans.** Cgt.)

    (2) $1 - \dfrac{1}{2} + \dfrac{1}{4} - \dfrac{1}{8} + \dfrac{1}{16} - \ldots$ **(Ans.** Cgt.)

    (3) $1 - \dfrac{1}{2\sqrt{2}} + \dfrac{1}{3\sqrt{3}} + \dfrac{1}{4\sqrt{4}} + \ldots$ **(May 2014)** **(Ans.** Cgt.)

    (4) $\log\left(\dfrac{2}{1}\right) - \log\left(\dfrac{3}{2}\right) + \log\left(\dfrac{4}{3}\right) - \log\left(\dfrac{5}{4}\right) + \ldots$ **(Ans.** Cgt.)

    (5) $\dfrac{1}{6} - \dfrac{2}{11} + \dfrac{3}{16} - \dfrac{4}{21} + \ldots\ldots$ **(Ans.** Oscillatory)

5. Explain the terms convergence of series and convergence of a sequence.
   Test for convergence of the series.

    $\dfrac{1}{1+2^{-1}} + \dfrac{2}{1+2^{-2}} + \dfrac{3}{1+2^{-3}} + \dfrac{4}{1+2^{-4}} + \ldots$ **(Ans.** divergent)

6. Test for convergence the following series stating the test of convergence you use.

    (a) $\sum\limits_{n=1}^{\infty} \left(\dfrac{n!}{2n!}\right)^2$ (b) $\sum\limits_{n=1}^{\infty} \left(\sqrt[3]{n^3+1} - n\right)$, (c) $\sum\limits_{n=1}^{\infty} \dfrac{1}{\left(1+\dfrac{1}{n}\right)^{n^2}}$.

7. Using the integral test, discuss the convergence of the following series :

    (a) $\sum \dfrac{1}{2n+3}$ **(Ans.** Div.) (b) $\sum \dfrac{1}{n(n+1)}$ **(Ans.** Cgt.)

    (c) $\sum \dfrac{1}{\sqrt{n}}$ **(Ans.** Div.) (d) $\sum \dfrac{1}{(n+1)^2}$ **(Ans.** Cgt.)

    (e) $\sum \dfrac{2n^3}{n^4+3}$ **(Ans.** Div.) (f) $\sum \dfrac{n}{(n^2+1)^2}$ **(Ans.** Cgt.)

    (g) $\sum\limits_{n=2}^{\infty} \dfrac{1}{n\sqrt{n^2-1}}$ **(Ans.** Cgt.) (h) $\sum n e^{-n^2}$ **(Ans.** Cgt.)

MULTIPLE CHOICE QUESTIONS

Type : Problems on P-series, Comparison test, Ratio test, n^{th} root test and Leibnitz's test :

1. If $\sum_{n=1}^{\infty} u_n$ series of positive terms is convergent then $\lim_{n \to \infty} u_n$ is (1)

   (A) less than 1   (B) 1
   (C) greater than 1   (D) 0

2. If $\lim_{n \to \infty} u_n = 0$ then infinite series $\sum_{n=1}^{\infty} u_n$ is (1)

   (A) convergent   (B) divergent
   (C) convergent or divergent   (D) oscillatory

3. If $\lim_{n \to \infty} u_n \neq 0$ then infinite seres $\sum_{n=1}^{\infty} u_n$ is (1)

   (A) convergent   (B) divergent
   (C) oscillatory   (D) none of these

4. For infinite series $\sum_{n=1}^{\infty} u_n$ with $s_n = u_1 + u_2 + u_3 + \ldots + u_n$, if $\lim_{n \to \infty} s_n = l$ (Finite quantity), then $\sum_{n=1}^{\infty} u_n$ is (1)

   (A) convergent   (B) divergent
   (C) oscillatory   (D) none of these

5. For infinite series $\sum_{n=1}^{\infty} u_n$ with $s_n = u_1 + u_2 + u_3 + \ldots + u_n$, if $\lim_{n \to \infty} s_n = \infty$ or $-\infty$, then $\sum_{n=1}^{\infty} u_n$ is (1)

   (A) convergent   (B) divergent
   (C) oscillatory   (D) none of these

6. The convergence of infinite series remains unaltered, then which of the following is not correct ? (1)

   (A) the sign of all terms in the series are changed
   (B) finite numbers of term are added to omitted from an infinite series
   (C) each term of the series is multiplied by non-zero constant
   (D) infinite number of terms are added to an infinite series

7. The geometric series $\sum_{n=1}^{\infty} ar^n$ with common ratio r is convergent if (1)

    (A) $|r| < 1$
    (B) $|r| > 1$
    (C) $|r| > 2$
    (D) none of these

8. The P-series $\sum_{n=1}^{\infty} \frac{1}{n^p}$ is convergent if (1)

    (A) $p < 1$
    (B) $p > 1$
    (C) $p = 1$
    (D) none of these

9. The P-series $\sum_{n=1}^{\infty} \frac{1}{n^p}$ is divergent if (1)

    (a) $p \leq 1$
    (B) $p \geq 1$
    (C) $p \geq 0$
    (D) none of these

10. In comparison test, if $\sum_{n=1}^{\infty} u_n$ and $\sum_{n=1}^{\infty} v_n$ are the series of positive terms such that $\lim_{n \to \infty} \frac{u_n}{v_n} = l$ (finite non-zero quantity) then (1)

    (A) if $\sum_{n=1}^{\infty} u_n$ is convergent then $\sum_{n=1}^{\infty} v_n$ is divergent

    (B) if $\sum_{n=1}^{\infty} v_n$ is convergent then $\sum_{n=1}^{\infty} u_n$ is divergent

    (C) both $\sum_{n=1}^{\infty} u_n$ and $\sum_{n=1}^{\infty} v_n$ are convergent or divergent together

    (D) none of these

11. In ratio test, if $\sum_{n=1}^{\infty} u_n$ is the series of positive terms such that $\lim_{n \to \infty} \frac{u_n}{u_{n+1}} = l$ then $\sum_{n=1}^{\infty} u_n$ is convergent for

    (A) $l > 1$
    (B) $l = 1$
    (C) $l < 1$
    (D) none of these

12. In ratio test, if $\sum_{n=1}^{\infty} u_n$ is the series of positive terms such that $\lim_{n \to \infty} \frac{u_n}{u_{n+1}} = l$ then $\sum_{n=1}^{\infty} u_n$ is divergent for (1)

    (A) $l > 1$
    (B) $l = 1$
    (C) $l < 1$
    (D) none of these

13. In Raabe's test if $\sum\limits_{n=1}^{\infty} u_n$ is the series of positive terms such that $\lim\limits_{n \to \infty} \left(\dfrac{u_n}{u_{n+1}} - 1\right) = l$ then $\sum\limits_{n=1}^{\infty} u_n$ is convergent for (1)

    (A) $l > 1$
    (B) $l = 1$
    (C) $l < 1$
    (D) none of these

14. In n^{th} root test, if $\sum\limits_{n=1}^{\infty} u_n$ is the series of positive terms such that $\lim\limits_{n \to \infty} (u_n)^{1/n} = l$ then $\sum\limits_{n=1}^{\infty} u_n$ is convergent for (1)

    (A) $l > 1$
    (B) $l = 1$
    (C) $l < 1$
    (D) none of these

15. In n^{th} root test, if $\sum\limits_{n=1}^{\infty} u_n$ is the series of positive terms such that $\lim\limits_{n \to \infty} (u_n)^{1/n} = l$ then $\sum\limits_{n=1}^{\infty} u_n$ is divergent for (1)

    (A) $l > 1$
    (B) $l = 1$
    (C) $l < 1$
    (D) none of these

16. For Leibnitz's test the conditions for the convergence of an alternating series $\sum\limits_{n=1}^{\infty} (-1)^{n-1} u_n$, ($u_n > 0$ for all n) are (1)

    (A) $u_n < u_{n+1}$ and $\lim\limits_{n \to \infty} (u_n) \neq 0$
    (B) $u_n < u_{n+1}$ and $\lim\limits_{n \to \infty} (u_n) = 0$
    (C) $u_n > u_{n+1}$ and $\lim\limits_{n \to \infty} (u_n) \neq 0$
    (D) $u_n > u_{n+1}$ and $\lim\limits_{n \to \infty} (u_n) = 0$

17. The given infinite series $\dfrac{1}{3} + \dfrac{1}{9} + \dfrac{1}{27} + \ldots + \dfrac{1}{3^n} + \ldots$ is (1)

    (A) P-series
    (B) alternating series
    (C) power series
    (D) geometric series

18. The given infinite series $1 + \dfrac{1}{4} + \dfrac{1}{9} + \dfrac{1}{16} + \ldots + \dfrac{1}{n^2} + \ldots$ is (1)

    (A) alternating series
    (B) P-series
    (C) power series
    (D) geometric series

19. The given infinite series $\dfrac{x}{1 \cdot 2} + \dfrac{x^2}{3 \cdot 4} + \dfrac{x^3}{5 \cdot 6} + \ldots + \dfrac{x^n}{(2n-1) \cdot (2n)} + \ldots$ is (1)

    (A) P-series
    (B) alternating series
    (C) power series
    (D) geometric series

20. The given infinite series $1 - \frac{1}{2} + \frac{1}{3} - \frac{1}{4} + \ldots + (-1)^{n+1}\frac{1}{n} + \ldots$ is (1)

    (A) P-series
    (B) alternating series
    (C) power series
    (D) geometric series

21. The nth term of infinite series $\frac{2}{1} + \frac{3}{8} + \frac{4}{27} + \frac{5}{64} \ldots$ is (1)

    (A) $\frac{n+1}{n^2}$
    (B) $\frac{2n+1}{n^3}$
    (C) $\frac{n^3}{n+1}$
    (D) $\frac{n+1}{n^3}$

22. The geometric series $\frac{1}{2} + \frac{1}{2^2} + \frac{1}{2^3} + \ldots + \frac{1}{2^n} + \ldots$ is (1)

    (A) oscillatory
    (B) divergent
    (C) convergent
    (D) none of these

23. The geometric series $1 + \frac{4}{3} + \left(\frac{4}{3}\right)^2 + \left(\frac{4}{3}\right)^3 + \ldots$ is (1)

    (A) convergent
    (B) divergent
    (C) oscillatory
    (D) none of these

24. The P-series $\sum_{n=1}^{\infty} \frac{1}{n^2}$ is (1)

    (A) divergent
    (B) convergent
    (C) oscillatory
    (D) none of these

25. The P-series $1 + \frac{1}{\sqrt{2}} + \frac{1}{\sqrt{3}} + \frac{1}{\sqrt{4}} + \ldots + \frac{1}{\sqrt{n}} + \ldots$ is (1)

    (A) convergent
    (B) oscillatory
    (C) divergent
    (D) none of these

26. Given P-series $1 + \frac{1}{2} + \frac{1}{3} + \frac{1}{4} + \ldots + \frac{1}{n} + \ldots$ is (1)

    (A) convergent
    (B) divergent
    (C) oscillatory
    (D) none of these

27. Which of the following series is convergent by P-series ? (2)

    (A) $\sum_{n=1}^{\infty} \frac{1}{n^{0.9}}$
    (B) $\sum_{n=1}^{\infty} \frac{1}{\sqrt{n}}$
    (C) $\sum_{n=1}^{\infty} \frac{1}{n^2}$
    (D) $\sum_{n=1}^{\infty} \frac{1}{n}$

28. The infinite series $\sum_{n=1}^{\infty} \cos\left(\frac{1}{n}\right)$ is (2)

   (A) divergent (B) convergent
   (C) oscillatory (D) none of these

29. The infinite series $\sum_{n=1}^{\infty} \left(2 + \frac{1}{n}\right)^n$ by n^{th} root test is (2)

   (A) divergent (B) convergent
   (C) oscillatory (D) none of these

30. The infinite series $\sum_{n=1}^{\infty} \left(1 + \frac{1}{n}\right)^{n^2}$ by n^{th} root rest is (2)

   (A) convergent (B) divergent
   (C) oscillatory (D) none of these

31. The infinite series $\sum_{n=1}^{\infty} \frac{1}{\left(1 + \frac{1}{n}\right)^{n^2}}$ by n^{th} root test is (2)

   (A) convergent (B) oscillatory
   (C) divergent (D) none of these

32. The infinite series $\sum_{n=1}^{\infty} \frac{3^n}{4^n}$ by n^{th} root test is (2)

   (A) divergent (B) convergent
   (C) oscillatory (D) none of these

33. The infinite series $\sum_{n=1}^{\infty} \frac{1}{n^n}$ by n^{th} root test is (2)

   (A) divergent (B) convergent
   (C) oscillatory (D) none of these

34. The infinite series $\sum_{n=1}^{\infty} \frac{x^n}{n^n}$ for $x > 0$ by n^{th} root test is (2)

   (A) divergent (B) convergent
   (C) oscillatory (D) none of these

35. The infinite series $\frac{2}{1} + \frac{3}{4} + \frac{4}{9} + \ldots + \frac{n+1}{n^3} + \ldots$ by comparison test is (2)

   (A) convergent (B) divergent
   (C) oscillatory (D) none of these

36. The infinite series $\sum_{n=1}^{\infty} \frac{1}{n^2+1}$ by comparison test is (2)

   (A) convergent (B) divergent
   (C) oscillatory (D) none of these

37. By comparison test, given infinite series $\sum_{n=1}^{\infty} \frac{\sqrt{n}}{n+\sqrt{n}}$ is (2)

   (A) convergent (B) divergent
   (C) oscillatory (D) none of these

38. By comparison test, given infinite series $\sum_{n=1}^{\infty} \frac{(n+1)^p}{n^q}$ where p and q are positive real numbers, is convergent for (2)

   (A) $1+p<q$ (B) $1+p>q$
   (C) $1+p=q$ (D) none of these

39. By ratio test, given infinite series $\sum_{n=1}^{\infty} \frac{n^2}{3^n}$ is (2)

   (A) oscillatory (B) divergent
   (C) convergent (D) none of these

40. By ratio test, given infinite series $\sum_{n=1}^{\infty} \frac{n^2}{n!}$ is (2)

   (A) oscillatory (B) divergent
   (C) convergent (D) none of these

41. By ratio test, given infinite series $\sum_{n=1}^{\infty} \frac{3n-1}{2^n}$ is (2)

   (A) oscillatory (B) convergent
   (C) divergent (D) none of these

42. By ratio rest, given infinite series $\sum_{n=1}^{\infty} \frac{1}{n!}$ is (2)

   (A) convergent (B) divergent
   (C) oscillatory (D) none of these

43. For appliation of ratio test, if $u_n = \frac{2 \cdot 5 \cdot 8 \cdot 11 \ldots (3n-1)}{1 \cdot 5 \cdot 9 \cdot 13 \ldots (4n-3)}$ then $\lim_{n \to \infty} \frac{u_n}{u_{n+1}}$ is (2)

   (A) $\frac{4}{3}$ (B) $\frac{3}{4}$
   (C) $\frac{1}{3}$ (D) 1

44. The power series $1 + \frac{x}{1!} + \frac{x^2}{2!} + \frac{x^3}{3!} + \ldots + \frac{x^n}{n!} + \ldots$ using ratio test is convergent if (2)

    (A) $x = -1$
    (B) $x > 0$
    (C) $x < 0$
    (D) none of these

45. The power series $\sum_{n=1}^{\infty} (3x)^n$ using ratio test is convergent if (2)

    (A) $x < \frac{1}{3}$
    (B) $x > \frac{1}{3}$
    (C) $x = \frac{1}{3}$
    (D) none of these

46. By ratio test, the power series $1 + 2x + 3x^2 + 4x^3 + \ldots + (n+1)x^n + \ldots$ where $0 < x < 1$ is (2)

    (A) oscillatory
    (B) divergent
    (C) convergent
    (D) none of these

47. The nth term of an alternating series $1 - \frac{1}{\sqrt{2}} + \frac{1}{\sqrt{3}} - \frac{1}{\sqrt{4}} + \ldots$ is (2)

    (A) $-\frac{1}{\sqrt{n}}$
    (B) $\frac{(-1)^{2n}}{\sqrt{n}}$
    (C) $\frac{1}{\sqrt{n}}$
    (D) $\frac{(-1)^{n+1}}{\sqrt{n}}$

48. The nth term of an alternating series $\log\left(\frac{2}{1}\right) - \log\left(\frac{3}{2}\right) + \log\left(\frac{4}{3}\right) - \log\left(\frac{5}{4}\right) + \ldots$ is

    (A) $(-1)^{n+1} \log\left(\frac{2n+1}{n}\right)$
    (B) $\log\left(\frac{n-1}{n}\right)$ (2)
    (C) $\log\left(\frac{n+1}{n}\right)$
    (D) $(-1)^{n+1} \log\left(\frac{n+1}{n}\right)$

49. By Leibnitz's test, given alternating series $1 - \frac{1}{2^2} + \frac{1}{3^2} - \frac{1}{4^2} + \ldots + \frac{(-1)^{n-1}}{n^2} + \ldots$ (2)

    (A) oscillatory
    (B) divergent
    (C) convergent
    (D) either divergent or oscillatory

50. By Leibnitz's test, given alternating series $\frac{2}{1^2} - \frac{3}{2^2} + \frac{4}{3^2} + \ldots + \frac{(n+1)(-1)^{n+1}}{n^2} + \ldots$ (2)

    (A) oscillatory
    (B) divergent
    (C) convergent
    (D) either divergent or oscillatory

51. By Leibnitz's test, an alternating series $\sum_{n=1}^{\infty} \frac{(-1)^{n-1}}{x+(n-1)a}$ where $x > 0$, $a > 0$ with each term of the series is numerially less than the preceding term is (2)

   (A) oscillatory
   (B) divergent
   (C) convergent
   (D) either divergent or oscillatory

52. By Leibnitz's test, an alternating series $\sum_{n=1}^{\infty} \frac{(-1)^n}{n^2+1}$ is (2)

   (A) oscillatory
   (B) convergent
   (C) divergent
   (D) either divergent or oscillatory

Answers

1. (D)	12. (C)	23. (B)	34. (B)	45. (A)
2. (C)	13. (A)	24. (B)	35. (A)	46. (C)
3. (B)	14. (C)	25. (C)	36. (A)	47. (D)
4. (A)	15. (A)	26. (B)	37. (B)	48. (D)
5. (B)	16. (D)	27. (C)	38. (A)	49. (C)
6. (D)	17. (D)	28. (A)	39. (C)	50. (C)
7. (A)	18. (B)	29. (A)	40. (C)	51. (C)
8. (B)	19. (C)	30. (B)	41. (B)	52. (B)
9. (A)	20. (B)	31. (A)	42. (A)	
10. (C)	21. (D)	32. (B)	43. (A)	
11. (A)	22. (C)	33. (B)	44. (B)	

CHAPTER SEVEN

SUCCESSIVE DIFFERENTIATION

7.1 INTRODUCTION

Successive Derivatives are used in finding Maxima and Minima of functions, in the expansion of functions by Taylor and Maclaurin series, in deciding the concavity and convexity of curves at certain points and in the determination of the points of inflexion which is important in tracing curves.

7.2 DEFINITION AND NOTATION

Definition : If y be a function of x, then its differential coefficient $\frac{dy}{dx}$ will be in general a function of x which can be differentiated further, $\frac{dy}{dx}$ is called the first differential coefficient (or first derivative) of y. The differential coefficient of $\frac{dy}{dx}$ with respect to x is called the second differential coefficient (or second derivative) of y and is written as $\frac{d^2y}{dx^2}$. Similarly, the differential coefficient of $\frac{d^2y}{dx^2}$ is called the third differential coefficient of y and is written as $\frac{d^3y}{dx^3}$ and so on.

Thus, the successive differential coefficients (derivatives) of y are denoted by

$$\frac{dy}{dx}, \frac{d^2y}{dx^2}, \frac{d^3y}{dx^3}, \ldots\ldots\ldots, \frac{d^ny}{dx^n}, \ldots\ldots$$

where each term is the derivative of the preceding one. The nth differential coefficient (n^{th} derivative) of y is denoted by $\frac{d^ny}{dx^n}$.

Notation :

(1) The following notations (symbols) are generally used for the successive differential coefficients of y with respect to x :

$$\frac{dy}{dx}, \frac{d^2y}{dx^2}, \frac{d^3y}{dx^3}, \ldots\ldots\ldots\ldots\frac{d^ny}{dx^n} \ldots$$

$$Dy, D^2y, D^3y, \ldots\ldots\ldots D^ny, \ldots \quad D = \frac{d}{dx}$$

$$f'(x), f''(x), f'''(x), \ldots\ldots \quad f^n(x), \ldots$$

$$y', y'', y''', \ldots\ldots\ldots\ldots\ldots \quad y^{(n)} \ldots$$

$$y_1, y_2, y_3, \ldots\ldots\ldots\ldots\ldots \quad y_{(n)} \ldots$$

(7.1)

(2) The value of nth differential coefficient at $x = a$ is usually denoted by $\left(\dfrac{d^n y}{dx^n}\right)_{x=a}$ or $(y_n)_a$. Sometimes, it is also written as $f^n(a)$ or $y^n(a)$.

7.3 n^{th} DIFFERENTIAL COEFFICIENTS OF SOME STANDARD FUNCTIONS

(A) To find the nth Derivative of $y = e^{ax}$:

We have $\qquad y = e^{ax}$,

then $\qquad y_1 = ae^{ax},\ y_2 = a^2 e^{ax},\ y_3 = a^3 e^{ax},\ \ldots,\ y_n = a^n e^{ax}$

$\therefore \qquad \dfrac{d^n}{dx^n}[e^{ax}] = a^n e^{ax}$ ... (1)

(B) To find the nth Derivative of $y = a^x$:

We have $\qquad y = a^x$,

then $\qquad y_1 = a^x (\log_e a),\ y_2 = a^x (\log_e a)^2$,

$\qquad y_3 = a^x (\log_e a)^3,\ \ldots,\ y_n = a^x (\log_e a)^n$

$\therefore \qquad \dfrac{d^n}{dx^n}[a^x] = a^x (\log_e a)^n$ ... (2)

(C) To find the nth Derivative of $y = (ax + b)^m$, where m is any Real number :

We have $\qquad y = (ax+b)^m$,

then $\qquad y_1 = ma(ax+b)^{m-1}$,

$\qquad y_2 = m(m-1)a^2(ax+b)^{m-2}$,

$\qquad y_3 = m(m-1)(m-2)a^3(ax+b)^{m-3}$

$\qquad \ldots \quad \ldots \quad \ldots \quad \ldots \quad \ldots$

Hence $\qquad y_n = m(m-1)(m-2)\ldots(m-n+1)a^n(ax+b)^{m-n}$

$\therefore \qquad \dfrac{d^n}{dx^n}[(ax+b)^m] = m(m-1)(m-2)\ldots(m-n+1)a^n(ax+b)^{m-n}$ ... (3)

(D) To find the nth Derivative of $y = (ax + b)^{-m}$, where m is any Positive Integer :

We have $\qquad y = (ax+b)^{-m}$

$\qquad y_1 = -ma(ax+b)^{-m-1} = (-1)ma(ax+b)^{-m-1}$

$\qquad y_2 = -m(-m-1)a^2(ax+b)^{-m-2}$

$\qquad \quad = (-1)^2 m(m+1)a^2(ax+b)^{-m-2}$

$\qquad y_3 = (-1)^3 m(m+1)(m+2)a^3(ax+b)^{-m-3}$

$\qquad \ldots \quad \ldots \quad \ldots \quad \ldots \quad \ldots \quad \ldots \quad \ldots$

$\qquad y_n = (-1)^n m(m+1)(m+2)\ldots(m+n-1)a^n(ax+b)^{-m-n}$

$$\therefore \quad \frac{d^n}{dx^n}\left[\frac{1}{(ax+b)^m}\right] = \frac{(-1)^n \, m \, (m+1)(m+2)\ldots(m+n-1) \, a^n}{(ax+b)^{m+n}} \quad \ldots (4)$$

Example: $\quad y = \dfrac{1}{(2x+1)^3}$, Here $a = 2$, $b = 1$, $m = 3$

$$y_n = \frac{(-1)^n \, 3 \cdot 4 \cdot 5 \ldots (3+n-1) \cdot 2^n}{(2x+1)^{n+3}}$$

$$= \frac{(-1)^n \, 1 \cdot 2 \cdot 3 \ldots (n+2) \cdot 2^n}{1 \cdot 2 \cdot (2x+1)^{n+3}} \quad \text{(Note this step)}$$

$$y_n = \frac{(-1)^n \, (n+2)! \, 2^n}{2 \cdot (2x+1)^{n+3}}$$

Special Cases:

Case I: n^{th} derivative of $y = (ax+b)^m$ when m is a positive integer and $m > n$.

We know that if $y = (ax+b)^m$ (m is real number) then,

$$y_n = m(m-1)(m-2)\ldots(m-n+1) \, a^n \, (ax+b)^{m-n}$$

This can be written as

$$y_n = \frac{m(m-1)(m-2)\ldots(m-n+1)\{(m-n)(m-n-1)\ldots 3\cdot 2\cdot 1\} \, a^n \, (ax+b)^{m-n}}{\{(m-n)(m-n-1)(m-n-2)\ldots 3\cdot 2\cdot 1\}}$$

$$y_n = \frac{m! \, a^n \, (ax+b)^{m-n}}{(m-n)!}$$

$$\therefore \quad \frac{d^n}{dx^n}[(ax+b)^m] = \frac{m! \, a^n \, (ax+b)^{m-n}}{(m-n)!} \quad \ldots (5)$$

Case II: n^{th} derivative of $y = (ax+b)^m$ when m is a positive integer and $m = n$.

Put $m = n$ in the above formula (5),

$$y_n = \frac{n! \, a^n \, (ax+b)^{n-n}}{(n-n)!} = \frac{n! \, a^n}{0!}(ax+b)^0$$

$$y_n = n! \, a^n \qquad [\because (ax+b)^0 = 1 \text{ and } 0! = 1]$$

$$\therefore \quad \frac{d^n}{dx^n}[(ax+b)^n] = n! \, a^n \quad \ldots (6)$$

If we put $a = 1$, $b = 0$ in (6), we get

$$\frac{d^n}{dx^n}[x^n] = n! \quad \ldots (7)$$

Note: If $y = x^n$ then $y_n = n!$, but $y_{n-1} \neq (n-1)!$

To find y_{n-1}, put $m = n$ and $n = n-1$ in the formula (5), with $a = 1$, $b = 0$,

$$y_{n-1} = \frac{n! \, 1^{n-1} \, x^{n-n+1}}{(n-n+1)!} = n! \, x$$

Similarly, we can obtain,

$$y_{n-2} = n! \cdot \frac{x^2}{2!}, \quad y_{n-3} = n! \, \frac{x^3}{3!} \text{ and so on.}$$

Case III : n^{th} derivative of $y = (ax + b)^m$ when m is a positive integer and $m < n$.
In this case, y_n becomes zero. Since m^{th} derivative of $y = (ax + b)^m$ will be constant,

$$\therefore \quad \frac{d^n}{dx^n}[(ax+b)^m] = 0 \qquad \ldots (8)$$

If we put $a = 1$, $b = 0$ in (8), we get

$$\frac{d^n}{dx^n}(x^m) = 0 \qquad \ldots (9)$$

Case IV : n^{th} derivative of $y = (ax + b)^{-m}$ when $m = 1$.

Here $\quad y = \dfrac{1}{ax+b}$ Put $m = 1$ in the formula (4),

$$y_n = \frac{(-1)^n \, 1 \cdot 2 \cdot 3 \ldots n \cdot a^n}{(ax+b)^{1+n}}$$

$$\therefore \quad \frac{d^n}{dx^n}\left[\frac{1}{ax+b}\right] = \frac{(-1)^n \, n! \, a^n}{(ax+b)^{n+1}} \qquad \ldots (10)$$

Example : If $\quad y = \dfrac{1}{2x+3}$, then $y_n = \dfrac{(-1)^n \cdot n! \cdot 2^n}{(2x+3)^{n+1}}$

If we put $a = 1$, $b = 0$ in equation (10), we get

$$\frac{d^n}{dx^n}\left[\frac{1}{x}\right] = \frac{(-1)^n \cdot n!}{x^{n+1}} \qquad \ldots (11)$$

(E) To find the nth Derivative of $y = \log(ax + b)$:

$$y = \log(ax+b)$$

$$y_1 = \frac{a}{ax+b} = a(ax+b)^{-1}$$

$$y_2 = -a^2(ax+b)^{-2} = (-1)\,a^2\,(ax+b)^{-2}$$

$$y_3 = (-1)(-2)\,a^3\,(ax+b)^{-3}$$

.. ..

$$y_n = \frac{(-1)^{n-1}(n-1)!\,a^n}{(ax+b)^n}$$

$$\therefore \quad \frac{d^n}{dx^n}[\log(ax+b)] = \frac{(-1)^{n-1}(n-1)!\,a^n}{(ax+b)^n} \qquad \ldots (12)$$

Example : If $\quad y = \log(2x+3)$ then, $y_n = \dfrac{(-1)^{n-1}(n-1)!\,2^n}{(2x+3)^n}$

(F) To find the nth Derivative of $y = \sin(bx + c)$:

We have $\quad y = \sin(bx+c)$

then $\quad y_1 = b\cos(bx+c) = b\sin\left(bx+c+\dfrac{\pi}{2}\right)$

$\quad y_2 = b^2\cos\left(bx+c+\dfrac{\pi}{2}\right) = b^2\sin\left(bx+c+\dfrac{\pi}{2}+\dfrac{\pi}{2}\right)$

$$y_3 = b^3 \sin\left(bx + c + \frac{3\pi}{2}\right)$$

$$\cdots \quad \cdots \quad \cdots \quad \cdots \quad \cdots$$

$$y_n = b^n \sin\left(bx + c + \frac{n\pi}{2}\right)$$

$$\therefore \quad \frac{d^n}{dx^n}[\sin(bx+c)] = b^n \sin\left(bx + c + \frac{n\pi}{2}\right) \quad \ldots (13)$$

If $c = 0$, $\quad \dfrac{d^n}{dx^n}[\sin bx] = b^n \sin\left(bx + \dfrac{n\pi}{2}\right)$

Similarly,

$$\frac{d^n}{dx^n}[\cos(bx+c)] = b^n \cos\left(bx + c + \frac{n\pi}{2}\right)$$

If $c = 0$, $\quad \dfrac{d^n}{dx^n}[\cos bx] = b^n \cos\left(bx + \dfrac{n\pi}{2}\right)$

Example : If $\quad y = \cos 3x$ then, $y_n = 3^n \cos\left(3x + \dfrac{n\pi}{2}\right)$

(G) To find the nth Derivative of $y = e^{ax} \sin(bx + c)$:

$$y = e^{ax} \sin(bx + c)$$
$$y_1 = e^{ax}[a \sin(bx+c) + b \cos(bx+c)]$$

Put $\quad a = r\cos\theta, \; b = r\sin\theta$ so that

$$r = \sqrt{a^2 + b^2} \text{ and } \theta = \tan^{-1}\frac{b}{a},$$

then $\quad y_1 = re^{ax}[\sin(bx+c)\cos\theta + \cos(bx+c)\sin\theta]$
$$= re^{ax}\sin(bx + c + \theta)$$

Similarly, $\quad y_2 = r^2 e^{ax} \sin(bx + c + 2\theta)$
$$y_3 = r^3 e^{ax} \sin(bx + c + 3\theta)$$
$$\cdots \quad \cdots \quad \cdots \quad \cdots \quad \cdots$$
$$y_n = r^n e^{ax} \sin(bx + c + n\theta)$$

$$\therefore \quad \frac{d^n}{dx^n}[e^{ax}\sin(bx+c)] = r^n e^{ax} \sin(bx + c + n\theta) \quad \ldots (14)$$

where, $\quad r = \sqrt{a^2 + b^2}, \quad \theta = \tan^{-1}\dfrac{b}{a}$

Similarly,

$$\frac{d^n}{dx^n}[e^{ax}\cos(bx+c)] = r^n e^{ax} \cos(bx + c + n\theta) \quad \ldots (15)$$

where $\quad r = \sqrt{a^2 + b^2}, \quad \theta = \tan^{-1}\dfrac{b}{a}$

Example: $y = e^x \sin x$
Here $a = 1, b = 1,$ then

$$r = \sqrt{a^2 + b^2} = \sqrt{2}, \quad \theta = \tan^{-1}\frac{b}{a} = \frac{\pi}{4}$$

$$\therefore \quad y_n = r^n e^x \sin(x + n\theta) = \left(\sqrt{2}\right)^n e^x \sin\left(x + \frac{n\pi}{4}\right)$$

7.4 ILLUSTRATIONS ON SUCCESSIVE DIFFERENTIATION

Type I : Examples on Higher Order Derivatives :

Ex. 1 : If $y = \dfrac{ax+b}{cx+d}$, show that $2y_1 y_3 = 3y_2^2$.

Sol. :
$$y = \frac{ax+b}{cx+d}$$

$$y_1 = \frac{a(cx+d) - c(ax+b)}{(cx+d)^2}$$

$$= \frac{ad-bc}{(cx+d)^2} = (ad-bc)(cx+d)^{-2}$$

$$y_2 = 2c(bc-ad)(cx+d)^{-3}$$

$$y_3 = -6c^2(bc-ad)(cx+d)^{-4}$$

$\therefore$ L.H.S. $= 2y_1 y_3 = 12c^2 (bc-ad)^2 (cx+d)^{-6}$

and R.H.S. $= 3y_2^2 = 12c^2 (bc-ad)^2 (cx+d)^{-6}$

Hence, $2y_1 y_3 = 3y_2^2$

Ex. 2 : If $y = \sin(\sin x)$, prove that $\dfrac{d^2y}{dx^2} + \dfrac{dy}{dx} \tan x + y \cos^2 x = 0$.

Sol. : $y = \sin(\sin x)$

Differentiating w.r.t. x

$$\frac{dy}{dx} = \cos(\sin x) \cos x$$

Differentiating again w.r.t. x

$$\frac{d^2y}{dx^2} = -\sin(\sin x) \cos^2 x - \sin x \cos(\sin x)$$

i.e. $\dfrac{d^2y}{dx^2} + \sin x \cos(\sin x) + \sin(\sin x) \cos^2 x = 0$

i.e. $\dfrac{d^2y}{dx^2} + \cos(\sin x) \cos x \dfrac{(\sin x)}{(\cos x)} + \sin(\sin x) \cos^2 x = 0$

$\therefore \quad \dfrac{d^2y}{dx^2} + \dfrac{dy}{dx} \tan x + y \cos^2 x = 0$

Ex. 3 : If $y = (1-x^2)^{1/2} \sin^{-1} x$, then show that $(1-x^2)\dfrac{d^2y}{dx^2} - x\dfrac{dy}{dy} + 2x + y = 0$.

Sol. : $\qquad y = (1-x^2)^{1/2} \sin^{-1} x$

Differentiating w.r.t. x,

$$\dfrac{dy}{dx} = \left\{\dfrac{1}{2}(1-x^2)^{-1/2}(-2x)\right\} \sin^{-1}x + (1-x^2)^{1/2} \dfrac{1}{\sqrt{1-x^2}}$$

$$= \dfrac{-x \sin^{-1}x}{(1-x^2)^{1/2}} + 1 = \dfrac{-x}{(1-x^2)} y + 1$$

$\therefore \qquad (1-x^2)\dfrac{dy}{dx} = -xy + 1 - x^2$

Differentiating again w.r.t. x,

$$(1-x^2)\dfrac{d^2y}{dx^2} + (-2x)\dfrac{dy}{dx} = -x\dfrac{dy}{dx} - y - 2x$$

$\therefore \qquad (1-x^2)\dfrac{d^2y}{dx^2} - x\dfrac{dy}{dx} + 2x + y = 0$

Ex. 4 : If $Y = sX$ and $Z = tX$, all the variables being functions of x, prove that

$$\begin{vmatrix} X & Y & Z \\ X_1 & Y_1 & Z_1 \\ X_2 & Y_2 & Z_2 \end{vmatrix} = X^3 \begin{vmatrix} s_1 & t_1 \\ s_2 & t_2 \end{vmatrix}$$

Sol. : $Y = sX \qquad \therefore Y_1 = sX_1 + s_1X, \qquad Y_2 = (sX_2 + 2s_1X_1 + s_2X)$
$Z = tX \qquad \therefore Z_1 = tX_1 + t_1X, \qquad Z_2 = (tX_2 + 2t_1X_1 + t_2X)$

$\therefore \qquad$ L.H.S. $= \begin{vmatrix} X & Y & Z \\ X_1 & Y_1 & Z_1 \\ X_2 & Y_2 & Z_2 \end{vmatrix}$

$$= \begin{vmatrix} X & sX & tX \\ X_1 & (sX_1 + s_1X) & (tX_1 + t_1X) \\ X_2 & (sX_2 + 2s_1X_1 + s_2X) & (tX_2 + 2t_1X_1 + t_2X) \end{vmatrix}$$

Perform $C_2 - (s)C_1$, $C_3 - (t)C_1$

$$= \begin{vmatrix} X & 0 & 0 \\ X_1 & s_1X & t_1X \\ X_2 & (s_2X + 2s_1X_1) & (t_2X + 2t_1X_1) \end{vmatrix}$$

$$= X \begin{vmatrix} s_1 X & t_1 X \\ s_2 X + 2s_1 X_1 & t_2 X + 2t_1 X_1 \end{vmatrix}$$

$$= X^2 \begin{vmatrix} s_1 & t_1 \\ s_2 X + 2s_1 X_1 & t_2 X + 2t_1 X_1 \end{vmatrix}$$

$$= X^2 [s_1 t_2 X + 2s_1 t_1 X_1 - t_1 s_2 X - 2s_1 t_1 X_1]$$

$$= X^2 [(s_1 t_2 - t_1 s_2) X]$$

$$= X^3 \begin{vmatrix} s_1 & t_1 \\ s_2 & t_2 \end{vmatrix} = \text{R.H.S.}$$

Ex. 5 : *Prove that the differential equation* $(1 + x^2) y_2 + xy_1 = m^2 y$ *is satisfied by*
$$y = \sinh(m \sinh^{-1} x)$$

Sol. : We have $\quad y = \sinh(m \sinh^{-1} x)$ ... (1)

Differentiating w.r.t. x

$$\frac{dy}{dx} = \cosh(m \sinh^{-1} x) \frac{m}{\sqrt{1 + x^2}}$$

$$\therefore \quad y_1 \left(\sqrt{1 + x^2}\right) = m \cosh[m \sinh^{-1} x]$$

Squaring both sides,

$$y_1^2 (1 + x^2) = m^2 \cosh^2 [m \sinh^{-1} x]$$

$$= m^2 [1 + \sinh^2(m \sinh^{-1} x)] \quad (\because \cosh^2 x - \sinh^2 x = 1)$$

$$= m^2 (1 + y^2) \qquad \text{(from 1)}$$

Hence, $\quad y_1^2 (1 + x^2) = m^2 (1 + y^2)$

Differentiating once again,

$$\therefore \quad 2y_1 y_2 (1 + x^2) + 2x y_1^2 = 2m^2 y y_1$$

Cancelling $2y_1$ throughout, we get

$$y_2 (1 + x^2) + xy_1 = m^2 y \qquad ... (2)$$

which proves that the equation (2) is satisfied by $y = \sinh(m \sinh^{-1} x)$.

Ex. 6 : *If* $p^2 = a^2 \cos^2 \theta + b^2 \sin^2 \theta$, *prove that* $p + \dfrac{d^2 p}{d\theta^2} = \dfrac{a^2 b^2}{p^3}$

Sol. : Differentiating given relation w.r.t. θ, we get

$$2p \frac{dp}{d\theta} = -2a^2 \cdot \cos\theta \sin\theta + 2b^2 \sin\theta \cos\theta$$

i.e. $\qquad p \dfrac{dp}{d\theta} = (b^2 - a^2) \sin\theta \cos\theta$ ... (i)

Differentiating again, we get

$$p\frac{d^2p}{d\theta^2} + \left(\frac{dp}{d\theta}\right)^2 = (b^2 - a^2)(\cos^2\theta - \sin^2\theta) \qquad \ldots \text{(ii)}$$

Putting in (ii) value of $\frac{dp}{d\theta}$ from (i),

$$p\frac{d^2p}{d\theta^2} + \frac{(b^2-a^2)^2 \sin^2\theta \cos^2\theta}{p^2} = (b^2 - a^2)(\cos^2\theta - \sin^2\theta)$$

$$p^3\frac{d^2p}{d\theta^2} = (b^2-a^2)[p^2(\cos^2\theta - \sin^2\theta) - (b^2-a^2)\sin^2\theta\cos^2\theta]$$

$$= (b^2-a^2)[(a^2\cos^2\theta + b^2\sin^2\theta)(\cos^2\theta - \sin^2\theta)$$
$$\quad - (b^2-a^2)\sin^2\theta\cos^2\theta] \quad (\because p^2 = a^2\cos^2\theta + b^2\sin^2\theta)$$

$$= (b^2-a^2)(a^2\cos^4\theta - b^2\sin^4\theta)$$

$$= a^2b^2(\cos^4\theta + \sin^4\theta) - (a^4\cos^4\theta + b^4\sin^4\theta)$$

$$= a^2b^2[(\cos^2\theta + \sin^2\theta)^2 - 2\sin^2\theta\cos^2\theta]$$
$$\quad - (a^4\cos^4\theta + b^4\sin^4\theta)$$

$$= (a^2b^2 - 2a^2b^2\sin^2\theta\cos^2\theta - a^4\cos^4\theta - b^4\sin^4\theta)$$

$$= a^2b^2 - (a^2\cos^2\theta + b^2\sin^2\theta)^2 = a^2b^2 - p^4$$

$$\therefore \quad p^3\frac{d^2p}{d\theta^2} + p^4 = a^2b^2$$

$$\therefore \quad \frac{d^2p}{d\theta^2} + p = \frac{a^2b^2}{p^3}.$$

Type II : n^{th} Derivative, Using Trigonometrical Transformations and Standard Results :

Ex. 7 : *Find the nth derivatives of :*

(i) $\sin 2x \cos 3x$, (ii) $\cos^4 x$, (iii) $\cos x \cos 2x \cos 3x$, (iv) $e^{ax} \sin bx \cos cx$,

(v) $e^{ax} \cos^2 x \sin x$, (vi) $e^{2x} \sin\frac{x}{2} \cos\frac{x}{2} \sin 3x$, (vii) $\cos^2 x \sin^3 x$, (viii) $\sin^5 x \cos^3 x$.

Sol. : (i) Let $\quad y = \sin 2x \cos 3x$

$$= \frac{1}{2}[2\cos 3x \sin 2x]$$

$$= \frac{1}{2}[\sin 5x - \sin x]$$

Differentiating n times, we have

$$y_n = \frac{1}{2}\left[5^n \sin\left(5x + \frac{n\pi}{2}\right) - \sin\left(x + \frac{n\pi}{2}\right)\right]$$

(ii) Let
$$y = \cos^4 x = \left(\frac{1+\cos 2x}{2}\right)^2$$
$$= \frac{1}{4}[1 + 2\cos 2x + \cos^2 2x]$$
$$= \frac{1}{4}\left[1 + 2\cos 2x + \frac{1+\cos 4x}{2}\right]$$
$$= \frac{1}{8}[3 + 4\cos 2x + \cos 4x]$$

Differentiating n times, we have
$$y_n = \frac{1}{8}\left[2^{n+2}\cos\left(2x + \frac{n\pi}{2}\right) + 4^n \cos\left(4x + \frac{n\pi}{2}\right)\right]$$

(iii) Let
$$y = \cos x \cos 2x \cos 3x$$
$$= \frac{1}{2}\cos 2x\,(2\cos x \cos 3x)$$
$$= \frac{1}{2}\cos 2x\,(\cos 4x + \cos 2x)$$
$$= \frac{1}{2}\cos 2x \cos 4x + \frac{1}{2}\cos^2 2x$$
$$= \frac{1}{4}(2\cos 2x \cos 4x) + \frac{1}{2}\cos^2 2x$$
$$= \frac{1}{4}(\cos 6x + \cos 2x) + \frac{1}{2}\left(\frac{1+\cos 4x}{2}\right)$$
$$= \frac{1}{4}[\cos 6x + \cos 4x + \cos 2x + 1]$$

Now, differentiating n times, we have
$$y_n = \frac{1}{4}\left[6^n \cos\left(6x + \frac{n\pi}{2}\right) + 4^n \cos\left(4x + \frac{n\pi}{2}\right) + 2^n \cos\left(2x + \frac{n\pi}{2}\right)\right]$$

(iv) Let
$$y = e^{ax} \sin bx \cos cx$$
$$= \frac{1}{2} e^{ax}(2 \sin bx \cos cx)$$
$$= \frac{1}{2} e^{ax}[\sin(b+c)x + \sin(b-c)x]$$
$$= \frac{1}{2}[e^{ax}\sin(b+c)x] + \frac{1}{2}[e^{ax}\sin(b-c)x]$$

Differentiating n times,
$$y_n = \frac{1}{2} r_1^n\, e^{ax} \sin\{(b+c)x + n\phi_1\} + \frac{1}{2} r_2^n\, e^{ax}\{\sin(b-c)x + n\phi_2\}$$

where $\quad r_1^2 = a^2 + (b+c)^2, \quad \phi_1 = \tan^{-1}\left\{\dfrac{(b+c)}{a}\right\}$

and $\quad r_2^2 = a^2 + (b+c)^2, \quad \phi_2 = \tan^{-1}\left\{\dfrac{(b-c)}{a}\right\}$

(v) Let $\quad y = e^{ax}\cos^2 x \sin x$

$$= e^{ax}\left[\frac{1+\cos 2x}{2}\right]\sin x = \frac{1}{2}e^{ax}\left[\sin x + \frac{1}{2}(\sin 3x - \sin x)\right]$$

$$= \frac{1}{4}[e^{ax}\sin x + e^{ax}\sin 3x]$$

Differentiating n times, we have

$$y_n = \frac{1}{4}\left[(a^2+1)^{n/2}e^{ax}\sin\left(x + n\tan^{-1}\frac{1}{a}\right) + (a^2+9)^{n/2}e^{ax}\cdot\sin\left(3x + n\tan^{-1}\frac{3}{a}\right)\right]$$

(vi) Let $\quad y = e^{2x}\sin\dfrac{x}{2}\cos\dfrac{x}{2}\sin 3x$

$$= e^{2x}\frac{\sin x}{2}\sin 3x$$

$$= \frac{1}{4}e^{2x}[2\sin x \sin 3x]$$

$$= \frac{e^{2x}}{4}[\cos 2x - \cos 4x]$$

$$= \frac{e^{2x}}{4}\cos 2x - \frac{e^{2x}}{4}\cos 4x$$

Differentiating n times, we have

$$y_n = \frac{e^{2x}}{4}(8)^{n/2}\cos\left(2x + n\frac{\pi}{4}\right) - \frac{e^{2x}}{4}(20)^{n/2}\cos(4x + n\theta)$$

$$= \frac{e^{2x}}{4}\left\{(8)^{n/2}\cos\left(2x + \frac{n\pi}{4}\right) - (20)^{n/2}\cos(4x + n\theta)\right\}$$

where $\quad \theta = \tan^{-1} 2$

(vii) Let $\quad y = \cos^2 x \sin^3 x$

$$= \left(\frac{1+\cos 2x}{2}\right)\left[\frac{1}{4}(3\sin x - \sin 3x)\right] \quad \{\because \sin 3x = 3\sin x - 4\sin^3 x\}$$

$$= \frac{1}{8}[3\sin x - \sin 3x + 3\sin x \cos 2x - \sin 3x \cos 2x]$$

$$= \frac{1}{8}\left[3\sin x - \sin 3x + \frac{3}{2}(2\sin x \cos 2x) - \frac{1}{2}(2\sin 3x \cos 2x)\right]$$

$$= \frac{1}{8}\left[3\sin x - \sin 3x + \frac{3}{2}(\sin 3x - \sin x) - \frac{1}{2}(\sin 5x + \sin x)\right]$$

$$= \frac{1}{8}\left[\sin x + \frac{1}{2}\sin 3x - \frac{1}{2}\sin 5x\right]$$

$$= \frac{1}{16}[2\sin x + \sin 3x - \sin 5x]$$

Differentiating n times, we have

$$y_n = \frac{1}{16}\left[2\sin\left(x + \frac{n\pi}{2}\right) + 3^n \sin\left(3x + \frac{n\pi}{2}\right) - 5^n \sin\left(5x + \frac{n\pi}{2}\right)\right]$$

(viii) First we express product $\sin^5 x \cos^3 x$ into a sum in terms of multiple angles.

Expansion of $\sin^n x$, $\cos^n x$ or $\sin^m x \cos^n x$ in series of sines or cosines of multiples of x : We use the following results.

Let $\quad z = \cos x + i \sin x \quad$ then $\quad \dfrac{1}{z} = \cos x - i \sin x$

$\therefore \quad z^m = \cos mx + i \sin mx \quad$ and $\quad \dfrac{1}{z^m} = \cos mx - i \sin mx$

Hence $\quad z + \dfrac{1}{z} = 2\cos x \qquad\qquad z - \dfrac{1}{z} = 2i \sin x$

$\qquad\quad z^m + \dfrac{1}{z^m} = 2\cos mx \qquad\quad z^m - \dfrac{1}{z^m} = 2i \sin mx$

These results are used to expand powers of sin x or cos x or their products in a series of sines or cosines of multiples of x.

$$(2i \sin x)^5 (2 \cos x)^3 = \left(z - \dfrac{1}{z}\right)^5 \left(z + \dfrac{1}{z}\right)^3$$

$\therefore \quad 2^8 i^5 \sin^5 x \cos^3 x = \left(z^8 - \dfrac{1}{z^8}\right) - 2\left(z^6 - \dfrac{1}{z^6}\right) - 2\left(z^4 - \dfrac{1}{z^4}\right) + 6\left(z^2 - \dfrac{1}{z^2}\right)$

$\qquad\qquad\qquad\qquad = 2i \sin 8x - 4i \sin 6x - 4i \sin 4x + 12i \sin 2x$

$\therefore \quad\quad \sin^5 x \cos^3 x = 2^{-7}[\sin 8x - 2\sin 6x - 2\sin 4x + 6\sin 2x]$

Differentiating n times, we have

$$D^n(\sin^5 x \cos^3 x) = 2^{-7}\left[8^n \sin\left(8x + \dfrac{n\pi}{2}\right) - 2 \cdot 6^n \sin\left(6x + \dfrac{n\pi}{2}\right)\right.$$
$$\left. - 2 \cdot 4^n \sin\left(4x + \dfrac{n\pi}{2}\right) + 6 \cdot 2^n \sin\left(2x + \dfrac{n\pi}{2}\right)\right]$$

Ex. 8 : If $y = e^x(\sin x + \cos x)$, prove that $y_n = 2^{\frac{n+1}{2}} e^x \sin\left[x + (n+1)\dfrac{\pi}{4}\right]$. **(May 2008)**

Sol. : $y = e^x (\sin x + \cos x) = \sqrt{2} \, e^x \left[\dfrac{1}{\sqrt{2}} \cdot \sin x + \cos x \cdot \dfrac{1}{\sqrt{2}}\right]$ (Note this step)

$\qquad\qquad\qquad\qquad = \sqrt{2} \, e^x \left[\sin x \cdot \cos \dfrac{\pi}{4} + \cos x \cdot \sin \dfrac{\pi}{4}\right] = \sqrt{2} \, e^x \sin\left[x + \dfrac{\pi}{4}\right]$

Differentiating n times w.r.t. x, we get

$$y_n = \sqrt{2} \, r^n e^x \sin\left[x + \dfrac{\pi}{4} + n\theta\right]$$

$$= \sqrt{2} \cdot (\sqrt{2})^n e^x \sin\left[x + \dfrac{\pi}{4} + \dfrac{n\pi}{4}\right] \qquad \begin{cases} \text{Here } a = 1, b = 1 \\ \therefore r = \sqrt{a^2 + b^2} = \sqrt{2} \\ \text{and } \theta = \tan^{-1}\dfrac{b}{a} = \dfrac{\pi}{4} \end{cases}$$

$$= (\sqrt{2})^{n+1} e^x \sin\left[x + (n+1)\dfrac{\pi}{4}\right]$$

$$y_n = 2^{\frac{n+1}{2}} e^x \sin\left[x + (n+1)\dfrac{\pi}{4}\right]$$

Ex. 9 : If $y = \sin px + \cos px$, prove that $y_n = p^n [1 + (-1)^n \sin 2px]^{1/2}$

(Jan. 2004, Dec. 2007)

Sol. : $\quad y = \sin px + \cos px$

Differentiating n times, w.r.t. x, we get

$$y_n = p^n \sin\left(px + \frac{n\pi}{2}\right) + p^n \cos\left(px + \frac{n\pi}{2}\right)$$

$$= p^n \left[\left\{\sin\left(px + \frac{n\pi}{2}\right) + \cos\left(px + \frac{n\pi}{2}\right)\right\}^2\right]^{1/2} \quad \text{(Note this step)}$$

$$= p^n \left[1 + 2\sin\left(px + \frac{n\pi}{2}\right)\cos\left(px + \frac{n\pi}{2}\right)\right]^{1/2}$$

$$= p^n [1 + \sin(2px + n\pi)]^{1/2}$$

$$= p^n [1 + (-1)^n \sin 2px]^{1/2} \quad \{\because \sin n\pi = 0 \text{ and } \cos n\pi = (-1)^n$$

Ex. 10 : If $y = (x - 1)^n$ then show that $y + y_1 + \dfrac{y_2}{2!} + \dfrac{y_3}{3!} + \ldots + \dfrac{y_n}{n!} = x^n$.

(Jan. 2005, Dec. 2006)

Sol. : We have,
$$y = (x - 1)^n$$
$$y_1 = n(x - 1)^{n-1}$$
$$y_2 = n(n - 1)(x - 1)^{n-2}$$
$$y_3 = n(n - 1)(n - 2)(x - 1)^{n-3}$$
$$\ldots \ldots \ldots \ldots \ldots$$
$$y_n = n(n - 1)(n - 2) \ldots \{n - (n - 1)\}(x - 1)^{n-n} = n!$$

$\therefore$ L.H.S. $= (x - 1)^n + n(x - 1)^n + \dfrac{n(n - 1)}{2!}(x - 1)^{n-2} + \dfrac{n(n - 1)(n - 2)}{3!}(x - 1)^{n-3} + \ldots \dfrac{n!}{n!}$

$$= (x - 1)^n + n_{C_1}(x - 1)^{n-1} + n_{C_2}(x - 1)^{n-2} + n_{C_3}(x - 1)^{n-3} + \ldots n_{C_n}(x - 1)^0$$

$$= [(x - 1) + 1]^n \quad \text{[By Binomial theorem]}$$

$$= x^n = \text{R.H.S.} \quad \text{which is the required result.}$$

Ex. 11 : If $y = x \log\left(\dfrac{x - 1}{x + 1}\right)$, then show that

$$y_n = (-1)^{n-2}(n - 2)! \left[\dfrac{(x - n)}{(x - 1)^n} - \dfrac{(x + n)}{(x + 1)^n}\right]$$

Sol. : Given that $\quad y = x \log\left(\dfrac{x - 1}{x + 1}\right) = x \log(x - 1) - x \log(x + 1)$

Differentiating with respect to x, we get

$$y_1 = \log(x - 1) + \dfrac{x}{(x - 1)} - \log(x + 1) - \dfrac{x}{(x + 1)}$$

$$= \log(x - 1) - \log(x + 1) + \dfrac{(x - 1 + 1)}{(x - 1)} - \dfrac{(x + 1 - 1)}{(x + 1)}$$

[Note this step]

$$= \log(x-1) - \log(x+1) + 1 + \frac{1}{(x-1)} - 1 + \frac{1}{(x+1)}$$

$$= \log(x-1) - \log(x+1) + \left[\frac{1}{(x-1)} + \frac{1}{(x+1)}\right]$$

Differentiating again with respect to x, we get

$$y_2 = \left[\frac{1}{(x-1)} - \frac{1}{(x+1)}\right] + \left[\frac{-1}{(x-1)^2} + \frac{-1}{(x+1)^2}\right]$$

Now differentiating (n – 2) times with respect to x, we get,

$$y_n = \left[\frac{(-1)^{n-2}(n-2)!}{(x-1)^{n-1}} - \frac{(-1)^{n-2}(n-2)!}{(x+1)^{n-1}}\right] - \left[\frac{(-1)^{n-2}(n-1)!}{(x-1)^n} + \frac{(-1)^{n-2}(n-1)!}{(x+1)^n}\right]$$

$$= (-1)^{n-2}(n-2)! \left[\frac{1}{(x-1)^{n-1}} - \frac{1}{(x+1)^{n-1}} - \frac{(n-1)}{(x-1)^n} - \frac{(n-1)}{(x+1)^n}\right]$$

$$\{\because (n-1)! = (n-1)(n-2)!\}$$

$$= (-1)^{n-2}(n-2)! \left[\frac{(x-1)-(n-1)}{(x-1)^n} - \frac{(x+1)+(n-1)}{(x+1)^n}\right]$$

$$= (-1)^{(n-2)}(n-2)! \left[\frac{(x-n)}{(x-1)^n} - \frac{(x+n)}{(x+1)^n}\right]$$

Ex. 12 : *Find n^{th} derivative of* $\frac{x}{(x+1)^4}$. **(May 2014)**

Sol. : Let $y = \frac{x}{(x+1)^4} = \frac{(x+1)}{(x+1)^4} - \frac{1}{(x+1)^4}$

$$= \frac{1}{(x+1)^3} - \frac{1}{(x+1)^4}$$

Differentiating n times w.r.t. x, we get,

$$y_n = \frac{(-1)^n (n+2)!}{2(x+1)^{n+3}} - \frac{(-1)^n (n+3)!}{6(x+1)^{n+4}}$$

$\begin{cases} \text{If } y = (ax+b)^{-m}, \text{ then} \\ y_n = \dfrac{(-1)^n m (m+1) \ldots (m+n-1) a^n}{(ax+b)^{m+n}} \end{cases}$

$$= \frac{(-1)^n (n+2)!}{6(x+1)^{n+3}} \left[3 - \frac{(n+3)}{(x+1)}\right]$$

$$= \frac{(-1)^n (n+2)!}{3! (x+1)^{n+4}} (3x-n)$$

Type III : n^{th} Derivative, Using Partial Fractions :

For finding the nth derivative of a fraction (rational function), we must decompose it into partial fractions, and then use standard results.

Ex. 13 : *Find the nth derivatives of*

(i) $\dfrac{1}{(1-5x+6x^2)}$, (ii) $\dfrac{1}{(x^3+6x^2+11x+6)}$, (iii) $\dfrac{2x+3}{5x+7}$,

(iv) $\dfrac{x^3}{(x-1)(x-2)}$ **(Jan. 2004)**, (v) $\dfrac{1}{(x-1)^2(x-2)}$.

Sol.: (i) Let $y = \dfrac{1}{(1 - 5x + 6x^2)} = \dfrac{1}{(2x - 1)(3x - 1)}$

$= \dfrac{A}{(2x - 1)} + \dfrac{B}{(3x - 1)}$

$= \dfrac{2}{(2x - 1)} - \dfrac{3}{(3x - 1)}$

Differentiating n times w.r.t. x, we get,

$$y_n = 2\left[\dfrac{(-1)^n n! \, 2^n}{(2x - 1)^{n+1}}\right] - 3\left[\dfrac{(-1)^n n! \, 3^n}{(3x - 1)^{n+1}}\right]$$

$$= (-1)^n n! \left[\dfrac{2^{n+1}}{(2x - 1)^{n+1}} - \dfrac{3^{n+1}}{(3x - 1)^{n+1}}\right]$$

$\left\{\because \dfrac{d^n}{dx^n} \dfrac{1}{(ax + b)} = \dfrac{(-1)^n n! \, a^n}{(ax + b)^{n+1}}\right\}$

(ii) Let $y = \dfrac{1}{x^3 + 6x^2 + 11x + 6}$

$= \dfrac{1}{(x + 1)(x + 2)(x + 3)} = \dfrac{A}{x + 1} + \dfrac{B}{x + 2} + \dfrac{C}{x + 3}$

$= \dfrac{\frac{1}{2}}{x + 1} + \dfrac{-1}{x + 2} + \dfrac{\frac{1}{2}}{x + 3}$

Differentiating n times successively using standard result, we get,

$$y_n = \dfrac{1}{2} \dfrac{(-1)^n n!}{(x + 1)^{n+1}} - \dfrac{(-1)^n n!}{(x + 2)^{n+1}} + \dfrac{1}{2} \dfrac{(-1)^n n!}{(x + 3)^{n+1}}$$

$$= (-1)^n n! \left[\dfrac{1}{2} \dfrac{1}{(x + 1)^{n+1}} - \dfrac{1}{(x + 2)^{n+1}} + \dfrac{1}{2} \dfrac{1}{(x + 3)^{n+1}}\right]$$

(iii) Let $y = \dfrac{2x + 3}{5x + 7}$

$= \dfrac{2}{5} \left[\dfrac{5x + \frac{15}{2}}{5x + 7}\right] = \dfrac{2}{5}\left[\dfrac{(5x + 7) + \frac{1}{2}}{(5x + 7)}\right]$

$= \dfrac{2}{5} + \dfrac{1}{5}\left(\dfrac{1}{5x + 7}\right)$

Differentiating n times w.r.t. x, we get

$$y_n = \dfrac{1}{5}\left[\dfrac{(-1)^n n! \, 5^n}{(5x + 7)^{n+1}}\right]$$

(iv) Let $y = \dfrac{x^3}{(x-1)(x-2)}$

Given fraction is not a proper fraction, therefore, we make it proper fraction by actual division.

∴ $y = \dfrac{x^3}{(x-1)(x-2)} = x + 3 + \dfrac{7x-6}{(x-1)(x-2)}$

$= x + 3 + \dfrac{A}{(x-1)} + \dfrac{B}{(x-2)}$

$= x + 3 - \dfrac{1}{x-1} + \dfrac{8}{x-2}$

Differentiating n times successively, we get

[for $n > 1$, $D^n(x) = 0$]

$y_n = -\left[\dfrac{(-1)^n n!}{(x-1)^{n+1}}\right] + 8\left[\dfrac{(-1)^n n!}{(x-2)^{n+1}}\right]$

$= (-1)^n n! \left[-\dfrac{1}{(x-1)^{n+1}} + \dfrac{8}{(x-2)^{n+1}}\right]$

(v) Let $y = \dfrac{1}{(x-1)^2(x-2)}$

$= \dfrac{A}{(x-1)} + \dfrac{B}{(x-1)^2} + \dfrac{C}{(x-2)}$

$= \dfrac{-1}{(x-1)} - \dfrac{1}{(x-1)^2} + \dfrac{1}{(x-2)}$

$= -\left[\dfrac{(-1)^n n!}{(x-1)^{n+1}}\right] - \dfrac{d^n}{dx^n}\left[\dfrac{1}{(x-1)^2}\right] + \left[\dfrac{(-1)^n n!}{(x-2)^{n+1}}\right]$

$= \dfrac{(-1)^{n+1} n!}{(x-1)^{n+1}} + \dfrac{(-1)^{n+1}(n+1)!}{(x-1)^{n+2}} + \dfrac{(-1)^n n!}{(x-2)^{n+1}}$

Ex. 14 : *Prove that the value of the nth differential coefficient of $\dfrac{x^3}{(x^2-1)}$, for $x = 0$ is zero if n is even and $-n!$ if n is odd and greater than 1.* **(May 2006, Dec. 2008, Dec. 2010)**

Sol. : Let $y = \dfrac{x^3}{x^2-1} = x + \dfrac{x}{x^2-1}$ (By actual division)

$= x + \dfrac{A}{(x-1)} + \dfrac{B}{(x+1)}$

$= x + \dfrac{1}{2}\left(\dfrac{1}{x-1} + \dfrac{1}{x+1}\right)$

Differentiating n times successively, we get

$y_n = +\dfrac{1}{2}\left[\dfrac{(-1)^n n!}{(x-1)^{n+1}} + \dfrac{(-1)^n n!}{(x+1)^{n+1}}\right]$ [For $n > 1$, $D^n(x) = 0$]

$= \dfrac{1}{2}(-1)^n n! \left[\dfrac{1}{(x-1)^{n+1}} + \dfrac{1}{(x+1)^{n+1}}\right]$

at $x = 0$, $(y_n)_{x=0} = \dfrac{1}{2} (-1)^n n! \left[\dfrac{1}{(-1)^{n+1}} + \dfrac{1}{(1)^{n+1}}\right]$

$\qquad\qquad\qquad\quad = \dfrac{1}{2} (-1)^n n! \left[\dfrac{1}{(-1)^{n+1}} + 1\right]$

if n is even,

$\qquad\qquad (y_n)_0 = \dfrac{1}{2} (+1) \, n! \, [-1 + 1] = 0 \qquad\qquad \{\because (-1)^{n+1} = -1 \text{ if n is even}$

if n is odd,

$\qquad\qquad (y_n)_0 = \dfrac{1}{2} (-1) \, n! \, [1 + 1] = -n! \qquad\qquad \{\because (-1)^{n+1} = 1 \text{ if n is odd}$

Type IV : n^{th} Derivative, Using Demoivre's Theorem :

When the denominator of a given algebraic fraction cannot be resolved into real linear factors, then they are resolved into linear imaginary factors, which are put into the form $r(\cos \theta + i \sin \theta)$ and then Demoivre's theorem is applied to simplify the result.

Ex. 15 : *Find the nth derivatives of* (i) $\dfrac{1}{x^2 + a^2}$, (ii) $\dfrac{x}{x^2 + a^2}$, (iii) $\tan^{-1} \dfrac{x}{a}$ **(May 10, Dec. 12)**

(iv) $\tan^{-1}\left(\dfrac{\sqrt{1 + x^2} - 1}{x}\right)$, (v) $\cos^{-1}\left(\dfrac{x - x^{-1}}{x + x^{-1}}\right)$ **(May 2004, 2007)**,

(vi) $\dfrac{1}{1 + x + x^2 + x^3}$ **(May 2006)**.

Sol. : (i) Let $\quad y = \dfrac{1}{x^2 + a^2}$

$\qquad\qquad\qquad = \dfrac{1}{(x + ia)(x - ia)}$

$\qquad\qquad\qquad = \dfrac{1}{2ia} \left[\dfrac{1}{x - ia} - \dfrac{1}{x + ia}\right]$ \qquad\qquad (By partial fraction)

Now differentiating n times w.r.t. x, we get

$\qquad\qquad y_n = \dfrac{1}{2ia} \left[\dfrac{(-1)^n n!}{(x - ia)^{n+1}} - \dfrac{(-1)^n n!}{(x + ia)^{n+1}}\right]$

$\qquad\qquad\quad = \dfrac{(-1)^n n!}{2ia} \left[\dfrac{1}{(x - ia)^{n+1}} - \dfrac{1}{(x + ia)^{n+1}}\right]$

Put $\qquad x + ia = r(\cos \theta + i \sin \theta) \quad \text{and} \quad x - ia = r(\cos \theta - i \sin \theta)$

$\therefore \qquad\qquad x = r \cos \theta, \quad a = r \sin \theta \quad \text{and} \quad \theta = \tan^{-1} \dfrac{a}{x}$

$\therefore \qquad\qquad y_n = \dfrac{(-1)^n n!}{2ia \, r^{n+1}} \left[\dfrac{1}{(\cos \theta - i \sin \theta)^{n+1}} - \dfrac{1}{(\cos \theta + i \sin \theta)^{n+1}}\right]$

$$= \frac{(-1)^n n!}{2ia\, r^{n+1}} \left[\frac{1}{\cos(n+1)\theta - i\sin(n+1)\theta} - \frac{1}{\cos(n+1)\theta + i\sin(n+1)\theta} \right]$$

(By Demoivre's theorem)

$$= \frac{(-1)^n n!}{2ia\, r^{n+1}} \Big[\{\cos(n+1)\theta + i\sin(n+1)\theta\} - \{\cos(n+1)\theta - i\sin(n+1)\theta\} \Big]$$

$$= \frac{(-1)^n n!}{2ia\, r^{n+1}} [2i\sin(n+1)\theta]$$

$$= \frac{(-1)^n n!\, \sin(n+1)\theta}{a \left(\dfrac{a^{n+1}}{\sin^{n+1}\theta}\right)} \qquad \left\{ \text{since } a = r\sin\theta \;\therefore\; r = \frac{a}{\sin\theta} \right\}$$

$$= \frac{(-1)^n n!\, \sin(n+1)\theta\, \sin^{n+1}\theta}{a^{n+2}}, \text{ where } \theta = \tan^{-1}\frac{a}{x}$$

(ii) Let $\quad y = \dfrac{x}{x^2 + a^2} = \dfrac{1}{2}\left[\dfrac{1}{x - ia} + \dfrac{1}{x + ia}\right]$ (By partial fraction)

Differentiating n times w.r.t. x, we get

$$y_n = \frac{1}{2}\left[\frac{(-1)^n n!}{(x - ia)^{n+1}} + \frac{(-1)^n n!}{(x + ia)^{n+1}}\right]$$

Put $\quad (x + ia) = r(\cos\theta + i\sin\theta)$ and $(x - ia) = r(\cos\theta - i\sin\theta)$

$$= \frac{(-1)^n n!}{2r^{n+1}} \left[\frac{1}{(\cos\theta - i\sin\theta)^{n+1}} + \frac{1}{(\cos\theta + i\sin\theta)^{n+1}}\right]$$

$$= \frac{(-1)^n n!}{2r^{n+1}} \left[\frac{1}{\cos(n+1)\theta - i\sin(n+1)\theta} + \frac{1}{\cos(n+1)\theta + i\sin(n+1)\theta}\right]$$

(By Demoivre's theorem)

$$= \frac{(-1)^n n!}{2r^{n+1}} \Big[\{\cos(n+1)\theta + i\sin(n+1)\theta\} + \{\cos(n+1)\theta - i\sin(n+1)\theta\} \Big]$$

$$= \frac{(-1)^n n!}{2r^{n+1}} [2\cos(n+1)\theta]$$

$$= \frac{(-1)^n n!\, \cos(n+1)\theta}{r^{n+1}}$$

$$= \frac{(-1)^n n!\, \cos(n+1)\theta}{a^{n+1} / \sin^{n+1}\theta} \qquad \left\{ \text{since } a = r\sin\theta \;\therefore\; r = \frac{a}{\sin\theta} \right\}$$

$$= \frac{(-1)^n n!\, \cos(n+1)\theta\, \sin^{n+1}\theta}{a^{n+1}}, \text{ where } \theta = \tan^{-1}\frac{a}{x}$$

(iii) Let $\quad y = \tan^{-1}\dfrac{x}{a}$

Differentiating w.r.t. x, we get

$$y_1 = \frac{a}{x^2 + a^2} = a\left(\frac{1}{x^2 + a^2}\right)$$

Differentiating $(n-1)$ times, w.r.t. x, we get

$$y_n = a\, D^{n-1}\left(\frac{1}{x^2+a^2}\right)$$

$$= a\left[\frac{(-1)^{n-1}(n-1)!\sin n\theta \sin^n\theta}{a^{n+1}}\right], \text{ where } \theta = \tan^{-1}\frac{a}{x}$$

$$= \frac{(-1)^{n-1}(n-1)!\sin n\theta \sin^n\theta}{a^n}$$

[**Note :** To obtain $D^{n-1}\left(\frac{1}{x^2+a^2}\right)$, replace n by $n-1$ in the result obtained in Ex. (i) above.]

(iv) Let $\quad y = \tan^{-1}\left(\frac{\sqrt{1+x^2}-1}{x}\right)$, put $x = \tan\theta$

$$= \tan^{-1}\left(\frac{\sqrt{1+\tan^2\theta}-1}{\tan\theta}\right)$$

$$= \tan^{-1}\left(\frac{\sec\theta - 1}{\tan\theta}\right)$$

$$= \tan^{-1}\left(\frac{1-\cos\theta}{\sin\theta}\right)$$

$$= \tan^{-1}\left(\frac{2\sin^2\theta/2}{2\sin\theta/2\cos\theta/2}\right)$$

$$= \tan^{-1}\left(\tan\frac{\theta}{2}\right)$$

$$= \frac{\theta}{2}$$

$$= \frac{1}{2}\tan^{-1}x$$

Using the result of Ex. (iii) with $a = 1$,

$\therefore \quad y_n = \frac{1}{2}(-1)^{n-1}(n-1)!\sin n\theta \sin^n\theta$, where $\theta = \tan^{-1}\frac{1}{x}$ or $x = \cot\theta$

(v) $\quad y = \cos^{-1}\left(\frac{x-x^{-1}}{x+x^{-1}}\right) = \cos^{-1}\left(\frac{x^2-1}{x^2+1}\right)$

Put $x = \tan\theta$

$\therefore \quad y = \cos^{-1}\left(\frac{\tan^2\theta - 1}{\tan^2\theta + 1}\right) = \cos^{-1}(-\cos 2\theta)$

$$= \cos^{-1}[\cos(\pi + 2\theta)]$$

$$= \pi + 2\tan^{-1}x$$

Using the result of Ex. (iii) with $a = 1$,

$\therefore \quad y_n = 2(-1)^{n-1}(n-1)!\sin^n\theta \sin n\theta$, where $\theta = \tan^{-1}\frac{1}{x}$.

(vi) Let $y = \dfrac{1}{1+x+x^2+x^3}$

$= \dfrac{1}{(1+x)(1+x^2)} = \dfrac{1}{(1+x)(x-i)(x+i)}$

$= \dfrac{1}{2(1+x)} + \dfrac{1}{2i(i+1)(x-i)} - \dfrac{1}{2i(1-i)(x+i)}$ (By partial fraction)

$= \dfrac{1}{2}\left[\dfrac{1}{(1+x)} - \dfrac{(1+i)}{2(x-i)} - \dfrac{(1-i)}{2(x+i)}\right]$ $\quad \left\{\begin{array}{l}\because \dfrac{1}{i(i+1)} = \dfrac{-(1+i)}{2} \\ \text{and } \dfrac{1}{i(1-i)} = \dfrac{(1-i)}{2}\end{array}\right.$

Differentiating n times w.r.t. x, we get

$y_n = \dfrac{1}{2}\left[\dfrac{(-1)^n n!}{(x+1)^{n+1}} - \dfrac{(1+i)(-1)^n n!}{2(x-i)^{n+1}} - \dfrac{(1-i)(-1)^n n!}{2(x+i)^{n+1}}\right]$

$= \dfrac{(-1)^n n!}{2}\left[\dfrac{1}{(x+1)^{n+1}} - \dfrac{(1+i)}{2(x-i)^{n+1}} - \dfrac{(1-i)}{2(x+i)^{n+1}}\right]$

$= \dfrac{(-1)^n n!}{2}\left[\dfrac{1}{(\cot\theta+1)^{n+1}} - \dfrac{(1+i)}{2(\cot\theta-i)^{n+1}} - \dfrac{(1-i)}{2(\cot\theta+i)^{n+1}}\right]$ on putting $x = \cot\theta$

$= \dfrac{(-1)^n n!}{2}\left[\dfrac{\sin^{n+1}\theta}{(\cos\theta+\sin\theta)^{n+1}} - \dfrac{(1+i)}{2}\left\{\dfrac{\sin^{n+1}\theta}{(\cos\theta - i\sin\theta)^{n+1}}\right\} - \dfrac{(1-i)}{2}\left\{\dfrac{\sin^{n+1}\theta}{(\cos\theta + i\sin\theta)^{n+1}}\right\}\right]$

$= \dfrac{(-1)^n n!}{2}\sin^{n+1}\theta\left[(\cos\theta+\sin\theta)^{-n-1} - \dfrac{(1+i)}{2}\{\cos(n+1)\theta + i\sin(n+1)\theta\}\right.$

$\left. - \dfrac{(1-i)}{2}\{\cos(n+1)\theta - i\sin(n+1)\theta\}\right]$

$= \dfrac{(-1)^n n!}{2}\sin^{n+1}\theta\left[(\cos\theta+\sin\theta)^{-n-1} - \dfrac{1}{2}\left\{\begin{array}{l}\cos(n+1)\theta + i\sin(n+1)\theta \\ + i\cos(n+1)\theta - \sin(n+1)\theta\end{array}\right\}\right.$

$\left.- \dfrac{1}{2}\left\{\begin{array}{l}\cos(n+1)\theta - i\sin(n+1)\theta \\ -i\cos(n+1)\theta - \sin(n+1)\theta\end{array}\right\}\right]$

$= \dfrac{(-1)^n n!}{2}\sin^{n+1}\theta\left[(\cos\theta+\sin\theta)^{-n-1} - \dfrac{1}{2}\{2\cos(n+1)\theta - 2\sin(n+1)\theta\}\right]$

$= \dfrac{(-1)^n n!}{2}\sin^{n+1}\theta\left[\{\sin(n+1)\theta - \cos(n+1)\theta\} + (\cos\theta+\sin\theta)^{-n-1}\right]$

where $\theta = \cot^{-1}x$

EXERCISE 7.1

1. Solve the following :

(i) If $y = Ae^{-kt}\cos(pt+c)$, prove that $\dfrac{d^2y}{dt^2} + 2k\dfrac{dy}{dt} + n^2y = 0$, where $n^2 = p^2 + k^2$.

(ii) If $x = a(\theta + \sin\theta)$ and $y = a(1 - \cos\theta)$, find $\dfrac{d^2y}{dx^2}$ in terms of θ. **Ans.** $\dfrac{1}{4a\cos^4\theta/2}$.

(iii) If $y = P\sin mx + Q\cos mx$, prove that $y_2 + m^2 y = 0$, P, Q being constants.

(iv) Find P and Q such that $y = P \sin 5x + Q \cos 5x$, satisfies the equation

$\dfrac{d^2y}{dx^2} + \dfrac{1}{5}\dfrac{dy}{dx} + 15y = 101 \sin 5x$. **Ans.** $P = -10, Q = -1$

(v) If $y = e^{ax} \sin bx$, prove that $y_2 - 2ay_1 + (a^2 + b^2)y = 0$.

(vi) If $x = \sin t, y = \sin pt$, prove that $(1 - x^2)\dfrac{d^2y}{dx^2} - x\dfrac{dy}{dx} + p^2 y = 0$.

(vii) If $y = \tan^{-1}(\sinh x)$, prove that $\dfrac{d^2y}{dx^2} + \tan y \left(\dfrac{dy}{dx}\right)^2 = 0$.

[**Hint**: $\tan y = \sinh x \quad \therefore \dfrac{dy}{dx} = \dfrac{\cosh x}{\sec^2 y} = \dfrac{\cosh x}{1 + \tan^2 y}$

$= \dfrac{\cosh x}{1 + \sinh^2 x} = \dfrac{\cosh x}{\cosh^2 x} = \text{sech } x$]

(viii) Verify that $y = \cos(k \cos^{-1} x)$ satisfy the differential equation

$(1 - x^2)\dfrac{d^2y}{dx^2} - x\dfrac{dy}{dx} + k^2 y = 0$ (k is a constant).

[**Hint**: Let $z = k \cos^{-1} x \quad \therefore y = \cos z$. Use $\dfrac{dy}{dx} = \dfrac{dy}{dz} \cdot \dfrac{dz}{dx}$]

(ix) If $x = \cos t, y = \cos 2nt$, prove that $(1 - x^2)\dfrac{d^2y}{dx^2} - x\dfrac{dy}{dx} + 4n^2 y = 0$.

(x) If $y = A \cos(\log x) + B \sin(\log x)$, prove that $x^2\dfrac{d^2y}{dx^2} + x\dfrac{dy}{dx} + y = 0$.

(xi) If $x^2 + 2xy + 3y^2 = 1$, show that $(x + 3y)^3 \dfrac{d^2y}{dx^2} + 2 = 0$.

[**Hint**: $(x + 3y)y_1 + (x + y) = 0$ and $(x + 3y)y_2 + 3y_1^2 + 2y_1 + 1 = 0$

Now put y_1 and multiply by $(x + 3y)^2$ throughout]

(xii) If $x^3 + y^3 = 3axy$, prove that $y_2 = 2a^3 xy / (ax - y^2)^3$.

[**Hint**: $\dfrac{dy}{dx} = \dfrac{x^2 - ay}{-y^2 + ax}$ and use $x^3 + y^3 - 3axy = 0$]

(xiii) If $y = x \log[x / (a + bx)]$, prove that $x^3 y_2 = (y - xy_1)^2$

[**Hint**: $xy_1 - y = ax/a + bx$]

(xiv) If $ax^2 + 2hxy + by^2 + 2gx + 2fy + c = 0$, prove that $D^2 y = \Delta (hx + by + f)^{-3}$,

where $\Delta = abc + 2fgh - af^2 - bg^2 - ch^2$.

[**Hint**: $\dfrac{dy}{dx} = \dfrac{-(ax + hy + g)}{(hx + by + f)}$ and use $ax^2 + 2hxy + by^2 + 2gx + 2fy = -c$]

(xv) If $f(x) = x^5$, prove that $f(1) + \dfrac{f'(1)}{1!} + \dfrac{f''(1)}{2!} + \dfrac{f'''(1)}{3!} + \dfrac{f^{iv}(1)}{4!} + \dfrac{f^{v}(1)}{5!} = 2^5$.

2. Find the nth derivatives of
   (i) e^{ax+b}, (ii) $(ax+b)^{p/q}$, (iii) $e^{ax}\cos^3 bx$,
   (iv) $e^x \cos x \cos 2x$, (v) $e^x \sin 4x \cos 6x$, (vi) $e^x \sin^4 x$.

   Ans. (i) $a^n e^{ax+b}$, (ii) $a^n (p/q)(p/q-1)(p/q-2) \ldots (p/q-n+1)(ax+b)^{p/q-n}$

   (iii) $\dfrac{1}{4}(a^2+9b^2)^{n/2} e^{ax} \cos\left(3bx + n\tan^{-1}\dfrac{3b}{a}\right) + \dfrac{3}{4}(a^2+b^2)^{n/2} e^{ax} \cos\left(bx + n\tan^{-1}\dfrac{b}{a}\right)$

   (iv) $\dfrac{1}{2}\left[(10)^{n/2} e^x \cos(3x + \tan^{-1} 3) + (2)^{n/2} e^x \cos\left(x + \dfrac{n\pi}{4}\right)\right]$

   (v) $\dfrac{1}{2}\left[(101)^{n/2} e^x \sin(10x + n\tan^{-1} 10) - (5)^{n/2} e^x \sin(2x + n\tan^{-1} 2)\right]$

   (vi) $\dfrac{1}{8} e^x [3 - 4(5)^{n/2} \cos(2x + n\tan^{-1} 2) + (17)^{n/2} \cos(4x + n\tan^{-1} 4)]$

3. Find the nth derivatives of
   (i) $\dfrac{1}{(x^2 - 4x + 3)}$ **(May 2013)**, (ii) $\dfrac{x}{(x-1)(x-2)(x-3)}$ **(May 2007, 2014)**,

   (iii) $\dfrac{x^4}{(x-1)(x-2)}$ **(Jan. 2005, May 2009)**

   (iv) $\dfrac{x}{(1-4x^2)(3x-5)}$, (v) $\dfrac{x^2}{(x+2)(2x+3)}$ **(Dec. 2008)** (vi) $\dfrac{x^2 + 4x + 1}{x^3 + 2x^2 - x - 2}$

   (May 2004)

   Ans. (i) $\dfrac{(-1)^n n!}{2}\left\{\dfrac{1}{(x-3)^{n+1}} - \dfrac{1}{(x-1)^{n+1}}\right\}$

   (ii) $(-1)^n n!\left\{\dfrac{1}{2(x-1)^{n+1}} - \dfrac{2}{(x-2)^{n+1}} + \dfrac{3}{2(x-3)^{n+1}}\right\}$

   (iii) $(-1)^n n!\left\{\dfrac{16}{(x-2)^{n+1}} - \dfrac{1}{(x-1)^{n+1}}\right\}$, $n > 2$

   (iv) $(-1)^n n!\left\{\dfrac{1}{26}\dfrac{2^n}{(2x+1)^{n+1}} + \dfrac{1}{14}\dfrac{2^n}{(2x-1)^{n+1}} - \dfrac{15}{91}\dfrac{3^n}{(3x-5)^{n+1}}\right\}$

   (v) $(-1)^n n! \dfrac{1}{2}\left\{\dfrac{9 \cdot 2^n}{(2x+3)^{n+1}} - \dfrac{8}{(x+2)^{n+1}}\right\}$

   (vi) $(-1)^n n!\left\{\dfrac{1}{(x-1)^{n+1}} + \dfrac{1}{(x+1)^{n+1}} - \dfrac{1}{(x+2)^{n+1}}\right\}$

4. Find y_n if $y = \tanh^{-1} x$.

   [Hint : Use $\tanh^{-1} x = \dfrac{1}{2} \log\left(\dfrac{1+x}{1-x}\right)$**]** **Ans.** $\dfrac{(n-1)!}{2}\left[\dfrac{1}{(1-x)^n} + \dfrac{(-1)^{n-1}}{(1+x)^n}\right]$

5. Prove that the nth derivative of $y = \tan^{-1} x$ is $(-1)^{n-1}(n-1)! \sin n\left(\dfrac{\pi}{2} - y\right) \sin^n\left(\dfrac{\pi}{2} - y\right)$. **(May 05)**

   [Hint : Let $\tan \theta = \dfrac{1}{x} = \dfrac{1}{\tan y} = \cot y = \tan\left(\dfrac{\pi}{2} - y\right)$ $\therefore$ $\theta = \dfrac{\pi}{2} - y$**]**

6. Find the nth derivative of $\cosh 4x \cos 3x$

[Hint: $y = \left(\dfrac{e^{4x} + e^{-4x}}{2}\right) \cos 3x = \dfrac{1}{2} e^{4x} \cos 3x + \dfrac{1}{2} e^{-4x} \cos 3x$]

Ans. $y_n = \dfrac{5^n}{2} \left\{ e^{4x} \cos\left(3x + n \tan^{-1}\dfrac{3}{4}\right) + e^{-4x} \cos\left(3x - n \tan^{-1}\dfrac{3}{4}\right) \right\}$

7. If $y = e^{x \cos \alpha} \cos(x \sin \alpha)$, prove that $y_n = e^{x \cos \alpha} \cos(x \sin \alpha + n\alpha)$.

8. Find the nth derivatives of (i) $\log(x^2 + a^2)$, (ii) $\tan^{-1}\dfrac{2x}{1-x^2}$, (iii) $\tan^{-1}\dfrac{1+x}{1-x}$,

   (iv) $\dfrac{1}{x^4 - a^4}$, (v) $\sin^{-1}\dfrac{2x}{1+x^2}$ **(Dec. 2005)**, (vi) $\tan^{-1}\dfrac{x \sin \alpha}{1 - x \cos \alpha}$ (α is constant)

Ans. (i) $\dfrac{2(-1)^{n-1}(n-1)! \cos n\theta \sin^n \theta}{a^n}$, where $\tan \theta = \dfrac{a}{x}$ or $x = a \cot \theta$.

(ii) $2(-1)^{n-1}(n-1)! \sin^n \theta \sin n\theta$, where $\cot \theta = x$.   [Hint: Put $x = \tan \theta$]

(iii) $(-1)^{(n-1)}(n-1)! \sin^n \theta \sin n\theta$, where $\cot \theta = x$.   [Hint: Put $x = \tan \theta$]

(iv) $\dfrac{(-1)^n n!}{4a^3} \left\{ \dfrac{1}{(x-a)^{n+1}} - \dfrac{1}{(x+a)^{n+1}} - \dfrac{2\sin(n+1)\theta}{r^{n+1}} \right\}$ where $r = \sqrt{x^2 + a^2}$ and $\theta = \tan^{-1}\dfrac{a}{x}$

(v) $2(-1)^{n-1}(n-1)! \sin^n \theta \sin n\theta$, where $\cot \theta = x$.   [Hint: P at $x = \tan \theta$]

(vi) [Hint: $y_1 = \dfrac{\sin \alpha}{(x - \cos \alpha)^2 + \sin^2 \alpha}$, then differentiating $(n-1)$ times]

Ans. $y_n = (-1)^{n-1}(n-1)! \csc^n \alpha \sin^n \theta \sin n\theta$, where $\cot \theta = \dfrac{x - \cos \alpha}{\sin \alpha}$

9. Find n^{th} derivatives of (i) $\dfrac{ax+b}{cx+d}$, (ii) $\log(x^2 + 3x + 2)$, (iii) $\log\{(ax+b)(cx+d)\}$

Hint: (i) $\left\{\dfrac{ax+b}{cx+d} = \dfrac{a(cx+d) + (bc - ad)}{c(cx+d)}\right\}$

Ans. (i) $\dfrac{(-1)^n n! c^{n-1}(bc - ad)}{(cx + d)^{n+1}}$

(ii) $(-1)^{n-1}(n-1)! \left[\dfrac{1}{(x+1)^n} + \dfrac{1}{(x+2)^n}\right]$, (iii) $(-1)^{n-1}(n-1)! \left[\dfrac{a^n}{(ax+b)^n} + \dfrac{c^n}{(cx+d)^n}\right]$

10. If $ac > b^2$, then prove that

$$D^n \left(\dfrac{b + cx}{a + 2bx + cx^2}\right) = (-1)^n n! \left(\dfrac{c}{a + 2bx + cx^2}\right)^{\frac{n+1}{2}} \times \cos\left\{(n+1) \tan^{-1}\left(\dfrac{\sqrt{ac - b^2}}{b + cx}\right)\right\}$$

[Hint : $y = \dfrac{b/c + x}{x^2 + \dfrac{2b}{c}x + \dfrac{a}{c}} = \dfrac{x + b/c}{\left(x + \dfrac{b}{c}\right)^2 + \left(\dfrac{ac - b^2}{c^2}\right)}$

$= \dfrac{x + b/c}{\left(x + \dfrac{b}{c}\right)^2 + k^2}$, where $k^2 = \dfrac{ac - b^2}{c^2}$

$= \dfrac{x + b/c}{\left(x + \dfrac{b}{c} + ik\right)\left(x + \dfrac{b}{c} - ik\right)} = \dfrac{1}{2}\left[\dfrac{1}{x + \dfrac{b}{c} + ik} + \dfrac{1}{x + \dfrac{b}{c} - ik}\right]$

Next, to find y_n, put $x + \dfrac{b}{c} = r \cos \theta$, $k = r \sin \theta$]

11. Find the nth derivative of $\tan^{-1} x$. Hence prove that value when $x = 0$ of $D^n (\tan^{-1} x)$ is 0, $(n - 1)!$ or $-(n - 1)!$ according as n is of the form $2p$, $(4p + 1)$ or $4p + 3$ respectively.

12. If $y = x \log (x + 1)$, prove that **(May 2011)**

$$y_n = \dfrac{(-1)^{n-2} (n - 2)! (x + n)}{(x + 1)^n}$$

[Hint : $y_1 = \dfrac{x}{x + 1} + \log (x + 1) = 1 - \dfrac{1}{x + 1} + \log (x + 1)$]

13. If $y = x (x + 1) \log (x + 1)^3$, prove that

$$y_n = \dfrac{3 (-1)^{n-1} (n - 3)! (2x + n)}{(x + 1)^{n-1}}.$$

7.5 LEIBNITZ'S THEOREM
(FOR FINDING n^{th} DERIVATIVE OF PRODUCT OF TWO FUNCTIONS)

Statement : If $y = uv$, where u and v are functions of x, possessing derivatives of nth order, then

$$y_n = n_{C_0} u_n v + n_{C_1} u_{n-1} v_1 + n_{C_2} u_{n-2} v_2 + \ldots + n_{C_r} u_{n-r} v_r + \ldots + n_{C_n} u v_n$$

where the suffixes denote the order of the derivatives and $n_{C_0}, n_{C_1} \ldots n_{C_r}$ are the Binomial coefficients.

Proof : We shall prove this theorem by mathematical induction. Let us assume that this theorem is true for particular value of n, say m, so that we have

$$y_m = m_{C_0} u_m v + m_{C_1} u_{m-1} v_1 + m_{C_2} u_{m-2} v_2 + \ldots + m_{C_r} u_{m-r} v_r + \ldots + m_{C_m} u v_m \quad \ldots \text{(i)}$$

Differentiating both sides of (i) w.r.t. x, we get

$$y_{m+1} = m_{C_0} (u_{m+1} v + u_m v_1) + m_{C_1} (u_m v_1 + u_{m-1} v_2) + m_{C_2} (u_{m-1} v_2 + u_{m-2} v_3)$$

$$+ \ldots + m_{C_{r-1}} (u_{m-r+2} v_{r-1} + u_{m=r+1} v_r) + m_{C_r} (u_{m-r +1} v_r + u_{m-r} v_{r+1})$$

$$+ \ldots + m_{C_m} (u_1 v_m + u v_{m+1})$$

$$= (m_{C_0}) u_{m+1} v + (m_{C_0} + m_{C_1}) u_m v_1 + (m_{C_1} + m_{C_2}) u_{m-1} v_2 + \ldots$$

$$+ (m_{C_{r-1}} + m_{C_r}) u_{m-r+1} v_r + \ldots + (m_{C_m}) u v_{m+1} \quad \ldots \text{(ii)}$$

But we know that $m_{C_{r-1}} + m_{C_r} = m+1_{C_r}$ and $m_{C_0} = 1 = m+1_{C_0}$, $m_{C_m} = 1 = m+1_{C_{m+1}}$

Also $(m_{C_0} + m_{C_1}) = m+1_{C_1}$ $(m_{C_1} + m_{C_2}) = m+1_{C_2}$, ... and so on.

Hence (ii) becomes,

$$y_{m+1} = m+1_{C_0}\, u_{m+1} v + m+1_{C_1}\, u_m v_1 + m+1_{C_2}\, u_{m-1} v_2 + \ldots$$
$$+ \ldots + m+1_{C_r}\, u_{m+1-r} v_r + \ldots + m+1_{C_{m+1}}\, u v_{m+1} \qquad \ldots \text{(iii)}$$

From (i) and (iii) we see that if the theorem is true for $n = m$, then it is also true for $n = m+1$.

Also by actual differentiation, we have

$$y_1 = u_1 v + u v_1 = 1_{C_0}\, u_1 v + 1_{C_1}\, u v_1$$
$$y_2 = u_2 v + u_1 v_1 + u_1 v_1 + u v_2 = u_2 v + 2 u_1 v_1 + u v_2$$
$$= 2_{C_0}\, u_2 v + 2_{C_1}\, u_1 v_1 + 2_{C_2}\, u v_2$$

Thus the theorem is true for $n = 1, 2$. Hence it must be true for $n = 2 + 1 = 3$ and so for $n = 3 + 1 = 4$ and so for every positive integral value of n.

This completes the proof of the theorem.

Note : While solving problems, choice of u and v is important. That function should be chosen as v whose successive derivatives vanish earlier and that function should be taken as u whose n^{th} derivative is known or can be easily evaluated.

7.6 ILLUSTRATIONS ON LEIBNITZ'S THEOREM

TYPE I :

Ex. 1 : *Find the nth derivatives of (i) $x^2 e^{ax}$, (ii) $x^2 \tan^{-1} x$.*

Sol. : (i) Let $y = x^2 e^{ax}$

Choose $\quad u = e^{ax} \quad$ and $\quad v = x^2$

$\therefore \quad u_n = a^n e^{ax} \qquad v_1 = 2x$

$\quad u_{n-1} = a^{n-1} e^{ax} \qquad v_2 = 2$

$\quad u_{n-2} = a^{n-2} e^{ax} \qquad v_3 = 0$

We know by Leibnitz's theorem,

$$y_n = {}^nC_0\, u_n v + {}^nC_1\, u_{n-1} v_1 + {}^nC_2\, u_{n-2} v_2 + \ldots + {}^nC_n\, u v_n$$

Substituting above results, we get,

$$y_n = (a^n e^{ax})(x^2) + n(a^{n-1} e^{ax})(2x) + \frac{n(n-1)}{2!}(a^{n-2} e^{ax})(2)$$

$$= a^n e^{ax} \left[x^2 + \frac{2n}{a} x + \frac{n(n-1)}{a^2} \right]$$

(ii) Let $y = x^2 \tan^{-1} x$, choose $u = \tan^{-1} x$, $v = x^2$.

We know that $u_n = (-1)^{n-1} (n-1)!\, \sin^n \theta \sin n\theta$, where $\cot \theta = x$

∴ By Leibnitz's theorem

$$y_n = [(-1)^{n-1}(n-1)!\sin^n\theta\sin n\theta](x^2) + n[(-1)^{n-2}(n-2)!\sin^{n-1}\theta\sin(n-1)\theta](2x)$$

$$+ \frac{n(n-1)}{2}[(-1)^{n-3}(n-3)!\sin^{n-2}\theta\sin(n-2)\theta](2)$$

$$= (-1)^{n-1}(n-3)![(n-1)(n-2)(x^2)\sin^n\theta\sin n\theta - n(2x)(n-2)\sin^{n-1}\theta\sin(n-1)\theta$$

$$+ n(n-1)\sin^{n-2}\theta\sin(n-2)\theta]$$

Ex. 2 : If $y = \dfrac{\log x}{x}$, prove that

$$y_n = (-1)^n \frac{n!}{x^{n+1}}\left\{\log x - \left(1 + \frac{1}{2} + \frac{1}{3} + \ldots + \frac{1}{n}\right)\right\}.$$

Sol. : Let $\quad u = \dfrac{1}{x}, \qquad v = \log x$

∴ $\quad u_n = \dfrac{(-1)^n n!}{x^{n+1}}$ and $\quad v_n = \dfrac{(-1)^{n-1}(n-1)!}{x^n}$

∴ By Leibnitz's theorem,

$$y_n = u_n v + n u_{n-1} v_1 + \frac{n(n-1)}{2!} u_{n-2} v_2 + \ldots \, uv_n$$

$$= \frac{(-1)^n n!}{x^{n+1}}(\log x) + \frac{n(-1)^{n-1}(n-1)!}{x^n}\left(\frac{1}{x}\right) + \frac{n(n-1)}{2!}\frac{(-1)^{n-2}(n-2)!}{x^{n-1}}\left(-\frac{1}{x^2}\right)$$

$$+ \frac{n(n-1)(n-2)}{3!}\frac{(-1)^{n-3}(n-3)!}{x^{n-2}}\left(\frac{2}{x^3}\right) + \ldots + \frac{1}{x}\frac{(-1)^{n-1}(n-1)!}{x^n}$$

$$= \frac{(-1)^n n!}{x^{n+1}}\left[\log x - \left(1 + \frac{1}{2} + \frac{1}{3} + \ldots + \frac{1}{n}\right)\right]$$

Ex. 3 : Find n^{th} derivative of $x^2 e^x \cos x$. **(Dec. 2012)**

Sol. : Let $\quad y = x^2 e^x \cos x, \quad$ choose $u = e^x \cos x, \quad v = x^2$

then, $\quad u_n = 2^{n/2} e^x \cos\left(x + \dfrac{n\pi}{4}\right)$

∴ By Leibnitz's theorem,

$$y_n = \left[2^{n/2} e^x \cos\left(x + \frac{n\pi}{4}\right)\right](x^2) + n\left[2^{\frac{n-1}{2}} e^x \cos\left\{x + (n-1)\frac{\pi}{4}\right\}\right](2x)$$

$$+ \frac{n(n-1)}{2!}\left[2^{\frac{n-2}{2}} e^x \cos\left\{x + (n-2)\frac{\pi}{4}\right\}\right](2)$$

$$= 2^{\left(\frac{n-2}{2}\right)} e^x \left[2x^2 \cos\left(x + \frac{n\pi}{4}\right) + 2\cdot 2^{1/2} nx \cos\left(x + \overline{n-1}\frac{\pi}{4}\right) + n(n-1)\cos\left(x + \overline{n-2}\frac{\pi}{4}\right)\right]$$

Ex. 4 : *Using Leibnitz's theorem, find n^{th} derivative of $y = x^3 e^{4x} \cos 3x$.*

Sol. : Let $\quad y = x^3 e^{4x} \cos 3x$, choose $u = e^{4x} \cos 3x$, $v = x^3$

then $\quad u_n = 5^n e^{4x} \cos\left(3x + n \tan^{-1}\dfrac{3}{4}\right)$

∴ By Leibnitz's theorem,

$$y_n = 5^n e^{4x} \cos\left(3x + n \tan^{-1}\dfrac{3}{4}\right)(x^3) +$$

$$n\left[5^{n-1} e^{4x} \cos\left\{3x + (n-1) \tan^{-1}\dfrac{3}{4}\right\}\right](3x^2) +$$

$$\dfrac{n(n-1)}{2!}\left[5^{n-2} e^{4x} \cos\left\{3x + (n-2) \tan^{-1}\dfrac{3}{4}\right\}\right](6x) +$$

$$\dfrac{n(n-1)(n-2)}{3!}\left[5^{n-3} e^{4x} \cos\left\{3x + (n-3) \tan^{-1}\dfrac{3}{4}\right\}\right](6)$$

Ex. 5 : *If $f(x) = \tan x$, then prove that*

$$f^n(0) - n_{C_2} f^{n-2}(0) + n_{C_4} f^{n-4}(0) \ldots = \sin\left(\dfrac{n\pi}{2}\right).$$ **(May 2005, 2007)**

Sol. : We have $\quad f(x) = \tan x = \dfrac{\sin x}{\cos x}$

∴ $\quad f(x) \cos x = \sin x$

Differentiating both the sides n times with respect to x, we have

$$n_{C_0} f^n(x) \cos x + n_{C_1} f^{n-1}(x)(-\sin x) + n_{C_2} f^{n-2}(x)(-\cos x)$$

$$+ n_{C_3} f^{n-3}(\sin x) + n_{C_4} f^{n-4}(x)(\cos x) + \ldots = \sin\left(x + \dfrac{n\pi}{2}\right)$$

Putting $x = 0$, we get

$$f^n(0)\cos(0) + n_{C_1} f^{n-1}(0)\{-\sin(0)\} + n_{C_2} f^{n-2}(0)\{-\cos(0)\}$$

$$+ n_{C_3} f^{n-3}(0)\{\sin(0)\} + n_{C_4} f^{n-4}(0)\{\cos(0)\} + \ldots = \sin\left(\dfrac{n\pi}{2}\right)$$

∴ $\quad f^n(0) - n_{C_2} f^{n-2}(0) + n_{C_4} f^{n-4}(0) \ldots = \sin\left(\dfrac{n\pi}{2}\right)$

Ex. 6 : *If $I_n = \dfrac{d^n}{dx^n}(x^n \log x)$, prove that $I_n = nI_{n-1} + (n-1)!$* **(May 2014)**

Also show that $\quad I_n = (n!)\left[\log x + 1 + \dfrac{1}{2} + \dfrac{1}{3} + \ldots + \dfrac{1}{n}\right]$

Sol. : Given that $\quad I_n = \dfrac{d^n}{dx^n}[x^n \log x] = \dfrac{d^{n-1}}{dx^{n-1}}\left\{\dfrac{d}{dx}(x^n \log x)\right\}$

$$\therefore \quad I_n = \frac{d^{n-1}}{dx^{n-1}}\left[nx^{n-1}\log x + \frac{x^n}{x}\right]$$

$$= \frac{d^{n-1}}{dx^{n-1}}(nx^{n-1}\log x) + \frac{d^{n-1}}{dx^{n-1}}(x^{n-1})$$

$$= n\frac{d^{n-1}}{dx^{n-1}}[x^{n-1}\log x] + (n-1)!$$

$$= n\,I_{n-1} + (n-1)!$$

$$I_n = n\,I_{n-1} + (n-1)! \qquad \text{This proves the first part.} \qquad \ldots \text{(i)}$$

For the second part, divide both sides of (i) by n!, then

$$\frac{I_n}{n!} = \frac{(n-1)!}{n!} + \frac{n\,I_{n-1}}{n!}$$

or $$\frac{I_n}{n!} = \frac{1}{n} + \frac{I_{n-1}}{(n-1)!} \qquad \ldots \text{(ii)}$$

Putting $n = 2, 3, 4, \ldots n$ successively in (ii), we have

$$\frac{I_2}{2!} = \frac{1}{2} + I_1$$

$$\frac{I_3}{3!} = \frac{1}{3} + \frac{I_2}{2!}$$

$$\frac{I_4}{4!} = \frac{1}{4} + \frac{I_3}{3!}$$

$$\ldots \ldots \quad \ldots \ldots$$

$$\frac{I_n}{n!} = \frac{1}{n} + \frac{I_{n-1}}{(n-1)!}$$

Adding all these equations and after cancellation, we have

$$\frac{I_n}{n!} = I_1 + \frac{1}{2} + \frac{1}{3} + \frac{1}{4} + \ldots \frac{1}{n}$$

But, $$I_1 = \frac{d}{dx}(x\log x) = (\log x + 1), \text{ hence}$$

$$\frac{I_n}{n!} = (\log x + 1) + \frac{1}{2} + \frac{1}{3} + \frac{1}{4} + \ldots + \frac{1}{n}$$

$$\therefore \quad I_n = (n!)\left[\log x + 1 + \frac{1}{2} + \frac{2}{3} + \ldots + \frac{1}{n}\right]$$

Ex. 7 : If $x + y = 1$, prove that

$$\frac{d^n}{dx^n}(x^n y^n) = n!\left[y^n - (n_{C_1})^2 y^{n-1} x + (n_{C_2})^2 y^{n-2} x^2 - (n_{C_3})^2 y^{n-3} x^3 + \ldots + (-1)^n x^n\right]$$

Sol.: We have $x + y = 1$ then $y = (1 - x)$

$\therefore \quad \dfrac{d^n}{dx^n}(x^n x^y) = \dfrac{d^n}{dx^n}[x^n(1-x)^n]$

Let $u = x^n$ and $v = (1 - x)^n$

Note:

$u_1 = nx^{n-1}$ $\qquad\qquad v_1 = n(1-x)^{n-1}(-1)$

$u_2 = n(n-1)x^{n-2}$ $\qquad v_2 = n(n-1)(1-x)^{n-2}(-1)^2$

$u_3 = n(n-1)(n-2)x^{n-3}$ $\quad v_3 = n(n-1)(n-2)(1-x)^{n-3}(-1)^3$

... ...

$u_{n-2} = n(n-1)(n-2)\ldots(n-n+3)x^{n-n+2}$ $\quad v_{n-1} = n(n-1)(n-2)\ldots 3\cdot 2$

$\qquad = \dfrac{n!}{2}x^2$ $\qquad\qquad\qquad\qquad (1-x)^{n-n+1}(-1)^{n-1}$

$u_{n-1} = n(n-1)(n-2)\ldots 3\cdot 2\cdot x = n!\, x$ $\quad v_n = n(n-1)(n-2)\ldots 3\cdot 2\cdot 1\,(-1)^n$

$u_n = n(n-1)(n-2)\ldots 3\cdot 2\cdot 1 = n!$ $\qquad\qquad = n!\,(-1)^n$

$\therefore$ By Leibnitz's theorem,

$\dfrac{d^n}{dx^n}(x^n y^n) = \dfrac{d^n}{dx^n}[x^n(1-x)^n]$

$\qquad = n_{C_0}(n!)(1-x)^n + n_{C_1}(n!\,x)[n(1-x)^{n-1}(-1)]$

$\qquad + n_{C_2}\left(\dfrac{n!}{2}x^2\right)[n(n-1)(1-x)^{n-2}(-1)^2]$

$\qquad + n_{C_3}\left(\dfrac{n!}{6}x^3\right)[n(n-1)(n-2)(1-x)^{n-3}(-1)^3] + \ldots$

$\qquad + n_{C_n}(x^n)[n!\,(-1)^n]$

$\qquad = n!\left[n_{C_0}y^n - n_{C_1}(n)y^{n-1}\cdot x + n_{C_2}\left\{\dfrac{n(n-1)}{2!}\right\}y^{n-2}\cdot x^2\right.$

$\qquad\qquad \left. - n_{C_3}\left\{\dfrac{n(n-1)(n-2)}{3!}\right\}y^{n-3}\cdot x^3 + \ldots + (-1)^n x^n\right]$

$\qquad = n!\left[y^n - (n_{C_1})^2 y^{n-1}\cdot x + (n_{C_2})^2 y^{n-2}\cdot x^2 - (n_{C_3})^2 y^{n-3}\cdot x^3 + \ldots + (-1)^n x^n\right]$

Ex. 8: *By finding two different ways the nth derivative of x^{2n}, prove that*

$$1 + \dfrac{n^2}{1^2} + \dfrac{n^2(n-1)^2}{1^2\cdot 2^2} + \dfrac{n^2(n-1)^2(n-2)^2}{1^2\cdot 2^2\cdot 3^2} + \ldots = \dfrac{2n!}{(n!)^2}$$

Sol. : **First way** : We know that

$D^n(ax+b)^m = m(m-1)(m-2)\ldots(m-n+1)a^n(ax+b)^{m-n}$

$$\therefore \quad D^n(x^{2n}) = (2n)(2n-1)(2n-2)\ldots(2n-n+1)(x)^{2n-n}$$
$$= (2n)(2n-1)(2n-2)\ldots(n+1)x^n$$
$$= \frac{2n!}{n!} x^n \qquad \ldots (1)$$

Second way : By Leibnitz's theorem,
$$D^n(x^{2n}) = D^n(x^n x^n)$$
$$= D^n(x^n) \cdot x^n + n_{C_1} D^{n-1}(x^n) \cdot D(x^n) + n_{C_2} D^{n-2}(x^n) D^2(x^n)$$
$$\qquad\qquad + n_{C_3} D^{n-3}(x^n) D^3(x^n) + \ldots$$
$$= (n!)\, x^n + n_{C_1}(n!\, x)(n\, x^{n-1}) + n_{C_2}\left(\frac{n!\, x^2}{2!}\right)(n(n-1)x^{n-2})$$
$$+ n_{C_3}\left(\frac{n!\, x^3}{3!}\right)\{n(n-1)(n-2)x^{n-3}\}\ldots\ldots$$
$$= (n!)\, x^n\left[1 + \frac{n^2}{1^2} + \frac{n^2(n-1)^2}{1^2 \cdot 2^2} + \frac{n^2(n-1)^2(n-2)^2}{1^2 \cdot 2^2 \cdot 3^2} + \ldots\ldots\right] \ldots (2)$$

Equating (1) and (2), we get
$$1 + \frac{n^2}{1^2} + \frac{n^2(n-1)^2}{1^2 \cdot 2^2} + \frac{n^2(n-1)^2(n-2)^2}{1^2 \cdot 2^2 \cdot 3^2} + \ldots\ldots = \frac{(2n)!}{(n!)^2}$$

TYPE II :

Ex. 9 : If $y = \sin^{-1} x$, prove that
$$(1-x^2)\, y_{n+2} - (2n+1)\, xy_{n+1} - n^2 y_n = 0.$$

Sol. : We have $\qquad y = \sin^{-1} x \qquad \ldots (1)$

Differentiating w.r.t. x, we get
$$y_1 = \frac{1}{\sqrt{1-x^2}}$$

Squaring both sides, we get
$$y_1^2(1-x^2) = 1 \qquad \ldots (2)$$

Differentiating (2) again w.r.t. x, we get
$$2y_1 y_2 (1-x^2) + y_1^2(-2x) = 0$$
i.e. $\qquad y_2(1-x^2) - xy_1 = 0 \qquad \ldots (3)$

Now differentiating (3) w.r.t. x, n times by Leibnitz's theorem
$$D^n[(1-x^2)\, y_2] - D^n[xy_1] = 0$$

i.e. $\left[y_{n+2}(1-x^2) + n\, y_{n+1}(-2x) + \dfrac{n(n-1)}{2} y_n(-2)\right] - [y_{n+1} x + n\, y_n] = 0$

$\therefore \quad (1-x^2)\, y_{n+2} - (2n+1)\, xy_{n+1} - n^2 y_n = 0$

Ex. 10 : If $y = \left(x + \sqrt{x^2-1}\right)^m$, show that (May 2006, Dec. 2010)
$(x^2-1) y_{n+2} + (2n+1) xy_{n+1} + (n^2-m^2) y_n = 0$.

Sol. : We have
$$y = \left(x + \sqrt{x^2-1}\right)^m \qquad \ldots (1)$$

then,
$$y_1 = m\left(x + \sqrt{x^2-1}\right)^{m-1} \left[1 + \frac{x}{\sqrt{x^2-1}}\right]$$

$$= m\left(x + \sqrt{x^2-1}\right)^{m-1} \frac{\left(x + \sqrt{x^2-1}\right)}{\sqrt{x^2-1}}$$

$\therefore \qquad y_1\left(\sqrt{x^2-1}\right) = m\left(x + \sqrt{x^2-1}\right)^m = my$

Squaring both sides,
$$y_1^2 (x^2-1) = m^2 (y^2) \qquad \ldots (2)$$

Differentiating (2) again w.r.t. x, we get

$2y_1 y_2 (x^2-1) + 2xy_1^2 - 2m^2 yy_1 = 0$

$\therefore \qquad y_2(x^2-1) + xy_1 - m^2 y = 0 \qquad \ldots (3)$

Differentiating (3) n times by Leibnitz's theorem

$D^n [y_2(x^2-1)] + D^n (xy_1) - m^2 D^n (y) = 0$

$[y_{n+2}(x^2-1) + 2n\, xy_{n+1} + n(n-1) y_n] + [xy_{n+1} + ny_n] - m^2 y_n = 0$

$\therefore \quad (x^2-1) y_{n+2} + (2n+1) xy_{n+1} + (n^2-m^2) y_n = 0$

Ex. 11 : If $y = \sin[\log(x^2 + 2x + 1)]$ then prove that,
$$(x+1)^2 y_{n+2} + (2n+1)(x+1) y_{n+1} + (n^2+4) y_n = 0 \qquad \text{(Dec. 2014)}$$

Sol. : We have $\qquad y = \sin[\log(x^2+2x+1)]$

i.e. $\qquad y = \sin[2 \log(x+1)] \qquad \ldots (1)$

$\therefore \qquad y_1 = \cos[2\log(x+1)] \dfrac{2}{(x+1)}$

i.e. $\qquad (x+1)^2 y_1^2 = 4\cos^2[2\log(x+1)]$

i.e. $\qquad (x+1)^2 y_1^2 = 4[1 - \sin^2\{2\log(x+1)\}]$

i.e. $\qquad (x+1)^2 y_1^2 = 4(1-y^2) \qquad \ldots (2)$

Differentiating (2) w.r.t. x again, we get

$(x+1)^2 2y_1 y_2 + 2(x+1) y_1^2 = -8yy_1$

i.e. $(x+1)^2 y_2 + (x+1) y_1 + 4y = 0 \qquad \ldots (3)$

Differentiating (3) n times successively and using Leibnitz's theorem for product, we have,

$$\left[(x+1)^2 y_{n+2} + n \cdot 2 (x+1) y_{n+1} + \frac{n(n-1)}{2!} (2) y_n\right] + [(x+1) y_{n+1} + n y_n] = 0$$

$$(x+1)^2 y_{n+2} + (2n+1)(x+1) y_{n+1} + (n^2 - n + n + 4) y_n = 0$$

∴ $\quad (x+1)^2 y_{n+2} + (2n+1)(x+1) y_{n+1} + (n^2 + 4) y_n = 0$

Ex. 12 : If $y = a \cos(\log x) + b \sin(\log x)$ then show that

$x^2 y_{n+2} + (2n+1) x y_{n+1} + (n^2 + 1) y_n = 0$ **(Dec. 2007, 2008, May 10, 11, 13)**

Sol. : We have $\quad y = a \cos(\log x) + b \sin(\log x) \quad$ ... (1)

Differentiating with respect to x,

$$y_1 = -a \sin(\log x) \frac{1}{x} + b \cos(\log x) \frac{1}{x}$$

∴ $\quad x y_1 = -a \sin(\log x) + b \cos(\log x) \quad$ ... (2)

Differentiating (2) again with respect to x

$$x y_2 + y_1 = -a \cos(\log x) \frac{1}{x} - b \sin(\log x) \frac{1}{x}$$

i.e. $\quad x^2 y_2 + x y_1 = -[a \cos(\log x) + b \sin(\log x)]$

i.e. $\quad x^2 y_2 + x y_1 = -y$

∴ $\quad y_2 x^2 + y_1 x + y = 0 \quad$ ... (3)

Differentiating (3) by Leibnitz's theorem n times

$$\left[y_{n+2} \cdot x^2 + {}^nC_1 y_{n+1} 2x + {}^nC_2 y_n \cdot 2\right] + [y_{n+1} x + {}^nC_1 y_n \cdot 1] + y_n = 0$$

i.e. $\quad x^2 y_{n+2} + 2nx y_{n+1} + x y_{n+1} + n(n-1) y_n + n y_n + y_n = 0$

i.e. $\quad x^2 y_{n+2} + (2n+1) x y_{n+1} + (n^2 - n + n + 1) y_n = 0$

i.e. $\quad x^2 y_{n+2} + (2n+1) x y_{n+1} + (n^2 + 1) y_n = 0$

Ex. 13 : If $x = \tan(\log y)$, prove that **(May 2007, 2009, 2011, 2015)**

$(1 + x^2) y_{n+1} + (2nx - 1) y_n + n(n-1) y_{n-1} = 0$

Sol. : We have $\quad x = \tan(\log y)$

∴ $\quad \tan^{-1} x = \log y$

∴ $\quad y = e^{\tan^{-1} x} \quad$ ... (1)

Differentiating (1) w.r.t. x, we get

$$y_1 = e^{\tan^{-1} x} \left(\frac{1}{1+x^2}\right)$$

i.e. $\quad (1 + x^2) y_1 = y \quad$ ... (2)

Differentiating (2) n times by Leibnitz's theorem, we get

$$(1 + x^2) y_{n+1} + n y_n (2x) + \frac{n(n-1)}{2} y_{n-1} (2) = y_n$$

$$(1 + x^2) y_{n+1} + (2nx - 1) y_n + n(n-1) y_{n-1} = 0$$

Ex. 14 : If $\cos^{-1}\left(\dfrac{y}{b}\right) = \log\left(\dfrac{x}{n}\right)^n$, prove that (Dec. 2006)

$$x^2 y_{n+2} + (2n + 1) xy_{n+1} + 2n^2 y_n = 0.$$

Sol. : We have $\cos^{-1}\left(\dfrac{y}{b}\right) = \log\left(\dfrac{x}{n}\right)^n$,

∴ $\qquad y = b \cos[n(\log x - \log n)]$ ... (1)

Differentiating (1) with respect to x, we have

$$y_1 = -b \sin[n(\log x - \log n)] \cdot \dfrac{n}{x}$$

i.e. $\qquad xy_1 = -bn \sin[n(\log x - \log n)]$ ... (2)

Again differentiating (2) with respect to x, we get,

$$xy_2 + y_1 = -bn \cos[n(\log x - \log n)] \dfrac{n}{x}$$

i.e. $\qquad x^2 y_2 + xy_1 = -n^2 y$ ... (3)

Now differentiating (3) n times by Leibnitz's theorem, we have,

$$\left[x^2 y_{n+2} + n(2x) y_{n+1} + \dfrac{n(n-1)}{2}(2) y_n\right] + [xy_{n+1} + n(1) y_n] + n^2 y_n = 0$$

∴ $\qquad x^2 y_{n+2} + (2n + 1) xy_{n+1} + 2n^2 y_n = 0$

Ex. 15 : If $y = \dfrac{\sin^{-1} x}{\sqrt{1 - x^2}}$, show that

$$y_2 (1 - x^2) - 3xy_1 - y = 0.$$

Hence prove that $(1 - x^2) y_{n+2} - (2n + 3) xy_{n+1} - (n + 1)^2 y_n = 0$.

Sol. : We have, $\qquad y = \dfrac{\sin^{-1} x}{\sqrt{1 - x^2}}$

∴ $\qquad (1 - x^2) y^2 = (\sin^{-1} x)^2$ ... (1)

Differentiating (1) with respect to x, we get,

$$(1 - x^2) 2yy_1 - 2xy^2 = 2 \sin^{-1} x \left(\dfrac{1}{\sqrt{1 - x^2}}\right)$$

i.e $\qquad (1 - x^2) 2yy_1 - 2xy^2 = 2y$

∴ $\qquad (1 - x^2) y_1 - xy - 1 = 0$ ... (2)

Differentiating (2) with respect to x, we get

$$(1 - x^2) y_2 - 2xy_1 - xy_1 - y = 0$$

i.e. $\qquad (1 - x^2) y_2 - 3xy_1 - y = 0$ ... (3)

Differentiating (3) n times by Leibnitz's theorem, we have,

$$\left[(1-x^2)\, y_{n+2} - n\, 2x\, y_{n+1} - \frac{2n(n-1)}{2}\, y_n\right] - [3xy_{n+1} + 3ny_n] - y_n = 0$$

i.e. $(1-x^2)\, y_{n+2} - (2n+3)\, xy_{n+1} - (n^2 - n + 3n + 1)\, y_n = 0$

i.e. $(1-x^2)\, y_{n+2} - (2n+3)\, xy_{n+1} - (n+1)^2\, y_n = 0$

Ex. 16 : If $y = \left[\log\left(x + \sqrt{1+x^2}\right)\right]^2$, show that

$$(y_{n+2})_0 = -n^2 (y_n)_0. \qquad \text{(Dec. 2006, 2008, May 2014)}$$

Sol. : Given, $\qquad y = \left[\log\left(x + \sqrt{1+x^2}\right)\right]^2 \qquad \ldots (1)$

Differentiating (1) with respect to x, we get

$$y_1 = 2\log\left(x+\sqrt{1+x^2}\right) \frac{1}{\left(x+\sqrt{1+x^2}\right)}\left[1 + \frac{x}{\sqrt{1+x^2}}\right]$$

i.e. $\qquad \left(\sqrt{1+x^2}\right) y_1 = 2\log\left(x+\sqrt{1+x^2}\right)$

Squaring both sides

$$(1+x^2)\, y_1^2 = 4\left[\log\left(x+\sqrt{1+x^2}\right)\right]^2$$

$\therefore \qquad (1+x^2)\, y_1^2 = 4y \qquad \ldots (2)$

Differentiating (2) again w.r.t. x, we get

$$2y_1 y_2 (1+x^2) + (2x)\, y_1^2 = 4y_1$$

$\therefore \qquad y_1(1+x^2) + y_1(x) - 2 = 0 \qquad \ldots (3)$

Differentiating (3) n times using Leibnitz's theorem, we get

$$\left[y_{n+2}(1+x^2) + n\, y_{n+1}(2x) + \frac{n(n-1)}{2}\, y_n(2)\right] + [y_{n+1}(x) + n\, y_n(1)] = 0$$

i.e. $(1+x^2)\, y_{n+2} + (2n+1)\, x\, y_{n+1} + n^2\, y_n = 0$

Putting $x = 0$, we get

$$(y_{n+2})_0 + n^2 (y_n)_0 = 0$$

$\therefore \qquad (y_{n+2})_0 = -n^2 (y_n)_0$

Ex. 17 : If $y = e^{a\sin^{-1} x}$, prove that

$$(1-x^2)\, y_{n+2} - (2n+1)\, xy_{n+1} - (n^2 + a^2)\, y_n = 0 \qquad \text{(May 2004)}$$

Also find the value of y_n at $x = 0$.

Sol. : We have $\qquad y = e^{a\sin^{-1} x} \qquad \ldots (1)$

$\therefore \qquad y_1 = \dfrac{a\, e^{a\sin^{-1} x}}{\sqrt{1-x^2}} = \dfrac{ay}{\sqrt{1-x^2}},$

$\therefore \qquad y_1^2 (1-x^2) = a^2 y^2 \qquad \ldots (2)$

Differentiating once again

$$2y_1 y_2 (1-x^2) - 2x\, y_1^2 - 2a^2 yy_1 = 0$$

$$\therefore \quad y_2 (1-x^2) - xy_1 - a^2 y = 0 \quad \ldots (3)$$

Differentiating n times by Leibnitz's theorem, we have

$$\left[(1-x^2) y_{n+2} - 2n\, xy_{n+2} + \frac{n(n-1)}{2} \cdot y_n (-2)\right] - [y_{n+1} x + ny_n] - a^2 y_n = 0$$

$$\therefore \quad (1-x^2) y_{n+2} - (2n+1) xy_{n+1} - (n^2 + a^2) y_n = 0 \quad \ldots (4)$$

To find $(y_n)_0$ i.e. the value of (y_n) at $x = 0$, we put $x = 0$ in (1), (2), (3) and (4), then

$$(y)_0 = e^0 = 1,\ (y_1)_0 = a,\ (y_2)_0 = a^2 \text{ and } (y_{n+2})_0 + (n^2 + a^2)(y_n)_0 \quad \ldots (5)$$

If n is odd : put $n = 1, 3, 5, 7 \ldots$ in (5)

$$(y_3)_0 = (1^2 + a^2)(y_1)_0$$
$$(y_5)_0 = (3^2 + a^2)(y_3)_0$$
$$(y_7)_0 = (5^2 + a^2)(y_5)_0$$
$$\vdots \qquad \vdots$$
$$(y_n)_0 = [(n-2)^2 + a^2](y_{n-2})_0$$

Multiplying all these equations, we get

$$(y_n)_0 = [(n-2)^2 + a^2][(n-4)^2 + a^2] \ldots$$
$$\ldots (5^2 + a^2)(3^2 + a^2)(1^2 + a^2) a$$

If n is even : put $n = 2, 4, 6, \ldots$ in (5)

$$(y_4)_0 = (2^2 + a^2)(y_2)_0$$
$$(y_6)_0 = (4^2 + a^2)(y_4)_0$$
$$(y_8)_0 = (6^2 + a^2)(y_6)_0$$
$$\vdots \qquad \vdots$$
$$(y_n)_0 = [(n-2)^2 + a^2](y_{n-2})_0$$

Multiplying all these equations, we get

$$(y_n)_0 = [(n-2)^2 + a^2][(n-4)^2 + a^2] \ldots$$
$$\ldots (6^2 + a^2)(4^2 + a^2)(2^2 + a^2) a^2$$

Ex. 18 : *If $y = \sin(m \sin^{-1} x)$, find $(y_n)_0$.* **(Jan. 2005, Dec. 2005)**

Sol. : We have

$$y = \sin(m \sin^{-1} x) \quad \ldots (1)$$

$$\therefore \quad y_1 = \cos(m \sin^{-1} x) \frac{m}{\sqrt{1-x^2}}$$

$$\therefore \quad y_1^2 (1-x^2) = (1-y^2) m^2 \quad \ldots (2)$$

Differentiating once again, we have

$$2y_1 y_2 (1-x^2) - 2xy_1^2 + 2m^2 yy_1 = 0$$

$$\therefore \quad y_2(1-x^2) - xy_1 + m^2 y = 0 \quad \ldots (3)$$

Differentiating n times by Leibnitz's theorem, we get

$$y_{n+2}(1-x^2) - (2n+1) xy_{n+1} - (n^2 - m^2) y_n = 0 \quad \ldots (4)$$

Put $x = 0$ in (1), (2), (3) and (4), then

$$(y)_0 = 0, \ (y_1)_0 = m, \ (y_2)_0 = 0$$

and

$$(y_{n+2})_0 = (n^2 - m^2)(y_n)_0 \quad \ldots (5)$$

When n is odd : put $n = 1, 3, 5, 7 \ldots$ in (5)

$$(y_3)_0 = (1^2 - m^2)(y_1)_0$$

$$(y_5)_0 = (3^2 - m^2)(y_3)_0$$

$$(y_7)_0 = (5^2 - m^2)(y_5)_0$$

$$\vdots \qquad \vdots$$

$$(y_n)_0 = [(n-2)^2 - m^2](y_{n-2})_0$$

Multiplying all these equations, we get

$$(y_n)_0 = [(n-2)^2 - m^2][(n-4)^2 - m^2] \ldots$$

$$\ldots (5^2 - m^2)(3^2 - m^2)(1^2 + m^2) m$$

When n is even : put $n = 2, 4, 6, \ldots$ in (5)

$$(y_4)_0 = (2^2 - m^2)(y_2)_0 = 0$$

$$(y_6)_0 = (4^2 - m^2)(y_4)_0 = 0$$

$$(y_8)_0 = (6^2 - m^2)(y_6)_0 = 0$$

Hence $\quad (y_n)_0 = 0$

Ex. 19 : If $y = (\sin^{-1} x)^2$, prove that $(y_n)_0 = 0$ for n odd
$= 2 \cdot 2^2 \cdot 4^2 \cdot 6^2 \ldots (n-2)^2$, $n \neq 2$ for n even. **(May 2010)**

Sol. : We have $\quad y = (\sin^{-1} x)^2 \quad \ldots (1)$

Differentiating (1) with respect to x, we have

$$y_1 = \frac{2 \sin^{-1} x}{\sqrt{1-x^2}}$$

$\therefore \quad (\sqrt{1-x^2}) y_1 = 2 \sin^{-1} x$

Squaring on both sides,

$$(1-x^2) y_1^2 = 4(\sin^{-1} x)^2$$

$$(1-x^2) y_1^2 = 4y \quad \ldots (2)$$

Differentiating (2) again with respect to x, we get

$$(1 - x^2)\, 2y_1 y_2 - 2xy_1^2 = 4y_1$$

$\therefore \quad (1 - x^2)\, y_2 - 4xy_1 - 2 = 0 \qquad \ldots (3)$

Differentiating (2) n times by Leibnitz's theorem, we have

$$\left[(1 - x^2)\, y_{n+2} + ny_{n+1}(-2x) + \frac{n(n-1)}{2}(-2y)\, y_n\right] - [xy_{n+1} + ny_n(1)] = 0$$

i.e. $(1 - x^2)\, y_{n+2} + (-2nx)\, y_{n+1} - xy_{n+1} - (n^2 - n)\, y_n - ny_n = 0$

$\therefore \quad (1 - x^2)\, y_{n+2} - (2n + 1)\, xy_{n+1} - n^2 y_n = 0 \qquad \ldots (4)$

Put $x = 0$ in (1), (2), (3) and (4)

$$(y)_0 = 0,\ (y_1)_0 = 0,\ (y_2)_0 = 2$$

and $\qquad (y_{n+2})_0 = n^2 (y_n)_0 \qquad \ldots (5)$

If n is odd : put $n = 1, 3, 5, \ldots$ in (5)

$$(y_3)_0 = 1^2 (y_1)_0 = 0$$
$$(y_5)_0 = 3^2 (y_3)_0 = 0$$
$$(y_7)_0 = 5^2 (y_5)_0 = 0$$
$$\vdots \qquad \vdots$$

Hence, in general, $(y_n)_0 = 0$, when n is odd.

If n is even : put $n = 2, 4, 6, \ldots$ in (5)

$$(y_4)_0 = 2^2 (y_2)_0 = 2^2 \cdot 2$$
$$(y_6)_0 = 4^2 (y_4)_0 = 4^2 \cdot 2^2 \cdot 2$$

Hence, in general, $(y_n)_0 = 2 \cdot 2^2 \cdot 4^2 \cdot 6^2 \ldots (n-2)^2$, $n \neq 2$ and n for n even.

EXERCISE 7.2

1. Find the nth derivatives of
   (i) $x^3 \cos x$ **(May 2010)**, (ii) $e^x (2x + 3)^3$ **(Jan. 2005)**,
   (iii) $e^{ax} [a^2 x^2 - 2n\, ax + n(n + 1)]$, (iv) $x^2 e^{3x} \sin 4x$ **(Jan. 2004, Dec. 2005, May 09, 11)**
   Ans. (i) $x^3 \cos(x + n\pi/2) + 3nx^2 \cos\{x + (n-2)\pi/2\}$
   $\qquad + 3n(n-1)\, x \cos\{x + (n-2)\pi/2\} + n(n-1)(n-2) \cos\{x + (n-3)\pi/2\}$
   (ii) $e^x [(2x + 3)^3 + 6n(2x + 3)^2 + 12n(n-1)(2x+3) - 8n(n-1)(n-2)]$
   (iii) $a^{n+2} e^{ax} x^2$
   (iv) $x^2 \left\{5^n e^{3x} \sin\left(4x + n \tan^{-1}\frac{4}{5}\right)\right\} + $
   $\qquad n(2x) \left\{5^{n-1} e^{3x} \sin\left(4x + (n-1)\tan^{-1}\frac{4}{5}\right)\right\} + n(n-1) \left\{5^{n-2} e^{3x} \sin 4x + (n-2) \tan^{-1}\frac{4}{5}\right\}$

2. Find the 4th differential coefficient of $x^2 \sin 3x$.

   Ans. $3^3 (3x^2 - 4) \sin 3x - 6^3 x \cos 3x$

3. Find the 5th differential coefficient of $\dfrac{\log x}{x}$.

   Ans. $\dfrac{5!}{x^6} \left(1 + \dfrac{1}{2} + \dfrac{1}{3} + \dfrac{1}{4} + \dfrac{1}{5} - \log x\right)$.

4. Prove that $\dfrac{d^n}{dx^n} \left(\dfrac{\sin x}{x}\right) = \dfrac{1}{x^{n+1}} \left[P \sin\left(x + \dfrac{n\pi}{2}\right) + Q \cos\left(x + \dfrac{n\pi}{2}\right)\right]$

   where $P = x^n - n(n-1) x^{n-2} + \ldots$ and $Q = nx^{n-1} - n(n-1)(n-2) x^{n-3} + \ldots$

5. If $y = x^2 e^x$, show that $y_n = \dfrac{1}{2} n(n-1) \dfrac{d^2 y}{dx^2} - n(n-2) \dfrac{dy}{dx} + \dfrac{1}{2}(n-1)(n-2) y$

   [**Hint:** L.H.S. $= e^x [x^2 + 2nx + n(n-1)] =$ R.H.S.]

6. Prove that the nth derivative of $x^n (1-x)^n$ is equal to

   $n! (1-x)^n \left[1 - \dfrac{n^2}{1^2} \dfrac{x}{(1-x)} + \dfrac{n^2(n-1)^2}{1^2 \cdot 2^2} \dfrac{x^2}{(1-x)^2} + \ldots\right]$

7. If $y = (\sin^{-1} x)^2$, prove that $(1 - x^2) y_{n+2} - (2n+1) x y_{n+1} - n^2 y_n = 0$

8. If $y = e^{\tan^{-1} x}$, prove that (i) $(1 + x^2) y_2 + (2x - 1) y_1 = 0$

   (ii) $(1 + x^2) y_{n+2} + [2(n+1) x - 1] y_{n+1} + n(n+1) y_n = 0$

9. If $y = A \left[x + \sqrt{x^2 - 1}\right]^n + B \left[x - \sqrt{x^2 - 1}\right]^n$, prove that

   (i) $(x^2 - 1) y_2 + xy_1 - n^2 y = 0$, (ii) $(x^2 - 1) y_{n+2} + (2n+1) xy_{n+1} = 0$

   [**Hint:** $y_1 \sqrt{x^2 - 1} = nA \left(x + \sqrt{x^2 - 1}\right)^n + nB \left(x - \sqrt{x^2 - 1}\right)^n$]

10. If $y = \sin^{-1}(3x - 4x^3)$, prove that (Dec. 2010)

    (i) $(1 - x^2) y_2 - xy_1 = 0$, (ii) $(1 - x^2) y_{n+2} - (2n+1) xy_{n+1} - n^2 y_n = 0$

11. If $x = \cos[\log(y^{1/\alpha})]$, then show that

    $(1 - x^2) y_{n+2} - (2n+1) x y_{n+1} - (n^2 + \alpha^2) y_n = 0$

    [**Hint:** Here $y = e^{\alpha \cos^{-1} x}$]

12. If $y = \dfrac{\sinh^{-1} x}{\sqrt{1 + x^2}}$, prove that

    $(1 + x^2) y_{n+2} + (2n+3) x y_{n+1} + (n+1)^2 y_n = 0$.

13. If $y = (x^2-1)^n$, prove that $(x^2-1) y_{n+2} + 2xy_{n+1} - n(n+1) y_n = 0$.

    Hence if $P_n = \dfrac{d^n}{dx^n} (x^2-1)^n$, show that $\dfrac{d}{dx}\left\{(1-x^2) \dfrac{dP_n}{dx}\right\} + n(n+1) P_n = 0$

    [Hint: Given $P_n = y_n$ $\therefore \dfrac{d}{dx}\left\{(1-x^2) \dfrac{dP_n}{dx}\right\} = \dfrac{d}{dx}\{(1-x^2) y_{n+1}\} = -n(n+1) P_n$]

14. If $x = \sin\theta$, $y = \sin 2\theta$, prove that $(1-x^2) y_{n+2} - (2n+1) x y_{n+1} - (n^2-4) y_n = 0$

    [Hint: $y = 2x\sqrt{1-x^2}$, differentiating w.r.t. x, we get,

    $(1-x^2) y_1^2 = 4(1-y^2)$, now differentiate n times.]   (Dec. 2007; May 2006, 2009)

15. If $x = \sin t$, $y = \sin at$, then show that

    $(1-x^2) y_{n+2} - (2n+1) x y_{n+1} - (n^2-a^2) y_n = 0$.

16. If $y = A \cosh(\log x^m) + B \sinh(\log x^m)$, show that

    $x^2 y'' + xy' - m^2 y = 0$ and differentiate n times.

17. If $y = \cos(m \log x)$, show that   (Jan. 2004)

    $x^2 y_{n+2} + (2n+1) x y_{n+1} + (m^2+n^2) y_n = 0$

18. If $y^{1/m} + y^{-1/m} = 2x$, prove that

    $(x^2-1) y_{n+2} + (2n+1) xy_{n+1} + (n^2-m^2) y_n = 0$

19. If $y = \sec^{-1} x$ then prove that

    $x(x^2-1) y_{n+2} + [(2+3n) x^2 - (n+1)] y_{n+1} + n(3n+1) xy_n + n^2(n-1) y_{n-1} = 0$

20. If $u_n = D^n(x^{n-1} \log x)$, then prove that

    $u_n = (n-1) u_{n-1}$ and hence deduce that $u_n = \dfrac{(n-1)!}{x}$.

21. Show that if $x(1-x) y_2 - (4-12x) y_1 - 36y = 0$, then

    $x(1-x) y_{n+2} - [4-n-(12-2n)x] y_{n+1} - (4-n)(9-n) y_n = 0$

22. If u_n denotes the nth derivative of $\dfrac{Lx+m}{x^2-2Bx+C}$, prove that

    $\left(\dfrac{x^2-2Bx+C}{(n+1)(n+2)}\right) u_{n+2} + \left(\dfrac{2(x-B)}{(n+1)}\right) u_{n+1} + u_n = 0$

    [Hint: $(x^2-2Bx+C) u = Lx+M$

    $\therefore$ $(x^2-2Bx+C) u_2 + 4(x-B) u_1 + 2u = 0$ and apply Leibnitz's theorem, then divide by $(n+1)(n+2)$]

23. If $y = e^{m\cos^{-1} x}$, prove that $(1 - x^2) y_{n+2} - (2n + 1) xy_{n+1} - (n^2 + m^2) y_n = 0$.
    Hence evaluate $y_n(0)$. **(Dec. 2009)**

    [**Hint** : $(y)_0 = e^{m(\pi/2)}$; $(y_1)_0 = -m e^{m(\pi/2)}$; $(y_2)_0 = m^2 e^{m(\pi/2)}$ and
    $$(y_{n+2})_0 = (n^2 + m^2) (y_n)_0]$$

    Ans. $(y_n)_0 = -\{(n - 2)^2 + m^2\} \{(n - 4)^2 + m^2\} \ldots (3^2 + m^2) (1^2 + m^2)\, m\, e^{m(\pi/2)}$ when n is odd

    $(y_n)_0 = -\{(n - 2)^2 + m^2\} \{(n - 4)^2 + m^2\} \ldots (2^2 + m^2)\, m^2 e^{m(\pi/2)}$ when n is even

24. If $y = \cosh(\sin^{-1} x)$, prove that
    (i) $(1 - x^2) y_2 - xy_1 - y = 0$
    (ii) $(1 - x^2) y_{n+2} - (2n + 1) xy_{n+1} - (n^2 + 1) y_n = 0$
    (iii) $(y_n)_0 = ((n - 2)^2 + 1) ((n - 4)^2 + 1) \ldots (4^2 + 1) (2^2 + 1)\, 1$, if n is even.
        $= 0$, if n is odd.

MULTIPLE CHOICE QUESTIONS

Type I : n^{th} Derivative using Trigonometric Transformation and Standard Results :

1. The nth derivative of $y = e^{ax}$ is (1)
    (A) $a^{-n} e^{ax}$ (B) e^{ax}
    (C) $a^n e^{ax}$ (D) $a^n e^{-ax}$

2. The nth derivative of $y = a^x$ is (1)
    (A) $a^n (\log a)^x$ (B) $\dfrac{a^x}{(\log a)^n}$
    (C) $\dfrac{(\log a)^n}{a^x}$ (D) $a^x (\log a)^n$

3. The nth derivative of $y = \sin(ax + b)$ is (1)
    (A) $a^n \sin(ax + b)$ (B) $a^n \sin\left(ax + b + \dfrac{n\pi}{2}\right)$
    (C) $b^n \cos(bx + a)$ (D) $b^n \sin\left(ax + b + \dfrac{n\pi}{2}\right)$

4. The nth derivative of $y = \cos(ax + b)$ is (1)
    (A) $a^n \cos\left(ax + b + \dfrac{n\pi}{2}\right)$ (B) $b^n \cos(bx + a)$
    (C) $a^n \cos(ax + b)$ (D) $b^n \cos\left(ax + b + \dfrac{n\pi}{2}\right)$

5. The nth derivative of $y = (ax + b)^{-m}$, where m is any positive integer is (1)

   (A) $\dfrac{a^n (m)(m+1)(m+2) \ldots (m+n-1)}{(ax+b)^{m-n}}$

   (B) $\dfrac{a^n (m)(m+1)(m+2) \ldots (m+n-1)}{(ax+b)^{-m-n}}$

   (C) $\dfrac{(-1)^n a^n (m)(m+1)(m+2) \ldots (m+n-1)}{(ax+b)^{m+n}}$

   (D) $\dfrac{a^n (m)(m+1)(m+2) \ldots (m+n-1)}{(ax+b)^{-m+n}}$

6. The nth derivative of $y = (ax + b)^m$, where m is any positive integer $m > n$ is (1)

   (A) $\dfrac{(-1)^n a^n n! (ax+b)^{m-n}}{(m-n)!}$

   (B) $\dfrac{b^n m! (ax+b)^{m-n}}{(m-n)!}$

   (C) $\dfrac{(-1)^n b^m n! (ax+b)^{m+n}}{(m+n)!}$

   (D) $\dfrac{a^n m! (ax+b)^{m-n}}{(m-n)!}$

7. The nth derivative of $y = (ax + b)^m$, where m is any positive integer and $m < n$ is (1)

   (A) $a^n m!$
   (B) $m!$
   (C) $a^n (ax+b)^{m+n}$
   (D) 0

8. The nth derivative of $y = (ax + b)^n$, where n is any positive integer is (1)

   (A) $n! \, b^n$
   (B) $\dfrac{n!}{b^n}$
   (C) $n! \, a^n$
   (D) 0

9. The nth derivative of $y = \dfrac{1}{(ax+b)}$ is (1)

   (A) $\dfrac{(-1)^n a^n n!}{(ax+b)^{n+1}}$

   (B) $\dfrac{a^n n!}{(ax+b)^{n+1}}$

   (C) $\dfrac{a^n n!}{(ax+b)^{n-1}}$

   (D) 0

10. The nth derivative of $y = \log(ax + b)$ is (1)

    (A) $\dfrac{(-1)^{n-1} a^n (n-1)!}{(ax+b)^n}$

    (B) $\dfrac{a^n (n-1)!}{(ax+b)^n}$

    (C) $\dfrac{a^n n!}{(ax+b)^n}$

    (D) 0

11. The nth derivative of $y = e^{ax} \sin(bx + c)$ with $r = \sqrt{a^2 + b^2}$ and $\theta = \tan^{-1} \dfrac{b}{a}$ is (1)

    (A) $r^n e^{ax} \cos(bx + c + n\theta)$
    (B) $r^n e^{ax} \sin(bx + c + n\theta)$
    (C) $e^{ax} \sin(bx + c + n\theta)$
    (D) $e^{ax} \cos(bx + c + n\theta)$

12. The nth derivative of $y = e^{ax} \cos(bx + c)$ with $r = \sqrt{a^2 + b^2}$ and $\theta = \tan^{-1}\dfrac{b}{a}$ is (1)

    (A) $r^n e^{ax} \sin(bx + c + n\theta)$ (B) $r^n e^{ax} \cos(bx + c + n\theta)$

    (C) $e^{ax} \sin(bx + c + n\theta)$ (D) $e^{ax} \cos(bx + c + n\theta)$

13. The nth derivative of the function $y = e^{2x}$ is (1)

    (A) $2^n e^{2x}$ (B) $2^{-n} e^{2x}$

    (C) e^{2x} (D) $2^n e^{-2x}$

14. The nth derivative of the function $y = e^{ax+b}$ is (1)

    (A) $(a^n b) e^{ax+b}$ (B) $(a^n b) e^{ax}$

    (C) $(a^n) e^{ax+b}$ (D) $(ab^n) e^{ax+b}$

15. The nth derivative of function of $y = 2^x$ is (1)

    (A) $2^n (\log 2)^x$ (B) $\dfrac{2^x}{(\log 2)^n}$

    (C) $\dfrac{(\log 2)^n}{2^x}$ (D) $2^x (\log 2)^n$

16. The nth derivative of $y = \sin px + \cos px$ is (2)

    (A) $\sin\left(px - \dfrac{n\pi}{2}\right) + \cos\left(px - \dfrac{n\pi}{2}\right)$

    (B) $p^{-n} \sin\left(px + \dfrac{n\pi}{2}\right) + p^{-n} \cos\left(px + \dfrac{n\pi}{2}\right)$

    (C) $p^n \sin\left(px + \dfrac{n\pi}{2}\right) - p^n \cos\left(px + \dfrac{n\pi}{2}\right)$

    (D) $p^n \sin\left(px + \dfrac{n\pi}{2}\right) + p^n \cos\left(px + \dfrac{n\pi}{2}\right)$

17. The nth derivative of $y = \sin x \cos x$ is (2)

    (A) $2^{n-1} \cos\left(2x + \dfrac{n\pi}{2}\right)$ (B) $2^{n-1} \sin\left(2x + \dfrac{n\pi}{2}\right) + 2^{n-1} \cos\left(2x + \dfrac{n\pi}{2}\right)$

    (C) $2^{n-1} \sin\left(2x + \dfrac{n\pi}{2}\right)$ (D) $2^{2n-2} \sin\left(2x + \dfrac{n\pi}{2}\right) \cos\left(2x + \dfrac{n\pi}{2}\right)$

18. The nth derivative of $y = 2 \sin 2x \cos 3x$ is (2)

    (A) $5^n \sin\left(5x + \dfrac{n\pi}{2}\right) - \sin\left(x + \dfrac{n\pi}{2}\right)$ (B) $\sin\left(5x + \dfrac{n\pi}{2}\right) + \sin\left(x + \dfrac{n\pi}{2}\right)$

    (C) $5^n \cos\left(5x + \dfrac{n\pi}{2}\right) - \cos\left(x + \dfrac{n\pi}{2}\right)$ (D) none of these

19. The nth derivative of $y = 2\cos x \cos 2x$ is (2)

    (A) $3^n \cos\left(3x + \dfrac{n\pi}{2}\right) + \cos\left(x + \dfrac{n\pi}{2}\right)$
    (B) $\cos\left(3x + \dfrac{n\pi}{2}\right) + \cos\left(x + \dfrac{n\pi}{2}\right)$
    (C) $3^n \cos\left(3x + \dfrac{n\pi}{2}\right) - \cos\left(x + \dfrac{n\pi}{2}\right)$
    (D) none of these

20. The nth derivative of $y = \cos^2 x$ is (2)

    (A) $2^n \cos^2\left(2x + \dfrac{n\pi}{2}\right)$
    (B) $2^{n-1} \sin\left(2x + \dfrac{n\pi}{2}\right)$
    (C) $\dfrac{1}{2} + 2^{n-1} \sin\left(2x + \dfrac{n\pi}{2}\right)$
    (D) $2^{n-1} \cos\left(2x + \dfrac{n\pi}{2}\right)$

21. The nth derivative of $y = \sin^2 x$ is (2)

    (A) $\cos\left(2x + \dfrac{n\pi}{2}\right)$
    (B) $2^{n-1} \sin\left(2x + \dfrac{n\pi}{2}\right)$
    (C) $-2^{n-1} \cos\left(2x + \dfrac{n\pi}{2}\right)$
    (D) $2^n \sin^2\left(2x + \dfrac{n\pi}{2}\right)$

22. The nth derivative of $y = \sin^3 x$ is (2)

    (A) $\dfrac{3}{4}\sin\left(x + \dfrac{n\pi}{2}\right) - \dfrac{3^n}{4}\sin\left(3x + \dfrac{n\pi}{2}\right)$
    (B) $\dfrac{3}{4}\sin\left(x + \dfrac{n\pi}{2}\right) + \dfrac{3^n}{4}\sin\left(3x + \dfrac{n\pi}{2}\right)$
    (C) $3\sin\left(x + \dfrac{n\pi}{2}\right) - 3^n \sin\left(3x + \dfrac{n\pi}{2}\right)$
    (D) none of these

23. The nth derivative of $y = x^n$ is (2)

    (A) $(n + 1)!$
    (B) $(n - 1)!$
    (C) $n!$
    (D) 0

24. The $(n-1)^{th}$ derivative of $y = x^n$ is (2)

    (A) $(n - 1)!$
    (B) $n!x$
    (C) $n!$
    (D) 0

25. The nth derivative of $y = x^{n-1}$ is (2)

    (A) $(n - 1)!$
    (B) $n!x$
    (C) $n!$
    (D) 0

26. The nth derivative of $y = \log(3x + 4)$ is (2)

    (A) $\dfrac{3^n \, n!}{(3x + 4)^n}$
    (B) $\dfrac{3^n (n - 1)!}{(3x + 4)^n}$
    (C) $\dfrac{(-1)^{n-1} 3^n (n - 1)!}{(3x + 4)^n}$
    (D) 0

27. The nth derivative of $y = e^x \sin x$ is (2)

   (A) $e^x \sin\left(x + n\frac{\pi}{4}\right)$
   (B) $(\sqrt{2})^n e^x \cos\left(x + n\frac{\pi}{4}\right)$
   (C) $(\sqrt{2})^n e^x \sin\left(x + n\frac{\pi}{3}\right)$
   (D) $(\sqrt{2})^n e^x \sin\left(x + n\frac{\pi}{4}\right)$

28. The nth derivative of $y = e^{2x} \cos(3x + 4)$ is (2)

   (A) $(\sqrt{13})^n e^{2x} \sin\left(3x + 4 + n\tan^{-1}\frac{3}{2}\right)$
   (B) $(\sqrt{13})^n e^{2x} \cos\left(3x + 4 + n\tan^{-1}\frac{3}{2}\right)$
   (C) $e^{2x} \cos\left(3x + 4 + n\tan^{-1}\frac{3}{2}\right)$
   (D) $e^{2x} \cos\left(3x + 4 + n\tan^{-1}\frac{2}{3}\right)$

29. The nth derivative of $y = \dfrac{1}{(x+1)^3}$ is (2)

   (A) $\dfrac{(-1)^n (n+2)!}{2(x+1)^{n+3}}$
   (B) $\dfrac{(-1)^n (n+3)!}{2(x+1)^{n+3}}$
   (C) $\dfrac{1}{2(x+1)^{n+3}}$
   (D) none of these

30. The value of nth derivative of y given by $y_n = \dfrac{1}{2}(-1)^n n!\left[\dfrac{1}{(x-1)^{n+1}} + \dfrac{1}{(x+1)^{n+1}}\right]$ at $x = 0$ when n is even is

   (A) 1
   (B) 0
   (C) n!
   (D) $-(n!)$

31. The value of nth derivative of y given by $y_n = \dfrac{1}{2}(-1)^n n!\left[\dfrac{1}{(x-1)^{n+1}} + \dfrac{1}{(x+1)^{n+1}}\right]$ at $x = 0$ when n is odd is (2)

   (A) 1
   (B) 0
   (C) n!
   (D) $-(n!)$

Type II : n^{th} Derivative using Partial Fractions :

32. If $y = \tan^{-1}\dfrac{x}{a}$, then the nth derivative of y is (1)

   (A) $\dfrac{(-1)^{n-1}(n-1)! \sin n\theta \sin^n \theta}{a^n}$ where $\theta = \tan^{-1}\dfrac{a}{x}$
   (B) $\dfrac{(-1)^{n-1}(n-1)! \cos n\theta \cos^n \theta}{a^n}$ where $\theta = \tan^{-1}\dfrac{a}{x}$
   (C) $\dfrac{\sin n\theta \sin^n \theta}{a^n}$ where $\theta = \tan^{-1}\dfrac{a}{x}$
   (D) $(-1)^{n-1}(n-1)! \sin n\theta \cos^n \theta$ where $\theta = \tan^{-1}\dfrac{a}{x}$

33. If $y = \dfrac{x}{(x-1)(x-2)}$, then for finding n^{th} derivative of y, simplified expression by using partial fraction is (2)

   (A) $\dfrac{1}{(x-1)} - \dfrac{2}{(x-2)}$
   (B) $-\dfrac{1}{(x-1)} + \dfrac{2}{(x-2)}$
   (B) $-\dfrac{2}{(x-1)} + \dfrac{1}{(x-2)}$
   (D) none of these

34. If $y = \dfrac{x^3}{(x-1)(x-2)}$, then for finding n^{th} derivative of y, simplified expression by using partial fraction is (2)

   (A) $-\dfrac{1}{(x-1)} + \dfrac{8}{(x-2)}$
   (B) $-\dfrac{8}{(x-1)} + \dfrac{1}{(x-2)}$
   (C) $(x+3) - \dfrac{1}{(x-1)} + \dfrac{8}{(x-2)}$
   (D) $(x+3) + \dfrac{1}{(x-1)} - \dfrac{8}{(x-2)}$

35. If $y = \dfrac{1}{(x-1)^2(x-2)}$, then for finding n^{th} derivative of y, simplified expression by using partial fraction is (2)

   (A) $+\dfrac{1}{(x-1)} + \dfrac{1}{(x-1)^2} - \dfrac{1}{(x-2)}$
   (B) $-\dfrac{1}{(x-1)} - \dfrac{1}{(x-1)^2} + \dfrac{1}{(x-2)}$
   (C) $-\dfrac{1}{(x-1)^2} + \dfrac{1}{(x-2)}$
   (D) none of these

36. If $y = \dfrac{x^3}{(x^2-1)}$, then for finding n^{th} derivative of y, simplified expression by using partial fraction is (2)

   (A) $\dfrac{x^2}{(x-1)} - \dfrac{x^2}{(x+1)}$
   (B) $x - \dfrac{1}{2}\dfrac{1}{(x-1)} - \dfrac{1}{2}\dfrac{1}{(x+1)}$
   (C) $\dfrac{1}{2}\dfrac{1}{(x-1)} + \dfrac{1}{2}\dfrac{1}{(x+1)}$
   (D) $x + \dfrac{1}{2}\dfrac{1}{(x-1)} + \dfrac{1}{2}\dfrac{1}{(x+1)}$

37. If $y = \dfrac{x}{(x+2)}$, then n^{th} derivative of y (2)

   (A) $-2\dfrac{(-1)^n}{(x+2)^{n+1}}$
   (B) $2\dfrac{(-1)^n n!}{(x+2)^{n+1}}$
   (C) $-2\dfrac{1}{(x+2)^{n+1}}$
   (D) $-2\dfrac{(-1)^n n!}{(x+2)^{n+1}}$

38. If $y = \dfrac{5x+3}{5x+7}$, then n^{th} derivative of y (2)

   (A) $-4\dfrac{(-1)^n n! 5^n}{(5x+7)^{n+1}}$
   (B) $-4\dfrac{1}{(5x+7)^{n+1}}$
   (C) $3\dfrac{(-1)^n n! 5^n}{(5x+7)^{n+1}}$
   (D) none of these

39. The nth derivative of $y = \dfrac{2}{(2x-1)} - \dfrac{3}{(3x-1)}$ is (2)

   (A) $2\left[\dfrac{2^n\, n!}{(2x-1)^n}\right] - 3\left[\dfrac{3^n\, n!}{(3x-1)^n}\right]$
   (B) $2\left[\dfrac{2^n\, n!}{(2x-1)^{n+1}}\right] - 3\left[\dfrac{3^n\, n!}{(3x-1)^{n+1}}\right]$
   (C) $2\left[\dfrac{(-1)^n\, 2^n\, n!}{(2x-1)^{n+1}}\right] - 3\left[\dfrac{(-1)^n\, 3^n\, n!}{(3x-1)^{n+1}}\right]$
   (D) $2\left[\dfrac{n!}{(2x-1)^{n+1}}\right] - 3\left[\dfrac{n!}{(3x-1)^{n+1}}\right]$

40. The nth derivative of $y = \dfrac{2}{5} + \dfrac{1}{5}\dfrac{1}{(5x+7)}$ is (2)

   (A) $\dfrac{1}{5}\left[\dfrac{(-1)^n\, 5^n\, n!}{(5x+7)^{n+1}}\right]$
   (B) $\dfrac{2}{5} + \dfrac{1}{5}\left[\dfrac{5^n\, n!}{(5x+7)^{n+1}}\right]$
   (C) $\left[\dfrac{5^n\, n!}{(5x+7)^{n+1}}\right]$
   (D) $\left[\dfrac{5^{n-1}\,(n-1)!}{(5x+7)^n}\right]$

41. If $y = (x^2 + 3x + 7) + \dfrac{16}{x-2} - \dfrac{1}{x-1}$, then n^{th} derivative of y for $n > 2$ is (2)

   (A) $16\dfrac{n!}{(x-2)^{n+1}} - \dfrac{n!}{(x-1)^{n+1}}$
   (B) $16\dfrac{(-1)^n\, n!}{(x-2)^{n+1}} - \dfrac{(-1)^n\, n!}{(x-1)^{n+1}}$
   (C) $\dfrac{(-1)^n\, n!}{(x-2)^{n+1}} - 16\dfrac{(-1)^n\, n!}{(x-1)^{n+1}}$
   (D) none of these

42. If $y = \dfrac{1}{x-1} + \dfrac{1}{(x-1)^2}$, then n^{th} derivative of y is (2)

   (A) $\dfrac{(-1)^n}{(x-1)^{n+1}} + \dfrac{(-1)^n}{(x-1)^{n+2}}$
   (B) $\dfrac{n!}{(x-1)^{n+1}} + \dfrac{(n+1)!}{(x-1)^{n+2}}$
   (C) $\dfrac{(-1)^n\, n!}{(x-1)^{n+1}} + \dfrac{(-1)^n\,(n+1)!}{(x-1)^{n+2}}$
   (D) none of these

43. If $y = \dfrac{1}{(x-2)(x-3)}$, then n^{th} derivative of y is (2)

   (A) $-\dfrac{(-1)^n\, n!}{(x-2)^{n+1}} + \dfrac{(-1)^n\, n!}{(x-3)^{n+1}}$
   (B) $-\dfrac{(-1)^n}{(x-2)^{n+1}} + \dfrac{(-1)^n}{(x-3)^{n+1}}$
   (C) $+\dfrac{n!}{(x-2)^{n+1}} - \dfrac{n!}{(x-3)^{n+1}}$
   (D) none of these

44. If $y = \cos^{-1}\left(\dfrac{x - x^{-1}}{x + x^{-1}}\right)$, then for finding n^{th} derivative of y, simplified expression by using $x = \tan\theta$ is (2)

   (A) $\pi - 2\tan^{-1}\left(\dfrac{1}{x}\right)$
   (B) $\pi - 2\tan^{-1} x$
   (C) $2\tan^{-1} x$
   (D) $\dfrac{\pi}{2} + \tan^{-1} x$

45. If $y = \tan^{-1}\left(\dfrac{2x}{1-x^2}\right)$, then for finding n^{th} derivative of y, simplified expression by using $x = \tan\theta$ is (2)

   (A) $\pi - 2\tan^{-1}\left(\dfrac{1}{x}\right)$
   (B) $\pi - 2\tan^{-1} x$
   (C) $2\tan^{-1} x$
   (D) $\pi + 2\tan^{-1} x$

46. If $y = \sin^{-1}\left(\dfrac{2x}{1+x^2}\right)$, then for finding n^{th} derivative of y, simplified expression by using $x = \tan\theta$ is (2)

   (A) $2\tan^{-1} x$
   (B) $\pi - 2\tan^{-1} x$
   (C) $\tan^{-1}\left(\dfrac{1}{x}\right)$
   (D) $\pi + 2\tan^{-1} x$

47. If $y = \sin^{-1}(3x - 4x^3)$, then using $x = \sin\theta$, which of the following is true ? (2)

   (A) $(1-x^2)y_2 + xy_1 + y = 0$
   (B) $x^2 y_2 + xy_1 + y = 0$
   (C) $(1-x^2)y_2 - xy_1 = 0$
   (D) $(1+x^2)y_2 + xy_1 = 0$

Type III : n^{th} Derivative using Leibnitz's theorem :

48. The nth derivative of product of two functions $y = uv$ by Leibnitz's theorem is (1)

   (A) ${}^nC_0 u_n v + {}^nC_1 u_{n-1} v_1 + {}^nC_2 u_{n-2} v_2 + \ldots + {}^nC_n u v_n$
   (B) ${}^nC_0 u_{n+1} v + {}^nC_1 u_{n+2} v_1 + {}^nC_2 u_{n+3} v_2 + \ldots + {}^nC_n u_{2n+1} v_n$
   (C) ${}^nC_0 v_{n+1} u + {}^nC_1 v_{n+2} u_1 + {}^nC_2 v_{n+3} u_2 + \ldots + {}^nC_n v_{2n+1} u_n$
   (D) $u_n v + u_{n-1} v_1 + u_{n-2} v_2 + \ldots + u v_n$

49. Using Leibnitz's theorem, the nth derivative of $y = xe^{4x}$ is (2)

   (A) $n\, 4^n e^{4x} + 4^{n-1} e^{4x} x$
   (B) $4^n e^{4x} x - n\, 4^{n-1} e^{4x}$
   (C) $e^{4x} x + n e^{4x}$
   (D) $4^n e^{4x} x + n\, 4^{n-1} e^{4x}$

50. Using Leibnitz's theorem, the nth derivative of $y = x\cos x$ is (2)

   (A) $n\cos\left(x + \dfrac{n\pi}{2}\right) + x\cos\left(x + \dfrac{(n-1)\pi}{2}\right)$
   (B) $x\cos\left(x + \dfrac{n\pi}{2}\right) - n\cos\left(x + \dfrac{(n-1)\pi}{2}\right)$
   (C) $x\cos\left(x + \dfrac{n\pi}{2}\right) + n\cos\left(x + \dfrac{(n-1)\pi}{2}\right)$
   (D) $x\cos\left(x + \dfrac{n\pi}{2}\right) - n\cos\left(x + \dfrac{(n+1)\pi}{2}\right)$

51. Using Leibnitz's theorem, the nth derivative of $y = x \sin x$ is (2)

    (A) $n \sin\left(x + \dfrac{n\pi}{2}\right) - x \sin\left(x - \dfrac{(n-1)\pi}{2}\right)$

    (B) $x \sin\left(x + \dfrac{n\pi}{2}\right) - n \sin\left(x + \dfrac{(n-1)\pi}{2}\right)$

    (C) $x \sin\left(x + \dfrac{n\pi}{2}\right) - n \sin\left(x + \dfrac{(n+1)\pi}{2}\right)$

    (D) $x \sin\left(x + \dfrac{n\pi}{2}\right) + n \sin\left(x + \dfrac{(n-1)\pi}{2}\right)$

52. Using Leibnitz's theorem, the nth derivative of $y = xe^x \cos x$ is (2)

    (A) $xe^x \cos\left(x + \dfrac{n\pi}{4}\right) + ne^x \cos\left(x + \dfrac{(n-1)\pi}{4}\right)$

    (B) $\left(\sqrt{2}\right)^n e^x \cos\left(x + \dfrac{n\pi}{4}\right) + \left(\sqrt{2}\right)^{n-1} xe^x \cos\left(x + \dfrac{(n-1)\pi}{4}\right)$

    (C) $\left(\sqrt{2}\right)^n xe^x \cos\left(x + \dfrac{n\pi}{4}\right) + n\left(\sqrt{2}\right)^{n-1} e^x \cos\left(x + \dfrac{(n-1)\pi}{4}\right)$

    (D) none of these

53. Using Leibnitz's theorem, the nth derivative of $y = xe^x \sin x$ is (2)

    (A) $xe^x \sin\left(x + \dfrac{n\pi}{4}\right) + ne^x \sin\left(x + \dfrac{(n-1)\pi}{4}\right)$

    (B) $\left(\sqrt{2}\right)^n e^x \sin\left(x + \dfrac{n\pi}{4}\right) + \left(\sqrt{2}\right)^{n-1} xe^x \sin\left(x + \dfrac{(n-1)\pi}{4}\right)$

    (C) $\left(\sqrt{2}\right)^n xe^x \sin\left(x + \dfrac{n\pi}{4}\right) + n\left(\sqrt{2}\right)^{n-1} e^x \sin\left(x + \dfrac{(n-1)\pi}{4}\right)$

    (D) none of these

54. Using Leibnitz's theorem, the nth derivative of $f(x) \cos x = \sin x$ is (2)

    (A) $f^n(x) \cos x + n f^{n-1}(x)(-\sin x) + \dfrac{n(n-1)}{2} f^{n-2}(x)(-\cos x) + \ldots = \cos\left(x + \dfrac{n\pi}{2}\right)$

    (B) $f^n(x) \cos x + n f^{n-1}(x)(-\sin x) + \dfrac{n(n-1)}{2} f^{n-2}(x)(-\cos x) + \ldots = \sin\left(x + \dfrac{n\pi}{2}\right)$

    (C) $f^n(x) \cos x + f^{n-1}(x)(-\sin x) + f^{n-2}(x)(-\cos x) + \ldots = \sin\left(x + \dfrac{n\pi}{2}\right)$

    (D) none of these

55. Using Leibnitz's theorem, the nth derivative of $(1 - x^2) y_2$ is (2)

    (A) $(1 - x^2) y_n + n (-2x) y_{n+1} - n(n - 1) y_{n+3}$
    (B) $(1 - x^2) y_{n+2} + n(-2x) y_{n+1} - n(n - 1) y_n$
    (C) $(1 - x^2) y_{n+1} + n(-2x) y_n - n(n - 1) y_{n-1}$
    (D) $(1 - x^2) y_{n+2} + (-2x) y_{n+1} - (2) y_n$

56. Using Leibnitz's theorem, the nth derivative of xy_1 is (2)

    (A) $xy_{n+1} + ny_n$
    (B) $xy_{n+1} - ny_n$
    (C) $xy_n + ny_{n-1}$
    (D) $xy_{n-1} + ny_n$

57. If $y = \sin^{-1} x$ then which of the following relation is true ? (2)

    (A) $(1 - x^2) y_2 + xy_1 + y = 0$
    (B) $x^2 y_2 + xy_1 + y = 0$
    (C) $(1 - x^2) y_2 - xy_1 = 0$
    (D) $(1 + x^2) y_2 + xy_1 = 0$

58. If $y = a \cos(\log x) + b \sin(\log x)$ then which of the following relation is true ? (2)

    (A) $(1 - x^2) y_2 + xy_1 + y = 0$
    (B) $x^2 y_2 - xy_1 - y = 0$
    (C) $(1 + x^2) y_2 + xy_1 = 0$
    (D) $x^2 y_2 + xy_1 + y = 0$

59. If $y = e^{\tan^{-1} x}$ then which of the following relation is true ? (2)

    (A) $(1 + x^2) y_1 - y = 0$
    (B) $(\sqrt{1 - x^2}) y_1 - y = 0$
    (C) $(1 + x^2) y_1 + xy = 0$
    (D) none of these

60. If $y = e^{a \sin^{-1} x}$ then which of the following relation is true ? (2)

    (A) $(1 - x^2) y_1 = ay$
    (B) $(\sqrt{1 - x^2}) y_1 = ay$
    (C) $\sqrt{(1 + x^2)} y_1 = ay$
    (D) none of these

61. If $y = e^{m \cos^{-1} x}$ then which of the following relation is true ? (2)

    (a) $(1 - x^2) y_1 = -my$
    (B) $(\sqrt{1 - x^2}) y_1 = -my$
    (C) $\sqrt{(1 + x^2)} y_1 = my$
    (D) none of these

62. If $y = (x + \sqrt{x^2 - 1})^m$ then which of the following relation is true ? (2)

    (A) $(x^2 - 1) y_1 = -my$
    (B) $\sqrt{(x^2 + 1)} y_1 = my$
    (C) $(\sqrt{x^2 - 1}) y_1 = my$
    (D) none of these

63. The relation between y_{n+2} and y_n at $x = 0$ from the equation
    $(1 - x^2) y_{n+2} - (2n + 1) xy_{n+1} - n^2 y_n = 0$ is (2)

    (A) $(y_{n+2})_{x=0} = n^2 (y_n)_{x=0}$
    (B) $(y_{n+2})_{x=0} = -n^2 (y_n)_{x=0}$
    (C) $(y_{n+2})_{x=0} = (y_n)_{x=0}$
    (D) none of these

64. If $y = (x+1)\log(x+1)$ then n^{th} order differential coefficient of y is (2)

(A) $\dfrac{(-1)^{n-2}(n-2)!}{(x+1)^n}$

(B) $\dfrac{(-1)^{n-1}(n-1)!}{(x+1)^{n+1}}$

(C) $\dfrac{(-1)^{n-1}(n-2)!\,x^n}{(x+1)^n}$

(D) $\dfrac{(-1)^{n-2}(n-2)!}{(x+1)^{n-1}}$

Answers

1. (C)	14. (C)	27. (D)	40. (A)	53. (C)
2. (D)	15. (D)	28. (B)	41. (B)	54. (B)
3. (B)	16. (D)	29. (A)	42. (C)	55. (B)
4. (A)	17. (C)	30. (B)	43. (A)	56. (A)
5. (C)	18. (A)	31. (D)	44. (B)	57. (C)
6. (D)	19. (A)	32. (A)	45. (C)	58. (D)
7. (D)	20. (D)	33. (B)	46. (A)	59. (A)
8. (C)	21. (C)	34. (C)	47. (B)	60. (B)
9. (A)	22. (A)	35. (B)	48. (A)	61. (B)
10. (A)	23. (C)	36. (D)	49. (D)	62. (C)
11. (B)	24. (B)	37. (D)	50. (C)	63. (A)
12. (B)	25. (D)	38. (A)	51. (D)	64. (D)
13. (A)	26. (C)	39. (C)	52. (C)	

CHAPTER EIGHT

TAYLOR'S AND MACLAURIN'S THEOREMS

8.1 MACLAURIN'S THEOREM

Statement : Let f(x) be a function of x which can be expanded in ascending powers (i.e. power series in x) and let the expansion be differentiable term by term any number of times, then

$$f(x) = f(0) + xf'(0) + \frac{x^2}{2!} f''(0) + \frac{x^3}{3!} f'''(0) + \ldots + \frac{x^n}{n!} f^n(0) + \ldots$$

Proof : Let $\quad f(x) = A_0 + A_1 x + A_2 x^2 + A_3 x^3 + A_4 x^4 + \ldots \quad \ldots$ (i)

where, A_0, A_1, A_2 are constants (independent of x) to be determined.

Differentiating (i) successively with respect to x, we get

$$f'(x) = A_1 + 2A_2 x + 3A_3 x^2 + 4A_4 x^3 + \ldots$$

$$f''(x) = 2.1\, A_2 + 3.2\, A_3 x + 4.3\, A_4 x^2 + \ldots$$

$$f'''(x) = 3.2\, A_3 + 4.3.2\, A_4 x + \ldots \text{ etc.}$$

Putting x = 0 in each of these, we get

$$f(0) = A_0,\ f'(0) = A_1,\ f''(0) = 2!A_2,\ f'''(0) = 3!A_3 \ \ldots \text{ etc.}$$

Substituting these values in (i), we get

$$f(x) = f(0) + xf'(0) + \frac{x^2}{2!} f''(0) + \frac{x^3}{3!} f'''(0) + \ldots + \frac{x^n}{n!} f^n(0) + \ldots$$

Note 1 : If y = f(x), then we write $f(0) = (y)_0, f'(0) = (y_1)_0, f''(0) = (y_2)_0 \ldots f^n(0) = (y_n)_0$, etc.

Hence the Maclaurin's theorem can also be stated as

$$y = (y)_0 + x\,(y_1)_0 + \frac{x^2}{2!} (y_2)_0 + \frac{x^3}{3!} (y_3)_0 + \ldots + \frac{x^n}{n!} (y_n)_0 + \ldots$$

Note 2 : The term $\frac{x^n}{n!} f^n(0)$, which is the $(n + 1)^{th}$ term in the expansion is called the general term.

8.2 ILLUSTRATIONS ON MACLAURIN'S THEOREM

Ex. 1 : *Expand $\log(1 + e^x)$ by Maclaurin's theorem as far as the term in x^4.*

Sol. : Let $\quad f(x) = \log(1 + e^x) \qquad \therefore f(0) = \log 2$

then, $\quad f'(x) = \dfrac{e^x}{1+e^x} \qquad \therefore f'(0) = \dfrac{1}{2}$

$$f''(x) = \dfrac{(1+e^x)e^x - e^x(e^x)}{(1+e^x)^2}$$

$$= \dfrac{e^x}{(1+e^x)^2} \qquad \therefore f''(0) = \dfrac{1}{4}$$

$$f'''(x) = \dfrac{(1+e^x)^2 e^x - 2(1+e^x)e^x e^x}{(1+e^x)^4}$$

$$= \dfrac{(1+e^x)e^x - 2e^{2x}}{(1+e^x)^3}$$

$$= \dfrac{e^x - e^{2x}}{(1+e^x)^3} \qquad \therefore f'''(0) = 0$$

$$f^{iv}(x) = \dfrac{(1+e^x)^3(e^x - 2e^{2x}) - 3(1+e^x)^2 e^x (e^x - e^{2x})}{(1+e^x)^6}$$

$$= \dfrac{(1+e^x)(e^x - 2e^{2x}) - 3e^x(e^x - e^{2x})}{(1+e^x)^4} \qquad \therefore f^{iv}(0) = -\dfrac{1}{8}$$

Substituting the values of $f(0)$, $f'(0)$, $f''(0)$, $f'''(0)$ in the Maclaurin's theorem etc.

$$f(x) = f(0) + xf'(0) + \dfrac{x^2}{2} f''(0) + \dfrac{x^3}{3} f'''(0) + \dfrac{x^4}{4} f^{iv}(0) + \ldots$$

We have $\quad f(x) = \log 2 + x\left(\dfrac{1}{2}\right) + \dfrac{x^2}{2}\left(\dfrac{1}{4}\right) + \dfrac{x^3}{6}(0) + \dfrac{x^4}{24}\left(\dfrac{-1}{8}\right) + \ldots$

$\therefore \quad \log(1 + e^x) = \log 2 + \dfrac{x}{2} + \dfrac{x^2}{8} - \dfrac{x^4}{192} + \ldots$

Ex. 2 : *Expand $\sec x$ by Maclaurin's theorem as far as the term in x^4.*

Sol. : Let $\quad f(x) = \sec x \qquad \therefore f(0) = 1$

then $\quad f'(x) = x \sec x \tan x \qquad \therefore f'(0) = 0$

$\quad f''(0) = \sec^3 x + \tan^2 x \sec x \qquad \therefore f''(0) = 1$

$\quad f'''(x) = 3 \sec^3 x \tan x + \sec x \tan^3 x + 2 \tan x \sec^3 x \qquad \therefore f'''(0) = 0$

$\quad f^{iv}(x) = 3[\sec^5 x + \tan^2 x \cdot 3 \sec^3 x] + \sec^3 x \cdot 3 \tan^2 x + \tan^4 x \sec x$

$\qquad + 2[\tan^2 x \cdot 3 \sec^3 x + \sec^5 x] \qquad \therefore f^{iv}(0) = 5$ etc.

Substituting the values of $f(0)$, $f'(0)$, $f''(0)$ ... etc. in the Maclaurin's theorem,

$$f(x) = f(0) + xf'(0) + \dfrac{x^2}{2!} f''(0) + \dfrac{x^3}{3!} f'''(0) + \dfrac{x^4}{4!} f^{iv}(0) + \ldots$$

We have $\quad f(x) = 1 + x(0) + \dfrac{x^2}{2!}(1) + \dfrac{x^3}{3!}(0) + \dfrac{x^4}{4!}(5) + \ldots$

$\therefore \quad \sec x = 1 + \dfrac{x^2}{2!} + \dfrac{5x^4}{4!} + \ldots$

Ex. 3 : *Expand tan x by Maclaurin's theorem as far as the term in x^5.*

Sol. : Let
$$f(x) = \tan x \qquad \therefore f(0) = 0$$
$$f'(x) = \sec^2 x = 1 + \tan^2 x \qquad \therefore f'(0) = 1$$
$$f''(x) = 2 \tan x \sec^2 x = 2 \tan x + 2 \tan^3 x \qquad \therefore f''(0) = 0$$
$$f'''(x) = 2 \sec^2 x + 6 \tan^2 x \sec^2 x \qquad \therefore f'''(0) = 2$$
$$= 2(1 + \tan^2 x) + 6 \tan^2 x (1 + \tan^2 x)$$
$$= 2 + 8 \tan^2 x + 6 \tan^4 x$$
$$f^{iv}(x) = 16 \tan x \sec^2 x + 24 \tan^3 x \sec^2 x \qquad \therefore f^{iv}(0) = 0$$
$$= 16 \tan x (1 + \tan^2 x) + 24 \tan^3 x (1 + \tan^2 x)$$
$$= 16 \tan x + 40 \tan^3 x + 24 \tan^5 x$$
$$f^v(x) = 16 \sec^2 x + 120 \tan^2 x \sec^2 x + 120 \tan^4 x \sec^2 x \qquad f^v(0) = 16$$

Substituting the values of $f(0)$, $f'(0)$, $f''(0)$, $f'''(0)$, $f^{iv}(0)$, $f^v(0)$, etc. in the Maclaurin's theorem,

$$f(x) = f(0) + xf'(0) + \frac{x^2}{2!} f''(0) + \frac{x^3}{3!} f'''(0) + \frac{x^4}{4!} f^{iv}(0) + \frac{x^5}{5!} f^v(0) + \ldots$$

$$\therefore \quad \tan x = x + \frac{1}{3} x^3 + \frac{2}{15} x^5 + \ldots$$

Ex. 4 : *If $x = (1-y)(1-2y)$ then show that $y = 1 + x - 2x^2 \ldots$*

Sol. : Assuming that y is a function of x, we first find $(y)_0$, $(y_1)_0$, $(y_2)_0$ … etc.

We have $x = (1-y)(1-2y) \quad \therefore$ at $x = 0$; $y = 1$ or $y = \frac{1}{2}$

We discard $y = \frac{1}{2}$, since it is not required in the expansion $\qquad \therefore (y)_0 = 1$

Again $\qquad x = 1 + 2y^2 - 3y$

Differentiating with respect to x, we get
$$1 = 4yy_1 - 3y_1 \qquad \therefore (y_1)_0 = 1$$

Differentiating again with respect to x, we get
$$0 = 4yy_2 + 4y_1^2 - 3y_2 \qquad \therefore (y_2)_0 = -4$$

Substituting these values in Maclaurin's theorem,
$$y = (y)_0 + x (y_1)_0 + \frac{x^2}{2!} (y_2)_0 + \ldots$$

We have $\qquad y = 1 + x(1) + \frac{x^2}{2}(-4) + \ldots$

$\therefore \qquad y = 1 + x - 2x^2 + \ldots$

Ex. 5 : *Expand $\tan^{-1} x$ in powers of x.*

Sol. : Let $\qquad f(x) = \tan^{-1} x$, then $f(0) = 0 \qquad \ldots (1)$

Now, we know that $f^n(x) = (-1)^{n-1} (n-1)! \sin n\theta \sin^n \theta$ where $\theta = \tan^{-1} \frac{1}{x}$

$$\theta = \frac{\pi}{2} \text{ at } x = 0$$

$\therefore \qquad f^n(0) = (-1)^{n-1}(n-1)! \sin \frac{n\pi}{2} \qquad \left(\because \sin^n \frac{\pi}{2} = 1 \right) \quad \ldots (2)$

Putting $n = 1, 2, 3, 4, \ldots$ in (2), we get

$f'(0) = 1$, $f''(0) = 0$, $f'''(0) = -2!$, $f^{iv}(0) = 0$, $f^{v}(0) = 4!$.

Hence by Maclaurin's theorem,

$$f(x) = f(0) + xf'(0) + \frac{x^2}{2} f''(0) + \ldots$$

We have, $\tan^{-1} x = x - \frac{x^3}{3} + \frac{x^5}{5} - \frac{x^7}{7} + \ldots$

Ex. 6 : *Obtain the Maclaurin's expansion of* $\tan\left(\frac{\pi}{4} + x\right)$ *and hence find the value of* $\tan (46.5°)$ *to three places of decimals.*

Sol. : Let $f(x) = \tan\left(\frac{\pi}{4} + x\right)$, $\qquad \therefore f(0) = \left(\tan \frac{\pi}{4}\right) = 1$

then $f'(x) = \sec^2\left(\frac{\pi}{4} + x\right)$, $\qquad \therefore f'(0) = \left(\sec \frac{\pi}{4}\right)^2 = 2$

$f''(x) = 2 \sec^2\left(\frac{\pi}{4} + x\right) \tan\left(\frac{\pi}{4} + x\right)$, $\quad \therefore f''(0) = 2 \left(\sec \frac{\pi}{4}\right)^2 \left(\tan \frac{\pi}{4}\right) = 4$

$f'''(x) = 4 \sec^2\left(\frac{\pi}{4} + x\right) \tan^2\left(\frac{\pi}{4} + x\right) + 2 \sec^4\left(\frac{\pi}{4} + x\right)$, $\quad \therefore f'''(0) = 16$

We know by Maclaurin's theorem,

$$f(x) = f(0) + xf'(0) + \frac{x^2}{2!} f''(0) + \frac{x^3}{3!} f'''(0) + \ldots \qquad \ldots (1)$$

Substituting the values of $f(0)$, $f'(0)$, $f''(0)$, $f'''(0)$ in (1), we get

$$\tan\left(\frac{\pi}{4} + x\right) = 1 + 2x + \frac{4}{2!} x^2 + \frac{16}{6} x^3 + \ldots$$

$$= 1 + 2x + 2x^2 + \frac{8}{3} x^3 + \ldots \qquad \ldots (2)$$

Now, $\tan (46.5°) = \tan (45° + 1.5°) = \tan\left(\frac{\pi}{4} + \frac{\pi}{120}\right)$

$= \tan\left(\frac{\pi}{4} + 0.02618\right) \qquad \left\{\because 1° = \frac{\pi}{180} \text{ Radian}\right\}$

$\therefore$ Putting $x = 0.02618$ in (2), we get

$\tan (46.5°) = \tan\left(\frac{\pi}{4} + 0.02618\right)$

$= 1 + 2 (0.02618) + 2 (0.02618)^2 + \frac{8}{3} (0.02618)^3 + \ldots$

$= 1 + 0.05236 + 0.00137 + 0.0000478 + \ldots$

$= 1.0537778$

Note : Only first three terms of the expansion are sufficient to find the value of $\tan (46.5°)$ correct to three places of decimals, because contribution of the fourth term is after fourth place of decimal.

Engineering Mathematics – I 8.5 Taylor's and Maclaurin's Theorems

EXERCISE 8.1

1. Expand by Maclaurin's theorem the following :

   (i) $\log(1 + \sin x)$ **(Dec. 2005)**,

   (ii) $e^x \sec x$, (iii) $\log \sec x$, (iv) $e^x \sin x$, (v) $\tan^{-1}(1+x)$

   Ans. (i) $x - \dfrac{x^2}{2} + \dfrac{x^3}{6} - \dfrac{x^4}{12} + \dfrac{x^5}{24} + \ldots$, (ii) $1 + x + x^2 + \dfrac{2}{3}x^3 + \ldots$,

   (iii) $\dfrac{1}{2}x^2 + \dfrac{1}{12}x^4 + \dfrac{1}{45}x^6 + \ldots$, (iv) $x + x^2 + \dfrac{2x^3}{3!} - \dfrac{4x^5}{5!} + \ldots$,

   (v) $\dfrac{\pi}{4} + \dfrac{x}{2} - \dfrac{x^2}{4} + \dfrac{x^3}{12} - \ldots$

2. If $x^3 + 2xy^2 - y^3 + x - 1 = 0$, expand y in ascending powers of x by Maclaurin's theorem.

   Ans. $-1 + x - \dfrac{1}{3}x^2 + \ldots$

3. By Maclaurin's theorem or otherwise, find the expansion of $y = \sin(e^x - 1)$ upto a term in x^4.

4. Expand $\log_e\left[x + \sqrt{x^2 + 1}\right]$ upto the first four terms by Maclaurin's theorem; by putting $x = 0.75$ in the expansion, calculate the value of $\log_e 2$ to four places of decimals.

   Ans. $x - \dfrac{x^3}{6} + \dfrac{9}{120}x^5 - \dfrac{225}{5040}x^7 + \ldots$; putting $x = 0.75 = \dfrac{3}{4}$, $\log_e 2 = 0.6915$

5. If $x^3 + y^3 + xy - 1 = 0$ then show that $y = 1 - \dfrac{x}{3} - \dfrac{26}{81}x^3 \ldots$ **(Dec. 2008)**

6. Using Maclaurin's theorem, show that $\log(1 + \tan x) = x - \dfrac{x^2}{2!} + \dfrac{4}{3!}x^3 + \ldots$

   (May 2014)

8.3 STANDARD EXPANSIONS

By the help of Maclaurin's theorem (or series), we shall now obtain the expansions for some standard functions such as $\sin x$, $\cos x$, e^x, etc.

1. Expansion of sin x :

Let $f(x) = \sin x$, then $f^n(x) = \sin\left(x + \dfrac{n\pi}{2}\right)$

∴ $f(0) = 0$, $f'(0) = 1$, $f''(0) = 0$, $f'''(0) = -1$, …… etc.

Substituting these values in Maclaurin's theorem, we get expansion (series) for $\sin x$ as

$$\sin x = x - \dfrac{x^3}{3!} + \dfrac{x^5}{5!} - \dfrac{x^7}{7!} + \dfrac{x^9}{9!} - \ldots$$

2. **Expansion of cos x :**

The expansion for cos x in ascending powers of x may either be obtained using Maclaurin's theorem as above, or by differentiating the expansion of sin x term by term $\left(\text{since, } \cos x = \frac{d}{dx} \sin x\right)$.

Thus,
$$\cos x = 1 - \frac{x^2}{2!} + \frac{x^4}{4!} - \frac{x^6}{6!} + \frac{x^8}{8!} - \ldots$$

3. **Expansion of tan x :**

The expansion for tan x may also be obtained by Maclaurin's theorem. But since we have calculated the expansion for sin x and cos x, we can use the fact

$$\tan x = \frac{\sin x}{\cos x} = \frac{x - \frac{x^3}{3!} + \frac{x^5}{5!} - \frac{x^7}{7!} + \frac{x^9}{9!} - \ldots}{1 - \frac{x^2}{2!} + \frac{x^4}{4!} - \frac{x^6}{6!} + \frac{x^8}{8!} - \ldots}$$

By actual division, we get
$$\tan x = x + \frac{x^3}{3} + \frac{2}{15} x^5 + \frac{17}{315} x^7 + \ldots$$

4. **Expansion of e^x:**

Let $\quad f(x) = e^x, \quad$ then $\quad f^n(x) = e^x$

$\therefore \quad f(0) = f'(0) = f''(0) = \ldots f^n(0) = \ldots = 1$

Substituting these values in Maclaurin's theorem, we get exponential series as
$$e^x = 1 + x + \frac{x^2}{2!} + \frac{x^3}{3!} + \frac{x^4}{4!} + \ldots$$

5. **Expansion of sinh x :**

The expansion of sinh x may be obtained using exponential series as $\sinh x = \frac{e^x - e^{-x}}{2}$ or may be obtained from Maclaurin's theorem directly.

Thus
$$\sinh x = x + \frac{x^3}{3!} + \frac{x^5}{5!} + \frac{x^7}{7!} + \ldots$$

Similarly, $\quad \cosh x = 1 + \frac{x^2}{2!} + \frac{x^4}{4!} + \frac{x^6}{6!} + \frac{x^8}{8!} + \ldots$

6. **Expansion of tanh x :**

We use the fact
$$\tanh x = \frac{\sinh x}{\cosh x} = \frac{x + \frac{x^3}{3!} + \frac{x^5}{5!} + \frac{x^7}{7!} + \ldots}{1 + \frac{x^2}{2!} + \frac{x^4}{4!} + \frac{x^6}{6!} + \ldots}$$

By actual division, we get

$$\tanh x = x - \frac{x^3}{3} + \frac{2}{15}x^5 - \frac{17}{315}x^7 + \ldots$$

7. Expansion of log (1 + x):

Let $f(x) = \log(1+x)$, then $f^n(x) = \dfrac{(-1)^{n-1}(n-1)!}{(1+x)^n}$

$\therefore \quad f(0) = 0,\ f'(0) = 1,\ f''(0) = -1,\ f'''(0) = 2!,\ f^{iv}(0) = -3!,\ \ldots$ etc.

Substituting these values in Maclaurin's theorem, we get logarithmic series as

$$\log(1+x) = x - \frac{x^2}{2} + \frac{x^3}{3} - \frac{x^4}{4} + \frac{x^5}{5} - \ldots$$

By replacing x by $-x$, we get the expansion for $\log(1-x)$ as

$$\log(1-x) = -x - \frac{x^2}{2} - \frac{x^3}{3} - \frac{x^4}{4} - \frac{x^5}{5} - \ldots$$

Differentiating above results w.r.t. x, we get

$$(1+x)^{-1} = 1 - x + x^2 - x^3 + x^4 - \ldots$$

$$(1-x)^{-1} = 1 + x + x^2 + x^3 + x^4 + \ldots$$

Also, $\log\left(\dfrac{1+x}{1-x}\right) = \log(1+x) - \log(1-x)$

and $\tanh^{-1} x = \dfrac{1}{2}\log\left(\dfrac{1+x}{1-x}\right)$

$\therefore \quad \tanh^{-1} x = x + \dfrac{x^3}{3} + \dfrac{x^5}{5} + \dfrac{x^7}{7} + \ldots$

8. Expansion of $(1 + x)^n$:

The expansion for $(1 + x)^n$ can also be obtained by Maclaurin's theorem which is known as **Binomial series.**

Thus, $(1+x)^n = 1 + nx + \dfrac{n(n-1)}{2!}x^2 + \dfrac{n(n-1)(n-2)}{3!}x^3 + \ldots$

Note: All the expansions obtained in this article are standard expansions and may be treated as formulae. The students are advised to remember these results.

Some Standard Expansion for Ready Reference:

1. $e^x = 1 + x + \dfrac{x^2}{2!} + \dfrac{x^3}{3!} + \dfrac{x^4}{4!} + \ldots = \sum\limits_{r=0}^{\infty} \dfrac{x^r}{r!}$

2. $e^{-x} = 1 - x + \dfrac{x^2}{2!} - \dfrac{x^3}{3!} + \dfrac{x^4}{4!} - \dfrac{x^5}{5!} + \ldots = \sum\limits_{r=0}^{\infty} \dfrac{(-1)^r x^r}{r!}$

3. $\sin x = x - \dfrac{x^3}{3!} + \dfrac{x^5}{5!} - \dfrac{x^7}{7!} + \ldots = \sum\limits_{r=0}^{\infty} \dfrac{(-1)^r x^{2r+1}}{(2r+1)!}$

4. $\cos x = 1 - \dfrac{x^2}{2!} + \dfrac{x^4}{4!} - \dfrac{x^6}{6!} + \ldots = \sum\limits_{r=0}^{\infty} \dfrac{(-1)^r x^{2r}}{(2r)!}$.

5. $\tan x = x + \dfrac{x^3}{3} + \dfrac{2x^5}{15} + \dfrac{17}{315} x^7 + \ldots$

6. $\sinh x = x + \dfrac{x^3}{3!} + \dfrac{x^5}{5!} + \dfrac{x^7}{7!} + \ldots = \sum\limits_{r=0}^{\infty} \dfrac{x^{2r+1}}{(2r+1)!}$.

7. $\cosh x = 1 + \dfrac{x^2}{2!} + \dfrac{x^4}{4!} + \dfrac{x^6}{6!} + \ldots = \sum\limits_{r=0}^{\infty} \dfrac{x^{2r}}{(2r)!}$.

8. $\tanh x = x - \dfrac{x^3}{3} + \dfrac{2}{15} x^5 - \dfrac{17}{315} x^7 + \ldots$

9. $\log(1+x) = x - \dfrac{x^2}{2} + \dfrac{x^3}{3} - \dfrac{x^4}{4} + \dfrac{x^5}{5} - \ldots = \sum\limits_{r=1}^{\infty} \dfrac{(-1)^{r-1} x^r}{r}$.

10. $\log(1-x) = -x - \dfrac{x^2}{2} - \dfrac{x^3}{3} - \dfrac{x^4}{4} - \dfrac{x^5}{5} - \ldots = -\sum\limits_{r=1}^{\infty} \dfrac{x^r}{r}$.

11. $(1+x)^n = 1 + nx + \dfrac{n(n-1)}{2!} x^2 + \dfrac{n(n-1)(n-2)}{3!} x^3 + \ldots$ Binomial series.

12. $\dfrac{1}{1+x} = (1+x)^{-1} = 1 - x + x^2 - x^3 + x^4 - x^5 + \ldots$ for $|x| < 1$.

13. $\dfrac{1}{1-x} = (1-x)^{-1} = 1 + x + x^2 + x^3 + x^4 + x^5 + \ldots$

8.4 METHODS OF EXPANSIONS OF FUNCTIONS

We have seen that a function to be expanded in powers of x by Maclaurin's theorem requires successive differentiation of function, which may not be always convenient. Other methods of expansions of functions may be classified as follows :

(I) Use of Standard Expansions.
(II) Use of Differentiation and Integration.
(III) Use of Substitutions.
(IV) Use of Complex Numbers.
(V) Use of Leibnitz's Theorem.

8.5 ILLUSTRATIONS ON EXPANSIONS OF FUNCTIONS

Type I : Use of Standard Expansion :

When we require only the first few terms of an expansion, it is often convenient to use standard expansions.

Note : Care should be taken not to omit any term of an order, lower than or the same as that of highest order term required.

Ex. 1 : *Expand $(1 + x)^x$ in ascending powers of x, expansion being correct upto fifth power of x.* **(Jan. 2004; Dec. 2007; May 2006, 2007)**

Sol. : Let
$$y = (1 + x)^x$$
$$\therefore \quad \log y = x \log (1 + x)$$
$$= x \left(x - \frac{x^2}{2} + \frac{x^3}{3} - \frac{x^4}{4} + \frac{x^5}{5} - \ldots \right) \quad \text{(by algorithmic series)}$$
$$= x^2 - \frac{x^3}{2} + \frac{x^4}{3} - \frac{x^5}{4} + \frac{x^6}{5} - \ldots$$
$$= z, \text{ say}$$
$$\therefore \quad y = e^z$$
$$= 1 + z + \frac{z^2}{2!} + \frac{z^3}{3!} + \ldots \quad \text{(by exponential series)}$$
$$= 1 + \left(x^2 - \frac{x^3}{2} + \frac{x^4}{3} - \frac{x^5}{4} - \ldots \right) + \frac{1}{2} \left(x^2 - \frac{x^3}{2} + \frac{x^4}{3} - \ldots \right)^2$$
$$+ \frac{1}{6} \left(x^2 - \frac{x^3}{2} + \ldots \right)^3 + \ldots$$

Neglecting x^6 and higher powers of x, we get
$$= 1 + \left(x^2 - \frac{x^3}{2} + \frac{x^4}{3} - \frac{x^5}{4} \right) + \frac{1}{2} (x^4 - x^5) + \ldots$$
$$= 1 + x^2 - \frac{1}{2} x^3 + \frac{5}{6} x^4 - \frac{3}{4} x^5 + \ldots$$

which is the required expansion.

Ex. 2 : *Expand $(1 + x)^{1/x}$ upto the term containing x^2.* **(May 2004, 2011)**

Sol. : Let
$$y = (1 + x)^{1/x}$$
$$\therefore \quad \log y = \frac{1}{x} \log (1 + x) = \frac{1}{x} \left(x - \frac{x^2}{2} + \frac{x^3}{3} - \ldots \right) \quad \text{(by logarithmic series)}$$
$$= \left(1 - \frac{x}{2} + \frac{x^2}{3} - \ldots \right)$$
$$\therefore \quad y = e^{\left(1 - \frac{x}{2} + \frac{x^2}{3} - \ldots \right)}$$
$$= e^1 e^z \qquad \text{where } z = \left(-\frac{x}{2} + \frac{x^2}{3} - \ldots \right)$$
$$= e \left[1 + z + \frac{z^2}{2!} + \ldots \right], \text{ by exponential series.}$$
$$= e \left[1 + \left(-\frac{x}{2} + \frac{x^2}{3} \ldots \right) + \frac{1}{2} \left(-\frac{x}{2} + \frac{x^2}{3} \ldots \right)^2 + \ldots \right]$$
$$= e \left[1 - \frac{x}{2} + \frac{x^2}{3} + \frac{x^2}{8} + \ldots \right] \quad \text{(on retaining terms upto } x^2\text{)}$$
$$= e \left[1 - \frac{x}{2} + \frac{11}{24} x^2 + \ldots \right]$$

Ex. 3 : If $x = y - \frac{1}{2}y^2 + \frac{1}{3}y^3 - \frac{1}{4}y^4 + \ldots\ldots$, prove that

$$y = x + \frac{x^2}{2!} + \frac{x^3}{3!} + \frac{x^4}{4!} + \ldots\ldots \text{ and conversely.}$$

Sol. : We know that the expression on the R.H.S. is a logarithmic series. Hence

$$x = \log(1+y)$$
$$\therefore \quad e^x = 1 + y$$
$$\therefore \quad y = e^x - 1$$
$$= \left(1 + x + \frac{x^2}{2!} + \frac{x^3}{3!} + \frac{x^4}{4!} + \ldots\ldots\right) - 1 \quad \text{(by exponential series)}$$
$$\therefore \quad y = x + \frac{x^2}{2!} + \frac{x^3}{3!} + \frac{x^4}{4!} + \ldots\ldots$$

Conversely : Let $\quad y = x + \frac{x^2}{2!} + \frac{x^3}{3!} + \frac{x^4}{4!} + \ldots\ldots$

Adding 1 on both sides, we get

$$1 + y = 1 + x + \frac{x^2}{2!} + \frac{x^3}{3!} + \frac{x^4}{4!} + \ldots\ldots$$
$$= e^x$$
$$\therefore \quad x = \log(1+y)$$
$$= y - \frac{y^2}{2} + \frac{y^3}{3} - \frac{y^4}{4} + \ldots\ldots \quad \text{(by logarithmic series)}$$

Ex. 4 : Prove that $\cos^2 x = 1 + \sum_{n=1}^{\infty} \frac{(-1)^n 2^{2n-1} x^{2n}}{(2n)!}$.

Sol. : We know that,

$$\cos^2 x = \frac{1}{2}(1 + \cos 2x)$$

Replacing x by 2x in the expansion of cos x,

$$\cos^2 x = \frac{1}{2}\left\{1 + \left(1 - \frac{2^2 x^2}{2!} + \frac{2^4 x^4}{4!} - \frac{2^6 x^6}{6!} + \ldots\right)\right\}$$

$$= \frac{1}{2}\left\{2 + \sum_{n=1}^{\infty} \frac{(-1)^n x^{2n} 2^{2n}}{2n!}\right\}$$

$$= \frac{2}{2} + \sum_{n=1}^{\infty} \frac{(-1)^n 2^{2n} x^{2n}}{2(2n)!}$$

$$= 1 + \sum_{n=1}^{\infty} \frac{(-1)^n 2^{2n-1} x^{2n}}{(2n)!}$$

Ex. 5 : *Show that* $e^{x \cos x} = 1 + x + \dfrac{x^2}{2} - \dfrac{x^3}{3} - \dfrac{11x^4}{24} + \ldots\ldots$ (Jan. 2005, Dec. 2006)

Sol. : Let $x \cos x = y$

$\therefore \quad e^{x \cos x} = e^y$

$= 1 + y + \dfrac{y^2}{2!} + \dfrac{y^3}{3!} + \dfrac{y^4}{4!} + \ldots\ldots$ (by exponential series)

$= 1 + x\left(1 - \dfrac{x^2}{2} + \dfrac{x^4}{24} + \ldots\right) + \dfrac{x^2}{2}\left(1 - \dfrac{x^2}{2} + \ldots\right)^2 \quad \begin{cases} \because x \cos x = \\ x\left(1 - \dfrac{x^2}{2} + \dfrac{x^4}{24} - \ldots\ldots\right) \end{cases}$

$+ \dfrac{x^3}{6}\left(1 - \dfrac{x^2}{2} + \ldots\right)^3 + \dfrac{x^4}{24}\left(1 - \dfrac{x^2}{2} + \ldots\right)^4 + \ldots\ldots$

$= 1 + \left(x - \dfrac{x^3}{2}\right) + \dfrac{x^2}{2}\left\{1 + 2\left(-\dfrac{x^2}{2} + \ldots\right) + (\ldots)^2\right\} + \dfrac{x^3}{6}(1) + \dfrac{x^4}{24}(1) + \ldots$

$= 1 + x - \dfrac{x^3}{2} + \dfrac{x^2}{2} - \dfrac{x^4}{2} + \dfrac{x^3}{6} + \dfrac{x^4}{24} + \ldots\ldots$

$= 1 + x + \dfrac{x^2}{2} - \dfrac{x^3}{3} - \dfrac{11}{24}x^4 + \ldots\ldots$

Note : We consider only those terms which contribute the expansion upto x^4.

Ex. 6 : *Show that* $e^{e^x} = e\left(1 + x + x^2 + \dfrac{5}{6}x^3 + \dfrac{5}{8}x^4 + \ldots\ldots\right)$ (Dec. 2005)

Sol. : By exponential series, we have

$e^x = 1 + x + \dfrac{x^2}{2!} + \dfrac{x^3}{3!} + \dfrac{x^4}{4!} + \ldots\ldots = 1 + y$, where

$y = x + \dfrac{1}{2}x^2 + \dfrac{1}{6}x^3 + \dfrac{1}{24}x^4 + \ldots\ldots$

$\therefore \quad e^{e^x} = e^{1+y} = e^1 \cdot e^y$ (Note this step)

$= e\left(1 + y + \dfrac{y^2}{2!} + \dfrac{y^3}{3!} + \ldots\right)$

$= e\left[1 + \left(x + \dfrac{1}{2}x^2 + \dfrac{1}{6}x^3 + \dfrac{1}{24}x^4 + \ldots\right) + \dfrac{1}{2}\left(x + \dfrac{1}{2}x^2 + \dfrac{1}{6}x^3 + \ldots\right)^2 \right.$

$\left. + \dfrac{1}{6}\left(x + \dfrac{1}{2}x^2 + \dfrac{1}{6}x^3 + \ldots\right)^3 + \dfrac{1}{24}(x + \ldots)^4 + \ldots\right]$

$= e\left[1 + \left(x + \dfrac{1}{2}x^2 + \dfrac{1}{6}x^3 + \dfrac{1}{24}x^4 + \ldots\right) + \dfrac{x^2}{2}\left(1 + \dfrac{x}{2} + \dfrac{x^2}{6} + \ldots\right)^2 \right.$

$\left. + \dfrac{x^3}{6}\left(1 + \dfrac{x}{2} + \dfrac{x^2}{6} + \ldots\right)^3 + \dfrac{x^4}{24}\left(1 + \dfrac{x}{2} + \ldots\right)^4 + \ldots\right]$

$$= e\left[1 + \left(x + \frac{x^2}{2} + \frac{x^3}{6} + \frac{x^4}{24} + \ldots\right) + \frac{x^2}{2}\left(1 + \frac{x^2}{4} + x + \frac{x^2}{3} \ldots\right)\right.$$

$$\left. + \frac{x^3}{6}\left(1 + \frac{3x}{2} + \ldots\right) + \frac{x^4}{24}\left(1 + \frac{x^4}{2}\right) + \ldots\right]$$

(on retaining terms upto x^4 only)

$$= e\left[1 + x + \left(\frac{1}{2} + \frac{1}{2}\right)x^2 + \left(\frac{1}{6} + \frac{1}{2} + \frac{1}{6}\right)x^3 + \left(\frac{1}{24} + \frac{7}{24} + \frac{1}{4} + \frac{1}{24}\right)x^4 + \ldots\right]$$

$$= e\left[1 + x + x^2 + \frac{5}{6}x^3 + \frac{5}{8}x^4 + \ldots\ldots\right]$$

Ex. 7 : *Show that* $\log\left[\dfrac{1 + e^{2x}}{e^x}\right] = \log 2 + \dfrac{x^2}{2} - \dfrac{x^4}{12} + \dfrac{x^6}{45} \ldots\ldots$

(May 2005; Dec. 2006, 2007, 2009)

Sol. : Let $\log\left[\dfrac{1 + e^{2x}}{e^x}\right] = \log\left\{(e^{-x} + e^{x})\dfrac{2}{2}\right\} = \log(2\cosh x)$

$$= \log 2 + \log \cosh x$$

$$= \log 2 + \log\left[1 + \left(\frac{x^2}{2!} + \frac{x^4}{4!} + \frac{x^6}{6!} + \ldots\right)\right]$$

$$= \log 2 + \left(\frac{x^2}{2} + \frac{x^4}{24} + \frac{x^6}{720} + \ldots\right) - \frac{1}{2}\left(x^2 + \frac{x^4}{24} + \frac{x^6}{720} + \ldots\ldots\right)^2$$

$$+ \frac{\left(\dfrac{x^2}{2} + \dfrac{x^4}{24} + \dfrac{x^6}{720} + \ldots\right)^3}{3} + \ldots\ldots$$

$$= \log 2 + \frac{x^2}{2} + \frac{x^4}{24} + \frac{x^6}{720} - \frac{x^6}{48} + \frac{x^6}{24} + \ldots\ldots$$

$$= \log 2 + \frac{x^2}{2} - \frac{x^4}{12} + \frac{x^6}{45} \ldots\ldots$$

Ex. 8 : *Expand* $\sqrt{1 + \sin x}$ *upto* x^6. (May 2004, 2005, 2009, 2013; Dec. 2006)

Sol. : Let

$$y = \sqrt{1 + \sin x} = \sqrt{\left(\sin^2\frac{x}{2} + \cos^2\frac{x}{2}\right) + 2\sin\frac{x}{2}\cos\frac{x}{2}}$$

$$= \sqrt{\left(\sin\frac{x}{2} + \cos\frac{x}{2}\right)^2}$$

$$= \sin\frac{x}{2} + \cos\frac{x}{2}$$

$$= \left[\left(\frac{x}{2}\right) - \frac{1}{3!}\left(\frac{x}{2}\right)^3 + \frac{1}{5!}\left(\frac{x}{2}\right)^5 - \ldots\right] + \left[1 - \frac{1}{2!}\left(\frac{x}{2}\right)^2 + \frac{1}{4!}\left(\frac{x}{2}\right)^4 - \ldots\right]$$

$$= 1 + \frac{x}{2} - \frac{x^2}{8} - \frac{x^3}{48} + \frac{x^4}{384} + \frac{x^5}{3840} - \frac{x^6}{46080} \ldots$$

Ex. 9 : Expand $\dfrac{x}{e^x-1}$ upto x^4. Hence prove that no odd powers of x occur in the expansion in ascending powers of x of the function $\dfrac{x}{2}\left(\dfrac{e^x+1}{e^x-1}\right)$. **(Dec. 2010)**

Sol. :
$$\dfrac{x}{e^x-1} = \dfrac{x}{\left(1+x+\dfrac{x^2}{2!}+\dfrac{x^3}{3!}+\dfrac{x^4}{4!}+\dfrac{x^5}{5!}+\ldots\right)-1}$$

$$= \dfrac{1}{\left(1+\dfrac{x}{2}+\dfrac{x^2}{6}+\dfrac{x^3}{24}+\dfrac{x^4}{120}+\ldots\right)}$$

$$= \left[1+\left(\dfrac{x}{2}+\dfrac{x^2}{6}+\dfrac{x^3}{24}+\dfrac{x^4}{120}+\ldots\right)\right]^{-1}$$

$$= 1-\left(\dfrac{x}{2}+\dfrac{x^2}{6}+\dfrac{x^3}{24}+\dfrac{x^4}{120}+\ldots\right)+\left(\dfrac{x}{2}+\dfrac{x^2}{6}+\dfrac{x^3}{24}+\dfrac{x^4}{120}+\ldots\right)^2$$

$$-\left(\dfrac{x}{2}+\dfrac{x^2}{6}+\dfrac{x^3}{24}+\dfrac{x^4}{120}+\ldots\right)^3+\left(\dfrac{x}{2}+\dfrac{x^2}{6}+\dfrac{x^3}{24}+\dfrac{x^4}{120}+\ldots\right)^4+\ldots$$

$$\{\because (1+x)^{-1}=1-x+x^2-x^3+\ldots\}$$

On retaining the terms upto fourth power of x, we get

$$= 1-\left(\dfrac{x}{2}+\dfrac{x^2}{6}+\dfrac{x^3}{24}+\dfrac{x^4}{120}\right)+\left\{\dfrac{x^2}{4}+\dfrac{x^4}{36}+2\left(\dfrac{x}{2}\cdot\dfrac{x^2}{6}+\dfrac{x}{2}\dfrac{x^3}{24}\right)\right\}$$

$$-\left\{\dfrac{x^3}{8}+3\left(\dfrac{x^2}{4}\right)\cdot\left(\dfrac{x^2}{6}\right)\right\}+\left\{\left(\dfrac{x^4}{16}\right)\right\}+\ldots\ldots$$

$$= 1-\dfrac{x}{2}-\left(-\dfrac{1}{6}+\dfrac{1}{4}\right)x^2+\left(-\dfrac{1}{24}+\dfrac{1}{6}-\dfrac{1}{8}\right)x^3$$

$$+\left(-\dfrac{1}{120}+\dfrac{1}{36}+\dfrac{1}{24}-\dfrac{1}{8}+\dfrac{1}{6}\right)x^4+\ldots\ldots$$

$$= 1-\dfrac{x}{2}+\dfrac{x^2}{12}-\dfrac{x^4}{720}+\ldots\ldots \qquad \ldots (1)$$

For the second part, we write

$$\dfrac{x}{2}\left(\dfrac{e^x+1}{e^x-1}\right) = \dfrac{x}{2}\left(1+\dfrac{2}{e^x-1}\right)$$

$$= \dfrac{x}{2}+\dfrac{x}{e^x-1} \qquad \ldots (2)$$

Substituting the result (1) in (2), we get

$$= \dfrac{x}{2}+\left(1-\dfrac{x}{2}+\dfrac{x^2}{12}-\dfrac{x^4}{720}\ldots\ldots\right)$$

$$= 1+\dfrac{x^2}{12}-\dfrac{x^4}{720}+\ldots\ldots$$

Hence no odd powers of x occur in the expansion.

Ex. 10 : *Prove that* $\tan^{-1}\left(\dfrac{x \sin \theta}{1 - x \cos \theta}\right) = x \sin \theta + \dfrac{x^2}{2} \sin 2\theta + \dfrac{x^3}{3} \sin 3\theta + \ldots$

Sol. : Let $\quad y = \tan^{-1}\left(\dfrac{x \sin \theta}{1 - x \cos \theta}\right)$

$\therefore \quad \tan y = \dfrac{x \sin \theta}{1 - x \cos \theta}$

$\therefore \quad \dfrac{e^{iy} - e^{-iy}}{i(e^{iy} + e^{-iy})} = \dfrac{x \sin \theta}{1 - x \cos \theta}$

i.e. $\quad \dfrac{e^{iy} - e^{-iy}}{e^{iy} + e^{-iy}} = \dfrac{xi \sin \theta}{1 - x \cos \theta} \quad \left\{\text{If } \dfrac{A}{B} = \dfrac{C}{D} \text{ then } \dfrac{A + B}{A - B} = \dfrac{C + D}{C - D}\right\}$

$\therefore \quad e^{2iy} = \dfrac{1 - xe^{-i\theta}}{1 - xe^{i\theta}}$

$\therefore \quad 2iy = \log\left(\dfrac{1 - xe^{-i\theta}}{1 - xe^{i\theta}}\right)$

$\qquad = \log(1 - xe^{-i\theta}) - \log(1 - xe^{i\theta})$

$\qquad = \left[-xe^{-i\theta} - \dfrac{x^2 e^{-2i\theta}}{2} - \ldots\right] - \left[-xe^{i\theta} - \dfrac{x^2 e^{2i\theta}}{2} - \ldots\right]$

$\qquad = x(e^{i\theta} - e^{-i\theta}) + \dfrac{x^2}{2}(e^{2i\theta} - e^{-2i\theta}) + \dfrac{x^3}{3}(e^{3i\theta} - e^{-3i\theta}) + \ldots$

$\qquad = x \cdot 2i \sin \theta + \dfrac{x^2}{2} 2i \sin 2\theta + \dfrac{x^3}{3} 2i \sin 3\theta + \ldots$

$\therefore \quad y = x \sin \theta + \dfrac{x^2}{2} \sin 2\theta + \dfrac{x^3}{3} \sin 3\theta + \ldots$

Ex. 11 : *Prove that* $\log x = \log 2 + \left(\dfrac{x}{2} - 1\right) - \dfrac{1}{2}\left(\dfrac{x}{2} - 1\right)^2 + \dfrac{1}{3}\left(\dfrac{x}{2} - 1\right)^3 + \ldots$

Sol. : $\log x = \log(x + 2 - 2)$

$\qquad = \log\left[2\left(\dfrac{x}{2} - 1 + 1\right)\right] = \log 2 + \log\left[1 + \left(\dfrac{x}{2} - 1\right)\right]$

$\qquad = \log 2 + \left(\dfrac{x}{2} - 1\right) - \dfrac{1}{2}\left(\dfrac{x}{2} - 1\right)^2 + \dfrac{1}{3}\left(\dfrac{x}{2} - 1\right)^3 + \ldots$

Ex. 12 : *Expand* $\log(1 + x + x^2 + x^3)$ *upto a term in* x^8. **(Jan. 2005)**

Sol. : Let $\quad f(x) = \log(1 + x + x^2 + x^3)$

$\qquad = \log\left[\dfrac{(1 + x + x^2 + x^3)(1 - x)}{(1 - x)}\right]$

$\qquad = \log\left[\dfrac{1 - x^4}{1 - x}\right]$

$\qquad = \log(1 - x^4) - \log(1 - x)$

$\qquad = \left[-x^4 - \dfrac{x^8}{2} - \ldots\right] - \left[-x - \dfrac{x^2}{2} - \dfrac{x^3}{3} - \dfrac{x^4}{4} - \dfrac{x^5}{5} - \dfrac{x^6}{6} - \dfrac{x^7}{7} - \dfrac{x^8}{8}\right]$

$\qquad = x + \dfrac{x^2}{2} + \dfrac{x^3}{3} - \dfrac{3}{4} x^4 + \dfrac{1}{5} x^5 + \dfrac{1}{6} x^6 + \dfrac{1}{7} x^7 - \dfrac{3}{8} x^8 \ldots$

Ex. 13 : *Prove that* $\cos x \cosh x = 1 - \dfrac{2^2 x^4}{4!} + \dfrac{2^4 x^8}{8!} \ldots\ldots\ldots$ (May 2004, Dec. 2005)

Sol. : $\cos x \cosh x = \left[1 - \dfrac{x^2}{2!} + \dfrac{x^4}{4!} - \dfrac{x^6}{6!} + \dfrac{x^8}{8!}\right] \times \left[1 + \dfrac{x^2}{2!} + \dfrac{x^4}{4!} + \dfrac{x^6}{6!} + \dfrac{x^8}{8!} + \ldots\right]$

$= \left[\left(1 + \dfrac{x^4}{4!} + \dfrac{x^8}{8!} + \ldots\right) - \left(\dfrac{x^2}{2!} + \dfrac{x^6}{6!} + \ldots\right) \times \right.$

$\left. \left(1 + \dfrac{x^4}{4!} + \dfrac{x^8}{8!} + \ldots\right) + \left(\dfrac{x^2}{2!} + \dfrac{x^6}{6!} + \ldots\right)\right]$

$= \left[1 + \dfrac{x^4}{4!} + \dfrac{x^8}{8!} + \ldots\right]^2 - \left[\dfrac{x^2}{2!} + \dfrac{x^6}{6!} + \ldots\right]^2$

$= \left[1 + \dfrac{x^8}{(4!)^2} + 2\dfrac{x^4}{(4!)} + 2\dfrac{x^8}{8!}\right] - \left[\dfrac{x^4}{(2!)^2} + \dfrac{x^8}{6!}\right],$

on retaining terms upto x^8

$= 1 + (2 - 6)\dfrac{x^4}{4!} + (70 + 2 - 56)\dfrac{x^8}{8!} + \ldots\ldots$

$= 1 - 4\dfrac{x^4}{4!} + 16\dfrac{x^8}{8!} + \ldots\ldots$

$= 1 - \dfrac{2^2 x^4}{4!} + \dfrac{2^4 x^8}{8!} + \ldots\ldots$

Ex. 14 : *Prove that* $\log\left[\log(1+x)^{1/x}\right] = -\dfrac{x}{2} + \dfrac{5}{24}x^2 - \dfrac{1}{8}x^3 + \dfrac{251}{2880}x^4 \ldots\ldots\ldots$

(May 2008)

Sol. : We have,

$\log(1+x)^{1/x} = \dfrac{1}{x}\log(1+x)$

$= \dfrac{1}{x}\left(x - \dfrac{x^2}{2} + \dfrac{x^3}{3} - \dfrac{x^4}{4} + \dfrac{x^5}{5} - \ldots\right)$ (By logarithmic series)

$= 1 - \dfrac{1}{2}x + \dfrac{1}{3}x^2 - \dfrac{1}{4}x^3 + \dfrac{1}{5}x^4 \ldots$

$= 1 - \dfrac{1}{2}x\left(1 - \dfrac{2}{3}x + \dfrac{x^2}{2} - \dfrac{2}{5}x^3 \ldots\right)$

$= 1 - y,$ where $y = \dfrac{x}{2}\left(1 - \dfrac{2}{3}x + \dfrac{x^2}{2} - \dfrac{2}{5}x^3 \ldots\right)$

$\therefore \quad \log\left[\log(1+x)^{1/x}\right] = \log(1 - y)$

$= -\left[y + \dfrac{y^2}{2} + \dfrac{y^3}{3} + \dfrac{y^4}{4} + \ldots\right]$

$= -\left[\dfrac{x}{2}\left(1 - \dfrac{2}{3}x + \dfrac{x^2}{2} - \dfrac{2}{5}x^3 \ldots\right) + \dfrac{1}{2}\dfrac{x^2}{4}\left(1 - \dfrac{2}{3}x + \dfrac{x^2}{2} \ldots\right)^2 \right.$

$\left. + \dfrac{1}{3}\dfrac{x^3}{8}\left(1 - \dfrac{2}{3}x + \dfrac{1}{2}x^2 \ldots\right)^3 + \dfrac{1}{4}\dfrac{x^4}{16}\left(1 - \dfrac{2}{3}x \ldots\right)^4 + \ldots\right]$

$$= -\left[\left(\frac{x}{2}-\frac{x^2}{3}+\frac{x^3}{4}-\frac{x^4}{5}\ldots\right)+\frac{x^2}{8}\left(1+\frac{4}{9}x^2-\frac{4}{3}x+x^2\ldots\right)-\frac{x^3}{24}(1-2x)-\frac{x^4}{64}\ldots\right]$$

$$= -\left[\frac{x}{2}+\left(-\frac{1}{3}+\frac{1}{8}\right)x^2+\left(\frac{1}{4}-\frac{1}{6}-\frac{1}{24}\right)x^3+\left(-\frac{1}{5}+\frac{13}{72}+\frac{1}{12}-\frac{1}{64}\right)x^4+\ldots\right]$$

$$= -\frac{x}{2}+\frac{5}{24}x^2-\frac{1}{8}x^3+\frac{251}{2880}x^4 \ldots\ldots$$

Type II : Use of Differentiation and Integration :

Sometimes the differentiation of the given function results into a function whose expansion can be easily obtained. Hence we expand this derivative result and then integrate it term by term between the limits 0 to x to obtain expansion of given function.

Ex. 15 : *Prove that* $\tan^{-1}x = x - \frac{x^3}{3}+\frac{x^5}{5}-\frac{x^7}{7}+\ldots\ldots$ **(Dec. 2006)**

Sol. : Let $\quad y = \tan^{-1}x,\quad$ then $\quad \frac{dy}{dx} = \frac{1}{1+x^2} = (1+x^2)^{-1}$

Expanding $(1+x^2)^{-1}$, we have

$$\frac{dy}{dx} = 1 - x^2 + x^4 - x^6 + x^8 - \ldots\ldots$$

Integrating both sides w.r.t. x, between 0 to x, we get

$$y = [\tan^{-1}x]_0^x = \left[x - \frac{x^3}{3}+\frac{x^5}{5}-\frac{x^7}{7}+\ldots\right]_0^x$$

$\therefore\quad \tan^{-1}x - 0 = x - \frac{x^3}{3}+\frac{x^5}{5}-\frac{x^7}{7}+\ldots\ldots \quad$ (Taking principal value)

$\therefore\quad \tan^{-1}x = x - \frac{x^3}{3}+\frac{x^5}{5}-\frac{x^7}{7}+\ldots\ldots$

Ex. 16 : *Expand* $\sin^{-1}x$ *in ascending powers of x.* **(May 2007, Dec. 2010)**

Sol. : Let $\quad y = \sin^{-1}x,\quad$ then $\quad \frac{dy}{dx} = \frac{1}{\sqrt{1-x^2}} = (1-x^2)^{-1/2}$

Expanding by Binomial theorem,

$$\frac{dy}{dx} = 1 + \left(-\frac{1}{2}\right)(-x^2) + \frac{\left(-\frac{1}{2}\right)\left(-\frac{1}{2}-1\right)}{2!}(-x^2)^2 + \frac{\left(-\frac{1}{2}\right)\left(-\frac{1}{2}-1\right)\left(-\frac{1}{2}-2\right)}{3!}(-x^2)^3 + \ldots$$

$\therefore\quad \frac{dy}{dx} = 1 + \frac{1}{2}x^2 + \frac{1.3}{2.4}x^4 + \frac{1.3.5}{2.4.6}x^6 + \ldots$

Integrating both sides w.r.t. x, between the limits 0 to x, we get

$$y = [\sin^{-1}x]_0^x = \left[x + \frac{1}{2}\frac{x^3}{3}+\frac{1.3}{2.4}\frac{x^5}{5}+\frac{1.3.5}{2.4.6}\frac{x^7}{7}+\ldots\right]_0^x$$

$\therefore\quad \sin^{-1}x = x + \frac{1}{2}\frac{x^3}{3}+\frac{1.3}{2.4}\frac{x^5}{5}+\frac{1.3.5}{2.4.6}\frac{x^7}{7}+\ldots\ldots$

$\left[\textbf{Note :}\text{ Similarly, we can obtain }\cos^{-1}x = \frac{\pi}{2}-\left(x+\frac{x^3}{6}+\frac{3}{40}x^5+\ldots\right)\right].$

Ex. 17 : *Prove that* $\log(\sec x) = \dfrac{x^2}{2} + \dfrac{1}{3}\dfrac{x^4}{4} + \dfrac{2}{15}\dfrac{x^6}{6} + \ldots\ldots$ (Dec. 2005, May 2008)

Sol. : Let $y = \log(\sec x)$, then $\dfrac{dy}{dx} = \tan x$

$\therefore \quad \dfrac{dy}{dx} = \tan x = x + \dfrac{x^3}{3} + \dfrac{2}{15}x^5 + \ldots\ldots$

Integrating both sides w.r.t. x, between the limits 0 to x, we get

$[\log(\sec x)]_0^x = \left[\dfrac{x^2}{2} + \dfrac{1}{3}\dfrac{x^4}{4} + \dfrac{2}{15}\dfrac{x^6}{6} + \ldots\ldots\right]_0^x$

$[\log(\sec x) - 0] = \dfrac{x^2}{2} + \dfrac{1}{3}\dfrac{x^4}{4} + \dfrac{2}{15}\dfrac{x^6}{6} + \ldots\ldots$

$\therefore \quad \log(\sec x) = \dfrac{x^2}{2} + \dfrac{1}{3}\dfrac{x^4}{4} + \dfrac{2}{15}\dfrac{x^6}{6} + \ldots\ldots$

Standard Expansions for Ready Reference :

1. $\sin^{-1} x = x + \dfrac{1}{2}\dfrac{x^3}{3} + \dfrac{1}{2}\dfrac{3}{4}\dfrac{x^5}{5} + \dfrac{1}{2}\dfrac{3}{4}\dfrac{5}{6}\dfrac{x^7}{7} + \ldots\ldots$

2. $\cos^{-1} x = \dfrac{\pi}{2} - \left[x + \dfrac{1}{2}\dfrac{x^3}{3} + \dfrac{1}{2}\dfrac{3}{4}\dfrac{x^5}{5} + \ldots\ldots\right]$

3. $\tan^{-1} x = x - \dfrac{x^3}{3} + \dfrac{x^5}{5} - \dfrac{x^7}{7} + \ldots\ldots$

4. $\sinh^{-1} x = x - \dfrac{1}{2}\dfrac{x^3}{3} + \dfrac{1}{2}\dfrac{3}{4}\dfrac{x^5}{5} - \dfrac{1}{2}\dfrac{3}{4}\cdot\dfrac{5}{6}\dfrac{x^7}{7} + \ldots\ldots$

5. $\tanh^{-1} x = \dfrac{1}{2}\log\left(\dfrac{1+x}{1-x}\right) = x + \dfrac{x^3}{3} + \dfrac{x^5}{5} + \dfrac{x^7}{7} + \ldots\ldots$

Type III : Use of Substitutions :

Sometimes by convenient substitution the function to be expanded can be reduced to the standard form. The following examples illustrate this method.

Ex. 18 : *Prove that* $\tan^{-1}\left(\dfrac{\sqrt{1+x^2}-1}{x}\right) = \dfrac{1}{2}\left[x - \dfrac{x^3}{3} + \dfrac{x^5}{5} \ldots\right]$. (Jan. 2005, May 2008)

Sol. : Put $x = \tan\theta$

$\therefore \quad \tan^{-1}\left(\dfrac{\sqrt{1+x^2}-1}{x}\right) = \tan^{-1}\left(\dfrac{\sqrt{1+\tan^2\theta}-1}{\tan\theta}\right)$

$= \tan^{-1}\left(\dfrac{\sec\theta - 1}{\tan\theta}\right) = \tan^{-1}\left(\dfrac{1-\cos\theta}{\sin\theta}\right)$

$= \tan^{-1}\left(\dfrac{2\sin^2\theta/2}{2\sin\theta/2\cos\theta/2}\right) = \tan^{-1}\left(\dfrac{\sin\theta/2}{\cos\theta/2}\right)$

$= \tan^{-1}(\tan\theta/2) = \dfrac{\theta}{2} = \dfrac{1}{2}\tan^{-1} x$

$= \dfrac{1}{2}\left[x - \dfrac{x^3}{3} + \dfrac{x^5}{5} \ldots\right]$ By standard expansion of $\tan^{-1} x$

Ex. 19 : *Prove that* $\tan^{-1}\left(\dfrac{p-qx}{q+px}\right) = \tan^{-1}\dfrac{p}{q} - \left[x - \dfrac{x^3}{3} + \dfrac{x^5}{5} - \dfrac{x^7}{7} \ldots\ldots\right]$ **(May 2007)**

Sol. : Let
$$y = \tan^{-1}\left(\dfrac{p-qx}{q+px}\right)$$
$$= \tan^{-1}\left(\dfrac{\dfrac{p}{q} - x}{1 + \dfrac{p}{q}x}\right)$$

Now put $\dfrac{p}{q} = \tan\theta$ and $x = \tan\phi$

$\therefore \quad y = \tan^{-1}\left[\dfrac{\tan\theta - \tan\phi}{1 + \tan\theta\cdot\tan\phi}\right]$

i.e. $\quad y = \tan^{-1}[\tan(\theta - \phi)]$

i.e. $\quad y = \theta - \phi$

$\therefore \quad y = \tan^{-1}\dfrac{p}{q} - \tan^{-1}x$

$\therefore \quad y = \tan^{-1}\dfrac{p}{q} - \left[x - \dfrac{x^3}{3} + \dfrac{x^5}{5} - \dfrac{x^7}{7} + \ldots\ldots\right]$

By standard expansion of $\tan^{-1}x$

Ex. 20 : *Expand* $\sin^{-1}\left(\dfrac{2x}{1+x^2}\right)$ *in ascending powers of x.* **(Dec. 2005, May 2010)**

Sol. : Let $\quad y = \sin^{-1}\dfrac{2x}{1+x^2}$

Put $\quad x = \tan\theta,$

$\therefore \quad y = \sin^{-1}\left(\dfrac{2x}{1+x^2}\right) = \sin^{-1}\left(\dfrac{2\tan\theta}{1+\tan^2\theta}\right)$

$\therefore \quad y = \sin^{-1}(\sin 2\theta) = 2\theta = 2\tan^{-1}x$

$\therefore \quad y = 2\left[x - \dfrac{x^3}{3} + \dfrac{x^5}{5} - \dfrac{x^7}{7} + \dfrac{x^9}{9} - \ldots\ldots\right]$ By standard result of $\tan^{-1}x$.

Ex. 21 : *Expand* $\cos^{-1}\dfrac{x - x^{-1}}{x + x^{-1}}$ *in ascending powers of x.* **(Dec. 2007, May 2009)**

Sol. : Let $\quad y = \cos^{-1}\dfrac{x - x^{-1}}{x + x^{-1}} = \cos^{-1}\left(\dfrac{x^2 - 1}{x^2 + 1}\right)$

Put $\quad x = \tan\theta$

$\therefore \quad y = \cos^{-1}\left(\dfrac{\tan^2\theta - 1}{\tan^2\theta + 1}\right) = \cos^{-1}\left[-\left(\dfrac{1 - \tan^2\theta}{1 + \tan^2\theta}\right)\right]$

$\quad y = \cos^{-1}[-\cos 2\theta] = \cos^{-1}[\cos(\pi - 2\theta)]$

$$y = \pi - 2\theta = \pi - 2\tan^{-1} x$$

$$\therefore \quad \cos^{-1}\left(\frac{x - x^{-1}}{x + x^{-1}}\right) = \pi - 2\left[x - \frac{x^3}{3} + \frac{x^5}{5} - \frac{x^7}{7} + \ldots\right]$$

Note : Above example can also be solved by substitution of $x = \cot\frac{\theta}{2}$.

Ex. 22 : *Obtain the expansion of* $\cos^{-1}(\tanh \log x)$. **(Jan. 2004, May 2005)**

Sol. : Since $(\tanh \log x) = \dfrac{e^{\log x} - e^{-\log x}}{e^{\log x} + e^{-\log x}} = \dfrac{x - x^{-1}}{x + x^{-1}} = \dfrac{x^2 - 1}{x^2 + 1}$

$\therefore \quad \cos^{-1}[\tanh \log x] = \cos^{-1}\left(\dfrac{x^2 - 1}{x^2 + 1}\right)$

Now put $\quad x = \tan\theta$

$\therefore \quad \cos^{-1}\left(\dfrac{x^2 - 1}{x^2 + 1}\right) = \cos^{-1}\left(\dfrac{\tan^2\theta - 1}{\tan^2\theta + 1}\right) = \cos(-\cos 2\theta)$

$\qquad\qquad\qquad = \cos^{-1}[\cos(\pi - 2\theta)] = \pi - 2\theta$

$\qquad\qquad\qquad = \pi - 2\tan^{-1} x$

$\therefore \quad \cos^{-1}[\tanh \log x] = \pi - 2\left(x - \dfrac{x^3}{3} + \dfrac{x^5}{5} - \dfrac{x^7}{7} + \ldots\right)$

Type IV : Use of Complex Numbers :

This method requires knowledge of complex numbers and separation of real and imaginary parts. This method can be used only when general term in the expansion of function is required, otherwise we use standard expansions. (i.e. when expansion is required upto limited terms).

Ex. 23 : *Expand* $e^x \cos x$ *in ascending powers of x upto a term in* x^4 *and also find general term of expansion.*

Sol. : We know that

$$e^x \cos x = \text{Real part of } e^x e^{ix} = \text{R.P. of } e^{(1+i)x}$$

$$= \text{R.P. of } \sum_{n=0}^{\infty} \frac{(1+i)^n x^n}{n!} \qquad \left(\because e^x = \sum_{n=0}^{\infty} \frac{x^n}{n!}\right)$$

$$= \sum_{n=0}^{\infty} [\text{R.P. of } (1+i)^n] \frac{x^n}{n!}$$

$$= \sum_{n=0}^{\infty} \left[\text{R.P. of } 2^{n/2}\left(\cos\frac{\pi}{4} + i\sin\frac{\pi}{4}\right)^n\right] \frac{x^n}{n!}$$

$$= \sum_{n=0}^{\infty} \left[\text{R.P. of } 2^{n/2}\left(\cos\frac{n\pi}{4} + i\sin\frac{n\pi}{4}\right)\right] \frac{x^n}{n!}$$

(By Demoivre's theorem)

$$= \sum_{n=0}^{\infty} \left(2^{n/2} \cos \frac{n\pi}{4}\right) \frac{x^n}{n!} \quad \text{(the general term of expansion)}$$

$$= 1 + 2^{1/2} \left(\cos \frac{\pi}{4}\right) x + 2^{2/2} \left(\cos \frac{2\pi}{4}\right) \frac{x^2}{2!} + 2^{3/2} \left(\cos \frac{3\pi}{4}\right) \frac{x^3}{3!}$$

$$+ 2^{4/2} \left(\cos \frac{4\pi}{4}\right) \frac{x^4}{4!} + \ldots\ldots$$

$$= 1 + x - \frac{x^3}{3} - \frac{x^4}{6} + \ldots\ldots$$

Note : If we consider I.P. of $(1 + i)^n$, we get expansion of $e^x \sin x$.

Ex. 24 : *Prove that* $\sin x \sinh x = x^2 - 8 \dfrac{x^6}{6!} + 32 \dfrac{x^{10}}{10!} \ldots\ldots$ **(May 2006)**

Sol. : We know that,

$$\cos(x - ix) = \cos x \cos(ix) + \sin x \sin(ix)$$

i.e. $\quad \cos(1-i)x = \cos x \cosh x + i \sin x \sinh x$

$\therefore \quad \sin x \sinh x = \text{I.P. of } [\cos(1-i)x]$

$$= \text{I.P. of } \sum_{n=0}^{\infty} \frac{(-1)^n (1-i)^{2n} x^{2n}}{(2n!)} \qquad \left(\because \cos x = \sum_{n=0}^{\infty} \frac{(-1)^n x^{2n}}{(2n!)}\right)$$

$$= \sum_{n=0}^{\infty} [\text{I.P. of } (1-i)^{2n}] \frac{(-1)^n x^{2n}}{(2n!)}$$

$$= \sum_{n=0}^{\infty} \left[\text{I.P. of } 2^n \left(\cos \frac{\pi}{2} - i \sin \frac{\pi}{2}\right)^n\right] \frac{(-1)^n x^{2n}}{(2n!)}$$

$$= \sum_{n=0}^{\infty} \left[\text{I.P. of } 2^n \left(\cos \frac{n\pi}{2} - i \sin \frac{n\pi}{2}\right)\right] \frac{(-1)^n x^{2n}}{(2n!)}$$

(By Demoivre's theorem)

$$= \sum_{n=0}^{\infty} \left(-2^n \sin \frac{n\pi}{2}\right) \frac{(-1)^n x^{2n}}{(2n)!}$$

$$= \sum_{n=0}^{\infty} (-1)^{n+1} 2^n \left(\sin \frac{n\pi}{2}\right) \left(\frac{x^{2n}}{(2n)!}\right)$$

$$= 2\left(\sin \frac{\pi}{2}\right) \frac{x^2}{2!} + 2^3 \left(\sin \frac{3\pi}{2}\right) \left(\frac{x^6}{6!}\right) + 2^5 \left(\sin \frac{5\pi}{2}\right) \left(\frac{x^{10}}{10!}\right) + \ldots$$

$$= x^2 - 8 \frac{x^6}{6!} + 32 \frac{x^{10}}{10!} \ldots \quad \left[\because \sin \frac{n\pi}{2} = 0 \text{ when } n \text{ is even.}\right]$$

Ex. 25 : *Prove that* $e^{x \cos \alpha} \cos (x \sin \alpha) = \sum_{n=0}^{\infty} \dfrac{x^n}{n!} \cos n\alpha$.

Sol. : We know that,
$$\cos (x \sin \alpha) = \text{R.P. of } e^{i(x \sin \alpha)}$$
$$\therefore \quad e^{x \cos \alpha} \cos (x \sin \alpha) = \text{R.P. of } e^{(x \cos \alpha)} e^{i(x \sin \alpha)}$$
$$= \text{R.P. of } e^{(\cos \alpha + i \sin \alpha) x}$$
$$= \text{R.P. of } \sum_{n=0}^{\infty} \dfrac{(\cos \alpha + i \sin \alpha)^n x^n}{n!}$$
$$= \sum_{n=0}^{\infty} \text{R.P. of } [(\cos n\alpha + i \sin n\alpha)] \dfrac{x^n}{n!}$$
(By Demoivre's theorem)
$$= \sum_{n=0}^{\infty} \dfrac{x^n}{n!} \cos n\alpha$$

Type V : Use of Leibnitz's theorem :

In this method we obtain a differential equation for the given function and then differentiate this equation n times by Leibnitz's theorem. Putting $x = 0$, in this result, we obtain a relation between successive derivatives at $x = 0$. These results are used to obtain expansion by Maclaurin's theorem.

Ex. 26 : *Expand* $e^{a \sin^{-1} x}$ *by Maclaurin's theorem and find the general term. Hence prove that* $e^\theta = 1 + \sin \theta + \dfrac{1}{2!} \sin^2 \theta + \dfrac{2}{3!} \sin^3 \theta + \dfrac{5}{4!} \sin^4 \theta + \ldots$

Sol. : Let
$$y = e^{a \sin^{-1} x} \quad \ldots (1)$$
$$\therefore \quad y_1 = \dfrac{a e^{a \sin^{-1} x}}{\sqrt{1 - x^2}}$$
i.e.
$$y_1^2 (1 - x^2) = a^2 y^2 \quad \ldots (2)$$
Differentiating and cancelling $2y_1$, we have
$$(1 - x^2) y_2 - x y_1 - a^2 y = 0 \quad \ldots (3)$$
Differentiating n times by Leibnitz's theorem,
$$(1 - x^2) y_{n+2} - (2n + 1) x y_{n+1} - (n^2 + a^2) y_n = 0 \quad \ldots (4)$$
If we put $x = 0$ in (1), (2) and (3) and (4), we get
$$(y)_0 = 1, \quad (y_1)_0 = a, \quad (y_2)_0 = a^2$$
and
$$(y_{n+2})_0 = (n^2 + a^2)(y_n)_0 \quad \ldots (5)$$
When n is odd, put $n = 1, 3, 5 \ldots$ in (5) for general term
$$(y_n)_0 = [(n-2)^2 + a^2] \ldots (3^2 + a^2)(1^2 + a^2) \cdot a$$
When n is even, put $n = 2, 4, 6 \ldots$ in (5)
$$(y_n)_0 = [(n-2)^2 + a^2] \ldots (4^2 + a^2)(2^2 + a^2) \cdot a^2$$
Hence
$$(y_3)_0 = (1^2 + a^2) a \quad \text{and} \quad (y_4)_0 = (2^2 + a^2) a^2$$

Now by Maclaurin's theorem, we have

$$y = y_0 + x(y_1)_0 + \frac{x^2}{2!}(y_2)_0 + \frac{x^3}{3!}(y_3)_0 + \frac{x^4}{4!}(y_4)_0 + \ldots + \frac{x^n}{n!}(y_n)_0 + \ldots$$

$$\therefore \quad e^{a \sin^{-1} x} = 1 + ax + \frac{a^2}{2!}x^2 + \frac{a(1^2 + a^2)}{3!}x^3 + \frac{a^2(2^2 + a^2)}{4!}x^4 + \ldots \quad \ldots (6)$$

General term $\frac{(y_n)_0}{n!} x^n$ can be found depending upon n, being odd or even.

Next, put $x = \sin \theta$ and $a = 1$ in (6)

$$e^{\theta} = 1 + \sin \theta + \frac{1}{2!} \sin^2 \theta + \frac{2}{3!} \sin^3 \theta + \frac{5}{4!} \sin^4 \theta + \ldots$$

Ex. 27 : *Prove that* $e^x = 1 + \tan x + \frac{1}{2!} \tan^2 x - \frac{1}{3!} \tan^3 x - \frac{7}{4!} \tan^4 x \ldots$

Sol. : Let $\tan x = \theta \qquad \therefore \quad x = \tan^{-1} \theta$

and $\qquad y = e^x = e^{\tan^{-1} \theta} \qquad \ldots (1)$

Differentiating (1) w.r.t. θ, we get

$$y_1 = \frac{e^{\tan^{-1} \theta}}{1 + \theta^2}$$

$$\therefore \quad y_1(\theta^2 + 1) = y \qquad \ldots (2)$$

Differentiating (2) n times w.r.t. θ using Leibnitz's theorem, we get

$$y_{n+1}(\theta^2 + 1) + ny_n(2\theta) + \frac{n(n-1)}{2!} y_{n-1}(2) = y_n$$

$$\therefore \quad (\theta^2 + 1) y_{n+1} + (2n\theta - 1) y_n + n(n-1) y_{n-1} = 0 \qquad \ldots (3)$$

If we put $\theta = 0$ in (1), (2), (3), we get

$$(y)_0 = 1, \qquad (y_1)_0 = 1$$

and $\qquad (y_{n+1})_0 = (y_n)_0 - n(n-1)(y_{n-1})_0 \qquad \ldots (4)$

If we put $n = 1, 2, 3 \ldots$ in (4), we get

$$(y_2)_0 = (y_1)_0 = 1, \quad (y_3)_0 = [(y_2)_0 - 2(2-1)(y_1)_0] = -1,$$
$$(y_4)_0 = [(y_3)_0 - 3(3-1)(y_2)_0] = -7, \ldots \text{etc.}$$

By Maclaurin's theorem, we have

$$y = (y)_0 + \theta(y_1)_0 + \frac{\theta^2}{2!}(y_2)_0 + \frac{\theta^3}{3!}(y_3)_0 + \frac{\theta^4}{4!}(y_4)_0 + \ldots \quad \ldots (5)$$

Substituting these results in (5), we get

$$y = e^{\tan^{-1} \theta} = 1 + \theta + \frac{\theta^2}{2!}(1) + \frac{\theta^3}{3!}(-1) + \frac{\theta^4}{4!}(-7) + \ldots$$

$$\therefore \quad e^x = 1 + \tan x + \frac{\tan^2 x}{2!} - \frac{\tan^3 x}{3!} - \frac{7}{4!} \tan^4 x \ldots$$

Note : Problems of this type can also be solved by an algebraic method, in which we assume $e^x = a_0 + a_1 \tan x + a_2 \tan^2 x + a_3 \tan^3 x + a_4 \tan^4 x + \ldots$. We now substitute for $e^x = 1 + x + \frac{x^2}{2!} + \frac{x^3}{3!} + \ldots$, and $\tan x = x + \frac{1}{3}x^3 + \frac{2}{15}x^5 + \ldots$ in the above equation, and equating coefficients of like powers of x on both sides, we get the same result as above.

Ex. 28 : If $y = f(x) = (\sin^{-1} x)^2$ prove that, $f^{n+2}(0) = n^2 f^n(0)$ and

$$y = \frac{2}{2!}x^2 + \frac{2.2^2}{4!}x^4 + \frac{2.2^2.4^2}{6!}x^6 + \ldots$$

Also if $(\sin^{-1} x)^2 = a_0 + a_1 x + a_2 x^2 + \ldots$, prove that $(n+1)(n+2)a_{n+2} = n^2 a_n$.

Sol. : We have $\qquad y = f(x) = (\sin^{-1} x)^2 \qquad \ldots (1)$

$\therefore \qquad y_1 = \dfrac{2 \sin^{-1} x}{\sqrt{1 - x^2}} \qquad \ldots (2)$

or $\qquad y_1^2 (1 - x^2) = 4y$

or $\qquad 2 y_1 y_2 (1 - x^2) - 2x y_1^2 = 4 y_1$

or $\qquad y_2 (1 - x^2) - x y_1 - 2 = 0 \qquad \ldots (3)$

Differentiating (3) n times by Leibnitz's theorem, we have

$$(1 - x^2) y_{n+2} - (2n + 1) x y_{n+1} - n^2 y_n = 0 \qquad \ldots (4)$$

Putting $x = 0$ in (1), (2), (3) and (4), we get

$$(y)_0 = 0, \quad (y_1)_0 = 0, \quad (y_2)_0 = 2 \quad \text{and} \quad (y_{n+2})_0 = n^2 (y_n)_0$$

$\therefore \qquad f^{n+2}(0) = n^2 f^n(0)$, the required first result. $\qquad \ldots (5)$

Next putting $n = 1, 2, 3, 4 \ldots$ in (5), we get

$$(y_3)_0 = 1^2 (y_1)_0 = 0, \quad (y_4)_0 = 2^2 (y_2)_0 = 2^2 \cdot 2, \quad (y_5)_0 = 3^2 (y_3)_0 = 0,$$
$$(y_6)_0 = 4^2 (y_4)_0 = 4^2 \cdot 2^2 \cdot 2 \ldots \text{etc.}$$

Hence by Maclaurin's theorem, we have

$$y = (y)_0 + x (y_1) + \frac{x^2}{2!}(y_2)_0 + \frac{x^3}{3!}(y_3)_0 + \ldots$$

$$= 0 + x(0) + \frac{x^2}{2!}(2) + \frac{x^3}{3!}(0) + \frac{x^4}{4!}(2^2 \cdot 2) + \frac{x^5}{5!}(0) + \frac{x^6}{6!}(4^2 \cdot 2^2 \cdot 2) \ldots$$

$$= \frac{2}{2!}x^2 + \frac{2 \cdot 2^2}{4!}x^4 + \frac{2 \cdot 2^2 \cdot 4^2}{6!}x^6 + \ldots, \text{ the required expansion } \ldots (6)$$

Also if $(\sin^{-1} x)^2 = a_0 + a_1 x + a_2 x^2 + a_3 x^3 + \ldots$ then by Maclaurin's theorem, we have $\qquad f(x) = f(0) + x f'(0) + \dfrac{x^2}{2!} f''(0) + \dfrac{x^3}{3!} f'''(0) \ldots$

Comparing the two, we get

$$a_n = \frac{f^n(0)}{n!} \qquad \ldots (7)$$

If we change n to n + 2, we have

$$a_{n+2} = \frac{f^{n+2}(0)}{(n+2)!} \quad \ldots (8)$$

Dividing (8) by (7),

$$\frac{a_{n+2}}{a_n} = \frac{f^{n+2}(0)}{(n+2)!} \cdot \frac{n!}{f^n(0)} = \frac{(n!)\, f^{n+2}(0)}{(n+2)(n+1)(n!)\, f^n(0)}$$

$$\frac{a_{n+2}}{a_n} = \frac{f^{n+2}(0)}{(n+2)(n+1)\, f^n(0)}$$

$$\therefore \quad (n+2)(n+1)\, a_{n+2} = \frac{f^{n+2}(0)}{f^n(0)}\, a_n = n^2 a_n \qquad \left\{\text{From (5)},\ \frac{f^{n+2}(0)}{f^n(0)} = n^2\right\}$$

Thus, $(n+2)(n+1)\, a_{n+2} = n^2 a_n$

EXERCISE 8.2

1. Prove that

   (i) $x \csc x = 1 + \dfrac{x^2}{6} + \dfrac{7}{360} x^4 + \ldots\ldots$ (Jan. 2004, Dec. 2012)

   (ii) Prove that $\log\left(\dfrac{\sinh x}{x}\right) = \dfrac{x^2}{6} + \dfrac{-x^4}{180} + \dfrac{x^6}{2835} \ldots\ldots$ (May 2004)

   (iii) Prove that $e^{ax} \cos bx = 1 + ax + \dfrac{1}{2}(a^2 - b^2) x^2 + \dfrac{1}{6} a(a^2 - 3b^2) x^3 + \ldots\ldots$

   (iv) Prove that $\log\left(\dfrac{\sin x}{x}\right) = \dfrac{-1}{6} x^2 - \dfrac{1}{180} x^4 - \dfrac{x^6}{2835} \ldots\ldots$

   (v) Prove that $\log \dfrac{xe^x}{e^x - 1} = \dfrac{x}{2} - \dfrac{x^2}{24} + \dfrac{x^4}{2880} \ldots\ldots$ (Dec. 2008)

   [**Hint**: Use simplification, $\log\left(\dfrac{xe^x}{e^x - 1}\right) = -\log\left(\dfrac{1 - e^{-x}}{x}\right)$]

   (vi) Show that $\sqrt{\dfrac{1 + e^x}{2e^x}} = 1 - \dfrac{1}{4} x + \dfrac{3}{32} x^2 \ldots\ldots$ (May 2007)

   [**Hint**: $\sqrt{\dfrac{1 + e^x}{2e^x}} = \dfrac{1}{\sqrt{2}}(1 + e^{-x})^{1/2}$]

   (vii) Prove that $e^x \cos x = 1 + x - \dfrac{x^3}{3} - \dfrac{x^4}{6} + \ldots\ldots$ (May 2004, May 2010)

   (viii) Prove that $\cosh^3 x = \dfrac{1}{4} \sum\limits_{n=0}^{\infty} \dfrac{3^{2n} + 3}{(2n)!} x^{2n}$.

   [**Hint**: $4 \cosh^3 x = \cosh 3x + 3 \cosh x$].

2. Expand $\sin x \cosh x$ in ascending powers of x upto x^5.

   Ans. $\sin x \cosh x = x - \dfrac{2}{3} x^3 - \dfrac{1}{30} x^5 + \ldots\ldots$ (Jan. 2005, May 2010, 2015)

3. Expand $[\log(1+x)]^2$ in the ascending powers of x, correct upto fourth power of x.

   Ans. $x^2 - x^3 + \dfrac{11}{12}x^4 \ldots\ldots$ (May 2008)

4. If $x = y - \dfrac{y^3}{3!} + \dfrac{y^5}{5!} \ldots\ldots$, prove that $y = x + \dfrac{x^3}{6} + \dfrac{3}{40}x^5 + \ldots\ldots$

5. Obtain the expansion of $\sinh^{-1} x$.

   [Hint : $y = \sinh^{-1} x = \log\left(x + \sqrt{x^2+1}\right)$ ∴ $\dfrac{dy}{dx} = (1+x^2)^{-1/2}$, expand by Binomial series and integrate.]

   Ans. $x - \dfrac{1}{2}\dfrac{x^3}{3} + \dfrac{1.3}{2.4}\dfrac{x^5}{5} - \dfrac{1.3.5}{2.4.6}\cdot\dfrac{x^7}{7} + \ldots\ldots$

6. Show that $\log(1 + \tan x) = x - \dfrac{x^2}{2} + \dfrac{2}{3}x^3 - \ldots\ldots$ (Dec. 2007)

7. Prove that

   (i) $\sin^{-1}(3x - 4x^3) = 3\left[x + \dfrac{1}{6}x^3 + \dfrac{3}{40}x^5 + \ldots\right]$ (Jan. 2004)

   [Hint : put $x = \sin\theta$]

   (ii) $\cot^{-1}\left(\dfrac{3x - x^3}{1 - 3x^2}\right) = \dfrac{\pi}{2} - 3\left(x - \dfrac{x^3}{3} + \dfrac{x^5}{5}\ldots\right)$. (May 2011)

   [Hint : put $x = \tan\theta$, $\dfrac{3x - x^3}{1 - 3x^2} = \tan 3\theta$]

   (iii) $\tan^{-1}\sqrt{\dfrac{1-x}{1+x}} = \dfrac{\pi}{4} - \dfrac{1}{2}\left[x + \dfrac{1}{6}x^3 + \dfrac{3}{40}x^5 + \ldots\right]$

   [Hint : put $x = \cos\theta$]

   (iv) $\sinh^{-1}(3x + 4x^3) = 3\left[x - \dfrac{1}{6}x^3 + \dfrac{3}{40}x^5\ldots\right]$

   [Hint : put $x = \sinh\theta$]

   (v) Prove that $\sec^{-1}\left(\dfrac{1}{1 - 2x^2}\right) = 2\left[x + \dfrac{1}{2}\cdot\dfrac{x^3}{3} + \dfrac{1.3}{2.4}\cdot\dfrac{x^5}{5} + \ldots\right]$ (Dec. 2008)

   [Hint : put $x = \sin\theta$]

8. Expand $\cos^{-1}(4x^3 - 3x)$ in ascending powers of x.
   [Hint : put $x = \cos\theta$]

9. If θ^6 is negligible then show that $\dfrac{\tan\theta}{\theta} - \dfrac{\theta^2}{\sin^2\theta} = \dfrac{\theta^4}{15}$.

10. Find the values of a and b such that the expansion of $\log(1+x) - \dfrac{x(1+ax)}{1+bx}$ in the ascending power of x may begin with the terms containing x^4 and hence show that the coefficient of x^4 is $\left(-\dfrac{1}{36}\right)$.

    Ans. $a = \dfrac{1}{6}$, $b = \dfrac{2}{3}$.

11. Show that $\log\left(1 + \dfrac{1}{x}\right) = 2\left\{\dfrac{1}{2x+1} + \dfrac{1}{3(2x+1)^3} + \dfrac{1}{5(2x+1)^5} + \ldots\right\}$.

[**Hint**: $1 + \dfrac{1}{x} = \dfrac{1 + 1/(2x+1)}{1 - 1/(2x+1)}$, now take log and then expand.]

12. Forming a differential equation, expand $\dfrac{\sinh^{-1} x}{\sqrt{1+x^2}}$ in a series of powers of x upto the term in x^7.

Ans. $x - \dfrac{2^2}{3}x^3 + \dfrac{2^2 \cdot 4^2}{5!}x^5 - \dfrac{2^2 \cdot 4^2 \cdot 6^2}{7!}x^7 \ldots$

13. If $y^{1/m} - y^{-1/m} = 2x$, prove that
$$y = 1 + mx + m^2\dfrac{x^2}{2!} - \dfrac{m(m^2-1^2)}{3!}x^3 + \dfrac{m^2(m^2-2^2)}{4!}x^4 \ldots$$

14. If $y = e^{m\tan^{-1} x} = a_0 + a_1 x + a_2 x^2 + \ldots$, then show that
(i) $y = 1 + mx + \dfrac{m^2}{2!}x^2 + \dfrac{m(m^2-2)}{3!}x^3 + \ldots$ (ii) $(n+1)a_n + (n-1)a_{n-1} = m a_n$

[**Hint**: $(y_{n+2})_0 = m(y_{n+1})_0 - n(n+1)(y_n)_0$. Also $a_n = \dfrac{(y_n)_0}{n!}$, $(y_n)_0 = n!\, a_n$,
$(y_{n+1})_0 = a_{n+1}(n+1)!$, $(y_{n-1})_0 = a_{n-1}(n-1)!$.
put $n = n-1$ in above relation, substitute these values.]

15. Show that $\dfrac{\sin^{-1} x}{\sqrt{1-x^2}} = x + \dfrac{2}{3}x^3 + \dfrac{2.4}{3.5}\cdot\dfrac{x^5}{5} + \ldots$

16. Show that $\sin(m\sin^{-1} x) = mx + \dfrac{m(1^2 - m^2)}{3!}x^3 + \dfrac{m(1^2-m^2)(3^2-m^2)}{5!}x^5 + \ldots$

8.6 TAYLOR'S THEOREM

Statement: Let $f(a+h)$ be a function of h, which can be expanded in powers of h and let the expansion be differentiable term by term any number of times with respect to h, then

$$f(a+h) = f(a) + h f'(a) + \dfrac{h^2}{2!}f''(a) + \dfrac{h^3}{3!}f'''(a) + \ldots + \dfrac{h^n}{n!}f^n(a) + \ldots$$

Proof: Let $\quad f(a+h) = A_0 + A_1 h + A_2 h^2 + A_3 h^3 + \ldots \qquad \ldots (1)$

Differentiating (1) successively w.r.t. h, we have
$$f'(a+h) = A_1 + 2A_2 h + 3A_3 h^2 + \ldots$$
$$f''(a+h) = 2.1.A_2 + 3.2.A_3 h + \ldots$$
$$f'''(a+h) = 3.2.1.A_3 + \ldots \text{ etc.}$$

Putting $h = 0$ in each of these, we get
$$A_0 = f(a),\ A_1 = f'(a),\ A_2 = \dfrac{f''(a)}{2!},\ A_3 = \dfrac{f'''(a)}{3!},\ \ldots \text{ etc.}$$

Substituting these values in (1), we get
$$f(a+h) = f(a) + h f'(a) + \dfrac{h^2}{2!}f''(a) + \dfrac{h^3}{3!}f'''(a) + \ldots + \dfrac{h^n}{n!}f^n(a) \ldots \qquad \ldots (2)$$

which proves the theorem.

Deductions:

(a) If we replace a by x in (2), we get expansion in powers of h as

$$f(x+h) = f(x) + h\,f'(x) + \frac{h^2}{2!}f''(x) + \frac{h^3}{3!}f'''(x) + \ldots + \frac{h^n}{n!}f^n(x) + \ldots \qquad \ldots (3)$$

Interchanging h and x in (3), we get expansion in powers of x as

$$f(x+h) = f(h) + x\,f'(h) + \frac{x^2}{2!}f''(h) + \frac{x^3}{3!}f'''(h) + \ldots + \frac{x^n}{n!}f^n(h) + \ldots \qquad \ldots (4)$$

(b) If we put $h = x - a$ in (2), we get more useful form of the Taylor's theorem as

$$f(x) = f(a) + (x-a)f'(a) + \frac{(x-a)^2}{2!}f''(a) + \ldots + \frac{(x-a)^n}{n!}f^n(a) + \ldots \qquad \ldots (5)$$

which is an expansion $f(x)$ in powers of $(x - a)$ or about a.

(c) If we put $a = 0$, $h = x$ in (2), we get Maclaurin's series

$$f(x) = f(0) + x\,f'(0) + \frac{x^2}{2!}f''(0) + \frac{x^3}{3!}f'''(0) + \ldots + \frac{x^n}{n!}f^n(0) + \ldots$$

For this reason, the Maclaurin's theorem is often referred to by the name of Taylor's theorem.

8.7 ILLUSTRATIONS ON TAYLOR'S THEOREM

Ex. 1: *Prove that* $\log(x+h) = \log h + \frac{x}{h} - \frac{x^2}{2h^2} + \frac{x^3}{3h^3} - \ldots$

Sol.: Here we have to expand $\log(x+h)$ in powers of x, hence we shall use the following form of Taylor's theorem.

$$f(x+h) = f(h) + x\,f'(h) + \frac{x^2}{2!}f''(h) + \frac{x^3}{3!}f'''(h) + \ldots$$

Let $\quad f(x+h) = \log(x+h) \qquad \ldots (1)$

$\therefore \quad f(x) = \log x \quad$ hence $\quad f(h) = \log h$

$\quad f'(x) = \frac{1}{x} \quad$ hence $\quad f'(h) = \frac{1}{h}$

$\quad f''(x) = -\frac{1}{x^2} \quad$ hence $\quad f''(h) = \frac{-1}{h^2}$

$\quad f'''(x) = \frac{1}{x^3}\,; \quad$ hence $\quad f'''(h) = \frac{2}{h^3}$ etc.

Putting these values of $f(h)$, $f'(h)$, $f''(h)$ etc. in (1), we get

$$\log(x+h) = \log h + x\left(\frac{1}{h}\right) + \frac{x^2}{2!}\left(-\frac{1}{h^2}\right) + \frac{x^3}{3!}\left(\frac{2}{h^3}\right) + \ldots$$

$$\therefore \quad \log(x+h) = \log h + \frac{x}{h} - \frac{x^2}{2h^3} + \frac{x^3}{3h^3} - \ldots$$

Ex. 2: *Use Taylor's theorem to prove*

$$\tan^{-1}(x+h) = \tan^{-1}x + h\sin z \cdot \frac{\sin z}{1} - (h\sin z)^2 \cdot \frac{\sin 2z}{2} + (h\sin z)^3 \frac{\sin 3z}{3} \ldots,$$

where $z = \cot^{-1}x$.

Sol. : Here we have to expand $\tan^{-1}(x+h)$ in powers of h. Hence we shall use the following form of Taylor's theorem.

$$f(x+h) = f(x) + h f'(x) + \frac{h^2}{2!} f''(x) + \frac{h^3}{3!} f'''(x) + \ldots \qquad \ldots (1)$$

Let $\quad f(x+h) = \tan^{-1}(x+h) \quad \therefore \quad f(x) = \tan^{-1} x$

then $\quad f^n(x) = (-1)^{n-1}(n-1)! \sin^n z \cdot \sin nz$, where $z = \cot^{-1} x$

Putting $n = 1, 2, 3, \ldots\ldots$, we have

$$f'(x) = \sin z \cdot \sin z$$
$$f''(x) = -\sin^2 z \cdot \sin 2z$$
$$f'''(x) = 2! \sin^3 z \cdot \sin 3z \text{ etc.}$$

Putting these values of $f(x), f'(x), f''(x)$ etc. in (1), we get

$$\tan^{-1}(x+h) = \tan^{-1} x + h (\sin z)(\sin z) - \frac{h^2}{2} \sin^2 z \sin 2z$$

$$+ \frac{h^2}{3!} (2 \sin^3 z \cdot \sin 3z) \ldots\ldots$$

$$= \tan^{-1} x + (h \sin z) \frac{\sin z}{1} - (h \sin z)^2 \cdot \frac{\sin 2z}{2}$$

$$+ (h \sin z)^3 \frac{\sin 3z}{3} \ldots\ldots \qquad \text{where } z = \cot^{-1} x \text{ proved.}$$

Ex. 3 : *Expand* $\log \tan\left(\frac{\pi}{4} + x\right)$ *in ascending powers of* x. **(Dec. 2009)**

Sol. : By Taylor's theorem, we have

$$f(x+h) = f(h) + x f'(h) + \frac{x^2}{2!} f''(h) + \frac{x^3}{3!} f'''(h) + \ldots\ldots \qquad \ldots (1)$$

Let $\quad f(x+h) = \log \tan\left(x + \frac{\pi}{4}\right) \quad \therefore \quad f(x) = \log \tan x$

and $\quad f(h) = \log \tan h$, where $h = \frac{\pi}{4}$

Differentiating successively w.r.t. h, we get

$$f'(h) = \frac{\sec^2 h}{\tan h} = 2 \operatorname{cosec} 2h$$

$$f''(h) = -4 \operatorname{cosec} 2h \cot 2h$$

$$f'''(h) = -8 [-\operatorname{cosec} 2h \cot^2 2h - \operatorname{cosec}^3 2h]$$

$$= 8 [\operatorname{cosec} 2h \cot^2 2h + \operatorname{cosec}^3 2h]$$

$$f^{iv}(h) = 16[-\cosec 2h \cot^3 2h - 2 \cot 2h \cosec^2 2h - 3 \cosec^2 2h \cot 2h]$$
$$= -16[\cosec 2h \cot^3 2h + 5 \cosec^3 2h \cot 2h]$$
$$f^{v}(h) = 32[\cosec 2h \cot^4 2h + 3 \cot^2 2h \cosec^3 2h + 5 \cosec^5 2h$$
$$+ 15 \cosec^3 2h \cot^2 2h]$$

Putting $h = \frac{\pi}{4}$, we get

$$f\left(\frac{\pi}{4}\right) = 0, \qquad f'\left(\frac{\pi}{4}\right) = 2, \qquad f''\left(\frac{\pi}{4}\right) = 0,$$
$$f'''\left(\frac{\pi}{4}\right) = 8, \qquad f^{iv}\left(\frac{\pi}{4}\right) = 0, \qquad f^{v}\left(\frac{\pi}{4}\right) = 160$$

Substituting these values in (1), we get

$$\log \tan\left(\frac{\pi}{4} + x\right) = 2x + \frac{4}{3}x^3 + \frac{4}{3}x^5 + \ldots\ldots$$

Note : We can also use standard series expansion as

$$\log \tan\left(\frac{\pi}{4} + x\right) = \log\left(\frac{1 + \tan x}{1 - \tan x}\right) = \log(1 + \tan x) - \log(1 - \tan x)$$
$$= 2 \tan x + 2 \frac{(\tan x)^3}{3} + \frac{2}{5}(\tan x)^5 + \ldots\ldots$$

and $\tan x = x + \frac{x^3}{3} + \frac{2}{15}x^5 + \ldots\ldots$

Ex. 4 : *Expand $2x^3 + 7x^2 + x - 6$ in powers of $(x - 2)$.* **(Jan. 2005, Dec. 2006, May 2009)**

Sol. : Let $f(x) = 2x^3 + 7x^2 + x - 6$

Adjust $f(x) = f[2 + (x - 2)]$

By Taylor's theorem,

$$f(x) = f[2 + (x-2)] = f(2) + (x-2)f'(2) + \frac{(x-2)^2}{2!}f''(2) + \frac{(x-2)^3}{3!}f'''(2) + \ldots \quad \ldots (1)$$

$\therefore \quad f(x) = 2x^3 + 7x^2 + x - 6 \qquad \therefore \quad f(2) = 40$
$\qquad f'(x) = 6x^2 + 14x + 1 \qquad \therefore \quad f'(2) = 53$
$\qquad f''(x) = 12x + 14 \qquad \therefore \quad f''(2) = 38$
$\qquad f'''(x) = 12 \qquad \therefore \quad f'''(2) = 12$
$\qquad f^{iv}(x) = 0 \qquad \therefore \quad f^{iv}(2) = 0 \text{ etc.}$

Substituting these values in (1), we get

$$f(x) = 40 + (x-2)(53) + \frac{(x-2)^2}{2!}(38) + \frac{(x-2)^3}{3!}(12) + \ldots$$
$$f(x) = 40 + 53(x-2) + 19(x-2)^2 + 2(x-2)^3$$

Ex. 5 : *Using Taylor's theorem, express* $(x-2)^4 - 3(x-2)^3 + 4(x-2)^2 + 5$ *in powers of x.*

(Jan. 2005; May 2006, 2009; Dec. 2007)

Sol. : Let $f(x+h) = (x-2)^4 - 3(x-2)^3 + 4(x-2)^2 + 5$, where $h = -2$.

$\therefore \quad f(h) = h^4 - 3h^3 + 4h^2 + 5 \qquad \therefore \quad f(-2) = 61$

$\quad f'(h) = 4h^3 - 9h^2 + 8h \qquad \therefore \quad f'(-2) = -84$

$\quad f''(h) = 12h^2 - 18h + 8 \qquad \therefore \quad f''(-2) = 92$

$\quad f'''(h) = 24h - 18 \qquad \therefore \quad f'''(-2) = -66$

$\quad f^{iv}(h) = 24 \qquad \therefore \quad f^{iv}(-2) = 24$

$\quad f^{v}(h) = 0 \qquad \therefore \quad f^{v}(-2) = 0$ etc.

Substituting these values in Taylor's theorem,

$$f(x+h) = f(h) + x f'(h) + \frac{x^2}{2!} f''(h) + \frac{x^3}{3!} f'''(h) + \ldots$$

$$= 61 - 84x + 92\frac{x^2}{2!} - 66\frac{x^3}{3!} + 24\frac{x^4}{4!}$$

$$= 61 - 84x + 46x^2 - 11x^3 + x^4$$

Ex. 6 : *Prove that* $f(mx) = f(x) + (m-1) x f'(x) + \frac{(m-1)^2}{2!} x^2 f''(x) + \ldots$

Sol. : Here we can write $f(mx) = f[x + (m-1)x]$ and so let $h = (m-1)x$

$\therefore \quad f(mx) = f(x+h)$

$$= f(x) + h f'(x) + \frac{h^2}{2!} f''(x) + \frac{h^3}{3!} f'''(x) + \ldots$$

Substituting for h, we have

$$f(mx) = f(x) + (m-1) x f'(x) + \frac{(m-1)^2 x^2}{2!} f''(x) + \ldots$$

Ex. 7 : *Show that* $\frac{1}{2}[f(x) - f(2a-x)] = (x-a) f'(a) + \frac{(x-a)^3}{3!} f'''(a) + \frac{(x-a)^5}{5!} f^{v}(a) + \ldots$

(May 2005)

Sol. : Let $f(x) = f[a + (x-a)]$

By Taylor's theorem, we have

$$f(x) = f(a) + (x-a) f'(a) + \frac{(x-a)^2}{2!} f''(a) + \frac{(x-a)^3}{3!} f'''(a) + \ldots$$

Also, let $f(2a-x) = f[a + (a-x)]$

By Taylor's theorem, we have

$$= f(a) + (a-x) f'(a) + \frac{(a-x)^2}{2!} f''(a) + \frac{(a-x)^3}{3!} f'''(a) + \ldots$$

$$\therefore \ [f(x) - f(2a-x)] = \left[f(a) + (x-a)f'(a) + \frac{(a-x)^2}{2} f''(a) + \ldots \right]$$
$$- \left[f(a) + (a-x)f'(a) + \frac{(x-a)^2}{2!} f''(a) + \ldots \right]$$
$$= 2\left[(x-a)f'(a) + \frac{(x-a)^2}{3!} f'''(a) + \ldots \right]$$
$$\therefore \ \frac{1}{2}[f(x) - f(2a-x)] = (x-a)f'(a) + \frac{(x-a)^3}{3!} f'''(a) + \frac{(x-a)^5}{5!} f^v(a) + \ldots$$

Ex. 8 : Use Taylor's theorem to find $\sqrt{25 \cdot 15}$. (Dec. 2006, May 2010)

Sol. : Here $f(x+h) = \sqrt{x+h}$, where $x = 25, \ h = 0.15$

$\therefore \quad f(x) = \sqrt{x}, \qquad f'(x) = \frac{1}{2\sqrt{x}} = \frac{1}{2} x^{-1/2}$

$\quad f''(x) = -\frac{1}{4} x^{-3/2}, \qquad f'''(x) = \frac{3}{8} x^{-5/2}$

Taylor's theorem in powers of h is

$$f(x+h) = f(x) + h f'(x) + \frac{h^2}{2!} f''(x) + \frac{h^3}{3!} f'''(x) + \ldots$$

$$\sqrt{x+h} = \sqrt{x} + \frac{h}{2}\frac{1}{\sqrt{x}} - \frac{h^2}{8(\sqrt{x})^3} + \frac{h^3}{16(\sqrt{x})^5} + \ldots$$

Put $\quad x = 25 \ \text{and} \ h = 0.15$

$\therefore \quad \sqrt{25.15} = \sqrt{25 + 0.15} = 5 + \frac{0.15}{2 \times 5} - \frac{(0.15)^2}{8 \times 125} + \frac{(0.15)^3}{16 \times 3125} + \ldots$

$\qquad \qquad = 5 + 0.015 - 0.000225 + 0.000000675 + \ldots$

$\qquad \qquad = 5.01478$ approximately.

Ex. 9 : Given $\sinh(1.5) = 2.1293, \ \cosh(1.5) = 2.3524$. Calculate approximately the value of $\cosh(1.505)$ by Taylor's theorem.

Sol. : Let $f(x+h) = \cosh(x+h)$, then $f(x) = \cosh x$

$\therefore \qquad f'(x) = \sinh x, \ f''(x) = \cosh x,$

$\qquad f'''(x) = \sinh x$ and so on.

By Taylor's theorem, we have

$$f(x+h) = f(x) + h f'(x) + \frac{h^2}{2!} f''(x) + \frac{h^3}{3!} f'''(x) + \ldots$$

$\therefore \quad \cosh(x+h) = \cosh x + h \sinh x + \frac{h^2}{2!} \cosh x + \frac{h^3}{3!} \sinh x + \ldots$

Put $\quad x = 1.5, \ h = 0.005$ in this result, then

$\qquad \cosh(1.505) = \cosh(1.5) + (0.005)\sinh(1.5) + \frac{(0.005)^2}{2!} \cosh(1.5) + \ldots$

$\qquad \qquad = (2.3524) + (0.005)(2.1293) + \frac{(0.005)^2}{2} (2.3524) + \ldots$

$\qquad \qquad = 2.3631$ Approximately.

Ex. 10 : *Using Taylor's theorem find expansion of* $\tan\left(x + \frac{\pi}{4}\right)$ *in ascending powers of x upto terms in x^4 and find approximately the value of tan (43°).* **(Jan. 2005, May 2007)**

Sol. : Let $f(x + h) = \tan\left(x + \frac{\pi}{4}\right)$, then $h = \frac{\pi}{4}$

$\therefore \quad f(h) = \tan h, \qquad \therefore f\left(\frac{\pi}{4}\right) = 1$

$f'(h) = \sec^2 h = 1 + \tan^2 h, \qquad \therefore f'\left(\frac{\pi}{4}\right) = 2$

$f''(h) = 2 \sec^2 h \tan h = 2 \tan h (1 + \tan^2 h)$

$= 2 (\tan h + \tan^3 h), \qquad \therefore f''\left(\frac{\pi}{4}\right) = 4$

$\therefore \quad f'''(h) = 2 (\sec^2 h + 3 \tan^2 h \sec^2 h)$

$= 2 [(1 + \tan^2 h) + 3 \tan^2 h (1 + \tan^2 h)]$

$= 2 [1 + 4 \tan^2 h + 3 \tan^4 h], \qquad \therefore f'''\left(\frac{\pi}{4}\right) = 16$

$\therefore \quad f^{iv}(h) = 2 [8 \tan h \sec^2 h + 12 \tan^3 h \sec^2 h]$

$= 2 [8 \tan h (1 + \tan^2 h) + 12 \tan^3 h (1 + \tan^2 h)]$

$= 2 [8 \tan h + 20 \tan^3 h + 12 \tan^5 h], \qquad \therefore f^{iv}\left(\frac{\pi}{4}\right) = 80$

Substituting these values in Taylor's theorem, we get

$$f(x + h) = f(h) + x f'(h) + \frac{x^2}{2!} f''(h) + \frac{x^3}{3!} f'''(h) + \ldots$$

$$= 1 + 2x + 4 \frac{x^2}{2!} + 16 \frac{x^3}{3!} + 80 \frac{x^4}{4!} + \ldots$$

$\therefore \quad \tan\left(x + \frac{\pi}{4}\right) = 1 + 2x + 2x^2 + \frac{8}{3} x^3 + \frac{10}{3} x^4 + \ldots \qquad \ldots (1)$

Now $\tan (43°) = \tan (x + h) = \tan (-2° + 45°) = \tan\left(-\frac{2\pi}{180} + \frac{\pi}{4}\right)$

$\therefore \quad x = -2° = -\frac{2\pi}{180} = -0.0349, \quad \text{where } h = \frac{\pi}{4}$

Putting $x = -0.09326$ in (1), we get

$\tan 43° = 1 - 2 (0.0349) + 2 (0.0349)^2 - \frac{8}{3} (0.0349)^3 + \frac{10}{3} (0.0349)^4 + \ldots$

$= 0.9326$ approximately.

EXERCISE 8.3

1. Prove that

   (i) $\log \sin(x+h) = \log \sin x + h \cot x - \dfrac{h^2}{2} \operatorname{cosec}^2 x + \dfrac{h^3}{3} \operatorname{cosec}^2 x \cot x \ldots$

   (ii) $\tan(x+h) = \tan x + h \sec^2 x + h^2 \sec^2 x \tan x + \ldots$

   (iii) $\sin\left(\dfrac{\pi}{6} + x\right) = \dfrac{1}{2}\left[1 + \sqrt{3}\, x - \dfrac{x^2}{2!} - \dfrac{\sqrt{3}\, x^3}{3!} \ldots\right]$

2. (i) Expand $3x^3 - 2x^2 + x - 4$ in powers of $(x+2)$. (Dec. 2012)

   Ans. $-38 + 45(x+2) - 20(x+2)^2 + 3(x+2)^3$.

   (ii) Expand $x^3 + 7x^2 + x - 6$ in powers of $(x-3)$ (May 2007, 2014)

   Ans. $87 + 70(x-3) + 16(x-3)^2 + (x-3)^3$

   (iii) Expand $x^4 - 3x^3 + 2x^2 - x + 1$ in powers of $(x-3)$. (Dec. 2008)

   Ans. $16 + 38(x-3) + 29(x-3)^2 + 9(x-3)^3 + (x-3)^4$

   (iv) Expand $2x^3 + 3x^2 - 8x + 7$ in powers of $(x-2)$. (May 2010, 2013, 2015)

   Ans. $19 + 28(x-2) + 15(x-2)^2 + 2(x-2)^3$.

   (v) Expand $\tan^{-1} x$ in powers of $(x-1)$. (May 2005)

   Ans. $\dfrac{\pi}{4} + \dfrac{1}{2}(x-1) + \dfrac{(x-1)^2}{4} + \dfrac{(x-1)^3}{12} + \ldots$

   (vi) Expand e^x in powers of $(x-2)$.

   Ans. $e^2 \left[1 + (x-2) + \dfrac{(x-2)^2}{2!} + \dfrac{(x-2)^3}{3!} + \ldots\right]$

   (vii) Expand $\sin x$ in powers of $\left(x - \dfrac{\pi}{2}\right)$.

   Ans. $1 - \dfrac{\left(x - \dfrac{\pi}{2}\right)^2}{2!} + \dfrac{\left(x - \dfrac{\pi}{2}\right)^4}{4!}$.

   (viii) Expand $\log \cos x$ about $\dfrac{\pi}{3}$ using Taylor's expansion. (Dec. 97, May 2011)

   Ans. $\log \cos x = \log \dfrac{1}{2} - \sqrt{3}\left(x - \dfrac{\pi}{3}\right) - 4\dfrac{(x-\pi/3)^2}{2!} - \dfrac{8\sqrt{3}(x-\pi/3)^3}{3!} \ldots$

   (ix) Expand $f(x) = (x+2)^4 + 5(x+2)^3 + 6(x+2)^2 + 7(x+2) + 8$ in ascending powers of $x - 1$.

   Ans. $299 + 286(x-1) + 105(x-1)^2 + 17(x-1)^3 + (x-1)^4$.

   (x) Expand $(1 + x + 2x^2)^{1/2}$ in powers of $(x-1)$. (May 2008)

3. (i) Using Taylor's theorem, express $7 + (x + 2) + 3(x + 2)^3 + (x + 2)^4$ in ascending powers of x. **(Jan. 2004, May 2011, Dec. 2014)**
   Ans. $49 + 69x + 42x^2 + 11x^3 + x^4$.

   (ii) Using Taylor's theorem, express $7 + (x + 2) + 3(x + 2)^3 + (x + 2)^4 - (x + 2)^5$ in ascending powers of x. **(May 2008)**
   Ans. $17 - 11x - 38x^2 - 29x^3 - 9x^4 - x^5$.

   (iii) Using Taylor's theorem, express $5 + 4(x - 1)^2 - 3(x - 1)^3 + (x - 1)^4$ in ascending powers of x. **(May 2004)**

4. Prove that $f\left(\dfrac{x^2}{1+x}\right) = f(x) - \dfrac{x}{1+x} f'(x) - \dfrac{x^2}{(1+x)^2} \dfrac{f'''(x)}{2!} \ldots\ldots$.

   [Hint : $\dfrac{x^2}{1+x} = x - \dfrac{x}{1+x}$]

5. Use Taylor's theorem to show that
   $(1 + x + 2x^2)^{1/2} = 1 + \dfrac{x}{2} + \dfrac{7}{8}x^2 - \dfrac{7}{16}x^3 \ldots$

6. Using Taylor's theorem, find $\sin(30° \, 30')$. **(Dec. 2008)**
   Ans. 0.50735.

7. Use Taylor's theorem to obtain approximate value of $\sqrt{10}$ to four decimal places.
   Ans. 3.1623 approximately. **(Dec. 2010)**

8. Use Taylor's theorem to obtain $\sqrt{9.12}$.
   Ans. 3.0146 approximately.

9. Using Taylor's theorem, obtain $\tan^{-1}(1.003)$ to 4 decimal places where $\pi = 3.1416$.
   (May 2006)

   [Hint : $\tan^{-1}(x + h) = \tan^{-1} x + h \dfrac{1}{1+x^2} + \dfrac{h^2}{2!} \dfrac{2x}{(1+x^2)^2} - \dfrac{h^3}{3!} \dfrac{2(1-3x^2)}{(1+x^2)^3} \ldots$]

10. Obtain the value of $\tan^{-1}(1.003)$ to five decimal places by using Taylor's theorem where $\pi = 3.141593$.
    Ans. 0.78690

11. Using Taylor's theorem, find the value of $\cos 64°$ correct to three decimal places.
    [Hint : $\cos(x + h) = \left(1 - \dfrac{h^2}{2!} \ldots\right) \cos x - \left(h - \dfrac{h^3}{3!} \ldots\right) \sin x$ and $64° = \dfrac{\pi}{3} + 0.06926$]
    Ans. $\cos 64° = 0.4384$

12. Expand $\log \cos\left(x + \dfrac{\pi}{4}\right)$ using Taylor's theorem in ascending powers of x and hence find the value of $\log \cos 48°$ correct upto four decimal places. **(Dec. 2005, 2008)**
    Ans. $-\dfrac{1}{2} \log 2 + x + x^2 + \dfrac{4}{3} x^3 + \dfrac{2}{3} x^4 + \ldots$ and $\log \cos 48° = -0.40178$

MULTIPLE CHOICE QUESTIONS

Type I : Maclaurin's Theorem and Expansion of Functions :

1. Expansion of f(x) in ascending powers of x by Maclaurin's theorem is (1)

   (A) $f(x) + xf'(x) + \dfrac{x^2}{2!} f''(x) + \ldots$
   (B) $1 + x + \dfrac{x^2}{2!} + \ldots$
   (C) $f(0) + xf'(0) + \dfrac{x^2}{2!} f''(0) + \ldots$
   (D) $f(x) - xf'(x) + \dfrac{x^2}{2!} f''(x) - \dfrac{x^3}{3!} f'''(x) + \ldots$

2. Expansion of sin x in ascending powers of x is (1)

   (A) $x + \dfrac{x^3}{3!} + \dfrac{x^5}{5!} + \ldots$
   (B) $x + \dfrac{x^2}{2!} + \dfrac{x^3}{3!} + \ldots$
   (C) $x - \dfrac{x^3}{3!} + \dfrac{x^5}{5!} - \dfrac{x^7}{7!} + \ldots$
   (D) $1 + x + \dfrac{x^2}{2!} + \dfrac{x^3}{3!} + \ldots$

3. Expansion of cos x in ascending powers of x is (1)

   (A) $1 + \dfrac{x^2}{2!} + \dfrac{x^4}{4!} + \dfrac{x^6}{6!} + \ldots$
   (B) $x - \dfrac{x^3}{3!} + \dfrac{x^5}{5!} - \dfrac{x^7}{7!} + \ldots$
   (C) $x + \dfrac{x^2}{2!} + \dfrac{x^4}{4!} + \dfrac{x^6}{6!} + \ldots$
   (D) $1 - \dfrac{x^2}{2!} + \dfrac{x^4}{4!} - \dfrac{x^6}{6!} + \ldots$

4. Expansion of tan x in ascending powers of x is (1)

   (A) $1 + x + \dfrac{1}{3} x^3 + \dfrac{2}{15} x^5 + \ldots$
   (B) $x - \dfrac{1}{3} x^3 + \dfrac{2}{15} x^5 - \ldots$
   (C) $x - \dfrac{x^3}{3!} + \dfrac{x^5}{5!} - \dfrac{x^7}{7!} + \ldots$
   (D) $x + \dfrac{1}{3} x^3 + \dfrac{2}{15} x^5 + \ldots$

5. Expansion of e^x in ascending powers of x is (1)

   (A) $1 + x + \dfrac{x^2}{2!} + \dfrac{x^3}{3!} + \ldots$
   (B) $1 - x + \dfrac{x^2}{2!} - \dfrac{x^3}{3!} + \ldots$
   (C) $1 - \dfrac{x^2}{2!} + \dfrac{x^4}{4!} - \dfrac{x^6}{6!} + \ldots$
   (D) $x - \dfrac{x^3}{3!} + \dfrac{x^5}{5!} - \dfrac{x^7}{7!} + \ldots$

6. Expansion of e^{-x} in ascending powers of x is (1)

   (A) $1 + x + \dfrac{x^2}{2!} + \dfrac{x^3}{3!} + \ldots$
   (B) $1 - x + \dfrac{x^2}{2!} - \dfrac{x^3}{3!} + \ldots$
   (C) $1 - \dfrac{x^2}{2!} + \dfrac{x^4}{4!} - \dfrac{x^6}{6!} + \ldots$
   (D) $x - \dfrac{x^3}{3!} + \dfrac{x^5}{5!} - \dfrac{x^7}{7!} + \ldots$

7. Expansion of sinh x in ascending powers of x is (1)

   (A) $1 + x + \dfrac{x^2}{2!} + \dfrac{x^3}{3!} + \ldots$
   (B) $x - \dfrac{x^3}{3!} + \dfrac{x^5}{5!} - \dfrac{x^7}{7!} + \ldots$
   (C) $1 + \dfrac{x^2}{2!} + \dfrac{x^4}{4!} + \dfrac{x^6}{6!} + \ldots$
   (D) $x + \dfrac{x^3}{3!} + \dfrac{x^5}{5!} + \dfrac{x^7}{7!} + \ldots$

8. Expansion of cosh x in ascending powers of x is (1)

   (A) $1 + x + \dfrac{x^2}{2!} + \dfrac{x^3}{3!} + \ldots$
   (B) $x - \dfrac{x^3}{3!} + \dfrac{x^5}{5!} - \dfrac{x^7}{7!} + \ldots$

   (C) $1 + \dfrac{x^2}{2!} + \dfrac{x^4}{4!} + \dfrac{x^6}{6!} + \ldots$
   (D) $x + \dfrac{x^3}{3!} + \dfrac{x^5}{5!} + \dfrac{x^7}{7!} + \ldots$

9. Expansion of tanh x in ascending powers of x is (1)

   (A) $1 + x + \dfrac{1}{3}x^3 + \dfrac{2}{15}x^5 + \ldots$
   (B) $x - \dfrac{1}{3}x^3 + \dfrac{2}{15}x^5 - \ldots$

   (C) $x - \dfrac{x^3}{3!} + \dfrac{x^5}{5!} - \dfrac{x^7}{7!} + \ldots$
   (D) $x + \dfrac{1}{3}x^3 + \dfrac{2}{15}x^5 + \ldots$

10. Expansion of log (1 + x) in ascending powers of x is (1)

    (A) $x - \dfrac{x^2}{2} + \dfrac{x^3}{3} - \dfrac{x^4}{4} + \ldots$
    (B) $-x - \dfrac{x^2}{2} - \dfrac{x^3}{3} - \dfrac{x^4}{4} + \ldots$

    (C) $1 + \dfrac{x^2}{2!} + \dfrac{x^4}{4!} + \dfrac{x^6}{6!} + \ldots$
    (D) $x + \dfrac{x^3}{3!} + \dfrac{x^5}{5!} + \dfrac{x^7}{7!} + \ldots$

11. Expansion of log (1 – x) in ascending powers of x is (1)

    (A) $-x - \dfrac{x^2}{2} - \dfrac{x^3}{3} - \dfrac{x^4}{4} - \ldots$
    (B) $x - \dfrac{x^2}{2} + \dfrac{x^3}{3} - \dfrac{x^4}{4} + \ldots$

    (C) $1 + \dfrac{x^2}{2!} + \dfrac{x^4}{4!} + \dfrac{x^6}{6!} + \ldots$
    (D) $x + \dfrac{x^3}{3!} + \dfrac{x^5}{5!} + \dfrac{x^7}{7!} + \ldots$

12. Expansion of $\dfrac{1}{(1-x)}$ in ascending powers of x is (1)

    (A) $-1 - x - x^2 - x^3 - \ldots$
    (B) $1 - x + x^2 - x^3 + \ldots$

    (C) $1 + \dfrac{x^2}{2!} + \dfrac{x^4}{4!} + \dfrac{x^6}{6!} + \ldots$
    (D) $1 + x + x^2 + x^3 + \ldots$

13. Expansion of $\dfrac{1}{(1+x)}$ in ascending powers of x is (1)

    (A) $-1 - x - x^2 - x^3 - \ldots$
    (B) $1 - x + x^2 - x^3 + \ldots$

    (C) $1 + \dfrac{x^2}{2!} + \dfrac{x^4}{4!} + \dfrac{x^6}{6!} + \ldots$
    (D) $1 + x + x^2 + x^3 + \ldots$

14. Expansion of $(1 + x)^n$ in ascending powers of x is (1)

    (A) $1 - nx + \dfrac{n(n-1)}{2!}x^2 - \dfrac{n(n-1)(n-2)}{3!}x^3 + \ldots$

    (B) $1 - nx + \dfrac{n(n+1)}{2!}x^2 - \dfrac{n(n+1)(n+2)}{3!}x^3 + \ldots$

    (C) $1 + nx + \dfrac{n(n+1)}{2!}x^2 + \dfrac{n(n+1)(n+2)}{3!}x^3 + \ldots$

    (D) $1 + nx + \dfrac{n(n-1)}{2!}x^2 + \dfrac{n(n-1)(n-2)}{3!}x^3 + \ldots$

15. The limit of the series $x - \dfrac{x^3}{3!} + \dfrac{x^5}{5!} - \dfrac{x^7}{7!} + \ldots$ as x approaches to $\dfrac{\pi}{2}$ is (2)

   (A) 0
   (B) $\dfrac{\pi}{2}$
   (C) 1
   (D) –1

16. First two terms in expansion of log (1 + e^x) by Maclaurin's theorem is (2)

   (A) $\log 2 + \dfrac{1}{2}x + \ldots$
   (B) $\log 2 - \dfrac{1}{2}x + \ldots$
   (C) $x - \dfrac{x^2}{2} + \ldots$
   (D) $x + \dfrac{x^2}{2} + \ldots$

17. First two terms in expansion of sec x by Maclaurin's theorem is (2)

   (A) $1 - \dfrac{x^2}{2!} + \ldots$
   (B) $x - \dfrac{x^3}{3!} + \ldots$
   (C) $1 + \dfrac{x^2}{2!} + \ldots$
   (D) $x + \dfrac{x^3}{3!} + \ldots$

18. First two terms in expansion of e^x sec x by Maclaurin's theorem is (2)

   (A) $x + x^2 + \ldots$
   (B) $x - x^2 + \ldots$
   (C) $1 + x + \ldots$
   (D) $1 - x + \ldots$

19. First two terms in expansion of tan⁻¹ (1 + x) by Maclaurin's theorem is (2)

   (A) $\dfrac{\pi}{4} + \dfrac{x}{2} - \ldots$
   (B) $\dfrac{\pi}{4} - \dfrac{x}{2} - \ldots$
   (C) $x - \dfrac{x^3}{3!} + \ldots$
   (D) $x + \dfrac{x^3}{3!} + \ldots$

20. Expansion of $\sin\left(\dfrac{x}{2}\right) + \cos\left(\dfrac{x}{2}\right)$ in ascending powers of x is (2)

   (A) $1 - \dfrac{x}{2} + \dfrac{x^2}{8} + \dfrac{x^3}{48} - \dfrac{x^4}{384} + \ldots$
   (B) $1 + \dfrac{x}{2} - \dfrac{x^2}{8} - \dfrac{x^3}{48} + \dfrac{x^4}{384} + \ldots$
   (C) $1 + \dfrac{x}{2} - \dfrac{x^2}{8} - \dfrac{x^3}{24} + \dfrac{x^4}{120} + \ldots$
   (D) $\dfrac{x^2}{8} - \dfrac{x^3}{48} + \dfrac{x^4}{384} + \ldots$

21. Expansion of log (1 – x⁴) – log (1 – x) in ascending powers of x is (2)

   (A) $-x - \dfrac{x^2}{2} - \dfrac{x^3}{3} - \dfrac{3}{4}x^4 + \ldots$
   (B) $x + \dfrac{x^2}{2} + \dfrac{x^3}{3} - \dfrac{3}{4}x^4 + \ldots$
   (C) $x + \dfrac{x^2}{2!} + \dfrac{x^3}{3!} - \dfrac{3}{4!}x^4 + \ldots$
   (D) $-x - \dfrac{x^2}{2!} - \dfrac{x^3}{3!} - \dfrac{3}{4!}x^4 + \ldots$

22. Expansion of log (1+ x)^(1/x) in ascending powers of x is (2)

   (A) $1 - \dfrac{x}{2} + \dfrac{x^2}{3} - \dfrac{x^3}{4} + \ldots$
   (B) $-1 - \dfrac{x}{2} - \dfrac{x^2}{3} - \dfrac{x^3}{4} - \ldots$
   (C) $1 - \dfrac{x}{2!} + \dfrac{x^2}{3!} - \dfrac{x^3}{4!} + \ldots$
   (D) $-1 - \dfrac{x}{2!} - \dfrac{x^2}{3!} - \dfrac{x^3}{4!} - \ldots$

23. Expansion of $\log(1+x)^x$ in ascending powers of x is (2)

   (A) $x^2 + \dfrac{x^3}{2} + \dfrac{x^4}{3} + \dfrac{x^5}{4} + \ldots$

   (B) $x^2 - \dfrac{x^3}{2!} + \dfrac{x^4}{3!} - \dfrac{x^5}{4!} + \ldots$

   (C) $1 + x + \dfrac{x^2}{2} - \dfrac{x^3}{3} + \dfrac{x^4}{4} - \dfrac{x^5}{5} + \ldots$

   (D) $x^2 - \dfrac{x^3}{2} + \dfrac{x^4}{3} - \dfrac{x^5}{4} + \ldots$

24. Expansion of $\cos^2 x$ in ascending powers of x is (2)

   (A) $\dfrac{1}{2}\left\{1 + \left(1 - \dfrac{2^2 x^2}{2!} + \dfrac{2^4 x^4}{4!} - \ldots\right)\right\}$

   (B) $\dfrac{1}{2}\left\{1 - \left(1 - \dfrac{2^2 x^2}{2!} + \dfrac{2^4 x^4}{4!} - \ldots\right)\right\}$

   (C) $\dfrac{1}{2}\left\{1 + \left(2x - \dfrac{2^3 x^3}{3!} + \dfrac{2^5 x^5}{5!} - \ldots\right)\right\}$

   (D) $\dfrac{1}{2}\left\{1 - \left(2x - \dfrac{2^3 x^3}{3!} + \dfrac{2^5 x^5}{5!} - \ldots\right)\right\}$

25. Expansion of $\sin x \cos x$ in ascending powers of x is (2)

   (A) $\dfrac{1}{2}\left(1 - \dfrac{2^2 x^2}{2!} + \dfrac{2^4 x^4}{4!} - \ldots\right)$

   (B) $\dfrac{1}{2}\left(1 - \dfrac{x^2}{2!} + \dfrac{x^4}{4!} - \ldots\right)$

   (C) $\dfrac{1}{2}\left(2x - \dfrac{2^3 x^3}{3!} + \dfrac{2^5 x^5}{5!} - \ldots\right)$

   (D) $\dfrac{1}{2}\left(x - \dfrac{x^3}{3!} + \dfrac{x^5}{5!} - \ldots\right)$

26. Expansion of $\sin 2x \cos 3x$ in ascending powers of x is (2)

   (A) $\dfrac{1}{2}\left[\left(5x - \dfrac{5^3 x^3}{3!} + \dfrac{5^5 x^5}{5!} - \ldots\right) - \left(x - \dfrac{x^3}{3!} + \dfrac{x^5}{5!} - \ldots\right)\right]$

   (B) $\dfrac{1}{2}\left[\left(5x - \dfrac{5^3 x^3}{3!} + \dfrac{5^5 x^5}{5!} - \ldots\right) + \left(x - \dfrac{x^3}{3!} + \dfrac{x^5}{5!} - \ldots\right)\right]$

   (C) $\dfrac{1}{2}\left[\left(1 - \dfrac{5^2 x^2}{2!} + \dfrac{5^4 x^4}{4!} - \ldots\right) - \left(1 - \dfrac{x^2}{2!} + \dfrac{x^4}{4!} - \ldots\right)\right]$

   (D) $\dfrac{1}{2}\left[\left(1 - \dfrac{5^2 x^2}{2!} + \dfrac{5^4 x^4}{4!} - \ldots\right) + \left(1 - \dfrac{x^2}{2!} + \dfrac{x^4}{4!} - \ldots\right)\right]$

27. Expansion of $\tan^{-1} x$ in ascending powers of x is (2)

   (A) $x + \dfrac{x^3}{3!} + \dfrac{x^5}{5!} + \ldots$

   (B) $x - \dfrac{x^3}{3!} + \dfrac{x^5}{5!} - \ldots$

   (C) $x - \dfrac{x^3}{3} + \dfrac{x^5}{5} - \ldots$

   (D) $x + \dfrac{x^3}{3} + \dfrac{x^5}{5} + \ldots$

28. Simplified expression of $1 + \left(x^2 - \dfrac{x^3}{2} + \dfrac{x^4}{3} - \ldots\right) + \dfrac{1}{2}\left(x^2 - \dfrac{x^3}{2} + \dfrac{x^4}{3} - \ldots\right)^2 + \ldots$ on neglecting x^5 and higher powers of x is (2)

   (A) $1 + x^2 + \dfrac{x^3}{2} + \dfrac{5x^4}{6} + \ldots$

   (B) $1 + x^2 - \dfrac{x^3}{2} - \dfrac{x^4}{6} - \ldots$

   (C) $x^2 - \dfrac{x^3}{2} + \dfrac{5x^4}{6} - \ldots$

   (D) $1 + x^2 - \dfrac{x^3}{2} + \dfrac{5x^4}{6} - \ldots$

29. By using substitution $x = \tan \theta$, simplified form of $\sin^{-1}\left(\dfrac{2x}{1+x^2}\right)$ is (2)

   (A) $\tan^{-1} x$

   (B) $2 \cot^{-1} x$

   (C) $2 \tan^{-1} x$

   (D) none of these

30. By using substitution $x = \tan \theta$, simplified form of $\cos^{-1}\left(\dfrac{x - x^{-1}}{x + x^{-1}}\right)$ is (2)

   (A) $\dfrac{\pi}{2} + 2 \tan^{-1} x$
   (B) $\pi - 2 \tan^{-1} x$
   (C) $2 \tan^{-1} x$
   (D) none of these

31. If $x = \log(1 + y)$, then expansion of y in ascending powers of x is (2)

   (A) $x + \dfrac{x^2}{2!} + \dfrac{x^3}{3!} + \ldots$
   (B) $x - \dfrac{x^2}{2!} + \dfrac{x^3}{3!} - \ldots$
   (C) $x + \dfrac{x^2}{2} + \dfrac{x^3}{3} + \ldots$
   (D) $-x - \dfrac{x^2}{2!} - \dfrac{x^3}{3!} - \ldots$

Type II : Taylor's Theorem and Expansion of Functions :

32. The Taylor's series expansion of $f(x + h)$ in ascending powers of h is (1)

   (A) $f(x) + hf'(x) + \dfrac{h^2}{2!} f''(x) + \ldots$
   (B) $-f(x) - hf'(x) - \dfrac{h^2}{2!} f''(x) - \ldots$
   (C) $f(0) + hf'(0) + \dfrac{h^2}{2!} f''(0) + \ldots$
   (D) $f(x) - hf'(x) + \dfrac{h^2}{2!} f''(x) - \dfrac{h^3}{3!} f'''(x) + \ldots$

33. The Taylor's series expansion of $f(x + h)$ in ascending powers of x is (1)

   (A) $f(h) - xf'(h) + \dfrac{x^2}{2!} f''(h) - \dfrac{x^3}{3!} f'''(h) + \ldots$
   (B) $f(x) + hf'(x) + \dfrac{h^2}{2!} f''(x) + \ldots$
   (C) $f(0) + xf'(0) + \dfrac{x^2}{2!} f''(0) + \ldots$
   (D) $f(h) + xf'(h) + \dfrac{x^2}{2!} f''(h) + \ldots$

34. The Taylor's series expansion of $f(a + h)$ in ascending powers of h is (1)

   (A) $f(a) + hf'(a) + \dfrac{h^2}{2!} f''(a) + \ldots$
   (B) $f(h) + af'(h) + \dfrac{a^2}{2!} f''(h) + \ldots$
   (C) $f(0) + hf'(0) + \dfrac{h^2}{2!} f''(0) + \ldots$
   (D) $f(a) - hf'(a) + \dfrac{h^2}{2!} f''(a) - \dfrac{h^3}{3!} f'''(a) + \ldots$

35. Expansion of $f(x)$ in ascending powers of $(x - a)$ by Taylor's theorem is (1)

   (A) $f(x) + af'(x) + \dfrac{a^2}{2!} f''(x) + \ldots$
   (B) $f(a) + (x - a) f'(a) + \dfrac{(x - a)^2}{2!} f''(a) + \ldots$
   (C) $f(0) - (x - a) f'(0) + \dfrac{(x - a)^2}{2!} f''(0) - \dfrac{(x - a)^3}{3!} f'''(0) + \ldots$
   (D) $f(a) - (x - a) f'(a) + \dfrac{(x - a)^2}{2!} f''(a) - \dfrac{(x - a)^3}{3!} f'''(a) + \ldots$

36. First two terms in expansion of log sec x by Taylor's theorem in ascending powers of $\left(x - \dfrac{\pi}{4}\right)$ is (2)

   (A) $\dfrac{1}{2}\log 2 - \left(x - \dfrac{\pi}{4}\right) + \ldots$
   (B) $\dfrac{1}{2}\log 2 + \left(x - \dfrac{\pi}{4}\right)\dfrac{1}{2} + \ldots$
   (C) $\dfrac{1}{2}\log 2 + \left(x - \dfrac{\pi}{4}\right) + \ldots$
   (D) $\dfrac{1}{2}\log 2 - \left(x - \dfrac{\pi}{4}\right)\dfrac{1}{2} \ldots$

37. First two terms in expansion of $\sqrt{x+h}$ by Taylor's theorem in ascending powers of h is (2)

   (A) $\sqrt{x} + h\dfrac{1}{\sqrt{x}} + \ldots$
   (B) $\sqrt{x} - \dfrac{h}{2}\dfrac{1}{\sqrt{x}} + \ldots$
   (C) $\dfrac{1}{\sqrt{x}} + \dfrac{h}{2}\dfrac{1}{\sqrt{x}} + \ldots$
   (D) $\sqrt{x} + \dfrac{h}{2}\dfrac{1}{\sqrt{x}} + \ldots$

38. First two terms in expansion of $\log \cos\left(x + \dfrac{\pi}{4}\right)$ by Taylor's theorem in ascending powers of x is (2)

   (A) $\log\dfrac{1}{\sqrt{2}} - x + \ldots$
   (B) $\log\dfrac{1}{\sqrt{2}} + x + \ldots$
   (C) $\log\dfrac{\sqrt{3}}{2} - x + \ldots$
   (D) $\log\dfrac{\sqrt{3}}{2} + x + \ldots$

39. First two terms in expansion of $(x + 2)^5 + 3(x + 2)^4$ by Taylor's theorem in ascending powers of x is (2)
   (A) $48 + 98x + \ldots$
   (B) $80 + 176x + \ldots$
   (C) $80 + 98x + \ldots$
   (D) $48 + 176x + \ldots$

40. First two terms in expansion of $(x - 1)^5 + 2(x - 1)^4$ by Taylor's theorem in ascending powers of x is (2)
   (A) $3 - 13x + \ldots$
   (B) $1 + 13x + \ldots$
   (C) $1 - 3x + \ldots$
   (D) $3 - 3x + \ldots$

41. First two terms in expansion of sinh (x + a) by Taylor's theorem in ascending powers of x is (2)
   (A) sinh a + x cosh a + ...
   (B) sinh a – x cosh a + ...
   (C) cosh a + x sinh a + ...
   (D) none of these

42. First two terms in expansion f (x + 2) + 3 (x + 2)³ + (x + 2)⁴ by Taylor's theorem in ascending powers of x is (2)
   (A) $42 + 68x + \ldots$
   (B) $42 + 66x + \ldots$
   (C) $42 + 69x + \ldots$
   (D) $40 + 69x + \ldots$

43. First two terms in expansion of e^x by Taylor's theorem in ascending powers of (x − 2) is (2)
   (A) $e^{-2} - e^2 (x - 2) + \ldots$
   (B) $e^{-2} + e^{-2} (x - 2) + \ldots$
   (C) $e^2 - e^2 (x - 2) + \ldots$
   (D) $e^2 + e^2 (x - 2) + \ldots$

44. First two terms in expansion of $\tan^{-1} x$ by Taylor's theorem in ascending powers of $(x-1)$ is (2)

   (A) $\dfrac{\pi}{4} - \dfrac{1}{2}(x-1) + \ldots$
   (B) $\dfrac{\pi}{4} + \dfrac{1}{2}(x-1) + \ldots$
   (C) $1 + \dfrac{1}{2}(x-1) + \ldots$
   (D) $1 - \dfrac{1}{2}(x-1) + \ldots$

45. First two terms in expansion of $\sin x$ by Taylor's theorem in ascending powers of $\left(x - \dfrac{\pi}{2}\right)$ is (2)

   (A) $\left(x - \dfrac{\pi}{2}\right) - \dfrac{1}{3!}\left(x - \dfrac{\pi}{2}\right)^3 + \ldots$
   (B) $1 + \dfrac{1}{2!}\left(x - \dfrac{\pi}{2}\right)^2 + \ldots$
   (C) $\left(x - \dfrac{\pi}{2}\right) + \dfrac{1}{3!}\left(x - \dfrac{\pi}{2}\right)^3 + \ldots$
   (D) $1 - \dfrac{1}{2!}\left(x - \dfrac{\pi}{2}\right)^2 + \ldots$

46. First two terms in expansion of $\log \cos x$ by Taylor's theorem in ascending powers of $\left(x - \dfrac{\pi}{4}\right)$ is (2)

   (A) $\log \dfrac{1}{2} - \left(x - \dfrac{\pi}{4}\right) + \ldots$
   (B) $\log \dfrac{1}{\sqrt{2}} + \left(x - \dfrac{\pi}{4}\right) + \ldots$
   (C) $\log \dfrac{1}{\sqrt{2}} - \left(x - \dfrac{\pi}{4}\right) + \ldots$
   (D) $\log \dfrac{1}{2} + \left(x - \dfrac{\pi}{4}\right) + \ldots$

47. First two terms in expansion of $\sin^{-1} x$ by Taylor's theorem in ascending powers of $\left(x - \dfrac{1}{2}\right)$ is (2)

   (A) $\dfrac{\pi}{6} + \left(x - \dfrac{1}{2}\right)\dfrac{2}{\sqrt{3}} + \ldots$
   (B) $\dfrac{\pi}{6} - \left(x - \dfrac{1}{2}\right)\dfrac{2}{\sqrt{3}} + \ldots$
   (C) $\dfrac{\pi}{6} + \left(x - \dfrac{1}{2}\right)\dfrac{1}{\sqrt{2}} + \ldots$
   (D) $\dfrac{\pi}{6} - \left(x - \dfrac{1}{2}\right)\dfrac{1}{\sqrt{2}} + \ldots$

48. First two terms in expansion of $x^{1/3}$ by Taylor's theorem in ascending powers of $(x-8)$ is (2)

   (A) $2 - (x-8)\dfrac{1}{12} + \ldots$
   (B) $2 + (x-8)\dfrac{1}{12} + \ldots$
   (C) $2 + (x-8)\dfrac{1}{24} + \ldots$
   (D) $2 - (x-8)\dfrac{1}{24} + \ldots$

49. First two terms in expansion of $\sqrt{x+2}$ by Taylor's theorem in ascending powers $(x-2)$ is (2)

   (A) $2 + (x-2)\dfrac{1}{4} + \ldots$
   (B) $2 - (x-2)\dfrac{1}{4} + \ldots$
   (C) $2 + (x-2)\dfrac{1}{8} + \ldots$
   (D) $2 - (x-2)\dfrac{1}{8} + \ldots$

50. In the Taylor's series expansion of $e^x + \sin x$ about the point $x = \pi$, the coefficient of $(x - \pi)^2$ is (2)

   (A) e^π
   (B) $e^\pi + 1$
   (C) $e^\pi - 1$
   (D) $\dfrac{1}{2} e^\pi$

51. Which of the following function will have only odd powers of x in its Taylor's series expansion about the point $x = 0$? (2)

   (A) $\sin(x^2)$
   (B) $\sin(x^3)$
   (C) $\cos(x^2)$
   (D) $\cos(x^3)$

Answers

1. (C)	11. (A)	22. (A)	33. (D)	44. (B)
2. (C)	12. (D)	23. (D)	34. (A)	45. (D)
3. (D)	13. (B)	24. (A)	35. (B)	46. (C)
4. (D)	14. (D)	25. (C)	36. (C)	47. (A)
5. (A)	15. (C)	26. (A)	37. (D)	48. (B)
6. (B)	16. (A)	27. (C)	38. (A)	49. (A)
7. (D)	17. (C)	28. (D)	39. (B)	50. (D)
8. (C)	18. (C)	29. (C)	40. (C)	51. (B)
9. (B)	19. (A)	30. (B)	41. (A)	
10. (A)	20. (B)	31. (A)	42. (C)	
	21. (B)	32. (A)	43. (D)	

CHAPTER NINE

INDETERMINATE FORMS

9.1 INDETERMINATE FORMS

Definition : Let $f(x)$ and $g(x)$ be any two functions of x such that $f(a) = 0$ and $g(a) = 0$; then the ratio $\dfrac{f(x)}{g(x)}$ is said to assume the indeterminate form $\dfrac{0}{0}$ at $x = a$.

There are seven indeterminate forms viz. $\dfrac{0}{0}, \dfrac{\infty}{\infty}, 0 \times \infty, \infty - \infty, 0^0, \infty^0, 1^\infty$.

True Value (Limit) :

The limiting value of an indeterminate form is called its true value, which is obtained by finding the limit of $\dfrac{f(x)}{g(x)}$ as x approaches a.

All the indeterminate forms by a suitable arrangement can be brought to the form $\dfrac{0}{0}$ and so we shall first discuss this form. In what follows it will always be assumed that the functions $f(x)$ and $g(x)$ possess continuous derivatives of every order in a certain interval enclosing $x = a$.

9.2 THE INDETERMINATE FORM $\dfrac{0}{0}$ (L'HOSPITAL RULE)

Statement : Let $f(x)$ and $g(x)$ be functions such that $f(a) = 0$ and $g(a) = 0$

or if $\quad \lim\limits_{x \to a} f(x) = 0$ and $\lim\limits_{x \to a} g(x) = 0$

then $\quad \lim\limits_{x \to a} \dfrac{f(x)}{g(x)} = \lim\limits_{x \to a} \dfrac{f'(x)}{g'(x)}$

Proof : By Taylor's theorem in the neighbourhood of $x = a$, we have

$$f(x) = f(a) + (x-a) f'(a) + \dfrac{(x-a)^2}{2!} f''(a) + \ldots\ldots$$

and

$$g(x) = g(a) + (x-a) g'(a) + \dfrac{(x-a)^2}{2!} g''(a) + \ldots\ldots$$

Hence
$$\frac{f(x)}{g(x)} = \frac{f(a) + (x-a)f'(a) + \frac{(x-a)^2}{2!}f''(a) + \ldots}{g(a) + (x-a)g'(a) + \frac{(x-a)^2}{2!}g''(a) + \ldots}$$

$$\therefore \quad \frac{f(x)}{g(x)} = \frac{(x-a)f'(a) + \frac{(x-a)^2}{2!}f''(a) + \ldots}{(x-a)g'(a) + \frac{(x-a)^2}{2!}g''(a) + \ldots} \qquad [\because f(a) = 0 = g(a)]$$

$$= \frac{f'(a) + (x-a)\frac{f''(a)}{2!} + \text{terms having higher powers of }(x-a)}{g'(a) + (x-a)\frac{g''(a)}{2!} + \text{terms with higher powers of }(x-a)}$$

Taking limit as $x \to a$, we have

$$\lim_{x \to a} \frac{f(x)}{g(x)} = \frac{f'(a) + 0 + 0 + 0 \ldots}{g'(a) + 0 + 0 + 0 \ldots} = \frac{f'(a)}{g'(a)} = \lim_{x \to a} \frac{f'(x)}{g'(x)}$$

Thus $$\lim_{x \to a} \frac{f(x)}{g(x)} = \lim_{x \to a} \frac{f'(x)}{g'(x)}$$

Note:

(1) If $f'(a), f''(a) \ldots f^{n-1}(a)$ and $g'(a), g''(a) \ldots g^{n-1}(a)$ are all zero, but $f^n(a)$ and $g^n(a)$ are not both zero, then

$$\lim_{x \to a} \frac{f(x)}{g(x)} = \lim_{x \to a} \frac{f^n(x)}{g^n(x)}$$

(2) If $\lim_{x \to \infty} f(x) = 0 = \lim_{x \to \infty} g(x)$, even then it can easily be shown that

$$\lim_{x \to \infty} \frac{f(x)}{g(x)} = \lim_{x \to \infty} \frac{f'(x)}{g'(x)}$$

(3) We can deduce L'Hospital rule for Cauchy's theorem, hence it is also called Cauchy's rule.

9.3 THE INDETERMINATE FORM $\frac{\infty}{\infty}$

If $\lim_{x \to a} f(x) = \infty$ and $\lim_{x \to a} g(x) = \infty$ then $\lim_{x \to a} \frac{f(x)}{g(x)}$ takes the form $\frac{\infty}{\infty}$.

Here we can write $\frac{f(x)}{g(x)}$ as $\frac{1/g(x)}{1/f(x)}$, in which case form reduces to $\frac{0}{0}$ and the L'Hospital Rule is applicable. However, it can be proved that L'Hospital Rule can be applied to the form $\frac{\infty}{\infty}$ without adjusting to the form $\frac{0}{0}$.

Thus $$\lim_{x \to a} \frac{f(x)}{g(x)} = \lim_{x \to a} \frac{f'(x)}{g'(x)}$$

9.4 THE INDETERMINATE FORM $0 \times \infty$

If $\lim_{x \to a} f(x) = 0$ and $\lim_{x \to a} g(x) = \infty$, then $\lim_{x \to a} f(x) \cdot g(x)$ takes the form $0 \times \infty$.

In this case we can write $f(x) \cdot g(x) = \dfrac{f(x)}{1/g(x)}$ or $\dfrac{g(x)}{1/f(x)}$ and the limit reduces to either $\dfrac{0}{0}$ form or $\dfrac{\infty}{\infty}$ form, where L'Hospital Rule is applicable.

9.5 THE INDETERMINATE FORM $\infty - \infty$

If $\lim_{x \to a} f(x) = \infty$ and $\lim_{x \to a} g(x) = \infty$ then $\lim_{x \to a} [f(x) - g(x)]$ takes the form $\infty - \infty$.

In this case, we simplify the expression $f(x) - g(x)$, by algebraic manipulation, so that either we get $\dfrac{0}{0}$ form or $\dfrac{\infty}{\infty}$ form, where L'Hospital Rule is applicable.

Working Rule:

1. **Use of L'Hospital Rule:** Differentiate numerator and denominator separately and then put $x = a$. If this reduces to indeterminate form then apply the rule again and follow the same procedure till the limit is obtain.

2. **Use of Standard Expansions:** In case where the expansions of some of the standard functions involved in indeterminate form then they are used either to simplify the process or shorten the process.

3. **Use of Standard Limits:** Sometimes use of standard limits simplifies the process. These limits may also be used to shorten the process at an intermediate stage.

Important Standard Limits:

$$\lim_{x \to 0} \frac{\sin x}{x} = 1; \qquad \lim_{x \to 0} \frac{\tan x}{x} = 1;$$

$$\lim_{x \to 0} \frac{\sin^{-1} x}{x} = 1; \qquad \lim_{x \to 0} (1+x)^{1/x} = e;$$

$$\lim_{x \to 0} \frac{a^x - 1}{x} = \log a; \qquad \lim_{x \to 0} \frac{e^x - 1}{x} = 1.$$

9.6 ILLUSTRATIONS ON INDETERMINATE FORMS $\dfrac{0}{0}$, $\dfrac{\infty}{\infty}$, $0 \times \infty$, $\infty - \infty$

Type 1 : Form $\dfrac{0}{0}$:

Ex. 1: *Evaluate* (i) $\lim\limits_{x \to 0} \dfrac{e^{ax} - e^{-ax}}{\log(1 + bx)}$ (ii) $\lim\limits_{x \to 0} \dfrac{(1+x)^n - 1}{x}$ **(May 2010).**

Sol.: (i) $\lim\limits_{x \to 0} \dfrac{e^{ax} - e^{-ax}}{\log(1 + bx)}$ $\left(\text{Form } \dfrac{0}{0}\right)$

Applying L'Hospital Rule, we get

$$= \lim_{x \to 0} \frac{ae^{ax} + ae^{-ax}}{\frac{b}{1+bx}}$$

Taking limit, we get

$$= \frac{a+a}{b/(1+0)} = \frac{2a}{b}. \text{ Hence the value.}$$

(ii) $\lim_{x \to 0} \frac{(1+x)^n - 1}{x}$ $\left(\text{Form } \frac{0}{0}\right)$

Applying L'Hospital Rule, we get

$$= \lim_{x \to 0} \frac{n(1+x)^{n-1}}{1}$$

Taking limit, we get

$$= n(1) = n. \text{ Hence the value.}$$

Ex. 2 : Evaluate $\lim_{x \to 0} \frac{e^{2x} - (1+x)^2}{x \log(1+x)}$. (Jan 2005, May 2009)

Sol. : $\lim_{x \to 0} \frac{e^{2x} - (1+x)^2}{x \log(1+x)}$ $\left(\text{Form } \frac{0}{0}\right)$

Applying L'Hospital Rule, we get

$$= \lim_{x \to 0} \frac{2e^{2x} - 2(1+x)}{x\left(\frac{1}{1+x}\right) + \log(1+x)} \quad \left(\text{Form } \frac{0}{0}\right)$$

Again, applying L'Hospital Rule, we get

$$= \lim_{x \to 0} \frac{4e^{2x} - 2}{\frac{1}{(1+x)} - \frac{x}{(1+x)^2} + \frac{1}{(1+x)}}$$

Taking limit, we get

$$= \frac{4(1) - (2)}{(1) - (0) + (1)} = \frac{2}{2}$$

$$= 1. \text{ Hence the value.}$$

Ex. 3 : Evaluate $\lim_{x \to 0} \frac{e^{x \sin x} - \cosh(x\sqrt{2})}{x^4}$

Sol. : $\lim_{x \to 0} \frac{e^{x \sin x} - \cosh(x\sqrt{2})}{x^4}$ $\left(\text{Form } \frac{0}{0}\right)$

We shall use standard expansions of $e^{x \sin x}$ and $\cosh(x\sqrt{2})$ to evaluate the limit.

$\therefore \quad e^{x \sin x} = 1 + x \sin x + \frac{x^2}{2!}(\sin x)^2 + \frac{x^3}{3!}(\sin x)^3 + \ldots$

$$= 1 + x\left(x - \frac{x^3}{3!} \ldots\right) + \frac{x^2}{2}\left(x - \frac{x^3}{3!} \ldots\right)^2 + \ldots$$

$$= 1 + x^2 + \left(-\frac{x^4}{6} + \frac{x^4}{2}\right) + \ldots\ldots$$

$$= 1 + x^2 + \frac{x^4}{3} + \ldots\ldots \qquad \ldots (1)$$

and $\quad \cosh(x\sqrt{2}) = 1 + \frac{(x\sqrt{2})^2}{2!} + \frac{(x\sqrt{2})^4}{4!} + \ldots\ldots$

$$= 1 + x^2 + \frac{x^4}{6} + \ldots\ldots \qquad \ldots (2)$$

$$\therefore \quad \lim_{x \to 0} \frac{e^{x \sin x} - \cosh(x\sqrt{2})}{x^4} = \lim_{x \to 0} \frac{\left(1 + x^2 + \frac{x^4}{3} + \ldots\right) - \left(1 + x^2 + \frac{x^4}{6} + \ldots\right)}{x^4}$$

$$= \lim_{x \to 0} \frac{x^4\left[\left(\frac{1}{3} - \frac{1}{6}\right) + \text{terms containing } x\right]}{x^4}$$

$$= \lim_{x \to 0} \left(\frac{1}{6} + \text{terms containing } x\right)$$

$$= \frac{1}{6}. \text{ Hence the value.}$$

Ex. 4 : *Evaluate* $\displaystyle\lim_{x \to 0} \left[\frac{2x^2 - 2e^{x^2} + 2\cos(x^{3/2}) + \sin^3 x}{x^4}\right]$

Sol. : We shall use standard expansions of e^{x^2}, $\cos(x^{3/2})$ and $\sin^3 x$ to evaluate the limit.

$$\therefore \quad e^{x^2} = 1 + x^2 + \frac{x^4}{2!} + \frac{x^6}{3!} + \ldots$$

$$(\cos x^{3/2}) = 1 - \frac{x^3}{2!} + \frac{x^6}{4!} - \ldots$$

$$\sin^3 x = \left(x - \frac{x^3}{2!} + \frac{x^5}{4!} - \ldots\right)^3 = x^3\left(1 - \frac{x^2}{6} + \frac{x^4}{120} - \ldots\right)^3 = x^3\left(1 - \frac{x^2}{2} + \ldots\right)$$

Numerator $= 2x^2 - 2e^{x^2} + 2\cos(x^{3/2}) + \sin^3 x$

$$= 2x^2 - 2\left(1 + x^2 + \frac{x^4}{2} + \frac{x^6}{6} + \ldots\right) + 2\left(1 - \frac{x^3}{2} + \frac{x^6}{24} - \ldots\right) + \left(x^3 - \frac{x^5}{2} + \ldots\right)$$

$$= (-2 + 2) + (2 - 2)x^2 + (-1 + 1)x^3$$

$$\quad + (-1)x^4 + \left(-\frac{1}{2}\right)x^5 + \left(-\frac{1}{3} + \frac{1}{12}\right)x^6 + \ldots$$

$$= -x^4 - \frac{1}{2}x^5 - \frac{1}{4}x^6 + \ldots$$

Hence given limit $= \lim\limits_{x \to 0} \dfrac{\left[-x^4 - \frac{1}{2}x^5 - \frac{1}{4}x^6 \ldots\right]}{x^4}$

$= \lim\limits_{x \to 0} -\dfrac{x^4[+1 + \text{terms containing } x]}{x^4}$

$= \lim\limits_{x \to 0} -[+1 + \text{terms containing } x]$

$= -1.$ Hence the value.

Ex. 5 : *Evaluate* $\lim\limits_{x \to y} \dfrac{x^y - y^x}{x^x - y^y}$.

Sol. : $\lim x \to y \Rightarrow$ regard y as constant.

$\lim\limits_{x \to y} \dfrac{x^y - y^x}{x^x - y^y}$ $\qquad \left(\text{Form } \dfrac{0}{0}\right)$

Applying L'Hospital Rule, we get

$= \lim\limits_{x \to y} \dfrac{y x^{y-1} - y^x \log y}{x^x(1 + \log x) - 0}$ $\qquad \because \dfrac{d}{dx}(x^y) = y x^{y-1},$

Taking limit,

$\qquad \dfrac{d}{dx}(y^x) = y^x \log y,$

$= \dfrac{y \cdot y^{y-1} - y^y \log y}{y^y(1 + \log y)}$ $\qquad$ let $z = x^x$

$\qquad \therefore \log z = x \log x$

$= \dfrac{y^y - y^y \log y}{y^y(1 + \log y)}$ $\qquad \therefore \dfrac{1}{z}\dfrac{dz}{dx} = (1 + \log x)$

$= \dfrac{1 - \log y}{1 + \log y}.$ Hence the value. $\qquad \dfrac{d}{dx}(x^x) = x^x(1 + \log x)$

Note : $\lim\limits_{y \to x} \dfrac{y^x - x^y}{y^y - x^x} = \dfrac{1 - \log x}{1 + \log x}$.

Ex. 6 : $\lim\limits_{x \to 1} \dfrac{x - x^x}{1 + \log x - x}$.

Sol. : $\lim\limits_{x \to 1} \dfrac{x - x^x}{1 + \log x - x}$ $\qquad \left(\text{Form } \dfrac{0}{0}\right)$

Applying L'Hospital Rule, we get

$= \lim\limits_{x \to 1} \dfrac{1 - x^x(1 + \log x)}{1/x - 1}$ $\qquad \left(\text{Form } \dfrac{0}{0}\right)$

Again, applying L'Hospital Rule, we get

$= \lim\limits_{x \to 1} \dfrac{-x^x(1/x) - x^x(1 + \log x)^2}{-1/x^2}$

$= 2.$ Hence the value.

Ex. 7 : Find $\lim_{x \to 0} \dfrac{1 + \sin x - \cos x + \log(1-x)}{x \tan^2 x}$.

Sol. : Inconvenience of continuously differentiating the denominator, which involves $\tan^2 x$ as a factor, may be partially avoided as follows :

$$\lim_{x \to 0} \dfrac{1 + \sin x - \cos x + \log(1-x)}{x^3} \cdot \lim_{x \to 0} \left(\dfrac{x}{\tan x}\right)^2$$

$$= \lim_{x \to 0} \dfrac{1 + \sin x - \cos x + \log(1-x)}{x^3} \cdot 1 \qquad \left(\text{Form } \dfrac{0}{0}\right)$$

Applying L'Hospital Rule

$$= \lim_{x \to 0} \dfrac{\cos x + \sin x - [1/(1-x)]}{3x^2} \qquad \left(\text{Form } \dfrac{0}{0}\right)$$

Again, applying L'Hospital Rule

$$= \lim_{x \to 0} \dfrac{-\sin x + \cos x - [1/(1-x)^2]}{6x}$$

Again, applying L'Hospital Rule

$$= \lim_{x \to 0} \dfrac{-\cos x - \sin x - [2/(1-x)^3]}{6}$$

$$= \dfrac{-3}{6} = -\dfrac{1}{2}$$

Ex. 8 : Prove that $\lim_{x \to 0} \dfrac{(\sqrt{1-x} - 1)^{2n}}{(1 - \cos x)^n} = 2^{-n}$.

Sol. : $\lim_{x \to 0} \dfrac{(\sqrt{1-x} - 1)^{2n}}{(1 - \cos x)^n}$ $\qquad \left(\text{Form } \dfrac{0}{0}\right)$

$$= \lim_{x \to 0} \dfrac{(\sqrt{1-x} - 1)^{2n}}{(1 - \cos x)^n} \cdot \dfrac{(\sqrt{1-x} + 1)^{2n}}{(\sqrt{1-x} + 1)^{2n}} \cdot \dfrac{(1 + \cos x)^n}{(1 + \cos x)^n}$$

$$= \lim_{x \to 0} \dfrac{(1 - x - 1)^{2n} (1 + \cos x)^n}{(1 - \cos^2 x)^n (\sqrt{1-x} + 1)^{2n}}$$

$$= \dfrac{(-x)^{2n} (1 + \cos x)^n}{\sin^{2n} x \, (\sqrt{1-x} + 1)^{2n}}$$

$$= \lim_{x \to 0} \dfrac{(-1)^{2n} (1 + \cos x)^n}{(\sin x / x)^{2n} (\sqrt{1-x} + 1)^{2n}} \qquad \left(\because \lim_{x \to 0} \dfrac{\sin x}{x} = 1\right)$$

$$= \dfrac{(1 + 1)^n}{(1)(2)^{2n}} = 2^{-n}. \quad \text{Hence the proof.}$$

Ex. 9 : *Prove that* $\lim_{x \to 0} \dfrac{\log_{\sec x/2} \cos x}{\log_{\sec x} \cos x/2} = 16.$ **(Jan. 2005, May 2007)**

Sol. : $\lim_{x \to 0} \dfrac{\log_{\sec x/2} \cos x}{\log_{\sec x} \cos x/2}$

$$= \lim_{x \to 0} \dfrac{\dfrac{\log \cos x}{\log \sec x/2}}{\dfrac{\log \cos x/2}{\log \sec x}} \quad \text{(Using change of base formula)}$$

$$= \lim_{x \to 0} \left(\dfrac{\log \cos x}{\log \sec x/2}\right)\left(\dfrac{\log \sec x}{\log \cos x/2}\right)$$

$$= \lim_{x \to 0} \left(\dfrac{\log \cos x}{\log \cos x/2}\right)^2 \quad \left(\text{Form} \dfrac{0}{0}\right)$$

Applying L'Hospital Rule, we have

$$= \lim_{x \to 0} \left[\dfrac{\dfrac{1}{\cos x}(-\sin x)}{\dfrac{1}{\cos x/2}(-1/2 \sin x/2)}\right]^2$$

$$= \lim_{x \to 0} \left[\dfrac{\cos x/2}{\cos x} \cdot \dfrac{2 \sin x/2 \cos x/2}{1/2 \sin x/2}\right]^2$$

$$= \lim_{x \to 0} \left[\dfrac{4 \cos^2 x/2}{\cos x}\right]^2 = 16. \text{ Hence the value.}$$

Ex. 10 : *If* $\lim_{x \to 0} \dfrac{\sin 2x + p \sin x}{x^3}$ *is finite then find the value of p and hence the value of the limit.* **(May 2004, 2009, 2010, 2014)**

Sol. : $\lim_{x \to 0} \dfrac{\sin 2x + p \sin x}{x^3}$

$$= \lim_{x \to 0} \dfrac{2 \sin x \cos x + p \sin x}{x^3}$$

$$= \lim_{x \to 0} \dfrac{\sin x}{x} \times \dfrac{2 \cos x + p}{x^2}$$

$$= \lim_{x \to 0} \dfrac{2 \cos x + p}{x^2} \quad \left(\because \lim_{x \to 0} \dfrac{\sin x}{x} = 1\right)$$

Here the denominator being zero for $x = 0$ and numerator becomes $2 + p$. Therefore, if the limit is to be finite, the numerator must be zero for $x = 0$. This requires

$$2 + p = 0 \quad \Rightarrow \quad p = -2 \quad \text{... (1)}$$

With this value of p, required limit

$$= \lim_{x \to 0} \frac{2\cos x - 2}{x^2} \quad \left(\text{Form } \frac{0}{0}\right)$$

$$= \lim_{x \to 0} \left(-\frac{\sin x}{x}\right) \quad \text{(by L'Hospital Rule)}$$

$$= -1 \quad \ldots (2)$$

Hence $\quad p = -2 \quad$ and $\quad \text{limit} = -1$

Ex. 11 : *Find the values of a and b if* $\lim_{x \to 0} \dfrac{x(1 + a\cos x) - b\sin x}{x^3} = 1.$ **(Dec. 2009)**

Sol. : $\lim_{x \to 0} \dfrac{x(1 + a\cos x) - b\sin x}{x^3} \quad \left(\text{Form } \dfrac{0}{0}\right)$

Applying L'Hospital Rule, we have

$$= \lim_{x \to 0} \frac{(1 + a\cos x) - ax\sin x - b\cos x}{3x^2} \quad \ldots (1)$$

In (1), the denominator being zero for $x = 0$ and numerator becomes $1 + a - b$. Therefore, the fraction will not tend to a finite limit unless numerator is also zero for $x = 0$. This requires

$$1 + a - b = 0 \quad \ldots (2)$$

With this relation between a and b, (1) is of the form $\dfrac{0}{0}$.

Again, applying L'Hospital Rule, we have, from (1),

$$= \lim_{x \to 0} \frac{-a\sin x - a\sin x - ax\cos x + b\sin x}{6x}$$

$$= \lim_{x \to 0} \frac{-2a\sin x - ax\cos x + b\sin x}{6x} \quad \left(\text{Form } \frac{0}{0}\right)$$

Again, applying L'Hospital Rule

$$= \lim_{x \to 0} \frac{-3a\cos x + ax\sin x + b\cos x}{6}$$

Taking the limit $= \dfrac{b - 3a}{6}$

But given that, limit of fraction is 1

$\therefore \quad \dfrac{b - 3a}{6} = 1 \quad \Rightarrow \quad -3a + b = 6 \quad \ldots (3)$

Solving (2) and (3), we get

$$a = -\frac{5}{2} \quad \text{and} \quad b = -\frac{3}{2}$$

Ex. 12 : *Find a, b and c if* $\lim_{x \to 0} \dfrac{ae^x - b\cos x + ce^{-x}}{x \sin x} = 2$.

Sol. : $\lim_{x \to 0} \dfrac{ae^x - b\cos x + ce^{-x}}{x \sin x}$ ... (1)

Here denominator in (1) being zero for $x = 0$ and numerator becomes $a - b + c$. Since the given limit is finite, numerator must be zero for $x = 0$. This requires

$$a - b + c = 0 \qquad \ldots (2)$$

With this relation between a, b and c, (1) is of the form $\dfrac{0}{0}$.

Applying L'Hospital Rule, we have

$$= \lim_{x \to 0} \dfrac{ae^x + b\sin x - ce^{-x}}{\sin x + x \cos x} \qquad \ldots (3)$$

Here again denominator in (3) being zero for $x = 0$ and numerator becomes $a - c$. Since the given limit is finite, numerator must be zero for $x = 0$. This requires

$$a - c = 0 \qquad \ldots (4)$$

With this relation, limit given by (3) takes the form $\dfrac{0}{0}$.

Again, applying L'Hospital Rule, we have

$$= \lim_{x \to 0} \dfrac{ae^x + b\cos x + ce^{-x}}{\cos x + \cos x - x \sin x} = \dfrac{a+b+c}{2}$$

But limit of the given fraction is 2.

$\therefore \qquad \dfrac{a+b+c}{2} = 2 \quad \Rightarrow \quad a + b + c = 4 \qquad \ldots (5)$

Solving (2), (4) and (5) for a, b, c, we get

$$a = 1, \quad b = 2, \quad \text{and} \quad c = 1$$

Type 2 : Form $\dfrac{\infty}{\infty}$:

Ex. 13 : *Evaluate* $\lim_{x \to 0} \dfrac{\log \tan x}{\log x}$. **(May 2010)**

Sol. : $\lim_{x \to 0} \dfrac{\log \tan x}{\log x}$ $\left(\text{Form } \dfrac{\infty}{\infty}\right)$

Applying L'Hospital Rule, we get

$$= \lim_{x \to 0} \dfrac{\dfrac{1}{\tan x} \sec^2 x}{\dfrac{1}{x}} \qquad \left(\text{Form } \dfrac{\infty}{\infty}\right)$$

$$= \lim_{x \to 0} \frac{x}{\sin x \cos x} \quad \text{(Note this step)} \quad \left(\text{Form } \frac{0}{0}\right)$$

$$= \lim_{x \to 0} \frac{2x}{\sin 2x}$$

$$= 1. \quad \text{Hence the value.}$$

Important Rule :

Indeterminate form of the type $\frac{\infty}{\infty}$ after applying L'Hospital Rule (once or number of times) reduces again to the form $\frac{\infty}{\infty}$ then change it to the form $\frac{0}{0}$ and apply L'Hospital Rule to evaluate the limit.

Ex. 14 : Determine $\lim_{x \to \pi/2} \frac{\tan 3x}{\tan x}$.

Sol. : $\lim_{x \to \pi/2} \frac{\tan 3x}{\tan x}$. $\qquad \left(\text{Form } \frac{\infty}{\infty}\right)$

Applying L'Hospital Rule

$$= \lim_{x \to \pi/2} \frac{3 \sec^2 3x}{\sec^2 x} \qquad \left(\text{Form } \frac{\infty}{\infty}\right)$$

$$= \lim_{x \to \pi/2} \frac{3 \cos^2 x}{\cos^2 3x} \quad \text{(Note this step)} \quad \left(\text{Form } \frac{0}{0}\right)$$

Again, applying L'Hospital Rule

$$= \lim_{x \to \pi/2} \frac{\sin 2x}{\sin 6x} \qquad \left(\text{Form } \frac{0}{0}\right)$$

Again, applying L'Hospital Rule

$$= \lim_{x \to \pi/2} \frac{2 \cos 2x}{6 \cos 6x}$$

$$= 1/3. \quad \text{Hence the value.}$$

Ex. 15 : Evaluate $\lim_{\theta \to \pi/2} \frac{\log\left(\theta - \frac{\pi}{2}\right)}{\tan \theta}$.

Sol. : $\lim_{\theta \to \pi/2} \frac{\log\left(\theta - \frac{\pi}{2}\right)}{\tan \theta}$ $\qquad \left(\text{Form } \frac{\infty}{\infty}\right)$

Applying L'Hospital Rule, we get

$$= \lim_{\theta \to \pi/2} \frac{1/(\theta - \pi/2)}{\sec^2 \theta} \qquad \left(\text{Form } \frac{\infty}{\infty}\right)$$

$$= \lim_{\theta \to \pi/2} \frac{\cos^2 \theta}{\theta - \pi/2} \qquad \left(\text{Form } \frac{0}{0}\right)$$

Again applying L'Hospital Rule, we get

$$= \lim_{\theta \to \frac{\pi}{2}} \frac{-2\cos\theta\sin\theta}{1}$$

$$= 0. \quad \text{Hence the value.}$$

Ex. 16 : Evaluate $\lim_{x \to 0} \frac{\log \sin 2x}{\log \sin x}$.

Sol. : $\lim_{x \to 0} \frac{\log \sin 2x}{\log \sin x}$ $\left(\text{Form } \frac{\infty}{\infty}\right)$

$$= \lim_{x \to 0} \frac{2 \cot 2x}{\cot x} \quad \left(\text{Form } \frac{\infty}{\infty}\right)$$

$$= 2 \lim_{x \to 0} \frac{\tan x}{\tan 2x} = 2 \lim_{x \to 0} \frac{x(\tan x / x)}{2x(\tan 2x / 2x)}$$

(Note this step)

$$= 1. \quad \text{Hence the value.}$$

Ex. 17 : Evaluate $\lim_{x \to 0} \log_{\tan x} \tan 2x$. **(Jan. 2004, Dec. 2014)**

Sol. : Changing the base to e, we have

$$\lim_{x \to 0} \log_{\tan x} \tan 2x = \lim_{x \to 0} \frac{\log_e \tan 2x}{\log_e \tan x} \quad \left(\text{Form } \frac{\infty}{\infty}\right)$$

$$= \lim_{x \to 0} \frac{\frac{2\sec^2 2x}{\tan 2x}}{\frac{\sec^2 x}{\tan x}} \quad \text{(By L'Hospital Rule)}$$

$$= 2 \left[\lim_{x \to 0} \frac{\tan x}{\tan 2x}\right] \cdot \left[\lim_{x \to 0} \frac{\sec^2 2x}{\sec^2 x}\right]$$

$$= 2 \left[\lim_{x \to 0} \frac{\tan x / x}{2 \tan 2x / 2x}\right] \times 1 = 2 \left[\frac{1}{2}\right]$$

$$= 1. \quad \text{Hence the value.}$$

Type 3 : Form $0 \times \infty$:

Ex. 18 : Evaluate $\lim_{x \to 0} \sin x \log x$.

Sol. : $\lim_{x \to 0} \sin x \log x$ (Form $0 \times \infty$)

$$= \lim_{x \to 0} \frac{\log x}{\cosec x} \quad \left(\text{Form } \frac{\infty}{\infty}\right)$$

$$= \lim_{x \to 0} \frac{1/x}{-\cosec x \cot x} = -\lim_{x \to 0} \frac{\sin^2 x}{x \cos x} \quad \left(\text{Form } \frac{0}{0}\right)$$

$$= -\lim_{x \to 0} \frac{2 \sin x \cos x}{\cos x - x \sin x} \quad \text{(By L'Hospital Rule)}$$

$$= -\left(\frac{0}{1-0}\right) = 0. \quad \text{Hence the value.}$$

Ex. 19 : Evaluate $\lim_{x \to 0} x \log x$. (May 2010)

Sol. :
$$\lim_{x \to 0} x \log x \quad \text{(Form } 0 \times \infty\text{)}$$
$$= \lim_{x \to 0} \frac{\log x}{1/x} \quad \left(\text{Form } \frac{\infty}{\infty}\right)$$
$$= \lim_{x \to 0} \frac{1/x}{-1/x^2} \quad \text{(By L'Hospital Rule)}$$
$$= \lim_{x \to 0} (-x)$$
$$= 0. \quad \text{Hence the value.}$$

Ex. 20 : Prove that $\lim_{x \to a} \sin^{-1} \sqrt{\frac{a-x}{a+x}} \operatorname{cosec} \sqrt{a^2 - x^2} = \frac{1}{2a}$. (Dec. 2009)

Sol. : The indeterminate form is $(0 \times \infty)$ and the limit can be arranged in the form

$$\lim_{x \to a} \frac{\sin^{-1}\sqrt{\frac{a-x}{a+x}}}{\sin \sqrt{a^2 - x^2}} \quad \left(\text{Form } \frac{0}{0}\right)$$

We can find the limit by L'Hospital Rule, however, use of $\lim_{\theta \to 0} \frac{\sin \theta}{\theta} = 1$ will be more convenient, hence the limit

$$= \lim_{x \to a} \frac{\left\{\dfrac{\sin^{-1}\sqrt{\frac{a-x}{a+x}}}{\sqrt{\frac{a-x}{a+x}}} \cdot \sqrt{\frac{a-x}{a+x}}\right\}}{\left\{\dfrac{\sin\sqrt{a^2-x^2}}{\sqrt{a^2-x^2}} \cdot \sqrt{a^2-x^2}\right\}} = \lim_{x \to a} \frac{\left[\dfrac{\sin^{-1}\alpha}{\alpha} \sqrt{\frac{a-x}{a+x}}\right]}{\left[\dfrac{\sin \beta}{\beta} \sqrt{a^2-x^2}\right]}$$

where $\quad \alpha = \sqrt{\dfrac{a-x}{a+x}} \to 0 \quad \text{as } x \to a$

and $\quad \beta = \sqrt{a^2 - x^2} \to 0 \quad \text{as } x \to a$

$\therefore \quad \dfrac{\sin^{-1}\alpha}{\alpha} \to 1 \quad \text{and} \quad \dfrac{\sin \beta}{\beta} \to 1 \quad \text{as } x \to a$

$$= \lim_{x \to a} \sqrt{\frac{a-x}{a+x}} \cdot \frac{1}{\sqrt{a^2 - x^2}} = \lim_{x \to a} \frac{1}{a+x}$$

$$= \frac{1}{2a}. \quad \text{Hence the proof.}$$

Ex. 21 : *Evaluate* $\lim_{x \to 0} x^m (\log x)^n$, where m and n are positive integers.

Sol. : $\lim_{x \to 0} x^m (\log x)^n$ (Form $0 \times \infty$)

$$= \lim_{x \to 0} \frac{(\log x)^n}{x^{-m}} \quad \left(\text{Form } \frac{\infty}{\infty}\right)$$

$$= \lim_{x \to 0} \frac{n (\log x)^{n-1} (1/x)}{-mx^{-m-1}} \quad \text{(By L'Hospital Rule)}$$

$$= \lim_{x \to 0} \left[(-1) \frac{n (\log x)^{n-1}}{m x^{-m}}\right] \quad \left(\text{Form } \frac{\infty}{\infty}\right)$$

$$= \lim_{x \to 0} \left[(-1)^2 \frac{n(n-1)}{m^2} \frac{(\log x)^{n-2}}{x^{-m}}\right] \quad \left(\text{Form } \frac{\infty}{\infty}\right)$$

Applying L'Hospital Rule (n – 2) times

$$= \lim_{x \to 0} \frac{(-1)^n n! (\log x)^0}{m^n (x^{-m})}$$

$$= \frac{(-1)^n n!}{m^n} \lim_{x \to 0} (x^m) = 0. \text{ Hence the value.}$$

Type 4 : Form $\infty - \infty$:

Ex. 22 : *Evaluate* $\lim_{x \to 1} \left[\frac{x}{x-1} - \frac{1}{\log x}\right]$.   **(Jan. 2004, May 2009)**

Sol. : $\lim_{x \to 1} \left[\frac{x}{x-1} - \frac{1}{\log x}\right]$ (Form $\infty - \infty$)

$$= \lim_{x \to 1} \left[\frac{x \log x - x + 1}{(x-1) \log x}\right] \quad \left(\text{Form } \frac{0}{0}\right)$$

$$= \lim_{x \to 1} \left[\frac{(1 + \log x) - 1}{\frac{(x-1)}{x} + \log x}\right] \quad \text{(By L'Hospital Rule)}$$

$$= \lim_{x \to 1} \left[\frac{\log x}{1 - \frac{1}{x} + \log x}\right] \quad \left(\text{Form } \frac{0}{0}\right)$$

$$= \lim_{x \to 1} \left[\frac{(1/x)}{\frac{1}{x^2} + \frac{1}{x}}\right] \quad \text{(By L'Hospital Rule)}$$

$$= \frac{1}{2}. \text{ Hence the limit.}$$

Ex. 23 : *Prove that* $\lim_{x \to 0} \left[\frac{a}{x} - \cot \frac{x}{a}\right] = 0$.   **(Jan. 2005, Dec. 2006, May 2009)**

Sol. : For simplicity, let $\frac{x}{a} = y$, then as $x \to 0$, $y \to 0$.

$$\text{Limit} = \lim_{y \to 0} \left[\frac{1}{y} - \cot y\right] \qquad \text{(Form } \infty - \infty\text{)}$$

$$= \lim_{y \to 0} \left[\frac{1}{y} - \frac{\cos y}{\sin y}\right]$$

$$= \lim_{y \to 0} \left[\frac{\sin y - y \cos y}{y \sin y}\right] \qquad \left(\text{Form } \frac{0}{0}\right)$$

$$= \lim_{y \to 0} \left[\frac{\cos y + y \sin y - \cos y}{\sin y + y \cos y}\right] \qquad \text{(By L'Hospital Rule)}$$

$$= \lim_{y \to 0} \left[\frac{y \sin y}{\sin y + y \cos y}\right] \qquad \left(\text{Form } \frac{0}{0}\right)$$

$$= \lim_{y \to 0} \left[\frac{\sin y + y \cos y}{\cos y - y \sin y + \cos y}\right] \qquad \text{(By L'Hospital Rule)}$$

$$= \frac{0 + 0}{1 - 0 + 1} = \frac{0}{2} = 0. \text{ Hence the proof.}$$

Ex. 24 : Evaluate $\lim_{x \to 0} \left(\frac{1}{x^2} - \cot^2 x\right)$.

Sol. : $\lim_{x \to 0} \left(\frac{1}{x^2} - \cot^2 x\right)$ \hfill (Form $\infty - \infty$)

Simplifying
$$= \lim_{x \to 0} \left(\frac{1}{x^2} - \frac{1}{\tan^2 x}\right) = \lim_{x \to 0} \left(\frac{\tan^2 x - x^2}{x^2 \tan^2 x}\right)$$

$$= \lim_{x \to 0} \frac{\tan^2 x - x^2}{x^4 \left(\frac{\tan x}{x}\right)^2} = \lim_{x \to 0} \frac{\tan^2 x - x^2}{x^4} \qquad \left(\text{Form } \frac{0}{0}\right)$$

Applying L'Hospital Rule,

$$= \lim_{x \to 0} \frac{2 \tan x \sec^2 x - 2x}{4x^3}$$

$$= \frac{1}{2} \lim_{x \to 0} \frac{\tan x \sec^2 x - x}{x^3} \qquad \left(\text{Form } \frac{0}{0}\right)$$

$$= \frac{1}{2} \lim_{x \to 0} \frac{\sec^4 x + 2 \tan^2 x \sec^2 x - 1}{3x^2}$$

$$= \frac{1}{6} \lim_{x \to 0} \frac{(\sec^4 x - 1) + 2 \tan^2 x \sec^2 x}{x^2}$$

$$= \frac{1}{6} \lim_{x \to 0} \frac{(\sec^2 x - 1)(\sec^2 x + 1) + 2 \sec^2 x \tan^2 x}{x^2}$$

$$= \frac{1}{6} \lim_{x \to 0} \frac{\tan^2 x (\sec^2 x + 1) + 2 \sec^2 x \tan^2 x}{x^2}$$

$$= \frac{1}{6} \lim_{x \to 0} \frac{\tan^2 x \{\sec^2 x + 1 + 2 \sec^2 x\}}{x^2}$$

$$= \frac{1}{6} \lim_{x \to 0} \left(\frac{\tan x}{x}\right)^2 (3 \sec^2 x + 1)$$

$$= \frac{1}{6} (1)^2 \cdot (3 \cdot 1 + 1) = \frac{2}{3} \quad \text{Hence the value.}$$

EXERCISE 9.1

1. Evaluate:

   (i) $\lim\limits_{x \to 1} \dfrac{\sqrt{1+x} - \sqrt{1+x^2}}{\sqrt{1-x} - \sqrt{1-x^2}}$

   (ii) $\lim\limits_{x \to 0} \dfrac{\sqrt{a+x} - \sqrt{a}}{x}$

   (iii) $\lim\limits_{x \to 1} \dfrac{\sqrt{x-1} + \sqrt{x-1}}{\sqrt{x^2-1}}$

   (iv) $\lim\limits_{x \to 0} \dfrac{xe^x - \log(1+x)}{x^2}$ (May 2008)

   (v) $\lim\limits_{x \to 0} \dfrac{e^x - 1 - x}{\log(1+x) - x}$

   (vi) $\lim\limits_{x \to 0} \dfrac{e^x - 2\cos x + e^{-x}}{x \sin x}$

   (vii) $\lim\limits_{x \to 0} \dfrac{\tan x - x}{x - \sin x}$

   (viii) $\lim\limits_{x \to 0} \dfrac{\tan x - x}{x^2 \tan x}$

   (ix) $\lim\limits_{x \to 0} \dfrac{x \cos x - \log(1+x)}{x^2}$

   (x) $\lim\limits_{x \to 0} \dfrac{e^x + \log\left(\dfrac{1-x}{e}\right)}{\tan x - x}$ (Dec. 2008)

   (xi) $\lim\limits_{x \to 0} \dfrac{x - \log(1+x)}{x^2}$

   (xii) $\lim\limits_{x \to 0} \dfrac{e^x - e^{-x} - 2\log(1+x)}{x \sin x}$ (May 2005)

   Ans. (i) 0, (ii) $\dfrac{1}{2\sqrt{a}}$, (iii) $\dfrac{1}{\sqrt{2}}$, (iv) $\dfrac{3}{2}$, (v) -1, (vi) 2, (vii) 2, (viii) $\dfrac{1}{3}$, (ix) $\dfrac{1}{2}$, (x) $-\dfrac{1}{2}$, (xi) $\dfrac{1}{2}$, (xii) 1.

2. Evaluate:

   (i) $\lim\limits_{x \to 0} \dfrac{a^x - 1 - x \log a}{x^2}$

   (ii) $\lim\limits_{x \to 0} \dfrac{a^x - b^x}{x}$

   (iii) $\lim\limits_{x \to a} \dfrac{x^a - a^x}{x^x - a^a}$

   (iv) $\lim\limits_{x \to 0} \left(\dfrac{5 \sin x - 7 \sin 2x + 3 \sin 3x}{\tan x - x}\right)$

(v) $\lim\limits_{x \to 0} \dfrac{\log(1+kx^2)}{1-\cos x}$ (Dec. 2005)

(vi) $\lim\limits_{y \to x} \dfrac{x^y - y^x}{y^y - x^x}$

(vii) $\lim\limits_{x \to 0} \dfrac{(1+x)^{1/x} - e}{x}$ (Jan. 2004)

(viii) $\lim\limits_{x \to 0} \left(\dfrac{e^x \sin x - x - x^2}{x^2 + x \log(1-x)}\right)$ (Dec. 2010)

(ix) $\lim\limits_{x \to 0} \dfrac{(1+x)^{1/x} - e + e^{x/2}}{x^2}$ (May 2008)

Ans. (i) $\dfrac{1}{2}(\log a)^2$, (ii) $\log\left(\dfrac{a}{b}\right)$, (iii) $\dfrac{1-\log a}{1+\log a}$, (iv) -15, (v) $2k$, (vi) $\dfrac{\log x - 1}{1 + \log x}$

(vii) $\left(-\dfrac{e}{2}\right)$, (viii) $\left(-\dfrac{2}{3}\right)$, (ix) $\dfrac{11e}{24}$

3. Prove that:

(i) $\lim\limits_{x \to 0} \dfrac{\sin x \sin^{-1} x - x^2}{x^6} = \dfrac{1}{18}$

(ii) $\lim\limits_{x \to 0} \dfrac{\tanh x - 2\sin x + x}{x^5} = \dfrac{7}{60}$ (Dec. 2010)

(iii) $\lim\limits_{x \to 0} \dfrac{x \sin(\sin x) - \sin^2 x}{x^6} = \dfrac{1}{18}$

(iv) $\lim\limits_{x \to a} \dfrac{\sqrt{x-a} + \sqrt{x} - \sqrt{a}}{\sqrt{x^2 - a^2}} = \dfrac{1}{\sqrt{2a}}$

(v) $\lim\limits_{x \to 1/2} \dfrac{(x - 4x^4)^{1/2} - \left(\dfrac{x}{4}\right)^{1/3}}{1 - (8x^3)^{1/4}} = \dfrac{8}{9}$

(vi) $\lim\limits_{\phi \to \alpha} \dfrac{1 - \cos(\phi - \alpha)}{(\sin \phi - \sin \alpha)^2} = \dfrac{1}{2}\sec^2 \alpha$

(vii) $\lim\limits_{x \to 0} (1 + \tan x)^{\cot x} = e$

(viii) $\lim\limits_{x \to 0} \dfrac{bx[\cosh bx - \cosh ax]}{bx \cosh bx - \sin bx} = \dfrac{3(b^2 - a^2)}{2b^2}$

(ix) $\lim\limits_{x \to 0} \dfrac{\sqrt{x} \tan x}{(e^x - 1)^{3/2}} = 1$,

(x) $\lim\limits_{x \to 0} \left(\dfrac{e^x - e^{\sin x}}{x - \sin x}\right) = 1$

4. Find a, b if $\lim\limits_{x \to 0} \dfrac{a \sin^2 x + b \log \cos x}{x^4} = -\dfrac{1}{2}$ (Jan. 04, Dec. 10) **Ans.** $a = 1, b = 2$.

5. Find the values of a and b if $\lim\limits_{x \to 0} (x^{-3} \sin x + ax^{-2} + b) = 0$. (Jan. 2005, May 2007)

(May 2013, Dec. 2014) **Ans.** $a = -1, b = \dfrac{1}{6}$.

6. Find a and b if $\lim_{x \to 0} \dfrac{a \sinh x + b \sin x}{x^3} = \dfrac{5}{3}$ (Dec. 08, 12) Ans. a = 5, b = −5

7. Find the values of a and b such that $\lim_{x \to 0} \dfrac{a \cos x - a + bx^2}{x^4} = \dfrac{1}{12}$ (May 2011, 2014)

   Ans. a = 2, b = 1.

8. Determine a, b, c so that $\lim_{x \to 0} \dfrac{(a + b \cos x) x - c \sin x}{x^5} = 1$. (May 2006, Dec. 2009)

   [Hint : a + b − c = 0, c − 3b = 0, 5b − c = 120.]   Ans. a = 120, b = 60, c = 180.

9. Determine a, b, c so that $\lim_{x \to 0} \dfrac{a \tanh x + b \sin x + cx}{x^5} = \dfrac{7}{60}$.

   [Hint : a + b + c = 0, 2a + b = 0, 16a + b = 14].   Ans. a = −1, b = −2, c = 3.

10. Evaluate :

    (i) $\lim_{x \to 0} \dfrac{\log x^2}{\cot x^2}$

    (ii) $\lim_{x \to 0} \dfrac{\log \sin x}{\cot x}$

    (iii) $\lim_{x \to 0} \dfrac{\log \tan 2x}{\log \tan x}$

    (iv) $\lim_{x \to 0} \dfrac{\log (x - a)}{(e^x - e^a)}$

    (v) $\lim_{x \to \pi/2} \dfrac{\tan x}{\tan 3x}$

    (vi) $\lim_{x \to 0} \dfrac{\log x}{\cosec x}$

    (vii) $\lim_{x \to 0} \dfrac{\log_{\sin x} \cos x}{\log_{\sin x/2} \cos x/2}$

Ans. (i) 0, (ii) 0, (iii) 1, (iv) 0, (v) 1, (vi) 0, (vii) 4.

11. Evaluate :

    (i) $\lim_{y \to \infty} y^2 \left(1 - e^{-\frac{2gx}{y^2}}\right)$

    (ii) $\lim_{x \to \infty} \left(x + \dfrac{1}{2}\right) \left\{\log\left(x + \dfrac{1}{2}\right) - \log x\right\}$ (Dec. 2008, May 2011)

    (iii) $\lim_{x \to \pi/2} (1 - \sin x) \tan x$

    (iv) $\lim_{x \to 1} (1 - x) \tan \dfrac{\pi x}{2}$

    (v) $\lim_{x \to 0} \cot x \cdot \log \left(\dfrac{1 + x}{1 - x}\right)$

    (vi) $\lim_{x \to 0} x \log \sin x$

    (vii) $\lim_{x \to a} \sqrt{\dfrac{a + x}{a - x}} \tan^{-1} \sqrt{a^2 - x^2}$ (May 2007, Dec. 2005)

(viii) $\lim\limits_{x \to a} \log\left(2 - \dfrac{x}{a}\right) \cot(x-a)$

Ans. (i) $2gx$, (ii) **Hint:** $\lim\limits_{x \to \infty} \left(x + \dfrac{1}{2}\right)\left[\log\left(1 + \dfrac{1}{2x}\right)\right]; \dfrac{1}{2}$ (iii) 0, (iv) $\dfrac{2}{\pi}$, (v) 2,

(vi) 0, (vii) 2a

12. Evaluate:

(i) $\lim\limits_{x \to 1} \left(\dfrac{1}{x-1} - \dfrac{2}{x^2-1}\right)$

(ii) $\lim\limits_{x \to 0} \left(\dfrac{1}{x} - \dfrac{1}{e^x - 1}\right)$

(iii) $\lim\limits_{x \to 2} \left[\dfrac{1}{x-2} - \dfrac{1}{\log(x-1)}\right]$

(iv) $\lim\limits_{x \to \pi/2} \left[\tan x - \dfrac{2x \sec x}{\pi}\right]$

(v) $\lim\limits_{x \to 0} \left(\dfrac{1}{\sin^2 x} - \dfrac{1}{x^2}\right)$,

(vi) $\lim\limits_{x \to \pi/2} \left(x \tan x - \dfrac{\pi}{2} \sec x\right)$,

(vii) $\lim\limits_{x \to \infty} \left[x - \sqrt{(x-a)(x-b)}\right]$

(viii) $\lim\limits_{x \to \infty} \left\{x - x^2 \log\left(1 + \dfrac{1}{x}\right)\right\}$ **(Dec. 2005)**

(ix) $\lim\limits_{x \to 0} \left(\dfrac{\pi}{4x} - \dfrac{\pi}{2x(e^{\pi x} + 1)}\right)$ **(May 2006)**

(x) $\lim\limits_{x \to 0} \left[\dfrac{1}{x} - \dfrac{1}{x^2} \log(1+x)\right]$ **(May 2007)**

(xi) $\lim\limits_{x \to \pi/2} (\sec x - \tan x)$ **(May 2015)**

(xii) $\lim\limits_{x \to 0} \left(\dfrac{1}{x} - \dfrac{1}{\sin x}\right)$

Ans. (i) $\dfrac{1}{2}$, (ii) $\dfrac{1}{2}$, (iii) $-\dfrac{1}{2}$, (iv) $\dfrac{2}{\pi}$, (v) $\dfrac{1}{3}$, (vi) -1 (vii) $\dfrac{1}{2}(a+b)$, (viii) $\dfrac{1}{2}$,

(ix) $\dfrac{\pi^2}{8}$, (x) $\dfrac{1}{2}$, (xi) 0, (xii) 0.

9.7 THE INDETERMINATE FORMS 0^0, ∞^0, 1^∞

Consider first the indeterminate form 0^0:

Thus, $\lim\limits_{x \to a} f(x) = 0$, $\lim\limits_{x \to a} g(x) = 0$,

then $\lim\limits_{x \to a} \{f(x)\}^{g(x)}$ takes the form 0^0.

In this case if the true value of the limit be denoted by L

then $\qquad L = \lim_{x \to a} \{f(x)\}^{g(x)}$

$\therefore \qquad \log L = \lim_{x \to a} g(x) \log f(x)$ which is of the form $(0 \times \infty)$ and hence its limit can be determined as in (9.6 Type III). If this true value be denoted by b, say then

$$\log L = b$$
$$\therefore \quad L = e^b$$

A similar method of taking logarithms of the given function, when the indeterminate form is ∞^0 or 1^∞ is used in getting the true value of the limits as it reduces again to indeterminate form $0 \times \infty$.

9.8 ILLUSTRATIONS ON INDETERMINATE FORMS 0^0, ∞^0, 1^∞

Type I : Form 0^0 :

Ex. 1 : Evaluate $\lim_{x \to \pi/2} (\cos x)^{\cos x}$. **(Dec. 2012, May 2014)**

Sol. : Let $\qquad L = \lim_{x \to \pi/2} (\cos x)^{\cos x}$ (Form 0^0)

$\therefore \qquad \log L = \lim_{x \to \pi/2} \cos x \log (\cos x)$ (Form $0 \times \infty$)

$\qquad = \lim_{x \to \pi/2} \dfrac{\log (\cos x)}{\sec x}$ $\left(\text{Form } \dfrac{\infty}{\infty}\right)$

$\qquad = \lim_{x \to \pi/2} \dfrac{(-\sin x / \cos x)}{(\sec x \tan x)} = \lim_{x \to \pi/2} (-\cos x) = 0$

$\therefore \qquad L = e^0 = 1.$ Hence the value.

Ex. 2 : Prove that $\lim_{x \to 1} (1 - x^2)^{1/\log (1-x)} = e$

Sol. : Let $\qquad L = \lim_{x \to 1} (1 - x^2)^{1/\log (1-x)}$ (Form 0^0)

$\therefore \qquad \log L = \lim_{x \to 1} \dfrac{\log (1 - x^2)}{\log (1 - x)}$ $\left(\text{Form } \dfrac{\infty}{\infty}\right)$

$\qquad = \lim_{x \to 1} \left[\dfrac{\log (1 - x) + \log (1 + x)}{\log (1 - x)}\right]$

$\qquad = \lim_{x \to 1} \left[1 + \dfrac{\log (1 + x)}{\log (1 - x)}\right]$

$\qquad = 1 + 0 = 1$

$\therefore \qquad L = e^1 = e.$ Hence the proof.

Ex. 3 : Evaluate $\lim_{x \to \infty} \left(\dfrac{1}{x}\right)^{1/x}$. **(May 2010)**

Sol. : Let $\qquad L = \lim_{x \to \infty} \left(\dfrac{1}{x}\right)^{1/x}$ (Form 0^0)

$$\therefore \quad \log L = \lim_{x \to \infty} \frac{1}{x} \log \frac{1}{x} \quad \text{(Form } 0 \times \infty\text{)}$$

$$= \lim_{x \to \infty} -\frac{\log x}{x} \quad \left(\text{Form } \frac{\infty}{\infty}\right)$$

$$= -\lim_{x \to \infty} \frac{(1/x)}{1} \quad \text{(By L'Hospital Rule)}$$

$$= 0$$

$$\therefore \quad L = e^0 = 1. \text{ Hence the value}$$

Type II : Form ∞^0 :

Ex. 4 : Evaluate $\lim_{x \to 0} \left(\frac{1}{x}\right)^{2 \sin x}$. **(Jan. 2004, May 2009)**

Sol. : Let
$$L = \lim_{x \to 0} \left(\frac{1}{x}\right)^{2 \sin x} \quad \text{(Form } \infty^0\text{)}$$

$$\therefore \quad \log L = \lim_{x \to 0} (2 \sin x) \log\left(\frac{1}{x}\right) \quad \text{(Form } 0 \times \infty\text{)}$$

$$= \lim_{x \to 0} -\frac{2 \log x}{\cosec x} \text{ (Note this step)} \quad \left(\text{Form } \frac{\infty}{\infty}\right)$$

$$= 2 \lim_{x \to 0} -\frac{1/x}{-\cosec x \cot x} \quad \text{(By L'Hospital Rule)}$$

$$= 2 \lim_{x \to 0} \frac{\sin^2 x}{x \cos x} \quad \left(\text{Form } \frac{0}{0}\right)$$

$$= 2 \lim_{x \to 0} \frac{2 \sin x \cos x}{\cos x - x \sin x} \quad \text{(By L'Hospital Rule)}$$

$$= 4 \cdot \frac{0}{1 - 0} = 0$$

$$\therefore \quad L = e^0 = 1. \text{ Hence the value.}$$

Ex. 5 : Evaluate $\lim_{x \to 0} (\cot x)^{\sin x}$. **(May 2007, 2010, 2014)**

Sol. : Let
$$L = \lim_{x \to 0} (\cot x)^{\sin x} \quad \text{(Form } \infty^0\text{)}$$

$$\therefore \quad \log L = \lim_{x \to 0} \sin x \log (\cot x) \quad \text{(Form } 0 \times \infty\text{)}$$

$$= \lim_{x \to 0} \frac{\log (\cot x)}{\cosec x} \quad \left(\text{Form } \frac{\infty}{\infty}\right)$$

$$= \lim_{x \to 0} \frac{\frac{1}{\cot x}(-\cosec^2 x)}{-\cosec x \cot x}$$

$$= \lim_{x \to 0} \frac{\cosec x}{\cot^2 x} \quad \left(\text{Form } \frac{\infty}{\infty}\right)$$

$$= \lim_{x \to 0} \frac{\sin x}{\cos^2 x} = 0$$

$$\therefore \quad L = e^0 = 1. \text{ Hence the value.}$$

Ex. 6 : *Evaluate* $\lim_{x \to 0} \left(\log \frac{1}{x}\right)^{\log(1-x)}$

Sol. : Let $L = \lim_{x \to 0} \left(\log \frac{1}{x}\right)^{\log(1-x)}$ (Form ∞^0)

$\therefore \quad \log L = \lim_{x \to 0} \log(1-x) \, [\log(-\log x)]$ $\quad\left(\text{Form } \dfrac{\infty}{\infty}\right)$

$= \lim_{x \to 0} \dfrac{\log(-\log x)}{\dfrac{1}{\log(1-x)}}$

$= \lim_{x \to 0} \dfrac{\dfrac{1}{-\log x}\left(-\dfrac{1}{x}\right)}{-\left[\dfrac{1}{\log(1-x)}\right]^2 \left(-\dfrac{1}{1-x}\right)}$ (By L'Hospital Rule)

$= \lim_{x \to 0} \dfrac{[\log(1-x)]^2}{x \log x} \cdot \lim_{x \to 0} \left(\dfrac{1}{1-x}\right)$

$= \lim_{x \to 0} \dfrac{[\log(1-x)]^2}{x \log x} \quad \left(\because \lim_{x \to 0} x \log x = 0 \therefore \text{ Form is } \dfrac{0}{0}\right)$

$= \lim_{x \to 0} \dfrac{2 \log(1-x) \cdot \left(-\dfrac{1}{1-x}\right)}{1 + \log x}$ (By L'Hospital Rule)

$= -2 \lim_{x \to 0} \dfrac{\log(1-x)}{1 + \log x} \cdot \lim_{x \to 0} \left(\dfrac{1}{1-x}\right)$

$= -2 \left(\dfrac{0}{-\infty}\right) = 0$

$\therefore \quad L = e^0 = 1.$ Hence the value.

Type III : Form 1^∞ :

Ex. 7 : *Evaluate* $\lim_{x \to 0} \left(\dfrac{\tan x}{x}\right)^{1/x^2}$ **(Dec. 2006, 2007)**

Sol. : Let $L = \lim_{x \to 0} \left(\dfrac{\tan x}{x}\right)^{1/x^2}$ (Form 1^∞)

$\therefore \quad \log L = \lim_{x \to 0} \dfrac{1}{x^2} \log\left(\dfrac{\tan x}{x}\right)$ (Form $\infty \times 0$)

$= \lim_{x \to 0} \dfrac{\log\left(\dfrac{\tan x}{x}\right)}{x^2}$ $\quad\left(\text{Form } \dfrac{0}{0}\right)$

$= \lim_{x \to 0} \dfrac{\left(\dfrac{x}{\tan x}\right)\left(\dfrac{x \sec^2 x - \tan x}{x^2}\right)}{2x}$ (By L'Hospital Rule)

$= \dfrac{1}{2} \lim_{x \to 0} \dfrac{(1)[x \sec^2 x - \tan x]}{x^3}$ $\quad\left(\text{Form } \dfrac{0}{0}\right)$

$$= \frac{1}{2} \lim_{x \to 0} \frac{\sec^2 x + 2x \sec^2 x \tan x - \sec^2 x}{3x^2}$$

(By L'Hospital Rule)

$$= \frac{1}{3} \lim_{x \to 0} (\sec^2 x) \left(\frac{\tan x}{x}\right) = \frac{1}{3}$$

$$\therefore \quad L = e^{1/3}$$

Ex. 8 : Evaluate $\lim_{x \to 0} \left(\frac{a^x + b^x}{2}\right)^{1/x}$ (Jan. 2005, Dec. 2005)

Sol. : Let $\quad L = \lim_{x \to 0} \left(\frac{a^x + b^x}{2}\right)^{1/x}$ (Form 1^∞)

$\therefore \quad \log L = \lim_{x \to 0} \frac{1}{x} \cdot \log\left(\frac{a^x + b^x}{2}\right)$ (Form $\infty \times 0$)

$$= \lim_{x \to 0} \frac{\log\left(\frac{a^x + b^x}{2}\right)}{x} \quad \left(\text{Form } \frac{0}{0}\right)$$

$$= \lim_{x \to 0} \frac{\left(\frac{2}{a^x + b^x}\right)\left(\frac{a^x \log a + b^x \log b}{2}\right)}{1} \quad \text{(By L'Hospital Rule)}$$

$$= \lim_{x \to 0} \frac{a^x \log a + b^x \log b}{(a^x + b^x)}$$

$$= \frac{\log a + \log b}{2} = \frac{1}{2} \log (ab) = \log \sqrt{ab}$$

$\therefore \quad L = e^{\log \sqrt{ab}} = \sqrt{ab} \qquad$ Hence the value.

Ex. 9 : Evaluate $\lim_{x \to e} (\log x)^{1/(1 - \log x)}$ (Dec. 2006)

Sol. : Let $\quad L = \lim_{x \to e} (\log x)^{1/(1 - \log x)}$ (Form 1^∞)

$\therefore \quad \log L = \lim_{x \to e} \frac{1}{(1 - \log x)} \log (\log x)$ (Form $\infty \times 0$)

$$= \lim_{x \to e} \frac{\log (\log x)}{(1 - \log x)} \quad \left(\text{Form } \frac{0}{0}\right)$$

$$= \lim_{x \to e} \frac{1/\log x \cdot 1/x}{-1/x} \quad \text{(By L'Hospital Rule)}$$

$$= - \lim_{x \to e} \frac{1}{\log x} = -1$$

$\therefore \quad L = e^{-1} = \frac{1}{e}$. Hence the value.

Ex. 10 : Evaluate $\lim_{x \to a} \left[\frac{1}{2}\left(\sqrt{\frac{a}{x}} + \sqrt{\frac{x}{a}}\right)\right]^{1/x - a}$ (Dec. 2006)

Sol. : Let $\quad L = \lim_{x \to a} \left[\frac{1}{2}\left(\sqrt{\frac{a}{x}} + \sqrt{\frac{x}{a}}\right)\right]^{1/x - a}$ (Form 1^∞)

$$\therefore \quad \log L = \lim_{x \to a} \left(\frac{1}{x-a}\right) \log\left[\frac{1}{2}\left(\sqrt{\frac{a}{x}} + \sqrt{\frac{x}{a}}\right)\right] \quad \text{(Form } \infty \times 0\text{)}$$

$$= \lim_{x \to a} \frac{\log\left[\frac{1}{2}\left(\sqrt{\frac{a}{x}} + \sqrt{\frac{x}{a}}\right)\right]}{x-a} \quad \left(\text{Form } \frac{0}{0}\right)$$

$$= \lim_{x \to a} \frac{\log\left[\frac{1}{2}\left(\frac{a+x}{\sqrt{x}\sqrt{a}}\right)\right]}{x-a} = \lim_{x \to a} \frac{\frac{1}{a+x} - \frac{1}{2x}}{1}$$

(By L'Hospital Rule)

$$= \frac{1}{2a} - \frac{1}{2a} = 0$$

$\therefore \quad L = e^0 = 1.$ Hence the value.

Ex. 11 : *Evaluate* $\lim\limits_{x \to \infty} \left(\dfrac{ax+1}{ax-1}\right)^x$. **(May 2008, 2009, 2011)**

Sol. : Put $x = \dfrac{1}{y}$, then $y \to 0$ as $x \to \infty$

$$\therefore \quad \lim_{x \to \infty} \left(\frac{ax+1}{ax-1}\right)^x = \lim_{y \to 0} \left(\frac{\frac{a}{y}+1}{\frac{a}{y}-1}\right)^{1/y}$$

$$= \lim_{y \to 0} \left(\frac{a+y}{a-y}\right)^{1/y}$$

Let $\quad L = \lim\limits_{y \to 0} \left(\dfrac{a+y}{a-y}\right)^{1/y}$ \quad (Form 1^∞)

$\therefore \quad \log L = \lim\limits_{y \to 0} \dfrac{1}{y} \log\left(\dfrac{a+y}{a-y}\right)$ \quad (Form $\infty \times 0$)

$$= \lim_{y \to 0} \frac{\log(a+y) - \log(a-y)}{y} \quad \left(\text{Form } \frac{0}{0}\right)$$

$$= \lim_{y \to 0} \frac{\frac{1}{a+y} + \frac{1}{a-y}}{1} \quad \text{(By L'Hospital Rule)}$$

$$= \frac{2}{a}$$

$\therefore \quad L = e^{2/a}.$ Hence the value.

Ex. 12 : *Evaluate* $\lim\limits_{x \to \infty} \left[\dfrac{1^{1/x} + 2^{1/x} + 3^{1/x}}{3}\right]^x$. **(May 2007, 2008)**

Sol. : Put $\dfrac{1}{x} = y$, then $y \to 0$ as $x \to \infty$ and

$$\lim_{x \to \infty} \left[\frac{1^{1/x} + 2^{1/x} + 3^{1/x}}{3}\right]^x = \lim_{y \to 0} \left[\frac{1^y + 2^y + 3^y}{3}\right]^{1/y}$$

Let
$$L = \lim_{y \to 0} \left[\frac{1^y + 2^y + 3^y}{3}\right]^{1/y} \quad \text{(Form } 1^\infty\text{)}$$

$\therefore$
$$\log L = \lim_{y \to 0} \frac{1}{y} \log \left[\frac{1^y + 2^y + 3^y}{3}\right] \quad \text{(Form } \infty \times 0\text{)}$$

$$= \lim_{y \to 0} \frac{\log\left[\frac{1^y + 2^y + 3^y}{3}\right]}{y} \quad \left(\text{Form } \frac{0}{0}\right)$$

$$= \lim_{y \to 0} \frac{\left(\frac{3}{1^y + 2^y + 3^y}\right)\left(\frac{1^y \log 1 + 2^y \log 2 + 3^y \log 3}{3}\right)}{1}$$

$$= \lim_{y \to 0} \left[\frac{1^y \log 1 + 2^y \log 2 + 3^y \log 3}{1^y + 2^y + 3^y}\right]$$

$$= \lim_{y \to 0} \frac{\log 1 + \log 2 + \log 3}{1 + 1 + 1} = \frac{\log 6}{3} = \log 6^{1/3}$$

$\therefore \quad L = 6^{1/3}$. Hence the value.

Ex. 13 : *Evaluate* $\displaystyle\lim_{x \to \infty} \left[\frac{a_1^{1/x} + a_2^{1/x} + a_3^{1/x} + \ldots + a_n^{1/x}}{n}\right]^{nx}$

Sol. : Put $\dfrac{1}{x} = y$, then $y \to 0$ as $x \to \infty$ and

let the limit of the expression be L, hence

$$L = \lim_{y \to 0} \left[\frac{a_1^y + a_2^y + a_3^y + \ldots + a_n^y}{n}\right]^{n/y} \quad \text{(Form } 1^\infty\text{)}$$

$\therefore$
$$\log L = \lim_{y \to 0} \left(\frac{n}{y}\right) \log \left[\frac{a_1^y + a_2^y + a_3^y + \ldots + a_n^y}{n}\right] \quad \text{(Form } \infty \times 0\text{)}$$

$$= n \lim_{y \to 0} \frac{\log\left[\frac{a_1^y + a_2^y + a_3^y + \ldots + a_n^y}{n}\right]}{y} \quad \left(\text{Form } \frac{0}{0}\right)$$

$$= n \lim_{y \to 0} \frac{\left(\frac{n}{a_1^y + a_2^y + a_3^y + \ldots + a_n^y}\right)\left[\frac{a_1^y \log a_1 + a_2^y \log a_2 + a_3^y \log a_3 + \ldots + a_n^y \log a_n}{n}\right]}{1}$$

(By L'Hospital Rule)

$$= n \left[\frac{\log a_1 + \log a_2 + \log a_3 + \ldots + \log a_n}{1 + 1 + 1 + \ldots + n \text{ times}}\right]$$

$$= n \left[\frac{\log (a_1 a_2 a_3 \ldots a_n)}{n}\right]$$

$$= \log (a_1 a_2 a_3 \ldots a_n)$$

$\therefore \quad L = a_1 a_2 a_3 \ldots a_n \qquad$ Hence the limit.

9.9 MISCELLANEOUS EXAMPLES

Ex. 14 : *Evaluate* $\lim\limits_{x \to \infty} \dfrac{e^{1/x} + e^{2/x} + \ldots + e^{x/x}}{x}$. (May 2008)

Sol. : Here numerator is a G.P. with first term $e^{1/x}$ and common ratio $e^{1/x}$.

$$\therefore e^{1/x} + e^{2/x} + \ldots + e^{x/x} = \dfrac{e^{1/x}[e^{x/x} - 1]}{e^{1/x} - 1} \qquad \left[S_n = \dfrac{a(r^n - 1)}{r - 1}\right]$$

$$\therefore \lim_{x \to \infty} \dfrac{e^{1/x} + e^{1/x} + \ldots + e^{x/x}}{x} \qquad \left(\text{Form } \dfrac{\infty}{\infty}\right)$$

$$= \lim_{x \to \infty} \dfrac{(e-1)\, e^{1/x}}{(e^{1/x} - 1)\, x} = (e-1) \lim_{x \to \infty} \dfrac{\frac{1}{x} e^{1/x}}{e^{1/x} - 1}$$

Put $\dfrac{1}{x} = y$, then $y \to 0$ as $x \to \infty$

$$= (e-1) \lim_{y \to 0} \dfrac{y\, e^y}{e^y - 1} \qquad \left(\text{Form } \dfrac{0}{0}\right)$$

$$= (e-1) \lim_{y \to 0} \dfrac{e^y + y\, e^y}{e^y} \qquad \text{(By L'Hospital Rule)}$$

$$= (e-1) \lim_{y \to 0} (1 + y)$$

$$= (e-1). \quad \text{Hence the value.}$$

Ex. 15 : *Evaluate* $\lim\limits_{x \to \infty} \dfrac{e^x}{\left[\left(1 + \dfrac{1}{x}\right)^x\right]^x}$.

Sol. : Let $\log L = \lim\limits_{x \to \infty} \log\left[\dfrac{e^x}{\left\{\left(1 + \dfrac{1}{x}\right)^x\right\}^x}\right]$

$$= \lim_{x \to \infty} \left[\log(e^x) - x^2 \log\left(1 + \dfrac{1}{x}\right)\right]$$

$$= \lim_{x \to \infty} \left[x - x^2 \log\left(1 + \dfrac{1}{x}\right)\right]$$

$$= \lim_{x \to \infty} \left[\dfrac{\dfrac{1}{x} - \log\left(1 + \dfrac{1}{x}\right)}{1/x^2}\right] \qquad \left(\text{Form } \dfrac{0}{0}\right)$$

$$= \lim_{x \to \infty} \left[\dfrac{\dfrac{-1}{x^2} - \dfrac{1}{(1 + 1/x)}(-1/x^2)}{-2/x^3}\right] \qquad \text{(By L'Hospital Rule)}$$

$$= \lim_{x \to \infty} \left[\frac{1 - \frac{1}{1+1/x}}{2/x} \right] \qquad \left(\text{Form } \frac{0}{0}\right)$$

$$= \lim_{x \to \infty} \left[\frac{\left(1+\frac{1}{x}\right)^{-2}(-1/x^2)}{-2/x^2} \right] \qquad \text{(By L'Hospital Rule)}$$

$$= \lim_{x \to \infty} \left[\frac{1}{2}\left(1+\frac{1}{x}\right)^{-2} \right]$$

$$= \frac{1}{2}$$

$\therefore \qquad L = e^{1/2}$. Hence the value.

Ex. 16 : *Evaluate* $\displaystyle \lim_{x \to 0} \frac{\int_1^{1+x} e^{t^2}\, dt}{\int_2^{2+x} e^{t^2}\, dt}$.

Sol. : $\displaystyle \lim_{x \to 0} \frac{\int_1^{1+x} e^{t^2}\, dt}{\int_2^{2+x} e^{t^2}\, dt}$ $\qquad \left(\text{Form } \frac{0}{0}\right)$

Applying L'Hospital Rule, we get

$$= \lim_{x \to 0} \frac{\frac{d}{dx}\left[\int_1^{1+x} e^{t^2}\, dt\right]}{\frac{d}{dx}\left[\int_2^{2+x} e^{t^2}\, dt\right]} = \lim_{x \to 0} \frac{e^{(1+x)^2}}{e^{(2+x)^2}}$$

Taking actual limit $= \dfrac{e^1}{e^4} = e^{-3}$. Hence the value.

Ex. 17 : *Evaluate* $\displaystyle \lim_{x \to 0} \frac{1 - x^x}{x \log x}$. **(May 2004)**

Sol. : We shall first evaluate $\displaystyle \lim_{x \to 0} x^x$ and $\displaystyle \lim_{x \to 0} x \log x$.

Let $y = \lim_{x \to 0} x^x$ (Form 0^0)

then $\log y = \lim_{x \to 0} x \log x = \lim_{x \to 0} \dfrac{\log x}{1/x}$ $\left(\text{Form } \dfrac{\infty}{\infty}\right)$

$= \lim_{x \to 0} \dfrac{1/x}{-1/x^2} = 0$

$\therefore \quad y = e^0 \Rightarrow \lim_{x \to 0} x^x = 1$

Also $\lim_{x \to 0} x \log x = 0$

$\therefore \quad \lim_{x \to 0} \dfrac{1 - x^x}{x \log x} = \lim_{x \to 0} \dfrac{-x^x(1 + \log x)}{(1 + \log x)}$ (By L'Hospital Rule) $\left(\text{Form } \dfrac{0}{0}\right)$

$= \lim_{x \to 0} (-x^x) = -1.$ Hence the value.

Ex. 18 : *In a $\triangle ABC$; $AB = r$; $BC = 1$; $AC = y$, $\angle B = \dfrac{\pi}{2}$ and $\angle C = \theta$.*

Find the following limits as $\theta \to \dfrac{\pi}{2}$: (i) $(r - y)$; (ii) $(r^2 - y^2)$ and (iii) $r^3 - y^3$.

Sol. : From Fig. 9.1, we have

$r = \sec \theta, \quad y = \tan \theta$

$\therefore$ (i) $\lim_{\theta \to \pi/2} (r - y) = \lim_{\theta \to \pi/2} (\sec \theta - \tan \theta)$

$= \lim_{\theta \to \pi/2} \left(\dfrac{1 - \sin \theta}{\cos \theta}\right)$ $\left(\text{Form } \dfrac{0}{0}\right)$

$= \lim_{\theta \to \pi/2} \dfrac{-\cos \theta}{-\sin \theta} = -\left[\dfrac{0}{1}\right] = 0$

(ii) $\lim_{\theta \to \pi/2} (r^2 - y^2) = \lim_{\theta \to \pi/2} (\sec^2 \theta - \tan^2 \theta)$

$= \lim_{\theta \to \pi/2} (1) = 1$

(iii) $\lim_{\theta \to \pi/2} (r^3 - y^3) = \lim_{\theta \to \pi/2} (\sec^3 \theta - \tan^3 \theta)$

$= \lim_{\theta \to \pi/2} \dfrac{1 - \sin^3 \theta}{\cos^3 \theta}$ $\left(\text{Form } \dfrac{0}{0}\right)$

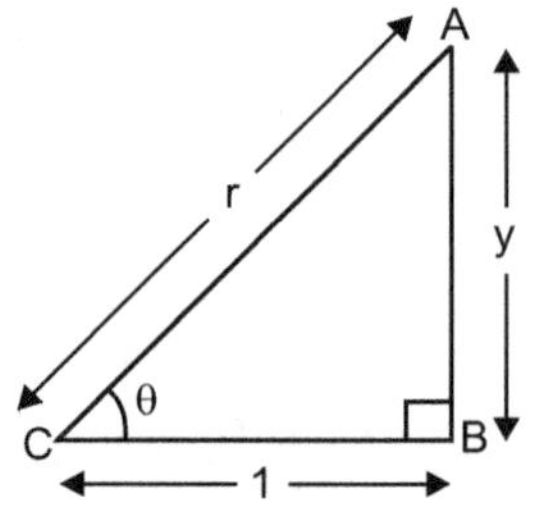

Fig. 9.1

$$= \lim_{\theta \to \pi/2} \frac{-3\sin^2\theta \cos\theta}{-3\cos^2\theta \sin\theta} = \lim_{\theta \to \pi/2} (\tan\theta)$$

$$= \tan\frac{\pi}{2} = \infty, \text{ limit does not exist.}$$

Ex. 19 : *Determine* y, $\frac{dy}{dx}$ *and* $\frac{d^2y}{dx^2}$ *at the origin for the curve* $y = x \cot x$ *studing respective indeterminate form.*

Sol. : We have
$$y = x \cot x = \frac{x}{\tan x}$$

$$\therefore \quad \lim_{x \to 0} y = \lim_{x \to 0} \frac{x}{\tan x} = 1$$

Now
$$\frac{dy}{dx} = \frac{\tan x - x\sec^2 x}{\tan^2 x}$$

$$\therefore \quad \lim_{x \to 0} \frac{dy}{dx} = \lim_{x \to 0} \frac{\tan x - x\sec^2 x}{\tan^2 x} \qquad \left(\text{Form } \frac{0}{0}\right)$$

$$= \lim_{x \to 0} \frac{\sec^2 x - \sec^2 x - 2x\sec^2 x \tan x}{2\tan x \sec^2 x}$$

(By L'Hospital Rule)

$$= \lim_{x \to 0} -\frac{2x}{2} = 0$$

Also
$$\frac{d^2y}{dx^2} = \frac{d}{dx}\left(\frac{1}{\tan x} - \frac{x}{\sin^2 x}\right)$$

$$= \frac{d}{dx}(\cot x - x\csc^2 x)$$

$$= -2\csc^2 x\,(1 - x\cot x)$$

$$\therefore \quad \lim_{x \to 0} \frac{d^2y}{dx^2} = -2\lim_{x \to 0} \frac{1 - x\cot x}{\sin^2 x} \qquad \left(\text{Form } \frac{0}{0}\right)$$

$$= -2\lim_{x \to 0} \frac{1 - \dfrac{x}{\tan x}}{\left(\dfrac{\sin^2 x}{x^2}\right) x^2} \qquad \text{(By L'Hospital Rule)}$$

$$= -2\lim_{x \to 0} \frac{\tan x - x}{x\left(\dfrac{\tan x}{x}\right) x^2}$$

$$= -2\lim_{x \to 0} \frac{\tan x - x}{x^3} \qquad \left(\text{Form } \frac{0}{0}\right)$$

$$= -2 \lim_{x \to 0} \frac{\sec^2 x - 1}{3x^2} \quad \text{(By L'Hospital Rule)}$$

$$= -2 \lim_{x \to 0} \frac{1}{3} \left(\frac{\tan x}{x}\right)^2 = -\frac{2}{3}$$

Hence y, $\frac{dy}{dx}$, $\frac{d^2y}{dx^2}$ at $x = 0$ for the given curve are $1, 0, -2/3$ respectively.

Ex. 20 : The current i in the circuit containing an inductance L, capacitance C and alternator of angular frequency ω and maximum e.m.f. E is given by

$$i = \frac{\omega E}{L(n^2 - \omega^2)} \{\cos \omega t - \cos nt\}, \text{ where } n = \frac{1}{\sqrt{LC}}.$$

Show that limiting form of expression for i when $\omega \to n$, is given by $\frac{E}{2L} t \sin nt$.

Sol. : We have here

$$\lim_{\omega \to n} i = \lim_{\omega \to n} \frac{\omega E}{L(n^2 - \omega^2)} \{\cos \omega t - \cos nt\}$$

$$= \frac{E}{L} \left(\lim_{\omega \to n} \omega\right) \lim_{\omega \to n} \frac{\cos \omega t - \cos nt}{n^2 - \omega^2}$$

$$= \frac{E}{L} (n) \lim_{\omega \to n} \frac{\cos \omega t - \cos nt}{n^2 - \omega^2} \quad \left(\text{Form } \frac{0}{0}\right)$$

$$= \frac{E}{L} (n) \lim_{\omega \to n} \frac{-t \sin \omega t}{-2\omega}$$

$$= \frac{Ent}{2L} \lim_{\omega \to n} \frac{\sin \omega t}{\omega}$$

$$= \frac{Ent}{2L} \left(\frac{\sin nt}{n}\right) = \frac{E}{2L} t \sin nt$$

Ex. 21 : A beam of length l is subjected to a uniformly distributed load of intensity ω and to an end thrust P, then the Central Deflection δ is given by

$$\delta = \frac{\omega EI}{P^2} \left[\sec\left(\frac{1}{2} ml\right) - 1\right] - \frac{\omega l^2}{8P} \text{ where } m^2 = \frac{P}{EI} \text{ find limit of } \delta \text{ as } P \to 0.$$

Sol. :
$$\lim_{p \to 0} \delta = \lim_{p \to 0} \frac{\omega EI}{P^2} \left[\sec\left(\frac{1}{2} ml\right) - 1\right] - \frac{\omega l^2}{8P}$$

$$= \lim_{m \to 0} \left\{\frac{\omega}{m^4 EI} \left[\sec\left(\frac{1}{2} ml\right) - 1\right] - \frac{\omega l^2}{8m^2 EI}\right\} \quad (\because P = m^2 EI)$$

Now,
$$\sec x = \frac{1}{\cos x} = \frac{1}{\left(1 - \frac{x^2}{2} + \frac{x^4}{24} \cdots\right)} = \left[1 - \left(\frac{x^2}{2} - \frac{x^4}{24} \cdots\right)\right]^{-1}$$

$$= 1 + \left(\frac{x^2}{2} + \frac{5x^4}{24} + \cdots\right) + \left(\frac{x^2}{2} - \frac{x^4}{24}\right)^2 + \cdots$$

$$= 1 + \frac{x^2}{2} + \frac{5x^4}{24} + \cdots$$

$\therefore \quad \sec(ml/2) = 1 + \frac{(ml/2)^2}{2} + \frac{5(ml/2)^4}{24} + \cdots$

$\therefore \quad \lim_{p \to 0} \delta = \lim_{m \to 0} \left\{\frac{\omega}{m^4 EI}\left[\left(1 + \frac{(ml/2)^2}{2} + 5\frac{(ml/2)^4}{24} \cdots\right) - 1\right] - \frac{\omega l^2}{8m^2 EI}\right\}$

$$= \lim_{m \to 0} \left\{\left[\frac{\omega l^2}{m^2 \, 8EI} + \frac{5\omega l^4}{384 \, EI} + \cdots\right] - \frac{\omega l^2}{8m^2 EI}\right\}$$

$$= \lim_{m \to 0} \left\{\frac{5\omega l^4}{384 \, EI} + \text{terms containing powers of } m\right\}$$

$$= \frac{5\omega l^4}{384 \, EI} \cdot \text{ Hence the value.}$$

Ex. 22 : *If the production function is given by* $y = k\left[\alpha x_1^{-\rho} + (1-\alpha)x_2^{-\rho}\right]^{-1/\rho}$
where k, α, x_1 *and* x_2 *are positive constants and* $\alpha < 1$*. Taking limits as* $\rho \to 0$*, show that* $\lim_{\rho \to 0} y = k \cdot x_1^\alpha \, x_2^{1-\alpha}$.

Sol. : We have $\quad y = k\left[\alpha x_1^{-\rho} + (1-\alpha)x_2^{-\rho}\right]^{-1/\rho}$

$\therefore \quad \log y = \log k - \frac{1}{\rho} \log\left[\alpha x_1^{-\rho} + (1-\alpha)x_2^{-\rho}\right]$

$\therefore \quad \lim_{\rho \to 0} \log y = \log k - \lim_{\rho \to 0} \frac{\log\left[\alpha x_1^{-\rho} + (1-\alpha)x_2^{-\rho}\right]}{\rho} \quad \left(\text{Form } \frac{0}{0}\right)$

$$= \log k - \lim_{\rho \to 0} \left[\frac{-\alpha x_1^{-\rho} \log x_1 - (1-\alpha)x_2^{-\rho} \log x_2}{\alpha x_1^{-\rho} + (1-\alpha)x_2^{-\rho}}\right]$$

$$= \log k + \frac{\alpha \log x_1 + (1-\alpha)\log x_2}{\alpha + (1-\alpha)}$$

$$= \log k + \alpha \log x_1 + (1-\alpha)\log x_2$$

$$= \log k + \log x_1^\alpha + \log x_2^{(1-\alpha)}$$

$$= \log k \, x_1^\alpha \, x_2^{(1-\alpha)}$$

$\therefore \quad \lim_{\rho \to 0} y = k \, x_1^\alpha \, x_2^{(1-\alpha)} \qquad \text{Hence the proof.}$

EXERCISE 9.2

1. Prove that:
   (i) $\lim_{x \to 0} (\sin x)^{\tan x} = 1$

   (ii) $\lim_{x \to \pi/2} (\cos x)^{\cos^2 x} = 1$ **(Dec. 2005)**

   (iii) $\lim_{x \to 0} x^{\tan\left(\frac{\pi x}{2}\right)} = e^{-2/\pi}$

2. Prove that:
   (i) $\lim_{x \to \infty} x^{1/x} = 0$

   (ii) $\lim_{x \to 0} (\cot x)^{1/\log x} = \frac{1}{e}$

   (iii) $\lim_{x \to \pi/2} (\sec x)^{\cot x} = 1$

   (iv) $\lim_{x \to 0} (\operatorname{cosec} x)^{\sin x} = 1$

3. Prove that:
   (i) $\lim_{x \to \pi/2} (\sin x)^{\tan^2 x} = e^{-1/2}$ **(Jan. 2005)**

   (ii) $\lim_{x \to 0} (\cos x)^{\cot x} = 1$

   (iii) $\lim_{x \to a} \left(2 - \frac{x}{a}\right)^{\tan\left(\frac{\pi x}{2a}\right)} = e^{2/\pi}$ **(Dec. 2005)**

   (iv) $\lim_{x \to \infty} \left(1 + \frac{a}{x}\right)^x = e^a$

   (v) $\lim_{n \to \infty} \left[\cos\left(\frac{\theta}{n}\right)^n\right] = e^{-\theta/2}$

   (vi) $\lim_{x \to 0} (a^x + x)^{1/x} = ae$

   (vii) $\lim_{x \to 0} \left(\sin^2 \frac{\pi}{2 - ax}\right)^{\sec^2 \frac{\pi}{2 - bx}} = e^{-a^2/b^2}$ **(Dec. 2010)**

   (viii) $\lim_{x \to 0} (1 + \sin x)^{\cot x} = e$

   (ix) $\lim_{x \to \pi/4} (\tan x)^{\tan 2x} = 1/e$

   (x) $\lim_{x \to 0} (\cos 2x)^{1/x^2} = e^{-2}$

(xi) $\lim_{x \to 0} (1 + \sin mx)^{\cot x} = 0$

(xii) $\lim_{x \to 1} x^{\frac{1}{x-1}} = 1/e$

(xiii) $\lim_{x \to \infty} \left(1 + \frac{1}{x^2}\right)^x = 1$

(xiv) $\lim_{x \to 0} (\cos mx)^{x^{n/2}} = e^{-\frac{m^2 n}{2}}$

(xv) $\lim_{x \to \infty} \left(1 + \frac{2}{x}\right)^x = e^2$

(xvi) $\lim_{x \to 0} x^{2 \sin x} = 1$

(xvii) $\lim_{x \to \pi/2} (\cosec x)^{\tan^2 x} = e^{1/2}$ **(Dec. 2008)**

4. Prove that (i) $\lim_{x \to \infty} e^{\left(\frac{\sinh^{-1} x}{\cosh^{-1} x}\right)} = e$

(ii) $\lim_{n \to \infty} \left[\cos\left(\frac{\theta}{n}\right)\right]^n = e^{-\theta/2}$ **(May 2006)**

5. Prove that $\lim_{n \to \infty} \frac{1^2 + 2^2 + 3^2 + \ldots + n^2}{n^3} = \frac{1}{3}$ **(May 2008)**

   [**Hint:** Use the formula $1^2 + 2^2 + 3^2 + \ldots n^2 = \frac{1}{6} n (n + 1) (2n + 1)$]

6. Prove that $\lim_{x \to 0} \left(\frac{1^x + 2^x + 3^x + 4^x}{4}\right)^{1/x} = (24)^{1/4}$ **(May 2011)**

7. A column of length l has a vertical load P and horizontal load F at the top and the transverse deflection δ is given by $\delta = \frac{Fl}{P} \left\{\frac{\tan ml}{ml} - 1\right\}$, where $m^2 = \frac{P}{EI}$, show that as $p \to 0$, $\delta = \frac{Fl^3}{8 \, EI}$.

8. The energy change $E(\alpha)$ in certain type of acid dissociation is related to the degree of dissociation α, by the formula $E(\alpha) = \log(1 - \alpha) + \alpha \log \frac{\alpha}{1 - \alpha} + k\alpha$, where k is a constant and $0 < \alpha < 1$. Prove that (i) $E(\alpha) \to k$ as $\alpha \to 1$, (ii) $E(\alpha) \to (0)$ as $\alpha \to 0$.

9. Prove that $\lim_{x \to \infty} \left(x \sin \frac{1}{x}\right)^{x^2} = e^{-1/6}$

10. If $x^3 + y^3 = 3axy$, find the value of $y'(0)$, $y''(0)$.

11. $\lim_{x \to 0} \left[\frac{2(\cosh x - 1)}{x^2}\right]^{1/x^2} = e^{1/12}$ **(Dec. 2008)**

MULTIPLE CHOICE QUESTIONS

Type I : Indeterminate Forms $\left(\dfrac{0}{0}, \dfrac{\infty}{\infty}, 0 \times \infty, \infty - \infty\right)$

1. If f(x) and g(x) be functions such that f(a) = 0 and g(a) = 0 then $\lim\limits_{x \to a} \dfrac{f(x)}{g(x)}$ is equal to (1)

   (A) $\lim\limits_{x \to a} \dfrac{f'(x)}{g'(x)}$
   (B) $\lim\limits_{x \to a} \dfrac{g'(x)}{f'(x)}$
   (C) $\dfrac{f(a)}{g(a)}$
   (D) none of these

2. If f(x) and g(x) be functions such that f(a) = 0, g(a) = 0 and f'(a) = 0, g'(a) = 0 then $\lim\limits_{x \to a} \dfrac{f(x)}{g(x)}$ is equal to (1)

   (A) $\dfrac{f'(a)}{g'(a)}$
   (B) $\lim\limits_{x \to a} \dfrac{g'(x)}{f'(x)}$
   (C) $\lim\limits_{x \to a} \dfrac{f''(x)}{g''(x)}$
   (D) none of these

3. If f(x) and g(x) be functions such that f(a) = ∞ and g(a) = ∞ then $\lim\limits_{x \to a} \dfrac{f(x)}{g(x)}$ is equal to (1)

   (A) $\lim\limits_{x \to a} \dfrac{f'(x)}{g'(x)}$
   (B) $\lim\limits_{x \to a} \dfrac{g'(x)}{f'(x)}$
   (C) $\dfrac{f(a)}{g(a)}$
   (D) none of these

4. $\lim\limits_{x \to \pi/2} \dfrac{1 - \sin x}{\cos x}$ is equal to (1)

   (A) 1
   (B) 0
   (C) $\dfrac{1}{2}$
   (D) −1

5. $\lim\limits_{x \to 0} \dfrac{\sin x}{x}$ is equal to (1)

   (A) 2
   (B) 0
   (C) −1
   (D) 1

6. $\lim_{x \to 0} \dfrac{\tan x}{x}$ is equal to (1)

   (A) 2
   (B) 1
   (C) $\dfrac{\pi}{2}$
   (D) $\dfrac{3}{2}$

7. $\lim_{x \to 0} \dfrac{\sin^{-1} x}{x}$ is equal to (1)

   (A) 1
   (B) −1
   (C) $\dfrac{1}{2}$
   (D) $\dfrac{\pi}{2}$

8. $\lim_{x \to 0} (1 + x)^{1/x}$ is equal to (1)

   (A) 1
   (B) e^2
   (C) $\dfrac{1}{e}$
   (D) e

9. $\lim_{x \to \infty} \left(1 + \dfrac{1}{x}\right)^x$ is equal to (1)

   (A) 1
   (B) e
   (C) $\dfrac{1}{e}$
   (D) e^2

10. $\lim_{x \to 0} \dfrac{e^x - 1}{x}$ is equal to (1)

    (A) 2
    (B) $\dfrac{1}{2}$
    (C) 1
    (D) none of these

11. $\lim_{x \to 0} \dfrac{a^x - 1}{x}$ is equal to (1)

    (A) a
    (B) $-\log a$
    (C) $\log a$
    (D) 1

12. $\lim_{\theta \to 0} \dfrac{\sin\left(\dfrac{\theta}{2}\right)}{\theta}$ is equal to (2)

    (A) 1
    (B) 2
    (C) $\dfrac{1}{2}$
    (D) not defined

13. $\lim\limits_{x \to 0} \dfrac{\sin^2 x}{x}$ is equal to (2)

   (A) −1
   (B) 1
   (C) 0
   (D) not defined

14. $\lim\limits_{x \to 0} \dfrac{1 - \cos x}{x}$ is equal to (2)

   (A) 0
   (B) 1
   (C) −1
   (D) 2

15. $\lim\limits_{x \to 3} \dfrac{2x^2 - 7x + 3}{5x^2 - 12x - 9}$ is equal to (2)

   (A) $-\dfrac{1}{3}$
   (B) $\dfrac{2}{5}$
   (C) $\dfrac{5}{18}$
   (D) 0

16. $\lim\limits_{x \to 0} \dfrac{a^x - b^x}{x}$ is equal to (2)

   (A) 0
   (B) 1
   (C) $\log \dfrac{b}{a}$
   (D) $\log \dfrac{a}{b}$

17. $\lim\limits_{x \to 0} \dfrac{\sin^2 x}{x \cos x}$ is equal to (2)

   (A) 0
   (B) 1
   (C) −1
   (D) 2

18. $\lim\limits_{x \to 0} \dfrac{e^{ax} - e^{-ax}}{\log(1 + bx)}$ is equal to (2)

   (A) $\dfrac{a}{2b}$
   (B) 0
   (C) $\dfrac{b}{2a}$
   (D) $\dfrac{2a}{b}$

19. $\lim\limits_{x \to 0} \dfrac{(1 + x)^n - 1}{x}$ is equal to (2)

   (A) n
   (B) 1
   (C) e
   (D) 0

20. $\lim_{x \to 0} \dfrac{2^x - 1}{\sqrt{(1 + x)} - 1}$ is equal to (2)

   (A) $\log 2$　　　　　　　　　　(B) $\dfrac{1}{2} \log 2$

   (C) 0　　　　　　　　　　　　(D) $2 \log 2$

21. $\lim_{x \to 0} \dfrac{\sqrt{(1 + x)} - \sqrt{(1 - x)}}{x}$ is equal to (2)

   (A) 0　　　　　　　　　　　　(B) -1

   (C) 1　　　　　　　　　　　　(D) 2

22. If $\lim_{x \to 0} \dfrac{\sin 2x + p \sin x}{x^3}$ is finite then value of p is equal to (2)

   (A) -2　　　　　　　　　　　(B) 2

   (C) 1　　　　　　　　　　　　(D) -1

23. If $\lim_{x \to 0} \dfrac{a \sinh x - 5 \sin x}{x^3}$ is finite then value of a is equal to (2)

   (A) -5　　　　　　　　　　　(B) 5

   (C) 0　　　　　　　　　　　　(D) 10

24. If $\lim_{x \to 0} \dfrac{a \sin 2x + \tan x}{x^3}$ is finite then value of a is equal to (2)

   (A) -2　　　　　　　　　　　(B) 2

   (C) $-\dfrac{1}{2}$　　　　　　　　　(D) $\dfrac{1}{2}$

25. If $\lim_{x \to 0} \dfrac{2 \cos x - 2 + bx^2}{x^4}$ is finite then value of b is equal to (2)

   (A) 2　　　　　　　　　　　　(B) 0

   (C) 1　　　　　　　　　　　　(D) -1

26. $\lim_{x \to \pi/4} \dfrac{1 - \tan x}{1 - \sqrt{2} \sin x}$ is equal to (2)

   (A) 2　　　　　　　　　　　　(B) 0

   (C) 1　　　　　　　　　　　　(D) -2

27. $\lim_{x \to \infty} \dfrac{\log x}{x^n}$ is equal to (2)

   (A) 2　　　　　　　　　　　　(B) -2

   (C) 1　　　　　　　　　　　　(D) 0

28. $\lim\limits_{x \to \infty} \dfrac{\log(1 + e^{3x})}{x}$ is equal to (2)

   (A) 9   (B) 3

   (C) $\dfrac{1}{3}$ (D) 0

29. $\lim\limits_{x \to 0} x \log x$ is equal to (2)

   (A) 2   (B) −1

   (C) 1   (D) 0

30. $\lim\limits_{x \to \infty} x \sin \dfrac{1}{x}$ is equal to (2)

   (A) 2   (B) 0

   (C) 1   (D) −1

31. $\lim\limits_{x \to 1} (1-x) \tan \dfrac{\pi x}{2}$ is equal to (2)

   (A) $\dfrac{2}{\pi}$ (B) $\dfrac{\pi}{2}$

   (C) π (D) 0

32. $\lim\limits_{x \to \pi/2} (1 - \sin x) \tan x$ is equal to (2)

   (A) 1   (B) −1

   (C) π (D) 0

33. $\lim\limits_{x \to \pi/2} (\sec x - \tan x)$ is equal to (2)

   (A) 1   (B) −1

   (C) π (D) 0

34. $\lim\limits_{x \to \pi/2} \left(x \tan x - \dfrac{\pi}{2} \sec x \right)$ is equal to (2)

   (A) 1   (B) −1

   (C) π (D) 0

35. $\lim\limits_{x \to \infty} \left[x - x^2 \log \left(1 + \frac{1}{x}\right) \right]$ is equal to (2)

   (A) 1 (B) $-\frac{1}{2}$

   (C) $\frac{1}{2}$ (D) 0

36. $\lim\limits_{x \to 0} \left[\frac{1}{x} - \frac{1}{x^2} \log (1 + x) \right]$ is equal to (2)

   (A) 1 (B) $-\frac{1}{2}$

   (C) $\frac{1}{2}$ (D) 0

37. $\lim\limits_{x \to 0} \left[\frac{1}{x} - \frac{1}{\sin x} \right]$ is equal to (2)

   (A) 1 (B) $-\frac{1}{2}$

   (C) $\frac{1}{2}$ (D) 0

38. $\lim\limits_{x \to 0} \left[\frac{1}{x} - \frac{1}{e^x - 1} \right]$ is equal to (2)

   (A) 1 (B) $-\frac{1}{2}$

   (C) $\frac{1}{2}$ (D) 0

39. $\lim\limits_{x \to \pi/2} \left[\tan x - \frac{2x \sec x}{\pi} \right]$ is equal to (2)

   (A) $\frac{2}{\pi}$ (B) $-\frac{2}{\pi}$

   (C) $\frac{\pi}{2}$ (D) 0

40. $\lim\limits_{x \to 1} \left[\frac{x}{\log x} - \frac{1}{\log x} \right]$ is equal to (2)

   (A) –1 (B) 1

   (C) $\frac{1}{2}$ (D) 0

Type II : Indeterminate Forms (0^0, ∞^0, 1^∞) :

41. $\lim\limits_{x \to \infty} \left(\dfrac{1}{x}\right)^{1/x}$ is equal to (2)

    (A) e (B) $-\dfrac{1}{2}$

    (C) $\dfrac{1}{2}$ (D) 1

42. $\lim\limits_{x \to 0} (\sin x)^{\tan x}$ is equal to (2)

    (A) 1 (B) e

    (C) -1 (D) $\dfrac{1}{e}$

43. $\lim\limits_{x \to \pi/2} (\cos x)^{\cos x}$ is equal to (2)

    (A) -1 (B) e

    (C) 1 (D) $\dfrac{1}{e}$

44. $\lim\limits_{x \to 0} (x)^x$ is equal to (2)

    (A) e (B) 1

    (C) -1 (D) none of these

45. $\lim\limits_{x \to \infty} (x)^{1/x}$ is equal to (2)

    (A) e (B) -1

    (C) 1 (D) none of these

46. $\lim\limits_{x \to \pi/2} (\sec x)^{\cot x}$ is equal to (2)

    (A) e (B) 1

    (C) $\dfrac{1}{e}$ (D) does not exist

47. $\lim\limits_{x \to \infty} \left(1 + \dfrac{a}{x}\right)^x$ is equal to (2)

    (A) e^{-a} (B) e^a

    (C) 1 (D) none of these

48. $\lim_{x \to 1} (x)^{\frac{1}{x-1}}$ is equal to (2)

   (A) e
   (B) 1
   (C) –1
   (D) none of these

49. $\lim_{x \to 0} (\cos x)^{1/x}$ is equal to (2)

   (A) e
   (B) 1
   (C) –1
   (D) none of these

50. $\lim_{x \to 0} (\cos x)^{\cot x}$ is equal to (2)

   (A) 1
   (B) e
   (C) –1
   (D) none of these

51. $\lim_{x \to 1} (1 - x^2)^{\frac{1}{\log(1-x)}}$ is equal to (2)

   (A) e
   (B) $\frac{1}{e}$
   (C) 1
   (D) e^2

52. $\lim_{x \to 0} \left(\frac{a+x}{a-x}\right)^{1/x}$ is equal to (2)

   (A) $e^{2/a}$
   (B) $e^{1/2a}$
   (C) 1
   (D) $e^{a/2}$

53. $\lim_{x \to 0} (1 + \sin x)^{\cot x}$ is equal to (2)

   (A) $e^{1/2}$
   (B) e^2
   (C) 1
   (D) e

54. $\lim_{x \to \pi/2} (\operatorname{cosec} x)^{\tan x}$ is equal to (2)

   (A) e^{-1}
   (B) e^2
   (C) 1
   (D) e

Answers

1. (A)	12. (C)	23. (C)	34. (B)	45. (C)
2. (C)	13. (C)	24. (C)	35. (C)	46. (B)
3. (A)	14. (A)	25. (C)	36. (C)	47. (B)
4. (B)	15. (C)	26. (A)	37. (D)	48. (A)
5. (D)	16. (D)	27. (D)	38. (C)	49. (B)
6. (B)	17. (A)	28. (B)	39. (A)	50. (A)
7. (A)	18. (D)	29. (D)	40. (B)	51. (A)
8. (D)	19. (A)	30. (C)	41. (D)	52. (A)
9. (B)	20. (D)	31. (A)	42. (A)	53. (D)
10. (C)	21. (C)	32. (D)	43. (C)	54. (C)
11. (C)	22. (A)	33. (D)	44. (B)	

CHAPTER TEN

PARTIAL DIFFERENTIATION AND APPLICATIONS

10.1 INTRODUCTION

In problems of maxima, minima, conduction of heat, vibration of strings, electromagnetic fields, theory of approximations, exact differential equations, vectors, multiple integrals, Boundary value problems, complex variables and in some problems of electrical engineering (transmission lines) we need the study of partial derivatives, which are different from the ordinary differential coefficients.

10.2 FUNCTION OF TWO OR MORE VARIABLES

In many applications, the values of the functions under study are determined by the values of more than one independent variable. The function may be as simple as $V = \pi r^2 h$ for calculating the volume of a right circular cylinder from its radius r of its base and height h. Here V will undergo a change if either r or h changes. Hence V is a function of two variables r (radius) and h (the height) because π is a constant. We can write V = f(r, h). Here V is the dependent variable and r, h are independent variables.

Definition : If Z has one definite value for each pair of values of x and y then Z is called a function of two variables x and y. We denote it by Z = f(x, y) or F(x, y) or ϕ(x, y).

Here Z is the dependent variable, x and y are independent variables.

e.g. $Z = x^3 + y^3 - 3axy$. Here Z is a function of two variables x and y.

Similarly, U = f(x, y, z) is a function of three variables x, y and z. Here U is the dependent variable and x, y, z are the independent variables.

e.g. $U = x^2 + y^2 + z^2$. Here U is a function of three independent variables x, y and z.

10.3 DOMAIN OF DEFINITION OF Z

Sometimes Z is defined only for those pairs of values of x and y for which the point (x, y) moves within a certain area in the x – y plane, then that area is called the Domain of definition of Z.

For example, Domain of the function defined by, $Z = f(x, y) = \sqrt{1 - \frac{x^2}{a^2} - \frac{y^2}{b^2}}$ has the domain bounded by the ellipse $\frac{x^2}{a^2} + \frac{y^2}{b^2} = 1$.

10.4 CONTINUITY OF A FUNCTION OF TWO VARIABLES

The function $Z = f(x, y)$ is said to be continuous at a point (a, b) of its domain if the limit of the function is equal to the value of the function i.e.

$$\lim_{\substack{x \to a \\ y \to b}} f(x, y) = f(a, b)$$

The limit being independent of the manner in which x approaches a and y approaches b. If the function is continuous at all points of some region R in the x − y plane, then it is said to be continuous in the entire region R.

10.5 PARTIAL DERIVATIVES OR PARTIAL DIFFERENTIAL COEFFICIENTS

Let $Z = f(x, y)$ be a function of two independent variables x and y.

Definition :

1. The partial derivative of Z with respect to x is nothing but the ordinary derivative of Z with respect to x treating the other variable y as constant. It is denoted by $\frac{\partial z}{\partial x}$ or $\frac{\partial f}{\partial x}$ or f_x or Z_x and we read it as dabba z by dabba x (or del z by del x).

$$\frac{\partial z}{\partial x} = \lim_{\Delta x \to 0} \left\{ \frac{f(x + \Delta x, y) - f(x, y)}{\Delta x} \right\} \text{ where } \Delta x \text{ is a small increment in x.}$$

2. The partial derivative of Z with respect to y is nothing but the ordinary derivative of Z with respect to y treating the other variable x as constant. It is denoted by $\frac{\partial z}{\partial y}$ or $\frac{\partial f}{\partial y}$ or f_y or Z_y and we read it as dabba z by dabba y (or del z by del y)

$$\frac{\partial z}{\partial y} = \lim_{\Delta y \to 0} \left\{ \frac{f(x, y + \Delta y) - f(x, y)}{\Delta y} \right\} \text{ where } \Delta y \text{ is small increment in y.}$$

Note 1 : $\frac{\partial z}{\partial x}$ and $\frac{\partial z}{\partial y}$ are called *first order partial derivatives of Z.*

Note 2 : Similarly if f is a function of n variables $x_1, x_2, x_3, \ldots x_n$, the partial derivative of f with respect to x_1, is the ordinary derivative of f when all the independent variables except x_1, are kept as constants, and is written as $\frac{\partial f}{\partial x_1}$.

10.6 GEOMETRICAL INTERPRETATION OF $\dfrac{\partial z}{\partial x}, \dfrac{\partial z}{\partial y}$

The function $z = f(x, y)$ represents a surface.

$\dfrac{\partial z}{\partial x}$ gives the slope of the tangent drawn to the curve of intersection of the surface $z = f(x, y)$ with a plane parallel to the ZOX plane.

$\dfrac{\partial z}{\partial y}$ gives the slope of the tangent drawn to the curve of intersection of the surface $z = f(x, y)$ with a plane parallel to the ZOY plane.

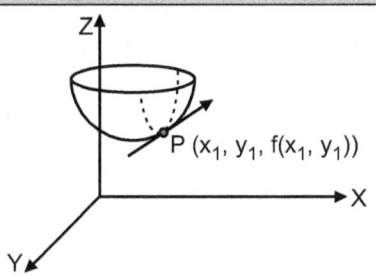

Fig. 10.1

10.7 RULES OF PARTIAL DIFFERENTIATION

Let u and v are functions of two independent variables x, y, therefore

1. **Derivative of Sum :**

$$\dfrac{\partial}{\partial x}(u \pm v) = \dfrac{\partial u}{\partial x} \pm \dfrac{\partial v}{\partial x}\ ; \qquad \dfrac{\partial}{\partial y}(u \pm v) = \dfrac{\partial u}{\partial y} \pm \dfrac{\partial v}{\partial y}$$

2. **Derivative of Product :**

$$\dfrac{\partial}{\partial x}(uv) = u\dfrac{\partial v}{\partial x} + v\dfrac{\partial u}{\partial x}\ ; \qquad \dfrac{\partial}{\partial y}(uv) = u\dfrac{\partial v}{\partial y} + v\dfrac{\partial u}{\partial y}$$

3. **Derivative of a Quotient :**

$$\dfrac{\partial}{\partial x}\left(\dfrac{u}{v}\right) = \dfrac{v\dfrac{\partial u}{\partial x} - u\dfrac{\partial v}{\partial x}}{v^2}\ ; \qquad \dfrac{\partial}{\partial y}\left(\dfrac{u}{v}\right) = \dfrac{v\dfrac{\partial u}{\partial y} - u\dfrac{\partial v}{\partial y}}{v^2}\ ;\ v \neq 0$$

4. If k is a constant, then

$$\dfrac{\partial}{\partial x}(ku) = k\dfrac{\partial u}{\partial x}\ ; \qquad \dfrac{\partial}{\partial y}(ku) = k\dfrac{\partial u}{\partial y}$$

5. **Derivative of a constant, say k :**

$$\dfrac{\partial}{\partial x}(k) = 0\ ; \qquad \dfrac{\partial}{\partial y}(k) = 0$$

6. $\dfrac{\partial}{\partial x}[f(y)] = 0 \qquad (\because f(y)$ does not contain any $x)$

$\dfrac{\partial}{\partial y}[\phi(x)] = 0 \qquad (\because \phi(x)$ does not contain any $y)$

7. $\dfrac{\partial}{\partial x}[f(x, y, z)]^n = n[f(x, y, z)]^{n-1}\dfrac{\partial f}{\partial x}\ ; \qquad \dfrac{\partial}{\partial y}[f(x, y, z)]^n = n[f(x, y, z)]^{n-1}\dfrac{\partial f}{\partial y}$

8. $\dfrac{\partial}{\partial x}\left[\dfrac{1}{f(x, y, z)}\right] = \dfrac{-1}{[f(x, y, z)]^2}\dfrac{\partial f}{\partial x}$; $\quad \dfrac{\partial}{\partial y}\left[\dfrac{1}{f(x, y, z)}\right] = \dfrac{-1}{[f(x, y, z)]^2}\dfrac{\partial f}{\partial y}$

9. $\dfrac{\partial}{\partial x}\left[\sqrt{f(x, y, z)}\right] = \dfrac{1}{2\sqrt{f(x, y, z)}}\cdot\dfrac{\partial f}{\partial x}$

$\dfrac{\partial}{\partial x}\left[\dfrac{1}{\sqrt{f(x, y, z)}}\right] = \dfrac{-1}{2[f(x, y, z)]^{3/2}}\cdot\dfrac{\partial f}{\partial x}$

10. $\dfrac{\partial}{\partial x}[\log f(x, y, z)] = \dfrac{1}{f(x, y, z)}\cdot\dfrac{\partial f}{\partial x}$

$\dfrac{\partial}{\partial x}[e^{f(x, y, z)}] = e^{f(x, y, z)}\cdot\dfrac{\partial f}{\partial x}$

11. $\dfrac{\partial}{\partial x}[a^{f(x, y, z)}] = a^{f(x, y, z)}\log a \cdot\dfrac{\partial f}{\partial x}$

12. $\dfrac{\partial}{\partial x}[\sin f(x, y, z)] = \cos f(x, y, z)\dfrac{\partial f}{\partial x}$

$\dfrac{\partial}{\partial x}[\cos f(x, y, z)] = -\sin f(x, y, z)\dfrac{\partial f}{\partial x}$

$\dfrac{\partial}{\partial x}[\tan f(x, y, z)] = \sec^2 f(x, y, z)\dfrac{\partial f}{\partial x}$

$\dfrac{\partial}{\partial x}[\cot f(x, y, z)] = -\csc^2 f(x, y, z)\cdot\dfrac{\partial f}{\partial x}$

$\dfrac{\partial}{\partial x}[\csc f(x, y, z)] = -\csc f(x, y, z)\cot f(x, y, z)\cdot\dfrac{\partial f}{\partial x}$

$\dfrac{\partial}{\partial x}[\sec f(x, y, z)] = \sec f(x, y, z)\tan f(x, y, z)\dfrac{\partial f}{\partial x}$

13. $\dfrac{\partial}{\partial x}[\sin^{-1} f(x, y, z)] = \dfrac{1}{\sqrt{1-[f(x, y, z)]^2}}\cdot\dfrac{\partial f}{\partial x}$

$\dfrac{\partial}{\partial x}[\tan^{-1} f(x, y, z)] = \dfrac{1}{1+[f(x, y, z)]^2}\cdot\dfrac{\partial f}{\partial x}$

14. Derivative of Composite function (or function of a function):

If $z = f(r)$ where r is again a function of two variables x and y then z becomes composite function of x and y.

To understand clearly the derivatives involved, we will make use of the following tree diagram.

$\dfrac{\partial z}{\partial x} = \dfrac{dz}{dr}\dfrac{\partial r}{\partial x}$ or $\dfrac{df}{dr}\dfrac{\partial r}{\partial x}$ or $f'(r)\dfrac{\partial r}{\partial x}$

$\dfrac{\partial z}{\partial y} = \dfrac{dz}{dr}\dfrac{\partial r}{\partial y}$ or $\dfrac{df}{dr}\dfrac{\partial r}{\partial y}$ or $f'(r)\dfrac{\partial r}{\partial y}$

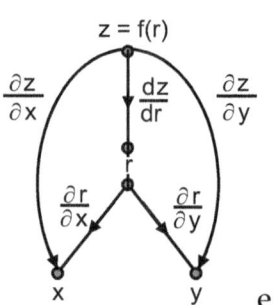

Fig. 10.2 : Tree diagram 1

10.8 PARTIAL DERIVATIVES OF HIGHER ORDER

If $Z = f(x, y)$, then the first order partial derivatives $\dfrac{\partial z}{\partial x}$ and $\dfrac{\partial z}{\partial y}$ may also be function of x and y, hence can be differentiated again partially both with respect to x as well as y. Thus there are four partial derivatives of the second order of a function of two variables.

These derivatives are denoted as follows :

$$\frac{\partial}{\partial x}\left(\frac{\partial z}{\partial x}\right) = \frac{\partial^2 z}{\partial x^2} \text{ or } \frac{\partial^2 f}{\partial x^2} \text{ or } Z_{xx} \text{ or } f_{xx}$$

$$\frac{\partial}{\partial y}\left(\frac{\partial z}{\partial x}\right) = \frac{\partial^2 z}{\partial y\, \partial x} \text{ or } \frac{\partial^2 f}{\partial y\, \partial x} \text{ or } Z_{yx} \text{ or } f_{yx}$$

$$\frac{\partial}{\partial x}\left(\frac{\partial z}{\partial y}\right) = \frac{\partial^2 z}{\partial x\, \partial y} \text{ or } \frac{\partial^2 f}{\partial x\, \partial y} \text{ or } Z_{xy} \text{ or } f_{xy}$$

$$\frac{\partial}{\partial y}\left(\frac{\partial z}{\partial y}\right) = \frac{\partial^2 z}{\partial y^2} \text{ or } \frac{\partial^2 f}{\partial y^2} \text{ or } Z_{yy} \text{ or } f_{yy}$$

Note : Here $\dfrac{\partial^2 z}{\partial x\, \partial y}$, $\dfrac{\partial^2 z}{\partial y\, \partial x}$ are called as Mixed Partial Derivatives.

Derivatives of the second order may again be differentiated both with respect to x and y.

We then get partial derivatives of the third order. Thus, possible eight types of third order partial derivatives are denoted as follows :

$$\frac{\partial^3 z}{\partial x^3} = \frac{\partial}{\partial x}\left[\frac{\partial}{\partial x}\left(\frac{\partial z}{\partial x}\right)\right] \text{ or } \frac{\partial^3 f}{\partial x^3} \text{ or } Z_{xxx} \text{ or } f_{xxx}$$

$$\frac{\partial^3 z}{\partial x^2\, \partial y} = \frac{\partial}{\partial x}\left[\frac{\partial}{\partial x}\left(\frac{\partial z}{\partial y}\right)\right] \text{ or } \frac{\partial^3 f}{\partial x^2\, \partial y} \text{ or } Z_{xxy} \text{ or } f_{xxy}$$

$$\frac{\partial^3 z}{\partial x\, \partial y\, \partial x} = \frac{\partial}{\partial x}\left[\frac{\partial}{\partial y}\left(\frac{\partial z}{\partial x}\right)\right] \text{ or } \frac{\partial^3 f}{\partial x\, \partial y\, \partial x} \text{ or } Z_{xyx} \text{ or } f_{xyx}$$

$$\frac{\partial^3 z}{\partial x\, \partial y^2} = \frac{\partial}{\partial x}\left[\frac{\partial}{\partial y}\left(\frac{\partial z}{\partial y}\right)\right] \text{ or } \frac{\partial^3 f}{\partial x\, \partial y^2} \text{ or } Z_{xyy} \text{ or } f_{xyy}$$

$$\frac{\partial^3 z}{\partial y\, \partial x^2} = \frac{\partial}{\partial y}\left[\frac{\partial}{\partial x}\left(\frac{\partial z}{\partial x}\right)\right] \text{ or } \frac{\partial^3 f}{\partial y\, \partial x^2} \text{ or } Z_{yxx} \text{ or } f_{yxx}$$

$$\frac{\partial^3 z}{\partial y\, \partial x\, \partial y} = \frac{\partial}{\partial y}\left[\frac{\partial}{\partial x}\left(\frac{\partial z}{\partial y}\right)\right] \text{ or } \frac{\partial^3 f}{\partial y\, \partial x\, \partial y} \text{ or } Z_{yxy} \text{ or } f_{yxy}$$

$$\frac{\partial^3 z}{\partial y^2\, \partial x} = \frac{\partial}{\partial y}\left[\frac{\partial}{\partial y}\left(\frac{\partial z}{\partial x}\right)\right] \text{ or } \frac{\partial^3 f}{\partial y^2\, \partial x} \text{ or } Z_{yyx} \text{ or } f_{yyx}$$

$$\frac{\partial^3 z}{\partial y^3} = \frac{\partial}{\partial y}\left[\frac{\partial}{\partial y}\left(\frac{\partial z}{\partial y}\right)\right] \text{ or } \frac{\partial^3 f}{\partial y^3} \text{ or } f_{yyy}$$

COMMUTATIVE PROPERTY OF MIXED PARTIAL DERIVATIVES

If $Z = f(x, y)$ is continuous and possesses continuous partial derivatives then second order mixed partial derivative follows the commutative property.

$$\boxed{\frac{\partial^2 z}{\partial x \, \partial y} = \frac{\partial^2 z}{\partial y \, \partial x}}$$

ILLUSTRATIONS ON PARTIAL DIFFERENTIATION

Illustrations on partial differentiations are classified into following five types:

Type 1: Examples on direct differentiation.

Type 2: Examples on verification of $\dfrac{\partial^2 z}{\partial x \, \partial y} = \dfrac{\partial^2 z}{\partial y \, \partial x}$.

Type 3: Examples on composite functions $z \to r \to x, y$ or $u \to r \to x, y, z$.

Type 4: Examples on variable to be treated as constant.

Type 5: Examples on finding the second order expression by using first order expression. (This type is to be studied after Euler's Theorem).

TYPE 1 : EXAMPLES ON DIRECT DIFFERENTIATION

Ex. 1: *If* $u = x^2 \tan^{-1} \dfrac{y}{x} - y^2 \tan^{-1} \dfrac{x}{y}$, *find* u_{xy}.

Sol. : **Step 1** : Let

$$u = x^2 \tan^{-1} \frac{y}{x} - y^2 \tan^{-1} \frac{x}{y} \qquad \ldots (1)$$

We have $\quad u_{xy} = \dfrac{\partial^2 u}{\partial x \, \partial y} = \dfrac{\partial}{\partial x}\left(\dfrac{\partial u}{\partial y}\right)$

Step 2 : First we will find $\dfrac{\partial u}{\partial y}$.

∴ Differentiating equation (1) partially with respect to y keeping x constant,

$$\frac{\partial u}{\partial y} = x^2 \frac{1}{1 + \frac{y^2}{x^2}} \left(\frac{1}{x}\right) - 2y \tan^{-1} \frac{x}{y} - y^2 \frac{1}{1 + \frac{x^2}{y^2}} \left(-\frac{x}{y^2}\right)$$

$$= \frac{x^3}{x^2 + y^2} - 2y \tan^{-1} \frac{x}{y} + \frac{xy^2}{x^2 + y^2}$$

$$= \frac{x(x^2 + y^2)}{x^2 + y^2} - 2y \tan^{-1} \frac{x}{y}$$

$$\frac{\partial u}{\partial y} = x - 2y \tan^{-1} \frac{x}{y}$$

Step 3:
$$\frac{\partial^2 u}{\partial x \, \partial y} = \frac{\partial}{\partial x}\left[x - 2y \tan^{-1}\frac{x}{y}\right] = 1 - 2y\left(\frac{1}{1+\frac{x^2}{y^2}}\right)\left(\frac{1}{y}\right)$$

$$= 1 - \frac{2y^2}{x^2+y^2} = \frac{x^2+y^2-2y^2}{x^2+y^2}$$

$$\frac{\partial^2 u}{\partial x \, \partial y} = \frac{x^2-y^2}{x^2+y^2}$$

Ex. 2 : If $u = \log(x^3 + y^3 - x^2 y - xy^2)$, prove that

$$\left(\frac{\partial}{\partial x} + \frac{\partial}{\partial y}\right)^2 u = \frac{-4}{(x+y)^2} \text{ or } \frac{\partial^2 u}{\partial x^2} + 2\frac{\partial^2 u}{\partial x \, \partial y} + \frac{\partial^2 u}{\partial y^2} = \frac{-4}{(x+y)^2}.$$ **(May 2009)**

Sol. : Step 1 :

We have
$$\left(\frac{\partial}{\partial x} + \frac{\partial}{\partial y}\right)^2 u = \left(\frac{\partial}{\partial x} + \frac{\partial}{\partial y}\right)\left(\frac{\partial}{\partial x} + \frac{\partial}{\partial y}\right) u = \left(\frac{\partial}{\partial x} + \frac{\partial}{\partial y}\right)\left(\frac{\partial u}{\partial x} + \frac{\partial u}{\partial y}\right)$$

$$\left(\frac{\partial}{\partial x} + \frac{\partial}{\partial y}\right)^2 u = \frac{\partial}{\partial x}\left(\frac{\partial u}{\partial x} + \frac{\partial u}{\partial y}\right) + \frac{\partial}{\partial y}\left(\frac{\partial u}{\partial x} + \frac{\partial u}{\partial y}\right) \qquad \ldots (1)$$

Step 2 : $\quad u = \log(x^3 + y^3 - x^2y - xy^2)$

Instead of finding $\frac{\partial u}{\partial x}, \frac{\partial u}{\partial y}$ directly first we will simplify the expression as follows :

$$u = \log(x^3 - x^2y + y^3 - xy^2) = \log[x^2(x-y) - y^2(x-y)]$$
or $\quad u = \log[(x-y)(x^2-y^2)] = \log(x-y)(x-y)(x+y)$
or $\quad u = \log(x-y)^2(x+y)$
$\therefore \quad u = 2\log(x-y) + \log(x+y) \qquad \ldots (2)$

Step 3 : Differentiating equation (2) partially with respect to x

$$\frac{\partial u}{\partial x} = \frac{2}{x-y}(1) + \frac{1}{x+y}(1)$$

Differentiating equation (2) partially with respect to y

$$\frac{\partial u}{\partial y} = \frac{2}{x-y}(-1) + \frac{1}{x+y}(1)$$

$\therefore \qquad \frac{\partial u}{\partial x} + \frac{\partial u}{\partial y} = \frac{2}{x+y}$

Step 4 : From equation (1),

$$\left(\frac{\partial}{\partial x} + \frac{\partial}{\partial y}\right)^2 u = \frac{\partial}{\partial x}\left(\frac{2}{x+y}\right) + \frac{\partial}{\partial y}\left(\frac{2}{x+y}\right) = -\frac{2}{(x+y)^2} - \frac{2}{(x+y)^2}$$

$\therefore \qquad \left(\frac{\partial}{\partial x} + \frac{\partial}{\partial y}\right)^2 u = \frac{-4}{(x+y)^2}$

Ex. 3 : If $v = (1 - 2xy + y^2)^{-1/2}$ then show that

(i) $xv_x - yv_y = y^2 v^3$, (ii) $\dfrac{\partial}{\partial x}[(1 - x^2) v_x] + \dfrac{\partial}{\partial y}[y^2 v_y] = 0$

Sol. : Step 1 : To prove (i), we have
$$v = (1 - 2xy + y^2)^{-1/2}$$

First we will remove fractional power or RHS by raising both sides to – 2.

$$\therefore \quad v^{-2} = 1 - 2xy + y^2 \qquad \ldots (1)$$

Step 2 : Differentiating equation (1) partially with respect to x on both sides keeping y constant, we have

$$-2v^{-3}\dfrac{\partial v}{\partial x} = -2y \quad \therefore \quad \dfrac{\partial v}{\partial x} = yv^3 \qquad \ldots (2)$$

Differentiating equation (1) partially with respect to y on both sides keeping x constant, we have

$$-2v^{-3}\dfrac{\partial v}{\partial y} = -2x + 2y = -2(x - y)$$

$$v^{-3}\dfrac{\partial v}{\partial y} = x - y \quad \therefore \quad \dfrac{\partial v}{\partial y} = (x - y)v^3 \qquad \ldots (3)$$

Step 3 : To prove (i), we consider

$$x v_x - y v_y = x(yv^3) - y(x - y)v^3 \qquad \text{[by equations (2) and (3)]}$$
$$= yv^3[x - x + y]$$
$$x v_x - y v_y = y^2 v^3$$

Step 4 : To prove (ii), we consider

$$\dfrac{\partial}{\partial x}[(1 - x^2)v_x] = \dfrac{\partial}{\partial x}[(1 - x^2)yv^3] = y\dfrac{\partial}{\partial x}[(1 - x^2)v^3]$$

$$= y[(1 - x^2)3v^2 \cdot v_x - 2x \cdot v^3] = y[3v^2(1 - x^2) \cdot yv^3 - 2xv^3]$$

$$\dfrac{\partial}{\partial x}[(1 - x^2)v_x] = 3y^2 v^5 (1 - x^2) - 2xyv^3 \qquad \ldots (4)$$

Consider $\dfrac{\partial}{\partial y}(y^2 v_y) = \dfrac{\partial}{\partial y}[y^2(x - y)v^3]$

$$= 2y(x - y)v^3 + y^2(-1)v^3 + y^2(x - y) \cdot 3v^2 \cdot v_y$$
$$= 2xy v^3 - 2y^2 v^3 - y^2 v^3 + 3v^2 y^2 (x - y) \cdot (x - y)v^3$$

$$\dfrac{\partial}{\partial y}(y^2 v_y) = 2xy v^3 - 3y^2 v^3 + 3y^2 v^5 (x - y)^2 \qquad \ldots (5)$$

Step 5 : By adding equations (4) and (5), we have

$$\frac{\partial}{\partial x}[(1-x^2)v_x] + \frac{\partial}{\partial y}[y^2 v_y] = 3y^2 v^5 (1-x^2) - 3y^2 v^3 + 3y^2 v^5 (x-y)^2$$

$$= 3y^2 v^5 [1 - x^2 + (x-y)^2] - 3y^2 v^3$$
$$= 3y^2 v^5 [1 - x^2 + x^2 - 2xy + y^2] - 3y^2 v^3$$
$$= 3y^2 v^5 [1 - 2xy + y^2] - 3y^2 v^3$$
$$= 3y^2 v^5 (v^{-2}) - 3y^2 v^3 \qquad \text{[by using (1)]}$$
$$= 3y^2 v^3 - 3y^2 v^3$$
$$= 0$$

Hence $\frac{\partial}{\partial x}[(1-x^2)v_x] + \frac{\partial}{\partial y}[y^2 v_y] = 0$

Ex. 4 : If $u = x^y$, show that $\dfrac{\partial^3 u}{\partial x^2 \partial y} = \dfrac{\partial^3 u}{\partial x \partial y \partial x}$.

Sol. : Given that $\quad u = x^y$

$$\frac{\partial u}{\partial x} = y \cdot x^{y-1} \qquad \ldots (1)$$

and $\qquad \dfrac{\partial u}{\partial y} = x^y \cdot \log x \qquad \ldots (2)$

Differentiating (2) partially with respect to x, we have

$$\frac{\partial^2 u}{\partial x \partial y} = x^y \cdot \frac{1}{x} + y \cdot x^{y-1} \cdot \log x = x^{y-1} + y\, x^{y-1} \cdot \log x$$

$$\frac{\partial^2 u}{\partial x \partial y} = x^{y-1}[1 + y \log x]$$

Differentiating again partially with respect to x on both sides, we have,

$$\frac{\partial^3 u}{\partial x^2 \partial y} = x^{y-1}\left(\frac{y}{x}\right) + (y-1)x^{y-2}(1 + y \log x)$$

$$= x^{y-2}[y + y - 1 + y(y-1)\log x]$$

$$\frac{\partial^3 u}{\partial x^2 \partial y} = x^{y-2}[2y - 1 + y(y-1)\log x] \qquad \ldots (3)$$

Now differentiating (1) partially with respect to y, we have

$$\frac{\partial^2 u}{\partial y \partial x} = x^{y-1} + y \cdot x^{y-1} \log x$$

$\therefore \qquad \dfrac{\partial^2 u}{\partial y \partial x} = x^{y-1}[1 + y \log x]$

Differentiating again with respect to x, we have,

$$\frac{\partial^3 u}{\partial x \partial y \partial x} = (y-1)x^{y-2}(1 + y \log x) + x^{y-1}\left(\frac{y}{x}\right)$$

$$= x^{y-2}[y - 1 + y(y-1)\log x + y]$$

$$\frac{\partial^3 u}{\partial x \, \partial y \, \partial x} = x^{y-2}\,[2y - 1 + y\,(y-1)\log x] \qquad \ldots (4)$$

From equations (3) and (4), we have,

$$\frac{\partial^3 u}{\partial x^2 \, \partial y} = \frac{\partial^3 u}{\partial x \, \partial y \, \partial x}$$

Ex. 5 : If $v = \dfrac{c}{\sqrt{t}}\, e^{-x^2/4a^2 t}$ then show that $\dfrac{\partial v}{\partial t} = a^2\, \dfrac{\partial^2 v}{\partial x^2}$.

Sol. : We have $\qquad v = \dfrac{c}{\sqrt{t}}\, e^{-x^2/4a^2 t}$

Taking logarithm, $\quad \log v = \log c - \dfrac{1}{2}\log t - \dfrac{x^2}{4a^2 t}$

$$\therefore \quad \frac{1}{v}\frac{\partial v}{\partial t} = -\frac{1}{2t} + \frac{x^2}{4a^2 t^2}$$

$$\therefore \quad \frac{\partial v}{\partial t} = v\left[-\frac{1}{2t} + \frac{x^2}{4a^2 t^2}\right] \qquad \ldots (1)$$

and $\qquad \dfrac{1}{v}\dfrac{\partial v}{\partial x} = -\dfrac{x}{2a^2 t} \qquad \therefore \quad \dfrac{\partial v}{\partial x} = -\dfrac{xv}{2a^2 t}$

$$\therefore \quad \frac{\partial^2 v}{\partial x^2} = -\frac{1}{2a^2 t}\left[v + x\frac{\partial v}{\partial x}\right] = -\frac{1}{2a^2 t}\left[v - \frac{vx^2}{2a^2 t}\right]$$

$$\therefore \quad a^2\frac{\partial^2 v}{\partial x^2} = v\left[-\frac{1}{2t} + \frac{x^2}{4a^2 t^2}\right] \qquad \ldots (2)$$

From equations (1) and (2), $\dfrac{\partial v}{\partial t} = a^2\, \dfrac{\partial^2 v}{\partial x^2}$.

Ex. 6 : If $u = \log(x^3 + y^3 + z^3 - 3xyz)$, prove that $\left(\dfrac{\partial}{\partial x} + \dfrac{\partial}{\partial y} + \dfrac{\partial}{\partial z}\right)^2 u = -\dfrac{9}{(x+y+z)^2}$.

Sol. :
$$\left(\frac{\partial}{\partial x} + \frac{\partial}{\partial y} + \frac{\partial}{\partial z}\right)^2 u = \left(\frac{\partial}{\partial x} + \frac{\partial}{\partial y} + \frac{\partial}{\partial z}\right)\left(\frac{\partial}{\partial x} + \frac{\partial}{\partial y} + \frac{\partial}{\partial z}\right) u$$

$$= \left(\frac{\partial}{\partial x} + \frac{\partial}{\partial y} + \frac{\partial}{\partial z}\right)\left(\frac{\partial u}{\partial x} + \frac{\partial u}{\partial y} + \frac{\partial u}{\partial z}\right)$$

$$= \left(\frac{\partial}{\partial x} + \frac{\partial}{\partial y} + \frac{\partial}{\partial z}\right) V$$

$$\left(\frac{\partial}{\partial x} + \frac{\partial}{\partial y} + \frac{\partial}{\partial z}\right)^2 u = \frac{\partial V}{\partial x} + \frac{\partial V}{\partial y} + \frac{\partial V}{\partial z} \qquad \ldots (1)$$

where $\qquad V = \dfrac{\partial u}{\partial x} + \dfrac{\partial u}{\partial y} + \dfrac{\partial u}{\partial z}$

$$u = \log(x^3 + y^3 + z^3 - 3xyz)$$

$$\frac{\partial u}{\partial x} = \frac{3(x^2 - yz)}{x^3 + y^3 + z^3 - 3xyz}$$

$$\frac{\partial u}{\partial y} = \frac{3(y^2 - xz)}{x^3 + y^3 + z^3 - 3xyz} \text{ and } \frac{\partial u}{\partial z} = \frac{3(z^2 - xy)}{x^3 + y^3 + z^3 - 3xyz}$$

$$V = \frac{3(x^2 + y^2 + z^2 - xy - yz - zx)}{x^3 + y^3 + z^3 - 3xyz}$$

$$V = \frac{3(x^2 + y^2 + z^2 - xy - yz - zx)}{(x + y + z)(x^2 + y^2 + z^2 - xy - yz - zx)}$$

$$(\because x^3 + y^3 + z^3 - 3xyz = (x + y + z)(x^2 + y^2 + z^2 - xy - yz - zx))$$

$$V = \frac{3}{x + y + z}$$

$$\frac{\partial V}{\partial x} = \frac{\partial V}{\partial y} = \frac{\partial V}{\partial z} = -\frac{3}{(x + y + z)^2}$$

Substituting in equation (1),

$$\therefore \left(\frac{\partial}{\partial x} + \frac{\partial}{\partial y} + \frac{\partial}{\partial z}\right)^2 u = -\frac{3}{(x + y + z)^2} - \frac{3}{(x + y + z)^2} - \frac{3}{(x + y + z)^2} = -\frac{9}{(x + y + z)^2}$$

Ex. 7 : *Prove that at a point of the surface $x^x \cdot y^y \cdot z^z = C$ where $x = y = z$*

$$\frac{\partial^2 z}{\partial x \, \partial y} = -(x \log ex)^{-1}.$$ **(Dec. 2009)**

Sol. : Given : $\quad x^x \cdot y^y \cdot z^z = C$

Taking logarithms, we have, $x \log x + y \log y + z \log z = \log c$ ... (1)

Differentiating (1) partially with respect to x considering y as constant and regarding z as a function of x and y, we have

$$x \cdot \frac{1}{x} + \log x \cdot (1) + z \cdot \frac{1}{z} \frac{\partial z}{\partial x} + \log z \cdot \frac{\partial z}{\partial x} = 0 \quad \text{or} \quad (\log x + 1) + (\log z + 1)\frac{\partial z}{\partial x} = 0$$

$$\therefore \quad \frac{\partial z}{\partial x} = -\left(\frac{1 + \log x}{1 + \log z}\right)$$

By symmetry $\quad \dfrac{\partial z}{\partial y} = -\left(\dfrac{1 + \log y}{1 + \log z}\right)$

$$\frac{\partial^2 z}{\partial x \, \partial y} = \frac{\partial}{\partial x}\left[-\left(\frac{1 + \log y}{1 + \log z}\right)\right] = -(1 + \log y)\frac{\partial}{\partial x}\left(\frac{1}{1 + \log z}\right)$$

$$= -(1 + \log y)\left\{-\frac{1}{(1 + \log z)^2}\right\} \cdot \frac{1}{z} \cdot \frac{\partial z}{\partial x} \quad \text{[Note this step]}$$

$$= \frac{1 + \log y}{z(1 + \log z)^2}\left[-\left(\frac{1 + \log x}{1 + \log z}\right)\right]$$

$$= \frac{-(1 + \log y)(1 + \log x)}{z(1 + \log z)^3}$$

But on the surface, $\quad x = y = z$

$$\left[\frac{\partial^2 z}{\partial x \, \partial y}\right]_{x=y=z} = -\frac{(1+\log x)^2}{x(1+\log x)^3} = -\frac{1}{x(1+\log x)}$$

$$= \frac{-1}{x(\log e + \log x)} = -\frac{1}{x \log e x}$$

$$= -(x \log e x)^{-1}$$

Ex. 8 : If $u = \tan^{-1}\left(\dfrac{xy}{\sqrt{1+x^2+y^2}}\right)$ then show that $\dfrac{\partial^2 u}{\partial x \, \partial y} = \dfrac{1}{(1+x^2+y^2)^{3/2}}$.

Sol. : Let $\qquad u = \tan^{-1}\left(\dfrac{xy}{\sqrt{1+x^2+y^2}}\right)$ ... (1)

Differentiating (1) partially with respect to y,

$$\frac{\partial u}{\partial y} = \left(\frac{1}{1+\dfrac{x^2 y^2}{1+x^2+y^2}}\right) \frac{\partial}{\partial y}\left(\frac{xy}{\sqrt{1+x^2+y^2}}\right)$$

$$= \left(\frac{1+x^2+y^2}{1+x^2+y^2+x^2 y^2}\right) \left[\frac{\sqrt{1+x^2+y^2} \cdot x - xy \cdot \dfrac{1}{2\sqrt{1+x^2+y^2}} \cdot 2y}{(1+x^2+y^2)}\right]$$

$$= \left(\frac{1+x^2+y^2}{1+x^2+y^2(1+x^2)}\right) \left[\frac{(1+x^2+y^2-y^2) x}{(1+x^2+y^2)\sqrt{1+x^2+y^2}}\right]$$

$$= \frac{(1+x^2) x}{(1+x^2)(1+y^2)\sqrt{1+x^2+y^2}}$$

$$\frac{\partial u}{\partial y} = \frac{x}{(1+y^2)\sqrt{1+x^2+y^2}} \qquad \text{... (2)}$$

Now differentiating (2) partially with respect to x

$$\frac{\partial^2 u}{\partial x \, \partial y} = \frac{\partial}{\partial x}\left(\frac{\partial u}{\partial y}\right) = \frac{\partial}{\partial x}\left[\frac{x}{(1+y^2)\sqrt{1+x^2+y^2}}\right]$$

$$= \frac{1}{1+y^2} \frac{\partial}{\partial x}\left(\frac{x}{\sqrt{1+x^2+y^2}}\right)$$

$$= \frac{1}{1+y^2}\left[\frac{\sqrt{1+x^2+y^2}\,(1) - x \cdot \dfrac{(2x)}{2\sqrt{1+x^2+y^2}}}{1+x^2+y^2}\right]$$

$$= \frac{1}{1+y^2}\left[\frac{1+x^2+y^2-x^2}{(1+x^2+y^2)\sqrt{1+x^2+y^2}}\right]$$

$$\frac{\partial^2 u}{\partial x \, \partial y} = \frac{1}{(1+x^2+y^2)^{3/2}}$$

Ex. 9 : *Find the value of n for which* $z = t^n e^{-r^2/4t}$ *satisfies the partial differential equation*
$\dfrac{1}{r^2}\left[\dfrac{\partial}{\partial r}\left(r^2 \dfrac{\partial z}{\partial r}\right)\right] = \dfrac{\partial z}{\partial t}$.

Sol. : Given, $\quad z = t^n e^{-r^2/4t}$

Taking logarithm, $\log z = n \log t - \dfrac{r^2}{4t}$ ... (1)

Differentiating (1) partially with respect to r,

$$\dfrac{1}{z}\dfrac{\partial z}{\partial r} = -\dfrac{2r}{4t} \quad \text{or} \quad \dfrac{\partial z}{\partial r} = -\dfrac{r \cdot z}{2t}$$

$\therefore \qquad r^2 \dfrac{\partial z}{\partial r} = -\dfrac{r^3 z}{2t}$

$\dfrac{\partial}{\partial r}\left(r^2 \dfrac{\partial z}{\partial r}\right) = -\dfrac{r^3}{2t}\dfrac{\partial z}{\partial r} - \dfrac{3r^2 z}{2t} = -\dfrac{r^3}{2t}\left(\dfrac{-rz}{2t}\right) - \dfrac{3r^2 z}{2t} = z\left[\dfrac{r^4}{4t^2} - \dfrac{3r^2}{2t}\right]$

$\dfrac{1}{r^2}\left[\dfrac{\partial}{\partial r}\left(r^2 \dfrac{\partial z}{\partial r}\right)\right] = z\left[\dfrac{r^2}{4t^2} - \dfrac{3}{2t}\right]$

Differentiating (1) partially with respect to t,

$$\dfrac{1}{z}\dfrac{\partial z}{\partial t} = \dfrac{n}{t} + \dfrac{r^2}{4t^2}$$

$\therefore \qquad \dfrac{\partial z}{\partial t} = z\left[\dfrac{r^2}{4t^2} + \dfrac{n}{t}\right]$

But $\quad \dfrac{1}{r^2}\left[\dfrac{\partial}{\partial r}\left(r^2 \dfrac{\partial z}{\partial r}\right)\right] = \dfrac{\partial z}{\partial t} \Rightarrow z\left[\dfrac{r^2}{4t^2} + \dfrac{n}{t}\right] = z\left[\dfrac{r^2}{4t^2} - \dfrac{3}{2t}\right]$

$\therefore \qquad \dfrac{n}{t} = -\dfrac{3}{2t} \Rightarrow n = -\dfrac{3}{2}.$

Ex. 10 : *If* $z = u(x, y) e^{ax + by}$ *where* $u(x, y)$ *is such that* $\dfrac{\partial^2 u}{\partial x \, \partial y} = 0$, *find the constants a, b such that* $\dfrac{\partial^2 z}{\partial x \, \partial y} - \dfrac{\partial z}{\partial x} - \dfrac{\partial z}{\partial y} + z = 0.$

Sol. : Note that since $u(x, y)$ is a function of x and y, hence partial derivatives with respect to x and y are denoted by $\dfrac{\partial u}{\partial x}$ and $\dfrac{\partial u}{\partial y}$ respectively.

$$z = u \cdot e^{ax + by} \qquad \qquad \ldots (1)$$

$\therefore$ Differentiating equation (1) partially with respect to x and y respectively, we have,

$$\dfrac{\partial z}{\partial x} = \dfrac{\partial u}{\partial x} e^{ax + by} + u \cdot e^{ax + by} \cdot a = e^{ax + by}\left(\dfrac{\partial u}{\partial x} + a \cdot u\right) \qquad \ldots (2)$$

$$\dfrac{\partial z}{\partial y} = \dfrac{\partial u}{\partial y} e^{ax + by} + u \cdot e^{ax + by} \cdot b = e^{ax + by}\left(\dfrac{\partial u}{\partial y} + b \cdot u\right) \qquad \ldots (3)$$

Now differentiating equation (3) partially with respect to x, we have

$$\frac{\partial^2 z}{\partial x \partial y} = e^{ax+by}\left(\frac{\partial^2 u}{\partial x \partial y} + b \cdot \frac{\partial u}{\partial x}\right) + \left(\frac{\partial u}{\partial y} + bu\right) e^{ax+by} \cdot a$$

But given that $\dfrac{\partial^2 u}{\partial x \partial y} = 0$

$\therefore \quad \dfrac{\partial^2 z}{\partial x \partial y} = e^{ax+by}\left(b\dfrac{\partial u}{\partial x} + a\dfrac{\partial u}{\partial y} + abu\right)$ ... (4)

By using equations (1), (2), (3) and (4), we have,

$$\frac{\partial^2 z}{\partial x \partial y} - \frac{\partial z}{\partial x} - \frac{\partial z}{\partial y} + z = 0$$

$$e^{ax+by}\left[b\frac{\partial u}{\partial x} + a\frac{\partial u}{\partial y} + abu - \frac{\partial u}{\partial x} - au - \frac{\partial u}{\partial y} - bu + u\right] = 0$$

or $\quad e^{ax+by}\left[(b-1)\dfrac{\partial u}{\partial x} + (a-1)\dfrac{\partial u}{\partial y} + au(b-1) - u(b-1)\right] = 0$

or $\quad e^{ax+by}\left[(b-1)\dfrac{\partial u}{\partial x} + (a-1)\dfrac{\partial u}{\partial y} + (b-1)u \cdot (a-1)\right] = 0$

$\because \quad e^{ax+by} \neq 0, \quad \dfrac{\partial u}{\partial x} \neq 0 \text{ and } \dfrac{\partial u}{\partial y} \neq 0,$

we must have, $\quad a - 1 = 0, \text{ and } b - 1 = 0$

$\therefore \quad a = 1 = b$

Note : For examples involving functions of the following types, use
(1) $\qquad u = f(x\ y)$

$$\frac{\partial u}{\partial x} = [f'(xy)]\,y \text{ and } \frac{\partial u}{\partial y}\,[f'(xy)]\,x$$

(2) $\qquad u = f\left(\dfrac{x}{y}\right)$, then

$$\frac{\partial u}{\partial x} = \left[f'\left(\frac{x}{y}\right)\right]\frac{1}{y} \text{ and } \frac{\partial u}{\partial y} = \left[f'\left(\frac{x}{y}\right)\right]\left(-\frac{x}{y^2}\right)$$

Ex. 11 : *Show that* $z = f(x+at) + \phi(x-at)$ *is a solution of* $a^2 \dfrac{\partial^2 z}{\partial x^2} = \dfrac{\partial^2 z}{\partial t^2}$ *for all f, ϕ and a being constant.*

Sol. : We have $\quad z = f(x+at) + \phi(x-at)$ ... (1)

$\dfrac{\partial z}{\partial x} = f'(x+at) + \phi'(x-at)$ and $\dfrac{\partial^2 z}{\partial x^2} = f''(x+at) + \phi''(x-at)$ ... (2)

Again $\quad \dfrac{\partial z}{\partial t} = af'(x+at) - a\,\phi'(x-at)$ and $\dfrac{\partial^2 z}{\partial t^2} = a^2 f''(x+at) + a^2 \phi''(x-at)$

$\qquad = a^2[f''(x+at) + \phi''(x-at)]$ ... (3)

Multiplying equation (2) by a^2, then

$$a^2 \frac{\partial^2 z}{\partial x^2} = a^2 [f''(x+at) + \phi''(x+at)] \qquad \ldots (4)$$

Hence from equations (3) and (4), we have the result

$$a^2 \frac{\partial^2 z}{\partial x^2} = \frac{\partial^2 z}{\partial t^2} \qquad \ldots (5)$$

Hence equation (1) is a solution of the differential equation (5).

Ex. 12 : If $v = (x^2 - y^2) f(xy)$ then show that $v_{xx} + v_{yy} = (x^4 - y^4) f''(xy)$. **(Dec. 2014)**

Sol. : $\qquad v = (x^2 - y^2) f(xy)$

Using product rule,

$$\frac{\partial v}{\partial x} = 2x\, f(xy) + (x^2 - y^2)\, f'(xy) \cdot y$$

$$\frac{\partial^2 v}{\partial x^2} = 2\, f(xy) + 2x\, f(xy) \cdot y + y\, [2x\, f'(xy) + (x^2 - y^2)\, f''(xy)\, y]$$

$$= 2\, f(xy) + 2xy\, f'(xy) + 2xy\, f'(xy) + (x^2 - y^2)\, f''(xy)\, y^2 \qquad \ldots (1)$$

Again, $\qquad \dfrac{\partial v}{\partial y} = -2y\, f(xy) + (x^2 - y^2)\, f'(xy) \cdot x$

$$\frac{\partial^2 v}{\partial y^2} = -2\, f(xy) - 2y\, f'(xy)\, x + x\, [-2y\, f'(xy) + (x^2 - y^2)\, f''(xy) \cdot x]$$

$$= -2f(xy) - 2xy\, f'(xy) - 2xy\, f'(xy) + x^2(x^2 - y^2)\, f''(xy) \qquad \ldots (2)$$

Adding equations (1) and (2), we get

$$\frac{\partial^2 v}{\partial x^2} + \frac{\partial^2 v}{\partial y^2} = (x^2 + y^2)(x^2 - y^2)\, f''(xy) = (x^4 - y^4)\, f''(xy)$$

Ex. 13 : Find the value of n so that $u = r^n\, (3\cos^2 \theta - 1)$ satisfies the partial differential equation $\dfrac{\partial}{\partial r}\left(r^2 \dfrac{\partial u}{\partial r}\right) + \dfrac{1}{\sin \theta} \dfrac{\partial}{\partial \theta} \left(\sin \theta \dfrac{\partial u}{\partial \theta}\right) = 0.$ **(Dec. 2010, May 2014)**

Sol. : $\qquad u = r^n\, (3\cos^2 \theta - 1) \qquad \ldots (1)$

$$\frac{\partial u}{\partial r} = n r^{n-1}\, (3\cos^2 \theta - 1) = \frac{n r^n\, (3\cos^2 \theta - 1)}{r}$$

$$\frac{\partial u}{\partial r} = n \frac{u}{r} \qquad \text{[by using equation (1)]}$$

$$r^2 \frac{\partial u}{\partial r} = nur$$

$$\frac{\partial}{\partial r}\left(r^2 \frac{\partial u}{\partial r}\right) = \frac{\partial}{\partial r}(nur) = nu + nr\, \frac{\partial u}{\partial r}$$

$$= nu + nr \left(\frac{nu}{r}\right)$$

$$\frac{\partial}{\partial r}\left(r^2 \frac{\partial u}{\partial r}\right) = nu + n^2 u \qquad \ldots (2)$$

$$\frac{\partial u}{\partial \theta} = r^n [6 \cos \theta (-\sin \theta)]$$

$$\sin \theta \frac{\partial u}{\partial \theta} = -6r^n \cos \theta \sin^2 \theta$$

$$\frac{\partial}{\partial \theta}\left(\sin \theta \frac{\partial u}{\partial \theta}\right) = -6r^n [-\sin^3 \theta + 2 \cos^2 \theta \sin \theta]$$

$$= -6r^n \sin \theta [2 \cos^2 \theta - (1 - \cos^2 \theta)]$$

$$= -6r^n \sin \theta [3 \cos^2 \theta - 1]$$

$$= -6 \sin \theta \cdot u \qquad \text{[by using (1)]}$$

$$\frac{1}{\sin \theta} \frac{\partial}{\partial \theta}\left(\sin \theta \frac{\partial u}{\partial \theta}\right) = -6u \qquad \ldots (3)$$

By adding equations (2) and (3), we get,

$$\frac{\partial}{\partial r}\left(r^2 \frac{\partial u}{\partial r}\right) + \frac{1}{\sin \theta} \frac{\partial}{\partial \theta}\left(\sin \theta \frac{\partial u}{\partial \theta}\right) = nu + n^2 u - 6u$$

$$= (n^2 + n - 6) u = 0 \text{ (given)}$$

$$\therefore \qquad n^2 + n - 6 = 0 \qquad (\because u \ne 0)$$

$$\therefore \qquad (n + 3)(n - 2) = 0$$

$$\therefore \qquad n = 2, -3.$$

Ex. 14 : If $z = \tan(y + ax) + (y - ax)^{3/2}$, find the value of $\dfrac{\partial^2 z}{\partial x^2} - a^2 \dfrac{\partial^2 z}{\partial y^2}$.

Sol. :

$$z = \tan(y + ax) + (y - ax)^{3/2}$$

$$\frac{\partial z}{\partial x} = a \sec^2(y + ax) + \frac{3}{2}(y - ax)^{1/2}(-a)$$

$$\frac{\partial^2 z}{\partial x^2} = 2a^2 \sec^2(y + ax) \tan(y + ax) + \frac{3}{4} a^2 (y - ax)^{-1/2} \qquad \ldots (1)$$

$$\frac{\partial z}{\partial y} = \sec^2(y + ax) + \frac{3}{2}(y - ax)^{1/2}$$

$$\frac{\partial^2 z}{\partial y^2} = 2 \sec^2(y + ax) \tan(y + ax) + \frac{3}{4}(y - ax)^{-1/2}$$

$$a^2 \frac{\partial^2 z}{\partial y^2} = 2a^2 \sec^2(y + ax) \tan(y + ax) + \frac{3}{4} a^2 (y - ax)^{-1/2} \qquad \ldots (2)$$

Subtracting (2) from (1), we get,

$$\frac{\partial^2 z}{\partial x^2} - a^2 \frac{\partial^2 z}{\partial y^2} = 0$$

Ex. 15 : If $u = x^m y^n$, show that $\dfrac{\partial^3 u}{\partial x \, \partial y \, \partial x} = \dfrac{\partial^3 u}{\partial y \, \partial x^2}$.

Sol. :
$$u = x^m y^n$$
$$\frac{\partial u}{\partial x} = m \, x^{m-1} y^n,$$
$$\frac{\partial^2 u}{\partial y \, \partial x} = m \cdot n \cdot x^{m-1} y^{n-1}$$
$$\frac{\partial^3 u}{\partial x \, \partial y \, \partial x} = m \cdot n \, (m-1) \, x^{m-2} \, y^{n-1} \qquad \ldots (1)$$

Also,
$$\frac{\partial^2 u}{\partial x^2} = m \, (m-1) \, x^{m-2} y^n$$
$$\frac{\partial^3 u}{\partial y \, \partial x^2} = m \cdot n \, (m-1) \, x^{m-2} \, y^{n-1} \qquad \ldots (2)$$

From equations (1) and (2),
$$\frac{\partial^3 u}{\partial x \, \partial y \, \partial x} = \frac{\partial^3 u}{\partial y \, \partial x^2}$$

Ex. 16 : If $z^3 - xz - y = 4$, find $\dfrac{\partial z}{\partial x}, \dfrac{\partial z}{\partial y}$.

Sol. : Here z is not expressed explicitly in terms of x and y and the derivatives $\dfrac{\partial z}{\partial x}, \dfrac{\partial z}{\partial y}$ required indicate that z must be dependent variable and x, y are independent variables.

Let
$$z^3 - xz - y = 4. \qquad \ldots (1)$$

Differentiating equation (1) partially with respect to x keeping y constant and regarding z as a function of x and y,

$$3z^2 \frac{\partial z}{\partial x} - x \frac{\partial z}{\partial x} - z(1) = 0 \text{ or } \frac{\partial z}{\partial x} (3z^2 - x) = z \quad \therefore \quad \frac{\partial z}{\partial x} = \frac{z}{3z^2 - x}$$

Differentiating equation (1) partially with respect to y keeping x constant and $z \to x, y$, we have,

$$3z^2 \frac{\partial z}{\partial y} - x \frac{\partial z}{\partial y} - 1 = 0 \quad \text{or} \quad \frac{\partial z}{\partial y} (3z^2 - x) = 1 \quad \therefore \quad \frac{\partial z}{\partial y} = \frac{1}{3z^2 - x}$$

Ex. 17 : If $z^3 - zx - y = 0$, prove that $\dfrac{\partial^2 z}{\partial x \, \partial y} = -\dfrac{(3z^2 + x)}{(3z^2 - x)^3}$. **(May 2009, 2011)**

Sol. : Given : $\quad z^3 - zx - y = 0 \qquad \ldots (1)$

Regarding z as a function of x and y and differentiating (1) partially w.r.t. y and x respectively, we have

$$3z^2 \frac{\partial z}{\partial y} - x \frac{\partial z}{\partial y} - 1 = 0 \quad \therefore \quad \frac{\partial z}{\partial y} = \frac{1}{3z^2 - x}$$

$$3z^2 \frac{\partial z}{\partial x} - x \frac{\partial z}{\partial x} - z = 0 \quad \therefore \frac{\partial z}{\partial x} = \frac{z}{3z^2 - x}$$

$$\therefore \quad \frac{\partial^2 z}{\partial x \, \partial y} = \frac{\partial}{\partial x} \left(\frac{1}{3z^2 - x} \right) = -\frac{1}{(3z^2 - x)^2} \cdot \left(6z \frac{\partial z}{\partial x} - 1 \right)$$

$$= -\frac{1}{(3z^2 - x)^2} \left[\frac{6z^2}{3z^2 - x} - 1 \right] = -\frac{(3z^2 + x)}{(3z^2 - x)^3}$$

EXERCISE 10.1

Problems on direct differentiation :

1. Find $\dfrac{\partial u}{\partial x}, \dfrac{\partial u}{\partial y}$ in the following cases :
   (a) $u = ax^2 + 2hxy + by^2$, (b) $u = x^y + y^x$, (c) $x^3 y - \sin z + z^3 = 0$.

2. Find $\dfrac{\partial z}{\partial x}$ and $\dfrac{\partial z}{\partial y}$ where (a) $z = \dfrac{x}{x^2 + y^2}$, (b) $z = \log(x^2 + y^2)$.

3. If $x = r \sin\theta \cos\phi$, $y = r \sin\theta \sin\phi$, $z = r \cos\theta$ find $\dfrac{\partial r}{\partial x}, \dfrac{\partial \theta}{\partial x}$ and $\dfrac{\partial \phi}{\partial x}$ in terms of r, θ, ϕ.

   [**Hint :** use $r^2 = x^2 + y^2 + z^2$, $\phi = \tan^{-1} \dfrac{y}{x}$, $\theta = \tan^{-1} \sqrt{(x^2 + y^2)/z^2}$]

   Ans. $\sin\theta \cos\phi, \dfrac{\cos\theta \cos\phi}{r}, \dfrac{-\sin\phi}{r \sin\theta}$]

4. Find the value of n for which $u = Ae^{-gx} \sin(nt - gx)$ satisfies the partial differential equation $\dfrac{\partial u}{\partial t} = m \dfrac{\partial^2 u}{\partial x^2}$ where A, g are constants. **(Dec. 2008, May 2015)**

   Ans. $n = 2m g^2$

5. Find the value of n for which $u = kt^{-1/2} \cdot e^{-x^2/na^2 t}$ satisfies the partial differential equation $\dfrac{\partial u}{\partial t} = a^2 \dfrac{\partial^2 u}{\partial x^2}$.
   Ans. $n = 4$

6. If $u = t^n e^{-r^2/4kt}$, find n for which $\dfrac{\partial u}{\partial t} = k \left(\dfrac{\partial^2 u}{\partial r^2} + \dfrac{2}{r} \dfrac{\partial u}{\partial r} \right)$ (k = constant).

7. If $u = e^{xyz}$ then show that $\dfrac{\partial^3 u}{\partial x \, \partial y \, \partial z} = (1 + 3xyz + x^2 y^2 z^2) e^{xyz}$.

8. If $u = x^p y^q$, show that $\dfrac{\partial^3 u}{\partial x \, \partial y^2} = \dfrac{\partial^3 u}{\partial y \, \partial x \, \partial y}$.

9. If $u = e^{x - pt} \cos(x - pt)$, prove that $\dfrac{\partial^2 u}{\partial t^2} = p^2 \dfrac{\partial^2 u}{\partial x^2}$.

10. If $u = \log(\tan x + \tan y + \tan z)$, show that $\sin 2x \, u_x + \sin 2y \, u_y + \sin 2z \, u_z = 2$.
    [**Hint :** L.H.S. $= (\sin 2x \sec^2 x + \sin 2y \sec^2 y + \sin 2z \sec^2 z)/\tan x + \tan y + \tan z$]

11. If $u = (x^2 - y^2) f(r)$ where $r = xy$ then show that $u_{xy} = (x^2 - y^2) [3 f'(r) + r f''(r)]$.

12. Prove that $u = \dfrac{1}{r}[f(ct + r) + \phi(ct - r)]$ satisfies the partial differential equation
$\dfrac{\partial^2 u}{\partial t^2} = \dfrac{c^2}{r^2} \dfrac{\partial}{\partial r}\left[r^2 \dfrac{\partial u}{\partial r}\right]$ where $c =$ constant.

13. If $u + iv = f(x + iy)$, prove that $u_{xx} + u_{yy} = 0$, $v_{xx} + v_{yy} = 0$.

14. If $z(x + y) = x^2 + y^2$, show that $\left(\dfrac{\partial z}{\partial x} - \dfrac{\partial z}{\partial y}\right)^2 = 4\left(1 - \dfrac{\partial z}{\partial x} - \dfrac{\partial z}{\partial y}\right)$.

15. If $u = x^y$ show that $\dfrac{\partial^3 u}{\partial x^2 \, \partial y} = \dfrac{\partial^3 u}{\partial x \, \partial y \, \partial z}$.

16. If $\dfrac{x^2}{a^2 + u} + \dfrac{y^2}{b^2 + u} + \dfrac{z^2}{c^2 + u} = 1$, show that $(u_x)^2 + (u_y)^2 + (u_z)^2 = 2(x\, u_x + y\, u_y + z\, u_z)$.

[**Hint**: $2x\, u_x = 2x \cdot [(2x/a^2 + u)/\Sigma\, (x^2/(a^2 + u)^2)]$.]

TYPE 2 : EXAMPLES ON VERIFICATION OF $\dfrac{\partial^2 z}{\partial x \, \partial y} = \dfrac{\partial^2 z}{\partial y \, \partial x}$

Ex. 1 : If $u = \log(x^2 + y^2)$, verify $u_{xy} = u_{yx}$. (May 2010)

Sol. :
$\dfrac{\partial u}{\partial x} = u_x = \dfrac{1}{x^2 + y^2} \times 2x = \dfrac{2x}{x^2 + y^2}$

$\dfrac{\partial u}{\partial y} = u_y = \dfrac{1}{x^2 + y^2} \times 2y = \dfrac{2y}{x^2 + y^2}$

$\dfrac{\partial^2 u}{\partial x \, \partial y} = u_{xy} = \dfrac{\partial}{\partial x}\left(\dfrac{\partial u}{\partial y}\right) = \dfrac{\partial}{\partial x}\left(\dfrac{2y}{x^2 + y^2}\right) = 2y\left[-\dfrac{1}{(x^2 + y^2)^2}\right] \times 2x$

$\therefore \quad u_{xy} = -\dfrac{4xy}{(x^2 + y^2)^2}$ ... (1)

$\dfrac{\partial^2 u}{\partial y \, \partial x} = u_{yx} = \dfrac{\partial}{\partial y}\left(\dfrac{\partial u}{\partial x}\right) = \dfrac{\partial}{\partial y}\left(\dfrac{2x}{x^2 + y^2}\right) = 2x\left[-\dfrac{1}{(x^2 + y^2)^2}\right] \times 2y$

$\therefore \quad u_{yx} = -\dfrac{4xy}{(x^2 + y^2)^2}$ ... (2)

From (1) and (2), we notice that
$u_{xy} = u_{yx}$

Ex. 2 : If $u = x^y$ then verify $\dfrac{\partial^2 u}{\partial x \, \partial y} = \dfrac{\partial^2 u}{\partial y \, \partial x}$.

Sol. : Here $u = x^y$, $\dfrac{\partial u}{\partial x} = y \cdot x^{y-1}$ (since y is constant)

$\dfrac{\partial^2 u}{\partial x^2} = y(y-1)x^{y-2}$ (again since y is constant)

$\dfrac{\partial^2 u}{\partial y \, \partial x} = \dfrac{\partial}{\partial y}\left(\dfrac{\partial u}{\partial x}\right) = \dfrac{\partial}{\partial y}[y \cdot x^{y-1}]$

$\dfrac{\partial^2 u}{\partial y \, \partial x} = y \cdot x^{y-1} \log x + x^{y-1}(1)$

(using product rule keeping x as constant)

Now,
$$u = x^y$$
$$\frac{\partial u}{\partial y} = x^y \log x \qquad \text{(since x is constant and } \frac{d}{dy} a^y = a^y \log a\text{)}$$
$$\frac{\partial^2 u}{\partial y^2} = \log x \cdot [x^y \cdot \log x] \qquad \text{(again since x is constant)}$$
$$\frac{\partial^2 u}{\partial x \, \partial y} = \frac{\partial}{\partial x}\left[\frac{\partial u}{\partial y}\right] = \frac{\partial}{\partial x}[x^y \log x] = x^y \left(\frac{1}{x}\right) + \log x \, (y \cdot x^{y-1})$$
(using product rule keeping y as constant)
$$\frac{\partial^2 u}{\partial x \, \partial y} = x^{y-1} + y x^{y-1} \log x$$

We note that, $\quad \dfrac{\partial^2 u}{\partial x \, \partial y} = \dfrac{\partial^2 u}{\partial y \, \partial x}$

Ex. 3 : *If $z = x^y + y^x$, verify that $\dfrac{\partial^2 z}{\partial x \, \partial y} = \dfrac{\partial^2 z}{\partial y \, \partial x}$.*

Sol. : Let $\quad z = x^y + y^x \qquad \ldots (1)$

Differentiating equation (1) partially with respect to x keeping y constant, we have
$$\frac{\partial z}{\partial x} = y x^{y-1} + y^x \log y \qquad \ldots (2)$$

Now differentiating equation (2) partially with respect to y keeping x constant, we have
$$\frac{\partial^2 z}{\partial y \, \partial x} = \frac{\partial}{\partial y}\left[\frac{\partial z}{\partial x}\right] = \frac{\partial}{\partial y}[y \, x^{y-1} + y^x \log y]$$
$$= \frac{\partial}{\partial y}(y \, x^{y-1}) + \frac{\partial}{\partial y}(y^x \log y)$$
$$= x^{y-1} + y \cdot x^{y-1} \log x + y^x \cdot \frac{1}{y} + x y^{x-1} \log y$$
$$\therefore \quad \frac{\partial^2 z}{\partial y \, \partial x} = x^{y-1} + y \, x^{y-1} \log x + y^{x-1} + x \, y^{x-1} \log y \qquad \ldots (3)$$

Differentiating equation (1) partially with respect to y keeping x constant, we have
$$\frac{\partial z}{\partial y} = x^y \log x + x \, y^{x-1} \qquad \ldots (4)$$

Now differentiating equation (4) partially with respect to x keeping y constant, we have
$$\frac{\partial^2 z}{\partial x \, \partial y} = \frac{\partial}{\partial x}\left(\frac{\partial z}{\partial y}\right) = \frac{\partial}{\partial x}[x^y \log x + x \, y^{x-1}]$$
$$= \frac{\partial}{\partial x}(x^y \log x) + \frac{\partial}{\partial x}(x y^{x-1})$$
$$= x^y \cdot \frac{1}{x} + y \, x^{y-1} \log x + x y^{x-1} \log y + y^{x-1}$$

$$\frac{\partial^2 z}{\partial x\, \partial y} = x^{y-1} + yx^{y-1}\log x + xy^{x-1}\log y + y^{x-1} \qquad \ldots (5)$$

From equations (3) and (5), we note that $\dfrac{\partial^2 z}{\partial x\, \partial y} = \dfrac{\partial^2 z}{\partial y\, \partial x}$.

EXERCISE 10.2

Verify that $\dfrac{\partial^2 u}{\partial x\, \partial y} = \dfrac{\partial^2 u}{\partial y\, \partial x}$ for

1. $u = \tan(y + ax) - (y - ax)^{3/2}$
2. $u = 3xy - y^3 + (y^2 - 2x)^{3/2}$
3. $u = \tan^{-1}\left(\dfrac{xy}{\sqrt{1 + x^2 + y^2}}\right)$
4. $u = \log\left(\dfrac{x^2 + y^2}{xy}\right)$
5. $u = \tan^{-1}\left(\dfrac{x}{y}\right)$ (May 2014)

TYPE 3 : EXAMPLES ON COMPOSITE FUNCTIONS

Note the following important results.

(1) Let $u = f(r)$ where r is again a function of two variables x and y.

Then u becomes composite function of x and y. i.e. $u \to r \to x, y$

$$\therefore \quad \frac{\partial u}{\partial x} = \frac{du}{dr}\frac{\partial r}{\partial x}, \quad \frac{\partial u}{\partial y} = \frac{du}{dr}\frac{\partial r}{\partial y}$$

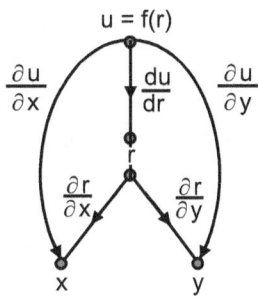

Fig. 10.3

(2) Let $v = f(r)$ where r is again a function of three variables x, y and z then v becomes composite function of x, y and z.

i.e. $v \to r \to x, y, z$

$$\frac{\partial v}{\partial x} = \frac{dv}{dr}\frac{\partial r}{\partial x}, \quad \frac{\partial v}{\partial y} = \frac{dv}{dr}\frac{\partial r}{\partial y}, \quad \frac{\partial v}{\partial z} = \frac{dv}{dr}\frac{\partial r}{\partial z}$$

(3) If $r = \sqrt{x^2 + y^2}$, $r^2 = x^2 + y^2$

then $2r \cdot \dfrac{\partial r}{\partial x} = 2x \Rightarrow \dfrac{\partial r}{\partial x} = \dfrac{x}{r}$ and $\dfrac{\partial r}{\partial y} = \dfrac{y}{r}$

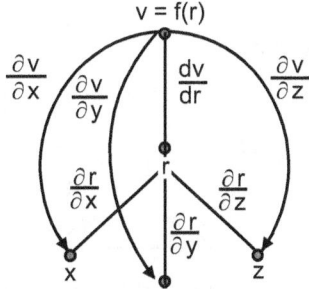

Fig. 10.4

(4) If $r = \sqrt{x^2 + y^2 + z^2}$, $r^2 = x^2 + y^2 + z^2$

then $2r\dfrac{\partial r}{\partial x} = 2x,\ \dfrac{\partial r}{\partial x} = \dfrac{x}{r},\ \dfrac{\partial r}{\partial y} = \dfrac{y}{r},\ \dfrac{\partial r}{\partial z} = \dfrac{z}{r}$

Ex. 1 : If $u = f(r)$ where $r = \sqrt{x^2 + y^2}$, prove that

$$\frac{\partial^2 u}{\partial x^2} + \frac{\partial^2 u}{\partial y^2} = f''(r) + \frac{1}{r}f'(r) \quad \text{or} \quad u_{xx} + u_{yy} = \frac{d^2 u}{dr^2} + \frac{1}{r}\frac{du}{dr}.$$ **(Dec. 2009)**

Sol. : Step 1 : Here $u \to r \to x, y$ i.e. u becomes composite function of x and y.

We have, $\quad \dfrac{\partial u}{\partial x} = \dfrac{du}{dr}\dfrac{\partial r}{\partial x}, \quad \dfrac{\partial u}{\partial y} = \dfrac{du}{dr}\dfrac{\partial r}{\partial y}$

Step 2 : We have, $\quad r = \sqrt{x^2 + y^2}, \quad r^2 = x^2 + y^2$

$$2r\frac{\partial r}{\partial x} = 2x \quad \therefore \quad \frac{\partial r}{\partial x} = \frac{x}{r} \; ; \; \frac{\partial r}{\partial y} = \frac{y}{r}$$

Make a note that for $u = f(r) \Rightarrow \dfrac{du}{dr}$ or $\dfrac{\partial f}{\partial r}$ or $f'(r)$ all mean the same thing.

Step 3 : $\quad \dfrac{\partial u}{\partial x} = \dfrac{du}{dr}\dfrac{x}{r} = f'(r)\dfrac{x}{r}$

Carefully note the second order partial derivative.

Step 4 : $\quad \dfrac{\partial^2 u}{\partial x^2} = f'(r)\left\{\dfrac{r(1) - x \cdot \dfrac{\partial r}{\partial x}}{r^2}\right\} + \dfrac{x}{r} f''(r) \dfrac{\partial r}{\partial x}.$

[**Note :** $\dfrac{\partial}{\partial x}\left(\dfrac{x}{r}\right) \neq \dfrac{1}{r}$ because r is a function of x and y. Also $\dfrac{\partial}{\partial x}[f'(r)] = \dfrac{d}{dr}[f'(r)]\dfrac{\partial r}{\partial x} = f''(r)\dfrac{\partial r}{\partial x}$].

$\therefore \quad \dfrac{\partial^2 u}{\partial x^2} = f'(r)\left\{\dfrac{r - x \cdot \dfrac{x}{r}}{r^2}\right\} + \dfrac{x^2}{r^2} f''(r)$

$\dfrac{\partial^2 u}{\partial x^2} = f'(r)\left(\dfrac{r^2 - x^2}{r^3}\right) + \dfrac{x^2}{r^2} f''(r)$

Similarly, $\quad \dfrac{\partial^2 u}{\partial y^2} = f'(r)\left(\dfrac{r^2 - y^2}{r^3}\right) + \dfrac{y^2}{r^2} f''(r)$

Step 5 : $\quad \dfrac{\partial^2 u}{\partial x^2} + \dfrac{\partial^2 u}{\partial y^2} = \dfrac{f'(r)}{r^3}[2r^2 - (x^2 + y^2)] + \dfrac{f''(r)}{r^2}(x^2 + y^2)$

$\dfrac{\partial^2 u}{\partial x^2} + \dfrac{\partial^2 u}{\partial y^2} = \dfrac{f'(r)}{r^3}(2r^2 - r^2) + \dfrac{f''(r)}{r^2}(r^2) \quad (\because x^2 + y^2 = r^2)$

$\dfrac{\partial^2 u}{\partial x^2} + \dfrac{\partial^2 u}{\partial y^2} = f''(r) + \dfrac{1}{r} f'(r).$

Ex. 2 : If $u = f(r)$ where $r = \sqrt{x^2 + y^2 + z^2}$, prove that $u_{xx} + u_{yy} + u_{zz} = f''(r) + \dfrac{2}{r}f'(r).$

(May 2005)

Sol. : Here $u \to r \to x, y, z$ hence u becomes composite function of x, y, z.

$$\frac{\partial u}{\partial x} = \frac{du}{dr}\frac{\partial r}{\partial x} = f'(r) \cdot \frac{x}{r}$$

$$u_{xx} = f'(r)\left(\frac{r - x\frac{\partial r}{\partial x}}{r^2}\right) + \frac{x}{r} f''(r) \frac{\partial r}{\partial x}$$

$$u_{xx} = f'(r)\left(\frac{r^2 - x^2}{r^3}\right) + \frac{x^2}{r^2} f''(r)$$

Similarly,
$$u_{yy} = f'(r)\left(\frac{r^2 - y^2}{r^3}\right) + \frac{y^2}{r^2} f''(r)$$

$$u_{zz} = f'(r)\left(\frac{r^2 - z^2}{r^3}\right) + \frac{z^2}{r^2} f''(r)$$

$$\therefore\ u_{xx} + u_{yy} + u_{zz} = \frac{f'(r)}{r^2}[3r^2 - (x^2 + y^2 + z^2)] + \frac{f''(r)}{r^2}(x^2 + y^2 + z^2)$$

$$= \frac{f'(r)}{r^2}(2r^2) + \frac{f''(r)}{r^2}(r^2)$$

$$\therefore\ u_{xx} + u_{yy} + u_{zz} = f''(r) + \frac{2}{r} f'(r)$$

Ex. 3 : If $u = x \cdot \log(x + r) - r$ where $r^2 = x^2 + y^2$, find $u_{xx} + u_{yy}$.

Sol. : Given
$$u = x \log(x + r) - r \qquad \ldots (1)$$

Differentiating (1) partially with respect to x and note that $\frac{\partial r}{\partial x} = \frac{x}{r}$, we have

$$\frac{\partial u}{\partial x} = x \cdot \frac{1}{x+r}\left(1 + \frac{\partial r}{\partial x}\right) + \log(x+r) \cdot 1 - \frac{\partial r}{\partial x}$$

$$= \frac{x}{x+r}\left(1 + \frac{x}{r}\right) + \log(x+r) - \frac{x}{r}$$

$$= \frac{x}{x+r}\left(\frac{r+x}{r}\right) + \log(x+r) - \frac{x}{r}$$

$$\frac{\partial u}{\partial x} = \log(x+r)$$

Differentiating again partially with respect to x,

$$\frac{\partial^2 u}{\partial x^2} = \frac{1}{x+r}\left(1 + \frac{\partial r}{\partial x}\right) = \frac{1}{x+r}\left(1 + \frac{x}{r}\right) = \frac{(x+r)}{(x+r)r}$$

$$\frac{\partial^2 u}{\partial x^2} = \frac{1}{r} \qquad \ldots (2)$$

Differentiating (1) partially with respect to y and note that $\frac{\partial r}{\partial y} = \frac{y}{r}$, we have

$$\frac{\partial u}{\partial y} = x \cdot \frac{1}{x+r}\left(\frac{\partial r}{\partial y}\right) - \frac{\partial r}{\partial y} = \frac{x}{x+r}\left(\frac{y}{r}\right) - \frac{y}{r}$$

$$= \frac{y}{r}\left(\frac{x}{x+r} - 1\right) = \frac{y}{r}\left(\frac{x-x-r}{x+r}\right)$$

$$\frac{\partial u}{\partial y} = -\frac{y}{(x+r)}$$

Differentiating again with respect to y

$$\frac{\partial^2 u}{\partial y^2} = -\left\{\frac{(x+r)(1) - y(\partial r/\partial y)}{(x+r)^2}\right\} = -\left\{\frac{x+r-y(y/r)}{(x+r)^2}\right\}$$

$$= -\left\{\frac{rx + r^2 - y^2}{r(x+r)^2}\right\} = -\left\{\frac{rx + x^2}{r(x+r)^2}\right\} \qquad (\because r^2 - y^2 = x^2)$$

$$= -\left\{\frac{x(r+x)}{r(x+r)^2}\right\}$$

$$\frac{\partial^2 u}{\partial y^2} = \frac{-x}{r(x+r)} \qquad \ldots (3)$$

By adding equations (2) and (3),

$$\frac{\partial^2 u}{\partial x^2} + \frac{\partial^2 u}{\partial y^2} = \frac{1}{r} - \frac{x}{r(x+r)} = \frac{1}{r}\left[1 - \frac{x}{x+r}\right] = \frac{1}{r}\left[\frac{x+r-x}{x+r}\right]$$

$$\frac{\partial^2 u}{\partial x^2} + \frac{\partial^2 u}{\partial y^2} = \frac{1}{x+r}$$

Ex. 4 : If $V = e^{\frac{r-x}{l}}$ where $r^2 = x^2 + y^2$; l is a constant, show that

$$V_{xx} + V_{yy} + \frac{2}{l}V_x = \frac{V}{lr}.$$

Sol. : Given $\quad V = e^{\frac{r-x}{l}}$

$\therefore \qquad V_x = e^{\frac{r-x}{l}} \cdot \frac{1}{l}\left(\frac{\partial r}{\partial x} - 1\right)$

$$V_x = \frac{V}{l}\left(\frac{x}{r} - 1\right)$$

$$V_{xx} = \frac{V_x}{l}\left(\frac{x}{r} - 1\right) + \frac{V}{l}\left(\frac{1}{r} - \frac{x}{r^2} \cdot \frac{\partial r}{\partial x}\right)$$

$$V_{xx} = \frac{V}{l^2}\left(\frac{x}{r} - 1\right)^2 + \frac{V}{lr} - \frac{V x^2}{lr^3}$$

$$V_y = e^{\frac{r-x}{l}} \cdot \frac{1}{l}\left(\frac{\partial r}{\partial y}\right) = \frac{V}{l}\left(\frac{y}{r}\right) = \frac{Vy}{lr}$$

$$V_{yy} = \frac{V}{lr} + \frac{yV_y}{lr} - \frac{Vy}{lr^2}\frac{\partial r}{\partial y} = \frac{V}{lr} + \frac{y^2 V}{l^2 r^2} - \frac{Vy^2}{lr^3}$$

$$V_{xx} + V_{yy} = \frac{V}{l^2}\left(\frac{x}{r}-1\right)^2 + \frac{V}{lr} - \frac{Vx^2}{lr^3} + \frac{V}{lr} + \frac{y^2V}{l^2r^2} - \frac{V\cdot y^2}{lr^3}$$

$$= \frac{V}{l^2}\left(\frac{x}{r}-1\right)^2 + \frac{2V}{lr} - \frac{V}{lr^3}(x^2+y^2) + \frac{Vy^2}{l^2r^2}$$

$$= \frac{V}{l^2}\left(\frac{x}{r}-1\right)^2 + \frac{V}{lr} + \frac{Vy^2}{l^2r^2}$$

$$\therefore \quad V_{xx} + V_{yy} + \frac{2}{l}V_x = \frac{V}{l^2}\left(\frac{x}{r}-1\right)^2 + \frac{V}{lr} + \frac{Vy^2}{l^2r^2} + \frac{2V}{l^2}\left(\frac{x}{r}-1\right)$$

$$= \frac{V}{l^2}\left(\frac{x^2}{r^2} - \frac{2x}{r} + 1\right) + \frac{V}{lr} + \frac{Vy^2}{l^2r^2} + \frac{2V\cdot x}{l^2r} - \frac{2V}{l^2}$$

$$= \frac{V}{l^2r^2}(x^2+y^2) - \frac{V}{l^2} + \frac{V}{lr} = \frac{V}{lr}$$

EXERCISE 10.3

1. If $u^2(x^2+y^2+z^2) = 1$, prove that $u_{xx} + u_{yy} + u_{zz} = 0$.
   [Hint : Let $x^2+y^2+z^2 = r^2$ $\therefore u^2 = r^{-2}$; $u \to r \to xyz$, use tree diagram.]

2. If $\theta = e^{r-x}$ and $r = \sqrt{x^2+y^2}$, show that $\dfrac{\partial^2\theta}{\partial y^2} = \left(\dfrac{x^2}{r^3} + \dfrac{y^2}{r^2}\right)e^{r-x}$.

3. If $u = \log r$ and $r = \sqrt{(x-a)^2+(y-b)^2}$, prove that $u_{xx} + u_{yy} = 0$ if a, b are constants.

4. If $u = \log\sqrt{x^2+y^2+z^2}$, show that $(x^2+y^2+z^2)(u_{xx}+u_{yy}+u_{zz}) = 1$. **(Dec. 12)**
   [Hint : set $x^2+y^2+z^2 = r^2$ $\therefore u = \log r$; $u \to r \to xyz$.]

5. If $u = r^m$ where $r = \sqrt{x^2+y^2+z^2}$ then find the value of $u_{xx} + u_{yy} + u_{zz}$. **(May 2013)**

6. If $u = \log r$ where $r^2 = (x-a)^2 + (y-b)^2 + (z-c)^2$ prove that $u_{xx} + u_{yy} + u_{zz} = 1/r^2$.

TYPE 4 : EXAMPLES ON VARIABLE TO BE TREATED AS CONSTANT

Let $x = r\cos\theta$, $r = r\sin\theta$. Then $r^2 = x^2 + y^2$.

Notation : $\left(\dfrac{\partial r}{\partial x}\right)_\theta$ means the partial derivative of r with respect to x, treating θ constant in a relation expressing r as a function of x and θ only.

Thus $\left(\dfrac{\partial r}{\partial x}\right)_\theta = \sec\theta$; and $2r\cdot\left(\dfrac{\partial r}{\partial x}\right)_y = 2x$. Hence $\left(\dfrac{\partial r}{\partial x}\right)_y = \dfrac{x}{r} = \cos\theta$.

When no indication is given regarding the variable to be kept constant, then by convention $\frac{\partial}{\partial x}$ always means $\left(\frac{\partial}{\partial x}\right)_y$ and $\left(\frac{\partial}{\partial y}\right)$ means $\left(\frac{\partial}{\partial y}\right)_x$. Similarly $\frac{\partial}{\partial r}$ means $\left(\frac{\partial}{\partial r}\right)_\theta$ and $\frac{\partial}{\partial \theta}$ means $\left(\frac{\partial}{\partial \theta}\right)_r$.

Ex. 1: If $x = r\cos\theta$, $y = r\sin\theta$, show that $\left[x\left(\frac{\partial x}{\partial r}\right)_\theta + y\left(\frac{\partial y}{\partial r}\right)_\theta\right]^2 = x^2 + y^2$,

Sol.: Here $x = r\cos\theta$, hence $\left(\frac{\partial x}{\partial r}\right)_\theta = \cos\theta$ and $y = r\sin\theta$, hence $\left(\frac{\partial y}{\partial r}\right)_\theta = \sin\theta$.

$$\therefore \quad x\left(\frac{\partial x}{\partial r}\right)_\theta + y\left(\frac{\partial y}{\partial r}\right)_\theta = x\cos\theta + y\sin\theta$$

$$= x\left(\frac{x}{r}\right) + y\left(\frac{y}{r}\right) = \frac{x^2 + y^2}{r} = r$$

$$\therefore \quad \left[x\left(\frac{\partial x}{\partial r}\right)_\theta + y\left(\frac{\partial y}{\partial r}\right)_\theta\right]^2 = \left(\frac{x^2+y^2}{r}\right)^2 = \frac{(x^2+y^2)^2}{r^2}$$

$$= r^2 = x^2 + y^2$$

Ex. 2: If $u = ax + by$, $v = bx - ay$, find the value of $\left(\frac{\partial u}{\partial x}\right)_y \cdot \left(\frac{\partial x}{\partial u}\right)_v \cdot \left(\frac{\partial y}{\partial v}\right)_x \cdot \left(\frac{\partial v}{\partial y}\right)_u$.

(Dec. 2009)

Sol.: Given that $u = ax + by$, hence $\left(\frac{\partial u}{\partial x}\right)_y = a$ ... (1)

and $v = bx - ay$ $\therefore y = \frac{b}{a}x - \frac{v}{a}$ $\therefore \left(\frac{\partial y}{\partial v}\right)_x = -\frac{1}{a}$ ... (2)

To find $\left(\frac{\partial x}{\partial u}\right)_v$, express x in terms of u and v, so we eliminate y between the given relations.

$$\frac{u - ax}{b} = \frac{bx - v}{a} \Rightarrow au - a^2x = b^2x - bv \Rightarrow x = \frac{au + bv}{a^2 + b^2}$$

Hence $\left(\frac{\partial x}{\partial u}\right)_v = \frac{a}{a^2 + b^2}$ ... (3)

Similarly to find $\left(\frac{\partial v}{\partial y}\right)_u$ eliminate x between the given relations.

$$\frac{u - by}{a} = \frac{v + ay}{b} \Rightarrow bu - b^2y = av + a^2y$$

$$\Rightarrow \quad v = \frac{bu - (a^2 + b^2)y}{a}$$

Hence $\left(\frac{\partial v}{\partial y}\right)_u = -\left(\frac{a^2 + b^2}{a}\right)$ ... (4)

From equations (1), (2), (3) and (4) on multiplication, we get,

$$\left(\frac{\partial u}{\partial x}\right)_y \cdot \left(\frac{\partial x}{\partial u}\right)_v \cdot \left(\frac{\partial y}{\partial v}\right)_x \cdot \left(\frac{\partial v}{\partial y}\right)_u = a\left(\frac{a}{a^2+b^2}\right) \cdot \left(-\frac{1}{a}\right)\left(-\frac{a^2+b^2}{a}\right) = 1$$

Ex. 3 : If $x = \dfrac{\cos\theta}{u}$; $y = \dfrac{\sin\theta}{u}$, evaluate $\left(\dfrac{\partial x}{\partial u}\right)_\theta \cdot \left(\dfrac{\partial u}{\partial x}\right)_y + \left(\dfrac{\partial y}{\partial u}\right)_\theta \cdot \left(\dfrac{\partial u}{\partial y}\right)_x$

(May 2013, 2015)

Sol. : $x = \dfrac{\cos\theta}{u}$ $\quad \therefore \left(\dfrac{\partial x}{\partial u}\right)_\theta = -\dfrac{\cos\theta}{u^2}$ ... (1)

$y = \dfrac{\sin\theta}{u}$ $\quad \therefore \left(\dfrac{\partial y}{\partial u}\right)_\theta = -\dfrac{\sin\theta}{u^2}$ ... (2)

To find $\left(\dfrac{\partial u}{\partial x}\right)_y$, we eliminate θ from given relations,

i.e. $\quad x^2 + y^2 = \dfrac{1}{u^2}$ $\quad$ or $\quad u^2 = \dfrac{1}{x^2+y^2}$

$\therefore \quad 2u\left(\dfrac{\partial u}{\partial x}\right)_y = -\dfrac{2x}{(x^2+y^2)^2}$ $\quad \therefore \left(\dfrac{\partial u}{\partial x}\right)_y = -\dfrac{x}{u(x^2+y^2)^2}$ ... (3)

and $\quad 2u\left(\dfrac{\partial u}{\partial y}\right)_x = -\dfrac{2y}{(x^2+y^2)^2}$ $\quad \therefore \left(\dfrac{\partial u}{\partial y}\right)_x = -\dfrac{y}{u(x^2+y^2)^2}$ ... (4)

From equations (1), (2), (3) and (4), we get,

Required expression $= \left(-\dfrac{\cos\theta}{u^2}\right)\left(-\dfrac{x}{(x^2+y^2)^2}\right) + \left(-\dfrac{\sin\theta}{u^2}\right)\left(-\dfrac{y}{u(x^2+y^2)^2}\right)$

$= \dfrac{x\cos\theta + y\sin\theta}{u^3(x^2+y^2)^2}$

but $\quad x\cos\theta + y\sin\theta = \dfrac{\cos^2\theta + \sin^2\theta}{u} = \dfrac{1}{u}$

$\therefore$ Required expression $= \dfrac{1}{u^4(x^2+y^2)^2}$

$= \dfrac{1}{u^4} \cdot u^4 = 1 \quad \because u^4 = \dfrac{1}{(x^2+y^2)^2}$

Ex. 4 : If $x = \dfrac{r}{2}(e^\theta + e^{-\theta})$, $y = \dfrac{r}{2}(e^\theta - e^{-\theta})$ then show that $\left(\dfrac{\partial x}{\partial r}\right)_\theta = \left(\dfrac{\partial r}{\partial x}\right)_y$.

(Jan 2004, May 2009)

Sol. : $\cosh\theta = \dfrac{e^\theta + e^{-\theta}}{2}$ and $\sinh\theta = \dfrac{e^\theta - e^{-\theta}}{2}$

$\therefore \quad x = r\cosh\theta, \ y = r\sinh\theta \quad \therefore x^2 - y^2 = r^2$

and $\quad \left(\dfrac{\partial x}{\partial r}\right)_\theta = \cosh\theta$ ... (1)

We have $r^2 = x^2 - y^2$

Differentiating with respect to x keeping y constant, we get,

$$2r \left(\frac{\partial r}{\partial x}\right)_y = 2x \qquad \therefore \left(\frac{\partial r}{\partial x}\right)_y = \frac{x}{r} = \cosh\theta \qquad \ldots (2)$$

From equations (1) and (2),

$$\left(\frac{\partial x}{\partial r}\right)_\theta = \left(\frac{\partial r}{\partial x}\right)_y$$

Ex. 5 : If $u \cdot x + v \cdot y = 0$, $\frac{u}{x} + \frac{v}{y} = 1$, prove that $\frac{u}{x}\left(\frac{\partial x}{\partial u}\right)_v + \frac{v}{y}\left(\frac{\partial y}{\partial v}\right)_u = 0$

Sol. : We have, $\quad y = -\frac{u \cdot x}{v}$

$\therefore \quad \frac{u}{x} + v \cdot \left[-\frac{v}{u \cdot x}\right] = 1$

$\quad \frac{u^2 - v^2}{u \cdot x} = 1 \qquad\qquad \therefore x = \frac{u^2 - v^2}{u}$

$\therefore \quad \left(\frac{\partial x}{\partial u}\right)_v = 1 + \frac{v^2}{u^2}$

We have $\quad x = -\frac{v \cdot y}{u}$

$\therefore \quad u\left(-\frac{u}{v \cdot y}\right) + \frac{v}{y} = 1$

$\therefore \quad y = \frac{v^2 - u^2}{v}$

$\left(\frac{\partial y}{\partial v}\right)_u = 1 + \frac{u^2}{v^2}$

$\frac{u}{x} \cdot \left(\frac{\partial x}{\partial u}\right)_v + \frac{v}{y}\left(\frac{\partial y}{\partial v}\right)_u = \frac{u}{x} + \frac{v^2}{xu} + \frac{v}{y} + \frac{u^2}{yv}$

$= \frac{u^2 + v^2}{xu} + \frac{v^2 + u^2}{yv}$

$= (u^2 + v^2)\left(\frac{yv + xu}{xu \cdot yv}\right)$

$= 0 \qquad \because xu + yv = 0$

Ex. 6 : If $x + y + z + u + v = a$, $x^2 + y^2 + z^2 + u^2 + v^2 = b^2$ where a, b are constant, prove that

$$\left(\frac{\partial u}{\partial x}\right)_{y,z}\left(\frac{\partial x}{\partial u}\right)_{v,z} = \left(\frac{\partial v}{\partial y}\right)_{x,z}\left(\frac{\partial y}{\partial v}\right)_{u,z}$$

Sol. : $\quad x + y + z + u + v = a \qquad \ldots (1)$

$\quad x^2 + y^2 + z^2 + u^2 + v^2 = b^2 \qquad \ldots (2)$

Regarding u and v as a function of x, y, z and differentiating equations (1) and (2) partially w.r.t. x keeping y, z constant, we get,

$$1 + u_x + v_x = 0$$
$$2x + 2u \cdot u_x + 2v \cdot v_x = 0$$

Eliminating v_x we have,

$$v - x + (v - u) u_x = 0 \qquad \therefore u_x = \frac{x - v}{v - u}$$

Also differentiating equations (1) and (2) w.r.t. y keeping z and x constant,

$$1 + u_y + v_y = 0$$
$$2y + 2u \cdot u_y + 2v \cdot v_y = 0$$

Eliminating u_y, we have

$$u - y + (u - v) v_y = 0 \qquad \therefore v_y = \frac{y - u}{u - v}$$

Regarding x and y as a function of u, v, z and differentiating equations (1) and (2) partially w.r.t. u keeping v, z constant, we have,

$$x_u + y_u + 1 = 0$$
$$2x \cdot x_u + 2y \cdot y_u + 2u = 0$$

Eliminating y_u, we have

$$(y - x) \cdot x_u + y - u = 0 \qquad \therefore x_u = \frac{u - y}{y - x}$$

Also differentiating equations (1) and (2) w.r.t. v keeping u, z as constant, we have

$$x_v + y_v + 1 = 0$$
$$2x \cdot x_v + 2y \cdot y_v + 2v = 0$$

Eliminating x_v, we have

$$(x - y) y_v + x - v = 0 \qquad \therefore y_v = \frac{v - x}{x - y}$$

$\therefore$
$$\left(\frac{\partial u}{\partial x}\right)_{y, z} \left(\frac{\partial x}{\partial u}\right)_{v, z} = \frac{x - v}{v - u} \cdot \frac{u - y}{y - x} \qquad \ldots (3)$$

$$\left(\frac{\partial v}{\partial y}\right)_{x, z} \left(\frac{\partial y}{\partial v}\right)_{u, z} = \frac{y - u}{u - v} \cdot \frac{v - x}{x - y}$$

$$= \frac{x - v}{v - u} \cdot \frac{u - y}{y - x} \qquad \ldots (4)$$

From (3) and (4), the required result follows.

EXERCISE 10.4

1. If $x = r \cos \theta$, $y = r \sin \theta$, show that

   (a) $\dfrac{\partial^2 r}{\partial x^2} + \dfrac{\partial^2 r}{\partial y^2} = \dfrac{1}{r}$ (b) $\left(\dfrac{\partial r}{\partial x}\right)^2 + \left(\dfrac{\partial r}{\partial y}\right)^2 = 1$ **(May 2010)**

   (c) $r_{xx} r_{yy} = (r_{xy})^2$ (d) $\left(\dfrac{\partial y}{\partial r}\right)_x \cdot \left(\dfrac{\partial y}{\partial r}\right)_\theta = 1$ **(May 2014)**

2. If $x^2 = a\sqrt{u} + b\sqrt{v}$ and $y^2 = a\sqrt{u} - b\sqrt{v}$ where a, b are constant, prove that

   $\left(\dfrac{\partial u}{\partial x}\right)_y \left(\dfrac{\partial x}{\partial u}\right)_v = \dfrac{1}{2} = \left(\dfrac{\partial v}{\partial y}\right)_x \left(\dfrac{\partial y}{\partial v}\right)_u$

3. If $x = e^{r \cos \theta} \cos(r \sin \theta)$, $y = e^{r \cos \theta} \sin(r \sin \theta)$, prove that

   (a) $\dfrac{\partial x}{\partial r} = \dfrac{1}{r} \dfrac{\partial y}{\partial \theta} = e^{r \cos \theta} \cos(\theta + r \sin \theta)$,   (b) $\dfrac{\partial y}{\partial r} = \dfrac{-1}{r} \dfrac{\partial x}{\partial \theta} = e^{r \cos \theta} \sin(\theta + r \sin \theta)$

4. If $u = ax + by$, $v = bx - ay$ prove that

   (a) $\left(\dfrac{\partial y}{\partial v}\right)_x \left(\dfrac{\partial v}{\partial y}\right)_u = \dfrac{a^2 + b^2}{a^2}$ (b) $\left(\dfrac{\partial u}{\partial x}\right)_y \left(\dfrac{\partial x}{\partial u}\right)_v = \dfrac{a^2}{a^2 + b^2}$.

5. If $ux + vy = 0$ and $\dfrac{u}{x} + \dfrac{v}{y} = 1$ then show that $\left(\dfrac{\partial u}{\partial x}\right)_y - \left(\dfrac{\partial v}{\partial y}\right)_x = \dfrac{x^2 + y^2}{y^2 - x^2}$ where suffixes denote constant.   **(May 2004; Dec. 2010, 2012, 2014)**

6. If $x = r \cos \theta$, $y = r \sin \theta$, prove that

   (a) $\left(\dfrac{\partial r}{\partial x}\right)_y = \left(\dfrac{\partial x}{\partial r}\right)_\theta$,   (b) $\dfrac{1}{r}\left(\dfrac{\partial x}{\partial \theta}\right)_r = r\left(\dfrac{\partial \theta}{\partial x}\right)_y$,   (c) $\dfrac{\partial^2 \theta}{\partial x^2} + \dfrac{\partial^2 \theta}{\partial y^2} = 0$.

7. If $x^2 = au + bv$, $y = au - bv$, prove that $\left(\dfrac{\partial u}{\partial x}\right)_y \left(\dfrac{\partial x}{\partial u}\right)_v = \left(\dfrac{\partial v}{\partial y}\right)_x \left(\dfrac{\partial y}{\partial v}\right)_x$.   **(May 2011)**

8. If $x = u \tan v$, $y = u \sec v$, prove that $\left(\dfrac{\partial u}{\partial x}\right)_y \left(\dfrac{\partial v}{\partial x}\right)_y = \left(\dfrac{\partial u}{\partial y}\right)_x \left(\dfrac{\partial v}{\partial y}\right)_x$.

   (Dec. 2008, May 2014)

10.9 HOMOGENEOUS FUNCTIONS

Definition : A rational integral, algebraic function of x and y is said to be *homogeneous function* of nth degree in x and y if the sum of the indices of x and y in each term is the same, and the sum being equal to n.

Thus $x^3 y - 4xy^3 + 2x^2 y^2 + y^4 - x^4$ is a homogeneous function of degree four.

An expression of the type

$z = f(x, y) = a_0 x^n + a_1 x^{n-1} y + a_2 x^{n-2} y^2 + a_3 x^{n-3} y^3 + \ldots + a_n y^n$ is a homogeneous function of nth degree in x and y. We can express it as

$$z = f(x, y) = x^n \left[a_0 + a_1 \left(\frac{y}{x}\right) + a_2 \left(\frac{y}{x}\right)^2 + a_3 \left(\frac{y}{x}\right)^3 + \ldots + a_n \left(\frac{y}{x}\right)^n \right]$$

$$z = x^n \left[a_0 \left(\frac{y}{x}\right)^0 + a_1 \left(\frac{y}{x}\right) + a_2 \left(\frac{y}{x}\right)^2 + a_3 \left(\frac{y}{x}\right)^3 + \ldots + a_n \left(\frac{y}{x}\right)^n \right]$$

$$z = x^n f(y/x)$$

We may express in the another form as

$$z = y^n \left[a_0 \left(\frac{x}{y}\right)^n + a_1 \left(\frac{x}{y}\right)^{n-1} + \ldots + a_n \left(\frac{x}{y}\right)^0 \right]$$

$$z = y^n \phi \left(\frac{x}{y}\right)$$

10.10 HOMOGENEOUS FUNCTIONS OF TWO VARIABLES

Definition : A function z of two variables x and y is said to be *homogeneous of degree n* if it is possible to express z in the form

$$z = x^n f\left(\frac{y}{x}\right), \quad z = y^n f\left(\frac{x}{y}\right)$$

e.g. (1) $\dfrac{x^2 + y^2}{\sqrt{x} + \sqrt{y}}$ is a homogeneous function of degree $\dfrac{3}{2}$ because it can be written as,

$$x^{3/2} \left[\frac{1 + \left(\frac{y}{x}\right)^2}{1 + \sqrt{\frac{y}{x}}} \right] = x^{3/2} f\left(\frac{y}{x}\right)$$

(2) The expression $4x^6 - 9x^4 y^2 + 12xy^5 + y^6$ can also be put as

$$x^6 \left[4 - 9 \left(\frac{y}{x}\right)^2 + 12 \left(\frac{y}{x}\right)^5 + \left(\frac{y}{x}\right)^6 \right]$$

or $x^6 f\left(\dfrac{y}{x}\right)$, where degree n = 6.

(3) The function $\sin^{-1}\left(\dfrac{y}{x}\right)$ is an homogeneous function of degree zero because we can write it as $x^0 \cdot \sin^{-1}\left(\dfrac{y}{x}\right)$.

(4) But $\sin\left(\dfrac{x^2 + y^2}{x + y}\right)$ is not a homogeneous function. It may at best be called a function of an homogeneous expression. Because it cannot be put in the form $x^n f\left(\dfrac{y}{x}\right)$, so that its degree may be pronounced.

(5) Similarly, $\operatorname{cosec}^{-1}\sqrt{\dfrac{x^{1/2}+y^{1/2}}{x^{1/3}+y^{1/3}}}$ is not a homogeneous function but is a function of homogeneous expression. Distinction must always be made between a homogeneous function and a function of a homogeneous expression.

(6) $$z = \dfrac{x^2 y^2}{x+y} = \dfrac{x^4(y^2/x^2)}{x(1+y/x)}$$
$$= x^3 f(y/x)$$

$\Rightarrow$ z is a homogeneous function of x and y of degree n = 3.

We shall state and prove a very important theorem on homogeneous function called *Euler's theorem on Homogeneous Functions*.

10.11 EULER'S THEOREM : STATEMENT

Euler's theorem on homogeneous functions of two variables states that if z is a homogeneous function of two variables x, y of degree n,

then $\quad x\dfrac{\partial z}{\partial x} + y\dfrac{\partial z}{\partial y} = nz$

Proof : By definition of a homogeneous function of two variables, we can write

$$z = x^n \cdot f\left(\dfrac{y}{x}\right)$$

$\therefore \quad \dfrac{\partial z}{\partial x} = x^n f'\left(\dfrac{y}{x}\right)\left(-\dfrac{y}{x^2}\right) + nx^{n-1} f\left(\dfrac{y}{x}\right)$

or $\quad \dfrac{\partial z}{\partial x} = -yx^{n-2} f'\left(\dfrac{y}{x}\right) + nx^{n-1} f\left(\dfrac{y}{x}\right)$

and $\quad \dfrac{\partial z}{\partial y} = x^n f'\left(\dfrac{y}{x}\right) \cdot \dfrac{1}{x} = x^{n-1} f'\left(\dfrac{y}{x}\right)$

$\therefore \quad x\dfrac{\partial z}{\partial x} + y\dfrac{\partial z}{\partial y} = -yx^{n-1} f'\left(\dfrac{y}{x}\right) + nx^n f\left(\dfrac{y}{x}\right) + yx^{n-1} f'\left(\dfrac{y}{x}\right)$

$\therefore \quad x\dfrac{\partial z}{\partial x} + y\dfrac{\partial z}{\partial y} = nx^n f\left(\dfrac{y}{x}\right) = nz$

DEDUCTIONS FROM EULER'S THEOREM

(1) If z is a homogeneous function of two variables x, y of degree n, then

$$x^2 \dfrac{\partial^2 z}{\partial x^2} + 2xy \dfrac{\partial^2 z}{\partial x\, \partial y} + y^2 \dfrac{\partial^2 z}{\partial y^2} = n(n-1) z$$

Proof : Since z is a homogeneous function of x, y of degree n, we have, by Euler's theorem,

$$x\dfrac{\partial z}{\partial x} + y\dfrac{\partial z}{\partial y} = nz \qquad \ldots (1)$$

Differentiating equation (1) partially with respect to x,

$$\left(x\frac{\partial^2 z}{\partial x^2} + \frac{\partial z}{\partial x} \cdot 1\right) + y\frac{\partial^2 z}{\partial x \partial y} = n\frac{\partial z}{\partial x} \Rightarrow x\frac{\partial^2 z}{\partial x^2} + y\frac{\partial^2 z}{\partial x \partial y} = (n-1)\frac{\partial z}{\partial x} \qquad \ldots (2)$$

Similarly, on differentiating equation (1) partially with respect to y, we shall get

$$y\frac{\partial^2 z}{\partial y^2} + y\frac{\partial^2 z}{\partial y \partial x} = (n-1)\frac{\partial z}{\partial y} \Rightarrow y\frac{\partial^2 z}{\partial y^2} + y\frac{\partial^2 z}{\partial x \partial y} = (n-1)\frac{\partial z}{\partial y} \qquad \ldots (3)$$

$$\left(\because \frac{\partial^2 z}{\partial x \partial y} = \frac{\partial^2 z}{\partial y \partial x}\right)$$

Multiplying equation (2) by x, equation (3) by y, and adding, we have

$$\left(x^2\frac{\partial^2 z}{\partial x^2} + xy\frac{\partial^2 z}{\partial x \partial y}\right) + \left(y^2\frac{\partial^2 z}{\partial y^2} + xy\frac{\partial^2 z}{\partial x \partial y}\right) = (n-1)\left[x\frac{\partial z}{\partial x} + y\frac{\partial z}{\partial y}\right]$$

$$\Rightarrow x^2\frac{\partial^2 z}{\partial x^2} + 2xy\frac{\partial^2 z}{\partial x \partial y} + y^2\frac{\partial^2 z}{\partial y^2} = (n-1)\,nz = n(n-1)\,z \qquad \text{[by (1)]}$$

(2) Statement : If z is a homogeneous function of x, y of degree n and z = f(u)

then $\qquad x\dfrac{\partial u}{\partial x} + y\dfrac{\partial u}{\partial y} = n\dfrac{f(u)}{f'(u)}$

and $x^2\dfrac{\partial^2 u}{\partial x^2} + 2xy\dfrac{\partial^2 u}{\partial x \partial y} + y^2\dfrac{\partial^2 u}{\partial y^2} = g(u)\,[g'(u) - 1]$ where $g(u) = n\dfrac{f(u)}{f'(u)}$

Proof : Since z is a homogeneous function of x, y of degree n, we have, by Euler's theorem,

$$x\frac{\partial z}{\partial x} + y\frac{\partial z}{\partial y} = nz \qquad \ldots (1)$$

Now $\qquad z = f(u)$ given,

$\therefore \qquad \dfrac{\partial z}{\partial x} = f'(u)\dfrac{\partial u}{\partial x}\,,\quad \dfrac{\partial z}{\partial y} = f'(u)\dfrac{\partial u}{\partial y}$

Substituting in equation (1),

$$x \cdot f'(u)\frac{\partial u}{\partial x} + y \cdot f'(u)\frac{\partial u}{\partial y} = n\,f(u)$$

$$x\frac{\partial u}{\partial x} + y\frac{\partial u}{\partial y} = n\frac{f(u)}{f'(u)}$$

To prove the next part, we have $x\dfrac{\partial u}{\partial x} + y\dfrac{\partial u}{\partial y} = g(u)$. ...(2)

Differentiating equation (2) partially w.r.t. x,

$$\left(x\dfrac{\partial^2 u}{\partial x^2} + \dfrac{\partial u}{\partial x}\cdot 1\right) + y\dfrac{\partial^2 u}{\partial x\,\partial y} = g'(u)\dfrac{\partial u}{\partial x}$$

$$\Rightarrow \quad x\dfrac{\partial^2 u}{\partial x^2} + y\dfrac{\partial^2 u}{\partial x\,\partial y} = [g'(u)-1]\dfrac{\partial u}{\partial x} \quad \ldots(3)$$

Similarly, on differentiating equation (2) partially w.r.t. y,

$$\Rightarrow \quad y\dfrac{\partial^2 u}{\partial y^2} + x\dfrac{\partial^2 u}{\partial x\,\partial y} = [g'(u)-1]\dfrac{\partial u}{\partial y} \quad \ldots(4)$$

Multiplying equation (3) by x and equation (4) by y and adding, we get,

$$x^2\dfrac{\partial^2 u}{\partial x^2} + 2xy\dfrac{\partial^2 u}{\partial x\,\partial y} + y^2\dfrac{\partial^2 u}{\partial y^2} = [g'(u)-1]\left(x\dfrac{\partial u}{\partial x} + y\dfrac{\partial u}{\partial y}\right)$$

$$= g(u)\,[g'(u)-1] \qquad \ldots \text{by (1)}$$

10.12 HOMOGENEOUS FUNCTION OF THREE VARIABLES

A function $u = f(x, y, z)$ is said to be a homogeneous function of x, y, z of degree n if it is possible to express u as $u = x^n f(y/x, z/x)$.

EULER'S THEOREM ON HOMOGENEOUS FUNCTIONS

Statement : Euler's theorem on homogeneous functions of three variables states that if u is a homogeneous function of x, y, z of degree n,

then $\quad x\dfrac{\partial u}{\partial x} + y\dfrac{\partial u}{\partial y} + z\dfrac{\partial u}{\partial z} = nu$

DEDUCTION FROM EULER'S THEOREM

If u is a homogeneous function of x, y, z of degree n and if $u = f(v)$,

then $\quad x\dfrac{\partial v}{\partial x} + y\dfrac{\partial v}{\partial y} + z\dfrac{\partial v}{\partial z} = n\dfrac{f(v)}{f'(v)}$

For the proof of Euler's theorem on homogeneous functions of three variables, we require the knowledge of composite function. Hence, the proof is given in ch. 10.

ILLUSTRATIONS ON EULER'S THEOREM

Ex. 1 : *If* $u = \sin^{-1}\left(\dfrac{\sqrt{x}-\sqrt{y}}{\sqrt{x}+\sqrt{y}}\right)$, *show that* $\dfrac{\partial u}{\partial x} = -\dfrac{y}{x}\cdot\dfrac{\partial u}{\partial y}$.

Sol. : $u = x^0 \cdot \sin^{-1}\left(\dfrac{\sqrt{x}-\sqrt{y}}{\sqrt{x}+\sqrt{y}}\right) = x^0 \sin^{-1}\left[\dfrac{1-\sqrt{y/x}}{1+\sqrt{y/x}}\right]$

$$= x^0 f\left(\dfrac{y}{x}\right)$$

Hence u is a homogeneous function of degree 0, hence by Euler's theorem,

$$x\frac{\partial u}{\partial x} + y\frac{\partial u}{\partial y} = 0\,(u) = 0$$

$$\Rightarrow \quad x\frac{\partial u}{\partial x} = -y\frac{\partial u}{\partial y}$$

$$\Rightarrow \quad \frac{\partial u}{\partial x} = -\frac{y}{x}\frac{\partial u}{\partial y} \qquad \text{Proved.}$$

Ex. 2 : If $x = e^u \tan v$, $y = e^u \sec v$, find the value of $\left(x\frac{\partial u}{\partial x} + y\frac{\partial u}{\partial y}\right) \cdot \left(x\frac{\partial v}{\partial x} + y\frac{\partial v}{\partial y}\right)$.

(Jan. 2005, May 2009)

Sol. : Eliminating v between the given relations, we have

$$y^2 - x^2 = e^{2u} = z, \quad \text{say}$$

Here $z = x^2\left[\left(\frac{y}{x}\right)^2 - 1\right] = x^2 f\left(\frac{y}{x}\right)$, so that z is a homogeneous function of x, y of degree n = 2. Also $z = f(u) = e^{2u}$.

$\therefore$ By deduction (2), $x\frac{\partial u}{\partial x} + y\frac{\partial u}{\partial y} = n\frac{f(u)}{f'(u)} = 2\frac{e^{2u}}{2e^{2u}} = 1$ ... (1)

Again eliminating u between the given relations,

$$\frac{y}{x} = \frac{\sec v}{\tan v} = \text{cosec } v = z, \quad \text{say.} \quad \text{Here } z = x^0\left(\frac{y}{x}\right) = x^0 f\left(\frac{y}{x}\right)$$

So that z is a homogeneous function of x, y of degree n = 0.

$\therefore$ By deduction (2), $x\frac{\partial v}{\partial x} + y\frac{\partial v}{\partial y} = n \cdot \frac{g(v)}{g'(v)} = 0$ ... (2)

On multiplication of (1) and (2) we see that the value of the given expression is zero.

Ex. 3 : If $u = \log V$ where V is a homogeneous function of degree n in x and y, show that $x\frac{\partial u}{\partial x} + y\frac{\partial u}{\partial y} = n$.

Sol. : We have $u = \log V$

$\therefore \quad \frac{\partial u}{\partial x} = \frac{1}{V}\frac{\partial V}{\partial x}, \quad \frac{\partial u}{\partial y} = \frac{1}{V}\frac{\partial V}{\partial y}$

$\therefore \quad x\frac{\partial u}{\partial x} + y\frac{\partial u}{\partial y} = \frac{1}{V}\left[x\frac{\partial V}{\partial x} + y\frac{\partial V}{\partial y}\right]$ ... (1)

Now V is given to be homogeneous of degree n in x, y.

$\therefore$ By Euler's theorem,

$$x\frac{\partial V}{\partial x} + y\frac{\partial V}{\partial y} = nV$$

Substituting in equation (1), we have

$$x\frac{\partial u}{\partial x} + y\frac{\partial u}{\partial y} = \frac{1}{V}(nV) = n$$

Ex. 4 : If $f(x, y)$ and $\phi(x, y)$ are homogeneous functions of x, y of degree p, q respectively and $u = f(x, y) + \phi(x, y)$, show that

$$f(x, y) = \frac{1}{p(p-q)}\left[x^2\frac{\partial^2 u}{\partial x^2} + 2xy\frac{\partial^2 u}{\partial x\,\partial y} + y^2\frac{\partial^2 u}{\partial y^2}\right] - \frac{q-1}{p(p-q)}\left[x\frac{\partial u}{\partial x} + y\frac{\partial u}{\partial y}\right].$$

Sol. : Let $\qquad f(x, y) \equiv f \qquad$ and $\qquad \phi(x, y) \equiv \phi \qquad \qquad \ldots (1)$

Then $\qquad\qquad u = f + \phi$

Since f and ϕ are homogeneous functions of degree p and q respectively, we have

$$x\frac{\partial f}{\partial x} + y\frac{\partial f}{\partial y} = p \cdot f$$

$$x\frac{\partial \phi}{\partial x} + y\frac{\partial \phi}{\partial y} = q \cdot \phi$$

On adding,

$$x\left(\frac{\partial f}{\partial x} + \frac{\partial \phi}{\partial x}\right) + y\left(\frac{\partial f}{\partial y} + \frac{\partial \phi}{\partial y}\right) = pf + q\phi$$

i.e. $\qquad\qquad x\dfrac{\partial u}{\partial x} + y\dfrac{\partial u}{\partial y} = pf + q\phi$, by (1)

Also $\qquad x^2\dfrac{\partial^2 f}{\partial x^2} + 2xy\dfrac{\partial^2 f}{\partial x\,\partial y} + y^2\dfrac{\partial^2 f}{\partial y^2} = p(p-1)\, f$

and $\qquad x^2\dfrac{\partial^2 \phi}{\partial x^2} + 2xy\dfrac{\partial^2 \phi}{\partial x\,\partial y} + y^2\dfrac{\partial^2 \phi}{\partial y^2} = q(q-1)\, \phi$

On adding and using equation (1), we have

$$x^2\frac{\partial^2 u}{\partial x^2} + 2xy\frac{\partial^2 u}{\partial x\,\partial y} + y^2\frac{\partial^2 u}{\partial y^2} = p(p-1)\,f + q(q-1)\,\phi$$

Hence

$$\frac{1}{p(p-q)}\left[x^2\frac{\partial^2 u}{\partial x^2} + 2xy\frac{\partial^2 u}{\partial x\,\partial y} + y^2\frac{\partial^2 u}{\partial y^2}\right] - \frac{q-1}{p(p-q)}\left[x\frac{\partial u}{\partial x} + y\frac{\partial u}{\partial y}\right]$$

$$= \frac{1}{p(p-q)}[p(p-1)\,f + q(q-1)\,\phi] - \frac{q-1}{p(p-q)}[pf + q\phi]$$

$$= \frac{1}{p(p-q)}[p(p-1)\,f + q(q-1)\,\phi - (q-1)(pf + q\phi)]$$

$$= \frac{1}{p(p-q)}[\{p(p-1) - p(q-1)\}f + \{q(q-1) - q(q-1)\}\phi]$$

$$= \frac{1}{p(p-q)} \cdot p(p-q)\,f = f(x, y)$$

Ex. 5 : If $u = \operatorname{cosec}^{-1}\sqrt{\dfrac{x^{1/2} + y^{1/2}}{x^{1/3} + y^{1/3}}}$, show that $\hfill$ (Jan. 2005)

$$x^2\frac{\partial^2 u}{\partial x^2} + 2xy\frac{\partial^2 u}{\partial x\,\partial y} + y^2\frac{\partial^2 u}{\partial y^2} = \frac{\tan u}{12}\left(\frac{13}{12} + \frac{\tan^2 u}{12}\right).$$

Sol. : Here $\qquad \text{cosec } u = \sqrt{\dfrac{x^{1/2} + y^{1/2}}{x^{1/3} + y^{1/3}}} = \sqrt{\dfrac{x^{1/2}[1 + (y/x)^{(1/2)}]}{x^{1/3}[1 + (y/x)^{(1/3)}]}}$

$$= x^{1/12} \left[\dfrac{1 + (y/x)^{1/2}}{1 + (y/x)^{1/3}}\right]^{1/2} = x^{1/12} \, \phi\left(\dfrac{y}{x}\right)$$

$$= \text{a homogeneous function of } x, y \text{ of degree } \dfrac{1}{12}$$

Also $f(u) = \text{cosec } u$

∴ By formula, $\quad x\dfrac{\partial u}{\partial x} + y\dfrac{\partial u}{\partial y} = n\dfrac{f(u)}{f'(u)} = \dfrac{1}{12} \dfrac{\text{cosec } u}{-\text{cosec } u \cdot \cot u} = -\dfrac{1}{12} \tan u \quad \ldots (1)$

Differentiating partially with respect to x and y respectively, we get

$$x\dfrac{\partial^2 u}{\partial x^2} + \dfrac{\partial u}{\partial x} + y\dfrac{\partial^2 u}{\partial x \partial y} = -\dfrac{1}{12} \sec^2 u \cdot \dfrac{\partial u}{\partial x} \qquad \ldots (2)$$

and $\quad x\dfrac{\partial^2 u}{\partial x \partial y} + y\dfrac{\partial^2 u}{\partial y^2} + \dfrac{\partial u}{\partial y} = -\dfrac{1}{12} \sec^2 u \cdot \dfrac{\partial u}{\partial y} \qquad \ldots (3)$

Multiplying equation (2) by x and equation (3) by y and adding,

$$x^2\dfrac{\partial^2 u}{\partial x^2} + 2xy\dfrac{\partial^2 u}{\partial x \partial y} + y^2\dfrac{\partial^2 u}{\partial y^2} + \left(x\dfrac{\partial u}{\partial x} + y\dfrac{\partial u}{\partial y}\right) = -\dfrac{\sec^2 u}{12} \left(x\dfrac{\partial u}{\partial x} + y\dfrac{\partial u}{\partial y}\right)$$

$$\Rightarrow \quad x^2\dfrac{\partial^2 u}{\partial x^2} + 2xy\dfrac{\partial^2 u}{\partial x \partial y} + y^2\dfrac{\partial^2 u}{\partial y^2} = \left(x\dfrac{\partial u}{\partial x} + y\dfrac{\partial u}{\partial y}\right) \times \left(-\dfrac{\sec^2 u}{12} - 1\right)$$

$$= -\dfrac{1}{12} \tan u \left[-\left(\dfrac{1 + \tan^2 u}{12}\right) - 1\right]$$

$$= \dfrac{\tan u}{12} \left(\dfrac{\tan^2 u}{12} + \dfrac{13}{12}\right)$$

Ex. 6 : If $u = \tan^{-1}\left(\dfrac{x^3 + y^3}{x - y}\right)$, prove that

$$x^2 \dfrac{\partial^2 u}{\partial x^2} + 2xy \dfrac{\partial^2 u}{\partial x \partial y} + y^2 \dfrac{\partial^2 u}{\partial y^2} = (1 - 4\sin^2 u) \sin 2u. \quad \textbf{(Jan. 2004, Dec. 2009)}$$

Sol. : Given : $\qquad \tan u = \dfrac{x^3 + y^3}{x - y} = x^2\left[\dfrac{1 + y^3/x^3}{1 - y/x}\right] = x^2 \phi\left(\dfrac{y}{x}\right)$

$$= \text{a homogeneous function of } x, y \text{ of degree 2.}$$

Also, $\qquad f(u) = \tan u$

By Euler's theorem,

$$x\dfrac{\partial u}{\partial x} + y\dfrac{\partial u}{\partial y} = n\dfrac{f(u)}{f'(u)} = 2\dfrac{\tan u}{\sec^2 u} = 2 \sin u \cos u = \sin 2u$$

$$= G(u), \text{ say}$$

$$\therefore \quad x^2 \frac{\partial^2 u}{\partial x^2} + 2xy \frac{\partial^2 u}{\partial x \partial y} + y^2 \frac{\partial^2 u}{\partial y^2} = G(u) [G'(u) - 1]$$

$$= \sin 2u [2 \cos 2u - 1]$$

$$= \sin 2u [2 (1 - 2 \sin^2 u) - 1]$$

$$= \sin 2u [1 - 4 \sin^2 u]$$

Ex. 7 : If $u = \sin^{-1} \left(\dfrac{x+y}{\sqrt{x}+\sqrt{y}} \right)$, prove that

$$x^2 \frac{\partial^2 u}{\partial x^2} + 2xy \frac{\partial^2 u}{\partial x \partial y} + y^2 \frac{\partial^2 u}{\partial y^2} = \frac{1}{4} (\tan^3 u - \tan u). \qquad \text{(May 04, 2011, 2015)}$$

Sol. : Given : $\sin u = \dfrac{x+y}{\sqrt{x}+\sqrt{y}} = x^{1/2} \left[\dfrac{1+y/x}{1+\sqrt{y/x}} \right] = x^{1/2} \phi (y/x)$.

$\qquad\qquad\qquad\quad$ = a homogeneous function of x, y of degree $\dfrac{1}{2}$

Also $\qquad\qquad f(u) = \sin u$

By Euler's theorem

$$x \frac{\partial u}{\partial x} + y \frac{\partial u}{\partial y} = n \frac{f(u)}{f'(u)} = \frac{1}{2} \frac{\sin u}{\cos u} = \frac{1}{2} \tan u = G(u), \text{ say}$$

$$\therefore \quad x^2 \frac{\partial^2 u}{\partial x^2} + 2xy \frac{\partial^2 u}{\partial x \partial y} + y^2 \frac{\partial^2 u}{\partial y^2} = G(u) [G'(u) - 1]$$

$$= \frac{1}{2} \tan u \left[\frac{1}{2} \sec^2 u - 1 \right]$$

$$= \frac{1}{2} \tan u \left[\frac{1}{2} + \frac{1}{2} \tan^2 u - 1 \right]$$

$$= \frac{1}{4} [\tan^3 u - \tan u]$$

Ex. 8 : If $u = \left(\dfrac{x^3 + y^3}{y\sqrt{x}} \right) + \dfrac{1}{x^7} \sin^{-1} \left[\dfrac{x^2 + y^2}{x^2 + 2xy} \right]$, find the value of $\qquad$ **(May 2014)**

$$x^2 \frac{\partial^2 u}{\partial x^2} + 2xy \frac{\partial^2 u}{\partial x \partial y} + y^2 \frac{\partial^2 u}{\partial y^2} + x \frac{\partial u}{\partial x} + y \frac{\partial u}{\partial y} \text{ at the point } (1, 2)$$

Sol. : We have $\quad u = \dfrac{x^3+y^3}{y\sqrt{x}} + \dfrac{1}{x^7} \sin^{-1} \left[\dfrac{x^2+y^2}{x^2+2xy} \right]$

Let $\qquad\qquad u = v + w \qquad\qquad\qquad\qquad\qquad\qquad\qquad\qquad\qquad\qquad\qquad\quad$ … (1)

where $\qquad v = x^{3/2} \left[\dfrac{1+(x/y)^{3/2}}{y/x} \right]$ is a homogeneous function of degree 3/2

$\qquad\qquad w = x^{-7} \sin^{-1} \left[\dfrac{1+(y/x)^2}{1+2(y/x)} \right]$ is a homogeneous function of degree -7.

∴ By Euler's theorem,

$$x\frac{\partial v}{\partial x} + y\frac{\partial v}{\partial y} = \frac{3}{2} v \qquad \ldots (2)$$

and $$x^2\frac{\partial^2 v}{\partial x^2} + 2xy\frac{\partial^2 v}{\partial x \partial y} + y^2\frac{\partial^2 v}{\partial y^2} = \frac{3}{2}\left(\frac{1}{2}\right)v = \frac{3}{4}v \qquad \ldots (3)$$

Also $$x\frac{\partial w}{\partial x} + y\frac{\partial w}{\partial y} = -7w \qquad \ldots (4)$$

and $$x^2\frac{\partial^2 w}{\partial x^2} + 2xy\frac{\partial^2 w}{\partial x \partial y} + y^2\frac{\partial^2 w}{\partial y^2} = -7(-8)w = 56w \qquad \ldots (5)$$

By adding equations (2) and (4) and using equation (1),

$$x\frac{\partial u}{\partial x} + y\frac{\partial u}{\partial y} = \frac{3}{2}v - 7w \qquad \ldots (6)$$

By adding equations (3) and (5) and using equation (1),

$$x^2\frac{\partial^2 u}{\partial x^2} + 2xy\frac{\partial^2 u}{\partial x \partial y} + y^2\frac{\partial^2 u}{\partial y^2} = \frac{3}{4}v + 56w \qquad \ldots (7)$$

Adding equations (6) and (7), we get

$$x^2\frac{\partial^2 u}{\partial x^2} + 2xy\frac{\partial^2 u}{\partial x \partial y} + y^2\frac{\partial^2 u}{\partial y^2} + x\frac{\partial u}{\partial x} + y\frac{\partial u}{\partial y} = \frac{3}{2}v + \frac{3}{4}v + 56w - 7w = \frac{9}{4}v + 49w$$

$$\ldots (8)$$

Now at the point $(1, 2)$, $v = \frac{9}{2}$, $w = \sin^{-1}\left[\frac{5}{1+4}\right] = \frac{\pi}{2}$.

∴ $$\frac{9}{4}v + 49w = \frac{9}{4}\left(\frac{9}{2}\right) + 49\frac{\pi}{2}$$

$$= \frac{81}{8} + 49\frac{\pi}{2}$$

From equation (8), we have

$$x^2\frac{\partial^2 u}{\partial x^2} + 2xy\frac{\partial^2 u}{\partial x \partial y} + y^2\frac{\partial^2 u}{\partial y^2} + x\frac{\partial u}{\partial x} + y\frac{\partial u}{\partial y} = \frac{81}{8} + 49\frac{\pi}{2}$$

Ex. 9 : If $z = x^n f(y/x) + y^{-n} \phi(x/y)$ then prove that **(May 2014)**

$$x^2\frac{\partial^2 z}{\partial x^2} + 2xy\frac{\partial^2 z}{\partial x \partial y} + y^2\frac{\partial^2 z}{\partial y^2} + x\frac{\partial z}{\partial x} + y\frac{\partial z}{\partial y} = n^2 z$$

Sol. : We have $$z = x^n f\left(\frac{y}{x}\right) + y^{-n}\phi\left(\frac{x}{y}\right)$$

$$z = u + v \qquad \ldots (1)$$

where $$u = x^n f(y/x) \text{ and } v = y^{-n}\phi\left(\frac{x}{y}\right)$$

$u = x^n f\left(\dfrac{y}{x}\right) \Rightarrow$ u is a homogeneous function of x and y of degree n, by Euler's theorem,

$$x \dfrac{\partial u}{\partial x} + y \dfrac{\partial u}{\partial y} = nu \qquad \ldots (2)$$

and $\quad x^2 \dfrac{\partial^2 u}{\partial x^2} + 2xy \dfrac{\partial^2 u}{\partial x \partial y} + y^2 \dfrac{\partial^2 u}{\partial y^2} = n(n-1)u \qquad \ldots (3)$

Also $v = y^{-n} \phi\left(\dfrac{x}{y}\right) \Rightarrow$ v is a homogeneous function of x and y of degree (–n), by Euler's theorem,

$$x \dfrac{\partial v}{\partial x} + y \dfrac{\partial v}{\partial y} = -nv \qquad \ldots (4)$$

and $x^2 \dfrac{\partial^2 v}{\partial x^2} + 2xy \dfrac{\partial^2 v}{\partial x \partial y} + y^2 \dfrac{\partial^2 v}{\partial y^2} = -n(-n-1)v$

i.e. $\quad x^2 \dfrac{\partial^2 v}{\partial x^2} + 2xy \dfrac{\partial^2 v}{\partial x \partial y} + y^2 \dfrac{\partial^2 y}{\partial y^2} = n(n+1)v \qquad \ldots (5)$

By adding equations (2) and (4),

$$x\left(\dfrac{\partial u}{\partial x} + \dfrac{\partial v}{\partial x}\right) + y\left(\dfrac{\partial u}{\partial y} + \dfrac{\partial u}{\partial y}\right) = nu - nv$$

From (1), $\qquad \dfrac{\partial z}{\partial x} = \dfrac{\partial u}{\partial x} + \dfrac{\partial v}{\partial x}, \ \dfrac{\partial z}{\partial y} = \dfrac{\partial u}{\partial y} + \dfrac{\partial v}{\partial y}$

$$x \dfrac{\partial z}{\partial x} + y \dfrac{\partial z}{\partial y} = nu - nv \qquad \ldots (6)$$

By adding equations (3) and (5),

$$x^2\left(\dfrac{\partial^2 u}{\partial x^2} + \dfrac{\partial^2 v}{\partial x^2}\right) + 2xy\left(\dfrac{\partial^2 u}{\partial x \partial y} + \dfrac{\partial^2 v}{\partial x \partial y}\right) + y^2\left(\dfrac{\partial^2 u}{\partial y^2} + \dfrac{\partial^2 v}{\partial y^2}\right) = n(n-1)u + n(n+1)v$$

From (1), $\quad \dfrac{\partial^2 z}{\partial x^2} = \dfrac{\partial^2 u}{\partial x^2} + \dfrac{\partial^2 v}{\partial x^2}, \ \dfrac{\partial^2 z}{\partial x \partial y} = \dfrac{\partial^2 u}{\partial x \partial y} + \dfrac{\partial^2 v}{\partial x \partial y}, \ \dfrac{\partial^2 z}{\partial y^2} = \dfrac{\partial^2 u}{\partial y^2} + \dfrac{\partial^2 v}{\partial y^2}$

$$x^2 \dfrac{\partial^2 z}{\partial x^2} + 2xy \dfrac{\partial^2 z}{\partial x \partial y} + y^2 \dfrac{\partial^2 z}{\partial y^2} = n(n+1)v + n(n-1)u \qquad \ldots (7)$$

By adding equations (6) and (7),

$$x^2 \dfrac{\partial^2 z}{\partial x^2} + 2xy \dfrac{\partial^2 z}{\partial x \partial y} + y^2 \dfrac{\partial^2 z}{\partial y^2} + x \dfrac{\partial z}{\partial x} + y \dfrac{\partial z}{\partial y} = n(n-1)u + n(n+1)v + nu - nv$$

$$= nu[n-1+1] + nv[n+1-1]$$
$$= n^2 u + n^2 v$$
$$= n^2(u+v) = n^2 z \qquad \ldots \text{by (1)}$$

$\therefore \quad x^2 \dfrac{\partial^2 z}{\partial x^2} + 2xy \dfrac{\partial^2 z}{\partial x \partial y} + y^2 \dfrac{\partial^2 z}{\partial y^2} + x \dfrac{\partial z}{\partial x} + y \dfrac{\partial z}{\partial y} = n^2 z$

Ex. 10 : If $u = \sin(\sqrt{x} + \sqrt{y})$, prove that $x\dfrac{\partial u}{\partial x} + y\dfrac{\partial u}{\partial y} = \dfrac{1}{2}(\sqrt{x} + \sqrt{y})\cos(\sqrt{x} + \sqrt{y})$

(May 2011, 2013)

Sol. : $u = \sin(\sqrt{x} + \sqrt{y})$ is not a homogeneous function. But u is a function of a homogeneous expression.

$$\sin^{-1} u = (\sqrt{x} + \sqrt{y})$$

Let
$$z = (\sqrt{x} + \sqrt{y}) = \sin^{-1} u$$

$$z = \sqrt{x} + \sqrt{y} = \sqrt{x}\,[1 + \sqrt{y/x}]$$

$z = x^{1/2} f(y/x) \Rightarrow Z$ is a homogeneous function of two variables x and y of degree $n = \dfrac{1}{2}$, by Euler's theorem, $x\dfrac{\partial z}{\partial x} + y\dfrac{\partial z}{\partial y} = \dfrac{1}{2} z.$

But
$$z = \sin^{-1} u, \quad \dfrac{\partial z}{\partial x} = \dfrac{1}{\sqrt{1-u^2}} \dfrac{\partial u}{\partial x}$$

$$\dfrac{\partial z}{\partial y} = \dfrac{1}{\sqrt{1-u^2}} \dfrac{\partial u}{\partial y}$$

$$x \dfrac{1}{\sqrt{1-u^2}} \dfrac{\partial u}{\partial x} + y \dfrac{1}{\sqrt{1-u^2}} \dfrac{\partial u}{\partial y} = \dfrac{1}{2} \sin^{-1} u$$

$$x \dfrac{\partial u}{\partial x} + y \dfrac{\partial u}{\partial y} = \dfrac{1}{2} (\sqrt{x} + \sqrt{y})(\sqrt{1-u^2}) \quad (\because \sin^{-1} u = \sqrt{x} + \sqrt{y})$$

$$= \dfrac{1}{2}(\sqrt{x} + \sqrt{y}) \sqrt{1 - \sin^2(\sqrt{x} + \sqrt{y})}$$

$$= \dfrac{1}{2}(\sqrt{x} + \sqrt{y}) \cos(\sqrt{x} + \sqrt{y})$$

Alternate method :

Here we will apply use of direct differentiation.

Let
$$u = \sin(\sqrt{x} + \sqrt{y})$$

Now
$$\dfrac{\partial u}{\partial x} = \cos(\sqrt{x} + \sqrt{y}) \dfrac{1}{2\sqrt{x}}$$

$$x \dfrac{\partial u}{\partial x} = \dfrac{\sqrt{x}}{2} \cos(\sqrt{x} + \sqrt{y}) \qquad \ldots (1)$$

$$\dfrac{\partial u}{\partial y} = \cos(\sqrt{x} + \sqrt{y}) \dfrac{1}{2\sqrt{y}}$$

$$y \dfrac{\partial u}{\partial y} = \dfrac{\sqrt{y}}{2} \cos(\sqrt{x} + \sqrt{y}) \qquad \ldots (2)$$

By adding equations (1) and (2),

$$x \dfrac{\partial u}{\partial x} + y \dfrac{\partial u}{\partial y} = \left(\dfrac{\sqrt{x} + \sqrt{y}}{2}\right) \cos(\sqrt{x} + \sqrt{y})$$

Ex. 11 : *Verify Euler's theorem on homogeneous function for* $u = \dfrac{x+y+z}{\sqrt{x}+\sqrt{y}+\sqrt{z}}$.

Sol. : We have $\dfrac{\partial u}{\partial x} = \dfrac{(\sqrt{x}+\sqrt{y}+\sqrt{z}) - (x+y+z)\cdot\dfrac{1}{2\sqrt{x}}}{(\sqrt{x}+\sqrt{y}+\sqrt{z})^2}$

and similar expression for $\dfrac{\partial u}{\partial y}, \dfrac{\partial u}{\partial z}$.

$$\therefore \quad x\dfrac{\partial u}{\partial x} + y\dfrac{\partial u}{\partial y} + z\dfrac{\partial u}{\partial z} = \dfrac{(\sqrt{x}+\sqrt{y}+\sqrt{z})(x+y+z) - \dfrac{1}{2}(x+y+z)(\sqrt{x}+\sqrt{y}+\sqrt{z})}{(\sqrt{x}+\sqrt{y}+\sqrt{z})^2}$$

$$= \dfrac{\dfrac{1}{2}(x+y+z)(\sqrt{x}+\sqrt{y}+\sqrt{z})}{(\sqrt{x}+\sqrt{y}+\sqrt{z})^2}$$

$$= \dfrac{1}{2}\dfrac{x+y+z}{\sqrt{x}+\sqrt{y}+\sqrt{z}} = \dfrac{1}{2}u \quad \ldots (1)$$

Also $\quad u = \dfrac{x\left(1+\dfrac{y}{x}+\dfrac{z}{x}\right)}{\sqrt{x}\left(1+\sqrt{\dfrac{y}{x}}+\sqrt{\dfrac{z}{x}}\right)} = x^{1/2} f\left(\dfrac{y}{x}, \dfrac{z}{x}\right)$

which is a homogeneous function of x, y, z of degree $n = \dfrac{1}{2}$.

∴ By Euler's theorem,

$$x\dfrac{\partial u}{\partial x} + y\dfrac{\partial u}{\partial y} + z\dfrac{\partial u}{\partial z} = nu = \dfrac{1}{2}u \quad \ldots (2)$$

From equations (1) and (2), we see that Euler's theorem is verified for the given function.

Ex. 12 : *If* $\dfrac{x^2}{a^2+u} + \dfrac{y^2}{b^2+u} + \dfrac{z^2}{c^2+u} = 1$, *where u is a homogeneous function of degree n in x, y, z show that* $u_x^2 + u_y^2 + u_z^2 = 2nu$.

Sol. : Since u is a homogeneous function of degree n in x, y, z we have by Euler's theorem,

$$xu_x + yu_y + zu_z = nu \quad \ldots (1)$$

Differentiating the given equation partially with respect to x, regarding u as a function of x, y, z we have

$$\left[x^2 \cdot \dfrac{-1}{(a^2+u)^2} u_x + \dfrac{2x}{a^2+u}\right] + y^2 \cdot \dfrac{-1}{(b^2+u)^2} u_x + z^2 \cdot \dfrac{-1}{(c^2+u)^2} u_x = 0$$

$$\Rightarrow u_x \left[\frac{x^2}{(a^2+u)^2} + \frac{y^2}{(b^2+u)^2} + \frac{z^2}{(c^2+u)^2} \right] = \frac{2x}{a^2+u}$$

$$\Rightarrow u_x \cdot p = \frac{2x}{a^2+u}, \text{ where } p \equiv \frac{x^2}{(a^2+u)^2} + \frac{y^2}{(b^2+u)^2} + \frac{z^2}{(c^2+u)^2}$$

Similarly, $u_y \cdot p = \frac{2y}{b^2+u}$ and $u_z p = \frac{2z}{c^2+u}$.

On squaring and adding, we have

$$p^2 \left(u_x^2 + u_y^2 + u_z^2 \right) = 4 \left[\frac{x^2}{(a^2+u)^2} + \frac{y^2}{(b^2+u)^2} + \frac{z^2}{(c^2+u)^2} \right]$$

$$= 4p$$

$$\therefore \quad u_x^2 + u_y^2 + u_z^2 = \frac{4}{p} \qquad \ldots (2)$$

Now, substituting for u_x, u_y, u_z in equation (1), we have

$$x \cdot \frac{2x}{p(a^2+u)} + y \cdot \frac{2y}{p(b^2+u)} + z \cdot \frac{2z}{p(c^2+u)} = nu \Rightarrow \frac{2}{p} \left[\frac{x^2}{a^2+u} + \frac{y^2}{b^2+u} + \frac{z^2}{c^2+u} \right] = nu$$

$$\Rightarrow \frac{2}{p} \cdot 1 = nu, \text{ from the given relation.}$$

$$\therefore \quad \frac{4}{p} = 2nu \qquad \ldots (3)$$

From equations (2) and (3), we have

$$u_x^2 + u_y^2 + u_z^2 = 2nu$$

Ex. 13 : If $u = \frac{x^2 y^2 z^2}{x^2+y^2+z^2} + \cos\left(\frac{xy+yz}{x^2+y^2+z^2}\right)$, show that

$$x \frac{\partial u}{\partial x} + y \frac{\partial u}{\partial y} + z \frac{\partial u}{\partial z} = 4 \left(\frac{x^2 y^2 z^2}{x^2+y^2+z^2} \right). \qquad \text{(Jan. 2004, Dec. 2012)}$$

Sol. : Let $\quad u = U + V$

where $\quad U = \left(\frac{x^2 y^2 z^2}{x^2+y^2+z^2} \right)$

and $\quad V = \cos\left(\frac{xy+yz}{x^2+y^2+z^2} \right)$

Now $\quad U = \dfrac{x^4 \left[\left(\dfrac{y}{x}\right)^2 \left(\dfrac{z}{x}\right)^2 \right]}{1 + \left(\dfrac{y}{x}\right)^2 + \left(\dfrac{z}{x}\right)^2}$

$$= x^4 \phi \left[\frac{y}{x}, \frac{z}{x} \right]$$

is a homogeneous function of x, y, z of degree 4.

Hence by Euler's theorem, we have,

$$x\frac{\partial U}{\partial x} + y\frac{\partial U}{\partial y} + z\frac{\partial U}{\partial z} = 4U$$

$$\Rightarrow x\frac{\partial U}{\partial x} + y\frac{\partial U}{\partial y} + z\frac{\partial U}{\partial z} = 4\left(\frac{x^2 y^2 z^2}{x^2 + y^2 + z^2}\right) \quad \ldots (1)$$

Again

$$V = \cos\left[\frac{\frac{y}{x} + \frac{y}{x}\cdot\frac{z}{x}}{1 + \left(\frac{y}{x}\right)^2 + \left(\frac{z}{x}\right)^2}\right] = x^0\,\psi\left(\frac{y}{x}, \frac{z}{x}\right)$$

Hence V is a homogeneous function of x, y and z of degree zero. Hence by Euler's theorem, we have

$$x\frac{\partial V}{\partial x} + y\frac{\partial V}{\partial y} + z\frac{\partial V}{\partial z} = 0\cdot V = 0 \quad \ldots (2)$$

Adding equations (1) and (2), we have

$$x\left(\frac{\partial U}{\partial x} + \frac{\partial V}{\partial x}\right) + y\left(\frac{\partial U}{\partial y} + \frac{\partial V}{\partial y}\right) + z\left(\frac{\partial U}{\partial z} + \frac{\partial V}{\partial z}\right) = 4\frac{x^2 y^2 z^2}{x^2 + y^2 + z^2} + 0$$

$$\Rightarrow x\frac{\partial}{\partial x}(U+V) + y\frac{\partial}{\partial y}(U+V) + z\frac{\partial}{\partial z}(U+V) = 4\frac{x^2 y^2 z^2}{x^2 + y^2 + z^2}$$

$$\Rightarrow x\frac{\partial u}{\partial x} + y\frac{\partial u}{\partial y} + z\frac{\partial u}{\partial z} = 4\frac{x^2 y^2 z^2}{x^2 + y^2 + z^2} \text{ Proved.}$$

Ex. 14 : *Verify Euler's theorem on homogeneous function when* **(May 2014)**
$f(x, y, z) = 3x^2 y z + 5xy^2 z + 4z^4$.

Sol. : $\quad \dfrac{\partial f}{\partial x} = 6xyz + 5y^2 z$

$\Rightarrow \quad x\dfrac{\partial f}{\partial x} = 6x^2 yz + 5xy^2 z$

Similarly $\quad y\dfrac{\partial f}{\partial y} = 3x^2 y + 10xy^2 z$

$\quad z\dfrac{\partial f}{\partial z} = 3x^2 yz + 5xy^2 z + 16z^4$

Hence

$$x\frac{\partial f}{\partial x} + y\frac{\partial f}{\partial y} + z\frac{\partial f}{\partial z} = 12x^2 y + 20xy^2 z + 16z^4 \quad \ldots (1)$$

Also $\quad f(x, y, z) = x^4\left[\left(\dfrac{y}{x}\right)\left(\dfrac{z}{x}\right) + 5\left(\dfrac{y}{x}\right)^2\left(\dfrac{z}{x}\right) + 4\left(\dfrac{z}{x}\right)^4\right]$

$$= x^4\,\phi\left[\frac{y}{x}, \frac{z}{x}\right]$$

Engineering Mathematics – I 10.45 Partial Differentiation and Applications

which is a homogeneous function of degree 4 in x, y and z. Hence by Euler's theorem,

$$x\frac{\partial f}{\partial x} + y\frac{\partial f}{\partial y} + z\frac{\partial f}{\partial z} = 4f$$

$$\Rightarrow x\frac{\partial f}{\partial x} + y\frac{\partial f}{\partial y} + z\frac{\partial f}{\partial z} = 4[3x^2yz + 5xy^2z + 4z^4]$$

$$= 12x^2yz + 20xy^2z + 16z^4 \qquad \ldots (2)$$

Hence from equations (1) and (2), Euler's theorem stands verified.

EXERCISE 10.5

1. Determine whether the following functions are homogeneous, non-homogeneous or function of homogeneous expression :

   (i) $\sqrt{\dfrac{x^2 + y^3}{x - y}}$ (ii) $\sqrt{\dfrac{x^{3/2} + y^{3/2}}{x^2 - y^2}}$

   (iii) $\sin^{-1}\dfrac{x - y}{x^5 + y^5}$ (iv) $\log\dfrac{x^2 + y^2}{x^2 - y^2}$

   (v) $\dfrac{x + y}{x^2 + y^2}$ (vi) $\tan^{-1}\dfrac{\sqrt{x^2 + y^2}}{y}$

   (vii) $\sin^{-1}\sqrt{x^2 + y^2}$ (viii) $\log\dfrac{x^3 + y^3}{x^2 + y^2}$

   (ix) $x^3 + y^3 - 3axy$ (x) $\sin^{-1}\left[\dfrac{x^{1/3} + y^{1/3}}{x^{1/3} - y^{1/3}}\right]^{1/2}$

2. If $u = \sin^{-1}\dfrac{x + y}{\sqrt{x} + \sqrt{y}}$, show that $2x\dfrac{\partial u}{\partial x} + 2y\dfrac{\partial u}{\partial y} = \tan u$.   **(May 2010)**

3. If $V = \dfrac{1}{r} f(\theta)$ where $x = r\cos\theta$, $y = r\sin\theta$, then show that $x\dfrac{\partial V}{\partial x} + y\dfrac{\partial V}{\partial y} + V = 0$.

   [Hint : $V = \dfrac{1}{\sqrt{x^2 + y^2}} f\left(\tan^{-1}\dfrac{y}{x}\right)$]

4. If $x = e^u \tan v$, $y = e^u \sec v$ and $z = e^{-2u} f(v)$ prove that $x\dfrac{\partial z}{\partial x} + y\dfrac{\partial z}{\partial y} + 2z = 0$.

   [Hint : $z = \dfrac{1}{y^2 - x^2} f\left(\mathrm{cosec}^{-1}\dfrac{y}{x}\right)$]

5. If $u = f(y/x) + \sqrt{x^2 + y^2}$, prove that $x\dfrac{\partial u}{\partial x} + y\dfrac{\partial u}{\partial y} = \sqrt{x^2 + y^2}$.

6. If $T = \sin\left(\dfrac{xy}{x^2 + y^2}\right) + \sqrt{x^2 + y^2} + \dfrac{x^2 y}{x + y}$, then find $x\dfrac{\partial T}{\partial x} + y\dfrac{\partial T}{\partial y}$. **(May 2004, Dec. 2014)**

Ans. $\sqrt{x^2 + y^2} + \dfrac{2x^2 y}{x + y}$

7. If $f(x, y) = \dfrac{1}{x^2} + \dfrac{1}{xy} + \dfrac{\log x - \log y}{x^2 + y^2}$, prove that $x\dfrac{\partial f}{\partial x} + y\dfrac{\partial f}{\partial y} + 2f = 0$.

8. Find $x^2 u_{xx} + 2xy\, u_{xy} + y^2 u_{yy}$ in the following cases: **(Dec. 2014)**

(i) $u = \operatorname{cosec}^{-1} \sqrt{\dfrac{x^{1/2} + y^{1/2}}{x^{1/3} + y^{1/3}}}$
Ans. $\dfrac{\tan u}{12}\left(\dfrac{13}{12} + \dfrac{\tan^2 u}{12}\right)$

(ii) $u = \sin^{-1}\left\{\dfrac{x^{1/3} + y^{1/3}}{x^{1/2} + y^{1/2}}\right\}^{1/2}$
Ans. $\dfrac{\tan u}{144}(13 + \tan^2 u)$.

(iii) $u = \log(x^3 + y^3 - x^2 y - xy^2)$
Ans. -3

(iv) $u = \sin^{-1}(x^3 + y^3)^{2/5}$
Ans. $\dfrac{6}{5}\tan u \left(\dfrac{6}{5}\sec^2 u - 1\right)$

(v) $u = \tan^{-1}\dfrac{\sqrt{x^3 + y^3}}{\sqrt{x} + \sqrt{y}}$
Ans. $-2\sin^3 u \cos u$

(vi) $u = \sin^{-1}(x^2 + y^2)^{1/5}$
Ans. $\dfrac{2}{25}\tan u\,(2\tan^2 u - 3)$

(vii) $u = \sin^{-1}\sqrt{x^2 + y^2}$ **(May 2013)**
Ans. $\tan^3 u$

(viii) $u = \sin^{-1}\dfrac{x + y}{\sqrt{x} + \sqrt{y}}$
Ans. $-\dfrac{\sin u \cos 2u}{4\cos^3 u}$

(ix) $\dfrac{(x^2 + y^2)^m}{2m(2m - 1)} + xf(y/x) + \phi(y/x)$.
Ans. $(x^2 + y^2)^m$

9. Verify Euler's theroem for (a) $u = \dfrac{\sqrt{x} + \sqrt{y} + \sqrt{z}}{x + y + z}$, (b) $u = \sqrt{x} + \sqrt{y} + \sqrt{z}$,

(c) $\dfrac{x^2 + y^2 + z^2}{x + y + z}$.

TYPE 5 : FINDING THE SECOND ORDER EXPRESSION BY USING FIRST ORDER EXPRESSION

Method 1: Let $V = f(x, y)$

To find a $x^2 \dfrac{\partial^2 v}{\partial x^2} + (a \pm b)\, xy \dfrac{\partial^2 v}{\partial x\, \partial y} + by^2 \dfrac{\partial^2 v}{\partial y^2}$ ... (1)

we will proceed as follows :

Step 1 : Solve first $a \cdot x \cdot \dfrac{\partial v}{\partial x} \pm by \dfrac{\partial v}{\partial y}$. ... (2)

Step 2 : Select the middle sign in equation (2) as +ve if sign of $\dfrac{\partial^2 v}{\partial x\, \partial y}$ in equation (1) is +ve.

Step 3 : Select the middle sign in equation (2) as –ve if sign of $\dfrac{\partial^2 v}{\partial x\, \partial y}$ in equation (1) is –ve.

Step 4 : Differentiate equation (2) partially with respect to x.
Step 5 : Differentiate equation (2) partially with respect to y.
Step 6 : Now use proper multipliers.
Step 7 : Finally combine these expressions to find equation (1).

Method 2 : Let $v = f(x, y)$. To find $a\dfrac{\partial^2 v}{\partial x^2} + (a \pm b)\dfrac{\partial^2 v}{\partial x\, \partial y} + b\dfrac{\partial^2 v}{\partial y^2}$ ... (1)

we will proceed as follows :

Step 1 : Solve first $a\dfrac{\partial v}{\partial x} \pm b\dfrac{\partial v}{\partial y}$. ... (2)

Step 2 : Select the middle sign in equation (2) as +ve (or –ve) if sign of $\dfrac{\partial^2 v}{\partial x\, \partial y}$ in equation (1) is +ve (or –ve).

Step 3 : Differentiate equation (2) partially with respect to x and y.
Step 4 : Use proper multipliers.
Step 5 : Finally combine these expressions to find equation (1).
The following illustrations will give a clear cut idea.

Ex. 1 : If $u = f\left(\dfrac{x^2}{y}\right)$ then show that $x^2 u_{xx} + 3xy\, u_{xy} + 2y^2 u_{yy} = 0$.

Sol. : Given expression is $x^2 u_{xx} + 3xy\, u_{xy} + 2y^2 u_{yy} = 0$. Comparing with

$ax^2 u_{xx} + (a \pm b)\, xy\, u_{xy} + by^2 u_{yy} = 0$. We have

$a = 1$, $b = 2$ and middle sign of u_{xy} is +ve.

Step 1 : We consider the first order expression $a \cdot x \cdot u_x + b \cdot y \cdot u_y$ i.e. $xu_x + 2y\, u_y$.

Now, $\quad u = f\left(\dfrac{x^2}{y}\right)$

$$u_x = f'\left(\dfrac{x^2}{y}\right)\dfrac{2x}{y} \quad \text{and} \quad u_y = f'\left(\dfrac{x^2}{y}\right)\left(\dfrac{-x^2}{y^2}\right)$$

$\therefore \quad xu_x + 2y\, u_y = x\left[f'\left(\dfrac{x^2}{y}\right)\cdot\dfrac{2x}{y}\right] + 2y\left[f'\left(\dfrac{x^2}{y}\right)\cdot\left(\dfrac{-x^2}{y^2}\right)\right]$

$$= \dfrac{2x^2}{y} f'\left(\dfrac{x^2}{y}\right) - \dfrac{2x^2}{y} f'\left(\dfrac{x^2}{y}\right)$$

$xu_x + 2yu_y = 0$ ... (1)

Step 2 : Differentiating (1) partially with respect to x, we get,

$$xu_{xx} + u_x + 2y\, u_{xy} = 0 \quad \ldots (2)$$

Differentiating (1) partially with respect to y, we get

$$xu_{yx} + 2y\, u_{yy} + 2u_y = 0 \quad \ldots (3)$$

Step 3 : Equation (2) xx + equation (3) xy $\Rightarrow$

$$\therefore\ x^2 u_{xx} + x\, u_x + 2xy\, u_{xy} + xy\, u_{yx} + 2y^2\, u_{yy} + 2y\, u_y = 0$$

$$(x^2 u_{xx} + 3xy\, u_{xy} + 2y^2\, u_{yy}) + (x\, u_x + 2y\, u_y) = 0$$

$$\therefore\ x^2 u_{xx} + 3xy\, u_{xy} + 2y^2\, u_{yy} = 0 \text{ by using equation (1).}$$

Ex. 2 : *If* $u = f(x^2 + y^2)$ *then show that* $y^2\, u_{xx} - 2xy\, u_{xy} + x^2\, u_{yy} = x \cdot u_x + y \cdot u_y$.

Sol. : Here $a = 1$, $b = 1$ and middle sign of u_{xy} is negative therefore.

Step 1 : We first consider $a \cdot yu_x - b \cdot x \cdot u_y$ (Role of x and y is changed)

i.e. $y \cdot u_x - x \cdot u_y$.

$$u = f(x^2 + y^2)$$

$$u_x = f'(x^2 + y^2) \cdot 2x \quad \text{and} \quad u_y = f'(x^2 + y^2) \cdot 2y$$

$$\therefore\ y \cdot u_x - x \cdot u_y = 2xy\, f'(x^2 + y^2) - 2xy\, f'(x^2 + y^2) = 0 \quad \therefore\ yu_x - xu_y = 0$$

$$\ldots (1)$$

Step 2 : Differentiating equation (1) partially with respect to x, we get,

$$yu_{xx} - xu_{xy} - u_y = 0 \quad \ldots (2)$$

Differentiating equation (1) partially with respect to y, we get,

$$yu_{yx} + u_x - xu_{yy} = 0 \quad \ldots (3)$$

Step 3 : Equation (2) × y − equation (3) × x $\Rightarrow$

$$y^2 u_{xx} - xy\, u_{xy} - yu_y - xy\, u_{xy} - xu_x + x^2\, u_{yy} = 0$$

$$\therefore\quad y^2 u_{xx} - 2xy\, u_{xy} + x^2\, u_{yy} = xu_x + yu_y.$$

EXERCISE 10.6

1. If $u = \tan^{-1}(xy)$ then show that $x^2 u_{xx} - 2xy\, u_{xy} + y^2 u_{yy} + xu_x + yu_y = 0$
2. If $u = x\, f(x + y) + y\, \phi(x + y)$ then show that $u_{xx} - 2u_{xy} + u_{yy} = 0$.
3. If $u = \log(x^3 + y^3 - x^2 y - y^2 x)$ then show that $\dfrac{\partial^2 u}{\partial x^2} + 2\dfrac{\partial^2 u}{\partial x\, \partial y} + \dfrac{\partial^2 u}{\partial y^2} = -\dfrac{4}{(x+y)^2}$.

10.13 COMPOSITE FUNCTION

1. If u be a function of two independent variables x and y, where x and y are separately functions of a single independent variable t, then u is called a *composite function of t*.

   For example, if $u = y \cos(x + y)$ where $x = e^t$ and $y = \log t$, then u becomes a composite function of t.

   i.e. $u \rightarrow xy \rightarrow t$.

2. If $u = f(x, y)$, where $x = \phi_1(t_1, t_2)$ and $y = \phi_2(t_1, t_2)$, then u is called the *composite function of two independent variables* t_1, t_2.

   For example, if $u = x^2 + y^2 - 2xy$ where $x = t_1 + t_2$ and $y = t_1 - t_2$ then u becomes a composite function of two independent variables t_1 and t_2.

   i.e. $u \to x, y \to t_1, t_2$.

3. If $u = f(x_1, x_2, x_3, \ldots, x_n)$ where $x_1, x_2, x_3, \ldots x_n$ are functions of a single independent variable t, then u is called a composite function of a single variable t.

   i.e. $u \to x_1, x_2, x_3, \ldots x_n \to t$.

4. If $u = f(x_1, x_2, x_3, \ldots x_n)$, where $x_1, x_2, x_3, \ldots x_n$ are functions of m independent variables $t_1, t_2, t_3, \ldots t_m$, then u is called the composite function of several independent variables $t_1, t_2, \ldots t_m$.

   i.e. $u \to x_1, x_2, \ldots x_n \to t_1, t_2, \ldots t_m$.

10.14 TOTAL DERIVATIVE

If $u = f(x, y)$, where $x = \phi(t)$ and $y = \psi(t)$, then u can be expressed as a function of a single variable t. Substituting for x and y in $u = f(x, y)$, the derivative of u with respect to t is the ordinary differential coefficient $\dfrac{du}{dt}$.

This $\dfrac{du}{dt}$ is called the *Total Derivative*. To distinguish it from the Partial Derivatives $\dfrac{\partial u}{\partial x}$ and $\dfrac{\partial u}{\partial y}$, we shall now establish a relation between $\dfrac{du}{dt}$ and the partial derivatives $\dfrac{\partial u}{\partial x}, \dfrac{\partial u}{\partial y}$.

THEOREM ON TOTAL DIFFERENTIAL COEFFICIENT

1. If u be a composite function of t given by the relation $u = f(x, y)$, $x = \phi(t)$ and $y = \psi(t)$, where u possesses continuous partial derivatives with respect to x and y and x, y possess derivatives with respect to t then to show that :

$$\frac{du}{dt} = \frac{\partial u}{\partial x}\frac{dx}{dt} + \frac{\partial u}{\partial y}\frac{dy}{dt}$$

Proof : We have $u = f(x, y)$, giving increment δt to t, let the corresponding increments in x, y and u be $\delta x, \delta y$ and δu respectively, then

$$u + \delta u = f(x + \delta x, y + \delta y)$$

Subtracting $\quad \delta u = f(x + \delta x, y + \delta y) - f(x, y)$

$$= \{f(x + \delta x, y + \delta y) - f(x, y + \delta y)\} + \{f(x, y + \delta y) - f(x, y)\}$$

$$\therefore \quad \frac{\delta u}{\delta t} = \frac{(x + \delta x, y + \delta y) - f(x, y + \delta y)}{\delta x} \frac{\delta x}{\delta t}$$

$$+ \frac{f(x, y + \delta y) - f(x, y)}{\delta y} \frac{\delta y}{\delta t}$$

Now taking limits, as $\delta t \to 0$, δx and δy also tend to zero, then

$$\frac{du}{dt} = \lim_{\delta x \to 0} \left[\left\{ \frac{f(x+\delta x, y+\delta y) - f(x, y+\delta y)}{\delta x} \right\} \right] \frac{dx}{dt}$$

$$+ \lim_{\delta y \to 0} \left\{ \frac{f(x, y+\delta y) - f(x, y)}{\delta y} \right\} \frac{dy}{dt}$$

$$= \frac{\partial f(x, y)}{\partial x} \frac{dx}{dt} + \frac{\partial f(x, y)}{\partial y} \frac{dy}{dt}$$

$$= \frac{\partial f}{\partial x} \cdot \frac{dx}{dt} + \frac{\partial f}{\partial y} \cdot \frac{dy}{dt}$$

Hence $\quad \dfrac{du}{dt} = \dfrac{\partial u}{\partial x} \cdot \dfrac{dx}{dt} + \dfrac{\partial u}{\partial y} \cdot \dfrac{dy}{dt}$ ... (1)

The required formula in terms of differentials only, can be written as :

$$du = \frac{\partial u}{\partial x} dx + \frac{\partial u}{\partial y} dy \qquad \ldots (2)$$

is called as total differential.

We will remember the formula given by equation (1) by using tree diagram 1 as :

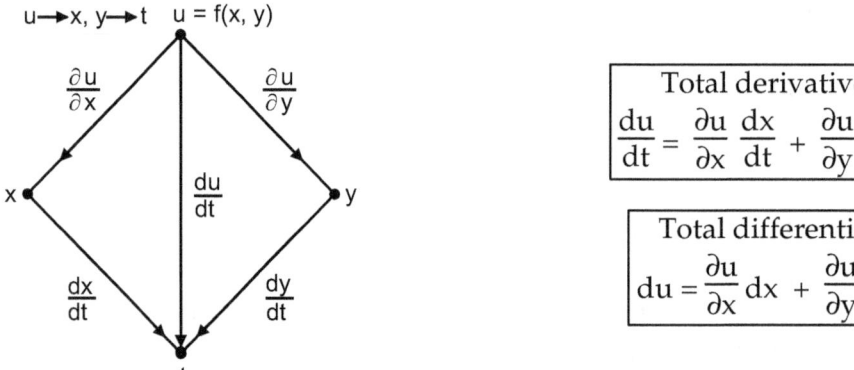

Fig. 10.5 : Tree diagram 1

2. If u be a composite function of t given by the relation $u = \phi(x, y, z)$, $x = \phi(t)$, $y = \psi(t)$, $z = \xi(t)$, where u possesses continuous partial derivatives with respect to x, y, z and x, y, z possess derivatives with respect to t, then

$$\frac{du}{dt} = \frac{\partial u}{\partial x} \frac{dx}{dt} + \frac{\partial u}{\partial y} \frac{dy}{dt} + \frac{\partial u}{\partial z} \frac{dz}{dt} \qquad \ldots (3)$$

We have $\quad du = \dfrac{\partial u}{\partial x} dx + \dfrac{\partial u}{\partial y} dy + \dfrac{\partial u}{\partial z} dz$ ... (4)

is called as total differential.

We will remember the formula given by equation (3) by using tree diagram 2.

u → x, y, z → t

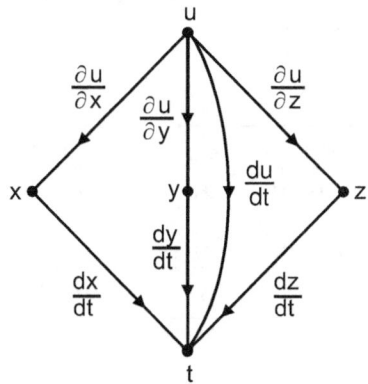

$$\text{Total derivative}$$
$$\frac{du}{dt} = \frac{\partial u}{\partial x}\frac{dx}{dt} + \frac{\partial u}{\partial y}\frac{dy}{dt} + \frac{\partial u}{\partial z}\frac{dz}{dt}$$

$$\text{Total differential}$$
$$du = \frac{\partial u}{\partial x}dx + \frac{\partial u}{\partial y}dy + \frac{\partial u}{\partial z}dz$$

Fig. 10.6 : Tree diagram 2

While dealing with a function of several variables, this can be generalised.

Thus if, $\qquad u = f(x_1, x_2, x_3, \ldots x_n)$

where $x_1, x_2, x_3, \ldots x_n$ are functions of a single variable t, then

$$\frac{du}{dt} = \frac{\partial u}{\partial x_1}\cdot\frac{dx_1}{dt} + \frac{\partial u}{\partial x_2}\cdot\frac{dx_2}{dt} + \ldots + \frac{\partial u}{\partial x_n}\cdot\frac{dx_n}{dt}$$

and $\qquad du = \frac{\partial u}{\partial x_1}\cdot dx_1 + \frac{\partial u}{\partial x_2}\cdot dx_2 + \ldots + \frac{\partial u}{\partial x_n}\cdot dx_n$

3. If $u = f(x, y)$ where $x = f_1(r, \theta)$, $y = f_2(r, \theta)$ then the differential coefficients of u with respect to r and θ, will be partial derivatives $\frac{\partial u}{\partial r}$, $\frac{\partial u}{\partial \theta}$, and are given by

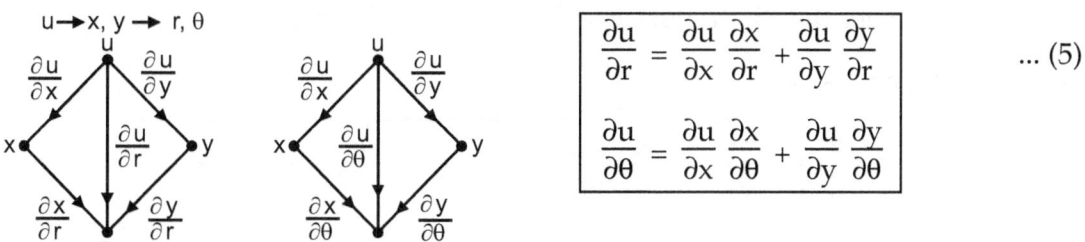

$$\frac{\partial u}{\partial r} = \frac{\partial u}{\partial x}\frac{\partial x}{\partial r} + \frac{\partial u}{\partial y}\frac{\partial y}{\partial r} \qquad \ldots (5)$$

$$\frac{\partial u}{\partial \theta} = \frac{\partial u}{\partial x}\frac{\partial x}{\partial \theta} + \frac{\partial u}{\partial y}\frac{\partial y}{\partial \theta}$$

Fig. 10.7 : Tree diagram 3

We will remember formulae given by equation (5) by using tree diagram 3.

4. If $u = f(x, y, z)$ where $x = f_1(r, \theta)$, $y = f_2(r, \theta)$ and $z = f_3(r, \theta)$ then the differential coefficients of u with respect to r and θ, will be partial derivatives $\dfrac{\partial u}{\partial r}, \dfrac{\partial u}{\partial \theta}$, and are given by

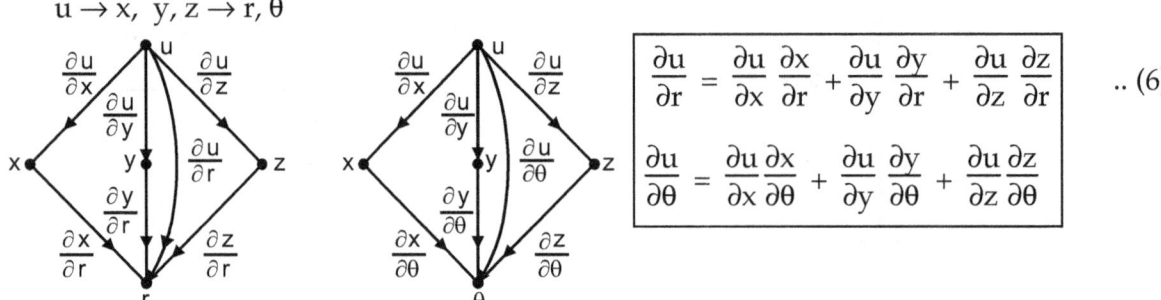

$$\dfrac{\partial u}{\partial r} = \dfrac{\partial u}{\partial x}\dfrac{\partial x}{\partial r} + \dfrac{\partial u}{\partial y}\dfrac{\partial y}{\partial r} + \dfrac{\partial u}{\partial z}\dfrac{\partial z}{\partial r} \quad \ldots (6)$$

$$\dfrac{\partial u}{\partial \theta} = \dfrac{\partial u}{\partial x}\dfrac{\partial x}{\partial \theta} + \dfrac{\partial u}{\partial y}\dfrac{\partial y}{\partial \theta} + \dfrac{\partial u}{\partial z}\dfrac{\partial z}{\partial \theta}$$

Fig. 10.8 : Tree diagram 4

We will remember formulae given by equation (6) by using tree diagram 4.

5. If $u = f(x, y, z)$ where $x = f_1(r, \theta, \phi)$, $y = f_2(r, \theta, \phi)$, $z = f_3(r, \theta, \phi)$ then the differential coefficients of u with respect to r, θ, ϕ will be partial derivatives $\dfrac{\partial u}{\partial r}, \dfrac{\partial u}{\partial \theta}, \dfrac{\partial u}{\partial \phi}$, and are given by

$$\dfrac{\partial u}{\partial r} = \dfrac{\partial u}{\partial x}\dfrac{\partial x}{\partial r} + \dfrac{\partial u}{\partial y}\dfrac{\partial y}{\partial r} + \dfrac{\partial u}{\partial z}\dfrac{\partial z}{\partial r}$$

$$\dfrac{\partial u}{\partial \theta} = \dfrac{\partial u}{\partial x}\dfrac{\partial x}{\partial \theta} + \dfrac{\partial u}{\partial y}\dfrac{\partial y}{\partial \theta} + \dfrac{\partial u}{\partial z}\dfrac{\partial z}{\partial \theta} \quad \ldots (7)$$

$$\dfrac{\partial u}{\partial \phi} = \dfrac{\partial u}{\partial x}\dfrac{\partial x}{\partial \phi} + \dfrac{\partial u}{\partial y}\dfrac{\partial y}{\partial \phi} + \dfrac{\partial u}{\partial z}\dfrac{\partial z}{\partial \phi}$$

6. If $u = f(x_1, x_2, x_3, \ldots, x_n)$ where $x_1, x_2, x_3, \ldots, x_n$ are function of m variables $t_1, t_2, t_3, \ldots, t_m$ then, the differential coefficient of u with respect to t_1, will be a partial derivative, $\dfrac{\partial u}{\partial t_1}$ and is given by

Also

$$\dfrac{\partial u}{\partial t_1} = \dfrac{\partial u}{\partial x_1}\dfrac{\partial x_1}{\partial t_1} + \dfrac{\partial u}{\partial x_2}\dfrac{\partial x_2}{\partial t_1} + \ldots + \dfrac{\partial u}{\partial x_n}\dfrac{\partial x_n}{\partial t_1}$$

$$\dfrac{\partial u}{\partial t_2} = \dfrac{\partial u}{\partial x_2}\dfrac{\partial x_2}{\partial t_2} + \dfrac{\partial u}{\partial x_2}\dfrac{\partial x_2}{\partial t_2} + \ldots + \dfrac{\partial u}{\partial x_n}\dfrac{\partial x_n}{\partial t_2} \quad \ldots (8)$$

$$\ldots\ldots\ldots\ldots\ldots\ldots\ldots\ldots\ldots\ldots\ldots\ldots\ldots\ldots\ldots$$

$$\dfrac{\partial u}{\partial t_m} = \dfrac{\partial u}{\partial x_1}\dfrac{\partial x_1}{\partial t_m} + \dfrac{\partial u}{\partial x_2}\dfrac{\partial x_2}{\partial t_m} + \ldots + \dfrac{\partial u}{\partial x_n}\dfrac{\partial x_n}{\partial t_m}$$

AN IMPORTANT RESULT

If we put t = x and t = y in result (1) respectively (Refer Article 10.13) then

$$\boxed{\frac{du}{dx} = \frac{\partial u}{\partial x} + \frac{\partial u}{\partial y} \cdot \frac{dy}{dx} \, , \, \frac{du}{dy} = \frac{\partial u}{\partial y} + \frac{\partial u}{\partial x} \cdot \frac{dx}{dy}} \qquad \ldots (9)$$

10.15 DIFFERENTIATION OF IMPLICIT FUNCTIONS

Implicit Function : Let $f(x, y) = 0$ represents an implicit relation

(e.g. $x^3 + y^3 - 3a\,xy = 0$).

Note : When y is expressed in terms of x i.e. $y = f(x)$, then y is called as explicit function.

Consider $z = f(x, y) = 0$, then

$$\frac{dz}{dx} = \frac{\partial z}{\partial x} \cdot \frac{dx}{dx} + \frac{\partial z}{\partial y} \cdot \frac{dy}{dx} \, , \, \frac{dz}{dx} = \frac{\partial z}{\partial x} + \frac{\partial z}{\partial y} \cdot \frac{dy}{dx} \qquad \ldots (1)$$

Since $z = f(x, y) = 0$ then $\frac{dz}{dx} = 0$ and therefore (1) becomes

$$\frac{\partial z}{\partial x} + \frac{\partial z}{\partial y} \cdot \frac{dy}{dx} = 0$$

$$\therefore \qquad \frac{dy}{dx} = -\frac{\partial z/\partial x}{\partial z/\partial y} = -\frac{\partial f/\partial x}{\partial f/\partial y}$$

We now introduce notations :

$$p = \frac{\partial f}{\partial x} \, ; \, q = \frac{\partial f}{\partial y} \, ; \, r = \frac{\partial^2 f}{\partial x^2} \, ; \, s = \frac{\partial^2 f}{\partial x \, \partial y} \, ; \, t = \frac{\partial^2 f}{\partial y^2} \, .$$

$$\boxed{\frac{dy}{dx} = -\frac{\partial f/\partial x}{\partial f/\partial y} = -\frac{p}{q}} \qquad \ldots (2)$$

Differentiating (2) w.r.t. x, we have

$$\frac{d^2 y}{dx^2} = -\left(\frac{q \cdot \frac{dp}{dx} - p \cdot \frac{dq}{dx}}{q^2}\right) \qquad \ldots (3)$$

Since $p = \frac{\partial f}{\partial x}$ is a function of x and y, therefore, p becomes composite function of x.

Similarly, q is also composite function of x, then

$$\frac{dp}{dx} = \frac{\partial p}{\partial x} \cdot \frac{dx}{dx} + \frac{\partial p}{\partial y} \cdot \frac{dy}{dx} = \frac{\partial}{\partial x}\left(\frac{\partial f}{\partial x}\right) + \frac{\partial}{\partial y}\left(\frac{\partial f}{\partial x}\right) \cdot \frac{dy}{dx}$$

$$\frac{dp}{dx} = \frac{\partial^2 f}{\partial x^2} + \frac{\partial^2 f}{\partial y\, \partial x} \cdot \frac{dy}{dx} = r + s\left(-\frac{p}{q}\right) = r - \frac{ps}{q}$$

Also,
$$\frac{dq}{dx} = \frac{\partial q}{\partial x} \cdot \frac{dx}{dx} + \frac{\partial q}{\partial y} \cdot \frac{dy}{dx}$$

$$= \frac{\partial}{\partial x}\left(\frac{\partial f}{\partial y}\right) + \frac{\partial}{\partial y}\left(\frac{\partial f}{\partial y}\right) \cdot \frac{dy}{dx}$$

$$\frac{dq}{dx} = \frac{\partial^2 f}{\partial x\, \partial y} + \frac{\partial^2 f}{\partial y^2} \cdot \frac{dy}{dx}$$

$$= s + t\left(-\frac{p}{q}\right) = s - \frac{pt}{q}$$

Substituting these values in equation (1), we have

$$\frac{d^2 y}{dx^2} = -\left[\frac{q\left(r - \frac{ps}{q}\right) - p\left(s - \frac{pt}{q}\right)}{q^2}\right]$$

Thus,
$$\boxed{\frac{d^2 y}{dx^2} = -\left[\frac{q^2 r - 2pqs + p^2 t}{q^3}\right]}$$

Note : The above result for $\frac{d^2 y}{dx^2}$ may be remembered as $q^3 \frac{d^2 y}{dx^2} = \begin{vmatrix} r & s & p \\ s & t & q \\ p & q & 0 \end{vmatrix}$.

ILLUSTRATIONS ON COMPOSITE FUNCTIONS
TYPE 1 : ILLUSTRATIONS ON IMPLICIT FUNCTION :

Ex. 1 : Find $\frac{du}{dx}$, given that $u = x \log xy$ and $x^3 + y^3 = -3xy$.

Sol. : u is a composite function of x, so that

$$\frac{du}{dx} = \frac{\partial u}{\partial x} \cdot \frac{dx}{dx} + \frac{\partial u}{\partial y} \cdot \frac{dy}{dx}$$

Now,
$$\frac{\partial u}{\partial x} = x \cdot \left(\frac{1}{xy}\right) \cdot y + \log(xy) = 1 + \log xy$$

$$\frac{\partial u}{\partial y} = x \cdot \frac{1}{xy} \cdot x = \frac{x}{y}$$

$$\frac{dy}{dx} = -\frac{p}{q} = -\frac{\partial f/\partial x}{\partial f/\partial y} = -\frac{3x^2 + 3y}{3y^2 + 3x} = -\frac{x^2 + y}{y^2 + x}$$

$\therefore$
$$\frac{du}{dx} = 1 + \log xy + \frac{x}{y}\left(-\frac{x^2 + y}{y^2 + x}\right) = 1 + \log xy - \left(\frac{x^3 + xy}{y^3 + xy}\right)$$

$$\frac{du}{dx} = \log xy + \frac{y^3 + xy - x^3 - xy}{y^3 + xy}$$

$$\frac{du}{dx} = \log xy + \frac{y^3 - x^3}{y(y^2 + x)}$$

Ex. 2 : If $\phi(x, y, z) = 0$, prove that $\left(\dfrac{\partial z}{\partial y}\right)_x \left(\dfrac{\partial x}{\partial z}\right)_y \left(\dfrac{\partial y}{\partial x}\right)_z = -1$. **(May 2005)**

Sol. : Given, $\phi(x, y, z) = 0$.

$$\therefore \quad \left(\dfrac{dx}{dz}\right)_y = \left(\dfrac{\partial x}{\partial z}\right)_y = -\dfrac{\partial \phi/\partial z}{\partial \phi/\partial x} \quad \ldots (1)$$

and $\left(\dfrac{dy}{dx}\right)_z = \left(\dfrac{\partial y}{\partial x}\right)_z = -\dfrac{\partial \phi/\partial x}{\partial \phi/\partial y} \quad \ldots (2)$

also $\left(\dfrac{dz}{dy}\right)_x = \left(\dfrac{\partial z}{\partial y}\right)_x = -\dfrac{\partial \phi/\partial y}{\partial \phi/\partial z} \quad \ldots (3)$

Multiplying equations (1), (2) and (3), we have

$$\left(\dfrac{\partial z}{\partial y}\right)_x \cdot \left(\dfrac{\partial x}{\partial z}\right)_y \cdot \left(\dfrac{\partial y}{\partial x}\right)_z = \left(-\dfrac{\partial \phi/\partial y}{\partial \phi/\partial z}\right)\left(-\dfrac{\partial \phi/\partial z}{\partial \phi/\partial x}\right)\left(-\dfrac{\partial \phi/\partial x}{\partial \phi/\partial y}\right) = -1$$

Ex. 3 : If $(\cos x)^y = (\sin y)^x$ then find $\dfrac{dy}{dx}$.

Sol. : Given, $(\cos x)^y = (\sin y)^x$

Taking logarithm, we have

$y \log \cos x = x \log \sin y$

Let $f(x, y) = y \log \cos x - x \log \sin y = 0$

$$\therefore \quad \dfrac{dy}{dx} = -\dfrac{\partial f/\partial x}{\partial f/\partial y} \quad \ldots (1)$$

Now, $\dfrac{\partial f}{\partial x} = y \cdot \dfrac{1}{\cos x}(-\sin x) - \log \sin y = -y \tan x - \log \sin y$

and $\dfrac{\partial f}{\partial y} = \log \cos x - x \dfrac{1}{\sin y} \cos y = \log \cos x - x \cot y$

$\therefore$ From (1),

$$\dfrac{dy}{dx} = \dfrac{y \tan x + \log \sin y}{\log \cos x - x \cot y}$$

Ex. 4 : If $f(x, y) = 0$ and $\phi(y, z) = 0$, show that $\dfrac{\partial f}{\partial y} \cdot \dfrac{\partial \phi}{\partial z} \cdot \dfrac{dz}{dx} = \dfrac{\partial f}{\partial x} \cdot \dfrac{\partial \phi}{\partial y}$. **(May 2014)**

Sol. : Given, $f(x, y) = 0$

$$\therefore \quad \dfrac{dy}{dx} = -\dfrac{\dfrac{\partial f}{\partial x}}{\dfrac{\partial f}{\partial y}} \quad \ldots (1)$$

Given, $\phi(y, z) = 0$

$$\therefore \quad \dfrac{dz}{dy} = -\dfrac{\dfrac{\partial \phi}{\partial y}}{\dfrac{\partial \phi}{\partial z}} \quad \ldots (2)$$

Multiplying (1) and (2), we have

$$\frac{dy}{dx} \cdot \frac{dz}{dy} = \frac{dz}{dx} = \frac{\frac{\partial \phi}{\partial y} \cdot \frac{\partial f}{\partial x}}{\frac{\partial \phi}{\partial z} \cdot \frac{\partial f}{\partial y}}$$

$$\frac{dz}{dx} \cdot \frac{\partial \phi}{\partial z} \cdot \frac{\partial f}{\partial y} = \frac{\partial \phi}{\partial y} \cdot \frac{\partial f}{\partial x}$$

$$\Rightarrow \quad \frac{\partial f}{\partial y} \cdot \frac{\partial \phi}{\partial z} \cdot \frac{dz}{dx} = \frac{\partial f}{\partial x} \cdot \frac{\partial \phi}{\partial y}$$

Ex. 5 : If $z = xy\, f(y/x)$, show that $x \dfrac{\partial z}{\partial x} + y \dfrac{\partial z}{\partial y} = 2z$. Further, show that if z is constant

then $\dfrac{f'(y/x)}{f(y/x)} = \dfrac{x\left(y + x\dfrac{dy}{dx}\right)}{y\left(y - x\dfrac{dy}{dx}\right)}$.

Sol. : Given : $z = xy\, f(y/x) = x^2 \left[\dfrac{y}{x} f(y/x)\right]$, z is a homogeneous function of degree 2.

By Euler's theorem, $x\dfrac{\partial z}{\partial x} + y\dfrac{\partial z}{\partial y} = 2z$.

Next, if z = constant = K (say) then

Let $F = xy\, f(y/x) - K = 0$ i.e. $F(x, y) = 0$

$$\therefore \quad \frac{dy}{dx} = -\frac{\partial F/\partial x}{\partial F/\partial y} = -\frac{y\, f(y/x) + xy\, f'(y/x)\, (-y/x^2)}{x\, f(y/x) + xy\, f'(y/x)\, (1/x)}$$

$$x\, [x\, f(y/x) + y\, f'(y/x)]\frac{dy}{dx} = -y\, [x\, f(y/x) - y\, f'(y/x)]$$

$$x\left[x\frac{dy}{dx} + y\right] f(y/x) = y\left(y - x\frac{dy}{dx}\right) \cdot f'(y/x)$$

$$\frac{f'(y/x)}{f(y/x)} = \frac{x\left(y + x\dfrac{dy}{dx}\right)}{y\left(y - x\dfrac{dy}{dx}\right)}$$

Ex. 6 : If $x^3 + y^3 = 3ax^2$, prove that $\dfrac{d^2y}{dx^2} + \dfrac{2a^2 x^2}{y^5} = 0$.

Sol. : Given : $f(x, y) = x^3 + y^3 - 3ax^2 = 0$ is an implicit relation. With usual notations, we use the formula,

$$\frac{d^2y}{dx^2} = -\left(\frac{q^2 r - 2pqs + p^2 t}{q^3}\right)$$

$$p = \frac{\partial f}{\partial x} = 3x^2 - 6ax, \quad q = \frac{\partial f}{\partial y} = 3y^2, \quad r = \frac{\partial^2 f}{\partial x^2} = 6x - 6a$$

$$s = \frac{\partial^2 f}{\partial x\, \partial y} = \frac{\partial}{\partial x}\left(\frac{\partial f}{\partial y}\right) = \frac{\partial}{\partial x}(3y^2) = 0, \quad t = \frac{\partial^2 f}{\partial y^2} = 6y$$

$$\therefore \quad \frac{d^2 y}{dx^2} = -\left(\frac{9y^4 \cdot 6(x-a) - 2(3x^2 - 6ax) \cdot 3y^2 \cdot (0) + [3(x^2 - 2ax)]^2 \cdot 6y}{27 \cdot y^6}\right)$$

$$= -\left(\frac{54 y^4 (x-a) + 54 y (x^4 - 4ax^3 + 4a^2 x^2)}{27 y^6}\right)$$

$$= -\frac{54 y}{27 y^6}\,[xy^3 - ay^3 + x^4 - 4ax^3 + 4a^2 x^2]$$

$$= \frac{-2}{y^5}\,[xy^3 + x^4 - ay^3 - ax^3 - 3ax^3 + 4a^2 x^2]$$

$$= \frac{-2}{y^5}\,[x(x^3 + y^3) - a(x^3 + y^3) - 3ax^3 + 4a^2 x^2]$$

$$= \frac{-2}{y^5}\,[(x-a)(3ax^2) - 3ax^3 + 4a^2 x^2]$$

$$= \frac{-2}{y^5}\,[3ax^3 - 3a^2 x^2 - 3ax^3 + 4a^2 x^2] = -\frac{2}{y^5}\,[a^2 x^2]$$

Ex. 7 : If $x^4 + y^4 = 4a^2 xy$, prove that $\dfrac{d^2 y}{dx^2} = \dfrac{2a^2 xy\,(3a^4 + x^2 y^2)}{(a^2 x - y^3)^3}$.

Sol. : Given : $f(x, y) = x^4 + y^4 - 4a^2 xy = 0$ is an implicit relation.

$$\therefore \quad \frac{d^2 y}{dx^2} = -\left(\frac{q^2 r - 2pqs + p^2 t}{q^3}\right)$$

$$p = 4x^3 - 4a^2 y; \quad q = 4y^3 - 4a^2 x; \quad r = 12x^2; \quad s = -4a^2; \quad t = 12y^2.$$

$$\frac{d^2 y}{dx^2} = -\,\frac{[4(y^3 - a^2 x)]^2 \cdot 12x^2 - 2 \cdot 4(x^3 - a^2 y)\,4(y^3 - a^2 x)(-4a^2) + [4(x^3 - a^2 y)]^2 \cdot 12 y^2}{64\,(y^3 - a^2 x)^3}$$

$$\frac{d^2 y}{dx^2} = -\,\frac{64\,\{(y^6 - 2a^2 xy^3 + a^4 x^2)\,3x^2 + 2a^2(x^3 y^3 - a^2 x^4 - a^2 y^4 + a^4 xy) + 3y^2(x^6 - 2a^2 yx^3 + a^4 y^2)\}}{-\,64\,(a^2 x - y^3)^3}$$

$$= \frac{3x^2 y^6 - 6a^2 x^3 y^3 + 3a^4 x^4 + 2a^2 x^3 y^3 - 2a^4 x^4 - 2a^4 y^4 + 2a^6 xy + 3y^2 x^6 - 6a^2 y^3 x^3 + 3a^4 y^4}{(a^2 x - y^3)^3}$$

$$= \frac{3x^2 y^2\,(y^4 + x^4) - 10 a^2 x^3 y^3 + a^4(x^4 + y^4) + 2a^6 xy}{(a^2 x - y^3)^3}$$

$$= \frac{12 x^3 y^3 a^2 - 10 a^2 x^3 y^3 + 4 a^6 xy + 2 a^6 xy}{(a^2 x - y^3)^3}$$

$$= \frac{2 a^2 x^3 y^3 + 6 a^6 xy}{(a^2 x - y^3)^3} = \frac{2 a^2 xy\,(3 a^4 + x^2 y^2)}{(a^2 x - y^3)^3}$$

EXERCISE 10.7

1. If $x^m + y^m = b^m$, show that $\dfrac{d^2y}{dx^2} = -(m-1) b^m \cdot \dfrac{x^{m-2}}{y^{2m-1}}$.

2. If the curves $f(x, y) = 0$ and $\phi(x, y) = 0$ touch, show that at their point of contact,
$$\dfrac{\partial f}{\partial x} \cdot \dfrac{\partial \phi}{\partial y} = \dfrac{\partial f}{\partial y} \cdot \dfrac{\partial \phi}{\partial x}.$$

3. Find $\dfrac{dy}{dx}$ and $\dfrac{d^2y}{dx^2}$ for $x^4 + y^4 = 5a^2 xy$.

4. Find $\dfrac{dy}{dx}$ in the following cases :
   (i) $x^y + y^x = a^b$ (ii) $(\tan x)^y + y^{\cot x} = a$
   (iii) $x^2 y^4 + \sin y = 0$ (iv) $\cos y = \dfrac{3 + 5 \cos x}{5 + 3 \cos x}$

   Ans. (i) $-\left(\dfrac{yx^{y-1} + y^x \log y}{xy^{x-1} + x^y \log x}\right)$ (ii) $-\left(\dfrac{y(\tan x)^{y-1} \sec^2 x - \cosec^2 x \log y \, y^{\cot x}}{\log \tan x \, (\tan x)^y + \cot x \, y^{\cot x - 1}}\right)$
   (iii) $-\left(\dfrac{2xy^4}{4x^2 y^3 + \cos y}\right)$ (iv) $\dfrac{4}{5 + 3 \cos x}$.

TYPE 2 : EXAMPLES ON FIRST ORDER PARTIAL DIFFERENTIAL COEFFICIENTS

Ex. 1 : If $z = f(x, y)$, where $x = e^u + e^{-v}$, $y = e^{-u} - e^v$, then prove that
$$\dfrac{\partial z}{\partial u} - \dfrac{\partial z}{\partial v} = x\dfrac{\partial z}{\partial x} - y\dfrac{\partial z}{\partial y}.$$

Sol. : Here $z \to x, y \to u, v$. Thus, z is a composite function of u and v.

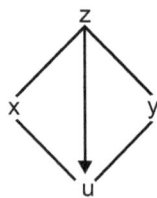
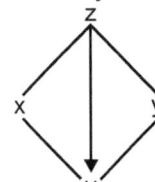

$$\dfrac{\partial z}{\partial u} = \dfrac{\partial z}{\partial x}\dfrac{\partial x}{\partial u} + \dfrac{\partial z}{\partial y}\dfrac{\partial y}{\partial u} = \dfrac{\partial z}{\partial x} e^u + \dfrac{\partial z}{\partial y}(-e^{-u})$$

$$\dfrac{\partial z}{\partial u} = e^u \dfrac{\partial z}{\partial x} - e^{-u}\dfrac{\partial z}{\partial y} \qquad \ldots (1)$$

Fig. 10.9

From second tree diagram,

$$\dfrac{\partial z}{\partial v} = \dfrac{\partial z}{\partial x}\dfrac{\partial x}{\partial v} + \dfrac{\partial z}{\partial y}\dfrac{\partial y}{\partial v} = \dfrac{\partial z}{\partial x}(-e^{-v}) + \dfrac{\partial z}{\partial y}(-e^v)$$

$$\dfrac{\partial z}{\partial v} = -e^{-v}\dfrac{\partial z}{\partial x} - e^v \dfrac{\partial z}{\partial y} \qquad \ldots (2)$$

On subtracting (2) from (1), we get

$$\dfrac{\partial z}{\partial u} - \dfrac{\partial z}{\partial v} = \dfrac{\partial z}{\partial x}(e^u + e^{-v}) - \dfrac{\partial z}{\partial y}(e^{-u} - e^v) = \dfrac{\partial z}{\partial x}(x) - \dfrac{\partial z}{\partial y}(y)$$

$\therefore \qquad \dfrac{\partial z}{\partial u} - \dfrac{\partial z}{\partial v} = x\dfrac{\partial z}{\partial x} - y\dfrac{\partial z}{\partial y}$

Ex. 2 : If $z = f(x, y)$ and u, v are homogeneous functions of degree n in x and y then show that $x\dfrac{\partial z}{\partial x} + y\dfrac{\partial z}{\partial y} = n\left(u\dfrac{\partial z}{\partial u} + v\dfrac{\partial z}{\partial v}\right)$.

Sol. : Given that u and v are homogeneous functions of degree n in x and y, therefore by Euler's theorem,

$$x\dfrac{\partial u}{\partial x} + y\dfrac{\partial u}{\partial y} = nu \qquad \ldots (1)$$

$$x\dfrac{\partial v}{\partial x} + y\dfrac{\partial v}{\partial y} = nv \qquad \ldots (2)$$

Treating z as a function of u and v where u and v are again functions of x and y, z becomes composite function of x and y i.e. $z \to u, v \to x, y$,

$$\dfrac{\partial z}{\partial x} = \dfrac{\partial z}{\partial u}\dfrac{\partial u}{\partial x} + \dfrac{\partial z}{\partial v}\dfrac{\partial v}{\partial x} \qquad \ldots (3)$$

$$\dfrac{\partial z}{\partial y} = \dfrac{\partial z}{\partial u}\dfrac{\partial u}{\partial y} + \dfrac{\partial z}{\partial v}\dfrac{\partial v}{\partial y} \qquad \ldots (4)$$

Multiplying (3) by x, (4) by y and adding,

$$x\dfrac{\partial z}{\partial x} + y\dfrac{\partial z}{\partial y} = \dfrac{\partial z}{\partial u}\left(x\dfrac{\partial u}{\partial x} + y\dfrac{\partial u}{\partial y}\right) + \dfrac{\partial z}{\partial v}\left(x\dfrac{\partial v}{\partial x} + y\dfrac{\partial v}{\partial y}\right)$$

$$= \dfrac{\partial z}{\partial u}(nu) + \dfrac{\partial z}{\partial v}(nv) \qquad \text{(Using (1) and (2))}$$

$$= n\left(u\dfrac{\partial z}{\partial u} + v\dfrac{\partial z}{\partial v}\right)$$

Ex. 3 : If $z = f(x, y)$ where $x = r\cos\theta, y = r\sin\theta$ then show that

$$\left(\dfrac{\partial z}{\partial x}\right)^2 + \left(\dfrac{\partial z}{\partial y}\right)^2 = \left(\dfrac{\partial z}{\partial r}\right)^2 + \dfrac{1}{r^2}\left(\dfrac{\partial z}{\partial \theta}\right)^2$$

Sol. : Here z is a function of x and y where x and y are again functions of r and θ. Thus, z becomes composite function of r and θ. i.e. $z \to xy \to r, \theta$

$$\dfrac{\partial z}{\partial r} = \dfrac{\partial z}{\partial x}\dfrac{\partial x}{\partial r} + \dfrac{\partial z}{\partial y}\dfrac{\partial y}{\partial r}$$

Given $\quad x = r\cos\theta \cdot \dfrac{\partial x}{\partial r} = \cos\theta \text{ and } \dfrac{\partial x}{\partial \theta} = -r\sin\theta$

and $\quad y = r\sin\theta \cdot \dfrac{\partial y}{\partial r} = \sin\theta \text{ and } \dfrac{\partial y}{\partial \theta} = r\cos\theta$

$\therefore \quad \dfrac{\partial z}{\partial r} = \dfrac{\partial z}{\partial x}(\cos\theta) + \dfrac{\partial z}{\partial y}(\sin\theta)$

$$\left(\dfrac{\partial z}{\partial r}\right)^2 = \cos^2\theta\left(\dfrac{\partial z}{\partial x}\right)^2 + 2\sin\theta\cos\theta\,\dfrac{\partial z}{\partial x}\cdot\dfrac{\partial z}{\partial y} + \sin^2\theta\left(\dfrac{\partial z}{\partial y}\right)^2 \quad \ldots (1)$$

$$\left[\text{Note}: \left(\dfrac{\partial z}{\partial x}\right)^2 \neq \dfrac{\partial^2 z}{\partial x^2}, \dfrac{\partial z}{\partial x}\cdot\dfrac{\partial z}{\partial y} \neq \dfrac{\partial^2 z}{\partial x\,\partial y} \text{ and } \left(\dfrac{\partial z}{\partial y}\right)^2 \neq \dfrac{\partial^2 z}{\partial y^2}\right]$$

Also
$$\frac{\partial z}{\partial \theta} = \frac{\partial z}{\partial x}\frac{\partial x}{\partial \theta} + \frac{\partial z}{\partial y}\frac{\partial y}{\partial \theta}$$

$\therefore \quad \dfrac{\partial z}{\partial \theta} = \dfrac{\partial z}{\partial x}(-r\sin\theta) + \dfrac{\partial z}{\partial y}(r\cos\theta)$

$$\left(\frac{\partial z}{\partial \theta}\right)^2 = r^2\sin^2\theta\left(\frac{\partial z}{\partial x}\right)^2 - 2r^2\sin\theta\cos\theta\,\frac{\partial z}{\partial x}\frac{\partial z}{\partial y} + r^2\cos^2\theta\left(\frac{\partial z}{\partial y}\right)^2$$

$$\frac{1}{r^2}\left(\frac{\partial z}{\partial \theta}\right)^2 = \sin^2\theta\left(\frac{\partial z}{\partial x}\right)^2 - 2\sin\theta\cos\theta\,\frac{\partial z}{\partial x}\cdot\frac{\partial z}{\partial y} + \cos^2\theta\left(\frac{\partial z}{\partial y}\right)^2 \quad \ldots (2)$$

By adding equations (1) and (2),

$$\left(\frac{\partial z}{\partial r}\right)^2 + \frac{1}{r^2}\left(\frac{\partial z}{\partial \theta}\right)^2 = (\cos^2\theta + \sin^2\theta)\left(\frac{\partial z}{\partial x}\right)^2 + (\sin^2\theta + \cos^2\theta)\left(\frac{\partial z}{\partial y}\right)^2$$

$$= \left(\frac{\partial z}{\partial x}\right)^2 + \left(\frac{\partial z}{\partial y}\right)^2$$

$\therefore \quad \left(\dfrac{\partial z}{\partial x}\right)^2 + \left(\dfrac{\partial z}{\partial y}\right)^2 = \left(\dfrac{\partial z}{\partial r}\right)^2 + \dfrac{1}{r^2}\left(\dfrac{\partial z}{\partial \theta}\right)^2$

Ex. 4 : If $u = x^2 + y^2$ where $x = s + 3t$, $y = 2s - t$, prove that $\dfrac{\partial^2 u}{\partial t^2} = 2\,\dfrac{\partial^2 u}{\partial s^2}$.

Sol. : Here u is a composite function of s, t.

$$\frac{\partial u}{\partial s} = \frac{\partial u}{\partial x}\frac{\partial x}{\partial s} + \frac{\partial u}{\partial y}\frac{\partial y}{\partial s}$$
$$= (2x)(1) + (2y)(2) = 2x + 4y$$

$$\frac{\partial^2 u}{\partial s^2} = \frac{\partial}{\partial s}(2x + 4y) = \frac{\partial}{\partial x}(2x)\cdot\frac{\partial x}{\partial s} + \frac{\partial}{\partial y}(4y)\frac{\partial y}{\partial s}$$
$$= (2)(1) + (4)(2) = 10 \quad \ldots (1)$$

$$\frac{\partial u}{\partial t} = \frac{\partial u}{\partial x}\frac{\partial x}{\partial t} + \frac{\partial u}{\partial y}\frac{\partial y}{\partial t}$$
$$= (2x)(3) + (2y)(-1) = 6x - 2y$$

$$\frac{\partial^2 u}{\partial t^2} = \frac{\partial}{\partial t}(6x - 2y) = \frac{\partial}{\partial x}(6x)\frac{\partial x}{\partial t} - \frac{\partial}{\partial y}(2y)\frac{\partial y}{\partial t}$$
$$= (6)(3) - (2)(-1) = 20 \quad \ldots (2)$$

From equations (1) and (2),

$$\frac{\partial^2 u}{\partial t^2} = 2\cdot\frac{\partial^2 u}{\partial s^2}$$

Ex. 5 : If $x = r\cos\theta$, $y = r\sin\theta$ where r and θ are functions of t, prove that

$$x\frac{dy}{dt} - y\frac{dx}{dt} = r^2\frac{d\theta}{dt} \quad \text{(Dec. 2012)}$$

Sol. : Here x and y are composite functions of t.

$\therefore \quad \dfrac{dx}{dt} = \dfrac{\partial x}{\partial r}\cdot\dfrac{dr}{dt} + \dfrac{\partial x}{\partial \theta}\cdot\dfrac{d\theta}{dt} = \cos\theta\,\dfrac{dr}{dt} - r\sin\theta\,\dfrac{d\theta}{dt}$

Also $\dfrac{dy}{dt} = \dfrac{\partial y}{\partial r} \cdot \dfrac{dr}{dt} + \dfrac{\partial y}{\partial \theta} \cdot \dfrac{d\theta}{dt} = \sin\theta \dfrac{dr}{dt} + r\cos\theta \dfrac{d\theta}{dt}$

$\therefore \quad x\dfrac{dy}{dt} - y\dfrac{dx}{dt} = r\cos\theta \left(\sin\theta \dfrac{dr}{dt} + r\cos\theta \dfrac{d\theta}{dt}\right)$

$\qquad\qquad\qquad - r\sin\theta \left(\cos\theta \dfrac{dr}{dt} - r\sin\theta \dfrac{d\theta}{dt}\right)$

$\qquad\qquad\qquad = r^2(\cos^2\theta + \sin^2\theta)\dfrac{d\theta}{dt} = r^2 \dfrac{d\theta}{dt}$

Ex. 6 : If $x = \sqrt{vw}$, $y = \sqrt{uw}$, $z = \sqrt{uv}$ and ϕ is a function of x, y, z then

$x\dfrac{\partial \phi}{\partial x} + y\dfrac{\partial \phi}{\partial y} + z\dfrac{\partial \phi}{\partial z} = u\dfrac{\partial \phi}{\partial u} + v\dfrac{\partial \phi}{\partial v} + w\dfrac{\partial \phi}{\partial w}$

Sol. : Here $\phi \to x, y, z \to u, v, w$, then we have

$\dfrac{\partial \phi}{\partial u} = \dfrac{\partial \phi}{\partial x} \cdot \dfrac{\partial x}{\partial u} + \dfrac{\partial \phi}{\partial y} \cdot \dfrac{\partial y}{\partial u} + \dfrac{\partial \phi}{\partial z} \cdot \dfrac{\partial z}{\partial u}$

$\qquad = \dfrac{\partial \phi}{\partial x} \cdot 0 + \dfrac{\partial \phi}{\partial y}\left(\dfrac{1}{2}u^{-1/2}w^{1/2}\right) + \dfrac{\partial \phi}{\partial z}\left(\dfrac{1}{2}u^{-1/2}v^{1/2}\right)$

$\therefore \quad u\dfrac{\partial \theta}{\partial u} = \dfrac{1}{2}u^{1/2}w^{1/2}\dfrac{\partial \phi}{\partial y} + \dfrac{1}{2}u^{1/2}v^{1/2}\dfrac{\partial \phi}{\partial z}$

$\qquad\qquad = \dfrac{1}{2}\left(y\dfrac{\partial \phi}{\partial y} + z\dfrac{\partial \phi}{\partial z}\right) \qquad\qquad\qquad \ldots (1)$

$\dfrac{\partial \phi}{\partial v} = \dfrac{\partial \phi}{\partial x} \cdot \dfrac{\partial x}{\partial v} + \dfrac{\partial \phi}{\partial y} \cdot \dfrac{\partial y}{\partial v} + \dfrac{\partial \phi}{\partial z} \cdot \dfrac{\partial z}{\partial v}$

$\qquad = \dfrac{\partial \phi}{\partial x}\left(\dfrac{1}{2}v^{-1/2}w^{1/2}\right) + \dfrac{\partial \phi}{\partial y}(0) + \dfrac{\partial \phi}{\partial z}\left(\dfrac{1}{2}u^{1/2}v^{-1/2}\right)$

$\therefore \quad v\dfrac{\partial \phi}{\partial v} = \dfrac{1}{2}v^{1/2}w^{1/2}\dfrac{\partial \phi}{\partial x} + \dfrac{1}{2}u^{1/2}v^{1/2}\dfrac{\partial \phi}{\partial z}$

$\qquad\qquad = \dfrac{1}{2}\left(x\dfrac{\partial \phi}{\partial x} + z\dfrac{\partial \phi}{\partial z}\right) \qquad\qquad\qquad \ldots (2)$

and $\dfrac{\partial \phi}{\partial w} = \dfrac{\partial \phi}{\partial x} \cdot \dfrac{\partial x}{\partial w} + \dfrac{\partial \phi}{\partial y} \cdot \dfrac{\partial y}{\partial w} + \dfrac{\partial \phi}{\partial z} \cdot \dfrac{\partial z}{\partial w}$

$\qquad = \dfrac{\partial \phi}{\partial x}\left(\dfrac{1}{2}w^{-1/2}v^{1/2}\right) + \dfrac{\partial \phi}{\partial y}\left(\dfrac{1}{2}u^{1/2}w^{-1/2}\right) + \dfrac{\partial \phi}{\partial z}(0)$

$\therefore \quad w\dfrac{\partial \phi}{\partial w} = \dfrac{1}{2}w^{1/2}v^{1/2} \cdot \dfrac{\partial \phi}{\partial x} + \dfrac{1}{2}u^{1/2}w^{1/2}\dfrac{\partial \phi}{\partial y}$

$\qquad\qquad = \dfrac{1}{2}x\dfrac{\partial \phi}{\partial x} + \dfrac{1}{2}y\dfrac{\partial \phi}{\partial y} \qquad\qquad\qquad \ldots (3)$

Adding (1), (2) and (3), we get

$u\dfrac{\partial \phi}{\partial u} + v\dfrac{\partial \phi}{\partial v} + w\dfrac{\partial \phi}{\partial w} = x\dfrac{\partial \phi}{\partial x} + y\dfrac{\partial \phi}{\partial y} + z\dfrac{\partial \phi}{\partial z}$

Ex. 7 : If $z = f(u, v)$ where $u = x^2 - 2xy - y^2$ and $v = y$, show that

$$(x+y)\frac{\partial z}{\partial x} + (x-y)\frac{\partial z}{\partial y} = (x-y)\frac{\partial z}{\partial v}. \qquad \text{(May 2011)}$$

Also prove that the equation $(x+y)\frac{\partial z}{\partial x} + (x-y)\frac{\partial z}{\partial y} = 0$ is equivalent to $\frac{\partial z}{\partial v} = 0$.

Hence show that $z = \phi(x^2 - y^2 - 2xy)$ where ϕ denotes an arbitrary function.

Sol. : $z \to u, v \to x, y \Rightarrow z$ is a composite function of x and y.

$$\frac{\partial z}{\partial x} = \frac{\partial z}{\partial u}\frac{\partial u}{\partial x} + \frac{\partial z}{\partial v}\frac{\partial v}{\partial x} = \frac{\partial z}{\partial u}(2x-2y) + \frac{\partial z}{\partial v}(0)$$

$$\frac{\partial z}{\partial x} = 2(x-y)\frac{\partial z}{\partial u}$$

$$(x+y)\frac{\partial z}{\partial x} = 2(x-y)(x+y)\frac{\partial z}{\partial u} = 2(x^2-y^2)\frac{\partial z}{\partial u} \qquad \ldots (1)$$

$$\frac{\partial z}{\partial y} = \frac{\partial z}{\partial u}\frac{\partial u}{\partial y} + \frac{\partial z}{\partial v}\frac{\partial v}{\partial y}$$

$$= \frac{\partial z}{\partial u}(-2x-2y) + \frac{\partial z}{\partial v}$$

$$(x-y)\frac{\partial z}{\partial y} = -2(x+y)(x-y)\frac{\partial z}{\partial u} + (x-y)\frac{\partial z}{\partial v} \qquad \ldots (2)$$

By adding (1) and (2), we obtain

$$(x+y)\frac{\partial z}{\partial x} + (x-y)\frac{\partial z}{\partial y} = (x-y)\frac{\partial z}{\partial v}$$

If $(x+y)\frac{\partial z}{\partial x} + (x-y)\frac{\partial z}{\partial y} = 0$ then $(x-y)\frac{\partial z}{\partial v} = 0 \Rightarrow \frac{\partial z}{\partial v} = 0 \qquad (\because x-y \neq 0)$

Again since $\frac{\partial z}{\partial v} = 0$, it follows that z can only be a function of u, say $\phi(u)$.

Hence $z = \phi(u) = \phi(x^2 - 2xy - y^2)$.

Ex. 8 : If u is a homogeneous function of x, y, z of degree n and $X = \frac{\partial u}{\partial x}$, $Y = \frac{\partial u}{\partial y}$, $Z = \frac{\partial u}{\partial z}$ and if $u = f(X, Y, Z)$, prove that $X\frac{\partial f}{\partial X} + Y\frac{\partial f}{\partial Y} + Z\frac{\partial f}{\partial Z} = \left(\frac{n}{n-1}\right)u$.

(May 2005, Dec. 2008)

Sol. : Since u is a homogeneous function of x, y, z of degree n, by Euler's theorem,

$$x\frac{\partial u}{\partial x} + y\frac{\partial u}{\partial y} + z\frac{\partial u}{\partial z} = nu \qquad \ldots (1)$$

$\frac{\partial u}{\partial x}, \frac{\partial u}{\partial y}, \frac{\partial u}{\partial z}$ are again a function of x, y, z. But given that $X = \frac{\partial u}{\partial x}$, $Y = \frac{\partial u}{\partial y}$, $Z = \frac{\partial u}{\partial z}$, therefore X, Y, Z are functions of x, y, z.

Also u = f(X, Y, Z) where X Y Z are functions of x, y, z i.e.

u → X Y Z → x, y, z ∴ u becomes composite function of x, y, z

$$\frac{\partial u}{\partial x} = \frac{\partial u}{\partial X}\frac{\partial X}{\partial x} + \frac{\partial u}{\partial Y}\frac{\partial Y}{\partial x} + \frac{\partial u}{\partial Z}\frac{\partial Z}{\partial x} \qquad \ldots (2)$$

$$\frac{\partial u}{\partial y} = \frac{\partial u}{\partial X}\frac{\partial X}{\partial y} + \frac{\partial u}{\partial Y}\frac{\partial Y}{\partial y} + \frac{\partial u}{\partial Z}\frac{\partial Z}{\partial y} \qquad \ldots (3)$$

$$\frac{\partial u}{\partial z} = \frac{\partial u}{\partial X}\frac{\partial X}{\partial z} + \frac{\partial u}{\partial Y}\frac{\partial Y}{\partial z} + \frac{\partial u}{\partial Z}\frac{\partial Z}{\partial z} \qquad \ldots (4)$$

equation (2) × x + equation (3) × y + equation (4) × z ⇒

$$x\frac{\partial u}{\partial x} + y\frac{\partial u}{\partial y} + z\frac{\partial u}{\partial z} = \frac{\partial u}{\partial X}\left[x\frac{\partial X}{\partial x} + y\frac{\partial X}{\partial y} + z\frac{\partial X}{\partial z}\right] + \frac{\partial u}{\partial Y}\left[x\frac{\partial Y}{\partial x} + y\frac{\partial Y}{\partial y} + z\frac{\partial Y}{\partial z}\right]$$

$$+ \frac{\partial u}{\partial Z}\left[x\frac{\partial Z}{\partial x} + y\frac{\partial Z}{\partial y} + z\frac{\partial Z}{\partial z}\right] \qquad \ldots (5)$$

Important Point : If u is homogeneous function of degree n in x, y, z and $X = \frac{\partial u}{\partial x}$, $Y = \frac{\partial u}{\partial y}$, $Z = \frac{\partial u}{\partial z}$ being first order differential coefficients of homogeneous function u of degree n, then X, Y, Z are homogeneous functions of degree (n – 1) in x, y, z.

$X = \frac{\partial u}{\partial x}$ is homogeneous function of degree (n – 1) in x, y, z by Euler's theorem,

$$x\frac{\partial X}{\partial x} + y\frac{\partial X}{\partial y} + z\frac{\partial X}{\partial z} = (n-1)\ X \qquad \ldots (6)$$

$Y = \frac{\partial u}{\partial y}$ is homogeneous function of degree (n – 1) in x, y, z by Euler's theorem,

$$x\frac{\partial Y}{\partial x} + y\frac{\partial Y}{\partial y} + z\frac{\partial Y}{\partial z} = (n-1)\ Y \qquad \ldots (7)$$

$Z = \frac{\partial u}{\partial z}$ is homogeneous function of degree (n – 1) in x, y, z by Euler's theorem,

$$x\frac{\partial Z}{\partial x} + y\frac{\partial Z}{\partial y} + z\frac{\partial Z}{\partial z} = (n-1)\ Z \qquad \ldots (8)$$

Substituting results (6), (7), and (8) in equation (5) and using equation (1),

$$nu = \frac{\partial u}{\partial X}[(n-1)X] + \frac{\partial u}{\partial Y}[(n-1)Y] + \frac{\partial u}{\partial Z}[(n-1)Z]$$

$$\left(\frac{n}{n-1}\right)u = X\frac{\partial u}{\partial X} + y\frac{\partial u}{\partial Y} + Z\frac{\partial u}{\partial Z}$$

EXERCISE 10.8

1. If $x = \frac{\cos\theta}{u}$, $y = \frac{\sin\theta}{u}$ then show that $u\frac{\partial z}{\partial u} - \frac{\partial z}{\partial \theta} = (y-x)\frac{\partial z}{\partial x} - (y+x)\frac{\partial z}{\partial y}$.
   [Hint : Here $Z = f(x, y)$, $z \to xy \to u, \theta$] (Dec. 2014)

2. If u is a homogeneous function of x, y of degree p and $X = \frac{\partial u}{\partial x}$, $Y = \frac{\partial u}{\partial y}$ and if $u = f(X, Y)$ prove that $X\frac{\partial u}{\partial X} + Y\frac{\partial u}{\partial Y} = \left(\frac{p}{p-1}\right)u$.

3. If $u = x^2 - y^2$, $v = 2xy$ and $z = f(u, v)$ then show that (May 2010, Dec. 2012)
   $x\frac{\partial z}{\partial x} - y\frac{\partial z}{\partial y} = 2\sqrt{u^2+v^2}\frac{\partial z}{\partial u}$.

4. If $u = f(r, s)$ where $r = x^2 + y^2$, $s = x^2 - y^2$ then show that
   (i) $y\frac{\partial u}{\partial x} + x\frac{\partial u}{\partial y} = 4xy\frac{\partial u}{\partial r}$.
   (ii) $\left(\frac{\partial u}{\partial x}\right)^2 + \left(\frac{\partial u}{\partial y}\right)^2 = 4r\left[\left(\frac{\partial u}{\partial r}\right)^2 + \left(\frac{\partial u}{\partial s}\right)^2\right] + 8s\frac{\partial u}{\partial r}\frac{\partial u}{\partial s}$.

5. If u is a homogeneous function of degree 4 in x, y, z and $u = f(X, Y, Z)$ where X, Y, Z are the first differential coefficients of u w.r.t. x, y, z respectively, prove that $3\left[X\frac{\partial f}{\partial X} + Y\frac{\partial f}{\partial Y} + Z\frac{\partial f}{\partial Z}\right] = 4u$.

6. Given Z is a function of x, y where $x = u + v$, $y = uv$, prove that
   (i) $(u-v)\frac{\partial z}{\partial x} = u\frac{\partial z}{\partial u} - v\frac{\partial z}{\partial v}$
   (ii) $(u-v)\frac{\partial z}{\partial y} = \frac{\partial z}{\partial v} - \frac{\partial z}{\partial u}$.
   (iii) $u\frac{\partial z}{\partial u} + v\frac{\partial z}{\partial v} = x\frac{\partial z}{\partial x} + 2y\frac{\partial z}{\partial y}$.

7. If $x = u + v + w$, $y = uv + vw + wu$, $z = uvw$ and F is a function of x, y, z show that
   $u\frac{\partial F}{\partial u} + v\frac{\partial F}{\partial v} + w \cdot \frac{\partial F}{\partial w} = x \cdot \frac{\partial F}{\partial x} + 2y\frac{\partial F}{\partial y} + 3z\frac{\partial F}{\partial Z}$. (May 2014, Dec. 2014)

8. If $z = f(u, v)$ and $u = x\cos\theta - y\sin\theta$, $v = x\sin\theta + y\cos\theta$, show that :
   $x\frac{\partial z}{\partial x} + y\frac{\partial z}{\partial y} = u\frac{\partial z}{\partial u} + v\frac{\partial z}{\partial v}$. (Jan. 2005, May 2015)

TYPE 3 : EXAMPLES INVOLVING SUBSTITUTION

Ex. 1 : If $u = f(x-y, y-z, z-x)$ then prove that $\dfrac{\partial u}{\partial x} + \dfrac{\partial u}{\partial y} + \dfrac{\partial u}{\partial z} = 0.$ (Dec. 2009)

Sol. : Given : $u = f(x-y, y-z, z-x)$

Put $l = x-y,\ m = y-z,\ n = z-x$ then $u = f(l, m, n)$

$\therefore\ u \to l, m, n \to x, y, z \Rightarrow u$ is composite function of x, y, z

$$\frac{\partial u}{\partial x} = \frac{\partial u}{\partial l}\frac{\partial l}{\partial x} + \frac{\partial u}{\partial m}\frac{\partial m}{\partial x} + \frac{\partial u}{\partial n}\frac{\partial n}{\partial x}$$

$$= \frac{\partial u}{\partial l}(1) + \frac{\partial u}{\partial m}(0) + \frac{\partial u}{\partial n}(-1)$$

$$\frac{\partial u}{\partial x} = \frac{\partial u}{\partial l} - \frac{\partial u}{\partial n} \qquad \ldots (1)$$

$$\frac{\partial u}{\partial y} = \frac{\partial u}{\partial l}\frac{\partial l}{\partial y} + \frac{\partial u}{\partial m}\frac{\partial m}{\partial y} + \frac{\partial u}{\partial n}\frac{\partial n}{\partial y}$$

$$= \frac{\partial u}{\partial l}(-1) + \frac{\partial u}{\partial m}(1) + \frac{\partial u}{\partial n}(0)$$

$$\frac{\partial u}{\partial y} = -\frac{\partial u}{\partial l} + \frac{\partial u}{\partial m} \qquad \ldots (2)$$

$$\frac{\partial u}{\partial z} = \frac{\partial u}{\partial l}\frac{\partial l}{\partial z} + \frac{\partial u}{\partial m}\frac{\partial m}{\partial z} + \frac{\partial u}{\partial n}\frac{\partial n}{\partial z}$$

$$= \frac{\partial u}{\partial l}(0) + \frac{\partial u}{\partial m}(-1) + \frac{\partial u}{\partial n}(1)$$

$$\frac{\partial u}{\partial z} = -\frac{\partial u}{\partial m} + \frac{\partial u}{\partial n} \qquad \ldots (3)$$

On adding (1), (2) and (3),

$$\frac{\partial u}{\partial x} + \frac{\partial u}{\partial y} + \frac{\partial u}{\partial z} = \frac{\partial u}{\partial l} - \frac{\partial u}{\partial n} - \frac{\partial u}{\partial l} + \frac{\partial u}{\partial m} - \frac{\partial u}{\partial m} + \frac{\partial u}{\partial n} = 0$$

Ex. 2 : If $z = e^{ax+by} f(ax-by)$, prove that $b\dfrac{\partial z}{\partial x} + a\dfrac{\partial z}{\partial y} = 2abz.$

Sol. : Let $u = ax + by$ and $v = ax - by$ then $z = e^u f(v)$

Hence z is a function of u and v and u, v are functions of x and y. Hence z is a composite function of x and y.

Now $\dfrac{\partial u}{\partial x} = a,\ \dfrac{\partial u}{\partial y} = b,\ \dfrac{\partial v}{\partial x} = a,\ \dfrac{\partial v}{\partial y} = -b.$

Hence
$$\frac{\partial z}{\partial x} = \frac{\partial z}{\partial u}\cdot\frac{\partial u}{\partial x} + \frac{\partial z}{\partial v}\frac{\partial v}{\partial x} = a\frac{\partial z}{\partial u} + a\frac{\partial z}{\partial v} = a\left(\frac{\partial z}{\partial u} + \frac{\partial z}{\partial v}\right)$$

$\therefore\qquad b\dfrac{\partial z}{\partial x} = ab\left(\dfrac{\partial z}{\partial u} + \dfrac{\partial z}{\partial v}\right) \qquad \ldots (1)$

Similarly, $\dfrac{\partial z}{\partial y} = \dfrac{\partial z}{\partial u}\dfrac{\partial u}{\partial y} + \dfrac{\partial z}{\partial v}\dfrac{\partial v}{\partial y} = b\dfrac{\partial z}{\partial u} - b\dfrac{\partial z}{\partial v} = b\left(\dfrac{\partial z}{\partial u} - \dfrac{\partial z}{\partial v}\right)$

$\therefore \quad a\dfrac{\partial z}{\partial y} = ab\left(\dfrac{\partial z}{\partial u} - \dfrac{\partial z}{\partial v}\right)$ ... (2)

Adding equations (1) and (2), we get

$$b\dfrac{\partial z}{\partial x} + a\dfrac{\partial z}{\partial y} = ab\left[\dfrac{\partial z}{\partial u} + \dfrac{\partial z}{\partial v} + \dfrac{\partial z}{\partial u} - \dfrac{\partial z}{\partial v}\right] = 2ab\dfrac{\partial z}{\partial u} = 2ab\,e^u f(v) = 2ab\,z$$

Hence $\quad b\dfrac{\partial z}{\partial x} + a\dfrac{\partial z}{\partial y} = 2ab\,z$

Ex. 3 : If $u = f(x^2 - y^2, y^2 - z^2, z^2 - x^2)$, prove that $\dfrac{1}{x}\dfrac{\partial u}{\partial x} + \dfrac{1}{y}\dfrac{\partial u}{\partial y} + \dfrac{1}{z}\dfrac{\partial u}{\partial z} = 0$. **(May 2010)**

Sol. : Let $x^2 - y^2 = l$, $y^2 - z^2 = m$, $z^2 - x^2 = n$. Then $u = f(l, m, n)$ where l, m, n themselves are functions of x, y, z. $\Rightarrow u$ be a composite function of x, y, z.

Thus $\quad \dfrac{\partial u}{\partial x} = \dfrac{\partial u}{\partial l}\cdot\dfrac{\partial l}{\partial x} + \dfrac{\partial u}{\partial m}\cdot\dfrac{\partial m}{\partial x} + \dfrac{\partial u}{\partial n}\cdot\dfrac{\partial n}{\partial x}$

$\qquad = \dfrac{\partial u}{\partial l}(2x) + \dfrac{\partial u}{\partial m}(0) + \dfrac{\partial u}{\partial n}(-2x)$ ... (1)

$\dfrac{\partial u}{\partial y} = \dfrac{\partial u}{\partial l}\cdot\dfrac{\partial l}{\partial y} + \dfrac{\partial u}{\partial m}\cdot\dfrac{\partial m}{\partial y} + \dfrac{\partial u}{\partial n}\cdot\dfrac{\partial n}{\partial y}$

$\qquad = \dfrac{\partial u}{\partial l}(-2y) + \dfrac{\partial u}{\partial m}(2y) + \dfrac{\partial u}{\partial n}(0)$ ... (2)

$\dfrac{\partial u}{\partial z} = \dfrac{\partial u}{\partial l}\cdot\dfrac{\partial l}{\partial z} + \dfrac{\partial u}{\partial m}\cdot\dfrac{\partial m}{\partial z} + \dfrac{\partial u}{\partial n}\cdot\dfrac{\partial n}{\partial z}$

$\qquad = \dfrac{\partial u}{\partial l}(0) + \dfrac{\partial u}{\partial m}(-2z) + \dfrac{\partial u}{\partial n}(2z)$ ... (3)

Multiplying (1) by $\dfrac{1}{x}$, (2) by $\dfrac{1}{y}$, (3) by $\dfrac{1}{z}$, and then adding, we have

$$\dfrac{1}{x}\dfrac{\partial u}{\partial x} + \dfrac{1}{y}\dfrac{\partial u}{\partial y} + \dfrac{1}{z}\dfrac{\partial u}{\partial z} = \dfrac{2\partial u}{\partial l} - \dfrac{2\partial u}{\partial n} - \dfrac{2\partial u}{\partial l} + \dfrac{2\partial u}{\partial m} - \dfrac{2\partial u}{\partial m} + \dfrac{2\partial u}{\partial n} = 0$$

Ex. 4 : If $f(lx + my + nz, x^2 + y^2 + z^2) = 0$ prove that

$$(mz - ny) + (lz - nx)\dfrac{\partial x}{\partial y} + (mx - ly)\dfrac{\partial x}{\partial z} = 0$$

Sol. : Given : $f(lx + my + nz, x^2 + y^2 + z^2) = 0$,

Let $u = lx + my + nz$ and $v = x^2 + y^2 + z^2$, then

$\qquad f(u, v) = 0$ ... (1)

Since (1) is implicit relation between u, v, i.e. between x, y, z, indicates that one of the three variables x, y, z can be expressed as a function of remaining two variables which are independent.

The result to be proved indicates that x is a function of y, z i.e. $f \to u, v \to y, z$.

$$\frac{\partial f}{\partial y} = \frac{\partial f}{\partial u}\frac{\partial u}{\partial y} + \frac{\partial f}{\partial v}\frac{\partial v}{\partial y} = 0 \qquad \ldots (2)$$

$$\frac{\partial f}{\partial z} = \frac{\partial f}{\partial u}\frac{\partial u}{\partial z} + \frac{\partial f}{\partial v}\frac{\partial v}{\partial z} = 0 \qquad \ldots (3)$$

From (2), $\quad \dfrac{\partial f/\partial u}{\partial f/\partial v} = \dfrac{-\partial v/\partial y}{\partial u/\partial y}$

From (3), $\quad \dfrac{\partial f/\partial u}{\partial f/\partial v} = -\dfrac{\partial v/\partial z}{\partial u/\partial z}$

$\therefore \quad \dfrac{\partial v/\partial y}{\partial u/\partial y} = \dfrac{\partial v/\partial z}{\partial u/\partial z}$

$$\frac{\partial u}{\partial z}\frac{\partial v}{\partial y} = \frac{\partial u}{\partial y}\frac{\partial v}{\partial z} \qquad \ldots (4)$$

Next $\quad u = lx + my + nz$

Differentiating partially w.r.t. y and noting that x is a function of y, z we have

$$\frac{\partial u}{\partial y} = l\frac{\partial x}{\partial y} + m \qquad \text{(z is constant)}$$

Differentiating partially w.r.t. z keeping y constant,

$$\frac{\partial u}{\partial z} = l\frac{\partial x}{\partial z} + n$$

and $\quad v = x^2 + y^2 + z^2$

$$\frac{\partial v}{\partial y} = 2x\frac{\partial x}{\partial y} + 2y$$

$$\frac{\partial v}{\partial z} = 2x\frac{\partial x}{\partial z} + 2z$$

Substituting in equation (4),

$$\left(l\frac{\partial x}{\partial z} + n\right)\left(2x\frac{\partial x}{\partial y} + 2y\right) = \left(l\frac{\partial x}{\partial y} + m\right)\left(2x\frac{\partial x}{\partial z} + 2z\right)$$

$$lx\frac{\partial x}{\partial z}\frac{\partial x}{\partial y} + ly\frac{\partial x}{\partial z} + nx\frac{\partial x}{\partial y} + ny = lx\frac{\partial x}{\partial y}\frac{\partial x}{\partial z} + lz\frac{\partial x}{\partial y} + mx\frac{\partial x}{\partial z} + mz$$

$$(mz - ny) + (lz - nx)\frac{\partial x}{\partial y} + (mx - ly)\frac{\partial x}{\partial z} = 0.$$

TYPE 4 : EXAMPLES ON TOTAL DERIVATIVE

Ex. 5 : If $u = \sin \dfrac{x}{y}$ and $x = e^t, y = t^2$, verify $\dfrac{du}{dt} = \dfrac{\partial u}{\partial x} \cdot \dfrac{dx}{dt} + \dfrac{\partial u}{\partial y} \cdot \dfrac{dy}{dt}$.

Sol. : By actual substitution, we have $u = \sin \dfrac{e^t}{t^2}$.

$$\therefore \quad \dfrac{du}{dt} = \left(\cos \dfrac{e^t}{t^2}\right) \cdot \dfrac{t^2 e^t - 2te^t}{t^4} = \left(\cos \dfrac{e^t}{t^2}\right) \cdot \left(\dfrac{1}{t^2} - \dfrac{2}{t^3}\right) e^t \quad \ldots (1)$$

Here $u \to xy \to t \Rightarrow u$ is a composite function of t i.e.

$$\dfrac{du}{dt} = \dfrac{\partial u}{\partial x} \cdot \dfrac{dx}{dt} + \dfrac{\partial u}{\partial y} \cdot \dfrac{dy}{dt}$$

$$= \left(\cos \dfrac{x}{y}\right) \cdot \dfrac{1}{y} \cdot e^t + \left(\cos \dfrac{x}{y}\right) \cdot \dfrac{-x}{y^2} \cdot 2t$$

$$= \left(\cos \dfrac{x}{y}\right) \left[\dfrac{1}{y} e^t - \dfrac{2x}{y^2} t\right]$$

$$= \left(\cos \dfrac{e^t}{t^2}\right) \left[\dfrac{1}{t^2} e^t - \dfrac{2e^t}{t^4} \cdot t\right]$$

$$= \left(\cos \dfrac{e^t}{t^2}\right) \cdot \left(\dfrac{1}{t^2} - \dfrac{2}{t^3}\right) \cdot e^t \quad \ldots (2)$$

From (1) and (2), the formula is verified.

Ex. 6 : If $u = x^2 + y^2$, where $x = at^2$, $y = 2at$, find $\dfrac{du}{dt}$.

Sol. : Here u is a composite function of t and $\dfrac{du}{dt}$, the total derivative is required.

Hence

$$\dfrac{du}{dt} = \dfrac{\partial u}{\partial x} \cdot \dfrac{dx}{dt} + \dfrac{\partial u}{\partial y} \cdot \dfrac{dy}{dt} = (2x)(2at) + 2y(2a)$$

$$= 4at(x) + 4ay = 4at(at^2) + 4a(2at)$$

$$= 4a^2 t^3 + 8a^2 t$$

Ex. 7 : If $x^2 y - e^z + x \sin z = 0$ and $x^2 + y^2 + z^2 = a^2$, evaluate $\dfrac{dy}{dx}$ and $\dfrac{dx}{dz}$. **(May 2011)**

Sol. : Let $\quad f(x, y, z) = x^2 y - e^z + x \sin z = 0$

We have $\quad df = \dfrac{\partial f}{\partial x} dx + \dfrac{\partial f}{\partial y} dy + \dfrac{\partial f}{\partial z} dz$

$$0 = (2xy + \sin z) dx + (x^2) dy + (x \cos z - e^z) dz \quad \ldots (1)$$

$\phi(x, y, z) = x^2 + y^2 + z^2 - a^2 = 0$

$$d\phi = \dfrac{\partial \phi}{\partial x} dx + \dfrac{\partial \phi}{\partial y} dy + \dfrac{\partial \phi}{\partial z} dz$$

$$0 = 2x\,dx + 2y\,dy + 2z\,dz$$
i.e. $\quad 0 = x\,dx + y\,dy + z\,dz \quad \ldots (2)$

Solving (1) and (2) by Cramer's rule for dx, dy and dz, we have

$$\frac{dx}{\begin{vmatrix} x^2 & x\cos z - e^z \\ y & z \end{vmatrix}} = \frac{-dy}{\begin{vmatrix} 2xy + \sin z & x\cos z - e^z \\ x & z \end{vmatrix}} = \frac{dz}{\begin{vmatrix} 2xy + \sin z & x^2 \\ x & y \end{vmatrix}}$$

$$\frac{dx}{x^2 z - y(x\cos z) - e^z} = \frac{-dy}{z(2xy + \sin z) - x(x\cos z - e^z)} = \frac{dz}{y(2xy + \sin z) - x^3}$$

$$\therefore \quad \frac{dy}{dx} = \frac{z(2xy + \sin z) - x(x\cos z - e^z)}{-x^2 z + y(x\cos z - e^z)} \quad \text{and} \quad \frac{dx}{dz} = \frac{x^2 z - y(x\cos z - e^z)}{y(2xy + \sin z) - x^3}$$

EXERCISE 10.9

1. If $v = f(e^{x-y}, e^{y-z}, e^{z-x})$ then show that $\frac{\partial v}{\partial x} + \frac{\partial v}{\partial y} + \frac{\partial v}{\partial z} = 0$.

2. If $f(lx + my + nz, x^2 + y^2 + z^2) = 0$ then show that
$$(ly - mx) + (ny - mz)\frac{\partial z}{\partial x} + (lz - nx)\frac{\partial z}{\partial y} = 0.$$

3. If $f(lx + my + nz, x^2 + y^2 + z^2) = 0$ then show that
$$(lz - nx) + (mz - ny)\frac{\partial y}{\partial x} + (ly - mx)\frac{\partial y}{\partial z} = 0.$$

4. If $f(x + y + z, x^2 + y^2 + z^2) = 0$ then show that $(z - x) + (z - y)\frac{\partial y}{\partial x} + (y - x)\frac{\partial y}{\partial z} = 0$.

5. If $f(x + y + z, x^2 + y^2 + z^2) = 0$ then show that $(z - y) + (z - x)\frac{\partial x}{\partial y} + (x - y)\frac{\partial x}{\partial z} = 0$.

6. If $u = f(ax^2 + 2hxy + by^2)$, $v = \phi(ax^2 + 2hxy + by^2)$ then show that
$$\frac{\partial}{\partial y}\left(u\frac{\partial v}{\partial x}\right) = \frac{\partial}{\partial x}\left(u\frac{\partial v}{\partial y}\right).$$

7. If $\frac{x^2}{a^2} + \frac{y^2}{b^2} + \frac{z^2}{c^2} = 1$ and $lx + my + nz = 0$ then prove that
$$\frac{dx}{\frac{ny}{b^2} - \frac{mz}{c^2}} = \frac{dy}{\frac{lz}{c^2} - \frac{nx}{a^2}} = \frac{dz}{\frac{mx}{a^2} - \frac{ly}{b^2}}.$$

8. Find $\frac{du}{dt}$ given $u = x^2 + y^2 + z^2$ where $x = e^t$, $y = e^t \sin t$ and $z = e^t \cos t$.

9. If $u = f(x^2 + 2yz, y^2 + 2zx)$, prove that
$$(y^2 - zx)\frac{\partial u}{\partial x} + (x^2 - yz)\frac{\partial u}{\partial y} + (z^2 - xy)\frac{\partial u}{\partial z} = 0. \qquad \text{(Dec. 2008)}$$

10. If $ax^2 + by^2 + cz^2 = 1$ and $lx + my + nz = 0$ prove that
$$\frac{dx}{bny - cmz} = \frac{dy}{clz - anx} = \frac{dz}{amx - bly}. \qquad \text{(May 2005)}$$

10.16 CHANGE OF INDEPENDENT VARIABLES

If $u = f(x, y)$, where $x = f_1(r, \theta)$ and $y = f_2(r, \theta)$. It is often necessary to change expressions involving u, x, y, $\frac{\partial u}{\partial x}$, $\frac{\partial u}{\partial y}$, $\frac{\partial^2 u}{\partial x^2}$ etc. into expressions involving u, r, θ, $\frac{\partial u}{\partial r}$, $\frac{\partial u}{\partial \theta}$ etc.

The necessary formulae of transformation of independent variables are easily obtained.

$$\frac{\partial u}{\partial r} = \frac{\partial u}{\partial x}\frac{\partial x}{\partial r} + \frac{\partial u}{\partial y}\frac{\partial y}{\partial r} \qquad \ldots (1)$$

$$\frac{\partial u}{\partial \theta} = \frac{\partial u}{\partial x}\frac{\partial x}{\partial \theta} + \frac{\partial u}{\partial y}\frac{\partial y}{\partial \theta} \qquad \ldots (2)$$

If we solve equations (1) and (2) simultaneously, we get values of $\frac{\partial u}{\partial x}$ and $\frac{\partial u}{\partial y}$ in terms of $\frac{\partial u}{\partial r}$, $\frac{\partial u}{\partial \theta}$ and the known quantities $\frac{\partial x}{\partial r}$, $\frac{\partial y}{\partial r}$, $\frac{\partial x}{\partial \theta}$, $\frac{\partial y}{\partial \theta}$.

Thus the two formulae for $\frac{\partial u}{\partial x}$ and $\frac{\partial u}{\partial y}$ are given by

$$\frac{\partial u}{\partial x} = \frac{\partial u}{\partial r}\frac{\partial r}{\partial x} + \frac{\partial u}{\partial \theta}\frac{\partial \theta}{\partial x} \qquad \ldots (3)$$

$$\frac{\partial u}{\partial y} = \frac{\partial u}{\partial r}\frac{\partial r}{\partial y} + \frac{\partial u}{\partial \theta}\frac{\partial \theta}{\partial y} \qquad \ldots (4)$$

A repeated application of equations (1), (2) and (3), (4) can give us the values of higher order partial differential coefficients of u such as

$$\frac{\partial^2 u}{\partial x^2}, \frac{\partial^2 u}{\partial y^2} \text{ or } \frac{\partial^2 u}{\partial r^2}, \frac{\partial^2 u}{\partial \theta^2} \text{ etc.}$$

The above formulae can easily be extended to the case of more than two independent variables.

Note : In case equations $x = f_1(r, \theta)$, $y = f_2(r, \theta)$ are easily solvable for r and θ in terms of x and y viz. $r = g_1(x, y)$, $\theta = g_2(x, y)$, then also we can use the formulae (3), (4) given above.

USE OF THE PRINCIPLE OF EQUIVALENT OPERATOR

(1) If $\frac{\partial z}{\partial x} = \frac{\partial z}{\partial u} + \frac{\partial z}{\partial v}$ then it can be written as

$$\frac{\partial}{\partial x}(z) = \frac{\partial}{\partial u}(z) + \frac{\partial}{\partial v}(z) \quad \text{or} \quad \frac{\partial}{\partial x}(z) = \left(\frac{\partial}{\partial u} + \frac{\partial}{\partial v}\right)(z)$$

Now z is any function of x and y or u and v, so the operator $\dfrac{\partial}{\partial x} \equiv \dfrac{\partial}{\partial u} + \dfrac{\partial}{\partial v}$

i.e. the differential operator $\dfrac{\partial}{\partial x}$ is equivalent to operator $\dfrac{\partial}{\partial u} + \dfrac{\partial}{\partial v}$.

We make use of this fact to find higher order partial derivatives.

$$\dfrac{\partial^2 z}{\partial x^2} = \dfrac{\partial}{\partial x}\left(\dfrac{\partial z}{\partial x}\right) = \left(\dfrac{\partial}{\partial u} + \dfrac{\partial}{\partial v}\right)\left(\dfrac{\partial z}{\partial u} + \dfrac{\partial z}{\partial v}\right)$$

$$= \dfrac{\partial}{\partial u}\left(\dfrac{\partial z}{\partial u} + \dfrac{\partial z}{\partial v}\right) + \dfrac{\partial}{\partial v}\left(\dfrac{\partial z}{\partial u} + \dfrac{\partial z}{\partial v}\right)$$

$$= \dfrac{\partial^2 z}{\partial u^2} + \dfrac{\partial^2 z}{\partial u\, \partial v} + \dfrac{\partial^2 z}{\partial v\, \partial u} + \dfrac{\partial^2 z}{\partial v^2}$$

$$\dfrac{\partial^2 z}{\partial x^2} = \dfrac{\partial^2 z}{\partial u^2} + 2\dfrac{\partial^2 z}{\partial u\, \partial v} + \dfrac{\partial^2 z}{\partial v^2}$$

(2) If $\dfrac{\partial z}{\partial u} = x\dfrac{\partial z}{\partial x} + y\dfrac{\partial z}{\partial y}$ then it can be written as

$$\dfrac{\partial}{\partial u}(z) = x\dfrac{\partial}{\partial x}(z) + y\dfrac{\partial}{\partial y}(z) \text{ or } \dfrac{\partial}{\partial u}(z) = \left(x\dfrac{\partial}{\partial x} + y\dfrac{\partial}{\partial y}\right)(z)$$

Now z is any function of u and v or x and y, so the operator $\dfrac{\partial}{\partial u} \equiv x\dfrac{\partial}{\partial x} + y\dfrac{\partial}{\partial y}$. i.e. the differential operator $\dfrac{\partial}{\partial u}$ is equivalent to operator $x\dfrac{\partial}{\partial x} + y\dfrac{\partial}{\partial y}$.

We make use of this fact to find higher order partial derivatives.

$$\dfrac{\partial^2 z}{\partial u^2} = \dfrac{\partial}{\partial u}\left(\dfrac{\partial z}{\partial u}\right)$$

$$= \left(x\dfrac{\partial}{\partial x} + y\dfrac{\partial}{\partial y}\right)\left(x\dfrac{\partial z}{\partial x} + y\dfrac{\partial z}{\partial y}\right)$$

$$= x\dfrac{\partial}{\partial x}\left[x\dfrac{\partial z}{\partial x} + y\dfrac{\partial z}{\partial y}\right] + y\dfrac{\partial}{\partial y}\left[x\dfrac{\partial z}{\partial x} + y\dfrac{\partial z}{\partial y}\right]$$

$$= x\left\{\dfrac{\partial}{\partial x}\left(x\dfrac{\partial z}{\partial x}\right) + y\dfrac{\partial}{\partial x}\left(\dfrac{\partial z}{\partial y}\right)\right\} + y\left\{x\dfrac{\partial}{\partial y}\left(\dfrac{\partial z}{\partial x}\right) + \dfrac{\partial}{\partial y}\left(y\cdot\dfrac{\partial z}{\partial y}\right)\right\}$$

$$= x\left\{x\cdot\dfrac{\partial^2 z}{\partial x^2} + \dfrac{\partial z}{\partial x}\cdot(1) + y\cdot\dfrac{\partial^2 z}{\partial x\, \partial y}\right\} + y\left\{x\dfrac{\partial^2 z}{\partial y\, \partial x} + y\dfrac{\partial^2 z}{\partial y^2} + \dfrac{\partial z}{\partial y}\cdot(1)\right\}$$

$$= x^2\dfrac{\partial^2 z}{\partial x^2} + x\dfrac{\partial z}{\partial x} + xy\dfrac{\partial^2 z}{\partial x\, \partial y} + yx\dfrac{\partial^2 z}{\partial y\, \partial x} + y^2\dfrac{\partial^2 z}{\partial y^2} + y\dfrac{\partial z}{\partial y}$$

$$\dfrac{\partial^2 z}{\partial u^2} = x^2\dfrac{\partial^2 z}{\partial x^2} + 2xy\dfrac{\partial^2 z}{\partial x\, \partial y} + y^2\dfrac{\partial^2 z}{\partial y^2} + x\dfrac{\partial z}{\partial x} + y\dfrac{\partial z}{\partial y}$$

TYPE 5 : EXAMPLES ON HIGHER ORDER PARTIAL DIFFERENTIAL COEFFICIENTS (CHANGE OF INDEPENDENT VARIABLE)

To obtain higher order partial derivatives we will make use of the principle of equivalent operator.

Ex. 1 : If $z = f(x, y)$ and $u = lx + my$, $v = ly - mx$, prove that

$$\frac{\partial^2 z}{\partial x^2} + \frac{\partial^2 z}{\partial y^2} = (l^2 + m^2)\left(\frac{\partial^2 z}{\partial u^2} + \frac{\partial^2 z}{\partial v^2}\right)$$

Sol. : Regard z as a function of u, v where u, v are functions of x, y. z becomes composite function of x, y. i.e. $z \rightarrow u\ v \rightarrow x, y$

From first tree diagram, we have

$$\frac{\partial z}{\partial x} = \frac{\partial z}{\partial u} \cdot \frac{\partial u}{\partial x} + \frac{\partial z}{\partial v} \cdot \frac{\partial v}{\partial x}$$

$$= l \cdot \frac{\partial z}{\partial u} - m \frac{\partial z}{\partial v}$$

or $\frac{\partial}{\partial x}(z) = \left(l\frac{\partial}{\partial u} - m\frac{\partial}{\partial v}\right) z$

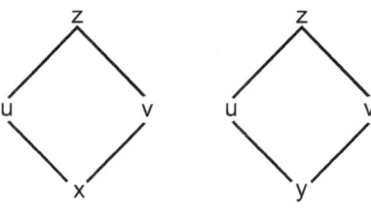

Fig. 10.10

Now z is any function of x and y or u and v, so the operator $\frac{\partial}{\partial x} \equiv l\frac{\partial}{\partial u} - m\frac{\partial}{\partial v}$, i.e. the differential operator $\frac{\partial}{\partial x}$ is equivalent to operator $l\frac{\partial}{\partial u} - m\frac{\partial}{\partial v}$. We make use of this to find $\frac{\partial^2 z}{\partial x^2}$.

Now,

$$\frac{\partial^2 z}{\partial x^2} = \frac{\partial}{\partial x}\left(\frac{\partial z}{\partial x}\right)$$

$$= \left(l\frac{\partial}{\partial u} - m\frac{\partial}{\partial v}\right)\left(l\frac{\partial z}{\partial u} - m\frac{\partial z}{\partial v}\right)$$

$$= l\frac{\partial}{\partial u}\left(l\frac{\partial z}{\partial u} - m\frac{\partial z}{\partial v}\right) - m\frac{\partial}{\partial v}\left(l\frac{\partial z}{\partial u} - m\frac{\partial z}{\partial v}\right)$$

$$= l\left\{l\frac{\partial^2 z}{\partial u^2} - m\frac{\partial^2 z}{\partial u\, \partial v}\right\} - m\left\{l\frac{\partial^2 z}{\partial v\, \partial u} - m\frac{\partial^2 z}{\partial v^2}\right\}$$

$$\frac{\partial^2 z}{\partial x^2} = l^2 \frac{\partial^2 z}{\partial u^2} - 2lm\frac{\partial^2 z}{\partial u\, \partial v} + m^2 \frac{\partial^2 z}{\partial v^2} \qquad \ldots (1)$$

From second tree diagram,

$$\frac{\partial z}{\partial y} = \frac{\partial z}{\partial u} \cdot \frac{\partial u}{\partial y} + \frac{\partial z}{\partial v} \cdot \frac{\partial v}{\partial y} = m\frac{\partial z}{\partial u} + l\frac{\partial z}{\partial v}$$

$$\frac{\partial}{\partial y}(z) = \left(m\frac{\partial}{\partial u} + l\frac{\partial}{\partial v}\right)(z)$$

Now z is any function of x and y and u and v, so the operator $\dfrac{\partial}{\partial y} \equiv m\dfrac{\partial}{\partial u} + l\dfrac{\partial}{\partial v}$.

i.e. the differential operator $\dfrac{\partial}{\partial y}$ is equivalent to the operator $m\dfrac{\partial}{\partial u} + l\dfrac{\partial}{\partial v}$.

We make use of this idea, to find $\dfrac{\partial^2 z}{\partial y^2}$.

Now,
$$\dfrac{\partial^2 z}{\partial y^2} = \dfrac{\partial}{\partial y}\left(\dfrac{\partial z}{\partial y}\right)$$

$$= m\left(\dfrac{\partial}{\partial u} + l\dfrac{\partial}{\partial v}\right)\left(m\dfrac{\partial z}{\partial u} + l\dfrac{\partial z}{\partial v}\right)$$

$$= m\dfrac{\partial}{\partial u}\left(m\dfrac{\partial z}{\partial u} + l\dfrac{\partial z}{\partial v}\right) + l\dfrac{\partial}{\partial v}\left(m\dfrac{\partial z}{\partial u} + l\dfrac{\partial z}{\partial v}\right)$$

$$= m\left\{m\dfrac{\partial^2 z}{\partial u^2} + l\dfrac{\partial^2 z}{\partial u\,\partial v}\right\} + l\left\{m\dfrac{\partial^2 z}{\partial v\,\partial u} + l\dfrac{\partial^2 z}{\partial v^2}\right\}$$

$$\dfrac{\partial^2 z}{\partial y^2} = m^2\dfrac{\partial^2 z}{\partial u^2} + 2lm\dfrac{\partial^2 z}{\partial u\,\partial v} + l^2\dfrac{\partial^2 z}{\partial v^2} \qquad \ldots (2)$$

By adding equations (1) and (2),

$$\dfrac{\partial^2 z}{\partial x^2} + \dfrac{\partial^2 z}{\partial y^2} = (l^2 + m^2)\dfrac{\partial^2 z}{\partial u^2} + (m^2 + l^2)\dfrac{\partial^2 z}{\partial v^2}$$

$$\dfrac{\partial^2 z}{\partial x^2} + \dfrac{\partial^2 z}{\partial y^2} = (l^2 + m^2)\left(\dfrac{\partial^2 z}{\partial u^2} + \dfrac{\partial^2 z}{\partial v^2}\right)$$

Ex. 2 : If $x + y = 2e^\theta \cos\phi$, $x - y = 2ie^\theta \sin\phi$, show that $\dfrac{\partial^2 u}{\partial \theta^2} + \dfrac{\partial^2 u}{\partial \phi^2} = 4xy\dfrac{\partial^2 u}{\partial x\,\partial y}$.

Sol. : $x + y = 2e^\theta \cos\phi$ $x - y = 2ie^\theta \sin\phi$

By adding $2x = 2e^\theta(\cos\phi + i\sin\phi)$ $x = e^\theta e^{i\phi} = e^{\theta + i\phi}$

By subtracting $2y = 2e^\theta(\cos\phi - i\sin\phi)$ $y = e^\theta e^{-i\phi} = e^{\theta - i\phi}$

Regard u as a function of x, y where x and y are functions of θ, ϕ, hence u becomes composite function of θ, ϕ i.e. $u \to x, y \to \theta, \phi$.

$$\dfrac{\partial u}{\partial \theta} = \dfrac{\partial u}{\partial x}\dfrac{\partial x}{\partial \theta} + \dfrac{\partial u}{\partial y}\dfrac{\partial y}{\partial \theta} = \dfrac{\partial u}{\partial x}e^{\theta + i\phi} + \dfrac{\partial u}{\partial y}e^{\theta - i\phi}$$

$$\dfrac{\partial u}{\partial \theta} = x\dfrac{\partial u}{\partial x} + y\dfrac{\partial u}{\partial y}$$

$$\dfrac{\partial}{\partial \theta}(u) = \left(x\dfrac{\partial}{\partial x} + y\dfrac{\partial}{\partial y}\right)(u) \quad \text{i.e.} \quad \dfrac{\partial}{\partial \theta} \equiv x\dfrac{\partial}{\partial x} + y\dfrac{\partial}{\partial y}$$

$$\frac{\partial^2 u}{\partial \theta^2} = \frac{\partial}{\partial \theta}\left(\frac{\partial u}{\partial \theta}\right) = \left(x\frac{\partial}{\partial x} + y\frac{\partial}{\partial y}\right)\left(x\frac{\partial u}{\partial x} + y\frac{\partial u}{\partial y}\right)$$

$$= x\frac{\partial}{\partial x}\left(x\frac{\partial u}{\partial x} + y\frac{\partial u}{\partial y}\right) + y\frac{\partial}{\partial y}\left(x\frac{\partial u}{\partial x} + y\frac{\partial u}{\partial y}\right)$$

$$= x\left\{x\frac{\partial^2 u}{\partial x^2} + \frac{\partial u}{\partial x} + y\frac{\partial^2 u}{\partial x \partial y}\right\} + y\left\{x\frac{\partial^2 u}{\partial y \partial x} + y\frac{\partial^2 u}{\partial y^2} + \frac{\partial u}{\partial y}\right\}$$

$$\frac{\partial^2 u}{\partial \theta^2} = x^2\frac{\partial^2 u}{\partial x^2} + x\frac{\partial u}{\partial x} + 2xy\frac{\partial^2 u}{\partial x \partial y} + y^2\frac{\partial^2 u}{\partial y^2} + y\frac{\partial u}{\partial y}$$

$$\frac{\partial^2 u}{\partial \theta^2} = x^2\frac{\partial^2 u}{\partial x^2} + 2xy\frac{\partial^2 u}{\partial x \partial y} + y^2\frac{\partial^2 u}{\partial y^2} + x\frac{\partial u}{\partial x} + y\frac{\partial u}{\partial y} \qquad \ldots (1)$$

$$\frac{\partial u}{\partial \phi} = \frac{\partial u}{\partial x}\frac{\partial x}{\partial \phi} + \frac{\partial u}{\partial y}\frac{\partial y}{\partial \phi} = \frac{\partial u}{\partial x} e^{\theta + i\phi} i + \frac{\partial u}{\partial y} \cdot e^{\theta - i\phi}(-i)$$

$$\frac{\partial u}{\partial \phi} = i\left[x\frac{\partial u}{\partial x} - y\frac{\partial u}{\partial y}\right]$$

$$\frac{\partial}{\partial \phi}(u) = i\left[x\frac{\partial}{\partial x} - y\frac{\partial}{\partial y}\right](u) \text{ i.e. } \frac{\partial}{\partial \phi} \equiv i\left(x\frac{\partial}{\partial x} - y\frac{\partial}{\partial y}\right)$$

$$\frac{\partial^2 u}{\partial \phi^2} = \frac{\partial}{\partial \phi}\left(\frac{\partial u}{\partial \phi}\right) = \left[i\left(x\frac{\partial}{\partial x} - y\frac{\partial}{\partial y}\right)\right]\left[i\left(x\frac{\partial u}{\partial x} - y\frac{\partial u}{\partial y}\right)\right]$$

$$= i^2\left\{x\frac{\partial}{\partial x}\left(x\frac{\partial u}{\partial x} - y\frac{\partial u}{\partial y}\right) - y\frac{\partial}{\partial y}\left(x\frac{\partial u}{\partial x} - y\frac{\partial u}{\partial y}\right)\right\}$$

$$= -\left\{x\left[x\frac{\partial^2 u}{\partial x^2} + \frac{\partial u}{\partial x} - y\frac{\partial^2 u}{\partial x \partial y}\right] - y\left[x\frac{\partial^2 u}{\partial y \partial x} - y\frac{\partial^2 u}{\partial y^2} - \frac{\partial u}{\partial y}\right]\right\}$$

$$= -\left\{x^2\frac{\partial^2 u}{\partial x^2} + x\frac{\partial u}{\partial x} - 2xy\frac{\partial^2 u}{\partial x \partial y} + y^2\frac{\partial^2 u}{\partial y^2} + y\frac{\partial u}{\partial y}\right\}$$

$$\frac{\partial^2 u}{\partial \phi^2} = -x^2\frac{\partial^2 u}{\partial x^2} + 2xy\frac{\partial^2 u}{\partial x \partial y} - y^2\frac{\partial^2 u}{\partial y^2} - x\frac{\partial u}{\partial x} - y\frac{\partial u}{\partial y} \qquad \ldots (2)$$

By adding equations (1) and (2), $\dfrac{\partial^2 u}{\partial \theta^2} + \dfrac{\partial^2 u}{\partial \phi^2} = 4xy\dfrac{\partial^2 y}{\partial x \partial y}$.

Ex. 3 : *If* $x = \dfrac{\cos \theta}{u}$, $y = \dfrac{\sin \theta}{u}$ *then show that* $\dfrac{\partial^2 z}{\partial x^2} + \dfrac{\partial^2 z}{\partial y^2} = u^4 \dfrac{\partial^2 u}{\partial u^2} + u^3 \dfrac{\partial z}{\partial u} + u^2 \dfrac{\partial^2 z}{\partial \theta^2}$.

Sol. : $z \to x, y \to u, \theta$ i.e. z is composite function of u and θ

$$\frac{\partial z}{\partial u} = \frac{\partial z}{\partial x}\frac{\partial x}{\partial u} + \frac{\partial z}{\partial y}\frac{\partial y}{\partial u}$$

$$\frac{\partial z}{\partial u} = \frac{\partial z}{\partial x}\left(\frac{-\cos \theta}{u^2}\right) + \frac{\partial z}{\partial y}\left(\frac{-\sin \theta}{u^2}\right)$$

Multiplying by u on both sides,

$$u\frac{\partial z}{\partial u} = -\frac{\cos\theta}{u}\frac{\partial z}{\partial x} - \frac{\sin\theta}{u}\frac{\partial z}{\partial y}$$

$$u\frac{\partial z}{\partial u} = -x\frac{\partial z}{\partial x} - y\frac{\partial z}{\partial y} \quad \text{i.e.} \quad u\frac{\partial}{\partial u} = -x\frac{\partial}{\partial x} - y\frac{\partial}{\partial y}$$

Important step : Consider

$$u\frac{\partial}{\partial u}\left(u\frac{\partial z}{\partial u}\right) = \left(-x\frac{\partial}{\partial x} - y\frac{\partial}{\partial y}\right)\left(-x\frac{\partial z}{\partial x} - y\frac{\partial z}{\partial y}\right)$$

$$u\left\{u\frac{\partial^2 z}{\partial u^2} + \frac{\partial z}{\partial u}\right\} = x\frac{\partial}{\partial x}\left(x\frac{\partial z}{\partial x} + y\frac{\partial z}{\partial y}\right) + y\frac{\partial}{\partial y}\left(x\frac{\partial z}{\partial x} + y\frac{\partial z}{\partial y}\right)$$

$$\left\{u^2\frac{\partial^2 z}{\partial u^2} + u\frac{\partial z}{\partial u}\right\} = x\left\{x\frac{\partial^2 z}{\partial x^2} + \frac{\partial z}{\partial x} + y\frac{\partial^2 z}{\partial x\,\partial y}\right\} + y\left\{x\frac{\partial^2 z}{\partial y\,\partial x} + y\frac{\partial^2 z}{\partial y^2} + \frac{\partial z}{\partial y}\right\}$$

$$= x^2\frac{\partial^2 z}{\partial x^2} + x\frac{\partial z}{\partial x} + 2xy\frac{\partial^2 z}{\partial x\,\partial y} + y^2\frac{\partial^2 z}{\partial y^2} + y\frac{\partial z}{\partial y}$$

$$u^2\frac{\partial^2 z}{\partial u^2} + u\frac{\partial z}{\partial u} = x^2\frac{\partial^2 z}{\partial x^2} + 2xy\frac{\partial^2 z}{\partial x\,\partial y} + y^2\frac{\partial^2 z}{\partial y^2} + x\frac{\partial z}{\partial x} + y\frac{\partial z}{\partial y} \qquad \ldots (1)$$

$$\frac{\partial z}{\partial \theta} = \frac{\partial z}{\partial x}\frac{\partial x}{\partial \theta} + \frac{\partial z}{\partial y}\frac{\partial y}{\partial \theta} = \frac{\partial z}{\partial x}\left(-\frac{\sin\theta}{u}\right) + \frac{\partial z}{\partial y}\left(\frac{\cos\theta}{u}\right)$$

$$\frac{\partial z}{\partial \theta} = -y\frac{\partial z}{\partial x} + x\frac{\partial z}{\partial y} \quad \text{i.e.} \quad \frac{\partial}{\partial \theta} = -y\frac{\partial}{\partial x} + x\frac{\partial}{\partial y}$$

$\therefore$ Similarly, $\quad \dfrac{\partial^2 z}{\partial \theta^2} = y^2\dfrac{\partial^2 z}{\partial x^2} - 2xy\dfrac{\partial^2 z}{\partial x\,\partial y} + x^2\dfrac{\partial^2 z}{\partial y^2} - x\dfrac{\partial z}{\partial x} - y\dfrac{\partial z}{\partial y} \qquad \ldots (2)$

By adding equations (1) and (2),

$$u^2\frac{\partial^2 z}{\partial u^2} + u\frac{\partial z}{\partial u} + \frac{\partial^2 z}{\partial \theta^2} = (x^2 + y^2)\frac{\partial^2 z}{\partial x^2} + (y^2 + x^2)\frac{\partial^2 z}{\partial y^2}$$

$$= (x^2 + y^2)\left(\frac{\partial^2 z}{\partial x^2} + \frac{\partial^2 z}{\partial y^2}\right)$$

But $\quad x^2 + y^2 = \dfrac{\cos^2\theta}{u^2} + \dfrac{\sin^2\theta}{u^2} = \dfrac{1}{u^2}$

$$u^2\frac{\partial^2 z}{\partial u^2} + u\frac{\partial z}{\partial u} + \frac{\partial^2 z}{\partial \theta^2} = \frac{1}{u^2}\left(\frac{\partial^2 z}{\partial x^2} + \frac{\partial^2 z}{\partial y^2}\right)$$

$$u^4\frac{\partial^2 z}{\partial u^2} + u^3\frac{\partial z}{\partial u} + u^2\frac{\partial^2 z}{\partial \theta^2} = \frac{\partial^2 z}{\partial x^2} + \frac{\partial^2 z}{\partial y^2}$$

Ex. 4 : *Find the values of the constants a and b such that the substitution* $u = x + ay$ *and* $v = x + by$. *Transform the equation* $9\dfrac{\partial^2 f}{\partial x^2} - 9\dfrac{\partial^2 f}{\partial x \partial y} + 2\dfrac{\partial^2 f}{\partial y^2} = 0$ *into* $\dfrac{\partial^2 f}{\partial u \partial v} = 0$ *where f is a function of x and y.*

Sol. : We have : $\dfrac{\partial u}{\partial x} = 1,\ \dfrac{\partial v}{\partial x} = 1,\ \dfrac{\partial u}{\partial y} = a,\ \dfrac{\partial v}{\partial y} = b.$

$$\dfrac{\partial f}{\partial x} = \dfrac{\partial f}{\partial u}\cdot\dfrac{\partial u}{\partial x} + \dfrac{\partial f}{\partial v}\cdot\dfrac{\partial v}{\partial x} = \dfrac{\partial f}{\partial u} + \dfrac{\partial f}{\partial v}$$

$$\Rightarrow \dfrac{\partial}{\partial x}(f) = \left(\dfrac{\partial}{\partial u} + \dfrac{\partial}{\partial v}\right) f \quad \text{i.e.} \quad \dfrac{\partial}{\partial x} = \dfrac{\partial}{\partial u} + \dfrac{\partial}{\partial v}$$

$$\dfrac{\partial^2 f}{\partial x^2} = \dfrac{\partial}{\partial x}\left(\dfrac{\partial f}{\partial x}\right)$$

$$= \left(\dfrac{\partial}{\partial u} + \dfrac{\partial}{\partial v}\right)\left(\dfrac{\partial f}{\partial u} + \dfrac{\partial f}{\partial v}\right)$$

$$= \dfrac{\partial}{\partial u}\left(\dfrac{\partial f}{\partial u} + \dfrac{\partial f}{\partial v}\right) + \dfrac{\partial}{\partial v}\left(\dfrac{\partial f}{\partial u} + \dfrac{\partial f}{\partial v}\right)$$

Hence $\dfrac{\partial^2 f}{\partial x^2} = \dfrac{\partial^2 f}{\partial u^2} + 2\dfrac{\partial^2 f}{\partial u \partial v} + \dfrac{\partial^2 f}{\partial v^2}$

$$\dfrac{\partial f}{\partial y} = \dfrac{\partial f}{\partial u}\cdot\dfrac{\partial u}{\partial y} + \dfrac{\partial f}{\partial v}\cdot\dfrac{\partial v}{\partial y}$$

$$= a\dfrac{\partial f}{\partial u} + b\dfrac{\partial f}{\partial v} \Rightarrow \dfrac{\partial}{\partial y} = a\dfrac{\partial}{\partial u} + b\dfrac{\partial}{\partial v}$$

$\therefore$ $\dfrac{\partial^2 f}{\partial y^2} = \dfrac{\partial}{\partial y}\left(\dfrac{\partial f}{\partial y}\right)$

$$= \left(a\dfrac{\partial}{\partial u} + b\dfrac{\partial}{\partial v}\right)\left(a\dfrac{\partial f}{\partial u} + b\dfrac{\partial f}{\partial v}\right)$$

$$= a\dfrac{\partial}{\partial u}\left(a\dfrac{\partial f}{\partial u} + b\dfrac{\partial f}{\partial v}\right) + b\dfrac{\partial}{\partial v}\left(a\dfrac{\partial f}{\partial u} + b\dfrac{\partial f}{\partial v}\right)$$

$$= a\left\{a\dfrac{\partial^2 f}{\partial u^2} + b\dfrac{\partial^2 f}{\partial u \partial v}\right\} + b\left\{a\dfrac{\partial^2 f}{\partial v \partial u} + b\dfrac{\partial^2 f}{\partial v^2}\right\}$$

i.e. $\dfrac{\partial^2 f}{\partial y^2} = a^2\dfrac{\partial^2 f}{\partial u^2} + 2ab\dfrac{\partial^2 f}{\partial u \partial v} + b^2\dfrac{\partial^2 f}{\partial v^2}$

Also we have : $\dfrac{\partial^2 f}{\partial x \partial y} = \dfrac{\partial}{\partial x}\left(\dfrac{\partial f}{\partial y}\right)$

$$= \left(\dfrac{\partial}{\partial u} + \dfrac{\partial}{\partial v}\right)\left[a\dfrac{\partial f}{\partial u} + b\dfrac{\partial f}{\partial v}\right]$$

Engineering Mathematics – I   Partial Differentiation and Applications

$$= \frac{\partial}{\partial u}\left(a\frac{\partial f}{\partial u} + b\frac{\partial f}{\partial v}\right) + \frac{\partial}{\partial v}\left(a\frac{\partial f}{\partial u} + b\frac{\partial f}{\partial v}\right)$$

$$= a\frac{\partial^2 f}{\partial u^2} + b\frac{\partial^2 f}{\partial u\,\partial v} + a\frac{\partial^2 f}{\partial u\,\partial v} + b\frac{\partial^2 f}{\partial v^2}$$

$$\frac{\partial^2 f}{\partial x\,\partial y} = a\frac{\partial^2 f}{\partial u^2} + b\frac{\partial^2 f}{\partial v^2} + (a+b)\frac{\partial^2 f}{\partial u\,\partial v}$$

$$9\frac{\partial^2 f}{\partial x^2} - 9\frac{\partial^2 f}{\partial x\,\partial y} + 2\frac{\partial^2 f}{\partial y^2} = 0 \qquad \ldots (1)$$

$$9\left[\frac{\partial^2 f}{\partial u^2} + 2\frac{\partial^2 f}{\partial u\,\partial v} + \frac{\partial^2 f}{\partial v^2}\right] - 9\left[a\frac{\partial^2 f}{\partial u^2} + b\frac{\partial^2 f}{\partial v^2} + (a+b)\frac{\partial^2 f}{\partial u\,\partial v}\right] + 2\left[a^2\frac{\partial^2 f}{\partial u^2} + 2ab\frac{\partial^2 f}{\partial u\,\partial v} + b^2\frac{\partial^2 f}{\partial v^2}\right] = 0$$

i.e. $(9 - 9a + 2a^2)\dfrac{\partial^2 f}{\partial u^2} + (18 - 9(a+b) + 4ab)\dfrac{\partial^2 f}{\partial u\,\partial v} + (9 - 9b + 2b^2)\dfrac{\partial^2 f}{\partial v^2} = 0$

Equation (1) will get transformed into $\dfrac{\partial^2 f}{\partial u\,\partial v} = 0$ provided

$$9 - 9a + 2a^2 = 0 \qquad \ldots (2)$$
$$9 - 9b + 2b^2 = 0 \qquad \ldots (3)$$
and $\quad 18 - 9(a+b) + 4ab \ne 0 \quad$ (Note this step) $\qquad \ldots (4)$

equation (2) $\Rightarrow (2a - 3)(a - 3) = 0 \Rightarrow a = \dfrac{3}{2}, 3;$ equation (3) $\Rightarrow (2b - 3)(b - 3) = 0 \Rightarrow b = \dfrac{3}{2}, 3$ $a = \dfrac{3}{2}, b = 3$ and $a = 3, b = \dfrac{3}{2}$ satisfy (4).

Hence required values of a and b are $a = \dfrac{3}{2}, b = 3$ and $a = 3, b = \dfrac{3}{2}$.

We reject the pair $a = 3, b = 3$ and $a = \dfrac{3}{2}, b = \dfrac{3}{2}$ because it does not satisfy (4).

Ex. 5 : *By using transformation $x = r\cos\theta,\ y = r\sin\theta$,*

show that $\dfrac{\partial^2 u}{\partial x^2} + \dfrac{\partial^2 u}{\partial y^2} = 0$ *gets transformed into* $\dfrac{\partial^2 u}{\partial r^2} + \dfrac{1}{r}\dfrac{\partial u}{\partial r} + \dfrac{1}{r^2}\dfrac{\partial^2 u}{\partial \theta^2} = 0.$

Sol. : The inverse relation can easily give : $r = \sqrt{x^2 + y^2}$ and $\theta = \tan^{-1}\left(\dfrac{y}{x}\right)$.

Hence $\quad \dfrac{\partial r}{\partial x} = \dfrac{x}{\sqrt{x^2 + y^2}} = \cos\theta; \quad \dfrac{\partial r}{\partial y} = \dfrac{y}{\sqrt{x^2 + y^2}} = \sin\theta$

$\quad \dfrac{\partial \theta}{\partial x} = -\dfrac{y}{\sqrt{x^2+y^2}} = -\dfrac{\sin\theta}{r}; \quad \dfrac{\partial\theta}{\partial y} = \dfrac{x}{\sqrt{x^2+y^2}} = \dfrac{\cos\theta}{r}$

Now $\quad \dfrac{\partial u}{\partial x} = \dfrac{\partial u}{\partial r}\cdot\dfrac{\partial r}{\partial x} + \dfrac{\partial u}{\partial \theta}\cdot\dfrac{\partial \theta}{\partial x}$

$\quad\quad = \cos\theta\,\dfrac{\partial u}{\partial r} - \dfrac{\sin\theta}{r}\cdot\dfrac{\partial u}{\partial \theta}$ or $\dfrac{\partial}{\partial x} = \left(\cos\theta\,\dfrac{\partial}{\partial r} - \dfrac{\sin\theta}{r}\dfrac{\partial}{\partial \theta}\right)$

Hence, it follows that :

$$\frac{\partial^2 u}{\partial x^2} = \frac{\partial}{\partial x}\left(\frac{\partial u}{\partial x}\right)$$

$$= \left(\cos\theta \frac{\partial}{\partial r} - \frac{\sin\theta}{r} \cdot \frac{\partial}{\partial \theta}\right)\left(\cos\theta \frac{\partial u}{\partial r} - \frac{\sin\theta}{r} \cdot \frac{\partial u}{\partial \theta}\right)$$

$$= \cos\theta \frac{\partial}{\partial r}\left[\cos\theta \frac{\partial u}{\partial r} - \frac{\sin\theta}{r} \cdot \frac{\partial u}{\partial \theta}\right] - \frac{\sin\theta}{r} \cdot \frac{\partial}{\partial \theta}\left[\cos\theta \frac{\partial u}{\partial r} - \frac{\sin\theta}{r} \cdot \frac{\partial u}{\partial \theta}\right]$$

$$= \cos\theta \left\{\cos\theta \frac{\partial^2 u}{\partial r^2} - \frac{\sin\theta}{r}\frac{\partial^2 u}{\partial r \partial\theta} - \sin\theta \frac{\partial u}{\partial \theta}\left(\frac{-1}{r^2}\right)\right\}$$

$$- \frac{\sin\theta}{r}\left\{\cos\theta \frac{\partial^2 u}{\partial \theta \partial r} - \sin\theta \frac{\partial u}{\partial r} - \frac{\sin\theta}{r}\frac{\partial^2 u}{\partial \theta^2} - \frac{\cos\theta}{r}\frac{\partial u}{\partial \theta}\right\}$$

$$= \cos^2\theta \frac{\partial^2 u}{\partial r^2} - \frac{\sin\theta \cos\theta}{r}\frac{\partial^2 u}{\partial r \partial \theta} + \frac{\sin\theta \cos\theta}{r^2}\frac{\partial u}{\partial \theta}$$

$$- \frac{\sin\theta \cos\theta}{r}\frac{\partial^2 u}{\partial \theta \partial r} + \frac{\sin^2\theta}{r}\frac{\partial u}{\partial r} + \frac{\sin^2\theta}{r^2}\frac{\partial^2 u}{\partial \theta^2} + \frac{\sin\theta \cos\theta}{r^2}\frac{\partial u}{\partial \theta}$$

$$\frac{\partial^2 u}{\partial x^2} = \cos^2\theta \frac{\partial^2 u}{\partial r^2} - \frac{2\sin\theta\cos\theta}{r} \cdot \frac{\partial^2 u}{\partial r \partial \theta} + \frac{\sin^2\theta}{r^2}\frac{\partial^2 u}{\partial \theta^2} \qquad \ldots (1)$$

$$+ \frac{\sin^2\theta}{r} \cdot \frac{\partial u}{\partial r} + \frac{2\sin\theta\cos\theta}{r^2} \cdot \frac{\partial u}{\partial \theta}$$

$$\frac{\partial u}{\partial y} = \frac{\partial u}{\partial r}\frac{\partial r}{\partial y} + \frac{\partial u}{\partial \theta}\frac{\partial \theta}{\partial y} = \sin\theta \frac{\partial u}{\partial r} + \frac{\cos\theta}{r}\frac{\partial u}{\partial \theta}$$

$$\frac{\partial}{\partial y} \equiv \sin\theta \frac{\partial}{\partial r} + \frac{\cos\theta}{r}\frac{\partial}{\partial \theta}$$

$$\frac{\partial^2 u}{\partial y^2} = \left(\sin\theta \frac{\partial}{\partial r} + \frac{\cos\theta}{r}\frac{\partial}{\partial \theta}\right)\left(\sin\theta \frac{\partial u}{\partial r} + \frac{\cos\theta}{r}\frac{\partial u}{\partial \theta}\right)$$

$$= \sin\theta \left\{\sin\theta \frac{\partial^2 u}{\partial r^2} + \frac{\cos\theta}{r}\frac{\partial^2 u}{\partial r \partial \theta} - \frac{\cos\theta}{r^2}\frac{\partial u}{\partial \theta}\right\}$$

$$+ \frac{\cos\theta}{r}\left\{\sin\theta \frac{\partial^2 u}{\partial \theta \partial r} + \cos\theta \frac{\partial u}{\partial r} + \frac{\cos\theta}{r}\frac{\partial^2 u}{\partial \theta^2} - \frac{\sin\theta}{r}\frac{\partial u}{\partial \theta}\right\}$$

$$= \sin^2\theta \frac{\partial^2 u}{\partial r^2} + \frac{\sin\theta \cos\theta}{r}\frac{\partial u}{\partial r \partial \theta} - \frac{\sin\theta \cos\theta}{r^2}\frac{\partial u}{\partial \theta}$$

$$+ \frac{\sin\theta \cos\theta}{r}\frac{\partial^2 u}{\partial \theta \partial r} + \frac{\cos^2\theta}{r}\frac{\partial u}{\partial r} + \frac{\cos^2\theta}{r^2}\frac{\partial^2 u}{\partial \theta^2} - \frac{\sin\theta \cos\theta}{r^2}\frac{\partial u}{\partial \theta}$$

$$\frac{\partial^2 u}{\partial y^2} = \sin^2\theta \frac{\partial^2 u}{\partial r^2} + \frac{2\sin\theta \cos\theta}{r} \cdot \frac{\partial^2 u}{\partial r \partial \theta} + \frac{\cos^2\theta}{r^2} \cdot \frac{\partial^2 u}{\partial \theta^2}$$

$$+ \frac{\cos^2\theta}{r} \cdot \frac{\partial u}{\partial r} - \frac{2\sin\theta \cos\theta}{r^2} \cdot \frac{\partial u}{\partial \theta} \qquad \ldots (2)$$

Adding (1) and (2), we get $\dfrac{\partial^2 u}{\partial x^2} + \dfrac{\partial^2 u}{\partial y^2} = \dfrac{\partial^2 u}{\partial r^2} + \dfrac{1}{r}\dfrac{\partial u}{\partial r} + \dfrac{1}{r^2}\dfrac{\partial^2 u}{\partial \theta^2}$.

Hence the transformed equation in terms of polar co-ordinate (r, θ) is

$$\dfrac{\partial^2 u}{\partial r^2} + \dfrac{1}{r}\dfrac{\partial u}{\partial r} + \dfrac{1}{r^2}\dfrac{\partial^2 u}{\partial \theta^2} = 0.$$

Additional Result :

Now

$$\dfrac{\partial^2 u}{\partial r^2} + \dfrac{1}{r}\dfrac{\partial u}{\partial r} + \dfrac{1}{r^2}\dfrac{\partial^2 u}{\partial \theta^2} = \dfrac{1}{r}\left[\left(r\dfrac{\partial^2 u}{\partial r^2} + \dfrac{\partial u}{\partial r}\right) + \dfrac{1}{r}\dfrac{\partial^2 u}{\partial \theta^2}\right] = \dfrac{1}{r}\left[\dfrac{\partial}{\partial r}\left(r\dfrac{\partial u}{\partial r}\right) + \dfrac{1}{r}\dfrac{\partial^2 u}{\partial \theta^2}\right]$$

Ex. 6 : *If $z = f(x, y)$ and if u and v are homogeneous functions of x and y of degree n, then show that*

(i) $x\dfrac{\partial z}{\partial x} + y\dfrac{\partial z}{\partial y} = n\left(u\dfrac{\partial z}{\partial u} + v\dfrac{\partial z}{\partial v}\right)$

(ii) $x^2\dfrac{\partial^2 z}{\partial x^2} + 2xy\dfrac{\partial^2 z}{\partial x \partial y} + y^2\dfrac{\partial^2 z}{\partial y^2} = n^2\left[u^2\dfrac{\partial^2 z}{\partial u^2} + 2uv\dfrac{\partial^2 z}{\partial u \partial v} + v^2\dfrac{\partial^2 z}{\partial v^2}\right]$

$$+ n(n-1)\left(u\dfrac{\partial z}{\partial u} + v\dfrac{\partial z}{\partial v}\right)$$

Sol. : Given $u = x^n f\left(\dfrac{y}{x}\right)$ and $v = x^n \phi\left(\dfrac{y}{x}\right)$ are homogeneous functions.

$\therefore \qquad x\dfrac{\partial u}{\partial x} + y\dfrac{\partial u}{\partial y} = nu$ ... (1)

and $\qquad x\dfrac{\partial v}{\partial x} + y\dfrac{\partial v}{\partial y} = nv$

Considering z as function of u and v, we have

$z \to u, \ v \to x, y$

$$\dfrac{\partial z}{\partial x} = \dfrac{\partial z}{\partial u}\dfrac{\partial u}{\partial x} + \dfrac{\partial z}{\partial v}\dfrac{\partial v}{\partial x} \qquad ... (2)$$

$$\dfrac{\partial z}{\partial y} = \dfrac{\partial z}{\partial u}\dfrac{\partial u}{\partial y} + \dfrac{\partial z}{\partial v}\dfrac{\partial v}{\partial y} \qquad ... (3)$$

equation (2) x + equation (3) $y \Rightarrow$

$$x\dfrac{\partial z}{\partial x} + y\dfrac{\partial z}{\partial y} = \dfrac{\partial z}{\partial u}\left(x\dfrac{\partial u}{\partial x} + y\dfrac{\partial u}{\partial y}\right) + \dfrac{\partial z}{\partial v}\left(x\dfrac{\partial v}{\partial x} + y\dfrac{\partial v}{\partial y}\right)$$

Using equation (1), we get

$$x\dfrac{\partial z}{\partial x} + y\dfrac{\partial z}{\partial y} = n\left(u\dfrac{\partial z}{\partial u} + v\dfrac{\partial z}{\partial v}\right) \qquad ... (4)$$

which proves the first part.

From equation (4),

$$\left(x\frac{\partial}{\partial x} + y\frac{\partial}{\partial y}\right)(z) = n\left(u\frac{\partial}{\partial u} + v\frac{\partial}{\partial v}\right)(z)$$

$$\Rightarrow x\frac{\partial}{\partial x} + y\frac{\partial}{\partial y} = n\left(u\frac{\partial}{\partial u} + v\frac{\partial}{\partial v}\right)$$

Important Step : Consider

$$\left(x\frac{\partial}{\partial x} + y\frac{\partial}{\partial y}\right)\left(x\frac{\partial z}{\partial x} + y\frac{\partial z}{\partial y}\right) = n\left(u\frac{\partial}{\partial u} + v\frac{\partial}{\partial v}\right)\left[n\left(u\frac{\partial z}{\partial u} + v\frac{\partial z}{\partial v}\right)\right]$$

$$x\frac{\partial}{\partial x}\left(x\frac{\partial z}{\partial x} + y\frac{\partial z}{\partial y}\right) + y\frac{\partial}{\partial y}\left(x\frac{\partial z}{\partial x} + y\frac{\partial z}{\partial y}\right)$$

$$= n^2\left\{u\frac{\partial}{\partial u}\left(u\frac{\partial z}{\partial u} + v\frac{\partial z}{\partial v}\right) + v\frac{\partial}{\partial v}\left(u\frac{\partial z}{\partial v} + v\frac{\partial z}{\partial v}\right)\right\}$$

$$x\left\{x\frac{\partial^2 z}{\partial x^2} + \frac{\partial z}{\partial x} + y\frac{\partial^2 z}{\partial x\,\partial y}\right\} + y\left\{x\frac{\partial^2 z}{\partial y\,\partial x} + y\frac{\partial^2 z}{\partial y^2} + \frac{\partial z}{\partial y}\right\}$$

$$= n^2\left\{u\left[u\frac{\partial^2 z}{\partial u^2} + \frac{\partial z}{\partial u} + v\frac{\partial^2 z}{\partial u\,\partial v}\right] + v\left[u\frac{\partial^2 z}{\partial v\,\partial u} + v\frac{\partial^2 z}{\partial v^2} + \frac{\partial z}{\partial v}\right]\right\}$$

$$x^2\frac{\partial^2 z}{\partial x^2} + x\frac{\partial z}{\partial x} + 2xy\frac{\partial^2 z}{\partial x\,\partial y} + y^2\frac{\partial^2 z}{\partial y^2} + y\frac{\partial z}{\partial y}$$

$$= n^2\left\{u^2\frac{\partial^2 z}{\partial u^2} + u\frac{\partial z}{\partial u} + 2uv\frac{\partial^2 z}{\partial u\,\partial v} + v^2\frac{\partial^2 z}{\partial v^2} + v\frac{\partial z}{\partial v}\right\}$$

$$\left(x^2\frac{\partial^2 z}{\partial x^2} + 2xy\frac{\partial^2 z}{\partial x\,\partial y} + y^2\frac{\partial^2 z}{\partial y^2}\right) + \left(x\frac{\partial z}{\partial x} + y\frac{\partial z}{\partial y}\right)$$

$$= n^2\left\{u^2\frac{\partial^2 z}{\partial u^2} + 2uv\frac{\partial^2 z}{\partial u\,\partial v} + v^2\frac{\partial^2 z}{\partial v^2}\right\} + n^2\left\{u\frac{\partial z}{\partial u} + v\frac{\partial z}{\partial v}\right\}$$

$$\left(x^2\frac{\partial^2 z}{\partial x^2} + 2xy\frac{\partial^2 z}{\partial x\,\partial y} + y^2\frac{\partial^2 z}{\partial y^2}\right) + n\left(u\frac{\partial z}{\partial u} + v\frac{\partial z}{\partial v}\right)$$

$$= n^2\left\{u^2\frac{\partial^2 z}{\partial u^2} + 2uv\frac{\partial^2 z}{\partial u\,\partial v} + v^2\frac{\partial^2 z}{\partial v^2}\right\} + n^2\left\{u\frac{\partial z}{\partial u} + v\frac{\partial z}{\partial v}\right\}$$

$$x^2\frac{\partial^2 z}{\partial x^2} + 2xy\frac{\partial^2 z}{\partial x\,\partial y} + y^2\frac{\partial^2 z}{\partial y^2}$$

$$= n^2\left\{u^2\frac{\partial^2 z}{\partial u^2} + 2uv\frac{\partial^2 z}{\partial u\,\partial v} + v^2\frac{\partial^2 z}{\partial v^2}\right\}$$

$$+ n^2\left\{u\frac{\partial z}{\partial u} + v\frac{\partial z}{\partial v}\right\} - n\left(u\frac{\partial z}{\partial u} + v\frac{\partial z}{\partial v}\right)$$

$$x^2\frac{\partial^2 z}{\partial x^2} + 2xy\frac{\partial^2 z}{\partial x\,\partial y} + y^2\frac{\partial^2 z}{\partial y^2}$$

$$= n^2\left\{u^2\frac{\partial^2 z}{\partial u^2} + 2uv\frac{\partial^2 z}{\partial u\,\partial v} + v^2\frac{\partial^2 z}{\partial v^2}\right\} + n(n-1)\left\{u\frac{\partial z}{\partial u} + v\frac{\partial z}{\partial v}\right\}$$

Ex. 7 : *Show that the transformation* $x = u^2 - v^2$, $y = 2uv$ *transforms* $\dfrac{\partial^2 f}{\partial u^2} + \dfrac{\partial^2 f}{\partial v^2}$

into $4(u^2 + v^2)\left(\dfrac{\partial^2 f}{\partial x^2} + \dfrac{\partial^2 f}{\partial y^2}\right)$.

Sol. : $f \to x, y \to u, v$ i.e. f becomes composite function of u, v

$$\frac{\partial f}{\partial u} = \frac{\partial f}{\partial x} \cdot \frac{\partial x}{\partial u} + \frac{\partial f}{\partial y} \cdot \frac{\partial y}{\partial u} = \frac{\partial f}{\partial x}(2u) + \frac{\partial f}{\partial y}(2v) \qquad \ldots (1)$$

$$\frac{\partial}{\partial u} = 2u\frac{\partial}{\partial x} + 2v\frac{\partial}{\partial y}$$

$$\frac{\partial^2 f}{\partial u^2} = \frac{\partial}{\partial u}\left(\frac{\partial f}{\partial u}\right)$$

Important Point :

Here $\dfrac{\partial}{\partial u}$ is not replaced by its equivalent operator and replace $\dfrac{\partial f}{\partial u}$ by equation (1).

$$\frac{\partial^2 f}{\partial u^2} = \frac{\partial}{\partial u}\left(2u\frac{\partial f}{\partial x} + 2v\frac{\partial f}{\partial y}\right)$$

$$= \frac{\partial}{\partial u}(2u) \cdot \frac{\partial f}{\partial x} + 2u \cdot \frac{\partial}{\partial u}\left(\frac{\partial f}{\partial x}\right) + 2v \cdot \frac{\partial}{\partial u}\left(\frac{\partial f}{\partial y}\right)$$

$$\frac{\partial^2 f}{\partial u^2} = 2\frac{\partial f}{\partial x} + 2u\frac{\partial}{\partial u}\left(\frac{\partial f}{\partial x}\right) + 2v\frac{\partial}{\partial u}\left(\frac{\partial f}{\partial y}\right)$$

Now we will replace $\dfrac{\partial}{\partial u}$ by its equivalent operator $2u\dfrac{\partial}{\partial x} + 2v\dfrac{\partial}{\partial y}$.

$$\frac{\partial^2 f}{\partial u^2} = 2 \cdot \frac{\partial f}{\partial x} + 2u\left\{\left(2u\frac{\partial}{\partial x} + 2v\frac{\partial}{\partial y}\right)\frac{\partial f}{\partial x}\right\} + 2v\left\{\left(2u\frac{\partial}{\partial x} + 2v\frac{\partial}{\partial y}\right)\frac{\partial f}{\partial y}\right\}$$

$$= 2\frac{\partial f}{\partial x} + 2u\left\{2u\frac{\partial^2 f}{\partial x^2} + 2v\frac{\partial^2 f}{\partial y \partial x}\right\} + 2v\left\{2u\frac{\partial^2 f}{\partial x \partial y} + 2v\frac{\partial^2 f}{\partial y^2}\right\}$$

$$= 2\frac{\partial f}{\partial x} + 4u^2\frac{\partial^2 f}{\partial x^2} + 4uv \cdot \frac{\partial^2 f}{\partial y \partial x} + 4uv\frac{\partial^2 f}{\partial x \partial y} + 4v^2\frac{\partial^2 f}{\partial y^2}$$

$$\frac{\partial^2 f}{\partial u^2} = 2\frac{\partial f}{\partial x} + 4u^2\frac{\partial^2 f}{\partial x^2} + 8uv\frac{\partial^2 f}{\partial x \partial y} + 4v^2\frac{\partial^2 f}{\partial y^2} \qquad \ldots (2)$$

$$\frac{\partial f}{\partial v} = \frac{\partial f}{\partial x} \cdot \frac{\partial x}{\partial v} + \frac{\partial f}{\partial y} \cdot \frac{\partial y}{\partial v} = \frac{\partial f}{\partial x}(-2v) + \frac{\partial f}{\partial y}2u \qquad \ldots (3)$$

$$\frac{\partial}{\partial v} = -2v\frac{\partial}{\partial x} + 2u\frac{\partial}{\partial y}$$

$$\frac{\partial^2 f}{\partial v^2} = \frac{\partial}{\partial v}\left(\frac{\partial f}{\partial v}\right)$$

Important Point :

Here $\frac{\partial}{\partial v}$ is not replaced by its equivalent operator and replace $\frac{\partial f}{\partial v}$ by equation (3).

$$\frac{\partial^2 f}{\partial v^2} = \frac{\partial}{\partial v}\left(-2v\frac{\partial f}{\partial x} + 2u\frac{\partial f}{\partial y}\right)$$

$$= \frac{\partial}{\partial v}(-2v) \cdot \frac{\partial f}{\partial x} - 2v\frac{\partial}{\partial v}\left(\frac{\partial f}{\partial x}\right) + 2u \cdot \frac{\partial}{\partial v}\left(\frac{\partial f}{\partial y}\right)$$

$$= -2\frac{\partial f}{\partial x} - 2v\frac{\partial}{\partial v}\left(\frac{\partial f}{\partial x}\right) + 2u\frac{\partial}{\partial v}\left(\frac{\partial f}{\partial y}\right)$$

Now we will replace $\frac{\partial}{\partial v}$ by its equivalent operator $\left(-2v\frac{\partial}{\partial x} + 2u\frac{\partial}{\partial y}\right)$.

$$\frac{\partial^2 f}{\partial v^2} = -2\frac{\partial f}{\partial x} - 2v\left\{\left(-2v\frac{\partial}{\partial x} + 2u\frac{\partial}{\partial y}\right)\frac{\partial f}{\partial x}\right\}$$

$$+ 2u\left\{\left(-2v\frac{\partial}{\partial x} + 2u\frac{\partial}{\partial y}\right)\frac{\partial f}{\partial y}\right\}$$

$$= -2\frac{\partial f}{\partial x} - 2v\left\{-2v\frac{\partial^2 f}{\partial x^2} + 2u\frac{\partial^2 f}{\partial y \partial x}\right\} + 2u\left\{-2v\frac{\partial^2 f}{\partial x \partial y} + 2u\frac{\partial^2 f}{\partial y^2}\right\}$$

$$\frac{\partial^2 f}{\partial v^2} = -2\frac{\partial f}{\partial x} + 4v^2\frac{\partial^2 f}{\partial x^2} - 8uv\frac{\partial^2 f}{\partial x \partial y} + 4u^2\frac{\partial^2 f}{\partial y^2} \qquad \ldots (4)$$

by adding (2) and (4), $\frac{\partial^2 f}{\partial u^2} + \frac{\partial^2 f}{\partial v^2} = 4(u^2 + v^2)\left(\frac{\partial^2 f}{\partial x^2} + \frac{\partial^2 f}{\partial y^2}\right)$.

Alternate Method : Show that the transformation $x = u^2 - v^2$, $y = 2uv$ transforms :
$\frac{\partial^2 f}{\partial u^2} + \frac{\partial^2 f}{\partial v^2}$ into $4(u^2 + v^2)\left(\frac{\partial^2 f}{\partial x^2} + \frac{\partial^2 f}{\partial y^2}\right)$

$$\frac{\partial f}{\partial u} = \frac{\partial f}{\partial x} \cdot \frac{\partial x}{\partial u} + \frac{\partial f}{\partial y} \cdot \frac{\partial y}{\partial u} = 2u\frac{\partial f}{\partial x} + 2v\frac{\partial f}{\partial y}$$

$$\frac{\partial^2 f}{\partial u^2} = \frac{\partial}{\partial u}\left[2u\frac{\partial f}{\partial x} + 2v\frac{\partial f}{\partial y}\right]$$

$$= 2\left[\frac{\partial}{\partial u}\left(u\frac{\partial f}{\partial x}\right) + \frac{\partial}{\partial u}\left(v\frac{\partial f}{\partial y}\right)\right]$$

$$= 2\left[\frac{\partial f}{\partial x} + u\left\{\frac{\partial^2 f}{\partial x^2} \cdot \frac{\partial x}{\partial u} + \frac{\partial^2 f}{\partial x \partial y} \cdot \frac{\partial y}{\partial u}\right\} + v\left\{\frac{\partial^2 f}{\partial x \partial y} \cdot \frac{\partial x}{\partial u} + \frac{\partial^2 f}{\partial y^2} \cdot \frac{\partial y}{\partial u}\right\}\right]$$

$$= 2\left[\frac{\partial f}{\partial x} + u\left\{2u\frac{\partial^2 f}{\partial x^2} + \frac{\partial^2 f}{\partial x \partial y}2v\right\} + v\left\{2u\frac{\partial^2 f}{\partial x \partial y} + 2v\frac{\partial^2 f}{\partial y^2}\right\}\right]$$

$$\frac{\partial^2 f}{\partial u^2} = 2\frac{\partial f}{\partial x} + 4u^2\frac{\partial^2 f}{\partial x^2} + 8uv\frac{\partial^2 f}{\partial x \partial y} + 4v^2\frac{\partial^2 f}{\partial y^2} \qquad \ldots (1)$$

$$\frac{\partial f}{\partial v} = \frac{\partial f}{\partial x} \cdot \frac{\partial x}{\partial v} + \frac{\partial f}{\partial y} \cdot \frac{\partial y}{\partial v}$$

$$= -2v \frac{\partial f}{\partial x} + 2u \frac{\partial f}{\partial y} \text{ and}$$

$$\frac{\partial^2 f}{\partial v^2} = \frac{\partial}{\partial v}\left[-2v \frac{\partial f}{\partial x} + 2u \frac{\partial f}{\partial y}\right]$$

$$= 2\left[-\frac{\partial}{\partial v}\left(v \frac{\partial f}{\partial x}\right) + \frac{\partial}{\partial v}\left(u \frac{\partial f}{\partial y}\right)\right]$$

$$= 2\left[-\frac{\partial f}{\partial x} - v\left\{\frac{\partial^2 f}{\partial x^2} \cdot \frac{\partial x}{\partial v} + \frac{\partial^2 f}{\partial x \partial y} \cdot \frac{\partial y}{\partial v}\right\} + u\left\{\frac{\partial^2 f}{\partial x \partial y} \cdot \frac{\partial x}{\partial v} + \frac{\partial^2 f}{\partial y^2} \cdot \frac{\partial y}{\partial v}\right\}\right]$$

$$= 2\left[-\frac{\partial f}{\partial x} - v\left\{-2v \frac{\partial^2 f}{\partial x^2} + 2u \frac{\partial^2 f}{\partial x \partial y}\right\} + u\left\{-2v \frac{\partial^2 f}{\partial x \partial y} + 2u \frac{\partial^2 f}{\partial y^2}\right\}\right]$$

$$\therefore \quad \frac{\partial^2 f}{\partial v^2} = -2 \frac{\partial f}{\partial x} + 4v^2 \frac{\partial^2 f}{\partial x^2} - 8uv \frac{\partial^2 f}{\partial x \partial y} + 4u^2 \frac{\partial^2 f}{\partial y^2} \qquad \ldots (2)$$

$$\therefore \quad \frac{\partial^2 f}{\partial u^2} + \frac{\partial^2 f}{\partial v^2} = 4 \frac{\partial^2 f}{\partial x^2}(u^2 + v^2) + 4 \frac{\partial^2 f}{\partial y^2}(u^2 + v^2)$$

$$= 4(u^2 + v^2)\left(\frac{\partial^2 f}{\partial x^2} + \frac{\partial^2 f}{\partial y^2}\right)$$

EXERCISE 10.10

1. Using $u = x^2 - y^2$, $v = 2xy$, prove that if $f(x, y) = \phi(u, v)$,

   $$\frac{\partial^2 f}{\partial x^2} + \frac{\partial^2 f}{\partial y^2} = 4(x^2 + y^2)\left(\frac{\partial^2 f}{\partial u^2} + \frac{\partial^2 f}{\partial v^2}\right) = 4(u^2 + v^2)^{1/2}\left[\frac{\partial^2 \phi}{\partial u^2} + \frac{\partial^2 \phi}{\partial v^2}\right].$$

2. If $u = x + ay$, $v = x + by$ changes $2f_{xx} - 5f_{xy} + 3f_{yy} = 0$ into $f_{uv} = 0$, find a and b.

   Ans. $a = 1$, $b = 2/3$ and $a = 2/3$, $b = 1$.

3. Transform the equation $(x - y)\left(x^2 \frac{\partial^2 z}{\partial x^2} - 2xy \frac{\partial^2 z}{\partial x \partial y} + y^2 \frac{\partial^2 z}{\partial y^2}\right) = 2xy\left(\frac{\partial z}{\partial x} - \frac{\partial z}{\partial y}\right)$

   to one in which the independent variables are u, v where $u = x + y$, $v = xy$.

4. If $z = f(x, y)$, $u = e^x$, $v = e^y$ then show that

   (i) $\dfrac{\partial^2 z}{\partial x \partial y} = uv \dfrac{\partial^2 z}{\partial u \partial v}$, (ii) $\dfrac{\partial^2 z}{\partial x^2} + \dfrac{\partial^2 z}{\partial y^2} = u^2 \dfrac{\partial^2 z}{\partial u^2} + v^2 \dfrac{\partial^2 z}{\partial v^2} + u \dfrac{\partial z}{\partial u} + v \dfrac{\partial z}{\partial u}$.

5. If $x = e^r \cos \theta$, $y = e^r \sin \theta$ show that $\dfrac{\partial^2 u}{\partial x^2} + \dfrac{\partial^2 u}{\partial y^2} = e^{-2r}\left(\dfrac{\partial^2 u}{\partial r^2} + \dfrac{\partial^2 u}{\partial \theta^2}\right)$.

6. Using $x = uv$, $y = \dfrac{1}{v}$ transform the equation

$$\dfrac{\partial^2 z}{\partial x^2} + 2xy^2 \cdot \dfrac{\partial z}{\partial x} + 2(y - y^3)\dfrac{\partial z}{\partial y} + x^2 y^2 z = 0$$ and hence show that z is same function of u, v as of x, y.

7. If $x = r\cosh\theta$, $y = r\sinh\theta$ and $z = f(x, y)$ then show that

  (i) $(x - y)\left(\dfrac{\partial z}{\partial x} - \dfrac{\partial z}{\partial y}\right) = r\dfrac{\partial z}{\partial r} - \dfrac{\partial z}{\partial \theta}$ (Dec. 2008, May 2013)

  (ii) $(x^2 - y^2)\left(\dfrac{\partial^2 z}{\partial x^2} - \dfrac{\partial^2 z}{\partial y^2}\right) = r^2 \dfrac{\partial^2 z}{\partial r^2} + r\dfrac{\partial z}{\partial r} - \dfrac{\partial^2 z}{\partial \theta^2}$.

8. If $x = e^v \sec u$, $y = e^v \tan u$ and $\phi = f(x, y)$ then show that

$$\cos u\left(\dfrac{\partial^2 \phi}{\partial u\, \partial v} - \dfrac{\partial \phi}{\partial u}\right) = xy\left(\dfrac{\partial^2 \phi}{\partial x^2} + \dfrac{\partial^2 \phi}{\partial y^2}\right) + (x^2 + y^2)\dfrac{\partial^2 \phi}{\partial x\, \partial y}.$$

9. If $u = f(x, y)$ where $x = \xi\cos\theta - \eta\sin\theta$, $y = \xi\sin\theta + \eta\cos\theta$

  then prove that $\dfrac{\partial^2 u}{\partial x^2} + \dfrac{\partial^2 u}{\partial y^2} = \dfrac{\partial^2 u}{\partial \xi^2} + \dfrac{\partial^2 u}{\partial \eta^2}$.

10. If $u = x^2 - y^2$ and $v = 2xy$, prove that $\dfrac{\partial^2 f}{\partial x^2} + \dfrac{\partial^2 f}{\partial y^2} = 4(x^2 + y^2)\left[\dfrac{\partial^2 f}{\partial u^2} + \dfrac{\partial^2 f}{\partial v^2}\right]$.

10.17 EULER'S THEOREM ON HOMOGENEOUS FUNCTIONS OF THREE VARIABLES

Definition : A function $u = f(x, y, z)$ is said to be a homogeneous function of three variables x, y, z of degree n if it is possible to express u as

$$u = x^n F\left(\dfrac{y}{x}, \dfrac{z}{x}\right)$$

Statement : Euler's Theorem on homogeneous functions of three variables :

This theorem states that if u is a homogeneous function of x, y, z of degree n, then

$$x\dfrac{\partial u}{\partial x} + y\dfrac{\partial u}{\partial y} + z\dfrac{\partial u}{\partial z} = nu$$

Proof : Since u is a homogeneous function of x, y, z of degree n, we have

$u = x^n f(y/x, z/x) = x^n (p, q)$ where $p = y/x$, $q = z/x$.

⇒ u is a composite function of x, y, z.

$$\therefore \quad u = x^n f(p, q) \Rightarrow \frac{\partial u}{\partial x} = x^n \frac{\partial f}{\partial x} + n x^{n-1} f$$

$$= x^n \left[\frac{\partial f}{\partial p} \frac{\partial p}{\partial x} + \frac{\partial f}{\partial q} \frac{\partial q}{\partial x} \right] + n x^{n-1} f$$

$$\frac{\partial u}{\partial x} = x^n \left[\frac{\partial f}{\partial p} \left(\frac{-y}{x^2} \right) + \frac{\partial f}{\partial p} \left(\frac{-z}{x^2} \right) \right] + n x^{n-1} \cdot f$$

$$= -x^{n-2} y \frac{\partial f}{\partial p} - x^{n-2} z \frac{\partial f}{\partial q} + n x^{n-1} \cdot f$$

Also, $\quad \dfrac{\partial u}{\partial y} = x^n \dfrac{\partial f}{\partial y} = x^n \left[\dfrac{\partial f}{\partial p} \cdot \dfrac{\partial p}{\partial y} + \dfrac{\partial f}{\partial q} \cdot \dfrac{\partial q}{\partial y} \right]$

$$\therefore \quad \frac{\partial u}{\partial y} = x^n \left[\frac{\partial f}{\partial p} \cdot \frac{1}{x} + \frac{\partial f}{\partial q} \cdot 0 \right]$$

$$= x^{n-1} \frac{\partial f}{\partial p}$$

Similarly, $\quad \dfrac{\partial u}{\partial z} = x^{n-1} \dfrac{\partial f}{\partial q}$

$$\therefore \quad x \frac{\partial u}{\partial x} + y \frac{\partial u}{\partial y} + z \frac{\partial u}{\partial z}$$

$$= -x^{n-1} y \frac{\partial f}{\partial p} - x^{n-1} z \frac{\partial f}{\partial q} + n x^n f + x^{n-1} y \frac{\partial f}{\partial p} + x^{n-1} z \frac{\partial f}{\partial q}$$

$$= n \cdot x^n f = n \cdot u$$

or $x u_x + y u_y + z u_z = n \cdot u$

Cor. 1 : If u is a homogeneous function of x, y, z of degree n and if u = f(v) then

$$x \frac{\partial v}{\partial x} + y \frac{\partial v}{\partial y} + z \frac{\partial z}{\partial z} = n \frac{f(v)}{f'(v)}.$$

Proof : Since u is a homogeneous function of x, y, z of degree n, by Euler's theorem, we have

$$x \frac{\partial u}{\partial x} + y \frac{\partial u}{\partial y} + z \frac{\partial u}{\partial z} = n \cdot u \qquad \ldots (1)$$

Since $u = f(v)$ $\therefore \dfrac{\partial u}{\partial x} = f'(v) \dfrac{\partial v}{\partial x}$

$$\dfrac{\partial u}{\partial y} = f'(v) \dfrac{\partial v}{\partial y}$$

$\dfrac{\partial u}{\partial z} = f'(v) \dfrac{\partial v}{\partial z}$ and substituting in (1), we have

$$x \cdot f'(v) \dfrac{\partial v}{\partial x} + y\, f'(v) \cdot \dfrac{\partial v}{\partial y} + z \cdot f'(v) \dfrac{\partial v}{\partial z} = n \cdot f(v)$$

$$\Rightarrow x \dfrac{\partial v}{\partial x} + y \dfrac{\partial v}{\partial y} + z \dfrac{\partial v}{\partial z} = \dfrac{n \cdot f(v)}{f'(v)}.$$

Cor. 2 : If u is a homogeneous function of x, y, z of degree n then by Euler's theorem, we have

$$x^2 \dfrac{\partial^2 u}{\partial x^2} + y^2 \dfrac{\partial^2 u}{\partial y^2} + z^2 \dfrac{\partial^2 u}{\partial z^2} + 2xy \dfrac{\partial^2 u}{\partial x\, \partial y} + 2yz \dfrac{\partial^2 u}{\partial y\, \partial z} + 2zx \dfrac{\partial^2 u}{\partial z\, \partial x} = n\,(n-1)\, u.$$

CHAPTER ELEVEN

JACOBIANS, ERRORS AND APPROXIMATIONS, MAXIMA AND MINIMA

11.1 JACOBIANS

Definition : If u and v be continuous and differentiable functions of two other independent variables x and y such as $u = \phi_1(x, y)$, $v = \phi_2(x, y)$ then we define the determinant

$$\begin{vmatrix} \dfrac{\partial u}{\partial x} & \dfrac{\partial u}{\partial y} \\ \dfrac{\partial v}{\partial x} & \dfrac{\partial v}{\partial y} \end{vmatrix}$$ as Jacobian of u, v with respect to x, y

and often denote this as $\dfrac{\partial(u, v)}{\partial(x, y)}$ or sometimes also as $J = \dfrac{\partial(u, v)}{\partial(x, y)} = \begin{vmatrix} u_x & u_y \\ v_x & v_y \end{vmatrix}$ ... (I)

In the same way if u, v, w be continuous and differentiable functions of other three variables x, y, z then we can define

$$\begin{vmatrix} u_x & u_y & u_z \\ v_x & v_y & v_z \\ w_x & w_y & w_z \end{vmatrix} = \dfrac{\partial(u, v, w)}{\partial(x, y, z)}$$ as Jacobian of u, v, w with respect to x, y, z

$$\therefore \quad J = \dfrac{\partial(u, v, w)}{\partial(x, y, z)} = \begin{vmatrix} u_x & u_y & u_z \\ v_x & v_y & v_z \\ w_x & w_y & w_z \end{vmatrix}$$

Actually, Jacobians are functional determinants.

ILLUSTRATIONS ON JACOBIANS

Ex. 1 : *Given* $u = x^2 - y^2$ *and* $v = 2xy$. *Calculate* $\dfrac{\partial(u, v)}{\partial(x, y)}$.

Sol. : Given : $u_x = 2x$, $u_y = -2y$, $v_x = 2y$, $v_y = 2x$

$$\therefore \quad J = \frac{\partial(u, v)}{\partial(x, y)} = \begin{vmatrix} u_x & u_y \\ v_x & v_y \end{vmatrix} = \begin{vmatrix} 2x & -2y \\ 2y & 2x \end{vmatrix}$$

$$= 4 \begin{vmatrix} x & -y \\ y & x \end{vmatrix} = 4[x^2 + y^2]$$

Ex. 2 : If $x = r \cos \theta$, $y = r \sin \theta$ then evaluate $\dfrac{\partial(x, y)}{\partial(r, \theta)}$ and $\dfrac{\partial(r, \theta)}{\partial(x, y)}$.

Sol. : Given that $x = r \cos \theta$, $y = r \sin \theta$ then $r^2 = x^2 + y^2$ and $\theta = \tan^{-1} \dfrac{y}{x}$. ...(1)

$$\therefore \quad \frac{\partial x}{\partial r} = \cos \theta, \quad \frac{\partial x}{\partial \theta} = -r \sin \theta, \quad \frac{\partial y}{\partial r} = \sin \theta, \quad \frac{\partial y}{\partial \theta} = r \cos \theta$$

Hence $\quad J = \dfrac{\partial(x, y)}{\partial(r, \theta)} = \begin{vmatrix} \dfrac{\partial x}{\partial r} & \dfrac{\partial x}{\partial \theta} \\ \dfrac{\partial y}{\partial r} & \dfrac{\partial y}{\partial \theta} \end{vmatrix} = \begin{vmatrix} \cos \theta & -r \sin \theta \\ \sin \theta & r \cos \theta \end{vmatrix}$

$$= r \cos^2 \theta + r \sin^2 \theta = r \qquad \ldots (2)$$

From equation (1), we can obtain

$$\frac{\partial r}{\partial x} = \frac{x}{r}, \quad \frac{\partial r}{\partial y} = \frac{y}{r}; \quad \frac{\partial \theta}{\partial x} = \frac{-y}{r^2}; \quad \frac{\partial \theta}{\partial y} = \frac{x}{x^2 + y^2} = \frac{x}{r^2}$$

$$J' = \begin{vmatrix} \dfrac{\partial r}{\partial x} & \dfrac{\partial r}{\partial y} \\ \dfrac{\partial \theta}{\partial x} & \dfrac{\partial \theta}{\partial y} \end{vmatrix} = \begin{vmatrix} \dfrac{x}{r} & \dfrac{y}{r} \\ \dfrac{-y}{r^2} & \dfrac{x}{r^2} \end{vmatrix} = \frac{1}{r^3} \begin{vmatrix} x & y \\ -y & x \end{vmatrix}$$

$$= \frac{1}{r^3} [x^2 + y^2] = \frac{1}{r^3} (r^2) = \frac{1}{r} \qquad \ldots (3)$$

We observe that from (2) and (3),

$$J J' = \frac{\partial(x, y)}{\partial(r, \theta)} \cdot \frac{\partial(r, \theta)}{\partial(x, y)} = r \cdot \frac{1}{r} = 1 \Rightarrow J J' = 1$$

Ex. 3 : If $x = r \sin \theta \cos \phi$, $y = r \sin \theta \sin \phi$, $z = r \cos \theta$, show that $\dfrac{\partial(x, y, z)}{\partial(r, \theta, \phi)} = r^2 \sin \theta$.

(Dec. 2014)

Sol. : Given that $x = r \sin \theta \cos \phi$, $y = r \sin \theta \sin \phi$, $z = r \cos \theta$. ... (1)

$$\therefore \quad \frac{\partial x}{\partial r} = \sin \theta \cos \phi, \quad \frac{\partial x}{\partial \theta} = r \cos \theta \cos \phi, \quad \frac{\partial x}{\partial \phi} = -z \sin \theta \sin \phi$$

$$\frac{\partial y}{\partial r} = \sin \theta \sin \phi, \quad \frac{\partial y}{\partial \theta} = r \cos \theta \sin \phi, \quad \frac{\partial y}{\partial \phi} = r \sin \theta \cos \phi$$

$$\frac{\partial z}{\partial r} = \cos \theta, \quad \frac{\partial z}{\partial \theta} = -r \sin \theta, \quad \frac{\partial z}{\partial \phi} = 0$$

$$J = \frac{\partial(x, y, z)}{\partial(r, \theta, \phi)} = \begin{vmatrix} \frac{\partial x}{\partial r} & \frac{\partial x}{\partial \theta} & \frac{\partial x}{\partial \phi} \\ \frac{\partial y}{\partial r} & \frac{\partial y}{\partial \theta} & \frac{\partial y}{\partial \phi} \\ \frac{\partial z}{\partial r} & \frac{\partial z}{\partial \theta} & \frac{\partial z}{\partial \phi} \end{vmatrix} = \begin{vmatrix} \sin\theta\cos\phi & r\cos\theta\cos\phi & -\sin\theta\sin\phi \\ \sin\theta\sin\phi & r\cos\theta\sin\phi & r\sin\theta\cos\phi \\ \cos\theta & -r\sin\theta & 0 \end{vmatrix}$$

$$= r^2 \begin{vmatrix} \sin\theta\cos\phi & \cos\theta\cos\phi & -\sin\theta\sin\phi \\ \sin\theta\sin\phi & \cos\theta\sin\phi & \sin\theta\cos\phi \\ \cos\theta & -\sin\theta & 0 \end{vmatrix}$$

$$= r^2 [\cos\theta \{\cos\theta\sin\theta\cos^2\phi + \sin\theta\cos\theta\sin^2\phi\}$$
$$\quad + \sin\theta \{\sin^2\theta\cos^2\phi + \sin^2\theta\sin^2\phi\}]$$
$$= r^2 [\sin\theta\cos^2\theta + \sin^3\theta] = r^2 \sin\theta [\cos^2\theta + \sin^2\theta]$$
$$= r^2 \sin\theta$$

Ex. 4 : If $x = a\cosh\theta\cos\phi$, $y = a\sinh\theta\sin\phi$,

show that $\dfrac{\partial(x, y)}{\partial(\theta, \phi)} = \dfrac{a^2}{2} [\cosh 2\theta - \cos 2\phi]$.

Sol. :
$$J = \frac{\partial(x, y)}{\partial(\theta, \phi)} = \begin{vmatrix} \frac{\partial x}{\partial \theta} & \frac{\partial x}{\partial \phi} \\ \frac{\partial y}{\partial \theta} & \frac{\partial y}{\partial \phi} \end{vmatrix} = \begin{vmatrix} a\sinh\theta\cos\phi & -a\cosh\theta\sin\phi \\ a\cosh\theta\sin\phi & a\sinh\theta\cos\phi \end{vmatrix}$$

$$= a^2 [\sinh^2\theta\cos^2\phi + \cosh^2\theta\sin^2\phi]$$
$$= a^2 [\sinh^2\theta (1 - \sin^2\phi) + (1 + \sinh^2\theta)\sin^2\phi]$$
$$= a^2 [\sinh^2\theta - \sinh^2\theta\sin^2\phi + \sin^2\phi + \sinh^2\theta\sin^2\phi]$$
$$= a^2 [\sinh^2\theta + \sin^2\phi] = \frac{a^2}{2} [\cosh 2\theta - 1 + 1 - \cos 2\phi]$$
$$= \frac{a^2}{2} [\cosh 2\theta - \cos 2\phi]$$

Ex. 5 : If $u = xyz$, $v = x^2 + y^2 + z^2$, $w = x + y + z$, find $\dfrac{\partial(u, v, w)}{\partial(x, y, z)}$.

Sol. :
$$J = \frac{\partial(u, v, w)}{\partial(x, y, z)} = \begin{vmatrix} \frac{\partial u}{\partial x} & \frac{\partial u}{\partial y} & \frac{\partial u}{\partial z} \\ \frac{\partial v}{\partial x} & \frac{\partial v}{\partial y} & \frac{\partial v}{\partial z} \\ \frac{\partial w}{\partial x} & \frac{\partial w}{\partial y} & \frac{\partial w}{\partial z} \end{vmatrix} = \begin{vmatrix} yz & zx & xy \\ 2x & 2y & 2z \\ 1 & 1 & 1 \end{vmatrix}$$

Perform $C_1 - C_2$, $C_2 - C_3$

$$= \begin{vmatrix} z(y-x) & x(z-y) & xy \\ 2(x-y) & 2(y-z) & 2z \\ 0 & 0 & 1 \end{vmatrix} = 2(x-y)(y-z) \begin{vmatrix} -z & -x & xy \\ 1 & 1 & z \\ 0 & 0 & 1 \end{vmatrix}$$

$$= 2(x-y)(y-z)(x-z) = -2(x-y)(y-z)(z-x)$$

Ex. 6 : If $x + y + z = u$, $y + z = uv$, $z = uvw$, find $\dfrac{\partial(x, y, z)}{\partial(u, v, w)}$.

Sol. : We note that $x = u - uv$, $y = uv - uvw$, $z = uvw$

$$\dfrac{\partial(x, y, z)}{\partial(u, v, w)} = \begin{vmatrix} \dfrac{\partial x}{\partial u} & \dfrac{\partial x}{\partial v} & \dfrac{\partial x}{\partial w} \\ \dfrac{\partial y}{\partial u} & \dfrac{\partial y}{\partial v} & \dfrac{\partial y}{\partial w} \\ \dfrac{\partial z}{\partial u} & \dfrac{\partial z}{\partial v} & \dfrac{\partial z}{\partial w} \end{vmatrix} = \begin{vmatrix} 1-v & -u & 0 \\ v-vw & u-uw & -uv \\ vw & uw & uv \end{vmatrix}$$

Perform $R_1 + R_2 + R_3$ $= \begin{vmatrix} 1 & 0 & 0 \\ v-vw & u-uw & -uv \\ vw & uw & uv \end{vmatrix} = 1[(u-uw)(uv) + (uv)(uw)]$

$$= u^2 v$$

Ex. 7 : If $u_1 = f_1(x_1)$, $u_2 = f_2(x_1, x_2)$, $u_3 = f_3(x_1, x_2, x_3)$, ..., $u_n = f_n(x_1, x_2, \ldots x_n)$

then show that $\dfrac{\partial(u_1, u_2, \ldots u_n)}{\partial(x_1, x_2, \ldots x_n)} = \dfrac{\partial u_1}{\partial x_1} \cdot \dfrac{\partial u_2}{\partial x_2} \cdot \dfrac{\partial u_3}{\partial x_3} \ldots \dfrac{\partial u_n}{\partial x_n}$ and hence if $x = \cos u$, $y = \sin u \cos v$, $z = \sin u \sin v \cos w$, find $\dfrac{\partial(x, y, z)}{\partial(u, v, w)}$.

Sol. : $\dfrac{\partial(u_1, u_2, \ldots, u_n)}{\partial(x_1, x_2, \ldots, x_n)} = \begin{vmatrix} \dfrac{\partial u_1}{\partial x_1} & 0 & 0 & \ldots & 0 \\ \dfrac{\partial u_2}{\partial x_1} & \dfrac{\partial u_2}{\partial x_2} & 0 & \ldots & 0 \\ \dfrac{\partial u_3}{\partial x_1} & \dfrac{\partial u_3}{\partial x_2} & \dfrac{\partial u_3}{\partial x_3} & \ldots & 0 \\ \ldots & \ldots & \ldots & \ldots & \ldots \\ \dfrac{\partial u_n}{\partial x_1} & \dfrac{\partial u_n}{\partial x_2} & \ldots & \ldots & \dfrac{\partial u_n}{\partial x_n} \end{vmatrix}$

$$= \dfrac{\partial u_1}{\partial x_1} \cdot \dfrac{\partial u_2}{\partial x_2} \cdot \dfrac{\partial u_3}{\partial x_3} \ldots \ldots \cdot \dfrac{\partial u_n}{\partial x_n} \qquad \ldots (1)$$

Next, if
$$x = f_1(u) = \cos u$$
$$y = f_2(u, v) = \sin u \cos v$$
$$z = f_3(u, v, w) = \sin u \sin v \cos w$$

From result (1) above

$$\therefore \quad \frac{\partial(x, y, z)}{\partial(u, v, w)} = \frac{\partial x}{\partial u} \cdot \frac{\partial y}{\partial v} \cdot \frac{\partial z}{\partial w}$$

$$= (-\sin u)(-\sin u \sin v)(-\sin u \sin v \sin w)$$

$$= -\sin^3 u \sin^2 v \sin w$$

EXERCISE 11.1

1. If in cylindrical coordinates $x = u \cos \phi$, $y = u \sin \phi$, $z = z$, find $\dfrac{\partial(x, y, z)}{\partial(u, \phi, z)}$.

2. If $y_1 = 1 - x_1$, $y_2 = x_1(1 - x_2)$, $y_3 = x_1 x_2 (1 - x_3)$, find $\dfrac{\partial(y_1, y_2, y_3)}{\partial(x_1, x_2, x_3)}$. **Ans.:** $(-1)^3 x_1^2 (x_2)$

3. If $x = ar \sin \theta \cos \phi$, $y = br \sin \theta \sin \phi$, $z = cr \cos \theta$, show that $\dfrac{\partial(x, y, z)}{\partial(r, \theta, \phi)} = abc\, r^2 \sin \theta$.

4. If $ux = yz$, $vy = zx$, $wz = xy$, find $\dfrac{\partial(u, v, w)}{\partial(x, y, z)}$. **(May 2010) Ans.:** 4

5. If $xu = vw$, $yv = wu$, $zw = uv$, find $\dfrac{\partial(x, y, z)}{\partial(u, v, w)}$. **Ans.:** 4

6. If $u = x + 2y^2 - z^3$, $v = x^2 yz$, $w = 2z^2 - xy$, find $\dfrac{\partial(u, v, w)}{\partial(x, y, z)}$ at $(1, -1, 0)$. **Ans.:** 6

7. If $x = u - v + w$, $y = u^2 - v^2 - w^2$, $z = u^3 v$, find $\dfrac{\partial(x, y, z)}{\partial(u, v, w)}$.

    Ans.: $6u^2 (v + w) + 2u + 2w$

8. If $u = \dfrac{x}{y - z}$, $v = \dfrac{y}{z - x}$, $w = \dfrac{z}{x - y}$, find $\dfrac{\partial(u, v, w)}{\partial(x, y, z)}$. **Ans.:** 0

9. If $u = 3x + 2y - z$, $v = x - 2y + z$, $w = x(x + 2y - z)$, find $\dfrac{\partial(u, v, w)}{\partial(x, y, z)}$. **Ans.:** 0

10. If $u = x + y + z$, $v = x^2 + y^2 + z^2$, $w = xy + yz + zx$, find $\dfrac{\partial(u, v, w)}{\partial(x, y, z)}$. **Ans.:** 0

11.2 JACOBIANS OF COMPOSITE FUNCTIONS

CHAIN RULE OF JACOBIANS

If x, y be functions of u, v and u, v functions of r, s such that

$$\left.\begin{array}{l} x = \phi_1(u, v);\ y = \phi_2(u, v) \\ u = \psi_1(r, s);\ v = \psi_2(r, s) \end{array}\right\} \qquad \ldots \text{(i)}$$

then

$$\frac{\partial(x, y)}{\partial(u, v)} \cdot \frac{\partial(u, v)}{\partial(r, s)} = \frac{\partial(x, y)}{\partial(r, s)} \qquad \ldots \text{(ii)}$$

Proof : From equation (i) it is quite obvious that x, y are composite functions of r and s. Thus we have,

$$\frac{\partial x}{\partial r} = \frac{\partial x}{\partial u} \cdot \frac{\partial u}{\partial r} + \frac{\partial x}{\partial v} \cdot \frac{\partial v}{\partial r}$$

$$\frac{\partial x}{\partial s} = \frac{\partial x}{\partial u} \cdot \frac{\partial u}{\partial s} + \frac{\partial x}{\partial v} \cdot \frac{\partial v}{\partial s} \quad \ldots \text{(iii)}$$

and

$$\frac{\partial y}{\partial r} = \frac{\partial y}{\partial u} \cdot \frac{\partial u}{\partial r} + \frac{\partial y}{\partial v} \cdot \frac{\partial v}{\partial r}$$

$$\frac{\partial y}{\partial s} = \frac{\partial y}{\partial u} \cdot \frac{\partial u}{\partial s} + \frac{\partial y}{\partial v} \cdot \frac{\partial v}{\partial s} \quad \ldots \text{(iv)}$$

Hence we have

$$\text{L.H.S.} = \frac{\partial(x, y)}{\partial(u, v)} \cdot \frac{\partial(u, v)}{\partial(r, s)} = \begin{vmatrix} \frac{\partial x}{\partial u} & \frac{\partial x}{\partial v} \\ \frac{\partial y}{\partial u} & \frac{\partial y}{\partial v} \end{vmatrix} \times \begin{vmatrix} \frac{\partial u}{\partial r} & \frac{\partial u}{\partial s} \\ \frac{\partial v}{\partial r} & \frac{\partial v}{\partial s} \end{vmatrix}$$

Interchanging the rows and columns of 2nd determinant

$$= \begin{vmatrix} \frac{\partial x}{\partial u} & \frac{\partial x}{\partial v} \\ \frac{\partial y}{\partial u} & \frac{\partial y}{\partial v} \end{vmatrix} \times \begin{vmatrix} \frac{\partial u}{\partial r} & \frac{\partial v}{\partial r} \\ \frac{\partial u}{\partial s} & \frac{\partial v}{\partial s} \end{vmatrix} = \begin{vmatrix} \frac{\partial x}{\partial u} \cdot \frac{\partial u}{\partial r} + \frac{\partial x}{\partial v} \cdot \frac{\partial v}{\partial r} & \frac{\partial x}{\partial u} \cdot \frac{\partial u}{\partial s} + \frac{\partial x}{\partial v} \cdot \frac{\partial v}{\partial s} \\ \frac{\partial y}{\partial u} \cdot \frac{\partial u}{\partial r} + \frac{\partial y}{\partial v} \cdot \frac{\partial v}{\partial r} & \frac{\partial y}{\partial u} \cdot \frac{\partial u}{\partial s} + \frac{\partial y}{\partial v} \cdot \frac{\partial v}{\partial s} \end{vmatrix}$$

$$= \begin{vmatrix} \frac{\partial x}{\partial r} & \frac{\partial x}{\partial s} \\ \frac{\partial y}{\partial r} & \frac{\partial y}{\partial s} \end{vmatrix} = \frac{\partial(x, y)}{\partial(r, s)} = \text{R.H.S.}$$

$$\frac{\partial(x, y)}{\partial(u, v)} \cdot \frac{\partial(u, v)}{\partial(r, s)} = \frac{\partial(x, y)}{\partial(r, s)} \quad \ldots \text{(v)}$$

Corollary : If in (v) above we put r = x and s = y then we get

$$\frac{\partial(x, y)}{\partial(u, v)} \cdot \frac{\partial(u, v)}{\partial(x, y)} = 1 \quad \text{which means } J \cdot J' = 1$$

Similarly,

$$\frac{\partial(x, y, z)}{\partial(u, v, w)} \cdot \frac{\partial(u, v, w)}{\partial(x, y, z)} = 1$$

Note : The above formula can be generalised as

$$\frac{\partial(x_1, x_2, \ldots, x_n)}{\partial(u_1, u_2, \ldots, u_n)} \cdot \frac{\partial(u_1, u_2, \ldots, u_n)}{\partial(v_1, v_2, \ldots, v_n)} = \frac{\partial(x_1, x_2, \ldots, x_n)}{\partial(v_1, v_2, \ldots, v_n)}$$

and

$$\frac{\partial(x_1, x_2, \ldots, x_n)}{\partial(u_1, u_2, \ldots, u_n)} \cdot \frac{\partial(u_1, u_2, \ldots, u_n)}{\partial(x_1, x_2, \ldots, x_n)} = 1.$$

ILLUSTRATIONS ON CHAIN RULE

Ex. 1 : If $u = e^x \cos y$, $v = e^x \sin y$, where $x = lr + sm$ and $y = mr - sl$, verify chain rule of Jacobians. l, m being constants.

Sol. : To verify that

$$\frac{\partial(u, v)}{\partial(x, y)} \cdot \frac{\partial(x, y)}{\partial(r, s)} = \frac{\partial(u, v)}{\partial(r, s)} \qquad \ldots (1)$$

$$\frac{\partial(u, v)}{\partial(x, y)} = \begin{vmatrix} u_x & u_y \\ v_x & v_y \end{vmatrix} = \begin{vmatrix} e^x \cos y & -e^x \sin y \\ e^x \sin y & e^x \cos y \end{vmatrix}$$

$$= e^{2x} \begin{vmatrix} \cos y & -\sin y \\ \sin y & \cos y \end{vmatrix} = e^{2x} \qquad \ldots (2)$$

$$\frac{\partial(x, y)}{\partial(r, s)} = \begin{vmatrix} x_r & x_s \\ y_r & y_s \end{vmatrix} = \begin{vmatrix} l & m \\ m & -l \end{vmatrix} = -(l^2 + m^2) \qquad \ldots (3)$$

Now $u = e^{lr + ms} \cos(mr - ls)$, $v = e^{lr + ms} \cdot \sin(mr - ls)$ ... (4)

Hence
$$\frac{\partial(u, v)}{\partial(r, s)} = \begin{vmatrix} u_r & u_s \\ v_r & v_s \end{vmatrix}$$

$$= \begin{vmatrix} le^x \cos y - me^x \sin y & me^x \cos y + le^x \sin y \\ le^x \sin y + me^x \cos y & me^x \sin y - le^x \cos y \end{vmatrix}$$

$$= e^{2x} \begin{vmatrix} l \cos y - m \sin y & m \cos y + l \sin y \\ l \sin y + m \cos y & m \sin y - l \cos y \end{vmatrix}$$

$$= e^{2x} [(l \cos y - m \sin y)(m \sin y - l \cos y)$$
$$\quad - (l \sin y + m \cos y)(m \cos y + l \sin y)]$$
$$= e^{2x} [lm \cos y \sin y - l^2 \cos^2 y - m^2 \sin^2 y + lm \sin y \cos y$$
$$\quad - lm \sin y \cos y - l^2 \sin^2 y - m^2 \cos^2 y - lm \sin y \cos y]$$
$$= e^{2x} [-l^2 (\cos^2 y + \sin^2 y) - m^2 (\cos^2 y + \sin^2 y)]$$
$$= -e^{2x} (l^2 + m^2)$$

$$\therefore \quad \frac{\partial(u, v)}{\partial(r, s)} = -e^{2x}(l^2 + m^2) \qquad \ldots (5)$$

If we multiply (2) and (3), we get

$$\frac{\partial(u, v)}{\partial(x, y)} \cdot \frac{\partial(x, y)}{\partial(r, s)} = -e^{2x}(l^2 + m^2) \qquad \ldots (6)$$

Hence from (5) and (6), we have

$$\frac{\partial(u, v)}{\partial(x, y)} \cdot \frac{\partial(x, y)}{\partial(r, s)} = \frac{\partial(u, v)}{\partial(r, s)}$$

Ex. 2 : *For the transformation $x = a(u + v)$, $y = b(u - v)$ where $u = r^2 \cos 2\theta$, $v = r^2 \sin 2\theta$, a and b being constants, find $\frac{\partial(x, y)}{\partial(r, \theta)}$.* **(Dec. 2005)**

Sol. : Here $x, y \to u, v \to r, \theta$.

$$\frac{\partial(x, y)}{\partial(r, \theta)} = \frac{\partial(x, y)}{\partial(u, v)} \cdot \frac{\partial(u, v)}{\partial(r, \theta)}$$

$$= \begin{vmatrix} \frac{\partial x}{\partial u} & \frac{\partial x}{\partial v} \\ \frac{\partial y}{\partial u} & \frac{\partial y}{\partial v} \end{vmatrix} \times \begin{vmatrix} \frac{\partial u}{\partial r} & \frac{\partial u}{\partial \theta} \\ \frac{\partial v}{\partial r} & \frac{\partial v}{\partial \theta} \end{vmatrix}$$

$$= \begin{vmatrix} a & a \\ b & -b \end{vmatrix} \cdot \begin{vmatrix} 2r \cos 2\theta & -2r^2 \sin 2\theta \\ 2r \sin 2\theta & 2r^2 \cos 2\theta \end{vmatrix}$$

$$= (-2ab) \times (4r^3) = -8abr^3$$

Ex. 3 : *If $u = e^x (x \cos y - y \sin y)$, $v = e^x (x \sin y + y \cos y)$ where $x = l\xi + m\eta$ and $y = l\eta - m\xi$, find $\frac{\partial(u, v)}{\partial(\xi, \eta)}$.*

Sol. : Here $u, v \to x, y \to \xi, \eta$

$$\frac{\partial(u, v)}{\partial(\xi, \eta)} = \frac{\partial(u, v)}{\partial(x, y)} \cdot \frac{\partial(x, y)}{\partial(\xi, \eta)}$$

$$= \begin{vmatrix} e^x (x \cos y - y \sin y + \cos y) & e^x (-x \sin y - y \cos y - \sin y) \\ e^x (x \sin y + y \cos y + \sin y) & e^x (x \cos y + \cos y - y \sin y) \end{vmatrix} \cdot \begin{vmatrix} l & m \\ -m & l \end{vmatrix}$$

$$= e^{2x} [(x \cos y - y \sin y + \cos y)^2 + (x \sin y + y \cos y + \sin y)^2] (l^2 + m^2)$$

$$= e^{2x} (x^2 + y^2 + 1 + 2x)(l^2 + m^2) = e^{2x} (l^2 + m^2)[(x + 1)^2 + y^2]$$

Ex. 4 : *If $x = \sqrt{vw}$, $y = \sqrt{uw}$, $z = \sqrt{uv}$ and $u = r \sin \theta \cos \phi$, $v = r \sin \theta \sin \phi$, $w = r \cos \theta$, find $\frac{\partial(x, y, z)}{\partial(r, \theta, \phi)}$.*

Sol. : Here $x, y, z \to u, v, w \to r, \theta, \phi$.

$$\frac{\partial(x, y, z)}{\partial(r, \theta, \phi)} = \frac{\partial(x, y, z)}{\partial(u, v, w)} \cdot \frac{\partial(u, v, w)}{\partial(r, \theta, \phi)} \qquad \dots (1)$$

We first calculate

$$\frac{\partial(x, y, z)}{\partial(u, v, w)} = \begin{vmatrix} 0 & \frac{1}{2}\sqrt{\frac{w}{v}} & \frac{1}{2}\sqrt{\frac{v}{w}} \\ \frac{1}{2}\sqrt{\frac{w}{u}} & 0 & \frac{1}{2}\sqrt{\frac{u}{w}} \\ \frac{1}{2}\sqrt{\frac{v}{u}} & \frac{1}{2}\sqrt{\frac{u}{v}} & 0 \end{vmatrix}$$

$$= \frac{1}{8} \frac{1}{uvw} \cdot \begin{vmatrix} 0 & \sqrt{vw} & \sqrt{vw} \\ \sqrt{uw} & 0 & \sqrt{uw} \\ \sqrt{uv} & \sqrt{uv} & 0 \end{vmatrix}$$

$$= \frac{1}{8} \frac{\sqrt{vw}\sqrt{uw}\sqrt{uv}}{uvw} \begin{vmatrix} 0 & 1 & 1 \\ 1 & 0 & 1 \\ 1 & 1 & 0 \end{vmatrix} = \frac{1}{4} \qquad \ldots (2)$$

and $\qquad \dfrac{\partial(u, v, w)}{\partial(r, \theta, \phi)} = r^2 \sin\theta \quad$ [Refer Ex. 3, Article 11.1] $\qquad \ldots (3)$

Substituting (2) and (3) in (1),

$\therefore \qquad \dfrac{\partial(x, y, z)}{\partial(r, \theta, \phi)} = \dfrac{1}{4} (r^2 \sin\theta)$

Ex. 5 : If $x = uv$ and $y = \dfrac{u+v}{u-v}$, find $\dfrac{\partial(u, v)}{\partial(x, y)}$. **(May 2009, 2013)**

Sol. : Here x, y are functions of u, v. Hence it is easier to find $J = \dfrac{\partial(x, y)}{\partial(u, v)}$ and then we shall apply the formula $J \cdot J' = 1$ to obtain $J' = \dfrac{\partial(u, v)}{\partial(x, y)}$.

$\dfrac{\partial x}{\partial u} = v, \quad \dfrac{\partial x}{\partial v} = u, \quad \dfrac{\partial y}{\partial u} = \dfrac{u - v - (u + v)}{(u - v)^2} = \dfrac{-2v}{(u - v)^2}, \quad \dfrac{\partial y}{\partial v} = \dfrac{u - v + (u + v)}{(u - v)^2} = \dfrac{2u}{(u - v)^2}$

$\therefore \qquad J = \dfrac{\partial(x, y)}{\partial(u, v)} = \begin{vmatrix} \dfrac{\partial x}{\partial u} & \dfrac{\partial x}{\partial v} \\ \dfrac{\partial y}{\partial u} & \dfrac{\partial y}{\partial v} \end{vmatrix} = \begin{vmatrix} v & u \\ \dfrac{-2v}{(u-v)^2} & \dfrac{2u}{(u-v)^2} \end{vmatrix}$

$$= \dfrac{uv}{(u-v)^2} \begin{vmatrix} 1 & 1 \\ -2 & 2 \end{vmatrix} = \dfrac{4uv}{(u-v)^2}$$

Hence $\qquad J' = \dfrac{\partial(u, v)}{\partial(x, y)} = \dfrac{(u-v)^2}{4uv}$

Ex. 6 : If $u = f(x, y)$ and $\phi(x, y) = 0$, then show that $\dfrac{du}{dx} = \dfrac{\partial(f, \phi) / \partial(x, y)}{\partial \phi / \partial y}$.

Sol. : Given $\qquad u = f(x, y) \qquad \therefore \; u \to x, y$
and $\qquad \phi(x, y) = 0 \qquad \therefore \; y \to x$
$\therefore \qquad u \to x, \; y \to x$

$\therefore \qquad \dfrac{du}{dx} = \dfrac{\partial u}{\partial x} \cdot (1) + \dfrac{\partial u}{\partial y} \cdot \dfrac{dy}{dx} \qquad \ldots (1)$

Given that $\phi(x, y) = 0 \quad \therefore \quad \dfrac{dy}{dx} = -\dfrac{\partial \phi / \partial x}{\partial \phi / \partial y}$

Putting in (1),

$$\frac{du}{dx} = \frac{\partial u}{\partial x} + \frac{\partial u}{\partial y}\left[-\frac{\partial \phi/\partial x}{\partial \phi/\partial y}\right] = \frac{\partial f}{\partial x} - \frac{\partial f}{\partial y}\left[\frac{\partial \phi/\partial x}{\partial \phi/\partial y}\right]$$

$$= \frac{\dfrac{\partial f}{\partial x}\cdot\dfrac{\partial \phi}{\partial y} - \dfrac{\partial f}{\partial y}\cdot\dfrac{\partial \phi}{\partial x}}{\partial \phi/\partial y} = \frac{\begin{vmatrix} f_x & f_y \\ \phi_x & \phi_y \end{vmatrix}}{\partial \phi/\partial y}$$

$$= \frac{\partial(f, \phi)/\partial(x, y)}{\partial \phi/\partial y}$$

Ex. 7 : *For the transformations* $x = e^u \cos v$, $y = e^u \sin v$,

prove that $\dfrac{\partial(x, y)}{\partial(u, v)} \cdot \dfrac{\partial(u, v)}{\partial(x, y)} = 1$. **(May 2006, 2008; Jan. 2004)**

Sol. : Given : $x = e^u \cos v$, $y = e^u \sin v$.
We first find

$$J = \frac{\partial(x, y)}{\partial(u, v)} = \begin{vmatrix} \dfrac{\partial x}{\partial u} & \dfrac{\partial x}{\partial v} \\ \dfrac{\partial y}{\partial u} & \dfrac{\partial y}{\partial v} \end{vmatrix} = \begin{vmatrix} e^u \cos v & -e^u \sin v \\ e^u \sin v & e^u \cos v \end{vmatrix}$$

$$= e^{2u} \begin{vmatrix} \cos v & -\sin v \\ \sin v & \cos v \end{vmatrix} = e^{2u}(\cos^2 v + \sin^2 v)$$

$$= e^{2u} \qquad \ldots (1)$$

Next, we find $\quad J' = \dfrac{\partial(u, v)}{\partial(x, y)} = \begin{vmatrix} \dfrac{\partial u}{\partial x} & \dfrac{\partial u}{\partial y} \\ \dfrac{\partial v}{\partial x} & \dfrac{\partial v}{\partial y} \end{vmatrix}$

We note from the given transformations,

$$\frac{y}{x} = \tan v \quad \text{and} \quad x^2 + y^2 = e^{2u}$$

or $\quad v = \tan^{-1}\dfrac{y}{x} \quad \text{and} \quad u = \dfrac{1}{2}\log(x^2 + y^2)$

$\therefore \quad J' = \dfrac{\partial(u, v)}{\partial(x, y)} = \begin{vmatrix} \dfrac{x}{x^2+y^2} & \dfrac{y}{x^2+y^2} \\ \dfrac{-y}{x^2+y^2} & \dfrac{x}{x^2+y^2} \end{vmatrix} = \dfrac{x^2+y^2}{(x^2+y^2)^2} = \dfrac{1}{x^2+y^2} = \dfrac{1}{e^{2u}} \quad \ldots (2)$

From (1) and (2), we have

$$JJ' = \frac{\partial(x, y)}{\partial(u, v)} \cdot \frac{\partial(u, v)}{\partial(x, y)} = e^{2u} \cdot \frac{1}{e^{2u}} = 1$$

EXERCISE 11.2

1. If $u = 2xy$, $v = x^2 - y^2$ where $x = r \cos \theta$, $y = r \sin \theta$, find $\dfrac{\partial(u, v)}{\partial(r, \theta)}$. **Ans. :** $4r^3$

2. For the transformations $x = e^v \sec u$, $y = e^v \tan u$, prove that $\dfrac{\partial(x, y)}{\partial(u, v)} \cdot \dfrac{\partial(u, v)}{\partial(x, y)} = 1$.

   [**Hint :** Use $v = \dfrac{1}{2} \log(x^2 - y^2)$, $u = \sin^{-1} \dfrac{y}{x}$] **(May 2004. 2014)**

3. Verify $JJ' = 1$ for the transformations $x = uv$, $y = u/v$.
   [**Hint :** $u^2 = xy$, $v^2 = x/y$]

4. If $x = v^2 + w^2$, $y = w^2 + u^2$, $z = u^2 + v^2$, prove that $JJ' = 1$.
   [**Hint :** $2u^2 = y + z - x$, $2v^2 = x - y + z$, $2w^2 = x + y - z$]

5. Verify $JJ' = 1$ in the following cases :
   (1) $x = u \cos v$, $\quad y = u \sin v$
   (2) $u = xy$, $\qquad\quad v = x + y$
   (3) $x = u(1 - v)$, $\quad y = uv$ **(Dec. 2009)**
   (4) $u = x^2$, $\qquad\quad v = y^2$
   (5) $x = \sin \theta \cos \phi$, $\quad y = \sin \theta \sin \phi$

6. If $u = x + y + z$, $u^2 v = y + z$, $u^3 w = z$, evaluate $\dfrac{\partial(u, v, w)}{\partial(x, y, z)}$.

   [**Hint :** Let $x + y + z = r$, $y + z = s$, $z = t$, then $r, s, t \to u, v, w \to x, y, z$.

   Thus $\dfrac{\partial(u, v, w)}{\partial(x, y, z)} = \dfrac{\partial(u, v, w)}{\partial(r, s, t)} \cdot \dfrac{\partial(r, s, t)}{\partial(x, y, z)} = \dfrac{1}{\dfrac{\partial(r, s, t)}{\partial(u, v, w)}} \cdot \dfrac{\partial(r, s, t)}{\partial(x, y, z)}$]

APPLICATIONS OF JACOBIANS

11.3 JACOBIAN OF IMPLICIT FUNCTIONS

If u_1, u_2, u_3 be implicit functions of the variables x_1, x_2, x_3 connected by f_1, f_2, f_3 such that $f_1(u_1, u_2, u_3, x_1, x_2, x_3) = 0$, $f_2(u_1, u_2, u_3, x_1, x_2, x_3) = 0$, $f_3(u_1, u_2, u_3, x_1, x_2, x_3) = 0$ then

$$\frac{\partial f_1}{\partial x_1} + \frac{\partial f_1}{\partial u_1} \frac{\partial u_1}{\partial x_1} + \frac{\partial f_1}{\partial u_2} \frac{\partial u_2}{\partial x_1} + \frac{\partial f_1}{\partial u_3} \frac{\partial u_3}{\partial x_1} = 0 \quad \text{or} \quad \frac{\partial f_1}{\partial x_1} + \sum_{r=1}^{3} \frac{\partial f_1}{\partial u_r} \frac{\partial u_r}{\partial x_1} = 0$$

$$\frac{\partial f_1}{\partial x_2} + \frac{\partial f_1}{\partial u_1} \frac{\partial u_1}{\partial x_2} + \frac{\partial f_1}{\partial u_2} \frac{\partial u_2}{\partial x_2} + \frac{\partial f_1}{\partial u_3} \frac{\partial u_3}{\partial x_2} = 0 \quad \text{or} \quad \frac{\partial f_1}{\partial x_2} + \sum_{r=1}^{3} \frac{\partial f_1}{\partial u_r} \frac{\partial u_r}{\partial x_2} = 0$$

$$\frac{\partial f_1}{\partial x_3} + \frac{\partial f_1}{\partial u_1} \frac{\partial u_1}{\partial x_3} + \frac{\partial f_1}{\partial u_2} \frac{\partial u_2}{\partial x_3} + \frac{\partial f_1}{\partial u_3} \frac{\partial u_3}{\partial x_3} = 0 \quad \text{or} \quad \frac{\partial f_1}{\partial x_3} + \sum_{r=1}^{3} \frac{\partial f_1}{\partial u_r} \frac{\partial u_r}{\partial x_3} = 0$$

Similarly,

$$\frac{\partial f_2}{\partial x_1} + \frac{\partial f_2}{\partial u_1}\frac{\partial u_1}{\partial x_1} + \frac{\partial f_2}{\partial u_2}\frac{\partial u_2}{\partial x_1} + \frac{\partial f_2}{\partial u_3}\frac{\partial u_3}{\partial x_3} = 0 \quad \text{or} \quad \frac{\partial f_2}{\partial x_1} + \sum_{1}^{3}\frac{\partial f_2}{\partial u_r}\frac{\partial u_r}{\partial x_1} = 0$$

$$\frac{\partial f_2}{\partial x_2} + \frac{\partial f_2}{\partial u_1}\frac{\partial u_1}{\partial x_2} + \frac{\partial f_2}{\partial u_2}\frac{\partial u_2}{\partial x_2} + \frac{\partial f_2}{\partial u_3}\frac{\partial u_3}{\partial x_2} = 0 \quad \text{or} \quad \frac{\partial f_2}{\partial x_2} + \sum_{r=1}^{3}\frac{\partial f_2}{\partial u_r}\frac{\partial u_r}{\partial x_2} = 0$$

$$\frac{\partial f_2}{\partial x_3} + \frac{\partial f_3}{\partial u_1}\frac{\partial u_1}{\partial x_3} + \frac{\partial f_2}{\partial u_2}\frac{\partial u_2}{\partial x_3} + \frac{\partial f_2}{\partial u_3}\frac{\partial u_3}{\partial x_3} = 0 \quad \text{or} \quad \frac{\partial f_2}{\partial x_3} + \sum_{r=1}^{3}\frac{\partial f_2}{\partial u_r}\frac{\partial u_r}{\partial x_3} = 0$$

Similarly,

$$\frac{\partial f_3}{\partial x_1} + \frac{\partial f_3}{\partial u_1}\frac{\partial u_1}{\partial x_1} + \frac{\partial f_3}{\partial u_2}\frac{\partial u_2}{\partial x_1} + \frac{\partial f_3}{\partial u_3}\frac{\partial u_3}{\partial x_1} = 0 \quad \text{or} \quad \frac{\partial f_3}{\partial x_1} + \sum_{1}^{3}\frac{\partial f_3}{\partial u_r}\frac{\partial u_r}{\partial x_1} = 0$$

$$\frac{\partial f_3}{\partial x_2} + \frac{\partial f_3}{\partial u_1}\frac{\partial u_1}{\partial x_2} + \frac{\partial f_3}{\partial u_2}\frac{\partial u_2}{\partial x_3} + \frac{\partial f_3}{\partial u_3}\frac{\partial u_3}{\partial x_3} = 0 \quad \text{or} \quad \frac{\partial f_3}{\partial x_2} + \sum_{r=1}^{3}\frac{\partial f_3}{\partial u_r}\frac{\partial u_r}{\partial x_2} = 0$$

$$\frac{\partial f_3}{\partial x_3} + \frac{\partial x_3}{\partial u_1}\frac{\partial u_1}{\partial x_3} + \frac{\partial f_3}{\partial u_2}\frac{\partial u_2}{\partial x_3} + \frac{\partial f_3}{\partial u_3}\frac{\partial u_3}{\partial x_3} = 0 \quad \text{or} \quad \frac{\partial f_3}{\partial x_3} + \sum_{r=1}^{3}\frac{\partial f_3}{\partial u_r}\frac{\partial u_r}{\partial x_3} = 0$$

Now, $\quad \dfrac{\partial(f_1, f_2, f_3)}{\partial(u_1, u_2, u_3)} \cdot \dfrac{\partial(u_1, u_2, u_3)}{\partial(x_1, x_2, x_3)}$

$$= \begin{vmatrix} \dfrac{\partial f_1}{\partial u_1} & \dfrac{\partial f_1}{\partial u_2} & \dfrac{\partial f_1}{\partial u_3} \\ \dfrac{\partial f_2}{\partial u_1} & \dfrac{\partial f_2}{\partial u_2} & \dfrac{\partial f_2}{\partial u_3} \\ \dfrac{\partial f_3}{\partial u_1} & \dfrac{\partial f_3}{\partial u_2} & \dfrac{\partial f_3}{\partial u_3} \end{vmatrix} \times \begin{vmatrix} \dfrac{\partial u_1}{\partial x_1} & \dfrac{\partial u_1}{\partial x_2} & \dfrac{\partial u_1}{\partial x_3} \\ \dfrac{\partial u_2}{\partial x_1} & \dfrac{\partial u_2}{\partial x_2} & \dfrac{\partial u_2}{\partial x_3} \\ \dfrac{\partial u_3}{\partial x_1} & \dfrac{\partial u_3}{\partial x_2} & \dfrac{\partial u_3}{\partial x_3} \end{vmatrix}$$

Interchanging of rows and columns of 2nd determinant

$$= \begin{vmatrix} \dfrac{\partial f_1}{\partial u_1} & \dfrac{\partial f_1}{\partial u_2} & \dfrac{\partial f_1}{\partial u_3} \\ \dfrac{\partial f_2}{\partial u_1} & \dfrac{\partial f_2}{\partial u_2} & \dfrac{\partial f_2}{\partial u_3} \\ \dfrac{\partial f_3}{\partial u_1} & \dfrac{\partial f_3}{\partial u_2} & \dfrac{\partial f_3}{\partial u_3} \end{vmatrix} \times \begin{vmatrix} \dfrac{\partial u_1}{\partial x_1} & \dfrac{\partial u_2}{\partial x_1} & \dfrac{\partial u_3}{\partial x_1} \\ \dfrac{\partial u_1}{\partial x_2} & \dfrac{\partial u_2}{\partial x_2} & \dfrac{\partial u_3}{\partial x_2} \\ \dfrac{\partial u_1}{\partial x_3} & \dfrac{\partial u_2}{\partial x_3} & \dfrac{\partial u_3}{\partial x_3} \end{vmatrix}$$

$$\frac{\partial(f_1, f_2, f_3)}{\partial(u_1, u_2, u_3)} \cdot \frac{\partial(u_1, u_2, u_3)}{\partial(x_1, x_2, x_3)} = \begin{vmatrix} \sum \frac{\partial f_1}{\partial u_r}\frac{\partial u_r}{\partial x_1} & \sum \frac{\partial f_1}{\partial u_r}\frac{\partial u_r}{\partial x_2} & \sum \frac{\partial f_1}{\partial u_r}\frac{\partial u_r}{\partial x_3} \\ \sum \frac{\partial f_2}{\partial u_r}\frac{\partial u_r}{\partial x_1} & \sum \frac{\partial f_2}{\partial u_r}\frac{\partial u_r}{\partial x_2} & \sum \frac{\partial f_2}{\partial u_r}\frac{\partial u_r}{\partial x_3} \\ \sum \frac{\partial f_3}{\partial u_r}\frac{\partial u_r}{\partial x_1} & \sum \frac{\partial f_3}{\partial u_r}\frac{\partial u_r}{\partial x_3} & \sum \frac{\partial f_3}{\partial u_r}\frac{\partial u_r}{\partial x_3} \end{vmatrix}$$

$$= \begin{vmatrix} -\frac{\partial f_1}{\partial x_1} & -\frac{\partial f_1}{\partial x_2} & -\frac{\partial f_1}{\partial x_3} \\ -\frac{\partial f_2}{\partial x_1} & -\frac{\partial f_2}{\partial x_2} & -\frac{\partial f_2}{\partial x_3} \\ -\frac{\partial f_3}{\partial x_1} & -\frac{\partial f_3}{\partial x_2} & -\frac{\partial f_3}{\partial x_3} \end{vmatrix} = (-1)^3 \frac{\partial(f_1, f_2, f_3)}{\partial(x_1, x_2, x_3)}$$

$$\therefore \quad \frac{\partial(u_1, u_2, u_3)}{\partial(x_1, x_2, x_3)} = (-1)^3 \frac{\frac{\partial(f_1, f_2, f_3)}{\partial(x_1, x_2, x_3)}}{\frac{\partial(f_1, f_2, f_3)}{\partial(u_1, u_2, u_3)}}$$

Similarly, if u_1, u_2 be implicit functions of the variables x_1, x_2 connected by f_1, f_2 such that $f_1(u_1, u_2, x_1, x_2) = 0$, $f_2(u_1, u_2, x_1, x_2) = 0$ then

$$\frac{\partial(u_1, u_2)}{\partial(x_1, x_2)} = (-1)^2 \frac{\frac{\partial(f_1, f_2)}{\partial(x_1, x_2)}}{\frac{\partial(f_1, f_2)}{\partial(u_1, u_2)}}$$

This result can be generalised as

$$\frac{\partial(u_1, u_2, u_3, \ldots, u_n)}{\partial(x_1, x_2, x_3, \ldots, x_n)} = (-1)^n \frac{\partial(f_1, f_2, f_3, \ldots f_n)/\partial(x_1, x_2, x_3, \ldots x_n)}{\partial(f_1, f_2, f_3, \ldots f_n)/\partial(u_1, u_2, u_3, \ldots u_n)}$$

ILLUSTRATIONS ON JACOBIAN OF IMPLICIT FUNCTION

Ex. 1 : If $u = \frac{x}{\sqrt{1-r^2}}$, $v = \frac{y}{\sqrt{1-r^2}}$, $w = \frac{z}{\sqrt{1-r^2}}$ then show that $\frac{\partial(u, v, w)}{\partial(x, y, z)} = \frac{1}{(1-r^2)^{5/2}}$ where $r^2 = x^2 + y^2 + z^2$.

Sol. : $u = \frac{x}{\sqrt{1-r^2}}$, on squaring and cross multiplying, we have $u^2(1-r^2) = x^2$

$\therefore \quad f_1(u, v, w, x, y, z) = u^2[1 - x^2 - y^2 - z^2] - x^2 = 0$

$f_2(u, v, w, x, y, z) = v^2[1 - x^2 - y^2 - z^2] - y^2 = 0$

$f_3(u, v, w, x, y, z) = w^2[1 - x^2 - y^2 - z^2] - z^2 = 0$

Now, $\dfrac{\partial(u, v, w)}{\partial(x, y, z)} = (-1)^3 \dfrac{\dfrac{\partial(f_1, f_2, f_3)}{\partial(x, y, z)}}{\dfrac{\partial(f_1, f_2, f_3)}{\partial(u, v, w)}} = -\dfrac{N}{D}$ (Say)

$$N = \dfrac{\partial(f_1, f_2, f_3)}{\partial(x, y, z)} = \begin{vmatrix} -2u^2x - 2x & -2u^2y & -2u^2z \\ -2v^2x & -2v^2y - 2y & -2v^2z \\ -2w^2x & -2w^2y & -2w^2z - 2z \end{vmatrix}$$

$$= -8xyz \begin{vmatrix} u^2 + 1 & u^2 & u^2 \\ v^2 & v^2 + 1 & v^2 \\ w^2 & w^2 & w^2 + 1 \end{vmatrix}$$

Perform $C_1 - C_2, C_2 - C_3$

$$= -8xyz \begin{vmatrix} 1 & 0 & u^2 \\ -1 & 1 & v^2 \\ 0 & -1 & 1 + w^2 \end{vmatrix} = -8xyz\,[u^2 + v^2 + w^2 + 1]$$

$$= -8xyz \left[\dfrac{x^2}{1-r^2} + \dfrac{y^2}{1-r^2} + \dfrac{z^2}{1-r^2} + 1\right] = -8xyz\left(\dfrac{1}{1-r^2}\right)$$

$$D = \dfrac{\partial(f_1, f_2, f_3)}{\partial(u, v, w)}$$

$$= \begin{vmatrix} 2u(1-r^2) & 0 & 0 \\ 0 & 2v(1-r^2) & 0 \\ 0 & 0 & 2w(1-r^2) \end{vmatrix}$$

$$= 8uvw\,(1 - x^2 - y^2 - z^2)^3$$

$$= 8 \left(\dfrac{x}{\sqrt{1-r^2}}\right)\left(\dfrac{y}{\sqrt{1-r^2}}\right)\left(\dfrac{z}{\sqrt{1-r^2}}\right)[1-r^2]^3$$

$$= 8xyz\,(1-r^2)^{3/2}, \text{ hence}$$

$$\dfrac{\partial(u, v, w)}{\partial(x, y, z)} = -\dfrac{N}{D} = \dfrac{8xyz/(1-r^2)}{8xyz\,(1-r^2)^{3/2}} = \dfrac{1}{(1-r^2)^{5/2}}$$

Ex. 2 : *If u, v, w are the roots of the equation $(\lambda - x)^3 + (\lambda - y)^3 + (\lambda - z)^3 = 0$ in λ, find $\dfrac{\partial(u, v, w)}{\partial(x, y, z)}$.*

Sol. : After simplifying the equation, we get

$$3\lambda^3 - 3(x + y + z)\lambda^2 + 3(x^2 + y^2 + z^2)\lambda - (x^3 + y^3 + z^3) = 0$$

From relation between roots and coefficients, we get

$$u + v + w = x + y + z$$
$$uv + vw + wu = x^2 + y^2 + z^2$$
$$uvw = \dfrac{1}{3}(x^3 + y^3 + z^3)$$

which yield the three implicit functions in u, v, w and x, y, z as
$$f_1 = u + v + w - x - y - z$$
$$f_2 = uv + vw + wu - x^2 - y^2 - z^2$$
$$f_3 = uvw - \frac{1}{3}(x^3 + y^3 + z^3)$$

Now, $\dfrac{\partial(u, v, w)}{\partial(x, y, z)} = (-1)^3 \dfrac{\dfrac{\partial(f_1, f_2, f_3)}{\partial(x, y, z)}}{\dfrac{\partial(f_1, f_2, f_3)}{\partial(u, v, w)}} = -\dfrac{N}{D}$ (say)

Now, $N = \begin{vmatrix} \dfrac{\partial f_1}{\partial x} & \dfrac{\partial f_1}{\partial y} & \dfrac{\partial f_1}{\partial z} \\ \dfrac{\partial f_2}{\partial x} & \dfrac{\partial f_2}{\partial y} & \dfrac{\partial f_2}{\partial z} \\ \dfrac{\partial f_3}{\partial x} & \dfrac{\partial f_3}{\partial y} & \dfrac{\partial f_3}{\partial z} \end{vmatrix} = \begin{vmatrix} -1 & -1 & -1 \\ -2x & -2y & -2z \\ -x^2 & -y^2 & -z^2 \end{vmatrix}$

$= (-1)(-2)(-1) \begin{vmatrix} 1 & 1 & 1 \\ x & y & z \\ x^2 & y^2 & z^2 \end{vmatrix}$

Perform $C_1 - C_2$, $C_2 - C_3$

$= -2 \begin{vmatrix} 0 & 0 & 1 \\ x - y & y - z & z \\ x^2 - y^2 & y^2 - z^2 & z^2 \end{vmatrix}$

$= -2 \begin{vmatrix} 0 & 0 & 1 \\ x - y & y - z & z \\ (x - y)(x + y) & (y - z)(y + z) & z^2 \end{vmatrix}$

$= -2(x - y)(y - z) \begin{vmatrix} 0 & 0 & 1 \\ 1 & 1 & z \\ x + y & y + z & z^2 \end{vmatrix}$

$= -2(x - y)(y - z)(y + z - x - y)$
$= -2(x - y)(y - z)(z - x)$

and $\quad D = \dfrac{\partial(f_1, f_2, f_3)}{\partial(u, v, w)} = \begin{vmatrix} \dfrac{\partial f_1}{\partial u} & \dfrac{\partial f_1}{\partial v} & \dfrac{\partial f_1}{\partial w} \\ \dfrac{\partial f_2}{\partial u} & \dfrac{\partial f_2}{\partial v} & \dfrac{\partial f_2}{\partial w} \\ \dfrac{\partial f_3}{\partial u} & \dfrac{\partial f_3}{\partial v} & \dfrac{\partial f_3}{\partial w} \end{vmatrix} = \begin{vmatrix} 1 & 1 & 1 \\ v+w & u+w & u+v \\ vw & wu & uv \end{vmatrix}$

Perform $C_1 - C_2$, $C_2 - C_3$

$$D = \begin{vmatrix} 0 & 0 & 1 \\ v-u & w-v & u+v \\ w(v-u) & u(w-v) & uv \end{vmatrix}$$

$$= (v-u)(w-v) \begin{vmatrix} 0 & 0 & 1 \\ 1 & 1 & u+v \\ w & u & uv \end{vmatrix}$$

$$= (v-u)(w-v)(u-w)$$
$$= -(u-v)(v-w)(w-u)$$

$\therefore \quad \dfrac{\partial(u, v, w)}{\partial(x, y, z)} = -\dfrac{N}{D} = \dfrac{2(x-y)(y-z)(z-x)}{(u-v)(v-w)(w-u)}$

Ex. 3 : If $x = u(1-v)$, $y = uv$, show that $JJ' = 1$. **(Dec. 2012)**

Sol. : We first find J : Here $x, y \to u, v$.

Let $\quad J = \dfrac{\partial(x, y)}{\partial(u, v)} = \begin{vmatrix} 1-v & -u \\ v & u \end{vmatrix} = u - uv + uv = u$

Next, we shall obtain $J' = \dfrac{\partial(u, v)}{\partial(x, y)}$ by the method of Implicit function.

From given relation, $f_1 = x - u + uv$, $f_2 = y - uv$

$$J' = \dfrac{\partial(u, v)}{\partial(x, y)} = (-1)^2 \dfrac{\dfrac{\partial(f_1, f_2)}{\partial(x, y)}}{\dfrac{\partial(f_1, f_2)}{\partial(u, v)}} \quad \ldots (1)$$

Here $\quad \dfrac{\partial(f_1, f_2)}{\partial(x, y)} = \begin{vmatrix} 1 & 0 \\ 0 & 1 \end{vmatrix} = 1$

and $\quad \dfrac{\partial(f_1, f_2)}{\partial(u, v)} = \begin{vmatrix} -1+v & u \\ -v & -u \end{vmatrix} = u$

Putting in equation (1) the values of these Jacobians, we have $J' = \dfrac{1}{u}$.

$\therefore \quad JJ' = u \cdot \dfrac{1}{u} = 1$

Ex. 4 : If $x + y = 2e^\theta \cos \phi$, $x - y = 2i \, e^\theta \sin \phi$, prove that $JJ' = 1$. (Jan. 2005)

Sol. : We first find J :

Adding the given relations, we get

$$2x = 2e^\theta (\cos \phi + i \sin \phi)$$

or $\qquad x = e^\theta e^{i\phi} = e^{\theta + i\phi}$ ... (i)

Subtracting the given relations, we get

$$2y = 2e^\theta (\cos \phi - i \sin \phi)$$

or $\qquad y = e^{\theta - i\phi}$ ... (ii)

$$\therefore \quad J = \frac{\partial(x, y)}{\partial(\theta, \phi)} = \begin{vmatrix} \frac{\partial x}{\partial \theta} & \frac{\partial x}{\partial \phi} \\ \frac{\partial y}{\partial \theta} & \frac{\partial y}{\partial \phi} \end{vmatrix}$$

$$= \begin{vmatrix} e^{\theta + i\phi} & e^{\theta + i\phi}(i) \\ e^{\theta - i\phi} & e^{\theta - i\phi}(-i) \end{vmatrix}$$

$$= i(e^{\theta + i\phi})(e^{\theta - i\phi}) \begin{vmatrix} 1 & 1 \\ 1 & -1 \end{vmatrix}$$

$$= -2i \, e^{2\theta} \qquad \ldots (1)$$

Next, we find J' :

From equations (i) and (ii), we get

$$f_1 = e^{\theta + i\phi} - x$$

$$f_2 = e^{\theta - i\phi} - y$$

$$\therefore \quad J' = \frac{\partial(\theta, \phi)}{\partial(x, y)} = (-1)^2 \frac{\partial(f_1, f_2)/\partial(x, y)}{\partial(f_1, f_2)/\partial(\theta, \phi)}$$

$$= \frac{\begin{vmatrix} -1 & 0 \\ 0 & -1 \end{vmatrix}}{\begin{vmatrix} e^{\theta + i\phi} & e^{\theta + i\phi}(i) \\ e^{\theta - i\phi} & e^{\theta - i\phi}(-i) \end{vmatrix}} = \frac{1}{-2i \, e^{2\theta}} \qquad \ldots (2)$$

Multiplying equations (1) and (2), we have

$$JJ' = 1.$$

Ex. 5 : If $x = v^2 + w^2$, $y = w^2 + u^2$, $z = u^2 + v^2$, prove that $JJ' = 1$. **(May 2015)**

Sol. : We first find J :

Here, $x, y, z \to u, v, w$

$$\therefore \quad J = \frac{\partial(x, y, z)}{\partial(u, v, w)} = \begin{vmatrix} 0 & 2v & 3w \\ 2u & 0 & 2w \\ 2u & 2v & 0 \end{vmatrix}$$

$$= 8uvw \begin{vmatrix} 0 & 1 & 1 \\ 1 & 0 & 1 \\ 1 & 1 & 0 \end{vmatrix} = 16\, uvw \quad \ldots (1)$$

We next find J' :

From given relations, we have,

$$f_1 = v^2 + w^2 - x$$
$$f_2 = w^2 + u^2 - y$$
$$f_3 = u^2 + v^2 - z$$

$$J' = \frac{\partial(u, v, w)}{\partial(x, y, z)} = (-1)^3 \frac{\partial(f_1, f_2, f_3)/\partial(x, y, z)}{\partial(f_1, f_2, f_3)/\partial(u, v, w)}$$

$$\therefore \quad J' = (-1)^3 \frac{\begin{vmatrix} -1 & 0 & 0 \\ 0 & -1 & 0 \\ 0 & 0 & -1 \end{vmatrix}}{\begin{vmatrix} 0 & 2v & 2w \\ 2u & 0 & 2w \\ 2u & 2v & 0 \end{vmatrix}}$$

$$= \frac{1}{16uvw} \quad \ldots (2)$$

Multiplying (1) and (2), we have

$$JJ' = 1$$

EXERCISE 11.3

1. If $u^3 + v^3 = x + y$, $u^2 + v^2 = x^3 + y^3$, show that $\dfrac{\partial(u, v)}{\partial(x, y)} = \dfrac{1}{2} \dfrac{y^2 - x^2}{uv\,(u - v)}$. **(May 2015)**

2. If $x^2 + y^2 + u^2 - v^2 = 0$ and $uv + xy = 0$, prove that $\dfrac{\partial(u, v)}{\partial(x, y)} = \dfrac{x^2 - y^2}{u^2 + v^2}$. **(May 2005)**

3. If $u^3 + v^3 + w^3 = x + y + z$, $u^2 + v^2 + w^2 = x^3 + y^3 + z^3$, $u + v + w = x^2 + y^2 + z^2$

show that $\dfrac{\partial(u, v, w)}{\partial(x, y, z)} = \dfrac{(x - y)\,(y - z)\,(z - x)}{(u - v)\,(v - w)\,(w - u)}$ **(May 2004)**

4. If $u = \dfrac{x}{k}$, $v = \dfrac{y}{k}$, $w = \dfrac{z}{k}$ where $k = \sqrt{1-x^2-y^2-z^2}$ find $\dfrac{\partial(x, y, z)}{\partial(u, v, w)}$ in terms of k.

   [Hint : Refer solved example 1]   (Jan. 2004, May 2007) **Ans. :** k^5

5. If $u^3 + v + w = x + y^2 + z^2$, $u + v^3 + w = x^2 + y + z^2$, $u + v + w^3 = x^2 + y^2 + z$

   find $\dfrac{\partial(u, v, w)}{\partial(x, y, z)}$.

6. If u, v, w are roots of equation in λ, $\dfrac{x}{a+\lambda} + \dfrac{y}{b+\lambda} + \dfrac{z}{c+\lambda} = 1$ then find $\dfrac{\partial(x, y, z)}{\partial(u, v, w)}$.   **Ans. :** $-\dfrac{(u-v)(v-w)(w-u)}{(a-b)(b-c)(c-a)}$

7. If $x + y + z = u$, $y + z = uv$, $z = uvw$, show that $\dfrac{\partial(x, y, z)}{\partial(u, v, w)} = u^2 v$.   (Dec. 2007)

8. If $u_1 = x_1 + x_2 + x_3 + x_4$, $u_1 u_2 = x_2 + x_3 + x_4$, $u_1 u_2 u_3 = x_3 + x_4$, $u_1 u_2 u_3 u_4 = x_4$

   show that $\dfrac{\partial(x_1, x_2, x_3, x_4)}{\partial(u_1, u_2, u_3, u_4)} = u_1^3 \cdot u_2^2 \cdot u_3$

9. Verify $JJ' = 1$ for the following transformations :

   (1) $x = uv$, $y = \dfrac{u}{v}$ **(May 2010)**, (2) $u = xy$, $v = x + y$, (3) $x = e^v \sec u$, $y = e^v \tan u$.

   [**Hint :** For J', use relations $f_1 = 0$ and $f_2 = 0$]

10. If $u^2 + v + w = x + y^2 + z^2$, $u + v^3 + w = x^2 + y + z^2$, $u + v + w^2 = x^2 + y^2 + z^2$,

    prove that $\dfrac{\partial(u, v, w)}{\partial(x, y, z)} = \dfrac{1 - 4(yz + zx + xy) + 16xyz}{2 - 3(u^2 + v^2 + w^2) + 27 u^2 v^2 w^2}$.

11. If $u + v + w = x + y + z$, $uv + vw + wu = x^2 + y^2 + z^2$

    and $uvw = \dfrac{1}{3}(x^3 + y^3 + z^3)$, find $\dfrac{\partial(u, v, w)}{\partial(x, y, z)}$.   (Dec. 2004, 2006)

    Ans. : $\dfrac{\partial(u, v, w)}{\partial(x, y, z)} = -\dfrac{N}{D} = \dfrac{2(x-y)(y-z)(z-x)}{(u-v)(v-w)(w-u)}$

11.4 PARTIAL DERIVATIVES OF IMPLICIT FUNCTIONS

Consider four variables u, v, x, y related by implicit functions :

$$f_1(u, v, x, y) = 0 \qquad \ldots (1)$$
$$f_2(u, v, x, y) = 0 \qquad \ldots (2)$$

These functions express u, v as functions of independent variables x, y, to find the partial derivatives :

$$\dfrac{\partial u}{\partial x}, \dfrac{\partial u}{\partial y}, \dfrac{\partial v}{\partial x}, \dfrac{\partial v}{\partial y}$$

If we differentiate partially the equations (1) and (2) w.r.t. x and y, we have

$$\frac{\partial f_1}{\partial x} + \frac{\partial f_1}{\partial u} \cdot \frac{\partial u}{\partial x} + \frac{\partial f_1}{\partial v} \cdot \frac{\partial v}{\partial x} = 0 \qquad \frac{\partial f_1}{\partial y} + \frac{\partial f_1}{\partial u} \cdot \frac{\partial u}{\partial y} + \frac{\partial f_1}{\partial v} \cdot \frac{\partial v}{\partial y} = 0$$

$$\frac{\partial f_2}{\partial x} + \frac{\partial f_2}{\partial u} \cdot \frac{\partial u}{\partial x} + \frac{\partial f_2}{\partial v} \cdot \frac{\partial v}{\partial x} = 0 \quad \ldots (3) \qquad \frac{\partial f_2}{\partial y} + \frac{\partial f_2}{\partial u} \cdot \frac{\partial u}{\partial y} + \frac{\partial f_2}{\partial v} \cdot \frac{\partial v}{\partial y} = 0 \quad \ldots (4)$$

If we solve simultaneous equation (3) for $\dfrac{\partial u}{\partial x}$ and $\dfrac{\partial v}{\partial x}$, we get by Cramer's rule.

$$\frac{\partial u}{\partial x} = -\frac{\begin{vmatrix} \dfrac{\partial f_1}{\partial x} & \dfrac{\partial f_1}{\partial v} \\ \dfrac{\partial f_2}{\partial x} & \dfrac{\partial f_2}{\partial v} \end{vmatrix}}{\begin{vmatrix} \dfrac{\partial f_1}{\partial u} & \dfrac{\partial f_1}{\partial v} \\ \dfrac{\partial f_2}{\partial u} & \dfrac{\partial f_2}{\partial v} \end{vmatrix}} = -\frac{\partial(f_1, f_2)/\partial(x, v)}{\partial(f_1, f_2)/\partial(u, v)} \qquad \ldots (5)$$

Also,

$$\frac{\partial v}{\partial x} = -\frac{\begin{vmatrix} \dfrac{\partial f_1}{\partial u} & \dfrac{\partial f_1}{\partial x} \\ \dfrac{\partial f_2}{\partial u} & \dfrac{\partial f_2}{\partial x} \end{vmatrix}}{\begin{vmatrix} \dfrac{\partial f_1}{\partial u} & \dfrac{\partial f_1}{\partial v} \\ \dfrac{\partial f_2}{\partial u} & \dfrac{\partial f_2}{\partial v} \end{vmatrix}} = -\frac{\partial(f_1, f_2)/\partial(u, x)}{\partial(f_1, f_2)/\partial(u, v)} \qquad \ldots (6)$$

Similarly, if we solve equation (4) simultaneously for $\dfrac{\partial u}{\partial y}$ and $\dfrac{\partial v}{\partial y}$, we get,

$$\frac{\partial u}{\partial y} = -\frac{\partial(f_1, f_2)/\partial(y, v)}{\partial(f_1, f_2)/\partial(u, v)} \qquad \ldots (7)$$

$$\frac{\partial v}{\partial y} = -\frac{\partial(f_1, f_2)/\partial(u, y)}{\partial(f_1, f_2)/\partial(u, v)} \qquad \ldots (8)$$

Provided $\dfrac{\partial(f_1, f_2)}{\partial(u, v)} \neq 0$ in all the four formulae.

Note 1 : In the formula $\dfrac{\partial u}{\partial x} = -\dfrac{\partial(f_1, f_2)/\partial(x, v)}{\partial(f_1, f_2)/\partial(u, v)}$

first we write the Jacobian in the Denominator and then to write for Numerator we change u to x. Similarly in all such formulae viz. $\dfrac{\partial u}{\partial y}$, $\dfrac{\partial v}{\partial x}$ and $\dfrac{\partial v}{\partial y}$ etc.

Note 2 : More generally if we have six variables u, v, w, x, y, z connected by three implicit functions f_r (u, v, w, x, y, z) = 0, r = 1, 2, 3.

we can obtain any partial derivative by the same rule.

viz. $\dfrac{\partial y}{\partial w} = -\dfrac{\partial(f_1, f_2, f_3)/\partial(x, w, z)}{\partial(f_1, f_2, f_3)/\partial(x, y, z)}$ and so on.

First we write the Jacobian in the Denominator and then to write for the Jacobian in Numerator, we simply replace y by w.

ILLUSTRATIONS ON PARTIAL DERIVATIVES OF IMPLICIT FUNCTIONS

Ex. 1 : If $u^2 + xv^2 - uxy = 0$, $v^2 - xy^2 + 2uv + u^2 = 0$, find $\dfrac{\partial u}{\partial x}$ by proper choice of dependent and independent variables. **(May 2013, Dec. 2014)**

Sol. : Let $f_1 = u^2 + xv^2 - uxy = 0$, $f_2 = v^2 - xy^2 + 2uv + u^2 = 0$.

Now, $\dfrac{\partial u}{\partial x} = -\dfrac{\dfrac{\partial(f_1, f_2)}{\partial(x, v)}}{\dfrac{\partial(f_1, f_2)}{\partial(u, v)}}$ ... (1)

$\dfrac{\partial(f_1, f_2)}{\partial(x, v)} = \begin{vmatrix} \dfrac{\partial f_1}{\partial x} & \dfrac{\partial f_1}{\partial v} \\ \dfrac{\partial f_2}{\partial x} & \dfrac{\partial f_2}{\partial v} \end{vmatrix} = \begin{vmatrix} v^2 - uy & 2xv \\ -y^2 & 2v + 2u \end{vmatrix}$

$= (v^2 - uy)(2v + 2u) + 2xy^2 v$ ... (2)

$\dfrac{\partial(f_1, f_2)}{\partial(u, v)} = \begin{vmatrix} 2u - xy & 2xv \\ 2v + 2u & 2v + 2u \end{vmatrix}$

$= 2(u + v)[2u - xy - 2xv]$ ... (3)

Putting these values in (1), we get,

$\dfrac{\partial u}{\partial x} = -\dfrac{(v^2 - uy)(2v + 2u) + 2xvy^2}{2(u + v)(2u - xy - 2xv)}$

Ex. 2 : If $u = x + y^2$, $v = y + z^2$, $w = z + x^2$, find the values of $\dfrac{\partial x}{\partial u}$, $\dfrac{\partial^2 x}{\partial u\, \partial v}$.

Sol. : Let $f_1 = u - x - y^2$, $f_2 = v - y - z^2$, $f_3 = w - z - x^2$.

Now,
$$\frac{\partial x}{\partial u} = -\frac{\dfrac{\partial(f_1, f_2, f_3)}{\partial(u, y, z)}}{\dfrac{\partial(f_1, f_2, f_3)}{\partial(x, y, z)}} = -\frac{N}{D} \text{ (say)} \qquad \ldots (1)$$

$$N = \frac{\partial(f_1, f_2, f_3)}{\partial(u, y, z)} = \begin{vmatrix} 1 & -2y & 0 \\ 0 & -1 & -2z \\ 0 & 0 & -1 \end{vmatrix} = 1 \qquad \ldots (2)$$

$$D = \frac{\partial(f_1, f_2, f_3)}{\partial(x, y, z)} = \begin{vmatrix} -1 & -2y & 0 \\ 0 & -1 & -2z \\ -2x & 0 & -1 \end{vmatrix}$$

$$= -1(1 + 0) + 2y(0 - 4zx) = -(1 + 8xyz) \qquad \ldots (3)$$

Hence
$$\frac{\partial x}{\partial u} = -\frac{N}{D} = -\frac{1}{-(1 + 8xyz)} = \frac{1}{1 + 8xyz} \qquad \ldots (4)$$

To calculate $\dfrac{\partial^2 x}{\partial u\, \partial v}$, we have

$$\frac{\partial^2 x}{\partial u\, \partial v} = \frac{\partial}{\partial v}\left(\frac{\partial x}{\partial u}\right) = \frac{\partial}{\partial v}\left[\frac{1}{1 + 8xyz}\right]$$

$$= -\frac{1}{(1 + 8xyz)^2} \frac{\partial}{\partial v}(1 + 8xyz)$$

$$\therefore \quad \frac{\partial^2 x}{\partial u\, \partial v} = -\frac{1}{(1 + 8xyz)^2}\left[0 + 8\left(\frac{\partial x}{\partial v}(yz) + \frac{\partial y}{\partial v}(zx) + \frac{\partial z}{\partial v}(xy)\right)\right]$$

$$= -\frac{8}{(1 + 8xyz)^2}\left[yz\frac{\partial x}{\partial v} + zx\frac{\partial y}{\partial v} + xy\frac{\partial z}{\partial v}\right] \qquad \ldots (5)$$

Now,
$$\frac{\partial x}{\partial v} = -\frac{\dfrac{\partial(f_1, f_2, f_3)}{\partial(v, y, z)}}{\dfrac{\partial(f_1, f_2, f_3)}{\partial(x, y, z)}} = -\frac{N_1}{D} \text{ (say)}$$

Now,
$$N_1 = \frac{\partial(f_1, f_2, f_3)}{\partial(v, y, z)} = \begin{vmatrix} 0 & -2y & 0 \\ 1 & -1 & -2z \\ 0 & 0 & -1 \end{vmatrix} = -2y$$

$$\therefore \quad \frac{\partial x}{\partial v} = -\frac{-2y}{-(1 + 8xyz)} = \frac{-2y}{1 + 8xyz} \qquad \ldots (6)$$

$$\frac{\partial y}{\partial v} = -\frac{\frac{\partial(f_1, f_2, f_3)}{\partial(x, v, z)}}{\frac{\partial(f_1, f_2, f_3)}{\partial(x, y, z)}} = -\frac{N_2}{D} \text{ (Say)}$$

$$N_2 = \frac{\partial(f_1, f_2, f_3)}{\partial(x, v, z)} = \begin{vmatrix} -1 & 0 & 0 \\ 0 & 1 & -2z \\ -2x & 0 & -1 \end{vmatrix} = -[-1-0] = 1$$

$$\therefore \quad \frac{\partial y}{\partial v} = -\frac{1}{-(1+8xyz)} = \frac{1}{1+8xyz} \quad \ldots (7)$$

Again
$$\frac{\partial z}{\partial v} = -\frac{\frac{\partial(f_1, f_2, f_3)}{\partial(x, y, v)}}{\frac{\partial(f_1, f_2, f_3)}{\partial(x, y, z)}} = -\frac{N_3}{D} \text{ (Say)}$$

$$N_3 = \frac{\partial(f_1, f_2, f_3)}{\partial(x, y, v)} = \begin{vmatrix} -1 & -2y & 0 \\ 0 & -1 & 1 \\ -2x & 0 & 0 \end{vmatrix}$$

$$= -1\,[0 - 4xy] = 4xy$$

$$\therefore \quad \frac{\partial z}{\partial v} = -\frac{4xy}{-(1+8xyz)} = \frac{4xy}{1+8xyz} \quad \ldots (8)$$

Putting the values of $\frac{\partial x}{\partial v}, \frac{\partial y}{\partial v}, \frac{\partial z}{\partial v}$ from (6), (7) and (8) in (5), we have

$$\frac{\partial^2 x}{\partial u \, \partial v} = -\frac{8}{(1+8xyz)^2}\left[yz\left(\frac{-2y}{1+8xyz}\right) + zx\left(\frac{1}{1+8xyz}\right) + xy\left(\frac{4xy}{1+8xyz}\right)\right]$$

$$= -\frac{8}{(1+8xyz)^3}\,[-2y^2z + zx + 4x^2y^2]$$

Ex. 3 : If $x + y + z + u + v = a$ and $x^2 + y^2 + z^2 + u^2 + v^2 = b$ where a, b are constants, use Jacobians to find $\left(\frac{\partial v}{\partial y}\right)_{x, u}$ and $\left(\frac{\partial y}{\partial v}\right)_{x, z}$.

Sol. :
$$f_1 = x + y + z + u + v - a = 0$$
$$f_2 = x^2 + y^2 + z^2 + u^2 + v^2 - b = 0$$

$$\left(\frac{\partial v}{\partial y}\right)_{x,u} = -\frac{\partial(f_1, f_2)/(y, z)}{\partial(f_1, f_2)/\partial(v, z)} = -\frac{\begin{vmatrix} 1 & 1 \\ 2y & 2z \\ 1 & 1 \\ 2v & 2z \end{vmatrix}}{} = \frac{y-z}{z-v}$$

$$\left(\frac{\partial y}{\partial v}\right)_{x,z} = -\frac{\partial(f_1, f_2)/(v, u)}{\partial(f_1, f_2)/\partial(y, u)} = -\frac{\begin{vmatrix} 1 & 1 \\ 2v & 2u \\ 1 & 1 \\ 2y & 2u \end{vmatrix}}{} = \frac{u-v}{y-u}$$

Ex. 4 : If $x = \cos\theta - r\sin\theta$, $y = \sin\theta + r\cos\theta$, prove that

(i) $\dfrac{\partial r}{\partial x} = \dfrac{x}{r}$, (ii) $\dfrac{\partial^2 \theta}{\partial x^2} = \dfrac{\cos\theta}{r^3}(\cos\theta - 2r\sin\theta)$.

Sol. : (i) Here $f_1 = x - \cos\theta + r\sin\theta$

$f_2 = y - \sin\theta - r\cos\theta$

$$\frac{\partial r}{\partial x} = -\frac{\partial(f_1, f_2)/\partial(x, \theta)}{\partial(f_1, f_2)/\partial(r, \theta)} = -\frac{\begin{vmatrix} 1 & \sin\theta + r\cos\theta \\ 0 & -\cos\theta + r\sin\theta \end{vmatrix}}{\begin{vmatrix} \sin\theta & \sin\theta + r\cos\theta \\ -\cos\theta & -\cos\theta + r\sin\theta \end{vmatrix}}$$

$$= -\frac{(-\cos\theta + r\sin\theta)}{-\sin\theta\cos\theta + r\sin^2\theta + \sin\theta\cos\theta + r\cos^2\theta}$$

$$= \frac{\cos\theta - r\sin\theta}{r} = \frac{x}{r}$$

$\therefore \quad \dfrac{\partial r}{\partial x} = \dfrac{x}{r}$ ... (1)

(ii) $$\frac{\partial \theta}{\partial x} = -\frac{\partial(f_1, f_2)/\partial(r, x)}{\partial(f_1, f_2)/\partial(r, \theta)} = -\frac{\begin{vmatrix} \sin\theta & 1 \\ -\cos\theta & 0 \end{vmatrix}}{r}$$

$$\frac{\partial \theta}{\partial x} = -\frac{\cos\theta}{r} \qquad \ldots (2)$$

Differentiating (2) w.r.t. x,

$$\frac{\partial}{\partial x}\left(\frac{\partial \theta}{\partial x}\right) = \frac{\partial}{\partial x}\left(-\frac{\cos\theta}{r}\right)$$

Engineering Mathematics – I 11.25 Jacobians, Errors & Approximations, Maxima & Minima

$$\therefore \quad \frac{\partial^2 \theta}{\partial x^2} = -\left[\frac{1}{r}(-\sin\theta)\frac{\partial\theta}{\partial x} + \cos\theta\left(-\frac{1}{r^2}\right)\frac{\partial r}{\partial x}\right]$$

$$= \frac{1}{r}\sin\theta\left(-\frac{\cos\theta}{r}\right) + \frac{\cos\theta}{r^2}\left(\frac{x}{r}\right) \quad \text{[using (1) and (2)]}$$

$$= \frac{-\sin\theta\cos\theta}{r^2} + \frac{x\cos\theta}{r^3}$$

$$= \frac{\cos\theta}{r^3}[-r\sin\theta + \cos\theta - r\sin\theta]$$

$$\therefore \quad \frac{\partial^2\theta}{\partial x^2} = \frac{\cos\theta}{r^3}[\cos\theta - 2r\sin\theta] \quad \ldots (3)$$

Ex. 5: If $x = u + v + w$, $y = u^2 + v^2 + w^2$, $z = u^3 + v^3 + w^3$ then show that

$$\frac{\partial u}{\partial x} = \frac{vw}{(u-v)(u-w)} \quad \text{(May 2006, 2015, Dec. 2007)}$$

Sol.: Here
$$f_1 = x - u - v - w$$
$$f_2 = y - u^2 - v^2 - w^2$$
$$f_3 = z - u^3 - v^3 - w^3$$

$$\frac{\partial u}{\partial x} = -\frac{\partial(f_1, f_2, f_3)/\partial(x, v, w)}{\partial(f_1, f_2, f_3)/\partial(u, v, w)} = -\frac{\begin{vmatrix} 1 & -1 & -1 \\ 0 & -2v & -2w \\ 0 & -3v^2 & -3w^2 \end{vmatrix}}{\begin{vmatrix} -1 & -1 & -1 \\ -2u & -2v & -2w \\ -3u^2 & -3v^2 & -3w^2 \end{vmatrix}}$$

$$= \frac{vw(w-v)}{(u-v)(v-w)(w-u)}$$

$$\therefore \quad \frac{\partial u}{\partial x} = \frac{vw}{(u-v)(u-w)}$$

Ex. 6: If $ux + vy = a$, $\frac{u}{x} + \frac{v}{y} = 1$, prove that

(i) $\left(\frac{\partial u}{\partial x}\right)_y - \left(\frac{\partial v}{\partial y}\right)_x = \frac{x^2 + y^2}{y^2 - x^2}$, (ii) $\frac{u}{x}\left(\frac{\partial x}{\partial u}\right)_v + \frac{v}{y}\left(\frac{\partial y}{\partial v}\right)_u = 0$. (Dec. 2008)

Sol.: Here $f_1 = ux + vy - a = 0$

$$f_2 = \frac{u}{x} + \frac{v}{y} - 1 = 0$$

(i) $\left(\frac{\partial u}{\partial x}\right)_y = -\frac{\partial(f_1, f_2)/\partial(x, v)}{\partial(f_1, f_2)/\partial(u, v)}$

$$= -\frac{\begin{vmatrix} u & y \\ -\dfrac{u}{x^2} & \dfrac{1}{y} \end{vmatrix}}{\begin{vmatrix} x & y \\ \dfrac{1}{x} & \dfrac{1}{y} \end{vmatrix}} = -\frac{u\left(\dfrac{1}{y}+\dfrac{y}{x^2}\right)}{\dfrac{(x^2-y^2)}{xy}}$$

$$= -\frac{u(x^2+y^2)/x^2 y}{(x^2-y^2)/xy} = -\frac{u}{x}\left(\frac{x^2+y^2}{x^2-y^2}\right) \qquad \ldots (1)$$

and $\left(\dfrac{\partial v}{\partial y}\right)_x = -\dfrac{\partial(f_1,f_2)/\partial(u,y)}{\partial(f_1,f_2)/\partial(u,v)}$

$$= \frac{-\begin{vmatrix} x & v \\ \dfrac{1}{x} & -\dfrac{v}{y^2} \end{vmatrix}}{\begin{vmatrix} x & y \\ \dfrac{1}{x} & \dfrac{1}{y} \end{vmatrix}} = -\frac{v\left(-\dfrac{x}{y^2}-\dfrac{1}{x}\right)}{(x^2-y^2)/xy}$$

$$= \frac{v(x^2+y^2)/xy^2}{(x^2-y^2)/xy} = \frac{v}{y}\left(\frac{x^2+y^2}{x^2-y^2}\right) \qquad \ldots (2)$$

From (1) and (2),

$$\left(\frac{\partial u}{\partial x}\right)_y - \left(\frac{\partial v}{\partial y}\right)_x = -\frac{u}{x}\left(\frac{x^2+y^2}{x^2-y^2}\right) - \frac{v}{y}\left(\frac{x^2+y^2}{x^2-y^2}\right)$$

$$= -\left(\frac{x^2+y^2}{x^2-y^2}\right)\left(\frac{u}{x}+\frac{v}{y}\right)$$

$$= \frac{x^2+y^2}{(y^2-x^2)} \qquad \left(\text{Given}: \frac{u}{x}+\frac{v}{y}=1\right)$$

(ii) $\dfrac{\partial(f_1,f_2)}{\partial(x,y)} = -\begin{vmatrix} u & v \\ -\dfrac{u}{x^2} & -\dfrac{v}{y^2} \end{vmatrix} = uv\left(-\dfrac{1}{y^2}+\dfrac{1}{x^2}\right) = \dfrac{uv(y^2-x^2)}{x^2 y^2} \qquad \ldots (i)$

$$\left(\frac{\partial x}{\partial u}\right)_v = -\frac{\partial(f_1,f_2)/\partial(u,y)}{\partial(f_1,f_2)/\partial(x,y)} = -\frac{-v(x^2+y^2)/y^2 x}{uv(y^2-x^2)/x^2 y^2}$$

$$= \frac{x}{u}\cdot\frac{x^2+y^2}{y^2-x^2} \qquad \ldots (3)$$

and $\left(\dfrac{\partial y}{\partial v}\right)_u = -\dfrac{\partial(f_1, f_2)/\partial(x, v)}{\partial(f_1, f_2)/\partial(x, y)}$

$= -\dfrac{u(x^2+y^2)/x^2 y}{uv(y^2-x^2)/x^2 y^2} = -\dfrac{y}{v}\left(\dfrac{x^2+y^2}{y^2-x^2}\right)$ ... (4)

From (3) and (4),

$\therefore \quad \dfrac{u}{x}\left(\dfrac{\partial x}{\partial u}\right)_v + \dfrac{v}{y}\left(\dfrac{\partial y}{\partial v}\right)_u = \dfrac{x^2+y^2}{y^2-x^2} - \dfrac{x^2+y^2}{y^2-x^2} = 0$

Ex. 7 : If $f(x, y, z) = 0$ and $g(x, y, z) = 0$, show that

$$\dfrac{dx}{\partial(f, g)/\partial(y, z)} = \dfrac{dy}{\partial(f, g)/\partial(z, x)} = \dfrac{dz}{\partial(f, g)/\partial(x, y)}$$

Sol. : Here $f_1 = f(x, y, z)$, $f_2 = g(x, y, z)$ ... (i)

We first find $\dfrac{dy}{dx}$ and $\dfrac{dz}{dx}$.

$\dfrac{dy}{dx} = -\dfrac{\partial(f_1, f_2)/\partial(x, z)}{\partial(f_1, f_2)/\partial(y, z)}$

$= -\dfrac{\begin{vmatrix} f_x & f_z \\ g_x & g_z \end{vmatrix}}{\begin{vmatrix} f_y & f_z \\ g_y & g_z \end{vmatrix}} = \dfrac{\partial(f, g)/\partial(z, x)}{\partial(f, g)/\partial(y, z)}$

$\therefore \quad \dfrac{dy}{\partial(f, g)/\partial(z, x)} = \dfrac{dx}{\partial(f, g)/\partial(z, x)}$ ... (1)

and $\dfrac{dz}{dx} = -\dfrac{\partial(f_1, f_2)/\partial(y, x)}{\partial(f_1, f_2)/\partial(y, z)}$

$= -\dfrac{\begin{vmatrix} f_y & f_x \\ g_y & g_x \end{vmatrix}}{\begin{vmatrix} f_y & f_z \\ g_y & g_z \end{vmatrix}} = \dfrac{\partial(f, g)/\partial(x, y)}{\partial(f, g)/\partial(y, z)}$

$\therefore \quad \dfrac{dz}{\partial(f, g)/\partial(x, y)} = \dfrac{dx}{\partial(f, g)/\partial(y, z)}$ ... (2)

From results (1) and (2),

$$\dfrac{dx}{\partial(f, g)/\partial(y, z)} = \dfrac{dy}{\partial(f, g)/\partial(z, x)} = \dfrac{dz}{\partial(f, g)/\partial(x, y)}$$

EXERCISE 11.4

1. If $x = u + e^{-v} \sin u$, $y = v + e^{-v} \cos u$, find $\dfrac{\partial u}{\partial y}$, $\dfrac{\partial v}{\partial x}$ and establish the relation between them. **Ans.**: $\dfrac{\partial u}{\partial y} = \dfrac{\partial v}{\partial x} = \dfrac{e^{-v} \sin u}{1 - e^{-2v}}$

2. If $x = u^2 - v^2$, $y = uv$ find $\dfrac{\partial u}{\partial x} \cdot \dfrac{\partial u}{\partial y} \cdot \dfrac{\partial v}{\partial x} \cdot \dfrac{\partial v}{\partial y}$ and also $\dfrac{\partial(u, v)}{\partial(x, y)}$.

   (Dec. 2012) Ans.: $\dfrac{u}{2(u^2 + v^2)} \cdot \dfrac{v}{2(u^2 + v^2)} \cdot \dfrac{-v}{2(u^2 + v^2)} \cdot \dfrac{u}{2(u^2 + v^2)}$ and $\dfrac{1}{4(u^2 + v^2)}$

3. If $u = xyz$, $v = x^2 + y^2 + z^2$, $w = x + y + z$ find $\dfrac{\partial x}{\partial u}$. **Ans.**: $\dfrac{1}{(x-y)(x-z)}$

   (May 2005, May 2007)

4. If $u = x + y^2$, $v = y + z^2$, $w = z + x^2$, prove that $\dfrac{\partial^2 x}{\partial u^2} = -8 \dfrac{(yz + 4z^2 x^2 - 2x^2 y)}{(1 + 8xyz)^2}$.

5. If $u + v^2 = x$, $v + w^2 = y$, $w + u^2 = z$, find $\dfrac{\partial u}{\partial x}$. **(May 2008)**

6. Use Jacobians to find $\dfrac{\partial u}{\partial x}$, if $u^2 + xv^2 - xy = 0$, $u^2 + xyv + v^2 = 0$.

   Ans.: $\dfrac{\partial u}{\partial x} = \dfrac{xyv^2 + xy^2 + 2vy - 2v^2}{2u(xy + 2v - 2xy)}$

7. If $u = x + y + z$, $v = x^2 + y^2 + z^2$, $w = x^3 + y^3 + z^3$, show that $\dfrac{\partial x}{\partial u} = \dfrac{-yz}{(x-y)(z-x)}$.

   (Dec. 2005)

8. If $u^2 + xv^2 = x + y$, $v^2 + yu^2 = x - y$, find $\dfrac{\partial u}{\partial x}$, $\dfrac{\partial v}{\partial y}$. **(Dec. 2013)**

   Ans.: $\dfrac{\partial u}{\partial x} = \dfrac{1 - x - v^2}{2u(1 - xy)}$, $\dfrac{\partial v}{\partial y} = \dfrac{1 + y + u^2}{-2v(1 - xy)}$.

11.5 FUNCTIONAL DEPENDENCE

Let $u = f_1(x, y)$ and $v = f_2(x, y)$ be any two functions of x and y. Sometimes we study under what conditions u and v will be functionally dependent or independent. If there exists a functional relation between u and v of the type $v = F(u)$ we say that u and v are functionally dependent or f_1, f_2 are functionally dependent.

Assuming that a relation of this type exists between f_1 and f_2 (say)

$$F(f_1, f_2) = 0 \qquad \ldots (1)$$

We have after differentiating (1) partially with respect to x, y and since

$$F(f_1, f_2) = 0, \quad \dfrac{\partial F}{\partial x} = 0, \quad \dfrac{\partial F}{\partial y} = 0$$

$$\frac{\partial F}{\partial f_1} \cdot \frac{\partial f_1}{\partial x} + \frac{\partial F}{\partial f_2} \cdot \frac{\partial f_2}{\partial x} = 0 \qquad \ldots (2)$$

$$\frac{\partial F}{\partial f_1} \cdot \frac{\partial f_1}{\partial y} + \frac{\partial F}{\partial f_2} \cdot \frac{\partial f_2}{\partial y} = 0 \qquad \ldots (3)$$

Eliminating $\dfrac{\partial F}{\partial f_1}$ and $\dfrac{\partial F}{\partial f_2}$ from equations (2) and (3), we get,

$$\begin{vmatrix} \dfrac{\partial f_1}{\partial x} & \dfrac{\partial f_2}{\partial x} \\ \dfrac{\partial f_1}{\partial y} & \dfrac{\partial f_2}{\partial y} \end{vmatrix} = 0 \Rightarrow \begin{vmatrix} \dfrac{\partial f_1}{\partial x} & \dfrac{\partial f_1}{\partial y} \\ \dfrac{\partial f_2}{\partial x} & \dfrac{\partial f_2}{\partial y} \end{vmatrix} = 0 \Rightarrow \dfrac{\partial(f_1, f_2)}{\partial(x, y)} = 0 \qquad \ldots (4)$$

From (4) it is clear that $f_1(x, y)$ and $f_2(x, y)$ are functionally dependent if their Jacobian vanishes identically.

i.e. $\qquad J = \dfrac{\partial(f_1, f_2)}{\partial(x, y)} = \dfrac{\partial(u, v)}{\partial(x, y)} = 0 \qquad \ldots (5)$

Note 1 : This fact can be generalised in case of n functions $f_r(x_1, x_2, \ldots, x_n)$ in $(r = 1, 2, 3 \ldots)$ n independent variables $x_1, x_2 \ldots x_n$ i.e. these n functions are functionally dependent if and only if their Jacobian $J = \dfrac{\partial(f_1, f_2, f_3, \ldots, f_n)}{\partial(x_1, x_2, x_3, \ldots, x_n)} = 0 \qquad \ldots (6)$

Note 2 : However, if number of functions are less than the number of variables then several relations of type (6) are required to be satisfied for the functional dependence. viz. for functions $f_1(x, y, z)$ and $f_2(x, y, z)$ of three variables it can be seen that for their functional dependence,

$$\dfrac{\partial(f_1, f_2)}{\partial(x, y)} = 0, \quad \dfrac{\partial(f_1, f_2)}{\partial(y, z)} = 0, \quad \text{and} \quad \dfrac{\partial(f_1, f_2)}{\partial(z, x)} = 0$$

ILLUSTRATIONS ON FUNCTIONAL DEPENDENCE

Ex. 1 : *Ascertain whether the following functions are functionally dependent, if so find the relation between them.* $u = \dfrac{x + y}{1 - xy}$, $v = \tan^{-1} x + \tan^{-1} y$.

(Jan. 2005, Dec. 2006, May 2009, Dec. 2009, 2014)

Sol. : $\qquad \dfrac{\partial u}{\partial x} = \dfrac{(1 - xy) - (x + y)(-y)}{(1 - xy)^2} = \dfrac{1 - xy + xy + y^2}{(1 - xy)^2} = \dfrac{1 + y^2}{(1 - xy)^2}$

$\qquad \dfrac{\partial u}{\partial y} = \dfrac{(1 - xy) - (x + y)(-x)}{(1 - xy)^2} = \dfrac{1 - xy + x^2 + xy}{(1 - xy)^2} = \dfrac{1 + x^2}{(1 - xy)^2}$

$\qquad \dfrac{\partial v}{\partial x} = \dfrac{1}{1 + x^2} + 0 = \dfrac{1}{1 + x^2}, \dfrac{\partial v}{\partial y} = \dfrac{1}{1 + y^2}$

$$\therefore \quad J = \frac{\partial(u, v)}{\partial(x, y)} = \begin{vmatrix} \frac{\partial u}{\partial x} & \frac{\partial u}{\partial y} \\ \frac{\partial v}{\partial x} & \frac{\partial v}{\partial y} \end{vmatrix} = \begin{vmatrix} \frac{1+y^2}{(1-xy)^2} & \frac{1+x^2}{(1-xy)^2} \\ \frac{1}{1+x^2} & \frac{1}{1+y^2} \end{vmatrix}$$

$$= \frac{1}{(1-xy)^2} - \frac{1}{(1-xy)^2} = 0$$

Thus $J = \dfrac{\partial(u,v)}{\partial(x,y)} = 0$, hence u and v are functionally dependent.

Relation between u and v : We have

$$v = \tan^{-1}x + \tan^{-1}y = \tan^{-1}\left(\frac{x+y}{1-xy}\right) = \tan^{-1}u$$

$$\therefore \quad v = \tan^{-1}u \qquad \ldots \text{Ans.}$$

Ex. 2 : *Are the following functions functionally dependent ? If so find the relation between them* $u = \dfrac{x-y}{x+z}, \ v = \dfrac{x+z}{y+z}$. **(Dec. 2010)**

Sol. : Here number of functions are less than the number of variables, hence for the functional dependence, we must have,

$$\frac{\partial(u,v)}{\partial(x,y)} = 0, \ \frac{\partial(u,v)}{\partial(y,z)} = 0 \text{ and } \frac{\partial(u,v)}{\partial(z,x)} = 0$$

$$\frac{\partial u}{\partial x} = \frac{(x+z)-(x-y)}{(x+z)^2} = \frac{y+z}{(x+z)^2},$$

$$\frac{\partial u}{\partial y} = \frac{1}{x+z}(-1) = -\frac{1}{(x+z)},$$

$$\frac{\partial u}{\partial z} = (x-y)\frac{-1}{(x+z)^2} = \frac{y-x}{(x+z)^2}$$

and $\quad \dfrac{\partial v}{\partial x} = \dfrac{1}{y+z}, \ \dfrac{\partial v}{\partial y} = -\dfrac{(x+z)}{(y+z)^2}$

$$\frac{\partial v}{\partial z} = \frac{(y+z)-(x+z)}{(y+z)^2} = \frac{y-x}{(y+z)^2}$$

Now, $\quad \dfrac{\partial(u,v)}{\partial(x,y)} = \begin{vmatrix} \dfrac{\partial u}{\partial x} & \dfrac{\partial u}{\partial y} \\ \dfrac{\partial v}{\partial x} & \dfrac{\partial v}{\partial y} \end{vmatrix} = \begin{vmatrix} \dfrac{y+z}{(x+z)^2} & \dfrac{-1}{x+z} \\ \dfrac{1}{y+z} & -\dfrac{x+z}{(y+z)^2} \end{vmatrix} = 0$

$$\frac{\partial(u, v)}{\partial(y, z)} = \begin{vmatrix} \frac{\partial u}{\partial y} & \frac{\partial u}{\partial z} \\ \frac{\partial v}{\partial y} & \frac{\partial v}{\partial z} \end{vmatrix} = \begin{vmatrix} -\frac{1}{x+z} & \frac{y-x}{(x+z)^2} \\ \frac{-(x+z)}{(y+z)^2} & \frac{y-x}{(y+z)^2} \end{vmatrix} = 0$$

$$\frac{\partial(u, v)}{\partial(z, x)} = \begin{vmatrix} \frac{\partial u}{\partial z} & \frac{\partial u}{\partial x} \\ \frac{\partial v}{\partial z} & \frac{\partial v}{\partial x} \end{vmatrix} = \begin{vmatrix} \frac{y-x}{(x+z)^2} & \frac{y+z}{(x+z)^2} \\ \frac{y-x}{(y+z)^2} & \frac{1}{y+z} \end{vmatrix} = 0$$

Hence $\quad \dfrac{\partial(u, v)}{\partial(x, y)} = \dfrac{\partial(u, v)}{\partial(y, z)} = \dfrac{\partial(u, v)}{\partial(z, x)} = 0$

Hence u and v are functionally dependent.

Relation between u and v : $\quad u = \dfrac{x-y}{x+z}, \quad v = \dfrac{x+z}{y+z} \quad \therefore \quad \dfrac{1}{v} = \dfrac{y+z}{x+z}$

$$u + \frac{1}{v} = \frac{x-y+y+z}{x+z} = \frac{x+z}{x+z} = 1$$

$\therefore \quad u + \dfrac{1}{v} = 1$

Ex. 3 : *Examine for the functional dependence $u = \sin^{-1} x + \sin^{-1} y$,*
$v = x\sqrt{1-y^2} + y\sqrt{1-x^2}$ and find the relation between them if it exist.

(May 06, 11, 13, Dec. 2014)

Sol. :
$$\frac{\partial u}{\partial x} = \frac{1}{\sqrt{1-x^2}}, \quad \frac{\partial u}{\partial y} = \frac{1}{\sqrt{1-y^2}}$$

$$\frac{\partial v}{\partial x} = \sqrt{1-y^2} + y \cdot \frac{-2x}{2\sqrt{1-x^2}} = \sqrt{1-y^2} - \frac{xy}{\sqrt{1-x^2}}$$

$$\frac{\partial v}{\partial y} = \frac{-2y}{2\sqrt{1-y^2}} + \sqrt{1-x^2} = -\frac{xy}{\sqrt{1-y^2}} + \sqrt{1-x^2}$$

$$J = \frac{\partial(u, v)}{\partial(x, y)} = \begin{vmatrix} \frac{\partial u}{\partial x} & \frac{\partial u}{\partial y} \\ \frac{\partial v}{\partial x} & \frac{\partial v}{\partial y} \end{vmatrix}$$

$$= \begin{vmatrix} \frac{1}{\sqrt{1-x^2}} & \frac{1}{\sqrt{1-y^2}} \\ \left(\sqrt{1-y^2} - \frac{xy}{\sqrt{1-x^2}}\right) & \left(-\frac{xy}{\sqrt{1-y^2}} + \sqrt{1-x^2}\right) \end{vmatrix}$$

$$= \left(\frac{-xy}{\sqrt{1-x^2}\sqrt{1-y^2}} + 1\right) - \left(1 - \frac{xy}{\sqrt{1-x^2}\sqrt{1-y^2}}\right) = 0$$

Hence u and v are functionally dependent.

Relation between u and v :

Let $\sin^{-1} x = \alpha \implies x = \sin \alpha$
$\sin^{-1} y = \beta \implies y = \sin \beta$
$v = \sin \alpha \cdot \cos \beta + \sin \beta \cos \alpha = \sin(\alpha + \beta)$
$ = \sin(\sin^{-1} x + \sin^{-1} y)$
$ = \sin u$

$\therefore \quad v = \sin u$

Ex. 4 : If $u = x + y + z$, $v = x^2 + y^2 + z^2$, $w = xy + yz + zx$ examine whether u, v, w are functionally dependent. If so find the relation between them. **(Jan. 2004)**

Sol. : For functional dependence, we must have $\dfrac{\partial(u, v, w)}{\partial(x, y, z)} = 0$.

$\dfrac{\partial u}{\partial x} = 1 \qquad \dfrac{\partial u}{\partial y} = 1 \qquad \dfrac{\partial u}{\partial z} = 1$

$\dfrac{\partial v}{\partial x} = 2x \qquad \dfrac{\partial v}{\partial y} = 2y \qquad \dfrac{\partial u}{\partial z} = 2z$

$\dfrac{\partial w}{\partial x} = y + z \qquad \dfrac{\partial w}{\partial y} = x + z \qquad \dfrac{\partial w}{\partial z} = x + y$

$$\dfrac{\partial(u, v, w)}{\partial(x, y, z)} = \begin{vmatrix} \dfrac{\partial u}{\partial x} & \dfrac{\partial u}{\partial y} & \dfrac{\partial u}{\partial z} \\ \dfrac{\partial v}{\partial x} & \dfrac{\partial v}{\partial y} & \dfrac{\partial v}{\partial z} \\ \dfrac{\partial w}{\partial x} & \dfrac{\partial w}{\partial y} & \dfrac{\partial w}{\partial z} \end{vmatrix} = \begin{vmatrix} 1 & 1 & 1 \\ 2x & 2y & 2z \\ y+z & z+x & x+y \end{vmatrix}$$

$$= 2 \begin{vmatrix} 1 & 1 & 1 \\ x & y & z \\ y+z & z+x & x+y \end{vmatrix}$$

Perform $R_3 + R_2$

$$= 2 \begin{vmatrix} 1 & 1 & 1 \\ x & y & z \\ x+y+z & x+y+z & x+y+z \end{vmatrix}$$

$$= 2(x + y + z) \begin{vmatrix} 1 & 1 & 1 \\ x & y & z \\ 1 & 1 & 1 \end{vmatrix} = 0$$

Hence u, v, w are functionally dependent.

Relation between u, v and w :

We have $\quad u^2 = (x + y + z)^2$

or $\quad u^2 = x^2 + y^2 + z^2 + 2(yz + zx + xy) = v + 2w$

$\therefore \quad u^2 = v + 2w$

Ex. 5 : *Find the condition that the functions*

$$f_1(x, y) = a_1 x + b_1 y + c_1 \quad \ldots (i)$$

$$f_2(x, y) = a_2 x + b_2 y + c_2 \quad \ldots (ii)$$

may be functionally dependent, and then find the relation between them if this condition is satisfied.

Sol. : For functional dependence, $\dfrac{\partial(f_1, f_2)}{\partial(x, y)} = 0$.

$$J = \frac{\partial(f_1, f_2)}{\partial(x, y)} = \begin{vmatrix} \dfrac{\partial f_1}{\partial x} & \dfrac{\partial f_1}{\partial y} \\ \dfrac{\partial f_2}{\partial x} & \dfrac{\partial f_2}{\partial y} \end{vmatrix} = \begin{vmatrix} a_1 & b_1 \\ a_2 & b_2 \end{vmatrix} = a_1 b_2 - a_2 b_1$$

Hence for functional dependence, $a_1 b_2 = a_2 b_1$.

Relation between f_1 and f_2 : For relation between f_1 and f_2 multiply (i) by b_2 and (ii) by b_1 and subtracting, we have

$$\begin{aligned} b_2 f_1 - b_1 f_2 &= b_2 (a_1 x + b_1 y + c_1) - b_1 (a_2 x + b_2 y + c_2) \\ &= (a_1 b_2 - a_2 b_1) x + (b_1 b_2 - b_1 b_2) y + b_2 c_1 - b_1 c_2 \\ &= 0 \cdot x + 0 \cdot y + b_2 c_1 - b_1 c_2 \end{aligned}$$

or $\quad b_2 f_1 - b_1 f_2 = b_2 c_1 - b_1 c_2$

Ex. 6 : *Examine $u = x + y - z$, $v = x - y + z$, $w = x^2 + y^2 + z^2 - 2yz$ are functionally dependent, if so, find the relation between them.*

Sol. : For functional dependence,

$$J = \frac{\partial(u, v, w)}{\partial(x, y, z)} = \begin{vmatrix} u_x & u_y & u_z \\ v_x & v_y & v_z \\ w_x & w_y & w_z \end{vmatrix}$$

$$= \begin{vmatrix} 1 & 1 & -1 \\ 1 & -1 & 1 \\ 2x & 2y - 2z & 2z - 2y \end{vmatrix}$$

Perform $(-1) C_3 = \begin{vmatrix} 1 & 1 & 1 \\ 1 & -1 & -1 \\ 2x & 2y - 2z & 2y - 2z \end{vmatrix} = 0 \qquad (\because C_2 \approx C_3)$

Hence, u and v are functionally dependent.

Relation between u, v, w :

$$u + v = 2x \quad \text{and} \quad u - v = 2y - 2z$$

$$\Rightarrow x = \frac{u+v}{2} \quad \text{and} \quad y - z = \frac{u-v}{2}$$

$$\therefore \quad \left(\frac{u+v}{2}\right)^2 + \left(\frac{u-v}{2}\right)^2 = x^2 + (y-z)^2$$

$$\frac{1}{4}[2u^2 + 2v^2] = x^2 + y^2 + z^2 - 2yz$$

$$\therefore \quad u^2 + v^2 = 2w$$

Ex. 7 : *Show that $ax^2 + 2hxy + by^2$ and $Ax^2 + 2Hxy + By^2$ are independent, unless*

$$\frac{a}{A} = \frac{h}{H} = \frac{b}{B}$$

Sol. : Let
$$u = ax^2 + 2hxy + by^2$$
$$v = Ax^2 + 2Hxy + By^2$$

If u and v are dependent then $J = \dfrac{\partial(u, v)}{\partial(x, y)} = 0$.

i.e. $\dfrac{\partial(u, v)}{\partial(x, y)} = \begin{vmatrix} 2(ax + hy) & 2(hx + by) \\ 2(Ax + Hy) & 2(Hx + By) \end{vmatrix} = 0$

or $(ax + hy)(Hx + By) - (hx + by)(Ax + Hy) = 0$

or $(aH - Ah)x^2 + (aB - Ab)xy + (Bh - bH)y^2 = 0$

i.e. $aH - Ah = 0, \quad Bh - bH = 0$

or $\dfrac{a}{A} = \dfrac{h}{H} = \dfrac{b}{B}$

Ex. 8 : *Find whether the following functions are functionally dependent. If so, find the relation between them.*

$$u = \frac{x}{y-z}, \quad v = \frac{y}{z-x}, \quad w = \frac{z}{x-y} \quad \text{(Dec. 2008, May 2014)}$$

Sol. : Taking logarithms, we have

$$\log u = \log x - \log(y - z)$$
$$\log v = \log y - \log(z - x)$$
$$\log w = \log z - \log(x - y)$$

$$\therefore \quad \frac{\partial(u, v, w)}{\partial(x, y, z)} = \begin{vmatrix} \dfrac{u}{x} & -\dfrac{u}{y-z} & \dfrac{u}{y-z} \\ \dfrac{v}{z-x} & \dfrac{v}{y} & -\dfrac{v}{z-x} \\ -\dfrac{w}{x-y} & \dfrac{w}{x-y} & \dfrac{w}{z} \end{vmatrix} = uvw \begin{vmatrix} \dfrac{1}{x} & -\dfrac{1}{y-z} & \dfrac{1}{y-z} \\ \dfrac{1}{z-x} & \dfrac{1}{y} & -\dfrac{1}{z-x} \\ -\dfrac{1}{x-y} & \dfrac{1}{x-y} & \dfrac{1}{z} \end{vmatrix}$$

$$= \frac{uvw}{(x-y)(y-z)(z-x)} \begin{vmatrix} \frac{y-z}{x} & -1 & 1 \\ 1 & \frac{z-x}{y} & -1 \\ -1 & 1 & \frac{x-y}{z} \end{vmatrix}$$

$$= 0$$

Hence u, v, w are functionally dependent.

Relation between u, v, w :

We note that $\quad u + v = \dfrac{x}{y-z} + \dfrac{y}{z-x} = \dfrac{(x-y)(z-x-y)}{(y-z)(z-x)}$ ... (1)

Similarly, $\quad v + w = \dfrac{(y-z)(x-y-z)}{(z-x)(x-y)}$ ... (2)

and $\quad w + u = \dfrac{(z-x)(y-z-x)}{(y-z)(x-y)}$ ... (3)

Again $\quad 1 - u = 1 - \dfrac{x}{y-z} = \dfrac{y-z-x}{y-z}$ ... (4)

Similarly, $\quad 1 - v = \dfrac{z-x-y}{z-x}$ ... (5)

and $\quad 1 - w = \dfrac{x-y-z}{x-y}$ ... (6)

From results (1), (2) and (3),

$$(u+v)(v+w)(w+u) = \frac{(x-y)(z-x-y)}{(y-z)(z-x)} \cdot \frac{(y-z)(x-y-z)}{(z-x)(x-y)} \cdot \frac{(z-x)(y-z-x)}{(y-z)(x-y)}$$

$$= \frac{(y-z-x)(z-x-y)(x-y-z)}{(y-z)(z-x)(x-y)}$$

$$= (1-u)(1-v)(1-w) \quad \text{[using results (4), (5) and (6)]}$$

$\therefore \quad (u+v)(v+w)(w+u) = (1-u)(1-v)(1-w)$ is the required relation.

EXERCISE 11.5

1. Examine for functional dependence $u = \dfrac{x-y}{x+y}$, $v = \dfrac{(x+y)}{x}$, if functionally dependent find the relation between them.

Ans. yes, $uv = 2 - v$ **(Dec. 2007, May 2007)**

2. Verify whether the following functions are functionally dependent, if so find relation between them. $u = \dfrac{x-y}{x+y}$, $v = \dfrac{xy}{(x+y)^2}$. **Ans.** yes, $4v = 1 - u^2$

3. Prove that the functions $u = y + z$, $v = x + 2z^2$, $w = x - 4yz - 2y^2$ are functionally dependent and find the relation between them. **Ans.** $w = v - 2u^2$ **(May 05, 08, Dec. 12)**

4. Examine for functional dependence $u = \dfrac{x-y}{1+xy}$, $v = \tan^{-1} x - \tan^{-1} y$, if dependent find the relation. **Ans.** yes, $u = \tan v$

5. Examine $u = x + y + z$, $v = x^2 + y^2 + z^2 - 2xy - 2yz - 2zx$, $w = x^3 + y^3 + z^3 - 3xyz$ for functional dependence, and find relation between them if functionally dependent. **Ans.** yes, $w = \dfrac{u}{4}(u^2 + 3v)$

6. Examine $u = x + y + z$, $v = x - y + z$, $w = x^2 + y^2 + z^2 + 2xz$ for functional dependence and find the relation between them if functionally dependent.
Ans. yes, $u^2 + v^2 = 2w$ **(May 2004)**

7. Examine $u = \dfrac{x+y}{z}$, $v = \dfrac{y+z}{x}$, $w = \dfrac{y(x+y+z)}{xz}$ for functional dependence, and find the relation between them if functionally dependent. **Ans.** yes, $1 + w = uv$

8. If $u = x + y + z$, $v = x^2 + y^2 + z^2$, $w = x^3 + y^3 + z^3 - 3xyz$, prove that u, v, w are not independent and find the relation between them.
Ans. dependent, $2w = u(3v - u^2)$ **(May 2014)**
[**Hint :** $w = (x + y + z)(x^2 + y^2 + z^2 - xy - yz - zx)$ and $u^2 - v = 2(xy + yz + zx)$]

9. Examine for functional dependence $u = x + y + z + t$, $v = x^2 + y^2 + z^2 + t^2$, $w = x^3 + y^3 + z^3 + t^3$, $r = xyz + yzt + zxt + txy$, if so find the relation between them.
Ans. yes, $u^3 = 3uv - 2w + 6r$

11.6 ERRORS AND APPROXIMATIONS

Let $f(x, y)$ be a continuous function of x and y. If δx and δy be the increments of x and y, then the new value of $f(x, y)$ will be $f(x + \delta x, y + \delta y)$. Hence change in $f(x, y)$ is given by

$$\delta f = f(x + \delta x, y + \delta y) - f(x, y) \qquad \ldots (1)$$

Expanding $f(x + \delta x, y + \delta y)$ by Taylor's theorem and supposing $\delta x, \delta y$ to be so small that their products, squares and higher powers can be neglected, we have

$$\delta f = \frac{\partial f}{\partial x} \delta x + \frac{\partial f}{\partial y} \delta y \text{ approximately}$$

or
$$df = \frac{\partial f}{\partial x} dx + \frac{\partial f}{\partial y} dy \qquad \ldots (2)$$

Similarly, if f be a function of variables $x, y, z, t \ldots$ etc. we may have

$$df = \frac{\partial f}{\partial x} dx + \frac{\partial f}{\partial y} dy + \frac{\partial f}{\partial z} dz + \ldots \text{ approximately} \qquad \ldots (3)$$

Formulae (2) and (3) are very useful in correcting the effect of small errors in measured quantities.

Note 1 : Actually in (2), dx, dy may be taken as actual errors or (increments) in x and y respectively, while df is approximate error in f.

Note 2 : If $z = f(x, y)$ we may have : $dz = \dfrac{\partial z}{\partial x} dx + \dfrac{\partial z}{\partial y} dy$.

Here dx, dy, dz are known as actual errors in x, y and z respectively,

$\dfrac{dx}{x}, \dfrac{dy}{y}, \dfrac{dz}{z}$ as relative errors in x, y and z respectively,

and $\dfrac{100\, dx}{x}, \dfrac{100\, dy}{y}, \dfrac{100\, dz}{z}$ are known as percentage errors in x, y and z respectively.

ILLUSTRATIONS ON ERRORS AND APPROXIMATIONS

Ex. 1 : *Find the percentage error in the area of an ellipse when an error of 1% is made in measuring its major and minor axes.* **(Dec. 2009)**

Sol. : If A is area and 2a and 2b are the major and minor axes of the ellipse having equation $\dfrac{x^2}{a^2} + \dfrac{y^2}{b^2} = 1$ then

$$A = \pi a b \qquad \ldots (1)$$

Taking log of both sides, $\log A = \log \pi + \log a + \log b$ ... (2)

Differentiating, we have

$$\dfrac{dA}{A} = 0 + \dfrac{da}{a} + \dfrac{db}{b}$$

$\therefore \quad \dfrac{100\, dA}{A} = \dfrac{100\, da}{a} + \dfrac{100\, db}{b}$

Given that percentage errors $\dfrac{100\, da}{a}$ and $\dfrac{100\, db}{b}$ each are equal to 1, hence

$$\dfrac{100\, dA}{A} = 1 + 1 = 2$$

$\therefore$ Percentage error in the area A = 2%.

Ex. 2 : *The deflection at the centre of a rod of length l and diameter d, supported at its ends and loaded at the centre with a weight w, varies as $wl^3 d^{-4}$. What is the percentage increase in the deflection corresponding to the percentage increase in w, l and d of 3, 2 and 1 respectively ?*

Sol. : Given that, Deflection $D \propto w l^3 d^{-4}$

Let the deflection at the centre be D, then $D = k \dfrac{w l^3}{d^4}$. ... (1)

Taking log of both sides, $\log D = \log k + \log w + 3 \log l - 4 \log d$.

Differentiating, we get

$$\dfrac{\delta D}{D} = \dfrac{\delta w}{w} + 3 \dfrac{\delta l}{l} - 4 \dfrac{\delta d}{d}$$

or $\quad \dfrac{100\, \delta D}{D} = \dfrac{100\, \delta w}{w} + 3 \cdot \dfrac{100\, \delta l}{l} - 4 \cdot \dfrac{100\, \delta d}{d}$

$\therefore \quad$ % increase in D $= 3 + 3 \times 2 - 4 \times 1 = 5\%$.

Ex. 3 : *The density ρ of a body is calculated from its weight W in air and w in water. If errors dW and dw are made in W and w, find the relative error in ρ.*

Sol. : We know that, $\rho = \dfrac{W}{W-w}$

Taking log of both sides and differentiating, we get

$$\log \rho = \log W - \log (W-w)$$

$\therefore \quad \dfrac{1}{\rho} d\rho = \dfrac{1}{W} dW - \dfrac{1}{W-w} (dW - dw)$

$$= \left(\dfrac{1}{W} - \dfrac{1}{W-w}\right) dW + \dfrac{dw}{W-w}$$

$$= -\dfrac{w}{W(W-w)} dW + \dfrac{dw}{W-w}$$

Hence $\quad d\rho = \rho \left[\dfrac{dw}{W-w} - \dfrac{w \, dW}{W(W-w)}\right]$

$\therefore \quad$ Relative error in $\rho = \dfrac{W}{W-w}\left[\dfrac{dw}{W-w} - \dfrac{w}{W(W-w)} dW\right]$

$$= \dfrac{W}{(W-w)^2}\left[dw - \dfrac{w}{W} dW\right]$$

$$= \dfrac{W \, dw - w \, dW}{(W-w)^2}$$

Ex. 4 : *In the manufacture of closed rectangular boxes with specified sides a, b, c ($a \neq b \neq c$) small changes of A %, B %, C % occurred in a, b, c respectively from box to box from the specified dimension. However, the volume and surface area of all boxes were according to the specification. Show that :* **(May 2011)**

$$\dfrac{A}{a(b-c)} = \dfrac{B}{b(c-a)} = \dfrac{C}{c(a-b)}$$

Sol. : Let V be the volume and S the surface area of the box, then

$$V = abc \qquad \ldots (1)$$
$$S = 2(ab + bc + ca) \qquad \ldots (2)$$

From (1), we get $\log V = \log a + \log b + \log c$

$$\dfrac{1}{V} dV = \dfrac{1}{a} da + \dfrac{1}{b} db + \dfrac{1}{c} dc$$

$$\dfrac{100 \, dV}{V} = \dfrac{100 \, da}{a} + \dfrac{100 \, db}{b} + \dfrac{100 \, dc}{c}$$

$$= A + B + C$$

But $\quad dV = 0 \quad$ (as there is no change in the volume of the box)

$\therefore \quad 0 = A + B + C \qquad \ldots (3)$

Similarly from (2),

$$dS = \frac{\partial S}{\partial a} da + \frac{\partial S}{\partial b} db + \frac{\partial S}{\partial c} dc$$

$$= 2(b+c) \cdot \frac{aA}{100} + 2(c+a)\frac{bB}{100} + 2(c+a)\frac{cC}{100}$$

because $\quad A = 100\dfrac{da}{a}$, etc.

But $\quad dS = 0,\quad$ (as there is no change in surface area)

$\therefore \quad 0 = a(b+c) \cdot A + b(c+a) \cdot B + c(c+a) \cdot C \quad \ldots (4)$

Apply Cramer's rule to (3) and (4) then

$$\frac{A}{c(a+b)-b(c+a)} = \frac{-B}{c(a+b)-a(b+c)} = \frac{C}{b(c+a)-a(b+c)}$$

$\Rightarrow \quad \dfrac{A}{a(c-b)} = \dfrac{-B}{b(c-a)} = \dfrac{C}{c(b-a)}$

$\Rightarrow \quad \dfrac{A}{a(b-c)} = \dfrac{B}{b(c-a)} = \dfrac{C}{c(a-b)} \quad$ ... Proved

Ex. 5 : *Find the possible percentage error in computing the parallel resistance r of three resistances r_1, r_2, r_3 from the formula $\dfrac{1}{r} = \dfrac{1}{r_1} + \dfrac{1}{r_2} + \dfrac{1}{r_3}$ if r_1, r_2, r_3 are each in error by plus 1.2%.* **(May 2005)**

Sol. : Here $\dfrac{1}{r} = \dfrac{1}{r_1} + \dfrac{1}{r_2} + \dfrac{1}{r_3}$. $\quad \ldots (1)$

Differentiating, we get

$$-\frac{1}{r^2} dr = -\frac{1}{r_1^2} dr_1 - \frac{1}{r_2^2} dr_2 - \frac{1}{r_3^2} dr_3$$

$\Rightarrow \quad \dfrac{1}{r}\left(\dfrac{100\, dr}{r}\right) = \dfrac{1}{r_1}\left(\dfrac{100\, dr_1}{r_1}\right) + \dfrac{1}{r_2}\left(\dfrac{100\, dr_2}{r_2}\right) + \dfrac{1}{r_3}\left(\dfrac{100\, dr_3}{r_3}\right)$

$$= \frac{1}{r_1}(1.2) + \frac{1}{r_2}(1.2) + \frac{1}{r_3}(1.2)$$

$$= (1.2)\left[\frac{1}{r_1} + \frac{1}{r_2} + \frac{1}{r_3}\right]$$

$$= 1.2\left(\frac{1}{r}\right) \text{ from (1)}.$$

$\therefore \quad \dfrac{100\, dr}{r} = 1.2\,\% = $ the % error in r.

Ex. 6 : *The voltage V, across a resistor is measured with error δV and the resistance R with error δR. Prove that the error in calculating the power $W = \dfrac{V^2}{R}$, generated in the resistor is $\dfrac{V}{R^2}(2R\,\delta V - V\,\delta R)$. If there are errors of 1% and 2% respectively in measuring the voltage V and resistance R, find % error in calculation of work $W = \dfrac{V^2}{R}$.*

Sol. : Given
$$W = \frac{V^2}{R} \qquad \ldots (1)$$

Hence, we have
$$\delta W = \frac{\partial W}{\partial V}\,\delta V + \frac{\partial W}{\partial R}\,\delta R$$

$$= \left(\frac{2V}{R}\right)\delta V - \left(\frac{V^2}{R^2}\right)\delta R = \frac{2VR\,\delta V - V^2\,\delta R}{R^2}$$

$$= \frac{V}{R^2}[2R\,\delta V - V\,\delta R] \qquad \ldots (2)$$

Now, we have
$$\delta W = \frac{V^2}{R^2}\left[2R\,\frac{\delta V}{V} - \delta R\right]$$

$\therefore$
$$\frac{\delta W}{\left(\dfrac{V^2}{R}\right)} = 2\,\frac{\delta V}{V} - \frac{\delta R}{R}$$

$\therefore$
$$\frac{100\,\delta W}{W} = 2\left(\frac{100\,\delta V}{V}\right) - \frac{100\,\delta R}{R}$$

$$= 2(1) - (2)$$
$$= 2 - 2 = 0$$

% Error in W $= 0 =$ No appreciable error.

Ex. 7 : *The area of a triangle ABC, is calculated from the formula $\Delta = \dfrac{1}{2}\cdot bc \cdot \sin A$. Errors of 1%, 2% and 3% respectively are made in measuring b, c, A. If the correct value of A is 45°, find the % error in the calculated value of Δ.* **(May 2004, Dec. 2010, 2014)**

Sol. : Given that $\Delta = \dfrac{1}{2}\,bc\sin A$.

Taking log of both sides and differentiating, we have

$$\log \Delta = \log \frac{1}{2} + \log b + \log c + \log \sin A$$

$\therefore$
$$\frac{1}{\Delta}\,d\Delta = 0 + \frac{1}{b}\,db + \frac{1}{c}\,dc + \cot A \cdot dA$$

or
$$\frac{100\,d\Delta}{\Delta} = \frac{100\,db}{b} + \frac{100\,dc}{c} + \cot A \cdot (100\,dA) \qquad \ldots (1)$$

Given
$$\frac{100\,db}{b} = 1,\ \frac{100\,dc}{c} = 2,\ \text{and}\ \frac{100\,dA}{A} = 3$$

So that $100\,dA = 3A.$

Putting these values in (1), we get

$$\frac{100\, d\Delta}{\Delta} = 1 + 2 + \cot A\, (3A) = 3 + 3A\, \cot A$$

$$= 3 + 3\frac{\pi}{4}\left(\cot\frac{\pi}{4}\right), \quad A = \frac{\pi}{4} \text{ (given)}$$

$$= 3 + \frac{3\pi}{4}$$

Ex. 8 : *In calculating volume of right circular cylinder, errors of 2% and 1% are found in measuring height and base radius respectively. Find the percentage error in calculating volume of the cylinder.*

Sol. : If r and h are base radius and height of the right circular cylinder, its volume V is given by

$$V = \pi r^2 h$$

Taking log of both sides,

$$\log V = \log \pi + 2 \log r + \log h$$

Taking differentials, we have

$$\frac{dV}{V} = 2\frac{dr}{r} + \frac{dh}{h}$$

$$\therefore \quad \frac{100\, dV}{V} = 2\left(\frac{100\, dr}{r}\right) + \left(\frac{100\, dh}{h}\right) = 2(1) + (2) = 4\%$$

$$\therefore \quad \% \text{ error in } V = \frac{100\, dV}{V} = 4\%$$

Ex. 9 : *In estimating the cost of a pile of bricks measured 2m × 15m × 1.2m, the top of the pile is stretched 1% beyond the standard length. If the count is 450 bricks pile cubic meter and bricks cost Rs. 450 per thousand, find the approximate error in cost.*

Sol. : Let l, b and h be the length, breadth and height of the pile, then $V = l \times b \times h$.

$$\therefore \quad \log V = \log l + \log b + \log h$$

$$\therefore \quad \frac{1}{V} dV = \frac{1}{l} dl + \frac{1}{b} db + \frac{1}{h} dh$$

Since the top of the pile is stretched 1% beyond the standard length,

$$\frac{100\, dl}{l} = 0, \quad \frac{100\, db}{b} = 0 \text{ and } \frac{100\, dh}{h} = 1$$

$$\therefore \quad \frac{100\, dV}{V} = \frac{100\, dh}{h} = 1$$

$$\therefore \quad dV = \frac{V}{100} = \frac{l \cdot b \cdot h}{100} = \frac{2 \times 15 \times 1.2}{100} = \frac{36}{100} \text{ cubic metres.}$$

$$\therefore \quad \text{Error in number of bricks} = \frac{36}{100} \times 450 = 162 \text{ bricks}$$

Given cost of bricks is Rs. 450 per thousand,

$$\therefore \quad \text{Error in cost} = 162 \times \frac{450}{1000} = 72.9 \text{ Rs.}$$

Ex. 10 : *In estimating the cost of a pile of bricks measured 2m × 15m × 1.2m, the tape is stretched 1% beyond the standard length. If the count in 450 bricks per cubic meter and bricks cost Rs. 130 per thousand, find the approximate error in cost. Is the brick seller gaining or losing ?*

Sol. : Let l, b and h be the length, breadth and height of the pile, then $V = l \times b \times h$.

$$\therefore \quad \text{Volume} = 2 \times 15 \times 1.2 = 36 \text{ cubic meters}$$

$$\therefore \quad \log V = \log l + \log b + \log h$$

$$\therefore \quad \frac{dV}{V} = \frac{dl}{l} + \frac{db}{b} + \frac{dz}{z}$$

$$\therefore \quad 100\frac{dV}{V} = 100\frac{dx}{x} + 100\frac{dy}{y} + 100\frac{dz}{z}$$

As the tape is stretched 1% beyond the standard length, each dimension is in error by 1%.

$$\therefore \quad 100\frac{dV}{V} = 3 \qquad \therefore\ dV = \frac{3V}{100} = \frac{3 \times 36}{100}$$

$$\therefore \quad \text{Number of bricks in error} = dV \times 450 = \frac{3 \times 36}{100} \times 450 = 486$$

Given cost of bricks is Rs. 130 per thousand,

$$\therefore \quad \text{Error in cost} = 486 \times \frac{130}{1000} = \text{Rs. } 63.18$$

Since the calculated volume V + dV = 37.08 cubic meter is more than the actual volume 36 cubic meter, seller is gaining.

Ex. 11 : *A power dissipated in a resistor is given by* $P = \frac{E^2}{R}$. *Using calculus, find the approximate percentage error in P when E is increased by 3% and R is decreased by 2%.*

Sol. : Given, $$P = \frac{E^2}{R}$$

Taking log and differentiating, we have

$$\log P = 2 \log E - \log R$$

$$\therefore \quad \frac{1}{P} dP = 2\frac{1}{E}\, dE - \frac{1}{R} dR$$

$$\therefore \quad \frac{100\ dP}{P} = 2\left(\frac{100\ dE}{E}\right) - \frac{100\ dR}{R}$$

$$= 2(3) - (2) = 4$$

$\therefore$ % Error in power, P = 4.

Ex. 12 : Find $[(3.82)^2 + 2(2.1)^3]^{1/5}$ by using the theory of approximations. **(May 2011)**

Sol. : Consider $z = (x^2 + 2y^3)^{1/5}$. ... (1)

Taking $x = 4$, $dx = 3.82 - 4 = -0.18$; $y = 2$, $dy = 2.1 - 2 = 0.1$.

Now
$$dz = \frac{\partial z}{\partial x} dx + \frac{\partial z}{\partial y} dy$$

$$= \frac{1}{5}(x^2 + 2y^3)^{-4/5} \cdot 2x \, dx + \frac{1}{5}(x^2 + 2y^3)^{-4/5} \cdot 6y^2 \, dy \quad [\text{from (1)}]$$

$$= \frac{1}{5}(16 + 16)^{-4/5} \cdot 8(-0.18) + \frac{1}{5}(16 + 16)^{-4/5} \cdot 24(0.1)$$

$$= \frac{1}{5} \cdot \frac{1}{16} \cdot 8(-0.18) + \frac{1}{5} \cdot \frac{1}{16} \cdot 24(0.1)$$

$$= -0.018 + 0.03 = 0.012$$

But $z = (16 + 16)^{1/5} = 2$. [from (1)]

Thus required value of the given expression $= z + dz = 2 + 0.012 = 2.012$

Ex. 13 : *A balloon is in the form of right circular cylinder of radius 1.5 m and length 4 m and is surrounded by hemispherical ends. If the radius is increased by 0.01 m and the length by 0.05 m, find the % change in the volume of a balloon.*

Sol. : Volume V of the balloon is

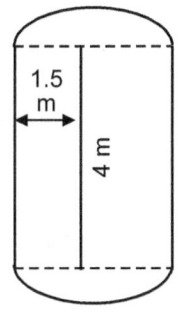

Fig. 11.1

$$V = \text{Volume of cylinder} + \text{Volume of two hemispheres}$$

$$= \pi r^2 h + \frac{2}{3}\pi r^3 + \frac{2}{3}\pi r^3$$

$$V = \pi r^2 h + \frac{4}{3}\pi r^3 \qquad ...(1)$$

$$dV = \pi \, 2r \, \delta r \cdot h + \pi r^2 \cdot \delta h + \frac{4}{3}\pi \, 3r^2 \, \delta r$$

$$\frac{dV}{V} = \frac{\pi r [2\delta r \cdot h + r \cdot \delta h + 4r \, \delta r]}{\pi r^2 h + \frac{4}{3}\pi r^3} = \frac{2\delta r h + r \delta h + 4r \, \delta r}{rh + \frac{4}{3} r^2}$$

$$= \frac{2 \times 0.01 \times 4 + 1.5 \times 0.05 + 4 \times 1.5 \times 0.01}{1.5 \times 4 \times \frac{4}{3}(1.5)^2} = \frac{0.215}{9}$$

$\therefore$ % Error in V $= \frac{100 \, dV}{V} = 100 \left(\frac{0.215}{9}\right) = 2.38$

Ex. 14 : *At a distance of 20 m from the foot of a tower, the elevation of its top is 60°. If the possible error in measuring distance and elevation are 1 cm and 1 minute, find the approximate error in the calculated height.*

Sol. : We note that, $d\theta = 1' = \left(\frac{1}{60}\right)^o = \left(\frac{\pi}{180} \times \frac{1}{60}\right)^c = \left(\frac{3.142}{180 \times 60}\right)$,

$$dx = 1 \text{ cm} = \frac{1}{100} \text{ m} = 0.01$$

and $\quad x = 20 \text{ m}$

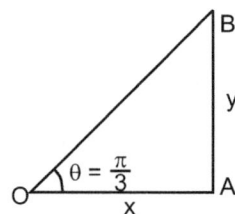

Fig. 11.2

We know that, $\quad y = x \tan \theta$

Taking differentials,

$$dy = dx \cdot \tan \theta + x \sec^2 \theta \cdot d\theta$$

$\therefore \quad dy = \left(\frac{1}{100}\right)(\sqrt{3}) + 20 \times 4 \times \frac{3.142}{180 \times 60}$

Error in calculated height,

$$dy = 0.0407 \text{ m}.$$

Ex. 15 : *The acceleration of a piston is calculated by $f = w^2 r \left(\cos \theta + \frac{r}{l} \cos 2\theta\right)$. It is calculated for the values of $\theta = 30°$, $\frac{r}{l} = \frac{1}{4}$. If the values of θ, w were each 1% small then show that the calculated value of f is about 1.5% too small.*

Sol. : We note here that r and l are constants and since the errors in values of θ and w are given to be small, they are considered to be negative.

Given $\frac{r}{l} = \frac{1}{4}$, $\theta = \frac{\pi}{6}$, $100 \frac{d\theta}{\theta} = -1$, and $100 \frac{dw}{w} = -1$

and $\quad f = w^2 r \left(\cos \theta + \frac{r}{l} \cos 2\theta\right) \quad \ldots (1)$

Taking log of (1), we have

$$\log f = 2 \log w + \log r + \log \left(\cos \theta + \frac{r}{l} \cos 2\theta\right)$$

Taking differentials, we get

$$\frac{df}{f} = 2\frac{dw}{w} + 0 + \frac{\left(-\sin\theta - \frac{2r}{l}\sin 2\theta\right)}{\left(\cos\theta + \frac{r}{l}\cos 2\theta\right)} \cdot d\theta$$

$$\therefore \quad 100\frac{df}{f} = 2\times 100\frac{dw}{w} - \left[\frac{\sin\theta + \frac{2r}{l}\sin 2\theta}{\cos\theta + \frac{r}{l}\cos 2\theta}\right](\theta)\left(100\frac{d\theta}{\theta}\right)$$

$$= 2(-1) - \left[\frac{\frac{1}{2} + 2\cdot\frac{1}{4}\cdot\frac{\sqrt{3}}{2}}{\frac{\sqrt{3}}{2} + \frac{1}{4}\cdot\frac{1}{2}}\right]\frac{\pi}{6}(-1) \qquad \left(\because \theta = \frac{\pi}{6}\right)$$

% error in $f = \frac{100\, df}{f} = -1.5$

Ex. 16 : If $(x, y) = (50 - x^2 - y^2)^{1/2}$ then find the approximate value of $f(3, 4) - f(2.9, 4.1)$.

Sol. : Given : $f(x, y) = (50 - x^2 - y^2)^{1/2}$, then, $f(3, 4) = 5$.

To find $f(2.9, 4.1)$, let,

$$x = 3, \quad y = 4$$
$$x + \delta x = 2.9, \quad y + \delta y = 4.1$$
$$\therefore \quad \delta x = -0.1, \quad \delta y = 0.1$$

Let u be the error value of $f(2.9, 4.1)$, and with $x = 3$, $y = 4$, $u = 5$.

$$\therefore \quad u^2 = 50 - x^2 - y^2$$

Taking differentials,

$$2u\,\delta u = -2x\,\delta x - 2y\,\delta y$$

$$\therefore \quad \delta u = \frac{-x\,\delta x - y\,\delta y}{u} = \frac{-3(-0.1) - 4(0.1)}{5} = -0.02$$

$\therefore$ Approximate value of $f(2.9, 4.1)$ is given by,

$$f(2.9, 4.1) = u + \delta u = 5 - 0.02$$

$$\therefore \quad f(3, 4) - f(2.9, 4.1) = 5 - (5 - 0.02) = 0.02$$

Ex. 17 : *If the kinetic energy is calculated by the formula $T = \frac{mv^2}{2}$ and 'm' change from 49 to 49.5 and 'v' change from 1600 to 1590, find (a) approximately the change in 'T', (b) percentage error in kinetic energy 'T'.* **(Dec. 2007, May 2013)**

Sol. : (a) We have, $T = \frac{1}{2}mv^2$, $m = 49$ and $v = 1600$ ... (i)

Also $m + dm = 49.5 \Rightarrow dm = 49.5 - 49 = 0.5$

and $v + dv = 1590 \Rightarrow dv = 1590 - 1600 = -10$

Taking log and differentials of (i),

$$\log T = -\log 2 + \log m + 2 \log v$$

$$\frac{1}{T} dT = \frac{1}{m} dm + \frac{2}{v} dv \qquad \ldots \text{(ii)}$$

$$dT = T\left(\frac{dm}{m} + \frac{2dv}{v}\right) = \frac{1}{2} mv^2 \left(\frac{dm}{m} + \frac{2dv}{v}\right)$$

$$= \frac{1}{2} (49)(1600)^2 \left[\frac{0.5}{49} + \frac{2(-10)}{1600}\right]$$

$$= -144000$$

∴ Approximate changes in T = -144000 ... (1)

(b) Now, from equation (ii),

$$100 \frac{dT}{T} = \frac{100 \, dm}{m} + 2 \frac{100 \, dv}{v}$$

$$= \frac{100}{49.5}(0.5) + 2\frac{100(-10)}{1590}$$

$$= 1.0101 + (-1.257) = -0.2469$$

∴ % error in T = -0.2469 ... (2)

Ex. 18 : $z = 2xy^2 - 3x^2y$, x increases at the rate of 2 cm/sec as it passes through 3 cm. Show that if y is passing through y = 1 cm, y must decrease at the rate of $\frac{32}{15}$ cm/sec in order that z shall remain constant. **(Dec. 2009)**

Sol. : Given $\quad z = 2xy^2 - 3x^2y \qquad \ldots \text{(i)}$

Also $x = 3$ cm, $y = 1$ cm, $\frac{dx}{dt} = 2$ cm/sec and $\frac{dz}{dt} = 0 \qquad \ldots \text{(ii)}$

∴
$$\frac{dz}{dt} = \frac{\partial z}{\partial x} \cdot \frac{dx}{dt} + \frac{\partial z}{\partial y} \cdot \frac{dy}{dt}$$

$$= (2y^2 - 6xy)\frac{dx}{dt} + (4xy - 3x^2)\frac{dy}{dt}$$

or $\qquad 0 = (2-18)(2) + (12-27)\frac{dy}{dt}$

or $\qquad 0 = -32 - 15 \frac{dy}{dt}$

or $\qquad \frac{dy}{dt} = -\frac{32}{15}.$

Hence, y decreases at the rate of $\frac{32}{15}$ cm/sec.

ILLUSTRATIONS ON SINE, COSINE AND PROJECTION FORMULAE

Note : We note the following trigonometric formulae for ready reference :

(I) Cosine rule :
$$a^2 = b^2 + c^2 - 2bc \cdot \cos A$$
$$b^2 = a^2 + c^2 - 2ac \cdot \cos B$$
$$c^2 = a^2 + b^2 - 2ab \cdot \cos C.$$

(II) Sine rule : $\dfrac{a}{\sin A} = \dfrac{b}{\sin B} = \dfrac{c}{\sin C} = 2R$

(III) Area of triangle ABC :
$$\Delta = \frac{1}{2} bc \sin A = \frac{1}{2} ac \sin B = \frac{1}{2} ab \sin C$$

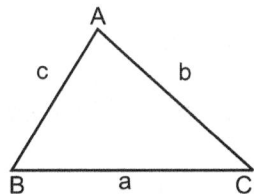

Fig. 11.3

(IV) Semi-perimeter of a triangle, $s = \dfrac{a+b+c}{2}$

and Area of triangle, $\Delta = \sqrt{s(s-a)(s-b)(s-c)}$

(V) Projection rule :
$$a = b \cos C + c \cos B$$
$$b = a \cos C + c \cos A$$
$$c = a \cos B + b \cos A$$

Ex. 19 : *If the sides and angles of a plane triangle vary in such a way that its circum radius remains constant, prove that* $\dfrac{da}{\cos A} + \dfrac{db}{\cos B} + \dfrac{dc}{\cos C} = 0$ *where da, db, dc are small increments in the sides a, b, c respectively.*

Sol. : We know from the sine rule,
$$\frac{a}{\sin A} = \frac{b}{\sin B} = \frac{c}{\sin C}$$

Considering $R = \dfrac{a}{2 \sin A}$

we have, $dR = \dfrac{\partial R}{\partial A} dA + \dfrac{\partial R}{\partial a} da$

$$0 = -\frac{a \cos A}{2 \sin^2 A} \cdot dA + \frac{1}{2 \sin A} \cdot da, \text{ R being constant}$$

∴ $\dfrac{da}{\cos A} = \dfrac{a}{\sin A} \cdot dA = 2R \cdot dA$

∴ $\dfrac{da}{\cos A} = 2R \, dA$ ... (1)

Similarly, $\dfrac{db}{\cos B} = 2R\, dB$ ... (2)

and $\dfrac{dc}{\cos C} = 2R\, dC$ ... (3)

Adding equations (1), (2) and (3), we have

$$\dfrac{da}{\cos A} + \dfrac{db}{\cos B} + \dfrac{dc}{\cos C} = 2R\,[dA + dB + dC] \quad ...(4)$$

But in any triangle ABC, $A + B + C = \pi$

hence $dA + dB + dC = 0$

Putting value of $dA + dB + dC = 0$ in equation (4),

$$\dfrac{da}{\cos A} + \dfrac{db}{\cos B} + \dfrac{dc}{\cos C} = 2R\,(0) = 0$$

Ex. 20 : *The angles of a triangle are calculated from the sides a, b, c. If small changes δa, δb, and δc are made in sides then show that,*

$$\delta A = \dfrac{a}{2\Delta}\,(\delta a - \delta b \cdot \cos C - \delta c \cdot \cos B) \quad \text{where } \Delta = \text{Area of } \triangle ABC$$

Hence show that $\delta A + \delta B + \delta C = 0$.

Sol. : Let A, B, C be the angles of a triangle.

∴ $A = f(a, b, c)$

Since changes in angles are due to changes in sides,

taking differentials, we get

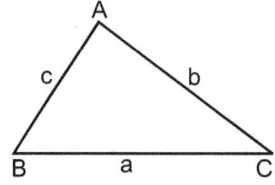

Fig. 11.4

$$\delta A = \dfrac{\partial A}{\partial a}\,\delta a + \dfrac{\partial A}{\partial b}\,\delta b + \dfrac{\partial A}{\partial c}\,\delta c \quad ...(1)$$

We first find expressions for $\dfrac{\partial A}{\partial a}$, $\dfrac{\partial A}{\partial b}$ and $\dfrac{\partial A}{\partial c}$.

∵ $a^2 = b^2 + c^2 - 2bc \cdot \cos A$ ... (2)

Differentiating (2) partially with respect to a, we get,

$$2a = 0 + 0 + 2bc \cdot \sin A \, \dfrac{\partial A}{\partial a}$$

∴ $\dfrac{\partial A}{\partial a} = \dfrac{a}{bc \sin A} = \dfrac{a}{2\Delta}$ $\left(\because \Delta = \dfrac{1}{2} bc \sin A\right)$ ... (3)

Again differentiating (2) partially with respect to b,

$$0 = 2b + 0 - 2c\left[\cos A - b \sin A \frac{\partial A}{\partial b}\right]$$

∴ $\dfrac{\partial A}{\partial b} = \dfrac{c \cos A - b}{bc \cdot \sin A} = -\dfrac{a \cos C}{2\Delta}$ ... (4)

$$\left(\because b = c \cos A + a \cos C \text{ and } \Delta = \frac{1}{2} bc \sin A\right)$$

Again differentiating (2) partially with respect to c,

$$0 = 0 + 2c - 2b\left[\cos A - c \sin A \frac{\partial A}{\partial c}\right]$$

∴ $\dfrac{\partial A}{\partial c} = \dfrac{b \cos A - c}{bc \sin A} = -\dfrac{a \cos B}{2\Delta}$ ... (5)

$$\left(\because c = b \cos A + a \cos B \text{ and } \Delta = \frac{1}{2} bc \sin A\right)$$

Substituting equations (3), (4), (5) in (1), we get

$$\delta A = \frac{a}{2\Delta} \delta a - \frac{a \cos C}{2\Delta} \delta b - \frac{a \cos B}{2\Delta} \delta c$$

$$= \frac{a}{2\Delta}[\delta a - \cos C \, \delta b - \cos B \, \delta c] \quad \ldots (6)$$

Similarly, it can be shown that,

$$\delta B = \frac{b}{2\Delta}[\delta b - \cos A \, \delta c - \cos C \, \delta a] \quad \ldots (7)$$

and $\delta C = \dfrac{c}{2\Delta}[\delta c - \cos B \, \delta a - \cos A \, \delta b]$ ... (8)

Adding equations (6), (7), and (8), we get,

$$\delta A + \delta B + \delta C = \frac{1}{2\Delta}[(a - b \cos C - c \cos B) \delta a + (b - a \cos C - c \cos A) \delta b$$

$$+ (c - a \cos B - b \cos A) \delta c]$$

$$= \frac{1}{2\Delta}[(0) \delta a + (0) \delta b + (0) \delta c] \quad \text{[Using projection formula]}$$

$$= 0$$

EXERCISE 11.6

1. In calculating the volume of a right circular cone, errors of 2% and 1% are made in measuring the height and radius of base respectively. Find the error in the calculated volume. **(Jan. 2004, May 2007, May 2010)**

$$\left[\text{Hint : Volume } V = \frac{1}{3} \pi r^2 h \quad \therefore \quad \frac{100 \, dV}{V} = 2 \frac{100 \, dr}{r} + \frac{100 \, dh}{h}\right] \quad \textbf{Ans. : 4\%}$$

2. The area of rectangular field is calculated by measuring its length and breadth. If there is an error of 2% in measuring the length and an error of 3% in measuring the breadth of the field, find the approximate % error in the calculated area of the field. **Ans. : 5%**

3. Find the possible % error in computing the parallel resistance r of two resistances r_1 and r_2 from the formula : $\dfrac{1}{r} = \dfrac{1}{r_1} + \dfrac{1}{r_2}$ where r_1 and r_2 are both in error by + 2% each. **(Dec. 2012) Ans. : 2%**

[Hint : $\dfrac{1}{r}\left(\dfrac{100\,dr}{r}\right) = \dfrac{1}{r_1}\dfrac{100\,dr_1}{r_1} + \dfrac{1}{r_2}\dfrac{100\,dr_2}{r_2} = 2\left(\dfrac{1}{r_1} + \dfrac{1}{r_2}\right) = 2\dfrac{1}{r}$]

4. The focal length of a mirror is found from the formula : $\dfrac{1}{v} - \dfrac{1}{u} = \dfrac{2}{f}$. Find the percentage error in f if u and v are both in error by p % each. **Ans. : p %**

[Hint : $-\dfrac{2}{f}\left(\dfrac{100\,df}{f}\right) = -\dfrac{1}{v}\left(\dfrac{100\,dv}{v}\right) + \dfrac{1}{u}\left(\dfrac{100\,du}{u}\right) = -p\left(\dfrac{1}{v} - \dfrac{1}{u}\right) = -p\dfrac{2}{f}$] **(May 2009)**

5. In estimating the cost of a pile of bricks measured as 6' × 50' × 4', the tape is stretched 1% beyond the standard length. If the count is 12 bricks to 1 ft³ and bricks cost Rs. 100 per 1000, find the approximate error in the cost.

Ans. : 720 bricks, Rs. 25.20

6. If the kinetic energy, $K = \dfrac{wv^2}{2g}$ where g is constant, find approximately the change in kinetic energy as w changes from 49 to 49.5 and v changes from 1600 to 1590.

Ans. : 60211.2/g

7. Find the approximate error in the surface area of a rectangular parallelopiped of sides a, b, c due to error δ in measuring each side. **Ans. : [4 (a + b + c) δ]**

8. The torsional rigidity N of a length l of a wire is obtained from the formula : $N = \dfrac{8\pi l}{r^4 t^2}$. Find the percentage error in N due to − 2% error in t, + 2% error in r and + 1.5% error in l. **Ans. : − 13%**

9. Show that the acceleration due to gravity is reduced by nearly 1% at an altitude equal to 5% of earth's radius, given that at an external point 'x' kilometers from the earth's centre such an acceleration is given by $g\left(\dfrac{r}{x}\right)^2$ where 'r' is the radius of the earth.

10. The period of a simple pendulum with small oscillations is $T = 2\pi\sqrt{\dfrac{l}{g}}$. If T is computed using l and g are 8.05 ft and 32.01 ft/sec² respectively, find % error in 'T' if the true values of l and g are 8 ft and 32 ft/sec² respectively. **(Dec. 2004, Jan. 2005)**

[Hint : $\dfrac{dT}{T} = \dfrac{1}{2}\dfrac{dl}{l} - \dfrac{1}{2}\dfrac{dg}{g}$, Given that : $l = 8$, $g = 32$ ∴ $T = \pi$ and $l + dl = 8.05$, $g + dg = 32.01$; $dl = 0.05$, $dg = 0.01$ ∴ $\dfrac{dT}{\pi} = \dfrac{0.05}{16} - \dfrac{0.01}{64} \Rightarrow dT = 0.00933\pi$]

11. If V is calculated from the formula $V = a^l b^m c^n$ with small errors $\delta a, \delta b, \delta c$ respectively in a, b, c find an approximate expression for the resulting error δV in V. If small errors in a, b, c are respectively p%, q%, r% then show the resulting % error in V is $pl + qm + rn$.

   [**Hint**: $\dfrac{dV}{v} = l\dfrac{da}{a} + m\dfrac{db}{b} + n\dfrac{dc}{c} \quad \therefore \quad \dfrac{100\,dV}{v} = (lp + mq + nr)\,\%$]

12. The H.P. required to propel a steamer varies as the cube of the velocity and square of the length. If there is 3% increase in velocity and 4% increase in length, find the % increase in H.P. **(May 2008, Dec. 2005) Ans. 17%**

    [**Hint**: Here $H = kv^3 l^2 \quad \therefore \quad \dfrac{100\,dH}{H} = 3\dfrac{100\,dv}{v} + 2\dfrac{100\,dl}{l} = 17\%$]

13. The resistance R of a circuit was found by using the formula $I = E/R$. If there is an error of 0.1 ampere in reading I and 0.5 volts in E, find the corresponding possible % error in R when readings are I = 15 amp and E = 100 volts. **(Dec. 2013)**

    [**Hint**: $\dfrac{dV}{v} = l\dfrac{da}{a} + m\dfrac{db}{b} + n\dfrac{dc}{c} \quad \therefore \quad \dfrac{100\,dV}{v} = (lp + mq + nr)\,\%$]

14. The quantity Q of water flowing over a triangular notch is given by the formula $Q = CH^{5/2}$ where H is head of water and C is constant. Find the % error in Q if the error in H is that it is measured 0.198 instead of 0.2.

15. The time of swing 't' of a pendulum of length l under certain conditions is given by $t = 2\pi\sqrt{l/g'}$, where $g' = g\left(\dfrac{r}{r+h}\right)^2$. Show that the % error in t due to error p% in h and q% in l is given by $\dfrac{1}{2}\left(q + \dfrac{2ph}{r+h}\right)$ where r is constant. **(May 2006)**

    [**Hint**: Here $t = 2\pi\left(\sqrt{\dfrac{l}{g} \cdot \dfrac{r+h}{r}}\right) \quad \therefore \quad \dfrac{100\,dt}{t} = \dfrac{1}{2}\dfrac{100\,dl}{l} + \dfrac{h}{r+h}\dfrac{100\,dh}{h} = \dfrac{1}{2}q + \dfrac{h}{r+h}p$]

16. The resonant frequency in a series electrical circuit is given by $f = \dfrac{1}{2\pi\sqrt{LC}}$. If the measurements in L and C are in error by +2% and −1% respectively, find the percentage error in f.

    [**Hint**: $\dfrac{100\,df}{f} = -\dfrac{1}{2}\dfrac{100\,dL}{L} - \dfrac{1}{2}\dfrac{100\,dc}{C} = -0.5\%$] **(May 2014)**

17. At a distance of 120 ft from the foot of a tower, the elevation of its top is 60°. If the possible error in measuring the distance and elevation are 1 inch and 1 minute, find the approximate error in the calculated height.

    [**Hint**: $h = x\tan\theta,\; x = 120,\; \theta = 60°,\; h = 120\sqrt{3}$ since $\delta x = \dfrac{1}{12}$ ft, $\delta\theta = \dfrac{1}{60}\dfrac{\pi}{180}$

    $\therefore \quad \delta h = 120\sqrt{3}\left[\dfrac{1}{120}\cdot\dfrac{1}{12} + 4\cdot\dfrac{1}{\sqrt{3}}\dfrac{1}{60}\dfrac{\pi}{180}\right] = 0.284$ approximately.]

18. In a plane triangle, if the sides a, b are constants, prove that the variations of its angles are given by the relations :

$$\frac{\delta A}{\sqrt{a^2 - b^2 \sin^2 A}} = \frac{\delta B}{\sqrt{b^2 - a^2 \sin^2 B}} = -\frac{\delta C}{C}$$

[Hint : By sine rule $\frac{a}{\sin A} = \frac{b}{\sin B}$ or $a \sin B = b \sin A$ ∴ $a \cos B\, \delta B = b \cos A\, \delta A$

or $\frac{\delta A}{a \cos B} = \frac{\delta B}{b \cos A} = \frac{\delta A + \delta B}{a \cos B + b \cos A}$. But $A + B = \pi - C$ or $\delta A + \delta B = -\delta C$

and use cosine rule, $a \cos B + b \cos A = c$].

19. If Δ is the area of a triangle, prove that the error in Δ resulting from a small error δc in c is given by

$$\Delta = \frac{\Delta}{4}\left[\frac{1}{s} + \frac{1}{s-a} + \frac{1}{s-b} - \frac{1}{s-c}\right] \delta c.$$

[Hint : $\frac{\delta \Delta}{\Delta} = \frac{1}{2}\left[\frac{\delta s}{s} + \frac{\delta(s-a)}{s-a} + \frac{\delta(s-b)}{s-b} + \frac{\delta(s-c)}{s-c}\right]$ ∵ a, b are constants, $\delta s = \delta c/2$

and $\delta(s-a) = \delta s = \frac{sc}{2}$, $\delta(s-b) = \delta s = \frac{\delta c}{2}$, $\delta(s-c) = \delta s - \delta c = \delta c/2 - \delta c = -\delta c/2$]

11.7 MAXIMA AND MINIMA OF A FUNCTION OF TWO INDEPENDENT VARIABLES

We are familiar with the definitions of maximum and minimum values of a function of single independent variable (i.e. for $y = f(x)$ with the following working rule.

(i) Find $f'(x)$ and equate it to zero. Solve this equation for x. Let the roots be $a_1, a_2, \ldots$ Find $f''(x)$ and substitute in it by terms $a_1, a_2, \ldots$

(ii) If $f''(a_1)$ is negative, we have a maximum at $x = a_1$.

If $f''(a_1)$ is positive, we have a minimum at $x = a_1$.

(iii) If $f''(a_1) = 0$, we must find $f'''(x)$ and substitute in it a_1. If $f'''(a_1) \neq 0$, there is neither a maximum nor a minimum at a_1. Buf if $f'''(a_1)$ is also zero, we must find $f^{iv}(x)$ and substitute in it a_1. If $f^{iv}(a_1)$ is negative, we have a maximum at $x = a_1$ and if it is positive we have a minimum. If it is zero, we must find $f^{v}(x)$ and so on.

In this section we extend the definition of maxima and minima to the function of two independent variables, conditions for $f(x, y)$ to be maximum or minimum (without proof) are also discussed.

Definitions : A function $z = f(x, y)$ of two independent variables is said to have a *maximum for* $x = a$, $y = b$, if $f(a, b)$ is greater than the value of the function for every other pair of values of x, y in a small neighbourhood of a, b, i.e. if

$$f(a, b) > f(a + h, b + k)$$

for all sufficient small independent values of h and k.

A function $z = f(x, y)$ is said to have a *minimum* or $x = a$, $y = b$, if $f(a, b)$ is less than the value of the function for every other pair of values of x, y in a small neighbourhood of a, b i.e. if
$$f(a, b) < f(a + h, b + k)$$
for all sufficiently small independent values of h and k.

Note 1 : A maximum or a minimum value of a function is called its *extreme value*.

Note 2 : A function $f(x, y)$ is said to be *stationary* at (a, b) or $f(a, b)$ is said to be *stationary value* of the function $f(x, y)$ if
$$f_x(a, b) = 0, \quad f_y(a, b) = 0$$

Thus every extreme value is a stationary value but converse may not be true.

Remark : If $z = f(x, y)$ is regarded as *surface*, then at a point of maximum the ordinate to the surface is the largest in the neighbourhood. It corresponds to a *'hill–top'* (or a dome) from which the surface descends in every direction. Similarly a minimum corresponds to *bottom of a cup–like depression (or a bowl)* from which the surface ascends in every direction. Sometimes the maximum or minimum values may form a *ridge* such that the surface falls (or rises) in all directions except that of ridge where it remains stationary.

Besides these, we can have such a point on the surface, where the tangent plane is horizontal and the surface falls for displacements in certain directions and rises for displacements in other directions. Such a point is called a *saddle point*.

Working rule of Determining the Maxima and Minima of Function $z = f(x, y)$:

Step I : Find $\dfrac{\partial f}{\partial x}$ and $\dfrac{\partial f}{\partial y}$, and equate them to zero. $\left(\text{i.e. put } \dfrac{\partial f}{\partial x} = 0 \text{ and } \dfrac{\partial f}{\partial y} = 0\right)$. Solve these simultaneous equations for x and y. Let a_1, b_1 ; a_2, b_2 ; ... be the pairs of values (roots).

Step II : Calculate the values of
$$r = \frac{\partial^2 f}{\partial x^2}, \quad s = \frac{\partial^2 f}{\partial x \, \partial y}, \quad t = \frac{\partial^2 f}{\partial y^2}$$
and substitute in them by terms a_1, b_1 ; a_2, b_2 ; ... for x, y.

Step III : (i) If $rt - s^2 > 0$ and $r < 0$ at (a_1, b_1), $f(x, y)$ is a maximum at (a_1, b_1) and $f(a_1, b_1)$ is maximum value.

(ii) If $rt - s^2 > 0$ and $r > 0$ at (a_1, b_1), $f(x, y)$ is a minimum at (a_1, b_1) and $f(a_1, b_1)$ is minimum value.

(iii) If $rt - s^2 < 0$ at (a_1, b_1), $f(x, y)$ is neither maximum nor minimum at (a_1, b_1) i.e. $f(a_1, b_1)$ is not an extreme value. Such a point is sometimes called a *saddle point*

(iv) If $rt - s^2 = 0$ at (a_1, b_1), the case is undecided (i.e. no conclusion can be drawn about a maximum or minimum value), and further investigation is necessary to decide it.

Similarly examine the other pairs of values one by one.

Remark : In order to solve $\frac{\partial f}{\partial x} = 0, \frac{\partial f}{\partial y} = 0$, we may either eliminate one of the variables or factorise the equations. In the latter case each factor of the first equation has to be solved in conjunction with each factor of the second equation. Sometimes it is easier to factorise a combination of the two equations. Each of these factors must then be taken with any one of the original equations.

Type I : Illustrations of Maxima and Minima of Function of Two Variables

Ex. 1 : *Determine the points where the function*
$$x^3 + y^3 - 3axy$$
has a maximum or minimum. (Jan. 2004, Dec. 2013, May 2007, 2014)

Sol. : Here $\quad f(x, y) = x^3 + y^3 - 3axy$

Step I : The points of maxima and minima are given by :

$$\frac{\partial f}{\partial x} = 0 \Rightarrow 3x^2 - 3ay = 0 \qquad \ldots (1)$$

$$\frac{\partial f}{\partial y} = 0 \Rightarrow 3y^2 - 3ax = 0 \qquad \ldots (2)$$

We now solve the equations (1) and (2) as simultaneous equations. From the equation (1), we have $y = x^2/a$. Substituting in the equation (2), we obtain
$$x^4 - a^3 x = 0, \quad \text{or} \quad x(x-a)(x^2 + ax + a^2) = 0$$

Hence $x = 0$ or a (on discarding the imaginary roots) and corresponding values of y are
$$y = 0 \text{ or } a \quad (\because y = x^2/a)$$

Therefore the function is stationary at $(0, 0)$ and (a, a).

Step II : Next we have

$$r = \frac{\partial^2 f}{\partial x^2} = 6x, \quad s = \frac{\partial^2 f}{\partial x \partial y} = -3a, \quad t = \frac{\partial^2 f}{\partial y^2} = 6y$$

Step III : (i) At $(0, 0)$, $\quad rt - s^2 = (0)(0) - (-3a)^2 = -9a^2 < 0$

Hence at the point $(0, 0)$, function $f(x, y)$ is neither maximum nor minimum and it is a saddle point.

(ii) At (a, a), $\quad rt - s^2 = (6a)(6a) - (-3a)^2 = 27 a^2 > 0$ and $r = 6a$

Hence at the point (a, a) function, $f(x, y)$ has maximum or minimum. Since $r = 6a$, it is a maximum if a is negative (i.e. $r < 0$) and minimum if a is positive (i.e. $r > 0$).

Ex. 2 : *Locate the stationary points of* $x^4 + y^4 - 2x^2 + 4xy - 2y^2$ *and determine their nature.*

Sol. : Step I : The stationary points are given by

$$\frac{\partial f}{\partial x} = 0 \Rightarrow 4x^3 - 4x + 4y = 0 \qquad \ldots (1)$$

$$\frac{\partial f}{\partial y} = 0 \Rightarrow 4y^3 + 4x - 4y = 0 \qquad \ldots (2)$$

We now solve equations (1) and (2) as simultaneous equations.

Adding (1) and (2), we get
$$4x^3 + 4y^3 = 0, \quad \text{or} \quad x = -y$$
Putting $y = -x$ in (1), we obtain $x^3 - 2x = 0$, which gives
$$x = 0, \quad \sqrt{2}, \quad -\sqrt{2}$$
and corresponding values of y are
$$y = 0, \quad -\sqrt{2}, \quad \sqrt{2}$$
Therefore $(0, 0)$, $(\sqrt{2}, -\sqrt{2})$ and $(-\sqrt{2}, \sqrt{2})$ are the stationary points of the given function.

Step II : Next, we have
$$r = \frac{\partial^2 f}{\partial x^2} = 12x^2 - 4, \quad s = \frac{\partial^2 f}{\partial x \partial y} = 4, \quad t = \frac{\partial^2 f}{\partial y^2} = 12y^2 - 4 \quad ...(3)$$

Step III : At $(0, 0)$, $rt - s^2 = (-4)(-4) = 0$
At $(\sqrt{2}, -\sqrt{2})$, $rt - s^2 = (20)(20) - (4)^2 > 0$ and $r = 20$
At $(-\sqrt{2}, \sqrt{2})$, $rt - s^2 = (20)(20) - (4)^2 > 0$ and $r = 20$

(i) We note that, at $(\pm\sqrt{2}, \pm\sqrt{2})$, condition $rt - s^2 > 0$ is satisfied and also $r > 0$. Hence at these two points, the function has minima. The minimum value of $f(x, y)$ being -8.

(ii) At $(0, 0)$, condition $rt - s^2 > 0$ is not satisfied, therefore further investigation is needed.

Remark : We note that, $f(0, 0) = 0$
and
$$\begin{aligned} f(x, y) &= x^4 + y^4 - 2x^2 + 4xy - 2y^2 \\ &= x^4 + y^4 - 2(x - y)^2 \\ &= -2(x - y)^2, \end{aligned}$$
approximately, for small values of x, y, which is *negative* (i.e. $< f(0, 0)$

Hence the function is 0 at $(0, 0)$ and negative for all values of x, y, n the neighbourhood of the point $(0, 0)$ except when $x \neq y$.

When $x = y$, the second order term vanish and $f(x, y) = x^4 + y^4$, which is *positive* (i.e. $> f(0, 0)$.

Hence there is no maxima or minima at $(0, 0)$ and the point $(0, 0)$ is *saddle point*.

Ex. 3 : *Find the extreme values of* $xy(a - x - y)$. **(May 97, 13; Dec. 2009)**

Sol. : We write $\quad f(x, y) = xy(a - x - y) = axy - x^2y - xy^2$

Step I : Extreme values of $f(x, y)$ are given by
$$\frac{\partial f}{\partial x} = 0 \Rightarrow ay - 2xy - y^2 = 0 \quad ...(1)$$
$$\frac{\partial f}{\partial y} = 0 \Rightarrow ax - x^2 - 2xy = 0 \quad ...(2)$$

We now solve the equations (1) and (2) simultaneously.

Equations (1) and (2) are equivalent to 0
$$y(a - 2x - y) = 0, \quad x(a - x - 2y) = 0$$
so that we have to consider four pairs of equations viz,
$$y = 0, \quad x = 0$$
$$a - 2x - y = 0, \quad x = 0$$
$$y = 0, \quad a - x - 2y = 0$$
$$a - 2x - y = 0, \quad a - x - 2y = 0$$

Solving these, we obtain the following pair of values of x and y which make the function stationary :

$(0, 0), (0, a), (a, 0), (a/3, a/3)$

Step II : Next, we have
$$r = \frac{\partial^2 f}{\partial x^2} = -2y, \quad s = \frac{\partial^2 f}{\partial x \partial y} = a - 2x - 2y, \quad t = \frac{\partial^2 f}{\partial y^2} = -2x$$

Step III : (i) At $(0, 0)$, $rt - s^2 = (0)(0) - (a)^2 < 0$

Hence $f(0, 0)$ is not an extreme value of $f(x, y)$

(ii) At $(0, a)$, $rt - s^2 = (-2a)(0) - (-a)^2 < 0$

Hence $f(0, a)$ is also not an extreme value of $f(x, y)$

(iii) At $(a, 0)$, $rt - s^2 = (0)(-2a) - (-a)^2 < 0$

Also $f(a, 0)$ is not an extreme value of $f(x, y)$

(iv) At $(a/3, a/3)$, $rt - s^2 = (-2a/3)(-2a/3) - (a - 2a/3 - 2a/3)^2$
$$= 4a^2/9 - a^2/9 = a^2/3 > 0 \text{ and } r = -\frac{2a}{3}$$

Hence $f(a/3, a/3)$ is an extreme value and will be maximum or a minimum according as, r is negative or positive, i.e. according as, a is positive or negative.

The extreme value $f(a/3, a/3) = a^3/27$.

Ex. 4 : *Discuss the maxima and minima of*
$$x^3 y^2 (1 - x - y) \hspace{3cm} \text{(Dec. 96)}$$

Sol. : Here $f(x, y) = x^3 y^2 (1 - x - y) = x^3 y^2 - x^4 y^2 - x^3 y^3$

Step I : The points of maxima and minima are given by
$$\frac{\partial f}{\partial x} = 3x^2 y^2 - 4x^3 y^2 - 3x^2 y^3 = 0 \hspace{2cm} \ldots (1)$$
$$\frac{\partial f}{\partial y} = 2x^3 y - 2x^4 y - 3x^3 y^2 = 0 \hspace{2cm} \ldots (2)$$

Equations (1) and (2) are equivalent to
$$x^2 y^2 (3 - 4x - 3xy) = 0 \quad \text{and} \quad x^3 y (2 - 2x - 3y) = 0$$
i.e. $x = 0, y = 0, 3 - 4x - 3y = 0$ and $x = 0, y = 0, 2 - 2x - 3y = 0$

Solving these equations, we obtain the following stationary points :
$$(0, 0) \text{ and } (1/2, 1/3)$$

Step II : We now calculate,

$$r = \frac{\partial^2 f}{\partial x^2} = 6xy^2 - 12x^2y^2 - 6xy^3$$

$$s = \frac{\partial^2 f}{\partial x \partial y} = 6x^2y - 8x^3y - 9x^2y^2$$

$$t = \frac{\partial^2 f}{\partial y^2} = 2x^3 - 2x^4 - 6x^3y$$

At $(1/2, 1/3)$, $r = 1/9$, $s = -1/12$, $t = -1/8$

At $(0, 0)$, $r = 0$, $s = 0$, $t = 0$

Step III : At $(1/2, 1/3)$, $rt - s^2 = (-1/9)(-1/8) - (1/12)^2 = \frac{1}{44} > 0$ and $r = -\frac{1}{9} < 0$

Hence $f(x, y)$ is maximum at $(1/2, 1/3)$ and $f_{max} = \frac{1}{432}$

At $(0, 0)$, $rt - s^2 = 0$

Here condition of maxima and minima is not satisfied. Hence the case is undecided (i.e. no conclusion can be drawn about maxima and minima) and further investigation is needed.

Ex. 5 : *Show that the minimum value of* $xy + a^3\left(\frac{1}{x} + \frac{1}{y}\right)$ *is* $3a^2$. **(May 2004, Dec. 2012)**

Sol. : Here $f(x, y) = xy + a^3/x + a^3/y$

Step I : Extreme values of $f(x, y)$ are given by

$$\frac{\partial f}{\partial x} = y - a^3/x^2 = 0 \qquad \ldots (1)$$

$$\frac{\partial f}{\partial y} = x - a^3/y^2 = 0 \qquad \ldots (2)$$

We now solve (1) and (2) simultaneously.

Equations (1) and (2) are equivalent to

$$x^2 y = a^3 \text{ and } xy^2 = a^3$$

Substituting the value of x from second equation into the first,

$$\frac{a^6}{y^4} y = a^3 \text{ or } y = a$$

From second equation, $x = a$.

Hence the stationary point is (a, a).

Step II : We have

$$r = \frac{\partial^2 f}{\partial x^2} = \frac{2a^3}{x^3}, \quad s = \frac{\partial^2 f}{\partial x \partial y} = 1, \quad t = \frac{\partial^2 f}{\partial y^2} = \frac{2a^3}{y^3}$$

At (a, a), $r = 2$, $s = 1$, $t = 2$

Step III :

At (a, a), $rt - s^2 = (2)(2) - (1)^2 = 3 > 0$ and $r = 2 > 0$

Hence at the point (a, a), function $f(x, y)$ has minimum value and

$f_{min} = (a)(a) + a^3 (1/a + 1/a) = 3a^2$, which is the required result.

Ex. 6 : *Find all the stationary points of the function* (Dec. 07, May 11, Dec. 2014)

$$x^3 + 3xy^2 - 15x^2 - 15y^2 + 72x$$

Examine whether the function is maximum or minimum at those points.

Sol. : Here $\quad f(x, y) = x^3 + 3xy^2 - 15x^2 - 15y^2 + 72x$

Step I : The stationary points are given by

$$\frac{\partial f}{\partial x} = 3x^2 + 3y^2 - 30x + 72 = 0 \qquad \ldots (1)$$

$$\frac{\partial f}{\partial y} = 6xy - 30y = 0 \qquad \ldots (2)$$

We now solve equations (1) and (2) simultaneously.

From equation (2), we have

$$6y(x - 5) = 0, \quad y = 0 \quad \text{or} \quad x = 5$$

(i) When $x = 5$, $3y^2 - 3 = 0 \Rightarrow y = \pm 1$

Therefore the stationary points are $(5, 1)$ and $(5, -1)$

(ii) When $y = 0$, $3x^2 - 30x + 72 = 0 \Rightarrow x = 4, 6$.

Therefore the stationary points are $(4, 0)$ and $(6, 0)$.

Thus $(5, 1), (5, -1), (4, 0), (6, 0)$ are the stationary points of the function.

Step II : We have

$$r = \frac{\partial^2 f}{\partial x^2} = 6x - 30, \quad s = \frac{\partial^2 f}{\partial x \partial y} = 6y, \quad t = \frac{\partial^2 f}{\partial y^2} = 6x - 30$$

Step III :

(i) At $(5, 1)$ and $(5, -1)$, $rt - s^2 = (0)(0) - (\pm 6)^2 = -36 < 0$

Hence at $(5, 1)$ and $(5, -1)$, function is neither maximum nor minimum.

(ii) At (4, 0), $rt - s^2 = (-6)(-6) - (0)^2 = 36 > 0$ and $r = -6 < 0$

Hence at (4, 0), function is maximum and $f_{max} = 112$.

(iii) At (6, 0), $rt - s^2 = (6)(6) - (0)^2 = 36 > 0$ and $r = 6 > 0$

Hence at (6, 0), function is minimum and $f_{min} = 108$.

Ex. 7 : *Find the maximum and minimum values of*

$$x^3 + 3xy^2 - 3x^2 - 3y^2 + 4 \quad \text{(Jan. 2003, Dec. 2006)}$$

Sol. : Step I : The stationary points are given by

$$\frac{\partial f}{\partial x} = 3x^2 + 3y^2 - 6x = 0 \quad \ldots (1)$$

$$\frac{\partial f}{\partial y} = 6xy - 6y = 0 \quad \ldots (2)$$

We now solve (1) and (2) simultaneously.

Equations (1) and (2) are equivalent to

$$x^2 + y^2 - x = 0 \quad \text{and} \quad y(x-1) = 0$$

From second equation, we have

$$y = 0 \quad \text{or} \quad x = 1$$

Using these results in first equation, we have

(i) When $y = 0$, $x^2 - 2x = 0 \Rightarrow x = 0$

Therefore the stationary points are (0, 0), (2, 0)

(ii) When $x = 1$, $y^2 - 1 = 0 \Rightarrow 1$ or -1

Therefore the stationary points are (1, 1), (1, -1)

Thus (0, 0), (2, 0), (1, 1) and (1 -1) are the stationary points of the function

Step II : We have $r = \dfrac{\partial^2 f}{\partial x^2} = 6x - 6$, $s = \dfrac{\partial^2 f}{\partial x \, \partial y} = 6y$, $t = \dfrac{\partial^2 f}{\partial y^2} = 6x - 6$

Step III :

(i) At (0, 0), $rt - s^2 = (-6)(-6) - (0)^2 = 36 > 0$ and $r = -6 < 0$

Hence at (0, 0), function is maximum and $f_{max} = 4$

(ii) At (2, 0), $rt - s^2 = (6)(6) - (0)^2 = 36 > 0$ and $r = +6 > 0$

Hence at (2, 0), function is minimum and $f_{min} = 0$

(iii) At (1, 1) and (1, -1), $rt - s^2 = (0)(0) - (\pm 6)^2 = -36 < 0$

Hence at (1, 1) and (1, -1), function is neither maximum nor minimum

Ex. 8 : *Examine for minimum and maximum values*

$$\sin x + \sin y + \sin(x+y) \quad \text{(Dec. 97)}$$

Sol. : Here $\quad f(x, y) = \sin x + \sin y + \sin(x+y)$

Step I : The stationary points are given by

$$\frac{\partial f}{\partial x} = \cos x + \cos(x+y) = 0 \qquad \ldots (1)$$

$$\frac{\partial f}{\partial y} = \cos y + \cos(x+y) = 0 \qquad \ldots (2)$$

Solving (1) and (2) for x and y as simultaneous equations.

Subtracting (2) from (1), we have

$$\cos x - \cos y = 0 \quad \text{or} \quad \cos x = \cos y \Rightarrow x = y$$

On substituting $y = x$ in (1), we obtain

$$\cos x + \cos 2x = 0 \quad \text{or} \quad \cos 2x = -\cos x = \cos(\pi - x)$$

$$\therefore \quad 2x = \pi - x \quad \text{or} \quad x = \frac{\pi}{3}$$

and since $\quad x = y \quad \Rightarrow \quad y = \frac{\pi}{3}$

Thus $\left(\frac{\pi}{3}, \frac{\pi}{3}\right)$ is the stationary point of the function.

Step II : We have

$$r = \frac{\partial^2 f}{\partial x \partial y} = -\sin x - \sin(x+y), \quad s = \frac{\partial^2 f}{\partial x \partial y} = -\sin(x+y),$$

$$t = \frac{\partial^2 f}{\partial y^2} = -\sin y - \sin(x+y)$$

At $\left(\frac{\pi}{3}, \frac{\pi}{3}\right)$, $\quad r = -\frac{\sqrt{3}}{2} - \frac{\sqrt{3}}{2} = -\sqrt{3}, \; s = -\frac{\sqrt{3}}{2}, \; t = -\frac{\sqrt{3}}{2} - \frac{\sqrt{3}}{2} = -\sqrt{3}$

Step III :

At $\left(\frac{\pi}{3}, \frac{\pi}{3}\right)$, $\; rt - s^2 = (-\sqrt{3})(-\sqrt{3}) - (-\sqrt{3}, 2)^2 = \frac{9}{4} > 0$ and $r = -\sqrt{3} < 0$

Hence at $\left(\frac{\pi}{3}, \frac{\pi}{3}\right)$, function is maximum.

$$\text{Maximum value} = f\left(\frac{\pi}{3}, \frac{\pi}{3}\right) = \sin\frac{\pi}{3} + \sin\frac{\pi}{3} + \sin\frac{2\pi}{3}$$

$$= \frac{\sqrt{3}}{2} + \frac{\sqrt{3}}{2} + \frac{3\sqrt{3}}{2}$$

Remark : Since $f(x, y) = \sin x + \sin y + \sin(x+y)$ is periodic with period π for both x and y, values of x and y between 0 and π is only considered.

Ex. 9 : *Find the stationary values of $\sin x \sin y \sin (x + y)$.* (May 2006, 2008)

Sol. : Here $f(x, y) = \sin x \sin y \sin (x + y)$

Step I : The stationary points are given by

$$\frac{\partial f}{\partial x} = \sin y [\cos x \sin (x + y) + \sin x \cos (x + y)]$$

$$= \sin y \sin (2x + y) = 0 \quad \ldots (1)$$

$$\frac{\partial f}{\partial y} = \sin x [\cos y \sin (x + y) + \sin y \cos (x + y)]$$

$$= \sin x \sin (x + 2y) = 0 \quad \ldots (2)$$

Solving (1) and (2) simultaneously, we obtain

$$x = 0, y = 0 \text{ or } 2x + y = \pi \text{ and}$$

$$x + 2y = \pi \text{ gives } x = \frac{\pi}{3}, y = \frac{\pi}{3}$$

Thus $(0, 0)$ and $\left(\frac{\pi}{3}, \frac{\pi}{3}\right)$ are the stationary points.

Step II : $r = \frac{\partial^2 f}{\partial x^2} = 2 \sin y \cos (2x + y)$,

$s = \frac{\partial^2 f}{\partial x \partial y} = \cos x \sin (x + 2y) + \sin x \cos (x + 2y) = \sin (2x + 2y)$,

$t = \frac{\partial^2 f}{\partial y^2} = 2 \sin x \cos (x + 2y)$

At $(0, 0)$, $r = 0, s = 0, t = 0$

At $\left(\frac{\pi}{3}, \frac{\pi}{3}\right)$, $r = 2\left(\frac{\sqrt{3}}{2}\right)(-1) = -\sqrt{3}$, $s = -\frac{\sqrt{3}}{2}$, $t = 2\left(\frac{\sqrt{3}}{2}\right)(-1) = -\sqrt{3}$

Step III :

(i) At $(0, 0)$, $rt - s^2 = 0$

Hence at the point $(0, 0)$, now conclusion can be drawn about maxima and minima (i.e. case is undecided) and further investigation is needed.

(ii) At $\left(\frac{\pi}{3}, \frac{\pi}{3}\right)$, $rt - s^2 = (-\sqrt{3})(-\sqrt{3}) - (\sqrt{3}/2)^2 = \frac{9}{4} > 0$ and $r = -\sqrt{3} < 0$

Hence at the point $\left(\frac{\pi}{3}, \frac{\pi}{3}\right)$, function is maximum.

Maximum value $= f\left(\frac{\pi}{3}, \frac{\pi}{3}\right) = \sin \frac{\pi}{3} \sin \frac{\pi}{3} \sin \frac{2\pi}{3}$

$$= \left(\frac{\sqrt{3}}{2}\right)\left(\frac{\sqrt{3}}{2}\right)\left(\frac{\sqrt{3}}{2}\right) = \frac{3\sqrt{3}}{8}$$

Type II : Illustrations on maxima and minima of function of three variables (which can be converted to function of two variables using the given condition)

Ex. 10 : *Divide 120 into three parts so that the sum of their products taken two at a time shall be maximum.*

Sol. : Consider x, y, z be the numbers whose sum is 120

i.e. $\quad x + y + z = 120 \quad$ ... (1)

Next, consider the sum of their products as

$$u = xy + yz + zx \quad \text{(function of three variables)} \quad ... (2)$$

Converting the function of two variables using condition (1), we have

$$u = xy + y(120 - x - y) + x(120 - x - y)$$
$$= 120x + 120y - xy - x^2 - y^2 = f(x, y) \text{ (function of two variables)} \quad ... (3)$$

Step I : Now for maximum value of u, we solve

$$\frac{\partial f}{\partial x} = 0 \implies 120 - y - 2x = 0 \quad ... (4)$$

$$\frac{\partial f}{\partial y} = 0 \implies 120 - x - 2y = 0 \quad ... (5)$$

Solving (4) and (5) simultaneously, we have

$$x = 40 \quad \text{and} \quad y = 40$$

Hence the point (40, 40) is the stationary point of the function.

Step II : We have

$$r = \frac{\partial^2 f}{\partial x^2} = -2, \quad s = \frac{\partial^2 f}{\partial x \partial y} = 1, \quad \frac{\partial^2 f}{\partial y^2} = -2$$

Step III : At (40, 40), $rt - s^2 = (-2)(-2) - (-1)^2 = 3 > 0$ and $r = -2 < 0$

Hence the function f(x, y) and therefore u is maximum at x = 40, y = 40 and z = 40

Ex. 11 : *Show that the rectangular solid of maximum volume that can be inscribed in a given sphere is a cube.*

Sol. : Let x, y, z be the length, breadth and height of the rectangular solid. If V is the volume of the solid, then

$$V = xyz \quad ... (1)$$

Since each diagonal of the solid passes through the centre of the sphere.

∴ each diagonal = diameter of the sphere = d (say)

i.e. $\quad \sqrt{x^2 + y^2 + z^2} = d \quad \text{or} \quad x^2 + y^2 + z^2 = d^2$

or $\quad z = \sqrt{d^2 - x^2 - y^2} \quad$ (d is constant)

Therefore from (1), we have

$$V = xy\sqrt{d^2 - x^2 - y^2}$$

or $$V^2 = x^2y^2(d^2 - x^2 - y^2)$$

or $$f(xy) = d^2x^2y^2 - x^4y^2 - x^2y^4 \quad \text{(function of two variables)}\ldots (2)$$

Step I : The stationary points are given by

$$\frac{\partial f}{\partial x} = 2d^2xy^2 - 4x^3y^2 - 2xy^4 = 0 \qquad \ldots (3)$$

$$\frac{\partial f}{\partial y} = 2d^2x^2y - 2x^4y - 4x^2y^3 = 0 \qquad \ldots (4)$$

Equations (3) and (4) are equivalent to

$$2xy^2(d^2 - 2x^2 - y^2) = 0 \qquad \ldots (5)$$
$$2x^2y(d^2 - x^2 - 2y^2) = 0 \qquad \ldots (6)$$

Solving (5) and (6), we have

$$x = \frac{d}{\sqrt{3}}, \quad y = \frac{d}{\sqrt{3}}, \quad z = \frac{d}{\sqrt{3}} \qquad (\because x \neq 0, y \neq 0)$$

Step II : We have $\quad r = \dfrac{\partial^2 f}{\partial x^2} = 2d^2y^2 - 12x^2y^2 - 2y^4$

$$s = \frac{\partial^2 f}{\partial x \partial y} = 4d^2xy - 8x^3y^2 - 8xy^3$$

$$t = \frac{\partial^2 f}{\partial y^2} = 2d^2x^2 - 2x^4 - 12x^2y^2$$

At $x = y = \dfrac{d}{\sqrt{3}}$, $\quad r = 2d^2 \cdot \dfrac{d^2}{3} - 12 \dfrac{d^2}{3} \cdot \dfrac{d^2}{3} - 2\dfrac{d^4}{9} = -\dfrac{8d^4}{9} < 0$

$$s = 4d^2 \cdot \frac{d^2}{3} - 8\frac{d^3}{3\sqrt{3}} \cdot \frac{d}{\sqrt{3}} - 8\frac{d}{\sqrt{3}} \cdot \frac{d^3}{3\sqrt{3}} = -\frac{4d^2}{9}$$

$$t = 2d^2 \cdot \frac{d^2}{3} - 2\frac{d^4}{9} - 12\frac{d^2}{3} \cdot \frac{d^2}{3} = -\frac{8d^4}{9}$$

Step III : At $x = y = \dfrac{d}{\sqrt{3}}$,

$$rt - s^2 = \frac{64 d^8}{81} - \frac{16 d^4}{81} = \frac{48 d^4}{81} > 0, \text{ Also } r < 0$$

Therefore $V^2 = f(x, y)$ and hence V is maximum when $x = y = z$ i.e. when the rectangular solid is a cube.

Ex. 12 : *Prove that if the perimeter of a triangle is constant, its area is maximum, when the triangle is equilateral.*

Sol. : Let a, b, c be the sides of the triangle whose perimeter 2s is constant.

Then $\quad\quad\quad\quad 2s = a + b + c \quad$ or $\quad c = 2s - a - b \quad\quad\quad\quad$ ... (1)

and area of the triangle is

$$\text{Area } A = \sqrt{s(s-d)(s-b)(s-c)}$$
$$= \sqrt{s(s-a)(s-b)(s+b-s)} \quad\quad [\text{Using (1)}]$$

Let $\quad\quad A^2 = s(s-a)(s-b)(a+b)-s) = f(a,b) \quad\quad$ ... (2)

Now for largest triangle, area must be maximum.

Step I : Condition for maxima or minima is

$$\frac{\partial f}{\partial a} = s(s-b)[-(a+b-s)+(s-a)] = s(s-b)(2s-a-2b) = 0 ... (3)$$

$$\frac{\partial f}{\partial b} = s(s-a)[-(a+b-s)+(s-b)] = s(s-a)(2s-a-2b) = 0 ... (4)$$

Solving (3) and (4), we have

$\quad\quad (s-b)(2s-2a-b) = 0 \quad$ and $\quad (s-a)(2s-a-2b) = 0 \quad\quad\quad (\because s \neq 0)$

When s = b, from second equation, we have

$\quad\quad (b-a)(-a) = 0 \quad$ or $\quad b = a \quad\quad\quad\quad\quad\quad\quad\quad\quad (\because a \neq 0)$

When 2s = 2a + b, from second equation, we have

$\quad\quad \left(\frac{b}{2}\right)(a-b) = 0 \quad$ or $\quad a = b \quad\quad\quad\quad\quad\quad\quad\quad\quad (\because b \neq 0)$

If we express A^2 as a function of b and c, we similarly get b = c.

$\therefore \quad\quad\quad\quad a = b = c = \frac{2s}{3}$

Step II : We have

$$r = \frac{\partial^2 f}{\partial a^2} = -2s(s-b), \quad s = \frac{\partial^2 f}{\partial a \partial b} = s[-(2s-a-2b)-(s-a)]$$
$$= s(2a + 2b - 35)$$
$$t = \frac{\partial^2 f}{\partial b^2} = -2s(s-a)$$

At $a = \frac{2s}{3}, b = \frac{2s}{3}$,

$$r = -2s\left(\frac{5}{3}\right) = -\frac{2s^2}{3} < 0, \quad s = s\left(-\frac{s}{3}\right) = -\frac{s^2}{3}, \quad t = -2s\left(\frac{3}{3}\right) = -\frac{2s^2}{3}$$

Step III : At $a = \frac{2s}{3}, b = \frac{2s}{3}$,

$$rt - s^2 = \left(-\frac{2s^2}{3}\right)\left(-\frac{2s^2}{3}\right) - \left(\frac{s^2}{3}\right)^2 = \frac{s^4}{3} > 0 \text{ and also } r < 0.$$

Therefore A^2 and hence A (area of triangle) is maximum when $a = b = c = \frac{2s}{3}$ i.e. when the triangle is equilateral.

Ex. 13 : *Find the volume of the largest rectangular parallelopiped that can be inscribed in an ellipsoid* $\frac{x^2}{a^2} + \frac{y^2}{b^2} + \frac{z^2}{c^2} = 1.$

Sol. : Let 2x, 2y, 2z are the dimensions of the parallelopiped so that the volume V is given by
$$V = (2x)(2y)(2z) = 8xyz \qquad \ldots (1)$$
and with the condition
$$\frac{x^2}{a^2} + \frac{y^2}{b^2} + \frac{z^2}{c^2} = 1 \qquad \ldots (2)$$

$$V = 8xy\left(1 - \frac{x^2}{a^2} - \frac{y^2}{b^2}\right)^{1/2} \cdot c$$

or
$$V^2 = 64 x^2 y^2 c^2 \left(1 - \frac{x^2}{a^2} - \frac{y^2}{b^2}\right)$$

$$= 64 c^2 \left(x^2 y^2 - \frac{x^4 y^2}{a^2} - \frac{x^2 y^4}{b^2}\right) = f(xy) \qquad \ldots (3)$$

Step I : The stationary points are given by

$$\frac{\partial f}{\partial x} = 64 c^2 \left(2xy^2 - \frac{4x^3 y^2}{a^2} - \frac{2xy^4}{b^2}\right) = 0$$

$$= 128 c^2 xy^2 \left(1 - \frac{2x^2}{a^2} - \frac{y^2}{b^2}\right) = 0 \qquad \ldots (4)$$

$$\frac{\partial f}{\partial y} = 64 c^2 \left(2x^2 y - \frac{2x^4 y}{a^2} - \frac{4x^2 y^3}{b^2}\right) = 0$$

$$= 64 c^2 x^2 y \left(1 - \frac{x^2}{a^2} - \frac{2y^2}{b^2}\right) = 0 \qquad \ldots (5)$$

Solving (4) and (5) and using (2), we have

$$x = \frac{a}{\sqrt{3}}, \quad y = \frac{b}{\sqrt{3}} \text{ and using (2),}$$

$$z = \frac{c}{\sqrt{3}} \qquad (\because x \neq 0, y \neq 0)$$

Thus $\quad x = \frac{a}{\sqrt{3}}, y = \frac{a}{\sqrt{3}}$ is a stationary point

Step II : We have

$$r = \frac{\partial^2 f}{\partial x^2} = 64c^2 \left(2y^2 - \frac{12x^2 2y^2}{a^2} - \frac{2y^4}{b^2}\right)$$

$$s = \frac{\partial^2 f}{\partial x \partial y} = 64c^2 \left(4xy - \frac{8x^3 y}{a^2} - \frac{8xy^3}{b^2}\right)$$

$$t = \frac{\partial^2 f}{\partial y^2} = 64c^2 \left(2x^2 - \frac{2x^4}{a^2} - \frac{12x^2 y^2}{b^2}\right)$$

At $x = \dfrac{a}{\sqrt{3}}, y = \dfrac{a}{\sqrt{3}}$,

$$r = 64c^2\left[\dfrac{2b^2}{3} - \dfrac{12}{a^2} \cdot \dfrac{a^2}{3} \cdot \dfrac{b^2}{3} - \dfrac{2}{b^2} \cdot \dfrac{b^4}{9}\right] = -\dfrac{512}{9}b^2c^2 < 0$$

$$s = 64c^2\left[4 \cdot \dfrac{a}{\sqrt{3}} \cdot \dfrac{b}{\sqrt{3}} - \dfrac{8}{a^2} \cdot \dfrac{a^3}{3\sqrt{3}} \cdot \dfrac{b}{\sqrt{3}} - \dfrac{8}{b^2} \cdot \dfrac{a}{\sqrt{3}} \cdot \dfrac{b^3}{3\sqrt{3}}\right] = -\dfrac{256}{9}abc^2$$

$$t = 64c^2\left[2 \cdot \dfrac{9^2}{3} - \dfrac{2}{a^2} \cdot \dfrac{a^4}{9} - \dfrac{12}{b^2} \cdot \dfrac{a^2}{3} \cdot \dfrac{b^2}{3}\right] = -\dfrac{512}{9}a^2c^2$$

Step III : At $\left(\dfrac{a}{\sqrt{3}}, \dfrac{b}{\sqrt{3}}\right)$,

$$rt - s^2 = \left(\dfrac{512}{9}\right)^2 a^2b^2c^4 - \left(\dfrac{256}{9}\right)^2 a^2b^2c^4$$

$$= \left(\dfrac{256}{9}\right)^2 a^2b^2c^4 (4-1) > 0 \text{ and } r < 0$$

Hence V^2 and therefore, V is maximum when $x = \dfrac{a}{\sqrt{3}}, y = \dfrac{b}{\sqrt{3}}, z = \dfrac{c}{\sqrt{3}}$

Also maximum volume $= 8 \cdot \dfrac{a}{\sqrt{3}} \cdot \dfrac{b}{\sqrt{3}} \cdot \dfrac{c}{\sqrt{3}} = \dfrac{8\,abc}{3\sqrt{3}}$.

EXERCISE 11.7

1. Discuss the maxima and minima of the following functions :

   (i) $x^2 + y^2 + 6x + 12$ **(Dec. 2005, May 2010, 2015)**

   Ans. Minimum at $x = -3, y = 0$ and minimum value is 3

   (ii) $x^2y^2 - 5x^2 - 8xy - 5y^2$

   Ans. Maximum at $x = 0, y = 0$ and maximum value is 0

   (iii) $x^2 + y^2 + 2/x + 2/y$

   Ans. Maximum at $x = 1, y = 1$ and maximum value is 6

   (iv) $3x^2 - y^2 + x^3$ **(May 2005)**

   Ans. Maximum at $(-2, 0)$ and maximum value is 4

2. Find the extreme values of the following functions : **(Dec. 2008)**

   (i) $x^3y^2(12 - x - y), x > 0, y > 0$

   Ans. Maximum at $(6, 4)$ and maximum value is 6912

   (ii) $x^2y^3(1 - x - y)$

   Ans. Maximum at $(1/3, 1/2)$ and maximum value is $1/432$

(iii) $xy(3-x-y)$

Ans. Maximum at (1, 1) and maximum value is 1. At the points (0, 0) (3, 0), (0, 3) function has no extreme values.

(iv) $x^3y^2(12-3x-4y)$

Ans. Maximum at (2, 1) and minimum value is 16

3. Find the stationary points of the following functions and examine their nature :

(i) $2a^2xy - 3ax^2y - ay^2 + x^2y + xy^2$

Ans. Maximum at $(a/2, a/2)$, $(3a/2, -a/2)$; Minimum at $(a/2, -a/2)$, $(3a/2, 3a/3)$

(ii) $x^4 + y^4 - x^2 - y^2 + 1$

Ans. Maximum value 1 at (0, 0) ; Minimum value 1/2 at four points $(\pm 1/\sqrt{2}, \pm 1/\sqrt{2})$

(iii) $x^3 + 3xy^2 - 3x^2 + 7$

Ans. Maximum value 7 at (0, 0) ; Minimum value 3 at (2, 0)

(iv) $x^3 + xy^2 + 21x - 12x^2 - 2y^2$

Ans. Maximum value 10 at (1, 0) ; Minimum value -98 at (7, 0)

4. Find maximum and minimum values of the following functions :

(i) $(x-y)(x^2+y^2)(x+y-1)$

Ans. No maxima ; No minima

(ii) $2(x^2-y^2) - x^4 + y^4$

Ans. Maximum at $(\pm 1, 0)$; Minimum at $(0, \pm 1)$

(iii) $x^4 + y^4 - 2(x-y)^2$

Ans. Minimum value -8 at $(-\sqrt{2}, \sqrt{2})$ and at $(\sqrt{2}, -\sqrt{2})$

(iv) $x^4 + y^4 - 4a^2 xy$, a is constant

Ans. Minimum value a^4 at (a, a) and (−a, −a)

(v) $(x^2+y^2)^2 - 2(x^2-y^2)$

Ans. Minimum value -1 at (1, 0) and (−1, 0)

(vi) $y^2 + 4xy + 3x^2 + x^3$

Ans. No maxima and No minima i.e. no stationary value

5. Show that the expression $2 \sin \frac{x+y}{2} \cos \frac{x-y}{2} + \cos(x+y)$ is a minimum when $x = y = \frac{3\pi}{2}$ and find for what value of x, y the expression is a maximum.

Ans. $x = y = n\pi + (-1)^n \frac{\pi}{6}$, n integer

6. A rectangular box, open at the top is to have a volume of 108 cubic meter. What must be the dimensions so that the total surface area is minimum ?

[**Hint :** Let the length, breadth and height of the box be x, y, z respectively

Volume $= V = xyz \therefore z = \frac{108}{xy}$ and $S = xy + 2xz + 2yz$.

Ans. Dimensions for minimum surface area are $x = 6, y = 6, z = 3$]

7. A rectangular box, open at the top is to have a volume of 32 c.c. Find the dimensions of the box requiring least material for its construction.

Ans. Length = Breadth = 4 cm and height = 2 cm

8. Find the dimensions of the rectangular box without a top of maximum capacity whose surface is 108 sq. cm.

Ans. Length = Breadth = 6 cm and height = 3 cm

9. In a plane triangle ABC, find the maximum value of cos A cos B cos C

    [**Hint :** Let $f(x, y) = \cos A$ and $\cos B \cos (\pi - A + B)$

Ans. Maximum at $A = B = C = \dfrac{\pi}{3}$ and maximum value is $\dfrac{1}{8}$]

10. Find the maximum volume of a parallelopiped inscribed in a sphere $x^2 + y^2 + z^2 = a^2$

11. Divide 24 into three parts such that the continued product of the first, square of the second and cube of the third is maximum. **(May 2009)**

    [**Hint :** Let three parts be x, y, z. Also let $u = xy^2 z^3$ and condition is $x + y + z = 24$

Ans. $x = 4, y = 8, z = 12$]

12. The sum of three positive numbers is a. Determine the maximum value of their product. **(Dec. 2010)**

Ans. $\dfrac{a^3}{27}$

11.8 LAGRANGE'S METHOD OF UNDETERMINED MULTIPLIERS

We use this method to find stationary values or extreme values or terminal values of a function of several variables (these variables are not all independent) which are connected by some given relations.

Here we shall consider a function of only 3 variables f(x, y, z) with either one or two conditions are given.

Note : The drawback of this method is that we cannot determine the nature of the stationary values i.e. whether they are maximum or minimum.

Method :

Type I : To find stationary value of f(x, y, z) under one condition $\phi(x, y, z) = 0$

Step I : Let $\quad u = f(x, y, z)$ be the given function ... (1)

Under the condition

$$\phi(x, y, z) = 0 \quad \ldots (2)$$

Construct the function $F = u + \lambda \phi$

where λ is non-zero constant which is called Lagrange's undetermined multiplier.

Form the equations :

$$\frac{\partial F}{\partial x} = 0 \qquad \ldots (3)$$

$$\frac{\partial F}{\partial y} = 0 \qquad \ldots (4)$$

$$\frac{\partial F}{\partial z} = 0 \qquad \ldots (5)$$

Step II : We eliminate x, y, z and λ using equations (1) to (5) and we get the equation in terms of u.

The roots of that equation give the stationary values.

ILLUSTRATIONS ON LAGRANGE'S METHOD OF UNDETERMINED MULTIPLIERS

Ex. 1 : *Prove that the stationary value of $x^m\, y^n\, z^p$ under the condition $x + y + z = a$ is*

$$m^m\, n^n\, p^p \left(\frac{a}{m+n+p}\right)^{m+n+p} \qquad \textbf{(May 2007)}$$

Sol. : Let $\qquad u = f(x, y, z) = x^m\, y^n\, z^p \qquad \ldots (1)$

Step I : Under the condition

$$\phi = x + y + z - a = 0 \qquad \ldots (2)$$

Construct the function

$$F = u + \lambda \phi$$
$$= x^m\, y^n\, z^p + \lambda\,[x + y + z - a]$$

Form the equations :

$$\frac{\partial F}{\partial x} = 0 \quad \therefore \quad m x^{m-1}\, y^n\, z^p + \lambda = 0 \qquad \ldots (3)$$

$$\frac{\partial F}{\partial y} = 0 \quad \therefore \quad n x^m\, y^{n-1}\, z^p + \lambda = 0 \qquad \ldots (4)$$

$$\frac{\partial F}{\partial z} = 0 \quad \therefore \quad p x^m\, y^n\, z^{p-1} + \lambda = 0 \qquad \ldots (5)$$

Step II : We eliminate x, y, z, λ using equations (1) to (5).

From equations (3), (4) and (5),

$$m x^{m-1}\, y^n\, z^p = n x^m\, y^{n-1}\, z^p = p x^m\, y^n\, z^{p-1}$$

Dividing each by $x^m\, y^n\, z^p$

$$\frac{m}{x} = \frac{n}{y} = \frac{p}{z}$$

Let $\qquad \dfrac{x}{m} = \dfrac{y}{n} = \dfrac{z}{p} = k$

$\therefore \quad x = km, \quad y = kn, \quad z = kp \qquad \ldots (6)$

Substituting in (2), we have

$$km + kn + kp = a$$

$$\therefore \quad k = \frac{a}{m+n+p}$$

$\therefore$ From (6) $\quad x = \dfrac{am}{m+n+p}, \quad y = \dfrac{an}{m+n+p}, \quad z = \dfrac{ap}{m+n+p}$

Substituting in (1), the stationary value of u is

$$\left(\frac{am}{m+n+p}\right)^m \left(\frac{an}{m+n+p}\right)^n \left(\frac{ap}{m+n+p}\right)^p$$

$$= m^m n^p p^p \left(\frac{a}{m+n+p}\right)^{m+n+p}$$

Ex. 2 : *As the dimensions of a triangle ABC are varied, show that the maximum value of $\cos A \cos B \cos C$ is obtained when the triangle is equilateral.* **(Dec. 2009)**

Sol. : Step I : Let $\quad u = f(A, B, C) = \cos A \cos B \cos C \quad \ldots (1)$

Under the condition $\quad \phi = A + B + C - \pi = 0 \quad \ldots (2)$

Construct the function $\quad F = u + \lambda \phi$

$$F = \cos A \cos B \cos C + \lambda(A + B + C - \pi)$$

Form the equations :

$$\frac{\partial F}{\partial A} = 0 \quad \therefore \quad -\sin A \cos B \cos C + \lambda = 0 \quad \ldots (3)$$

$$\frac{\partial F}{\partial B} = 0 \quad \therefore \quad -\cos A \sin B \cos C + \lambda = 0 \quad \ldots (4)$$

$$\frac{\partial F}{\partial C} = 0 \quad \therefore \quad -\cos A \cos B \sin C + \lambda = 0 \quad \ldots (5)$$

Step II : We eliminate A, B, C and λ using equations (1) to (5).

From equations (3), (4) and (5)

$$\sin A \cos B \cos C = \cos A \sin B \cos C = \cos A \cos B \sin C$$

Dividing by $\cos A \cos B \cos C$, we have

$$\tan A = \tan B = \tan C$$

$$\Rightarrow \quad A = B = C$$

$\Rightarrow \quad \triangle ABC$ is equilateral.

Ex. 3 : *Use Lagrange's method to find the minimum distance from origin to the plane $3x + 2y + z = 12$.* **(Jan. 2004; May 2006, 2013, 2015)**

Sol. : Step I : Let $P(x, y, z)$ be any point on the plane $3x + 2y + z = 12$

$$\therefore \quad d(O, P) = \sqrt{x^2 + y^2 + z^2}$$

$$\therefore \quad [d(O, P)]^2 = x^2 + y^2 + z^2$$

Let $u = f(x, y, z) = x^2 + y^2 + z^2$ ... (1)
Under the condition $\phi = 3x + 2y + z - 12 = 0$ ... (2)
Construct the function $F = u + \lambda \phi$
$= x^2 + y^2 + z^2 + \lambda [3x + 2y + z - 12]$

Form the equations :

$$\frac{\partial F}{\partial x} = 0 \quad \therefore \quad 2x + 3\lambda = 0 \quad ...(3)$$

$$\frac{\partial F}{\partial y} = 0 \quad \therefore \quad 2y + 2\lambda = 0$$

$$y + \lambda = 0 \quad ...(4)$$

$$\frac{\partial F}{\partial z} = 0 \quad \therefore \quad 2z + \lambda = 0 \quad ...(5)$$

Step II : We eliminate x, y, z and λ using equations (1) to (5).
From equations (3), (4) and (5),

$$\frac{2x}{3} = y = 2z$$

Let $\frac{2x}{3} = y = 2z = k$

$\therefore \quad x = \frac{3k}{2}, \quad y = k, \quad z = \frac{k}{2}$ ... (6)

Substituting in (2)

$$\frac{9k}{2} + 2k + \frac{k}{2} = 12$$

$\therefore \quad k = \frac{12}{7}$

From (6), $x = \frac{18}{7}$

$y = \frac{12}{7}$

$z = \frac{6}{7} \quad \therefore \quad P \equiv \left(\frac{18}{7}, \frac{12}{7}, \frac{6}{7}\right)$

$\therefore \quad d(OP) = \sqrt{\left(\frac{18}{7}\right)^2 + \left(\frac{12}{7}\right)^2 + \left(\frac{6}{7}\right)^2} = \frac{\sqrt{504}}{7}$

Ex. 4 : If $u = \frac{x^2}{a^3} + \frac{y^2}{b^3} + \frac{z^2}{c^3}$, where $x + y + z = 1$ then prove that the stationary value of u is given by $x = \frac{a^3}{a^3 + b^3 + c^3}$, $y = \frac{b^3}{a^3 + b^3 + c^3}$, $z = \frac{c^3}{a^3 + b^3 + c^3}$ **(Dec. 2005, May 2010, 2014)**

Sol. : Step I : Let $u = f(x, y, z) = \frac{x^2}{a^3} + \frac{y^2}{b^3} + \frac{z^2}{c^3}$ ... (1)

Under the condition $\phi = x + y + z - 1 = 0$ ...(2)

Construct the function $F = u + \lambda \phi$

$$= \frac{x^2}{a^3} + \frac{y^2}{b^3} + \frac{z^2}{c^3} + \lambda(x + y + z - 1)$$

Form the equations: $\frac{\partial F}{\partial x} = 0$ $\therefore$ $\frac{2x}{a^3} + \lambda = 0$ ...(3)

$\frac{\partial F}{\partial y} = 0$ $\therefore$ $\frac{2y}{b^3} + \lambda = 0$ ...(4)

$\frac{\partial F}{\partial z} = 0$ $\therefore$ $\frac{2x}{c^3} + \lambda = 0$ ...(5)

Step II : We eliminate x, y, z and λ using equations (1) to (5).

From equations (3), (4) and (5)

$$\frac{x}{a^3} = \frac{y}{b^3} = \frac{z}{c^3} = \frac{-\lambda}{2}$$

Let $\frac{x}{a^3} = \frac{y}{b^3} = \frac{z}{c^3} = k$ (constant)

$\therefore$ $x = a^3 k, \quad y = b^3 k, \quad z = c^3 k$ ...(6)

Substituting in (2),

$$a^3 k + b^3 k + c^3 k = 1$$

$$k = \frac{1}{a^3 + b^3 + c^3}$$

From (6), $x = \frac{a^3}{a^3 + b^3 + c^3}, \quad y = \frac{b^3}{a^3 + b^3 + c^3}, \quad z = \frac{c^3}{a^3 + b^3 + c^3}$

which are the stationary values of u.

Ex. 5 : *If $ax^2 + by^2 = ab$, show that the extreme values of $u = x^2 + y^2 + xy$ are the roots of $4(u - a)(u - b) = ab$.*

Sol. : Step I : Let $u = f(x, y) = x^2 + y^2 + xy$ ...(1)

Under the condition $\phi = ax^2 + by^2 - ab = 0$ ...(2)

Construct the function $F = u + \lambda \phi$

$$= x^2 + y^2 + xy + \lambda(ax^2 + by^2 - ab)$$

Form the equations :

$\frac{\partial F}{\partial x} = 0$ $\therefore$ $2x + y + \lambda 2ax = 0$ ...(3)

$\frac{\partial F}{\partial y} = 0$ $\therefore$ $2y + x + \lambda 2by = 0$ ...(4)

Step II : We eliminate x, y and λ using equations (1) to (4)

equation (3) × x + (4) × y

$$2(x^2 + y^2 + xy) + 2\lambda(ax^2 + by^2) = 0$$

$$2u + 2\lambda ab = 0 \quad \text{using (1) and (2)}$$

$$\therefore \quad \lambda = \frac{-u}{ab}$$

Substituting in (3)

$$\therefore \quad 2x + y - \frac{2ux}{b} = 0$$

$$\Rightarrow \quad 2x\left(1 - \frac{u}{b}\right) + y = 0 \qquad \ldots (5)$$

Substituting the values of λ in (4)

$$2y + x - \frac{2uy}{a} = 0$$

$$\Rightarrow \quad x + 2y\left(1 - \frac{u}{b}\right) = 0 \qquad \ldots (6)$$

Eliminating x, y using equations (5) and (6)

$$2\left(1 - \frac{u}{b}\right) = \frac{1}{2\left(1 - \frac{u}{a}\right)}$$

$$\Rightarrow \quad \frac{4(b-u)}{b} \cdot \frac{(a-u)}{a} = 1$$

$$\Rightarrow \quad 4(u-a)(u-b) = ab$$

which is quadratic in u, giving the extreme values of u.

Ex. 6 : *A space probe in the shape of the ellipsoid $4x^2 + y^2 + 4z^2 = 16$ enters the earth's atmosphere and its surface begins to heat. After one hour, the temperature at the point (x, y, z) on the surface of the probe is*

$$T(x, y, z) = 8x^2 + 4yz - 16z + 600$$

Find the hottest points on the probe's surface by using Lagrange's method. **(Jan. 2005)**

Sol. : Step I : Let $\quad u = f(x, y, z) = 8x^2 + 4yz - 16z + 600 \qquad \ldots (1)$

Under the condition $\quad \phi = 4x^2 + y^2 + 4z^2 - 16 = 0 \qquad \ldots (2)$

Construct the function $\quad F = u + \lambda\phi$

$$= 8x^2 + 4yz - 16z + 600 + \lambda(4x^2 + y^2 + 4z^2 - 16)$$

Form the equations :

$$\frac{\partial F}{\partial x} = 0 \quad \therefore \quad 16x + \lambda\, 8x = 0 \qquad \ldots (3)$$

$$\frac{\partial F}{\partial y} = 0 \quad \therefore \quad 4z + 2\lambda y = 0 \qquad \ldots (4)$$

$$\frac{\partial F}{\partial z} = 0 \quad \therefore \quad 4y - 16 + 8\lambda z = 0 \qquad \ldots (5)$$

Step II : We eliminate x, y, z and λ using equations (1) to (5).

From (3) $\quad 8x(2+\lambda) = 0$

$\therefore \quad \lambda = -2$

From (4) $\quad 4z + 4y = 0$

$\Rightarrow \quad y = -z$

From (5) $\quad 4y - 16 - 16z = 0$

$\quad y - 4z = 4$

$\therefore$ Solving for y and z,

$$y = -\frac{4}{3} \text{ and } z = -\frac{4}{3}$$

Substituting in (2)

$$4x^2 + \frac{16}{9} + \frac{64}{9} = 16$$

$\therefore \quad 4x^2 = \frac{64}{9} \quad \therefore \quad x = \pm\frac{4}{3}$

$\therefore$ The required points are $\left(\pm\frac{4}{3}, -\frac{4}{3}, -\frac{4}{3}\right)$

Ex. 7 : *Show that the stationary value of $a^3 x^2 + b^3 y^2 + c^3 z^2$, where*

$\frac{1}{x} + \frac{1}{y} + \frac{1}{z} = 1$ *is given by*

$x = \frac{a+b+c}{a}, \quad y = \frac{a+b+c}{b}, \quad z = \frac{a+b+c}{c}$ **(Dec. 2006)**

Sol. : Step I : Let $\quad u = f(x, y, z) = a^3 x^2 + b^3 y^2 + c^3 z^2 \quad\quad \ldots (1)$

Under the condition $\quad \phi = \frac{1}{x} + \frac{1}{y} + \frac{1}{z} - 1 = 0 \quad\quad \ldots (2)$

Construct the function $\quad F = u + \lambda\phi$

$\quad = a^3 x^2 + b^3 y^2 + c^3 z^2 + \lambda\left(\frac{1}{x} + \frac{1}{y} + \frac{1}{z} - 1\right)$

Form the equations :

$\frac{\partial F}{\partial x} = 0 \quad\quad \therefore \quad 2a^3 x + \lambda\left(-\frac{1}{x^2}\right) = 0$

$\quad\quad\quad\quad \therefore \quad 2a^3 x^3 - \lambda = 0 \quad\quad \ldots (3)$

$\frac{\partial F}{\partial y} = 0 \quad\quad \therefore \quad 2b^3 y + \lambda\left(-\frac{1}{y^2}\right) = 0$

$\quad\quad\quad\quad \quad 2b^3 y^3 - \lambda = 0 \quad\quad \ldots (4)$

$\frac{\partial F}{\partial z} = 0 \quad\quad \therefore \quad 2c^3 z + \lambda\left(-\frac{1}{z^2}\right) = 0$

$\quad\quad\quad\quad \therefore \quad 2c^3 z^3 - \lambda = 0 \quad\quad \ldots (5)$

Step II : We eliminate x, y, z and λ using equations (1) to (5).
From equations (3), (4) and (5)

$$2a^3x^3 = 2b^3y^3 = 2c^3z^3 = \lambda$$

$\Rightarrow \quad ax = by = cz = k$

$$\left.\begin{array}{rcl} ax = k & \therefore & x = \dfrac{k}{a} \\[4pt] by = k & \therefore & y = \dfrac{k}{b} \\[4pt] cz = k & \therefore & z = \dfrac{k}{c} \end{array}\right\} \quad \ldots (6)$$

Substituting in equation (2),

$$\dfrac{a}{k} + \dfrac{b}{k} + \dfrac{c}{k} = 1$$

$\therefore \quad \dfrac{1}{k} = \dfrac{1}{a+b+c}$

$\Rightarrow \quad k = a+b+c$

From (6), $\quad x = \dfrac{a+b+c}{a}, \quad y = \dfrac{a+b+c}{b}, \quad z = \dfrac{a+b+c}{c}$

which are the required stationary value.

Ex. 8 : *Divide 24 into three parts such that the continued product of the first, square of the second and cube of the third may be maximum.* **(Dec. 2013, May 2004, 2009)**

Sol. : Step I : Divide 24 into three parts as

$$\begin{array}{rcl} \text{first part} &=& x \\ \text{second part} &=& y \\ \text{third part} &=& z \end{array}$$

Let $\quad u = f(x, y, z) = xy^2z^3 \quad \ldots (1)$

Under the condition $\quad \phi = x + y + z - 24 = 0 \quad \ldots (2)$

Construct the function $\quad F = u + \lambda\phi$

$\therefore \quad F = xy^2z^3 + \lambda(x + y + z - 24)$

Form the equations :

$\dfrac{\partial F}{\partial x} = 0 \quad \therefore \quad y^2z^3 + \lambda = 0 \quad \ldots (3)$

$\dfrac{\partial F}{\partial y} = 0 \quad \therefore \quad 2xyz^3 + \lambda = 0 \quad \ldots (4)$

$\dfrac{\partial F}{\partial z} = 0 \quad \therefore \quad 3xy^2z^2 + \lambda = 0 \quad \ldots (5)$

Step II : We eliminate x, y, z and λ using equations (1) and (5).

From equations (3), (4) and (5)
$$y^2 z^3 = 2xyz^3 = 3xy^2 z^2$$

Dividing by $xy^2 z^3$

$$\Rightarrow \quad \frac{1}{x} = \frac{2}{y} = \frac{3}{z} = k$$

$$\left.\begin{array}{lll} \dfrac{1}{x} = k & \therefore & x = \dfrac{1}{k} \\[4pt] \dfrac{2}{y} = k & \therefore & y = \dfrac{2}{k} \\[4pt] \dfrac{3}{z} = k & \therefore & z = \dfrac{3}{k} \end{array}\right\} \quad \ldots (6)$$

Substituting in equation (2),
$$\frac{1}{k} + \frac{2}{k} + \frac{3}{k} = 24$$

$\therefore \quad 6 = 24k$

$\therefore \quad k = \dfrac{1}{4}$

From equation (6) $x = 4$

$y = 8$

$z = 12$

$\therefore$ We divide 24 into three parts 4, 8, 12.

Ex. 9 : *Find the points on the surface $z^2 = xy + 1$ nearest to the origin, by using Lagrange's method.* **(May 2005, 2009, 2011; Dec. 2012)**

Sol. : Step I : Let P (x, y, z) be any point on the surface $z^2 = xy + 1$

$\therefore \quad d(O, P) = \sqrt{x^2 + y^2 + z^2}$

$[d(O, P)]^2 = x^2 + y^2 + z^2$

Let $\quad u = f(x, y, z) = x^2 + y^2 + z^2$ ... (1)

Under the condition $\quad \phi = z^2 - xy - 1 = 0$ ... (2)

Construct the function $\quad F = u + \lambda \phi$

$= x^2 + y^2 + z^2 + \lambda (z^2 - xy - 1)$

Form the equations :

$\dfrac{\partial F}{\partial x} = 0 \quad \therefore \quad 2x - \lambda y = 0$ ... (3)

$\dfrac{\partial F}{\partial y} = 0 \quad \therefore \quad 2y - \lambda x = 0$ ... (4)

$\dfrac{\partial F}{\partial z} = 0 \quad \therefore \quad 2z + 2\lambda z = 0$ ... (5)

Step II : We eliminate x, y, z and λ using equations (1) to (5).
From equation (5),
$$z(1+\lambda) = 0$$
$$\therefore \quad \lambda = -1$$
Put in equations (3) and (4)
$$\therefore \quad 2x + y = 0$$
$$2y + x = 0$$
$$\therefore \Rightarrow \quad x = 0, \quad y = 0$$
Substituting in (2), $\quad z^2 = 1$
$$\therefore \quad z = \pm 1$$
∴ (0, 0, ± 1) are the nearest points on the surface from the origin.

Ex. 10 : If $x^2 + y^2 + z^2 = r^2$ then maximum value of $yz + zx + xy$ is r^2 and minimum value is $-\dfrac{1}{2}r^2$.

Sol. : Type I : Step I : Let $u = f(x, y, z) = xy + yz + zx$ ... (1)
Under the condition $\quad \phi = x^2 + y^2 + z^2 - r^2 = 0$ ... (2)
Construct the function $\quad F = u + \lambda\phi$
$$= xy + yz + zx + \lambda[x^2 + y^2 + z^2 - r^2]$$

Form the equations :

$$\dfrac{\partial F}{\partial x} = 0 \quad \therefore \quad y + z + 2x\lambda = 0 \quad \text{... (3)}$$

$$\dfrac{\partial F}{\partial y} = 0 \quad \therefore \quad x + z + 2y\lambda = 0 \quad \text{... (4)}$$

$$\dfrac{\partial F}{\partial z} = 0 \quad \therefore \quad x + y + 2z\lambda = 0 \quad \text{... (5)}$$

Step II : We eliminate x, y, z and λ using equations (1) to (5).
Taking (3) × x + (4) × y + (5) × z
we get $\quad 2(xy + yz + zx) + 2\lambda(x^2 + y^2 + z^2) = 0$
$$2u + 2\lambda r^2 = 0 \quad \text{using equations (1) and (2)}$$
$$\Rightarrow \quad u + \lambda r^2 = 0$$
$$\therefore \quad \lambda = -\dfrac{u}{r^2}$$

Substituting in equations (3), (4) and (5)
we have
$$y + z - \dfrac{2xu}{r^2} = 0 \quad \text{... (6)}$$

$$x + z - \dfrac{2yu}{r^2} = 0 \quad \text{... (7)}$$

$$y + x - \dfrac{2zu}{r^2} = 0 \quad \text{... (8)}$$

Equations (6), (7) and (8) squaring and adding,

$$\therefore (y+z)^2 + (x+z)^2 + (y+x)^2 = \frac{4u^2}{r^4}(x^2+y^2+z^2)$$

$$\therefore 2(x^2+y^2+z^2) + 2(xy+yz+zx) = \frac{4u^2}{r^4}r^2$$

$$2u + 2r^2 = \frac{4u^2}{r^2}$$

$$\therefore 2u^2 - ur^2 - r^4 = 0$$
$$\therefore (2u+r^2)(u-r^2) = 0$$
$$\therefore 2u + r^2 = 0 \quad \text{or} \quad u - r^2 = 0$$

$$u = -\frac{1}{2}r^2, \quad r^2$$

$$\therefore \text{Maximum value} = r^2$$

$$\text{Minimum value} = -\frac{1}{2}r^2$$

Type II : To find stationary value of f(x, y, z) under two conditions

$$\phi(x, y, z) = 0$$
$$\psi(x, y, z) = 0$$

Method : Step I : Let $u = f(x, y, z)$ be the given function. ... (1)

Under the conditions

$$\phi(x, y, z) = 0 \qquad \ldots (2)$$
$$\psi(x, y, z) = 0 \qquad \ldots (3)$$

Construct the function

$$F = u + \lambda_1 \phi + \lambda_2 \psi$$

where λ_1, λ_2 are non zero constants which is called Lagrange's undetermined multiplier.

Form the equations :
$$\frac{\partial F}{\partial x} = 0 \qquad \ldots (4)$$

$$\frac{\partial F}{\partial y} = 0 \qquad \ldots (5)$$

$$\frac{\partial F}{\partial z} = 0 \qquad \ldots (6)$$

Step II : We eliminate x, y, z, λ_1 and λ_2 using equations (1) to (6) and we get the equation in terms of u.

The roots of that equation give the stationary values.

Ex. 11 : *Find the extreme values of $x^2 + y^2 + z^2$ if $3x + 2y + z = 0$, $6x^2 + 3y^2 + 2z^2 = 12$.*

Sol. : Step I : Let $u = f(x, y, z) = x^2 + y^2 + z^2$ ... (1)

Under the conditions

$$\phi = 3x + 2y + z = 0 \qquad \ldots (2)$$
$$\psi = 6x^2 + 3y^2 + 2z^2 - 12 = 0 \qquad \ldots (3)$$

Construct the function $F = u + \lambda_1 \phi + \lambda_2 \psi$

$$F = x^2 + y^2 + z^2 + \lambda_1(3x + 2y + z) + \lambda_2(6x^2 + 3y^2 + 2z^2 - 12)$$

Form the equations :

$$\frac{\partial F}{\partial x} = 0 \quad \therefore \quad 2x + 3\lambda_1 + 12\lambda_2 x = 0 \quad \ldots (4)$$

$$\frac{\partial F}{\partial y} = 0 \quad \therefore \quad 2y + 2\lambda_1 + 6\lambda_2 y = 0 \quad \ldots (5)$$

$$\frac{\partial F}{\partial z} = 0 \quad \therefore \quad 2z + \lambda_1 + 4\lambda_2 z = 0 \quad \ldots (6)$$

Step II : We eliminate $x, y, z, \lambda_1, \lambda_2$ using equations (1) to (6).

Equation (4) × x + (5) × y + (6) × z and adding

$$2(x^2 + y^2 + z^2) + \lambda_1(3x + 2y + z) + 2\lambda_2(6x^2 + 3y^2 + 2z^2) = 0$$

$$2u + \lambda_1 \cdot 0 + 2\lambda_2(12) = 0 \quad \text{using equations (1), (2), (3)}$$

$$\lambda_2 = -\frac{u}{12}$$

From equation (4),

$$2x + 3\lambda_1 - \frac{12ux}{12} = 0$$

$\therefore \quad 2x + 3\lambda - ux = 0$

$\therefore \quad x(2 - u) + 3\lambda_1 = 0$

$\therefore \quad x + \frac{3\lambda_1}{2-u} = 0 \quad \ldots (7)$

Similarly from (5), $\quad y + \frac{4\lambda_1}{4-u} = 0 \quad \ldots (8)$

From (6) $\quad z + \frac{3\lambda_1}{6-u} = 0 \quad \ldots (9)$

Equation (7) × 3 + (8) × 2 + (9) and adding

$$3x + 2y + z + \lambda_1 \left[\frac{9}{2-u} + \frac{8}{4-u} + \frac{3}{6-u}\right] = 0$$

$$0 + \lambda_1 \left[\frac{9}{2-u} + \frac{8}{4-u} + \frac{3}{6-u}\right] = 0 \quad \text{using (1)}$$

But $\lambda \neq 0$

$\Rightarrow \quad \frac{9}{2-u} + \frac{8}{4-u} + \frac{3}{6-u} = 0$

Multiply by $(2-u)(4-u)(6-u)$

$9(4-u)(6-u) + 8(2-u)(6-u) + 3(2-u)(4-u) = 0$

$\therefore \quad 9[24 - 10u + u^2] + 8[12 - 8u + u^2] + 3[8 - 6u + u^2] = 0$

$\therefore \quad (9 + 8 + 3)u^2 + (-90 - 64 - 18)u + (216 + 96 + 24) = 0$

$20u^2 - 172u + 336 = 0$

Dividing by 4
$$5u^2 - 43u + 84 = 0$$
$$(u - 3)(5u - 28) = 0$$
$$\therefore \quad u = 3 \quad \text{or} \quad u = \frac{28}{5}$$

$\therefore$ Stationary values are $3, \dfrac{28}{5}$

Ex. 12 : *Find the extreme values of $x^2 + y^2 + z^2$ and subject to the condition*
$ax^2 + by^2 + cz^2 = 1, \; lx + my + nz = 0$

Sol. : Step I : Let
$$u = f(x, y, z) = x^2 + y^2 + z^2 \qquad \ldots (1)$$
Under the conditions
$$\phi = ax^2 + by^2 + cz^2 - 1 = 0 \qquad \ldots (2)$$
$$\psi = lx + my + nz = 0 \qquad \ldots (3)$$

Construct the function
$$F = u + \lambda_1 \phi + \lambda_2 \psi$$
$$\therefore \quad F = x^2 + y^2 + z^2 + \lambda_1(ax^2 + by^2 + cz^2 - 1) + \lambda_2(lx + my + nz)$$

Form the equations :
$$\frac{\partial F}{\partial x} = 0 \quad \therefore \quad 2x + 2\lambda_1 ax + \lambda_2 l = 0 \qquad \ldots (4)$$
$$\frac{\partial F}{\partial y} = 0 \quad \therefore \quad 2y + 2\lambda_1 by + \lambda_2 m = 0 \qquad \ldots (5)$$
$$\frac{\partial F}{\partial z} = 0 \quad \therefore \quad 2z + 2\lambda_1 cy + \lambda_2 n = 0 \qquad \ldots (6)$$

Step II : We eliminate x, y, z, λ_1 and λ_2 using equations (1) to (5).

Equation $(4) \times x + (5) \times y + (6) \times z$

We have
$$2(x^2 + y^2 + z^2) + 2\lambda_1(ax^2 + by^2 + cz^2) + \lambda_2(lx + my + nz) = 0$$
$$2u + 2\lambda_1 + \lambda_2 \times 0 = 0 \text{ using equations (1) to (3)}$$
$$\Rightarrow \quad 2u + 2\lambda_1 = 0$$
$$\Rightarrow \quad \lambda_1 = -u$$

Substituting in equation (4)
$$2x - 2uax + \lambda_2 l = 0$$
$$2x(1 - au) + \lambda_2 l = 0$$
$$\therefore \quad x + \frac{\lambda_2 l}{2(1 - au)} = 0 \qquad \ldots (7)$$

Similarly from (5) $\; y + \dfrac{\lambda_2 m}{2(1 - bu)} = 0 \qquad \ldots (8)$

From (6) $\quad z + \dfrac{\lambda_2 n}{2(1 - cu)} = 0 \qquad \ldots (9)$

Equation $(7) \times l + (8) \times m + (9) \times n$
$$lx + my + nz + \frac{\lambda_2}{2}\left[\frac{l^2}{1 - au} + \frac{m^2}{1 - bu} + \frac{n^2}{1 - cu}\right] = 0$$

$$0 + \frac{\lambda_2}{2}\left[\frac{l^2}{1-au} + \frac{m^2}{1-bu} + \frac{n^2}{1-cu}\right] = 0 \quad \text{using equation (3)}$$

But $\lambda_2 \neq 0$

$$\Rightarrow \qquad \frac{l^2}{1-au} + \frac{m^2}{1-bu} + \frac{n^2}{1-cu} = 0$$

The roots of this equation give the stationary values.

Ex. 13 : *Prove that the stationary values of* $\frac{x^2}{a^4} + \frac{y^2}{b^4} + \frac{z^2}{c^4}$, *where* $lx + my + nz = 0$ *and* $\frac{x^2}{a^2} + \frac{y^2}{b^2} + \frac{z^2}{c^2} = 1$ *are the roots of* $\frac{l^2 a^4}{1-a^2u} + \frac{m^2 b^4}{1-b^2u} + \frac{n^2 c^4}{1-c^2u} = 0.$ **(June 2008)**

Sol. : Step I : Let
$$u = f(x, y, z) = \frac{x^2}{a^4} + \frac{y^2}{b^4} + \frac{z^2}{c^4} \qquad \ldots (1)$$

Under the conditions
$$\phi = lx + my + nz = 0 \qquad \ldots (2)$$
$$\psi = \frac{x^2}{a^2} + \frac{y^2}{b^2} + \frac{z^2}{c^2} - 1 = 0 \qquad \ldots (3)$$

Construct the function
$$F = u + \lambda_1 \phi + \lambda_2 \psi$$

$\therefore \qquad F = \frac{x^2}{a^4} + \frac{y^2}{b^4} + \frac{z^2}{c^4} + \lambda_1 (lx + my + nz)$

$$+ \lambda_2 \left(\frac{x^2}{a^2} + \frac{y^2}{b^2} + \frac{z^2}{c^2} - 1\right)$$

Form the equations:

$\frac{\partial F}{\partial x} = 0 \qquad \therefore \qquad \frac{2x}{a^4} + \lambda_1 l + \frac{2\lambda_2 x}{a^2} = 0 \qquad \ldots (4)$

$\frac{\partial F}{\partial y} = 0 \qquad \therefore \qquad \frac{2y}{b^4} + \lambda_1 m + \frac{2\lambda_2 y}{b^2} = 0 \qquad \ldots (5)$

$\frac{\partial F}{\partial z} = 0 \qquad \therefore \qquad \frac{2z}{c^4} + \lambda_1 n + \frac{2\lambda_2 z}{c^2} = 0 \qquad \ldots (6)$

Step II : We eliminate x, y, z, λ_1 and λ_2 using equations (1) to (6).

Equation (4) $\times x +$ (5) $\times y +$ (6) $\times z$
we get
$$2\left(\frac{x^2}{a^4} + \frac{y^2}{b^4} + \frac{z^2}{c^4}\right) + \lambda_1 (lx + my + nz) + 2\lambda_2\left(\frac{x^2}{a^2} + \frac{y^2}{b^2} + \frac{z^2}{c^2}\right)$$

$\therefore \qquad 2u + \lambda_1 0 + 2\lambda_2 \cdot 1 = 0$ using equations (1) to (3)

$\therefore \qquad \lambda_2 = -u$

From equation (4)
$$\frac{2x}{a^4} + \lambda_1 l - \frac{2xu}{a^2} = 0$$
$$2x\left(\frac{1-a^2u}{a^4}\right) + \lambda_1 l = 0$$

$\therefore \qquad x + \frac{\lambda_1 l a^4}{2(1-a^2u)} = 0 \qquad \ldots (7)$

Similarly, from equation (5)

$$y + \frac{\lambda_1 b^4 m}{2(1-b^2 u)} = 0 \qquad \ldots (8)$$

From (6)
$$z + \frac{\lambda_1 c^4 n}{2(1-c^2 u)} = 0 \qquad \ldots (9)$$

Equation (7) × l + (8) × m + (9) × n

$$lx + my + nz + \frac{\lambda_1}{2}\left[\frac{a^4 l^2}{1-a^2 u} + \frac{b^4 m^2}{1-b^2 u} + \frac{c^4 n^2}{1-c^2 u}\right] = 0$$

But $\lambda_1 \neq 0$

$$\Rightarrow \qquad \frac{a^4 l^2}{1-a^2 u} + \frac{b^4 m^2}{1-b^2 u} + \frac{c^4 n^2}{1-c^2 u} = 0$$

The roots of this equation give stationary values.

EXERCISE 11.8

1. Find maximum and minimum distances of the point (3, 4, 12) from the sphere $x^2 + y^2 + z^2 = 1$, using Lagrange's method.

Ans. Maximum distance = 14

Minimum distance = 12

2. If $x_1 > 0, x_2 > 0, \ldots x_3 > 0$, determine the maximum value of the nth root of the product of the numbers $x_1, x_2, \ldots x_n$, provided their sum is equal to a given number a. Hence show that their G.M. < A.M.

3. Show that the maximum and minimum distances from the origin to the section of the surface $(x^2 + y^2 + z^2)^2 = x^2 + 2y^2 + 3z^2$ made by the plane $x + y + z = 0$ are the root of the equation $3r^4 - 12r^2 + 11 = 0$.

4. If $u = \frac{a^3}{x^2} + \frac{b^3}{y^2} + \frac{c^3}{z^2}$, where $x + y + z = 1$, prove that the stationary value of u is given by $x = \frac{a}{\Sigma a}, \ y = \frac{b}{\Sigma a}, \ z = \frac{c}{\Sigma a}$ where $\Sigma a = a + b + c$.

5. Find stationary value of $u = x + y + z$ if $xy + yz + zx = 3a^2$. **(Dec. 2010)**

Ans. 3a

6. Find the greatest rectangular parallelopiped which can be inscribed in the ellipsoid $\frac{x^2}{a^2} + \frac{y^2}{b^2} + \frac{z^2}{c^2} = 1$.

Ans. $\frac{2a}{\sqrt{3}} \times \frac{2b}{\sqrt{3}} \times \frac{2c}{\sqrt{3}}$.

7. Find the maximum and minimum values of $x^2 + y^2$ when $3x^2 + 4xy + 6y^2 = 140$.

Ans. Maximum value = 70

Minimum value = 20

8. If $\dfrac{3}{x} + \dfrac{4}{y} + \dfrac{5}{z} = 6$, find the values of x, y, z which make $x + y + z$ maximum.

Ans. $x = k\sqrt{3}$, $y = 2k$, $z = k\sqrt{5}$ where $k = \dfrac{\sqrt{3} + 2 + \sqrt{5}}{6}$

9. Find the maximum value of $u = (x+1)(y+1)(z+1)$ under the condition $a^x b^y c^z = A$.

Ans. Maximum value of $u = \dfrac{[\log(Aabc)]^3}{\log a^3 \log b^3 \log c^3}$.

10. Find a point within a triangle such that the sum of the squares of its distances from the sides of the triangle is minimum.

Ans. $x = \dfrac{2a\Delta}{a^2 + b^2 + c^2}$, $y = \dfrac{2b\Delta}{a^2 + b^2 + c^2}$, $z = \dfrac{2c\Delta}{a^2 + b^2 + c^2}$.

where Δ = area of triangle.

11. If r is the distance of the point on the conic $ax^2 + by^2 + cz^2 = 1$, $lx + my + nz = 0$ from origin, then the stationary values of r are given by

$$\dfrac{l^2}{1 - ar^2} + \dfrac{m^2}{1 - br^2} + \dfrac{n^2}{1 - cr^2} = 0$$

12. Find the maximum value of $u = x^2 y^3 z^4$ such that $2x + 3y + 4z = a$. **(Dec. 2008)**

Ans. $u = \left(\dfrac{a}{9}\right)^9$

13. Find the extreme value of $x^l y^m z^n$ subject to the conditions

$ax + by + cz = l + m + n$

Ans. $u_{max} = \left(\dfrac{l}{a}\right)^l \left(\dfrac{m}{b}\right)^m \left(\dfrac{n}{c}\right)^n$

14. Discuss the maximum and minimum values of r, where $r^2 = \dfrac{x^2}{a} + \dfrac{y^2}{b} + \dfrac{z^2}{c}$

and $ax^2 + by^2 + cz^2 = 1$ and $a^2x + b^2y + c^2z = 0$.

Ans. Roots of the equation $\dfrac{a^5}{1 - a^2 r^2} + \dfrac{b^5}{1 - b^2 r^2} + \dfrac{c^5}{1 - c^2 r^2} = 0$.

15. Find extreme values of $x^2 + y^2 + z^2$, subject to the conditions $x + y + z = 1$ and $xyz + 1 = 0$.

Ans. Minimum of $u = 3$ for $z = 1$.

16. If $x + y + z = 1$ then show that the expression $ayz + bzx + cxy$ has a stationary solution given by $\dfrac{abc}{2bc + 2ca + 2ab - a^2 - b^2 - c^2}$.

17. Find the maximum and minimum distances from the origin to the conic $5x^3 + 6xy + 5y^2 = 8$.

Ans. 4, 1.

18. Find the stationary values of $x^2 + y^2 + z^2$, subject to the conditions $ax^2 + by^2 + cz^2 + 2fyz + 2gzx + 2hxy = 1$ and $lx + my + nz = 0$.

Ans.
$$\begin{vmatrix} 1-au & -uh & -ug & l \\ -uh & 1-bu & -uf & m \\ -ug & -uf & 1-cu & n \\ l & m & n & o \end{vmatrix} = 0$$

The roots of which give the stationary values of u.

19. Find the maximum and minimum radii vectors of the section of the surface of elasticity $(x^2 + y^2 + z^2)^2 = a^2 x^2 + b^2 y^2 + c^2 z^2$ made by the plane $lx + my + nz = 0$.

Ans. $\dfrac{l^2}{a^2 - u} + \dfrac{m^2}{b^2 - u} + \dfrac{n^2}{c^2 - u} = 0$ whose roots give maximum and minimum values.

20. Divide 120 into three parts so that the sum of their products taken two at a time shall be maximum.

Ans. 40, 40, 40.

ENGINEERING MATHEMATICS – I
MODEL QUESTION PAPER : FIRST ONLINE EXAM.

1. The rank of matrix $A = \begin{bmatrix} 1 & 2 & 3 \\ 2 & 2 & 2 \\ 3 & 3 & 3 \end{bmatrix}$ is equal to (2)

    (A) 4   (B) 3

    (C) 2   (D) 1

2. Given system of linear equation $x + y + z = 1$, $x + 2y + 4z = 2$, $x + 4y + 10z = 4$ has (2)

    (A) unique solution   (B) no solution

    (C) infinitely many solutions   (D) n-r solutions

3. For what value of 'b' the matrix $A = \dfrac{1}{13}\begin{bmatrix} b & -5 \\ 5 & b \end{bmatrix}$ is an orthogonal matrix ? (2)

    (A) ± 5 (B) ± 13

    (C) ± 12 (D) ± 16

4. For matrix $A = \begin{bmatrix} 1 & -2 & -1 \\ 0 & 3 & 2 \\ 0 & 0 & 5 \end{bmatrix}$ the eigen values of A are (2)

    (A) $1, -2, -1$ (B) $1, -3, -5$

    (C) $-1, -3, -5$ (D) $1, 3, 5$

5. If characteristic equation of matrix A of order 3×3 is $\lambda^3 - 3\lambda^2 - 3\lambda^2 + 3\lambda - 1 = 0$ then by Cayley-Hamilton theorem A^{-1} is equal to (2)

    (A) $A^3 - 3A^2 + 3A - I$ (B) $A^2 - 3A - 3I$

    (C) $3A^2 - 3A - I$ (D) $A^2 - 3A + 3I$

6. If a matrix A has all its minor of order $r + 1$ are zero then (1)

    (A) rank of $A \geq r$ (B) rank of $A = r$

    (C) rank of $A \leq r$ (D) none of these

7. The condition for unique solution of $m \times n$ non-homogenous system of linear equation $AX = B$ is (1)

    (A) rank of $A = r =$ number of unknowns   (B) rank of $A = r <$ number of unknowns

    (C) rank of $A = r >$ number of unknowns   (D) none of these

8. The sum of eigen values of a matrix is equal to (1)

    (A) trace of matrix   (B) determine of matrix

    (C) rank of matrix   (D) none of these

9. The real part of the complex number $z = e^{5 + i\frac{\pi}{2}}$ is (2)
   (A) e^5
   (B) $-e^5$
   (C) 0
   (D) e^{-5}

10. Using DeMoivre's theorem, simplified form of $(1 + i)^8 + (1 - i)^8$ is equal to (2)
    (A) 2^8
    (B) 2^5
    (C) $2^4 \cos\frac{\pi}{4}$
    (D) $2^8 \cos\frac{\pi}{8}$

11. The roots of equation $x^3 + 1 = 0$ are (2)
    (A) $\cos\frac{(2k + 1)\pi}{3} + i \sin\frac{(2k + 1)\pi}{3}$, $k = 0, 1, 2$
    (B) $\cos\frac{(2k - 1)\pi}{3} + i \sin\frac{(2k - 1)\pi}{3}$, $k = 0, 1, 2$
    (C) $\cos\frac{2k\pi}{3} + i \sin\frac{2k\pi}{3}$, $k = 0, 1, 2$
    (D) None of these

12. If $\sin(\alpha + i\beta) = x + iy$ then $\dfrac{x^2}{\cosh^2 \beta} + \dfrac{y^2}{\sinh^2 \beta}$ is equal to (2)
    (A) 1
    (B) 0
    (C) -1
    (D) none of these

13. The value of i^i is (2)
    (A) $\dfrac{\pi}{2}$
    (B) $-\dfrac{\pi}{2}$
    (C) $e^{\pi/2}$
    (D) $e^{-\pi/2}$

14. If $z = 1 + i$ then $\arg(z)$ is equal to (1)
    (A) $\dfrac{\pi}{4}$
    (B) $\pi + \dfrac{\pi}{4}$
    (C) $\pi - \dfrac{\pi}{4}$
    (D) π

15. If $y = \sinh x$ then $\dfrac{dy}{dx}$ is equal to (1)
    (A) $\sinh x$
    (B) $\cosh x$
    (C) $-\sinh x$
    (D) $-\cosh x$

ENGINEERING MATHEMATICS – I
MODEL QUESTION PAPER : SECOND ONLINE EXAM. (25 MARKS)

1. The P-series $1 + \frac{1}{\sqrt{2}} + \frac{1}{\sqrt{3}} + \ldots$ is (2)
   (A) convergent (B) divergent
   (C) oscillatory (D) none of these

2. The infinite series $\frac{2}{1} + \frac{3}{4} + \frac{4}{9} + \ldots \frac{n+1}{n^3} + \ldots$ by comparison test is (2)
   (A) convergent (B) divergent
   (C) oscillatory (D) none of these

3. The nth derivative of $y = \log(3x + 4)$ is (2)
   (A) $\frac{3^n \, n!}{(3x+4)^n}$ (B) $\frac{3^n (n-1)!}{(3x+4)^n}$
   (C) $\frac{(-1)^{n-1} 3^n (n-1)!}{(3x+4)^n}$ (D) 0

4. If $y = \frac{5x+3}{5x+7}$ then n^{th} derivative of y is
   (A) $-4 \frac{(-1)^n n! \, 5^n}{(5x+7)^{n+1}}$ (B) $-4 \frac{(-1)^n n! \, 5^n}{(5x+7)^{n+1}}$
   (C) $3 \frac{(-1)^n n! \, 5^n}{(5x+7)^{n+1}}$ (D) none of these

5. Using Leibnitz's theorem, the nth derivative of $y = x \, e^{4x}$ is (2)
   (A) $4^n e^{4x} n + 4^{n-1} e^{4x} x$ (B) $4^n e^{4x} x - 4^{n-1} e^{4x}$
   (C) $e^{4x} x + n e^{4x}$ (D) $4^n e^{4x} x + n 4^{n-1} e^{4x}$

6. In ratio test, if $\sum_{n=1}^{\infty} u_n$ is series of positive terms such that $\lim_{n \to \infty} \frac{u_n}{u_{n+1}} = l$, then $\sum_{n=1}^{\infty} u_n$ is convergent for
   (A) $l > 1$ (B) $l < 1$
   (C) $l = 1$ (D) none of these

7. The nth derivative of $y = \sin(ax + b)$ is (1)
   (A) $a^n \sin(ax + b)$ (B) $a^n \sin\left(ax + b + \frac{n\pi}{2}\right)$
   (C) $b^n \cos(bx + c)$ (D) $b^n \sin\left(ax + b + \frac{n\pi}{2}\right)$

8. The nth derivative of $y = \frac{1}{2x+3}$ is (1)
   (A) $\frac{(-1)^n 2^n n!}{(2x+3)^{n+1}}$ (B) $\frac{2^n n!}{(2x+3)^{n+1}}$
   (C) $\frac{2^n n!}{(2x+3)^{n-1}}$ (D) 0

9. Expanding of $\log(1-x)^4 - \log(1-x)$ in ascending powers of x is (2)

    (A) $-x - \dfrac{x^2}{2} - \dfrac{x^3}{3} - \dfrac{3}{2}x^4 - \ldots$

    (B) $x + \dfrac{x^2}{2} + \dfrac{x^3}{3} - \dfrac{3}{4}x^4 + \ldots$

    (C) $x + \dfrac{x^2}{2!} + \dfrac{x^3}{3!} - \dfrac{3}{4!}x^4 + \ldots$

    (D) $-x - \dfrac{x^2}{2!} - \dfrac{x^3}{3!} - \dfrac{3}{4!}x^4 - \ldots$

10. Expansion of $\sin\dfrac{x}{2} + \cos\dfrac{x}{2}$ in ascending powers of x is (2)

    (A) $1 - \dfrac{x}{2} + \dfrac{x^2}{8} + \dfrac{x^3}{48} - \dfrac{x^4}{384} + \ldots$

    (B) $1 + \dfrac{x}{2} - \dfrac{x^2}{8} - \dfrac{x^3}{48} - \dfrac{x^4}{384} + \ldots$

    (C) $1 + \dfrac{x}{2} - \dfrac{x^2}{8} - \dfrac{x^3}{24} - \dfrac{x^4}{120} + \ldots$

    (D) $\dfrac{x^2}{8} - \dfrac{x^3}{48} + \dfrac{x^4}{384} - \ldots$

11. First two terms in the expansion of $\sqrt{x+h}$ by Taylors theorem in ascending powers of h is (2)

    (A) $\sqrt{x} + \dfrac{h}{\sqrt{x}} + \ldots$

    (B) $\sqrt{x} - \dfrac{h}{2}\dfrac{1}{\sqrt{x}} + \ldots$

    (C) $\dfrac{1}{\sqrt{x}} + \dfrac{h}{2}\dfrac{1}{\sqrt{x}}$

    (D) $\sqrt{x} + \dfrac{h}{2}\dfrac{1}{\sqrt{x}} + \ldots$

12. $\displaystyle\lim_{x \to 0} \dfrac{(1+x)^n - 1}{x}$ is equal to (2)

    (A) n

    (B) 1

    (C) e

    (D) 0

13. $\displaystyle\lim_{x \to 0} \sin x^{\tan x}$ is equal to (2)

    (A) 1

    (B) e

    (C) -1

    (D) $\dfrac{1}{e}$

14. Expansion of $\cosh x$ in ascending powers of x is (1)

    (A) $1 + x + \dfrac{x^2}{2!} + \dfrac{x^3}{3!} + \ldots$

    (B) $x - \dfrac{x^2}{3!} + \dfrac{x^3}{5!} - \ldots$

    (C) $1 + \dfrac{x^2}{2!} + \dfrac{x^3}{4!} + \ldots$

    (D) $x + \dfrac{x^2}{3!} + \dfrac{x^3}{5!} + \ldots$

15. $\displaystyle\lim_{x \to 0} \dfrac{e^x - 1}{x}$ is equal to (1)

    (A) 2

    (B) $\dfrac{1}{2}$

    (C) 1

    (D) -1

□□□

ENGINEERING MATHEMATICS – I
MODEL QUESTION PAPER : THEORY EXAM.

1. (a) Reduce the following matrix A to its normal form and hence find its rank, (4)
$$A = \begin{bmatrix} 2 & -1 & -1 & -3 \\ 2 & 4 & -1 & 0 \\ 4 & -3 & 2 & -1 \end{bmatrix}$$
   (b) Find Eigen values for the matrix A and Eigen vectors corresponding to largest eigen value. (4)
$$A = \begin{bmatrix} 4 & 0 & 1 \\ -2 & 1 & 0 \\ -2 & 0 & 1 \end{bmatrix}$$
   (c) Solve : $x^4 - x^3 + x^2 - x + 1 = 0$ (4)

OR

2. (a) If z_1 and z_2 and origin represent on the Argand diagram, vertices of an equilateral triangle, show that $\dfrac{1}{z_1^2} + \dfrac{1}{z_2^2} = \dfrac{1}{z_1 z_2}$. (4)
   (b) Express $\cos^{-1}\left(\dfrac{3i}{4}\right)$ in the form $a + ib$. (4)
   (c) Examine the consistency of the system of linear equations and solve if consistent : (4)
$$x + y + z = 6$$
$$2x - 2y + 3z = 7$$
$$x - y + 2z = 5$$
$$3x + y + z = 8$$

3. (a) If $y = (x^2 - 1)^n$ then prove that $(x^2 - 1) y_{n+2} + 2xy_{n+1} - n(n+1) y_n = 0$. (4)
   (b) Test convergence of the series (Any one) : (4)
   (1) $\dfrac{x}{1.2} + \dfrac{x^2}{3.4} + \dfrac{x^3}{5.6} + \cdots$
   (2) $1 - \dfrac{1}{2} + \dfrac{1}{4} - \dfrac{1}{8} + \dfrac{1}{16} - \cdots$
   (c) Using Taylors theorem, express $7 + (x+2) + 3(x+2)^3 + (x+2)^4$ in ascending powers of x. (4)

OR

4. (a) Prove that : $\cot^{-1}\left[\dfrac{3x - x^3}{1 - 3x^2}\right] = \dfrac{\pi}{2} - 3\left(x - \dfrac{x^3}{3} + \dfrac{x^5}{5} \cdots\right)$ (4)
   (b) Solve (Any one) : (4)
   (1) Evaluate : $\displaystyle\lim_{x \to \infty} \left(\dfrac{ax+1}{ax-1}\right)^x$
   (2) Find a and b if $\displaystyle\lim_{x \to 0} \dfrac{a \cos x - a + bx^2}{x^4} = \dfrac{1}{12}$
   (c) Find n^{th} derivative of $\dfrac{x^3}{x^2 - 1}$. (4)

5. Solve (Any two) :

   (a) If $x^2 = au + bv$, $y^2 = au - bv$, prove that $\left(\dfrac{\partial u}{\partial x}\right)_y \left(\dfrac{\partial x}{\partial u}\right)_v = \left(\dfrac{\partial v}{\partial y}\right)_x \left(\dfrac{\partial y}{\partial v}\right)_u$ (6)

   (b) If $u = \sin^{-1}\left(\dfrac{x+y}{\sqrt{x}+\sqrt{y}}\right)$, prove that $x^2 \dfrac{\partial^2 u}{\partial x^2} + 2xy \dfrac{\partial^2 u}{\partial x \partial y} + y^2 \dfrac{\partial^2 u}{\partial y^2} = \dfrac{1}{4}(\tan^3 u - \tan u)$ (7)

   (c) If $z = f(u, v)$, where $u = x^2 - 2xy - y^2$ and $v = y$ show that (6)

   $(x + y) \dfrac{\partial z}{\partial x} + (x - y) \dfrac{\partial z}{\partial y} = (x - y) \dfrac{\partial z}{\partial v}$

OR

6. Solve (Any two) :

   (a) If $z^3 - xz - y = 0$, prove that $\dfrac{\partial^2 z}{\partial x \partial y} = -\dfrac{(3z^2 + x)}{(3z^2 - x)^3}$. (7)

   (b) If $u = \sin(\sqrt{x} + \sqrt{y})$, prove that, $x \dfrac{\partial u}{\partial x} + y \dfrac{\partial y}{\partial y} = \dfrac{1}{2}(\sqrt{x} + \sqrt{y}) \cos(\sqrt{x} + \sqrt{y})$ (6)

   (c) If $x^2 y - e^z + x \sin z = 0$ and $x^2 + y^2 + z^2 = a^2$, evaluate $\dfrac{dy}{dx}$ and $\dfrac{dx}{dz}$. (6)

7. Solve any two

   (a) Examine for the functional dependence (6)
   $u = \sin^{-1}x + \sin^{-1}y$, $v = x\sqrt{1-y^2} + y\sqrt{1-x^2}$ find the relation between them if exist.

   (b) Find $[(3.82)^2 + 2(2.1)^3]^{1/5}$ by 6 using the theory of approximations. (6)

   (c) Find the point on the surface $Z^2 = xy + 1$ nearest to the origin by using Lagrange's method. (7)

OR

8. Solve any two :

   (a) If $x = v^2 + w^2$, $y = w^2 + u^2$, $z = u^2 + v^2$ prove that $JJ' = 1$ (6)

   (b) In the manufacture of closed rectangular boxes with specified sides a, b, c, (a ≠ b ≠ c), small changes of A%, B%, C% occurred in a, b, c respectively from box to box from the specified dimension. However, the volume and surface area of all boxes were according to the specification. Show that : $\dfrac{A}{a(b-c)} = \dfrac{B}{b(c-a)} = \dfrac{C}{c(a-B)}$. (6)

   (c) Find all the stationary points of the function $x^2 + 3xy^2 - 15x^2 - 15y^2 + 72x$. (7)
   Examine whether the function is maximum or minimum at those points.

UNIVERSITY QUESTION PAPERS

Engineering Mathematics – I
(2012 Pattern)

Time : 2 Hours   December 2012   Max. Marks : 50

1. (A) Examine the consistency of the system of the following equations. If consistent, solve system of equations :   (04)

$$x + y + z = 3$$
$$x + 2y + 3z = 4$$
$$x + 4y + 9z = 6$$

   (B) Find Eigen Values and Eigen Vector corresponding to highest Eigen Value for the matrix :   (04)

$$A = \begin{bmatrix} 1 & 1 & -2 \\ -1 & 2 & 1 \\ 0 & 1 & -1 \end{bmatrix}$$

   (C) If $\tan\log(x - iy) = a - ib$ and $a^2 + b^2 \neq 1$, then prove that $\tan\log(x^2 + y^2) = \dfrac{2a}{1 - a^2 - b^2}$.   (04)

OR

2. (A) Examine for Linear Dependence or Independence of Vectors $(2, 2, 7, -1)$, $(3, -1, 2, 4)$ and $(1, 1, 3, 1)$.   (04)

   (B) Solve : $x^7 + x^4 + i(x^3 + 1) = 0$.   (04)

   (C) A square lies above real axis in Argand diagram and two of its adjacent vertices are the origin and the point $2 + 3i$. Find the complex number representing other vertices.   (04)

3. (A) Test convergence of the series : (Any One)   (04)

     (a) $\dfrac{2}{9} + \dfrac{2 \cdot 5}{9 \cdot 13} + \dfrac{2 \cdot 5 \cdot 8}{9 \cdot 13 \cdot 17} + \cdots$

     (B) $\displaystyle\sum_{n=1}^{\infty} \left(\dfrac{1}{n}\right) \sin\left(\dfrac{1}{n}\right)$.

   (B) Expand $3x^3 - 2x^2 + x - 6$ in powers of $(x - 2)$.   (04)

   (C) Find n^{th} derivative of $x^2 e^x \cos x$.   (04)

OR

4. (A) Solve : (Any one)   (04)

     (a) $\displaystyle\lim_{x \to 1} (1 - x^2)^{\frac{1}{\log(1-x)}}$

     (b) Find a and b, if $\displaystyle\lim_{x \to 0} \dfrac{a \sinh x + b \sin x}{2x^3} = \dfrac{8}{6}$.

(UQP.1)

(B) Show that : $x \csc x = 1 + \dfrac{x^2}{6} + \dfrac{7}{360}x^4 + \ldots$ (04)

(C) Prove that n^{th} derivative of $y = \tan^{-1} x$ is $(-1)^{n-1}(n-1)!\sin n\left(\dfrac{\pi}{2} - y\right)\sin^n\left(\dfrac{\pi}{2} - y\right)$. (04)

5. Solve any two :

   (a) If $u = \log\left(\sqrt{x^2 + y^2 + z^2}\right)$, then prove that $(x^2 + y^2 + z^2)\left(\dfrac{\partial^2 u}{\partial x^2} + \dfrac{\partial^2 u}{\partial y^2} + \dfrac{\partial^2 u}{\partial z^2}\right) = 1$. (06)

   (b) If $u = \dfrac{x^2 y^2 z^2}{x^2 + y^2 + z^2} + \cos\left(\dfrac{xy + xy}{x^2 + y^2 + z^2}\right)$, then find the value of $x\dfrac{\partial u}{\partial x} + y\dfrac{\partial u}{\partial y} + z\dfrac{\partial u}{\partial z}$. (07)

   (c) If $u = x^2 - y^2$, $v = 2xy$ and $z = f(u, v)$, then show that $x\dfrac{\partial z}{\partial x} - y\dfrac{\partial z}{\partial y} = 2\sqrt{u^2 + v^2}\dfrac{\partial z}{\partial u}$. (06)

OR

6. Solve any two :

   (a) If $ux + vy = 0$ and $\dfrac{u}{x} + \dfrac{v}{y} = 1$, then show that $\left(\dfrac{\partial u}{\partial x}\right)_y - \left(\dfrac{\partial v}{\partial y}\right)_x = \dfrac{x^2 + y^2}{y^2 - x^2}$. (06)

   (b) If $u = \csc^{-1}\left(\sqrt{\dfrac{x^{1/2} + y^{1/2}}{x^{1/3} + y^{1/3}}}\right)$, then show that $x^2 u_{xx} + 2xy u_{xy} + y^2 u_{yy} = \dfrac{\tan u}{12}\left(\dfrac{13}{12} + \dfrac{\tan^2 u}{12}\right)$. (07)

   (c) If $x = r\cos\theta$, $y = r\sin\theta$, where r and θ are functions of t, then prove that :
   $x\dfrac{dy}{dt} - y\dfrac{dx}{dt} = r^2\dfrac{d\theta}{dt}$. (06)

7. (A) If $u = x(1 - y)$ and $v = xy$, find $\dfrac{\partial(x, y)}{\partial(u, v)}$. (04)

   (B) Examine for functional dependence for $u = y + z$, $v = x + 2z^2$, $w = x - 4yz - 2y^2$. (04)

   (C) Discuss the maxima and minima of $f(x, y) = xy + a^3\left(\dfrac{1}{x} + \dfrac{1}{y}\right)$. (05)

OR

8. (A) If $x = u^2 - v^2$, $y = uv$, find $\dfrac{\partial u}{\partial x}$. (04)

   (B) Find the percentage error in computing the parallel resistance r of two resistances r_1 and r_2 from the formula $\dfrac{1}{r} = \dfrac{1}{r_1} + \dfrac{1}{r_2}$, where r_1 and r_2 are both in error by 2% each. (04)

   (C) Find the points on the surface $z^2 = xy + 1$ nearest to the origin, by using Lagrange's method. (05)

ENGINEERING MATHEMATICS – I
(2012 Pattern)

Time : 2 Hours **May 2013** **Max. Marks : 50**

1. (a) Find the values of λ for which the following system of equations : (04)
$$x + 2y + z = 3$$
$$x + y + z = \lambda$$
$$3x + y + 3z = \lambda^2$$
Are consistent.

   (b) Find Eigen values and Eigen vector for lowest Eigen value of the matrix. (04)
$$A = \begin{bmatrix} 4 & 2 & -2 \\ -5 & 3 & 2 \\ -2 & 4 & 1 \end{bmatrix}$$

   (c) Find the value of $(1 + i)^{1/5}$. (04)

OR

2. (a) Examine for linear dependence or independence of vectors (04)
$$x_1 = (1, -1, 0), \ x_2 = (0, 1, -1), \ x_3 = (0, 0, 1)$$

   (b) If $\log(\log(x + iy)) = p + qi$ prove that $y = x \tan[\tan q \cdot \log\sqrt{x^2 + y^2}]$. (04)

   (c) If $\dfrac{z - 2i}{2z - 1}$ is purely imaginary prove that locus of z in the Argand diagram is circle. (04)

3. (a) Test convergence of the series (any one) : (04)

   (1) $\dfrac{1}{1 \cdot 2 \cdot 3} + \dfrac{3}{2 \cdot 3 \cdot 4} + \dfrac{5}{3 \cdot 4 \cdot 5} + \cdots$

   (2) $\sum\limits_{n=1}^{\infty} \dfrac{1}{(\log n)^n}$.

   (b) Expand $2x^3 + 3x^2 - 8x + 7$ in powers of $(x - 2)$. (04)

   (c) Find n^{th} derivative of $\dfrac{1}{x^2 - 4x + 3}$. (04)

OR

4. (A) Solve (any one) : (04)

   (a) $\lim\limits_{x \to 0} \dfrac{xe^x - \log(1 + x)}{x^2}$.

   (b) Find the values of a and b if $\lim\limits_{x \to 0} \left[\dfrac{\sin x}{x^3} + \dfrac{a}{x^2} + b \right] = 0$.

   (B) Show that $\sqrt{1 + \sin x} = 1 + \dfrac{x}{2} - \dfrac{x^2}{8} - \dfrac{x^3}{48} + \dfrac{x^4}{384} \cdots$ (04)

   (C) If $y = a \cos \log x + b \sin \log x$, then show that
$$x^2 y_{n+2} + (2n + 1) x y_{n+1} + (n^2 + 1) y_n = 0.$$ (04)

5. Solve any two :

(a) If $u = r^m$ where, $r = \sqrt{x^2 + y^2 + z^2}$.

Then show that $\dfrac{\partial^2 u}{\partial x^2} + \dfrac{\partial^2 u}{\partial y^2} + \dfrac{\partial^2 u}{\partial z^2} = m(m+1) r^{m-2}$. (06)

(b) If $u = \sin(\sqrt{x} + \sqrt{y})$ then prove that $x\dfrac{\partial u}{\partial x} + y\dfrac{\partial u}{\partial y} = \dfrac{1}{2}(\sqrt{x} + \sqrt{y}) \cos(\sqrt{x} + \sqrt{y})$. (07)

(c) If $z = f(x, y)$ where $x = e^u \cos v$, $y = e^u \sin v$ then prove that :

$$y\dfrac{\partial z}{\partial u} + x\dfrac{\partial z}{\partial v} = e^{2u}\dfrac{\partial z}{\partial y}$$ (06)

OR

6. Solve any two :

(a) If $x = \dfrac{\cos\theta}{u}, y = \dfrac{\sin\theta}{u}$ then, evaluate $\left(\dfrac{\partial x}{\partial u}\right)_\theta \left(\dfrac{\partial u}{\partial x}\right)_y + \left(\dfrac{\partial y}{\partial u}\right)_\theta \left(\dfrac{\partial u}{\partial y}\right)_x$. (06)

(b) If $u = \sin^{-1}\sqrt{x^2 + y^2}$ then prove that $x^2\dfrac{\partial^2 u}{\partial x^2} + 2xy\dfrac{\partial^2 u}{\partial x \partial y} + y^2\dfrac{\partial^2 u}{\partial y^2} = \tan^3 u$. (07)

(c) If $z = f(x, y)$ and $x = r\cosh\theta$ and $y = r\sinh\theta$ then show that $(x - y)(Z_n - Z_y) = rZ_r = Z_\theta$. (06)

7. If $x = uv$ and $y = \dfrac{u+v}{u-v}$. Find $\dfrac{\partial(u, v)}{\partial(x, y)}$. (04)

(b) Examine the functional dependence of

$u = \sin^{-1} x + \sin^{-1} y$ and $v = x\sqrt{1-y^2} + y\sqrt{1-x^2}$. (04)

(c) Find the extreme values of, $f(x, y) = xy(a - x - y)$, $x > 0, y > 0, a > 0$. (04)

8. (a) If $u^2 + xv^2 - uxy = 0$ and $v^2 - xy^2 + 2uv + u^2 = 0$ find $\left(\dfrac{\partial u}{\partial x}\right)_y$. (04)

(b) If the kinetic energy is given by $T = \dfrac{mv^2}{2}$ and m changes from 49 to 49.5 and v changes from 1600 to 1590, find approximate change in T. (04)

(c) Use the Lagrange's method to find the minimum distance from origin to the plane $3x + 2y + z = 12$. (05)

Engineering Mathematics – I
(2012 Pattern)
Nov. 2013

Time : 2 Hours   Max. Marks : 50

1. (a) Examine the following system of equations for consistency and solve it, if consistent. (4)

    $4x - 2y + 6z = 8$, $x + y - 3z = -1$, $15x - 3y + 9z = 21$

    (b) Examine the following vectors for Linear dependence. Find the relation between them, if dependent. (2, –1, 3, 2), (1, 3, 4, 2) and (3, –5, 2, 2) (4)

    (c) If $2 \cos \phi = x + 1/x$, $2 \cos \psi = y + 1/y$ (4)

    Prove that, $x^p y^q + 1/x^p y^q = 2 \cos(p\phi + q\psi)$

OR

2. (a) Use De Moivres theorem, to solve the equation (4)

    $X^7 + X^4 + (x^3 + 1) = = 0$

    (b) If $(1 + ai)(1 + bi) = p + iq$, then prove that, (4)

    (i) $p \tan[\tan^{-1} a + \tan^{-1} b] = q$

    (ii) $(1 + a^2)(1 + b^2) = p^2 + q^2$

    (c) Reduce the following matrix A to its normal and hence find its rank, where (4)

    $A = \begin{bmatrix} 2 & -3 & 4 & 4 \\ 1 & 1 & 1 & 2 \\ 3 & -2 & 3 & 6 \end{bmatrix}$

3. (a) Test convergence of the series (Any one) (4)

    (i) $\sum_{n=1}^{\infty} \frac{2^n + 1}{3^n + 1}$

    (ii) $\frac{1*2}{3^2 * 4^2} + \frac{3*4}{5^2 * 6^2} + \frac{5*6}{7^2 * 8^2} + \ldots$

    (b) Expand $40 + 53(x-2) + 19(x-2)^2 + 2(x-2)^3$ in ascending powers of x. (4)

    (c) If $y = x^n \log x$ then, prove that (4)

    $Y_{n+1} = \dfrac{n!}{x}$

OR

4. (a) Solve any one (4)

(i) Evaluate $\lim_{x \to \infty} (\cot x)^{\sin x}$

(ii) Find the values of a and b such that,
$$\lim_{x \to \infty} \frac{a \cos x - a + bx^2}{x^4} = \frac{1}{12}$$

(b) Prove that, $e^x \tan x = x + x^2 + \frac{5x^3}{6} + \frac{x^4}{2} + \ldots$ (4)

(c) If $Y = \frac{x}{(x+1)}$ find Y_n (4)

5. (a) Solve any two of the following (13)

(i) Verify $\frac{\partial^2 u}{\partial x \partial y} = \frac{\partial^2 u}{\partial y \partial x}$ for $u = \tan^{-1}\left[\frac{y}{x}\right]$

(ii) If $x = u \tan v$, $y = u \sec v$

Prove that, $\left(\frac{\partial u}{\partial x}\right)_y \left(\frac{\partial v}{\partial x}\right)_y = \left(\frac{\partial u}{\partial y}\right)_x \left(\frac{\partial v}{\partial y}\right)_x$

(iii) If $u = \frac{x^3 + y^3}{y\sqrt{x}} + \frac{1}{x^7} \sin^{-1}\left(\frac{x^2 + y^2}{2xy}\right)$

Then find the value of

$x^2 \frac{\partial^2 u}{\partial x^2} + 2xy \frac{\partial^2 u}{\partial x \partial y} + y^2 \frac{\partial^2 u}{\partial y^2}$. At point $(1, 1)$.

OR

6. Solve any Two of the following (13)

(a) If $u = (x^2 - y^2) f(xy)$ then show that

$u_{xx} + u_{yy} = (x^4 - y^4) f''(xy)$

(b) Verify Eulers theorem for homogeneous functions $F(x, y, z) = 3x^2 yz + 5xy^2 z + 4z^4$

(c) If $x = u + v + w$, $y = uv + uw + vw$, $Z = uvw$ and F is function of x, y, z then prove that $x \frac{\partial F}{\partial x} + 2y \frac{\partial F}{\partial y} + 3z \frac{\partial F}{\partial z} = u \frac{\partial F}{\partial u} + v \frac{\partial F}{\partial v} + w \frac{\partial F}{\partial w}$

7. (a) If $x = v^2 + w^2, y = w^3 + u^2, z = u^2 + v^2$. Find $\dfrac{\partial(u, v, w)}{\partial(x, y, z)}$

(b) Examine for functional dependence for

$u = x + y + z, v = x^2 + y^2 + z^2, w = x^3 + y^3 + z^3 - 3xyz$ (4)

(c) Find the extreme values of $f(x, y) = x^3 + y^3 - 3axy, a > 0$ (5)

OR

8. (a) If $u^2 + xv^2 = x + y$ and $v^2 + yu^2 = x - y$ find $\dfrac{\partial v}{\partial y}$. (4)

(b) The resistance R of a circuit was calculated was calculated using the formula I = E/R. If there is an error of 0.1 Amp in reading I and 0.5 volts in E, find the corresponding percentage error in R When I = 15 Amp and E = 100 Volts. (4)

(c) Divide 24 into three parts such that, the continued product of the first, square of the second and cube of the third may be maximum. Use Lagrange's method. (5)

Engineering Mathematics – I
(2012 Pattern)

May 2014

Time : 2 Hours Max. Marks : 50

1. (a) Show that the system of equations. (4)

$3x + 4y + 5z = \alpha \qquad 4x + 5y + 6z = \beta \qquad 5x + 6y + 7z = \gamma$

is consistent only of α, β and γ are in arithmetic progression.

(b) Verify Cayley-Hamilton theorem for A and hence find A^{-1}. (4)

$$A = \begin{bmatrix} 1 & 0 & -2 \\ 2 & 2 & 4 \\ 0 & 0 & 2 \end{bmatrix}$$

(c) If $\alpha = 1 + i$, $\beta + 1 - i$ and $\cot \phi = x + 1$ then prove that

$$\frac{(x + \alpha)^n - (x + \beta)^n}{\alpha - \beta} = \sin n\phi \, \csc^n \phi \qquad (4)$$

OR

2. (a) Examine whether the following vectors are linearly dependent or independent. If dependent, find the relation between them (4)

$X_1 = [1, 2, 3]$, $X_2 = [3, -2, 1]$, $X_3 = [1, -6, -5]$

(b) Show that $\log = 2i \tan^{-1}(\cot x \tan hy)$ (4)

(c) Prove that $\tan^{-1}\left[i\left(\dfrac{x-a}{x+a}\right)\right] = -\dfrac{i}{2} \log\left(\dfrac{a}{x}\right)$ (4)

3. (a) Test the convergence of the series (Any one) (4)

(i) $\dfrac{2}{1} + \dfrac{3}{8} + \dfrac{4}{27} + \dfrac{5}{64} + \ldots + \dfrac{n+1}{n^3} + \ldots$ (ii) $1 - \dfrac{1}{2\sqrt{2}} + \dfrac{1}{3\sqrt{3}} - \dfrac{1}{4\sqrt{4}} + \ldots$

(b) Expand $x^3 + 7x^2 + x - 6$ in powers of $(x - 3)$ (4)

(c) If $y = \log(x + \sqrt{x^2 + 1})$, prove that

$(1 + x^2) y_{n+2} + (2n + 1) x y_{n+1} + n^2 y_n = 0$ (4)

Engineering Mathematics – I UQP.9 May 2014

OR

4. (a) Solve any one (4)

   (i) Evaluate $\lim_{x \to \pi/2} (\cos x)^{\cos x}$

   (ii) If $\lim_{x \to 0} \dfrac{\sin 2x + p \sin x}{x^3}$ is finite, find the value of p and hence evaluate the limit.

  (b) Prove that $\log(1 + \tan x) = x - \dfrac{x^2}{2} + \dfrac{2x^3}{3} - \ldots$ (4)

  (c) Find n^{th} derivative of $y = \dfrac{x}{(x+1)(x-2)(x-3)}$. (4)

5. Solve any two of the following : (4)

  (a) Find the value of n such that $u = x^n (3 \cos^2 y - 1)$ satisfies the partial differential equation. (6)

$$\frac{\partial}{\partial x}\left(x^2 \frac{\partial u}{\partial x}\right) + \frac{1}{\sin y} \frac{\partial}{\partial y}\left(\sin y \frac{\partial u}{\partial y}\right) = 0$$

  (b) If $x = r \cos \theta$, $y = r \sin \theta$ then prove that (6)

   (i) $\left(\dfrac{\partial y}{\partial r}\right)_x \left(\dfrac{\partial y}{\partial r}\right)_\theta = 1$ (ii) $\left(\dfrac{\partial x}{\partial \theta}\right)_r = r^2 \left(\dfrac{\partial \theta}{\partial x}\right)_y$

  (c) If $u = x^8 \left(\dfrac{y}{x}\right) + \dfrac{1}{y^8} \phi \left(\dfrac{x}{y}\right)$ then prove that (7)

$$x^2 \frac{\partial^2 u}{\partial x^2} + 2xy \frac{\partial^2 u}{\partial x \partial y} + y^2 \frac{\partial^2 u}{\partial y^2} + x \frac{\partial u}{\partial x} + y \frac{\partial u}{\partial y} = 64u$$

OR

6. Solve any two of the following :

  (a) If $u = \cos^{-1}\left[\dfrac{x^3 y^2 + 4y^3 x^2}{\sqrt{x^4 + 6y^4}}\right]$ find the value of

   (i) $x \dfrac{\partial u}{\partial x} + y \dfrac{\partial u}{\partial y}$ (ii) $x^2 \dfrac{\partial^2 u}{\partial x^2} + 2xy \dfrac{\partial^2 u}{\partial x \partial y} + y^2 \dfrac{\partial^2 u}{\partial y^2}$

  (b) If $u = f\left(\dfrac{x}{y}, \dfrac{y}{z}, \dfrac{z}{x}\right)$

   Prove that $x \dfrac{\partial u}{\partial x} + y \dfrac{\partial u}{\partial y} + z \dfrac{\partial u}{\partial z} = 0$ (6)

  (b) If $u = f(x, y)$, $\phi(x, z) = 0$ the prove that

$$\frac{\partial \phi}{\partial x} \frac{\partial f}{\partial y} \frac{dy}{dz} = \frac{\partial f}{\partial x} \frac{\partial \phi}{\partial z}$$ (6)

7. (a) I $x = e^v \sec u$, $y = e^v \tan u$, find $\dfrac{\partial (u, v)}{\partial (x, y)}$. (4)

   (b) Examine for functional dependence for $u = \dfrac{x}{y-z}$, $v = \dfrac{y}{z-x}$, $w = \dfrac{z}{x-y}$ (4)

   (c) Find extreme values of $f(x, y) = x^3 + y^3 - 3axy$, $a > 0$ (5)

   OR

8. (a) If $x = \cos \theta - r \sin \theta$, $y = \sin \theta + r \cos \theta$ find $\dfrac{\partial r}{\partial x}$. (4)

   (b) The resonant frequency in a series electrical circuit is given by $f = \dfrac{1}{2\pi \sqrt{LC}}$. If the measurement in L and C are in error by 2% and – 1% respectively. Find the percentage error in f. (4)

   (c) Use Lagrange's method to find stationary value of $u = \dfrac{x^2}{a^3} + \dfrac{y^2}{b^3} + \dfrac{z^2}{c^3}$ where $x + y + z = 1$. (5)

Engineering Mathematics – I
(2012 Pattern)
Nov. / Dec. 2014

Time : 2 Hours   Max. Marks : 50

1. (a) Examine for consistency the system of equations (4)

   $x - y - z = 2,\ x + 2y + z = 2,\ 4x - 7y - 5z = 2$

   and solve it if consistent.

   (b) Examine whether the following vectors are linearly dependent or independent. If dependent, find the relation between them, (4)

   $X_1 = [1\ -1\ 2]\ X_2 = [2\ 3\ 5]\ X_3 = [3\ 2\ 1]$

   (c) If $\operatorname{cosec}(x + iy) = u + iv$, prove that

   (i) $\dfrac{u^2}{\sin^2 x} - \dfrac{v^2}{\cos^2 x} = (u^2 + v^2)^2$

   (ii) $\dfrac{u^2}{\cosh^2 x} - \dfrac{v^2}{\sinh^2 x} = (u^2 + v^2)^2$ (4)

OR

2. (a) A square lies above real axis in Argand diagram and two of its adjacent vertices are the origin and the point $2 + 3i$. Find the complex numbers representing other two vertices. (4)

   (b) If $\arg(z + 1) = \dfrac{\pi}{6}$ and $\arg(z - 1) = \dfrac{2\pi}{3}$ then find z. (4)

   (c) Find the eigen values and eigen vectors of following matrix, (4)

   $$A = \begin{bmatrix} 1 & 1 & 1 \\ 0 & 2 & 1 \\ 0 & 0 & 3 \end{bmatrix}$$

3. (a) Test the convergence of the series (Any one) (4)

   (i) $\dfrac{1}{\sqrt{2}} + \dfrac{1}{\sqrt{9}} + \dfrac{1}{\sqrt{28}} + \dfrac{1}{\sqrt{65}} + \ldots$ (ii) $1 - \dfrac{1}{\sqrt{2}} + \dfrac{1}{\sqrt{3}} - \dfrac{1}{\sqrt{4}} + \ldots$

   (b) Prove that $\log(1 + \sin x) = x - \dfrac{x^2}{2} + \dfrac{x^3}{6} - \dfrac{x^4}{12} + \ldots$ (4)

   (c) Find n^{th} derivative of $\dfrac{x^2}{(x-1)(x-2)}$ (4)

OR

4. (a) Solve any one (4)

  (i) Evaluate $\lim_{x \to 0} \log_{\tan x} \tan 4x$

  (ii) Find the values of a and b if $\lim_{x \to 0} [x^{-3} \sin x + ax^{-2} + b] = 0$

  (b) Using Taylor's theorem expand $49 + 69x + 42x^2 + 11x^3 + x^4$ in powers of $(x + 2)$. (4)

  (c) If $y = \sin \log(x^2 + 2x + 1)$, then prove that (4)
  $(x + 1)^2 y_{n+2} + (2n + 1)(x + 1) y_{n+1} + (n^2 + 4) y_n = 0$.

5. Solve any two of the following : (4)

  (a) If $u = \log(x^3 + y^3 - x^2y - xy^2)$ then prove that $x^2 u_{xx} + 2xy\, u_{xy} + y^2 u_{yy} = -3$. (7)

  (b) If $x = u + v + w$, $y = uv + vw + wu$, $z = uvw$ and ϕ is a function of x, y, z then prove that

  $$u\frac{\partial \phi}{\partial u} + v\frac{\partial \phi}{\partial v} + w\frac{\partial \phi}{\partial w} = x\frac{\partial \phi}{\partial x} + 2y\frac{\partial \phi}{\partial y} + 3z\frac{\partial \phi}{\partial z}$$ (6)

  (c) If $ux + vy = 0$ and $\frac{u}{x} + \frac{v}{y} = 1$, then prove that $\left(\frac{\partial u}{\partial x}\right)y - \left(\frac{\partial v}{\partial y}\right)x = \frac{x^2 + y^2}{y^2 - x^2}$ (6)

OR

6. Solve any two of the following :

  (a) If $u = \cos\left(\frac{xy}{x^2 + y^2}\right) + \sqrt{x^2 + y^2} + \frac{xy^2}{x + y}$, then find the value of $xu_x + yu_y$ at $(3, 4)$. (7)

  (b) If $x = \frac{\cos \theta}{u}$, $y = \frac{\sin \theta}{u}$, then prove that $u\frac{\partial z}{\partial u} - \frac{\partial z}{\partial \theta} = (y - x)\frac{\partial z}{\partial x} - (y - x)\frac{\partial z}{\partial y}$ (6)

  (c) If $u = (x^2 - y^2) f(xy)$, then show that $u_{xx} + u_{yy} = (x^4 - y^4) f''(xy)$ (6)

7. (a) If $x = r \sin \theta \cos \phi$, $y = r \sin \theta \sin \phi$, $z = r \cos \theta$ find $\frac{\partial(x, y, z)}{\partial(r, \theta, \phi)}$ (4)

  (b) Examine for functional dependence $u = \sin^{-1} x + \sin^{-1} y$, $v = x\sqrt{1 - y^2} + y\sqrt{1 - x^2}$ if dependent find the the relation between them. (4)

  (c) The area of a triangle ABC is calculated from the formula $\Delta = \frac{1}{2} bc \sin A$. Errors or 1%, 2% and 3% respectively are made in measuring b, c, A. If the correct value of A is 30°, find the percentage error in the calculated value of area of triangle. (5)

OR

8. (a) If $u^2 + xv^2 - uxy = 0$, $v^2 - xy^2 + 2uv + u^2 = 0$ find $\frac{\partial u}{\partial x}$ by choosing u, v as dependent and x, y as independent variables. (4)

  (b) Show that $u = \frac{x + y}{1 - xy}$, $v = \tan^{-1} x + \tan^{-1} y$ are functionally dependent and find the relation between them. (4)

  (c) Find all the stationary values of the function $f(x, y) = x^3 + 3xy^2 - 15x^2 - 15y^2 + 72x$. Find maximum value of $f(x, y)$ at suitable point. (5)

Engineering Mathematics – I
(2012 Pattern)
May 2015

Time : 2 Hours
Max. Marks : 50

1. (a) Find the eigen values and eigen vector corresponding to minimum eigen value for the matrix : (4)

$$A = \begin{bmatrix} 1 & 0 & -1 \\ 1 & 2 & 1 \\ 2 & 2 & 3 \end{bmatrix}$$

(b) Determine the value of λ for which the equations :
$$3x_1 + 2x_2 + 4x_3 = 3$$
$$x_1 + x_2 + x_3 = \lambda$$
$$5x_1 + 4x_2 + 6x_3 = 15$$
are consistent. Find also the corresponding solution. (4)

(c) If z_1, z_2, z_3 are the vertices of an isosceles triangle right angled at z_2, prove that : (4)
$$z_1^2 + z_3^2 + 2z_2^2 = 2z_2(z_1 + z_3)$$

OR

2. (a) If $2\cos\theta = x + \dfrac{1}{x}$ (4)

prove that : $2\cos r\theta = x^r + \dfrac{1}{x^r}$

(b) If $Y = \log \tan x$, prove that : (4)
(i) $\sinh ny = \dfrac{1}{2}(\tan^n x - \cot^n x)$
(ii) $2\cosh ny \csc 2x = \cosh(n+1)y + \cosh(n-1)y$

(c) Examine for linear dependence or independence for the given vectors and if dependence, find the relation between them : (4)
$$X_1 = (1, -1, 2, 2)$$
$$X_2 = (2, -3, 4, -1)$$
$$X_3 = (-1, 2, -2, 3)$$

3. (a) Test convergence of the series (any one) : (4)

(i) $\sum\limits_{n=1}^{\infty} \left(\dfrac{2n+1}{3n+4}\right) 5^n$
(ii) $\dfrac{1}{1+\sqrt{2}} + \dfrac{2}{1+2\sqrt{3}} + \dfrac{3}{1+3\sqrt{4}} + \ldots$

(b) Prove that : (4)
$$\sin x \cosh x = x + \dfrac{1}{3}x^3 - \dfrac{1}{30}x^5 - \ldots$$

(c) Find n^{th} derivative of : $e^{2x} \sinh 3x \cos 4x$ (4)

OR

4. (a) Solve any one : (4)
   (i) $\lim_{x \to a} (x-a)^{(x-a)}$
   (ii) $\lim_{x \to \pi/2} (\sec x - \tan x)$

(b) Using Taylor's theorem, expand : $2x^3 + 3x^2 - 8x + 7$ in powers of $x - 2$. (4)

(c) If $y = e^{\tan^{-1}x}$, then show that $(1+x^2)y_{n+1} + (2nx-1)y_n + n(n-1)y_{n-1} = 0$. (4)

5. Solve any two :

(a) Find the value of n for which : $z = A e^{-gx} \sin(nt - gx)$ (6)
satisfies the partial differential equation : $\dfrac{\partial z}{\partial t} = \dfrac{\partial^2 z}{\partial x^2}$

(b) If $u = \dfrac{x^4 + y^4}{x^2 y^2} + x^6 \tan^{-1}\left[\dfrac{x^2 + y^2}{x^2 + 2xy}\right]$
find the value of : $x^2 \dfrac{\partial^2 u}{\partial x^2} + 2xy \dfrac{\partial^2 u}{\partial x \partial y} + y^2 \dfrac{\partial^2 u}{\partial y^2} + x \dfrac{\partial u}{\partial x} + y \dfrac{\partial u}{\partial y}$ at $x=1, y=2$. (7)

(c) If $z = f(u,v)$ and $u = \log(x^2 + y^2)$, $v = \dfrac{y}{x}$ show that : $x\dfrac{\partial z}{\partial y} - y\dfrac{\partial z}{\partial x} = (1+v^2)\dfrac{\partial z}{\partial v}$ (6)

OR

6. Solve any two : (6)

(a) If $x = \dfrac{\cos\theta}{r}, y = \dfrac{\sin\theta}{r}$. Find the value of : $\left(\dfrac{\partial x}{\partial r}\right)_\theta \left(\dfrac{\partial r}{\partial x}\right)_y + \left(\dfrac{\partial y}{\partial r}\right)_\theta \left(\dfrac{\partial r}{\partial y}\right)_x$

(b) If $u = \sin^{-1}\sqrt{\dfrac{x^2+y^2}{x+y}}$ (7)
Show that $x^2 \dfrac{\partial^2 u}{\partial x^2} + 2xy \dfrac{\partial^2 u}{\partial x \partial y} + y^2 \dfrac{\partial^2 u}{\partial y^2} = \dfrac{1}{4}\tan u [\tan^2 u - 1]$

(c) If $z = f(u,v)$ and $u = x\cos t - y\sin t$, $v = x\sin t + y\cos t$, where t is a constant, prove that : $x\dfrac{\partial z}{\partial x} + y\dfrac{\partial z}{\partial y} = u\dfrac{\partial z}{\partial u} + v\dfrac{\partial z}{\partial v}$ (6)

7. (a) If $u^3 + v^3 = x + y$, $u^2 + v^2 = x^3 + y^3$, find $\dfrac{\partial(u,v)}{\partial(x,y)}$. (4)

(b) Determine whether the following functions are functionally dependent. If functionally dependent, find the relation between them : (4)
$u = \sin x + \sin y, \quad v = \sin(x+y)$

(c) Examine maxima and minima of the following function and find their extreme values : $(x^2 + y^2 + 6x + 12)$ (5) **OR**

8. (a) If $x = u + v, y = v^2 + w^2, z = w^3 + u^3$, show that $\dfrac{\partial u}{\partial x} = \dfrac{vw}{vw + u^2}$ (4)

(b) If $e^z = \sec x \cos y$ and errors of magnitude h and $-h$ are made in estimating x and y, where x and y are found to be $\dfrac{\pi}{3}$ and $\dfrac{\pi}{6}$ respectively, find the corresponding error in z. (5)

(c) Find the minimum distance from origin to the plane : $3x + 2y + z = 12$ (4)

www.ingramcontent.com/pod-product-compliance
Lightning Source LLC
Chambersburg PA
CBHW080542300426
44111CB00017B/2836